COMPUTER SECURITY HANDBOOK

COMPUTER SECURITY HANDBOOK

Sixth Edition

Volume 2

Edited by

SEYMOUR BOSWORTH

MICHEL E. KABAY

ERIC WHYNE

Cover image: ©iStockphoto.com/Jimmy Anderson
Cover design: Wiley

Published by John Wiley & Sons, Inc., Hoboken, New Jersey.

Published simultaneously in Canada.

For general information on our other products and services or for technical support, please contact our Customer Care Department within the United States at (800) 762-2974, outside the United States at (317) 572-3993 or fax (317) 572-4002.

Wiley publishes in a variety of print and electronic formats and by print-on-demand. Some material included with standard print versions of this book may not be included in e-books or in print-on-demand. If this book refers to media such as a CD or DVD that is not included in the version you purchased, you may download this material at http://booksupport.wiley.com. For more information about Wiley products, visit www.wiley.com.

Library of Congress Cataloging-in-Publication Data

Computer security handbook / [edited by] Seymour Bosworth, Michel E. Kabay,
Eric Whyne. – Sixth edition.
volumes cm
Includes index.
ISBN 978-1-118-13410-8 (vol. 1 : pbk.) – ISBN 978-1-118-13411-5 (vol. 2 : pbk.) –
ISBN 978-1-118-12706-3 (2 volume set : pbk.); ISBN 978-1-118-85174-6 (ebk);
ISBN 978-1-118-85179-1 (ebk) 1. Electronic data processing departments–Security measures.
I. Bosworth, Seymour. II. Kabay, Michel E. III. Whyne, Eric, 1981–
HF5548.37.C64 2014
658.4′78–dc23

2013041083

Printed in the United States of America

10 9 8 7 6 5 4 3

CONTENTS

PREFACE

Computers are an integral part of our economic, social, professional, governmental, and military infrastructures. They have become necessities in virtually every area of modern life, but their vulnerability is of increasing concern. Computer-based systems are constantly under threats of inadvertent error and acts of nature, as well as those attributable to unethical, immoral, and criminal activities. It is the purpose of *The Computer Security Handbook* to provide guidance in recognizing these threats, eliminating them where possible and, if not, then reducing any losses attributable to them.

The Handbook will be most valuable to those directly responsible for computer, network, or information security, as well as those who must design, install, and maintain secure systems. It will be equally important to those managers whose operating functions can be affected by breaches in security and to those executives who are responsible for protecting the assets that have been entrusted to them.

With the advent of desktop, laptop, and handheld computers, and with the vast international networks that interconnect them, the nature and extent of threats to computer security have grown almost beyond measure. In order to encompass this unprecedented expansion, *The Computer Security Handbook* has grown apace.

When the first edition of the *Handbook* was published, its entire focus was on mainframe computers, the only type then in widespread use. The second edition recognized the advent of small computers, while the third edition placed increased emphasis on PCs and networks.

Edition	Publication Date	Chapters	Text Pages
First	1973	12	162
Second	1988	19	383
Third	1995	23	571
Fourth	2002	54	1,184
Fifth	2009	77	2,040
Sixth	2014	75	2224

The fourth edition of *The Computer Security Handbook* gave almost equal attention to mainframes and microcomputers, requiring more than twice the number of chapters and pages as the third.

The fifth edition was as great a step forward as the fourth. With 77 chapters and the work of 86 authors, we increased coverage in both breadth and depth. In this sixth edition, we updated all chapters while continuing to cover all 10 domains of the Common Body of Knowledge, as defined by the International Information Systems Security Certification Consortium $(ISC)^2$:

1. Security Management Practices: Chapters 10, 12, 13, 14, 15, 19, 10, 31, 43, 44, 45, 46, 47, 48, 49, 50, 51, 54, 55, 62, 63, 64, 65, 66, 67, 68, 74, 75
2. Security Architecture and Models: Chapters 1, 2, 3, 8, 9, 24, 26, 27, 51
3. Access Control Systems and Methodology: Chapters 15, 19, 28, 29, 32
4. Application Development Security: Chapters 13, 19, 21, 30, 38, 39, 52, 53
5. Operations Security: Chapters 13, 14, 15, 19, 21, 24, 36, 40, 47, 53, 57
6. Physical Security: Chapters 4, 13, 15, 19, 22, 23, 28, 29
7. Cryptography: Chapters 7, 32, 37, 42
8. Telecomm, Networks, and Internet Security: Chapters 4, 5, 6, 13, 14, 15, 16, 17, 18, 20, 21, 24, 25, 26, 27, 30, 31, 32, 33, 34, 35, 41, 48
9. Business Continuity Planning: Chapters 22, 23, 56, 57, 58, 59, 60
10. Law, Investigations, and Ethics: Chapters 11, 12, 13, 31, 42, 61

We have continued our practice from the fourth and fifth editions of inviting a security luminary to write the final chapter, "The Future of Information Assurance." We are pleased to include this stellar contribution from Jeremy A. Hansen.

SEYMOUR BOSWORTH
Editor-in-Chief
February 2014

ACKNOWLEDGMENTS

Seymour Bosworth, Editor-in-Chief. I would like to give grateful recognition to Arthur Hutt and Douglas Hoyt, my coeditors of the first, second, and third editions of this *Handbook.* Although both Art and Doug are deceased, their commitment and their competence remain as constant reminders that nothing less than excellence is acceptable. Mich Kabay, my coeditor from the fourth and fifth editions, and Eric Whyne, our fellow editor from the fifth and now sixth editions, continue in that tradition. I would not have wanted to undertake this project without them.

Thanks are also due to our colleagues at John Wiley & Sons: Tim Burgard as former Acquisitions Editor, Helen Cho as Editorial Program Coordinator, Sheck Ho as Executive Editor, Kimberly Kappmeyer as Production Editor, Natasha Andrews as Senior Production Editor, and Darice Moore as Copyeditor. All have performed their duties in an exemplary manner and with unfailing kindness, courtesy, and professionalism.

M. E. Kabay, Technical Editor. I want to thank my beloved wife, Deborah Black, light of my life, for her support and understanding over the years that this project has taken away from our time together. I am also grateful to the authors who have selflessly contributed so much to updating the material presented in this text.

Eric Whyne, Administrative Editor. An undertaking as big as pulling together this handbook would not be possible without my wife Lindsay and the love and support she gives to me and to our son Colton. I'd also like to thank the friends and mentors that have helped me most in my career: Mich and Sy, Tom Aldrich, Tom Payne, Frank Vanecek, and my parents Len and Terri. Any successful undertakings I've had, including this book, have been from listening to the advice they've given and aspiring to internalize the virtues that they exemplify. The authors who have contributed to this book also deserve many thanks for sharing their experience and wisdom. It is something for which I, myself, and the readers are extremely grateful.

A NOTE TO THE INSTRUCTOR

This two-volume text will serve the interests of practitioners and teachers of information assurance. The fourth edition and fifth editions of the *Handbook* were well received in academia; at least one-quarter of all copies were bought by university and college bookstores. The design of this sixth edition continues in the same vein and includes many updates to the material.

University professors looking for texts appropriate for a two-semester sequence of undergraduate courses in information assurance will find the *Handbook* most suitable. In my own work at Norwich University in Vermont, Volume I is the text for our *IS340 Introduction to Information Assurance* and Volume II is the basis for our *IS342 Management of Information Assurance* courses.

The text will also be useful as a resource in graduate courses. In the School of Graduate and Continuing Studies at Norwich University, both volumes have been used as required and supplementary reading for the 18-month, 36-credit Master's of Science in Information Security and Assurance program (MISA).

I will continue to create, update, and post PowerPoint lecture slides based on the chapters of the *Handbook* on my Website for free access by anyone applying them to noncommercial use (e.g., for self-study, for courses in academic institutions, and for unpaid industry training); the materials will be available in the IS340 and IS342 sections:

www.mekabay.com/courses/academic/norwich/is340/index.htm
www.mekabay.com/courses/academic/norwich/is342/index.htm

M. E. Kabay
Technical Editor
October 2013

INTRODUCTION TO PART IV

PREVENTION: HUMAN FACTORS

Human factors underlie all the mechanisms invented by technical experts. Without human awareness, training, education, and motivation, technical defenses inevitably fail. This part details a number of valuable areas of knowledge for security practitioners, including these chapters and topics:

43. **Ethical Decision Making and High Technology.** A strategy for setting a high priority on ethical behavior and a framework for making ethical decisions
44. **Security Policy Guidelines.** Guidelines for how to express security policies effectively
45. **Employment Practices and Policies.** Policy guidelines on hiring, managing, and firing employees
46. **Vulnerability Assessment.** Methods for smoothly integrating vulnerability assessments into the corporate culture
47. **Operations Security and Production Controls.** Running computer operations securely, and controlling production for service levels and quality
48. **E-Mail and Internet Use Policies.** Guidelines for setting expectations about employee use of the Web and e-mail at work
49. **Implementing a Security-Awareness Program.** Methods for ensuring that all employees are aware of security requirements and policies
50. **Using Social Psychology to Implement Security Policies.** Drawing on the science of social psychology for effective implementation of security policies
51. **Security Standards for Products.** Established standards for evaluating the trustworthiness and effectiveness of security products

CHAPTER 43

ETHICAL DECISION MAKING AND HIGH TECHNOLOGY

James Landon Linderman

43.1 INTRODUCTION: THE ABCs OF COMPUTER ETHICS

43.1.1 Why an Ethics Chapter in a Computer Security Handbook? In an information age, many potential misuses and abuses of information create privacy and security problems. In addition to possible legal issues, ethical issues affect many groups and individuals—including employees and customers, vendors, consultants, bankers, and stockholders—who have enough at stake in the matter to confront and even destroy an organization over ethical lapses. As is so often the case, consciousness raising is at the heart of maintaining control.

In this chapter, the term "ethics" refers to a system of moral principles that relate to the benefits and harms of particular actions and to the rightness and wrongness of motives and ends of these actions. The major sections cover principles of ethics, tests to help recognize ethical and unethical behavior, and approaches to help ensure good ethical conduct.

43.1.2 How Much Time Do You Have for This Chapter? Section 43.2 requires only one minute to read, but it forms the foundation of this chapter and of a lifelong concern for one of the most important requisites of a valued career and of a civilized society. Ethics matters, and here are the ABCs:

Section 43.2 **A**wareness (a one-minute primer)
Section 43.3 **B**asics (a 10-minute summary)
Section 43.4 **C**onsiderations (a 100-minute study)
Section 43.5 **D**etails (a lifetime of ongoing commitment)

43.2 AWARENESS.

The sections that follow distill some of the most important issues.

43.2.1 Principle 1: Ethics Counts. Increasingly, society is holding individuals and organizations to higher ethical standards than in the past; for example, in recent years, many countries have passed privacy legislation, conflict-of-interest restrictions for public officials, and full-disclosure laws for candidates for a variety of public offices. People, individually and collectively, really want to trust others. Two corollaries to the principle that ethics counts are:

1. Good ethical standards are usually good for business.
2. Violations of ethics are almost always bad for business.

In other words, good ethical behavior usually is appreciated by society, and bad ethical behavior almost always is frowned on and punished—sooner or later.

43.2.2 Principle 2: Ethics Is Everybody's Business. A second important principle is that good ethics flourishes best when everyone works at it, both in practicing good ethics and in holding others to do so. The reverse of this is also true: Those who practice bad ethics, or choose to ignore the bad ethics of others, are truly part of the problem. Ethics is inescapably everybody's business.

43.2.3 A Test: Put Yourself in Another's Shoes. One of the best evaluators of whether certain behavior is ethical or not invites you to put yourself in the other person's shoes and ask the role-reversal question: "What if I were on the receiving end of the behavior in question?" This variant of the time-honored golden rule translates to "If I wouldn't like it done to me, I probably shouldn't do it to others."

43.2.4 An Approach: Disclose! One of the best guidelines to help ensure good ethical behavior is to let your stakeholders in on what you are doing or are about to do. Good ethics flourishes in the light of day; bad ethics ultimately relies on concealment.

Disclosure buys you two forms of peace of mind: First, you're being openly honest; second, if others do not like it, you have at least given them the opportunity to express their concerns.

For example, consider organizational policy about managers reading employee email. Almost any policy (anywhere from aggressive intervention to complete hands off) is likely to be ethical if and only if employees are made aware of it.

43.3 BASICS.

The expansion of Section 43.2 that follows elaborates on the basic principles enunciated there.

43.3.1 Principle 3: Stakeholders Dictate Ethics.

Stakeholders are defined as any individuals or groups with something at stake in the outcome of a decision. In the world of business, stockholders are almost always stakeholders; employees, customers, suppliers, and even competitors are often stakeholders too. How a decision harms or benefits stakeholders is a major ethical consideration. Effects on stakeholders are so important that the best place to start looking at the ethics of a decision is to identify stakeholders and just what it is they have at stake. Decisions will invariably affect individuals and groups, often in opposite ways: Some may stand to gain, others to lose or suffer. The effects and trade-offs raise the principal ethics concerns.

43.3.2 Principle 4: Traditional Principles Still Apply.

Recent generations are not the first to raise questions and develop ideas about ethics, although the concept of business ethics has been mocked as an oxymoron and only recently promoted in academia as a valuable area of study. High technology has complicated some issues, but these fundamental principles still apply:

- The Golden Rule ("Do unto others as you would have them do unto you") and its variants have already been mentioned. These principles remain timeless and fundamental.
- Consideration of the interplay of duties, rights, and responsibilities remains important. When making ethical decisions, we normally examine the legal, professional, and customary constraints on behavior that apply to our situation.
- Traditional reasons for good ethical behavior, such as religious principles, egoism, utilitarianism, and altruism, still provide us with a useful taxonomy for discussions about ethics.

The point is that even though modern technology has created new opportunities for unethical behavior and new motivations for good ethical behavior, it has not been necessary to develop new principles to deal with ethics. For example, many of the principles (including politeness) governing the behavior of door-to-door sales still apply to Internet push technology.

43.3.3 More Tests.

In Section 43.2.3, we suggested the "other's shoes test" as an excellent evaluator of whether certain behavior is ethical or not. Here we introduce three other tests. The first two are negative in the sense of suggesting that behavior is inappropriate; the third is positive and suggests that the behavior in question is ethical.

1. The "mom test" asks how your mom (spouse, children, best friend, etc.) would react if aware of your actions. If you would be embarrassed having someone close to you know what is going on, the odds are pretty good it is unethical.
2. The "eye-team test" takes this a step further and considers the results of exposing your actions to the whole world as part of an investigative team broadcast. Again, the more embarrassment, the more likely the unethical nature of the actions.
3. The "market test" asks you to think about openly publicizing your actions as a competitive customer relations strategy. Never mind whether such a marketing strategy is actually feasible; if such exposure could impress others favorably, chances are you are on solid ethical ground.

43.3.4 A Guideline Approach: Ask! Section 43.2.4 endorsed disclosure as one of the best guidelines to help ensure good ethical behavior. This simply means letting your stakeholders in on what you are doing, or about to do. Having done so, it then becomes an appropriate guideline to ask those stakeholders for their permission (or acquiescence, or at least acknowledgment) before you proceed. This can be in the form of allowing stakeholders to opt out of certain policies. Many stakeholders prefer an opt-in approach rather than a default assumption of acceptability, particularly if that assumption is nonintuitive or otherwise obscure.

An example of this approach to ethical behavior is the legally enforced requirement in many countries to ask customers for permission to use their personally identifiable information for purposes other than the original defined functions. Typically, customers have either to opt out of information sharing or opt in to such use of their information.

In other cases, stakeholders such as employees or shareholders may disagree with the ethical implications of proposed actions. They can then argue against the proposals to the extent possible. The ultimate option for such stakeholders is to withdraw; employees can resign and shareholders can sell their shares. If the proposed actions are perceived as illegal, critics can become whistle-blowers and report the suspected illegality to law enforcement and regulatory officials.

43.3.5 Another Guideline Approach: An Ethics Officer. Designating an individual to serve as a full- or part-time ethics officer in an enterprise is a powerful, proactive way to help ensure good ethical behavior. Many large organizations now consider this a position on the top management team. But even small organizations can formally delegate such responsibilities on a part-time basis; they need not require much time and energy of the individual involved. In all cases, the common objectives include:

- Clear management commitment to good business ethics, including adequate resources to support this position
- Organizational recognition that this individual has appropriate authority and responsibility, and is a conduit of information into and within the organization
- Hassle-free avenues of access to this person

43.4 CONSIDERATIONS. This section discusses some issues of management style in promulgating and enforcing ethics.

43.4.1 Principle 5: Ethics Need Not and Should Not Be a Hassle. The last thing one wants with business ethics is hassle. An organization's ethics policies should not be obscure, complicated, onerous, or an obstacle to getting things done. The keys to avoiding hassles include:

- Clear and straightforward articulation of ethics policies
- Consciousness raising as a prime objective of ethics policies
- Clear, comfortable, and safe access to interpretation, for example, by an ethics officer
- Consistency in promulgation, education, application, and enforcement

Employees should not have to guess what constitutes acceptable behavior, nor should they be encumbered by anxiety, guilt, or fear. Individuals should be able to gain clarification on matters before, during, or after events without delay and without fear of being considered a nuisance. Questions about ethics issues deserve unbiased answers, without the presumption that there has been a breach of ethical conduct or that ulterior motives are involved.

Whenever an individual is uncomfortable with a situation or a potential situation, whether he or she is directly involved or not, and particularly if "whistle-blowing" implicates others or even organizational policy, that discomfort needs to be addressed. Even if the individual is wrong and should not be concerned, the discomfort should be dispelled. If the individual is right and there is a legitimate concern, the organization should resolve the issue in a way that does not put the whistle-blower on the spot but rather indicates support for such disclosure.

43.4.2 Principle 6: Ethics Policies Deserve Formality. Like other important policies, an organization's ethics policies deserve formality:

- Clear documentation
- Clear motivation
- Clear sanctions
- Clear management support at every level, including the top

Anything less than the foregoing suggests confusion at best and lip service at worst. Formality should not mean bureaucracy or piles of manuals. Consistent with the fifth principle of avoiding hassles, documentation should be brief and clear, and directed at simplifying matters rather than complicating them. The preparation and presentation of policies should reflect a process of thoughtful, high-priority consideration.

A corollary of this principle is peer participation. Policies that ultimately rely on organizational support are best developed and disseminated with peer involvement.

43.4.3 Principle 7: Ethics Policies Deserve Review. Perhaps the only thing as dangerous as ignorance when it comes to policy is complacency. This is as true of ethics policies as it is of any other organizational policy. In particular, to assume everyone in an organization is on board with policy is naïve at best. Review offers a type of preventive maintenance whereby policies and their promulgation are reconsidered with an eye to improvement.

Any organizational policy requires subscription on the part of the members of the organization. Understanding of and compliance with any policy suffers a dangerous tendency to lapse when a policy simply gathers dust. Even an occasional mention and discussion of ethical issues or principles during meetings can breathe new life into old policy.

Just as a corollary of Principle 6 was peer participation in the formalization of policy, so is peer involvement a corollary of policy review. Such peer review not only facilitates fresh insights into policy, but the process itself represents a powerful educational opportunity.

43.4.4 Principle 8: Anticipate. Few people relish the prospect of a serious breach of organizational ethics, particularly if matters reach the point of embarrassing publicity or even legal action. It is better to contemplate the worst scenarios in advance rather than to deal with them without preparation and after the fact. Wishful thinking often deters an organization from including appropriate issues in formal policy. This must not be permitted to happen.

It is better to address tough issues head on than to take anything for granted. The two best ways of doing so are to:

1. Have comprehensive policies that cover any foreseeable eventuality.
2. Have a full- or part-time ethics officer in place to stay on top of things.

43.4.5 The Smell Test. Sometimes the other tests discussed (other's shoes, mom, eye-team, market) can result in fuzzy or ambiguous analysis. It may be hard to put yourself in someone else's shoes, especially if different individuals would have widely different reactions to your behavior. And sometimes your family and friends, the general public, or your customers could be neutral or divided in their reactions. The so-called smell test does not require quantitative or even qualitative estimations; it simply relies on your intuition as to whether the behavior in question "smells fishy." In other words, if you catch yourself seeking justifications, or feel a bit uncomfortable even thinking about the implications, the ethics may be as bad or poor as they smell.

43.4.6 An Approach: Stocktaking. Where can an organization start with all this if it has not already done so? Things usually start with a concerned individual (you?) doing some stocktaking and consciousness raising. Questions for you and others in your organization to consider follow. If you like the answers, then your organization is ethically aware. If you do not like the answers, your organization must deal with the issues you have uncovered.

- If you felt that a fellow employee was misusing company resources or harassing someone, is it obvious what you should do? Is there someone in the organization you could comfortably talk with?
- Do you have the sense that top management in your organization is aware of ethics issues? Do you have the sense that they care?
- Do you know if your organization monitors employee email or computer usage? How much personal business, such as email and net surfing, is permissible on company time?
- How important is quality to your company's products and services? Are marketing claims consistent with quality?
- What, if any, information does your company capture about customers, suppliers, or employees without their permission? Without even their knowledge? What, if

any, information does your company provide to entities outside the organization about customers, suppliers, or employees without their permission? Without even their knowledge?

- Does your organization fully comply with license arrangements and payments for software and hardware?
- Are customers, suppliers, and employees always treated with dignity and respect? How would a stakeholder (e.g., a new employee) become aware of organizational ethics policies?

For each of these questions, the issue of how one knows must be raised. Ambiguous, confusing, or unreliable knowledge of what is or is not going on should raise red flags of concern. Discomfort with such knowledge may be symptomatic of underlying problems with ethics.

The stocktaking just suggested should translate into action steps for your organization. Here are a few suggested actions to get started.

- Ask some of your peers to consider the same stock-taking questions, and compare their thoughts with yours.
- Itemize and prioritize any concerns.
- Make an appointment with someone fairly high up in management to discuss those concerns. If you are that someone, make an appointment with two or three peers and with subordinates who represent the staff.
- Examine the feasibility of appointing a full- or part-time ethics officer while considering the downside of not having one.
- Ask your internal or external auditors to consider an audit of your ethics policies the next time they do a financial or operational audit.

43.5 CONCLUDING REMARKS.

As with security awareness, ethical awareness needs freshness and repetition.

43.5.1 How to Keep Up.

One of the best ways for individuals and organizations to keep up with matters of good ethics is to spread the job around. Do not try to shoulder the effort alone; it will likely overwhelm any one individual, and collective thinking is valuable in these matters. Without abrogating individual responsibilities, charging the right person with the job of ethics officer will certainly help to keep the enterprise on an appropriate ethical course. A growing number of periodicals, both professional and of general interest, include articles involving ethics. Reading and then discussing them with your peers can be invaluable. Additionally, there has been an increase in the number of Websites addressing ethical issues. See Section 43.6.

43.5.2 Why to Keep Up.

Keeping on top of organizational ethics is important because it is the right thing to do. Contemporary business practice embraces the idea of an extended value chain where entities such as customers and suppliers, traditionally seen as outside organizational boundaries, are now viewed as partners. Strategic alliances are being formed with these entities, and keeping business partners satisfied and confident is now a strategic necessity. Souring the relationship by a breach of ethics is completely inconsistent with sound business practices. Even if customers and suppliers are not formally viewed as business partners, they are still essential to doing business and are not to be taken for granted. At the very least, given the range of alternative choices available today, unfair exploitation and other forms of unethical practice expose an organization to outright abandonment.

Finally, in the spirit of total quality management, whereby everyone in the enterprise is seen to contribute to its success or failure, your enterprise can be said to be counting on you. The converse may also be true: Your job and your future career may well depend on the success of your enterprise. The good ethics of your organization reflect favorably on you and your colleagues, but bad ethics will have an opposite effect.

43.6 FURTHER READING.

A list follows of some books and Websites that will be helpful to readers seeking further discussion of ethical decision making in general, and ethics in business and high technology.

Barger, R. N. "In Search of a Common Rationale for Computer Ethics," 1994; www.nd.edu/~rbarger/common-rat.html

Computer Ethics Institute. www.computerethicsinstitute.org

Cavazos, E., and G. Morin. *Cyberspace and the Law: Your Rights and Duties in the On-Line World.* Cambridge, MA: MIT Press, 1996.

Computer & Information Ethics Resources on Center for Applied Ethics, University of British Columbia. www.ethicsweb.ca/resources

Vance, David (ed.). "Information System Ethics." http://cyberethics.cbi.msstate.edu

Cyber Citizen Partnership. Information Technology Association of America (ITAA) & Department of Justice (DoJ). www.cybercitizenship.org

Cyberangels. www.cyberangels.org

Cyberspacers (kids' site). www.cyberspacers.com/home.html

EpistemeLinks. Philosophy Resources on the Internet—Computer Ethics. http://tinyurl.com/33kduz (URL inactive).

Ess, C. *Digital Media Ethics.* Polity, 2013.

Ethics and Information Technology (journal). www.springer.com/computer/programming/journal/10676

Floridi, L. "Information Ethics: On the Philosophical Foundations of Computer Ethics." Version 2.0, 1998; www.philosophyofinformation.net/publications/pdf/ieotpfoce2.pdf

Forester, T., and P. Morrison. *Computer Ethics: Cautionary Tales and Ethical Dilemmas in Computing.* Cambridge, MA: MIT Press, 1990.

Gaskin, S., and A. Evans. *GO! Ethics in Cyberspace: Getting Started* 2nd Ed. Prentice-Hall, 2013.

Gotterbarn, D. K. W. Miller, J. Impagliazzo, and A. Z. B. A. Bakar. *Computing Ethics: A Multicultural Approach.* Chapman & Hall, 2013.

Institute for Global Ethics. www.globalethics.org

Johnson, D. O. *Computer Ethics*, 3rd ed. New York: Prentice-Hall, 2000.

Kabay, M. E. "Hacker Tips Published in *Wall Street Journal*." *Network World Security Strategies*, August 28, 2007; www.networkworld.com/newsletters/sec/2007/0827sec1.html

Kabay, M. E. "Ethical Decision-Making: Identifying the Ethical Issue," *Network World Security Strategies*, August 30, 2007; www.networkworld.com/newsletters/sec/2007/0827sec2.html

Kabay, M. E. "Ethical Decision-Making: Using Formal and Informal Guidelines," *Network World Security Strategies*, September 4, 2007; www.networkworld.com/newsletters/sec/2007/0903sec1.html

Kabay, M. E. "Ethical Decision-Making: Principles, Rights and Duties, and Intuitive Cues," *Network World Security Strategies*, September 6, 2007; www.networkworld.com/newsletters/sec/2007/0903sec2.html

Kabay, M. E. "Ethics." Section of Website. www.mekabay.com/ethics/index.htm

Kabay, M. E. "Incident Response: Don't Lie," *Network World Security Strategies*, October 23, 20/07; www.networkworld.com/newsletters/sec/2007/1022sec1.html

Kallman, E. A., and J. P. Grillo. *Ethical Decision Making and Information Technology: An Introduction with Cases*, 2nd ed. New York: McGraw-Hill, 1996.

Kizza, M. *Ethical and Social Issues in the Information Age*, 5th ed. Springer, 2013.

Lessig, L., D. Post, and E. Volokh. "Cyberspace Law for Non-Lawyers." Published via email, 1997; www.ssrn.com/update/lsn/cyberspace/csl_lessons.html (URL inactive).

Online Ethics Center for Engineering and Science. http://onlineethics.org

Orlando, J., and M. E. Kabay. "Social Engineering in Penetration Testing: Cases," *Network World Security Strategies*, October 25, 2007; www.networkworld.com/newsletters/2007/1022sec2.html

Pimple, K. *Emerging Pervasive Information and Communication Technologies (PICT): Ethical Challenges, Opportunities and Safeguards*. Springer, 2013.

Project NEThics at the University of Maryland. www.inform.umd.edu/CompRes/NEThics/ethics (URL inactive).

Schumacher, P., and M. E. Kabay. "Social Engineering in Penetration Testing: Intimidation," *Network World Security Strategies*, November 8, 2007; www.networkworld.com/newsletters/sec/2007/1105sec2.html

Schumacher, P., and M. E. Kabay. "Social Engineering in Penetration Testing: Overload and Fascination," *Network World Security Strategies*, November 13, 2007; www.networkworld.com/newsletters/sec/2007/1112sec1.html

Spinello, R. *Cyberethics: Morality and Law in Cyberspace*, 5th ed. Jones & Bartlett Learning, 2013

Tavani, H. T. *Ethics and Technology: Controversies, Questions, and Strategies for Ethical Computing*. 4th ed. Hoboken, NJ: Wiley, 2012.

Thies, C. *Computer Law and Ethics*. Mercury Learning & Information, 2013.

Thinkquest. "Computer Ethics." http://library.thinkquest.org/26658/?tqskip=1

University of British Columbia Centre for Applied Ethics. www.ethics.ubc.ca

Web Wise Kids. www.webwisekids.com

CHAPTER 44

SECURITY POLICY GUIDELINES

M. E. Kabay and Bridgitt Robertson

44.1 INTRODUCTION. This chapter reviews principles, topics, and resources for creating effective security policies. It does not propose specific guidelines except as examples. Many of the chapters in this *Handbook* discuss policy; examples include:

- Chapter 23 provides an extensive overview of physical security policies
- Chapter 25 discusses local area network security issues and policies
- Chapter 38 reviews software development policies
- Chapter 39 surveys quality assurance policies
- Chapter 43 discusses ethics
- Chapter 45 provides guidance on employment policies from a security standpoint

- Chapter 47 includes policies for improving operations security and production
- Chapter 48 reviews specific recommendations for email and Internet usage
- Chapter 49 looks at methods for enhancing security awareness
- Chapter 52 offers policies for secure application design
- Chapters 56 through 59 deal with policies for emergency response, backup, and recovery
- Chapter 61 presents policies for working effectively with law enforcement
- Chapter 66 discusses effective methods for developing security policies in specific organizations

44.2 TERMINOLOGY.

One of the preeminent leaders in security policy development, Charles Cresson Wood, has emphasized that when developing policy, it helps to segregate information that has different purposes. Specifically, one should create different documents for policy, standards, and procedures.[1]

44.2.1 Policy.

The term "policy" is defined as the rules and regulations set by the organization. Policies are laid down by management in compliance with applicable law, industry regulations, and the decisions of enterprise leaders. Policies are mandatory; they are expressed in definite language and require compliance. Failure to conform to policy can result in disciplinary action, termination of employment, and even legal action. Familiar examples of policy include requirements for background checks when hiring employees, the obligation to follow laws governing the duplication of proprietary software, and restrictions on the use of corporate vehicles for private purposes.

Security policy governs how an organization's information is to be protected against breaches of security; examples include policies on identification and authentication, authorization for specific kinds of access to specific data, responsibilities for data protection, limitations on the use of corporate resources for email and Internet access, and restrictions on installation of programs on corporate systems. Policies are the basis for security awareness, training, and education; they are a necessary underpinning for security audits. Without policies, it is impossible to demonstrate due diligence in the protection of corporate assets.

Policies are focused on the desired results, not on the means for achieving those results. The methods for achieving policies are defined in the next sections on controls, standards, and procedures.

44.2.2 Controls.

When developing a framework for implementing security policies, controls are the measures used to protect systems against specific threats. For example, a policy might stipulate that all production systems must be protected against unauthorized modification of data by programmers; a specific control that could be named in the policy might be that test data extracted by programmers from the production databases must be anonymized to protect confidential data.

44.2.3 Standards.

A standard in computing can be an accepted specification for hardware, software, or human actions. An example of a technical standard is the Transmission Control Protocol/Internet Protocol (TCP/IP) that governs how systems can be interconnected into the Internet.

Standards can be de facto when they are so widely used that new applications routinely respect their conventions; an example is the Hewlett-Packard interface bus

(HP-IB), which became so popular that it was eventually turned into a *de jure* standard when the Institute of Electrical and Electronics Engineers (IEEE) based its formal IEEE-488 standard on the HP-IB. In contrast, the Centronix parallel interface, although equally popular and universally used, remained proprietary.

In a corporate environment, the term "standard" refers to specific technical choices for implementing particular policies. For example, a corporate policy might stipulate that strong identification and authentication, selected by the technical staff, must be used when gaining access to restricted data; the corresponding standard might specify that a particular brand and model of a microprocessor-equipped smart card should be used in satisfying access control restrictions. Typically, standards are of concern to those who must implement policies; not all standards need be made known to all personnel. Standards also must change in response to a changing technical environment; typically standards change much more rapidly than policies.

44.2.4 Procedures. Procedures prescribe how people are to behave in implementing policies. For example, a policy might stipulate that all confidential communications from employees traveling outside the enterprise must be encrypted; the corresponding standard might define the proprietary virtual private network (VPN) software and hardware needed to implement that policy; and the corresponding procedure would explain in detail each step required to initiate a secure connection using that particular VPN.

44.3 RESOURCES FOR POLICY WRITERS.

If one is setting out to create policy *de novo* (i.e., without a preexisting policy document), it is critically important to use an existing policy template. Creating policies without guidance from experienced policy writers is a time-consuming, frustrating job that can consume thousands of hours of time, cause dissension within the enterprise, and leave everyone so disgusted that the policies end up turning into *shelfware*: stored, but never used. There are several well-recognized resources for helping policy writers structure their work, avoid pitfalls, and save enormous amounts of time. In the review that follows, readers will find information about these resources:

- ISO 17799
- COBIT®
- CERT-CC documentation
- NSA Security Guidelines
- U.S. Federal Best Security Practices
- RFC 2196
- IT Baseline Protection Manual
- Commercial policy guides

44.3.1 ISO/IEC 27002:2005. An increasingly popular standard for writing and implementing security policies, especially in Europe, is ISO/IEC 27002:2005, which is the current version of ISO/IEC 17799:2005, in turn based on the old BS7799.

The British Standard 7799 (BS7799) originated in the U.K. Department of Trade and Industry as a code of practice; it was formally renamed the BS7799 in February 1995. BS7799 was not adopted quickly in Great Britain because it was not flexible enough, it used a simplistic security model, and there were more pressing issues, such as the imminent arrival of the Y2K problem.[2] In addition, BS7799 was a proprietary standard for which users had to pay the equivalent of several hundred dollars before accessing the full documentation.

Version 2 of BS7799 was published in May 1999, and that year also saw the establishment of formal certification and accreditation methods. At that point, the International Organization for Standardization (ISO) began the process of defining BS7799 as an international standard; ISO 17799 was published in 1999. In 2005, the standard was renamed as ISO/IEC 17799:2005 in collaboration with the International Electrochemical Commission (IEC). It was then renamed in 2007.[3]

With the increasing interest in security, ISO/IEC 27002:2005 certification has been established as a goal for many organizations throughout the world. Major consultancies have trained their auditing staff for compliance with ISO/IEC 27002:2005; e-commerce is also a driving force behind the push for certification. One possible motivation is the experience of the ISO 9000 (quality) certification process in the 1980s; certification soon became a competitive edge and then a competitive requirement to maintain and develop market share.

In the context of policy development, ISO/IEC 27002:2005 offers a convenient framework to help policy writers structure their project in accordance with an international standard. The abstract from the ISO follows.

> ISO/IEC 27002:2005 comprises ISO/IEC 17799:2005 and ISO/IEC 17799:2005/Cor.1:2007. Its technical content is identical to that of ISO/IEC 17799:2005. ISO/IEC 17799:2005/Cor.1: 2007 changes the reference number of the standard from 17799 to 27002.
>
> ISO/IEC 27002:2005 establishes guidelines and general principles for initiating, implementing, maintaining, and improving information security management in an organization. The objectives outlined provide general guidance on the commonly accepted goals of information security management. ISO/IEC 27002:2005 contains best practices of control objectives and controls in the following areas of information security management:
>
> - security policy;
> - organization of information security;
> - asset management;
> - human resources security;
> - physical and environmental security;
> - communications and operations management;
> - access control;
> - information systems acquisition, development and maintenance;
> - information security incident management;
> - business continuity management;
> - compliance.
>
> The control objectives and controls in ISO/IEC 27002:2005 are intended to be implemented to meet the requirements identified by a risk assessment. ISO/IEC 27002:2005 is intended as a common basis and practical guideline for developing organizational security standards and effective security management practices, and to help build confidence in inter-organizational activities.

The full text of ISO/IEC 27002:2005 is available in electronic format or on paper from the ISO. In addition, a variety of guides are available to help organizations to develop ISO/IEC 27002:2005–compliant policies with minimal rewriting.[4]

44.3.2 COBIT. The *Control Objectives for Information and related Technology* (COBIT) provide a business-oriented set of standards for guiding management in the sound use of information technology.[5] COBIT was developed by volunteers working under the aegis of the IT Governance Institute (ITGI), which was itself founded by the Information Systems Audit and Control Association (ISACA).

COBIT is an information technology (IT) governance framework and supporting tool set that allows managers to bridge the gap between control requirements, technical issues, and business risks. COBIT enables clear policy development and good practice for IT control throughout organizations. COBIT was first published by ITGI in April 1996. ITGI's latest update—COBIT 5, published in 2012—emphasizes regulatory compliance, helps organizations to increase the value attained from IT, highlights links between business and IT goals, and simplifies implementation of the COBIT framework. COBIT 5 is a fine-tuning of the COBIT framework and can be used to enhance work already done based on earlier versions of COBIT. When major activities are planned for IT governance initiatives, or when an overhaul of the enterprise control framework is anticipated, it is recommended to start fresh with COBIT 5. COBIT 5 presents activities in a more streamlined and practical manner so continuous improvement in IT governance is easier than ever to achieve.[6]

COBIT Case Studies provide specific examples of how the framework has been applied.[7] The extensive *Frequently Asked Questions* provide detailed guidance for managers beginning their study of the standard.[8] ISACA also provides an interactive, Web-enabled version of COBIT that allows registered users to "construct and download [their] own, personalized version of COBIT for use on the desktop in MS Word or Access format."[9] Different levels of detail are available for visitors, ISACA members, and purchasers. ISACA also offers training courses[10] as shown:

- COBIT 5 Foundation
- COBIT 5 Implementation
- COBIT 5 Assessor Course

44.3.3 Informal Security Standards. In addition to the formal standards just discussed, several sets of guidelines have garnered a degree of acceptance as the basis for exercising due diligence in the protection of information systems. These informal standards include:

- CERT-CC security improvement modules
- Security guidelines handbook from the U.S. National Security Agency (NSA)
- RFC 2196 from the Internet Engineering Task Force
- IT baseline protection manual from the German Information Security Department

44.3.3.1 CERT-CC® Documentation. The Computer Emergency Response Team Coordination Center (CERT-CC)® at the Software Engineering Institute (SEI) of Carnegie Mellon University (CMU) has compiled a series of security improvement modules (www.cert.org/certcc.html) on these topics:

Vulnerability Remediation

- Current Vulnerability Work
- Vulnerability Notes Database

CSIRT Community

- CSIRT Development
- National CSIRTs

Secure Coding

- Secure Coding Project Page
- Secure Coding Standards

Artifact Analysis

In addition, CERT expert Julia H. Allen published an excellent guide in 2001 that has retained its value.[11] Chapter headings for this 480-page text are listed next.

1. The CERT Guide to System and Network Security Practices
2. Securing Network Servers and User Workstations
3. Securing Public Web Servers
4. Deploying Firewalls
5. Setting Up Intrusion Detection and Response Preparation
6. Detecting Signs of Intrusion
7. Responding to Intrusions
8. Appendix A: Security Implementations
9. Appendix B: Practice-Level Policy Considerations

44.3.3.2 NSA Security Guidelines. The National Security Agency (NSA) of the United States has published a freely available *Security Guidelines Handbook*.[12] The preface describes it in this way:

> This handbook is designed to introduce you to some of the basic security principles and procedures with which all NSA employees must comply. It highlights some of your security responsibilities, and provides guidelines for answering questions you may be asked concerning your association with this Agency. Although you will be busy during the forthcoming weeks learning your job, meeting co-workers, and becoming accustomed to a new work environment, you are urged to become familiar with the security information contained in this handbook.

This set of employee policies is tailored to the needs of the high-security NSA, but it provides useful information that all organizations can adapt to their own requirements. According to the table of contents, these topics are included:

Initial Security Responsibilities

- Anonymity
- Answering Questions about Your Employment
- Answering Questions about Your Agency Training
- Verifying Your Employment
- The Agency and Public News Media

General Responsibilities

- Espionage and Terrorism
- Classification

- Need-to-Know
- For Official Use Only
- Prepublication Review
- Personnel Security Responsibilities
- Association with Foreign Nationals
- Correspondence with Foreign Nationals
- Embassy Visits
- Amateur Radio Activities
- Unofficial Foreign Travel
- Membership in Organizations
- Changes in Marital Status/Cohabitation/Names
- Use and Abuse of Drugs
- Physical Security Policies
- The NSA Badge
- Area Control
- Items Treated as Classified
- Prohibited Items
- Exit Inspection
- Removal of Material from NSA Spaces
- External Protection of Classified Information
- Reporting Loss or Disclosure of Classified Information
- Use of Secure and Nonsecure Telephones

Helpful Information

- Security Resources

44.3.3.3 U.S. Federal Best Security Practices. The United States Federal Chief Information Officers (CIO) Council has created a Best Practices Committee that provides extensive free documentation for policy makers.[13] The committee is defined in this way:

> The Best Practices Committee (BPC) is established by the CIO Council Charter to serve as a focal point for promoting information management/information technology (IM/IT) best practices within the federal government. The BPC brings together a team of IT professionals committed to identifying the most successful of IM/IT practices being implemented in industry, government, and academia, and sharing them with agency CIOs as best practices, to be considered for emulation throughout the Federal government. It is about sharing the successes of others, and *not reinventing the wheel.* It is about constantly learning and applying working models to reduce complexity and achieve results. It is also about cost avoidance and sound stewardship of the taxpayers' dollars.

There is an extensive collection of documents freely available in PDF format for downloading.[14] Some of the topics in the collection of particular interest for this chapter's context include:

- Best Practices
- Enterprise Architecture

- IT Security/Privacy
- GAO Reports
- IT-Related Laws and Regulations

44.3.3.4 RFC 2196 (Site Security Handbook). The Internet Engineering Task Force (IETF) has an extensive list of informational documents called Requests for Comments (RFCs) governing all aspects of the Internet.[15] One document of particular value to any organization trying to improve its security practices is the classic *Site Security Handbook*, RFC 2196, edited by B. Fraser of the Software Engineering Institute at Carnegie Mellon University, the same body that hosts the CERT-CC.[16] The *Handbook* has this structure:

Introduction

- Purpose of this Work
- Audience
- Definitions
- Related Work
- Basic Approach
- Risk Assessment

Security Policies

- What Is a Security Policy and Why Have One?
- What Makes a Good Security Policy?
- Keeping the Policy Flexible

Architecture

- Objectives
- Network and Service Configuration
- Firewalls

Security Services and Procedures

- Authentication
- Confidentiality
- Integrity
- Authorization
- Access
- Auditing
- Securing Backups

Security Incident Handling

- Preparing and Planning for Incident Handling
- Notification and Points of Contact
- Identifying an Incident

- Handling an Incident
- Aftermath of an Incident
- Responsibilities

Ongoing Activities
Tools and Locations
Mailing Lists and Other Resources
References

44.3.3.5 *IT-Grundschutz Catalogues.* The German government's computer security arm, the *Bundesamt für Sicherheit in der Informationstechnik*, has published a useful set of guidelines since 1997, the *IT-Grundschutzhandbuch.* Originally known in English as the *IT Baseline Protection Manual*, the most recent version as of this writing was published in 2005 and is available free in English as the *IT-Grundschutz Catalogues.*[17] The work is freely available in PDF in German, English, Swedish, and Estonian.

In general, each module presents concepts, threats and vulnerabilities, and countermeasures. This work is easy to understand and provides a sound basis for effective information security protection.

44.3.4 Commercially Available Policy Guides. There are several commercially available policy templates that save time when developing new policies or improving existing policies. Three of the particular values are discussed next.

44.3.4.1 *Charles Cresson Wood's* ISPME. The most widely used commercially available collection of security standards is the work by Charles Cresson Wood, *Information Security Policies Made Easy* (*ISPME*). The text includes a CD-ROM for easy access to the text so that users can avoid tedious retyping of existing materials.

Wood integrates the perspectives of both management and technical staff when making recommendations. He was one of the original promoters of information security as a way to achieve a competitive advantage and a coauthor of the first computer crime investigation manual. He was one of the first to advocate and document integration of information resource management concepts with information security activities, use of head-count ratio analysis to determine appropriate levels of information security staffing, an information security document life cycle for planning and budgeting purposes, and network management tools to achieve consistent and centralized systems security. He has also developed and successfully marketed two unique software packages that automate information security administration activities. In addition, he evaluated and recommended U.S. Government policies on open versus classified cryptographic research for Frank Press, President Carter's technology advisor.

One of the outstanding features of *ISPME* is that Wood explains every policy and sometimes provides opposing policies for use in different environments. His text is not only a set of templates but an excellent basis for teaching security principles by looking at the practice of security.

44.3.4.2 *Tom Peltier's Practitioner's Reference.* Tom Peltier is the Year 2001 Hall of Fame Award Recipient from the Information Systems Security Association (www.issa.org). The citation provides the background that explains why Peltier is so highly regarded in the field of security:

> Tom Peltier is in his fifth decade working with computer technology. During this time he has garnered numerous industry honors for sharing his experiences with follow professionals. Because of his work he was given the 1993 Computer Security Institute's (CSI) Lifetime Achievement Award. In 1999, the Information Systems Security Association (ISSA) bestowed on him its Individual Contribution to the Profession Award, and in 2001 he was inducted into the ISSA Hall of Fame. Tom was also awarded the CSI Lifetime Emeritus Membership Award.

Peltier's policy text is *Information Security Policies and Procedures*. He provides you with the tools you need to develop policies, procedures, and standards. He demonstrates the importance of a clear, concise, and well-written security program. His examination of recommended industry best practices illustrates how they can be customized to fit any organization's needs.

44.3.4.3 SANS Resources. The System Administration and Network Security (SANS) Institute is well known for the excellent security resources it makes available to members and the general public.

44.3.4.3.1 Security Essentials Courses. The SANS Security Essentials Courses (www.sans.org) provide a solid foundation for understanding the issues underlying security policies. Level 524, *Security Policy & Awareness* (www.sans.org), highlights this objective:

> This course is designed to offer an individual a comprehensive approach to understanding security awareness and developing security policy. Business needs change, the business environment changes, and critical systems are continually exposed to new and developing vulnerabilities. Security awareness training is an effective business strategy that reduces the overall risk to an organization, therefore minimizing user-related faults and errors that lead to destructive and costly security incidents. Security awareness and policy development and assessment are a never-ending process.

44.3.4.3.2 Free Resources. The SANS Institute offers many free resources. For details, see www.sans.org/free_resources.php?utm_source=web-sans&utm_medium=ImageReplace&utm_content=Main_resource_button_green&utm_campaign=Home Page&ref=3601. Topics include:

- Reading Room: Over 1,600 computer security white papers in over 70 categories
- Top 20: The Twenty Most Critical Internet Security Vulnerabilities
- Newsletters: Latest Security News

44.4 WRITING THE POLICIES.

How should one write security policies? Should they be suggestions? Orders? Positive? Negative? This section affirms that policies should be definite, unambiguous, and directive. In addition, all policies should have (preferably optional) explanations for the reasons behind them.

44.4.1 Orientation: Prescriptive and Proscriptive. Security policies should be written with clear indications that all employees are expected to conform to them. Language should be definite and unambiguous (e.g., "All employees must..." or "No employees shall..."). Some policies require people to do something—these are *prescriptive* (e.g., "Employees must follow the password procedures defined by the Information Protection Group at all times."). Other policies prohibit certain actions—these are *proscriptive* (e.g., "No employee shall make or order illegal copies of proprietary software under any circumstances.").

44.4.2 Writing Style. Each policy should be short. Simple declarative sentences are best; writers should avoid long compound sentences with multiple clauses. Details of implementation are appropriate for standards and procedures, not for policies. Policies can refer users to the appropriate documents for implementation details; for example, "Passwords shall be changed on a schedule defined in the *Security Procedures* from the Information Protection Group."

For more details on developing policy, see Chapter 45 in this *Handbook*.

44.4.3 Reasons. Few people like to be ordered about with arbitrary rules. Trying to impose what appear to be senseless injunctions can generate a tide of rebellion among employees. It is far better to provide explanations of why policies make sense for the particular enterprise; however, such explanations can make the policies tedious to read for more experienced users. A solution is to provide optional explanations. One approach is to summarize policies in one part of the document and then to provide an extensive expansion of all the policies in a separate section or a separate document. Another approach is to use hypertext, as explained in Section 44.6.3 of this chapter.

44.5 ORGANIZING THE POLICIES.

Policies are distinct from the sequence in which they are presented. It is useful to have two distinct presentation sequences for policies: topical and organizational.

44.5.1 Topical Organization. Security involves a multitude of details; how one organizes these details depends on the purpose of the policy document. The most common format puts policies in a sequence that corresponds to some reasonable model of how people perceive security. For example, employees can look at security with a rough correspondence to the physical world. Under this model, one might have a policy document with a table of contents that looks like this:

Principles
Organizational Reporting Structure
Physical Security

- Servers
- Workstations
- Portable computers

Hiring, Management, and Firing Data Protection

- Classifying information
- Data access controls
- Encryption
- Countering industrial espionage

Communications Security

- Perimeter controls
- Web usage and content filtering
- Email usage and privacy
- Telephone and fax usage

Software

- Authorized products only
- Proprietary (purchased) software
- Development standards
- Quality assurance and testing

Operating Systems

- Access controls
- Logging

Technical Support

- Service-level agreements
- Helpdesk functions

44.5.2 Organizational. The complete set of policies may be comprehensive, concise, and well written, but they will still likely be a daunting document, especially for nontechnical staff. To avoid distressing employees with huge tomes of incomprehensible materials, it makes sense to create special-purpose documents aimed at particular groups. For example, one could have guides like these:

- General Guide for Protecting Corporate Information Assets
- Guide for Users of Portable Computers
- A Manager's Guide to Security Policies
- Human Resources and Security
- Network Administration Security Policies
- Programmer's Guide to Security and Quality Assurance
- The Operator's Security Responsibilities
- Security and the Helpdesk

Each of these volumes or files can present just enough information to be useful and interesting to the readers without overwhelming them with detail. Each can make reference to the full policy document.

44.6 PRESENTING THE POLICIES.

What options do policy makers have for publishing their policies? This section discusses printing them on paper versus publishing them electronically.

44.6.1 Printed Text. Policies are not inherently interesting. Large volumes full of policies quickly become shelfware. Short paper documents, however, are familiar to people; they can be carried around, or placed at hand for easy reference anywhere. Reference cards, summary sheets, stickers, and posters are some of the printed media that can be useful in security awareness, training, and education programs. Printed text, like its electronic versions, provides the opportunity for typeface and color to be used in clarifying and emphasizing specific ideas. However, printed copies of policies share a universal disadvantage: They are difficult to update.

Updating dozens, hundreds, or thousands of individual copies of policy documents can be such a headache that organizations simply reprint the entire document rather than struggle with updates. Updates on individual sheets require the cooperation of every user to insert the new sheets and remove the old ones; experience teaches that many people simply defer such a task, sometimes indefinitely, and that others have an apparently limited understanding of the sequential nature of page numbers. Badly updated policy guides may be worse than none at all, especially from a legal standpoint. If an employee violates a new policy that has been promulgated verbally, but available manuals fail to reflect that new policy, it may be difficult to justify dismissal for wrongdoing.

44.6.2 Electronic One-Dimensional Text. Despite the familiarity and ubiquity of paper, in today's world of near-universal access to computers in the work environment, there is a place for electronic documentation of policies. Such publication has enormous advantages from an administrative standpoint. All access to the policies can be controlled centrally, at least in theory. Making the current version of the policies (and subsets of the policies, as explained in Section 44.5.2) available for reference on a server obviates the problem of updating countless independent copies and avoids the normal situation when using paper: chaotic differences among copies of different ages.

How can one cope with employees stubbornly determined to have their own local copies of the policies on their workstations? One solution to this problem of enforcing a single version is to alert every user to changes in the central copy, or to send every user copies of the appropriate documents by email, with a request to replace their copies of lower version number. Although this solution is not perfect, it does help to keep most people up to date.

44.6.3 Hypertext. Perhaps the most valuable contribution from electronic publication of policies is the availability of hypertext. Hypertext allows a reader to jump to a different section of text and then come back to the original place easily. On paper, forward and backward references are cumbersome, and most readers do not follow such links unless they are particularly keen on the extra information promised in the reference. In electronic files, however, additional information may be as easy to obtain as placing the cursor over a link and clicking.

The most important function of hypertext for policy documents is to provide definitions of technical terms and explanations of the reasons for specific policies.

Some users are more comfortable with printed policies. Hypertext, like other formats of text, generally permits users to print out their own copies of all or part of their policy documentation. Many of the tools also allow annotations by users on their own copy of a file.

44.6.3.1 HTML and XML. The most widely used hypertext format today is Hypertext Markup Language (HTML). Its variant Extensible Markup Language (XML), provides additional functionality for programmers, but from the user's perspective, the hyperlinks are the same. A simple click of the mouse in a Web browser (e.g., Microsoft Internet Explorer, Netscape Communicator, or Firefox) branches to a different page. More sophisticated programming allows the use of frames and, with Java or ActiveX, pop-up windows. Navigation buttons allow the user to move backward to a previous page or forward to another page. Links also can be used to open new windows so that several pages are visible at once. All of these techniques allow users to move freely through a text with full control over the degree of detail they wish to pursue.

44.6.3.2 Rich Text Format and Proprietary Word Processor Files. Some people prefer to use word processor files for hypertext. As long as everyone uses the same word processing software, this approach can work acceptably. For example, it is usually possible to insert a hyperlink to a section of a single document, to a location in a different file on disk, or to a page on the Web. Some word processors, such as Microsoft Word and Corel WordPerfect, allow one to insert pop-up comments; floating the cursor over highlighted text brings up a text box that can provide definitions and commentary.

In addition to explicit links, Microsoft Word and other modern word processing programs can display a table of headings that allows instant movement to any section of the document.

Rich text format (RTF) is a general format for interchanging documents among word processors, but the results are not always comparable. For example, a comment created using Microsoft Word shows up as a pop-up box with a word or phrase highlighted in the text; the same comment and marker read from an RTF file by Corel WordPerfect shows up as a balloon symbol in the left margin of the document.

44.6.3.3 Portable Document Format. Adobe Acrobat's portable document format (PDF) provides all the hyperlinking that HTML offers, but it does so in a form that is universally readable and that can be controlled more easily. The free Acrobat reader is available for multiple operating systems from www.adobe.com. PDF documents can be locked easily, for example, so that no unauthorized changes can be made. In addition, unlike HTML and word processor documents, PDF files can be constructed to provide near-perfect reproduction of their original appearance, even if not all the fonts used by the author are present on the target computer system.

44.6.3.4 Help Files. Help files also provide hypertext capability. In the Windows environment, one can create help files using utilities such as *Help & Manual* from EC Software GmbH. Entering the search string "create help files" into an Internet search engine brings up many pages of such tools. Windows Help files can be distributed easily to any Windows user because they are relatively small, and they are loaded almost instantly by the Help subsystem. In addition, users are permitted to add their own notes to such documents and can easily print out sections if they wish.

44.7 MAINTAINING POLICIES. No fixed policy document can cover all eventualities. The information security field changes constantly and so must policies. Information security is a process much like total quality management: For success, both require a thoroughgoing integration into corporate culture.

Above all, some named individuals must see maintaining security policies as an explicit part of their job descriptions. Hoping that someone will spontaneously maintain security policies is like hoping that someone will spontaneously maintain financial records. However, as explained in Chapter 45 of this *Handbook*, security policies should represent the best efforts of people from throughout the organization, not the arbitrary dictates of just one person.

44.7.1 Review Process. An information protection working group can meet regularly—quarterly is a good frequency to try—to review all or part of the policies. Employees can be encouraged to suggest improvements in policies or to propose new policies. The working group can identify key areas of greatest change and work on those first, leaving minor policy changes to subcommittees. Members of the working group should discuss ideas with their colleagues from throughout the enterprise, not just with each other. Every effort should contribute to increasing the legitimate sense of involvement in security policy by all employees, including managers and executives.

44.7.2 Announcing Changes. Drafts of the new versions can be circulated to the people principally affected by changes, so that their responses can improve the new edition. Truly respectful inquiry will result in a greater sense of ownership of the policies by employees, although few of them will rejoice in the new policies. Some employees will see new security policies merely as a mild irritant, while others may view them as a tremendous obstacle to productivity and a general nuisance.

Ideally, major changes in policy should be described and explained in several ways. For example, a letter or email (digitally signed, for security) from the president, chair of the board of directors, chief officers, or chief information security officer can announce important changes in policy and the reasons for the changes. A brief article in the organization's internal newsletter, or a spot on the intranet, can also provide channels for communicating the policy decisions to everyone involved.

Finally, the updated policies can be made available or distributed to all employees using some of the channels discussed in Section 44.6.

44.8 SUMMARY.

These 10 recommendations will help in preparing to create and implement security policies:

1. Distinguish among policies, controls, standards, and procedures.
2. Use all resources from government, industry bodies, and commercial organizations in preparing to create policies.
3. Use unambiguous prose when defining policies: Tell people what to *do* and what *not* to do.
4. Use short sentences.
5. Give reasons for policies.
6. Provide different views of policies—topical and organizational.
7. Provide several ways of reading the policies, including printed text, electronic text, and hypertext.
8. Review and improve or adapt policies regularly.
9. Circulate drafts showing changes in policies to interested participants before publishing them.
10. Announce major changes using high-level authorities within the enterprise.

44.9 FURTHER READING

Allen, J. H. *The CERT® Guide to System and Network Security Practices*. Reading, MA: Addison-Wesley, 2001.

Atkinson, J. M. "NSA Security Guidelines Handbook," National Security Agency Central Security Service, 2002. www.tscm.com/NSAsecmanual1.html

Barman, S. *Writing Information Security Policies*. Indianapolis: New Riders, 2001.

Boran, S. "IT Security Cookbook." 2009. www.boran.com/security/index.html

Clarke, R. "Best Practice Guidelines: Controls over the Security of Personal Information," 1993, www.anu.edu.au/people/Roger.Clarke/DV/PDSecy.html

Dubin, J. *The Little Black Book of Computer Security*, 2nd ed. 29th Street Press, 2008.

Flynn, N. *The E-Policy Handbook: Designing and Implementing Effective E-Mail, Internet, and Software Policies*, 2nd ed. AMACOM, 2009.

Greene, S. *Security Program and Policies: Principles and Practices*, 2nd ed. Pearson IT Certification, 2013.

Peltier, T. R. *Information Security Policies and Procedures: A Practitioner's Reference*, 2nd ed. Auerbach, 2004.

Portela, I. M., and F. Almeida, eds. *Organizational, Legal, and Technological Dimensions of Information System Administration*. IGI Global, 2013.

Wood, C. C. *Information Security Policies Made Easy, version 12*. Houston: Information Shield, 2012. www.informationshield.com/ispmemain.htm

44.10 NOTES

1. C. C. Wood, *Information Security Policies Made Easy,* version 12 (Houston: Information Shield, 2012), www.informationshield.com/ispmemain.htm
2. *ISO 17799 Information Security Portal,* www.computersecuritynow.com
3. ISO/IEC 27002:2005, "Information Technology—Security Techniques—Code of Practice for Information Security Management," www.iso.org/iso/home/store/catalogue_ics/catalogue_detail_ics.htm?csnumber=50297
4. Sites that provide free evaluation versions of policy guides include: "Information Security Policy World," www.information-security-policies-and-standards.com, and "Computer Security Policy Directory," www.computer-security-policies.com/index.htm
5. ISACA, "COBIT 5 Product Family," 2013, www.isaca.org/COBIT/Pages/Product-Family.aspx
6. ISACA, "COBIT 5: A Business Framework for the Governance and Management of Enterprise IT," 2013, www.isaca.org/COBIT/Pages/default.aspx
7. ISACA, "COBIT Recognition," 2013, www.isaca.org/COBIT/Pages/Recognition.aspx
8. ISACA, "COBIT FAQs," 2013, www.isaca.org/Knowledge-Center/cobit/Pages/FAQ.aspx
9. ISACA, COBIT Online: www.isaca.org/Template.cfm?Section=COBIT_Online&Template=/ContentManagement/ContentDisplay.cfm&ContentID=15633
10. ISACA, "COBIT 5 Training," 2013, www.isaca.org/Education/COBIT-Education/Pages/COBIT-Training.aspx
11. J. H. Allen, *The CERT® Guide to System and Network Security Practices* (Reading, MA: Addison-Wesley, 2001).

12. NSA, "NSA Security Guidelines Handbook" (Fort Meade, MD: National Security Agency Central Security Service, 2002), www.tscm.com/NSAsecmanual1.html
13. CIO Council BPC: https://cio.gov/about/committees/management-best-practices-committee (URL inactive).
14. CIO Council Documents: https://cio.gov/resources/document-library
15. IETF RFCs: www.ietf.org/rfc.html
16. B. Fraser, "Site Security Handbook," IETF RFC 2196, 1997; www.ietf.org/rfc/rfc2196.txt?number=2196
17. BSI, "IT-Grundschutz," Bundesamt für Sicherheit in der Informationstechnik (German Federal Office for Information Security), 2005; https://www.bsi.bund.de/EN/Topics/ITGrundschutz/itgrundschutz.html

CHAPTER 45

EMPLOYMENT PRACTICES AND POLICIES

M. E. Kabay and Bridgitt Robertson

45.1 INTRODUCTION.

Crime is a human issue, not merely a technological one. True, technology can reduce the incidence of computer crimes, but the fundamental problem is that people can be tempted to take advantage of flaws in our information systems. The most spectacular biometric access control in the world will not stop someone from getting into the computer room if the janitor believes it is "just to pick up a listing."

People are the key to effective information security, and disaffected employees and angry ex-employees are important threats according to many current studies. Chapter 13 in this *Handbook* provides detailed information about insider crime.

This chapter presents principles for integrating human resources (HR) management and information security into corporate culture.[1]

45.2 HIRING.

The quality of employees is the foundation of success for all enterprises; it is also the basis for effective information security.

45.2.1 Checking Candidate's Background. Hiring new employees poses a particular problem; growing evidence suggests that many people inflate their résumés with unfounded claims. According to Edward Andler, author of *The Complete Reference Checking Handbook*, "cheating on résumés has become distressingly common. And many people are getting by with it, which appears to be making others follow suit." His research shows that up to 10 percent "seriously misrepresent" their background or work histories. A research project run by the Port Authority of New York and New Jersey used an advertisement asking for electricians who were expert at using "Sontag Connectors." They received 170 responses claiming such expertise, even though there was no such device.[2]

Reviewers should be especially careful of vague words such as "monitored" and "initiated." During interviews or background checking, HR staff should find out what the candidate did in specific detail, if possible. All references should be followed up, at least to verify that the candidates really worked where the résumé claims they did.

Unfortunately, there is a civil liberties problem when considering someone's criminal record. Once people have suffered the legally mandated punishment for a crime, whether fines, community service, or imprisonment, discriminating against them in hiring may be a violation of their civil rights. Can one exclude convicted felons from any job openings? From job openings similar to areas in which they abused their former employers' trust? Are employers permitted in law to require that prospective employees approve background checks? Can one legally require polygraph tests? Drug tests? Personality tests?

In some jurisdictions, "negligent hiring" that results in harm to third parties is being punished in civil litigation. Imagine, for example, that a firm were to hire an active criminal hacker as a system administrator without adequate background checking and interviews; if the hacker were then to use his position and corporate resources to break into or sabotage another organization's systems, it is reasonable to suppose that the victim could claim damages from the criminal's employer on the basis of negligent hiring. In addition, "negligent retention" could hold an employer liable when an employee, who may pose a risk to coworkers or the public, is not terminated immediately.

Employers should consult their corporate legal staffs to ensure that they know, and exercise, their rights and obligations in the specific legal context of their work.

Even checking references from previous employers is fraught with uncertainty. Employers may hesitate to give bad references for incompetent or unethical employees for fear of lawsuits if their comments become known, or if the employee fails to get a new job. Today, one cannot rely on getting an answer to the simple question "Would you rehire this employee?"

Ex-employers must also be careful not to inflate their evaluation of an ex-employee. Sterling praise for a scoundrel could lead to a lawsuit from the disgruntled new employer.

For these reasons, a growing number of employers have corporate policies that forbid discussing a former employee's performance in any way, positive or negative. All one gets from a contact in such cases is "Your candidate did work as an Engineer Class 3 from 1991 to 1992. I am forbidden to provide any further information."

It is commonplace in the security field that some people who have successfully committed crimes have been rewarded by a "golden handshake" (a special payment in return for leaving), sometimes even with positive references. The criminals can then move on to victimize a new employer. However, no one knows how often this takes place.

To work around such distortions, interviewers should question candidates closely about details of their education and work experience. The answers can then be checked for internal consistency and compared with the candidate's written submissions. Liars hate details: It is so much harder to remember which lie to repeat to which person than it is to tell the truth.

There are commercial services specializing in background checking (e.g., Achievement Tec). They provide the necessary forms to allow employers to query credit records and other background information. Companies such as Kroll and Securitas Security Services also conduct extensive background checks.

Another way to conduct an employee background check can be done for free or at modest cost via Internet search engines. By entering someone's name into one of these search engines, there is a good possibility that some aspect of the applicant's life will be retrieved. Of particular interest might be a search of messages from a particular blog to see what information is being disseminated.

Experienced employees should interview the candidate and compare notes in meetings to spot inconsistencies. A director of technical support at a large computer service bureau questioned a new employee who claimed to have worked on a particular platform for several years—but did not know how to log on. Had he chatted with any of the programmers on staff before being hired, his deception would have been discovered quickly enough. Ironically, had he told the truth, he might have been hired anyway.

45.2.2 Employment Agreements. Before allowing new employees to start work, they should sign an employment agreement stipulating that they will not disclose confidential information or trade secrets of their previous employers. Another clause must state that they understand that the new employer is explicitly *not* requesting access to information misappropriated from their previous employer, or from any other source. The Uniform Trade Secrets Act, which is enforced in many jurisdictions in the United States, provides penalties that are up to triple the demonstrated financial damages, plus attorney's fees, caused by such data leakage. One high-profile case involved three employees who were found guilty of stealing and trying to sell Coca-Cola secrets to its rival Pepsi.[3]

45.3 MANAGEMENT.

Security is the result of corporate culture; therefore, management practices are critically important for successful information protection. External attacks through Internet connections and damage from malicious software are certainly important threats; nonetheless, insider damage due to errors and omissions as well as through dishonesty or a desire for revenge are still major problems for information security.[4] These problems are compounded when there are collaborative threats involving insiders working with those outside the enterprise.

45.3.1 Identify Opportunities for Abuse. Security managers do not have to be paranoid, they just have to act as if they are paranoid. Managers must treat people with scrupulously fair attention to written policies and procedures. Selective or capricious enforcement of procedures may constitute harassment. If some individuals are permitted to be alone in the printer room as salary checks are printed, while other employees of equivalent rank must be accompanied, the latter can justifiably interpret the inconsistency as an implicit indication of distrust. Such treatment may move certain employees to initiate grievances and civil lawsuits, to lay complaints under criminal statutes for discrimination, or even to commit vengeful acts.

45.3.2 Access Is Neither a Privilege Nor a Right. When management removes access rights to the network server room from a system analyst who has no reason to enter that area, the response may be resentment, sulking, and abuse. People sometimes treat access controls as status symbols; why else would a CEO who has no technical training demand that his access code include the tape library and the wiring closet? Managers can overcome these psychological barriers to better security by introducing a different way of looking at vulnerabilities and access. After identifying an opportunity for a particular employee to use the system in unauthorized ways, one should turn the discussion into a question of protecting the person who has unnecessary access against undue suspicion. For example, an employee having more access to secured files than is required is put at risk. If anything ever did go wrong with the secured files, that employee would be a suspect. There is no need to frame the problem in terms of suspicion and distrust.

With these principles in mind, managers should be alert to such dangers as permitting an employee to remain alone in a sensitive area, allowing unsupervised access to unencrypted backups, or having only one programmer who knows anything about the internals of the accounting package.

As for language, it would be better to stop referring to access *privileges*. The very word connotes superiority and status—the last things management should imply. Access is a function and a responsibility, not a privilege or a right; it should be referred to simply as *access functions* or *access authorizations*.

45.3.3 The Indispensable Employee. In many areas of information processing, redundancy is generally viewed as either a bad thing or an unavoidable but regrettable cost paid for specific advantages. For example, in a database, indexing may require identical fields (items, columns) to be placed in separate files (data sets, tables) for links (views, joins) to be established. However, in managing personnel for better security, redundancy is a requirement. Without shared knowledge, an organization is at constant risk of a breach of availability.

Redundancy in this context means having more than one person who can accomplish a given task. Another way of looking at it is that no knowledge should belong to only one person in an organization. Putting the keys to the kingdom in the hands of one employee invites disaster.

Unique resources always put systems at risk; that is why companies such as Tandem, Stratus, and others have so successfully provided redundant and fault-tolerant computer systems for critical task functions, such as stock exchanges and banking networks. These computer systems and networks have twin processors, channels, memory arrays, disk drives, and controllers. Similarly, a fault-tolerant organization will invest in cross-training of all its personnel. Every task should have at least one other person who knows how to do it—even if less well than the primary resource. This principle does not imply that managers have to create clones of all their employees; it is in fact preferable to have several people who can accomplish various parts of any one person's job. Spreading knowledge throughout the organization makes it possible to reduce the damage caused by absence or unavailability of key people.

It is dangerous to allow a single employee to be the only person who knows about a critical function in the enterprise. Operations will suffer if the key person is away, and the enterprise will certainly suffer if this unique resource person decides to behave in unauthorized and harmful ways. Managers should ask themselves if there is anyone in their department whose absence they dread. Are there any critical yet undocumented procedures for which everyone has to ask a particular person?

A client in a data center operations management class volunteered the following story. There was a programming wizard responsible for maintaining a key production program; unfortunately, he had poor communication skills and preferred to solve problems himself rather than to train and involve his colleagues. "It'll be faster for me to do it myself," he used to say. During one of his rare vacations, something went wrong with "his" production program, shutting down the company's operations. The wizard was in the north woods, out of reach of all communications; the disaster lasted until he returned.

Not only does the organization suffer, but also the indispensable persons suffer from the imbalance of knowledge and skill when no one else knows what they know. Some indispensable employees are dedicated to the welfare of their employer and of their colleagues. They may hesitate to take holidays. If their skills are needed from hour to hour, it becomes more difficult for them to participate in committee meetings. These are the people who wear beepers and cannot sit undisturbed even in a two-hour class. If the indispensable employees' skills affect day-to-day operations, they may find it hard to go to offsite training courses, conferences, and conventions. Despite their suitability for promotion, indispensable people may be delayed in their career change because the organization finds it difficult or expensive to train their replacements. In extreme cases, newly promoted managers may find themselves continuing to perform specialized duties that ought to be done by their staff. Sometimes even a VP of Operations is the only person who can make the changes to a production system that should be performed by a programmer three or four levels down.

A particular kind of indispensability occurs when an employee becomes the *de facto* technical support resource for a particular software package or system. Without authorization from their managers, these employees can find themselves in difficulty. They may be fired because their productivity drops too low according to their job descriptions, which do not include providing undocumented technical support to other people. They may burn out and quit because of overwork and criticism. Or they may cause resentment among their colleagues and neighbors by declining to help them, or by complaining about overwork. Alternatively, they may enjoy the situation, and manage to meet all the demands on their time quite successfully, until others in the information technology department begin to feel threatened, and someone either complains to the higher-ups or begins spreading nasty comments about these unauthorized support technicians.

Looking at this situation from a management point of view, there are problems for the recipients of all this free aid. The longer they persist in getting apparently free help from their unofficial benefactor, the longer they can avoid letting upper management know they need help. Then when the bubble bursts and the expert becomes unavailable, managers are confronted with a sudden demand for unplanned resources. In most organizations, unexpected staffing requirements are difficult to satisfy. Managers have a hard time explaining how it is that they were unable to predict the need and to budget for it.

Sometimes persons continue to be indispensable because of fear that their value to their employers resides in their private knowledge. Such employees resent training others. The best way to change their counterproductive attitude is to set a good example; managers should share knowledge with them and with everyone else in their group. Education should be a normal part of the way everyone in the enterprise works. Managers can encourage cross-training by allocating time for it. Cross-training can be a factor in employee evaluations. Current topics from the trade press and academic journals, for example, can be discussed in a journal club, or at informal, scheduled meetings, where people take turns presenting the findings from recent research in areas of interest.

Reluctance to explain their jobs to someone else may also mask unauthorized or illegal activity. Take, for example, the case of Lloyd Benjamin Lewis, assistant operations officer at Wells Fargo Bank in Beverly Hills, California. He arranged with a confederate outside the bank to cash fraudulent checks for up to $250,000 each on selected legitimate accounts at Lewis's branch. Using a secret code stolen from another branch, Lewis would scrupulously encode a credit for the exact amount of the theft, thus giving the illusion of correcting a transaction error. Lewis stole $21.3 million from his employer between September 1978 and January 1981, when he was caught by accident. For unknown reasons, a computer program flagged one of his fraudulent transactions so that another employee was notified of an irregularity. It did not take long to discover the fraud, and Lewis was convicted of embezzlement. He was sentenced to five years in a federal prison.[5]

Because Lewis was obliged to be physically present to trap the fraudulent checks as they came through the system, he could not afford to have anyone with him watching what he did. Lewis would have been less than enthusiastic about having to train a backup to do his job. If anyone had been cross-trained, the embezzlement would probably not have continued so long, or have become so serious.

45.3.4 Career Advancement. In a topic related to avoiding indispensability, managers can improve the security climate through accepted principles of good human resources management, such as career advancement for all employees. By promoting individuals to new responsibilities, managers can also increase the number of people with expertise in critical functions. As managers carry out their regular employee performance reviews, they should include discussions of each person's career goals. Here, based on a summary by employment expert Lee Kushner, are some practical questions to discuss with employees as part of their interviews.[67]

1. What are your long-term plans?
2. What are your strengths and weaknesses?
3. What skills do you need to develop?
4. Have you acquired a new skill in the past year?
5. What are your most significant career accomplishments, and will you soon achieve another one?
6. Have you been promoted over the past three years?
7. What investments have you made in your own career?

When managers support individuals' interests and aspirations, they foster a climate of respect and appreciation and concurrently support positive feelings about the organization.

45.3.5 Vacation Time. In the example presented in Section 45.3.3, Lloyd Benjamin Lewis took his unauthorized duties (stealing money from his bank) so seriously that during the entire period of his embezzlement, about 850 days, he was never late, never absent, and never took a single vacation day in over two years. Any data center manager should have been quite alarmed at having an employee who had failed to be absent or late a single day in more than two years. The usual rule in companies is that unused vacation days can be carried over for only a limited time, and then they expire. This is intended to be an incentive to take vacation time; for normal, honest employees, it probably works fine. For dishonest employees who have to be present to control a scam, losing vacation days is intolerable.

Every employee should be required to take scheduled vacations within a definite—and short—time limit. No exceptions should be permitted. Excessive resistance to taking vacations should be investigated to find out why the employee insists on being at work all the time.

Unfortunately, this suspicious attitude toward perfect attendance can cause problems for the devoted, dedicated, and honest employee. An innocent person can get caught up in a web of suspicion precisely because of exceptional commitment. One may be able to avoid difficulties of this kind by:

1. Making the reasons for the policy well known to all employees so no one feels singled out;
2. Relying on the judgment, discretion, and goodwill of the investigating manager to avoid hurt feelings in their most loyal employees; and
3. Switching such an employee's functions temporarily to see if anything breaks.

45.3.6 Responding to Changes in Behavior. Any kind of unusual behavior can pique the curiosity of a manager. Even more important from a security management standpoint, any consistent change in behavior should stimulate interest. Is a normally punctual person suddenly late, day after day? Did an employee start showing up regularly in hand-tailored suits? Why is a usually charming person snarling obscenities at subordinates these days? What accounts for someone's suddenly working overtime every day, in the absence of any known special project? Is a competent person now producing obvious errors in simple reports? How is it that a formerly complacent staffer is now a demanding and bitter complainer?

With so much of the enterprise's financial affairs controlled by information systems, it is not surprising that sudden wealth may be a clue that someone is committing a computer crime. A participant in an information systems security course reported that an accounting clerk at a government agency in Washington, DC, was arrested for massive embezzlement. The tip-off? He arrived at work one day in a Porsche sports car and boasted of the expensive real estate he was buying in a wealthy area of the capital region—all completely beyond any reasonable estimate of his income.

Not all thieves are that stupid. A healthy curiosity is perfectly justified if you see an employee sporting unusually expensive clothes, driving a sleek car after years with a rust bucket, and chatting pleasantly about the latest trip to Acapulco when that person's salary does not appear to explain such expenditures. Unsolicited inquiries into people's private lives, however, will usually win no friends. There is a delicate line to walk, but ignoring the issue does not make it disappear.

The other kind of change—toward the negative—also may indicate trouble. Why is the system manager looking both dejected and threadbare these days? Is he in the throes of a personal debt crisis? In the grip of a blackmailer? Beset with a family medical emergency? A compulsive gambler on a losing streak? On humane grounds alone, one would want to know what is up in order to help; however, a manager concerned with security would be compelled to investigate. In these days of explosive rage and ready access to weapons, ignoring employees with a dark cloud hovering over their heads may be irresponsible and dangerous.

Any radical change in personality should elicit concern. If the normally relaxed head accountant now has beads of sweat on her forehead whenever you discuss the audit trails, perhaps it is time to look into her work more closely. Why does a good family man begin returning from long lunches with whiskey on his breath? A formerly grim manager now waltzes through the office with a perpetual smile on his face. What happened? Or what is happening?

All of these changes should alert managers to the possibility of changes in the lives of their employees. Although these changes do indeed affect the security of an organization, they also concern managers as human beings who can help other human beings. Mood swings, irritability, depression, euphoria—these can be signs of psychological stress. Is an employee becoming alcoholic? A drug addict? Abused at home? Going through financial difficulties? Having trouble with teenagers? Falling in love with a colleague? Of course managers cannot help everyone, and in some cases, help should involve qualified mental health professionals; but at least everyone can express concern and support in a sensitive and gentle way. Such discussions should take place in private, and without alarming the subject or exciting other employees. At any time, a manager should feel free to involve the HR or personnel department. They will either have a psychologist or trained counselor on staff or be able to provide appropriate help in some other way, such as an employee crisis line.

There are sad cases in which employees have shown signs of stress but have been ignored, with disastrous consequences: suicides, murders, theft, and sabotage. Be alert to the indicators and take action quickly.

Australian human resources expert Laura Stack offers this analysis of signs of extreme stress:

> People don't normally all of a sudden flip out; they give off early warning signals. Luckily, managers can observe signs of stress in employee behaviour, beginning with milder signs and culminating in desk rage. Be observant for the following stress stages:
>
> - Physical stage: Headaches, illness, fatigue.
> - Social stage: Negativity, blaming things on others, missed deadlines, working through lunch.
> - Cerebral stage: Clock-watching, errors in assignments, minor accidents, absentmindedness and indecisiveness.
> - Emotional stage: Anger, sadness, crying, yelling, feelings of being overwhelmed, depression.
> - Spiritual stage: Brooding, crying, wanting to make drastic changes in life, not relating well with people, distancing themselves from personal relationships.[7]

The manager's job in probing behavioral changes is difficult; one must walk the thin and possibly invisible line between laissez-faire uninvolvement, risking lifelong regrets or even prosecution for dereliction of duty, and overt interference in the private affairs of the staff, risking embarrassment and possible prosecution for harassment.

Written policies will help; so will a strong and ongoing working relationship with the HR staff. Making it clear to all employees that managers are available for support, but are also expected to investigate unusual behavior, will also help avoid misunderstandings.

45.3.7 Separation of Duties. The same principles that apply to the control of money should apply to control of data. Tellers at a bank, when someone deposits a large check, will always go to a supervisor and have that person look the check over and initial the transaction. When bank tellers empty the automatic teller machines at night and fill the cash hoppers, there are always two people present. In most organizations, the person who creates a check is not the person who signs it.

In well-run information systems departments, with good operations security, data entry is distinct from validation and verification.[8] For example, a data entry supervisor can check on the accuracy of data entry but should not be allowed to enter a new transaction without having a direct supervisor check the work. There is no excuse for allowing the data entry supervisor to enter a transaction and then, effectively, to authorize it. What if the entry were in error—or fraudulent? Where would the control be?

In quality assurance for program development, the principles of separation of duty are well established. For example, the person who designs or codes a program must not be the only one to test the design or the code.[9] Test systems are separate from production systems; programmers must not have access to confidential and critical data that are controlled by the production staff. Programmers must not enter the computer room if they have no authorized business there; operators must not modify production programs and batch jobs without authorization.[10]

Managers should consider giving up access to functions that have been delegated to two or more subordinates. Maintaining such access could cause more problems than it solves, but in an emergency, access and control could easily be restored. This attitude exemplifies the concept of separation of duties.

In early 1995, the financial world was rocked by the collapse of the Barings PLC investment banking firm. The Singapore office chief, Nicholas Leeson, was accused of having played the futures market with disastrous consequences.[11] The significant point is that he managed to carry out all the orders without independent overview. Had there been effective separation of duties, the collapse would not have occurred.

Another shocking example occurred when a system administrator at UBS PaineWebber, upset about the poor salary bonus he received, deployed malicious code on the company's network. But before quitting his job, he wrote a program that would delete files and wreak havoc on the company's network. By creating a logic bomb, he was able to impact over 1,000 servers and 17,000 individual workstations. Additionally, buying puts against UBS, he would profit from that attack.

A related approach is called dual control. As an example of dual control, consider the perennial problem of having secret passwords not known to managers who sometimes need emergency access to those passwords. This problem does not generally apply to ordinary users' passwords, which normally can be reset by a security administrator without having to know the old password. This temporary password should be changed to a truly secret string by the user, after a single logon. However, to guard against the absence of the only person who has the root password for a system, possibly because the others are on vacation, it is advisable to arrange for dual-access to backup copies of the password. The principle of dual control dictates that such a copy of the root password should be accessible only if two officers of the organization simultaneously sign for it when taking it out of the secure storage:

- One can store a written copy of the root password in a truly opaque envelope, seal it, sign the seal, tape over the seal with nonremovable tape, and then store the envelope in a corporate safe or strongbox
- The password can be encrypted twice using the public keys of two officers; the dual encryption requires the officers to decrypt the ciphertext in the reverse order of encryption (see Chapter 7 in this *Handbook*).

In conclusion, managers should think about the structure of control over information as they design security policies, so that the safeguards afforded by separation of duties or dual control are present throughout all systems.

45.3.8 The Capability and Responsibility Matrices. One of the tools that can help evaluate and improve the resilience of organizations is the capabilities matrix.[12] One starts by listing (or brainstorming, perhaps using Computer-Aided Consensus™)[13] all the critical functions that the organization requires and all the people in the team. The group then has to decide on a way of rating the capabilities of each person; the figure suggests one way to do it, but in no sense is this suggestion meant to constrain users. The group can come to a consensus on which of the team members can do which tasks at which level of competence and then examine the overall pattern of skills. Exhibit 45.1 shows such a matrix with made-up information.

Problems may be highlighted when no one has high-level capabilities or when too few people can effectively carry out those tasks. Another problem is that some people

CAPABILITIES MATRIX FOR UNTELECOM CORPORATION

Total points ≤	0	1	3	6	9	12
EVALUATION	*ACK!!!*	*DANGER!*	*URGENT*	*IMPROVE*	*GOOD*	*EXCELLENT*

Capabilities & Assignments			
0	1	2	3
NO CAP.	NOVICE	IS/CAN BE BACKUP	CAN BE IN CHARGE

	PERSONNEL CAPABILITIES								TOTAL	NEED
Task	Albert	Betty	Charlie	Dahlia	Edward	Frannie	Golamo	Hur'dath		
application monitoring	3			3			2	2	10	*GOOD*
application security vulnerabilities	3			3			2	2	10	*GOOD*
business impact analysis		3		1				2	6	*IMPROVE*
computer security incident response team			3		3			2	8	*IMPROVE*
coordination with corporate counsel		3	1		1	2		2	9	*GOOD*
coordination with human resources group		3	1		1	2		2	9	*GOOD*
Database performance	1			3			2	3	9	*GOOD*
Database support	2			3			2	2	9	*GOOD*
denial-of-service monitoring				1	3			3	7	*IMPROVE*
denial-of-service response				1	3			2	6	*IMPROVE*
detect cyber-attacks					3			3	6	*IMPROVE*
enterprise antivirus									0	*ACK!!!*
governance decisions		3	1	1		2		2	9	*GOOD*
identification and authentication			2		2		2	3	9	*GOOD*
intellectual property protection				2		2		3	7	*IMPROVE*
intrusion detection systems					3		2	3	8	*IMPROVE*
intrusion prevention systems			2		3		2	2	9	*GOOD*
log management systems	1		2	3	3			2	11	*GOOD*
manage cyber-attacks		2		1	3	2	1	2	11	*GOOD*
monitor dashboard			2	2	3			2	9	*GOOD*
network behavior analysis			1	3	2			3	9	*GOOD*
network discovery			1	2	2			2	7	*IMPROVE*
penetration testing			1	1	2			3	7	*IMPROVE*
quality of service measures	1	3		3	1	2		2	12	*EXCELLENT*
respond to system alarms		2	3	1	3			3	12	*EXCELLENT*
risk analysis and management				1		3		3	7	*IMPROVE*
security awareness				1		3		2	6	*IMPROVE*
security information and event management			3	2				3	8	*IMPROVE*
service level agreements	2	3	1	3		3		2	14	*EXCELLENT*
system firewalls			2		3		3	2	10	*GOOD*
training				1		3		2	6	*IMPROVE*
unified threat management					3		2	3	8	*IMPROVE*
vulnerability assessment			2		3		1	2	8	*IMPROVE*
Web site assessment					2		1	2	5	*URGENT*
Web site monitoring					3		1	3	7	*IMPROVE*
wireless intrusion prevention									0	*ACK!!!*
TOTAL SCORE	13	22	28	42	55	24	23	81		

EXHIBIT 45.1 Capabilities Matrix For Untelecom Corporation

may have so much knowledge compared with others that the organization is in danger were they to be absent; such cases should lead to training efforts to bring others up to an appropriate level of knowledge and skill. Individuals may also be noticeably lacking in skills; again, training may help solve such problems.

A similar matrix should be developed showing the responsibilities of every team member, with indicators of who has primary responsibility and the names of two or more members who can serve as backups (in prioritized order). It is important that every team member fill out their matrix by themselves, because conflicts may be discovered that way.[14]

The responsibility matrix can identify problems in the management structure. For example

- Some tasks may have no one assigned formally or have nobody assigned primary responsibility, leading to breakdowns in response, especially in emergencies.
- There may be tasks where two or more people believe that they are primary decision makers or leaders for a task, leading to conflicts.
- Some people may be identified with far too many assigned tasks; others may have too few.

45.3.9 No Unauthorized Security Probes. In general, all managers—not just security officers—should always be looking for vulnerabilities and opportunities for improving security. However, no one should ever *test* production systems for vulnerabilities without the full cooperation of the corporate information protection group, and only with authorization of the right executives. Written approval for explicit tests of security are informally known as *get-out-of-jail cards*, because without them, employees can go to jail for unauthorized probes of system security.

The case of Randal Schwartz, a consultant to Intel Corporation in Beaverton, Oregon, is a salutary example for employees of the dangers of unauthorized security probes. He was convicted of hacking his way into Intel Corporation computer networks in what he claimed was an effort to point out security flaws while he was working there as a consultant. The would-be security expert failed to notify his employers of his intentions and forgot to get authorization for stealing passwords and making unauthorized changes in system software. He was convicted of three felony counts in July 1995 and was fined $68,000 in restitution as well as being put under five years of probation and having to perform 480 hours of community service.[15]

A counterexample to warn managers of misplaced zeal in suppressing cooperation with law enforcement is the case of Shawn Carpenter, a network intrusion detection security analyst at Sandia National Laboratories. He was fired by publicity-shy administrators when he worked with law enforcement officials to track down extensive penetrations of U.S. national security assets. An investigation code-named TITAN RAIN began in late 2003.[16] Carpenter noted a flood of expert hacker activity focusing on data theft from a wide range of national security interests. Carpenter discovered that "the attacks emanated from just three Chinese routers that acted as the first connection point from a local network to the Internet."[17] Carpenter worked with U.S. Army Counterintelligence and FBI investigators to learn more about the attacks and the attackers. Carpenter never used Sandia's or government-owned equipment or network resources in his investigations. Administrators applied Sandia Internal Directive 12 ISNL ID012, which "specifically prohibits employees from speaking with local, state, or Federally elected officials." In 2007, Carpenter was awarded $4.3 million for wrongful termination.[18]

In February 2012, police and courthouse managers in Vienna, Austria, staged a theatrically convincing terrorist attack as a training exercise. The staging included "one simulated death, apparently by a gunshot to the head. Makeup was used to simulate injuries, and several officers were placed in the building as if they were injured persons. The supposed death was staged in front of courthouse staff who were evacuating offices." Because none of the ordinary staff members was informed (and nothing was announced to the public), "By the next day 40 staff members were in treatment for severe trauma and an undisclosed number had taken sick leave. We must assume that some will suffer from post-traumatic stress disorder (PTSD) in the weeks and months to come."[19] See Chapter 46 in this *Handbook* for more discussion of how to prepare for tests of this sort.

45.4 TERMINATION OF EMPLOYMENT.

Taking our security mandate in the widest sense, we have to protect our employer and ourselves against potential damage from unethical, disgruntled, or incompetent employees, and against the legal consequences of improper firing procedures. Common sense and common decency argue for humane and sensitive treatment of people being fired and those who are resigning. Firing people is a stressful time for everyone concerned, and it usually leads to increased security risks.[20] Managers should do everything in their power to ensure a courteous, respectful, and supportive experience when terminating employment.

45.4.1 Resignations.

Potentially the most dangerous form of employment termination is a resignation. The problem is summed up in the caption of a cartoon where a savage attack is in progress against a medieval town that is in flames; a clan war chieftain confronts a singed and dirty warrior. "No, no, Thor! Pillage, THEN burn!" Like the war chieftain, employees rarely resign without planning. An employee may have an indefinite period during which the action is imminent, while the employer may remain unaware of the situation. If the employee has bad feelings toward, or evil designs on, the current employer, there is a period of vulnerability frequently unknown to management. Dishonest or unbalanced employees could steal information or equipment, cause immediate or delayed damage using programmatic techniques, or introduce faulty data into the system.

The policies discussed in previous sections of this chapter should reduce the risks associated with resignations. The manager's goal should be to make resignations rare and reasonable. By staying in touch with employees' feelings, moods, and morale, managers can identify sources of strain and perhaps resolve problems before they lead to resignations and their associated security risks.

45.4.2 Firings.

Firings appear to give the advantage to employers, but there may be complications.

45.4.2.1 Timing.

One advantage is that the time of notification to a fired employee can be controlled to minimize effects on the organization and its business. For example, employers might find it best to fire an incompetent, or no longer acceptable, employee before beginning an important new project or after a particular project has finished.

Some people argue that to reduce the psychological impact on other employees, they should fire people at the end of the day, perhaps even before a long weekend.

The theory is that the practice gives everyone a cooling-off period outside working hours. These managers say they do not want the buzz of conversation and speculation that often follow a firing to intrude on the workday. This policy fails to regard the psychological stress to employees who have a ruined weekend and no way of responding constructively to their potentially catastrophic loss of a regular income.

A better approach to this stressful task is to fire people early on Monday morning in order to provide an unrushed exit interview and, if appropriate, job counseling to help the employee prepare for job hunting. In this scenario, the regrettable necessity (from the manager's point of view) of terminating employment is buffered by professionals in the HR department, who can give the departing employee a sense of hope and some practical as well as emotional support in this difficult time. A humane attitude is particularly important during downsizing, or when plants are closed, and many people are being fired—one of the worst experiences possible for both employees and managers, and an event that has serious security implications.

In one large company, the personnel department asked their information security staff to suspend the access codes for more than 100 people who were to be fired at 6:00 PM on Tuesday. On Wednesday at 8:00 AM, the security staff began receiving phone calls asking why the callers' logon IDs no longer worked. It turned out that the personnel staff had failed to inform the terminated employees on time. The psychological trauma to both the employees who were fired and to the security staff was severe. Several security staff members were sent home in tears to recuperate from their unfortunate experience. The harm done to the fired employees was even more serious, and the effect on morale of the remaining employees was a disaster. There could well have been violence in that situation.

45.4.2.2 Procedures upon Termination. In both resignations and firings, security consultants unanimously advise instant action. Not for them the leisurely grace period during which employees wind down their projects, or hand them off to other staff members. Security officers are a hard lot, and they usually advise this scenario: In a formal exit interview, and in the presence of at least two managers, an officer of the employer informs the employee politely that his or her employment is at an end. During the exit interview, the officer explains the reasons for termination of employment. The officer gives the employee a check for the period of notification required by law or by contract, plus any severance pay due. Under supervision, preferably in the presence of at least one security guard, the employee is escorted to the accustomed work area and invited to remove all personal belongings and place them in a container provided by the employer. The employee returns all company badges, IDs, business cards, credit cards, and keys, and is then ushered politely outside the building.

At the same time all this is happening, all security arrangements must be changed to exclude the ex-employee from access to the building and to all information systems. Such restrictions can include:

- Striking the person's name from all security post lists of authorized access
- Explicitly informing guards that the ex-employee may not be allowed into the building, whether unaccompanied or accompanied by an employee, without special authorization by named authorities
- Changing the combinations, reprogramming access card systems, and replacing physical keys if necessary for all secure areas to which the individual used to have authorized access

- Removing or changing all personal access codes known to have been used by the ex-employee on all secured computer systems, including microcomputers, networks, and mainframes
- Informing all outside agencies (e.g., tape storage facilities and outsourced functions) that the ex-employee is no longer authorized to access any of the employer's information or to initiate security or disaster recovery procedures
- Requesting cooperation from outside agencies in informing the employer if ex-employees attempt to exercise unauthorized functions on behalf of their former employer

The task is made more difficult by seniority, or if the ex-employee played an important role in disaster recovery or security. The employer should be assiduous in searching out all possible avenues of entry resulting from the person's position of responsibility and familiarity with security procedures.

In one story circulating in the security literature, an employee was fired without the safeguards just suggested. He returned to the workplace the next Saturday with his station wagon and greeted the security guard with the usual friendliness and confidence. The guard, who had known him for years, was unaware that the man had been fired. The ex-employee still had access codes and copies of keys to secure areas. He entered the unattended computer room, destroyed all the files on the system, and then opened the tape vault. He engaged the guard's help in loading all the company's backup tapes into his station wagon. The thief even complained about how he had to work on weekends. This criminal then tried to extort money from the company by threatening to destroy the backup tapes, but he was found by police and arrested in time to prevent a disaster for his ex-employer.

This story emphasizes the importance of reaching *everyone* who needs to know that an employee no longer works for the enterprise.

45.4.2.3 Support in Involuntary Terminations. Security does sometimes prevent a farewell party, one obvious sign of friendliness. The problem with a farewell party at work is that employees leaving under a cloud may feel humiliated when other people get a party but they do not. Generally, it makes sense to treat all departing employees the same, even if the termination is involuntary.

However, nothing stops a humane and sensitive employer from encouraging employees to arrange an after-hours party even for people who have been fired. If a *resignation* is on good terms, however, the employer may even arrange a celebration, possibly during working hours and perhaps at company cost, without having to worry about possible negative repercussions.

A firing, or a resignation on poor terms, has two psychological dangers: effects on the individual concerned of embarrassment, shame, and anger, and effects on the remaining staff of rumors, resentment, and fear. Both kinds of problems can be minimized by publishing termination procedures in organization documents provided to all employees; by requiring all employees to sign a statement confirming that they have read and agreed to the termination procedures; and by consistent application of the termination procedures.

The personal shock of being fired can be reduced by politeness and consideration consistent with the nature of the reasons for being fired, although even nasty people should not be subject to verbal or physical abuse, no matter how bad their behavior. Their treatment should be consistent with that meted out to other fired employees, and there should be generous severance arrangements, if possible.

Organizational turmoil can be reduced by convening organization-wide or departmental meetings to brief remaining employees on the details of a significant termination. Open discussions, including how people feel about the rupture of relationships, can be helpful. The remaining employees may have to suffer grief, as a process, not a state. Grief is a normal and healthy response to disruption of relationships (e.g., death of a loved one, divorce, and even the loss of a coworker). Some people value social relationships more than other aspects of their work, and they may be especially affected by firings. Grief involves stages of denial, anger, mourning, and recovery. Trying to forestall such responses by denying that people legitimately have feelings is foolish and counterproductive. It is far better to encourage those who are upset to voice their feelings, and to engage in constructive discussion, than to clamp down in a futile attempt to suppress discussion.

45.4.2.4 Style of Termination. The way an organization handles job termination affects more than internal relations; it also influences its image in the outside world. Prospective employees will think twice about accepting job offers from an organization that mistreats departing employees. Clients may form a negative impression of a company's stability if it abuses its own people. Investors also may look askance at a firm that gets a reputation for shoddy treatment of employees. Bad relations among managers and employees are a warning sign of long-term difficulties.

45.4.2.5 Legal Issues. There is another dimension to employment termination that depends on local laws and the litigation environment. The United States, for example, is said to be one of the most litigious nations on the planet, perhaps because of the high number of lawyers compared with the total population.

The list that follows is not legal advice; for legal advice, consult an attorney. However, simple experience does teach some principles, even without going to law school. Here are some pragmatic guidelines for preventing legal problems related to firings for cause:

- Build a solid, documented case for firing someone before acting.
- Keep good records, be objective, and get the opinions of several trustworthy people on record.
- Offer the delinquent employee all reasonable chances to correct his or her behavior.
- Give the employee clear feedback long before considering firing.

Timing is important in employee relations, as it is in almost everything else we do. In particular, if an employee is found to be behaving improperly or illegally, there must be no marked delay in dealing with the problem. Such persons could sue the employer and individual managers. They could argue in court that the very fact that there was a delay in firing them was proof that the firing was due to other factors such as personality conflicts, racism, or sexism. A well-defined procedure for progressing through the decision will minimize such problems.

The critical legal issue is consistency. If rules such as those just described for the day of the firing are applied haphazardly, there could easily be grounds for complaining of unfairness. Those to whom the rules were strictly applied would justifiably feel implicitly criticized. How would we feel if we were singled out by having guards check what we took home from our desk—if everyone else got a party and two weeks' notice? Such inconsistency would be grounds for legal proceedings for defamation of character. The company might lose and it might win, but what nonlawyer wants to spend time in court?

Another issue that arises in connection with firings and resignations involves nondisclosure agreements. All such agreements must be included in a contract signed before the prospective employee begins work; it is almost impossible to force an existing employee to sign such an agreement.

Managers, the legal department, and the personnel department should study the necessity and feasibility of instituting a legally binding contractual obligation to protect their company's confidential information for a specified period of time after leaving. One typically does not impose indefinite gags on people, as one year seems to be normal. (However, there are exceptions. Oprah Winfrey insists that all employees who work at Harpo sign a lifelong confidentiality agreement, which an Illinois appeals court upheld when a former employee tried to write a book about the media mogul.) For this measure to be meaningful, the initial employment contract should stipulate that departing employees must reveal their new employer, if there is one at that time.

Noncompetition agreements require the employee to refrain from working for direct competitors for perhaps a year after termination of employment. The key to a successful clause here is that there be a strict, operational definition of "direct competitors." Because this limitation can be an onerous impediment to earning a living, many jurisdictions forbid such clauses.

45.5 SUMMARY.

Some of the key recommendations from this chapter follow:

Hiring

- Investigate the accuracy of every likely job candidate's résumé.
- Perform background investigations when hiring for sensitive positions.
- Arrange for experienced staff members to interview candidates and discuss inconsistencies.
- Require signing of a legally appropriate employment contract.

Ongoing Management

- Identify and resolve opportunities for abuse.
- Assign access functions on the basis of need, not social status.
- Identify indispensable employees, and arrange for cross-training of other staff.
- Require employees to take their vacations, or to rotate their job functions periodically, so as to assure operational continuity and as a possible indication of fraud.
- Note and respond to sudden changes in behavior and mood; involve human resources as appropriate.
- Enforce separation of duties and dual control for sensitive functions.
- Do not engage in, or tolerate, unauthorized probes of system security.

Termination of Employment

- Provide an opportunity for fired employees to receive counseling and support.
- Ensure that the HR department collaborates with the information technology group to take all appropriate security measures when anyone leaves the employment of the enterprise.

- Ensure that firings do not cause long-term morale problems.
- Follow the guidance of corporate counsel to avoid wrongful dismissal suits.
- Use legally appropriate nondisclosure and noncompetition clauses in employment contracts.

In summary, information security depends on coordination with HR personnel to ensure consistent policies for hiring, ongoing management, and termination of employment.

45.6 FURTHER READING

Armstrong, M. *Armstrong's Handbook of Human Resource Management Practice*, 12th ed. Kogan Page, 2012.

Cascarino, R. E. *Corporate Fraud and Internal Control + Software Demo: A Framework for Prevention*. Wiley, 2012.

Dresang, D. L. *Personnel Management in Government Agencies and Nonprofit Organizations*, 5th ed. Pearson, 2009.

Girgenti, R. H., and T. P. Hedley. *Managing the Risk of Fraud and Misconduct: Meeting the Challenges of a Global, Regulated and Digital Environment*. McGraw-Hill, 2011.

Mathis, R. L., and J. H. Jackson. *Human Resources Management*, 13th ed. South-Western Cengage Learning, 2010.

McNamara, C. "All About Human Resources and TalentManagement." 2013, http://managementhelp.org/humanresources/index.htm

NAPA (National Academy of Public Administration). "Browse Publications by Category." 2013. www.napawash.org/publications-reports/browse-publications-by-keyword

NOLO. "Human Resources." 2013. www.nolo.com/info/human-resources

SHRM (Society for Human Resource Management). "Publications." 2013. www.shrm.org/PUBLICATIONS/pages/default.aspx

Wells, J. T. *Corporate Fraud Handbook: Prevention and Detection*. 3rd ed. Wiley, 2011.

45.7 NOTES

1. For guidance on setting policies, see Chapter 44 in this *Handbook*; for details of email and Internet usage policies, see Chapter 48; for security awareness advice, see Chapter 49; and for applications of the principles of social psychology in reinforcing a culture of security, see Chapter 50 in this *Handbook*.
2. Peter Levine, quoted in www.virtualhrscreening.com/background/whybackground.htm (URL inactive).
3. Department of Justice Press Release, "Jury Finds Former Coke Employee Guilty in Conspiracy to Steal and sell Coca-Cola Trade Secrets," February 2, 2007, http://atlanta.fbi.gov/dojpressrel/pressrel07/tradesecrets020207.htm (URL inactive).
4. See Chapter 10 in this *Handbook* for more details on understanding computer crime statistics.
5. "Around the Nation: 2d Man Pleads Guilty in Wells Fargo Case," *The New York Times*, August 12, 1981, p A.10 (fee required), http://tinyurl.com/5byd6c

6. L. J. Kushner, "Career Management 101 for Information Security Pros," SearchSecurity Website, June 29, 2006, http://searchsecurity.techtarget.com/generic/0,295582,sid14_gci1196912,00.html
7. L. Stack, "Employees Behaving Badly: Combating Desk Rage," HC Online Website, October 5, 2004, www.hcamag.com/resources/learning-and-development/employees-behaving-badly-combating-desk-rage-110891.aspx
8. See Chapter 47 in this *Handbook*.
9. See Chapter 39 in this *Handbook*.
10. See Chapter 47 in this *Handbook*.
11. Nicholas Leeson's official Website: www.nickleeson.com/biography/index.html
12. M. E. Kabay, "Continuity of Operations and the Capability Matrix," *InfoSec Perception*, February 1, 2013, http://resources.infosecskills.com/perception/continuity-of-operations-and-the-capability-matrix (URL inactive).
13. M. E. Kabay, "Computer-Aided Consensus," 2009, www.mekabay.com/methodology/cac.pdf
14. M. Jacka, and P. Keller, *Business Process Mapping: Improving Customer Satisfaction*. Wiley, 2009.
15. S. Pacenka, "Computer Crime?" State of Oregon v. Randal Schwartz, Washington County Circuit Court C94-0322CR, 2007. Complaint brought by Mr. Schwart's client, the Intel Corporation; www.lightlink.com/spacenka/fors
16. I. Winkler, "Guard against Titan Rain Hackers," *Computerworld*, October 20, 2005, www.computerworld.com/securitytopics/security/story/0,10801,105585,00.html
17. N. Thornburgh, "The Invasion of the Chinese Cyberspies (and the Man Who Tried to Stop Them)," *Time*, August 29, 2005, www.time.com/time/magazine/printout/0,8816,1098961,00.html (URL inactive).
18. J. Vijayan, "Reverse Hacker Wins $4.3M in suit against Sandia Labs: Shawn Carpenter used his own hacking techniques to probe outside breach," *Computerworld*, February 14, 2007, www.computerworld.com/action/article.do?command=viewArticleBasic&articleId=9011283
19. M. Krausz, "Terrifying Your Employees: Not Recommended for Training," InfoSec Perception Website, March 12, 2012, http://resources.infosecskills.com/perception/terrifying-your-employees-not-recommended-for-training (URL inactive).
20. S. Terlap and E. Morath, "Final Day at Ford Bittersweet for Scores of Salaried Workers," *Detroit News*, March 1, 2007, http://detroitnews.com/apps/pbcs.dll/article?AID=/20070301/AUTO01/703010359/1148

CHAPTER 46

VULNERABILITY ASSESSMENT

Rebecca Gurley Bace and Jason Sinchak

46.1 THE SCOREKEEPER OF SECURITY MANAGEMENT.

Information security has, over time, evolved from a collection of esoteric security issues and technical remedies to its current state, in which it is more tightly integrated with the area of enterprise risk management. One hallmark of this evolution from technology to management discipline is the emphasis placed on the deployment and use of vulnerability management practices. Vulnerability management has three complementary functional components, *vulnerability assessment* (VA), *penetration testing*, and *remediation*. Vulnerability management is considered fundamental to modern information security practice, and its components have adapted in architecture, features, and interfaces to accommodate the changing landscape of modern enterprises.

46.1.1 What Is Vulnerability Management?

Vulnerability management is the process of assessing deployed IT systems in order to determine the security state of those systems. It includes the automated scanning of system attributes (vulnerability assessment), the manual testing and exploitation of systems in search of illicit authorization or access (penetration testing), and the determination of corrective measures to mitigate issues identified that represent exposures for the enterprise, as well as managing the application of those measures (remediation). Vulnerability assessment is considered by many the key technology component of vulnerability management. However, there is a synergy between VA and the other elements of vulnerability management such that these elements drive what features are supported by VA technology (i.e., vulnerabilities that arise in the course of penetration testing may be reflected in future versions of VA scanners). Although early vulnerability management systems focused on vulnerabilities in operating systems and network configuration of IT enterprise systems, over time, the scope of VM coverage has grown to include applications as well.

The vulnerability management process is often defined in terms of four key functions. They are as follows:

- ***Inventory.*** Before an examiner can determine the extent of testing, she must identify all systems that are resident within the domain of interest. At this time, the operating system platforms and functions associated with each system are articulated and documented; furthermore any unauthorized or unmanaged systems are identified.
- ***Focus.*** Once an examiner has an idea of the systems that reside within the network, he must determine what information he (or his assessment tools) needs to see in order to find those vulnerabilities that are relevant to him and the enterprise. Some include the tuning of VA tools as a part of this step. When VA is driven by compliance requirements, such information is often specified in the regulations or policies in question.
- ***Assess.*** The examiner performs any testing (both automated and manual) necessary to identify vulnerabilities resident on the systems. She then assesses the results of these tests. Finally, she evaluates (and ranks) the actual risk to her organization's systems security, making that judgment guided by security policy and current risk management criteria.
- ***Respond.*** Finally, the examiner must execute procedures that act on the results of the assessment in order to address the problems identified. As much of current vulnerability management is performed as part of regulatory compliance, formal reporting of the results of VA, including remediation status, is an important part of this step.

Now that we've laid the cornerstones of the vulnerability management process, let's proceed to the technology particulars of VA.

46.1.2 What Is Vulnerability Assessment? VA is the analysis of the security state of a system on the basis of system information collected on demand. The four-step strategy for VA is as follows:

1. A predetermined set of target system attributes (for example, specific parameters for particular firewalls), are sampled.
2. The sampled information is placed in a data store.
3. The data store is organized and compared to a reference set of attributes.
4. The differences between the data store and the reference set are documented and reported.

46.1.3 Where Does Vulnerability Assessment Fit in Security Management? Vulnerability assessment and its parent function, vulnerability management are key elements of virtually all modern system security management strategies. There are many reasons for the popularity and acceptance of these functions, including:

- When systems are first deployed, VA allows you to baseline the security state of those systems.
- When security breaches are suspected, VA may allow you to quickly identify likely paths of attack and furthermore, determine whether they have been exercised.
- When new vulnerabilities are reported, VA can allow you to identify systems that are subject to the vulnerabilities so that you can patch or otherwise address the exposures.
- The results of individual VAs can be archived and used to document the security state of systems at a specific time. This is often used to satisfy regulatory audit or other oversight requirements.

Although VA and vulnerability management are accepted as important system security functions, they are not sufficient to protect systems from all security threats. Such measures should be included in a more comprehensive security strategy that includes security policy and procedural controls (see Chapters 44, 47, 50, 51, 52, and 53 in this *Handbook*), network firewalls and other perimeter defenses (Chapters 26 and 27), strong identification and authentication mechanisms (Chapters 28 and 29), access control mechanisms (Chapter 32), file and link encryption (Chapters 7, 32, and 33), file integrity checking (Chapters 7, 24, and 37), physical security measures (Chapters 22 and 23), and security training and education (Chapters 43, 45, 48, and 49). There are references and insight into building the rest of a comprehensive security strategy throughout this *Handbook*.

46.1.4 Brief History of Vulnerability Assessment. Early vulnerability assessment systems (VASs) include the COPS system, developed in the late 1980s by Eugene H. Spafford and Daniel Farmer at Purdue University.[1] COPS was a UNIX-targeted credentialed VA product that gained wide acceptance in security circles. The initial freeware version of the Internet Security Scanner (ISS) was also released in the early 1990s, as was Farmer's and Wietse Venema's VA software, SATAN.[2]

Subsequent trends of note include the advent of open-source tools for performing various forms of VA (e.g., NESSUS,[3] which provides vulnerability scanning capabilities, and NMAP,[4] which provides an inventory of the systems on a specific network, along with the network services resident on those systems).

Also of note is the move of VA from individual systems to the network infrastructure (i.e., dedicated network-connected appliances) and to the cloud (i.e., the VA is actually performed over the network, controlled by the security administrator over a Web interface, with results stored offsite).

Finally, as endpoints have become more mobile and application-centric than classic workstations, VA coverage has grown to cover software applications. The solution provider market for VA has adapted to these trends, and modern VA practice usually involves a mix of application software, dedicated appliances, managed services, and expert professional services (especially in areas such as penetration testing.)

46.2 A TAXONOMY OF VULNERABILITY ASSESSMENT TECHNOLOGIES.

VA products snapshot the security state of systems, diagnosing problems that indicate that the system is vulnerable to specific attacks.

VA performs an examination of key indicators within systems that are known to correspond to security vulnerabilities. Some consider some types of VAs a special case of a host-based, interval-based intrusion detection process and describe it in terms of the intrusion detection process model outlined in Chapter 27 in this *Handbook*.

46.2.1 Vulnerability Assessment Strategy and Techniques.

As noted above, there is a four-stage high-level strategy for conducting VA: Sample, Store, Compare, and Report. This four-stage process becomes quite complex when fleshed out to cover the full range of vulnerabilities that are commonly exploited by modern adversaries. A standard VA process may involve the use of any or all of the following techniques:

- ***Network Scanning.*** Maps network nodes and associated services by use of a "port scanner." This articulates issues at a network and network services layer of abstraction.
- ***Vulnerability Scanning.*** Takes the port scanning functions of network scanners to the next level by testing for operating system and application software system vulnerabilities resident on hosts connected to the network.
- ***Password Cracking.*** Identifies weak passwords.
- ***Log Review.*** A feature rooted in the earliest production computing platforms, log review remains one of the most powerful means of identifying weaknesses in systems.
- ***Integrity Checking.*** Uses checksums, hash totals, and digital signatures to allow quick and reliable detection of tampered files and system objects.
- ***Virus Detection.*** Scans for known viruses infecting systems.
- ***War Dialing.*** Scans enterprise systems for unauthorized modems.
- ***War Driving.*** Scans enterprise systems for unauthorized wireless LAN connections.
- ***Penetration Testing.*** Reenacts attackers' behavior in order to gain access and thereby test technical and procedural security measures.[5]

As many of these techniques are complex enough to merit a full chapter of their own (and are covered in specific chapters in this *Handbook*), we focus on only three of them in this chapter: network scanning, vulnerability scanning, and penetration testing.

46.2.2 Network Scanning.

Network scanners run a function called a *port scanner*, which uses a feature of ICMP, part of TCP/IP, in order to identify hosts available in a specified network address range. The port scanner then scans identified systems for open network ports and associated services.

Some network scanners use inference and other techniques to make intelligent guesses about the operating systems being run on open systems. These inferences are based on the combinations of active ports observed on a specific host (e.g., if Port 80 is open on a given host, it is likely running a Web server). Some scanners listen to ports for traffic that provides additional information about the system connected to that port.

One example of this type of surveillance is called *banner grabbing*, and can provide a great deal of detail about the connected system. The scanner collects information that is routinely sent to any process on connection; this *banner* often includes details of the name and version of the application.[6]

As a primary security policy decision involves specifying what systems are allowed on an enterprise network, network scanners provide a vital piece of information for VA. They also provide collateral information regarding the connected systems on a network, which is critical for tuning and refining the VA process. It is important, however, to understand that although the operation of a network scanner is automated, the identification of vulnerabilities discovered by network scanning is not. There is minimal, if any, decision support in network scanning products—some will identify certain port numbers as associated with a known Trojan attack. Therefore, it is important that the results from a network scanner be evaluated by someone familiar with the assessed network and associated security policy.

Increasingly, VA products include passive network scanning in addition to active network scanning. This involves placing passive network monitors to sniff traffic between target systems, inferring vulnerabilities from the traffic patterns observed between the target systems. This is useful in certain enterprise situations when protective mechanisms interfere with more classic active scanning (e.g., personal firewall agents on endpoints) but provides insights versus actionable results.

46.2.3 Vulnerability Scanning. Vulnerability scanning is the heart of traditional VA systems. In some ways vulnerability scanning appears to be the same as port scanning, but it differs in a critical way—it takes the additional step of not only collecting data regarding traffic, connections, and system attributes, but also analyzes the data to determine whether it matches a known vulnerability. Many systems (credentialed; see below) also attempt to correct the vulnerabilities identified in the scan, either automatically or overseen by human operators.

As vulnerability scanning usually targets specific hosts, it often conducts a deeper inspection than network scanners, identifying software versions, specific software applications, and configuration attributes of systems. The policy checks available to host-based vulnerability scanners can include usage patterns for software.

Perhaps the most valuable feature of vulnerability scanners is the current database of known vulnerabilities. Virtually all commercial offerings in this area include updates to these vulnerability databases as a core feature of the product. Many products offer features that assist security managers in configuring scanners to fit their environments, including a wide variety of configuration, reporting, and support features.

Vulnerability scanners can perform extremely fine-grained security assessment, in far more detail than network port scanners. However, this degree of detail comes at a price. Vulnerability scanners are typically slower and more resource greedy than network port scanners. The range of available assessment techniques is usually richer for vulnerability scanners; some (e.g., DDoS testing) can disrupt the normal operation of an enterprise network. False-positive rates (i.e., vulnerabilities spotted where none exist), can be high for many vulnerability scanners, requiring more human intervention. Finally as the value of the vulnerability scanner resides in its vulnerability database, it is critical that the database be updated frequently. A vulnerability scanner with a noncurrent database leaves users open to compromise.

46.2.4 Assessment Strategies. As in intrusion detection systems, VASs have features that allow differentiation between individual systems. The primary descriptors for VASs involve the information sources and how those information sources are generated.

46.2.4.1 Credentialed Monitoring. Credentialed monitoring approaches for VAs are those that utilize system data sources such as file contents, installed applications, configuration information, and status information. This information is gained from nonintrusive sources; that is, it is gained by performing standard system status queries and inspection of system attributes. These sources are accessible only when the entity gathering them has legitimate access to the system (i.e., the entity possesses access credentials). In UNIX systems, this information is gathered at the host or device level; therefore, *credentialed approaches* are also *host-based* approaches. As many modern operating systems (e.g., Windows) handle status information differently, often providing it in the form of Application Programming Interfaces (APIs), the *credentialed* = *host-based* equivalence does not always apply in those environments.

46.2.4.2 Noncredentialed Monitors. Noncredentialed monitoring approaches are those approaches that stage system attacks and record target system responses to the attacks. These approaches are much more intrusive than credentialed attacks and do not assume (nor do they require) any legitimate access to the target system; they are launched from an attacker's perspective. Noncredentialed approaches are often called *active* approaches and have detection and monitoring features that complement those of credentialed approaches. In particular, noncredentialed approaches are usually superior for diagnosing vulnerabilities associated with network services. As noted, in UNIX systems, noncredentialed assessments are usually considered *network-based* assessments. For instance, network scanning is a noncredentialed monitoring process. It bears repeating that here, as in credentialed approached, the equivalence relationship does not necessarily apply in Windows and other modern operating system environments that provide status information in API form.[7]

46.2.5 Strengths and Weaknesses of VASs. Knowing that security point products (e.g., firewalls, NIDS, and access-control systems) that defend particular features of a security perimeter cannot be perfect in the dynamic world of network and system attack, VASs serve an important function in the overall strategy for protecting information assets.

The benefits associated with vulnerability analysis are as follows:

- VASs conserve time and resources, as they allow even nonexpert personnel to check systems automatically for literally thousands of problems, any one of each might result in an intrusion.
- VASs can be extremely helpful in training security novices to make systems more secure.
- VASs can be updated to reflect new knowledge of vulnerabilities found by vendors and researchers.
- VASs can be configured to address specific vulnerabilities and configurations affected by regulatory requirements. They are a critical component in IT security regulatory compliance.

As VASs are used in more environments as a part of a risk-management regime, they are helpful for benchmarking the security state of systems in order to document progress toward a protection goal.

As security problems have become an item of broad interest to customer and regulatory communities, the capabilities of VASs may be a fundamental requirement for operating in certain IT markets. This inclusion of VA as a requirement for doing business is likely to not only remain stable over time, but grow at an appreciable rate.

VASs are systematic and therefore consistent. These attributes allow them to be used as quality assurance measures for network or security managers. Many security professionals routinely recommend that operational security policies include provisions for using VASs to check systems for problems after major changes have occurred (as might be the case whenever software is updated or system recovery is required).

Weaknesses in VA include the following:

- Although VA is necessary for system security, it is not in and of itself sufficient to secure a system.
- Many VASs serve only to diagnose problems, not to correct them. They are part of a more comprehensive vulnerability management process. User follow-through is still required.
- If the VASs are not kept up to date, they may mislead users into underestimating the risk of penetration.
- VAS can negatively impact the performance of an operational network. It is critical to balance demand for the network with the performance hits associated with running some types of VAS.

As in many other knowledge-based security tools, VA can be used for either productive or malicious purposes. In the hands of a security manager, VA is a valuable diagnostic technique. In the hands of an attacker, VA may optimize efforts to identify targets of attack and provide insight as to exactly how those targets might be compromised.

46.2.6 Roles for Vulnerability Assessment in System Security Management. VA products can be used at several points in the system security management life cycle.

First, when a new program is put into place, a VA can baseline the security state of the system. This application is particularly valuable in establishing the case for a security program, as it provides hard evidence that security problems exist.

Next, when an operational system changes (as might be the case when software updates are installed or new equipment is connected), a VA can help. It can find specific security vulnerabilities that occur as side effects of such changes.

Finally, when security incidents occur or are suspected, VA results can assist investigators in diagnosing possible paths of entry for attackers, locating artifacts of attacks (such as back doors or Trojan horses), and identifying the system resources affected by an attack so that they may be restored to their original states.

46.3 PENETRATION TESTING. A penetration assessment is used to augment the vulnerability management program's reoccurring and baseline VA by iteratively exploiting known and unknown vulnerabilities with the intent of demonstrating business impact and risk across technical, physical, and personnel environments. The goal of a VA and underlying automated vulnerability scanning activities is to identify and prioritize *known* technical vulnerabilities. A penetration assessment will test the effectiveness of the VA through the objective identification of vulnerabilities in the environment and the ensuing exploitation of them. The exploitation of known vulnerabilities demonstrates the real-life impact and business risk associated with the VA's ability to effectively identify known vulnerabilities and remediate them in the environment. The exploitation of *unknown* vulnerabilities or "stacked" known vulnerabilities will assess the organization's ability to respond to an incident or mitigate the impact caused by unforeseen vulnerabilities. Exploitation is performed in a manner that closely simulates actions that a real-life attacker is capable of performing outside and within the targeted environment.

Penetration assessments are performed by professional, ethical hackers using automated and manual techniques in conventional and unconventional ways. A penetration assessment should be leveraged to augment a VA and not as a replacement for the vulnerability scanning component. Assessments are performed by a *team* of qualified practitioners, ensuring well-rounded subject matter expertise in diverse areas.

Human penetration ("pen") testers have several advantages over purely automated methods:

- Automated VA tools, such as vulnerability scanners, are incapable of leveraging a vulnerability, component, or specification through a sequence of iterative and adaptive actions which may produce a high-impact outcome.
- A VA is only capable of testing and assessing the organization's susceptibility to known vulnerabilities; a penetration test is inclusive of unknown vulnerabilities and the exploitation of both.
- Pen testers possess an out-of-the-box mentality combined with a continuous strive to adapt circumvention efforts and pivot around preventative controls.
- Penetration tester activities are very difficult to mirror through automated means primarily due to human intuition.
- A pen tester thinks very differently than a traditional system or network administrator, making a large effort to solve problems in an *untraditional* way using *traditional* tools or methods.

46.3.1 Testing Goals

46.3.1.1 Demonstration of Impact and Risk. As penetration testers, our hearts thrive on the ability to compromise a target and received the coveted command level access. Although this may appear successful in the short term, the ultimate goal of a penetration test is to determine, demonstrate, and explain the risk as it applies to the organization, with accompanying steps to mitigate it or adequately manage it in the future.

Management should discuss with the penetration team what the assessment's end goal should be. *Goal-oriented* penetration testing aims to maximize value by demonstrating impact and risk appropriately for the organization's unique business. Goals include things that are important to the organization outside of security controls, such as the theft of intellectual property, theft of client base information, or a reduction in availability for core business processes thereby affecting an organization's bottom line.

46.3.1.2 Attestation and Compliance. The result of the penetration assessment can be provided to management, business partners, or regulators as an attestation to organizations point-in-time level of susceptibility to impact as a result of the current effectiveness of the vulnerability management program and underlying assessment capabilities.

A penetration assessment is a point-in-time assessment. Due to the fluid nature of information security advancement, a penetration testing team can never provide any level of assurance relating to the audit of vulnerabilities currently present in the environment. The primary goal of a penetration assessment is to demonstrate business impact and risk to management and business partners for the threats they face at a specific point in time.

46.3.2 Testing Perspectives. Penetration assessments provide a vehicle for evaluating the security of technical, physical, personnel, and procedural controls at a holistic level through the objective perspective of a third party mimicking the actions of an external attacker or malicious internal user. A VA is typically managed by an internal office and is therefore subject to bias during the assessment phase and compounded by resistance to the advancement in skillsets required to align with an advancing security field.

A malicious user and external attacker are different perspectives and approaches to the assessment which result in different perceived levels of impact and risk. It is important to understand the difference in order to properly develop the scope of the assessment to cover VA and management's objective for the assessment.

External Attacker

- An external attacker mimics the capabilities of an outsider with no internal knowledge of the target environment.
- The capabilities of an external attacker are greatly limited to publicly available resources.
- This type of test typically involves attacks against perimeter network devices and applications, which may result in internal connectivity.

Malicious User

- A malicious user mimics the capabilities of an authenticated or authorized user who possesses knowledge of internal operations.
- The capabilities of a malicious user are only afforded to trusted employees or contractors inside the network perimeter or within an application's authenticated or authorized zone.
- This type of test typically poses a greater risk of impact than an external attack, primarily due to the intricate knowledge pertaining to the location of and adequacy of preventive controls around sensitive data.

46.3.3 Testing Types. Penetration testing can be utilized to expand the scope of a technical VA to include the physical, personnel, and procedural controls that may be targeted by an adversary in an attack. Additionally, penetration tests can be used to increase focus on a particularly weak technical area within the over-arching assessment.

External Assessment: Penetration efforts originate from the Internet and target Internet-facing devices with the primary goal of gaining internal access to systems and acquiring business trophies such as client information or intellectual property.

Application Assessment: Application level assessments are increasingly common as organizations continue to remove Internet-accessible external services and heavily leverage Web services. Application assessments involve user-based attacks such as manipulating user input or client-controlled parameters. Goals include accessing administrative panels, extracting sensitive database information, masquerading as authorized users, or compromising the underlying Web or backend database server.

Internal Assessment: Internal penetration assessments target vulnerabilities within the organization. This assessment assumes the role of an attacker or malicious users who has been provided access to a network port within the facility. Goals of this assessment mirror those of an external or application assessment with the inclusion of a reduced level of accessibility controls.

Wireless Assessment: Wireless penetration assessments involve internally and externally surveying the organization's physical facilities for authorized and unauthorized wireless communications (e.g., 802.11) and attempting to circumvent or exploit controls to gain access. The primary goal of this assessment is to gain internal access to resources. Secondary goals of a wireless assessment include those of an internal assessment on achieving connectivity.

Physical Assessment: Physical security assessments focus testing activities on bypassing controls designed to prevent access to the facility and access to physical electronic data such as computing areas or telecommunication closet.

Personnel and Social Engineering: Personnel and social engineering assessments aim to test an organization's security awareness training and ability of personnel to follow procedures designed to safeguard their interactions with external parties.

46.3.4 Social Engineering.

Security depends on people; therefore, people are the single weakest link in any penetration assessment and overarching VA. People possess the power to assist an attacker in covertly bypassing any security control in the environment with a minimal amount of resources. Social engineering is defined as the use of persuasive techniques to abuse an inherent trust relationship and induce personnel to divulge information or perform an action used to gain illicit access to systems or data. Social engineering attacks can be performed through multiple mediums of communication, such as telephone conversations, convincing emails, or spoofed Websites.

Social engineering attacks have historically been leveraged in many high-profile security breaches involving Advanced Persistent Threats (APTs). This is primarily due to the level of effectiveness, covert nature, high impact of return, and ease of execution. Including social engineering as a component of a penetration assessment should be considered to evaluate policies, procedures, and security awareness programs designed to protect the business and inform personal of this particular threat.

Practical recommendations

- The decision to include Social Engineering as part of the assessment should align with objectives and goals.
- Precautionary measures should be taken to protect the testing team from unnecessary harm if they are identified; this can be provided through a "get-out-of-jail-free" document provided by upper management.

Common assessment scenarios

The following are example scenarios commonly executed during penetration assessments inclusive of Social Engineering tests:

- *USB/CD Drops*: The testing team stages a series of USB thumb drives or CDs with an auto-run or convincing "click me" executable. This executable "calls home" to an Internet rendezvous point once executed. This test is benign and rudimentary but a valuable determination of the susceptibility of authorized personnel to executing attacker provided code on internal systems.
- *Email Phishing/Pharming*: Hoaxes or scams are sent to a subset of targeted personal groups by an attacker masquerading as an internal employee or department with the intent of coercing them into responding, visiting a malicious Web page, or executing an attachment.
- *Call Masquerading*: The testing team contacts a provided list of phone numbers for a subset of personal groups within the organization to elicit information or perform an action by posing as an employee or contractor.

46.3.5 Managing a Penetration Assessment. Varying testing models can used to fine-tune the impact of the penetration assessment and align it with the vulnerability management and assessment goals.

46.3.5.1 Announced versus Unannounced Testing. Announced testing introduces awareness to internal IT staff prior to the beginning of the assessment. The primary motivation behind announced testing is to reduce any perceived impact from testing activities.

- Due to heightened awareness, announced testing reduces the effectiveness of the assessment to accurately evaluate security monitoring and incident response processes.
- Announced testing can provide educational value by presenting a learning opportunity to internal security staff through the real-time observation of controls, which are attacked or circumvented.

Unannounced testing involves the covert performance of testing activities under the sole knowledge and authorization from upper management to perform the agreed-upon assessment. Unannounced testing will deliver the most accurate assessment of all tested security controls.

Due to the covert nature of unannounced testing, activities are commonly focused on demonstrating impact through only exploiting vulnerabilities, which will quickly and covertly lead to a desired trophy.

46.3.5.2 Testing Scope. The penetration testing scope should be developed so that it aligns with the objectives of the assessment and its purpose within the vulnerability management program. It should be noted that regulatory requirements may dictate the scope to include specific network segments or applications (e.g., the Payment Card Industry Data Security Standard, or PCI DSS).

Penetration assessments can be scoped to allow social engineering attacks and specify to what degree these attacks will proceed, such as targets for phishing campaigns or locations for USB/CD drive drops.

Scope should ensure the assessment covers all intended areas within the VA, such as physical, personnel, and procedural controls.

- Scope should be reduced to a manageable number of targets within the environment for the allocated time period to ensure proper assessment of critical components.
- Scope reduction may eliminate a subset of vulnerabilities but may be necessary to ensure adequate time is available to test the environment and important assets using the provided methodology.

46.3.5.3 Testing Methodology. A penetration assessment should be performed under a consistent and repeatable methodology to ensure it can be operated in a repeatable manner for each VA.

Penetration testing activities involve a large variety of techniques and tools. The best way to harness and document the range of activities is through a vetted and documented methodology.

A structured methodology is crucial to accurately document the scope and depth for which testing activities should be performed.

- The assessment must be performed under a proven and structured methodology to be accepted by many third-party auditors or regulatory agencies.
- A structured methodology enables the ability to transition testing resources into and out of the assessment and provides results in a comparative manner between testing periods.

46.4 FUTURE READING

Abraham, J. "Goal-Oriented Penetration Testing—The New Process for Penetration Testing." Personal Website, November 16, 2009. http://spl0it.wordpress.com/2009/11/16/goal-oriented-pentesting-the-new-process-for-penetration-testing

Abraham, J. "Goal-Oriented Penetration Testing (Part 2)." Personal Website, November 17, 2009. http://spl0it.wordpress.com/2009/11/17/goal-oriented-pentesting—the-new-process-for-penetration-testing-part-2/

Foster, J. C., and V. T. Liu. *Writing Security Tools and Exploits*. Syngress, 2006.

Fischer, M., and Kabay, M. E. "Penetration Testing, Part 3," Network World Security Strategies, February 11, 2003, www.networkworld.com/newsletters/sec/2003/0210sec1.html

Faircloth, J. *Penetration Tester's Open Source Toolkit*, 3rd ed. Syngress, 2011.

Hurley, C., R. Rogers, F. Thornton, and B. Baker. *Wardriving & Wireless Penetration Testing*. Syngress, 2007.

Kabay, M. E. "Social Engineering in Penetration Testing: Cases." *Network World Security Strategies Alert*, October 25, 2007. www.networkworld.com/newsletters/2007/1022sec2.html

Manzuik, S., A. Gold, and C. Gatford. *Network Security Assessment: From Vulnerability to Patch*. Syngress, 2006.

McGraw, G., "Is Penetration Testing a Good Idea?" Network Magazine, July 2005, www.cigital.com/papers/download/0507sec.penetration.pdf

Orlando, J., and Kabay, M. E., "Social Engineering in Penetration Testing: Analysis," Network World Security Strategies, October 30, 2007, www.networkworld.com/newsletters/sec/2007/1029sec1.html

PCI Security Standards Council. *Information Supplement: Requirement 11.3 Penetration Testing*. 2008. https://www.pcisecuritystandards.org/pdfs/infosupp_11_3_penetration_testing.pdf

Schumacher, P., and Kabay, M. E. "Social Engineering in Penetration Testing: Intimidation," Network World Security Strategies, November 8, 2007, www.networkworld.com/newsletters/sec/2007/1105sec2.html

Siemens Insight Consulting, "Penetration Testing," April 2006, www.insight.co.uk/files/datasheets/ Penetration%20Testing%20(Datasheet).pdf

Skoudis, E. "Maximizing Value in Pen Testing." *SANS Penetration Testing*, February 9, 2012. http://pen-testing.sans.org/blog/2012/02/09/maximizing-value-in-pen-testing (URL inactive).

Van Der Walt, C., H. D. Moore, R. Temmingh, H. Meer, J. Long, C. Hurley, and J. Foster. *Penetration Tester's Open Source Toolkit*. Norwell, MA: Syngress, 2005.

46.5 NOTES

1. D. Farmer and E. H. Spafford, "The COPS Security Checker System," *Proceedings of the Summer USENIX Conference,* Anaheim, California, June 1990, pp. 165–170, http://docs.lib.purdue.edu/cgi/viewcontent.cgi?article=1844&context=cstech
2. D. Farmer and W. Venema, "Improving the Security of Your Site by Breaking into It," Internet white paper, 1993, www.csm.ornl.gov/~dunigan/cracking.html
3. Nessus Vulnerability Scanner. www.nessus.org
4. NMAP.ORG. http://nmap.org/
5. J. Wack, M. Tracy, and M. Souppaya, "Guideline on Network Security Testing," NIST Special Publication 800-42, National Institute of Standards and Technology, October, 2003, http://csrc.nist.gov/publications/nistpubs/800-42/NIST-SP800-42.pdf (URL inactive).
6. wiseGEEK, "What is Banner Grabbing?" wiseGeek Website, 2013, www.wisegeek.com/what-is-banner-grabbing.htm
7. A. Shostack and S. Blake, "Towards a Taxonomy of Network Security Assessment Techniques." *Proceedings of 1999 Black Hat Briefings,* Las Vegas, NV, July 1999, www.blackhat.com/presentations/bh-usa-99/AdamS/shostack-blackhat.pdf

CHAPTER 47

OPERATIONS SECURITY AND PRODUCTION CONTROLS

M. E. Kabay, Don Holden, and Myles Walsh

47.1 INTRODUCTION.

Despite the enormous increase in individual computing on personal computers and workstations in the years since the first edition of this *Handbook* was published in 1975, centralized arrays of dozens, hundreds, or thousands of computers used in computational arrays and cloud services are still used for enterprise computing in applications devoted to the core business of the enterprise. This chapter focuses on how to run vital computers and networks safely and effectively.

Readers with a military background will note that operations security in the civilian sector is different from the OPSEC (a military acronym for "operational security") designation used in military discourse. As defined by the Joint Chiefs of Staff of the United States military, "OPSEC seeks to deny real information to an adversary, and prevent correct deduction of friendly plans."[1]

In determining what operations security and production controls are required for any system, a thorough risk analysis should be conducted; you will find references throughout this *Handbook*. For a quick analysis, it may be helpful to use a few other common military acronyms and list the threats from their perspectives.

EMPCOA—enemy's most probable course of action. What is the most likely course of action an attacker will take against your systems?

EMDCOA—enemy's most dangerous course of action. What is the worst possible thing an attacker could accomplish?

Weighing these as part of a risk analysis can help tremendously to decide how to employ limited resources. The acronym *METT-TC*, which is essentially a larger version of the engineering triad of cost, time, and quality, may help. There are various versions of the METT-TC acronym, but perhaps the most useful stands for

- Mission (what we need to do),
- Equipment (what we have),
- Time (by when we need to do it),
- Troops (whom we have to do it),
- Terrain (where are we doing it), and
- Culture (the possible cultural considerations).

Each part of our METT-TC analysis should be self-evident, except for perhaps culture. Ignoring the management, political, and community cultures of the locations in which to install security controls is a frequent mistake, usually with dire consequences for both security and the careers of security professionals.

It is critical to be able to define precisely the terms associated with operations security and production controls before engaging in a discourse about them.

47.1.1 What Are Production Systems?

A *production system* is one on which an enterprise depends for critically important functions. Examples include systems for handling accounts receivable, accounts payable, payroll, inventory, manufacturing systems, real-time process control, data-entry systems, Web-based client interfaces for e-commerce, critical information systems, portable data-handling systems, and management information systems. What is defined as critical is a function of the mission, not a uniform prescription. Thus, the accounts receivable may be a critically important function for a manufacturing company working on a tight profit margin, with receivables needed to pay immediately for crucial supplies, but it may be less critical for a small group of successful partners running a consulting firm.

47.1.2 What Are Operations? *Operations* consist of the requirements for control, maintenance, and support of production systems. Operations staff are responsible for such functions as:

- Integrating new software systems into an existing configuration
- Running programs and batch jobs to update databases and create reports
- Installing new versions of production programs
- Maintaining production databases for maximal efficiency
- Managing backups (creation, labeling, storage, and disposal)
- Responding to emergencies and recovering functionality
- Mounting storage volumes of tapes, cartridges, or disks in response to user or program requests
- Handling special forms for particular printouts (e.g., check blanks)
- Managing all aspects of production networks, such as configuring routers, bridges, gateways, wireless propagation, and firewalls

47.1.3 What Are Computer Programs? A *computer program* is a set of instructions that tells a computer what to do to perform a task. Computer programs may be acquired, or they may be internally developed.

Internally developed programs are stored in computer systems in two basic forms. *Source* programs are in the form in which they were written (coded) by computer programmers. The statements in source programs are in languages such as COBOL, Visual BASIC, C++, and Java. Source language programs are kept in files and stored on disk folders called *source libraries* or *program libraries.*

Executable programs have been converted from source code, by *compilation* or *interpretation*, into a program that the computer can execute. Executable programs may be maintained in two separate forms: *object* and *load.*

An object program is a partially executable module that must be linked to other executable modules, such as input/output modules, to become a load module. As load modules, the programs are said to be in executable form. Executable programs are kept in *production libraries*, from which they are called when needed. Acquired programs are generally in object and load form. The source code is proprietary to the organization that developed it and is rarely given to the acquiring enterprise.

When internally developed programs have to be changed, programmers work with copies of the source programs. The copies are stored in another type of library, referred to as *programmer libraries.* The programmers make changes to their copy of the source programs, and go through a process of recompiling and testing until the modified program is working properly. When acquired programs require changes, often a contract to make the modifications is issued to the organization from which the programs were acquired. In some situations, internal programmers generate new programs and interfaces to the original acquired programs. The same libraries are used: source libraries for source code, production libraries for executable modules, and programmer libraries for work in progress. These libraries need to be protected. Loss or damage can entail huge costs and considerable inconvenience; recovering them can require a long time and great expense.

47.1.4 What Are Procedures? *Procedures* are sets of statements that tell a computer what to do in certain situations. They are unlike programs in that they are not compiled. Stored in files or databases, they are invoked and interpreted as needed. Procedural statements are made up of operational commands and parameters. The operational commands tell the computer what to do, and the parameters tell the computer which entity to act upon. *Job Control Language* (JCL) is an example of a procedural language. Procedural language statements often are used in database management systems and in security software products. On personal computers, *batch files* (.BAT) are a form of simple procedure.

47.1.5 What Are Data Files? Almost everything stored and maintained in a computer system takes the form of a *file*.[2] Programs, procedures, information, all are stored in files, using the concept of a file in its broadest sense; that is, a collection of related items. This usage has become most apparent with the ubiquitous personal computer (PC). Data files, as distinguished from program files and other types, are those that store information. In a PC environment, data files may be called documents. Documents are created by word processors, spreadsheet programs, graphics generators, and other application programs. In mainframe and midsize computer environments, data files are those created and maintained by applications such as payroll, accounting, inventory, order entry, and sales.

Some data files are transient; that is, they are created, used, and deleted within a short period of time. If lost or damaged, they can be reconstructed quickly, with little difficulty. There is usually no need to protect transient files. Other files, such as *master files* or organizational *databases* (groups of files that are linked to one another using a database management system or DBMS), contain information that is vital, confidential, or virtually irreplaceable. These files, generated by PCs, mainframes, and midsize computer systems, must be protected by security software and backup procedures to ensure against loss, destruction, theft, interference, and unauthorized disclosure.

47.2 OPERATIONS MANAGEMENT.

The processes for effective and efficient management of operations have direct benefits on information assurance. In particular, these aspects of operations management are of special value for improving and maintaining security:

- Separation of duties
- Defining the role of the security officer or security administrator
- Limiting access to the operations center
- Defining secure change-control processes
- Careful controls over externally supplied software
- Managing quality assurance and quality control

47.2.1 Separation of Duties. *Separation of duties* (also discussed in Chapter 45 in this *Handbook*) is a key control that should be applied to development and modification of programs. In enterprises where there are systems and programming departments that create and maintain custom programs, each individual programmer is assigned a user ID and a password. In these enterprises, where programs are developed and maintained internally, changes are constantly made to programs in order to meet changing business requirements. Modified executable programs, after recompilation and testing by programmers, are moved from their libraries into production libraries. Modified source programs are moved into source libraries. The programmers are responsible for keeping the source libraries current, while computer operations, or some other functional group separated from programming, may be responsible for maintaining the production libraries. When an updated executable program is transferred from the programmer's library to the production library, a transmittal is included, signed off by a manager in the programming department.

A particular consequence of the separation of duties is that a member of the operations staff should always be involved in the functional analysis and requirements definition phases for changes to production programs. The operations perspective is not always clear to programmers, and such issues as logging, backout, and recovery, as discussed later in this chapter, need to be brought to their attention early in the development and maintenance cycles.

It is critically important that programmers and operations staff understand that under no circumstances are programmers to install changes into production systems without adequate testing and authorization. Patch management is discussed in detail in Chapter 40 in this *Handbook*.

47.2.2 Security Officer or Security Administrator. Contemporary enterprises typically include a mix of external cloud-computing services, mainframes, mid-size computers, and local area networks (LANs) comprising hundreds or thousands of workstations, PCs, terminals, and other devices, all interconnected with one another, and often connected with the same mix in other enterprises throughout the world via the Internet.

A department, or an individual or small group in smaller enterprises, has the responsibility for providing and maintaining the security of files, databases, and programs. The title that is often associated with this function is *information security officer* (ISO) or *information systems security officer* (ISSO). This individual or department has the mandate to carry out the security policy as set down by the senior management of the enterprise. The security officer is empowered to allow or to disallow access to files, databases, and programs. In the language of the security officer, procedures are set up and maintained that establish relationships among individuals, programs, and files. Users, programmers, and technicians are granted privileges for full access, update only, or even read only. The security officer has the power to change or to revoke privileges (see Chapter 24 in this *Handbook* for details of operating-system security mechanisms; see Chapters 28 and 29 for discussions of identification and authentication).

47.2.3 Limit Access to Operations Center. Physical access to the operations center grants a person enormous power to disrupt production systems. Such access must be tightly controlled.

47.2.3.1 Need, Not Status, Determines Access. A fundamental principle for effective security is that access to restricted areas is granted on the basis of roles. Employees whose roles do not justify access should be excluded from autonomous access to production systems. In particular, high-placed executives, such as the president, chief executive officer, chief financial officer, chief operating officer, chief technical officer, and all vice presidents, should examine their own roles and determine if they should be able to enter the operations center unaccompanied; in most cases, such access is unjustified. Limiting their own access sets an important model for other aspects of security policy and demonstrates that need, not social status or position within the corporate hierarchy, determines access to restricted areas. This issue is also discussed in Chapter 45 on employment practices and policies in this *Handbook*.

47.2.3.2 Basic Methods of Access Control. As explained in Chapters 28 and 29 in this *Handbook*, access control depends on identification and authentication (I&A). I&A can be based on:

- What one has that others lack (tokens such as physical keys or smart cards)
- What one knows that others don't know (user IDs and passwords or passphrases)
- What one is that differs from what others are (static biometric attributes, such as fingerprints, iris patterns, retinal patterns, and facial features)
- What one does differently from how others do it (dynamic biometrics, such as voice patterns, typing patterns, and signature dynamics)

A typical arrangement for secure access to an operations center may involve keypads for entry of a particular code or card readers programmed to admit the holders of specific magnetic-stripe cards, smart cards, or radio-frequency identification (RFID) tokens. If the operations center is a 24-hour operation with full-time staffing, the presence of operators provides an additional layer of security to preclude unauthorized access. Remote monitoring of sensitive areas increases security by discouraging unauthorized access or unauthorized behavior and speeds up the response to possible sabotage. For extensive discussion of physical and facilities security, see Chapters 22 and 23 in this *Handbook*.

47.2.3.3 Log In and Badge Visitors. Visitors to a facility that houses sensitive systems should be logged in (that is, their identification checked and recorded in writing) at a controlled entrance and provided with visitor badges.

In high-security applications, an additional login may be required when entering the operations center itself. To encourage return of visitor badges, some security policies require the visitor to deposit a valuable document, such as a driver's license, with the security guards at the main entrance.

The effectiveness of visitor badges as a means of identifying nonemployees depends entirely on the use of badges by all personnel at all times; if *not* wearing a badge is acceptable and common, a malicious visitor could simply hide a visitor badge to pass as an authorized employee.

The time of login and of logout can be valuable forensic evidence if malfeasance is detected. However, such records can be shown to be reliable only if the guards responsible for keeping the logs consistently verify the completeness and correctness of all information written into the logs. Video recordings of the entrance to capture the face of each visitor as well as the exact time of arrival and departure can be of great value both for identifying imposters and also for verifying that the security guards are doing their job properly.

47.2.3.4 Accompany Visitors. No unaccompanied visitors should be permitted to circulate in the operations center or in the facility housing such a center. In high-security facilities, someone must even accompany the visitor to the washroom and wait for the visitor outside the door.

If a consultant or temporary employee is to work on a project for longer than a day, it may be acceptable to grant that person a restricted pass for low-security areas; however, high-security areas, such as the operations center, would still require such a person to be accompanied.

When one of the authors (Kabay) was director of technical services for a large service bureau in Montreal in the mid-1980s, the president of the company arrived unannounced on a Saturday evening at the door of the operations center with a visitor to show him around the computer center. The young operator explained with some trepidation that the president's name was not on the list of approved solo visitors, and so he would not grant entry (although he offered to call his boss for authorization). To his credit, the president accepted the restriction gracefully—and wrote a letter of commendation for the operator on Monday morning.

47.2.4 Change-Control Procedures from the Operations Perspective. When programmers have made changes to production programs and all documentation and testing procedures are complete, the new versions are formally turned over to the operations staff for integration into production.

47.2.4.1 Moving New Versions of Software into Production. Operations managers and staff must meet these demands when moving new versions of software into production:

- Identification—tracking which software is in use
- Authorization—controlling changes
- Scheduling—minimizing disruptions to production
- Backups—ensuring that all requisite information is available to restore a prior state
- Logging—keeping track of data input for recovery, and of errors for diagnosis of problems
- Backout—returning to a prior production version in case of catastrophic errors

47.2.4.1.1 Identification. Knowing precisely which versions of all production software are in use is the basis of production controls. Every module must have a unique identification that allows immediate tracking between executable code and source code; all changes to a particular module must be fully documented by the programming group. Unique identifiers allow the quality assurance process to ensure that the only modules that go into production are those that have been properly tested.

Most production shops use a three-level numbering scheme to track versions. Typically, version *a.b.c* (e.g., 7.13.201) is defined in this way:

- *c* changes every time anything at all—even a spelling mistake—is changed.
- *b* changes when program managers decide to group a number of fixes to errors into a new version for release to production.
- *a* changes when significant new functions are added; often the source code is completely renumbered if the changes are great enough.

The version number of object code must match the number of its source code. All object code should include internal documentation of its version number so that the version can be ascertained instantly, without having to consult possibly inaccurate external documentation.

47.2.4.1.2 Authorization. Strict procedures must be in place to preclude rogue programmers from introducing modified code into the production suite. In addition to the dangers of introducing untested or undocumented changes, allowing any individual to modify production processes without verification and authorization by an appropriate chain of responsibility can allow hostile code, such as Trojan horses and backdoors (see Chapters 13, 16, and 20 in this *Handbook*), to be introduced into the systems.

47.2.4.1.3 Scheduling. Implementing any new version of a production system requires careful planning and scheduling. Operations staff must prepare for changes in all aspects of production that depend on the system in question; for example, there may be requirements for new printer forms, additional magnetic tapes, and other supplies that must be ordered in advance. New requests for operator intervention, or changes in status and error messages during production, necessitate appropriate documentation and training. Effects on other programs may require special preparations that must take into account the scheduling requirements of the other systems that are affected. In addition, new versions of software often are implemented immediately after major production jobs, such as end-of-year or quarterly processing, to maintain consistency within an accounting period. For all these reasons, scheduling is critically important for trouble-free operations.

47.2.4.1.4 Backups. When modifying production systems, operations staffs usually take one or more complete backups (see Chapter 57 in this Handbook) of the software and data to be modified. This procedure is essential to allow complete restoration of the previous working environment should there be catastrophic failure of the new software and data structures.

System managers and operators should be aware that if their proposed changes require reformatting disk drives on the production system, they must make at least *two* full backups to ensure that an error in one of the backups won't cause a catastrophe when the entire system has to be restored.

47.2.4.1.5 Logging. To allow recovery or backout without losing the new data and changes to existing data that may have been carried out using new software and data structures, all production programs should include a logging facility. Logging keeps a journal of all information required to track changes in data and to regenerate a valid version of the data by applying all changes to an initial starting condition. Logging requires synchronization with backups to avoid data loss or data corruption. Special requirements may exist when a new version of the production system involves changes to data structures; in such cases, applying the information about changes to the older data structures may require special-purpose application programs. Since programmers sometimes forget about such possibilities, operations staff should be prepared to remind the programming staff about such requirements during the design phases for all changes.

47.2.4.1.6 Backout and Recovery. Sometimes a new version of production software is unacceptable and must be removed from the production environment. This decision may be made immediately, or it may occur after a significant amount of data entry and data manipulation has taken place. In either case, operations should be able to return to the previous version of a production system without data loss. This process involves restoring the earlier complete operating environment, with software and data in synchrony, and then using log files to repeat the data input and data modifications from the moment of changeover to the moment of fallback (see Chapter 52 in this *Handbook*).

Not all of the changes that were made using a new version will necessarily be applicable to the previous data; for example, if new fields were added to a database, the data stored in those fields would not be usable for an older, simpler data structure. Similarly, if fields were removed in the newer database, recovery will involve providing values for those fields in the older database. All of these functions must be available in the recovery programs and backups that should accompany any version change in production systems.

47.2.4.2 Using Digital Signatures to Validate Production Programs. If an unauthorized intruder or a disgruntled employee were discovered to have gained access to the production libraries, it would be necessary to determine if there had been unauthorized modifications to the production programs.

Date and time stamps on programs can record the timing of changes, but many operating environments allow such information to be modified using system utilities that read and write directly to disk without passing through normal system calls. In those instances, there would be no time stamp or log entry.

One approach that has been used successfully is to apply checksums to all production components. Checksum software applies computations to programs as if the codes were simply numbers; the results can be sensitive to changes as small as a single bit. However, if the checksums are computed the same way for all programs, access to the checksum utility could allow a malefactor to change a module and then run the checksum utility to create the appropriate new checksum, thus concealing the evidence of change. To make such subterfuge harder, the checksums can be stored in a database. Naturally, this database of checksums itself must be protected against unauthorized changes, for example, using encryption. Storing checksums may make unauthorized changes more difficult to disguise, but it also extends the chain of vulnerabilities.

A better way of determining whether object code or source code has been modified is to use digital signatures. Digital signatures are similar to checksums, but they require input of a *private key* that can, and must, be protected against disclosure. Verifying the digital signature may be done using a corresponding *public key* that can be made available without compromising the secrecy of the private key. For more information on public and private keys, see Chapter 7 on encryption and Chapter 37 on PKI and certificate authorities in this *Handbook*.

When digital signatures are used to authenticate code, it may be possible to validate production systems routinely, provided that the process is not too arduous to be accomplished as part of the normal production process. For example, it should be possible to validate all digital signatures in no more than a few minutes, before allowing the daily production cycle to start.

47.2.5 Using Externally Supplied Software. Production often uses software from outside the organization; such software may be commercial off-the-shelf (COTS) programs or it may consist of programs modified for, or written especially for, the organization by a software supplier. In any case, external software poses special problems of trust for the production team. There have been documented cases in which production versions of software from reputable software houses have contained viruses or Easter eggs (undocumented features, such as the well-known flight simulator in MS-Excel 97, which popped up a graphic landscape that included a monitor showing the names of the Excel development team). In addition, some consultants have publicly admitted that they deliberately include Trojan horse code (undocumented malicious programming) that allows them to damage data or inactivate the programs they have installed at client sites if their fees are not paid.

In large data centers, it may be possible to run quality-assurance procedures on externally supplied code (see Chapter 39 in this *Handbook*). Such tests should include coverage monitoring, in which a test suite exercises all the compiled code corresponding to every line of source code. However, it is rare that an operations group has the resources necessary for such testing.

The trustworthiness of proprietary external software written or adapted especially for a client ultimately may depend on the legal contracts between supplier and user. Such legal constraints may not prevent a disgruntled or dishonest employee in the supplier organization from including harmful code, but at least they may offer a basis for compensation should there be trouble.

47.2.5.1 Verify Digital Signatures on Source Code If Possible. If externally supplied code is provided with its source library as well as with compiled modules, operations should try to have the supplier provide digital signatures for all such programs. Digital signatures will permit authentication of the code's origins and may make it harder for malefactors to supply modified code to the user. In addition, the digital signatures can support nonrepudiation of the code (i.e., the supplier will be unable credibly to claim that it did not supply the code) and therefore the signatures may be useful in legal action, if necessary.

47.2.5.2 Compile from Source When Possible. Wherever possible, it is highly desirable to be able to compile executables from source code on the target machine. Compiling from source allows quality assurance processes to check the source for undocumented features that might be security violations and to couple the executables tightly to the verified source. In addition, compiling on the local system ensures that all calls to system routines will be satisfied by linking to executables such as dynamic link libraries (DLLs) supplied in the current version of the operating system.

However, compilation on a local system has additional implications that complicate implementation of new applications: Because the system routines being linked to the compiled code may not be identical to those used during the manufacturer's quality assurance tests, the customer organization must plan for its own quality assurance testing.

Operations staff should express this preference for source code clearly to the person or group controlling acquisition of external software. For more information about writing secure code, see Chapter 38 in this *Handbook*; for information about secure software development and software quality assurance, see Chapter 39.

47.2.6 Quality Control versus Quality Assurance. Throughout this chapter, quality assurance has been mentioned as an essential underpinning for operations security. *Quality assurance* refers to the processes designed to ensure and to verify the validity of production programs. However, another aspect of quality concerns the operations group: the quality of output. The process of verifying and ensuring the quality of output is known as *quality control.*

47.2.6.1 *Service-Level Agreements.* Unlike mathematical truth, there is no absolute standard of quality for computing operations. Every organization must define the level of quality that is suitable for a particular application. A commonly quoted principle in programming and operations is that there is a complex relationship among quality, cost, and development time: Increasing quality increases both cost and development time; shortening development time increases cost, if quality is to be maintained. It follows that every system should include a definition of acceptable performance; such definitions are known as *service-level agreements* (SLAs).

SLAs typically include minimum and maximum limits for performance, resource utilization, and output quality. The limits should be expressed in statistical terms; for example, "The response time measured as the time between pressing ENTER and seeing the completed response appear on screen shall be less than three seconds in 95 percent of all transactions and shall not exceed four seconds at any time." SLAs may define different standards for different types of transactions if the business needs of the users so dictate.

47.2.6.2 *Monitoring Performance.* Computer-system performance depends on five elements:

1. Access time and speed of the central processing unit(s) (CPU)
2. Access time and speed of mass storage (disks)
3. Access time and speed of fast memory (RAM)
4. Application design
5. Available network bandwidth

Operations groups should monitor performance to ensure that the requirements of the SLAs are met. There are two approaches to such monitoring: (1) analysis of log files and (2) real-time data capture and analysis.

Log files that are designed with performance analysis in mind can capture the precise times of any events of interest; for example, one might have a record in the log file to show when a particular user initiated a read request for specific data and another record to show when the data were displayed on the user's screen. Such level of detail is invaluable for performance analysis because the data permit analysts to look at any kind of transaction and compute statistics about the distribution of response times. In turn, these data may be used for trend analysis that sometimes can highlight problems in program or data structure, design, or maintenance. For example, an excessively long lookup time in a data table may indicate that the system is using serial data access because it had been designed without an appropriate index that would permit rapid random access to the needed records.

Another approach to performance monitoring and analysis is to use real-time monitors that can alert operations staff to abnormal performance. For example, an application program may be designed to calculate response times on the fly; the results may be displayed numerically or graphically on a *dashboard* for the operations staff. Values falling below a specified parameter may signal an abnormal condition, using color or sound to alert the operators to the drop in performance. Such *integrated performance metrics* allow the fastest possible response to performance problems. Extensive sets of real-time measures are sometimes called *situational awareness* tools.

Even if the application programs lack integrated performance metrics, it is sometimes possible to use system-level online performance tools to analyze system activity. In one instance in the experience of one of the authors (Kabay), for example, a software supplier in the mid-1980s had promised a response time of 10 seconds or less for all transactions, but one particular operation was taking 43 minutes. Because the SLA was violated, the client was threatening to sue the supplier for the entire development cost and the three years of maintenance payments—a total of $3.8 million (about $12 million in 2013 dollars). Using an online performance tool, it quickly became obvious that the transaction in question was generating an enormous amount of disk I/O (read and write operations): 80,000 random-access reads in a particular data set to filter out a few target records using a nonindex field. Installing and using an appropriate index and compacting the data set on that field as the primary key to provide rapid access to blocks of related records reduced response time to 6 seconds.

47.2.6.3 Monitoring Resources. Consistent monitoring of resource utilization is one of the most valuable roles of the operations staff. Data center operations should include regular analysis of system log files to track changes in the number of files, amount of disk free space available, number of CPU cycles consumed, number of virtual memory swap operations, and less esoteric resource demands, such as numbers of lines or pages printed, number of tape mounts requested, number of backup tapes in use, and so on. These data should be graphed and subjected to trend analysis to project when particular resources will be saturated if the trend continues. Even a simple spreadsheet program such as Excel can produce regression lines in graphs easily. Operations can then reduce demand either by improving aspects of production (e.g., optimizing programs to require fewer resources) or by increasing available resources (e.g., installing a memory upgrade).

Another level of analysis focuses on specific users and groups of users. Each functional group using the production systems should be analyzed separately to see if there are discontinuities in their trends of resource utilization. For example, a specific department might show a relatively slow and stable rise in CPU cycles consumed per month—until the rate of increase suddenly increases tenfold. If such a rate of increase were to continue, it could surpass all the rest of the system demands combined; operations therefore would investigate the situation before it caused problems. The cause of the discontinuity might be a programming error; for example, there might be a logical loop in one of the programs or a repeated computation that ought to have its result stored for reuse. However, the change in slope in CPU utilization might be due to introduction of new programs with a rapidly growing database; in such cases, operations would have to act to meet heavy new demands.

Disk space is often a key resource that can cause problems. If users fail to clean up unwanted files, disk space can disappear at an astounding rate. This problem is exacerbated by poor programming practices that allow temporary work files to remain permanently in place. Systems have been designed with tens of thousands of sequentially numbered temporary work files that had no function whatsoever after a production run was completed but that were accumulated over several years.

One of the methods widely used to reduce resource waste is *chargeback.* Using system and application log files, system administration charges the users of particular systems a fee based on their use of various resources. Sometimes these chargebacks are viewed as *funny money* because they are an accounting fiction—no money actually changes hands. However, requiring managers to budget carefully for computing resources can greatly improve attention to mundane housekeeping matters such as cleaning up useless files. If the chargeback system extends to aspects of program performance such as number of disk I/Os, it can even influence programmers to optimize their design and their code appropriately. Optimization is appropriate when the total costs of optimization are less than the savings in resources and the increases in productivity that result from optimization efforts, measured over the lifetime of the application.

47.2.6.4 *Monitoring Output Quality.* The final component of quality control is the meticulous monitoring of everything that is produced in the data center and sent to users or clients. Although much printing is now performed on local printers controlled by users, in many situations the operations group is responsible for documents such as payroll checks, invoices, and account status reports. Every operations group must explicitly assign responsibility for verifying the quality of such output before it leaves the data center. Operators should keep careful logs that record various types of error (e.g., torn paper, misaligned forms, or poor print quality) so that management can identify areas requiring explicit attention or repairs to improve quality.

47.3 PROVIDING A TRUSTED OPERATING SYSTEM.

The operating system (OS) is usually the single biggest and most important example of externally supplied software in a data center. Because the OS affects everything that is done in production, it is essential to know that the software is trustworthy. To this effect, operations staff use procedures to ensure that *known-good* software is always available to reinstall on the system. Systems with such software are known as *trustworthy computing platforms.*

47.3.1 Creating Known-Good Boot Medium.

The simple principle that underlies known-good operating software is that there shall be an unbroken chain of copies of the OS that have never run any other software. That is, operations will create a boot medium (tape, cartridge, CD-ROM) immediately after installing known-good software.

For example, if boot-medium V1B0 is defined as version 1 of the OS as it is delivered from the manufacturer; its installation would require specific settings and parameters for the particular configuration of the system. Immediately after installing V1B0, but before running any other software, operations would create medium V1B1 and set it aside for later use if V1B0 had to be replaced.

47.3.2 Installing a New Version of the Operating System.

Continuing this example of how to maintain known-good operating software, it might become necessary to install a new version of the operating system—say, version 2 on medium V2B0. Before using V2B0, operations would reinstall the current known-good OS, say from V1B1. Only then would V2B0 be installed, and the new boot medium V2B1 would be created immediately.

47.3.3 Patching the Operating System.

Often, when it is necessary to modify a small part of the OS, rather than installing a whole new version, manufacturers ask users to *patch* the OS. The patch programs modify the compiled code in place. If checksums or digital signatures are in use to maintain OS integrity, these codes will have to be regenerated after the patch is applied. However, to maintain a known-good status, applying a patch should follow a rigid sequence:

1. Load the current known-good software from the appropriate medium (e.g., V2B1).
2. Install the patch.
3. Immediately create a known-good boot medium before running any other software (in our example, this medium would be V2B2).

For extensive discussion of managing patches for production systems, see Chapter 40 in this *Handbook*.

47.4 PROTECTION OF DATA

47.4.1 Access to Production Programs and Control Data. Just as the operations center needs restricted access, so do production programs and data. From a functional point of view, there are three categories of people who might be allowed access to programs and data on which the enterprise depends: users, programmers, and operations staff.

47.4.1.1 Users. The only people who should have read and write access to production *data* are those users assigned to the particular systems who have been granted specific access privileges. For example, normally only the human resources staff would have access to personnel records; only the finance department staff would have full access to all accounts payable and accounts receivable records. Managers and other executive users would have access to particular subsets of data, such as productivity records or budget figures. Of course, *no* user should ever have write access to production *programs.*

47.4.1.2 Programming Staff. Programmers create and maintain production programs; they naturally have to be able to access the versions of those programs on which they currently are working. However, programmers must not be able to modify the programs currently used in *production*. All changes to production programs must be documented, tested, and integrated into the production environment with the supervision of quality assurance, operations, and security personnel.

Programmers need to be able to use realistic data in their development, maintenance, and testing functions; however, programmers should *not* have privileged access to restricted data. For example, programmers should not be allowed to read confidential files from personnel or medical records or to modify production data in the accounts payable system. Programmers can use extracts from the production databases, but particular fields may have to be randomized to prevent breaches of confidentiality. Programmers generally resent such constraints, but usually an effective process of education can convince them that maintaining barriers between production systems and systems under development is a wise policy.

47.4.1.3 Operations Staff. Much as the programmers are responsible for developing and maintaining systems, so the operations staff are responsible for using and controlling these systems. Operations staff perform tasks such as scheduling, error handling, quality control, backups, recovery, and version management. However, operations staff should not be able to modify production programs or to access sensitive data in production databases.

47.4.2 Separating Production, Development, and Test Data. For obvious reasons, testing with production data and production programs is an unacceptable practice, except in emergency situations. Therefore, programmers who develop new programs or modify existing programs must perform tests using their own libraries. These are frequently referred to as test libraries. Experienced programmers keep copies of the source programs for which they are responsible as well as copies of some of the data files that are used by the programs and subsets of others in their own test libraries. To avoid security violations, such copies and subsets of privileged data should be anonymized to the degree necessary to protect confidentiality. For example, a system using personnel data might substitute random numbers and strings for the employee identifiers, names, and addresses.

It is important to include time stamps on all files and programs, including both production and test versions. This practice serves to resolve problems that arise about program malfunctions. If all programs and files have time stamps, it can be helpful in determining whether the most current version of the load program is in the production library and whether test files and production files have been synchronized.

Final testing prior to production release may entail more formal review by an independent quality assurance section or department; the quality assurance group may also control transfers of programs to the production library.

47.4.3 Controlling User Access to Files and Databases. Access to files has to be controlled for two reasons:

1. There is confidential information in files that is not to be made accessible to everyone.
2. There are other files that are considered auditable.

The information in these files may be confidential, but that is not the reason for controlling access to them. The information in these files must be controlled because changing it is illegal. An example would be an enterprise's general ledger file once the books have been closed. Changing the information in these files gave birth to the pejorative phrase *cooking the books*. The original copies of these files are developed on the computer that handles the day-to-day transactions of an enterprise. Some time after the month-end closing of the books, copies of these files are archived. In this form they are the recorded history of the enterprise and cannot be changed. Storing this chiseled-in-stone historical information, combining details and summaries in database format so as to be accessible for the purpose of analysis is known as data warehousing.

In most large enterprises, these files are created on mainframe and midsize computers, although microcomputer database servers in LANs are increasingly in use today. In any event, controlling user access to files is performed in several ways depending on what types of access are allowed. Remote access to online production databases and files is often done over leased lines—dedicated communication facilities paid for on a monthly basis as opposed to dial-up or switched lines paid for on a when-used basis. Access control may be readily accomplished through the use of front-end security software modules, which in turn feed into database and file handling software and finally into the application software. For example, in an environment using a software product for handling queries and updates of online databases and files, a number of different security software products could be installed. Such products use what are called rules or schemas to validate user IDs and passwords, to authorize types of transactions, and to allow access to files and databases.

Many information system installations allow remote communications for many kinds of transactions. Various individuals, including sales representatives entering order information and traveling executives wishing to access current information from databases or files, use public networks, such as wired or wireless Internet service providers at hotels, airports, and coffee shops. This type of access increases the potential for security breaches. The usual practice today is to use *virtual private networks* (VPNs), which consist of encrypted channels between the portable equipment and the enterprise networks. Even so, some inadequate implementations of VPNs allow cleartext transmission of the initial logon information, allowing the identification and authentication data to be captured and used for unauthorized access. Poorly secured network access also allows *man-in-the-middle* attacks on the user's traffic.

For more information about encryption, see Chapters 7 and 37 in this *Handbook*; for more about network and communications security, see Chapters 5, 25, 32, 33, and 34.

47.5 DATA VALIDATION. Just as it is essential to have trusted operating systems and application software for production, the operations group must be able to demonstrate that data used for production are valid.

Validation controls normally are carried out dynamically throughout data entry and other processing tasks. Some validity checks are carried out automatically by database software; for example, inconsistencies between header records and details may be reported as errors by the database subsystems. Bad pointers are usually flagged immediately as errors by the database software; examples include:

- Pointers from a particular master record to a detail record with the wrong key value or to a nonexistent location
- Forward or backward pointers from a detail record to records that have the wrong key value for the chain or that do not exist at all

However, many errors cannot be caught by database subsystems because they involve specific constraints particular to the application rather than errors in the database itself. For example, it may be improper to allow two chemical substances to be mixed in a processing vat, yet there is nothing in the data themselves that the database software would recognize as precluding those two values to be recorded in the input variables. The programmers must include such restrictions in edit checks; often these relations among variables can be coded in a data dictionary. If the programming environment does not allow such dependencies, the programmers must incorporate the restrictions in lookup tables or in initialization of variables.

From a production point of view, operations staff must run appropriate validation programs created by the database suppliers and by the application programmers to assure the quality of all production data. The next sections review in more detail what is involved in such validation programs.

47.5.1 Edit Checks. Operations should have access to diagnostic programs that scan entire databases looking for violations of edit criteria. For example, if a field is designated as requiring only alphanumeric characters but not special characters such as "#" and "@," then part of the diagnostic sweep should be checking every occurrence of the field for compliance with those rules. Similarly, range checks (greater than, less than, greater than or equal, equal, less than or equal, between) are a normal part of such scans. Lookup tables listing allowed and forbidden data and combinations of data provide further sophistication for more complex relations and restrictions. In any case, the role of operations staff is to run the diagnostics and identify errors; correction of the errors should fall to authorized personnel, such as the database administrators.

Diagnostic programs should provide detailed information about every error located in the production files. Such details include:

- Configurable view of the record or records constituting an error, showing some or all of the fields
- Unique identification of such records by file name or number, record number, and optionally by physical location (cylinder, sector) on disk
- Error code and optional full-text descriptions of the error, including exactly which constraints have been violated

A diagnostic program should, ideally, also allow for repair of the error. Such repair could be automatic, as, for example, insertion of the correct total in an order-header, or manual, by providing for the database administrator to correct a detail record known to be wrong.

47.5.2 Check Digits and Log Files. Another form of verification relies on check digits. Programs can add the numerical or alphanumeric results of data manipulations to each record or to groups of records when transactions are completed properly. Finding records with the wrong check digits will signal inconsistencies and potential errors in the processing. Check digits are particularly useful to identify changes in production databases and other files that have been accomplished through utilities that bypass the constraints of application programs. For example, most databases come with a relatively simple *ad hoc* query tool that permits lookups, serial searches, views, and simple reporting. However, such tools often include the power to modify records in compliance with database subsystem constraints, but completely free of application program constraints.

An even more powerful type of utility bypasses the file system entirely, and works by issuing commands directly to the low-level drivers or to the firmware responsible for memory and disk I/O. In the hands of the wrong people, both database and system utilities can damage data integrity. However, it is usually difficult for the users of these utilities to compute the correct checksums to hide evidence of their modifications. A diagnostic routine that recomputes checksums and compares the new values with the stored values can spot such unauthorized data manipulations immediately.

If possible, checksums in log files should be *chained* from one record to the next so that the checksum for every record is calculated using the checksum from the previous record in addition to the data in the current record. Changing, adding, or deleting any record in the log file then requires the criminal to modify all subsequent checksums, and comparison of the modified log file with the backup of the original log file may easily identify the tampering because there are so many discrepancies in evidence.

A similar technique for validating and repairing data uses database and application log files to record information such as before and after images of modified records.

Such log files also can include special marker records to flag different steps in complex transactions; these flags can allow diagnostic programs to identify precisely when transactions have been interrupted or subjected to other forms of failure. Using these log files, it is often possible to identify which defective transactions need to be removed, repeated, or completed.

Commercial data-integrity software is available for a wide range of platforms and databases. Searching on "data integrity software" in the Google search engine (www.google.com) locates many references to such products.[3]

For more information on integrating security into application design, see Chapter 52 in this *Handbook*. For more about log files and other monitoring and control systems, see Chapter 53.

47.5.3 Handling External Data. Before using data provided by external organizations, operations should routinely check for data purity. Diagnostic routines from the programming group should be available to check on all data before they are used in batch processing to update a production database. The same principles of data validation used in checking production databases should apply to all data received from clients, suppliers, governments, and any other organization. Special validation programs can and should be written or obtained to test the data received on any medium, including tapes, cartridges, removable discs, CD-ROMs, DVDs, and data communications channels.

47.6 CLOUD COMPUTING AND PRODUCTION SYSTEMS.

The history of production computing is repeating itself: In the 1960s through the 1980s, computers were so physically large and hugely expensive that many smaller organizations contracted with *service bureaus* to access computing resources. Connections in physically close locations (e.g., city cores) were often through physical coaxial cable or twisted pair connections. For more distant connections, clients linked their *dumb terminals* to the *mainframes* through telephone lines using *modems*. Sometimes the switched telephone connections through the *plain old telephone service* (POTS) were fixed in place and dedicated to the connection—hence they were called *dedicated lines*.

Today, as we approach the middle of the 2010s, the speed of Internet connections is reaching 10 Gbps—an enormous bandwidth that facilitates remote access to banks of computing power of almost unimaginable power.[4] Organizations are capitalizing on the possibility of creating virtual machines (*virtualization*) that insulate concurrent processes from each other, allowing far more efficient sharing of centralized resources than running processes on dedicated systems in-house. Inexpensive computers (*thin clients*) with relatively little application software and local disk storage can be used to access all the necessary programs and data required for the organization's business through access to cloud services.

In March 2013, industry analysts said, "More than 60% of all enterprises will have adopted some form of cloud computing in 2013, according to Gartner Research. The cloud market is slated to grow to $131 billion worldwide this year, or 18.5% over the $111 billion last year. In its 2013 *State of the Cloud Report* that surveyed over 1200 IT professionals, IT-reseller CDW found 39% of organizations are already using some form of cloud solution, an 11% increase over 2011."[5]

IDC reported that "In coming years, the economic impact of cloud computing will be vast. Each year a greater percentage of businesses IT budgets are earmarked for cloud. An expansive study by the International Data Corporation (IDC) … reported that, in 2011, businesses spent $28 billion on public cloud IT services. Amazingly, the spending on public cloud expected to surpass $207 billion worldwide by 2016 … ." The researchers analyzed trends in specific industries:

- Banking: increasing use of cloud computing
- Healthcare: slower adoption
- Manufacturing: particularly strong growth for customer relationship management (CRM) and among smaller businesses
- Insurance: increasing use
- Communications/media: particularly strong user of *storage-on-demand*[6]

Gartner also predicted that, "… by 2015, 10% of overall IT security enterprise capabilities will be delivered in the cloud, with the focus today clearly on messaging, Web security, and remote vulnerability assessment. However, there's also the expectation there will be more on the way, such as data-loss prevention, encryption, authentication available too as technologies aimed to support cloud computing mature."[7]

As with service bureaus of yesteryear, cloud computing poses special challenges for operations security and production controls.

- The reliability of employees hired to handle confidential and critically important data is out of the hands of the client organization.
- Management policies, monitoring, software maintenance, audits—all are potentially handled exclusively by employees of the cloud-computing provider.
- Bring-your-own-device (BYOD) practices are facilitated by access to remote cloud services.
- Quality of service (QOS) issues and details of the service-level agreements (SLAs) complicate the contractual relations between providers and customers.

Cloud computing, like service bureaus, can provide cost-effective growth paths for smaller business and can offload information technology used for IT functions that are not viewed as mission critical, allowing IT staff to concentrate on innovative, highly productive applications that can differentiate an organization in its marketplace. They allow for graded increases in computing power without forcing organizations to follow step-functions with large investments in much bigger equipment and increased operational costs. However, extending one's IT infrastructure into centers run by separate entities with their own profit motives requires careful attention to security. At a minimum, organizations should implement the following recommendations for maintaining adequate controls over their production environment when it is in a remote site using cloud computing:

1. During evaluations of multiple vendors, be sure to contact clients of each firm to have personal discussions of their experience with the providers' service-level agreements and performance, openness of communications about production controls, cooperation in site visits, and adequacy and cooperation in resolving problems.
2. Examine the adequacy of encryption for all stored proprietary data. No cleartext data should be accessible to employees of the cloud-hosting company at any time—including while decrypted on the virtual machines running on their servers.

3. Be sure that virtual private networks are in place for all Internet-based data transfers.
4. Explicitly discuss update standards for all the software your organization plans to run on the cloud service. Are you responsible for such updates or is the cloud vendor?
5. Be sure that all software running in the cloud on behalf of the customer organization respects the terms of the vendors' licenses. For example, be sure that a one-user license is not being applied to a thousand concurrent virtual machines on your behalf.
6. Understand and analyze the business-continuity planning (BCP) and disaster-recovery planning (DRP) in place to ensure continued operations on your behalf should there be problems at the cloud vendor's site(s). Are the exact terms spelled out to your satisfaction in the contracts? Are there provisions for testing the adequacy of the BCP and DRP?
7. Ensure that the contract allows for external audits which can be initiated by the client. Independent evaluation of the security, QOS and continuity of operations (CoO) is essential for the protection of the client.
8. Discuss the vendors' security policies and practices, including real-time monitoring for breaches (*situational awareness*), handling malware, and vulnerability analysis, including penetration testing.
9. Evaluate the billing processes carefully: what determines the periodic invoicing—concurrent users? Total number of sessions? Detailed algorithms measuring such elements as disk I/O, CPU cycles, swapping to and from virtual memory, or bandwidth utilization? Model the costs if possible using detailed information from your own existing systems.

47.7 CONCLUDING REMARKS. Up until the mid-1980s, the world of mainframes and minicomputers differed from that of PCs. However, from the mid-1980s and into the millennium, these worlds have merged. LANs have proliferated, the Internet has changed the way business is conducted, and bridges, routers, and gateways make it possible for information to move among computer platforms, regardless of type. Security requirements are now universal in scope. Numerous layers of software and hardware separate the user and the technician from the information to which they require access. These layers themselves contribute to security because they require some technical skill to get at the information. As this is being written in 2008, computer literacy is increasing rapidly. Children are taught to use computers in grade school, and tens of millions of workers routinely use PCs or workstations daily, so the security provided by the technology is not as significant as it once was.

Security is also an economic issue. If an individual with the requisite skill is determined to gain access to online files or databases, it is extremely expensive to prevent such access. Even with high expenditures, success in achieving complete security is never guaranteed. Nevertheless, if the value of the information and its confidentiality justifies additional expense, there are software products available that employ complex schemes to support security. When necessary, information security can be extended down to the field level in records of online files and databases.

Other related security measures, such as physical protection, communication security, encryption of data, auditing techniques, system application controls, and other topics, are covered in other chapters of this *Handbook*. No one measure can stand alone or provide the ultimate protection for security, but with a proper balance of measures, the exposures can be contained and managed.

47.8 FURTHER READING

Baumann, W. J., J.T. Fritsch, and K. J. Dooley. *Network Maturity Model: An Integrated Process Framework for the Management, Development and Operation of High Quality Computer Networks*. Outskirts Press, 2007.

Benyon, R., and R. Johnston *Service Agreements: A Management Guide*. Van Haren Publishing, 2006.

Blanding, S. *Enterprise Operations Management Handbook*, 2nd ed. Auerbach, 1999.

Cisco. "Cisco on Cisco Best Practices: Data Center Operations Management." White paper, 2008. www.cisco.com/web/about/ciscoitatwork/downloads/ciscoitatwork/pdf/Cisco_IT_Operational_Overview_Data_Center_Management.pdf

Erl, T., R. Puttini, and Z. Mahmood. *Cloud Computing: Concepts, Technology & Architecture*. Prentice-Hall, 2013.

Franklin, C., and B. Chee. *Securing the Cloud: Security Strategies for the Ubiquitous Data Center*. Auerbach, 2013.

Halpert, B. *Auditing Cloud Computing: A Security and Privacy Guide*. Wiley, 2011.

Hoesing, M. T. *Virtualization Security Audit and Assessment*. Auerbach, 2014.

Mather, T., S. Kumaraswamy, and S. Latif. *Cloud Security and Privacy: An Enterprise Perspective on Risks and Compliance*. O'Reilly Media, 2009.

McCrie, R. *Security Operations Management*, 2nd ed. Upper Saddle River, NJ: Prentice-Hall, 2006.

Nielsen, L. *The Little Book of Cloud Computing Security, 2013 Edition*. New Street Communications, 2013.

Rhoton, J., J. De Clercq, and D. Graves. *Cloud Computing Protected: Security Assessment Handbook*. Recursive, 2013.

Rosado, D. G., D. Mellado, E. Fernandez-Medina, and M. Piattini, eds. *Security Engineering for Cloud Computing: Approaches and Tools*. IGI Global, 2012

Winkler, J. R. *Securing the Cloud: Cloud Computer Security Techniques and Tactics*. Syngress, 2011.

47.9 NOTES

1. United States Joint Chiefs of Staff, "Information Operations," Joint Publication 3–13, 2006, p. II-2, www.dtic.mil/doctrine/jel/new_pubs/jp3_13.pdf (URL inactive).
2. There are some forms of data that don't reside in files, but they are transient. For example, memory buffers, stacks, and registers contain data used during execution of programs, but they are not normally accessible to users except through special tools such as *privileged-mode debug* utilities or special forensic programs.
3. The site http://dmoz.org/Computers/Software/Databases/Data_Warehousing/Data_Integrity_and_Cleansing_Tools listed 38 such tools at the time of writing (May 2013).
4. L. Bandoim, "Growth of Cloud Computing and ERP Continues to Accelerate," *Technorati | Technology | Cloud Computing*, May 4, 2013, http://technorati.com/technology/cloud-computing/article/growth-of-cloud-computing-and-erp
5. A. Nain, "With The Cloud Market Set To Flirt With 20% Growth In 2013, How Can You Play It?" *Seeking Alpha*, March 20, 2013, http://seekingalpha.com/article/

1291461-with-the-cloud-market-set-to-flirt-with-20-growth-in-2013-how-can-you-play-it

6. J. Weeks, "Vertical Markets—2013 Growth Predictions for Cloud Computing," *US Signal Blog*, January 16, 2013, http://ussignalcom.com/blog/vertical-markets-2013-growth-predictions-for-cloud-computing
7. E. Messmer, "Gartner: Growth in Cloud Computing To Shape 2013 Security Trends: Gartner Predicts by 2015, 10% of Overall IT Security Enterprise Capabilities Will Be Delivered in the Cloud," *Network World*, December 6, 2012, www.networkworld.com/news/2012/120612-gartner-cloud-security-264873.html

CHAPTER 48

EMAIL AND INTERNET USE POLICIES

M. E. Kabay and Nicholas Takacs

48.1 INTRODUCTION.[1] The Internet offers every enterprise exciting opportunities to find timely information and to reach potential clients. This very power brings with it risks of damaging corporate and professional reputations. Nontechnical problems in cyberspace include bad information, fraud, loss of productivity, and violations of civil and criminal law as well as violations of the conventions of proper behavior established by custom in cyberspace.

In addition, widespread abuse of Internet access while at work is forcing recognition that clear policies are essential to guide employees in appropriate use of these corporate resources. The consensus in our profession—despite the dreadful lack of hard statistics—is that something like two-thirds of all the damage caused to our information systems is from insiders who are poorly trained, careless, or malicious. (For a detailed discussion of security statistics, see Chapter 10 in this *Handbook.*) For example, a study published in late 2005 reported that:

> Sixty-nine percent of 110 senior executives at Fortune 1,000 companies say they are "very concerned" about insider network attacks or data theft, according to a study by Caymas Systems, a network security technology firm based in San Jose, Calif. And 25 percent say they are so concerned they can't sleep at night, Sanjay Uppal, a vice president at Caymas Systems, told eSecurityPlanet.[2]

A McAfee-sponsored survey in Europe showed that (in the words of the Department of Homeland Security *Daily Open Source Infrastructure Report*[3]):

> Workers across Europe are continuing to place their own companies at risk from information security attacks. This "threat from within" is undermining the investments organizations make to defend against security threats, according to a study by security firm McAfee. The survey, conducted by ICM Research, produced evidence of both ignorance and negligence over the use of company IT resources. One in five workers let family and friends use company laptops and PCs to access the Internet. More than half connect their own devices or gadgets to their work PC and a quarter of these do so every day. Around 60 percent admit to storing personal content on their work PC. One in ten confessed to downloading content at work they shouldn't. Most errant workers put their firms at risk through either complacency or ignorance, but a small minority are believed to be actively seeking to damage the company from within. Five percent of those questioned say they have accessed areas of their IT system they shouldn't have while a very small number admitted to stealing information from company servers.[4]

Another topic of growing significance is saturation by floods of email sent by well-intentioned employees who do not know how to use email effectively.

Finally, some of the information in this chapter may help security administrators involve their users in a more active role by giving them take-home messages that can help them protect their own families and friends. Getting employees to care about security for their families is a good step to involving them in corporate security.

For more information on effective security awareness and corporate culture change, see Chapters 49 and 50 in this *Handbook*.

48.2 DAMAGING THE REPUTATION OF THE ENTERPRISE. When someone posts information to the 'Net, the message header normally indicates who the sender is. In particular, all employees using a corporate email account identify their employer in every posting. It follows that when an employee—for example, joe@acme.com—misbehaves on the 'Net, it is likely that everyone seeing the misbehavior will associate it with the employer, regardless of futile attempts to dissociate the employee from the employer by statements such as "The opinions above are not necessarily those of my employer."

Employees can embarrass their employers by using their corporate email identifiers in these ways:

- **Flaming.** Launching rude verbal attacks on others.
- **Spamming.** Sending junk email (spam), unsolicited advertising, and sales promotions, to multiple, often unrelated, Usenet groups and mailing lists and to people's email addresses without their permission.
- **Mail-bombing.** Sending many email messages to a single email address to annoy its user, or in extreme cases, to cause a denial of service.

In addition, employees can violate laws, send out embarrassing content via email, implicate their employers in personal affairs, and spread falsehoods with actionable consequences.

48.2.1 Violating Laws.

Employees may engage in illegal activities that can seriously compromise their employer; examples include:

- Industrial espionage
- Stock manipulation
- Criminal hacking, unauthorized penetration of other systems
- Sabotage, denial of service attacks
- Vandalism, defacement of Websites
- Creating, transmitting, or storing child pornography
- Sending threats (e.g., of harm to the President of the United States)
- Credit card fraud, using stolen or fraudulently generated credit card numbers for purchases made using corporate resources

Corporate Internet usage policies should explicitly forbid any of these actions.

48.2.2 Ill-Advised Email.

There have been too many cases of foolish use of email in recent years. Employees have created a hostile working environment by sending internal email with lewd or hateful jokes and images; staff members have insulted their bosses or their employees in email that later became public; people have made libelous accusations about other workers or about competing companies. All of these uses are wholly inappropriate for a medium that takes control of distribution away from the originators and produces records that can be backed up and archived for indefinite periods of possible retrieval.

Common sense dictates that anything sent via email should not be illegal or even embarrassing if it were published in a newspaper.

Users should also be aware that it is a poor idea to insult people using email. Sending *flames* that belittle, ridicule, and demean other people is likely to generate more of the same in response, and flaming is an ugly practice that distorts standards for public and private discourse. If a user or employee chooses to respond to a rude or demeaning email, he or she should refrain from replying with the same rude or demeaning tone. In one case reported in a security management class to author Kabay in 2013, an employee noted that a young intern responded to an email memorandum by hitting REPLY ALL and sending a contemptuous, arrogant, demeaning, and ungrammatical criticism of the message. That message had been sent to all employees by the CEO. The intern was fired that day.

Employees should work to maintain the moral high ground by refraining from obscenity, profanity, and vulgarity in written as well as in oral discourse. Not only is this a good habit in general, but it also avoids the possibility of enraging total strangers who may be physically or electronically dangerous.

These best practices also apply to the home and family life. Criminal hackers have been known to damage credit ratings, participate in identity theft to rack up large bills in the victims' names, and even tamper with phone company accounts. In one notorious prank, hackers forwarded all incoming phone calls for the famous security expert Donn Parker, who is quite bald, to a hair restoration business.

Anonymizers are services that strip identifying information from email and then forward the text to the indicated targets. However, even anonymizers respond to subpoenas demanding the identity of people involved in libel or threats. The Website called *annoy.com* consistently posts messages that will annoy a substantial number of people as an exercise of United States First Amendment rights; however, even that service once had a particularly clear message on its refusal to tolerate abuse:

> WARNING
>
> It has come to our attention that certain people have been using annoy.com to deliver what some might consider to be threats of physical violence or harm to others.
>
> Do not mistake our commitment to freedom of speech for a license to abuse our service in this manner.
>
> We plan to cooperate fully with law enforcement agencies in whatever efforts they make to find you and punish you—even if it's some renegade authoritarian dictatorship ... Free speech and annoy.com are not about harassment and definitely not about harm or violence. If you think for a second we will allow cowardly idiots to spoil our free speech party you are making a mistake. A huge mistake.

For both USENET, a global Internet discussion system, and for discussion groups on the Web, a message may be forever. There are archives of USENET messages stretching back for decades, and the Wayback Machine (named for a time machine run by Mr. Peabody [a scholarly dog] in Hanna-Barbara's *Rocky* [a flying squirrel] *and Bullwinkle* [an engaging moose] TV cartoon show of the 1960s) for the Web has records back to 1996. Sending abusive or degrading messages online may not permanently damage the sender's reputation, but it is not likely to *improve* anyone's prospects for getting or keeping a good job, especially if the sender's email address includes a corporate affiliation.

48.2.3 Inappropriate Use of Corporate Identifiers. Considerable controversy exists as to whether corporate policy should forbid corporate IDs for any personal use on the Internet. There is little reason for posting messages to newsgroups in the .alt hierarchy, and especially not to groups catering to or sympathetic to criminal activity. If employees of an organization want to participate in vigorous political discussion, conversations about sexual activity, and any other topic unrelated to their work, they are free to do so using their own Internet identities. Employers pay for corporate email identities; people who want to post opinions—especially political opinions—about, say, basket-weaving techniques should pay for their own access and leave their employer out of the postings.

The risks of damaging an organization's reputation by violating netiquette are high. Some abusers have themselves been abused by angry and unscrupulous Internauts. In one notorious early case, back in 1994, a naïve executive spammed the 'Net—he posted messages in a couple of dozen newsgroups. In retaliation, his company's 800-number was posted to phone-sex discussion groups in the .alt hierarchy, resulting in thousands of irate and expensive phone calls by seekers of aural sex. Regular customers were unable to get through, and some staff resigned because of the offensive calls. The executive nearly lost his job.

An additional risk is that employees will inadvertently post company-confidential information to what they erroneously perceive as closed, private groups. Competitors or troublemakers can then exploit the information for competitive advantage or publicize it to harm the enterprise. Even if a discussion group or mailing really is closed, nothing prevents a participant from using or disseminating confidential information without permission. By the time the breach of security is discovered, it can be too late for remediation. Such breaches are an invitation for spear-phishing attacks, as discussed in Chapter 20 in this *Handbook*.

48.2.4 Blogs, Personal Websites, and Social Networking Sites. Should employers be concerned about the creation of blogs, personal Websites, and social-networking pages by employees? There have been cases in which employees made unwise or frankly derogatory comments about their current employers, with predictable consequences. It is much better to prevent such conflicts by establishing clear policies for employees that explicitly ban mention of the employer's name in personal publications and media such as blogs and Websites. A variation can require corporate approval by the public relations or communications departments before material is published. Such policies are commonplace for control over what employees publish in interviews, newsletters, and other publications.

Some employees likely have personal pages in social-networking sites such as Facebook, Twitter, and Tumblr. The same issues arise when employees make reference to their employer by name as part of their profile: How would an employer feel about seeing an indecently dressed pictured on their Facebook page with the individual's profile displaying their corporate name? Employment agreements can, and should, stipulate limitations on the use of corporate identity. There is nothing wrong with stipulating that social-networking pages not include the name of an employer.

Further complicating the matter is the growth of professional social networking sites such as LinkedIn. These sites encourage posting a *digital resume*, which includes basic information about an individual's employment history. Much like personal networking sites, companies must set clear expectations on use and periodically monitor compliance through searches and visual inspection. In contrast with Facebook, though, LinkedIn tends not to have many users who post unprofessional information and comments on their own pages.

48.2.5 Disseminating and Using Incorrect Information. The Internet and in particular the World Wide Web are in some ways as great a change in information distribution as the invention of writing 6,000 years ago and the invention of movable type 600 years ago. In all these cases, the inventions involved *disintermediation*: the elimination of intermediaries in the transmission of knowledge. Writing eliminated the oral historians; one could read information from far away and long ago without having to speak to a person who had personally memorized that knowledge. Print allowed a far greater distribution of knowledge than handwritten books and scrolls, eliminating an entire class of scribes who controlled access to the precious and rare records. The 'Net and the Web have continued this trend, with a radical increase in the number of people capable of being publishers. Where publishing once required printing presses, capital, and extensive administrative infrastructure, or at least relatively expensive mimeographs (1950s), photocopiers (1960s), and printers (1970s), today an individual can publish material relatively inexpensively, if not free. Many Internet Service Providers (ISPs) offer free Web-hosting services and places for people to join electronic communities of every imaginable type. Even if the individual does not have access to the Internet at home, and follows work policies on use, free access can be obtained from local libraries or the increasing number of free Internet hot spots.

Web pages can lead to visibility unheard of even a decade ago. For example, one young exhibitionist named Jennifer Kaye Ringley put up a Website to display images of her home taken through Web-enabled cameras (Webcams); this "jennycam.org" site received up to *half a million hits per day* while it was in operation. Another young woman decided to put up a Website devoted to one of her favorite literary characters, Nero Wolfe, in the mid-1990s. Within a few years, her site was so well respected that she was hired by a Hollywood filmmaker as a technical consultant on a series of Nero Wolfe movies. The fees she was paid, despite offering to help for free, helped her get through her Ph.D. studies in social psychology. It would have been virtually impossible for her to achieve this recognition by trying to publish her own hard-copy fan magazine; the paper might have reached a few hundred people, but the Website reached many thousands.

Unfortunately, all of this disintermediation has negative implications as well as positive ones. Freedom from publishers has liberated the independent thinker from corporate influence, editorial limitations, and standards for house style. However, this freedom also liberated many people from responsible reporting, adequate research, and even the rudimentary principles of spelling and grammar. The dictum "Don't believe everything you read" is even more important when reading Web-based information. Individuals may publish incorrect versions of technical information (e.g., health sites that claim that massaging parts of the earlobe can cure many known diseases), unsubstantiated theories about historical and natural events (e.g., the Tungska Impact of 1908 was caused by an antimatter meteorite), and off-the-wall revisionist history (e.g., slavery in the United States was good for black people, and Hitler never persecuted Jews).

Wikipedia, although it has become the first line of information for some users, suffers from the possibility of temporary or even long-term modifications of content as pranks or for other purposes. For example, supporters of the failed right-wing candidate Sarah Palin are thought to have tried to alter the *Wikipedia* entry on Paul Revere to force it to conform to her incorrect statements about his famous ride.[5] Because there is no guarantee that the content of a reference to *Wikipedia* is legitimate or will be legitimate or even the same the next time the reference is followed, academic institutions tend to reject references to *Wikipedia* in term papers.

48.2.6 Hoaxes. Pranksters have been using email to fool gullible people for years using a particular sort of incorrect information: deliberate *hoaxes*. A hoax is a mischievous trick based on a made-up story. There are two major kinds of hoaxes circulating on the Internet: urban myths and false information about viruses. The archives in the urban myths Websites are full of hilarious hoaxes, some of which have been circulating for years. Why don't they die out?

The problem is the nature of the Internet. Information is not distributed solely from a centrally controlled site; on the contrary, anyone can broadcast, or rebroadcast, any kind of data at any time. There is neither reliable creation dates nor obligatory expiry dates on files, so those receiving a five-year-old document may have no obvious way of recognizing its age, and they almost certainly have no simple way of identifying obsolete or incorrect information. All they see is that the document has been sent to them recently, often by someone they know personally.

48.2.6.1 *Urban Myths.* Here are some notorious examples of the bizarre and sometimes disturbing urban myths that are thoroughly debunked on the Snopes.com Website:

- **Expensive cookies.** Someone claims that a Neiman-Marcus employee charged $250 to a credit card for the recipe to some good chocolate chip cookies. This story has been traced to a false claim dating back to 1948 in which a store was accused of charging $25 for the recipe to a fudge cake.
- **Do not flash your car lights.** In a gang-initiation ritual, hoodlums drive down a highway with their car lights off. Innocent drivers, flashing their lights as a reminder, would become the new target victims, usually resulting in their deaths by the gang.
- **Watch out for poisoned needles.** Insane, vengeful druggies leave needles tipped with HIV+ blood in movie theater seats, gas pump handles, and telephone change-return slots.
- **Lose your kidneys.** The victim visits a foreign city, goes drinking with strangers, and wakes up in the morning in a bathtub of ice with two neat incisions through which both kidneys have been removed. No one ever seems to explain why criminals who remove kidneys would bother packing the victim in ice.
- **Poor little guy wants postcards.** Craig Shergold is just one of the many real or imaginary children about whom well-meaning people circulate chain letters asking for postcards, business cards, prayers, and even money. Shergold was born in 1980; when he was nine, he was diagnosed with brain cancer, and friends started a project to cheer him up—they circulated messages asking people to send him postcards so he could be listed in the *Guinness Book of World Records.* By 1991, he had received 30 million cards and an American philanthropist arranged for brain surgery, which worked: Shergold went into remission. The postcard deluge did not. By 1997, the local post office had received over *250 million* postcards for him, and he was long since sick of the whole project.
- **Wish you would stop Making a Wish.** Around the mid-1990s, some prankster inserted false information about the Make-a-Wish Foundation into the outdated chain letters concerning Shergold. The unfortunate organization was promptly inundated with email and postal mail, none of which was in any way useful or relevant to its work. They had to post disclaimers on the Website to try to dissociate themselves from the outdated information.

48.2.6.2 *Virus Myths.* One category of hoaxes has become a perennial nuisance on the 'Net: virus myths. There is something wonderful about the willingness of gullible, well-meaning people to pass on ridiculous news about nonexistent viruses with impossible effects. One of the most famous is the Good Times "virus," which appeared around 1994. The myth and numerous variants have been circulating uninterruptedly for years. Every few years, there is a new outburst as some newcomers to the Internet encounter an old copy of the warnings and send it to everyone they know.

The original very short warning was as follows, including the incorrect punctuation:

> Here is some important information. Beware of a file called Goodtimes.
>
> Happy Chanukah everyone, and be careful out there. There is a virus on America Online being sent by E-Mail. If you get anything called "Good Times", DON'T read it or download it. It is a virus that will erase your hard drive. Forward this to all your friends. It may help them a lot.

The Good Times virus claimed that downloading a document or reading a document could cause harm; at that time, such a claim was impossible. Ironically, within a couple of years, it did in fact become possible to cause harm via documents because of the macro-language capabilities of Microsoft Word and other programs enabled for scripting. Over the rest of the 1990s, foolish people modified the name of the imaginary virus and added more details, sometimes claiming impossible effects such as destruction of computer hardware.

By 1997, the warnings were so ridiculous that an anonymous author distributed the following Monty Pythonesque satire:

> It turns out that this so-called hoax virus is very dangerous after all. Goodtimes will re-write your hard drive. Not only that, it will scramble any disks that are even close to your computer. It will recalibrate your refrigerator's coolness setting so all your ice cream goes melty. It will demagnetize the strips on all your credit cards, screw up the tracking on your television and use subspace field harmonics to scratch any CDs you try to play.
>
> It will give your ex-girlfriend your new phone number. It will mix Kool-aid into your fish tank. It will drink all your beer and leave dirty socks on the coffee table when company comes over. It will put a dead kitten in the back pocket of your good suit pants and hide your car keys when you are late for work.
>
> Goodtimes will make you fall in love with a penguin. It will give you nightmares about circus midgets. It will pour sugar in your gas tank and shave off both your eyebrows while dating your girlfriend behind your back and billing the dinner and hotel room to your Discover card.
>
> It will seduce your grandmother. It does not matter if she is dead, such is the power of Goodtimes, it reaches out beyond the grave to sully those things we hold most dear.
>
> It moves your car randomly around parking lots so you can't find it. It will kick your dog. It will leave libidinous messages on your boss's voice mail in your voice! It is insidious and subtle. It is dangerous and terrifying to behold. It is also a rather interesting shade of mauve.
>
> Goodtimes will give you Dutch Elm disease. It will leave the toilet seat up. It will make a batch of Methamphetamine in your bathtub and then leave bacon cooking on the stove while it goes out to chase gradeschoolers with your new snowblower.

Unaware people circulate virus hoaxes because they receive the hoax from someone they know. Unfortunately, a personal friendship with a sender is no guarantee of the accuracy of their message. Some awfully nice people are gullible, well-meaning dupes of social engineers. Transmitting technical information about viruses (or any apprehended danger) without verifying that information's legitimacy and accuracy is a disservice to everyone. It makes it harder for experts to reach the public with warnings of real dangers, and it clutters up recipients' email in-baskets with alarming information of limited or no use whatever. Teach employees, family, and friends to consult snopes.com or an equivalent before forwarding alarming messages—and don't forward any messages about malware: Make sure everyone you know uses up-to-date antimalware software.

48.2.6.3 Junk Email. Unsolicited commercial email (UCE) is derisively known as *junk* email and also as *spam*. Junk email is spawned by foolish (in the early days) or criminal (today) people who send out thousands or millions of identical messages to unwilling recipients. Junk email clogs victims' in-baskets and wastes their time as they open these unwanted messages and take a few seconds to realize that they are junk. Junk email containing pornographic images or advertising pornography may be highly offensive to the recipients. Junk may even push people's email systems over their server limits if they are not picking up their messages regularly; in such cases, wanted email may bounce because the mailbox is full. Today, junk email is the primary vector for social engineering attacks such as *phishing* designed to trick recipients into compromising their privacy or their identification and authentication codes. (See Chapter 20 in this *Handbook* for more details of spam, phishing, and other tricks.)

Most junk email uses forged headers; that is, the senders deliberately put misleading information in the FROM and REPLY fields to avoid receiving angry responses from the victims of their criminal behavior. Forging email headers is illegal in the states of Massachusetts, Virginia, and Washington. In these states, if the perpetrators are identified, it can lead to court cases and financial penalties for each message involved in the fraud.

In one famous, groundbreaking case, college student Craig Nowak sent out a few thousand junk email messages and followed the instructions in his spam kit by putting a made-up REPLY address using "@flowers.com" without checking to see if there really was such a domain. Indeed there was, and the owner of this reputable floral delivery service, Tracy LaQuey Parker, was none too pleased when her system was flooded with over 5,000 bounce messages and angry letters from customers saying that they would never do business with her again. She sued the student for damages and was awarded over $18,000 by a judge who said he wished he could have been even more punitive.[6]

In general, spam has become a mechanism for tricking unaware vendors into paying for illusory marketing services. It is sad to see email advertising for Chinese industrial piping being sent to North American university professors; the victims are the hard-working Chinese industrialists who have been cheated by assurances from criminals promising to send their advertising to willing and well-qualified recipients.

Much of the remaining junk is sent out in the hope that a tiny proportion of the recipients of the misspelled, absurd claims will be gulled into sending money—or their email addresses—to drop boxes. For more information about such social engineering attacks, see Chapters 19 and 20 in this *Handbook*.

If you are involved in an email discussion group, especially an unmoderated group, about a specific topic, do not post email to members of the list on a subject that is outside the topic area. A typical class of inappropriate posting is an appeal for support of a worthy cause that has no, or only a tenuous, relation to the subject area. For example, someone might appeal for support to save whales in a discussion group about gardening: bad idea. The reasoning is "They like plants; probably environmentally sensitive; likely to be interested in conservation; therefore they will be glad to hear about whales." The problem is that such reasoning could be extended to practically any topic, disrupting the focus of the group. Such messages often cause angry retorts, which are typically sent by naïve members to the entire list instead of only to the sender of the inappropriate mail. Then the angry retorts cause further angry responses about burdening the list with useless messages and soon the gardening group is mired in dissension and wasted effort, generating bad feeling and distrust.

As suggested in the preceding paragraph, if you see inappropriate messages on an email list you care about, do not reply to the entire list; reply *nicely* and only to the sender, with possibly a copy to the moderator, if there is one. The reply should be temperate and polite.

48.2.6.4 Chain Letters and Ponzi Schemes. A particularly annoying form of junk email is the chain letter. Some chain letters include ridiculous stories about terrible diseases and accidents that have befallen people who refused to forward the message (ridiculous on the face of it, but apparently appealing to the irrational enough to keep the nonsense circulating). Others focus on getting victims to send money to someone at the top of a list of names, while adding their names to the bottom of the list, before sending it on to a specified number of recipients. Depending on the length of the list and the amount to be sent to the person on top, the theoretical return could be in the hundreds of thousands of dollars. In practice, only the originators of the scheme profit. After a while, all possible participants have been solicited with disappointing results, and the chains are broken in many places.

Another type of pyramid is known as a Ponzi scheme, which is an investment swindle in which high profits are promised and early investors are paid off with funds raised from later ones. The scam is named after Charles Ponzi (1882–1949), a speculator who organized such a scheme in 1919 and 1920. The Ponzi scheme tricked thousands of people in Boston when Ponzi guaranteed a 50 percent profit on contributions in 45 days and a doubling of value in 90 days. The con man claimed he was redeeming 1-cent Spanish postal certificates for 6-cent U.S. stamps—a claim ridiculed by financial analysts at the time. Nonetheless, Ponzi took in around $15 million in 1920 dollars and stole around $8 million, paying out the rest to the early participants in order to develop credibility. Six banks collapsed because they invested their depositors' funds in the scheme. Ponzi eventually served over three years in jail but escaped in 1925.[7]

The modern-day email Ponzi scheme typically includes passionate assurances from vaguely identified people about how skeptical they were about the scheme, but how they succumbed to curiosity, participated in the scheme, and earned vast amounts of money (e.g., $50,000) within a couple of weeks. The letters often include assurances that everything is legal and point to nonexistent postal information phone lines or claim "As Seen on TV" at various points in the letter.

These letters instruct the victim to send a small amount of money (typically $1 or $2) to a short list of about four people to receive their "reports." The victim is then instructed to add his or her name and address to the list, while removing the first one, before sending a copy of the new letter to as many people as possible. Some letters go through computations involving such assumptions as "Imagine you send out a hundred, a thousand, or ten thousand messages and get a mere 1%, 2%, or 10% response," and then promise enormous returns. In fact, the "reports" are nothing but one-page, meaningless blurbs about chain letters. The scammers are trying to get around regulations such as the U.S. Post Office's bar against fraudulent uses of the mail.

Here is the exact text of a letter sent on December 1, 2000, by V. J. Bellinger of the Operations Support Group of the United States Postal Inspection Service in Newark, New Jersey. It has some interesting information that should be helpful to readers attempting to convince employees (or family and friends) that such chain email involving postal addresses is illegal.

> A chain letter or a multi-level marketing program is actionable under the Postal Lottery, False Representation, and/or Mail Fraud Statutes if it contains three elements: prize, consideration and chance. Prize is usually in the form of money, commissions, or something else of value that the solicitation claims you will receive. Consideration is the required payment to the sponsor in order to obtain the prize. Chance is determined by the activities of participants over whom the mailer has no control. These types of schemes constitute lotteries are barred from the mails because they violate the following statutes: Title 18, United States Code, Sections 1302 and 1341 and Title 39, United States Code, Section 3005.
>
> In attempts to appear legal, many chain letter or multi-level marketing mailings offer, for a fee, a product, or "report." However, since the success of the program is dependent on the number of people willing to participate, all three elements that constitute a violation continue to be present.
>
> The promoter of this scheme has been advised of the potential violations involved and has been requested to discontinue this type of mailing activity. ...

A superficially similar phenomenon is known as multilevel marketing. In this non-fraudulent, legitimate system of selling products and services, people are encouraged to recruit distributors from among their friends and acquaintances, but the emphasis is on the value of the products. No one claims that anyone is going to become wealthy without work, and there is no demand for investments. The products have an established market, and the company makes money through sales, not through recruitment.

Here are some practical guidelines for employees and individuals:

- Do not participate in any scheme that relies on forwarding large numbers of letters or email messages to everyone you know or to strangers.
- Differentiate between pyramid frauds and legitimate multilevel marketing systems: The former emphasize enrolling participants, whereas the latter emphasize the value of products and services.
- Do not participate in alleged multilevel marketing systems if they require substantial investments.
- If you are interested in a multilevel marketing operation:
  - Check out the owners and officers.
  - Talk to people who have bought the products to see if they are happy with their purchases.
  - Contact your local Better Business Bureau to see if there have been any complaints.
- Do not send money to suspected pyramid frauds.
- Work with your colleagues to demonstrate how a pyramid fraud takes money from a growing number of later victims and shifts it to people who participate earlier in the fraud. Reinforce the fact that fraud is illegal, even though the prospect of early participation might seem to yield results.

48.2.6.5 Get-Rich-Quick Schemes. Other get-rich-quick schemes on the 'Net play on the victims' wishful thinking, their lack of skepticism, and usually on a lack of common sense. There have been claims that you can earn a quarter of a million dollars a year by grooming poodles in your home. Or that you can become a millionaire by working four hours a week, sending out promotional literature for products you do not even have to sell. Often, dangerous people promulgate some such schemes; for example, some extremist militia groups have been charging people hundreds of dollars to learn how to defraud the government by claiming liens on government property and then pledging the nonsensical liens as collateral for loans. Other criminals circulate programs for generating fraudulent credit card numbers and using them to steal goods. In other cases, criminals charge money to teach victims how to falsify their bad credit records so they can obtain yet more fraudulent credit, all the while claiming that their criminal methods are 100 percent legal.

From a corporate standpoint, such chain letters and schemes waste bandwidth and pose a potential for serious embarrassment when enterprise resources are used to spread the nonsensical material. However, corporate security can win favor with users by helping them avoid the pitfalls of such fraud, even when using their own computer systems. The benefits are particularly strong when helping employees to teach their own children how to avoid this kind of trouble.

To illustrate the trouble kids can get into using these techniques, consider the case of Drew Henry Madden. In 1996, this 16-year-old Australian boy from Brisbane, just after leaving school, started defrauding businesses using stolen and forged credit card numbers. He stole $18,000 of goods and, in February 1997, pled guilty to 104 counts of fraud and was sentenced to a year in jail. However, investigators uncovered additional fraud, and it turned out that he had stolen an additional $100,000 in goods and services. In October 1997, he pled guilty to another 294 counts of fraud and was given an additional suspended sentence. His defense attorney blamed poor security for the losses: "Madden started with very minor credit card fraud, but it escalated alarmingly, because the safeguards were so inadequate." Despite the youngster's unusual revenue stream, his mother appeared to have accepted his globetrotting ways and massive purchases of lottery tickets without comment. At one point, she told reporters, "If we were a wealthy family he'd be at a private school, where his talents could be directed properly."

A relatively new kind of fraud on the Internet is the diploma mill. These organizations pretend to be educational institutions; actually, they are one or more fraudulent individuals who sell bogus diplomas purporting to represent recognized degrees but that fool no one but the purchaser. While diploma mills are not accredited, the lack of accreditation does not automatically implicate a school as a fraudulent entity.

48.3 THREATS TO PEOPLE AND SYSTEMS.

One particular class of email deserves a special mention: threats. Threatening emails may target people, systems, organizations, or the processes that these entities rely on. As with the other types of illegal activity on the Internet, proper education, awareness, and response can limit the number of future victims.

48.3.1 Threats of Physical Harm.

Anyone who receives threats through email has a right, and possibly a duty, to inform local law enforcements officials. In today's climate of fear and violence, any threat warrants attention. In addition to the distress such messages can generate, they may be warning signs of serious trouble. In particular, threats about violence at work, at school, or against any definable group may be the early warning that allows authorities to step in to defuse a potentially explosive situation.

Sending threatening email is not an acceptable joke or a minor prank, especially if the threat involves violence. Some people, believing that they can mask their real identity, have foolishly sent death threats to the White House; because the Secret Service is obligated by law to investigate *all* threats to the president and the first family, agents show up within a few hours to interrogate the miscreants. For example, youngsters in the tenth grade at Profile High School in Bethlehem, New Hampshire, sent death threats to the White House Website from their school computers. The messages were traced within minutes by the Secret Service, the children were suspended from school, and they lost their Internet privileges for the next two years.

48.3.2 Pedophiles Online. This section applies primarily to training users for protection of their children.

Pedophilia is defined as sexual arousal in response to contact with or images of prepubescent children. Some pedophiles misrepresent themselves as youngsters in chat rooms or via email and trick children into forming friendships with what they believe are peers. In one notorious case, Paul Brown Jr., a 47-year-old man, misrepresented himself as a 15-year-old boy in email to a 12-year-old girl in New Jersey. The victim's mother stumbled onto the long-range relationship when she found sitting on her own doorstep a package from her daughter to a man she did not know; the child had put the wrong postage on it and the post office had sent it back. Opening the package, she found a videotape that showed her daughter cavorting naked in front of the family video camera. The distraught mother searched her daughter's room and discovered a pair of size 44 men's underpants in one of the child's bureau drawers.

Brown was arrested in February 1997. Police found correspondence with at least 10 other teenage girls across the country, through which Brown convinced his young victims, some as young as 12, to perform various sexual acts in front of cameras and to send him the pictures and videotapes. He pleaded guilty in June to enticing a minor into making pornography. In August 1997, at his sentencing hearing, one of his many victims told the court that she had suffered ridicule and humiliation as a result of her entrapment and had left her school to escape the trauma. She accused Brown of emotional rape. Displaying an astonishing interpretation of his own behavior, Brown said at his sentencing hearing, "It was just bad judgment on my part." Using good judgment, the court sentenced him to five years of incarceration.

In March 2000, Patrick Naughton, a former executive of the INFOSEEK online company, pled guilty to having crossed state lines to commit statutory rape of a child. In August, FBI officials said that Naughton had been providing help in law enforcement investigations of pedophilia on the 'Net. In return for his cooperation, prosecutors asked the court for five years of probation (instead of a possible 15 years in prison), counseling, a $20,000 fine (instead of the maximum $250,000), and an agreement not to have unapproved contact with children and to stay out of sex chat rooms online.

The problem of Internet-enabled pedophile stalking has reached international dimensions. In January 1999, police forces around the world cooperated to track and close down a worldwide ring of pedophiles trafficking in child pornography through the 'Net. Child safety experts have warned the U.S. congressional committee on child online protection that with the average age of online users declining (children between the ages of two and seven are among the fastest-growing user cohorts on the Internet), children increasingly are put at risk by their careless or ignorant online activities.

48.3.3 Viruses and Other Malicious Code. As of 2008, the WildList (www.wildlist.org) reports over 2,000 distinct forms of malicious program code commonly circulating in cyberspace. There are many more types recorded by antivirus researchers, but they have not been seen infecting significant numbers of user computers. Most of these harmful programs are limited to antivirus laboratories and to the computers of virus hobbyists—people who derive pleasure from playing with danger. For more information about viruses and other malware, see Chapters 16, 17, 18, and 41 in this *Handbook*.

Employers should have policies clearly forbidding the creation, exchange, and storage of malicious software on corporate systems.

48.3.4 Spyware and Adware. In December 1999, computer scientist, cybercrime investigator, and writer Richard Smith became curious about a program called *zBubbles* that he had installed on his system to improve online shopping. Created by Alexa, a subsidiary of e-tailer Amazon.com, the program provided competitive information about alternative and possibly cheaper sources for particular products. However, Smith discovered that there was more going on than met the eye.

Smith monitored his own Internet traffic while he was using zBubbles by using a packet sniffer, a tool that displays details of every piece of information being transmitted through a network connection. He found that zBubbles was sending a steady stream of information about him and his surfing habits to Alexa, including his home address, the titles of DVDs he had browsed on Buy.com, and the details of an airline ticket he had verified online. In addition, the program even continued to send information regularly to Alexa's servers even when Smith was not using his browser. It was learned that zBubbles was not the only program sending information back to its makers.

Many programs are available that, once installed, report on the Websites you visit, which banner advertisements you click, what products you search for, and any other information the programs have been designed to acquire. Even widely used downloading software, such as NetZip, has been shown to report to its providers on the names of every file downloaded by each user.

Sometimes these programs are informally known as *E.T.* applications, in a reference to Steven Spielberg's movie of that name, in which an extraterrestrial strives to "phone home"—exactly what the spyware programs are doing.

The term *spyware* is applied to any technology that transmits information without the knowledge of its user. Several programs distributed without charge through the Internet secretly collect information about the user, monitor user behavior, and then send those data to advertisers. The more general class of monitoring software that collects information for use by advertisers is known as *advertising-supported software* or *adware*. These programs allow freeware to make money for its creators by generating revenue based on how many users transmit information to the advertisers about their habits.

Although defenders of the advertising-supported programs claim that they are harmless, privacy advocates argue that the issue is control: Do users know what these programs are doing, or are they collecting and transmitting information covertly? Some adware comes with complicated contracts containing complex legal language to bury the fact that they will monitor and report user behavior. Worse yet, many such contracts explicitly authorize the software supplier to alter the privacy conditions without notification and, preposterously, instruct the user to check the contracts on the Web frequently. No one has the time to monitor countless suppliers to see if privacy conditions have been altered, especially if there is no attempt to highlight changes.

Another issue is that some spyware modules have used *stealth* technology characteristic of viruses, Trojan horses, and other malicious software. For example, some adware (e.g., TSADBOT) installs itself as a system process and is not listed in the Windows task list. Therefore, it cannot easily by aborted by a user. TSADBOT also resists removal; even if the carrier product is uninstalled, TSADBOT persists. If a user's firewall blocks outbound transmission by the TSADBOT process, the spyware initiates attempts to reach its target at a rate of 10 per second, potentially leading to central processing unit (CPU) and network resource overload.

Spyware, like any software, can contain errors that cause system problems. In particular, components of the Aureate/Radiate spyware have been shown to cause system instability and crashes.

One of the most egregious cases of spyware erupted in 1999, when it was discovered that CometCursor, a supplier of cute cartoon-character cursors aimed at children, was sending information back to its servers about what the children were browsing on the 'Net. According to some attorneys, this kind of covert data gathering about children may be a violation of the U.S. Federal Child Online Privacy Protection Act.

Several free software programs have been written to help users identify and remove spyware. In addition, personal firewalls can usually identify and block unauthorized outbound communications; the free version of ZoneAlarm, for example, does so effectively. Today's antimalware programs (e.g., Bitdefender) include antispyware functions. There are also many specialized programs (e.g., Lavasoft's Ad-Aware) available that run in the background to monitor and thwart attempts to install spyware and adware.

48.4 THREATS TO PRODUCTIVITY.

Some activities and phenomena are nuisances to employers principally because of their noxious effects on productivity and their abuse of corporate resources. Junk email and mailstorms, for example, are a problem because they saturate resources, not because they cause specific harm to the organization or to its employees. However, chain letters, get-rich-quick schemes, online auctions, online gambling, excessive online shopping, and Internet addiction can be directly harmful to employees and others.

48.4.1 Inefficient Use of Corporate Email.

The next sections focus on problems caused by mistakes in the use of email—mistakes that can cause annoyance, inefficiency, and potential disruption of critical business processes.

48.4.1.1 Forwarding Email to Personal Accounts.

Employees may be tempted to forward their corporate email traffic to their personal email addresses for convenience, or when they have no convenient way of accessing their corporate email system from outside the office. Such forwarding should be forbidden by policy unless virtual private networks (VPNs) or other strongly encrypted channels are used for the employee's private email.

Email and other traffic on the Internet have no inherent confidentiality. In theory, anyone capable of intercepting TCP/IP packets anywhere during transmission can breach confidentiality. Thus, again in theory, anyone with access to the equipment of ISPs, Internet backbone transmission lines, and even to the public switched telephone network can intercept packets. With downlink footprints from satellite relays amounting to square miles, practically anything can in theory be intercepted from much of the traffic circulating on the Internet.

However, in practice, reported breaches of confidentiality have almost all resulted from data access at the endpoints, not in transit. Insider attacks and breaches of server security have been responsible for most of the data interceptions that have reached the press and the courts.

A practical impediment to effective interception of meaningful data in transit is the datagram routing that underlies the Internet: Datagrams are packets of information with origin and destination information; store-and-forward transmission allows these datagrams to be sent through the Internet via different routes from other packets in a message stream. Routing tables can be updated in real time to reflect changes in traffic density or availability of specific links to other destinations on the Internet, so there is no guarantee that packets from the same message will travel the same route or arrive in the proper sequence (sequence numbers allow reassembly of the original message). Therefore, seizing individual packets at random anywhere other than the origin and destination of packets is unlikely to result in very much result for the effort.

Nonetheless, best practices do recommend that encryption be used for communication of sensitive data; therefore, many organizations install virtual private networks (VPN) for communication with established trading partners. VPN software is also available for *tunneling* through the Internet from a remote workstation over nonsecure communications lines. A simple example of such a link-encryption function is the Web-based email services that use SSL to establish a secure link to the email server (i.e., they use https instead of just plain http). The user can pick up email from the corporate server without having it forwarded in the clear to an insecure external email service. Some of the email products include facilities for direct communication between a secure email server and the users' email client.

Using *VPN tunneling software* as a search string in the Google search engine brings up almost half a million hits (in May 2013), many of them for specific products and data sheets, so readers will be able to find a solution that fits their needs.

48.4.1.2 Mislabeling the Subject Line.

Many people make the mistake of creating new messages to a correspondent by finding any old message from that person and replying to it. The problem is that these people usually leave the old subject intact, resulting in ridiculous situations such as finding a critically important message in July in an email labeled "Birthday party 12 May."

Not all email messages are created equal; some are destined for the trash heap, if not of history, at least of the email system. That decision is sometimes made automatically as a function of the subject line. For example, a user adds the subject line of a joke to an email filter, resulting in future messages with that subject ending up in the junk mail folder. Someone replies to the joke message with important information, and the mail filter sees the subject and automatically moves the message to the recipient's junk mail folder. The recipient may never see the important information, as most people do not actively monitor their junk folders.

Another problem with mislabeled subjects occurs when someone embeds more than one distinct topic in an email message whose subject line implies otherwise. For example, suppose an email message subject reads "Next week's meeting," but the sender includes an urgent request for action today on some critical issue; there is a good chance the receiver may not open the message right away if other messages seem more important.

Employees should make their subject line as descriptive as possible without turning it into a paragraph. Some email systems truncate subject lines in the display of messages that a user sees; it makes sense to put keywords at the front of the subject. Encourage staff to use prefixes such as "MISA:" or "ABCv2.0.1:" to help organize their messages. Using standard formats in subject lines can help too. For example, faculty and staff in the MISA program at Norwich University refer to an issue in a particular seminar by using the form "MISA c.s" in their subject line, where c represents the class (e.g., 40 for students starting in December 2013) and s represents the seminar number (e.g., 1 through 6).

These simple suggestions can make email more effective as a communications tool.

48.4.1.3 First e-Impressions. When you receive an email message from a stranger, do you care whether it has spelling mistakes and grammar mistakes? What about offensive language and off-color humor? Does the context matter? For example, do you apply the same standards to email referring to business matters as to informal communications about a hobby?

Researchers at the University of Chicago have been investigating the effects of email on perceptions of character. Psychologist Nicholas Epley and colleagues examined oral exchanges on conversational topics by phone between randomly selected people using six assigned questions. They then transcribed the oral conversations and used exactly the same answers for the written, email version of the question and answer sessions.[8]

Their results were interesting. The questioners had been given false biographical sketches of the people they were communicating with, indicating substandard intelligence or normal intelligence, as well as different pictures showing neat people or slobs. Subjects who used the phone to listen to the prescribed responses had favorable impressions of their interlocutor's intelligence, regardless of the bios and pictures. In contrast, "Via email, however, students held onto their first impressions, continuing to assume their partners had substandard intelligence, for example, if that's what the biographical sketch indicated."

If this research is confirmed, the lesson is that when using email, first impressions really do count. Professionals should carefully review email messages for acceptable writing, including word choice, punctuation, capitalization, and spelling.

48.4.1.4 Email Disclaimers. Author Kabay once received a 30-word email message from a very nice reader in Britain and noticed that his email system added the following astonishing disclaimer, which is quoted in its sonorous totality, including British spelling, after scrubbing it of identifying details:

> This email, its contents and any files or attachments transmitted with it are intended solely for the addressee(s) and may be legally privileged and/or confidential. Access by any other party is unauthorised without the express written permission of the sender.
>
> If you have received this email in error you may not copy or use the contents, files, attachments, or information in any way nor disclose the same to any other person. Please destroy it and contact the sender on the number printed above, via the <Name of Bank> switchboard on +44 (0) nnnn nnnnnn for <place1> and + 44 (0) nnnn nnnnnn for <place2> or via email by return.
>
> Internet communications are not secure unless protected using strong cryptography. This email has been prepared using information believed by the author to be reliable and accurate, but <Name of Bank> makes no warranty or representation, express or implied, as to its accuracy or completeness and is not liable to you or to anyone else for any loss or damage in connection with any transmission sent by the Bank to you over the Internet. <Name of Bank> makes no warranty that any information or material is free from any defects or viruses.
>
> In particular <Name of Bank> does not accept responsibility for changes made to this email after it was sent. If you suspect that this email may have been amended or intercepted, please contact the sender in the manner stated above. If this transmission includes files or attachments, please ensure that they are opened within the relevant application to ensure full receipt. If you experience difficulties, please refer back to the sender in the manner stated above.
>
> Any opinions expressed in this transmission are those of the author and do not necessarily reflect the opinions of the Bank and may be subject to change without notice.
>
> Please note that for the purposes of this document all references to <Name of Bank> or the Bank shall be taken to mean <Name of Bank> (place) Limited or any other member of the <Bigger> Bank Group. Nothing in this transmission shall or shall be deemed to constitute an offer or acceptance of an offer or otherwise have the effect of forming a contract by electronic communication.

Kabay commented in his response, "Did you know that your message has 30 words (152 bytes including spaces) whereas your disclaimer has 367 words (2,177 bytes)? That's the lowest signal-to-noise ratio (6.5 percent useful information out of the total and a 1:73 signal:noise ratio) I've ever seen outside a copy-of-copy-of-copy chain. Please congratulate your attorneys on using maximum of bandwidth for minimum content!"

Cluttering up email messages this way is a waste of bandwidth. It is worse in offices where people copy entire messages without editing the contents, resulting in copy-of-copy-of-copy chains that spread like cancerous eruptions through in-baskets throughout the organization. Some well-meaning folks even include the detailed headers in their copies.

As a matter of courtesy and good sense, when one replies to a message, it is a simple matter to strip nonessentials out of the copy of the original. Senders can use ellipses (… for cuts within a sentence, …. for cuts crossing sentence boundaries) to signal gaps, but usually one or two snips are enough to clean up the copy so that the reader can get the gist of the conversation without having to wade through reams of superfluous stuff. Unfortunately, this recommendation does not seem to be used much in practice.

48.4.1.5 *Centralized Distribution Lists.* Organizations may grow large enough that there is significant turnover among the staff. Not only do new staff members periodically join the group, but also staff members move from one functional group to another; for example, a staff member may change from being an assistant director in one program to being an administrative director in another. Occasionally, staff members may leave the group altogether.

A primitive way of maintaining distribution lists is to name a "Keeper-of-the-Lists" to maintain the list of all staff members; however, there is no link between the file and the mailing lists that each member of the group must maintain to be able to distribute email to appropriate individuals or groups. The independent files are almost certain to diverge from a centralized and accurate list. For example, a message that should be sent to all current employees may end up missing several new members and including staff members who no longer work in the target group.

Trying to make many people maintain their own copies of several distribution lists is a hopeless cause: Even with the best will in the world, people will inevitably forget to update their lists and therefore:

- Some mailings will miss legitimate recipients.
- Some people will receive messages they have no business reading.

There are at least four solutions that would rectify such a problem.

1. One can implement a central email sever (e.g., Microsoft Exchange Server), switch all users to a centrally controlled email client (e.g., Microsoft Outlook), and define corporate distribution lists maintained by the Keeper-of-the-Lists. All users will automatically access the one and only distribution list for each group without manual intervention.
2. One can install widely available list-server software to allow centralized creation and maintenance of specific lists; for example, SGS-ALL, SGS-DIRECTORS, MSIA-STAFF, MSIA-INSTRUCTORS, and the like create lists that all employees can use in addressing email.

3. One can switch all users to any email client that supports exportable mailing lists. Updated corporate distribution lists can then be sent to all users. However, this solution still requires manual intervention by users: Everyone has to replace an old list by the new list.
4. One can create a discussion group on a public server (e.g., Yahoo Groups) to define closed groups. These groups provide automatic access to mailing lists. Unfortunately, this approach has serious problems:
   - There are security concerns about using such groups for corporate communications.
   - It seems inappropriate to put a necessary production application on a free resource completely out of the control of the organization.

48.4.1.6 HTML Email. One of the six fundamental attributes of information that we protect is integrity, one aspect of which is consistency with the originally stored data (see Chapter 3 in this *Handbook*). When someone goes to the trouble of producing an elegantly formatted memorandum or other document and sends it out to recipients, everyone would like to preserve data integrity by seeing the same appearance on all the systems sharing that document.

Unfortunately, sending formatted messages as email messages (as distinct from attachments) does not guarantee preservation of the exact appearance of the source material.

Attractive, well-formatted email messages with boldface, italics, different point sizes, and the like usually get transmitted as HTML (hypertext markup language) to recipients' mailboxes, where most people's email clients (Eudora, Netscape, Outlook, etc.) allow the funny-looking code to be reconstituted into something similar to the original.

The word *similar* is mentioned rather than *exactly like* because HTML does not necessarily control the final appearance of text on a recipient's system. The codes refer to types, not exact matches, of fonts; thus, a sender might want to use, say, 24-point Arial as a Heading 1 display but a particular recipient might have defined Heading 1 as, say, Times Roman 14 point. A two-page original document may appear to be a three-page document to one recipient and a one-page document to another.

More significantly, though, many people turn off HTML email for security reasons. All such formatted email gets converted automatically into plain ASCII text. A correspondent once sent author Kabay a message that read: "Note: The on-line course evaluation system may be used from room, lab, and home—anywhere Internet access is available. / Overview: .... Failure to complete a course evaluation will result in a 'hold' being placed on the student's final grades."

The fragment of message that follows shows the result of MS-Outlook auto-conversion of the original formatted HTML message to ASCII: "Note: The on-line course evaluation system may be used from room, lab, and home ? anywhere Internet access is available./Overview: .... Failure to complete a course evaluation will result in a ?hold? being placed on the student?s final grades."

- In the conversion process, the original apostrophes turned into question marks ("?hold?") because the sender was using "curly" quotation marks instead of the straight ones in the word-processing package or email editor. If one cares to prevent this peculiarity when using earlier versions of Microsoft Word, one has to turn off the option in the {Tools | AutoCorrect | AutoFormat As You Type} screen by unchecking the box labeled {"Straight quotes" with "smart quotes"}. In later versions, turn off the option by clicking {Word Options} in the main menu, selecting {Proofing}, and then clicking the {AutoCorrect Options} button at the top of the box. {AutoFormat As You Type} is one of the available tabs, and you can then uncheck the box labeled {"Straight quotes" with "smart quotes"}.

- In addition, it looks like a dash character may have been in the text in the first section (labeled "Note"). One can turn that conversion off in the same menus by unchecking {Hyphens (–) with dash (—)}.

A much simpler solution to prevent the mess is simply to send unformatted ASCII text in all outbound messages by selecting that option in one's email package.

Some people try to send files that should look the same on a recipient system and the originating system by attaching word processing documents: for example, Word (DOC) files, WordPerfect (WPD) files, or Rich Text Format (RTF) files (and so on). Unfortunately, even these attempts do not necessarily work as planned, since lack of shared fonts, different default paper sizes (different countries may use different sizes), and different printing margins (resulting from installation of different printers) may cause the documents not to look precisely the same on all systems.

So if the exact appearance of a message one is sending via email is critically important, one should send the content *and* its format in a way that is (largely) platform independent; for example, Acrobat PDF (Portable Document Format) files. Although even they do not necessarily result in perfect rendition of the author's intentions across systems, PDF files are far more likely to succeed than the other methods mentioned. One can create PDF files in a number of ways; some systems have Adobe Acrobat installed so that one can either send to an Acrobat driver to create the PDF files or even just click a toolbar button to do so from within the word processor. Microsoft Office 2007 and later versions, for example, provide the ability to Save as PDF in all of its major components. Other packages exist that are less expensive (and generally less feature-rich) than the full Adobe Acrobat software, but nonetheless allow users to create PDF files easily. One can type "create PDF" into a Web search engine to find lots of choices.

48.4.1.7 Distribution Lists in Email. As for confidentiality, consider that using the *To* and *CC* (*carbon copy*—a bit of historical detritus) fields in email makes all recipient addresses visible to all recipients. This situation is usually helpful in internal email because team members can see who has gotten the message, but it can be annoying in external email. Why should a list of dozens, or even hundreds, of names of strangers be distributed freely among them, without the explicit permission of all concerned? Who knows where that information will end up? Use of the *BCC* (blind carbon copy) field eliminates the ability of recipients to see all of the intended recipients for the original message. This extra step is a good piece of email etiquette, whether the message is business or personal. The *BCC* field is also useful for internal email when the list of recipients is very large, but it is not important for people to know exactly who received the message.

In one case, a nice lady in the human resources (HR) department at a university sent out a note to a dozen people reminding recipients that they had not yet finished signing up for their new medical insurance coverage.

Unfortunately, she put all the email addresses into the *CC* (carbon copy) line where they were visible to everyone in the list. Predictably, someone on the list composed a response to her, hit *REPLY ALL*, and sent some mildly personal information about the state of her medical concerns to all the recipients on the original list, none of whom had any interest in her problems.

Luckily, there was not a lot of private information in that message, but it did prompt the realization that many people unthinkingly use the *CC* line for addresses to a distribution list and that many people unthinkingly use REPLY ALL for replies to every email message.

The combination can lead to embarrassing violations of confidentiality; when the HR department staff use *CC* instead of *BCC* (the Blind Carbon Copy function that conceals the distribution list), the REPLY ALL function can inadvertently violate privacy.

In this case, there was no particularly sensitive material revealed, but a different case could easily violate HIPAA (Health Information Portability and Accountability Act) and the university's rules on employee confidentiality.

Once employees understand the issue, they will learn not to use *CC* for distribution lists when the intention is to communicate with individuals; by default, everyone should use the *BCC* list unless there is a need to stimulate group discussion of an issue or it is important for the members of the group to know who received the message.

It is important not to dismiss this issue as too easy or too obvious to bother with. "Against stupidity, the gods themselves contend in vain," wrote Friedrich von Schiller in his *Maid of Orleans* (*Die Jungfrau von Orleans*) in 1801. Nonetheless, the *CC* + REPLY ALL habit becomes a covert channel for release of confidential information for people who refuse to keep an address book, and simply look up any old email and REPLY ALL to it as a lazy way of sending a new message.

If you doubt the seriousness of the problem, take some time to look through your own archives of email and count how many obvious cases there are of emails with inappropriate subject lines and inappropriate distribution lists sitting in your received folders. Unfortunately, you may be dismayed by the results of your research. If you look into your own SENT folder, you may be even more dismayed.

48.4.1.8 Effective Use of BCC. As discussed, the problems caused by *CC* are worse when the recipients do not know each other. One often receives messages from technically unsophisticated correspondents who put dozens of email addresses in the *CC* field even though many of the recipients are total strangers to each other. Such exposure of email addresses always makes security staff nervous; who knows whether everyone on the list is trustworthy? Even if the list is not misused for outright spam, people often REPLY ALL with useless information, effectively adding people to discussion lists that they never wanted to be on.

One particularly annoying habit is to REPLY ALL with a comment stemming from some initial message. People then generate a series of increasingly long messages including copies of all the previous copies of the ostensibly clever repartee, driving some users to generate an addition to their junk mail filters.

The habit of using REPLY ALL is annoying enough when a reply does not in fact have to go to everyone on the original distribution list. However, REPLY ALL is a positive menace if it is coupled with the abhorrent practice of using an existing email message as a shortcut to creating a new one with a completely different topic, as discussed in Section 48.4.1.2.

48.4.1.9 Managing Private Email at Work. What is wrong with using corporate email for jokes, invitations, and the like? One issue is the waste of bandwidth. Some people find the quality of the jokes, hoaxes, and cheering sessions low enough to be irritating. Worst yet, the tolerance level for what is considered appropriate in the workplace may vary by individual, requiring the utmost care and consideration for everyone. Another problem arises with politically sensitive messages, such as announcements or viewpoints that some members of a group may find offensive. Why should everyone in the group be subjected to a barrage of unsolicited email just because they work somewhere?

The question also raises some valuable and instructive points about appropriate-use policies for email. Corporations must have a formal written policy on appropriate use of official email. Managers should frame clear written policies that any of the staff members can easily consult for guidance about suitable and unsuitable content for personal messages using corporate mailing addresses. Such policies will reduce possible disappointments and resentments resulting from decisions based on unwritten expectations. In addition, any hint of discrimination based on particular political or religious biases will have to be scrutinized to ensure that the organization is not subject to legal repercussions.

An easy tool that employees can develop is a voluntary mailing list of nonwork email addresses for nonwork email. A Yahoo! group (http://groups.yahoo.com/), for example, offers many benefits over an informal list in the *CC*: or To: field. Jokes and the like can thus be distributed only to willing recipients, since joining can be purely optional. However, employees must always remember that any activities occurring on company equipment, or using company computing resources, may be viewed by authorized parties and could potentially hurt their reputation or, even worse, set them up for legal problems.

48.4.2 Mail Storms.

A peculiar kind of junk email is sent by accident. These flurries of unwanted messages are called *mail storms.*

Most of us belong to mailing lists; many of us have more than one email address; some of us use autoforwarding to shift email from one address to another automatically; and a few of us use automated responses on our email accounts to let correspondents know when we are out of the office or unable to respond quickly.

All of these factors can contribute to mail storms.

48.4.2.1 Autoforwarding.

A mail storm occurs when computers begin sending mail to each other without human intervention. Sometimes mail storms can become a denial of service by saturating communications channels and other resources. The email-enabled worms such as Melissa, the I-love-you message, and others, are examples of malicious software programs whose authors deliberately wrote them to create mail storms.

A simple situation occurred in the 1990s:

- An employee leaving on vacation decided to receive company email using a personal account on an ISP with a global presence. By setting an autoforward command on the company account, all incoming mail was sent to the personal email account.
- Unfortunately, on the remote tropical island where the vacationer spent two weeks, it was impossible to access the worldwide ISP without paying a surcharge of $6 a minute for long-distance service to the nearest dial-up node. This proved too expensive, and no emails were received or sent.

- Meanwhile, the company account dutifully forwarded every message it received to the proper personal account—which had a tiny storage limit of 250 messages. That limit was reached within a few days. At that point, every inbound message generated a bounce informing the sender that the recipient's mailbox was full.
- The very first full-mailbox message sent to the company account was autoforwarded back to the vacationer's personal mailbox.
- That copy of the full-mailbox message generated a second mailbox-full message, which then got bounced back to the company account, and so on without letup.
- Eventually, even the company mailbox filled up, and then the two email systems continued chattering at each other indefinitely. In this particular case, system administrators noticed the problem when the user's mailbox reached 20,000 messages and crashed the mail server.

The number of email messages that can be generated by this kind of infinite loop is a function of the latency of the positive feedback system that the user has accidentally created. For example, if it takes exactly one minute for a bounce message to be returned to the originating site, then each message causing an initial error can create 60 additional messages per hour. However, every new message from another sender that arrives at the originating mailbox will generate its own new set of bouncing messages in infinite loops. It is not uncommon to see tens of thousands of messages accumulating in the recipient's mailbox if nobody notices the loops with traffic mounting steadily into hundreds or thousands of messages per hour bouncing between the accounts, potentially generating a denial of service on corporate email through bandwidth saturation alone. The mail servers may also crash because of the overwhelming traffic.

An out-of-office message can also inadvertently create mail storms through a *race condition* (see Chapter 39 in this *Handbook*). For example, two employees (Albert and Bob) both enable out-of-office messages, and Albert sends an email to Bob. Bob's email service sends Albert back its out-of-office message, which in turn generates another out-of-office message from Albert to Bob. A mail storm results.

48.4.2.2 Poorly Configured List Servers. The user of an autoresponder may belong to a list where the FROM address is actually the broadcast address that sends a response to the entire list. The very first automated out-of-office response to the list will generate a message to everyone on that list, producing an infinite sequence of to-and-from messages. This situation is very embarrassing for the list administrator and intensely annoying for everyone else.

48.4.2.3 Human Error. Something analogous to a mail storm results from thoughtless behavior when using a public list. A typical instance occurs when a list member posts to an entire list comments relevant only to one individual. For example, a member asks for a reprint of an article and another answers on the list: "I'll send you a reprint tomorrow." Several thousand unwilling readers now know about this projected email message. One of these irritated people posts a message saying, "Did you really have to post that message to the entire list?" This second message is so irritating that at least one other person posts a third message to the entire list, criticizing the originator of the second letter for criticizing the writer of the first. This useless tempest of email continues via the public list, creating thousands of copies of useless information.

Another form of inconsiderate behavior is to quote entire messages when responding to email. Only the fragments of text that have elicited a response should be copied to the new message. This principle is particularly important on public lists, where messages have been observed containing the entire text, including Internet headers, for up to seven levels of previous messages. Often, the amount of new information contained in messages posted to Usenet groups is extremely small; the rest was quotations of quotations of quotations.

48.4.3 Buying on the Web. Employers may decide to allow reasonable (however they decide the term) use of corporate resources for non–work-related activities, including buying services and products through the Internet. However, it is in the interests of employers to educate employees to avoid becoming victims of criminals. An employee distraught over the loss of significant sums due to foolish credulity will not be as productive as usual; in any case, no one wants to see friends and colleagues cheated.

Buying from known merchants through the Web can be as satisfying as buying in their stores. If you know the organizations selling goods and services, there is no more reason to be worried about buying from them through a Web connection than buying from them over the phone or in person at a store. Websites belonging to recognized merchants or organizations, such as nonprofit charities, are trustworthy, especially if they show any of several symbols representing compliance with various standards of security for customer data. Some of the safety seals in common use include SSL SiteSafe Certificates, TRUSTe, McAfee SECURE, and WhiteHat Security Certification.

48.4.3.1 Dynamic Pricing. One controversial technique that some firms have been studying is *dynamic pricing*. Dynamic pricing presents different prices to different customers. By building a profile of a specific customer's buying habits, vendors can inflate prices for people who appear to be more willing to buy higher-priced goods and lower prices for those who are cost conscious. Many brick-and-mortar stores do the same, in that stores in some parts of town may cater to richer people than in other areas; similarly, some chains of stores have been documented as charging higher prices to poor people in ghettos than in suburbs, in part because there is less competition in poor neighborhoods and the cost of doing business may be higher there. A different kind of dynamic pricing occurs in the airline industry, where seats on planes vary in price according to when they are booked and how many seats are expected to be sold. However, unlike these examples, dynamic pricing on the Web resembles traditional automobile sales, where research confirms that women and racial minorities are consistently offered higher prices than the deals for white males. In both automobile sales and dynamic pricing on the Web, the fundamental difference from the normal free-market model is that the prices are varied secretly so that only the victim of the predatory pricing sees the offered price. Without mechanisms for sharing information among purchasers, this model of pricing seems to put the buyers at an immense disadvantage with respect to the seller. It will be interesting to see how it develops over time.

48.4.3.2 Privacy. Another key area of concern when buying products on the Web is privacy. Many consumers prefer their buying habits to remain their own business. Receiving unwanted paper mail or email, because of past purchases, seems intrusive and irritating to them; they classify all such promotions as junk mail. Other consumers appreciate the convenience of receiving targeted information about new products and special sale prices for items they have previously bought. In either case, it is important to pay attention to the privacy policies offered by online vendors.

Marketers must decide whether to set up their systems on an opt-in or opt-out basis. If marketers choose the former, then all individuals actually must *agree* to have information about themselves included on lists that may be used within the organization or sold to or traded with third parties. If the system is set up for opt-out, then everyone's information may be freely disclosed, except for those who specifically state that they do not want the list keepers to do so. These are broad general outlines; the privacy policy of each organization must be spelled out in detail.

Some sites such as online bookstores and music services may keep detailed records of what each person buys from them and even what items are simply looked at. These Websites can then tailor their sales presentations to products that are appropriate to each customer's interests. Amazon.com, for example, tries to be helpful to visitors by suggesting books that may interest the returning visitor based on previous behavior. However, one of the unexpected consequences of customer profiling is that the practice may reveal more than users would wish; if you watch one of your employees enter such a Website and discover that the predominant theme is, say, weapons and techniques of terrorism, you might want to have some serious discussions with your human resources staff. A less positive application of profiling caused a flurry of interest when information about the purchasing habits of employees of specific companies was accidentally made available to those companies' competitors.

Another issue often raised in discussions of privacy involves *cookies*. Cookies are small text files that a site stores on a visitor's hard disk to store information that can be used the next time the user visits the site. Properly defined cookies can be used only by the site that deposited them. The information stored can include the sequence of Web pages the visitor saw, or personal identifiers that allow the Web software to recognize the visitor so that the Website can build up a preference profile for each visitor or client and to enable those cheery greetings like "Welcome back, Bob! We have a special deal for you on the newest title in *The Real Man's Guide to Heavy Artillery* series!" Cookies also may be used to accumulate items in a shopping cart; without cookies, each purchase would have to be concluded separately.

In general, cookies are harmless. If you do not like the idea of having identifiers stored on your system, you can block cookies in your browser settings, block them globally or on a site-by-site basis using a personal firewall, or install cookie sweepers that get rid of all cookies whenever you activate them.

For a review of legal aspects of privacy in cyberspace, see Chapter 69 in this *Handbook*.

48.4.3.3 Online Auctions. The theory behind an auction is that the competition for an object or service helps participants determine a fair price. This process can be corrupted in a real-world, physical auction if the seller conspires with confederates to bid up the price artificially. Unfortunately, this is even easier online, where anyone can have as many identities as he or she wants. The ease with which browsers and email systems allow forged headers and forged identifiers means that sellers can inflate the price of their own offerings.

The Federal Trade Commission of the United States reports that online auctions cause the largest number of complaints they receive annually about fraud.

This theoretical discussion does not even begin to address such questions as whether the auctioned items really exist, are as described, or will ever be delivered. A case of such fraud occurred on eBay, where Robert Guest of Los Angeles admitted in court in July 1999 that he defrauded victims of about $37,000 by offering goods for auction via eBay but failed to deliver anything. The customers of Mr. Guest certainly found out the hard way that they were being cheated, but it appears that they could not have known in advance that he was untrustworthy. Although eBay maintains a system whereby potential bidders can see reviews and comments posted by earlier customers of each seller, new sellers such as Mr. Guest have no record, and anyone with a bad record can assume a new identity.

eBay has further responded to these concerns by suggesting the use of escrow services and by warning its users that it does not guarantee the legitimacy of the transactions it facilitates.

There are also concerns about the legality of some of the items put up for auction. Someone offered items made from endangered species, in violation of the Convention on International Traffic in Endangered Species (CITES). The products included dried feet of elephants and gorillas caught in snares and allowed to die excruciating deaths before being hacked into pieces. In the United States, buying, selling, and possessing such contraband can lead to arrest, prosecution, fines, or imprisonment.

More ludicrously, someone put up a human kidney for sale through eBay in September 1999 and received bids of up to $5.8 million. The auction service canceled the sale because selling human organs is a federal felony punishable by up to $250,000 in fines and at least five years in jail. A week later eBay had to shut down an auction for an unborn human baby. Prices for the supposed baby had risen into the $100,000 range before eBay shut down that auction. Finally, a fool or a prankster—it is unclear which—tried to sell 500 pounds of fresh marijuana online. The auction was shut down after 21 hours, during which prices offered had reached $10 million. In August 2001, a couple offered to name their baby in accordance with the wishes of a high bidder. That auction, too, was ended prematurely.

Most of the bids probably were not legitimate. It is unlikely that everyone who bid for kidneys, pot, and babies really expected to pay for what they were bidding on. They may have been treating the auction like a video game, with no element of reality. Situations such as these invite other abuses, and ordinary users are often at a loss as to how to proceed.

Even if the items being offered for sale online are ordinary things such as software or physical products, they may have been obtained illegally. Online auctions are a frequently used channel for fencing stolen goods.

Corporate users should probably not be using Internet auctions to buy or sell products, except in those closely guarded, industry-specific sites that have proven their worth. Certainly, employees should not be using corporate Internet access to engage in such activities for their private purposes.

48.4.4 Online Gambling.

It is hard to imagine that any enterprise would authorize employees to gamble online using corporate resources, but providing employees with the following guidance may be a valuable service.

48.4.4.1 Fraud and Error.

In 1998, the Arizona lottery discovered that no winning number in its Pick 3 game had ever included even one numeral 9.[9] It turned out that the pseudorandom number generator algorithm had an elementary programming error that generated only the digits 0 through 8. All those who had used a 9 in their lottery numbers felt justifiable anger—especially when they were told they could have a refund, but only if they had kept their old losing tickets.

The Arizona lottery used a simulated random process to provide the illusion to gamblers that they were betting on a physical process such as balls mixing together in a barrel and falling out of a tube. One of the problems with the Arizona simulation is similar to a genuine vulnerability in proprietary (i.e., secret) cryptographic algorithms.

As cryptographers have stressed over many decades, the security of an encryption scheme should not depend on the secrecy of its algorithm. Had the lottery algorithm been exposed to public scrutiny, its flaws would have been detected sooner. For example, in the 1980s, there was much excitement over a new encryption scheme called the *knapsack algorithm*; after extensive examination by cryptographers, it proved to be flawed. It is conceivable that someone detecting the flaw in the Arizona lottery might have made bets with a higher probability of winning than those of uninformed people, but exposing the algorithm and its implementation to scrutiny before it went into production would have made that less likely.

These examples demonstrate that electronic gambling, as in older, conventional types, is subject to more than the rules of chance. Lack of conformity to good security practices lays both the gambler and the house open to abuse and to inadvertent errors.

48.4.4.2 Lack of Control. Physical gaming devices are located in real-world establishments under the nominal control of regulatory and law enforcement officials. Even so, they are always adjusted for a certain predetermined payout. Gambling based on the results of actual sports events or contests is validated by external news reports, although the contests themselves can be rigged. But there is no basis for a gambler to trust the results of computer-generated pseudorandom numbers displayed on a browser screen.

Most individual gamblers will never know if a long-range analysis of the pseudorandom numbers would support their hopes for fairness in the odds. No one is keeping track of these data except the people making money from the participants, and they are not distributing the results.

The disclaimer at one Internet gambling portal, findinternetcasino.com, is not very encouraging:

> Although every attempt has been made to ensure fairness and security toward the player at each of the links that can be found in the directories, FindInternetCASINO® cannot be held responsible if discrepancies occur between an Online Gambling operation and you, the player, after following a link from this WWW site. Consult your local authorities prior to registering with any online wagering service. U.S. Citizens: The information at this site is for entertainment and news purposes only. Use of this information in violation of any federal, state, or local laws is prohibited.

48.4.4.3 Legal Issues. In some jurisdictions, betting online is illegal. In the United States, for example, it is already illegal to use interstate telecommunications to place bets; in addition, Internet betting is illegal in the United States even if the host is outside the United States. At the same time, due to ambiguities in the current laws and the inability to clearly enforce them, the use of overseas betting sites has driven this business to a total of over $15.5 billion a year, over half of that income coming from the United States. The ambiguities stem from a lack of a clear definition on what constitutes illegal online gambling. This resulted in certain groups of individuals believing that they were exempt from the law, poker players being the most common. In addition, online horse racing receives a specific exemption from the law, but without accompanying clarification on whether the wagering process constitutes online gambling.

Unfortunately, in the United Kingdom and many other countries, online gambling is for the most part legal. This creates numerous conflicts of interest, and international tension, between various betting companies in legalized countries, all advertising to Americans eager to risk their money for a chance at a big payout. It appears that until clear definitions are included in the law, the blurred line between legal and illegal gambling activities using online resources will continue.[10]

48.4.5 Internet Addiction. Any activity can become the basis of compulsive exaggeration. A small proportion, around 5 percent, of Internet users may qualify as addicted to any of these computer-mediated activities:

- An uncontrollable desire to find and organize more and more information about an enormous range of topics
- Excessive involvement in games, gambling, and buying things on the Internet
- Excessive concentration on relationships mediated through email and chat rooms, to the detriment of real-life relationships
- Involvement in long sessions of viewing pornography, or of being sexually stimulated via email, chat rooms, pornographic sites, or sexual-fantasy games

None of these activities is a suitable use of corporate computing resources, and employees should be alerted to the policies prohibiting such activities at work. In addition, everyone should be aware of the dangers of Internet addiction.

The issue here is what constitutes *excessive* involvement in these activities. Professional psychologists such as Dr. Kimberly Young have identified some of the diagnostic criteria for these disorders, including these based on her *Internet Addiction Test*[11]:

- Regularly staying online longer than intended
- Often neglecting obligations to spend more time online
- Consistently preferring to spend time online instead of with one's partner
- Frequent complaints by friends and family about excessive Internet use
- Suffering consequences at school or at work because of time spent online
- Giving email a higher priority than other important issues
- Concealing the extent of Internet usage
- Turning to the Internet as a substitute for dealing with disturbing issues
- Feeling that life without the Internet would be devoid of meaning and pleasure
- Getting angry when disturbed during Internet usage
- Losing sleep due to late-night Internet activity
- Yearning to be back online

Those who feel uncomfortable about their level of involvement with the Internet would do well to take this test offered by Dr. Young, and, if several of their answers are positive, to seek counseling to prevent possibly tragic consequences of untreated addiction.

48.4.6 Online Dating and Cybersex. As in other topics in this chapter, it is unlikely that corporate policy would allow users to engage in online dating and cybersex. Nonetheless, in line with the overall orientation of this chapter, the next sections will help employees understand the issues in these online activities.

48.4.6.1 Dating Online. Thousands of sites on the Web specialize in helping people meet each other. In a sense, chat rooms and bulletin board systems are ways for people with similar interests to communicate about their hobbies and lifestyles. There are also sites that specialize in helping people find others who match particular profiles.

Some of these sites are free; others charge fees for participation. Dating service sites usually explicitly restrict participation to people over 18 years old, and most of them depend on possession of a credit card as their sole mechanism for authenticating age. It is very difficult to exclude teenagers, or even younger children, from such sites if they have access to credit card numbers.

Parents, teachers, and employers who want to get a sense of what is going on can type "online dating" in the search field of a search engine such as Google (www.google.com) and then visit a few of the sites. If children post information about themselves in such a cyberspace locale, even with false information claiming that they are adults, there is a real risk of attracting unsavory characters or perhaps ordinary people who can become angry at being tricked into exposing their feelings to an imposter.

48.4.6.2 *Sex Talk Online.* In addition to matchmaking, users of the Internet also can get involved in *cybersex*. People chatting online can describe themselves or each other in sexual interactions that are inappropriate for youngsters. Such online chat also has been implicated in a number of divorces, since many spouses find it wholly inappropriate that their beloved is getting sexually excited with a stranger via the Internet.

In August 2001, a 15-year-old girl from Massachusetts was alleged to have been kept captive for at least a week during which she was repeatedly sexually abused by the couple who had brought her to Long Island. According to the criminal complaint, she was also loaned out for two days to another man and further abused. The couple had met the teenager in an Internet chat room, where their conversation was explicitly sexual.

In the work environment, circulating sexually charged messages or outright pornography can justifiably be perceived and described as fostering a *hostile work environment* and can lead to lawsuits by the affected employees.

Employers should promulgate policies to prevent such abuse and monitor corporate email and instant messaging to ensure that no one in their employ engage in these activities using corporate resources.

48.4.6.3 *Traffic in Women.* A number of sites on the Web, particularly some situated in the former Soviet bloc, advertise services for introducing men to willing candidates for marriage. The evidence is strong that much of the information communicated about the supposedly nubile and marriage-oriented women is false. Many of the pictures are taken from public Websites and include actresses and people who have posted their photos on social networking groups. Sometimes the same picture has dozens of names associated with it. Much as in the phone-based sex-talk services, people claiming to be youthful, attractive, persons of marriageable age may be nothing of the sort, and may be copy/pasting responses from prepared scripts. When men travel to visit their potential mates, they can be charged high rates for the privilege of taking their dates to expensive restaurants. Some of the women who actually do go through with marriages later divorce their hapless victims once they are admitted to their husband's country of residence in what appears to be systematic fraud.

48.4.7 Games and Virtual Reality. Some enterprises allow their employees to play games at various times during the day—usually low-usage times such as lunch, or before and after the normal workday. However, some Internet-enabled multiuser games can consume enormous bandwidth; the shoot-'em-up (*first-person shooter*, or FPS) game called Quake was notorious in its day for saturating all available connectivity.

When helping employees understand how to negotiate the perils of the Internet, you might recommend that parents read reviews of video games before allowing their young children to play them. Some games have astonishing levels of graphic violence ("Brilliant Bleeding! Detailed Decapitations!") and unusual values ("Win points by burning as many residents to death as possible!"). This latter example is based on a notorious case in which a video-game vendor was apparently surprised by the public wave of revulsion over a game that glorified arson. Some military and police shoot-'em-up games explicitly take points off for hitting innocent bystanders; others do not. Some games use graphic nudity; others are more modest. The main point is that relying on the judgment of eight-year-olds to choose their own entertainment may be unwise.

From a corporate perspective, it would be unusual to find employers encouraging the use of local or networked games during working hours; however, some may allow use of their resources in off-hours, assuming the corporation does not maintain around-the-clock operations. However, issues of suitability persist; some games may contribute to a hostile work environment and lead to complaints and lawsuits from offended employees.

A development that started in the 1990s has become a potentially valuable tool in the first decades of the twenty-first century: virtual reality or virtual worlds, such as Second Life (http://secondlife.com). These services use controllable representations called *avatars,* which allow some degree of expressiveness when communicating. Participants see a representation of a three-dimensional world, complete with viewpoint and perspective, that includes their interlocutors in a shared virtual reality that can be creative and fun. Some companies are using resources in these virtual worlds for advertising, delivery of services (e.g., training and education), and internal remote meetings or training. Organizations must determine appropriate policies about the use of such services.

48.4.8 Changing Email Addresses. Employees may leave a company, change organizational units, or change their own names. All of these changes may result in new email addresses. Handling such changes poorly can lead to trouble.

One reaction to such a change is to delete the original email address without notification to anyone. Email sent to the original address is returned with an *undeliverable (no such user)* error. The sender must then find out what happened—or may simply drop the connection altogether, possibly losing a company a client or leaving important information undelivered.

If the disappearing email address is due to the user's change of name (for example, resulting from marriage or divorce), it is even possible that the corporate directory will have the original name wiped, making it difficult for correspondents unaware of the new name to reach the person at all by email or by phone.

A wiser response to any such change is to autoforward the incoming mail to the correct address. For example, if Farid Hallings's original email address was fhallings@company.com and is now fmalteso@company.com, any mail sent to the first address would automatically end up in the mailbox for the second address. If Farid no longer works for the company at all, the email can be forwarded to the appropriate replacement's address. Such forwarding can be maintained for whatever period seems appropriate.

In addition to the autoforward, it may be helpful to send automatic notifications to the sender of the outdated email. "Farid Halling's new email address is fmalteso@company.com; your message has automatically been forwarded. Please make a note of the change in your email address book."

48.5 LEGAL LIABILITY.

This section briefly reviews some of the legal issues that may arise as a result of misuse of email and Internet resources. For more detailed information, see Chapters 63, 64, 69, 70, 71, and 72 in this *Handbook*.

48.5.1 Libel.

Some people have taken advantage of the freedom to publish whatever they want by crossing the boundaries of libel. For example, the self-styled reporter Matt Drudge went too far in postings on his electronic scandal sheet in 1997, when he made unsubstantiated accusations about White House advisor Sidney Blumenthal's marriage. Professional journalists pounced on him for shoddy journalism. Blumenthal and his wife filed a $30 million libel suit against Drudge even after he apologized for failing to verify the gossip he disseminated. Drudge then claimed that public White House support for Blumenthal amounted to a threat against free speech.

In another notorious case, Walter Cronkite, whom polls revealed to be the most respected man in the United States in the 1980s, was appalled to discover a page of lies about him on the Web in 1997. A 28-year-old programmer, Tim Hughes, invented and posted a scurrilous story about Cronkite's becoming enraged at the author, shrieking imprecations at Hughes and his wife, boasting about his own infidelity, and spitting in their spice cake at a Florida restaurant. In addition, the anti-Cronkite Web page included falsified photographs purporting to show Cronkite at a Ku Klux Klan meeting. Cronkite threatened to sue for libel; Hughes took the page down and weakly protested that it was all a joke.

The effect of this kind of misinformation on children or immature employees, untrained in critical thinking and lacking in skepticism about information on the Internet, can be damaging.

Another source of information is the Usenet—that collection of thousands of discussion groups on every conceivable topic. These discussion groups fall into two major classes: moderated and unmoderated. In a moderated group, messages are passed through a *moderator* who decides either to post them for participants or to delete offensive or otherwise inappropriate messages. Not all moderated groups are reliable, and not all unmoderated groups are unreliable. However, many unmoderated groups distribute unsubstantiated information from people who appear to derive their major pleasure in life by insulting other participants and by making outrageous statements about any topic that comes up. Everyone should be trained to recognize emotional and inflammatory language, and should be encouraged to apply skeptical analysis to all statements, especially to those published in rants.

In the first decades of the twenty-first century, *blogs*—commentaries published on the Web by individuals or groups—have exploded into common awareness. The same principles of critical evaluation apply to blogs as to any other source of disintermediated information. In one case involving author Kabay, a lunatic conspiracy site illegally reposted the entire text of one of his columns describing InfraGard with pictures of victims of Nazi atrocities in concentration camps between each paragraph. A Digital Millennium Copyright Act (DMCA) *takedown request* was obeyed, but the incident was disgusting to the author.

48.5.2 Stolen Software, Music, and Videos.

Organizations cannot permit employees to download and make illegal copies of intellectual property of any kind. Security policies must explicitly address these issues; security monitoring must explicitly control for abuse of corporate resources in such activities. The risks to organizations by tolerating such violations of law are severe. For more details of intellectual property law, see Chapter 11 in this *Handbook*.

48.5.3 Plagiarism. A different kind of fraud involving intellectual property occurs when people misrepresent someone else's work as their own. Older students know intellectually that this is supposed to be bad, but for young children, the issue is completely abstract. The problem today is that plagiarism is easier than ever and harder for teachers to detect.

Academic guidelines try to make it clear to students that copying other people's work without attribution is called *plagiarism* and is severely frowned on. Plagiarism includes not only direct quotation without indications of origin but also paraphrasing that merely shuffles the ideas around a little or substitutes synonyms for the original words. In many institutions, plagiarism is grounds for suspension or expulsion. In all cases, plagiarism defeats the purpose of writing assignments by eliminating the opportunity for critical thinking and creative expression. Few plagiarists remember what they have copied from others after they hand their material in.

Assuredly, students have traded term papers and other assignments for centuries. However, the availability of electronic documents and of the World Wide Web has enormously increased both the fund of material that can be plagiarized and the ease of copying. Worse still, some people are profiting from easy accessibility by selling papers specifically for plagiarism and even writing papers to order. In one study by Peggy Bates and Margaret Fain of the Kimbel Library at Coastal Carolina University, the authors easily located over 100 sites on the Web selling or donating papers to students for plagiarism.[12]

To combat this problem, science has come to the aid of beleaguered instructors by providing automated similarity analysis of any paper submitted electronically. The system uses a bank of more than 100,000 term papers and essays as well as documents located on the Web; analysis uses pattern recognition to measure similarities among different documents and to estimate the probability of plagiarism. According to the turnitin.com documentation:

> Our system is now being used in the majority of universities in the United States and the U.K., as well as a large number of schools around the world. Many of these institutions, among them UC Berkeley and the fifty-eight member schools of the Consortium of Liberal Arts Colleges, an association of the most respected liberal arts schools in the US, have chosen to ensure the academic integrity of all their students by selecting institution-wide subscriptions to our service. Other universities, such as Harvard and Cornell, have elected to make use of our system on a departmental or single-instructor basis.

Plagiarism is also a risk to the enterprise; having employees misuse other people's or other organization's materials without attribution can lead to lawsuits, embarrassing publicity, and serious financial penalties. In one notorious case from 2003, a policy paper about Iraqi intelligence organizations distributed by the Prime Minister's Office in the United Kingdom was discovered to include large swathes of verbatim material, including typographical errors, copied and pasted without quotation marks and without indication of its source.[13]

Practical guidelines:

- Discuss plagiarism clearly at work, at home, and at school.
- Use examples to illustrate the difference between plagiarism and a legitimate use of other people's work.
- Encourage children to practice summarizing information in their own words.
- Practice writing references to quoted material.

- Have a student submit their term paper to one of the online services that verify originality.
- Discuss how antiplagiarism sites analyze documents to measure similarities and help teachers identify plagiarism.

48.5.4 Criminal Hacking and Hacktivism. As discussed in Chapter 45 in this *Handbook*, it is important that all employees understand and agree that using corporate systems for unauthorized access to computers and networks is grounds for dismissal, and possibly criminal prosecution. In particular, no employee should ever imagine that testing for security weaknesses in the enterprise's systems without authorization is a contribution to security.

The motivation for illegal actions does not mitigate the seriousness of computer trespass. Employees should be informed explicitly that regardless of the excuse, no violations of law will be tolerated. For example, hacking into systems in another country to support a war effort is not excusable; nor is destroying child pornography sites a good idea. Cybervigilantes can destroy evidence needed for prosecution.

48.5.5 Creating a Hostile Work Environment. In today's society, there are numerous activities and language constructs that individuals of a certain race, gender, sexual orientation, national origin, religious affiliation, or other legally protected characteristics may find offensive. Any type of harassment, most especially comments or actions based on these protected characteristics, toward another employee may create a hostile work environment. The two most common situations created by a hostile work environment are:

1. A reduction or loss of productivity due to the harassment, whether physical, verbal, or psychological
2. A reduction in salary, bonus, job level, responsibilities, or other components of compensation due to one or more of the legally protected characteristics

Although there are no formal laws barring hostile work environments, Title VII of the Civil Rights Act of 1964 covers these types of situations. These laws are written in such a way that an individual comment or action does not usually constitute harassment. Rather, a pattern of frequent, severe, and pervasive abuse may constitute a hostile work environment. It is important to distinguish between *quid pro quo* harassment, where an employee is required to tolerate such harassment in order to maintain job status or compensation levels, and a hostile work environment. Both are very serious and potentially illegal activities, but this section focuses on the hostile environment.[14]

Employers are obligated by law to set appropriate expectations around employee behavior, and confidentially and swiftly to investigate any complaint of harassment from an employee. Employees are granted some legal protections such that retaliation by an employer for sounding the alarm on a hostile environment is illegal.

These issues become even more important when office romances occur. Although many employers forbid couples from working together in the same department, in part to avoid any perception of favoritism or future harassment cases, should the romance fail, there is still the potential for romantically linked coworkers to create a hostile environment for others. In this case, employers have an obligation to define in policy that coworkers should maintain a professional relationship while on company business. Even though two individuals may feel that their words or actions are seemingly innocuous, it is the perception of others around them that creates the basis for a harassment complaint. The best solution is to keep personal lives out of the office, which is a difficult but appropriate recommendation for everyone.

48.5.5.1 Hate Groups. Another source of concern for employers and parents is the easy accessibility of hate literature on the Web. Hatemongers have taken full advantage of the largely unregulated nature of the 'Net to spread their pernicious messages. One can find Websites devoted to hatred of every imaginable identifiable group. Race, ethnicity, religion, gender, sexual orientation, immigration status, and political ideology—anything can spark hatred in susceptible personalities. Unfortunately, some of the hate groups have been quite successful in recruiting young people through the Web; they publish propaganda such as pro-Nazi revisionist history that may fool uncritical people into believing their rants. Neo-Nazi and racist skinhead groups have formed hate-rock groups that take advantage of kids' enthusiasm for very loud music with aggressive lyrics.

Employers cannot tolerate the slightest involvement of their employees in such activities using corporate resources. Aside from their possible personal revulsion at such hatemongering, managers also should be aware that toleration of intolerance can lead to a hostile work environment in which targets of hate or contempt can legitimately appeal to the courts for compensatory and punitive damages. Employees must understand and agree that using any corporate resources for participation in hate groups is a serious infraction of Internet usage policy.

According to the Simon Wiesenthal Center, there are over 2,300 Websites advocating hatred, of which over 500 are extremist sites hosted on American servers but authored by Europeans; most European countries have strict antihate laws. Using more stringent criteria, the Hate Watch group estimates more than 500 extremist hate sites on the Web; it distinguishes between hate propaganda and those pages that consist largely of racial epithets, dismissed as mere graffiti.

The Southern Poverty Law Center monitors 500 active hate organizations in the United States. It has regularly reported on the growing number and stridency of such sites. In comments about the center's paper for the United Nations Commission on Human Rights, spokesperson Mark Potok said at a conference in 2000:

> A few years ago, a Klansman needed to put out substantial effort and money to produce and distribute a shoddy pamphlet that might reach a few hundred people. Today, with a $500 computer and negligible other costs, that same Klansman can put up a slickly produced Web site with a potential audience in the millions.[15]

A fundamental reality is that human beings are gregarious. They find it very easy to affiliate with others to form *in-groups,* groups to which they feel entitled to belong. Unfortunately, defining in-groups naturally means it is equally easy to define *out-groups*: groups to which we *do not* want to belong. Grade school and high school cliques are examples of in- and out-groups. A wealth of study in social psychology confirms the validity of the universal impression that we tend to inflate our esteem for in-groups and to reduce our respect and liking for out-groups. However, research also shows that social norms against discrimination can reduce hostility toward out-groups; thus it seems likely that parental and teacher articulation of norms of tolerance can significantly reduce children's susceptibility to the blandishments of hate groups.

48.5.5.2 Pornography. Pornography—even with the most restrictive definitions—is widespread on the Internet. Observers of 'Net culture have commented that the sure-fire way of telling if new technology is going to be a success on the Internet is to see how quickly pornographers can apply it. For example, the appearance in July 2000 of the first WAP (wireless application protocol) pornography sites signaled the adoption of WAP technology into the mainstream. Although the sites offered only tiny grainy images of naked Japanese models, sociologists said that the same expected sequence of rapid technological advances had occurred with photography and video cameras.

48.5.5.2.1 Prevalence of Porn. Some studies of Internet traffic have claimed that more than half of the total 'Net bandwidth is used for transfer of pornography or solicitations for purchase of pornography.

48.5.5.2.2 Trickery. Pornographers use various tricks to get people onto their Websites:

- Using a different domain, like the old whitehouse.com, which used to take advantage of interest in "whitehouse.gov" by showing porn (it is now a directory with several paid links for dating).
- Misspellings, such as the now-inactive micosoft.com, which traded on the likelihood of mistyping "Microsoft.com."
- Junk email invitations with innocent-looking labels for URLs that do not match the actual link but instead take the viewer to a pornography site.
- Padding porn-site metatags (normally invisible text used to describe a Website) with inoffensive keywords that place the site high on search engine lists where they can appeal to children.
- Disabling normal features of a browser to trap victims in the porn site. One perpetrator who was shut down by the Federal Trade Commission (FTC) actually ran Java applets that disabled the back arrow and defeated the ability to close the browsers. People trapped in porno-hell had to reboot their computers to get out.

Porn sites are notorious for using deceit to defraud their victims. One widely used scam is to demand a credit card number from a visitor as proof of their age (it is nothing of the sort), then to charge the card even though the site clearly states that there is a period of free use.

In 1996, viewers of pornographic pictures on the sexygirls.com site were in for a surprise when they got their next phone bills. Victims who downloaded a *special viewer* were actually installing a Trojan horse program that silently disconnected their connection to their normal ISP and reconnected them (with the modem speaker turned off) to a number in Moldova in central Europe. The long-distance charges then ratcheted up until the user disconnected the session—sometimes hours later, even when the victims switched to other, perhaps less prurient, sites. Some victims who stayed online for a long time paid more than $1,000 in long-distance charges. In February 1997 in New York City, a federal judge ordered the scam shut down. An interesting note is that AT&T staff spotted the scam because of unusually high volume of traffic to Moldova, not usually a destination for many U.S. phone calls. In November 1997, the FTC won $2.74 million from the Moldovan telephone company to refund to the cheated customers—or the ones willing to admit to having been cheated.

Both of the scams just described relied in part on the reluctance of porn-seeking victims to admit to their socially disapproved interest. Few victims were willing to pursue the matter until the damages mounted into the thousands of dollars.

48.5.5.2.3 Filtering. An entire industry has grown up to try to shield (or block) children from seeing pornography or other materials deemed offensive by their parents or by the makers of the blocking software. The popular blocking systems are reviled by many free-speech advocates, and often ridiculed for what are described as clumsy, keyword-oriented algorithms. The classic examples of ludicrous blocking include trapping access to any site that uses the word *breast*—including even possibly this very page if you are reading it on the Web. Other simple-minded traps have blocked users from accessing information pages for geographical locations ending in the old British suffix *-sex* such as Wessex, Sussex, Middlesex, and so on. The village of Scunthorpe in England was blocked by software used by a major Internet service provider because its internal filters prevented anyone from using vulgar words in their mailing address.

Some of the blocking software products use hidden assumptions about the unsuitability of a wide range of topics, including abortion rights, civil rights, political ideology, and gay liberation. Any parent is entitled to express opinions about any topic; however, parents will want to check on whether a particular program is imposing its makers' political agenda by stealth. In the workplace, employers who use broad-spectrum blocking software may interfere with legitimate research by their employees.

48.5.5.2.4 Monitoring. A different approach to interfering with the nefarious deeds of pornographers is to install monitoring software on the computers that employees use at work or that children will use at home. These products keep a log, or audit trail, that allows employers and parents to see exactly what users have been doing with their computers.

In the family context, most important, however, is the principle that machines and programs cannot by themselves teach values. Instead of relying only on passive barriers or on snoopware, parents would do well to make surfing the Internet a family activity rather than a private hobby. When kids express interest in pornography—because our popular culture is full of sexual innuendo that children read, hear, and see—it makes sense to discuss the issues rather than try to pretend that they do not exist. One approach for reducing the power of the forbidden fruit offered by pornographers is to explain to children in a supportive and nonpunitive way why sexual exploitation and degradation are bad for people. Children who stumble on porn sites by accident or at their friends' houses may be better prepared to cope with the sometimes disturbing images and words if their parents have prepared them for this aspect of today's world.

48.5.6 Archiving Email. Organizations must remember that email may be demanded as evidence in court cases. There is a fiduciary duty to maintain business records appropriately for each type of business, and that obligation extends to electronic records. Policies should stipulate how long email records should be maintained. Destruction of email should never be selective, especially if there is an anticipated threat of legal action. Selective destruction of particular records, or premature wholesale destruction of email, may be interpreted by the courts as grounds for charges of interference with the judicial process.

For details of backup and archiving policies, see Chapter 57 in this *Handbook*.

48.6 RECOMMENDATIONS.

This section summarizes some practical recommendations for employees and their families. Framing policies in a way that supports employees' concern about their own families is a helpful way of increasing the perceived value of the guidelines.

48.6.1 Protecting Children

- Explain the dangers of communicating with strangers via the 'Net in the same terms that you discuss the dangers of talking to strangers anywhere else.
- Alert children to the questionable identity of anyone they meet exclusively through the 'Net or via email. Discuss the possibility that people are not what they claim to be in their online persona.
- It is important that children feel confident of a supportive response from their parents when raising these issues. Establish a calm atmosphere so that children will not fear your reactions if they are troubled by what they encounter online. Worst of all would be to punish a child for reporting a disturbing incident.
- Tell children not to give their address to strangers they meet electronically.
- Children should not send pictures of themselves to strangers.
- Make a practice of discussing online relationships in a friendly and open way at home. Show interest in the new friends without expressing hostility or suspicion; ask to participate in some of the online chats and email correspondence. Invite your children to sit in with you during your own online interactions.
- If a child feels that another child met online is becoming a good friend, parents should contact the child's parents by phone and, eventually, in person before allowing contacts.
- If a child wants to meet someone encountered on the Internet, be sure that a parent is involved at all stages. Never let a child meet anyone in the real world whom he or she has met only on the 'Net. Any attempt to induce a child to meet the correspondent alone or secretly should be reported to local police authorities for investigation.
- Make it clear that anyone who suggests hiding an online relationship from the child's parents is already doing something wrong.
- Make it clear to your children that no one has the right to send them age-inappropriate, sexually suggestive, or frankly pornographic materials, whether written or pictorial. Suggestions on the Internet that children engage in virtual sex play or sexual fantasies should be reported to parents right away. Making, transmitting, and storing child pornography is a felony; report such cases to local police authorities at once.
- Children receiving a request for anything unusual (e.g., a request for a piece of clothing or for nude pictures) should immediately report the incident to their parents. Teachers and other caregivers can adapt these principles for the specific circumstances of their relationship with the children they are taking care of.

48.6.2 Threats

- Employers, parents, and teachers should clearly enunciate policies preventing anyone—including children—from uttering threats of violence or other harm, even in email messages or chat rooms.
- Employees should be instructed to report all threats directed at them, or at others, to the security officers in their organization; similarly, parents, teachers, or librarians should ensure that children know to report any threats immediately to the appropriate adult.

48.6.3 Hate Sites

- To protect children against the wiles of these hateful people, the most important step is to discuss the issue of hate speech and hate groups with them openly. Parents may even want to visit some of the sites listed below *with your kids* to give them a sense of the problem and possible countermeasures.
- Discuss your children's feelings about out-groups in their own lives; for example, encourage them to speak freely, without fear of punishment or reprimand, about whatever groups they do not like. Then pursue the discussion with explanations of such issues as cultural differences, history, or whatever else you feel will help your children gain perspective on their own feelings and behavior. Of course, this positive attitude cannot be applied to hate groups or similar outlaws.
- Provide positive social role models for children with respect to hate groups. Speak out firmly in opposition to intolerance rather than sit silently by when bigots display their hatred for other groups.

48.6.4 Pornography

- Place young children's Internet-access computers in a family area of the home rather than in their bedrooms.
- Interact with your children while they are using the Internet; treat the Web browser like a window on the world, and be present to help your children interpret that world in a way consistent with your values.
- Talk with your children about the existence and nature of pornography; as they reach puberty, assure them that there is nothing wrong with being interested in sex, but that pornography is not a healthy way of learning about wholesome, loving relations.
- Warn your children about some of the tricks used by pornographers to get traffic on their Websites, such as telling them to download special readers. Tell them about the Moldovan porn scam.
- Discuss the issue of junk email that advertises porn sites. Warn children that no one should ever click on a URL from any kind of junk email because it can easily be a trick to get them into dangerous territory.
- Teach your children to keep an eye on the actual URL that appears in the browser window; any discrepancy between the visible URL shown on a page and the actual URL should alert them to the possibility of fraud.
- Explain that pornographers sometimes charge for access to their sites without permission; be sure your children understand how dangerous it would be to give your credit card number to these people for any reason.

48.6.5 Internet Addiction

- Know the warning signs of Internet addiction and self-monitor.
- Discuss Internet addiction and its warning signs with your employees and your children.
- Encourage open discussion of feelings about the 'Net, so that children feel free to turn to you for help if they become uncomfortable or unhappy about their own experiences on the 'Net.

48.6.6 Online Dating

- Do not build online profiles or give out addresses, phone numbers, or school names.
- Do share email accounts with your children, and oversee their messages.
- Keep the computer in a family room where children's activities can be monitored.
- Remember that people may lie when describing themselves online.
- Do not allow children to meet online users without permission, and make all meetings in public places with adult supervision.
- Forward copies of suggestive or obscene messages to your Internet service provider.
- Find ways to block objectionable material.
- Discuss online dating with kids so they understand what is involved.
- Ensure that kids understand why it is inappropriate and even dangerous for them to masquerade as adults in online dating services.
- Do not rush into face-to-face contact; you need to be sure that you are meeting someone who is on the level, not an imposter who has ulterior motives.
- You may want to take advantage of anonymizing services offered by some dating sites to avoid handing out your real email address to complete strangers.
- Be suspicious of anyone who tries to pressure you in any way, including demanding money or insisting on a meeting, before you feel confident of the person's good intentions.
- As you are getting to know someone online, ask questions about lots of things you are interested in—for example, hobbies, politics, religion, education, birth date, family background, and marital history and status.
- Keep the answers you receive and beware of people who provide inconsistent or contradictory information as they are communicating with you—any lie is a danger signal.
- Be suspicious of anyone who seems to be too good to be true; if someone matches you on every single preference or interest you mention, try mentioning the very opposite of what you said earlier in the communications and see if the person agrees with *that* too. Trying too hard to please by lying may mark a manipulative and potentially dangerous personality.
- Be honest about yourself; state your own interests and characteristics fairly, including things you think might be less attractive than stereotypes and cultural norms dictate. A mature, good person will not necessarily be turned off if you do not look like a movie star, or if you do not play four musical instruments perfectly, or if you lisp.
- If you get to the point of exchanging pictures, be sure that you see the person in a wide variety of situations and with other people; some online daters send false pictures to misrepresent themselves.
- Talk to the person you are getting interested in over the phone; be suspicious if the person resists such a request for a long time or always has excuses for not being available when you have agreed to talk.
- Listen carefully to how the person sounds on the phone, and be suspicious if you now receive information that contradicts something the person wrote to you about. Any lie should alert you to potential problems.

- Before you agree to meet, get your date's full name, address, and telephone number. Be suspicious if the person refuses to give you a home number: Could he or her have a spouse or a current live-in friend that he or she is trying to deceive? Call the home number a couple of times to see if someone else answers.
- Give the person's information, and the exact details of where and when you are going to meet, to friends and family. Do not ever accept a date with someone who wants to keep the location and time a secret. Be sure the meeting place is well lighted and in a public place such as a coffee shop.
- Do not allow a stranger to pick you up at your house, and be sure you can get home by yourself.
- Before considering further involvement, for safety's sake think about having a background check done on the person you like, using a professional service.

48.6.7 Online Games

- Learn to play some of the games your kids are enthusiastic about. Take the time to immerse yourself in the imaginary worlds they play in, and study the underlying values that are being communicated by the game creators.
- Use published reviews from online or other media that reflect your own family's values before allowing games into your home.
- Accompany your children to the stores when buying video games. Check for parental warning labels. Talk to the salespeople if you think they are reliable.
- Know the characteristics of your hardware and software before buying recently released games. Do not buy a new game only to discover that it does not run on your obsolescent system. A disappointed child can apply intense pressure to spend money on a new system. Some games are computationally intensive and require expensive, advanced computer hardware and modern sound systems, complete with a high-powered amplifier driving woofers and subwoofers.
- Try making game playing an opportunity for family fun or parent–child bonding instead of the isolating experience games can sometimes be. See if you can all have fun with puzzle- and exploration-oriented games such as *Myst* and *Riven*, neither of which involves violence, and both of which are visually beautiful.

48.6.8 Online Purchases

- Before spending a considerable amount of money on a new online merchant's site, do some basic research into the site's reliability. Check the company's reputation; see if it belongs to the Better Business Bureau (BBB), and contact the appropriate chapter of the BBB to see if there have been complaints about the vendor.
- Do a Web search using a good search engine, such as Google, to see if there are any up-to-date reports about customer experience on the site you are interested in.
- Pretend that you already have a problem and look for the customer service pages. Are there clear instructions on how to communicate problems? Would you have the choice of email, letters, or phone communications? If you have the time, you may even want to try calling customer service and find out just how they handle calls. If you hit a company that hangs up on you when its lines are busy ("We are sorry, but all our agents are busy; please call back later."), you might want to give serious thought as to whether it is safe doing business with them.

- Read the company's return policy; how does it handle breakage in transit, or defective goods? Does it offer guarantees on delivery time? What happens if the company is out of stock on a specific item—does it ship partial shipments or wait for everything to be ready? When out of stock, does it charge your credit card immediately, or only after the shipment is made? If it splits your shipment, does it charge extra for delivery of the later parts?
- Read the site's privacy policy. If the text is practically invisible 6-point yellow on white, be suspicious. Look for weasel-words in the clauses that say, for instance, that their policies can be changed at any time without notice. You must check the site regularly to see if the policy has changed, but this is unrealistic. Instead, look for firm, clear assurances that your personal information will not be sold, traded, or given away without your permission. Usually, Website owners state that they may have to divulge information to partnering organizations that handle such normal functions as billing and order fulfillment. There can be little objection to this provided the partners are bound by acceptable security policies.
- Keep a detailed record of your transactions. Use the browser functions to save copies of, or print out, the relevant Web pages with descriptions of the products, prices, a summary of your order, the order number, promised delivery date, and method of shipment.

48.6.9 Online Auctions

- Before becoming involved with online auctions, research the value of goods you are interested in buying. Check bricks-and-mortar stores, online retail outlets, and comparative shopping sites that provide you with specific prices.
- Examine the policies and costs on shipping, warrantees, and refunds.
- Set your upper limit before you get involved in an auction. Do not be influenced by the value other people appear to place on a particular product or service, and certainly do not be caught up in a bidding frenzy.
- Do not treat online auctions as a competition you have to win.
- Look for auction services that provide a guarantee of support if you are cheated in a transaction. For example, check for language in the terms of service that covers losses up to a suitable limit. Check for insurance policies, costs, terms, and limits. Use search engines to evaluate the trustworthiness of the service you are thinking of using.
- If possible, use a service that provides an escrow function so that you pay money to the service and then release it only when the product is received in good condition.
- Use the browser functions to print documents, and save Web pages to disk at every stage of each transaction.

48.6.10 Online Gambling

- Do not gamble with money you cannot afford to lose.
- Do not gamble online, except at well-known sites.
- If you do gamble online, do not gamble with money at sites hosted outside your own country.
- Do not give your credit card number to online gambling centers that are outside your own country.

- Before you gamble online, do some research to find out if there have been complaints about that casino. Contact your Better Business Bureau, or equivalent, and see if you can find friends or acquaintances who have played on the site you are considering.

48.6.11 Preventing Malware Infections

- Keep your virus strings up to date (automatic daily updates are good).
- Do not download or use software that purports to help you break the law or cheat people and businesses.
- Do not download or use software that has been copied without permission or in violation of license restrictions. That is software piracy, copyright infringement, or plain theft.
- Do not execute software that anyone sends you through email even if you know and like the person who sent it to you. Just because the person is nice does not mean he or she is qualified to inspect programs for safety.
- Before sending someone an attachment such as a picture or any other kind of file by email, let your recipient know what to expect via a preliminary message; if you do not know the person personally, send an email requesting permission to send the attachment.
- Never open attachments you have received without advance notice, regardless of who sent them or what the subject line or text says. Be especially suspicious of generic subjects such as "FYI" without details or "You'll like this." If you are really curious about the attachment, phone or email the supposed sender to find out whether it is legitimate. However, remember that you should not run programs you receive as attachments, regardless of what the sender thinks.
- Do not forward programs, even reliable programs, to anyone; instead, tell your friends where to download useful programs from a trustworthy source, such as a legitimate Website.
- Before sending anyone a Microsoft Word document as an attachment, save the document as an RTF file instead of as the usual DOC file. RTF files do not include document macros and therefore cannot carry macroviruses.
- Disable macros in Microsoft Word.
- Use the options offered by your email client to shut off automatic opening or execution of attachments.
- Do not circulate virus warnings; if you insist on doing so, personally check their validity on any of a number of virus-information and hoax sites on the Web.

48.6.12 Guarding against Spyware

- Before installing freeware or adware, read the terms and conditions carefully to see if they currently include language permitting automatic transfer of information to the supplier or to third parties. Be aware that these contracts often include language authorizing the supplier to change the terms and conditions at any time and without notifying you.

- Install and use a spyware scanner and removal program, such as the free Ad-Aware program from Lavasoft, PestPatrol from Computer Associates, or ZoneAlarm firewall.
- If you are particularly irritated by spyware, install a real-time spyware monitor and blocker such as those just mentioned.
- Support legislative attempts to force software manufacturers to disclose their use of spyware.

48.6.13 Junk Email

- Do not buy products or services from anyone who has sent you junk email. If the company is unprofessional or inconsiderate enough to use such methods of advertising, it does not deserve either your business or your trust.
- Do not assume that the FROM address is correct, because often it is either nonexistent or, worse, fraudulently misrepresents the origin by pointing to a legitimate business that is completely innocent of wrongdoing. Never bombard the owner of a FROM address with multiple copies, or even one copy, of abusive email. Such messages, known as *mail-bombs,* will probably reach the wrong target—some innocent addressee.
- Never respond to the address listed for removal from an email distribution list unless you initiated the contact or are confident that you know the organization that sent you the message (e.g., publications you already subscribe to). Since bounces (returned email due to bad addresses) never reach them and there is no incremental cost for sending out addresses to unwilling people, these operators really do not care how you feel about the junk they send. Therefore, the unethical people who send junk email use the REMOVE function primarily to harvest correct email addresses so they can sell them to someone else.
- Even if you trust the organization that sent you a junk email, never click on a link contained in the message. Instead, visit the company's Website and request removal from their official contact address, which any reputable company has.
- Do not visit the URLs listed in junk email messages. Some of them are deliberately mislabeled and may bring you to offensive Websites.
- If you *really* feel angry about a particular email and it has a dropbox (a real address in the body of the message where you are supposed to reply), then if you have nothing better to do, you may want to send a copy of the spam to the appropriate address (usually in the form abuse@ISPname.domain where you have to fill in the variables *ISPname* and *domain*) address running the dropbox. However, the chances are high that your message will be one of hundreds or thousands of similar reports.
- Do not send any junk email yourself. Encourage those around you (friends, neighbors, children) not to send junk email either.

48.6.14 Mail Storms. Here are some simple suggestions for reducing the likelihood of mail storms:

- Minimize the use of automated responses on your email accounts.
- If you do autoforward your email, do not let your target mailbox fill up.

- If you are receiving autoforwarded email from your primary mailbox, do not autoforward back to the original mailbox.
- Email system administrators should receive exception reports identifying accounts with excessive numbers of email messages or excessive traffic, so that they can investigate for mail storms.
- Firewalls that inspect the content of email messages should be able to react to an excessive number of bounce messages from a single originating address by deleting the traffic or informing the system administrator of a likely mail storm.
- Managers of unmoderated lists should configure a FROM address different from the address that participants use to post messages to the list.
- Users of list servers who want to send personal messages should reply to the sender, not to the entire list.

48.6.15 Detecting Hoaxes. Key indicators that a message is a hoax:

- Use of exclamation marks. No official warning uses them.
- Use of lots of uppercase text, typical of youngsters.
- Misspellings and bad grammar.
- No date of origination or expiration.
- Inclusion of words like "yesterday" when there is no date on the message.
- References to official-sounding sources such as Microsoft, Computer Incident Advisory Capability (CIAC), Computer Emergency Response Team Coordination Center CERT-CC) but no specific document URLs for details. URLs for a site's home page do not count.
- No valid digital signature from a known security organization.
- Requests to circulate widely. No such request is ever made in official documents.
- Claims that someone is counting the number of email messages containing copies of the hoax.
- Threats about dire consequences if someone breaks the chain by refusing to forward the message.
- Claims of monetary rewards that make no sense. For example, the Disney organization will send you $5,000—for forwarding an email message.
- Use of complicated technical language such as "*n*-th dimensional infinite complexity control loops" that do not make sense.
- Claims of damage to computer hardware from viruses or other computer software.

48.6.16 Get-Rich-Quick Schemes

- Remind everyone to use common sense: Earning lots of money with little or no effort usually results in uncovering something impossible or illegal.
- Teach users the mantra of the skeptic: "If it sounds too good to be true, it usually is."
- Explain how dangerous it is to get involved with criminal schemes like using stolen or falsified credit cards. Talk about the victims of such fraud: everyone who

pays higher interest rates on unpaid credit card bills and innocent shopkeepers who lose merchandise to e-commerce crooks.

- Especially when talking to children, discuss Internet-mediated theft in the same terms as you discuss shoplifting. Explain how commerce works; point out that everyone suffers from all kinds of theft, including electronic shoplifting.

48.6.17 Hacking

- Contact your local FBI office and find out if they can send a speaker to your company or to a local meeting of a professional security association for a discussion of computer crime.
- If you or specific authorized staff (e.g., from the security group) do visit Websites that support criminal hacking, be sure to use a personal firewall and set the parameters to deny access to personal information and to refuse cookies and active code (ActiveX, Java) from such sites.

48.7 CONCLUDING REMARKS. This chapter focuses specifically on the use and abuse of Internet and email resources. However, it becomes clear that both of these technologies are simply extensions of the human being behind the computer. Whether it is pornography, online gambling, deceitful emails, or simply posting inappropriate material to a public Website, the potential for damage to an individual, family, or organization is high. Taking a proactive stance through education and awareness is one major tool to combat these deceptive and unethical practices.

Employers have an ethical, and in many cases legal, responsibility to develop and implement policies around the appropriate use of the Internet and email at work. Unfortunately, simply putting the policies out for employee consumption is not enough. Employers must continually remind employees about both the dangers of misuse and the potential consequences to their employment. And when an employee chooses to violate the policy, employers must have a clearly defined process for encouraging proper behavior.

The scope of impact for these issues does not simply end when the employees leaves the office. Because of the widespread use of Internet and email into nearly every facet of our lives, taking the message home to the family is an important responsibility for everyone. Child predators use the Internet to prey on unsuspecting or naïve children, in an effort to exploit them for whatever immoral activity they wish. Parents then have an obligation to put their own family policies in place regarding what is, or is not, acceptable use of the Internet and email in the home.

Unfortunately, there is no easy answer to the problems described in this chapter. Both the Internet and email are neither good nor bad. They only become good or bad by the users and their actions. As technology continues to increase in speed, and in the ability to store more data in less space, everyone must take an active role in protecting each other at the corporate level and in the home.

48.8 FURTHER READING

Blanpain, R., and M. Van Gestel. *Use and Monitoring of Email, Intranet, and Internet Facilities at Work: Law and Practice*. The Hague: Kluwer Law International, 2004.

Cavanaugh, C. *Managing Your E-Mail: Thinking Outside the Inbox*. Hoboken, NJ: John Wiley & Sons, 2003.

Criddle, L. *Look Both Ways: Help Protect Your Family on the Internet*. Redmond, WA: Microsoft Press, 2006.

Fraser, J. M. *Email Etiquette for Business Success: Use Emotional Intelligence to Communicate Effectively in the Business World*. [self-published], 2011.

Flynn, N., and R. Kahn. *E-Mail Rules: A Business Guide to Managing Policies, Security, and Legal Issues for E-Mail and Digital Communication*. New York: AMACOM, 2003.

Goldsmith, J., and T. Wu. *Who Controls the Internet? Illusions of a Borderless World*. New York: Oxford University Press, 2006.

Holtz, S. *Corporate Communications: A Guide to Crafting Effective and Appropriate Internal Communication*. New York: AMACOM, 2004.

Jovin, E. *Email Etiquette for Business Professionals*. New York: Syntaxis Press, 2007.

Payne, T. P., and A. Proops. *Employee Surveillance*. Jordan Publishing, 2013.

Spinello, R. A. *Regulating Cyberspace: The Policies and Technologies of Control*. Westport, CT: Quorum Books, 2002.

Stanton, J. M., and K. R. Stam. *The Visible Employee: Using Workplace Monitoring and Surveillance to Protect Information Assets—Without Compromising Employee Privacy or Trust*. Information Today, 2006.

Willard, N. E. *Cyberbullying and Cyberthreats: Responding to the Challenge of Online Social Aggression, Threats, and Distress*, 2nd ed. Champaign, IL: Research Press, 2007.

48.9 NOTES

1. Parts of this article are based on materials originally published by M. E. Kabay in a series of articles in his Network World Security Strategies column between 2001 and 2011 and in older writings. To avoid cluttering the text with nonessential endnotes, no quotation marks or references are provided for such material. A complete archive is available. www.mekabay.com/nwss
2. Gaudin, "Insider Threats Giving IT Execs Nightmares," eSecurityplanet, November 4, 2005, www.esecurityplanet.com/prevention/article.php/3561761
3. http://search.dhs.gov/search?query=daily+report&affiliate=dhs
4. J. Leyden, "The Enemy Within: Geeks, Squatters and Saboteurs Threaten Corporate Security," *The Register*, December 15, 2005, www.theregister.co.uk/2005/12/15/mcafee_internal_security_survey
5. S. Gaudin, "Sarah Palin fans try to rewrite history on Wikipedia: Former governor's supporters battle with Wikipedia editors over Paul Revere page," *Computerworld*, June 6, 2011, www.computerworld.com/s/article/9217359/Sarah_Palin_fans_try_to_rewrite_history_on_Wikipedia
6. *Parker v. C. N. Enterprises Order, District Court of Travis County, Texas*. Final Judgment, www.loundy.com/CASES/Parker_v_CN_Enterprises.html
7. Information on the Ponzi scheme is taken from James Trager, *The People's Chronology* (Henry Holt & Co. 1995, 1996), made available through the Microsoft Encarta 2007 CD. All rights reserved.
8. C. Tran, "Reading Is Believing." ScienceNow, July 19, 2005; http://news.sciencemag.org/sciencenow/2005/07/19-01.html
9. A. Hamilton, "Arizona Lottery Pick 3 Random Number Bug," *RISKS Forum Digest* 19, No. 83 (1998); http://catless.ncl.ac.uk/Risks/19.83.html=subj5#subj5

10. E. Werner, "Feds Say Vague Law Makes Ban on Internet Gambling Tough to Enforce," Associated Press, April 2, 2008; www.sddt.com/News/article.cfm?SourceCode=20080402fac
11. K. Young, "Internet Addiction Test," Center for Internet Addiction Recovery, 2008, www.globaladdiction.org/dldocs/GLOBALADDICTION-Scales-InternetAddictionTest.pdf
12. P. Bates and M. Fain, "Cheating 101: Paper Mills and You," Coastal Carolina University, 2000, www.coastal.edu/library/presentations/papermil.html
13. J. Rush, "Downing St Dossier Plagiarised," Channel Four News, February 6, 2003, www.channel4.com/news/articles/politics/domestic_politics/downing%2Bst%2Bdossier%2Bplagiarised%2B%2B%2B/253293.html
14. A. Larson, "Sexual Harassment Law," ExpertLaw, 2003, www.expertlaw.com/library/employment/sexual_harassment.html#FN1
15. M. Potok, "Internet Hate and the Law: The First Amendment Protects Most Hateful Speech on the World Wide Web, but There Are Exceptions," Southern Poverty Law Center Intelligence Report 97 (Winter 2000), www.splcenter.org/get-informed/intelligence-report/browse-all-issues/2000/winter/internet-hate-and-the-law

CHAPTER 49

IMPLEMENTING A SECURITY-AWARENESS PROGRAM

K. Rudolph

49.1 INTRODUCTION. An active security-awareness program is not a luxury: It is a business necessity. Losses from security failures are growing at an increasing rate. Some examples of such failures include:

- A 2012 New Year's Eve California office building burglary led to the March collapse and bankruptcy of a national medical records firm because it allowed medical records and social security numbers of14,000 people to be exposed[1];
- As of March 2012, BlueCross BlueShield had spent $18.5 million resolving a 2009 hard drive heist, not including the value of the data itself[2]; and
- An attack on Sony's PlayStation Network exposed personal details of 90,000 customers, which analysts say will cost as much as $2 billion to fix.[3]

According to the Government Accountability Office, the number of reported security breaches increased from 5,503 in 2006 to 41,776 in 2010, an increase of 650 percent.[4] The number of compromised records reported in 2011 was 174 million in Verizon's 2012 data-breach report.[5]

Information security is the translation of the instinctive ability to recognize and react to physical threats into an ability to recognize and respond to threats to information assets (e.g., hardware, software, data, and information).

The purpose of an information-security awareness program is to prevent loss and to ensure compliance with laws and regulations. Security awareness helps to instantiate security policies—to convert theoretical advice and instructions on protecting information assets into observable, positive behavior.

Information-security awareness leads people to:

- Pay attention to what is happening around them;
- Recognize suspicious circumstances that may be security violations;
- Know the initial actions to take in response to their suspicions; and
- Take the appropriate actions in response (people often know what they should do, but are reluctant to get involved).

Security awareness is the result of activities, tools, and techniques that help a target audience focus on identifying what in their environment has value that must be protected (physical assets such as a laptop or mobile phone and intangibles such as data/information) and what they can do to provide that protection. For a business, the target audience must include owners, employees, contractors, suppliers, partners, customers, and any other individuals who have or require access to the organization's information or information systems. A well-trained workforce is inarguably the most cost-effective security control.

The most important security-awareness messages are:

- What must be protected and why should I care?
- Why am I important to security?
- What do security incidents look like?
- What do I do about security?

Effective awareness programs motivate people, provide measurable benefits, and measure those benefits. Awareness materials must compete to gain people's attention. They must also be tailored to an audience, their work environment, and the technologies they use to achieve maximum impact. This chapter outlines a practical approach for implementing an effective security-awareness program.

49.2 KEY CONCEPTS.

Key concepts for this chapter are that security awareness is part of a learning continuum, awareness relates more to common knowledge than common sense, and effective security awareness focuses on behavior modification.

49.2.1 Learning Continuum.

"Information Security Training Requirements: A Role- and Performance-Based Model (Draft)," National Institute of Standards and Technology (NIST) Special Publication (SP) 800-16 Revision 1, addresses security awareness and role-based training. This document defines an information-security learning continuum:

- Awareness,
- Awareness training,
- Role-based training, and
- Education and professional development.[6]

Awareness applies to all employees whether or not they have access to information systems (e.g., a groundskeeper who notices someone carrying boxes out of the office after hours needs to recognize that he or she may be witnessing a security incident and must know how to report the potential incident). Awareness training addresses security basics and literacy, and serves as a transition from awareness to role-based training.

SP 800-16 REV1 states:

> Awareness training strives to build in an organization's information system user population a foundation of information-security terms and concepts upon which later role-based training, if required, can be based. Awareness training informs users of the threats and vulnerabilities that impact their organization and personal work environments by explaining the "what" but not the "how" of security, and communicating what is and what is not allowed. Awareness training not only communicates information-security policies and procedures that need to be followed, but also provides the foundation for any sanctions and disciplinary actions imposed for noncompliance. Awareness training is used to explain the rules of behavior for using a department's or agency's information systems and information and establishes a level of expectation on the acceptable use of the information and information systems.[7]

Awareness programs, as used in this chapter, include the first two levels of the continuum: awareness and basics and literacy. Awareness intends to focus attention on security. Awareness sets the stage for additional learning by changing individual perceptions and organizational culture so that security is recognized as critical and necessary. Security failures can keep individuals from successfully completing their work and can threaten organizational survival. Security-awareness activities have the following characteristics:

- Learning tends to be short term, immediate, and specific.
- Learners are information recipients.
- Learning can occur at the same time everywhere throughout an organization, and it can be continuous.
- Awareness activities are directed at broad audiences with attractive, attention-getting techniques, similar to those used in advertising and cause-marketing.

Basics and literacy applies to workers who use an organization's computers or access nonpublic information. Basics and literacy should direct the workforce regarding compliance with security controls and appropriate responses to attacks in process. Characteristics of basics and literacy are:

- Basics and literacy activities are more formal than awareness activities. The purpose of basics and literacy is to build knowledge and to change attitudes. Specifically, these activities "promote personal responsibility and positive behavioral change throughout an organization's information and information system user population, beyond what is disseminated in the organization's basic awareness efforts."[8]
- Basics and literacy activities use a variety of techniques to address different learning personalities and styles.
- Basics and literacy activities often include a course or presentation and a statement of acceptance of responsibilities.
- Basics and literacy activities typically start with an employee orientation, usually completed before the employee is placed in a work environment.
- Basics and literacy activities include periodic refresher activities on at least an annual schedule.

Awareness materials are generally broad in coverage, but limited in depth (that is, awareness covers a lot of ground, but does not dig very deep holes). Role-based training and education and professional development apply to staff with significant security-related roles or functions, including:

- Executives, such as the chief information officer (CIO) and the chief information security officer (CISO)
- Information system security officers (ISSOs) and staff
- Program and functional managers (e.g., system owners, information owners, network administrators, system administrators, security administrators)
- Application designers and developers

Role-based training takes longer than awareness, and involves establishing and enhancing skills and competency for those involved in functional specialties (e.g., management, systems design, and acquisition). Training is provided selectively based on an individual's job functions (roles) and is most effective when tailored to the business environment. Education and professional development are appropriate for those pursuing a security career, and include college-level courses and professional certifications, such as the Certified Information Systems Security Professional (CISSP) and the Certified Data Protection (CDP) specialist. Role-based training and education and professional development are beyond the scope of this chapter.

49.2.2 Awareness: Common Sense or Common Knowledge? Ira Winkler, president of the Internet Security Advisors Group, writes, "The fundamental issue is that of common sense vs. common knowledge. You cannot expect people to behave with common sense if they do not have a common knowledge."[9] Consider the following security-awareness messages. Are the messages below common sense?

- Do not share your password
- Do not discuss sensitive or protected information in public
- Create long, strong passwords
- Report actual or suspected incidents
- Delete email chain messages

Some would say that these messages are nothing but common sense. If these security messages are common sense, then why do we need to publish tips telling people not to share their passwords, not to let others tailgate into secure work areas, and not to talk about sensitive information in public? Perhaps these messages are "common sense waiting to happen." Or, possibly, these are common-sense items only within a particular environment or background, such as individuals who are computer literate.

In 2007, IRS workers familiar with the policy of not sharing passwords, disclosed their passwords because they did not understand that changing their password to one provided by a caller was the same as disclosing it.[10]An IRS audit group, posing as computer help desk staff, called 102 IRS employees asking each to help them "correct a computer problem" by providing their user name and temporarily changing their password to one the caller suggested.

- Sixty-one of the 102 employees did as requested.
- Managers were more lax than nonmanagers.
- A follow-up survey asking why the employees gave up their passwords so easily found that about one-third believed what they had been told by the unknown caller.
- *Ten percent believed that changing their password was not the same as disclosing it, which they knew was against the rules.*[11]

The 10 percent of respondents who did not recognize their actions as disclosure demonstrate a need for improved security-awareness activities. While most (but unfortunately not all) security professionals know to never change their password to one that someone else knows, this principle is not common knowledge among all computer users. "When there are widespread problems, there is clearly a failure in how the security community is delivering the message."[12] An awareness program should instill common knowledge, and by using material that grabs attention and maintains interest, transform that common knowledge into common sense.

49.2.3 Focus on Behavior. An organization's workforce is generally among the first to be affected by a security incident. Their compliance with security policy can make or break a security program. A staff that is security-aware can detect and prevent many incidents and mitigate damage when incidents do occur. Thus, the need for awareness programs that focus on behaviors.

The need to focus on behaviors is critical, especially with younger workers. "Seven out of ten young employees who are aware of their companies' IT policies acknowledge breaking those rules with varying regularity, according to a Cisco survey of more than 2,800 college students and young professionals in 14 countries."[13]

The most common reasons for this are:

- The employees' belief that they aren't doing anything wrong (33 percent)
- The need to access unauthorized applications for their jobs (22 percent)
- Lack of enforcement (19 percent)
- Lack of time to think about policies (18 percent)
- Inconvenience of adhering to policies (16 percent)
- Forgetting to follow policies (15 percent)

Nearly two-thirds (61 percent) said that the responsibility for protecting information and devices is on IT or service providers and not on individual employees. As this example illustrates, security is too important to sacrifice to the status quo.

Security-related behaviors can be classed as good, bad, or ugly[14]: Good behavior complies with the letter of the law or better, the spirit of the law; bad behavior includes naïve mistakes or dangerous tinkering for example, sharing a password, writing a packet-spoofing application to test one's programming ability, or scanning the organization network to see how it works; and ugly behavior consists of intentional misuse or destruction for example, building script that disables other users' terminal sessions, forging email header information, using a file decryption program to access trade secrets without authorization, or introducing a Trojan horse program into the network.

Within an organization, good security behaviors include compliance with security policy, such as:

- Releasing nonpublic information only with appropriate authorization
- Promptly reporting a potential security vulnerability such as a lost mobile device
- Politely terminating and then reporting a suspected social engineering attempt
- Creating and using strong, unique passwords for critical systems

Bad security typically experienced includes:

- Sharing passwords
- Deploying a wireless network gateway that allows noncompany personnel to use the company's network

- Setting up a packet-spoofing application to test the user's programming ability
- Setting up a network monitoring scanner on the user's PC

Ugly security behaviors include intentional misuse such as:

- Building a script to disable other users' terminal sessions
- Forging email header information
- Intentionally introducing malicious code into the organization computing infrastructure
- Using someone else's email to send messages

Behaviors directly affect the ability of the organization to meet its business objectives. Good behaviors promote business objectives and allow resources to be focused on achieving organizational goals (e.g., improved profitability and reduced costs). Bad and ugly behaviors result in wasted resources and loss of workforce focus on business objectives (that is, increased costs and reduced performance). Bad and ugly behaviors, carried to their extreme, can result in organizational failure (e.g., intentionally compromising customer financial records could result in a financial liability so large that the company goes bankrupt). Exhibits 49.1 and 49.2 illustrate a table showing measurable end user security behaviors, whether the behaviors are good, bad, or ugly, and how they could be measured.

Effective security-awareness programs encourage people to treat mistakes as "portals of discovery" where they can learn how to avoid similar mistakes. Employees should recognize that it is in everyone's best interest to limit damage from a mistake and, more importantly, to learn from it, and report it quickly rather than fixing it quietly. Mistakes often have side effects, and pretending that a mistake didn't happen is dangerous. In a *Harvard Business Review* interview, former Toyota chairman Katsuaki Watanabe said, "Hidden problems are the ones that become serious threats eventually. If problems are revealed for everyone to see, I will feel reassured. Because once problems have been visualized, even if our people didn't notice them earlier, they will rack their brains to find solutions to them."[15] Sharing what you learned can prevent loss. In her research on learning in hospitals, Amy Edmondson of Harvard University discovered that the highest-performing nursing units had reported the largest number of mistakes. Not because they made more mistakes, but because they felt safe to report and share the ones they did make.[16] Learning the cause and how to avoid mistakes is vital to security.

Technologists typically try to control workforce behaviors by adding layers of technical controls. As demonstrated by the increasing number of reported information compromises, technological approaches alone cannot solve a people problem. The workforce needs access to data and computing functions to do their job. Technology cannot effectively distinguish between the instances when an individual employs a capability they are authorized to use to accommodate a good behavior versus a bad behavior. Technology cannot adequately address the human factor of intent.

The rise of mobile computing in the work environment has brought increased importance to the human factor. The network perimeter now extends from a defined physical area to wherever data might be at any given time (e.g., an employee's home, a laptop at an offsite meeting). Building good computing habits at home is as important, if not more important, than building those behaviors at work. Secure computing habits will

Security Awareness Program Metrics Internal User Behaviors *Examples to be tailored should be based on goals and then questions.*	G · B · U*	Survey	Observation	Helpdesk Incid. Rpts	Manual Tests or Audits	Software (Automated)
% of users recognizing a security event scenario	G	✓				
% of users susceptible to social engineering (compare mid-week at mid-day to Friday afternoon)	B				✓	
% of users revealing their password when tested	B				✓	
% of users activating a "test virus"	B				✓	
% of security incidents having human behavior as a major factor/involving behaviors covered in awareness materials	BU			✓		
Storage of unauthorized file content on desktop or network resources, such as audio, video, or other multimedia files	B					✓
Number of attempts to access inappropriate/blocked Websites	B					✓
Nonpublic information found in dumpsters outside of facilities	B		✓			
% of systems having unapproved software installed	BU				✓	✓
% of systems having unapproved hardware installed	B				✓	✓
% of emails (random sample) with inappropriate content	B				✓	
% of passwords visible or in common locations (e.g., under lamp)	B		✓			
% of PCs logged on and unattended	B		✓			
% of laptops, portable devices/media, sensitive data unsecured	B		✓			
% of laptops, portable devices/media, stolen (office/travel)	B			✓		
Number of attempts to use unauthorized resources, e.g., VPN	B					✓
% of emails sent via Internet containing nonpublic/sensitive data that are not encrypted	B				✓	
% of users wearing badges with picture facing out	G		✓			
% of monitors positioned to be easily seen from hallways, doors, or windows (especially on the ground floor)	B		✓			

EXHIBIT 49.1 Awareness Metrics, continued as Exhibit 49.2

transfer across environments, as individuals recognize good behaviors are beneficial to them regardless of whether they are at home or at work.

49.3 CRITICAL SUCCESS FACTORS.

Critical success factors for implementing a security-awareness program include:

- An information security policy
- Senior-level management commitment and buy-in, to demonstrate the importance of security
- Resources with subject matter, communications, and training expertise

Security Awareness Program Metrics Internal User Behaviors *Examples to be tailored should be based on goals and then questions.*	G · B · U*	Survey	Observation	Helpdesk Incid. Rpts	Manual Tests or Audits	Software (Automated)
% of users who challenge unknown visitor with no access badge	G		✓	✓		
% of users who open a test email with a questionable subject	B				✓	✓
% of users activating a "test virus"	B				✓	✓
% of users who click a link in a test email (instead of typing the URL into their browsers)	B				✓	✓
% of users responding to a test email via an "unsubscribe" link	B				✓	✓
% of crackable user passwords	B				✓	✓
% of user systems having spyware or malware installed	B				✓	✓
Number of incidents of unauthorized use of administrator privileges	U			✓	✓	
% of users sending Internet email to multiple recipients who do not use the BCC field	B				✓	
% who have actively acknowledged policies/security responsibilities	G					✓
Number of major findings from internal and external security audits	B				✓	
% viewing optional security materials in online courses	G					✓
% participating in contests, suggestion programs, bonus questions	G					✓

***G·B·U** = Good, Bad, or Ugly
G: Good behavior complies with the 'letter or the law' or better, the 'spirit of the law,' e.g., not releasing nonpublic information inappropriately, discovering and reporting a security vulnerability.
B: Bad behavior includes **naïve mistakes** or **dangerous tinkering** — e.g., sharing a password, deploying a wireless network gateway that allows noncompany personnel to use the company's network, setting up a packet spoofing application to test one's programming ability, or setting up a network monitoring scanner on one's PC.
U: Ugly behavior consists of **detrimental mususe** or **intentional destruction** — e.g., someone builds a special script that disabled other users' terminal sessions, forges email header information to make it look like someone else sent a message, uses a file decryption program to discover the contents of a file containing trade secrets, or intentionally introduces a Trojan horse program into the network.

(Behavior categories inspired by "Analysis of End User Security Behaviors" - by Jeffrey M. Stanton, Kathryn R. Stam, Paul Mastrangelo, and Jeffrey Jolton, July 12, 2004.)

EXHIBIT 49.2 Awareness Metrics, continued from Exhibit 49.1

- Visibility, audience appeal, and participation to address all subgroups within the workforce
- Destinations and road maps to guide and monitor program activities

49.3.1 Information Security Policy. Effective information security policies are in-place, credible, comprehensive, and current. Security objectives must be embodied in policies that clarify and document management's intentions and concerns. Policies are an organization's laws. They set expectations for employee performance and guide behaviors. Information security policies include statements of goals and responsibilities, and delineate what activities are allowed, what activities are not allowed, and what penalties may be imposed for failure to comply.

Effective information security policies show that management expects a focus on security. Well-defined security policies show what is expected of the workforce and make it easier to take disciplinary action against those who ignore policy and compromise security.

A cohesive security-awareness policy provides credibility and visibility to the information-security program. It shows that management recognizes that security is important and that individuals should and will be held accountable for their actions. As Daryl White, chief information officer for the U.S. Department of the Interior, said, "You can't hold firewalls and intrusion detection systems accountable; you can only hold people accountable."[17] Credibility also requires that management back employees who do the right thing.

An awareness policy should address three basic concepts:

1. **Participation** in the awareness program is required for everyone, including senior management, part-time and full-time staff, new hires, contractors, and other outsiders who have access to the organization's information systems. New hires might be required to receive a security-awareness orientation briefing within a specific time (e.g., 30 days after hire) or before being allowed system access. Existing employees might be required to attend an awareness activity or take a course within one month of program initiation, and periodically thereafter (e.g., semiannually or annually).
2. Everyone will be given sufficient **time to participate** in awareness activities. In many organizations, security policy also requires that employees sign a statement indicating that they understand the material presented and will comply with security policies.
3. **Responsibility** for conducting awareness program activities is assigned. The program might be created and implemented by one or a combination of: the training department, and the security staff, or an outside organization, consultant, or security-awareness specialist.

49.3.2 Senior Level Management Commitment. Senior management must be committed to information security and visibly demonstrate that commitment by example (e.g., signing the awareness program or activity launch announcement, participating in awareness activities), providing an adequate budget, and supporting the security staff. Saying security is important but failing to follow organizational policies will have negative consequences.

Executives set the standard for organizational behavior. For example, in Colombia, when there was a water shortage, the mayor of Bogotá, Antanas Mockus, appeared on television programs taking a shower and turning off the water as he soaped, asking his fellow citizens to do the same. In just two months people were using 14 percent less water, a savings that increased when people realized how much money they were also saving because of economic incentives approved by Mockus. Water use is now 40 percent less than before the shortage.[18]

Organizational leaders must understand and support the program as well as provide oversight. Program responsibility has shifted in recent years from a collateral duty of a compliance or information-security officer to the highest levels of the organization.

Poor security measures can be costly in damage to the organization's brand or reputation, in impact on operations, and in actual and potential lawsuits. The media will not hesitate to report a security threat or breach. Such stories are a wake-up call and highlight the need for senior executive commitment to the security function.

Wise senior managers know that security is not just about reducing risk, it's also a tool to protect the organization's reputation. It also builds customer confidence and market valuations, and delivers a competitive edge. In today's e-commerce environment, effective information security can increase business and profits. Top management should understand that security is not solely a risk avoidance measure and should see the security-awareness program as a business enabler.[19]

Senior-management compliance provides credibility. If security policy prohibits installation of personal software on organization infrastructure, even senior executives must comply. Doing otherwise undermines the policy and creates a perception of inconsistence, unfairness, or unimportance. Senior managers must stand behind the organization's policies and the security staff charged with enforcing those policies. Consistent enforcement is especially important in areas where security and convenience conflict, such as changing passwords frequently or enforcing denial of system access for users who have not completed a required awareness refresher activity. In addition, human beings tend to imitate those with higher social status, so executives who see their superiors refusing to wear name badges will soon be doing the same—and the breach of security policy will propagate downward through the entire organization.[20]

Implementing an awareness program is always a management challenge. Senior managers generally appear to recognize the benefits of an awareness program, but are often still reluctant to allocate the financial and staff resources necessary to make it effective. Awareness programs must compete against other organizational needs. It is relatively easy to identify the cost of an awareness program, but it is difficult to quantify its benefits. Thus, awareness programs often lose when competing against programs where benefits are more tangible (e.g., programs that return a profit). The difficulty in quantifying benefits is a primary reason why the U.S. Government made maintenance of a computer security-awareness program mandatory for federal organizations[21] and why security awareness is required by laws and regulation in specific industries such as finance and healthcare.

Management resistance is often tied to viewing security awareness as "nice to have" but not as important as other needs vying for limited funds. Although the time and effort to build a strong security program is not trivial, it is far less than the time and effort required to deal with just one serious incident. Some security professionals recommend equating awareness with insurance policies. Insurance policies require continuous funding but are not often used (and the hope is not to use them); however, few organizations choose to forego those costs.

When common sense and fiduciary responsibilities are not enough, legal requirements provide another incentive for awareness programs. The Federal Information Security Management Act and the Computer Security Act require such programs for federal organizations. State and federal laws (e.g., the Sarbanes-Oxley Act and the Gramm-Leach-Bliley Act for financial information, and the Health Insurance Portability and Accountability Act for healthcare information) require security-awareness components in information-security programs for state agencies and public companies. Requirements to maintain effective security programs are also included in state and federal contracts that impact critical infrastructures (e.g., healthcare, public safety) and contracts that require retention of sensitive customer information.[22]

49.3.3 Resources with Security, Communications, and Training Expertise. Ideally, responsibility for an awareness program should be assigned to one individual who has a defined budget and has security subject matter expertise, communications skills (such as marketing), and knowledge of training principles. This individual should be a member of senior management and performance of the awareness program should be a factor in his or her performance evaluation. Program activities and materials may be created and deployed by one or more individuals drawn from internal or external resources.

The mix of skills needed to successfully maintain a security-awareness program include:

1. **Subject matter expertise**—Individuals attempting to infuse security awareness into the business processes should be knowledgeable of those business processes. This ensures that awareness messages support the business and are delivered using terminology and content that are accurate and aligned with other organizational initiatives and activities (e.g., a professional security certification is valuable when working with a technical audience to establish credibility).
2. **Communications expertise**—Awareness activities often require translation of technical, security-oriented information into tips, discussions, presentations, posters, job aids, and other tools that average computer users can understand and apply in their daily work. Communications skills facilitate development of these awareness materials.
3. **Training expertise**—Training is its own discipline. People learn in different ways. Knowledge of training techniques, how people learn, and how to match training techniques to learning styles will improve the potential success of an awareness program.

The awareness team also needs to include an individual with deep information security experience. This individual serves to validate material for the general workforce and to help avoid the *curse of knowledge*. Once we know something—say, the melody of a song—we find it hard to imagine not knowing it. Our knowledge has metaphorically cursed us. We have difficulty sharing our own knowledge because we cannot readily relate to our audience's state of mind.[23]

The curse of knowledge was identified in a 1990 study by Elizabeth Newton, a graduate student at Stanford University. Study participants were divided into two groups: tappers and listeners. The experimenters chose 120 well-known songs such as "Happy Birthday" and the tappers tapped out the rhythm on a table while the listeners tried to guess the song. Before they started, the tappers were asked to predict listener success. Most predicted about 50 percent. The actual success ratio was 2.5 percent. The tappers conveyed the message successfully one time in 40, but thought that they would get the message across one time in two. This discrepancy resulted from the fact that the tappers hear the tune internally while they tap, but the listeners only hear what sounds like random taps.[24]

49.3.4 Visibility, Audience Appeal, and Participation. An effective awareness program cultivates a professional, positive, and visible image. A visible program demonstrates the value of the awareness activities, raises employee morale, and encourages the support of the general workforce. The more methods used to spread the message, the more visible the program. An awareness program that uses computer-based courses, videos, posters, acknowledgment statements, newsletters, contests, events, daily tips, and checklists will reach more people and have a greater impact than a program that consists of posting security policies to the organization's intranet and sending a memo advising staff to read the policies.

Everyone should receive sufficient time to participate in awareness activities; this includes those who are responsible for planning and developing awareness activities. These activities should occur on compensated time. Organizations that require employees to only obtain or develop security awareness and training on their own time effectively state that security is not important.

Security-awareness programs that show the organization's concern for employees' IT security well-being at home (for telecommuters and others who use computers at home) and while traveling are better received than programs that ignore such issues. Practical topics that cross between home and office might include "what to do if your Twitter account is hacked," "how to use Apple iOS5 securely," or "how to protect your personal email account." Whether the target audience is all end users or senior management, showing them how they will personally benefit from improved security awareness contributes to program success. Viewing security as a service, with the entire organization as a customer, highlights the importance of marketing security to management and staff.

Computer behaviors and habits from home transfer to work. Security professional Donna Mattick put it this way,

> Just knowing that my elderly relatives are using the Internet causes me to stay up at night worrying, but it also drives me to find ways to protect them automatically. On the other end of the scale, I have a teenage daughter who has an iPad, cell phone, and exposure to computers at school. She can find a way around every protection measure I put in place. So I have to stay current to keep up with her. ... Children, parents, and elders all need to be cyberaware and we security professionals need to step up and help. For every person we educate how to stay safe we chip away at the criminals' ability to take advantage of us.[25]

49.3.5 Destination and Road Maps. When a psychologist was invited to give a talk at the Pentagon on managing time and resources, he decided to warm up the group of generals with a short exercise. He asked them all to write a summary of their strategic approach in no more than 25 words. The exercise stumped most of them. The only general who managed a response was one who had worked her way through the ranks and been wounded in combat in Iraq. Her approach was as follows: "First I make a list of priorities: one, two, three, and so on. Then I cross out everything from three down."[26]

Create a security-awareness program plan that contains these elements:

- A description of the organization and its IT culture (culture is the instinctive behavior of individuals within an organization), including assigned roles and responsibilities
- Program goals and the status of the organization's current efforts with a security baseline
- A determination of awareness needs by audience
- A description of methods and materials to be acquired, created, and/or modified
- A schedule showing actions to be completed and who is responsible for ensuring their completion (including program evaluation and updates)

49.3.5.1 Goals. A security-awareness program should have goals and a plan for achieving the goals that includes measureable criteria. The goals and objectives should be related to improvements in workforce performance and security risk. For example, the following might be appropriate goals for a security-awareness program:

- Improve employees' ability to recognize potential threats and vulnerabilities
- Improve the level of compliance with company physical and computer security controls
- Reduce the occurrence of security failures resulting from employee action or inaction
- Reduce the severity of the security incidents that do occur

Specific, realistic, and measurable goals are best. If possible, establish a baseline prior to implementing your awareness program or launching a new campaign. A baseline defines where the organization stands with regard to its security-awareness efforts and program. It may be that the baseline is zero and a program has not been implemented. In that case, the organization may take a survey to find out how people in the organization view security and how familiar they are with security policies. The results of the survey would become the baseline. Where a program has been implemented, the organization may choose to document the level of awareness so that over time, other measurements can be taken to show changes.

Victor Basili of the University of Maryland developed an approach for metrics where the metric is created as the final step of a process called Goal-Question-Metric.[27] He recommends defining a goal, for example: "Goal—decrease inappropriate Website visits." Next, create a question that will indicate whether the goal is being met or not: "Are staff continuing to visit Websites that they should not?" Then, and only then, create a metric that will support the goal. The metric would be the number of attempts to access inappropriate Websites, such as illegal or pornographic material. This information can be extracted from Web filtering products. This approach offers several benefits:

- It leads to an automated metric
- The information for the metric is easy to collect
- The metric will give a constantly updated idea of what the organization's users are doing

49.3.5.2 Audiences and Messages. Awareness programs need to be planned to ensure they address the intended target audience in the appropriate manner. If you are directing your message to your total workforce, then you should consider consultants, contractors, subcontractors, vendors, suppliers, and other third parties. When your audience is employees, don't forget temporary hires and interns. If you divide your audience by technical skill, you can provide detailed information to your technical staff and less detail to your clerical staff.

Once you decide on your audience and how to segment that audience, you can develop messages and delivery methods specific to each segment. The following are audience breakdowns for a typical business:

- **Executives**—are generally interested in return on investment and risk reduction, have a moderate level of technical literacy, and are key targets for spear phishing and social engineering.

- **Information technology staff**—should be interested in building security into applications, networks, and systems, should have specific security responsibilities, and are expected to have moderate to high computer literacy.
- **Business users**—primarily focus on getting the business process completed regardless of the security impact. They can be easily frustrated when security controls are time consuming or inhibit "real work," but they can be motivated when they can see the benefits to themselves and their families, and will respond positively once they understand the value of security controls, especially if they handle sensitive or protected customer data.
- **New hires**—for those for whom this is their first "real" job, awareness will need to focus on the fundamentals (what needs protection, from whom or what, why they should care, and what is their role in the organization). For new hires who have been in the job market, awareness messages generally need to focus on how security is addressed in this organization.
- **Mobile device and smart phone users**—often associate risk with the smallness and low cost of the device instead of the adverse impact their compromise or loss could have on themselves as well as on the company.
- **People who travel**—whether they travel locally or abroad, travelers have removed themselves and their computer devices from the friendly surroundings of the office and home. An unattended device, in a hotel room, in the trunk of a car, or even at airport screening, is an invitation for theft and data compromise.

These messages should be delivered using a mix of tools (e.g., posters, screen savers, presentations, events, computer-based courseware, classroom training, and one-on-one training). The more times the same message is delivered using different approaches, the greater the likelihood the information will be retained.

49.3.5.3 Methods and Frequency.

Some companies use a perpetual calendar for their security program. The calendar is used to create a communications plan that covers the type and frequency of message by audience. A calendar-oriented plan shows what security-awareness materials and activities are produced monthly, quarterly, or annually. Calendars need to be periodically updated to add special events, such as security-awareness days or weeks.

A security-awareness program should be an ongoing effort. Some organizations offer a security-awareness orientation to new employees and regular reinforcement for all employees at various times throughout the year. Doing so provides spaced repetition of the material, and reinforces learning. Some organizations address security awareness on a monthly basis with newsletters, posters, screen savers, contests, surveys, and online modules. Other organizations offer awareness courses that are updated annually and provide reinforcement at various times, such as on November 30, International Computer Security Awareness Day. NIST SP 800-50, "Building an Information Technology Security Awareness and Training Program"[28] presents a detailed approach for establishing and maintaining a security-awareness program, including an appendix with a sample awareness program plan template.

49.3.6 Common Challenges and Mistakes.

Awareness program planning should consider common obstacles and constraints such as keeping management informed, changing material language to relevant business terminology, gaining union support, and overcoming audience resistance. The program should also be structured to address significant, but less recognized challenges of diffusion of responsibility (where a person is less likely to act when others are present because they assume that others will take action or have already done so); and attenuation (when a message loses its strength and the learners tune out, usually because the message has been reused, overused, or doesn't capture the student's interest). Wildlife managers describe attenuation as "getting used to something we shouldn't." They say: "A fed bear is a dead bear."[29] When bears in parks get used to campers and carelessly stored food, they adapt, resulting in dangerous encounters or mailings and the destruction of the bear. Bad things can happen when your awareness messages lose their signal strength.

A common mistake is not fitting the program to the environment. Build an awareness program around your business environment. If you take materials from other organizations, be sure to tailor the content to your environment and target audience. Free training materials can have significant costs in terms of wasted audience time and can increase security risks by providing a false sense of security if the training doesn't meet your program objectives.

Security program planners often overlook the learners. This typically occurs because those charged with planning and building the program were selected for their technical competence, but have limited experience in selecting learning methods and techniques. Programs that don't consider the learner often fail. Learners should be able to relate to the awareness materials and apply the materials to their jobs.[30]

Joseph A. Grau, former chief of the Information Security Division at the Department of Defense Security Institute, believed in the importance of marketing security and often stated that customers actually pay for security services. For example, managers pay for enforcing the requirement to lock a classified document in a safe rather than leaving it on a desk, with labor hours. Other methods of payment are in the form of energy, attention, and concern for security matters, such as taking time to identify and report a potential security incident. Even egos are part of the payment for security. There is an "ego cost" when "scientists, researchers, technical specialists, engineers, and management personnel must refrain from communicating their successes to friends, family, and peers to protect sensitive, company private or classified information."[31]

Be sure that your awareness program plan clearly defines your objective (how to know when you are successful) and how you can monitor your progress toward your stated objective. Successful performance is always easier to achieve when you have a road map or plan that tells you where you are, where you are going, and how to tell that you have reached your destination. Abraham Lincoln related planning to sharpening an ax. If he was asked to cut down a tree in eight hours, he would spend the first six sharpening his ax. It takes great effort to chop down a tree with a dull ax, but cutting a tree down with a sharp ax goes much more quickly. Similarly it is much harder to create, manage, and measure the effect of an unplanned awareness program than a planned program with defined objectives, assigned responsibilities, and management direction.

Careful planning promotes awareness activities that elicit specific, positive responses. Flexible plans allow timely changes to address changes in the organizational structure, objectives, new technologies, and applicable threats and vulnerabilities. Flexibility also allows incorporation of relevant current events, events that use external sources to emphasize your security message. Microsoft's policy of issuing awards for help in capturing virus writers is evidence that security issues are now getting high-level attention.

49.4 TOPICS. In planning an awareness program, you should have an understanding of the topics that you want to address. NIST SP 800-16, "Information Security Training Requirements: A Role- and Performance-Based Model (Draft)," identifies the following security-awareness topics:

- Roles and responsibilities in information security
- Ways to protect shared data (e.g., encryption, backups)
- Examples of internal and external threats (e.g., social engineering, hackers)
- Malicious code (e.g., viruses, worms)
- Security controls
- Ways to recognize an information-security incident
- Principles of information security
- Passwords
- Social engineering
- Data backup and storage
- Computer viruses and worms
- Incident response
- Personal use and gain
- Privacy
- Personally identifiable information (PII)
- Identity theft
- Internet surfing
- Inventory control
- Physical security
- Spyware
- Phishing
- Scams and spam
- Mobile devices (e.g., laptops, smartphones, tablet computers)
- Portable storage devices (e.g., CDs, USB drives)
- Remote access
- Copyright infringement and software piracy
- Use and abuse of email
- Email do's and don'ts
- Peer-to-peer file sharing threats
- National security information systems, where applicable[32]

Although these topics may not be directly relevant to a specific organization, they do provide a catalog to which you can add or subtract based on your industry, technology, and assets that need protection. For example, healthcare providers should address personal health information (PHI), both paper and electronic (ePHI); organizations that accept credit cards should include topics linked to the Payment Card Industry Data

Security Standards (PCI DSS); and organizations that deal extensively with intellectual property (IP) should consider adding topics that include advanced persistent threats (APT) and related social engineering techniques.

Exploiting technology weaknesses to gain financial reward is a significant threat, but less obvious data thefts can cause substantial harm to your organization's reputation and require significant clean-up costs. Identity theft can affect organizations as well as individuals, and stealing the ideas for a new marketing program or product can damage a firm's ability to effectively compete for new business.

Including the impact of data theft is a key topic in your awareness list. The impact of data theft was often not well understood, even though it could result in a firm's bankruptcy. It wasn't too long ago that a court held that a data theft could not be prosecuted because nothing was actually taken. Today's judges are more knowledgeable and recognize that the knowledge the data conveys (e.g., a person's identity) can be more damaging than stealing a person's money. Linking your awareness messages to impact on the organization is an effective approach to explaining impact and increasing acceptance of your security message.

Another way to identify appropriate topics is to ask managers, helpdesk, and incident response personnel to identify recurring problems or review the problem reports to identify recurring issues. Awareness topics can then be structured to help resolve these problems by surfacing their cause and how to avoid them. Also, topics that are of personal relevance are good for gaining attention. Data mining, mobile device location awareness, cyberbullying, identity theft, travel precautions, and the latest frauds, scams, and malware are of interest to most computer users.

49.5 TECHNIQUES FOR GETTING AND HOLDING ATTENTION.

> *If you want to build a ship, don't drum up the men to gather wood, divide the work, and give orders. Instead, teach them to yearn for the vast and endless sea.*[33]
>
> —Antoine de Saint-Exupery

If you want to secure information and computer systems, don't dictate orders or make commandments for employees to follow. Teach them why they are crucial to the security process. Learning methods that are interactive, demonstrative, and rewarding get the most attention. Work with the brain to capture and maintain attention. Before you can teach your audience anything, you must have their attention. The strongest messages have a visual and visceral impact and use images, surprise, novelty, emotional involvement, and empathy.

> Most of the events that predict whether something learned will also be remembered occur in the first few seconds of learning. The more elaborately we encode a memory during its initial moments, the stronger it will be.[34]

Emotional context plays a large role in memory retention. Emotional arousal helps the brain learn. People remember things that they feel, such as empathy when they learn about a person who accidentally reformatted a hard drive and did not have a backup. (Are my files backed up? Could I accidentally reformat my disk?) Other feelings that awareness program materials and events can convey include surprise, curiosity, and satisfaction (e.g., correctly answering a difficult quiz question or solving a security puzzle). Scenarios are a good way to create empathy because they allow choice of action to be directly associated with consequences.

Anything that increases brain activity causes deeper learning. The more different types of brain activity involved, the better the results of the awareness program. In short, design and implement awareness activities and messages that use as much of the brain (especially both sides) as possible.

49.5.1 Images. "We do not see with our eyes. We see with our brains."[35] Half the brain is set up for visual processing. The more visual the input, the more likely it is to be remembered and recalled. This phenomenon is called the Pictorial Superiority Effect (PSE). The potency of the PSE was described definitively in 1976 by neuroscientist Douglas Nelson. "He and others have shown that our brains are essentially hard-wired for visuals—the very architecture of our visual cortex allows graphics a unique mainline into our consciousness."[36] People pay attention to color, size, and orientation. People pay special attention to objects that are moving. This is why animations (e.g., our computer game-oriented culture) are so effective.

Imagery stimulates both verbal and visual representations. Language is primarily processed through only the verbal channel. Experiments have shown that imagery activates multiple, powerful neural pathways of memory recall. While our access to raw information has grown, our time to process this information has declined (we are reduced to communicating in sound bites and 140 character Tweets). This places a premium on meaning-making. Given our brain's preference for the visual and the current complexity of our world, "we've learned that the very best shortcuts usually come in graphical form … consequently, today's visual storytellers have considerable power."[37]

Graphics that incorporate the message in the image (e.g., speech boxes) are more effective than graphics that described the message or image in an accompanying narrative or that have the message as a caption or title below the image. Exhibit 49.3 shows two images of a vulnerability caused by a modem. Learners were observed to glance at the first one for a short period of time and many "tuned it out." When the speech boxes were added, learners looked at the image longer and expressed excitement, saying, "Oh, I get it. The modem goes around the firewall and circumvents the control."

49.5.2 Video. While some educational professionals say the future of online learning is gamification[38] (learning through games), video is arguably the future of online security awareness. YouTube is the second most popular search engine online—today. Humanity watches more than 80 million hours of YouTube every day, according to Chris Anderson, TED[39] founder. Our brains are wired for video more that print. Video offers a greater density of information. Anderson points out that print and reading are relatively new compared to face to face communication. Print was scalable, which was an advantage that has been overtaken by video. Anderson's TED talk addressed crowd-accelerated innovation and learning where cycles of improvement are driven by people watching Web video. He uses the examples of street dancers and TED talks. As a result of being able to see what others in their fields are doing, people are stepping up their game. Anderson identified three concepts that fuel accelerated learning and performance:

1. A crowd, such as a global Internet community—the bigger the crowd, the more potential innovators there are, as well as commenters, trendspotters, cheerleaders, skeptics, mavericks, and super-spreaders. These people are creating the ecosystem through which innovation emerges.

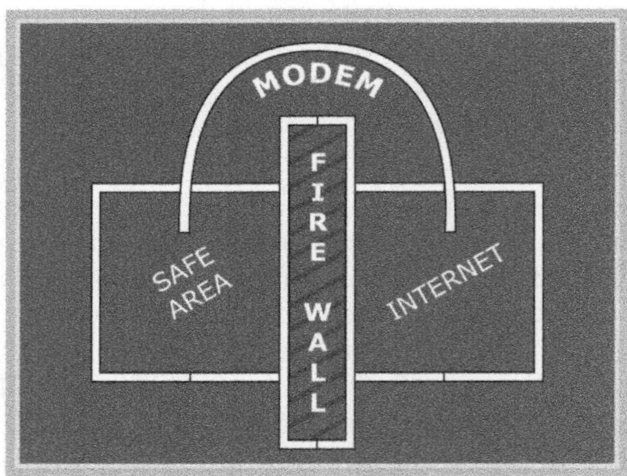

Graphic showing vulnerability. "Tuned out" by many learners.

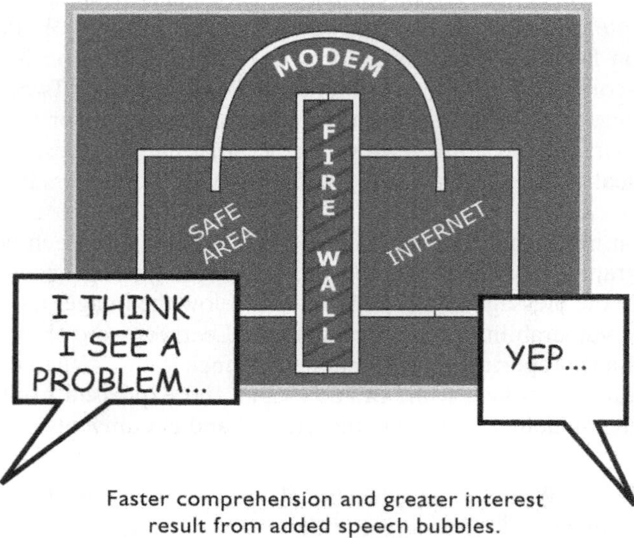

Faster comprehension and greater interest result from added speech bubbles.

EXHIBIT 49.3

2. Light, clear, open visibility of what the best are doing—this empowers others to participate. A light shines on the innovators, either directly through comments, ratings, email, Facebook, and Twitter, or indirectly through numbers of views and links (that point Google there).
3. Desire for social status—where the best walks tall and is recognized—"You might just be a kid with a Webcam, but if you can do something that goes viral, you can be seen by the equivalent of sports stadiums crammed with people." This global recognition drives huge amounts of effort. The light and desire are self-fueling and attract new people to the crowd.[40]

Here's an example of how well video can work for security awareness described by Chip and Dan Heath. Russ Berland was tasked with redesigning BearingPoint's ethics and compliance training program. He inherited a code of conduct which might have been repurposed from a law firm. A principal challenge was the need to influence the behavior of employees across the country, operating in different organizational cultures. Berland interviewed associates about real-world "gray areas" and uncovered dramatic stories of strained relationships and ethical quandaries. This inspired his team to create a humorous fictional series based on *The Office* featuring a fictional company designed to be the "evil doppelganger" of BearingPoint. The fictional company, Aggrieva, used the motto: "Aggrieva says yes when everyone else says no." Berland hired a film maker and shot 10 short episodes over a weekend. The films included topics such as bosses "hitting on" subordinates, teams misrepresenting their expertise, and managers trying to pass along inappropriate expenses to the client.

The episodes created a sensation and employees said that this was the best training they had ever had. The characters and situations became part of the company's vocabulary. "New episodes debuted each Monday, but employees were so ravenous for the next episode that they started tracking them down on the company's staging server, where the videos were posted on the preceding Friday. Thousands of employees watched the videos before they were released."[41]

The videos started conversations about ethics and compliance, and after the videos aired more people called the hotline to discuss difficult topics and situations. The videos were so well-received that people chose to watch them. Awareness programs should aim to create or locate materials so engaging that people are eager to watch.

49.5.3 Surprise, Novelty, and Expectation Failure. Vital information about potential threats and resources is likelier to be identified from things that are new or unfamiliar. Nature ensures that all living creatures react to novelty and change because novelty and change often results in danger. A swerving car on the highway, a jump in your bad cholesterol, or a drop in a stock's value rivets your attention and jangles your nerves, events which prime you to protect yourself from harm. Basically, our brains are surprise detectors.[42]

Use surprise and expectation failure to deepen security-awareness experiences. Humans crave novelty from evolution and for survival and will respond to the unique and unusual. Anything that is counter-expectational will tweak the arousal–adaptation cycle.

Ask questions such as, "Did You Know?" Ask learners with mobile phones how long their data (multimedia pieces of communication like photos, videos, and texts) is stored by their cell phone network provider and if their data can be sold to third parties. Not many people know that nearly four years' worth of their digital identity is stored by AT&T, which holds the data for 84 months. Verizon holds this data for 12 months, Sprint for 24 months, and T-Mobile for 60 months. "28,000 MMS messages are sent into the world every second, and cell phone companies record much of the metadata that travels with them, like location, receiver identity, amount of data transferred, and the cost of the transmission. The average user has 736 pieces of this personal data collected every day."[43]

Another innovative idea from the mayor of Bogotá, Antanas Mockus, was to use mimes to improve both traffic and citizens' behavior. Initially, 20 professional mimes shadowed pedestrians who didn't follow crossing rules: A pedestrian running across the road would be tracked by a mime who mocked his every move. Mimes also poked fun at reckless drivers. The program was so popular that another 400 people were trained as mimes.[44] What would happen if mimes followed people in your organization around their offices for a day and mocked people who talked about sensitive information in public areas or left their computers logged on while they were away from their desks?

Social psychologist Robert Cialdini states, "Mysteries are powerful because they create a need for closure."[45] Mysteries exist wherever there are questions without obvious answers. "Why do criminals attack personal home computers?" "How was the source of the cyberattacks on Estonia discovered?" "What does the encrypted message in this week's security awareness contest say?"

Another way to maintain interest is to pose a question or puzzle that confronts people with a gap in their knowledge. As part of a security-awareness program, newsletters, an intranet site, posters, and online courses can ask challenging quiz questions. This creates two knowledge gaps: "What's the correct answer?" and "Was I right?" Providing hints and clues for more difficult security-awareness questions or contests also helps to maintain interest. Remember, the objective is to make people think about the problem, not to guess a single right answer.

Note: Don't expect people to remember much about security from an initiation day presentation when all stimuli are new.

49.5.4 Conversational Style. Use a conversational and personal style. A conversational style is useful because "people tend to pay more attention when they perceive that they're in conversation, since they're expected to follow along and hold up their end." The brain does this even when the learner is reading (e.g., the conversation is between the learner and a book, magazine, Website, or an eLearning module).[46]

First- and second-person constructions (involving "I," "we," and "you") create a feeling of conversation between the content and the reader. In five out of five studies performed in 2000, students who received material with personalized, conversational text performed better on subsequent transfer tests than those who learned with formal text.[47] Studies found that "students performed up to forty percent better on post-learning tests if the content spoke directly to the reader using a first person, conversational style rather than taking a formal tone."[48]

In addition, Dr. Roger Schank, author and expert in workplace learning, states that conversation is a form of learning by doing.[49]

49.5.5 Analogies and Examples. To better engage people with a new topic, start by highlighting things that the audience already knows. As an example, your target audience may know that the Storm worm was widely spread malicious code, but they may not know that the controlling computer changes the malicious code it sends every 30 minutes, or that the Storm worm contained new defensive techniques that shut down the efforts of researchers who were attempting to learn more about it. Use analogies and examples to tie ideas your audience knows to what you want them to learn:

- Backups are like flossing—everyone knows it's important, but few devote enough thought or energy to it.
- A dynamic IP address is like moving your house several times a day so that burglars can't find it.
- Sensitive information is like prescription medicine: it should be used only by those who need it and are authorized to have it; it should not be transferred, sold, or given to people who are not authorized to have it (this is illegal and penalties apply); it can cause damage if given to people who are not authorized to have it.[50]
- Passwords are like bubble gum; strongest when fresh; should be used by an individual and not a group; and if laying around, will create a sticky mess.[51]

49.5.6 Stories and Empathy. The number-one story commandment, according to Pixar is: "Make me care."[52] Include stories in awareness materials to increase people's attention and retention. Stories energize powers of recall and communicate priorities effectively. Stories are powerful because they provide the content missing from abstract prose. Stories captivate people. They survive the test of time, and they become part of the popular culture. Audiences are typically more receptive to someone who tells stories than to someone who lectures.

Relating a story is different from making a reasoned argument because the way the message is delivered determines how the audience will react. When the audience hears an argument, they evaluate it and usually argue back, even if only in their minds. Stories engage the audience and involve people with the idea. When an audience hears a story, they are likely to think of similar situations that they have experienced. Stories can suggest a course of action to someone who is at a decision-making point.

Stories should be about situations that are realistic and related to the lives of the learners; otherwise, stories may backfire and cause a loss of credibility. The stories should relate to situations and decisions the audience may face. Stories about hackers accessing medical records would be useful to organizations that process medical data, whereas stories about fraud or identity theft would be of interest to personnel involved in the financial industry or the accounting function of an organization.

Effective security-awareness stories are short (a few paragraphs), have two or three characters at the most, and have a singular message. Stories that show more than one point of view increase retention because the brain is tuned to learn more deeply when it is forced to make evaluations and judgments. Stories should contain a surprising element and they must be true. Lack of credibility in a story is a single point of failure.

Stories about real people and real consequences (people being praised, disciplined, or fired) are useful in presentations and courses. Sources of stories include individuals who have been with the organization for a long time and have a "corporate memory," news events, Internet special interest bulletin boards, and security personnel who attend special interest group meetings and conferences.

Organizations should collect stories about security incidents, security heroes, mistakes made, and lessons learned. Having a story collection prepared allows for quick response to trigger events, such as when an incident similar to ones from the story collection occurs at the organization. "The secret is to gather, gather, gather—and do it in advance of any pressing need.... Gather things that get a response in you.... Anything that displays or evokes energy. Storage is cheap."[53]

49.5.7 Currency. Awareness material must be fresh and current. Chef Oscar Gizelt of Delmonico's Restaurant in New York said, "Fish should smell like the tide. Once they smell like fish, it's too late." If awareness material is not changed frequently, it too begins to smell old and becomes boring.

Take advantage of circumstances. Prepare material to be ready to launch a campaign alerting people to respond quickly after a disaster or major news event. For example, after a disaster such as the tsunami in Japan there are always scams and malware that use sensational news headlines to entice potential victims to click on links to sites that contain drive-by malware.

Another idea is to prepare messages in advance for specific times of the year. November 30 is International Computer Security Day. In October, educate about scareware. During the holiday season in November and December, laptop and mobile-device theft peaks, so offer tips on securing mobile devices. For tax time, offer tips about keeping track of your credit and information regarding fraud resolution specialists to contact for victims of fraud (e.g., remind staff that if the IRS wants more information from them, they will receive a letter, not an email. When an email claims to be from the IRS, it's best not to click on any links—and to report it to phishing@irs.gov).

Current events can be an excellent source of material and can add credibility to an awareness program. Review current news reports for events that can be used to emphasize security messages. For example, newscasters who make statements when they do not know that their microphones are live or a show on the impact of ID theft can provide good examples for use in an awareness program. Also, several Internet security and technology sites offer subscriptions to electronic security alerts and news clippings. One of the more useful newsletters reporting on information-security breaches is from INFOWAR.[54] Some organizations have established a news-hawk program, in which rewards are given to the first employee to bring in a new relevant story that can be used as part of the awareness program. This is also a good technique to gain buy-in from the end user community.

One of the best times to raise awareness is right after a breach at the organization or at a similar organization (one in the same industry, in the same location, or using the same technology). The news is full of stories about information security and data breaches.

49.5.8 Credibility. Credibility is crucial for an awareness program. The message must be clear, relevant, and appropriate to the real world. If the audience is required to use 15 different passwords as a part of day-to-day functions, prohibiting them from writing their passwords may not be as realistic as providing strategies for protecting the written list.

Show consequences. Some organizations send memos to all staff that describe specific examples of personnel who have violated policy. The memos cover a set time period (e.g., the previous quarter) and include the number of individuals, the nature of the violations, and the penalties, such as loss of Internet privileges or leave without pay, displayed in dollars, and based on the average salary.

While all messages should have a call to action, credible messages avoid fear, uncertainty, and doubt (FUD). FUD isn't the best choice for communication, and it will backfire if the material creates a scare and then doesn't offer a practical solution.

Comedian Chris Bliss explains why FUD doesn't work:

> A great piece of comedy is a verbal magic trick... there's this mental delight that's followed by the physical response of laughter, which, not coincidentally, releases endorphins in the brain. And just like that, you've been seduced into a different way of looking at something because the endorphins have brought down your defenses. This is the exact opposite of the way that anger and fear and panic, all of the flight-or-fight responses, operate. Flight-or-fight releases adrenalin, which throws our walls up sky-high. And the comedy comes along, dealing with a lot of the same areas where our defenses are the strongest—race, religion, politics, sexuality—only by approaching them through humor instead of adrenalin, we get endorphins and the alchemy of laughter turns our walls into windows, revealing a fresh and unexpected point of view.[55]

The use of appropriate humor such as the advertising technique of exaggerated consequences works because humor is a door into the serious. To spoof the popular advertisements that show a chain reaction of consequences, you could do a similar ad that says:

1. If you don't teach your employees about security awareness, they will post their vacation plans on social media sites.

2. If your employees post their vacation plans on social media sites, the bad guys will know when your employees aren't home.
3. If the bad guys know when your employees aren't home, the bad guys will clean them out.
4. If your employees' homes are cleaned out, they will come to work naked.
5. Don't let your employees come to work naked.

Another point that Chris Bliss makes is that comedy is a powerful way to communicate because it's inherently viral; people can't wait to pass along a great new joke. He adds, "But it's when you put all of these elements together—when you get the viral appeal of a great joke with a powerful punch line that's crafted from honesty and integrity, it can have a real world impact at changing a conversation."[56]

49.5.9 Social Proof. Robert B. Cialdini is considered an expert on influence. He studies and writes about the science of persuasion. He describes a common mistake that causes messages to self-destruct. It's the story of a former graduate student who had visited the Petrified Forest National Park in Arizona with his fiancée. At the park's entrance a sign stated, "Your heritage is being vandalized every day by theft losses of petrified wood of 14 tons a year, mostly a small piece at a time." The student was shocked when after reading the sign, his normally ultra-honest fiancée whispered, "We'd better get ours now."[57]

This incident inspired Cialdini and his colleagues to design an experiment where they posted two different signs. One used the concept of "negative social proof." It read, "Many past visitors have removed the petrified wood from the park, changing the natural state of the Petrified Forest." That sign also showed a picture of several visitors taking pieces of wood. The experiments placed a second sign to simply convey that stealing wood was not appropriate. The second sign said, "Please don't remove the petrified wood from the park, in order to preserve the natural state of the Petrified Forest." The accompanying image showed a lone visitor stealing a piece of wood, covered by the universal "No" symbol of a red circle with a slash through it.

The experimenters placed marked pieces of wood along various pathways and observed how the signs affected the rate of theft. They switched the signs at the entrance to the pathways, and they also used pathways with no signs posted as a control condition. The results:

- Where there was no sign, 3 percent of the wood pieces were stolen. Where the social proof sign (stating that many visitors had removed wood) was posted, the theft rate increased to 8 percent. Where the sign asked people not to steal the wood and depicted a single thief, the theft rate decreased to 1.7 percent.
- Put simply, social proof refers to our tendency to go along with the crowd and follow the most popular course of action. We do things that we see other people like us doing.
- Using negative social proof, for example, communicating the popularity of an undesirable behavior, focuses the audience on the prevalence, rather than the undesirability, of the behavior.
- The authors recommended that the park management reframe the statistics to focus attention on the number of people who respect the park's rules, which turned out to be more than 97 percent.[58]

Here's an example of how to apply this to security awareness. Todd Snapp, President of RocketReady, speaks to audiences about the human side of security. He often asks the audience to guess the most common passwords that his team of penetration testers finds in organizations where the passwords requirements include using characters from at least three sets (e.g., uppercase, lowercase, and numbers) and the passwords had to be changed every 90 days.

Audience members usually call out with guesses, but they rarely guess the answer. When Todd tells them, there is usually a collective groan and head slap as audience wonders why such a simple and retrospectively obvious answer didn't occur to them.

The answer? The season and the year: Fall2011, Winter2011, or Spring2012.

One way to present this information would be to start with "Did You Know? The most common passwords we find are…" This approach would catch attention, but it would also convey the wrong message. Despite the implied disapproval of choosing passwords that are easy to guess, the message is that such behavior is common. Putting the information out in a neutral way would act as strong social proof that many people just like the audience choose these easily guessed passwords.

A better way to present the information would be to advise people not to choose the season and year for passwords and to focus their attention on a positive behavior (e.g., use an image showing people who had chosen strong passwords speaking disapprovingly of a person in the organization who used the season and year). This makes it clear that people who use weak passwords are in the minority and have the disapproval of their co-workers. The take-away is that it's more effective to emphasize the deviance, not the popularity, of insecure behavior.[59]

49.5.10 Accessibility, Diversity, and Culture. Effective awareness materials are accessible, diverse, and culture specific. Guidelines for creating Web pages that are accessible to people with vision or hearing impairments are published by the World Wide Web Consortium (W3C). To be accessible, the Web pages should not rely on vision or sound alone to impart meaning; for example, all graphics should be labeled with text that explains the graphic, and the contrast between the text and the background should be maximized.[60] An alternative is to create and maintain two versions of an online course.

Accessible content is easy to understand. Check written program materials for ease of reading and understanding with Flesch–Kincaid readability levels or the Gunning Fog Index. Some word processors have the ability to perform two Flesch–Kincaid readability tests to indicate how difficult a passage is to read. The Flesch Reading Ease and the Flesch–Kincaid Grade Level use the same core measures (word length and sentence length), but different weighting factors. A text with a comparatively high score on the Reading Ease test should have a lower score on the Grade Level test.[61]

The Gunning Fog Index measures the readability of English writing. The index estimates the years of formal education needed to understand the text on a first reading. A Fog Index of 12 requires the reading level of a U.S. high school senior (around 18 years old). The Fog Index is commonly used to confirm that text can be read easily by the intended audience. Texts for a wide audience generally need a Fog Index less than 12. Awareness material requiring near-universal understanding should have an Index less than 8.[62]

Diversity is important to address cultural and other differences among staff. Awareness materials should suit the culture of the organization. Images of people in awareness materials should show different genders and races, with the subjects dressed similarly to the way that people within the organization dress. People relate to pictures of other people who are similar to themselves. In a global awareness program, language and cultural differences should be addressed. Materials should avoid the use of local idioms such as (in the United States), "In a nutshell."

Awareness materials designed for use in an Islamic country might address differences in techniques used by social engineers. For example, high-pressure techniques (as are often used in America) would likely be counterproductive in an Islamic culture. Instead, social engineers are likely to concentrate on the techniques that emphasize trust and relationship building. Also, since many social engineers are most active when they expect the target company to have fewer resources, instead of noting that an attack is most likely on a Friday afternoon (as in the United States), the materials should note that attacks are most likely on Thursday afternoons and that organizations might receive a higher volume of social engineering calls during Ramadan or around the Eids when the organization may have fewer staff available.

Awareness materials designed for Japan might address threats that are targeted to the Japanese culture, where privacy, reputation, family, and a desire to stay out of trouble, such as the "It's me, It's me" fraud where a young-sounding person calls a senior and claims to be in trouble and need money to avoid a scandal, and the "One click contract" fraud, where a Website visitor to a dating or pornography site receives the message that by clicking on the previous page they have entered a contract and must now deposit money into a specified account to avoid fines or scandal. By keeping the amount affordable (e.g., the equivalent of about $100 U.S. dollars), many Japanese people simply make the deposit to avoid the potential trouble.[63]

When designing material for a company in Qatar, which has a rich history and industry of pearl diving, a memorable approach is to use a pearl to illustrate the value of data. Exhibit 49.4 shows a poster image of an oyster with a data disc in place of the pearl with the caption, "How Valuable Is Your Data?"

49.5.11 Spaced Repetition. The technique of spaced repetition was identified by Hermann Ebbinghaus about a hundred years ago. He observed that learning and memory are the strongest if you spread the repetition of information over a long period of time—for example, days, weeks, and months. He also proposed a "forgetting curve," which are like radioactive half-lives: Each review of the information to be learned increases memory in strength by about 50 percent, but immediate review does not increase memory very much because the memory hasn't decayed much.[64]

A meta-analysis in 1999 suggested that those who learn information by spaced repetition will outperform 67 percent of those who learn by mass presentation given the same number of practice episodes. This varies according to the "nature of the task being practiced, the inter-trial time interval, and the interaction between these two variables."[65]

For awareness, this means exposure to awareness once a year likely not enough to effect behavior changes. For awareness, a best practice is to follow John Medina's Brain Rules: "Repeat to remember" and "Remember to repeat."

49.5.12 Pretest and Refine Messages and Methods Before Distributing Them. Pretest and refine materials before distributing them. Pretesting provides evidence that materials are reaching your target audience with the intended message. It can also avoid embarrassing situations, such as occur after distributing a poster on which punctuation or the lack of punctuation changes the message (e.g., "Slow Work Zone" instead of "Slow, Work Zone").

EXHIBIT 49.4 "How Valuable Is Your Data?"

Pretesting may be accomplished using focus groups, providing materials to a single unit within the organization, or through group or individual interviews. All evaluations should include a set of multiple-choice or ranking questions with one or two open-ended questions. This analysis approach facilitates data comparison and aggregation. The question set should be structured to determine the message received and the level of experience (novice, beginner, user, power user) required to understand the material. The questions should also be structured to avoid leading the respondent. A useful approach for coordinating input from larger focus groups is Computer-Aided Consensus™, which uses a shared spreadsheet to identify hidden assumptions and divergent values among the respondents.[66]

49.6 TOOLS.

When choosing tools to convey an awareness message, address these questions:

1. What tools are most appropriate for the message?
2. What methods are most likely to be credible to and accessible by the target audience?
3. Which methods (and how many methods) are feasible, considering the available budget and the time frame?
4. How often should each method and messages be delivered?

Use as many methods and tools as possible, with a consistent message, to reinforce the material and increase the likelihood that the audience will be exposed to it often enough and long enough to absorb it. Some methods are suited to daily updates, such as tips or questions of the day. Some material, such as simplified policies, frequently asked questions (FAQs), and incident reporting information will be received best if it's available on demand and just in time when needed. Newsletters are best received monthly or quarterly. Online courses can be provided monthly (short content pieces or modules), quarterly, biannually, or annually. Regular updates to content on an intranet Website, including contests, will drive repeat visits and increase awareness; stale information will lose viewers.

49.6.1 Intranet Website.

An intranet Website focused on security can contain checklists (e.g., what to post on social media, how to protect mobile devices, how to manage privacy on Facebook), one-line policies (the most important concept of each policy distilled to a single line) linked to full policies, identify–react charts, and interactive technologies such as password visualizers that illustrate the relationships of your passwords and password strength meters.

Security-awareness activities that use the Internet or an intranet offer the advantages of ease of use, scalability (can be used for various audience sizes and in distributed locations), accountability (can capture use statistics, quiz or test scoring, and other metrics), accommodation of individual learning rates, and even interaction among members of a community or among students and instructors.

Websites (public or private) can be used in these ways:

- As a research tool for gathering information
- To present policies and other documents
- To post alerts
- To collect data for security-awareness surveys or incident reporting
- For self-assessments to identify at-risk security practices
- For anonymous reporting of security concerns
- For Webcasts of security conferences or presentations

49.6.2 Social Media and Crowd Sourcing. Use social marketing techniques such as Twitter and social networking, email, daily tips, questions, contests, surveys, and suggestion programs that help achieve buy-in. Your social media strategy can be used to push and pull. Use social media as a channel for delivering messages to an audience as a push. Use social media as a way to listen and learn and to create relationships as a pull. Test and learn. Focus on understanding, run experiments (for new benefits and services) and analyze the results (for audience engagement). Where traditional companies push out messages and products, these companies pull customers in. Instead of treating customers as passive targets, they treat them as active participants. Like the sun in a solar system, they create a gravitational field that pulls customers into their orbit. They go beyond customer loyalty to building customer gravity.[67]

If your organization is a nonprofit, you can use virtual volunteers to help with your awareness program. One example is Sparked.com, a micro-volunteering network, in which nonprofits post challenges to the network and volunteers respond with ideas. Challenges range from requesting user input on a logo to creating promotional materials. This brings together the talents and ideas of many to find a single solution, and gives nonprofits a way to get valuable work for free. Volunteers might design newsletters, illustrate online courses, or create Website pages. Volunteers search for opportunities by skill, interest area, development topic, or geographic region.

49.6.3 Videos and Podcasts. Videos can be delivered on DVDs, VHS tapes, CD-ROMs, or over the Web in various formats including podcasts (videos formatted to play on iPods or other portable media players). Most security-awareness videos are less than 20 minutes long. They can be used at orientation briefings and brown-bag lunches for staff where popcorn can be provided in bags preprinted with security messages. Videos are useful starting points for discussions and for briefings. They provide a consistent message throughout the organization and can be shown to staff at distributed locations, saving instructor travel time and costs. They can also be used to demonstrate cost effectively the impact of security failures, such as a fire at a data center or how sensitive data were found in the trash. Security-awareness videos are available commercially for various fees and from the U.S. Government often at no charge or for a nominal fee.

Produce awareness videos in digital format in segments that allow for updates as the environment or organizational needs change.

49.6.4 Compliance Statements. Compliance statements and policy reading sign-offs are among the most effective security-awareness offerings. After computer-based instruction, according to the Security-Awareness Index report, the most effective methods were:

- Tracking whether workers read policies or not
- Requiring a compliance statement
- Requiring full-time employees (FTEs) to read policies
- Making policies available in electronic format
- Require workers to read policies annually
- Requiring a compliance statement prior to issuing a user ID[68]

49.6.5 Sign-on Messages, Networked Screen Savers. With some systems, it is possible to add a text message to the log-on or sign-on screen. These messages should be short, to the point, and changed frequently.

Screen savers are a graphic form of communication and should be eye-catching for maximum impact. Involving a professional artist will improve message delivery. Screen savers should contain contact information for the organization's security and incident-handling functions. Animations or trivia questions and answers may make the screen saver more interesting. Screen savers should be updated periodically to keep the message fresh. Commercially produced security screen savers are available, as are screen savers that can be easily tailored to deliver a security message.

Software programs such as BroadcastIT offer a centrally managed screen saver that can show images and videos. This software updates in the background and doesn't require much space.

49.6.6 Publications. Publications, such as newsletters, brochures, pamphlets, comic books, tip sheets, identify and react sheets (documents that list signs of an incident and steps for the end user to take), whitepapers, and checklists of behaviors organized by topic, can be targeted to specific audiences. They may be security focused or may be generalized publications that contain articles on security-related events or items of interest. Newsletters should be short, one to two pages, tailored to the organization's industry or business. Newsletters should use attention-getting graphics, headlines, and white space to appeal to readers. Audience interaction can be generated by encouraging questions, answered in future newsletters, or by including contests, inviting readers to submit news items, tips, trivia, or reviews of security books or products.

49.6.7 Posters and Digital Signage. A poster series with themes or related designs can be used to highlight specific security issues. A poster should be colorful, present a single message or idea, and include a "call to action." Using a professional artist to design the posters will increase their impact. Posters should be larger than standard letter size to stand out and gain attention. They should be changed or rotated regularly and placed at eye level in multiple locations. Posters can be printed on both sides of the paper, saving paper and shipping costs for organizations with multiple locations. Signs can make a difference in behavior. In Kenya, inexpensive messages urging minibus passengers to heckle and criticize their drivers for being reckless caused a 50–60 percent reduction in insurance claims involving injury or death. The stickers had messages such as "Don't just sit there as he drives dangerously! Stand up. Speak up. Now!" and were illustrated with severed feet and legs. Drivers were given incentives to leave the stickers in place. The messages encouraging passengers to speak up were placed in a random sample of over 1,000 long-distance Kenyan minibuses. In those buses, insurance claims fell by a half to two-thirds, from 10 to less than 5 percent annually. "Results of a driver survey eight months into the intervention indicated that passenger heckling contributed to the safety"[69] improvement.

49.6.8 eLearning Courses. Web-based awareness courses are useful for geographically dispersed staff members and staff who need to take training at a time that is convenient for them (e.g., after normal work hours). Web-based courses are especially well suited for use by individuals who have diverse backgrounds and different technology experience levels. Online courses offer the following advantages over traditional place-based, classroom training:

- Feedback—Feedback is essential to motivation and performance. Feedback is immediate, so learners do not build on early misunderstandings. Well-designed Web-based training takes cultural and personality differences into account and reassures timid trainees while allowing more confident ones to progress at a faster pace. "Why," "How," "Show me an example," and "Give me an alternative" buttons or links can be used to let learners with different needs and personalities use the course to learn in ways that are comfortable for them.
- User convenience—Web-based awareness courses are convenient for the learners because they can be taken at any time. Those with variable or hectic schedules can arrange to take the course after hours or whenever they have a convenient time in their schedule.
- Nonthreatening—Web-based courses allow users to make mistakes and learn from them in a safe, nonthreatening environment.
- Flexibility—Web-based courses are flexible and can be customized to accommodate learners with different levels of experience and different interests. By placing detailed information in subordinate, linked pages, users are able to choose between the "need-to-know" main pages and the "nice-to-know" hyperlinked pages.
- Web-based courses can reduce costs and training time. Placing updates to courses on the Web eliminates the work involved with distributing the current version and materials to multiple locations. This can be more efficient and consistent because the content has been reviewed, edited, and tested to make it clear and concise. Courseware can also be directly linked to specific organizational policies and procedures.
- Web-based courses are self-paced, so that more experienced users can race through without getting bored while novice users can ponder and explore.

A potential problem to watch for in Web-based courses is the tendency to get lost in the technology. Just because an awareness course could have three dozen animated, singing computers decorating the pages does not mean that it should. The technology must be used appropriately; bigger buildings do not make better scholars, and more impressive technology does not necessarily result in a better learning experience. A Web-based course that is overloaded with animations and graphics that do not relate to course content or that has a poorly designed user interface will lose user acceptance.

49.6.9 Classroom Training and Clickers. A study by the European Network and Information Security Agency (ENISA) found that:

> The most effective technique has been face-to-face time with staff through workshops and training sessions. Being able to put a face to a name or function is more personable and people are more receptive to messages being face-to-face. The training is mandatory. Senior management actively supports the awareness schemes, making sure that training events are at convenient times for the business and promoting them to staff. There is good attendance at sessions since missing the events results in escalation to the employee's manager. This senior management support across the business has proved to be critical to the success of the awareness program.[70]

A downside to in-person, instructor-led training is cost. Instructor-led training must have an audience that is collocated. Instructor-led training is not cost effective for organizations with a large, distributed workforce—unless they have an in-place audio/visual conference capability.

Use audience response systems (e.g., clickers) to enhance feedback and audience interaction. Audience response systems can be used to take attendance, instant polls, and multiple-choice tests. You can also use the devices to survey audience awareness of security topics and instantly show the correct answers and a response breakdown. Clickers allow online crowdsourcing for offline crowds. These devices have a fun factor and have been described as "efficient, eco-friendly and techno-tickling." Clickers allow audiences to participate in the same way as TV game-show contestants and help shy people "speak up." Professor James Katz, Director of the Center for Mobile Communication Studies at Rutgers said: "If people feel their opinions really count, they'll be happy and likely to give more opinions."[71] With the prevalence of cell phones, text messages can now be used for in-class responses.

49.6.10 People Penetration Tests and Spear Phishing Exercises. Demonstrations of penetration tests and spear phishing exercises are a good way to generate interest in security among the technical staff and power users. You can also incorporate vendors and other business partners into internal tests to evaluate and strengthen your organization's ability to respond to a cyberattack. Consulting firms may offer social engineering and penetration testing includes email phishing tests and phone calls from social engineers. The goals are to test employees' awareness of fraudulent email messages and incident response effectiveness. It must be made clear that penetration tests are intended as training exercises, not as employee evaluations.

You can also test awareness by checking the strength of passwords or simulating social engineering attacks to gauge responses. You can develop penetration exercises internally or acquire external support. Products such as Metasploit, Core Impact, and Canvass can be used to simulate a wide range of vulnerability tests, including email and Web phishing exercises. Before conducting any phishing or other vulnerability exercise, obtain permission in writing (often termed Rules of Engagement). Without permission, such activities may be considered hacking, even when performed by security personnel as part of an awareness exercise.

All testing works best when in support of defined policies and procedures. The same is true of penetration exercises. A well-designed test will include techniques for recognizing an attack as well as remedial actions that "victims" of an attack should take (e.g., reporting spear phishing attacks to organization security).

Testing can provide an estimate of the likelihood that a member of your workforce will:

- Click on an embedded hyperlink in a suspect email message,
- Enter Social Security numbers,
- Open an attachment without checking to see if it might include malware,
- Verify their network account,
- Register at an unknown site to download a whitepaper and receive a free product, or
- Download a suspicious file.

After the exercise, collect follow-up information by sending a message to recipients for feedback asking, "Why did you click or not click" or other questions to assess their thought processes.

Metrics to evaluate testing might include:

- Emails that were deleted and not read,
- Email forwarded to security personnel,
- Reports as spam,
- Emails that were read,
- Replies to email,
- Forwards to colleagues,
- "Victims" who clicked on the link, and
- "Victims" who provided personal information.

Real-world simulation exercises add to but do not replace traditional awareness techniques. Classroom instruction can explain and describe attack approaches, but exercises provide students with a "touch, feel, and experience" that expands their understanding of security attack approaches and aids in content retention. The goal of a security-awareness exercise is to make security a natural concern within the organization, campus, or university. Periodic security-awareness exercises will help minimize network downtime and maximize network performance as students become more judicious about handling emails.[72]

49.6.11 Contests and Incentive Prizes. Contests, incentive prizes, rewards, and giveaways help achieve buy-in. People like to win and most love a good contest. A contest can be a simple prize draw or a competition with rules for entry and criteria for winning.

Contests can be used to ask questions, collect data, conduct research, inspire ideas, or drive traffic to your security Website. The 3 Ps of contests are:

- **Planning.** Decide on the goal of your contest, then create a theme. Establish clear rules, including entry procedures and criteria for judging competition entries. You may need to consider your country or state-specific regulations (e.g., some contests and competitions may require a permit, if open to the public and the competition is a random chance draw).
- **Prizes.** Prizes can be anything from bragging rights to security-themed DVDs (such as *Catch Me If You Can* or *Swordfish*) or books (such as *The Cuckoos' Egg* by Clifford Stoll, *Kingpin* by Kevin Poulsen, or *The Lure* by Steve Schroeder) to cash awards, lunch with a senior executive, or time off. At presentations, speakers can tape prizes or awards under seats in the front row to encourage people to come early and sit up front.

  Prizes don't have to be expensive to be valuable to your audience. Time off, lunch with the boss, gift certificates, shredders, security-themed T-shirts, mugs, certificates, and trophies all work. Shiny prizes, such as the latest technology (e.g., an iPad) or money, have mass appeal. You may want to poll your audience to find out what would be valuable to them. The prize might be intangible (e.g., an honor, such as announcing the winner in the organization newsletter).

- **Promotion.** Announce your contest with email, posts on the security intranet site, and posters. Also, if it's a public contest, consider tweeting it, enlisting coworkers to help spread the word, putting links to the contest on the organization's Facebook Page, and writing press releases.

If you run the contest on social media, such as Facebook, Twitter, or Google+, use applications (many are available) to help administer the contest. To win, people may simply have to follow, retweet, or answer trivia questions. This type of campaign is often successful because of the ease of entry. Your security "brand" will benefit from the increased engagement.

Here are some contest ideas:

- **What's That Number?** Post a number that relates to security and have people guess how the number relates to security. The number might be the number of password reset requests the helpdesk receives in a week, the number of malware-infested sites blocked by the corporate firewall, or the number of records exposed or dollars lost as a result of a breach experienced by a company in your industry.
- **Catch the Red Team**. A red team is a group of individuals assigned to test the security of an organization. Staff are told that a red team will be testing security (e.g., making social engineering calls). Staff members who catch the red team and report the potential security violations win a prize. Often, these contests result in identifying security vulnerabilities and sometimes in catching intrusion attempts by cybercriminals and not just the attempts of the red team.
- **Nooo Face!** A security-awareness video or photo contest, such as the Annual Security Video Contest held by Educause or Trend Micro's "Nooo! Face" Contest, provide awards for photos that capture the feeling one gets when they realize they are a cyber, victim: precious data has vanished, destroyed, or been taken by an attack.
- **Awareness Materials Contests**. Award prizes and recognition for awareness materials, such as the annual contests held by the Federal Information Systems Security Educators' Association (FISSEA) and the International Information Systems Security Certification Consortium, Inc., ((ISC)^2)'s CyberExchange. FISSEA's contest has categories: Awareness Posters, Motivational Items (trinkets—pens, stress relief items, T-shirts, etc.), Awareness Websites, Awareness Newsletters, and Role-Based Training & Education. The CyberExchange accepts posters, presentations, best practices, flyers, white papers, and more.
- **Security Song, Jingle, and Verse Contests.** Contests could be for the best security haiku or six-word security stories. The six-word stories are based on the challenge issued to Ernest Hemingway to write an entire story in six words. His story: "For sale: baby shoes, never worn." A security-related six-word story might be "I never checked my offsite backup…"
- **Top Ten Lists**. Award a prize for the best (funniest) Security Top Ten list. Examples are the "Top Ten Places Not to Hide Your Password" (such as written with a permanent marker on a light bulb in the office lamp, on a white board, as a tattoo) and "Top Ten Security Headlines We'll Never See" such as, "White House Painted Purple to Confuse Terrorists" or "Courts Close Due to Lack of Lawsuits over Security Breaches."

- **Security Stories**. Invite people to share their security stories—for example, how a person was affected by identity theft, or how someone refused to share personal data when it wasn't necessary to do so, such as when a healthcare provider's form asks for a Social Security number. The emotional content makes stories prime material for sharing.
- **Security Trivia**. Ask security-related questions, such as:
  - "What color is Whitfield Diffie's hair?" (or, "Who is Whitfield Diffie and why is he important to security?")
  - "What is the name of the 1983 movie where Mathew Broderick played a young hacker who gained access to a government nuclear war simulator?" (*War Games*)

    Or, for more technically advanced audiences,
  - "What type of attack against database-driven applications involves the intruder manipulating a site's Web-based interfaces to force the database to execute undesirable code?" (SQL injection)
  - "What hardware protocol caused the vulnerability where a Firewire device, when plugged in, can overwrite anywhere in memory?" (DMA or Direct Memory Access)
- **Security Fact or Fiction Contests.** Contestants must decide if statements are true or not. For example: "In fiscal year 2011, the Electronic Crimes Special Agent program processed 1,066 terabytes of data on 8,525 units" (fact).[73]

Contests can boost morale, motivate people, and contribute to team spirit. Vince Lombardi, former head coach of the Green Bay Packers, understood this. He once said, "Winning isn't everything. It's the only thing." After criticizing him for this statement, some of his critics put together a new kind of baseball league for children in a Texas community: "It was like the Little League—the same ball, same bat, same number of innings, same playing field—everything was the same except that they didn't keep score. The idea was that there wouldn't be any losers because nobody would know who won." The game lasted one and a half innings. After that "the kids went across the street to play sand-lot ball where they could keep score."[74]

49.6.12 Awards and Recognition. Rewarding good security behaviors contributes to good security. Security is part of everyone's job and often management believes no special recognition or incentives should be provided. This approach does not work well because in a poorly managed organization, security tends to be outside the normal business process (i.e., security measures are often viewed as an impediment to getting a job done).

Security is a special concern that must be emphasized if assets are to be adequately protected. Security should be integrated with performance appraisals. "Personnel become motivated to actively support information security and privacy initiatives when they know that their job advancement, compensation, and benefits will be impacted. If this does not exist, then an organization is destined to depend only upon technology for information security assurance."[75]

Awards can be given for extraordinary security behaviors, participation in security events, achieving a security certification, or providing a security service such as speaking to local groups about cybersecurity. Awards work best if they are publicized, support desired behaviors, and are immediate (close to the act for which the award is being given).

49.6.13 Human Libraries. A Human Library is a technique to promote dialogue, information interchange, reduce prejudices, and encourage understanding. A Human Library consists of a group of individuals ("books") who have agreed to share their knowledge (i.e., the information that's in their head) with others. Living Books are people you have recruited because they have experiences of interest to the audience. A Human Library can be established as a single event with defined start and end times or an ongoing activity (long-term resource), where the Living Books come and go much as books are checked in and out from a conventional library; it may be established in a single physical location where the "books" are available for a fixed time frame, or it may be a virtual library where the books may be checked out by accessing a database.[76] For security awareness, a Human Library can serve as a resource where members of the workforce can learn about security from people who understand their work environment their specific policies and procedures.

Living Books should be volunteers who are recruited with care to ensure that they are committed and willing to talk with strangers about important and sometimes very personal issues. Interview book candidates to ensure the quality of books. Ask the book about its title (subject area) and motivation to be a book. This is to ensure that books are focused on supporting awareness. A reader can safely ask any question without fear of ridicule. A Human Library provides an opportunity to ask the information security questions you always wanted to ask, but were afraid that asking would make you appear naïve.

The best sellers are defined as the books that have the most requests for loans. For metrics, ask books, readers, and librarians for their comments on their Human Library experience. Ask the books if they would be a book again. Ask if people felt that they benefited from the library. Ask the books if they learned anything from the readers.

The experiences that might increase security awareness in living books include:

- Victim of identity theft
- Computer gaming addict
- Computer Incident Response Team member
- Penetration tester
- Social engineer
- Digital forensics expert
- Hacker
- Ethical hacker
- Helpdesk staff member
- Biometric expert
- Reformed cyberbully
- Someone who lost their job as a result of something posted on the Internet
- Information system security officer
- Senior executive responsible for security policy
- Privacy expert
- Electronic Frontier Foundation member
- Information-security blogger

- HIPAA expert
- Malware researcher
- Computer programmer

49.6.14 Volunteer Activities. Strengthen your security-minded workforce through volunteer programs. Volunteerism increases engagement. Data from the Center for Talent Innovation (CTI) shows that the vast majority of college graduates want to amplify their commitment to good causes through their employer.[77] According to the Deloitte Volunteer Impact Survey,[78] Generation Ys who frequently participate in their company's volunteer activities are more likely to be very proud to work for their company, feel very loyal, and be very satisfied with the progression of their careers. These sentiments hold true across generational cohorts—91 percent of Gen X women and 76 percent of Gen X men, and 90 percent of female and 79 percent of male Baby Boomers, feel it is important to contribute to their community or the wider world through work.[79]

There are many programs that allow individuals with security interests to give back to the community:

- Attending the FBI Citizens Academy, which shows how dedicated our FBI is to protecting our freedom. Most individuals not exposed to computer crime get a rude awakening of just how bad cybercrime is, especially when they see in real-time the innocent images of victims of pedophile activity in their own neighborhood.
- Individuals with CISSP certification can join the (ISC)^2 Safe and Secure Online Program to teach children how to be cyberaware.
- Volunteering to be a living book at a Human Library event.
- Participating in National Teach-In day to promote cyberawareness for elementary students.
- Cyberawareness training for seniors can be arranged through libraries, religious organizations, and other groups.

49.6.15 Inspections and Audits. Inspections and audits raise awareness among the staff being reviewed, at least for the duration of the inspection. Audits and inspections are typically viewed as negative events. However, there are approaches that can turn an audit/inspection from a negative to a positive experience. Using a technique called "security by wandering around" (SBWA), a security staff member tours the work area, identifies staff members doing something correctly, and leaves certificates of congratulations, thank-you notes, or trinkets on their desks. One audit technique is to treat each encounter with a staff member as a training opportunity, explanations are provided as to "why" a policy is important instead of just rating compliance as pass or fail. Security personnel might periodically demonstrate social engineering by attempting to smooth-talk users into providing their passwords. The number of people who fall for the scheme might be used as an example for the next awareness session.

49.7 EVALUATION AND METRICS. Security consultant Gary Hinson compared security to the brakes on a car. The brakes slow you down, but they also make it possible for you to go a lot faster. A good metrics program takes time to set up, but once you have it set up and working well, it can save you time in the long run by making your program more effective. Metrics aid in decision making. Without a solid metrics program, it is hard to know whether the program is effective, or if the organization should spend more money on doing the same thing, or if the resources would be better used elsewhere.

49.7.1 Baseline. As with any tool, it is important to know how to use metrics. Metrics are best used when they compare measurements over time to a baseline. Defining appropriate metrics and immediately gathering data on the current state of those metrics is an essential first phase for all future evaluation of security-awareness programs.

49.7.2 Metrics. Security metrics are evolving, and different organizations have put forth different tools, different guidance, and different frameworks for evaluating IT security. For example, organizations may use metrics based on such standards as:

- COBIT[80]
- FISMA[81]
- FITSAF[82]
- GLBA[83]
- HIPAA[84]
- ISO 27002:2005[85]
- NIST SP 800-55[86]
- PCI DSS[87]
- SANS[88]
- SOX[89]

or combinations of such guidance.

Few organizations currently use security metrics or even a common vocabulary. Also, many of the tools and guides for measuring IT security metrics only consider security awareness as a small portion of overall security program metrics. Metrics regarding security-awareness programs are high level and not specific. It is easy to collect quantitative measures of data, such as the number of virus infections, server patches performed, or program costs. It is difficult to measure behavioral change.

A commonly used metric is the number of people who participated in awareness orientations and refreshers. This figure can be determined through attendance sheets, course registrations, or completion notifications for online courses, and signed user "acceptance of responsibilities" statements. Another common metric is seat time—how long this person spent in front of a computer, clicking through the screens, soaking up the knowledge that was there. Attendance and seat time may indicate that a program is *not* effective, but they are not the best measures of awareness program *effectiveness*. Better measurements focus on the end users and measure behaviors that are a part of normal business operations, including user perceptions, activities, and response to anomalous occurrences.

An effective, measured awareness program can ensure that the workforce serves as a staff firewall, protecting the organization's information assets, and ensuring that there exists a gold-standard or best-in-class security environment. It also provides decision makers who are allocating resources with assurances that the security-awareness programs are cost-effective control measures. Also, using objectives such as "ensuring that 100 percent of employees take the awareness course" is a statement regarding the program process, not impact, and should be avoided. When it comes to making a decision between a business case supported by hard numbers and one based on subjective feelings and unsupported statements such as "workforce training is the most cost-effective security control," the hard numbers will win.

Once the performance measures are adopted, the next step in building the business case solution is to establish at least one metric for each of the supporting goals and objectives. These metrics may be hard numbers (e.g., number of security incidents), estimates (e.g., the average cost per security incident), or the results of testing (e.g., annual testing of a sample of the workforce). Examples of metrics that might be used for the four awareness goals presented above include:

- Goal: The awareness program will improve employees' ability to recognize and report potential threats and vulnerabilities.
  - Metric: The number of security events as measured by the number of incident reports.
  - What to expect: When an awareness program is first introduced, the expectation is that the number of reported incidents will increase as employees become more aware of potential threats, vulnerabilities, and the need to report. Over time, the number of reported events should stabilize and decline as the security environment is strengthened.
- Goal: The awareness program will improve the level of compliance with company physical and computer security controls.
  - Metric: The number of sanctions of individuals for failure to comply with security policy.
  - Metric: The number of incidents resulting from employee action or inaction as determined through incident analysis.
  - What to expect: The number of employees sanctioned for compliance failures should decrease as the awareness program reaches more individuals. Similarly, the awareness program should make individuals more diligent in performing security-related responsibilities, thus resulting in a reduced number of incidents.
- Goal: The awareness program will reduce the occurrence of security failures resulting from employee action or inaction.
  - Metric: The number of incidents resulting from employee action or inaction as determined through incident analysis.
  - Metric: The number of security incidents resulting from employee actions or inactions declines over time as individuals recognize the importance of fulfilling their security responsibilities.
- Goal: The awareness program will reduce the severity of the security incidents that do occur.
  - Metric: The cost per incident as determined through incident analysis.
  - What to expect: The cost per incident decreases as individuals react more quickly to identify a potential security incident and take action to mitigate its impact.

Two other issues should be addressed relative to an awareness program's goals and metrics. First, an awareness program seeks to make a *behavioral* change in the workforce. Behavioral change takes time, so the metrics should have an established time frame where management should expect to see performance improvement. The time frame should be realistic (e.g., quarterly, semi-annual, annual), avoid immediate impacts (e.g., "After a course on viruses, the number of virus incidents should decrease within a week") and avoid time frames that are too long (e.g., "The number of virus incidents should decrease over the next five years").

Second, solicit and use employee feedback. Employee feedback should be analyzed because it provides indicators of the level of security awareness and the importance employees ascribe to information security. Analysis of employee feedback could be used to generate other performance metrics for an awareness program.

Automated metrics are useful to help measure changes in behavior.

- Filtering software that monitors content (e.g., 9- or 16-digit strings of numbers for Social Security numbers and credit card account numbers) or specific words can indicate how often people try to email this information;
- Web statistics and firewall monitoring software can indicate how often people visit or attempt to visit specific Websites, such as the security intranet page;
- Helpdesk call log summaries can identify problems related to security issues; and
- Performance appraisals, participation in contests, and results of quizzes are indicators of interest in security-related behaviors.

49.8 CONCLUDING REMARKS.

Awareness among an organization's staff is vital to maintaining the integrity of data and systems. Although organizations often view computer security as a technological problem and use sophisticated hardware and software solutions to control access, detect potential security incidents, and prevent fraud, the reality is that computer security is as much a people problem as a technological problem. End users are closer to potential problems; therefore, they need to be aware of potential risks, threats, vulnerabilities, and their own security responsibilities.

People are major contributors to the IT security problem, and they are also crucial to its solution. People are perceptive and adaptive, and if trained and motivated to be aware, they can be the strongest and most effective security countermeasure. Individuals often are the first to detect security incidents. The actions they take or fail to take determine the level of damage. An aware workforce often can compensate for deficiencies in technical controls. The intent of the awareness program is to make recognition of and reaction to security threats a reflexive behavior.

Awareness takes time. It also requires the organization to have an in-place information security policy, the support of the senior-level managers, and clear goals and plans for achieving awareness. The importance of establishing measurable goals cannot be overestimated and is critical to obtaining support and funding.

The goal of an awareness program is often to change attitudes and behaviors that may be embedded in long-term procedures or habits. To effect awareness, the program must appeal to the audience and be tailored to the workforce and to the technology of the organization. The primary message of a security-awareness program should be that security is everyone's responsibility. Actions taken by end users make a significant difference; thus, a well-trained and motivated workforce is a critical and necessary security control.

49.9 GLOSSARY

Awareness—being conscious of what is going on around one; security awareness specifically focuses attention on security. Security awareness is the individual's understanding that security is important and that everyone has a role in ensuring the security of information and information technology.

Awareness campaign—the activities associated with conveying a specific awareness message (e.g., telling people "log off when away from your computer").

Awareness program—the planned implementation and control of a mix of awareness activities over a period of time, with measurable goals and multiple topics. An awareness program may encompass several campaigns.

Basics and literacy—a transitional stage between awareness and role-based training.

Education—the process of integrating all security skills and competencies into a common body of knowledge, adding a multidisciplinary study of concepts, issues, and principles.

End user (also computer user or user)—any person who uses an information system.

Focus group—a small group of end users (or of individuals from the target audience) who review and discuss awareness activities, courses, products, and the like, often under the guidance of an awareness material developer or training specialist.

FUD factor—the effects of fear, uncertainty, and doubt (FUD).

Gamification—the concept of applying game-design thinking to nongame applications to make them more fun and engaging.

Malicious code (also malware)—hardware, software, or firmware that is intentionally included in a system for an unauthorized purpose (e.g., a Trojan horse).

Orientation briefing—a presentation that provides new employees, contractors, and the like with basic security information and information on the organization's security policies and programs. Usually these presentations are conducted on arrival or shortly thereafter.

Refresher—an awareness activity, such as a briefing, intended to reinforce and update awareness of security controls and policies and to remind individuals of their security responsibilities.

Role-based training—the process of producing relevant and needed security skills and competency. Security awareness is the "what." Role-based training is the "how."

Safe failure—the opportunity to learn from mistakes privately, such as with a computer simulation or course.

Social engineering—social methods (e.g., threats, misrepresentations) that deceive a victim so that the victim does what the attacker wants him or her to do. Often the goal is to get the victim to provide private or sensitive information, such as account numbers or passwords. An example of a social engineering attack is the use of "phishing" emails.

Social marketing—an approach to security awareness using attraction and persuasion techniques designed to encourage a group of people to alter old ideas, understand and accept new ideas, and value their new awareness enough to change attitudes and take positive actions to improve IT security.

Target audience—a specified audience or demographic group for which a security-awareness message is designed.

Threat—anything that can potentially harm a system or its associated assets (hardware, software, data, operations). Threats may be man-made or natural occurrences. Awareness programs do little to address threats; instead, they seek to reduce vulnerabilities.

Vulnerability—a weakness in automated system security procedures, administrative controls, physical layout, internal controls, and so forth, which could be exploited by a threat to gain unauthorized access to information or disrupt critical processing. A goal of security-awareness programs is to reduce behavior-related vulnerabilities.

49.10 NOTES

1. Katy Stech, "Burglary Triggers Medical Records Firm's Collapse," *The Wall Street Journal*, March 12, 2012, http://blogs.wsj.com/bankruptcy/2012/03/12/burglary-triggers-medical-records-firm%E2%80%99s-collapse
2. Ellis Smith, "BlueCross Burglary Could be Chattanooga's Costliest Caper," *Times Free Press*, March 13, 2012, http://timesfreepress.com/news/2012/mar/13/bluecross-burglary-could-be-citys-costliest
3. Alex Pham, "Sony Expects Much Wider Annual Loss," *Los Angeles Times*, February 3, 2012, http://articles.latimes.com/2012/feb/03/business/la-fi-ct-sony-earns-20120203
4. Tony Busseri, "It's Time to Take Cybersecurity Seriously," *Wired*, March 12, 2012, www.wired.com/threatlevel/2012/03/opinion-busseri-cybersecurity
5. "Verizon 2012 Data Breach Investigations Report," p. 2, www.verizonbusiness.com/resources/reports/rp_data-breach-investigations-report-2012-ebk_en_xg.pdf (url inactive).
6. Mark Wilson, Kevin Stine, and Pauline Bowen, "Information Security Training Requirements: A Role- and Performance-Based Model (Draft)," NIST Special Publication 800-16 Rev. 1 (Draft), March 2009, http://csrc.nist.gov/publications/drafts/800-16-rev1/Draft-SP800-16-Rev1.pdf
7. Wilson et al., "Information Security Training Requirements," NIST Special Publication 800-16 Rev. 1 (Draft)
8. Wilson et al., "Information Security Training Requirements," NIST Special Publication 800-16 Rev. 1 (Draft)
9. Ira Winkler, *Zen and the Art of Information Security* (Rockland: Syngress, 2007).
10. Mary Kirwan, "Education May Not Be Enough to Ensure Compliance," *The Globe and Mail*, March 31, 2012, http://v1.theglobeandmail.com/servlet/story/RTGAM.20070911.WBsecurityblog20070911120000/WBStory/WBsecurityblog
11. WebCPA staff, "IRS Security Still Lax," *Accounting Today*, Washington, D.C., August 6, 2007, www.accountingtoday.com/news/25009-1.html
12. Winkler, *Zen and the Art of Information Security.*
13. "Many Young Workers Are IT Rule-Breakers," *Harvard Business Review* | The Daily Stat, January 10, 2012, http://web.hbr.org/email/archive/dailystat.php?date=011012

14. Jeffrey M. Stanton, Kathryn R. Stam, Paul Mastrangelo, and Jeffrey Jolton, "Analysis of End User Security Behaviors," *Computers & Security* 24, no. 2 (March 2005): 124–133, www.sciencedirect.com/science/article/pii/S0167404804001841
15. Thomas Steward and Anand Raman, "Lessons from Toyota's Long Drive, An Interview with Katsuaki Watanabe," *Harvard Business Review*, July 2007, http://hbr.org/2007/07/lessons-from-toyotas-long-drive/ar/1
16. John Caddell, "How to Bounce Back from a Big Mistake," *99U*, approximately November 2011, http://99u.com/articles/7089/how-to-bounce-back-from-a-big-mistake
17. D. Verton, "Federal Agency Faces Judicial Ultimatum," *Computerworld*, 2002, www.computerworld.com/securitytopics/security/story/0,10801,69937,00.html
18. María Cristina Caballero, "Academic Turns City into a Social Experiment: Mayor Mockus of Bogotá and His Spectacularly Applied Theory," *Harvard University Gazette*, March 11, 2004, www.news.harvard.edu/gazette/2004/03.11/01-mockus.html
19. M. E. Kabay, "The Net Present Value of Information Security: A Paradigm Shift for INFOSEC and E-commerce," 2006, www.mekabay.com/infosecmgmt/npvsec.pdf
20. Additional note: See also Chapter 50, "Using Social Psychology to Implement Security Policies."
21. The Federal Information Security Management Act of 2002, Section 3544, "Federal Agency Responsibilities," http://csrc.nist.gov/drivers/documents/FISMA-final.pdf
22. See Chapter 64, "U.S. Legal and Regulatory Security Issues"
23. Dan Heath and Chip Heath. *Made to Stick* (New York: Random House, 2007).
24. C. Heath and D. Heath, "The Curse of Knowledge." *Harvard Business Review*, December 2006, http://hbr.org/2006/12/the-curse-of-knowledge/ar/1
25. Donna Mattick, personal correspondence, March 2012.
26. John Tierney and Roy Baumeister, *Willpower: Rediscovering the Greatest Human Strength* (The Penguin Press HC, 2011).
27. V. Basili, G. Caldiera, and H. D. Rombach, "The Goal Question Metric Approach," *Encyclopedia of Software Engineering* (New York: John Wiley & Sons, 1994), 528–532 www.cs.umd.edu/~basili/publications/technical/T87.pdf (url inactive).
28. Mark Wilson and Joan Hash, "Building an Information Technology Security Awareness and Training Program," NIST SP 800-50, October 2003, http://csrc.nist.gov/publications/nistpubs/800-50/NIST-SP800-50.pdf
29. K. Sanders, "Bears in Your Backyard? Guidelines for Bear-Proofing Your Property, and Living *with* Bears," 2000, www.yellowstone-bearman.com/B_housesafe.html
30. Rebecca Herold, *Managing an Information Security and Privacy Awareness and Training Program*, 2nd ed. (CRC Press, 2011).
31. K. Hall and the SE SIG Steering Committee, "A System for Gaining Management Support for Your Safeguards and Security Awareness Program," 2002, www.orau.gov/se/Products/SE%20SIG%20Gaining%20Mgmt%20Support.doc
32. Wilson et al., "Information Security Training Requirements," NIST Special Publication 800-16 Rev. 1 (Draft).
33. de Saint-Exupery, Antoine. *The Wisdom of the Sands* (Amereon Ltd., October 2003).
34. John Medina, *Brain Rules* (Pear Press, 2008).

35. Medina, *Brain Rules*.
36. Reif Larson, "This Chart Is a Lonely Hunter: The Narrative Eros of the Infographic," *The Millions*, February 7, 2012, www.themillions.com/2012/02/this-chart-is-a-lonely-hunter-the-narrative-eros-of-the-infographic.html
37. Larson, "This Chart Is a Lonely Hunter."
38. Brenda Oldfield, "Game-Changing Technologies for Cybersecurity Awareness and Training" (presentation, FISSEA Conference, Gaithersburg, MD, March 29, 2012).
39. Anderson, Chris. "How Web Video Powers Global Innovation," Technology, Entertainment, Design (TED) Talks, TEDGlobal 2010, Filmed July 2010, Posted September 2010; www.ted.com/talks/chris_anderson_how_web_video_powers_global_innovation.html
40. Anderson, "How Web Video Powers Global Innovation."
41. Chip Heath and Dan Heath, *The Myth of the Garage* (Crown Business, 2011).
42. Winifred Gallagher, *New: Understanding Our Need for Novelty and Change* (Penguin Press HC: 2011).
43. Maria Popova, "Network: The Secret Life of Your Personal Data," January 10, 2012; www.brainpickings.org/index.php/2012/01/10/network-michael-rigley/ contains embedded video, "Network," by Michael Rigley
44. Caballero, "Academic Turns City into a Social Experiment."
45. Heath and Heath, *Made to Stick*.
46. Elisabeth Freeman and Eric Freeman, *Head First HTML with CSS & XHTML* (O'Reilly Media, 2005).
47. Ruth Colvin Clark and Richard E. Mayer, *eLearning and the Science of Instruction*. (San Francisco: Pfeiffer, 2003).
48. Freeman and Freeman, *Head First HTML.*
49. Roger, C. Schank, *Lessons in Learning, e-Learning, and Training: Perspectives and Guidance for the Enlightened Trainer* (Pfeiffer, 2005).
50. Native Intelligence, Poster 153A, www.nativeintelligence.com/ni-posters/posters.asp
51. Native Intelligence, Poster 115, www.nativeintelligence.com/ni-posters/posters.asp
52. Andrew Stanton, "The Clues to a Great Story," Technology, Entertainment, Design (TED)Talks, TED2012, Filmed February 2012, Posted March 2012; www.ted.com/talks/andrew_stanton_the_clues_to_a_great_story.html
53. Gerald Weinberg, *Weinberg on Writing: The Fieldstone Method* (Dorset House, 2005).
54. INFOWAR: The Nexus of Technology and Security in Cyberspace, www.infowar.com
55. Bliss, Chris. "Comedy Is Translation," Technology, Entertainment, Design (TED)Talks, TEDX Talk, www.ted.com/talks/chris_bliss_comedy_is_translation.html
56. Bliss, "Comedy Is Translation."
57. Robert B. Cialdini, Noah J. Goldstein, and Steve Martin, *Yes!: 50 Scientifically Proven Ways to Be Persuasive* (Free Press, 2009).
58. R. B. Cialdini, *Influence: The Psychology of Persuasion* (HarperBusiness, 2006).

59. M. E. Kabay, "Applying the Science of Persuasion to Security Awareness," *Network World Security Strategies Newsletters*, 2009, www.mekabay.com/nwss/725_applying_the_science_of_persuasion_to_security_awareness.pdf
60. W3C, "Accessibility," 2012, www.w3.org/standards/webdesign/accessibility
61. Rudolph Flesch, *The Art of Readable Writing* (Wiley, 1994).
62. Robert Gunning, *The Technique of Clear Writing* (McGraw-Hill, 1952).
63. Carnegie Mellon University Information Networking Institute (INI) "Confronting One-Click Fraud in Japan," www.ini.cmu.edu/news/features/one-click.html
64. Gwern.net, "Spaced Repetition," March 12, 2012, www.gwern.net/Spaced%20 repetition
65. J. J. Donovan and D. J. Radosevich, "A Meta-analytic Review of the Distribution of Practice Effect: Now You See It, Now You Don't." *Journal of Applied Psychology* 84, no. 5 (1999): 795–805.
66. M. E. Kabay, "CAC: Computer-Aided Consensus™," 2009, www.mekabay.com/methodology/cac_ppt.zip
67. Mark Bonchek, "How Top Brands Pull Customers into Orbit," *Harvard Business Review* | Blogs, March 5, 2012, http://blogs.hbr.org/cs/2012/03/how_top_brands_pull_customers.html
68. PentaSafe. "Security Awareness Index Report: Worldwide State of Security Awareness," 2002.
69. James Habyarimana and William Jack, "Heckle and Chide: Results of a Randomized Road Safety Intervention in Kenya," Center for Global Development, Working Paper No. 169, April 2009, http://www.cgdev.org/files/1421541_file_Habyarimana_Jack_Heckle_FINAL.pdf
70. The European Network and Information Security Agency (ENISA), "Information Security Awareness Initiatives: Current Practice and the Measurement of Success," www.enisa.europa.eu/doc/pdf/deliverables/enisa_measuring_awareness.pdf
71. Jan Hoffman, "Speak Up? Raise Your Hand? That May No Longer Be Necessary," *The New York Times*, March 30, 2012, www.nytimes.com/2012/03/31/us/clickers-offer-instant-interactions-in-more-venues.html
72. Aaron Ferguson, "Fostering E-Mail Security Awareness: The West Point Carronade," EDUCAUSE, 2004, www.educause.edu/ir/library/pdf/EQM0517.pdf
73. United States Secret Service, "Fiscal Year 2011 Annual Report," 2011, p. 40, www.secretservice.gov/USSS_FY2011AR.pdf
74. C. Coonradt, *The Game of Work* (Park City, 1997).
75. Herold, *Managing an Information Security and Privacy Awareness and Training Program.*
76. Human Library Website, 2012, http://humanlibrary.org
77. Sylvia Ann Hewlett, "Strengthen Your Workforce Through Volunteer Programs," *Harvard Business Review* | Blogs, March 5, 2012, http://blogs.hbr.org/hbr/hewlett/2012/03/strengthen_your_workforce_thro.html
78. Deloitte Website, "2011 Deloitte Volunteer Impact Survey," 2011 www.deloitte.com/view/en_US/us/About/Community-Involvement/volunteerism/impact-day/f98eec97e6650310VgnVCM2000001b56f00aRCRD.htm
79. Hewlett, Sylvia Ann. "Strengthen Your Workforce Through Volunteer Programs," 2012; http://blogs.hbr.org/hbr/hewlett/2012/03/strengthen_your_workforce_thro.html

80. Information Systems Audit and Control Association (ISACA) "COBIT 5: A Business Framework for the Governance and Management of Enterprise IT," ISACA Website, 2012, www.isaca.org/COBIT/Pages/default.aspx

81. National Institute of Standards and Technology (NIST), "FISMA FAQs," NIST Website, 2012, http://csrc.nist.gov/groups/SMA/fisma/faqs.html

82. National Institute of Standards and Technology (NIST), "The Federal Information Technology Security Assessment Framework," 2000, http://csrc.nist.gov/drivers/documents/Federal-IT-Security-Assessment-Framework.pdf

83. Bureau of Consumer Protection, "Gramm-Leach-Bliley Act," 2012, http://business.ftc.gov/privacy-and-security/gramm-leach-bliley-act

84. U.S. Department of Health & Human Services, "Health Information Privacy," 2012, www.hhs.gov/ocr/privacy

85. ISO/IEC 27002:2005, "Information Technology—Security Techniques—Code of Practice for Information Security Management," 2005, www.iso.org/iso/home/store/catalogue_ics/catalogue_detail_ics.htm?csnumber=50297

86. E. Chew, M. Swanson, K. Stine, N. Bartol, A. Brown, and W. Robinson, "Performance Measurement Guide for Information Security," NIST SP-800-55, rev. 1, 2008, http://csrc.nist.gov/publications/nistpubs/800-55-Rev1/SP800-55-rev1.pdf

87. VISA Data Security Bulletin, "Visa PCI DSS Compliance Validation Framework," 2008, < http://usa.visa.com/download/merchants/cisp-bulletin-visa-pci-dss-framework-111808.pdf

88. SANS (2012). "Standards," SANS | Reading Room, 2012 www.sans.org/reading_room/whitepapers/standards

89. U.S. Securities and Exchange Commission, "The Laws That Govern the Securities Industry," U.S. SEC Website, 2012, www.sec.gov/about/laws.shtml

CHAPTER 50

USING SOCIAL PSYCHOLOGY TO IMPLEMENT SECURITY POLICIES

M. E. Kabay, Bridgitt Robertson, Mani Akella, and D. T. Lang

50.1 INTRODUCTION.[1] Most security personnel have commiserated with colleagues about the difficulty of getting people to pay attention to security policies—to comply with what seems like good common sense. They shake their heads in disbelief as they recount tales of employees who hold secured doors open for their workmates—or for total strangers, thereby rendering million-dollar card-access systems useless. In large organizations, upper managers who decline to wear their identification badges discover that soon no one else will either. In trying to implement security policies, practitioners sometimes feel that they are involved in turf wars and personal vendettas rather than rational discourse.

These problems reflect the social nature of human beings; however, they also reflect the fact that although people involved in information systems security and network management have a wide variety of backgrounds, many lack training in social or organizational psychology.

Security policies and procedures affect not only what people do, but also how they see themselves, their colleagues, and their world. Despite these psychosocial issues, security personnel pay little or no attention to what is known about social psychology. The established principles of human social behavior have much to teach in any attempts to improve corporate and institutional information assurance (IA).

IA specialists concur that security depends on people more than on technology. Another commonplace is that employees are a far greater threat to IA than outsiders (see Chapter 13 in this *Handbook*).

It follows from these observations that improving security necessarily involves changing beliefs, attitudes, and behavior, both of individuals and of groups. Social psychology can help us understand how best to work with human predilections and predispositions to achieve our goals of improving security:

- Research on social cognition looks at how people form impressions about reality. Knowing these principles, we can better teach our colleagues and clients about effective security.
- Work on attitude formation and beliefs helps to present information effectively and so convince employees and others to cooperate in improving security.
- Scientists studying persuasion and attitude change have learned how best to change people's minds about unpopular views, such as those regarding the security community.
- Studies of factors enhancing prosocial behavior provide insights on how to foster an environment where corporate information is willingly protected.
- Knowledge of the phenomena underlying conformity, compliance, and obedience can help to enhance security by encouraging compliance and by protecting staff against social pressure to breach security.
- Group psychology research provides warnings about group pathology and about hints for working better with groups in establishing and maintaining IA in the face of ingrained resistance.

This chapter reviews well-established principles of social psychology that help security and network management personnel implement security policies more effectively. Any recent introductory social psychology college textbook will provide ample references to the research underpinning the principles applied here to security policy implementation.[2]

50.2 RATIONALITY IS NOT ENOUGH. IA policies sometimes evoke strong emotions. People can get very angry about what they perceive as interference with their way of getting their work done. From the perspective of the traditional information security professional, information security is still perceived as a technical problem, but as recent research reveals, it is more of a management problem, and the prevalent security culture offers insight into how management handles this problem.

To put the discussion in context, here is a definition of rationality from a respected academic, Jonathan Baron: Rationality is "the kind of thinking we would all want to do, if we were aware of our own best interests, in order to achieve our goals."[3]

Applying this definition to the concept of security, it seems to imply that rational thought would direct us to what appears to be the best compromise between what we perceive as our security needs and what appears to be the most convenient process.

50.2.1 Schema.

Psychologists use the word *schema* to summarize the complex picture of reality on which we base our judgments. The schema is what social psychologists call the way people make sense of their social interactions. IA practitioners must often change their colleagues' schemata.

Schemata are self-consistent views of reality. They help us pay attention to what we expect to be important and to ignore irrelevant data. They also help us organize our behavior. For example, our schema for relations at the office includes polite greetings, civil discussions, written communications, and businesslike clothes. The schema excludes obscene shrieks, abusive verbal attacks, spray-painted graffiti, and colleagues dressed in swimsuits. It is the schema that lets people know what is appropriate or inappropriate in a given situation.

Unfortunately, security policies and procedures conflict with most people's schemata. Office workers' schemata includes sharing office supplies ("Lend me your stapler, please?"), trusting their team members to share information ("Take a look at these figures, Sally"), and letting their papers stay openly visible when they leave their desks.

Sharing user IDs, showing sensitive information to someone who lacks the appropriate clearance, and leaving workstations logged on without protection are gross breaches of a different schema—that of the IA specialist. Think about access controls: Normal politeness dictates that when a colleague approaches the door we have just opened, we hold the door open for the person; when we see a visitor, we smile politely—after all, it might be a customer. In contrast, access-control policies require that we refuse to let even well-liked colleagues piggyback their way through an access-card system; security policies insist that unbadged strangers be challenged or reported to security personnel. Common sense tells us that when the chief executive officer (CEO) of the company wants something, we do not oppose it; yet good IA dictates that we train computer room operators to forbid entry to anyone without documented authorization—including the CEO.

Sometimes people subvert IA by systematically getting around the rules because their normal social schema supersedes the security schema. It is not uncommon for naïve staff to give keys or the door lock combination for access into secured areas to regularly schedule outside delivery and maintenance persons. Such delivery people are rarely subjected to security checks, and yet their potential for intentional or inadvertent damage is great; nonetheless, the naïve staff members are acting without authorization, subverting normal security controls, and entrusting the safety and security of corporate resources to relative unknowns: Why? Are they deliberately violating security policy with evil intent? Of course not: The employees are simply acting in a friendly fashion and extending trust that might be appropriate in other circumstances—but they are using the wrong schema for a high-security corporate environment. In contrast, an IA specialist's schema in the same circumstances includes all the potentially untrustworthy friends of those outsiders. Until the security administration group alters the employees' perception of the appropriateness of the security regulations, the conflict between different schemata will continue to cause security violations and fuel resentment on all sides.

Indeed, a common response to attempts at enforcing existing policies and procedures, or to new security rules, is a charge of paranoia leveled against security personnel. Other accusations include authoritarian behavior and undue interference with job functions. These responses usually indicate a conflict between accepted norms of behavior and the need to change behavior to conform to security principles. They imply that social and cultural needs and behavior were not accounted for in the design of the principles. They also indicate a need for security personnel to understand that basic social graces and accepted norms of social activity conflict with the basic needs of security—and that the employees violating security rules are not inherently bad people.

Some redesign might allow for better security by recognizing that security rules can violate accepted social norms. For example, in the case of security-locked doors, one could allow for relatively free access to common areas (thus allowing people to hold the door for colleagues following them) while forbidding such actions in secured locations. A posted explanation of both the reasons for, and consequences of, the policy explicitly addressing the difference between the needs of normal politeness and the needs of high security could lead to better adherence to stated policy. The text might read something like this:

> This is a high-security area. Preventing anyone from entering without swiping their owned access card is not rude: it's common sense. Entering secured areas without using each employee's access card could put employees who did not use their access cards to enter at risk in an emergency if security staff didn't know that they were still in the secured areas. You are welcome to exercise normal politeness by holding the doors open for your colleagues and badge-wearing visitors in the nonsecured areas.

If we persist in assuming that we can influence our colleagues to change their perception of IA solely by informing, cajoling, nagging, or browbeating them, we will continue to fail. IA must be integrated into the corporate culture by changing our colleagues' schemata, a process that needs to use all of the techniques that social psychology can teach us.

A simple measure of this reality is to be found in the persistent avoidance practiced by many U.S. Government agencies in applying the information security program requirements of the Federal Information Security Management Act of 2002 (FISMA). It took almost five years and a series of undesirable security incidents before the various agencies woke up to the reality of the need to implement appropriate protection.[4] Another illustration of the reluctance to implement security policies is the Veterans Affairs debacle in the late 2000s involving loss of control over personally identifiable information on unencrypted disk drives.[5]

50.2.2 Theories of Personality. One of the most pervasive obstacles to cooperation in organizations is interpersonal conflict. Many conflicts are rooted in differences of *personality style*. For example, one widely used set of categories for describing people's personalities uses this schema:

- Extroversion
  - High: active, assertive, energetic, outgoing, talkative
  - Low: quiet, reserved, shy, silent, withdrawn
- Agreeableness
  - High: affectionate, appreciative, kind, soft-hearted, sympathetic
  - Low: cold, fault-finding, hard-hearted, quarrelsome, unfriendly

- Conscientiousness
  - High: efficient, organized, planful, responsible, thorough
  - Low: careless, disorderly, frivolous, irresponsible, slipshod
- Emotional stability
  - High: calm, contented, stable, unemotional
  - Low: anxious, moody, nervous, tense, worrying
- Openness or culturedness
  - High: imaginative, insightful, intelligent, original, wide interests
  - Low: commonplace, shallow, simple, narrow interests, unintelligent

The adjectives used in this summary are positive for the high side of each trait and negative for the low side. However, the assumption that different personality types are easily characterized as superior and inferior seriously interferes with respectful communications among colleagues. For example, people with low characteristics might view the preceding summary in this way:

- Extroversion
  - High: nervous, aggressive, excitable, pushy, chattering
  - Low: dignified, respectful, unassuming, attentive, self-sufficient
- Agreeableness
  - High: clinging, gushy, soft-headed, knee-jerk reactive, uncritical
  - Low: stately, analytical, rational, principled, reserved
- Conscientiousness
  - High: obsessive, compulsive, unspontaneous, pompous, slavish
  - Low: free, spontaneous, creative, fun, youthful, having perspective
- Emotional stability
  - High: frozen, ambitionless, boring, dead
  - Low: vibrant, romantic, alive, strong, sensible
- Openness or culturedness
  - High: flaky, theoretical, complicated, off-the-wall, dilettante
  - Low: earthy, smart, grounded, focused, practical

In discussing corporate culture change, leaders must be on guard to defuse conflicts based on the misperception that one particular response or view of an issue is necessarily good and another necessarily bad. The conflict may be rooted in personality styles rather than in problems of understanding. If the security working group proposes that all employees must challenge anyone in the secured areas who is not wearing a badge, some people—those who have low extroversion, for example—may have a great deal of difficulty with the concept that they should tell anyone else what to do, especially a manager of a higher rank than their own. Arguing only over the reasons why such a policy would be *useful* would sidestep the fundamental problem: that the required behavior is in direct conflict with possibly lifelong and firmly held views on appropriate behavior.

Security personnel must remember that failure to comply with policy is not necessarily the result of a bad attitude. When it becomes obvious that conflicts are rooted in personality, security personnel will have to try to arrive at a useful compromise. Instead of requiring that everyone confront the unbadged individual personally, the security policies could include a proviso allowing for individuals to choose simply to inform security personnel immediately.

Role-playing exercises sometimes can defuse a problem in accepting security policies by desensitizing resistant personnel. Going through the motions of what they fear or dislike sometimes can help them come to realize that the proposed change in behavior is not as bad as they originally thought. Returning to the example of confronting violations of security, many people have difficulty imagining that they could tell a superior in the management hierarchy not to *piggyback*. This term, like *hitchhiking* and *tailgating*, describes entering through a secured door that has been opened by someone else using a valid access code or token. Going through exercises in which each person pretends in turn to be the upper manager and then the challenger helps to break down resistance to this particular security policy. Trainers can emphasize that the challenge must be seen using a different schema from the normal situation:

- It is socially acceptable to apply security policies within the organization.
- Higher-status employees can encourage lower-status employees by articulating their support for the policy and showing that they are not offended by the request.
- Participants of all hierarchical levels can introspect to see that they themselves do not feel offended when they are politely asked to use their badge during the role-playing exercise.

In general, leaders of the security team responsible for implementing security policies should be on the lookout for conflicts of style that interfere with the central task of making the enterprise more secure. If an individual likes short, direct instructions without chitchat about nonessentials, the security team member should adapt and stick to essentials; if an individual is known to like getting to know a stranger and wants to spend a few minutes learning about family background, it should not be opposed. Communicating ideas in a way that is likely to be acceptable is more important than imposing one's own interpersonal style preferences on others.

Above all, security personnel—and management in general—ought to be doing a great deal more *listening* and a great deal less *commanding*.

Some important psychological issues for security leaders to consider include:

- Digital security is extremely complicated, and the explanations can be very technical—both attributes that are unfavorable to fostering management attention.
- Most security incidents stem from insiders rather than from outsiders, so prevention requires consistent nagging—not something management or anyone else normally regards favorably.
- Success in digital security (in fact, all of security) is best shown by having *nothing* happen, which is a tough thing to measure and tougher to sell. So the personal payoff for a well-executed security strategy is often little to nothing—and no management executive wants to put up *nothing* as a true measure of success.

The practical implications of these observations include:

- Discussions of IA should be down-to-earth and practical whenever possible.
- Awareness can be achieved by more positive means than nagging.

- One can create metrics of success by using security games and competitions that are fun as well as informative and effective at maintaining security awareness.

Here is an abstract of an article on the general manager's contribution to security:

> Few senior executives pay much attention to computer security. They either hand off responsibility to their technical people or bring in consultants. But given the stakes involved, an arm's-length approach is extremely unwise. According to industry estimates, security breaches affect 90% of all businesses every year and cost some $17 billion. Fortunately ... senior executives don't need to learn about the more arcane aspects of their company's IT systems to take a hands-on approach. Instead, they should focus on the familiar task of managing risk. Their role should be to assess the business value of their information assets, determine the likelihood that those assets will be compromised, and then tailor a set of risk abatement processes to their company's particular vulnerabilities. *This approach, which views computer security as an operational rather than a technical challenge, is akin to a classic quality assurance program in that it attempts to avoid problems rather than fix them and involves all employees, not just IT staffers.* The goal is not to make computer systems completely secure—that's impossible—but to reduce the business risk to an acceptable level...[6]

We have italicized the key sentence in the quote to emphasize the critical role of changing corporate culture in successful security management.[7]

50.2.3 Explanations of Behavior. In practice, trying to change corporate culture can be a frustrating and long-drawn-out project. One aspect of this process that security group leaders should monitor closely is the interpretation of employee behavior (called *attribution* theory in the social psychology literature) by members of the security team. In general, people can be viewed as interpreting (i.e., explaining) other people's behavior according to two independent dimensions: *internal or external* and *stable or unstable*. Here are some explanations of why Betty has failed to log off her session for the fourth time this week before leaving the office:

- **Internal, stable.** "That's just the way she is—she never pays attention to these rules."
- **Internal, unstable.** "She's been under strain lately because her child is sick—that's why she's forgotten."
- **External, stable.** "The system doesn't respond properly to the logoff command."
- **External, unstable.** "This week, the system has not been responding properly to the logoff command."

This simple four-way classification is useful for leaders in understanding and avoiding classic errors of attribution. Such attribution errors can cause conflicts between the security staff and other employees, or even among employees with different degrees of compliance to policy.

50.2.4 Errors of Attribution. Some well-established misinterpretations of others' behavior can interfere with the acceptance of security policies. Such errors interfere with the ability of security personnel to communicate the value of security policies. Security group leaders should sensitize their staff to the consequences of these errors.

50.2.4.1 Fundamental Attribution Error. The most important error people use when explaining other people's behavior is to assume that a person's actions are stable, internal features; a typical example of this error is the naïve belief that an actor's personality is essentially what that person portrays in performance. Anyone who has ever experienced surprise at the demeanor and speech of a favorite actor who is being interviewed has committed the *fundamental attribution error*. Some actors who play bad characters in fictional situations have even been verbally and physically assaulted by viewers who cannot resist the fundamental attribution error, and who genuinely believe that the actors are as bad as the nasty people they portray. The abstract of a conference presentation in 2008 summarized some significant findings illustrating this point:

> Two studies attempted to document the occurrence of the psychological phenomenon known as the fundamental attribution error (FAE) in the audiovisual medium. The FAE refers to the human tendency to attribute people's behavior to internal attributes more than external factors. In Study 1, we demonstrated that in the audiovisual medium, viewers tend to attribute an actor's behavior in television dramas to the actor's personality, ignoring the existence of a script dictating the actor's behavior. Study 2 replicated this finding, and also demonstrated that the tendency to make the FAE is related to the degree to which the person reports being transported into the narrative of the TV drama. Furthermore, we showed that the tendency to attribute character traits to the actor is not diminished following exposure to the same actor playing two opposing roles. The last scene viewed was found to determine the evaluation of the actor's characteristics.[8]

In security work, being on guard against the fundamental attribution error helps to smooth relations with other employees. For example, if a security group member sees an employee, Jill, who is not wearing her badge, it is easy to assume that she never wears her badge and is refusing to wear it because of a character flaw. The security officer may act according to these assumptions by being harsh or unfriendly in correcting Jill's behavior. The harshness generates resentment, and Jill may come to associate security with unpleasant people, thus reducing the likelihood that she will comply with policy or encourage others to do so.

In fact, however, most people's behavior is far less stable and internal than unstable and externally based. For example, if the security officer simply smiled and pointed gently to the lack of a badge instead of jumping to conclusions, he might discover that Jill's lack of a badge today was due simply to her having taken her jacket off just before an urgent call from the vice president, interrupting her normal procedure of moving the badge from jacket to shirt pocket. Thus, her lack of a badge would not be stable behavior at all—it would be a temporary aberration of no longlasting significance. A solution would be to get used to clipping the badge to her trousers or her skirt instead of her jacket or her blouse. Similarly, just by asking nicely, the security officer might learn that Jill normally does wear her badge, but today her four-year-old son took it off her jacket to play with it, without his mother's noticing the change. In this example, Jill's behavior is externally based and has nothing to do with character. The kindly interactions between Jill and the security guard *increase* the sense of social relation and make it more likely that she will remember the incident positively and comply with the security policy in the future.

In summary, by being aware of the fundamental attribution error, security personnel can be trained to adopt a less judgmental, or quick-draw, mentality that can alienate other employees and damage security programs.

50.2.4.2 Actor-Observer Effect. The *actor-observer effect* consists of interpreting one's own behavior as appropriate unstable, externally motivated responses to environmental conditions, whereas other people's behavior is viewed in the light of the fundamental attribution error as stable, internally motivated expressions of character traits. Becoming aware of this tendency helps security personnel resist the fundamental attribution error.

50.2.4.3 Self-Serving Bias. The counterpart of the actor-observer effect is the *self-serving bias*, which fools people into believing that their own behavior is due to stable, internal aspects of their character. Security officers who are unaware of this dangerous error may come to feel that they are in some sense superior to other people who do not know as much about security as they do or who do not comply as fully as they do with security policy. The officers may have failed to integrate the fact that hours of training and coaching by their security group leaders are at least as responsible for their own knowledge of, and compliance with, security policies as any innate superiority.

By bringing this kind of erroneous thinking to light during training and supervision of security staff, managers can help reduce the conflicts that naturally result from an air of assumed superiority.

50.2.4.4 Salience and Prejudice. When people are asked to guess which person in a group is the most influential (or least influential) person, social psychologists find that whichever person stands out the most, for whatever reason, is more often attributed with the special properties in question. Such effects apply to any characteristic that the psychologists ask about: most (or least) intelligent, aggressive, sympathetic, and so on. This phenomenon is known as the *salience effect.*

An application of the salience effect might occur if security officers see a group of employees who are violating security policies. A natural and counterproductive tendency is to leap to the conclusion that the tallest or shortest, the thinnest or fattest, the whitest or blackest person in the group must be to blame. This error can result in unfair treatment of perfectly innocent people.

This problem of misinterpreting salience is exacerbated by prejudice; for example, imagine there were an identifiable group called the *Ogunians* (as far as we can determine, there is no such group) who traditionally wear, say, a seven-sided symbol of their identity. If an anti-Ogunian security officer sees a noncompliant group where one of the members is wearing the characteristic heptagon of Ogun, it may be hard for the officer to resist blaming the noncompliance on the Ogunian even if, in fact, the Ogunian was waiting to use a valid access card in full compliance with security policy.

Worse, people can be so strongly influenced by expectation—part of their schema—that they actually misperceive a situation altogether. For example, in some classic experiments studying prejudice in the 1950s, psychologists showed subjects a drawing of two people, one light-colored and the other dark-colored, standing in a tramway car. One was holding a knife. When questioned about the image afterward, white subjects consistently reported that the black figure had been holding the knife, but actually it was the white figure in the drawing who had the knife.

Thus, even observation itself can be twisted by prejudice and expectations; for example, if the anti-Ogunian security officer sees a group of people passing through an open doorway into a secured area without using their badges, the officer may incorrectly report that it was the fault of an Ogunian even if there was no Ogunian in the group. Such a mistaken report would not only infuriate innocent Ogunians and possibly cause general Ogunian resentment or hostility toward security efforts in general, but it also could mislead the security group itself into trying to correct the behavior of the wrong person or people.

Similarly, any minority—whether in terms of gender, gender orientation, religion, race, or disability—can be the focus of a prejudiced security officer's blame when a group disobeys policy. Security leaders should make their staff aware of the danger of applying this erroneous method of explaining group behavior. In many organizations, such discrimination is a violation of corporate policy and may even be illegal. In any case, prejudice is not constructive and must be monitored and overcome.

50.2.5 Intercultural Differences. Many countries in the world are experiencing changes in their population due to immigration. Especially in areas where people have heretofore been largely homogeneous, cultural, religious, and racial diversity can lead to interpersonal and intergroup conflicts. Such conflicts may be based in part on prejudice, but they also may be the result of differing values and assumptions.

This definition of culture helps define the discussion:

> **Culture as Mental Programming**
> Every person carries within him- or herself patterns of thinking, feeling, and potential acting that were learned throughout their lifetime. Much of it has been acquired in early childhood, because at that time a person is most susceptible to learning and assimilating. As soon as certain patterns of thinking, feeling, and acting have established themselves within a person's mind, he or she must unlearn these before being able to learn something different, and unlearning is more difficult than learning for the first time.
>
> Using the analogy of the way computers are programmed, this book will call such patterns of thinking, feeling and acting *mental programs,* or … *software of the mind…*
>
> A customary term for such mental software is *culture.*[9]

Security personnel engaged in the process of corporate culture change should be sensitive to the possibility that people with different real-world cultural backgrounds can respond differently to proposed security policies. For example, in 2001 the fundamentalist extremists of the Taliban in Afghanistan decreed that non-Muslim people would have to wear badges in public.[10] One can imagine that a Hindu Afghan refugee in the United States who is told to wear a badge for security reasons might have an unexpectedly emotional response to the order. Before pressuring (or becoming hostile to) anyone who seems to be resisting a policy, it is valuable to inquire about the person's beliefs and attitudes and to explain the foundation for the policies in question. Especially where there are intercultural differences, such inquiry and discussion can forestall difficulties and dissension and assuage unexpected, culturally rooted anxiety.

Security professionals need to be acutely aware of the cultural differences of individuals in their target audiences. For example, in some cultures (mostly the new world and western), reality is directly related to facts and verifiable calculations. Other cultures may put a stronger emphasis on personal feelings, intuition, and culturally ingrained beliefs into their comprehension of reality. Hence different people may not share the same understanding of reality or implement policies by the same principles unless they make their assumptions known and discuss them with the intention of coming to agreement.

When considering culture, the changing dynamics of modern society also need to be accounted for. Any modern city or leading public institution today is a complex combination of people from different cultural and social backgrounds. Working together for large parts of their active days together as a group leads to a melting pot situation, with all the individual cultures and social leanings being added into the mix and emerging as a (mostly) different culture. The individuals then take this new culture back home, where it mixes in with their family and friends' contributions, resulting in often more modifications and variation. The organization itself is constantly changing, as people join and leave. All of this leads to culture being a dynamic phenomenon, albeit not as rapidly changing as the technology front. Hence, any security policy or framework needs to be able to account for and accommodate this changing paradigm if it has to be successful in securing the enterprise.

50.2.6 Framing Reality. How can we make the corporate culture more supportive of IA?

Schemata influence what we perceive. For example, an employee refuses to take vacations, works late every night, is never late, and is never sick. A model employee? Perhaps, in one schema. From the security point of view, the employee's behavior is suspect. There have been cases where such people have been embezzlers unable to leave their employment: Even a day away might result in discovery of their crimes. Saint or sinner? Our expectations determine what we see.[11]

To change the schema so that people take IA seriously, we should provide participants in training and security awareness with real-life examples of computer crime and security breaches, so that security policies make obvious sense rather than seeming to be arbitrary.

Schemata influence what we remember. When information inconsistent with our preconceptions is mixed with details that fit our existing schemata, we selectively retain what fits and discard what conflicts. When we have been fed a diet of movies and television shows illustrating the premise that information is most at risk from brilliant hackers, why should we remember the truth: that carelessness and incompetence by authorized users of information systems cause far more harm than evil intentions and outsiders ever do?

Instructors should emphasize the practical side of IA by showing how policies protect all employees against false accusations, prevent damage to the organization's reputation and profits, and even play a role in national security. This is especially true where business touches the technical infrastructure on which we all depend.

Most important of all, teaching others about IA cannot be an occasional and haphazard affair. Before attempting to implement policies and procedures (aside from emergency measures that are needed at once), we should ensure that we build up a consistent view of IA among our colleagues. In light of the complexity of social cognition, our usual attempts to implement security policies and procedures seem pathetically inept. A couple of hours of lectures followed by a video, a yearly ritual of signing a security policy that seems to have been written by Martians—these are not methods that will improve security. These efforts merely pay lip service to the idea of security.

According to research on counterintuitive information, people's judgment is influenced by the manner in which information is presented. For example, even information contrary to established schemata can be assimilated if people have enough time to integrate the new knowledge into their worldviews. It follows that nonemergency security policies should be introduced over a long time, not rushed into place.

An effective IA program includes frequent reminders of security. To change the corporate culture, practitioners should use methods such as a security corner in the corporate publication, security bulletins detailing the latest computer crime or security breach that has hit the news, contests for identifying the problems in realistic scenarios, and write-in columns to handle questions about policies. IA has to become part of the framework of reality, not just an imposition from management.

In every security course or awareness program, instructors and facilitators should explicitly address the question of corporate culture, expectations, and social schemata. Do not rely solely on intellectual discourse when addressing a question of complex perceptions and feelings. Use simulations, videos, and role-playing exercises to bridge the gap between intellect and emotion.

Address the feelings and perceptions of all participants as they learn about the counterintuitive behaviors that improved security will demand. Encourage learners to think about how they might feel and respond in various situations that can arise during the transition to a more secure environment. For example, ask participants to imagine:

- Asking colleagues not to step through a secured entrance without passing through the access-control system with their own identity
- Telling their boss that they will not copy software without a license to do so
- Questioning a visitor or employee who is not wearing an identity badge[12]

50.2.7 Getting Your Security Policies Across. What are some ways to change our colleagues' schemata so that they become more receptive to IA policies?

- **Initial exposure.** Preliminary information may influence people's responses to information presented later. For example, merely exposing experimental subjects to words such as *reckless* or *adventurous* affects their judgment of risk-taking behavior in a later test.

  It follows that when preparing to increase employee awareness of security issues, presenting case studies is likely to have a beneficial effect on participants' readiness to examine security requirements.
- **Counterexamples.** Preexisting schemata can be challenged by several counterexamples, each of which challenges a component of the schema. For example, prejudice about an ethnic group is more likely to be changed by contact with several people, each of whom contradicts a different aspect of the prejudiced schema.

  It follows that security awareness programs should include many realistic examples of security requirements and breaches. In a counterexample, students in college IA courses have commented on the unrealistic scenario in a training video they were shown: a series of disastrous security breaches occurring in the same company. Based on the findings of cognitive social psychologists, the film would be more effective for training if the incidents had been dramatized as occurring in different companies.

  In practical terms, practitioners should stay current and update their materials. Many IA publications provide useful case studies that will help make awareness and training more effective.
- **Choice of wording.** Perceptions of risks and benefits are profoundly influenced by the wording in which situations and options are presented. For example, experimental subjects responded far more positively to reports of a drug with "50 percent success" than to the same drug described as having "50 percent failure."

  It follows that practitioners should choose their language carefully during security awareness campaigns. Instead of focusing on reducing failure rates (violations of policy), we should emphasize improvements in our success rates. Unfortunately, some rates cannot be expressed in positive terms; for example, it is not easy to measure the success rate of security measures designed to foil attacks on systems.

Judgments are easily distorted by the tendency to rely on personal anecdotes, small samples, easily available information, and faulty interpretation of statistical information. Basically, we humans are not always rational processors of factual information. If security awareness programs rely strictly on presentation of factual information about risks and proposed policies and procedures, they are likely to run up against a stubborn refusal to act logically. Security program implementation must engage more than the rational mind. We must appeal to our colleagues' imagination and emotion as well. We must inspire a commitment to security rather than merely describing it.

50.2.8 Reward versus Punishment. When enforcing security policies, too many organizations focus entirely on punishing those who break the rules. However, everything we know about modifying behavior teaches us to use reward rather than punishment. Punishing people who do not comply with security rules often generates resentment and hostility that carry over into future interactions. Instead of seeing information assurance as a benefit to the organization and to their interests, victims of harsh treatment can resist even well-intentioned, sensible changes in security policies simply because of the emotional overlay associated with the embarrassment and frustration generated by criticism and penalties.

In addition to avoiding negativity and push-back, reward may simply work better than punishment at changing behavior. For example, a security officer from a large corporation experimented with reward and punishment in implementing security policies. Employees were supposed to log off their mainframe terminals when leaving the office, but compliance rates were only around 40 percent. In one department, the security officer used the usual techniques recommended in the literature and common among security professionals; for example, she put up nasty notes on terminals that were not logged off, changed the passwords on delinquent accounts, and humiliated violators by forcing them to report to their bosses for authorization to obtain a new password. However, in a different department, she simply left a Hershey's Chocolate Kiss on the keyboard of every terminal whose user had indeed logged off before leaving. After one month of these two strategies, compliance rates in the department subject to punishment had climbed to around 60 percent. Compliance in the department getting chocolates had reached around 80 percent—and their feelings toward security were much more favorable than the norm.

This case illustrates some of the benefits of reward:

- Compliance rates were significantly higher than in the group subjected to punishment.
- Attitudes (see Section 50.3) are more likely to be positive.
- Costs can be lower because small rewards delivered en masse may be much cheaper and quicker to apply than administrative procedures applied one by one through management intervention.

50.3 BELIEFS AND ATTITUDES.

Psychologists distinguish between beliefs and attitudes. A *belief* refers to cognitive information that need not have an emotional component. An *attitude* refers to an evaluation or emotional response. Thus, a person may believe correctly that copying a large number of proprietary software packages without authorization is a felony while nonetheless having the attitude that it does not matter to him. A rational employee may *believe* that malware can be downloaded onto company computers through unauthorized software available on unvetted Websites (and thus answer a questionnaire evaluating security awareness correctly) yet have the *attitude* that the risk is negligible—and cheerfully go on downloading unauthorized software at work.

50.3.1 Beliefs. Beliefs can change when contradictory information is presented, but some research suggests that it can take up to a week before significant shifts are measurable. Other studies suggest that when people hold contradictory beliefs, providing an opportunity to articulate and evaluate those beliefs may lead to changes that reduce inconsistency.

These findings imply that corporate security must explore the current structure of beliefs among employees and managers. Questionnaires, focus groups, and interviews may not only help the security practitioner, they actually may help move the corporate culture in the right direction. The *Hawthorne Effect* is the name given to improvements in measured behavior resulting simply from employee responses to being studied; done correctly, honestly, and nonpunitively, inquiring into employee beliefs and attitudes may communicate a genuine interest by management in improving security policy and practice with input from everyone involved.

50.3.2 Attitudes. An attitude, in the classical definition, is a learned evaluative response, directed at specific objects, which is relatively enduring and influences behavior in a generally motivating way. The advertising industry spends over $50 billion yearly to influence public attitudes in the hope that these attitudes will lead to changes in spending habits—that is, in behavior.

Research on classical conditioning suggests that attitudes can be learned even through simple word association. If we wish to move our colleagues toward a more negative view of computer criminals, it is important not to portray computer crime using positive images and words. Movies that show criminal hackers as pleasant, smart, physically attractive, and likable people may do harm by minimizing the seriousness of industrial espionage and cybervandalism. When teaching security, we should avoid praising the criminals we describe in case studies.

Studies of how attitudes are developed consistently show that rewards and punishments are important motivators of behavior. Studies show that even apparently minor encouragement can influence attitudes. A supervisor or instructor should praise any comments that are critical of computer crime or that support the established security policies. Employees who dismiss security concerns, or who flout the regulations, should be challenged on their attitudes, not ignored. Such challenges are best carried out in private to avoid causing embarrassment to the skeptics and possibly generating resistance due to pride or a sense of machismo.

50.3.3 Changing Attitudes toward Security. Persuasion—changing someone's attitudes—has been described in terms of communications. The four areas of research include:

1. **Communicator variables.** Who is trying to persuade?
2. **Message variables.** What is being presented?

3. **Channel variables.** By what means is the attempt taking place?
4. **Audience variables.** At whom is the persuasion aimed?

50.3.3.1 Communicator Variables. Attractiveness, credibility, and social status have strong effects immediately after the speaker or writer has communicated with the target audience; however, over a period of weeks to a month, the effects decline until the predominant issue is message content. We can use this phenomenon by identifying the senior executives most likely to succeed in setting a positive tone for subsequent security training. We should look for respected, likable people who understand the issues and sincerely believe in the policies they are advocating.

One personality style in particular can threaten the success of security policies: the *authoritarian personality*. A body of research suggests that some people, often those raised by punitive parents highly concerned with social status, become rigidly devoted to conventional beliefs, submit to authority, exercise authority harshly themselves, and are hostile to groups they perceive as unpopular. An authoritarian person might make a terrible security officer. Such an officer might derive more satisfaction from ordering people around and punishing them than from long-term success in implementing security policies.

50.3.3.2 Message Variables. Fear can work to change attitudes only if judiciously applied. Excessive emphasis on the terrible results of poor security is likely to backfire, with participants in the awareness program rejecting the message altogether. Frightening consequences should be coupled immediately with effective and achievable security measures.

Some studies suggest that presenting a balanced argument helps convince those who initially disagree with a proposal. Presenting objections to a proposal and offering counterarguments is more effective than one-sided diatribes. Popular training videos from the Software & Information Industry Association use this technique: they show people such as "college students, college faculty and publishers of all types of media discuss[ing] the legal and ethical implications of copying other people's works" and fairly present the arguments of copyright violators before rebutting them.[13]

Modest repetition of a message can help generate a more positive response. Thus, security awareness programs that include imaginative posters, mugs, special newsletters, audio and videotapes, and lectures are more likely to build and sustain support for security than occasional intense sessions of indoctrination. The use of multiple communications channels (discussed in the next section) also increases the effectiveness of the message.

50.3.3.3 Channel Variables. The channel through which we communicate has a strong effect on attitudes and on the importance of superficial attributes of the communicator. In modern organizations, most people assume that a meeting is the ideal way to communicate new information. However, the most effective medium for convincing someone to pay attention to any topic is face-to-face persuasion. Security training should include more than tapes and books; a charismatic teacher or leader can help generate enthusiasm for—or at least reduce resistance to—better security.

In addition, security educators should not introduce new ideas to decision makers in a meeting. There is too much danger of confounding responses to policy with nonpolicy matters rooted in relationships among the participants. It is not uncommon for one executive to oppose a new policy simply because another has supported it. A good way to introduce security policies is to have individual meetings with one executive at a time in order to explain the issues and proposals and to ask for support.

Psychologists testing cognitive response theory have studied many subtle aspects of persuasion. Experiments have shown that rhetorical questions, such as "Are we to accept invasions of our computer systems?" are effective when the arguments are solid but counterproductive when arguments are weak. Security officers should not ask rhetorical questions unless they are certain that almost everybody will inevitably have the same answer—the one the security officers are looking for.

Consideration of facts and logical arguments, as the central route to persuasion, has been found to lead to more lasting attitudes and attitude changes than the peripheral influences from logically unrelated factors, such as physical attractiveness of a speaker.

50.3.3.4 *Audience Variables.* As mentioned, questionnaires and interviews may help cement a favorable change in attitude by leading to commitment. Once employees have publicly avowed support for better security, some will begin to change their perception of themselves. Specific employees should be encouraged to take on various areas of public responsibility for IA within their work group. These roles should periodically be rotated among the employees to give everyone the experience of public commitment to improved security.

To keep up interest in security, regular meetings of enthusiasts to discuss recent security news can keep the subject fresh and interesting. New cases can help security officers explain policies with up-to-date references that will interest their fellow employees and motivate managers to pay attention to security policies.

50.4 ENCOURAGING INITIATIVE.

The ideal situation would be for everyone actually to help enforce security policies. Actually, however, some people are cooperative and helpful whereas others—or even the same people in different circumstances—are reluctant and suspicious about new policies. What can we do to increase cooperation and reduce rejection?

50.4.1 Prosocial Behavior. Studies of people who have come to the aid of others can help to encourage everyone in an organization to do the right thing. Some people intervene to stop crimes; others ignore crimes or watch passively. Social psychologists have devised a schema that describes the steps leading to prosocial behavior:

1. People have to notice the emergency or the crime before they can act. Thus, security training has to include information on how to tell that someone may be engaging in computer crime.
2. The situation has to be defined as an emergency—something requiring action. Security training that provides facts about the effects of computer crime on society and solid information about the need for security within the organization can help employees recognize security violations as emergencies.
3. Everyone must take responsibility for acting, but the larger the number of people in a group confronted with an emergency, the slower the average response time. Larger groups seem to lead to a *diffusion of responsibility*; each person feels that someone else is more responsible for dealing with the emergency. Another possible factor is uncertainty about the social climate; people fear appearing foolish or overly emotional in the eyes of those present. To overcome this effect, a corporate

culture must be established that rewards responsible individual behavior, such as reporting security violations.

4. Once responsibility for solving a problem has been accepted, appropriate decisions and actions must be taken. Clearly written security policies and procedures will make it more likely that employees act to improve security. In contrast, contradictory policies, poorly documented procedures, and inconsistent support from management will interfere with the decision to act.

Another analysis proposes that people implicitly analyze costs of helping and of not helping when deciding whether to act prosocially. The combination of factors most conducive to prosociality is low cost for helping and high cost for not helping.

Security procedures should make it easy to act in accordance with security policy. There should be a hotline for reporting security violations, and anonymity should be respected if desired. Psychological counseling and follow-up should be available if people feel upset about their involvement. Conversely, failing to act responsibly should be a serious matter; personnel policies should document clear and meaningful sanctions for failing to act when a security violation is observed. Penalties would include critical remarks in employment reviews and, where appropriate, even dismissal.

One method that does *not* work to increase prosocial behavior is *exhortation*; merely lecturing people in the abstract about what they ought to do has little or no positive effect.

Significantly, the general level of stress and pressure to focus on difficult tasks with seemingly impossible deadlines can greatly reduce the likelihood that people will act on their moral and ethical principles. Security is likely to flourish in an environment that provides sufficient time and support for employees to work professionally. Offices where everyone responds to a continuing series of apparent emergencies will not be likely to pay attention to security violations.

Some findings from research confirm common sense. For example, guilt motivates many people to act more prosocially. This effect works best when people are forced to assume responsibility. Thus, enforcing standards of security using reprimands and sanctions can indeed increase the likelihood that employees subsequently will act more cooperatively; however, as suggested earlier, punishment should not replace reward.

In addition, mood affects susceptibility to prosocial pressures. Bad moods make prosocial behavior less likely, whereas good moods increase prosociality. A working environment in which employees are respected is more conducive to good security than one that devalues and abuses them.

Even cursory acquaintance with other people makes it more likely that we will help them; it thus makes sense for security supervisors to get to know the staff from whom they need support. Encouraging social activities in an office (e.g., lunchtime discussion groups, occasional parties, and charitable projects) enhances interpersonal relationships and can improve the climate for effective security training. *Management by walking around* is an excellent practice at many levels, including fostering at least the first stage of interpersonal relationship among coworkers.[14]

50.4.2 Conformity, Compliance, and Obedience.

Some people react negatively to the words *conformity*, *compliance*, and *obedience*, but ignoring social phenomena will not help security practitioners to attain their goals. Despite the unpopularity of this subject area, it is valuable to understand how people can work together in reinforcing security policies. The next sections look at how to increase conformity with a culture of cooperation for increased security, compliance with rational security rules, and a bias toward obedience to IA authorities in security matters.

50.4.2.1 *Social Pressure and Behavior Change.* Turning a group into a community provides a framework within which social pressures can operate to improve an organization's IA. Most people respond to the opinions of others by shifting their own opinions, sometimes unconsciously, toward what statisticians call the *mode*—the most popular opinion. Security programs must aim to shift the normative values, the sense of what one should do, toward protecting confidentiality, possession or control, integrity, authenticity, availability, and utility of data.

According to an informal survey conducted by Mani Akella, a coauthor of this Chapter, at three leading financial firms on Wall Street, these inferences resulted from a test group of 80 respondents:

- Older employees prefer to model their reactions based on common group preferences, even if some of the reactions go against their own gut feeling. The rationale here seems to be that the group provides anonymity and even insulates them from management reaction. Younger employees, however, tend to buck the group trend when they disagree with proposed concepts.
- Leadership has a large role to play—and the group modifies its reactions very quickly to adapt to leadership changes. If the leader likes to follow a specific path and not ask questions, the entire group tends to let issues lie and not disturb the even tenor of the organization for fear of disturbing the leader, even at the cost of risking serious potential security lapses (see Section 50.5.4 on groupthink). If the leader fosters a dynamic, open, and collaborative environment with a measured adaptability to evolving threats, however, the group enlivens itself with innovation and puts out additional effort to stay abreast (or even ahead) of the current threat landscape.
- When the leaders challenge the individuals to greater achievement without threats of punitive reaction, the *group* reacts with positive response. Leadership can create a security environment that can exceed the enterprise's security expectations by encouraging the individual to increase productivity and to reward oneself with greater job satisfaction. Security, like most other organizational management efforts, is all about people. Responsible, satisfied, and aware personnel naturally lead to better overall security for the organization.

50.4.2.2 *Changing Expectations.* As has been evident in public campaigns aimed at eliminating drunken driving, it *is* possible to shift the mode. In the United States in the mid-twentieth century, many people believed that driving while intoxicated was amusing; today, a drunken driver is a social pariah. High school children used to kill themselves in large numbers on the nights of their high school proms; today, many children spontaneously are arranging for safe rides home. In much the same way, we must move toward making computer crime as distasteful as public drunkenness.

The trend toward similar behavior increases when people within the group like or admire each other. In addition, the social status of an individual within a group influences that individual's willingness to conform to group standards. High-status people (those liked by most people in the group) and low-status people (those disliked by the group) both tend to be more autonomous and less compliant than people liked by some and disliked by others. Therefore, security officers should pay special attention to those outliers during instruction programs. Managers should monitor compliance more closely at both ends of the popularity range. If security practices are currently poor, and allies are needed to change the norm, working with the outliers to resist the majority's anti-security bias may be the most effective approach. The most popular people may be disastrous agents of rebellion if they do not sign on to the security program; paradoxically, the most unpopular people may be helpful if they can be persuaded to comply.

50.4.2.3 Norm of Reciprocity. According to social psychologists, the norm of reciprocity indicates that, in social relations, favors are usually returned. Even a small, unexpected, unsolicited, or even unwanted gift increases the likelihood that we will respond to requests. For example, members of various religious cults often hand out flowers or books at airports, knowing that the norm of reciprocity will increase the frequency and amount of donations from basically uninterested passersby.

A security awareness program that includes small gifts, such as an attractive mug labeled "SECURITY IS EVERYONE'S BUSINESS" or an inexpensive but useful booklet summarizing security policies, can help get people involved in security. The combination of such programs with rewards for compliance can be a powerful tool for improving security.

Combining a token of appreciation with direct personal contact starting with the statement "I need your help" followed by a frank exposition of the security situation can be positive at all levels. This approach works at multiple levels—establishing personal relations, building on the norm of reciprocity, and changing the schema.

50.4.2.4 Incremental Change. The foot-in-the-door technique suggests that a small initial request should be followed by an even larger second one. Political field workers, for example, know that they can start small by asking people to let them put candidate stickers in their window; then they ask to put a candidate's poster on their lawn; eventually they can ask for volunteer time or money. Every compliance with a request increases the likelihood that the person will agree to the next step in an escalating series. It is as if agreeing to one step helps to change the targets' sense of themselves. To reduce discomfort about their beliefs and their behavior (what psychologists call *cognitive dissonance*), people change their beliefs to conform with their behavior.

Employees can be asked personally to set a good example by blanking screens and locking terminals when leaving their desks. Later, once they have begun the process of redefining themselves ("I am a person who cares about computer security"), they can be asked for something more intense, such as participating in security training by asking others to blank their screens and lock their terminals—or rewarding those who do with the famous chocolate tidbit. By applying the same methods to various tasks, the corporate culture can change so that a majority of people feel personally committed to good security practices.

Some security specialists have proposed that we should not ask the audience to think. The reasoning is that each incremental policy step should not require the target audience to reason or explain behavior. Rather, focus on building conditioned reflexes to specific environmental and usage factors. The organization and the security team should be more assured of a common and predictable reaction to any security threat from each individual internal person. However, a countervailing view is that every behavior proposed to improve security *must* be grounded in an understandable schema. In other words, although one need not force the members of the audience to *articulate* the rationale, the rules must make sense if they are to be integrated, remembered, and applied in the long term.

50.5 GROUP BEHAVIOR.

Some groups of people are referred to as *teams*, while others are called *gangs*. Social psychological insights into group behavior can improve success rates for IA policies.

50.5.1 Social Arousal.

Studies on the behavioral effects of being in groups produced contradictory results; sometimes people did better at their tasks when there were other people around, and sometimes they did worse. Eventually, psychologists realized that the presence of other people is *socially arousing*; that is, people become more aware both of their own behavior and of social norms when they are in groups. Social arousal *facilitates well-learned habits, but it inhibits poorly learned habits*. Thus, when trying to teach employees new habits to improve security, it is counterproductive to put them into large groups. Individualized learning (e.g., by means of computer-based training and videotapes) can overcome inhibitory effects of groups in the early stages of behavioral change.

50.5.2 Locus of Control.

Another factor that interferes with implementation of security policies is the *locus of control*. People do not like feeling that they have no control over their environment. For example, in a classic experiment reported in social psychology textbooks, two equivalent teams of people were both subjected to loud and disruptive noise coming through a loudspeaker in their work area. One group had no control whatever over the noise, whereas the other had a large button with which they could stop the noise at once. The group with the stop button did noticeably better at their complex task than the other group—yet in no case did anyone actually press the button. Simply feeling that they *could* exert control, if they wanted to, significantly altered the performance of the experimental subjects.

Similarly, in studies of healing among older patients, three groups were defined: (1) controls, (2) people given a plant in a pot, and (3) people given a plant in a pot plus instructions to water it regularly. The third group did significantly better than the second in their recovery. Once again, the sense of control over the environment appeared to influence outcomes.

In security policy implementation, experience confirms that those organizations with the most participation and involvement by all sectors do best at developing and implementing information protection plans. A common phrase that refers to this phenomenon is *buy-in*, as in: "The different departmental representatives felt that they could genuinely buy into the new policies because they had fully participated in framing them."[15]

50.5.3 Group Polarization.

Another branch of research into group psychology deals with group polarization. Groups tend to take more extreme decisions than would individuals in the group acting alone. In group discussions of the need for security, polarization can involve deciding to take more risks—by reducing or ignoring security concerns—than any individual would have judged reasonable. Again, one-on-one discussions of the need for security will generally be more effective in building a consensus that supports cost-effective security provisions than will large meetings.

50.5.4 Groupthink.

In the extreme, a group can display groupthink, in which a consensus is reached because of strong desires for social cohesion. When groupthink prevails, evidence contrary to the received view is discounted; opposition is viewed as disloyal; dissenters are discredited. Especially worrisome for security professionals, those people in the grip of groupthink tend to ignore risks and contingencies. To prevent such aberrations, the leader must remain impartial and encourage open debate. Respected security consultants from the outside could be invited to address the group, bringing their own experiences to bear on the group's requirements. After a consensus—not the imposition of a dominant person's opinions—has been achieved, the group should meet again and focus on playing devil's advocate to try to come up with additional challenges and alternatives.

In summary, security experts should pay attention to group dynamics and be prepared to counter possible dysfunctional responses that interfere with acceptance of IA policies.

50.6 TECHNOLOGICAL GENERATION GAPS.

In our society there are growing societal gaps between the social groups that grew up interacting in real-world communities (unwired), groups that grew up with the Internet (wired), and the newest group growing up with the always-on technology of our complex and content-rich wireless social networks.

- **The unwired generation.** In today's always-on world of ubiquitous wireless communications, we sometimes forget about the unwired generation, those born in the early 1960s or before, who grew up actually playing outside with their friends and communicating face to face. For these older employees, online discussion groups, streaming video training, blogs, and email may not be as effective as with other, more technological groups. The unwired generation may see the use of impersonal technology in training as an indicator of management apathy toward a topic that is not worth taking the time for real-world interaction. To this generation, if security training is important, someone should take the time to deliver it face to face. The unwired generation is also the most susceptible to many of the social psychology techniques and pitfalls discussed in this chapter.
- **The wired generation.** Those born from the early 1960s to the late 1970s comprise the wired generation. This transitional generation grew up at the dawn of the Internet from 300 baud dial-up access to ISDN. From MS DOS to Windows 98 and from Cobol to C++, this generation is the bridge from the real world to the cyberworld. This generation is also the generation currently coming to power in both business and government. Although accustomed to meeting face to face for important business, the wired generation lives by email and cell phones, tolerating both the unwired and wired methods of communicating and learning.
- **The always-on generation.** Those born after 1980 comprise the always-on generation. This generation grew up with high-speed Internet, cell phones, video games, portable electronics, and online virtual communities. This is the connected, networked, Facebook, video-game generation. It is this generation that seems to confound traditional security screening and implementation policy.

Although the unwired and wired generations shared psychological roots in the real world, the always-on generation has two homes: the real world and the cyberworld. With instant messaging (IM), texting (Short Message Service, or SMS), and cellular wireless, this generation moves in and out of cyberspace as the previous generation moved between the worlds of work and home. Moreover, like the previous generations, the always-on generation has different psychological and sociological frameworks for their worlds—a serious information assurance concern.

To the unwired and wired generations, personal communication meant face to face. To the always-on generation personal, communication means IM, email, and smart phones. In addition, social interaction often means social networking, blogs, Web pages, message boards, and wikis. Add to this the fact that the always-on generation has a keen ability to quickly transfer information between their tightly integrated worlds, and you have the ingredients for a security officer's nightmare.

Recognizing these differences and reacting accordingly can pay sizable dividends in both security compliance and general management success. As a first step, one can ensure that security teams include members from more than the oldest generation in the enterprise; younger people may be able to act as intermediaries or translators between increasingly disparate cultures.

50.7 SUMMARY OF RECOMMENDATIONS.

This chapter has reviewed the major findings of social psychology that can help to improve IA programs. These ideas can prove useful to readers who think about social psychology as they work to implement security policies:

- Recognize that IA policies often conflict with the schema for trusting, polite behavior in situations outside the work arena.
- Train IA personnel to recognize that failure to comply with security policies may be rooted in many other factors than simply bad attitude.
- Listen more than you command.
- Teach security personnel to avoid the classic errors of attribution when trying to understand their colleagues' motivations.
- Openly discuss and counter prejudice before it causes conflicts.
- Take intercultural differences into account when setting and implementing security policies.
- Before attempting to implement policies and procedures, ensure a consistent view of IA among colleagues.
- Whenever possible, security policies should be introduced over a long time, not rushed into place.
- Presenting case studies is likely to have a beneficial effect on participants' readiness to examine security requirements.
- Security awareness programs should include many realistic examples of security requirements and breaches.
- Attempt to inspire a commitment to security rather than merely describing it.
- Emphasize improvements rather than reduction of failure.
- Create a new concern for corporate security by exploring the current structure of beliefs among employees and managers.
- Never portray computer crime using positive images and words.
- Praise any comments that are critical of computer crime or that support the established security policies.
- Employees who dismiss security concerns or flout the regulations should be challenged on their attitudes, not ignored.
- Identify the senior executives most likely to succeed in setting a positive tone for subsequent security training and engage their cooperation to act as role models.

- Examples of frightening consequences used in awareness and training materials should be coupled immediately with descriptions of effective and achievable security measures to forestall such consequences.
- Presenting objections to a proposal and offering counterarguments is more effective than one-sided diatribes.
- Security-awareness programs should include many, frequent, and preferably novel and entertaining reminders of security issues.
- In addition to tapes and books, rely on a charismatic teacher or leader to help generate enthusiasm for better security.
- Encourage specific employees to take on public responsibility for IA within their work groups.
- Rotate security roles periodically.
- Security training should include information on how to tell that someone may be engaging in computer crime.
- Build a corporate culture that rewards responsible behavior, such as reporting security violations.
- Develop clearly written security policies and procedures.
- Security procedures should make it easy to act in accordance with security policy.
- Treat failures to act in accordance with security policies and procedures as very serious matters.
- Enforcing standards of security can increase the likelihood that employees will subsequently act more cooperatively.
- A working environment in which employees are respected is more conducive to good security than one that devalues and abuses them.
- Get to know the staff from whom you need support.
- Encourage social activities in the office.
- Pay special attention to social outliers during instruction programs.
- Monitor compliance more closely at both ends of the popularity range.
- Work with the outliers to resist a group's antisecurity bias.
- Include small gifts in your security-awareness program.
- Start improving security a little at a time, and work up to more intrusive procedures.
- Before discussing security at a meeting, have one-on-one discussions with the participants.
- Remain impartial, and encourage open debate in security meetings.
- Bring in experts from the outside when faced with groupthink.
- Meet again after a consensus has been built, and play devil's advocate.
- Recognize the generational technology gaps in our culture and communicate accordingly; therefore, include people from different generations in your security teams.

None of these suggestions is essential; none of them is appropriate in all situations. However, building on the accumulated experience and wisdom of social psychologists will support the smooth integration of information assurance into any corporate culture. We hope that readers will explore the literature of social and organizational psychology and will try out new ideas that will enrich the field of information assurance in years to come.

50.8 FURTHER READING

Adler, N. J., and A. Gunderson. *International Dimensions of Organizational Behavior*, 5th ed. South-Western College Publications, 2007.

Bik, O. *The Behavior of Assurance Professionals: A Cross-Cultural Perspective.* Eburon Academic Publishers, 2010.

Greenberg, J. *Managing Behavior in Organizations*, 6th ed. Prentice-Hall, 2012.

Kreitner, R., and A. Kinicki. *Organizational Behavior*, 9th ed. McGraw-Hill, 2009.

Kowert, P. *Groupthink or Deadlock: When Do Leaders Learn from Their Advisors?* State University of New York Press, 2002.

Lesko, W. A. ed. *Readings in Social Psychology: General, Classic, and Contemporary Selections*, 8th ed. Pearson, 2011.

Mills, J. H., K. Dye, and Al. J. Mills. *Understanding Organizational Change*. Routledge, 2008.

Myers, D. G. *Social Psychology*, 11th ed. McGraw-Hill Humanities, 2012.

Myers, D. G. *Exploring Social Psychology*, 7th ed. McGraw-Hill Higher Education, 2014.

Prestwich, A., and M. Conner. *Applied Social Psychology.* Wiley-Blackwell, 2014.

Senior, C., and M. Butler. *Social Cognitive Neuroscience of Organizations*. Wiley-Blackwell, 2008.

Smith, E. R., and D. M. Mackie. *Social Psychology*, 3rd ed. Psychology Press, 2007.

50.9 NOTES

1. This chapter is based on original work by M. E. Kabay as a contributed paper at the Sixteenth National Computer Security Conference organized in 1993 by the National Computer Security Center. That work was updated over the years and became a chapter in the fourth edition of this *Handbook.* It was updated for the fifth edition with contributions from colleagues teaching and studying in the MSIA (now MISA) program at the School of Graduate and Continuing Studies at Norwich University. This version includes minor updates and new suggested readings.
2. Few specific references to the scholarly literature of social psychology research are included in this chapter except for quoted materials. For details of the information presented, consult any college-level introduction to social psychology.
3. J. Baron, *Thinking and Deciding*, 4th ed. Cambridge University Press, 2007
4. Government Accountability Office, "Information Security: Emerging Cybersecurity Issues Threaten Federal Information Systems," United States Government Accountability Office Report GAO-05-231 (May 2005); www.gao.gov/new.items/d05231.pdf
5. M. E. Kabay, "The VA Data Insecurity Saga." (2008), www.mekabay.com/infosecmgmt/vasaga.pdf
6. R. D. Austin and C. A. R. Darby, "The Myth of Secure Computing," *Harvard Business Review* (June 2003); http://cb.hbsp.harvard.edu/cb/web/product_detail.seam;?E=71608&R=R0306J-PDF-ENG

7. For an in-depth discussion of the manager's role in IA, see Chapter 63 in this *Handbook*; for a discussion of the role of the chief information security officer, see Chapter 65.
8. N. Tal-Or and Y. Papirman, "The Fundamental Attribution Error in Attributing Fictional Figures' Characteristics to the Actors." Paper presented at the annual meeting of the International Communication Association, Sheraton New York, New York, NY, April 13, 2008; www.allacademic.com/meta/p13476_index.html
9. G. Hofstede, G. J. Hofstede, and M. Minkov, *Cultures and Organizations: Software of the Mind,* 3rd ed., McGraw-Hill, 2010.
10. S. Salahuddin, "Taliban Defend Yellow Badges for Non-Muslim Afghans," Reuters, May 23, 2001; www.afghanistannewscenter.com/news/2001/may/may23c2001.html
11. See Chapter 45 in this *Handbook* for a discussion of such an example.
12. For more ideas on effective security-awareness programs, see Chapter 49.
13. SIIA Resource eStore: www.siia.net/estore/10browse.asp and choose Category=Anti-piracy
14. See FUTURECents, "Management by Walking Around, www.futurecents.com/mainmbwa.htm; and A. Fisher, "Management by Walking Around: 6 Tips to Make it Work," CNNMoney, August 23, 2012, http://management.fortune.cnn.com/2012/08/23/management-by-walking-around-mbwa/
15. See Chapter 66 in this *Handbook* for a discussion of the importance of widespread participation in security-policy development.

CHAPTER 51

SECURITY STANDARDS FOR PRODUCTS

Paul Brusil and Noel Zakin

51.1 INTRODUCTION. Organizations, people, devices, tests, software, and products have defining characteristics. Standards are established for the purpose of providing uniformity of essential characteristics among different instantiations of such entities. Standards thus allow different parties to understand and to compare the defining characteristics of different entities.

There are many types of standards depending on the characteristic being addressed. There are also many different bodies or authorities that develop and issue standards.

A particular goal of standardization in the security arena is to evolve toward an information technology (IT)–driven economy where security products, and secured products, approach plug-and-play status. They should be comparably trusted, be available for purchase from multiple competing vendors, and be able to be mixed, matched, and integrated to provide requisite secure, trusted IT infrastructures that reduce the risks of greatest concern.

In the U.S. Government sector, product security and software quality assurance has been important for years. However, security became of top concern to government agency chief information security officers as a result of the *Federal Information Security Management Act* (FISMA).[1] FISMA applies to the security of systems.

The security of *systems* such as those impacted by FISMA and other industry-specific standards applicable to secure systems is not considered in this chapter. But such standards have certainly increased the attention to security associated with an individual *product*.

Although several different categories of security-relevant standards exist, this chapter provides insights about the field of security standards by considering only a representative sample of the multitude of standards that pertain to product security. Standards associated with developing product trust are especially important in the electronically interwoven world. As such, the primary focus herein is on standards pertaining to product trust.

The chapter begins by providing a general introduction to standards. Section 51.2 addresses why standards are important. Section 51.3 summarizes what types of security-relevant standards exist, what bodies create standards, and what security characteristics, features, or capabilities are addressed in examples of different standards.

Then attention turns to considering examples of some of the many types of standards that apply specifically to enhancing trust in products. Section 51.4 describes several standards-based product development approaches ranging (for example) from consensus-based standards for security specifications and product development processes to formal capability-based standards and ISO secure software development processes. Section 51.4 also summarizes several different product assessment approaches that rely on informal standards ranging from vendor self-declarations to third-party assessments via *de jure* methods.

In Section 51.5 three standards-based approaches for assessing the security of products are described, for products ranging from cryptographic modules and products, to general classes of products, to cloud service offerings.

51.2 IMPORTANCE OF STANDARDS.

The value of standards is considered in Section 51.2.1. The motivation for using standards to establish trust and to manage risks associated with products is discussed in Section 51.2.2. The difficulties of establishing trust in systems consisting of many individual products are briefly examined in Section 51.2.3

51.2.1 Value of Standards.

Many parties benefit from standards pertaining to security: customers, vendors, software developers, testing houses, product reviewers in the media, consultants, and more.

For example, customers find standards helpful in several ways. Standards help specify their needs for various security functionalities and the degrees of assurance they require in the products they buy. Standards help customers understand what security functionality and assurances a product builder claims to provide. Standards help consumers select commercial off-the-shelf products that they can trust will conform to their security and assurance requirements and that, as needed, will interoperate with comparable products. Procurement standards help customers buy appropriately trusted products that meet customer requirements. Customers under the mandates of the security-relevant regulations imposed by federal regulations such as the *Health Insurance Portability and Accountability Act* (HIPAA) and the *Sarbanes-Oxley Act* (SOX) often look to establishing due diligence by leveraging products that have established trust in their security and assurance functionality in a standard way. Standard security certifications of customer staff and hired consultants help customers employ appropriately knowledgeable people to protect customers' facilities and information or to help deal with certain vendors or regulators.

Vendors and service providers find standards helpful in several ways. Use of standards provides evidence that vendors have migrated their product development to a paradigm wherein security is built in from the start. Use of standards provides evidence that security is not some afterthought that is patched or bolted on. Use of implementation-related standards and standard personnel certifications shows that security is the foundation on which a vendor is building a product or a service provider is providing a service. Use of standards helps to open global marketplaces to vendors and service providers. By using standard, third-party verification of security capabilities, vendors are making their products (and service providers are making their services) either stand out from, or be comparable to, their competitors.

51.2.2 Motivation for Establishing Trust and Managing Risk in Products. Trust in the electronic processing, storage, and interactions among customers, businesses, business partners, suppliers, service organizations, and governments is key to electronic economy, electronic healthcare, and electronic government models. The need for trust will only increase as new IT paradigms and technologies proliferate, mutate business and IT support models, and introduce new risks and vulnerabilities. For electronic service models to succeed, all e-business, e-health, and e-government players need confidence in the IT products used by interacting players as well as products used in the intervening IT infrastructure.

Another key notion besides trust is the notion of risk management. When electronic relationships are established between parties, there are quantifiable risks associated with such relationships.

Risks are quantifiable in many ways. For example, they can be quantified in terms of the types of possible adverse events. They can be quantified in terms of the likelihood of different types of adverse events and by the value of what is to be protected by IT security solutions during an adverse event. They can be quantified in terms of the consequences of adverse events, such as the liability that may be exposed via compromises, or the entities that may be hurt by compromises.

Risks then can be mitigated in a number of possible ways. For example, risks can be mitigated by using products that reduce the occurrence or impacts of the adverse events of most concern. When assets of increasing value need to be protected, risks can be reduced by using products that have increased assurance. Risks also can be mitigated by using products that decrease the specific, deleterious liabilities and undesired consequences of greatest concern. Being able to specify the risks of concern and to identify security solutions that mitigate those risks is a powerful strategy used within certain standards-based approaches such as the *Common Criteria* (CC) paradigm.

Linking notions of trust together with notions of risk reduction makes for a powerful strategy. Establishing trust among interacting electronic parties that all parties are using products with appropriate security quality is akin to the role of face-to-face handshakes in older business models. In the e-business marketplace, trust, like the old handshake, is key to increased revenues via increased business transaction volumes. Furthermore, by mitigating risks, business losses and costs can be reduced. When trust enhancement is coupled with risk management, the resulting increased revenues, combined with decreased losses and lower costs, make for significant profit multiplication.

The CC paradigm is an example of a standards-based product assessment strategy that provides for both establishing appropriate levels of trust in products and for specifying, managing, and mitigating risks of most concern.

Various standard-based ways have been developed and used over the years to build confidence about the quality of security implementations. The focus of such efforts includes establishing trust via one or both of two perspectives: (1) that a product performs its claimed security functionality completely and correctly and (2) that the product builder's processes (from design, to development, to delivery, to maintenance) are sound. Typically, trust is established either by testing in a standard way just the implementation or by evaluating in a standard way both the product and its implementer.

Not all approaches to establishing trust via product assessment necessarily address trust via formal standards–based assessment of implemented security functionality as well as the assurance of the soundness of the builder's abilities and processes. That is, many of the testing and evaluation approaches are based on informal, de facto or de jure standards[2]—not on formal, nationally recognized standards.

51.2.3 Motivation for Establishing Trust in Systems.

Recent U.S. Government administrations have recognized the importance of establishing trust in IT. They have issued directives and guidance to elevate awareness of the central, critical nature of IT and to help to preserve trust in national IT infrastructures.

National IT infrastructures are typically large IT systems often composed of many individual products. Standards-based methods for establishing trust in products do not necessarily work for establishing trust in systems. Standards-based methods of establishing trust in IT systems exist. They include, for example, standards and testing activities associated with the original U.S. *Department of Defense* (DoD) *Information Technology Security Certification and Accreditation Process* (DITSCAP)[3] and the *Department of Defense Information Assurance Certification and Accreditation Process* (DIACAP)[4] which replaced it, the U.S Government's FISMA, and the financial community's *Payment Card Industry Data Security Standard* (PCI DSS).[5]

Such systems-focused, trust-development methods tend to be employed only by large enterprises. Furthermore, the problem of establishing a quantitative measure of trust in a very large, heterogeneous system like a national IT infrastructure is evolving. At a minimum, it requires coordination and cooperation among all who contribute to or use the infrastructure. Security requirements and security testing approaches applicable to IT systems, per se, are not considered herein.

Although still argued among security professionals, many believe a step in the right direction is to build IT systems with products and components that are individually assessed to be trustworthy, with some specified degree of confidence. What is most difficult, however, in a product assessment is to test the product's security aspects in an environment that perfectly mimics the environment in which the product is to be used.

51.3 TYPES, SOURCES, AND EXAMPLES OF STANDARDS.

In today's heterogeneous, multidisciplinary, multitechnology, multiparty, interconnected IT environments, different types of security standards are essential for a variety of reasons. Several formal, informal, and ad hoc bodies develop and issue standards. The significance and acceptance of any given standard tends to depend on the notoriety of the body that creates the standard. A high-level taxonomy for what types of security standards exist appears in Section 51.3.1. The various types of bodies involved with security standardization efforts are listed in Section 51.3.2. Examples of the standards developed and issued by various bodies are presented in Section 51.3.3

51.3.1 Types of Standards. In the security world, there are a many different types of standards. The types of standards pertinent to security include, for example, the following:

- Capability standards
- Personnel certifications
- Risk assessment criteria
- Requirements specifications
- Functional specifications
- Assurance specifications
- Performance criteria
- Product development standards
- Testing, evaluation, and assessment standards/criteria[6]
- Product review criteria
- Interoperability standards
- Procurement standards
- Ancillary standards

51.3.2 Sources of Standards. Some of the bodies that issue formal nation-recognized standards, organizational standards, or proprietary standards, or that use de jure approaches pertinent to security, include the following:

- Recognized national bodies
- International organizations
- Governments
- Military
- Consortia
- Like-minded communities
- Vendors
- Consulting houses
- Trade press
- Commercial testing houses
- Private testing contractors

Formal standards relevant to information assurance (IA) are created, published, and maintained by recognized standards bodies. There are various recognized standards bodies including technology-specific working groups associated with professional organizations like the IEEE (Institute of Electrical and Electronics Engineers) and the IETF (Internet Engineering Task Force). Standards are also created by working groups associated with recognized, country-specific, national standards bodies, such as the ASC (American Standards Committee, formerly ANSI) in the United States, the BSI (British Standards Institute) in the United Kingdom, and the *Bundesamt für Sicherheit in der Informationstechnik* (also BSI) in Germany. Such national standards bodies create either country-specific standards or they collaborate and harmonize with other peer national standards bodies to create international, globally applicable standards, such as those associated with International Organization for Standardization (ISO).[7]

Recognized organizations within national governments also create standards. For example, the National Institute of Standards and Technology (NIST)—a U.S. federal agency under the U.S. Department of Commerce—creates and issues standards called *Federal Information Processing Standards* (FIPS). It also issues standards called SPs (*Special Publications*) that delineate security, privacy, and assurance best practices guidance. FIPS and SPs often apply not only to the U.S. Government but are widely used as references in other nongovernmental organizations and may even apply formally to some. For example, a 2005 amendment to the *Federal Acquisition Regulation* to implement the IT security provisions of FISMA requires all federal procurements to adhere to pertinent NIST standards and publications.

National governments also form bodies to collaborate and to harmonize international standards for use by governments within several nations. The CC Project is an example of such a cross-government standardization body. Standards developed by this particular cross-government standards body are also fed to recognized international standards bodies such as the ISO to create even broader-reaching standards.

In the military area, the U.S. DoD publishes military standard directives such as *Mil Standard 8500*,[8,9] that must be followed when procuring security-related products, as well as *Department of Defense Directive 8570*[10] that pertains to training, certification, and management of employees performing IA functions.

Technology-specific and industry-specific consortia have large, broad-based, international membership; examples include

- Cloud Security Alliance (CSA)[11]
- Security Standards Council (SSC)[12] of the Payment Card Industry (PCI) consortium
- Software Assurance Forum for Excellence in Code (SAFECode)[13]
- Object Management Group (OMG)[14]
- Web Application Security Consortium (WASC)[15]
- TM (formerly TeleManagement) Forum[16]

Often they are considered to be creators of informal, security-relevant standards for use within specific industries or technology sectors. Small consortia or individual entities also claim to create standards, but such efforts are generally not accepted by as broad constituencies as are the legitimate, recognized, formal, and informal standards.

Other like-minded communities like the *SANS* (formerly *System Administration and Network Security*) *Institute*[17] promulgate de facto best-practices security standards, such as the *20 Critical Controls*,[18] claimed to reflect community consensus within a certain community of security practitioners.

Vendors such as Microsoft develop standard-like documents such as the *PCI DSS Compliance Planning Guide*[19] or the *Secure Development Lifecycle*[20] framework and strategy for secure coding that they presumably hope will be adopted by large communities.

Consulting houses such as Gartner, Forrester, and Frost & Sullivan develop private product review criteria pertaining to security and security features. They use such criteria to evaluate security-relevant products. Gartner and others also produce product reviews based on user interviews.

The trade press includes media outlets such as *Computerworld, CSO, IT Business Edge, Network World, SC Magazine*, and *Security Management* that create yet other private product review criteria that they use to examine security-relevant products.

Commercial testing houses such as *ICSA Labs, NSS Labs*, and *West Coast Labs* create and use private, independent, product-testing criteria and methodologies to evaluate product security and performance. Some of the commercial testing houses, such as AV-Test, develop private, independent, product-testing criteria and methods to certify tested products.

Private contractors conduct product security testing via a variety of informally standard techniques that rely on private criteria and test procedures. Such techniques include vulnerability scanning, vulnerability assessment, penetration testing, security auditing, ISO 27001 auditing, security reviews, ethical hacking, and more. Academic organizations are also beginning to establish security product-evaluation laboratories that rely on various published vulnerability and assurance test procedures and criteria.

51.3.3 Examples of Security Standards. Examples of the types of security-relevant standards issued by examples of the different standards issuing bodies are provided in this section below. Detailed summaries of a number of these standards are provided later in this chapter.

Capability standards such as the Capability Maturity Model (CMM) and ISO 9000 exist to measure the competency of organizations that build products—in particular, security-related products.

General personnel certifications such as the Certified Information Systems Security Professional (CISSP) from the International Information Systems Security Certification Consortium ($(ISC)^2$) measure, among other things, the competency of staff specifying, building, procuring, installing, or maintaining security-related products. Other certifications like the IEEE Computer Society's Certified Software Development Associate (or Professional) or the $(ISC)^2$ Certified Secure Software Lifecycle Professional (CSSLP) or the Electronic Commerce Council Certified Secure Programmer are examples of certifications more directly useful in certain product software development areas involving security. The Cloud Security Alliance's Certificate of Cloud Security Knowledge assesses an individual's competency in major matters related to cloud security.

Standards exist to provide consistent ways to stipulate security needs and requirements in both security products and secured products. Some standards specify the security functionality appearing within products. Standards like IETF's IPSec not only specify security functionality, but they also foster interoperability of separately built security implementations. Other standards specify security-related software interfaces, naming conventions, and data structures such as for Common Object Request Broker Architecture (CORBA) middleware products.

Standards like FIPS 140 can specify security requirements, evaluation methods, and validation concepts for a single specific type of security-relevant component or product. The CC series of standards can specify the security functionality and security assurance characteristics to be incorporated into any class of products.

De jure standards like SANS 20 Critical Controls, which compete with certain national and international standards, specify a single, small, essential core of security functionality. This de jure, consensus-based standard may be growing in popularity.

Product development standards like ISO/IEC 27034-1 specify requirements for secure software development processes while the Building Security in Maturity Model (BSIMM) de facto industry standard provides an ability to compare secure coding environments and to identify best development practices.

Vendor standards like Microsoft's Security Development Lifecycle also specify software development and assurance processes to increase reliability of software security.

Standards also exist to govern the testing of products. It is essential that vendors and buyers of security and security-enhanced products (a) verify that a product under test implements functionality that addresses the stipulated security functional requirements desired, and (b) demonstrate how well the product and the vendor's product development processes meet stipulated requirements. There are national and international standards such as FIPS 140 and the CC that stipulate such conformance testing and that stipulate testing methods to accomplish such testing. The FedRAMP standard approach applies to validation of the security capabilities associated with a specific class of service providers.

Conformance of different security-relevant products to the same functional standard, however, does not necessarily ensure that these products will interoperate. Interoperability of separately manufactured security solutions is possible if implementation standards can specify precise, interoperable profiles of selected security capabilities from within a security functional standard. Interoperability testing can assure secure interoperation between comparable products built by autonomous vendors and used between autonomous parties. Conformance implies only that interoperability is possible; but interoperability needs to be verified by pair-wise testing. Standards exist to specify how to examine conformance of implementations to functional standards and how to assure the interoperability of implementations that must meet the same functional standard.

Interoperating, conformant, secured products and security products cannot necessarily be trusted to provide or to support sound security, or to mitigate the risks of greatest concern. Key to developing trust is to build confidence that products mitigate the risks of concern, that products are properly built and behave according to specification, and that products do no more or no less than advertised. Standards like the CC exist for establishing and testing the degree to which risks and vulnerabilities are mitigated to a specified level of confidence. These standards specify implementation assurance requirements and associated tests and testing methods to verify the quality of implemented security within the products under test.

Regarding private, de jure standards, different trade press media and others develop private product review criteria and methodologies. These private standards are used to create reviews of specific security or security-enhanced products, or to develop buyer's guides that compare the individual product reviews of several products within a class of products. Certain metrics created by such criteria can provide measures of security performance.

Some media outlets operate awards programs that use question-driven surveys for identifying readers' choice picks of best products within certain classes of products. Popularity-based product leadership awards also exist.

In the area of procurement standards, standards like DoD's *8500.1* and *8500.2* stipulate standard policy and policy implementation directives, respectively, for what types of products DoD must procure. These standards also specify what must be done by DoD entities to meet a need or what constraints DoD organizations must follow when procuring IT products.

In the area of ancillary standards, standards such as companion standards within the suite of CC standards specify how to become a product tester and how to accredit organizations to conduct conformance, trust, or interoperability testing in a standard way.

Other ancillary standards—not considered in this chapter—like the DITSCAP[21] (replaced by DIACAP in November 2007) for U.S. DoD, the National Information Assurance Certification and Accreditation Process (NIACAP),[22] and the NIST Certification & Accreditation (C&A)[23] methodologies for U.S. federal civilian departments and agencies specify how to certify and how to accredit systems composed of secure products and secure components. Standards like ISO 17799[24] and NIST SP 800-53[25] can specify guidelines or best practices for users assembling and using secure components.

In aggregate, standards promote consistent security, end-to-end as well as across different public and private domains and computing environments.

51.4 PRODUCT DEVELOPMENT AND ASSESSMENT APPROACHES.

This chapter focuses on standards for enhancing trust in security-related products. There are two classes of products of interest: "security" products and "security-enabled" products. Security products directly provide security services or prevent penetrations. Security products include, for example, intrusion detection products and firewalls. Security-enabled products are secured products that do not exist solely to provide security services; instead they provide other services that are protected. Examples include operating systems, database management systems, and virtual private networking gear that incorporate security functionality such as identification and authentication or IPSec to protect either the product or the services provided by the product.

The remainder of this chapter summarizes various approaches that support increasing trust in such products. The historical approaches for establishing trust in certain classes of products are summarized in Section 51.4.1. A sampling of community-based consensus standards that specify security controls are described in Section 51.4.2. The chapter then summarizes numerous other current approaches for developing product trust, including standard product development approaches used during the design and building of products (Section 51.4.3), informal product assessment criteria and approaches (Section 51.4.4), and formal, internationally recognized, standard product assessment criteria and approaches (Sections 51.4.5 and 51.5).

The U.S. Government had hoped that all public sector and private-sector consumers, vendors, and testers of security-related products would rally around the formal, internationally recognized standards that pertain to specification, development, and testing and evaluation of such products. With formal standards being produced by national and international standards bodies, it was anticipated that consumers could understand with greater certainty the security and assurance features offered by a product or a service provider. It was hoped that the confidence obtained by using universal, internationally accepted standards would contrast sharply with nonstandard approaches that, because of their sheer numbers of competing approaches, would confront and befuddle consumers.

In today's actuality, the government and military sectors frequently rely on the formal standards-based approaches. But, in contrast—despite the expectations associated with such formal standards-based approaches—the entire marketplace has not necessarily coalesced around the formal standards approach.

Many informal private product assessment alternatives that do not rely on formal standards came into being and are being used with greater or less frequency than the alternatives based on formal standards. There is no shortage of alternative approaches and alternative frameworks on which such approaches are based. Correspondingly, there is no shortage in approaches stipulated in user procurement directives. The marketplace is fractured among many alternatives. A sampling of these alternatives is examined below.

51.4.1 Historical, Sunsetted Approaches. To introduce consistency in describing the security features and levels of trust of a limited set of security-enhanced products, and to facilitate comprehensive testing and evaluation of such products, the U.S. DoD developed the *Trusted Computer System Evaluation Criteria* (TCSEC).[26] The TCSEC—often called the *Orange Book*—defined a small set of classes (C1 to A1) of increasing security functionality and increasing assurance applying to operating systems. The TCSEC was extended to networking devices[27] and database management systems.[28] Government in-house evaluations were offered first, followed by comparable government-sponsored commercial evaluation services.

Partly because of large testing delays and costs, other countries developed other criteria that were more flexible and adaptable to accommodate rapidly evolving IT. The *Information Technology Security Evaluation Criteria*[29] (ITSEC) arose from the combined inputs of earlier German criteria, French criteria, and U.K. confidence levels. The *Canadian Trusted Computer Product Evaluation Criteria* (CTCPEC) were then developed as a combination of the TCSEC and ITSEC approaches. The U.S. Federal Criteria development then attempted to combine the CTCPEC and ITSEC with the TCSEC.

With growth of the international market for trusted IT products, all these historical, competing, national criteria had the potential to fracture the marketplace. They were sunsetted after efforts were completed to harmonize the various criteria into common, standards-based, internationally accepted criteria.

The result of the harmonization effort was a single, wide-ranging CC program (Section 51.5.3). These standard criteria provide a fully flexible, highly tailorable approach to the standardization of security functionality, evaluation assurance requirements, specification, and testing of implementations of security-related products.

51.4.2 Consensus Security Specification Approaches

51.4.2.1 SANS Institute. The SANS Institute has issued a de jure standard[30] that specifies what is believed to be the core set of the most critical, baseline security controls deemed essential for virtually any organization. These security controls are colloquially called the *20 Critical Controls*. They provide a feasible, implementable, best-practice, security approach based on providing what is purported to be the greatest risk-reduction, the best protection against actual, in-the-field threats, and the best techniques to stop the most dangerous, common, regularly occurring attacks. The SANS approach provides for continuous, automated monitoring of key portions of an organization's IT infrastructure to ensure security effectiveness.

SANS has published a guideline of the steps for how to implement these critical controls.[31] The guideline provides a tabulation of many real attacks and provides a mapping that identifies which of the 20 Critical Controls provide the best defenses against each of these attacks.

The SANS Critical Controls map to a certain subset of the security controls specified in NIST Special Publication 800-53, Revision 3 (see Appendix A of the SANS Critical Controls guidelines). In some sense, the SANS critical controls may be considered as a specific profile of the most essential security controls in NIST SP 800-53. Some security professionals feel the SANS 20 Critical Controls will provide the necessary (but not necessarily sufficient) due diligence to become the de facto yardstick for measuring the standard of care for security.

51.4.2.2 *Cloud Security Alliance (CSA).* The CSA has developed a guideline explaining cloud computing and identifying the best risk-based practices for transitioning to secure cloud operations provided by different cloud service models in cloud computing environments. Partitioning of security responsibilities between cloud customers and cloud service providers depends on the cloud service being offered, for example, cloud Software as a Service (SaaS), cloud Infrastructure as a Service (IaaS), cloud Platform as a Service (PaaS). The stipulated security controls and technologies apply to (a) protecting data migrating to clouds, (b) protecting data in transit to the cloud and in transit between different cloud providers/cloud environments, (c) protecting data within clouds, (d) privacy preservation, (e) application security, (f) data loss prevention, and more. The version 3 edition of this guideline is available at the time of this writing (July 2013).[32]

51.4.3 Standard Product Development Approaches. A key that can lead to a productive product assessment is for product builders to rely on high-quality, highly capable product developers and to use product development standards, such as software design and testing standards, during product design and creation. Such product developer capability standards that can apply to builders of security products include the Capability Maturity Model (Section 51.4.3.1) and the ISO 9000 series of standards (Section 51.4.3.2). Standards and approaches used during product development to enhance the quality and inherent security offered by products are examined in Section 51.4.3.3.

51.4.3.1 *Capability Maturity Model.* The Systems Security Engineering Capability Maturity Model (SSE-CMM) has been standardized as ISO/IEC 21827. This standard provides a way to assess the soundness of a security product builder's engineering practices, as well as a way for continuously improving such practices up a hierarchy of increasingly mature software process levels, during the many stages of product development, such as during:

- Product requirements capture and analysis
- Product concept definition, including accurate translation of security requirements into product requirements
- Product architecting
- Product design
- Product implementation

A security product developer can demonstrate competence in building products by means of recognized, so-called capability maturity assessments of the developer's software and security engineering processes. Security-enhanced products built by organizations with demonstrated expertise and maturity can merit greater trust than products built by organizations that do not demonstrate mature, competent, software design, and security engineering capabilities.

The SSE-CMM establishes a framework of generally accepted security engineering principles and a standard way of measuring (and improving) the effectiveness of an organization's security engineering practices. The SSE-CMM describes the essential characteristics of, and provides tools for, assessing an organization's security engineering process that must exist to ensure good security engineering. These characteristics are graded by a set of security metrics that assess specific attributes about a vendor's processes, and the security effectiveness of the results of vendor's processes.

When the level of the SSE-CMM security metrics associated with a specific builder shows the builder to have mature security engineering capabilities and effective security engineering practices, then confidence is increased that the builder can build sound security products.

Trust in, and assurance about, a product can be inferred, to some degree, for measurably competent vendors that use sound security engineering processes as assessed by the SSE-CMM. The quantitative comparability of assurance developed via the SSE-CMM approach to the assurance developed via other approaches such as evaluation of assurance requirements stipulated from the CC paradigm is not well understood. For now, it appears possible to assess the assurance of a vendor's capability to build quality products by both the SSE-CMM and CC approaches; but, perhaps both approaches should be integrated to form a more comprehensive assurance assessment model.

51.4.3.2 *ISO 9000 Standards.* The ISO 9000 standard[33] is used as a guide to conduct a broad, high-level, horizontal assessment of the quality of systems and of the competence of an organization (typically a manufacturing or service organization) across all its facets. Although not specific to organizations that build security products, it does provide some amount of basic information about the potential for quality and repeatability in an organization's ability to meet its mission. In fact, derivative standards such as in the CC, in part inspired by ISO 9000, are used to accredit the quality associated with security testing laboratories.

The ISO 9001 standard has applicability to software development. Although not specific to organizations that build security products, it nevertheless specifies in general an acceptable, minimum quality level for software processes.

51.4.3.3 *Product Development Standards and Approaches.* There is great need to focus on secure software development as new products are brought to market. The current situation for secure software development is not stellar. Annually, about 5,000 new software vulnerabilities—many exploitable by real-world threats and attacks—are discovered per year. Unfortunately, software sabotage also incorporates intentional, sinister flaws. Studies indicate that up to 99 percent of coded applications contain vulnerabilities. Industrial control, so-called supervisory control and data acquisition (SCADA) software, is equally vulnerable. Indeed, while slightly better than these statics for general applications, even software within security appliances is not immune to software development flaws and is not—as many customers might believe—inherently secure.[34]

To overcome threats to software, security software scientists are trying to move secure software development practices from an art to a science based on standards. Common mitigation strategies include establishing appropriate and rather specific policies and procedures (that should include coding examples) to govern secure software development. Specific tactics include, for example, reliance on commonly available, standard, checks-and-balances–oriented technologies such as

- Code signing by developers,
- Code check-in audit monitors and audit trails,
- Multiparty mutually monitoring code reviews,
- Automated code and vulnerability scanning with acceptable false-positive/negative detection rates,
- Live attack scanning, and
- Use of antitampering technology for code integrity checking.

Guidelines for secure software development exist.[35,36] Commercial development testing tools such as static and dynamic code analyzers can also be used to find defects and vulnerabilities in code being developed.

The key to secure software development efforts[37] is to establish standard corporate culture and appropriate policies that:

- Put software security developers at the table when software project requirements are established,
- Incorporate security into software by design,
- Incorporate only vulnerability-scanned, third-party software components[38] and use dynamically linked libraries so that the newest, less vulnerable, updated software components automatically replace older, outdated, more vulnerable software,
- Foster collaborative mutually cross-checking software development,
- Incorporate better testing early in, and throughout, the software development life cycle so as to manage security and quality defects as the code is being written, and
- Establish formal processes for upstream feedback aimed at eliminating root causes of software vulnerabilities, defects, and flaws.

Such actions increase code quality before code is released for manufacturing. Higher quality code tends to have fewer security vulnerabilities, smaller attack surfaces, and fewer holes that need to be plugged after software reaches production status. If internal testing resources are limited, secure software testing services can be outsourced to external firms such as Coverity that provides a Development Testing Platform or the NCC Group that provides direct testing services.

Going even further than just focusing on software development science, many are looking toward more formal product development standards that provide repeatable, proactive, product development and testing processes. Certain vendors such as Microsoft (in 2002), via its *Trustworthy Computing Initiative*, and Adobe (in 2009) initiated leading-edge, standard, internal initiatives to incorporate security into their software designs prior to mass production and sales of their software. Microsoft's *Security Development Lifecycle*[39] (SDL) specifies processes for developing secure software.

More recently, the 2011 international standard *ISO/IEC 27034-1* specifies requirements for, and describes processes and practices for, secure software development. Several large software companies are starting to use this standard to start comprehensive programs for necessarily incorporating security into their products right from the start of the software design stage. This standard is valuable to both buyers and builders of security-related products. Software builders display due diligence in using the standard to create quality, secure code. Buyers understand that compliant software builders are committed to secure development processes.

The *Software Assurance Forum for Excellence in Code* (SAFECode) consortium's training material allows product developers to stay current with the best practices, principles, and methods in secure software engineering and development. Other organizations such as the *Association for Software Testing* are also trying to build a developer community knowledgeable in software development and testing sciences.

The *Building Security in Maturity Model* (BSIMM) program provides an ability for enterprises—as a combined community—to survey its members to discern a common core of secure software development best practices. The BSIMM has created a de facto secure software development standard by comparing the real-life secure coding environments and practices of its membership to identify best secure software development practices. The model is free under a Creative Commons license.

51.4.3.4 Problems in Development Practices. A disappointing observation related to secure development practices is that a 2013 survey[40] indicated that only about a third of product developers are focused on building security into their software; nearly two-thirds are not necessarily focused on security and do not consider using application attack mitigation standard technologies like Data Execution Prevention (DEP) and Address Space Layout Randomization (ASLR). The situation has the potential to worsen as

- New so-called agile software development and testing methodologies emerge,
- Demands for more complex, cloud-based or mobile software rise—often with greater vulnerability densities, and
- Fielded software is upgraded—often by a patchwork of code created by different software developers with differing skills, with differing knowledge of the software being upgraded, and at differing points in times.

Consumers seem to want products with more features; and vendors seem to have little incentives or liability exposures to invest much time or resources into building solid products.

51.4.4 Informal Product Assessment Approaches. A variety of product assessment approaches are not dependent on formal, standard, internationally recognized, security testing and evaluation approaches. Indeed, most have not reached the status of even a de facto standard, but they are considered, nonetheless, for completeness purposes. Such approaches include:

- Vendor self-declarations (Section 51.4.4.1)
- Consumer assessments (Section 51.4.4.2)
- Consortium-based assessments (Section 51.4.4.3)
- Implicit assessments via open-source code development (Section 51.4.4.4)
- Implicit assessments via hacking (Section 51.4.4.5)
- Assessments by magazines and trade press publications (Section 51.4.4.6)
- Third-party commercial assessments using de jure methods (Section 51.4.4.7)

There are shortcomings to most of these approaches. Some are not considered to offer much value. One of the basic shortcomings is that lack of reliance on formal standards makes for difficulty in comparing the product assessment results:

- Of different products,
- For products tested and evaluated via different approaches, and
- For products tested and evaluated by different testing facilities that all purportedly use the same product assessment approach.

51.4.4.1 *Vendor Self-Declarations.* An approach to establishing trust is based on the notion of vendor self-declarations. A vendor can unilaterally claim that a specific product meets the security needs of a class of customers and that an appropriate amount of customer-desired confidence can be placed in the product's implemented security features. In part, the confidence associated with this approach is implicitly tied to the past reputation of a vendor or to the customer's past experience in dealing with the vendor. If the vendor's reputation or customer's experiences are good, there is some sense that the vendor may have again done an adequate job of implementing security. This approach, however, lacks measurable ways of quantifying the degree of trust that can be associated with a product. It also lacks measurable ways of comparing the relative degrees of trust that can be associated with different products.

An example of such a self-declaration was recently created by the consulting division of a large computer company.[41] In this example, the vendor stipulated what were identified as the most important criteria in selecting a Managed Security Services Provider (MSSP) and revealed why the vendor's services are the best in the marketplace.

This self-declaration approach may have some merit in establishing a sense of continuing confidence in products that have been updated since an earlier version of the product that has undergone rigorous, standards-based security testing and evaluation. If a vendor is known to have good security engineering capabilities—such as can be assessed, in part, by standard Capability Maturity Model approaches (see Section 51.4.2.1)—and if the vendor can provide reasonable evidence as to the nature of the upgrade or revision since the product version that underwent rigorous assessment, then there can be some qualitative (albeit, quantitatively unknown) degree of confidence about the upgraded or revised product. Under these conditions, customers who have innate trust in the vendor can believe that the quality of the changed product is similar to the quality of the version of the product that was formally assessed.

51.4.4.2 *Consumer Assessments.* It has been reported that less than 20 percent of software consumers are assessing the security attendant with the application software they buy. Product consumers can, however, develop the requisite substantial technical expertise in-house to test and to evaluate specific security-enhanced products directly.

Vendor standard tools are available to help consumers in specific security technology areas. For example, a GFI Software division has developed an *Antivirus Evaluation Guide* that stipulates a repeatable, readily deployable, testing criteria for customers to evaluate vendor antivirus products.[42] For another example, Ixia has developed an attack simulator that a user of security products can run in a safe environment to emulate a range of attack or configuration scenarios so as to evaluate how well the security products in question detect and block certain attacks.[43] For example, attacks by zombie botnets as well as the full life cycle of DDoS attack scenarios can be simulated.

Alternatively, because of lack of in-house expertise or available staff, consumers may hire a consultant to perform limited security assessments via techniques such as penetration testing or source code analysis or binary analysis when source code is not available. Consumers with more resources may contract a private third-party evaluator, such as a commercial security testing provider (such as Veracode, see Section 51.4.4.7.3) or one of the big consulting houses or systems integrators, to do third-party security testing and evaluation. Many of the third-party approaches are private and tend to be unique.

Some financial institutions have used the in-house assessment approach. Financial institutions as a whole are very careful to make sure that products they use are trustworthy. The security, integrity, and soundness of all products and systems supporting financial institutions must be consistent and verifiable. These institutions fear that any breach of IT security anywhere within their systems will result in a loss of confidence in the entire institution, not just in the specific, subverted IT product.

Many financial institutions developed their own internal standard security specifications and evaluation processes as well as an evaluation methodology to quantify, to compare, to approve, and to certify general security aspects of competing products. One of the consequences of this approach to the customer community at large is that it requires substantial, costly duplication of testing infrastructure across the financial industry as well as the costly duplication of testing support efforts by vendors for those products that are candidates for purchase by multiple customers. With each financial entity funding the establishment of its own testing program, the aggregate testing expenses are raised across all entities within the financial industry.

Furthermore, as the volume of financial devices, such as credit card platforms, operating systems, and thousands of applications, continues to increase dramatically, in-house resources are finding it difficult to keep up. Product customers find this kind of do-it-yourself, in-house testing approach to be a tremendous undertaking in terms of development, implementation, legitimacy demonstration, maintenance, and rejustification. They have found it to be expensive, time consuming, resource intensive, hard to maintain, always open to interpretation and to debate, and always in need of justification to regulators and principals in new markets.

51.4.4.3 Consortium-Based Assessment Approaches. Many consortium-directed approaches exist, or have existed, to demonstrate product interoperability, or conformance of a product to stated security features or to specific security technology standards.

In the Internet world, the notion of implementation bake-offs among trial (preproduct) implementations of emerging IETF standards has been a mainstay in the community for quite some time. For example, the IETF initiated a series of *IPSec VPN Interoperability Workshops* upon culmination of the *Internet Key Exchange Version 2* (IKEv2) standard. Vendors of IKEv2-based preproducts gathered in a common testing facility to test the functionality and interoperability of their preproducts against those of their competitors. Initial test scenarios focused on basic functionality and secure tunnel maintenance.

Other consortia use either their own or standard testing approaches. Examples of assessment efforts of an example set of consortia are summarized below. The consortia herein include the *VPN Consortium* (Section 51.4.4.3.1), the *Cloud Security Alliance* (Section 51.4.4.3.2), and the *Smart Card Security Users Group* (Section 51.4.4.3.3).

51.4.4.3.1 Virtual Private Network Consortium. The *Virtual Private Network (VPN) Consortium* developed an approach for demonstrating conformance of a product to a specific security standard.[44] The VPN Consortium conducts testing of the IPSec and Secure Sockets Layer (SSL) implementations built by its consortium members.

In the early 2000s, the consortium provided three specific profiles of conformance tests of VPN products implementing the IETF's IPSec standard. For each type of test profile, predefined tasks had to be performed successfully against two different reference test gateways. Due to the nonexhaustive set of tests, passing a VPN Consortium conformance test provided only indications that tested products conform, in limited part, to various standard parts of the IPSec standard. Such tests also provided indications that interoperability may be possible with other products that pass the same tests under the same environmental situations.

The consortium has since focused on interoperability testing. It conducts several classes of IPSec interoperability tests: Basic Interoperability, AES Interoperability, IKEv2 Basic Interoperability, IPv6 Interoperability and Authentication with Certificates Interoperability. The types of capabilities being tested, and the profiles by which tested systems are set up for each class of interoperability testing, are specified. The tests help assure VPN users that IPSec systems configured according to the specified profile are generally interoperable with other IPSec systems also configured according to the same profile.

The consortium also provides interoperability testing for profiles of a variety of SSL VPN features in SSL implementations.

The consortium issues logos for member company products that interoperate with at least 75 percent of the other products in an interoperability test. A list of member companies that offer products that pass any of the specific interoperability tests is maintained.[45]

51.4.4.3.2 Cloud Security Alliance. The CSA has established a publically available Security, Trust & Assurance Registry.[46] Any cloud provider can post self-assessments that document the cloud provider's security practices and their compliance to CSA best practices. Cloud providers' self-assessments are documented either (a) according to a CSA standard Cloud Assessment Initiative Questionnaire, or (c) via a CSA Cloud Controls Matrix that details a cloud provider's security concepts and principles in accordance with the CSA's security guidelines (as described in Section 51.4.2.2).

51.4.4.3.3 Smart Card Security Users Group. Although proprietary, in-house approaches were originally used by individual financial institutions to assess thousands of financial IT products, components, and systems, the financial community banded together as a whole in the *Smart Card Security Users Group.* Through this group, financial institutions can use a single standard—the CC—for product assessments and avoid duplication of their individual product assessment efforts. Benefits of such an alliance included:

- Financial institutions can replace their internal, custom product assessment approaches with a common, universally accepted approach.
- They can pool their resources to address common security testing and evaluation needs by using standards-based, CC security specification and testing schemes recognized across all major financial players.
- They can develop profiles of security requirements for the various common elements of smart cards (e.g., chips, operating systems, applications, crypto engines).

- They can develop common test suites to unify the current hodgepodge of fragmented customer-specific and vendor-specific testing of smart cards.
- They can outsource security testing and evaluation to competent, accredited testing laboratories whose expertise can be used by all financial institutions.

The alliance produced a CC profile—a so-called *Smart Card Protection Profile*—of standard security functional requirements and assurance requirements to be addressed by smart cards used in conjunction with sensitive applications such as those encountered in banking industry payment systems. This standard requirements profile was validated and certified by the *Canadian CC Scheme*, and can be used across the financial community.[47] Since then a *UK smart card Protection Profile* for dual-interface authentication cards was developed for uses such as passports.[48]

Consumers can reference such profiles to state their requirements. Vendors can reference such profiles to indicate what they built. Accredited testing laboratories use standard methods to test individual products once for the entire consumer community (not once per consumer institution). The standard tests assess a vendor's claim that its product meets the standard requirements profile. With known confidence, a consumer can then purchase any assessed product that has been independently certified to comply with a specific Protection Profile.

51.4.4.4 Open Source Approach. One approach for software development is use of the Open Source model. According to this approach, software is made publicly available for inspection, for modification of flaws and inefficiencies, and for potential upgrading of capabilities and features. In theory, by the continuous and collective—but uncoordinated and seemingly semirandom—efforts of potentially thousands of autonomous software developers and testers, the public review will improve the quality of the software over time.

The downside of the open source approach is that the degree of trustworthiness achieved by the process is unmeasurable. In certain cases it has been observed that remediation of security flaws is pursued aggressively by major software contributors (especially those that have products that depend on the open source software being remediated); whereas, other software contributors are more inclined to expand open source software functionality rather than fixing discovered security flaws.[49]

To help identify security issues in open source code, the U.S. Department of Homeland Security initiated the *Vulnerability Discovery and Remediation Open Source Hardening Project*. In this project, new approaches for finding critical defects in complex software code sets were developed and used to test open source code to isolate defects and root causes.

In a more recent similar effort,[50] the *Eliminate Vulnerable Code* (eVc) Project[51] uses Internet crawler tools, as well as volunteer identification and/or submissions of bad code, to discover examples of, or citations to, vulnerable open source code. Such discoveries are added to a list shared with eVc members and with developers of the discovered flawed software. The eVc Project hopes that eVc members, sponsors, academia, and more might work with the developers of the discovered flawed software to remediate or to remove the flawed, vulnerable software. By eliminating faulty open source code, it will be easier for other open source projects to reuse higher-quality code that does not contain security flaws such as those identified in the *Open Web Application Security Project* (OWASP) *Top 10* flaws list for Web application security flaws[52] or in the SANS *Top 25* flaws list.[53]

However, the trustworthiness of a product is more than just improved code. Although the open source code will have some degree of trustworthiness developed by the open source process, the incorporation of such code into a product still leads to other factors that influence trustworthiness in the product. Product trustworthiness also depends on vendor processes, such as the quality of design, the protection provided to security features during the delivery of a product from the vendor to the consumer, vendor strategies for maintaining or upgrading security in the face of new threats, and so on.

Several vendors have relied on the standard CC testing and evaluation approach to assess the security and assurance features of their Linux software products. A listing of evaluated Linux products that are certified according to the CC approach can be found online.[54]

51.4.4.5 Hacking. De facto assurance of the underlying security in a product can arise from those who actively probe new products for security flaws. Such probing may arise from internally sanctioned security probing or from unsanctioned, unexpected probing by individuals of ill will. Hacking approaches (ethical or otherwise) do not necessarily follow a consistent or comprehensive approach to evaluating the quality of the security functions and services that are implemented. Hence, the level of assurance achieved is unknown and typically very low.

51.4.4.6 Trade Press. Many trade press publications and magazines conduct reviews of products that pertain to security. Products are tested in ad hoc environments and against private, ad hoc, de jure criteria that vary from product to product and magazine to magazine. Such magazines may rely on unaccredited consultants, staff, or private labs to review products. Some reviews may focus on examining quantitative product details other than security, such as performance or throughput of a product. Tests performed often fall short of assessing the real security aspects of a product. Some reviews rate qualitative parameters, such as product *innovativeness*. Because of the potential lack of quantified testing rigor and potential dissimilarity of evaluation metrics, comparisons of trade press reviews from different sources are difficult. Perhaps most important, no evaluations are made of the confidence (assurance) that can be associated with the soundness of the security implementation.

Examples of publications that provide reviews of security products include *SC* (formerly *Secure Computing) Magazine*,[55] *Network Computing*,[56] *Security Management* magazine,[57] *InfoWorld*,[58] and many more. Some of these trade press initiatives are summarized below.

51.4.4.6.1 SC Magazine. In its general test process for individual security-relevant products, *SC Magazine* uses about 50 private criteria codeveloped by SC Lab and the Center for Regional and National Security at Eastern Michigan University. Tests of groups of products focus on operational characteristics. Test and evaluation methods are similar to those used for the CC's lowest assurance levels. *SC Magazine* has also established overall ratings values to indicate how well a product has done against the test criteria and whether the product should be considered for purchase.

Examples of the types of products, or groups of products that have been reviewed by *SC Magazine* include: SIEM, network forensic appliances, multifactor authentication, unified threat managers, risk manager, network sentry, identity enforcement platform, application security manager, password manager, Web application firewall, database activity monitors, secure email gateway, and more. More complete lists of tested items are identified at the magazine's Website.[59]

SC has also produced buyers' guides for groups of products, such as Universal Single Sign-On solutions.

SC Magazine also publishes privately created evaluations of products within certain classes such as cloud identity and access control products, unified threat management solutions, next-generation firewalls, and more.

51.4.4.6.2 Other Publications. *ComputerWorld* and *IT Business Edge* obtain privately created evaluations (often from the same evaluation house) of products from various classes of security-relevant products such as endpoint security products. Individual product evaluations are compared to other products in the same class of products. For security-enabled products, test criteria include performance metrics indicating how security-related processes may impact the overall performance of the system being security-enabled.

NetworkWorld obtains privately created buyers' guides for security-related technology such as identity management in clouds, SSL/VPN tools, and more. Evaluation is based on (a) vendor self-declarations to private, evaluation survey questions in part oriented to security functionality, and (b) evaluator hands-on set up of products.

InformationWeek creates buyers' guides for technology such as gateway antimalware products. Evaluation is based on vendor self-declarations in response to private, evaluation survey questions in part oriented to security functionality.

IT Whitepapers obtains privately created comparisons of security-relevant products or services. Recent evaluation comparisons included, for example, (a) security provisions in major mobile platforms and (b) Managed Security Service Providers.

51.4.4.7 Third-Party Commercial De Jure Assessment Approaches. Early on in the security assessment arena, third-party, commercial, security assessment approaches were sometimes conducted by unaccredited testing houses or consulting houses. These third parties provided relatively low-confidence, so-called surface-level testing. Such testing resulted in vendors of security-relevant products receiving either a *brand mark* or an independent third-party white paper evaluation report that could be referenced in vendors' product brochures and advertisements. Such commercial activities began at a time when there needed to be a lower-cost—albeit lower confidence—alternative to expensive, lengthy, economically inappropriate, government evaluations such as the so-called *Orange Book* evaluations (see Section 51.4.1). These commercial assessment activities were also available to support trade press surveys and magazine reviews of products.

Such nonstandard, third-party approaches are still prevalent. There is a certain qualitative amount of risk reduction achievable by relying on such approaches. They are typically based on simple, one-size-fits-all testing that usually provides minimal, cursory checks of some of the implemented security functions. Some of these tests focus on product details other than security, such as performance or throughput. No evaluation is made of the confidence (assurance) that can be associated with the soundness of the security implementation. At best, these are *black box* approaches wherein products may be examined based only on their outputs relative to stimuli. These approaches have no assessment capabilities based on the fundamental design of the product, or of the engineering principles used by the vendor to build the product.

Many vendors, nonetheless, undergo these types of commercial testing because of the pressures from their competitors' products being so tested. Testing costs are reasonable, but such testing provides no inputs (e.g., evaluation reports) to consumers that can be analyzed to differentiate products. More comprehensive products are not examined for any of their differentiating capabilities. Instead, such check-mark testing programs merely provide a common-denominator assessment floor for products.

Typical vendor reaction to these types of these nonstandard third-party evaluations and branding programs is that they are often not very good and are often distracting nuisances. Vendors also indicate that unlike a more rigorous, standards-based testing paradigm, such as that based on the CC, these nonstandard, third-party programs do not have processes to help improve the quality of the product under test. Unlike CC testing labs, many vendors do not see these nonstandard testing labs as strategic partners looking to improve the product under test.

Examples of these types of product assessment approaches include the *West Coast Labs Check Mark Program* (Section 51.4.4.7.1), the *ICSA Labs Certified Program* (Section 51.4.4.7.2), and several others (Section 51.4.4.7.3).

51.4.4.7.1 Check Mark Program. The Check Mark program is a private testing service provided by West Coast Labs (www.westcoastlabs.org). Although touted to use *standard* testing criteria in a *standard* testing approach, the Check Mark program establishes private criteria and a private testing methodology that are not recognized by legitimate standards bodies such as ISO. West Coast's private criteria and testing approaches apply to certain types of computer-security products, such as antivirus products, firewall products, and VPN products. The criteria are designed to achieve a basic level of protection against a number of common hostile attacks. West Coast Labs tests products against the applicable Check Mark criteria and, if successfully tested, produces a certificate that shows that specific releases of products meet specific Check Mark criteria.

51.4.4.7.2 ICSA Labs Certified. Another well-known, commercial, security-relevant product branding service is the product certification program conducted by ICSA Labs.[60]

The ICSA approach is similar to the West Coast Labs testing approach. Product performance is tested against specified criteria to assess whether the product can resist the types of common threats and risks specified in the testing criteria. Product testing is typically a checklist-oriented approach geared for nonexpert testers. Testing criteria are developed for a number of classes of products, such as firewalls and antivirus (AV) software. While Check Mark uses private testing criteria, ICSA uses so-called *public criteria.* These public criteria are, however, nonstandard like those of Check Mark since they are created outside the recognized national or international standards-development communities. Instead, ICSA's testing criteria are developed via invited participation.

Products that pass ICSA criteria are entitled to display the ICSA brand mark. Products that fail are reported to their vendors with detailed analysis of the criteria they failed.

Unlike the West Coast certificate, once products are awarded an ICSA certificate, vendors take on the obligation to self-check and to self-declare continued certification of evolutions of the specific version product that passed ICSA testing. Spot checks by ICSA are used to verify that currently shipping products still can pass the ICSA tests.[61]

51.4.4.7.3 Other Third-Party Assessments and Assessors. There are several other organizations that use private, informal methods to create third-party assessments of certain types of security products or security services. Examples follow.

- Gartner issues Magic Quadrant analyses that evaluate how well a product compares to other products in the same class of products and where a product is positioned in the Magic Quadrant of characteristics. Examples of Magic Quadrant analyses exist for product classes such as Unified Threat Management.

- Forrester issues evaluations of products as well as services in the same class of services. For example, a 15-criteria evaluation of 10 Managed Security Service Providers was conducted using private evaluation criteria.
- NSS Labs uses its own testing laboratory, rather than surveys and questionnaires, to produce best-practices guides, product reviews, comparative test reports, buyer's guides, and more. Such materials pertain to security or security-enabled devices such as, for example, Web browsers, Web application firewalls, next-generation firewalls, endpoint solutions, breach detection systems, intrusion prevention systems, antivirus products, and more. Test criteria are private and tailored to the evaluation to be performed. They may include tests that verify a device's stability, performance, and security effectiveness (e.g., for a firewall not blocking legitimate traffic). Tests may determine the accuracy of a device's security coverage, as well as the usability of the device. NSS Labs publishes its test methodologies for specific devices as well as its own research about security effectiveness. It also publishes vulnerability threat reports. NSS research materials are primarily available to subscription clients.
- Veracode is another third-party assessor available for consumers who are unable to operate a meaningful program for testing the security aspects of vendor products. To support consumer security testing needs, Veracode has established the Veracode Vendor Application Security Testing (VAST) program. In conjunction with a cloud-based testing platform, Veracode provides analysis of security worthiness of vendor application software and its compliance with the customer's security policies and requirements for the application software they buy. It also provides de jure, standards-based, assurance level score requirements that dictate the minimal set of testing that is necessary to be performed. Like the CC paradigm, Veracode looks to establish a partnering relationship with vendors. It discloses its testing results to vendors and feeds remediation guidance back to the software developer. An excellent description of the security evaluation processes to be performed in conjunction with the VAST program is available.[62]
- The AV-Test Institute performs analyses of security products or constituent components.[63] It also performs comparative tests or tests of beta software. Evaluations use AV-Test's own daily-expanding malicious and safe test data samples, and its own analysis tools, as well as private test criteria. The criteria are based on protection (including, e.g., protection against zero-day malware attacks), repair (e.g., in terms of performance in detecting and removing hidden malware), and usability (including, e.g., performance slow-downs of computers using tested products). Based on a scoring system that depends on test results, the Institute awards certification seals of approval. Recertification occurs periodically. Comparative test results for different product classes often appear in the trade press. For example, test results for several Windows 8 virus scanners were recently summarized in the trade press.[64]

51.4.5 Security Assessment Standards for Products. In contrast to the informal, nonstandard product assessment approaches just discussed, formal standards exist for assessing various aspects of security associated with products or services. As detailed earlier, standards exist to assess the overall quality and soundness of product builders (Section 51.4.3.1) and their organization (Section 51.4.3.2) and to stipulate sound development methods for product builders (Section 51.4.3.3). A determination of security soundness based on these standards typically yield generalized conclusions such as "good" vendors build "good" products.

As detailed in the following sections, other standards can be followed to assess product quality, service quality, or a combination of both the quality of product builders as well as the quality of their products. The latter standards can be used to quantify how well "good" vendors build "good" products (with identifiable and demonstrable assurance levels), how much "better" specific vendors can build even "better" products (with identifiable and demonstrable, generally higher assurance levels), and how comprehensive are the security functionalities within the specific classes of products these vendors build. Similarly, at least one standard exists for verifying that "good" service providers offer "good" services.

Examples of product assessment and service assessment approaches that rely on formal standards are described in Section 51.5 below.

51.5 STANDARD PRODUCT AND SERVICES ASSESSMENT APPROACHES

51.5.1 Government Standard Cryptographic Validation Programs. The evolving FIPS 140 series of standards[65] specify requirements that are to be satisfied by cryptographic modules. In computer and telecommunications systems used or outsourced by the federal government, the U.S. Government mandates use of validated cryptographic modules for all uses of cryptography that protect "sensitive but unclassified" information. FISMA removes any possibility of receiving a waiver to the government FIPS 140 mandate. The Canadian government requires use of such modules for protection of "designated information." Other nongovernment organizations also look to use validated commercially available, crypto modules.

The FIPS 140 standards provide the basis for the long-standing, popular Cryptographic Module Validation Program (CMVP).[66] This program is focused on testing, evaluating, validating, and certifying hardware and software cryptographic modules. A crypto module may be an embedded component within a product or application; or, it may be a standalone product in and of itself.

A prerequisite to cryptographic module validation is the validation of the correct and complete implementation of the standard cryptographic algorithms used in cryptographic modules. The FIPS-approved standard symmetric key algorithms for encryption include the Advanced Encryption Standard which is the current algorithm of choice, Triple-DES and Skipjack. The Cryptographic Algorithm Validation Program (CAVP)[67] uses CAVP-designed validation test suites for testing, evaluating, and validating standard cryptographic algorithms using processes and methodologies similar to those described for the CMVP below. (Specific tests are described in companion NIST standards.) Details about the CAVP are not offered herein. Suffice it to indicate that thousands of cryptographic algorithm implementations have received algorithm validations to date.

FIPS 140-1 defines four increasing, qualitative levels of security assurance ranging from rock-bottom requirements stipulated in Level 1 to more, sequentially additive, security requirements in each of the subsequently higher levels. Security requirements address 11 different areas that pertain to the design and implementation of a cryptographic module.

FIPS 140-2 and the emerging FIPS 140-3 apply to more contemporary cryptographic module implementations. They incorporate changes in crypto module technology, and in the case of FIPS 140-3 add new requirements and an additional assurance Level 5.

Special security testing laboratories conduct standard cryptographic module conformance testing against requirements stated in FIPS 140-2 or FIPS 140-1. There are numerous such independent, commercial, third-party, so-called Cryptographic and Security Testing laboratories—each individually accredited by NIST's National Voluntary Laboratory Accreditation Program (NVLAP).

Entities that are looking to have crypto module validations performed must contract with any of these laboratories for the service of testing crypto modules and having such evaluations validated. Against the specific crypto module under test, these labs can perform appropriate, standardized conformance tests from a suite of standard conformance tests[68] tailored to the four FIPS 140 security levels.

After validation that the test results from an accredited testing laboratory correctly and completely demonstrate that the crypto module under test conforms to either of the FIPS 140 standards, a CMVP certificate can be issued by either NIST or the Communications Security Establishment Canada (CSEC). The certificate includes an evaluation score determined from the above testing.

NIST maintains a repository list of cryptographic modules—past and present—that have been tested and validated.[69] It should be noted that more products than appear in the repository of validated crypto modules may embed a validated module that is listed in the repository. NIST also maintains a list of crypto modules that are in the process of being evaluated.[70]

The FIPS 140 testing and validation scheme is not as broad, flexible and far-reaching as the CC scheme (Section 51.5.3) that is also used for product evaluation and certification. Why? Because the FIPS 140 scheme is focused on just one class of entities—cryptographic modules—whereas the CC scheme is applicable to any and every class of products as well as to a wider set of possible assurance requirements on the design, implementation, deployment, and maintenance of products. Furthermore, the FIPS 140 security requirements do not map directly to any specific CC security requirements. As such, when an FIPS 140 certificate is required, a CC certificate cannot be substituted.

51.5.2 FedRAMP. The FedRAMP program is a U.S. Government program that supports federal government agencies' adoption of commercial or government cloud services.[71] Such cloud services may be provided according to any one of several different service delivery models, such as Infrastructure as a Service (IaaS) or Platform as a Service (PaaS). FedRAMP is a different type of U.S. Government security assessment and certification program. It is not oriented specifically to security-relevant products. Instead, it is oriented to evaluating service providers and the systems they employ—in particular, cloud service providers.

FedRAMP's standard processes benefit both cloud service providers and cloud service customers. A single, third-party assessment of a cloud service provider's security claims reduces cloud service provider security evaluation costs by eliminating re-assessment for different cloud customers. Successful assessments receive government authorization that allows any or all government agencies to use the authorized cloud service provider's offering.

FedRAMP uses a standards-based and risk-based approach that relies on:

1. **Security Requirements Standards** that require cloud providers to implement security capabilities that address standard FedRAMP security requirements.

2. **Security Assessment Standards** that require approved, independent, third parties to audit and to assess cloud service provider offerings and to develop a security assessment report.
3. **Government Authorization Standards** that are used by the FedRAMP Joint Authorization Board to review the security assessment reports and to achieve and to issue consistent standardized authorizations for government agencies to use approved cloud service provider offerings.
4. **Continuous Monitoring Standards** that require specified, standard "Ongoing Assessment & Authorization" activities that include ongoing, periodic reassessment of cloud service provider systems to reaffirm compliance with FedRAMP security requirements, to reaffirm that required security controls are still effective, and, therefore, to retain ongoing authorization.
5. **Authorized Services Lists** that identify cloud service providers that have achieved either an "Authority to Operate" certificate from the authorizing government agency or a "Provisional Authority to Operate" certificate from the FedRAMP Joint Authorization Board and therefore are available for use by any government agency. (Lists of authorized cloud service providers are available at the GSA's Website).[72]

FedRAMP security requirements to be addressed by cloud providers are compliant with FISMA. They are based on security controls enumerated in NITS Special Publication 800-53, Revision 3, which adds cloud-oriented security controls not found in earlier versions of this standard. FedRAMP security assessments add additional controls to FedRAMP assessments that are not included in FISMA assessments.

FedRAMP assessments are initiated either by individual cloud service providers or by government agencies that wish to use cloud services.

A cloud service provider (or the government agency interested in obtaining cloud services) hires a FedRAMP-accredited, commercial, third-party security assessment organization, a so-called Third Party Assessment Organization (3PAO). 3PAOs use FedRAMP standards:

(a) To develop a security assessment plan that is specific to the cloud service provider to be assessed and that specifies the security controls to be assessed, how the controls are implemented within the cloud service provider's environment, security and privacy behavior rules, the boundaries of the cloud service provider's environment, and other security-related plans,

(b) To conduct a security assessment of the cloud service provider's security controls to determine the effectiveness of the implementations of all security controls identified in the security assessment plan, and

(c) To develop a security assessment report to be submitted for authorization approval of the cloud service provider being assessed.

If necessary, the cloud service provider will develop and execute a plan for correcting any weaknesses or flaws identified during the 3PAO security assessment.

If authorization is awarded, then according to FedRAMP's continuous monitoring standard, a 3PAO may conduct annual, follow-up, security reassessments of the cloud service provider's systems in order for the cloud service provider to maintain FedRAMP authorization to continue to be used by government agencies as an approved cloud service provider.

Parties wishing to become FedRAMP 3PAOs must be rigorously evaluated according to FedRAMP standard quality and acceptability criteria used to ensure 3PAO security assessment competency as well as conformity among 3PAOs' security assessment processes.

To leverage the benefits of using an assessed and authorized cloud service provider, government agencies are being encouraged to require, contractually, that their prospective cloud service provider meets FedRAMP security requirements.

Details about FedRAMP, its processes and guidance on how to use the FedRAMP processes are available.[73]

In an effort to be watched, the Cloud Security Alliance is contemplating though its Open Certification Framework (OCF) and Security, Trust & Assurance Registry (STAR) efforts (Section 51.4.4.3.2) to develop what appears could be an international version of a FedRAMP style of cloud service provider assessment and certification.

51.5.3 Common Criteria. Out of the experiences gleaned from the *Orange Book* and other national criteria (Section 51.4.1), a new, commercially driven, standard strategy emerged for testing products and for demonstrating confidence that their security features behave properly. This best-of-all-previous-breeds strategy is based on an international standard, ISO Standard 15408, the *Common Criteria for Information Technology Security Evaluation*, referred to colloquially as the *Common Criteria* (CC).[74]

The CC strategy offers a single, internationally recognized, approach for specification of consumer security requirements and for commercial evaluation of IT product security. Products can be built in any country, evaluated in any other country, and bought with confidence in yet any other country. This CC approach is useful within several international communities. In the United States, it is embraced by the DoD market sector and other communities such as the financial sector.

The CC paradigm presents a standard strategy that overcomes shortcomings of other approaches. It provides a standard way for stipulating (1) the risks of concern, (2) the security functional requirements that must be met in order to mitigate stated risks, and (3) the security assurance requirements that must be met to provide confidence that products are built with desired quality. It provides a recognized, reliable, maintained mechanism to develop trust that:

1. Security requirements are specified correctly,
2. Vendors do not misunderstand the requirements, and
3. Vendors design and manufacture products that address the requirements and provide risk integrity.

The CC provides a flexible process for specifying and testing security requirements for any and all classes, and specific instances, of all existing or future IT products.

In the CC paradigm, consumers' risks and protection requirements are stipulated so that product builders' security solutions can be tested (in a standard way) so as to be able to verify (in a standard way) product compliance with stipulated standard security requirements. Testing is performed by any one of the testing laboratories that are accredited (in a standard way).

Unlike other approaches, the CC provides a way to specify assurance requirements and to evaluate how well they are met. Assurance requirements are extremely important and are typically not considered in other product assessment approaches. Assurance requirements are the essential ingredients in establishing confidence in implementations of security and in providing the level of trust necessary for economies and governments to rely on new e-business and e-government models.

Trust in products is established by gaining confidence that the security functionalities claimed to be implemented to address specific security functional requirements (1) are effective in satisfying specified security objectives and (2) are implemented correctly and completely and operate as expected. Through security assurance requirements, trust is further established by ensuring that product developers have sound processes and take specified actions to ensure specified quality throughout the life cycle of the product they build, test, deliver, and maintain.

The CC also establishes a standard method to develop common tests and evaluation methods and to use them to verify the security aspects of products via competent, accredited laboratories. CC-based testing helps manufacturers reduce costs by providing a pool of private, licensed, competitive, security testing labs that have consistent, accredited testing quality and competence. Because testing is standardized and recognized worldwide, testing costs are, in effect, capped because product vendors are spared costly country-specific or customer-specific retesting campaigns.

Assessments of products are composed of both analysis and testing of the product. Use of standard evaluation criteria and standard evaluation methodology leads to repeatable, objective test and evaluation results. To remedy assessment-discovered shortcomings and flaws in products, CC testing labs feed back testing results to product vendors and work collaboratively to resolve discovered flaws and shortcomings.

Independent review and validation of CC-based testing and evaluation by accredited, country-specific, national CC validation bodies boosts consumers' confidence even further. Such CC validation bodies verify test results and certify that products were successfully assessed according to the standard testing and evaluation performed by accredited CC testing labs. These bodies are also responsible for maintaining national security testing and evaluation infrastructures that include (a) correct, consistent, credible, competent, and commercial application of CC standards and methodologies by accredited CC testing labs within their country, (b) a government oversight body, and (c) a government security evaluation certificate issuing authority.

The CC specification and testing approach is equally applicable to any and all types of security-relevant products, such as:

- **(a)** Products that implement security technologies (e.g., crypto boxes, intrusion detection/prevention systems, boundary protection devices and systems, audit tools, access control devices, digital signature products, and much more),
- **(b)** Products that are security-enabled (e.g., messaging systems, database management systems, Web e-commerce packages, telecom switches, industrial control systems, and much more), or
- **(c)** Products that support security (e.g., operating systems, certificate management systems, network management systems, smart cards, and more).

An ever-growing list of thousands of products that have been evaluated according to CC-based standard testing and that have received CC certifications is available online.[75] In short, the CC paradigm grows the pool of better-engineered, more acceptable products.

As certified products are altered or upgraded, vendors of such products can pursue a standard assurance maintenance process to retain the assurance level associated with initial certifications of such products. Information about this process appears elsewhere.[76]

The CC is today's unified choice for developing trust in products. The use of standards tends to increase the product appeal to various nonrelated consumer constituencies. A product builder's security culture is significantly improved because of the required verification of the builder's meticulous and clear focus on security, as well as the builder's security design, development, testing, and maintenance disciplines. Such culture improvement tends to benefit other products built by the vendor.

Some—especially proponents of the 20 Critical Controls paradigm (Section 51.4.2.1)—seem to feel that the CC approach is too flexible, requires too much expertise to capitalize on its flexibility, and would be better if it specified a small, mandatory set of "common-sense" controls of value in "most" situations.

Reciprocally, well-respected consulting houses have concluded that CC evaluation provides a substantial improvement over the nonstandard or informal testing approaches that typically result in seriously undertested software and that, as a group of inconsistent approaches, provide only "apples-to-oranges" comparisons of tested products. The CC paradigm provides an extra level of due diligence. It improves and differentiates products and allows buyers to compare products objectively. It is accepted by mutual agreement in most of the world's largest IT-building and IT-buying countries.

More details about the CC paradigm are given in Section 51.5.3.1. An overview of the two types of security profiles that can be developed by product consumers and product vendors appears in Section 51.5.3.2. A summary for using the CC to document consumers' security needs for products is given in Section 51.5.3.3. Section 51.5.3.4 provides a summary for using the CC to document the security features built into vendor products. More details about the CC testing and evaluation approach appear in Section 51.5.3.5. More detailed descriptions of the underlying CC standards and how to use them appear elsewhere.[77]

51.5.3.1 Common Criteria Paradigm Overview. The CC paradigm uses international standards, processes, and procedures to specify, to test, to validate, and to certify security-related products.

The CC paradigm is a multipurpose scheme for:

- Stipulating security requirements that can be used in product procurements,
- Specifying companion security solutions in products,
- Testing products according to product-tailored—but standard—criteria and testing methodologies using accredited, third-party, commercial testing laboratories,
- Independently validating test results, and
- Providing certificates to tested and validated products that obviate any need for further product retesting for differing consumer constituencies or in all countries that mutually recognize each other's commercial testing capabilities and testing results.

Consumers use a standard methodology, a standard language, and a catalog of standard security requirements to develop security profiles (see Section 51.5.3.3) tailored to the types of products they want to purchase. The profiles stipulate the security functional needs. They also stipulate the confidence or assurance desired in products as well as in product builders' processes from product design through maintenance.

Product builders use the same standard methodology, language, and catalog to develop different types of security profiles (see Section 51.5.3.4) to define their products' security specifications. They define product security specifications in terms of both security functionality and security assurance about the product and the builders' processes. The builders' specifications show how their products meet stated consumer security functionality and assurance needs. Builders' specifications may also show how their products meet any additional builder-claimed security features that go beyond the consumers' stated needs.

51.5.3.2 Specification Elements of the CC Paradigm. The CC standard defines the language used within, the methodologies used to construct, and structures for two types of security profiles that specify security requirements: protection profiles (PPs) and security targets (STs).

PPs help consumers articulate what risks and vulnerabilities are important, while STs help vendors articulate what risks and vulnerabilities are addressed by their products. PPs help consumers articulate what level of protection and confidence they want in products, while STs help vendors articulate what level of protection and confidence are provided by their products. PPs provide a standard and flexible way to transform consumers' security needs and policies into unambiguous, product-neutral, security requirements for the desired security behavior and quality for *any class of IT product*.

Both security functional requirements and assurance requirements are included in these two types of profiles. Functional requirements define desired security behavior and are extracted from a standard CC catalog of hundreds of such requirements. Assurance requirements provide the basis for establishing trust by putting constraints on how well a product or a profile is built. Assurance requirements are also catalogued in a CC standard as requirements that pertain to, for example, (a) configuration management of the product, (b) design, development, delivery, and operation of the product, (c) maintaining assurance throughout the product's life cycle, and (d) much more.

Assurance requirements are bundled into seven standard predefined packages called *Evaluation Assurance Levels* (EALs). Higher assurance level bundles (e.g., EAL4) contain more rigorous assurance requirements needing more rigorous methodologically design and testing than lower, entry-level bundles (e.g., EAL1) that need only functional testing. EALs are enumerated in a monotonically increasing scale that balances (a) the increasing levels of confidence that can be obtained, with (b) the increasing cost and decreasing feasibility of conducting the testing and evaluation necessary to develop a specific, higher level of confidence. The higher the assurance level, the more aspects of a vendor's development process will need to be examined during product test and evaluation.

At the low end, EAL1 can be used, for example, to support the contention that baseline due care has been exercised with regard to protection of personal information and to establish some minimal degree of confidence in correct operation of a product in an environment where the threats to security are not considered very serious. At the highest extreme, EAL7 requires a formally verified design and extensive formal analysis. EAL7 may be applicable to certain highly specific, perhaps one-of-a-kind products, targeted for extremely high-risk situations or where the high value of the assets being protected justifies the extraordinary costs of an evaluation to this level of confidence. Typical commercial products fall in the range from EAL1 to EAL4.

When specifying assurance requirements, the desired level of assurance—and the cost to attain such assurance—should be balanced against factors, such as (1) the value of the resources to be protected, (2) the risk and extent of possible losses, (3) the level of confidence desired, and (4) any reasonably expected cost and delay factors that may accompany the development, and any subsequent testing, evaluation, and validation of a product at a specific level of assurance.

While a PP stipulates generic, *product-neutral*, security functional and assurance requirements for some specific class of IT product that meets the needs of prospective buyers, an ST is a *product-specific* stipulation of the security functional and assurance requirements addressed by a single, specific product along with information as to how the implemented product meets the stated security requirements.

As stipulated in its accompanying ST, a specific product may claim conformance to one or more PPs as well as to additional product-specific security requirements enumerated within its ST.

Given the breadth, depth, and changeability of possible security requirements that can be stipulated within PPs or STs, the CC provides the ability to stipulate the user requirements and product requirements of virtually an unlimited number of existing and yet-to-be-conceived consumer security needs (PPs) and security product solutions (STs).

The purpose of CC-based testing and evaluation of a product is to evaluate and to confirm that the product meets the product-specific requirements and evaluation criteria contained in the product's ST. The STs' assurance requirements impact the requisite depth and breadth of testing and evaluation.

Many products that are successfully tested and evaluated will go further and have their test and evaluation results validated by a formal, recognized, CC national validation body. Products can then be certified by a government certificate issuing authority and added to the publicly viewable repository that lists CC-certified products.

51.5.3.3 Constructing Protection Profiles.

PPs enumerate consumers' security functional and assurance needs that are appropriate and valuable for a specific type of product to mitigate specific risks in a specific threat environment. Each PP states the security problem that a PP-compliant product is intended to solve. It stipulates the security functional requirements that are known to be useful and effective in meeting specific security objectives. It also stipulates the security assurance requirements that provide the confidence desired that products are built with desired quality.

The main contents of a PP include statements about the:

1. **Threats and Vulnerabilities** to which a product will be exposed,
2. **Security Environment** within which a product is to reside, including (a) descriptions of both the IT and non-IT aspects of the environment, (b) assumptions about the product's usage, administration, and management, and (c) all policies, laws, regulations, and rules to which the product must comply within the intended environment,
3. **Security Objectives** to be met either by a product or the environment within which the product operates, including descriptions of which threats and policies are to be addressed by the product and which are to be addressed by the environment,
4. **Security Requirements**, both functional and assurance requirements, selected and refined from the standard CC requirements catalogs, to meet each security objective and assumption, indicating which requirements are addressed by a product and which by the environment within which it operates, and

5. **Rationale** that is provided to justify all decisions and choices made in developing the content within a PP. Rationale includes statements such as how selected security requirements are suitable to counter the enumerated threats, how they comply with enumerated policies and assumptions, and how they map back to the original, underlying, driving needs and threats.

Guidance for developing PPs is available.[78] A list of PPs that were formally validated for correctness is maintained at the CC Website.[79]

51.5.3.4 Constructing Security Target Profiles. Product developers create STs to document detailed information about the security aspects of products they build and to specify how implemented security functions and assurance measures meet consumers' needs.

A ST provides the basis and the evaluation criteria against which testing and evaluation of the product are performed. It also specifies the configuration in which a product is to be tested.

The contents of an ST are similar to a PP. The ST describes the environment within which the product described via an ST is intended to operate. The ST enumerates the (a) threats to the product, (b) policies, laws, and regulations with which the product is claimed to conform, and (c) assumptions about the security aspects of the IT and non-IT environment within which the product is intended to be used. STs delineate the security objectives that the builder of a specific product claims are addressed by the product. STs also enumerate the security requirements that the product builder claims are addressed by the product as well as those requirements to be addressed by the environment within which the product is intended to operate. Some of these requirements may be refinements of generic or product-neutral requirements stipulated in a PP to which the ST claims compliance; and some may be additional security requirements over and above those stipulated in any PPs to which the product claims to be conformant.

However, the ST goes beyond a PP because it also specifies the security functions offered by the product to meet each of the stated security requirements in the ST. It also specifies the assurance measures taken by the product builder to meet all the stated assurance requirements in the ST.

Rationale is also provided for all decisions and choices made in developing the ST content. Rationale justifies all claims made in an ST about the PPs with which the product conforms. In essence, the rationale provided demonstrates that the ST contains an effective and suitable set of countermeasures and that this set of countermeasures is consistent, complete, and cohesive.

By comparing the STs of different products, consumers are better able to compare the security features of competing products. Consumers are able to understand what types of tests and evaluations that a specific product underwent. They also are able to determine whether the configuration in which a product was tested is consistent with the environment into which the product will be deployed.

51.5.3.5 Common Testing of Products. Products characterized by associated product-specific STs can undergo standard CC testing and evaluation using standard testing methodology by any officially accredited/licensed CC testing and evaluation laboratory anywhere in the world. Testing assures that products are correct, complete, well built, and compliant to their security specifications. Testing is conducted under conditions appropriate to the intended normal operation of the product so as to verify that the implemented security is correct, complete, and compliant under normal operations. Since CC-based testing can demonstrate the traceability of the security aspects of a product back to product user requirements as well as to applicable policies, laws, and regulations, such testing can reduce product users' exposure to potential penalties for noncompliance to security-relevant laws or regulations.

Testing labs and their staff are accredited for their security assessment competence, as specified in a security-testing-laboratory extension[80,81] to an ISO standard[82] specifying general testing laboratory competency requirements. As defined in the CC's *Common Evaluation Methodology* (CEM)[83] standard, evaluators use a standard methodology with structured, formal assessment processes and evaluation actions to carry out a series of standard testing and evaluation activities.

Since testing is done according to standards, consumers get a strong sense that testing is objective and not slanted to benefit the product that was tested. With the additional trust created by CC testing, customers reduce their product acquisition costs by minimizing acceptance testing that duplicates testing already performed on a product by an accredited CC testing lab. Studies indicate that CC testing improves products by eliminating exploitable security flaws and adding or extending necessary security features.

The CEM standard provides a common base for independent, autonomous CC testing laboratories to assess CC profiles and vendor products in the same ways, regardless of the CC testing lab being used. Use of the CEM by all CC testing labs provides a common floor of confidence in similar products that may have been assessed by different CC testing labs. Indeed, the *Common Criteria Arrangement on the Mutual Recognition of the Common Criteria Certifications in the Field of Information Technology Security*, often called just the *Mutual Recognition Arrangement* (MRA), is the multicountry, treaty-level declaration that different countries will recognize the CEM/CC-based assessments that may be conducted by CC testing labs in each other's jurisdictions.

Because the CEM is internationally recognized, the use of customer-unique or country-unique assessment is minimized, if not avoided all together. Assessment costs are minimized, since vendors need only prepare for one testing campaign rather than for a battery of different testing campaigns conducted against different customer-specific, consulting-house-specific, or country-specific, assessment criteria.

Although some consumers and vendors believe that the CC paradigm is complicated, inefficient, or costly, the many who do build and buy validated products see the CC paradigm as the best, proactive way to improve the security and assurance of products bought and sold in the marketplace.

51.6 NOTES

1. "Federal Information Security Management Act of 2002" (Title III of the E-Government Act of 2002), U.S. Public Law 107-347, Section III, December 2002, http://csrc.nist.gov/drivers/documents/FISMA-final.pdf
2. In this chapter, de facto means *accepted as a matter of common practice*; de jure is used idiosyncratically to mean *accepted under written standards* (but not the usual meaning of *according to law*).
3. U.S. Department of Defense Instruction, "DoD Information Technology Security Certification and Accreditation Process (DITSCAP)," 5200.40, December 30, 1997, http://iase.disa.mil/ditscap/i520040.pdf (URL inactive).
4. www.diacap.org

5. PCI Security Standards Council, PCI Standards & Documents, "PCI SSC Data Security Standards Overview," see link for PCI Data Security Standard: https://www.pcisecuritystandards.org/security_standards/
6. The terms *testing*, *evaluation*, and *assessment* are a source of ambiguity and discrepancy in the community. In this chapter, these terms are used interchangeably.
7. ISO is not an acronym; it is a reference to the Greek prefix isos (equal) and ensures that the abbreviation for the organization is identical in all languages. See "Our name" in the page www.iso.org/iso/home/about.htm
8. U.S. Department of Defense Directive 8500.1, "Information Assurance (IA)," October 24, 2002, www.acq.osd.mil/ie/bei/pm/ref-library/dodd/d85001p.pdf
9. Department of Defense Instruction 8500.2, "Information Assurance (IA) Implementation," February 6, 2003, www.dtic.mil/whs/directives/corres/pdf/850002p.pdf
10. www.dtic.mil/whs/directives/corres/pdf/857001m.pdf
11. https://cloudsecurityalliance.org
12. https://www.pcisecuritystandards.org/
13. www.safecode.org/index.php
14. http://omg.org
15. www.webappsec.org
16. www.tmforum.org
17. www.sans.org
18. www.sans.org/critical-security-controls
19. www.microsoft.com/en-us/download/details.aspx?id=18015
20. www.microsoft.com/security/sdl/default.aspx
21. U.S. Department of Defense Instruction, "DoD Information Technology Security Certification and Accreditation Process (DITSCAP)," 5200.40, December 30, 1997, http://iase.disa.mil/ditscap/i520040.pdf (URL inactive).
22. National Security Telecommunications and Information Systems Security Instruction (NSTISSI) No. 1000, "National Information Assurance Certification and Accreditation Process (NIACAP)" (April 2000), www.cnss.gov/Assets/pdf/nstissi_1000.pdf
23. NIST Special Publication 800-37, "Guide for the Security Certification and Accreditation of Federal Information Systems (May 2004), http://csrc.nist.gov/publications/nistpubs/800-37/SP800-37-final.pdf
24. "Information Technology—Security Techniques—Code of Practice for Information Security Management," ISO/IEC 17799 (2005), www.iso.org/iso/catalogue_detail?csnumber=50297
25. Joint Task Force Transformation Initiative (Ron Ross, JTF Leader), "Security and Privacy Controls for Federal Information Systems and Organizations," NIST Special Publication 800-53, Revision 4, April 2013, http://nvlpubs.nist.gov/nistpubs/SpecialPublications/NIST.SP.800-53r4.pdf
26. U.S. Department of Defense, "Trusted Computer System Evaluation Criteria," (TCSEC or Orange Book), DOD5200.28-STD (December 1985), http://csrc.nist.gov/publications/history/dod85.pdf
27. National Computer Security Center, National Security Agency, "Trusted Network Interpretation of the Trusted Computer System Evaluation Criteria"

(TNI), 9800 Savage Rd., Ft. Meade, MD 20755, July 31, 1987, www.ntis.gov/search/product.aspx?ABBR=ADA255422 See also "Trusted Network Interpretation Environments Guideline," www.fas.org/irp/nsa/rainbow/tg011.htm

28. National Computer Security Center, National Security Agency, "Trusted Database Management System Interpretation of the Trusted Computer System Evaluation Criteria," NCSC-TG-021, 9800 Savage Rd., Ft. Meade, MD 20755, April 1991, www.ntis.gov/search/product.aspx?ABBR=ADA393253
29. Office for Official Publications of the European Communities, "Information Technology Security Evaluation Criteria" (ITSEC), Luxembourg (June 1991), www.ssi.gouv.fr/site_documents/ITSEC/ITSEC-uk.pdf
30. www.sans.org/critical-security-controls/cag4.pdf
31. www.sans.org/critical-security-controls/guidelines.php
32. https://cloudsecurityalliance.org/guidance/csaguide.v3.0.pdf
33. ISO 9000—Quality Management, www.iso.org/iso/iso_9000
34. L. Constantin, "Security Appliances are Riddled with Serious Vulnerabilities, Researcher Says," *PCWorld*, March 15, 2013, www.pcworld.com/article/2030965/researcher-security-appliances-are-riddled-with-serious-vulnerabilities.html
35. for example, P. Wayner, "17 Security Tips for Developers to Safeguard Code," *CIO Newsletter*, February 4, 2013, www.cio.com/article/728207/17_Security_Tips_for_Developers_to_Safeguard_Code?page=2&taxonomyId=3089
36. Mead, N., and B. Hawthorne, "Transitioning from Software to Software Assurance," IEEE Computer Society, *CN Computing Now News Letter*, October 17, 2012, www.computer.org/portal/web/computingnow/security/content?g=53319&type=article&urlTitle=transitioning-from-software-to-software-assurance or http://tinyurl.com/ld4fq5k
37. Summary guidelines for secure software design in cloud and Web environments are available in D. Radcliff, "Code Surety: Secure by Design," *SC Magazine*, March 1, 2012, www.scmagazine.com//code-surety-secure-by-design/article/228646/4/
38. An ambitious *Eliminate Vulnerable Code* project (http://www.digitsec.com/evc.htm) was initiated to crawl the Internet to find pieces of vulnerable, publically available code and to work remove such vulnerable code from the public domain (see Section 51.4.4.4). It is not clear such an effort will succeed.
39. Microsoft, "Security Development Lifecycle," www.microsoft.com/security/sdl/default.aspx
40. K. J. Higgins, "Secure Software Standard In the Spotlight," *Security Dark Reading Applications News Letter*, May 15, 2013, www.darkreading.com/vulnerability/secure-software-standard-in-the-spotligh/240154983
41. IBM Global Technology Services, Thought Leadership White Paper, "Selecting a Managed Security Services Provider: The 10 Most Important Criteria to Consider," May 2011, http://www-03.ibm.com/innovation/us/engines/assets/Selecting_MSS_provider_whitepaper_SEW03026-USEN-00.pdf
42. TechRepublic, "Antivirus Evaluation Guide" provided by GFI Software, January 2013, www.techrepublic.com/resource-library/whitepapers/antivirus-evaluation-guide/
43. L. Musthaler, "Ixia Models Attacks on Your Systems so You Can Test Your Defenses," *Network World Infrastructure Management Newsletter*, February 28, 2013,

www.networkworld.com/newsletters/techexec/2013/030113bestpractices.html?source=NWWNLE_nlt_it_best_practices_2013-03-04

44. www.vpnc.org
45. www.vpnc.org/testing.html
46. https://cloudsecurityalliance.org/star
47. www.cse-cst.gc.ca/its-sti/services/cc/smartcard-sug-v30-eng.html
48. www.commoncriteriaportal.org/files/ppfiles/UNKT-DO-0002%20v1-0.pdf
49. E. Messmer, "Security of Open-Source Software Again Being Scrutinized," *Network World Security News Letter*, March 13, 2013, www. networkworld.com/news/2013/031313-opensource-security-267636.html?source=NWWNLE_nlt_compliance_2013-03-15
50. K. J. Higgins, "Project Finds, Purges Vulnerable Code Snippets From the NET," *Security Dark Reading Database Security News*, May 23, 2012, www.darkreading.com/applications/project-finds-purges-vulnerable-code-sni/240000936
51. https://evc.digitsec.com
52. www.owasp.org/index.php/Category:OWASP_Top_Ten_Project
53. www.sans.org/top25-software-errors
54. www.commoncriteriaportal.org/products
55. www.scmagazine.com
56. www.networkcomputing.com
57. www.securitymagazine.com/
58. www.infoworld.com/
59. www.scmagazine.com/group-tests/section/108/
60. www.icsalabs.com
61. M. E. Kabay was the first Secretary of the Anti-virus Product Developers' (AVPD) Consortium created in the early 1990s by the NCSA (the National Computer Security Association, later renamed ICSA and then TruSecure). In a personal communication, he reported that anti-virus vendors were using radically different standards for their definition of anti-virus coverage; with a few thousand known viruses in the world, some vendors claimed to combat thousands and others only hundreds. When the NCSA told the new AVPD members that the first test would require them to identify and block only 75 percent of Joe Wells' WildList, many of the technical staff from the companies laughed. They didn't laugh so much when many of their products failed the initial round! Over the next rounds of testing (4 per year), the percentage of coverage of the WildList rose to 100 percent and then went on to include other viruses in the "zoo" of laboratory-identified viruses that had not yet spread to ordinary computer users' computers. According to Kabay, the NCSA program led to major improvements in the quality of anti-virus products and increased clarity. He argues that the insights and methods developed in the AVPD were then applied successfully to other security products.
62. Veracode, "Five Best Practices of Vendor Application Security Management," White Paper, available in "The Secure Software Supply Chain Toolkit," *All Things Security* Blog, September 20, 2012, www.veracode.com/blog/2012/09/the-secure-software-supply-chain-toolkit
63. www.av-test.org

64. "Ms. Smith," "AV-Test issues first Windows 8 antivirus solution ratings," *Network World*, April 8, 2013, www.networkworld.com/community/blog/av-test-issues-first-windows-8-antivirus-solution-ratings?source=NWWNLE_nlt_daily_pm_2013-04-09_testA6
65. NIST, Computer Security Division, Computer Security Resource Center, CMVP, "Standards," http://csrc.nist.gov/groups/STM/cmvp/standards.html
66. NIST, Computer Security Division, Computer Security Resource Center, CMVP, "Cryptographic Module Validation Program," http://csrc.nist.gov/groups/STM/cmvp/ index.html
67. NIST, Computer Security Division, Computer Security Resource Center, CAVP, "Cryptographic Algorithm Validation Program," http://csrc.nist.gov/groups/STM/cavp/ index.html
68. CMVP Program Staff, "Derived Test Requirements for FIPS PUB 140-2, *Security Requirements for Cryptographic Modules*" (draft), published by NIST, January 4, 2011, http://csrc.nist.gov/groups/STM/cmvp/documents/fips140-2/FIPS1402DTR.pdf
69. NIST, Computer Security Division, Computer Security Resource Center, CMVP, "Module Validation Lists," updated periodically as new validations emerge, last updated August 27, 2013, http://csrc.nist.gov/groups/STM/cmvp/validation.html
70. http://csrc.nist.gov/groups/STM/cmvp/documents/140-1/140InProcess.pdf
71. www.gsa.gov/portal/category/102371
72. www.gsa.gov/portal/content/131931
73. U.S. DoD, DHS, GSA, NIST, "Guide to Understanding FedRAMP," Version 1.2, April 22, 2013 (and subsequent versions), www.gsa.gov/portal/category/102375 ("Key Documents" link on "About FedRAMP")
74. The Common Criteria Portal, www.commoncriteriaportal.org
75. Common Criteria Certified Products, www.commoncriteriaportal.org/products
76. S. Amiri, "Significance of Common Criteria Assurance Maintenance (AMA)," *SC Magazine* (September 22, 2004). www.scmagazine.com/significance-of-common-criteria-assurance-maintenance-ama/article/31385
77. P. Brusil, "Security Standards for Products," Chapter 51 in *Computer Security Handbook* (5th ed.), ed. S. Bosworth, M. E. Kabay, and E. Whyne (Wiley, 2009).
78. Technical Report ISO/IEC TR 15446, "Information Technology—Security Techniques—Guide for the Production of Protection Profiles and Security Targets" ISO/IEC TR 15446:2004, July 2004, http://standards.iso.org/ittf/PubliclyAvailableStandards/c039690_ISO_IEC_TR_15446_2004(E).zip [Available in the extensive list of "Freely Available Standards" http://isotc.iso.org/livelink/livelink/fetch/2000/2489/Ittf_Home/PubliclyAvailableStandards.htm]
79. Common Criteria Certified Products, www.commoncriteriaportal.org/products
80. ISO/IEC Technical Report 13233, "Information Technology Interpretation of Accreditation Requirements in Guide 25 Accreditation of Information Technology and Telecommunications Testing Laboratories for Software and Protocol Testing Services," available for purchase online, www.iso.org/iso/iso_catalogue/catalogue_tc/catalogue_detail.htm?csnumber=21468
81. NIST Handbook 150-20, "Information Technology Security Testing—Common Criteria," www.nist.gov/nvlap/upload/NIST-HB-150-20-2005-1.pdf—a technology-specific extension to J. L. Cigler and V. R. White, eds., NIST Handbook 150,

"National Voluntary Laboratory Accreditation Program—Procedures and General Requirements," U.S. Department of Commerce, Technology Administration, National Institute of Standards and Technology (Washington, DC: US Government Printing Office, 1994), www.nist.gov/nvlap/upload/nist-handbook-150.pdf

82. ISO/IEC/EN Guide 17025, "General Requirements for the Competence of Calibration and Testing Laboratories," 2011, www.fasor.com/iso25
83. Common Evaluation Methodology Editorial Board, "Common Methodology for Information Technology Security Evaluation: Evaluation Methodology," Version 3.1, Revision 3, July 2009, www.commoncriteriaportal.org/files/ccfiles/CEMV3.1R3.pdf

INTRODUCTION TO PART V

DETECTING SECURITY BREACHES

No matter how well we implement security mechanisms, we are facing human opponents who may counter our best efforts until we can respond appropriately. How do security and network administrators find out if there has been a breach of security? How can they evaluate their own defenses before they are penetrated? This part includes chapters on:

52. **Application Controls.** Application-software security and logging
53. **Monitoring and Control Systems.** System logging and data reduction methods
54. **Security Audits.** Measuring compliance with explicit policies and with industry standards
55. **Cyberinvestigation.** Organizing effective digital forensic studies of observed or suspected security breaches, for internal use, and for cooperation with law enforcement

CHAPTER 52

APPLICATION CONTROLS

Myles Walsh and Susan Baumes

52.1 INTRODUCTION. Application controls can be broad and multifaceted. Given the complexity of many applications, no single system can provide all of the controls needed. As part of the design of a new or changes to an existing application, there are a number of controls that must be considered to ensure that the underlying data is protected against threats to the six fundamental attributes of information (confidentiality, control, integrity, authenticity, availability, and utility) as discussed in Chapter 3 in this *Handbook*. As with all other information security areas, a defense-in-depth strategy for application controls is a necessity. As an example, should a Web server be publically available? If not, then that control would have to be considered in the design of the application.

The basis of application controls fall into three areas:

1. Systems architecture and design
2. User input and entitlements
3. Database and underlying data controls

There is tremendous complexity in modern systems due to architecture changes and cost pressure on IT departments. Because of this complexity, there is the potential to have so many controls that they end up overriding one another and in some cases limiting their usefulness. It is easiest to design a net new application and consider all of the controls necessary, but the same due diligence is required for changes to existing applications whether new functionality is being added or there are changes to business processes that may require large entitlement changes. All changes in applications need to follow a strict design method whether using agile, waterfall, or some other methodology.

It should be noted that every architecture tier plays a role in applications and each tier must have some controls in place.

Although this chapter focuses on data-processing applications, similar issues arise in supervisory control and data acquisition (SCADA) systems for real-time process control.

52.2 SYSTEMS ARCHITECTURE AND DESIGN.

Architecture and design provides the first line of defense for applications. The configuration of the design and systems are paramount. Protection of and how the controls effect an application must be considered in the underlying architecture and design.

Architecture controls fall into a number of categories, but they encompass all of the tiers of a system supporting an application. These are standard best practices for systems.

Things to consider when designing system controls for applications include:

1. What underlying processes need to run on the system in support of the application? **Recommendation**: Limit processes to only those that are required.
2. What ports need to be open in order for the system to run correctly in support of the application? **Recommendation**: Limit ports to only those that are required. See Chapter 26 in this *Handbook* for further discussion of gateway security.
3. Who has direct access to the system and why? **Recommendations**: Practice least privilege and require special approval for higher risk or administrative access. Regularly review all access, but if access is higher risk, more frequent review and validation of access may be required.
4. What controls and processes will be in place for support of the application? Similarly, what controls will be in place for change control or patching? **Recommendations**: Define, follow, and validate change control processes for the systems and applications that those systems require. See Chapter 40 in this *Handbook* for more details of patch management.
5. How are the interacting systems validated with each other to ensure they are who they say they are? **Recommendations**: Digital certificates and two-way SSL can be used to ensure the validity of the underlying systems. Know and understand what systems can communicate with other systems and why.

52.3 INPUT AND ENTITLEMENTS.

From an application development perspective, the biggest control that must be considered is user input. User input falls into two distinct areas. What rights or entitlements does or should the user have and what are the limits for the input that the user is allowed to have? Business requirements of the applications generally drive these specifications. An example could be the input field of an address. The business may stipulate that the field be 50 characters and that only certain types of users be granted access to input, change, or delete the field.

Questions to ask regarding entitlements include:

- What is a user or groups of users allowed to do in the application?
- What should the user be able to view, create, update, or delete?
- Are there specific functionalities that a particular user or groups of user are not allowed to perform because of their current role within an organization?
- From a reporting perspective, the same questions need to be asked.

As part of application design all of those questions need to be answered based on the business requirements.

On the other hand, each input field within those entitlements must be defined within certain limits and those limits must be carried from the initial input to the underlying data structure. Both the application and the underlying database can control the limits and data entered.

Continuing with the above example, the 50-character address field should only accept 50 characters. The field length should be 50 and there must be input validation completed to ensure only valid or approved characters are entered. This control can be based both at the field level of the application as well as the database where the data will be stored. Limiting the length of inputs is a key defense against injection attacks and buffer overflows.

Typically, data validation has occurred closer to user input simply due to speed of networks, and more recently, real-time user validation provides a better experience for the user (e.g., validation as the field is being entered versus at the "submit" button of a Web-based form). Best practice requires server-based validation of input prior to processing. Initial checks can be completed on a Web form or field within a desktop application, but server-side validation is better since it is closer to internal systems.

Systems can accept input from both users and systems; for example, a batch process may take input from one source, manipulate it, and carry it to another source. Input, whether by a user or system, must be validated.

Database controls work in support of application controls. If, for example, field-level validation were not occurring in an application, the underlying database could be used to protect against bad data. As with the example above, if the field-level validation and the server-side validation failed, the database field can be defined as a 50-character field. Most database systems will truncate and ignore additional data that is entered into a field.

52.3.1 Input. As stated above, all input must be cleansed and validated to ensure that only acceptable values are received and processed. This is true for user input as well as systems input. The same thought must be used for a database perspective. Obviously, there are challenges with this method. If all 50-character fields for addresses must be updated to accept 60, multiple changes and more thorough testing are required.

Organizations may decide that the applications data is not critical and design it with looser controls. This can lead to issues simply because an attacker may use an application with fewer controls as a jumping point to get to an application with more sensitive data.

One cannot stress enough the importance of data validation for all user input. Many attacks on systems could have been prevented if proper and comprehensive data validation were completed (e.g., many cross-site scripting (XSS) and cross-site request forgery (XSRF) attacks [see Chapter 16 in this *Handbook*] can be prevented with validation). Not accepting certain known malicious characters, encoding certain characters, blocking certain string combinations, and understanding application attack vectors are important to keep applications secure and maintain integrity. Application designers need to work with their business partners and explain the issues with allowing certain types and sequences of characters.

As with all information security controls, multiple levels of control are needed. It is not appropriate to build an application where there is only field-level validation of input. Multiple controls need to be used in order to provide a defense-in-depth strategy for applications.

52.3.2 User Entitlements. Especially daunting are user entitlements for applications. Defining and limiting access while enabling users to complete their required tasks can be a formidable challenge. Application controls are paramount when considering what a user can do when within an application. Entitlements are also important when considering segregation of duties within the same application, as users change roles within an organization, or even what, if any, access a developer would have to a production environment.

User access rights are the entitlements granted to users or groups to perform functions within an application. As an example, a user that is supposed to have read only access to data should not be granted rights to an account that allows updates. Good design uses systems, application, and database controls to allow or restrict users to perform different functions.

If an individual's role within an organization is as a developer, should they be allowed to migrate code to production? Best practices tell us that they should not; however, every organization is different and development teams may also migrate code to production. The important thing is to:

1. Understand where entitlements are granted, to whom, and why.
2. Verify entitlements on a cyclical basis.
3. From a development perspective, have entitlements listed as requirements, in the test plan, and validate that the tests were successful.

52.3.2.1 Practice Least Privilege. As a best practice, apply least privilege to user entitlements, as it should be applied in all other areas of technology in order to maintain control over data and processes. How the underlying system is architected, the size of the organization, and regulatory controls will dictate the feasibility of achieving the best-practice state.

In many instances, business requirements do not consider which specific types of users should have access to which functionality. This lack is not sustainable, simply because applications are constantly changing, functionality being added, legacy architecture being updated, and new technologies being included.

Careful consideration must be given to grant users only the permissions required to do their job function(s) and controls. Comprehensive testing must also be conducted to ensure access creep does not occur as changes are made to the application.

52.3.2.2 Solving the Problem. For smaller applications, one can easily define the different business requirements with the functions that should have access. A simple matrix may do, for example:

Business Function	Business Role	Technology	Application or database role
Add new account	Phone representative	Insert into certain tables	App: phone rep DB: phone rep
Update account	Phone rep (with review) or data input associate	Update certain tables	App: update account DB: update account
Confirm phone representative	Phone rep manager	Read certain tables Update certain tables	App: phone rep manager DB: phone rep manager

Once the business requirements are defined and put into a matrix, it becomes much easier to manage existing functions and any future changes and to understand where the critical functions are to grant only the required privileges.

52.4 DATABASES AND UNDERLYING DATA CONTROLS.

Database technology allows for granular control of information though the use of role-based access controls (RBAC), as discussed in Chapter 9 in this *Handbook*. In addition, databases provide a multifaceted approach to application control. Not only can all users be segregated based on business need, but the database design can provide a level of control using table design and layout. Good database design and use can help protect data security. Relational databases are based on an underlying theoretical model by E. F. Codd, developed in the 1970s, and widely used today and for the foreseeable future.

Relational database management systems (RDBMS) are sets of programs that provide database administrators (DBAs) with the tools to perform the following tasks:

- Create database structures (file or table layouts, and screens or forms).
- Enter information into the structures.
- Establish cross-references among the files or tables.
- Manipulate (sort, index, and summarize) the information in the structures.
- Import information from nonrelational database structures and export information to nondatabase structures. This allows for interfaces between applications using an RDBMS, and applications using conventional files structures
- Data-repository and data-dictionary tools. These tools document databases and may include descriptive information (*metadata*) about all of the resources included in an information-systems environment. Data dictionaries can support documentation standards. Common file or table structures, common program modules, and common field definitions contribute significantly to the reduction of confusion, and of communication breakdowns in an enterprise
- Databases move much of the dynamically changing requirements for data formats and data edits out of the source code of application programs and into easily localized and edited single criteria. Instead of having programmers hunt down and alter multiple occurrences of data restrictions, DBAs can collaborate with the programmers to change individual criteria with the assurance that all programs using the RDBMS will successfully execute the changes.

All of these tools help maintain the security and the integrity of the database.

There are two primary methods of organizing files and databases for access and processing: *batch* and *online*. Batch files, which can be written in various *job-control languages* (JCLs), carry out instructions without further human intervention once they are set in execution, whereas online methods involve human interaction with the programs at multiple points. Protection of online files and databases requires additional planning when the systems using them are being architected and special precautions when they are being used. Protection of batch files is more straightforward because the creation of backup copies is an inherent part of the batch process.

As previously discussed, data validation prior to entering information into a database must be completed regardless if the entry is via user or system. Every attempt should be made to assure that data are entered or transferred and validated expeditiously. Failure to get correct data into a system quickly delays the creation and display of the information, the very purpose of almost all systems. When improper attention is directed to validation of the data as it enters the system, incorrect information is created by the system. The acronym *GIGO* (*garbage in, garbage out*) has long become part of the national lexicon of everyday language. Improper validation and allowing of garbage into a database may have downstream impact to other applications or processes that use the data. Validation at all tiers of an application is critical.

For related topics, see Chapter 38 in this *Handbook* on writing secure code, Chapter 39 on software development and quality assurance, Chapter 40 on managing software patches, and Chapter 47 on operations security and production controls.

52.4.1 Data Corruption. Data corruption implies incorrect data—a violation of the *integrity* of the data. Corruption can occur because of physical factors or logical errors in programs. Good application controls dictate that databases and their underlying architecture be protected from data corruption. Data can be damaged through hardware problems, errors in software, or during concurrent access by two or more users or processes.

52.4.1.1 Physical Data Corruption. Physical corruption occurs through breakdown or other failures of hardware such as computers and network equipment, especially of mass-storage devices such as magnetic disks, tapes and cartridges, or optical drives. Data corruption during transmission can occur through electromagnetic perturbations of communications cables or radio-frequency noise that affects wireless transmission. Fiber-optic cables are susceptible to cross-talk and to disruption caused by physical bends or kinks in the cables; optical disks are susceptible to dirt and abrasion; magnetic disk drives can be harmed by physical jolts (dropping, intense vibration); solid-state drives do not do well when immersed in liquid.

In addition to problems in the transmission or storage media, improper settings or the effects of wear in the equipment can cause errors. Examples include misalignment of magnetic heads on disks and tapes; bad contacts in wireless transmission equipment, causing noise; and improper positioning of lasers in optical media. See Chapters 22 and 23 for extensive discussion of physical factors that can cause data corruption.

Physical corruption characteristically shows data written inappropriately across blocks, rather than in single fields defined by software applications. Such physical corruption usually has no relationship with the damaged records other than physical proximity on the disk; therefore, a cardinal sign of physical corruption is damage to files from completely different applications—a block of database records contiguous to a block of text files, for example.

52.4.1.2 *Logical Data Corruption.* Logical corruption occurs through programming errors such as incorrect sums, bad arithmetic formulas, incorrect logical conditions, bad data in look-up tables, out-of-bounds conditions allowing reading and writing in the wrong areas of memory, lack of data validation, and the effects of malicious software. See Chapter 38 in this *Handbook* for a discussion of many types of such errors.

Logical corruption characteristically shows errors in the same field in multiple records. Another class of logical errors shows bad values for boundary conditions (e.g., the smallest or largest possible value) but correct data within the range. Such errors rarely cross application boundaries unless there is a logical relationship among the damaged files; for example, an error in a spreadsheet (almost always due to input or programming errors by the user) may propagate to text files if object linking and embedding are used to insert the spreadsheet results into the document. Other documents will remain unaffected by such logical errors.

For more extensive discussion of preventing, locating, and correcting logical errors, see Chapter 39 on software development and quality assurance.

52.4.2 Database Management Subsystems. In the 1960s, complex systems, such as those based on accounting records, forced programmers to define their own file structures to represent relationships among the data; for example, an order header file would be linked to the corresponding order detail records through hard-coded relationships in the application programs. Each programmer or programming team had to define its own data access paths and code them explicitly. Coordinating access to multiple individually named files caused headaches for programmers. For example, it was easy to make errors such as forgetting to increment counters representing how many detail records corresponded to a master (index) record (e.g., line counts in order headers disagreeing with the actual number of detail lines). Because there was no particular protection for the files in such systems, it was easy to replace or delete individual files by mistake, leading to massive logical corruption. Deletion of header records could leave a fragment of inaccessible details (*orphans*) in associated files. Programs had to keep pointers up-to-date for forward and backward chaining. Backups sometimes failed through operator error so that not all related files were included. Furthermore, every system had its own unique methods for managing the data, causing maintenance and learning headaches.

The late 1960s saw many large programming shops defining their data access methods by using library routines that all programmers could share, but there was still a heavy investment in learning the new rules whenever a programmer changed jobs. Following the publication of E. F. Codd's model for relational databases in the early 1970s, the programming field saw explosive growth in implementation of database management subsystems, where the interface to the database controlled utility functions such as indexing, pointing, and chaining.

With proper configuration a typical DBMS protects all files, called *datasets,* against accidental erasure, and would force all reads, writes, appends, and locks to be mediated by the DBMS routines. General users should not have access to a DB's underlying infrastructure—only to the data through the DBMS.

The DBMS provides controlled access to data and also typically provides backup utilities to ensure that all datasets are copied together and to prevent accidental restoration of the wrong version of a dataset. Finally, a DBMS usually provides logging facilities to keep records of different types of access to the database. All of this functionality provides control to the data.

One of the most important rules enforced by a DBMS is *referential integrity* to prevent common logical data corruption, automatic *uniqueness constraints* to preclude duplicate and conflicting records, and *locking* for safe concurrent access.

- ***Referential Integrity.*** Referential integrity in DBMS design ensures that every dependent record has a primary key value that matches an existing primary key in the master file.
  - In an order database, for example, order numbers in a header file (often called the *order master*) are the primary keys.
  - Each order header record contains unique information about an order, such as customer number, date placed, total price of materials, taxes, and shipping costs.
  - The order detail file contains the dependent records, each of which can be located using its order number as the primary key.
  - Each detail record contains information about a specific part of the corresponding order such as an item number, quantity ordered, price, extended price, and special charges or discounts.
  - If an order header record is to be deleted, all the order detail records must first be deleted; otherwise, the detail records would be left with no way to locate them through their primary key value.
  - Similarly, no detail record can be added unless the master record with the same primary key already exists.
- ***Uniqueness Constraints.*** A modern DBMS allows configuration of nonrepeating primary keys; for example, in an order database, the order number would typically be a nonrepeating or unique key because there should never be two orders with the same identifying number. Setting the uniqueness property would preclude adding a second header record with the same value in the order number field as another order.

52.4.3 Distributed Databases.

A *distributed database* is one that is stored in different databases on different computer platforms. Databases can be distributed over many sites, using several different architectures.

The simplest and most susceptible to failure is the single database server that houses the database and shares its contents among several local area networks. Whenever the server or the database is offline, or during a crash, all clients lose access to the database. The backup and recovery of a single-server database follows the procedures described earlier.

A second architecture is the *replicated database server*, in which there are duplicate copies of the database on multiple servers. This type of system allows clients to access information from any of several copies of the database. With a replicated server environment, clients can still have access to the database, when one of the servers is offline. Such replicated systems usually have an additional benefit of being able to balance transaction traffic so as to keep any one server from being overwhelmed. The trade-off is the database synchronization process that increases the complexity of the replicated server architecture. Although the backup and recovery of a distributed database can also follow the procedures described earlier, it is complicated by the synchronization requirement.

A third architecture is known as a *partitioned database server*, in which specific subsets of a database are on two or more database servers. There could be a marketing database on one server, an accounting and finance database on a second server, and an inventory database on a third server. Because it is generally not possible to have mutually exclusive subsets of databases, synchronization must still be part of this architecture. Backup and recovery of partitioned databases requires application of the procedures described above for each of the subsets.

There is another distributed architecture known as *federated database servers*. This architecture is used in support of databases on two or more servers, made up of ordinarily incompatible storage models such as hierarchical and relational models supported by different DBMSs. With the federated architecture, a single unified database definition, or schema, is created and stored on a combined database server. That server acts as an interface between application programs and the databases residing on the other servers. Queries and other transactions are sent to the combined database server, which translates these into queries and transactions to the underlying databases. Responses then return from the underlying databases to the unified schema to formulate a response to the user. Backup and recovery procedures such as those described above are used for the underlying databases.

Although federated database architecture can be complex and expensive to maintain, it can be less complex and less expensive than the process of supporting application programs for each of the underlying DBMSs. Federated architecture is often used in the implementation of data warehouses, which are used to extract information from multiple internal databases, as well as external databases, to support management decision making.

52.4.3.1 Database Controls to Maintain Integrity. Concurrent access to data can cause problems of integrity unless the access is *serialized* to ensure that one process at a time accesses any given resource.

52.4.3.2 Lock on Update. When more than one user accesses a database, it is possible to experience conflicts over the use of specific records. A classic example occurs in an inventory database, where there are 15 units of part 1 in the inventory.

- User Albert needs to take five units of part 1 out of inventory, leaving a total of 10. The inventory program reads the inventory record for part 1 and modifies record 1 to show only 10 units.
- However, if while this is going on user Betty needs three units of part 1, the inventory record still shows 15 units available because user Albert has not yet updated that record.
- After user Albert's program completes its update, the record shows 10 units available, but after user Betty's program overwrites that record to show 12 available units for part 1, the inventory total is off by five units.
- This situation is an example of a *race condition* as described in Section 39.4.1.6 of Chapter 39 in this *Handbook*.

To avoid this kind of logical corruption, a DBMS provides facilities for *locking* parts of the database. In the inventory example, user A's program would lock the inventory record for part 1 (or the entire inventory dataset) until the update is completed. That way, user B's program would have to wait for user A's program to *unlock* the data before being able to act on the inventory record.

The obvious symptom of a bad locking strategy is a discrepancy between the database value and the real-world value. However, such a discrepancy is not by itself proof of logical corruption, because the same divergence could arise from events in the real world not reflected in the database. In the inventory example, the actual inventory may have been reduced by theft, or increased by an unrecorded addition of materials.

52.4.3.3 Unconditional versus Conditional Locking. There are two types of locking strategy: *conditional* locking and *unconditional* locking.

- Conditional locking attempts to obtain a lock, but if the required record or the entire dataset is already locked, the DBMS returns control to the calling program with a status indicator of this condition. The application program can then be written to loop until the lock is obtained.
- The unconditional lock request hangs the program until the lock is granted. The DBMS or the operating system provides automatic queuing using a first-in, first-out queue.

52.4.3.4 Deadlocks. Unconditional locking carries risks if multiple resources are locked by programs.

- For example, if program A unconditionally locks resource 1 and program B locks resource 2, trouble will occur when program A then attempts to lock resource 2, while program B tries to lock resource 1.
- Neither program will release the resource it has locked until it is released, and so both will wait forever or until one of the programs is forcibly terminated.
- Such a situation is known as a *deadlock* or more colorfully as a *deadly embrace.*
- If programmers insist on using unconditional locking, the deadlock prevention strategy is to ensure that all programs accessing the database must lock resources in the same order (e.g., lock 1, then lock 2) and must unlock in the reverse order (unlock 2, then unlock 1).

Other strategies are to keep transactions as short as possible, and to avoid the necessity for operator interactions that would keep the records locked for long periods of time.

52.4.3.5 Two-Phase Commit. Sometimes many records or datasets must be locked for complex transactions to be completed. For example, in a hospital's clinical systems database, discharging a patient could require modifications in datasets such as the patient-master, treatment-detail, nursing assignment master and details, doctor assignment master and details, and datasets for the financial functions. Locking everything that might be needed and waiting for a human being to enter all the appropriate data could take seconds to minutes, during which all the affected records would be locked and unavailable to everyone else on the system. In the extreme, if an operator were to leave in the middle of a transaction, other users could be blocked out of large parts of the database for an indeterminate length of time, even for hours. The delays resulting from such locking around human intervention led to the principle that *no transaction can be allowed to lock around a human intervention.*

Another problem with locking around human intervention is that a system failure could terminate processing while the database was in an inconsistent state. For example, in the inventory case, the DBMS might have updated the order detail by adding an item, but not yet updated the order header to show the new total cost of the order. To reduce the likelihood of such an occurrence, a DBMS can support the two-phase commit as an aid to making changes as fast as possible, and thus reducing the window of vulnerability for interruption.

- In the two-phase commit, the DBMS obtains copies of all the records needed when the operator begins a transaction.
- Once the operator has taken all necessary steps for completing the transaction, the DBMS locks and reads all the changed records again and compares the current values with the initial values; if there are no differences, the DBMS makes all the required changes and immediately unlocks all the records.
- However, if the current values have been modified since the operator requested the initial copies, then some other process has been active and so the DBMS reports that verification is needed.
- The operator is typically given the choice of how to proceed; for example, if there are no items left in inventory, the order may have to be delayed or canceled, whereas if there are enough items, the operator need merely reinitiate the transaction with the new initial values.

52.4.3.6 Database Backup Files and System Logs. When information in an online file or database is updated, the old information, that is, the information that was in the record before the change was made, is overlaid; unless steps are taken, it disappears without a trace. For this reason, many DBMSs allow an image of the original record to be copied to the *transaction log file*. In other cases, where the exact history of a particular group of records must be preserved, as with insurance and medical data, an application may append new records but not delete old ones.

If online files and databases were never damaged or lost, data loss would be of no concern with proper database configuration. However, in an imperfect world, steps must be taken so that damaged or lost online files and databases can be recovered. For further details of data backup and recovery, see Chapter 57 in this *Handbook.*

In order to recover online files and databases, it is first necessary to make periodic backup copies, and to make log copies of records that have been updated in the time between making the backups. How often a backup copy is made depends on how dynamic the files or databases are. In most enterprises, a significant number of total or partial files and databases are copied daily. It is not uncommon for computer operations departments to spend several hours each day doing backups. Whenever a backup copy of a file or database is created, there are two correct copies at that point in time. To explain how online file and database backup and system logging work, think of a single online file. The file is taken offline, and is no longer accessible to online transactions at 4 AM, and a copy is made. Both copies of this file are identical at that time. At 6 AM, the backup is complete and the original disk file is put back online. Transactions start to update that file again. From that point on, with each update transaction, the differences between that file and its backup increase.

At 2 PM, if for some reason the file is no longer usable, the backup file is then eight hours behind. At this point, the log file becomes critical in the restoration process. The log file is in sequence by time and contains copies of the updated records both before and after update was performed. It also contains copies of the transaction record.

52.4.4 Recovery and Restart. After it has been determined that an online file or database has been corrupted or destroyed, a procedure known as recovery and restart is initiated. The first step in this procedure is to copy the backup back to disk to create a new original as of the time of that backup. The next step uses the log file to reapply, in time sequence, all the transactions that had been executed since the backup copy was made.

Contemporary database systems may have files that cannot be taken offline. They are online 24 hours a day, seven days a week. In order to make backup copies, parts of the database are copied periodically (dynamic backup). Conceptually, a database can be broken up into parts. Each part can be backed up separately at different time periods. A number of schemes can be devised to back up some of the records. For example, copy to a backup file every fifth record of the database in one time period, say records 5, 10, 15, 20, etc. A bit later, copy to another backup file records 1, 6, 11, 16, 21, and so on. If a conflict occurs between copying the record for backup and a transaction attempting to update the record, have an appropriate procedure established to let one or the other take place first. Recovery and restart, as well as backout procedures, work the same way, with the additional complexity of establishing priorities for which gets done first when conflicts occur. Even though these conflicts increase complexity, they are resolved when the procedures for recovery, restart, and backout are created.

Another approach to backups of such critical files is the *shadow copy*, which copies data even when files are in use. Shadow copy software bypasses elements of the file system to be able to access locked records.

52.4.4.1 Backout. The log file is also used in a process known as *backout*. This process is initiated when online update transactions fail to complete after making incomplete or partial updates to files or databases. For example, an update transaction in which there are additions to three fields in three separate files is supposed to take place. After making two out of the three updates, the transaction terminates abnormally because of a program malfunction. Eventually, the program gets corrected, but something has to be done to undo the two partial updates. Otherwise, when the program is fixed and the transaction is rerun, those two updates would be reapplied, which would result in erroneous duplication. The backout procedure is initiated for those transactions which, if they had not completed properly, would generate errors.

Recovery, using log files, requires marking the start and end of every transaction; if the log file records show a transaction start without the corresponding transaction end, recovery processes can recognize the transaction as incomplete. Such markers correspond to what are called *checkpoints* in the program design.

52.4.4.2 Roll-Forward Recovery. Another approach to recovery is to start from a known good state and redo all transactions that are known to have been accomplished correctly. This roll-forward recovery requires a database backup and a transaction log file to be synchronized, so that the first record in the transaction log file represents the first transaction immediately following a database backup. With these data in hand, it is possible to reconstruct all the modifications up to, but not including, the last complete transaction. All incomplete transactions are discarded, although the recovery program typically prints out all the details available for transactions that were not completed.

52.5 BATCH FILES.

Operating systems have their own facilities for writing and executing batch files, sometimes called *scripts*. Batch files can be complex enough that they look like programs, with logical tests, branching, and so on.

52.5.1 Backup File Creation.

The protection of files that are updated by batch processing programs is automatic, because the file is completely recopied and the original is left in the form it was in before the program executed. Therefore, each processing cycle leaves its own backup. The name *batch processing* comes from the idea of sequentially processing transactions in a group. There are always two or more files involved. There is the master file that is being updated, and one or more transaction files that contain the information used to update the master. The process copies master file records that have no update activity into a new master file, updates the master records that do have activity and copies them into the new master file, and does not copy those master records that are flagged as deletions in the activity file. When the process completes, there are at least three files: the original master, the activity file(s), and the new master. Backups are the original master and the activity file(s). In the next processing cycle, the new master becomes input, together with that cycle's activity file(s). If a problem is encountered with the master file, the prior cycle's master file and all subsequent activity files can be used to generate an updated master. Keeping two or three generations of master and activity files is a common practice. The term *generation* is often applied to the batch processing cycles—generation 0, generation 1, generation 2—or as *grandfather*, *father*, and *son*. In recent decades, these latter terms have been replaced by *grandparent*, *parent*, and *child*.

52.5.2 Audit Controls.

Another security measure applied when working with batch files involves using control totals to assure that the batch process has executed with accuracy. Specific controls may include counts of records. There also may be control totals of the values in specific fields of the input records to compare with totals in the output, after processing additions and subtractions. For example, in a payroll system, information from time cards is submitted to a computer for processing. Along with the time cards is a transmittal that contains a count of the time cards, and totals of all the straight time and overtime hours compiled by the department that originated the time cards. A procedure is run in which the control totals on the transmittal are checked against the totals actually input from the time cards, to assure correctness before initiating the payroll process. If discrepancies are encountered, they need to be investigated and corrected before taking the next step in processing the payroll.

52.6 DATA INTEGRITY AND VALIDATION.

The following sections present a brief overview of validation; however, for more extensive coverage of this topic, see Chapter 47 in this *Handbook* on operations security and production controls.

52.6.1 Validation Controls.

Whether an application updates its files by means of batch or online processing, or in some combination of both, validation of input is paramount. The term *GIGO* (garbage in, garbage out) is not heard as often as it used to be, yet it is as true as ever. Most contemporary systems use online files and databases, with information entered interactively, allowing for validation at the source. There are several specific validation techniques that have been applied to reduce the amount of incorrect information input into files and databases.

52.6.1.1 Methods for Identifying Input Errors and Unauthorized Modifications

Data input errors are common.

- Fours and nines, ones and sevens, and sixes and zeros can easily be mistaken for one another.
- Operators can leave out a digit or insert an extraneous one.
- Transposition is another type of mistake that is made from time to time. For example, an order entry operator may key in 3286 instead of 3826 (a transposition error), or perhaps 7790 instead of 7796 (a transcription error).
- Such errors would be reported when the *check digit* calculation produces a number that differs from the input check digit.
- A check digit is an extra digit that is added to a generated variable as a suffix.
- For example, a five-digit stock number could have an extra digit; the sixth digit or *check digit*, as it is called, is calculated by applying an algorithm (performing some arithmetic) on the first five digits, resulting in a single-digit result.
- To minimize input errors, check digits can be used on any variables that are program generated; for example, part numbers, employee numbers, and codes of various types.

A single check digit can sometimes conceal the existence of double or multiple input errors in an input string because of the relatively simple arithmetic schemes. More complex versions of the check digit generate a sequence of digits called a *checksum*, which provides greater power to help identify input errors or fraud; credit card numbers typically include a four-digit checksum at the end of the number. For example, a typical VISA credit card number has the format 1111 2222 3333 4444; the fourth block (4444 in our example) is calculated using a secret algorithm as a function of the other three blocks. Computer criminals have often tried (and sometimes succeeded) to reverse engineer the checksum algorithm to create VISA numbers that actually belong to unknown victims. Credit card security organizations have learned to apply complex *heuristic methods* to identify unlikely transactions; e.g., if the legitimate owner has just filled up her gas tank at an often-used filling station in Vermont, it is unlikely that a transaction five minutes later for 1,000 wool blankets at a manufacturing firm in Italy is legitimate, regardless of the accurate-looking VISA number.

An extension of the checksum, the *hash total*, is a common tool for identifying logical or physical data corruption. A hash total is simply the meaningless sum of numerical values, such as part numbers, rather than the meaningful sum of quantities. Recalculation of a hash total can usually indicate if the data have been corrupted since the last time the hash total was computed.

A digital signature is a cryptographically generated value based on an encryption key. Applying the same digital signature process to the data should generate an identical signature. In addition, as described in Chapters 7 and 37 in this *Handbook*, using the public key cryptosystem allows one to verify the authenticity as well as the integrity of signed data.

52.6.1.2 Range Checks. Range checks offer another way of validating information at its source. In situations where quantities and currency values are being entered, lower and upper limits can be established. For example, a range check could be used on quantity ordered to ensure that the value entered is within specific bounds, such as no less than 10 or no more than 60 of a certain item. Although not completely error proof, such limits can at least eliminate obvious errors and reduce those not so blatant. Range checking with values of 10 and 40 will eliminate the extra 0 error, where an operator enters 100 or 600, or 1 or 4.

52.6.1.3 *Validity Checks Using Tables.* Using tables of values or valid codes is one of the best ways to ensure that only correct information is entered into files and databases. In contemporary files and databases, data type is specified as a property of the field during the design phase, and these properties can be used to make sure that text information is not entered into numeric fields and vice versa. Properties are also used to filter out invalid data configurations. Although impossible to filter out misspelled last names and other open-ended types of information, it is possible to filter out invalid state codes and other violations of standards. For example, a table containing the valid state codes in a country can be used to assure that none but those codes can be entered in the state field. Other such entities (e.g., department codes, product codes or types, and price classes) are primary candidates for table validation.

With tables, it is also possible to make combination tables. For example, if a certain product code fell within a specific range, then only four price classes might be allowable. To be concrete, suppose that when a product code falls within the 600 to 699 range, then the price class could only be R, PR, OC, and CD. Such tables are used to validate information as it is initially entered into files and databases. Entry of invalid information, whether intentional or inadvertent, is inhibited.

Tables of forbidden combinations are particularly important in real-time control systems for processes that can go seriously wrong as a result of bad inputs. For example, in December 1992, an explosion at a chemical plant in the Netherlands was traced to a data input error that could have been prevented by an edit check that verified a table of forbidden chemical mixtures. The following is an excerpt from a report published in RISKS 14.22 (January 4, 1993) by Meine van der Meulen of The Netherlands Organization for Applied Scientific Research, Department of Industrial Safety:

> The accident started with a typing error in a prescription by a Laboratory worker. Instead of tank 632 he typed tank 634. In tank 632 there was stored resin feed classic (UN-1268) and normally used in the batch process. In tank 634 DCDP (dicyclopentadiene) was stored. The operator, who had to check if the tank contents was [*sic*] equal with the prescription, filled the reactor with the wrong chemicals.
>
> ... a heavy explosion occurred which caused the death of 3 firemen of the works fire brigade and injured 11 workers [including] 4 firemen of the works fire brigade. The damage was estimated at several [10s] of millions NL guilders.

Tables should generally be used only for information that is relatively static, because of the need for maintenance. Frequent table maintenance can lead to errors that have a cascading effect. If a table is incorrect, then all the information supposedly validated by that table could be incorrect throughout the files and databases.

52.6.1.4 *Diagnostic Utilities.* Production programs need to operate on verifiably correct data. Every production program should include diagnostic utilities to scan databases for logically impossible values or deviations from reality. For example, a diagnostic routine might check to be sure that every header total matches the total computed from the linked line item values. Because older data may have been accepted under older range-validation rules, all records should be checked to ensure that they conform to the current range constraints. Similarly, any other logical constraints in an application system should be explicitly addressed in the diagnostic program. The output from the program should give all the details appropriate for identifying and correcting the incorrect data. For example, instead of simply indicating "BAD VALUE IN PRICE FIELD, RECORD 1234," the output should explain something like, "PRICE FOR ITEM 234 = $45.67 WHICH EXCEEDS CONFIGURED LIMIT OF $40.00 SHOWN IN INVENTORY MASTER RECORD 78999."

52.7 CONCLUDING REMARKS. In another application of the 80/20 rule, 20 percent of the design and development work is expended in handling 80 percent of the data (the normal and the correct) going through a system, whereas 80 percent of the design and development work is expended for handling 20 percent of the data (the errors, the exceptions, and the unusual situations) going through the system. It is safe to say that more effort should be expended on validation, and on backup and recovery procedures, than is spent on those processes that handle validated data and the routine tasks of application processing.

Good application controls involve data validation at all tiers of an architecture as well as careful consideration of the entitlements granted to users from an application, systems, and database perspective. It is not enough to focus only on user input and trust input from other systems. In today's complex systems there are too many areas where data can be modified either accidentally or maliciously to trust any input without validation.

In addition, organizations need to leverage all of the features of database systems to help not only maintain integrity, but understand data backup and recovery mechanisms. Adequate backup and recovery processes and procedures have to be put in place to handle system failures. These processes and procedures range from disaster recovery to single system or application recovery. To ensure that sites, enterprises, or applications can be brought back after failures requires that processes and procedures be put in place during the design and development process and kept up to date as the situation requires.

52.8 FURTHER READING

Basta, A., and M. Zgola. *Database Security*. Cengage Learning, 2011.

Chadli, M., and H. Coppier. *Command-control for Real-time Systems*. Wiley-ISTE, 2013.

Jones, C. *Software Engineering Best Practices: Lessons from Successful Projects in the Top Companies*. McGraw-Hill Osborne Media, 2009.

Kroenke, D. M., and D. Auer. *Database Processing*, 12th ed. Prentice-Hall, 2011.

Lublinksy, B., K. T. Smith, and A. Yakubovich. *Professional Hadoop Solutions*. Wrox, 2013.

Ottenheimer, D. *Big Data Security*. Wiley, 2014.

Post, G. V. *Database Management Systems: Designing and Building Business Applications*, 5th ed. Self-published, 2010. http://jerrypost.com/Books/DBBookSummary.html

Radvanovsky, R., and J. Brodsky, eds. *Handbook of SCADA/Control Systems Security*. CRC Press, 2013.

Romney, M. B., and P. J. Steinbart. *Accounting Information Systems*, 12th ed. Prentice-Hall, 2011.

Shelley, G. B., and H. J. Rosenblatt. *Systems Analysis and Design*, 10th ed. Cengage Learning, 2013.
Sommerville, I. *Software Engineering*, 9th ed. Addison Wesley, 2010.
Stair, R. M., and G. W. Reynolds. *Principles of Information Systems*, 11th ed. Cengage Learning, 2013.
Van Wyk, K. R., and M. G. Graf. *Enterprise Software Security: A Confluence of Disciplines*. Addison-Wesley Professional, 2014.

CHAPTER 53

MONITORING AND CONTROL SYSTEMS

Caleb S. Coggins and Diane E. Levine

53.1 INTRODUCTION. Monitoring and control (M&C) systems provide critical services to computing operations through prevention, detection, and response. When aligned with security policy and appropriately implemented, these systems enable organizations to detect security incidents, mitigate risk, and analyze trends. M&C systems may prevent persistent unauthorized login attempts from a remote location, detect performance issues on a storage network, or alert an incident responder to the attempted theft of intellectual property. Automation is a key factor for proactive, real-time, and scalable M&C system implementations. Although it is possible to review individual log files within a limited scope, manual log review remains impractical and inefficient for modern enterprises processing millions of events on a routine basis. Although the scope of M&C systems may vary in size and complexity, the central components remain the same: data collection, data reduction, and system response.

Data collection includes log file generation and storage. Computer systems use *log files* to store records of events. Logged information includes system time, relevant user accounts, system identifiers, and the actions performed. Programs write or append data to log files that are often stored in local directory structures and forwarded to central log collectors for aggregation.

Data reduction is the process of using predefined or on-demand rules and logic to generate relevant, filtered, and actionable views of aggregate log data. Exception reports such as failed or unauthorized login attempts filter out acceptable events, enabling analysts and automated alert processes to focus on anomalies for additional follow-up. Visual *dashboards,* including performance metrics and risk-ranked events, provide information managers and production operators with an enterprise view of current production activities that may impact service delivery objectives.

System response encompasses the actions resulting from the data reduction phase. Actions include alert notification, corrective actions, and recovery procedures. Depending on several factors, the response may be automated or involve feedback through a human–machine interface (HMI).

The following self-assessment questionnaire is based on the areas covered in this chapter; it identifies elements to review for an existing or planned M&C system:

- What is the purpose and goal of the M&C system, from a business and technical service perspective?
- What are the security, compliance, business, and legal requirements?
- What systems, components, or processes need to be monitored or controlled?
- What model will be used to monitor or control the target?
- Where will the data be stored?
- How will the data records be retained and secured?
- What kind of data reduction and reporting is required?
- Who or what will respond to detected events and incidents?
- What self-defense mechanisms exist for the M&C system?

53.1.1 Prevention, Detection, and Response. M&C system capabilities generally include the ability to prevent, detect, and respond to a wide number of events. However, not all events and challenges need to be met with costly control systems or dedicated sensors. Some activities may be more suited for monitoring than control. You may also want to alert on activities that may not be alarming on an individual basis but may be significant in aggregate or at specific thresholds. Decisions to implement and configure monitoring and control systems should be founded on a risk-based approach.

Prevention refers to the system's ability to prohibit an undesirable action. Common tools used in network security include in-line intrusion prevention systems (IPSs) and unified threat management (UTM) appliances. Deploying these systems at choke points, between enclaves, and at the network edge can restrict the proliferation of malware across an enterprise network as well as block Command and Control (C&C or C2) channels for botnet clients. In the physical-security realm, single-person mantraps prevent individuals from tailgating into secure facilities.[1]

Detection refers to the ability to identify attacks and other security concerns through sensory input. Systems rely on automated detection mechanisms and human observation. M&C systems must have reliable detection mechanisms in order to manage security events and provide meaningful metrics on the state of the information infrastructure. Proactive detection may involve the authorized use of a vulnerability scanner by security controls testers. Reactive detection may include the identification of source IP addresses and VPN users who participated in a distributed denial of service (DDoS) attack on an Internet-facing network.[2]

Response refers to the output of M&C systems. A monitoring system may detect remote attempts to enable FTP and Telnet on production servers, log the activity, and send an administrative alert to an operator or centralized correlation engine. A control system, however, would correct the configuration files and service states or prohibit the changes from occurring in the first place. Additional human response may occur after the administrative alert or dashboard refresh, such as escalation to an incident-response team for resolution and postmortem analysis.[3]

Failure to detect and report security breaches within mandated time frames may have legal ramifications, as many states require breach notification.[4] Implementing *defense in depth* (layered defenses) increases the likelihood of threat detection, incident prevention, and response. For example, AC power loss at a secure facility and a nonresponsive battery or generator backup may render a closed-circuit television (CCTV) system incapable of recording a physical attack. An additional layer, such as physical security guards, can provide a degraded level of monitoring while technicians restore power and monitoring systems to normal functionality.[5]

53.1.2 Controlling versus Monitoring. *Monitoring* refers to the observation, logging, and reporting of systems, components, and events. Data collected from monitoring systems may identify intruders, locate system vulnerabilities, confirm operational status, and provide confirmation that controls are online and in place. In a network environment, a vulnerability scanner can perform authenticated scans on specific devices to identify missing patches and configuration issues without necessarily modifying or controlling the targets. M&C systems operate in two modes, *continuous* and *batch*.

1. **Continuous mode** provides ongoing measurement and compliance assurance. Systems that operate in real-time, continuous mode present a more accurate, up-to-the-second view of an organization's operational environment.

2. **Batch mode** takes place at specific points in time. An annual audit often utilizes batch mode analysis, to determine the effectiveness of system controls and processes. The results provide limited assurance for a specific point in time or historical range based on available data.

Control refers to what we can manipulate and audit. Rather than merely observing and recording information about an unauthorized change in the operational environment, controls can restrict such activities based on predefined configurations and processes. Controls may be *prohibitive* or *corrective* in action.

- *Prohibitive* controls prevent the change from occurring.
- *Corrective* controls return or restore a control target to its approved state. A host intrusion prevention system (HIPS) may prevent modification to critical system files, while logging and alerting on failed attempts to do so.

Control systems ensure that the operational environment reflects stated policies and standards. The Control Objectives for Information and Related Technology (COBIT) section AI1.9 and ISO 17799 section 9.7 identify the need to monitor system access and use (see Chapters 44 and 54 in this *Handbook* for discussion of these standards).

Organizations that still depend on passwords for authentication should not only establish policies and draft procedures to meet those requirements but also need to implement technical controls to enforce compliance. If the standard includes a 15-character minimum password length, with specific complexity requirements and a mandated limit on the period of validity, technical password controls should prevent users and administrators from defining nonexpiring, short, trivial passwords such as *abcde*.[6]

Auditors inspect the operational environment to provide objective assurance of an organization's control environment. Typically, auditors evaluate a sample of control sets at scheduled intervals. These point-in-time, manual efforts provide insight into the infrastructure's degree of compliance. However, they do not provide the same level of efficiency as integrating automation into a framework that supports continuous information assurance.

The environment directly affects system security. Temperature, humidity, air quality, and other variables may introduce unscheduled system failures in a work environment. Such variables which may be outside our direct control also require monitoring. Computer system–management applications monitor internal components as well as environmental and equipment temperature and power-supply voltage levels. Most organizations may not be able to control the temperature of an overheating processor or a lack of electricity provided by the utility company, but sensory thresholds in a monitoring application may trigger automated scripts or notify local personnel to initiate a system shutdown. In these situations, the monitoring thresholds and alerts provide systems and operators the opportunity to gracefully stop running processes or revert processing to an alternate system or location.

Organizations decide to implement systems with monitoring or control capabilities for a number of reasons including perceived risk, financial costs, logistical difficulties, and business value. For organizations with an immature security program and limited visibility into the operational environment, monitoring can also provide a means of transition to future controls. For example, monitoring can provide baseline data and allow reports on an organization's resource utilization (e.g., disk space, Internet usage) and provide a basis for effective planning ("We will run out of disk space between

August and November of next year") as well as indicating areas for better awareness, training, education, and compliance efforts ("Four of our employees are collectively responsible for 60 percent of our Internet bandwidth utilization—and half of their activity involves watching pornographic videos during working hours!").

53.1.3 Control Loop.

For most environments, humans remain in the control loop. The *control loop* consists of the *controller*, the *target system*, a two-way *communication path*, and the *transmitted data*.

The control loop is considered a *closed* loop when the process is automated and does not require human interaction; an *open* loop involves human interaction.

The requirements of the system determine the loop type. When gas-pipeline sensors detect a sudden decrease in pressure, an automated control system may need to perform an immediate lockdown to isolate the leak and send alert notifications. Leaving the loop open and waiting for human response may result in undesirable product loss and environmental and legal challenges. For operating-system patch deployment, an open loop would allow a system to interrogate hosts, determine patch levels, and report status for further review and action. A supervisor could then approve specific patches to particular systems after sufficient testing on noncritical, nonproduction systems and coordination with system stakeholders. Although fully automated software patching may seem like a viable process, it introduces additional risk (through system and process disruptions) and compatibility concerns. For industrial automation and controls, specific updates may not be certified for use and require follow-up with the vendor or verification on a support Website.

53.1.4 Defining the Scope and System Requirements.

For M&C systems to operate effectively, management must clearly define the *scope* and the *system requirements*.

The *scope* specifically refers to the relevant processes and the people who interact with the computing environment. For example, to monitor the research and development (R&D) department for network communications regarding intellectual property, the scope may include IT/IS support staff, shared network resources, and existing processes to communicate with remote sites and external departments.

The *system requirements* refer to the capabilities necessary to perform the desired functions of M&C. In working through the requirements, it is important to remember that prevention mechanisms and controls in real-world environments can eventually fail or become obsolete due to technological changes. The requirements for monitoring R&D may include the need for real-time packet captures, an algorithm to identify intellectual property, automated alerts, and a reasonably secured collection device. Installing a network test access port (TAP) on the network uplink and then writing the captured traffic to a data collector for future analysis may seem logical. However, if a site survey identifies the use of undocumented cellular modems, unencrypted wireless hot spots, and personal email accounts for sensitive communications, the network TAP will fail to address the original goal. In this case, the M&C requirements expand to include signal limiters (Faraday caging), mandatory device restrictions, network access control (NAC), enforced IPSec communication policies, and Web filters. Periodic security awareness training and a policy refresh may also be necessary to ensure the organization clearly communicates expectations on the use of personal email and other electronic communications and devices.

We also need to take into consideration the capabilities of the M&C system, including the unintended consequences of unnecessary features and capabilities on a deployed system. For example, a PC-based system used to manage a physical security badge system could also be used by an operator to attach USB devices, play video games, and connect to the Internet for peer-to-peer (P2P) file sharing. These issues can be partially mitigated through system security hardening, agent-based tools, and network design. Distribution panels connected to badge readers perform more specific, restrictive processing functions than a PC or commodity server; for panels, the attention would be directed toward physical access to the devices and communication path.

Compliance requirements and an organization's security program influence the implementation of M&C systems. Regulations may require access controls to restrict information to authorized users and sufficient monitoring to detect unauthorized attempts to gain access to information resources. In response to HIPAA, an organization may need to integrate additional log review procedures as well as appropriate measures to control all systems and processes that touch or potentially transfer personally identifiable information (PII). A public company needs adequate controls, to ensure accurate financial reporting. A security policy may reference the need to comply with Sarbanes-Oxley Section 404. The scope of an M&C system would then need to include computing resources, information process flows, and personnel with access to the financial information system. M&C systems should reflect the expectations of an organization's security policy and should fit into a relevant framework, such as COBIT. Utilizing a control framework provides logical management of M&C systems. The framework enables management to further understand enterprise processes and determine the need for risk mitigation or acceptance. PO9.7 in COBIT identifies control systems as part of the safeguard selection portion of risk management.

53.2 SYSTEM MODELS

53.2.1 Internal, One-to-One, One-to-Many, and Distributed.

M&C systems fit into four general models: internal, one-to-one, one-to-many, and distributed. The type of model used depends on the complexity of the system and the type of information required. These models may include autonomous systems as well as those that require human interaction.

1. An *internal system* is one of the simplest forms of M&C; it monitors or controls itself. A single server or network device may monitor processor utilization or other system components to evaluate system performance issues. From a control perspective, an internal system may prohibit specific actions, such as unauthorized attempts to modify system files or to log on locally to the system.
2. The *one-to-one model* enables one system to monitor or control another independent system. When scaled out across a large environment, this model can become cumbersome and result in unnecessary duplication of IT services and processing. For example, an enterprise job scheduler monitoring a single financial application server can identify when files are available for processing. If other systems within the same environment are operating independent job schedulers, operators will require additional time to monitor and troubleshoot the duplicate functions. However, the one-to-one model can be quite useful in specific, high-availability situations that require failover. A network firewall, or critical server, would continually monitor and mirror the configuration and session information of the primary system. Once the primary system faults, the monitoring system would assume production functions, to avoid significant disruptions to the business environment.

3. The *one-to-many model* is most common in enterprise environments. A central monitor and control system remotely manages a number of systems. From a central point, all targets may be interrogated and updated, without the need for manual, one-to-one changes. Centralized M&C can also reduce cost by simplifying M&C functions of multiple resources at various sites. This model also improves audit efficiency, as fewer sources of information must be reviewed to validate controls and changes within an environment.

4. The *distributed* model involves sensors and controls dispersed throughout the environment. The control elements may operate independently or remotely with input from a central control system. Nodes may serve as a local proxy or feed information directly to a central collector for secure log management, reporting, and data reduction. For organizations attempting to manage heterogeneous devices, a distributed model enables staff to implement the best M&C components for specific systems while still maintaining the ability to aggregate data into a centralized repository. This level of aggregation provides a wider view of change in the infrastructure.

53.2.2 Automation and the Human–Machine Interface. Automation enables M&C systems to collect sensory information and to initiate a response without the need for human interaction. Many information systems operate round the clock and generate large volumes of event logs. Delegating to operations staff the tasks of manually reviewing millions of log entries and correlating them into meaningful information is impractical. The purpose of M&C systems is to obtain meaningful intelligence from target systems and to report and correct anomalies. By automating data collection and reduction, managers and staff can review consolidated event summaries and respond to situations that have not already been automatically filtered or controlled.

The *human–machine interface* (HMI) is the point at which an operator communicates with a monitoring or control system. In industrial environments, HMI middleware transforms system activities into interactive screens, with enough capabilities for staff to perform specific job functions. The presentation of data is an important factor for HMI. Operators must have the ability to perform their job functions and to maintain adequate situational awareness, without access to unnecessary or distracting system elements. In common network operational environments, interactive Web interfaces serve as the HMI. An analyst may review stoplight coded alerts (red, yellow, green) in a Web interface and perform investigative steps to triage and resolve open issues.

In some situations, organizations leveraging automation may benefit from improved workforce safety and response time. Autonomous vehicles and devices continue to proliferate. The U.S. Department of the Navy utilizes unmanned undersea vehicles (UUVs)[7] which reflect the distributed model, performing autonomous actions, with information exchange through a sensor grid within the Global Information Grid (GIG).[8] These systems can monitor environmental variables, detect threats such as unexploded ordinance, respond to change, and communicate with system owners. Much like intrusion detection and prevention systems in a network environment, UUVs can perform functions that may be unsuitable for direct human interaction. Both can perform continuous monitoring and collect a large volume of information that could not be collected through manual efforts. Also, similar to intrusion prevention systems in a network environment, a UUV may detect a threat, alert nearby UUVs, and report status back via the GIG.

The expanding use of artificial intelligence (AI) and robotic resources provide additional opportunities for mobile and autonomous M&C. The U.S. Naval Research Laboratory's humanoid firefighting robot, SAFFiR, is another example of responding to environmental threats without exposing the traditional workforce to hazardous tasks while operating as part of a team. While SAFFiR may not replace a data center's gas suppression system, artificial intelligence within a data center has been seen in the fight against unsolicited commercial email and spam.

When deploying automated resources, implementing artificial intelligence, or remotely commanding unmanned vehicles, the integrity of the system and security of the communication paths are critical. Improper physical access, software buffer overflows, weak administrative credentials, and USB malware infections are common ways to compromise the integrity of an M&C system. In network environments, a network engineer may use out-of-band communication paths to connect to the HMI via a console port, in order to avoid common network attacks against a management interface. Using insecure communication methods to update or manage M&C systems across untrusted paths is another common way to expose M&Cs to unauthorized access and compromise. Migrating from FTP, Telnet, and password authentication to Secure Shell (SSHv2) with key pair authentication is one practical way to reduce some of this risk to a more acceptable level.

For network IPSs in a properly baselined network environment, wormlike traffic anomalies may be detected, routed to network tarpits, and cross-reported to additional sensors. In this situation, the automated response is significantly faster and potentially less disruptive than using an intrusion detection system (IDS; monitoring only) with alerts routing to an on-duty analyst for additional follow-up.

53.2.3 Snapshots versus Real Time. *Snapshots* provide a point-in-time view of a target system. Auditors use these for regularly scheduled audits. Scanning the environment on a monthly basis to confirm compliance can also unearth security trends within an environment. Trend reports identify security performance over time. An organization may notice a sharp decline in vulnerabilities after an external audit. Over time, without a stable vulnerability management program, the number of vulnerabilities will return to preaudit levels. Snapshots do not provide immediate or ongoing information on changes or corrective actions made to production systems. Additionally, snapshots will not verify that a control is working all of the time, only during the time that the snapshot was taken. Using monthly snapshots to review a system that frequently changes on a daily basis will not provide the same level of assurance as real-time M&C.

Real-time monitoring refers to persistent, ongoing observation of a target. *Real-time control* refers to a control system's ability actively to influence its target. Industrial environments depend on information gathered through real-time M&C. When liquefied natural gas (LNG) travels through an LNG terminal,[9] operators should not have to wait until the tanker is empty in order to confirm that any of the product successfully transferred to the storage tanks. An M&C system can continually monitor the volume of product leaving the vessel, compare that data to the volume entering the storage container, trigger alerts if a leak is detected, and initiate a shutoff to avoid product loss.

When allocating and distributing resources to meet demand, real-time monitoring provides overseers with an immediate understanding of the areas of need. In a network environment, this may include peak network usage during an accounting cycle or online shopping trends due to holidays. An Internet-facing shopping portal that uses cloud computing for resource allocation can use real-time monitoring to transparently detect and provision or deprovision computing and storage resources based on customer demand. Internet sites facing distributed denial of service (DDoS) attacks may use real-time monitoring to identify the incident and real-time control to block or throttle undesirable traffic. A Web-caching service or content delivery network (CDN) may also be leveraged to minimize the impact. In industrial areas, real-time monitoring can detect where electric grid managers should route additional power resources to meet demand, how much to pull from reserves, as well as when to implement real-time controls to enforce rolling blackouts and ensure grid integrity.[10]

DS13.3 in COBIT 4.1 identifies the need for adequate event logging to analyze activities over time. However, without well-planned automated processes and data reduction, the volume of data generated from snapshots and real-time activities will overwhelm staff. Through centralized data collection and reduction, designated actors can evaluate the results of both real-time and snapshot reporting. This combination can identify general trends, ensure that M&C systems continually operate, and preserve evidence from an identified attack.

53.2.4 Memory Dumps. Memory dumps are representations of the data in memory at a specific point in time. Memory dumps are used most typically after a system failure, but they are also useful in forensic research when investigators want the maximum amount of information possible from the system. There are two approaches to obtaining copies of memory: online, using diagnostic utilities while the system is running, and offline, from magnetic storage media to which memory regions are copied.

53.2.4.1 Diagnostic Utilities. Diagnostic utilities are system software routines that that can be used for debugging purposes. Also known as *debug* utilities, these programs run at maximum privilege (*root* or *supervisor* level, or their equivalents) and allow the privileged user to see or modify any portion of memory. The utilities usually print or display the contents of memory regions in a variety of formats such as binary, octal (base 8), or hexadecimal (base 16), with conversion to ASCII for easier readability. The utilities generally can provide immediate access to memory structures such as terminal buffers that allow the analyst to see what specific users are typing or seeing on their screens, file buffers that contain data in transit to or from specific open files, spoolers (print buffers), and program-specific regions such as data stacks. Because debug utilities also allow modification of memory regions, they are to be used with the utmost circumspection; for security reasons, it is wise to formulate a policy that no debug utility with root access can be run without having two people present. In high-security operations, the output of debug utilities should be logged to paper files for proof that no unauthorized operations were carried out using these programs. Access to privileged debug programs should be tightly controlled, such as by strict access-control lists or even by encryption using restricted keys.

53.2.4.2 Output to Magnetic Media or Paper. One method of doing a memory dump and follow-up analysis is by copying the data from memory onto magnetic media such as tape, removable disks, or rewriteable DVDs. Although it was once practical to print the entire contents of memory to paper, the explosive growth of memory sizes makes such printing impractical in today's systems. In 1980, for example, a large multiuser minicomputer might have 1MB (megabyte) of RAM available, resulting in a manageable, half-inch-thick stack of paper. At the time of this writing, it is more common to see business systems with 64-bit processors and over 4 GB (4,000 MB) of memory. For perspective, a relatively older PC with only 256 MB of memory would generate a single printout that could be several feet thick.

Copying memory to a static storage medium is, therefore, preferred for future analysis of memory dumps following system crashes, unknown malware infections, and incidents requiring forensic response.

53.2.4.3 *Navigating the Dump Using Exploratory Utilities.* On production systems using reliable operating systems, crashes are rare and generally explored thoroughly to identify the causes of the anomaly. Generally after creating a dump it is necessary to study it looking for the problem and then correcting it. For large-memory systems, exploratory utilities are used to speed the search for problems in the dump by allowing the analyst to find any named system table or other memory region. At a forensic level, hashing may also be used to filter for known-good and known-bad elements within the memory archive.

53.2.4.4 *Understanding System Tables.* System tables are directories of system data where each datum is identified by an assigned label, by its position in the table, or by pointers from other tables. An understanding of system tables is essential in analyzing system problems.

Regardless of the details of the operating system and the system-specific names of tables, some of the important system tables include:

- **Process control table.** Pointers to the process tables for each process that is running on the system or that was running when the copy of memory was obtained
- **Process tables.** Detailed information about each process, with pointers to all the tables for that particular process
- **Data stacks.** All the variables used by specific processes
- **Buffers.** Data in transit to or from files and devices, such as disks and terminals
- **Memory management tables.** Lists of available memory blocks
- **Inter-process communications tables.** For example, information about resources locking or any logical flags used by multiple processes

Working with someone who understands the detailed structure of the operating system tables can be critically important for security work in which investigators must determine exactly what happened during an intrusion or other unauthorized use of a system.

53.2.4.5 *Security Considerations for Dump Data.* Memory dumps must be secured while in use and destroyed when appropriate. The dump contains the totality of a system's information in memory, including such data as:

- Passwords that had just been typed into terminal buffers for use in changing logons or for accessing restricted subsystems and applications
- Encryption keys
- Confidential data obtained from restricted files and not authorized for visualization by operations staff (e.g., medical data from personnel files)

- Financial data that could be used in frauds
- National security information restricted to higher levels of clearance than the system administration

53.3 LOG MANAGEMENT

53.3.1 Log Generation. A *log file* contains a record of events. This record is the basic building block for M&C systems. These files serve as a digital audit trail for system activities. Operating systems, databases, and applications may contain built-in logging capabilities. However, logging is not always enabled or configured for use and aggregation. The system monitors activities and writes relevant information as a log file entry. Operating system log files track application issues, access attempts, and system-wide problems. Thresholds and file sizes can be adjusted to meet the requirements of the environment. It may be unnecessary to write a log entry every time a user successfully opens or closes a file on a network share hosted on a storage volume, but it may be necessary to log and report on privileged access attempts to a management console or remote connections via Secure Shell (SSH).

Transaction logs take logging one step further, by storing copies of the actual changes made to a system. They have a fixed size, automatically generating a new file for future transactions. Most common in databases, transaction logs can be used to rebuild a corrupt database. Using a known-good database backup and the transaction logs from the database backup to the present time, databases can be rolled forward to a reliable point in time prior to the failure. Transaction logs should be actively monitored, as they can quickly consume large amounts of storage. Normally, committed transaction logs are purged after a successful backup. Other log types, such as Website traffic, may automatically generate new log files once per day; these logs may not contain entire Website transactions, but they will identify the visitor based on predefined criteria. The key here is the flexibility in determining what will be monitored and what format will work best for log generation.

Data retention policies must clearly define how long data should be retained, according to external requirements and internally driven policy. Retention requirements could range from 1 to 6 years, while some data may need to be retained indefinitely on backup media due to a legal hold. Log file archiving and storage become problematic over time: system-level log files may reach maximum size and overwrite existing log data or trigger a system shutdown; centralized log management systems may slow to a crawl when querying a relational database for data to export to a flat file. Log collection and analysis systems must be scalable as event rates and volumes may increase or burst over time. Some organizations address these variances through incorporation of cloud-based logging and storage services, while others rely on more traditional, internal storage solutions.

53.3.2 Types of Log File Records. A *log file* (also known as an *audit trail*) traditionally contains records about transactions that have updated online files or otherwise represent events of interest (e.g., logging on to the system or initiating a process). Some database or application log files also may contain copies of records that were affected before or after the logged transaction. There are a number of different types of log file records and each contains a specific kind of information. Typically, all of the operating system log records are stored in files with a maximum configured size, and that are identified by monotonically increasing file numbers. When the file fills up, the operating system opens another one with the next number in sequence as its identifier. Because log file records of different types have different sizes, on some operating systems the log file is defined with a variable record length.

53.3.2.1 System Boot. The system boot log record contains information on booting up, or starting, the machine. Since this is related to a specific activity and generally to a specific area of the hardware or media, information on the boot can prove helpful when the boot fails and analysis needs to take place.

53.3.2.2 System Shutdown. The system shutdown log record contains information on when the system was shut down and by whom. This information can be invaluable when attempting to analyze a problem or find a saboteur. On systems that include emergency shutdowns (e.g., by calling routines such as *suddendeath* when system parameters fall outside the range of allowable values), the shutdown record may contain specific information about the cause of the emergency shutdown.

From a security standpoint, trustworthy system boot and system shutdown records can prevent a malefactor from concealing a shutdown followed by unauthorized boot to a diagnostic subsystem that would allow file manipulations without log records to track the operations. The boot records would show an unexplained gap between shutdown and boot.

53.3.2.3 Process Initiation. A *process* begins when a specific program is loaded and run by a particular user at a particular time. Log records for process initiation show when the various processes were initiated and who initiated them. These files provide a method of tracking employee activity as well as monitoring events that occur. In addition, such records allow cost recovery using chargeback at different rates for different programs or for program launches at different times of day. More important, the record of which programs were executed by whom at which times can be invaluable in forensic research.

53.3.2.4 Process Termination. When reviewing the process termination log record, an administrator will be able to tell when each process completed or was terminated for some other reason. Some systems may provide more information, such as why an unscheduled or abrupt termination occurred, but not all process termination log records provide that information. Process termination records typically include valuable statistical information such as:

- Which process spawned or forked the process in question
- Identification of any processes spawned by the processes
- Number of milliseconds of CPU used
- Number of files opened and closed by the process
- Total number of input/output (I/O) operations completed by the process
- Total size of the memory partitions allocated to the process
- Maximum size of the data stack
- Number and maximum size of extra data segments in memory
- How many swaps to virtual memory were needed during the existence of the process
- Maximum priority assigned to the process for scheduling by the task manager

53.3.2.5 Session Initiation. A *session* consists of the communications between a particular user and a particular server during a particular time period. Whenever a user logs on to a system and initiates a session, a record of that event can be found in the session initiation log record. Frequent review of these records provides important information to alert administrators that an intruder is in the system. For instance, if an administrator knows that an authorized user is on vacation and the session initiation log file shows that a session was initiated for that particular user's ID, chances are significant that an unauthorized party used the system via a borrowed or stolen user ID. These records are particularly valuable during forensic work.

53.3.2.6 Session Termination. When a session terminates, for whatever reason, a copy of the time when it terminated is generally stored in the session termination log record. Much like the process termination record, the session termination record can include a great deal of aggregated information about the activities carried out during the session, such as total I/O, total number of processes launched and terminated, total number of files opened and closed, and so forth.

53.3.2.7 Invalid Logon Attempts. The invalid logon attempt file can prove invaluable in cases where logon attempts do not succeed. In some instances, the file can tell if the user attempted to log on with an incorrect password, if the user exceeded the allowed number of failed attempts, or if the user was attempting to log on at a seemingly unusual time. These log records can provide important information in cases where an administrator is attempting to track specific actions to a user or to ascertain if the logon failure was due to a simple error or to an attempted impersonation by an unwanted outsider. In hardwired networks, where every device has a unique identifier, the records usually include a specific identifier that allows administrators to track down the physical device used for the attempted logons.

53.3.2.8 File Open. The file open log record provides information on when each specific file was opened and by which process; in addition, the record generally records the mode in which the file was opened: for example, exclusive read and write, exclusive read, exclusive write with concurrent read, append only, or concurrent read and write.

53.3.2.9 File Close. The file close log record provides an administrator with information regarding when the file was closed, by which process, and by what means. The file usually captures information on whether the user specifically closed the file or whether some other type of interruption occurred. The records usually include details of total read and write operations, including how many physical blocks were transferred to accomplish the total number of logical I/O operations.

53.3.2.10 Invalid File Access Attempts. An important log record in the M&C effort, the invalid file access attempt shows the administrator when and to which files there were invalid file access attempts. The records generally show which process attempted the I/O and why it was refused by the file system (e.g., attempted write to a file opened for read-only access, violation of access control list, or violation of file-access barriers).

53.3.2.11 File I/O. Whenever information is placed into, read out of, or deleted from a file (input/output), the information regarding those changes is captured in the file I/O log. As mentioned earlier, the log includes images of a record before and after it was accessed. The I/O log can be used in file recovery after system or application crashes. Coupled with transaction-initiation and termination records, such data can be used for automatic roll-back or roll-forward recovery systems.

The activities recorded here can prove especially helpful when trying to validate actions that were taken and to attribute them to specific individuals. Detailed logs are typical for databases, where a subsystem provides optional logging of all I/O. Application log records, designed and programmed by application developers, also typically allow administrators to enable such detailed logging.

53.3.2.12 System Console Activity. The system console activity file provides information on any actions that originate from or are viewed at the system console. Typically, the system console includes not only logon and logoff records but also special requests, such as printer form mounts, specific tape or cartridge mounts, comments sent to the console by batch jobs, and free-form communications from users. The console file records all such activity as well as every command from the system operator, and the system responses to those commands. These records provide an excellent tool for investigators tracking down the specific events in a computer incident.

53.3.2.13 Network Activity. Network activity files provide valuable information on activity taking place on the network. Depending on the sophistication and settings of the system an administrator is using, the information derived can be plentiful or scant. Specific devices may generate their own records on network activity; for example, routers, gateways, and firewalls may all keep their own log files. However, typically these are circular files in which records to be entered after the file is full are shifted to the start of the file, where they overwrite the oldest records. In forensic work, it is essential to capture such data before the information of interest is obliterated. Unfortunately, in many systems, the volume of network activity is so high that log files contain only the most recent minutes of traffic.

53.3.2.14 Resource Utilization. A review of the resource utilization log records will show all of the system's resources and the level of utilization for each. By monitoring this file, administrators frequently make important decisions regarding modifying system configuration or expanding the system.

53.3.2.15 Central Processing Unit. The CPU file shows the capacity and usage of the central processing unit for whichever system is being used and monitored. Based on this information, administrators can monitor when usage is heaviest and the CPU is most stressed, and can decide on utilization rules and requirements as well as on possible CPU upgrades. As in all log file analyses, any outliers (unusual values) and any unexpected change in usage can be investigated. Global CPU utilization records can be compared with the sum of CPU usage collected from process termination records; discrepancies may indicate stealth operation of unauthorized processes, such as malicious software.

53.3.2.16 Disk Space. The log records for disk space show the amount of disk space originally available on a system, the amount of disk space used (and generally what type of files it is being used for), and the amount of disk space that remains free and available. Comparison of total disk space utilization with the total space allocated to all files can reveal problems such as *lost disk space* (i.e., space allocated to files that were never closed properly; such space is unusable by the file system because there are no pointers indicating that the disk sectors are actually supposed to be free). Such unallocated sectors or clusters also may be where malefactors hide data they have stored without authorization by bypassing the file system.

53.3.2.17 *Memory Consumption.* Important information on the amount of memory in a system and the amount actually being used can be obtained from the memory consumption log records. Such records typically also include information on virtual memory usage. Therefore, they can provide warning of *thrashing* conditions, where memory segments are being copied to disk and read back from disk too often. Details of memory consumption may be useful in tracking down unauthorized processes such as worms.

53.3.2.18 *System Level versus Job Level.* Different levels of monitoring, logging, and auditing may take place. Some of this may be preprogrammed, but in most environments it is possible to select the log records and related reports that are desired. For instance, a regular system level audit log may be produced at intervals, just to provide information that the system is up and running without any extraordinary problems. But an in-depth job level audit may take place more frequently in order to monitor the specific job and ensure that it is running correctly and providing the information needed.

53.3.3 Automation and Resource Allocation. Utilizing secure, well-organized log management systems to monitor and respond to events can lower the administrative effort required to manage an infrastructure. With the growing demands of compliance and costs associated with data retention, it is important to include log management within the scope of the enterprise data retention policy. E-discovery laws and postmortem attack analysis rely on efficient access to accurate log information. Logs require system resources, ranging from media storage to CPU cycles and memory utilization. Trade-offs must be considered when setting aside potential business-generating resources for the purpose of logging and reporting.

Manually reviewing millions of log files on various systems, in different time zones, and inconsistent formats is unrealistic for staff. For geographically dispersed sites, real-time log transfers may be delayed due to limited bandwidth over slow links. Not all logged information is of equal value. Some data records may tie directly to compliance issues, while others provide noncritical benefits to daily operations. Based on policy, management must determine what types of data must be aggregated and reduced in order to monitor and to ensure ongoing compliance. This is part of the scope definition process of M&C systems. Planners and implementers must not only scope current requirements but must ensure that the log management plan will scale to address perceived resource demands for operational, security, and compliance requirements.

53.3.4 Log Record Security. An organization must protect its log records from unauthorized access and modification. The four most common methods of log record security are: access control lists, checksums, encryption, and digital signatures. Combining these methods, based on the system requirements, can adequately protect most log data. Attackers with unfettered access to unencrypted email log files could download copies of the files and search them for sensitive information as well as modify or delete message content directly from the target server. This type of attack threatens every element of the Parkerian hexad.[11] In addition to the common concerns of confidentiality breaches and loss of data integrity, unauthorized access to log files may provide an attacker with additional information on the network environment. Vulnerability scanners may run at scheduled intervals and log detected issues to a central database. Leveraging aggregated data, an attacker can more efficiently compromise a network environment and evade detection routines accustomed to high-footprint reconnaissance.

Operating system and application-level access control lists (ACLs) restrict access to files. Some log files may be written to write-once, ready-many (WORM) media for auditors or legal staff. Operations staff may have no legitimate need to access such data. However, they may need to ensure that the communication flow operates continually. Databases can implement even more granular controls on specific records and fields, to avoid unnecessary information disclosure. Physical access controls to the media while in storage or in transit must also be considered when planning an M&C system for log data. Properly implemented ACLs can limit the level of log data exposure to authorized personnel and system processes.

Organizations subject to PCI DSS are required to implement integrity controls on log data. Historically, 32-bit cyclic redundancy checks (CRCs) generated checksums to guard against file alteration. Today, stronger cryptographic checksums, such as those generated by the SHA-2 family, provide a more reasonable level of assurance.[12] Checksums do not require constant human interaction. For tamper protection, a monitoring system may baseline a system and store copies of files or their hash equivalents for periodic or real-time file comparison. Changes to logs or other critical files could then be centrally reported for manual investigation. A control system could automatically quarantine the unauthorized file and restore a copy of the original file.

Digital signatures use public key cryptography to provide data integrity and nonrepudiation. These build on standard cryptographic checksums because they not only confirm file integrity but also identify who or what entity is providing that assurance. For organizations that must submit reports to external recipients, such as government offices, digital signatures can decrease the paper trail and provide a more efficient, digital means of meeting regulatory requirements.

Encryption must be considered for log data in transit and at rest. Encrypting entire log files reduces the ability to view or alter the contents. It also increases the resource usage on the target system during the encryption process. Like checksums, the keys required for decryption should be stored in a secure location, to increase the difficulty in defeating the control. Utilizing whole-disk encryption and then transferring a log file over a network in plaintext is not a consistent method of log security. Establishing secure network links, such as implementing IPSec, provides end-to-end link security. A combination of network and system-level encryption may be necessary to secure log files and other sensitive information properly.

The chain of custody should also be considered when planning a log management system. Some log data may need to be used in court. Without a verifiable audit trail, the contents may be inadmissible. A documented chain of custody for media transfers between staff and sites can validate physical controls. Implementing cipher block chaining (CBC) can further protect against unauthorized changes to log data. The previous log file ciphertext would Exclusive-Or (XOR) with the current plaintext to create a new value for encryption operations. This concept can also be useful for record sets within log files and database applications, as it will identify record deletions and other data modifications. See Chapter 7 in this *Handbook* for more information on cryptography.

53.4 GENERAL LOGGING CLASSES

53.4.1 Overview. M&C activities vary, based on the business scope, objectives, and target system functions. Targets can be grouped into general classes including: process flow, job scheduling, network connectivity, environmental measurement, system state assurance, system component status, process activities, configuration settings, file system information, and access control. Current regulations may include only a subset of an organization's information systems in the scope of compliance. Changes to the infrastructure and compliance requirements are inevitable. It is important to implement scalable and flexible M&C in order to accommodate future needs.

53.4.2 Process Flow and Job Scheduling. Some organizations use a combination of mainframe and distributed system resources. The mainframe group may use a particular batch job scheduler to process and monitor job status and output. Other distributed systems throughout the organization might use their own schedulers and logging capabilities. The complexity of this design, however, does not facilitate enterprise-wide monitoring and auditing. A centralized job scheduler may be necessary to monitor and control job flow. The centralized system will need to connect to disparate systems to collect job status and initiate commands. For management, an enterprise view of job scheduling can identify unnecessary complexity and redundancy, leading to future process improvement. When shifting to a central job scheduling system, it may seem desirable to shift the entire environment immediately or possibly to revert to a central mainframe. However, a gradual migration to centralized M&C would be a more ideal method of change.

53.4.3 Network Connectivity. *Network connectivity* refers to the devices, protocols, and communication media (wired or wireless) used in a computing environment. A network operations center will want to monitor the status of network links, health indicators of critical devices, and data streams traversing the network. In a layered environment, physical access to the network cabling may be secured in cable raceways and network closets or at distribution points. Devices will be up to date and configured according to best practices. Unnecessary protocols will be controlled by blocking or routing suspicious traffic to network black holes and honeynets for further analysis. Network intrusion prevention systems (IPSs) can identify a communications anomaly, block the communication exchange, log the event, and trigger an administrative alert. Prevention requires planning and sufficient controls to deny an attack from achieving its goal. A method to implement M&C for sensitive network nodes may involve moving nodes to isolated segments, deploying in-line network IPSs, and utilizing host-based security agents. Additional enterprise security assessment tools may also scan, report, generate tickets, propose remediation measures, and analyze security trends over time.

In addition to monitoring general network connectivity, some networks are specifically deployed for the purpose of M&C. Legacy industrial systems now integrate common Ethernet networking elements into mechanical, electromechanical, and electronic environments. Wireless M&C options are also available. The ZigBee[13] specification utilizes the IEEE 802.15.4 standard to provide ad hoc local networking connectivity.

ZigBee is primarily used for M&C. In a plant floor or outdoor facility, additional cabling for M&C systems may be infeasible. A potential solution may be to integrate inexpensive, robust ZigBee control points. For geographically dispersed sites, high-bandwidth, secure connection services such as satellite, leased-line, and virtual private (VPN) network connections bring sites together to manage M&C data centrally.

53.4.4 Environmental Concerns. Some environmental variables are easier to monitor than control. Whether we are using ZigBee to transmit sensory information or a software package to measure AC voltage irregularities, environmental measures provide additional situational awareness for information systems and staff. Humidity, temperature, smoke, and leaking water directly impact computing systems in a data center. Dedicated air-conditioning units and dehumidifiers can monitor and control humidity and temperature. Indeterminate sources of smoke or water leakage may be difficult to control with automated response, but monitoring and alert notification may trigger corrective procedures by staff in order to mitigate risk.

Environmental factors may also impact the quality of an organization's products. M&C systems can enhance an organization's quality control efforts, ensuring consistent product manufacturing within predefined tolerances.

As part of a business-continuity plan, it may become necessary for an organization to monitor and prepare for environmental threats such as floods, structural collapse, and power loss. A monitoring system, with early warning capability, could notify staff to report to an alternate work site or to prepare for contingency operations. In the event that an environmental threat disrupts control systems, staff must be capable of manual override. The EPA recommends familiarity with manual operations, in the event of a supervisory control and data acquisition (SCADA) system failure.[14] In addition to manual override, integrating redundant M&C systems with seamless failover can decrease the likelihood of operational disruptions.

53.4.5 System State. The *system state* refers to a collection of critical variables on the target system. A monitoring system may need to track running processes in memory, services, open port connections, system files, hardware status, and log data. In industrial control systems, the system state may reflect the overall picture of an electrical grid, or it may reduce to whether or not a set of valves are open or closed. When an antivirus application process fails to start, resulting in a subsequent malware infection, the monitoring system can trigger an alert so that staff or an automated control system can isolate the infection. One method of monitoring the system state is to run an *agent* on the host system. Software agents monitor a predefined list of items and report status on a regular basis to a central monitoring hub. When the agent fails to respond or "check in," the monitoring system can issue an alert to investigate the issue.

Host intrusion prevention systems (HIPS) protect the system state of nodes in a network environment. HIPS analyze activities based on signature and heuristic detection routines. They provide a reasonable means of Monitoring and Control (M&C), with the potential for centralized reporting and attack correlation. For postmortem analysis, memory dumps can be useful in analyzing problems with the system state. If a network monitoring system detected botnet-related activity originating from a system in human resources, capturing the live system state may be advantageous to an investigation. As part of the evidence collection process of forensics, controlling and preserving the system state requires specialized training and tools.[15]

53.4.6 System Components. Monitoring applications can track the usage and overall performance of system components, including CPU, memory, and storage media. Operating systems also have built-in tools to monitor components and store results in log files. Inventory management systems collect component-level information as well as software information as configured by operations staff. Six months after an equipment refresh, an audit may identify systems operating with only half of the originally purchased memory. The logged information will help to determine the scope of the issue.

Monitoring the performance of system components can also identify changes in business need or system abuse. With the deployment of a new Web portal, existing Web proxy servers may no longer be capable of handling the heavier load. Logged performance data would corroborate the need to expand the infrastructure or add additional capacity to existing systems. Performance set points trigger alerts when components depart from normal operating levels. The alerts may identify externally driven changes, such as voltage drops, or internal limits, such as maximum memory utilization. Heavy resource utilization on a historically idle PC running HMI may even point to misuse of the system for non-SCADA-related activities, such as internal network scanning, password cracking tools, or gaming.

System component monitors most often attempt to identify overutilized CPUs, heavy memory consumption, and full storage media. However, identifying routinely underutilized resources gives management the ability to reallocate resources to areas of need rather than purchase unnecessary additions to the infrastructure. Disk quotas control the allowable amount of usable media for users and applications. To protect a system from unintentional or malicious overutilization, quotas should be reviewed as part of a layered strategy. Virtual machines use storage, memory, and processor quotas to control the resources utilized on a host system. With large virtualization environments, an enterprise virtual manager system may be necessary to ensure adequate load balancing across all of the virtual system hosts as well as to determine if additional tuning is required to improve virtual machine performance.

53.4.7 Process Activities. A *process* refers to a running program in a computing device. Processes may initiate at the system or user level and may contain multiple threads. M&C processes can prevent malware infections and identify abnormal process activities. Antivirus systems typically address this area. The SQL Slammer worm targeted a vulnerable process over a network connection, injecting code into memory without writing to disk storage.[16] In addition to process monitoring, network traffic analysis and network IPSs could mitigate this type of activity. Using enterprise monitoring tools to aggregate critical process information on a number of systems will help to identify application issues, such as runaway processes. For performance tuning and resource evaluation, agents can also monitor the CPU time of running programs for high utilization.

Monitoring process activities can also play a role in software metering and reporting. Organizations may want to identify application usage for different departments, in order to avoid deploying unnecessary applications and paying licensing fees for *shelfware*. Agents can centrally report elapsed time for target processes, for data aggregation, and for management report generation. Monitoring the use of specific types of software utilities, such as those used primarily by administrative and security personnel (e.g., nmap, tcpdump, hping, Wireshark, and Microsoft SysInternals), could also indicate unauthorized network reconnaissance. Blocking the execution of known applications by file name or hash value can limit the level of follow-up required to locate and kill remote processes. Monitoring for uncategorized or unapproved processes may further help in identifying the cause of performance degradation on remote systems.

53.4.8 File System. File system activities provide a wealth of auditing information. File systems store log data ranging from application errors to unauthorized authentication attempts. Just like IDS logging, file system logging requires performance tuning to aggregate the data and to avoid data loss. Logging every file access attempt and data modification on a system will fill up event logs with generally useless information. If system owners configure the log file to overwrite when full, actual critical events may be lost. The volume of log entries also impacts network resources. A constant flow of file system activity logs may negatively impact the performance of the log collector. Focusing on critical system files, sensitive data, and configuration settings will decrease the number of log entries and provide a more targeted set of results.

The configuration files for operating systems and applications require layers of protection to avoid unauthorized modification. Much like the layers discussed in Section 53.3.4, regarding log-record security, Access Control Lists (ACLs), encryption, digital signatures, and checksums can play a critical role in protecting objects within the file system. Attempts to bypass M&C systems may begin with configuration files and settings. End users attempting to bypass Internet Web filters may reconfigure their Web browsers to use a rogue proxy server. Attackers attempting to modify the configuration of a poorly secured Web server may leverage the security lapses to target additional systems connected to the internal network. Controlling changes to configuration settings via system policies and HIPS will mitigate these kinds of attacks.

53.4.9 Access Controls. Access control is a central part of security management and compliance efforts. Organizations often rely on more than one stand-alone system for identification and authentication, including applications, network operating systems, and building security. As a result, they face significant challenges when attempting to communicate, aggregate, and manage access control events. Adding and removing staff to a secure environment may involve badge identification, security tokens, and passwords. An M&C system targeting access control will need to ensure that unauthorized personnel do not have access to any physical or digital resources. Management may first need to develop a process flow with support from operations staff and business stakeholders.

Aggregating access logs and detailing failed login attempts and multiple user instances aid in the identification of system abuse. When users log on to network resources, they establish a *session* with the target system. Multiple sessions for the same user, at multiple sites, may indicate that a user account has been compromised or is being shared. Depending on the level of importance, this information may surface in an exception report, trigger an administrative alert, or result in an automated account lockout. Similarly, a series of invalid login attempts may reach a threshold and automatically disable the user account for a predefined period of time. This control minimizes the effort required to actively monitor system accounts while ensuring that attackers are not able to perform a brute-force attack on the credentials of an authorized user.

See Chapters 28 and 29 in this *Handbook* for further discussion of identification and authentication.

53.5 DATA AGGREGATION AND REDUCTION

53.5.1 Centralized Data Stores. Systems generate logs in a variety of formats that are not always easy to access. The first phase in data aggregation is ensuring that logging is working properly on the target system. This may require installation of additional log collection software, in order to push or pull data in a standard *syslog* format. The second phase, gradually connecting logging points to a centralized data store, builds on individual logging mechanisms to create an enterprise view of events. Centralized data storage provides a single point of analysis and audit, without the time-consuming process of manually interrogating individual systems throughout the environment.

Log data must be communicated in a secure manner. An agent-based system needs to establish a secure communication channel with the primary collector, to avoid distributing log details to an unauthorized collector. It may also be advantageous to prohibit the log aggregator from collecting unsolicited syslog messages. This security measure may be built into the log forwarding or aggregating mechanism, or it may utilize IPSec over controlled network links.

A major problem with large volume data stores is processing time. Log processing can potentially delay or otherwise inhibit incident response. Depending on the resources available, it may be more economically advantageous to store secured log data in compressed archives while using agent-based monitoring only to report critical security issues or operational problems to central storage. The time and effort to log, parse, and report on every data block received by the central collector may exceed internal security-policy requirements and the perceived cost benefit. Filtering out noncritical events and alerts would then be part of the baseline process for the central M&C system. Storing and analyzing entire log files may serve as a secondary (slower) monitoring mechanism, while the security-specific alerts are handled on an immediate basis.

53.5.2 Filtered Queries. The volume of log file records can be overwhelming and generally impossible for operations staff to review individually and on a regular basis. Centrally storing the data does not change the infeasibility of the task. It does, however, lend itself toward improved data reduction. Transforming raw data into a meaningful, reduced form can minimize the noise and enable staff and automated processes to target higher-priority activities. Running filtered queries against log records can provide more immediate results on potential attacks or system issues. A scheduled query may list all failed logon attempts. Additional filtering may drill down to a set of computing assets (e.g., servers processing credit card data) or user types such as root-level accounts. Another more specific query may only list network traffic anomalies between the R&D department and an array of Internet proxy servers.

53.5.3 Analyzing Log Records. Log records can be valuable to the system administrator, but only if they are put to use. Properly using a log file requires monitoring and reviewing its records and then taking actions based on the findings. Such analysis typically uses utilities provided by the supplier of the operating system or by third parties, such as commercial software companies or freeware distributors.

53.5.3.1 Volume Considerations. Someone must make a decision regarding how big log files should be. Such a decision is generally made by the system administrator and is based on what is considered useful and manageable. If money is involved—for instance, if additional storage capacity is needed—the chief technology officer (CTO), chief information officer (CIO), chief operating officer (COO), system auditor, and a variety of other stakeholders might be called on to participate in the decision-making process. However, in the three and a half decades from 1980 to the time of this writing in June 2013, disk-space costs fell about 37 percent per year compounded annually—from approximately $853,000 per gigabyte (in 2013 dollars) to approximately $0.04 per gigabyte in constant dollars, so disk space is not much of an issue anymore.[17] More important is that log files, like any file, may be left in an inconsistent state if the system crashes; closing a log file and opening a new one in the series is a prophylactic measure that ensures that less information will be lost in disk I/O buffers if there is a system crash. In addition, it is wise to put log files on a separate disk controlled by a separate processor; that way, one can disable write-behind (delayed writes) and force completion of I/O for every record of the log file.

53.5.3.2 *Archiving Log Files.* Archiving is a very important part of making and using log files. Every organization needs to decide how long to keep its log files and where to keep them. Decisions of this nature sometimes are made based on space considerations but more frequently are made based on legal requirements within specific industries. Some companies may decide to keep materials for a year or two, while others may be mandated by law to retain archived log files for seven or eight years.

The decisions regarding the archiving of log files should never be made arbitrarily; in every instance a careful review and check of company, legal, and industry requirements should be conducted. Based on the findings of that review, a written policy and procedures should be produced. Every organization needs to tell its employees what these policies and procedures are, so they can be aware of what materials are being kept, where they can be found, and how they can be accessed.

53.5.3.3 *Platform-Specific Programs for Log File Analysis.* Many operating systems are in existence, and although there are certain similarities in how they function, there are also differences. Special training on each specific operating system may be necessary in order to do a correct analysis of the platform-specific log files it generates.

53.5.3.4 *Exception Reports.* The volume of log file records can be overwhelming. For example, a customer-facing banking portal could generate log entries for logons, logoffs, financial transactions, and other record changes. It may also log attempts to penetrate Web application defenses or detect hijacked banking sessions. Exception reports allow the analyst to focus on specific characteristics (e.g., unusual wire transfer activities to foreign countries). Such tools greatly simplify detection and analysis of anomalies and are particularly helpful in tracking down unauthorized and undesirable activities.

53.6 NOTIFICATIONS AND REPORTING

53.6.1 Alerts. Log management must include layers of automation to reduce the time required to review and respond to events in the environment. How an M&C system deals with alerts will directly impact the security of the target system. Overwhelming operators with too many alerts will result in slower problem-response time as well as the potential to ignore critical issues. The purpose of alerts is to improve responsiveness to major issues, such as a leaking pipeline or multisite network outage. Alerts may be configured at specific set points so that a responder will be notified only when the attack threshold is reached. Elements that are controlled in the environment may have a higher threshold for alert notification. A sudden influx of malware from the Internet may be immediately detected and filtered at the network edge. Notifying operations staff of a large volume of malware may be useful. However, spamming security administrators with alerts on every blocked attack would be an inefficient use of alert notification resources.

Additionally, the means of alert notification play an important role in business continuity and disaster recovery. Out-of-band monitoring systems may detect a network equipment error that could not otherwise be detected by the failing device itself. For alert recipients, multiple notification means may be necessary. Email, pager, cell phone, and SMS messaging are the most common forms. Alert visualization is another valuable means for operators actively monitoring the environment. Similar to the dashboard concept, visualization can reduce data collected from sensors into a visual map, with graphical indicators to identify system issues. A combination of dashboard-style alert monitoring and targeted message delivery may provide the best coverage for issues of high importance.

In industrial environments, operators utilize HMI tools to maintain situational awareness with field equipment. HMI uses virtual buttons and other visual elements to simplify industrial functions. If alerts are frequently generated for noncritical activities, staff will clear the alert list and ignore them over time. Ignoring alerts for critical issues can directly impact production and lead to costly repairs. In this situation, a management dashboard could display performance statistics that may trigger a field investigation into the root cause of declines in production performance.

53.6.2 Trend Analysis and Reporting. Data aggregation, reduction, and correlation lay the foundation for trend analysis. Data related to compliance requirements can be analyzed to determine the pace of security improvements within the organization. Further analysis may identify the level of consistency of an internal security program as well as the true drivers of audit compliance. If system vulnerabilities and business risk continually peak in between scheduled external audits, management will need to investigate the root cause of this unstable, cyclic behavior.

Chargeback refers to the ability to charge for the use of IT services. Some organizations include these costs in the overhead of doing business rather than billing individuals and departments. Regardless of the financial preference, enabling chargeback monitoring in an environment provides an understanding of how information resources are used. If the marketing department utilization has grown from 40 to 70 percent of the Internet bandwidth, and the helpdesk use has expanded from 30 to 50 percent of the cloud computing resources, the trends may encourage management to realign resources to meet business demand or investigate resource abuse. Monitoring resource utilization and demand can also benefit development and testing cycles, so that production resources are properly allocated.

Chargeback systems, such as internal billing services and those used by external service bureaus, prove valuable in monitoring and tracing system activities through their logs. In some states and cities, legislation requires that these types of services keep accurate logs for audit purposes. The original records are used not only for tracking but also in court cases as evidence. In most situations, both internal and external services are the secondary "proof" of transactions, while the initial system logs provide the primary proof.

The log file records provide the basis for sophisticated billing algorithms that encourage rational use of resources. In addition, because unexpected changes in expenses can stimulate interest by accounting staff and managers, billing systems can sometimes aide in the identification of unauthorized usage, based on historical patterns.

Exception reports focus on specific data anomalies, such as employee expense reports that suddenly exceed US$9,000. Managers may want to employ continuous monitoring of the financial system to evaluate exception report trends. In addition to misuse and fraud, exception reports can identify system problems. Generating exception reports for systems that regularly operate below acceptable performance levels may point to a failing component. Management, at an industrial site that regularly fails to account for missing product, may uncover procedural issues that result in wasted material or defective equipment that must be repaired to resolve the ongoing product loss. Exception reports may also identify an isolated issue or a widespread problem. If change management recorded the replacement of hardware on five pipeline segments and they all started leaking at the same time, aggregated log data and exception reports would support the need for hardware and procedural reviews. Or an exception report, based on sensor data collected in November 2002 along the Denali Fault,[18] may correlate with an environmental issue (e.g., earthquake) that would possibly explain the cause of an equipment malfunction.

See Chapter 10 in this *Handbook* for basic information about statistical methods.

53.6.3 Dashboards.

Dashboards consolidate information into a relevant and easily understood summary. Text, visual, and auditory elements may be employed, depending on management needs and system capability. Dashboards build on Web-based technology with a database backend to present a high-level overview of operational status at near-real-time refresh rates. Charts, graphs, stoplight indicators (red, yellow, green), system visualizations, and alert banners enhance the dashboard experience when used in moderation. Employees typically reference dashboards from a standard Web browser or through large video screens mounted in command centers and common areas.

Department and management-specific dashboards should also be considered when implementing specialty M&C systems. Depending on the sensitivity of the information, rotating the dashboards on common screens or within the Web portal itself may provide an opportunity to increase employee awareness of organization-wide and department-specific performance. Associates may learn more about the current level of business risk, of current operational performance (e.g., system uptime, and product generated, or sales volume), or even of the current state of cybersecurity.[19]

In addition to dashboards, organizations continue to use a number of system management consoles to monitor and control specific elements within an infrastructure. System management consoles often cater more to technical operations staff than to upper management. System management consoles and dashboards will likely continue to coexist, due to functional needs.

53.7 CHANGE AND SECURITY IMPLICATIONS

53.7.1 Change Management.

M&C systems enhance an organization's ability to identify and manage change in the information infrastructure. Environment isolation (Development, Test, & Production), source code control, and separation of duties are fundamental prerequisites for effective change management. Knowing when authorized and unauthorized changes occur can improve problem resolution and assist in incident response. In a data center environment, centralized system monitors track operational status. When running configurations are updated on core network equipment, a monitoring system could alert site staff in the event that the changes were not authorized. The cause may trace back to the remote exploitation of a known vulnerability or to an unintended change by a network engineer connecting to the production environment instead of a test lab. In either case, the information reported enables management to assess the situation and to implement corrective actions to reduce the likelihood of future attacks or procedural oversights.[20]

53.7.2 Configuration Protection. When new systems are deployed or legacy systems are brought up to specific compliance levels, configuration concerns surface. Although policy-based standards may correctly define the appropriate configurations to protect the information assets, failure to consistently apply configuration templates or checklists introduces unnecessary complexity to vulnerability and configuration management. To address this challenge, M&C systems can identify anomalies and bring systems back into compliance using predefined criteria. The Payment Card Industry Data Security Standard (PCI DSS) requires file integrity detection and alerting. However, an organization may also find it advantageous to deploy a system that will automatically detect, alert, and correct system integrity discrepancies while reporting on the noncompliant files or settings.

In industrial control systems (ICSs), programmable logic controllers (PLCs) store and run ladder logic programs to control hardware devices in the field. Programmers or automation specialists update these programs using specialized software for industrial networks. Modifying the program will directly affect the output of the actuators connected to the PLC. For example, incorrectly modifying a tank sensor's set point to a value greater than the tank's capacity could result in product loss, requiring manual override. For that reason, the program must be protected from malicious and accidental alteration. Using a password to protect the running program and layered network defenses such as a network IPS contribute to configuration protection in this scenario.

53.7.3 Performance Considerations. Like all systems, M&C systems require resources to operate. Depending on the operational model, these resources may come from the same host system, a network connection, or a remote device. Failing to gauge the performance impact of a monitoring system could leave the operational environment in a degraded state. Additionally, deploying new systems during heavy loads in a business cycle may disrupt normal operations. Installing an enterprise file integrity monitoring system and performing a baseline on production systems during peak hours could lead to overutilization of system resources and could halt critical production jobs. Changes in M&C require planning and coordination with relevant business units and technical staff, to ensure that new systems meet both the business needs and the technical requirements to operate efficiently.

53.8 MONITORING AND CONTROL CHALLENGES

53.8.1 Overview. Legacy systems do not always possess sufficient M&C for today's business and regulatory requirements. The art of retrofitting security into a legacy system requires overcoming physical, technical, and psychosocial barriers. Physical barriers range from wired ICS installations to wireless mobile communications. Technical issues include learning to detect and monitor unique communication protocols, understanding the production performance requirements, and managing systems that historically operated in isolated locations with limited security oversight. Psychosocial challenges are often the most difficult. Organizations and business sectors unaccustomed to mature M&C systems typically deny the need for such systems. Rationalization attempts generally include denial that an attacker would ever target their systems, claims that the business is running well, and concerns that additional changes or complexity will likely disrupt production. Security-awareness training and changes in leadership can partially address these misconceptions while pointing to the lack of M&C data available to support any claims that operations is running as efficiently and securely as it should.

53.8.2 Industrial Control Systems. Industrial control systems (ICSs) operate in a number of industries, including oil, water, and power. ICSs are generally divided into distributed control systems (DCSs) and supervisory control and data acquisition (SCADA) systems. DCSs are more commonly associated with processes such as oil refining. SCADA systems involve more human interaction via HMI, and they collect data from a number of remote devices. Some systems contain elements of both DCS and SCADA. Security issues have increased, due to network connectivity and risks to critical infrastructure. These systems are expected to continue to integrate on a global scale, with improved, centralized data aggregation and reporting. Management will find value not only in aggregating their own organization's data but in collaborating in industry forums to implement more stable, interoperable, and secure industrial M&C systems. Like mainframes, SCADA systems no longer operate in an isolated environment. Sites often communicate via leased lines, satellite, and dial-up modems. Some industrial sites utilize ZigBee wireless equipment rather than installing standard cabling to monitor and control remote devices. Technicians dial in with a modem or through a virtual private network (VPN) tunnel over the Internet to manage industrial systems remotely. Other direct connections from the Internet (via Remote Desktop or VNC) may also exist but are not recommended.

M&C challenges for these systems include authentication, network security, configuration protection, and physical security. Historically, authentication has not been required to use a PC to communicate directly with a PLC over an SCADA network. Some vendors now attempt to build authentication into the HMI. However, the network protocols used in SCADA (e.g., MODBUS/TCP, DNP3) can still send unsolicited messages to the PLC to execute arbitrary commands. Configuration protection is typically associated with the running program on a PLC, which may have a weak or nonexistent password. From the operator standpoint, HMI usually runs on an unpatched PC with application-level security controls. These controls are typically bypassed by attacking the improperly secured operating system or inserting an infected USB drive. Laptops used by engineers to manage and update PLC programs cross legacy air gap boundaries and are often connected to untrusted external networks, used for Internet and email, and exposed to off-site physical attacks. Physical security remains a challenge, as equipment may not be located in a secured area, or operators may lack adequate security awareness training to implement proper security procedures. Fortunately, these M&C systems may leverage existing information security resources to mitigate risk in a layered architecture. NIST SPEC PUB 800-82 clearly describes the security landscape surrounding these systems. Network firewalls, intrusion prevention systems, and more robust physical security would all contribute to a more secure SCADA environment. Vulnerability detection tools now integrate SCADA protocols, with the goal of detecting vulnerabilities and mitigating risk. Continuing to develop more secure communication protocols, and establishing configuration protection guidelines, would further improve the authentication weaknesses in SCADA deployments.

M&Cs in an ICS environment become more complex due to ownership and responsibilities. Traditional IT organizations often support networks up to a network port but often lack the expertise and knowledge specific to industrial control environments. Control engineers may implement specific network elements based on production demands, without necessarily aligning configurations with security and policy requirements.

53.8.3 Mobile Computing. As we continue to integrate mobile and distributed computing systems, the complexity and difficulty required to secure systems increases. We have more variables to address. Information flows even further from the traditional network perimeter. Organizations continue to support bring your own device (BYOD) policies that introduce untrusted and insecure network nodes into the environment; these personal devices storing company data should be addressed through very clearly defined policies and standards. With advances in de-perimeterization, M&C systems must ensure that data remains secure while in transit and at rest, as determined by organizational policy. Mobile technologies communicate over wireless links, invisible to traditional M&C systems. Some wireless devices require centralized system management but rarely connect to the corporate network. Mobile encryption and mandatory VPN connectivity help to control data storage and transmission. With centralized policies, these systems promote more consistent data communications throughout an organization.

Radio-frequency identification (RFID) monitoring systems wirelessly identify and collect information from the target system. NIST 800-98 describes the technological benefits and risks related to implementing this technology. M&C systems often collect sensitive information. The privacy issues inherent in RFID will require thorough risk assessment to avoid potential data loss. Tagging all of an organization's employees with RFID badges that contain PII subject to HIPAA regulations would be unwise, as the RFID tags could potentially be accessed from over one meter away without the holder's knowledge. From an inventory perspective, RFID tags provide a means to automate site audits of company assets or to collect asset information without manually writing it down. To avoid compromise, the device standards use integrity checks (CRC) and require a password to render them nonresponsive.

53.8.4 Virtualization. Organizations use a variety of computing equipment to meet their business needs. Some equipment may remain underutilized, while critical database servers require additional storage space and working memory. Virtualization provides the ability to slice and pool computing resources into more efficient, targeted, and often portable business resources. Virtual systems generally consist of physical hardware, a virtualization interface (VI), and a virtual machine (VM). The VM may be an application or an entire operating system. Since the VI oversees the VMs, we must implement appropriate M&C at the VI layer as well as within and around the VMs.

Users of a virtualized operating system may not be able to detect that it is virtualized. For example, a Web hosting company may wish to provide dedicated virtual servers to its customers without the additional expense of dedicated hardware. In this situation, the organization could deploy FreeBSD servers and implement a degree of virtualization using "jails"[21] to provide a high level of compartmentalized, system-level access to customers. An operator with root access to a jailed environment should not see the processes executed by other jails nor the underlying system hosting the jails. However, the host system owner may monitor or control elements of the host system as well as those within jailed environments. Additional monitoring of the host system may also be necessary, to detect jailbreak attempts.

Another type of virtualization, *paravirtualization*, utilizes a *hypervisor* as the VI between the hardware and the VM. Rather than create identical jailed environments, a hypervisor can be used to support more than one type of guest VM, such as Ubuntu, Fedora, and PC-BSD. This configuration is possible because the hypervisor handles all communications (hypercalls) between the hardware and the VMs. Along the same lines as a FreeBSD host with jails, the hypervisor can monitor and control activities within and around the VMs with varying degrees of transparency to the VM user. The capability of stealth VM monitoring makes virtualization a useful monitoring tool for honeypot research. For a greater level of system assurance, organizations will need tools to detect and prevent attacks against the hypervisor.

Portability, an advantage of virtualization, poses a challenge for M&C systems. VMs can migrate from one hardware device to another frequently, while the integrity of an off-line VM is unknown. In a managed, virtualized infrastructure, performance degradation issues detected in the VI may trigger VMs to migrate from one physical server to a less utilized resource. An unstable VM may also be manually forced off line and rapidly redeployed using a backup virtual disk, without disrupting other VMs sharing the same physical hardware. Tracking these moving targets requires reliable access to the virtual pool of resources, documentation mapping virtual to physical resources, as well as a clearly defined policy for virtual system provisioning. For example, an organization with policies that require clear separations between confidential and public systems should prohibit the same hypervisors from managing both payroll applications and public kiosk VMs on the same hosts.

53.8.5 Cloud Computing. Cloud computing uses several deployment and service models to provision flexible computing and storage resources. However, M&C in the cloud introduces additional challenges, due to the deployment variations and additional parties involved in functional tasks. In public clouds, the physical environment and network infrastructure M&C responsibilities belong to the hosting provider. As a result, organizations have significantly less visibility into daily network operations and incident handling activities, and must rely on third-party attestations and standard reports (e.g., SAS 70, SSAE 16). Decreased M&C visibility places increased reliance on contractual agreements between the cloud provider and the cloud tenant. Guidance published by ENISA and the Cloud Security Alliance can assist in the cost and risk benefit analyses.

In addition to standard computing and storage resource needs, organizations may also leverage cloud resources for log management, disaster recovery, and development environment isolation.

Security responsibilities and M&C capabilities are greater for an organization utilizing the infrastructure as a service (Iaas) model than other service models. Virtual system *instances* can be configured with standard logging capabilities at the operating system and application level. However, some of the hardware elements such as memory may be shared with neighboring cloud tenants. Platform (PaaS) and software as a service (SaaS) models provide customers with less visibility outside the application environment.

Management of cloud resources may be handled through a standard Web interface and APIs. While many of the monitoring and control elements may still exist, the approach to accessing and storing the data may vary. For example, an administrator may create a snapshot of a running instance without impacting the production system. Additionally, the snapshot may be mounted in cloud storage for forensic follow-up.

Controlling access to keys, management interfaces, virtual machines, and storage volumes are important targets for M&C in the cloud. Additionally, data encryption should also be considered where possible.

53.9 SUMMARY.

Monitoring and control systems provide technology stakeholders with additional assurance related to system operations. M&Cs enable visibility into production operations and may also detect and prevent undesirable events and operational inefficiency. Controlling every element of an information system is generally impractical from a cost and risk-based standpoint. However, in taking a risk-based approach, we can identify what should be monitored, controlled, or accepted as a residual risk. Regulations, internal policies, industry frameworks, business requirements, and operational needs all contribute to the decision process in selecting and implementing M&C systems and functions.

Defined scope and business requirements drive the selection of an appropriate M&C model. While human interaction continues to play a critical role in legacy systems, increased sophistication in automation can lead to improved reporting capability and continuous assurance. Unique challenges related to automation surface in environments with specific requirements including industrial controls.

Monitoring, control, and auditing interrogate information systems, identify problems, initiate corrective measures, and generate meaningful information on the state of various systems and processes. The systems may involve human interaction or function in an automated, closed-loop format. Systems generate log files based on system activities, store them in secure locations, and enable aggregators to collect and reduce the data into actionable information. Although log aggregation improves the analysis process, the resources required to store and manipulate the data can become problematic. Not all events are useful. In order to manage reasonable data volumes, only specific activities should be logged or collected by the central management system. Log file data provides a means to analyze events historically at any measured point in time—a necessary part of infrastructure management. Organizations need to understand the value of assets, align business with regulatory requirements, and find new ways to leverage M&C to improve operational performance.

53.9.1 M&C Checklist.

M&C systems may be reviewed at any phase of the lifecycle (e.g., planning, implementing, maintaining, and decommissioning). Assessing the appropriateness of M&C systems and components involves multiple actors. Enterprise Architecture may sit down and define the requirements and identify a short list of potential solutions, while Risk Management, Audit, and Information Security provide feedback based on their areas of focus. In larger environments, Risk Management may also consult with Legal, Senior Management, and IT Governance board members to ensure that M&C investments adequately align with business objectives, maintain acceptable risk levels, and integrate with the evolving maturity and direction of IT services.

Working through an M&C checklist should result in the identification of key elements for a current or future M&C implementation. The information may serve as an input to broader functions including risk management, information security, and enterprise planning. At a minimum, an M&C checklist should include:

- Identification of vision and goals for M&Cs
- Definition of how M&C will align with business
- Mapping of security, compliance, business, and legal requirements
- Scope, architecture, M&C model, and deliverables

- Components to be monitored or controlled
- Storage methods (store/forward)
- Data storage resources and security levels
- Data reduction and reporting outputs
- Response methods
- Self-defending M&C items (e.g., log blackouts/variance as a detective measure)

53.10 FURTHER READING

Badger, L., D. Bernstein, R. Bohn, F. de Vaulx, M. Hogan, J. Mao, J. Mesina, K. Mills, A. Sokol, J. Tong, F. Whiteside, and D. Leaf. U.S. Government Cloud Computing Technology Roadmap Volume I Release 1.0 (Draft) High-Priority Requirements to Further USG Agency Cloud Computing Adoption. NIST Special Publication SP 500-293. www.nist.gov/itl/cloud/upload/SP_500_293_volumeI-2.pdf

Badger, L., R. Bohn, S. Chu, M. Hogan, F. Liu, W. Kaufmann, J. Mao, J. Messina, K. Mills, A. Sokol, J. Tong, F. Whiteside, and D. Leaf. US Government Cloud Computing Technology Roadmap, Release 1.0 (Draft), Volume II Useful Information for Cloud Adopters. NIST Special Publication SP 500-293. www.nist.gov/itl/cloud/upload/SP_500_293_volumeII.pdf

Catteddu, D., and G. Hogben. "Cloud Computing: Benefits, Risks and Recommendations for Information Security." European Network and Information Security Agency (ENISA). November 20, 2009. www.enisa.europa.eu/activities/risk-management/files/deliverables/cloud-computing-risk-assessment

Cloud Security Alliance. "Security Guidance for Critical Areas of Cloud Computing Version 3.0." November 14, 2011. https://cloudsecurityalliance.org/research/security-guidance

ISACA. Control Objectives for Information and Related Technology (COBIT) v5: http://www.isaca.org/cobit

ISO/IEC 17799:200527002:2005: "Information Technology—Security Techniques—Code of Practice for Information Security Management." www.iso.org/iso/home/store/catalogue_ics/catalogue_detail_ics.htm?csnumber=50297; http://www.iso.org/iso/iso_catalogue/catalogue_ics/catalogue_detail_ics.htm?csnumber=39612 (URL inactive).

Karygiannis, T., B. Eydt, G. Barber, L. Bunn, and T. Phillips. Guidelines for Securing Radio Frequency Identification (RFID) Systems. NIST Special Publication 800-98. U.S. Department of Commerce, April 2007, http://csrc.nist.gov/publications/nistpubs/800-98/SP800-98_RFID-2007.pdf

McKinney, D. U.S. Naval Research Laboratory, "NRL Designs Robot for Shipboard Firefighting.," March 7, 2012. U.S. Naval Research Laboratory. www.nrl.navy.mil/media/news-releases/2012/nrl-designs-robot-for-shipboard-firefighting

NIST Cloud Computing: Information Technology Laboratory. www.nist.gov/itl/cloud/index.cfm

Payment Card Industry Data Security Standard (PCI DSS): https://www.pcisecuritystandards.org

Sarbanes-Oxley Act of 2002. 15 U.S.C. 7201. Public Law 107-204. 107th Congress; www.sec.gov/about/laws/soa2002.pdf

Stouffer, K., J. Falco, and K. Scarfone. Guide to Industrial Control Systems (ICS) Security, Rev. 1. NIST Special Publication SP 800-82. U.S. Department of

Commerce, June, 2011. http://csrc.nist.gov/publications/nistpubs/800-82/SP800-82-final.pdf

Ylonen, T., and C. Lonvick. "The Secure Shell (SSH) Protocol Architecture". The Internet Engineering Task Force (IETF) Network Working Group RFC 4251. http://datatracker.ietf.org/doc/rfc4251 and http://tools.ietf.org/html/rfc4251

53.11 NOTES

1. For more information on intrusion detection systems and unified threat management appliances, see Chapter 27 in this *Handbook*.
2. For more information about DoS attacks, see Chapter 18 in this *Handbook*.
3. For more information on incident response, see Chapter 56 in this *Handbook*.
4. Legislation on Notice of Security Breaches, National Conference of State Legislatures, www.ncsl.org/programs/lis/cip/priv/breach.htm
5. For more information on physical and facilities security, see Chapters 22 and 23 in this *Handbook*.
6. See Chapter 28 in this *Handbook* for discussion of identification and authentication.
7. U.S. Department of Navy, "The Navy Unmanned Undersea Vehicle (UUV) Master Plan," November 9, 2004, www.navy.mil/navydata/technology/uuvmp.pdf
8. Department of Defense Directive No. 8100.1, "Global Information Grid (GIG) Overarching Policy," September 19, 2002, www.acq.osd.mil/ie/bei/pm/ref-library/dodd/d81001p.pdf
9. Federal Energy Regulatory Commission, "Existing LNG Terminals," www.ferc.gov/industries/gas/indus-act/lng/exist-term/everett.asp
10. Consortium for Electric Reliability Technology Solutions, "Demand-Response, Spinning-Reserve Demonstration—A New Tool to Reduce the Likelihood of Outages," news release, July 26, 2006, http://certs.lbl.gov/press/press-7-26-06.html
11. See Chapter 3, page 3 in this *Handbook*.
12. K. Scarfone, M. Souppaya, A. Cody, and A. Orebaugh. NIST Special Publication 800-115, Technical Guide to Information Security Testing and Assessment, U.S. Department of Commerce, September 2008, http://csrc.nist.gov/publications/nistpubs/800-115/SP800-115.pdf Keccak was announced as the winner of the five-year SHA-3 competition on October 3, 2012: http://csrc.nist.gov/groups/ST/hash/sha-3
13. ZigBee Alliance: www.zigbee.org
14. U.S. Environmental Protection Agency, "Suggested Pre-Hurricane Activities for Water and Wastewater Facilities," http://water.epa.gov/infrastructure/watersecurity/emergencyinfo/pre-hurricane.cfm
15. Helix by e-Fense: www.e-fense.com/h3-enterprise.php
16. CERT® Advisory CA-2003-04 MS-SQL Server Worm, January 27, 2003, www.cert.org/advisories/CA-2003-04.html
17. An HP7925 120MB disk drive cost $25,000 in 1980, about $100,000 in 2013 currency. The cost per GB in 1980 was ~$853,000 in 2008 dollars. In 2013, a Western Digital Caviar Green 3 TB SATA III 64 MB Cache Bare/OEM Desktop Hard Drive—WD30EZRX for sale at consumer stores cost ~$123, or about $0.04/GB. The ratio of the change in cost is $\sim 4 \times 10–7$. Taking the 33rd root (2013–1980) of the change gives an annual cost change of ~64 percent per year (37 percent decline per year compounded annually).

18. U.S. Geological Survey, Fact Sheet 017-03, "The USGS Earthquake Hazards Program in NEHRP—Investing in a Safer Future," by J. R. Filson, J. McCarthy, W. L. Ellsworth, and M. L. Zoback. Last modified May 17, 2005. http://pubs.usgs.gov/fs/2003/fs017-03
19. Talisker Security Wizardry, The Computer Network Defence Internet Operational Picture, http://securitywizardry.com/radar.htm
20. For more information on software development and quality assurance, see Chapter 39 in this *Handbook*; for information on managing software patches, see Chapter 40.
21. For more information on jails, see Chapter 15 of the FreeBSD Documentation Project's *FreeBSD Handbook*, contributed by Matteo Riondato: www.freebsd.org/doc/en_US.ISO8859-1/books/handbook/jails.html

CHAPTER 54

SECURITY AUDITS

Donald Glass, Richard O. Moore III, Chris Davis, John Mason, David Gursky, James Thomas, Wendy Carr, M. E. Kabay, and Diane Levine

54.1 INTRODUCTION. Traditional auditing focused on reviewing organizational financial records and controls to validate the accuracy and integrity of financial data. External auditors typically focused on material or macro-level issues, and internal auditors focused primarily on transaction-level controls, protecting assets, and validating information adequacy and validity. However, changes in the regulatory environment over the past several years have caused a significant increase in the scope and depth of these responsibilities.

With the changed environment, the extent, focus, reliance, and quality of the audit work has increased significantly in quantity, depth, and reliance. Thus, the current business environment, whether global or domestic, increasingly requires routine, periodic security audits, and inspections that include compliance with:

- Legal requirements; e.g., U.S. Federal laws such as Sarbanes-Oxley (SOX), the Health Insurance Portability and Accountability Act (HIPAA), and the Gramm-Leach-Bliley Act (GLBA)
- Industry standards such as the Payment Card Industry Data Security Standard (PCI DSS) for organizations accepting credit card payments
- Auditing Standards, such as ISO 17799, ISO 27001, and ISO 27002, Statement of Auditing Standards (SAS) 70 audits, both Type I and Type II; and Statement on Standards for Attestation Engagements (SSAE) No. 16

These audits typically address networks, host systems, Internet-related connectivity, protection and detection devices, physical premises, and policy-related items on a recurring basis, since a static posture may unwittingly leave the organization vulnerable.

These reviews and audits may be regarded by an organization's management with attitudes varying between two extremes:

1. They are a cost of doing business, one required by a regulator or governmental law.
2. It's nice to have, but don't spend too much money.

Both extremes, particularly the latter, ignore the value to the organization from such reviews, since the expense may be the primary (or only) criterion evaluated by senior management.

Sarah Abelow summarized the value of information technology (IT) audits as follows:

> 1. **Reduce risk.** IT audits that are planned and executed based on best practices will identify and assess the risks in an organization's IT environment. … Once risks are assessed, there can be clear vision on what course to take—to reduce or mitigate the risks through controls, to transfer the risk through insurance or to simply accept the risk as part of the operating environment …
> 2. **Strengthen controls (and improve security).** Based on the assessed risks as discussed above, the next step is to identify and assess corresponding controls. If controls are assessed to be poorly designed or ineffective, corrective action can be taken.
> 3. **Comply with regulations.** Wide ranging regulations at the federal and state levels include specific requirements for information security. The IT auditor serves a critical function in ensuring that specific requirements are met, risks are assessed and controls implemented. … It is critical to an organization to have assurance that all requirements are met.
> 4. **Facilitate communication between business and technology management.** An audit opens channels of communication between an organization's business and technology management. Auditors spend time interviewing, observing, and testing what is happening in reality and in practice. An audit can provide valuable information in written reports and oral presentations. Senior management needs to know firsthand how their organization is functioning.

The reverse communication from senior management to the technology professionals is also critical. Senior management's objectives and expectations are communicated to the technology staff. Auditors can facilitate this communication through participation in technical meetings and through review of the current implementations of policies, standards, and guidelines. . . .

5. **Improve IT Governance.** The IT Governance Institute (ITGI) provides this definition:

   "IT Governance is the responsibility of executives and board of directors, and consists of the leadership, organizational structures, and processes that ensure that the enterprise's IT sustains and extends the organization's strategies and objectives."

   The leadership, organizational structures, and processes mentioned in the definition point to IT auditors as key players. IT auditing and overall IT management are focused on the value, risks, and controls around an organization's technology environment. IT auditors review the value, risks, and controls in all of the key components of technology—applications, information, infrastructure, and people.[1]

In addition, IT and security audits can help ensure that the organization is not unwittingly posing an IT-related risk for or threat to other organizations, whether related, foreign, competitor, peer, or unrelated, by becoming involved, even unwittingly, in national security breaches, industrial espionage or sabotage, computer trespass, privacy violations, spam, or harassment because of inadequate controls.

Recent developments in government regulation and oversight have reduced auditors' gray areas; that is, the number of ambiguities and exceptions to requirements for reporting and compliance have been reduced. Perhaps as a result of increasing public awareness of leaks of personally identifiable information (PII), several undergraduate and graduate programs have been developed in universities and colleges around the world to train students in the discipline of IT, security, and compliance auditing.

Finally, it is useful to remind readers of the difference between an *audit* and an *assessment:*

- An *audit* is a formal process, usually carried out by a certified audit professional, focusing on verifying compliance with stated internal policies, external formal standards, and legal requirements. An audit report usually provides detailed lists of exactly which formal requirements have been met or not met.
- An *assessment* is an informal process, usually carried out by an industry expert who may or may not be certified by a professional body, focusing on improving efficiency and effectiveness, often using informal industry best practices and the expertise of the evaluator. An assessment report usually provides detailed analysis of failings and concrete recommendations for specific ways to improve what has been assessed.[2]

This chapter focuses on security audits.

54.2 ADDRESSING MULTIPLE REGULATIONS FOR INFORMATION SECURITY. Federal regulations and industry standards increasingly recognize the need to address controls related to information security. However, because of continual advances in technology and the diversity of equipment and structures available for use, regulations and standards have continued to be vague in stating specifically how security configurations should be implemented, tested, and monitored. Although there are many different clients from diverse industries, with various regulations, legislation, or industry specific standards, all of them have a fundamental source of their best practices.

During the 1980s, the Defense Computer Security Center began to create a series of standards related to securing computer systems for governmental and subcontracted entities. The series of documents relating to the configuration, auditing, and securing of systems is commonly referred to as the "Rainbow Series" because each cover in the series is a different color.[3] Systems that followed the procedures of the series were considered *trusted* systems, due to the rigid requirements for following the configuration criteria contained within this series. The Rainbow Series documents have evolved into today's *Common Criteria Evaluation and Validation Scheme* (CCEVS)[4] to meet the demands of processing and computer systems of today; however, the fundamentals of how to secure and audit systems and information have remained semiconstant and have begun to be defined as best practices.

The term *best practices* is vague, but the concept comprises a set of standards, experiences, and after-action reports (lessons learned) that are intended to help meet the information security controls most commonly expected of trusted organizations. These best practices were derived from standards that were developed for secure or trusted systems. Today, information assurance best practices have evolved from the rigid requirements of the Rainbow Series standards. Best practices can now be found contained in various documents, including:

- Auditing checklists that can be obtained from the Information Systems Audit and Control Association (ISACA) as discussed in Section 54.4.3.3 in this chapter
- Defense Information Systems Agency's Security Technical Implementation Guides (DISA-STIG)[5]
- National Institute of Standards and Technology (NIST) Computer Security Division's Special Publications (SP) series—800 documents[6]

Another way to address the multiple regulations is to incorporate one of the more comprehensive frameworks, such as Control Objectives for Information and related Technology (COBIT, Section 54.4.3.3 in this chapter), Information Technology Infrastructure Library (ITIL),[7] and the International Organization for Standardization (ISO)[8] 27000 series (Section 54.3.2), with many relying on the others for ensuring that the information security areas have appropriate controls. Sections relevant to information security vary on the types of framework that should be incorporated but have value in that they identify areas that should have manual or technology controls pertinent to those areas.

For example, the Federal Information Security Management Act (FISMA) of 2002, the Sarbanes-Oxley Act of 2002, and the Health Insurance Portability and Accountability Act of 1996 all address security policy, logical access controls, and methods for the handling and storage of sensitive information.

In the past, if help was needed to classify information, the *Yellow Book*, or the CSC-STD-003-85, was the reference or standard. Once information was appropriately classified, an information security classification policy was developed by the organization and was applied to securing that data in information systems.

Today, legislative and industry specific requirements sometimes define what is critical or sensitive information; for many organizations looking for answers, the starting reference is the NIST SP 800-60, *Guide for Mapping Types of Information and Information Systems to Security Categories*. The NIST SP 800 series provide a wealth of information to support effective IT and security audits.

54.2.1 Gramm-Leach-Bliley Act. The Financial Services Modernization Act of 1999, more commonly known as the Gramm-Leach-Bliley Act (GLBA), regulates the security of consumers' personal financial information and nonpublic personal information (NPI). Major provisions of the GLBA address privacy requirements for information, disclosures of personal and financial information to third parties, rules regarding the safeguarding of information, and protections against the use of pretexting to illegally acquire personal information.[9] Financial information may include names of financial institution customers, account numbers, and information related to balances and transactions. NPI may include date of birth, Social Security number, driver's license number, financial account numbers, balances, home address, telephone numbers, and so on.

GLBA also governs the disclosure of such information to third parties. Institutions that are affected by GLBA must disclose to customers, in the form of a privacy notice, when and how their information is released. Additionally, institutions must provide for customers the opportunity to opt out of having their information shared with some third parties. Customers may not use the opt-out privileges to stop the release of their information to law enforcement agencies that are performing an authorized investigation.

GLBA regulations also protect consumers against the increasingly used form of social engineering called "pretexting." Pretexting is the act of using false statements or impersonation to obtain access to the information of another individual. An example would be a perpetrator calling a financial institution and pretending to be an authorized account holder requesting to make a funds transfer by telephone. In the absence of face-to-face verification of a drivers' license or some other token, banks are allowing such transactions to occur after the caller has verified some "known" information, be it date of birth, address, Social Security number, and so on. GLBA makes the act of pretexting illegal and encourages institutions to use more stringent methods for confirming a customer's identity.

Internal auditing to determine compliance with GLBA protects organizations and ensures the proper handling of NPI. Because mishandling or unauthorized release of NPI can lead to incidents of fraud and identity theft, institutions that are required to use and maintain such information must be very diligent in their security processes. Periodic audits of business and network processes that control the storage, transmission, and use of NPI will aid in alerting organizations to weaknesses in their security and will document due diligence efforts in the protection of customer information.

For more details of compliance with GLBA, see Chapter 64 in this *Handbook*.

54.2.2 Federal Information Systems Management Act. FISMA affects almost all U.S. Governmental entities and was created as part of the E-Government Act (Public Law 107-347)[10] passed by the 108th Congress in 2002 and signed into law by then President George W. Bush. The resolution recognized the importance of information security to the economic and national security interests of the United States. Title III of the E-Government Act entitled the FISMA[11] to require each federal agency to develop, document, and implement an agency-wide information assurance program that would provide security controls for the information and systems that support the operations and assets of the agency. This measure should also include security controls for information-handling services or systems that are provided, or managed, by third-party agencies, contractors, or other sources.

FISMA defined what should be included in an information-security program to be effective:

- Periodic assessments of risk, including the magnitude of harm that could result from the unauthorized access, use, disclosure, disruption, modification, or destruction of information and information systems that support the operations and assets of the organization (Many corporate entities may refer to this as a business impact analysis [BIA].)
- Policies and procedures that are based on the information provided by risk assessments, that would cost effectively reduce information security risks to an acceptable level, and that would ensure that information security is addressed throughout the life cycle of each organizational information system
- Subordinate plans for providing adequate information security for networks, facilities, information systems, or groups of information systems, as appropriate
- Security awareness training to inform personnel (including contractors and other users of information systems that support the operations and assets of the organization) of the information-security risks associated with their activities and their responsibilities in complying with organizational policies and procedures designed to reduce these risks
- Periodic testing and evaluation of the effectiveness of information-security policies, procedures, practices, and security controls will be performed, with frequency determined by the level of risk, but no less than annually
- A process for planning, implementing, evaluating, and documenting remedial actions to address any deficiencies in the information-security policies, procedures, and practices of the organization
- Procedures for detecting, reporting, and responding to security incidents
- Plans and procedures to ensure continuity of operations for information systems that support the operations and assets of the organization

FISMA, along with the Paperwork Reduction Act of 1995 and the Information Technology Management Reform Act of 1996 (Clinger-Cohen Act), explicitly emphasizes a risk-based policy for cost-effective security. In supporting and reinforcing this legislation, the Office of Management and Budget (OMB) through Circular A-130, Appendix III, Security of Federal Automated Information Resources,[12] requires executive agencies within the federal government to:

- Plan for security
- Ensure that appropriate officials are assigned security responsibility
- Periodically review the security controls in their information systems
- Authorize system processing prior to operations and periodically thereafter

These management requirements presume that responsible agency officials understand the risks and other factors that could adversely affect their objectives. Moreover, these officials must understand the status of their security programs, and the security controls planned or in place to protect their information and information systems, in order to make informed judgments and investments that appropriately mitigate risk to an acceptable level.

The ultimate objective is to conduct the day-to-day operations of the agency and to accomplish the agency's stated missions with security commensurate with level of risk, while acknowledging the magnitude of harm that could result from the unauthorized access, use, disclosure, disruption, modification, or destruction of information. As a key element of the FISMA Implementation Project, NIST also developed an integrated risk framework[13] that effectively brings together all of the FISMA-related security standards and guidance, in order to promote the development of comprehensive and balanced information-security programs by agencies.[14]

54.2.3 Health Insurance Portability and Accountability Act of 1996.

The Health Insurance Portability and Accountability Act (HIPAA),[15] 42 USC 201 et seq., includes specific provisions affecting information security:

> The Office for Civil Rights enforces the HIPAA Privacy Rule, which protects the privacy of individually identifiable health information; the HIPAA Security Rule, which sets national standards for the security of electronic protected health information; the HIPAA Breach Notification Rule, which requires covered entities and business associates to provide notification following a breach of unsecured protected health information; and the confidentiality provisions of the Patient Safety Rule, which protect identifiable information being used to analyze patient safety events and improve patient safety.[16]

For extensive discussion of HIPAA, see Chapter 71 in this *Handbook.*

54.2.4 Payment Card Industry Data Security Standards.

The Payment Card Industry Security Standards Council was formed in 2006 by collaboration of American Express, Discover Financial Services, JCB International, MasterCard Worldwide, and Visa Inc. The Council has promulgated the

- Payment Card Industry Data Security Standard (PCI DSS) for "merchants and entities that store, process, or transmit cardholder data"
- Payment Application Data Security Standard (PA-DSS) for software developers
- PIN Transaction Security (PTS) requirements for manufacturers of card-reading equipment.[17,18]

The core goals of the PCI DSS are summarized in the organization's table of goals and requirements as shown in Exhibit 54.1.[18]

The official site[19] has an extensive range of documents available at no cost (simple registration required), including (as of July 2013):

- FAQs for use with ROC [Report on Compliance] Reporting Instructions for PCI DSS v2.0
- Glossary v2.0
- Navigating the PCI DSS v2.0
- PCI DSS AOC—Merchants v2.0
- PCI DSS AOC—Service Providers v2.0
- PCI DSS Quick Reference Guide v2.0
- PCI DSS Summary of Changes Version 1.2.1 to 2.0
- PCI Quick Reference Order Form

Exhibit 54.1 Organization's Goals and Responsibilities

Goals	PCI DSS Requirements
Building and Maintain a Secure Network	**1.** Install and maintain a firewall configuration to protect cardholder data **2.** Do not use vendor-supplied defaults for system passwords and other security parameters
Protect Cardholder Data	**3.** Protect stored cardholder data **4.** Encrypt transmission of cardholder data across open public networks
Maintain a Vulnerability Management Program	**5.** Use and regularly update anti-virus software or program **6.** Develop and maintain secure systems and applications
Implement Strong Access Control Measures	**7.** Restrict access to cardholder data by business need to know **8.** Assign a unique ID to each person with computer access **9.** Restrict physical access to cardholder data
Regularly Monitor and Test Network	**10.** Track and monitor all access to network resources and cardholder data **11.** Regularly test security systems and processes
Maintain an Information Security Policy	**12.** Maintain a policy that addresses information security for all personnel

- Prioritized Approach for PCI DSS Version 2.0
- Prioritized Approach Tool Version 2.0
- ROC Reporting Instructions for PCI DSS v2.0
- Summary of Changes from Prioritized Approach for PCI DSS Version 1.2 to 2.0
- Summary of PCI DSS and PA-DSS Feedback 2012

The specific guidelines can be integrated into audit patterns adapted for the requirements of each organization handling credit card data.

54.2.5 Publicly Available Security Publications. The NIST SP (SP) 800-53 Revision 1 is the "Recommended Security Controls for Federal Information Systems."[20] The purpose of SP 800-53 is to provide guidelines for selecting and specifying what should be security controls for information systems supporting the executive agencies of the federal government. The guidelines have been developed to help achieve secure system requirements by:

- Facilitating a more consistent, comparable, and repeatable approach for selecting and specifying security controls for information systems

- Providing a recommendation for minimum security controls for information systems categorized in accordance with Federal Information Processing Standard (FIPS) 199,[21] *Standards for Security Categorization of Federal Information and Information Systems*
- Providing a stable yet flexible catalog of security controls for information systems to meet current organizational protection needs and the demands of future protection needs based on changing requirements and technologies
- Creating a foundation for the development of assessment methods and procedures for determining security control effectiveness

The guidelines provided in SP 800-53 are applicable to all federal information systems[22] with the exception of systems designated as national security systems as defined by 44 USC Section 3542.[23] The guidelines have been broadly developed from a technical perspective to complement similar guidelines for national security systems. This publication is intended to provide guidance to federal agencies implementing FIPS 200,[24] *Minimum Security Requirements for Federal Information and Information Systems*. In addition to the agencies of the federal government, the state, local, tribal governments, and private-sector organizations that comprise the critical infrastructure of the United States are also encouraged to use these guidelines as appropriate.

The security controls in SP 800-53 have been developed using inputs from a variety of sources including NIST SP 800-26, Department of Defense (DoD) Policy 8500, Director of Central Intelligence Directive (DCID) 6/3, ISO/IEC Standard 17799, General Accounting Office (GAO) Federal Information System Controls Audit Manual (FISCAM), and Health and Human Services (HHS) Centers for Medicare and Medicaid Services (CMS) Core Security Requirements. The security controls cover these topic areas[25]:

- Access control
- Accountability and audit
- Awareness and training
- Certification, accreditation, and security assessments
- Configuration management
- Contingency planning
- Identification and authentication
- Incident response
- Maintenance
- Media protection
- Personnel security
- Physical and environmental protection
- Risk assessment
- Security planning
- System and communications protection
- System and information integrity
- System services and acquisition

54.2.6 Risk Framework. The following list illustrates an example of how to create a security-audit framework that draws on a wide array of audit standards:

1. Categorize the information system and the information resident within that system based on impact. (FIPS 199iii and NIST SP 800-60[26])
2. Select an initial set of security controls for the information system based on the FIPS 199 security categorization and apply tailoring guidance, as appropriate, to obtain a starting point for required controls. (FIPS 200 and NIST SP 800-53)
3. Supplement the initial set of tailored security controls based on an assessment of risk and local conditions, including organization-specific security requirements, specific threat information, cost-benefit analyses, and special circumstances. (NIST SP 800-53 and SP 800-30[27])
4. Document the agreed-on set of security controls in the system security plan, including the organization's justification for any refinements or adjustments to the initial set of controls. (NIST SP 800-18[28])
5. Implement the security controls in the information system
6. Assess the security controls using appropriate methods and procedures to determine the extent to which the controls are implemented correctly, operating as intended, and producing the desired outcome with respect to meeting the security requirements for the system. (NIST SP 800-53A[29])
7. Authorize information system operation based on a determination of the risk to organizational operations, organizational assets, or to individuals resulting from the operation of the information system and the decision that this risk is acceptable. (NIST SP 800-37[30])
8. Monitor and assess selected security controls in the information system on a continuous basis including documenting changes to the system, conducting security impact analyses of the associated changes, and reporting the security status of the system to appropriate organizational officials on a regular basis.[31]

54.3 AUDITING STANDARDS.

Auditing standards and practices assist organizations in meeting regulatory requirements and provide industry guidance for ensuring due diligence, certification, and ensuring stakeholder security. As discussed in the preceding section, standard-setting entities include international organizations, federal and state levels of government, and industry-specific groups or associations whose focus includes regulatory compliance. Guiding principles and information published by these entities may be required or, at the very least, provide managers with the newest information regarding industry advances. Managers must not only be aware of new developments in auditing methodology; they must also be adept in identifying and applying the best solution available to their unique physical and logical architecture.

54.3.1 Introduction to ISO. ISO[32] is a nongovernmental cooperative of international members who work together to create, identify, and publish industry standards as they relate to business and technology. Membership comprises member bodies, correspondent members, and subscriber members.

- A *member body* is a group that represents the accepted standards of a specific country.

- *Correspondent members* represent a country that does not yet have fully developed standards.
- *Subscriber members* represent countries with developing economies.[33]

Level of membership determines technical and policy participation and voting privileges, but members all are equally represented in international standardization and are encouraged to contribute.

Standards are developed based on industry interest; needs of vendors, governments, and consumers; and initiatives of the ISO where it sees market interest. Once the idea of a standard has been recognized by the ISO, member committees begin the process of defining the technical requirements necessary for the standard. Committee members include technical experts representing countries interested in the potential new standard. Once the technical requirements have been defined, interested members and countries work toward agreement on detailed specifications for the standard. When final details have met committee approval, a draft of the international standard is released for review. Final release of an official ISO standard[34] requires approval of two-thirds of the members who participated in the development process and 75 percent of all members who vote.[35]

Standards established by ISO are not regulator; they represent best-practice guidance that is globally consistent for a given trade or line of business. Widespread acceptance and implementation of ISO standards and guidance further elevates them as identifiers of distinction within a given industry. Similar to worldwide recognition of ISO 9000 and ISO 14000 as standards for Quality and for Environmental Management (respectively), the ISO 27000 series is quickly becoming accepted as the measurement of excellence in information-security management.

54.3.2 ISO/IEC 27000 Series. Information and network security has been a concern since the early days of worms and viruses; however, it has only been in the past 15 to 20 years that structures have been defined to integrate security with network use and risk management. Introduction of BS7799 and its acceptance by ISO have given administrators the long-needed tools to identify and manage these domains. Additionally, regulations such as the Sarbanes-Oxley Act of 2002 (SOX), the Gramm-Leach-Bliley Act (GLBA), Health Insurance Portability and Accountability Act (HIPAA), and the Federal Information Security Management Act (FISMA) have set down compliance requirements that are more easily achievable with a comprehensive information-security management system in place.

British Standard 7799, representing best practices for information security, was first published in February 1995. This three-part standard encompasses security objectives and controls as well as the development methodology necessary to create an information-security management system (ISMS).[36]

- BS7799: Part 1, Best Practices for Information Security Management
- BS7799: Part 2, Defines specifications for information-security management systems
- BS7799: Part 3, Guidelines for information-security risk management

In the past decade, British Standard 7799 was the basis for the ISO 17799 and then into the ISO 27000 series, which continues to evolve as a widely accepted standard for information-security management and for operational procedure guidance. Both agencies (and their collective members) understood the need for a comprehensive program that addressed the risk management and auditing needs of organizations while defining a framework for programs and policies to support this concept. Partial or full implementation of these standards not only prepares organizations for audits and risk assessments but can also help them meet regulatory requirements.

The ISMS defined by BS7799 and further improved on by ISO 17799 and ISO/IEC 27000 is a means to ensure the best environment not only for security practices but also for objective auditing and assessments. An organization's interpretation of, and adherence to, the ISMS model can be a major indicator of the security climate of the organization as well as of management's support of policies and procedures. Programs that support ISMS functions must be promoted and used by management to demonstrate their significance to employees and to encourage participation. Audits typically consist of a planning phase, the actual audit process, and the final report to the audit committee presenting the details of audits or assessments.

In December 2000, BS7799 Part 1 (Best Practices for Information Security Management) was revised and released as ISO 17799.[37] The ISO 17799 standard comprises 10 domains:

1. Business continuity planning
2. System access control
3. System development and maintenance
4. Physical and environmental security
5. Compliance
6. Personnel security
7. Security organization
8. Computer and operations management
9. Asset classification and control
10. Security policy

In 2005, ISO completed a cooperative effort with the International Electrotechnical Commission to release ISO/IEC 17799:2005. This release, entitled *Information Technology—Security Techniques—Code of Practice for Information Security Management*, added objectives and controls for information-security management and updated the previous release to include advances in technology (mobile and wireless) and in applications and uses of the Internet.[38]

BS7799 and ISO 17799 established widely implemented guidance for the information-security management systems standard, but the evolutionary path of their published standards has made them nearly obsolete. The ISO/IEC 27000[39] set of standards not only incorporates the guidance of BS7799 and ISO 17799[40] but also provides a more thorough explanation and understanding of each domain by partitioning them into distinctly separate standards. The ISO/IEC ISMS family includes the following International Standards (as of July 2013):

- ISO/IEC 27000:2009, Information security management systems—Overview and vocabulary
- ISO/IEC 27001:2005, Information security management systems—Requirements
- ISO/IEC 27002:2005, Code of practice for information-security management

- ISO/IEC 27003:2010, Information-security management system implementation guidance
- ISO/IEC 27004:2009, Information-security management—Measurement
- ISO/IEC 27005:2011, Information-security risk management
- ISO/IEC 27006:2011, Requirements for bodies providing audit and certification of information-security management systems
- ISO/IEC 27007:2011, Guidelines for information-security management systems auditing
- ISO/IEC 27010:2012, Information-security management guidelines for inter-sector and interorganizational communications
- ISO 27799:2008, Health informatics—Information-security management in health using ISO/IEC 27002
- ISO/IEC FDIS 27013, Guidance on the integrated implementation of ISO/IEC 27001 and ISO/IEC 20000-1
- ISO/IEC TR 27008:2011, Guidelines for auditors on information-security management systems controls
- ISO/IEC TR 27015, Information-security management guidelines for financial services
- ISO/IEC WD 27016, Information-security management—Organizational economics
- ITU-T X.1051 | ISO/IEC 27011:2008, Information-security management guidelines for telecommunications organizations based on ISO/IEC 27002
- ITU-T X.1054 | ISO/IEC FDIS 27014, Governance of information security

Some ISO standards are freely available in electronic form from http://standards.iso.org/ittf/PubliclyAvailableStandards/index.html and they may also be purchased as electronic or printed documents from http://www.iso.org/iso/home/store.htm

ISO/IEC 27001 (ISMS Requirements) closely models the Organization for Economic Cooperation and Developments (OECD)[41] guidance on the security of information systems and networks, and is driven by the Plan-Do-Check-Act (PDCA) cycle.[42]

The PDCA cycle, developed by W. Edwards Deming in the 1950s, asks managers to view business processes as being in a constant feedback loop.[43] This method allows managers to be involved more thoroughly in the entire change control and improvement process.

Organizations may implement some or all of the standards of ISO/IEC 27001 or take their program a step further by applying for ISMS certification. Certification provides both auditors and stakeholders with the assurance that a comprehensive program is in place for information-security and business systems. Whether an organization seeks recognized ISMS certification or not, there are several advantages to adopting the objectives and controls outlined in ISO/IEC 27001. As stated earlier, having a comprehensive ISMS program in place can greatly contribute to compliance in other areas. An ISO/IEC 27001-certified ISMS will ensure compliance with the whole range of information-security–related legislation, including HIPAA, GLBA, and FISMA regulations, as well as the conditions for a successful Sarbanes-Oxley Section 404 report.[44]

Documented ISMS policies and programs, a security climate including both management and employees, and adherence to policy are not only necessary for an information-security management system to be effective, but will ensure a successful, constructive, and effective audit process.

54.3.3 AICPA Security Audit Standards. Companies and government agencies are under constant pressure to improve efficiencies and to reduce operational costs. In addition, public companies are being driven by investors and shareholders to improve profitability, contributing in a small way to IT outsourcing in the 2000s. The U.S. Bureau of Labor Statistics began including "Cost control/cost cutting/increase profitability" as a reason for mass layoffs starting with the 2007 studies; the proportions of respondents using this entry as a reason for the layoffs were stable at approximately 3 percent of total yearly layoffs between 2007 and 2011.[45]

Outsourcing has not been limited to public companies; government agencies have also embraced outsourcing to contain costs. In 2013, data from the U.S. Federal Office of Management and Budget suggested that about one-third of all U.S. Government discretionary spending was outsourced.[46]

With the drive for more companies to focus on their core competencies, these types of business functions are being outsourced:

- Claims processing
- Customer service and helpdesk
- Data processing
- Financial and accounting
- Human resources and benefit plans
- Web hosting

Executive officers of organizations considering outsourcing must understand both the benefits and the risks; they also have to mitigate the risk to a level acceptable for their organizations.

The American Institute of Certified Public Accountants (AICPA) has defined three widely used security-audit standards, discussed in the following sections:

- SAS 70
- SSAE 16

ISAE 3402 is an international standard with which SSAE 16 complies.

54.3.3.1 Introduction to SSAE 16 Audits. The *Statement of Auditing Standards No. 70 (SAS 70): Service Organizations*, was originally created by the American Institute of Certified Public Accountants (AICPA) for financial-service reporting and was a key method of ensuring that a company being considering for supplying outsourced services met security requirements.[47]

The security-audit industry's need to report on security controls has led to the replacement of SAS 70 by the *Statement on Standards for Attestation Engagements No. 16 (SSAE 16), Reporting on Controls at a Service Organization*, which replaced the guidance for service auditors in SAS 70 for all such engagements ending on or after June 15, 2011.

Exhibit 54.2 Types of SSAE 16 Audits

SSAE 16 Report Content	Type I	Type II
Independent service audits report	Included	Included
Service organization's description of controls	Included	Included
Information provided by the independent service auditor; includes a description of the service auditor's tests of operating effectiveness and the results of those tests	Optional	Included
Other service relevant information	Optional	Included

SSAE 16 was also "drafted with the intention and purpose of updating the US service organization reporting standard so that it mirrors and complies with the new international service organization reporting standard—ISAE 3402."[48]

In addition to being used for evaluating outsourcing suppliers, the SSAE 16 can be used when *partnering* with companies that may have access to your IT resources and data—especially personally identifiable information (PII) about customers.

In this section, the two types of SSAE 16 audits and their components are described.

Terminology associated with SSAE 16 audits:

Service organization—the company that will process information or transactions on behalf of the user organization

Service auditor—retained by the service organization to conduct an SSAE 16 audit and provide a certification of audit results

User organization—the company that outsourced services and is the customer of the service organization

Users' auditors—either an internal or external auditing group that provides auditing services to the user organization

SOC—service organization controls; there are three types of SOC reports

The SSAE 16 defines the professional standards that are used by the service auditor, who will be assessing the internal controls that a service organization has implemented.

An SSAE 16 audit provides authoritative guidance that allows a service organization to disclose its control processes and activities to potential customers and to external auditors; the information is presented in a standard reporting format. There are three different types (SOC-1, -2, and -3) and two different levels of SSAE 16 audits (Type I and Type II), as illustrated in Exhibit 54.2.

- **SOC-1**: Controls at a service organization that are relevant to the user entity's internal controls over financial reporting; these can include both IT-related as well as financial controls. This report can be used by all types of service organizations; data centers may use this type of report in place of a SOC-2 if one or more financially related controls are reviewed.
- **SOC-2**: Strictly an IT-focused report with the controls preestablished and organized into the categories of security, availability, processing integrity, confidentiality, and privacy. The service organization may choose to have the audit focus on selected categories; all controls within the selected category/categories must be reviewed. Typically, these apply to data centers, ISPs, and ASPs.

- **SOC-3**: Similar to a SOC-2, this report focuses on trust services and principles; e.g., a Web trust audit. If the service organization elects to include the privacy principle in the audit scope, the criteria for the content of a privacy notice is included. This typically includes information about collecting the information, the choices that the individuals have regarding their personal information, the security of the information, and how the individuals can contact the service organization for inquiries, complaints, or disputes.

Each report contains several key sections:

- Opinion letter from the CPA firm.
- Management assertion regarding the description of the service organization's system and the suitability of the design of the controls; if the report is a Type II, then the assertion also includes the operating effectiveness of the controls in achieving the control objectives.
- Description of the controls and control environment.
- Results of the controls' testing.
- Key subservice organizations (e.g., outsourced IT monitoring) whose activities affect the controls.

A critical difference between an SSAE 16 Type I audit and Type II is that a Type I audit tests the control design effectiveness and tests one sample transaction for each control; this, to prove that the design of the control functions appropriately in at least one instance. For a Type II audit, the control design is tested as well as the controls' effectiveness over the audit period. Because of this testing, Type II audits are more costly but provide a detailed report and provide more value and reliance to the service organizations' users.

An SSAE 16 audit starts with the service auditor conducting an initial risk assessment and evaluation of the processing system and of the transaction systems processing controls, and a review of the policies and procedures that govern IT system and processes. Next, the auditor will develop a statement of work (SOW) that will be presented to the service organization with completion date, details of the audit, audit scope, and cost.

An SSAE 16 audit team usually will be managed by a CPA; a CPA must review the audit report and work and must sign the opinion. This individual will be the primary interface with the customer executive management and will certify the audit results. The audit team performing the work may be a single person or a team of perhaps two to four auditors. The technical lead is responsible for evaluation and testing of systems and network devices.

If a SOC-1 audit is being performed, there may be two to five IT-related control objectives, and within each control objective, there may be one to fifteen controls tested. Typically, there is more granularity in the testing of the controls, so that if a particular control fails (e.g., not disabling a terminated user's access promptly), then it would not cause other controls bundled together to fail (e.g., if user provisioning—add, change, or remove users—is listed as a single control instead of three controls). For an SOC-1 audit, the service organization is responsible for identifying and approving the control objectives and the controls; the service auditor often provides information as to best practices and controls that typically are tested. For the SOC-2 and SOC-3 reports, the controls are preestablished, and the service organization may select which of the key categories are to be reviewed in the audit.

In addition to reviewing hardware and software configurations, IT policies and procedures typically are included to be evaluated, reviewed, and verified. Management, including system and network administrators, will be interviewed in the walkthrough phase to determine how certain tasks are performed; a sample item will be tested at that time to verify that the control's design is effective (i.e., that the control works for a sample transaction). For example, who approves a user account request form, and how does the form flow through the approval process? System or application administrators will be asked to explain what they do from the time they receive an account request form until the account is created. The auditor will use the information gathered from the interviews to determine if account policies and procedures are being followed and if they are adequate for the customer's environment.

A brief overview of what an auditor would review for a user request policy and how the results would be reported follows:

- **Policy statement**. All users who require a new computer account or modification to an existing account, on any system at the company will be required to complete User Account Request Form UA-09.
- **Policies and procedures**. User Account Request Policy "IT-23 November 1, 2011." All requests for a new account or for modification of an existing account must be submitted on a UA-09 Form.
- **Test procedure**. Conduct a sample review of user request forms and review the forms for proper authorized signatures and completeness. Interview authorized signers for compliance with user request policy; ensure that users are only given roles consistent with their job position's least privileges.
- **Test results**. Collect statistical samples of user request forms and interview the supervisors of the individuals making the requests to determine that least privileges needed to perform their job have been requested and approved. Check forms for completeness and accuracy of information.
- **Analysis of test results**. The auditor will provide both the positive test results and negative results with commentary. A sample of a positive or negative test results:
  - **Positive test result**. All forms that were reviewed were completed in accordance with User Account Request Policy "IT-23 November 1, 2011," and all interviews indicated that all policies and procedures were correctly followed. No discrepancies were found.
  - **Negative test result**. After reviewing the User Account Request Form and interviewing supervisors and authorized signers, it was determined that User Account Request Policy "IT-23 November 1, 2011" was not followed. Users were given privileges beyond what was required to perform their job.

Exceptions and findings are reported in the final SSAE 16 report sent to management in these ways:

- If the auditor deems that it is relevant, an exception is reported, including a description of the exception.
- The auditor will consider any mitigating controls or any management responses to the exception.
- If, in the auditor's opinion, the finding has an impact on the control objectives, then it would be reported with a qualified opinion and potential impact; if not, it would be reported as an exception.

The final document that a SSAE 16 will provide is the conclusion and summary report, which will clearly state whether the description of the controls is accurately and fairly presented. The report will also state whether the controls were adequately designed to meet their control objectives. The report for a Type II audit would also include the results of tests that were performed and would evaluate whether they provide reasonable assurance that controls were operating correctly during a period of time, normally no less than six months and no more than 12 months; however, for the first SSAE 16, a service organization must have a minimum review period of three months.

54.3.3.2 Cost and Benefits of SSAE 16 Audits. Before undertaking an SSAE 16 audit, any organization, whether a service provider or an outsourcing company, must decide whether such a procedure is worth the costs. For example, a small service organization whose customer requests an SSAE 16 audit must determine whether to keep that customer: an initial audit Type II SSAE 16 audit's cost can range from $15,000 to over $1 million, in addition to the annual cost to keep the audit current. Because of the reduced testing, a Type I may be engaged for $10,000 to $13,000, depending on the number of controls, the control objectives, and the extent that the service auditor (SSAE 16 auditor) can rely on the service organization's internal audit work.

User organizations have quickly embraced the SSAE 16 audit because of the benefits in complying with the SOX and GLBA requirements. Depending on the scope and timing of the audit, regulators and/or financial auditors may be able to place reliance on the audit and reduce their own audit scopes; this can translate into time and expense savings.

The audit can help foster business development activities, since an SSAE 16 audit is frequently regarded as an affirmation of the service organization's commitment to quality and security; the audit report can also provide benefits and reduce paperwork when responding to requests for proposal (RFPs) or similar offerings.

SSAE 16 has adopted the *Committee of Sponsoring Organizations of the Treadway Commission* (COSO) as its standard for reviewing internal controls.[49] The COSO definition of internal control is "a process, effected by an entity's board of directors, management and other personnel, designed to provide reasonable assurance regarding the achievement of objectives." Also, COSO is the same standard that Sarbanes-Oxley Section 404 has adopted for how to review internal controls. See Section 54.5.3.2 for further details of COSO.

The SSAE 16 has pros and cons for both the service organization and user organization; these issues must be understood so that management can perform a cost-benefit analysis (see Exhibit 54.3).

54.3.3.3 SSAE 16 Audits Conclusion. In conclusion, an SSAE 16 audit is not a 100 percent guarantee of assurance that all security-related controls and processes have been correctly designed and implemented; after all, the service organization selects the controls to be tested in an SOC-1 engagement. For SOC-2 or SOC-3 engagements, high-value control objectives and controls are included; however, they do not cover all possible controls. Nonetheless, an SSAE 16 audit provides a high-level of confidence that risks have been assessed and mitigated.

The SSAE 16 audit results can also provide information about areas for further investigation. A major benefit of an SSAE 16 audit is that it can be used to meet the reporting requirements for SOX Section 404 reporting, help in meeting GLBA and

EXHIBIT 54.3 Pros and Cons for Service and User Organizations

Factor	Service Organization	User Organization
Independent assessment of controls	Pro	Pro
Lower cost for evaluation of controls	Con	Pro
No additional review of controls required	Con	Con
SSAE 16 audits are forward looking	Con	Con
SSAE 16 audits must be continuously reviewed and updated	Con	Pro
SSAE 16 audits increase the value of services	Pro	Pro
Disruption to service organization is reduced by eliminating user organization auditors from visiting service organization to conduct audit	Pro	Pro
The SSAE 16 audit can be used to build a strong working relationship between organizations	Pro	Pro
Audit results can provide opportunities for improvements	Pro	Pro

HIPAA compliance, and may provide benefits as a marketing tool regarding service quality.

54.3.4 ISAE 3402 Standards. The *International Standard on Assurance Engagements (ISAE) No. 3402, Assurance Reports on Controls at a Service Organization*, is the international standard under which SSAE 16 has been approved:

> [ISAE 3402] was issued in December 2009 by the International Auditing and Assurance Standards Board (IAASB), which is part of the International Federation of Accountants (IFAC). ISAE 3402 was developed to provide an international assurance standard for allowing public accountants to issue a report for use by user organizations and their auditors (user auditors) on the controls at a service organization that are likely to impact or be a part of the user organization's system of internal control over financial reporting.[50]

Ernst & Young describe ISAE 3402 as follows in a 2013 brochure:

> Although many businesses have been outsourcing portions of their work for years now, outsourcing is still becoming more popular by the day. This is especially driven by increased globalization, technological evolutions, and the need for standardised business processes. Outsourcing is any task, operation, job, or process that could be performed by employees within the user organisation, but is instead contracted to a third party (service organisation) or another group company for a period of time.
>
> Some examples for the financial sector are:
>
> - Asset managers that perform asset management services for different parties within the group company.
> - Pension administrators who perform the administration for pension funds.
> - Claim service companies that perform claim handling services for large insurers.
>
> The widespread use of outsourcing requires organizations to better manage their risks associated with the outsourced services. More specifically, the user organisation requires a degree of assurance that the service organisation has a well-established internal control framework that is operating effectively. New regulations, regulatory authorities and supervisory boards also ask for specific controls over outsourced procedures.[51]

54.4 SARBANES-OXLEY ACT

54.4.1 Introduction. This section focuses on the practicalities of SOX compliance in the real world and introduces concepts that the practitioner is sure to encounter.

Sarbanes-Oxley is the financial reporting act enacted into U.S. law in July 2002.[52] It was the U.S. Government's response to a number of major public-company accounting failures, including Enron[53] and WorldCom.[54]

SOX is designed to reduce fraud and conflicts of interest while increasing financial transparency and public confidence in the market and in companies' internal control systems. The act is intended to encourage honesty and integrity in financial reporting and to place responsibility directly with owners, managers, and executives. The act requires that the executive officers certify that they are "responsible for establishing and maintaining internal controls" and "have designed such internal controls to ensure that material information relating to the company and its consolidated subsidiaries is made known to such officers by others within those entities, particularly during the period in which the periodic reports are being prepared." SOX allows for the possibility of both *civil* litigation and *criminal* prosecution.[55] Thus, noncompliance is likely to result in fines, imprisonment, or both for those who fail to ensure the accuracy of their organization's financial reporting.

Bearing in mind that SOX currently applies only to *publicly traded* companies with a market capitalization (or public debt) *exceeding $75 million*, many companies delisted themselves from U.S. stock exchanges or reverted to private status to avoid inclusion in the act.

More significantly, many non-U.S.-held companies now find themselves SOX-applicable because they or their subsidiaries are listed on the U.S. stock exchanges.[56] Compliance is necessary for the entire organization, not just for the listed subsidiary. Thus, from humble beginnings, the act now has global market penetration.

SOX may originally have been the driver for complying with stricture regulations; however, in the decade since it was passed, "SOX compliance has moved beyond being just a regulatory obligation. Today it is viewed in the context of a larger Governance, Risk, and Compliance (GRC) program that is closely integrated with strategic decision-making, aligned with business goals, and enabled by technology."[57]

It is in the best interests of an organization to design and implement a comprehensive governance program, to assess and implement internal processes and controls, and to set targets beyond that of mere regulatory compliance. The entire compliance effort should be repeatable, as compliance is not a one-off activity; rather it will be repeated annually for the life of the organization (or until such time as the law is materially revised or repealed).

54.4.2 Section 404. SOX consist of a number of sections; most are beyond the scope of this chapter. From an information assurance professional's viewpoint however, Section 404 is the most significant and most widely discussed. It is the area that directly addresses the impact of information technology on financial reporting and the adequacy and effectiveness of associated internal controls.

Section 404 reads as follows:

SEC. 404. MANAGEMENT <<NOTE: 15 USC 7262.>> ASSESSMENT OF INTERNAL CONTROLS.

(a) Rules Required.–The Commission shall prescribe rules requiring each annual report required by section 13(a) or 15(d) of the Securities Exchange Act of 1934 (15 USC 78m or 78o(d)) to contain an internal control report, which shall—

(1) state the responsibility of management for establishing and maintaining an adequate internal control structure and procedures for financial reporting; and

(2) contain an assessment, as of the end of the most recent fiscal year of the issuer, of the effectiveness of the internal control structure and procedures of the issuer for financial reporting.

(b) Internal Control Evaluation and Reporting.–With respect to the internal control assessment required by subsection (a), each registered public accounting firm that prepares or issues the audit report for the issuer shall attest to, and report on, the assessment made by the management of the issuer. An attestation made under this subsection shall be made in accordance with standards for attestation engagements issued or adopted by the Board. Any such attestation shall not be the subject of a separate engagement.

With widespread reliance on IT for financial and operational management systems, it is now accepted within U.S. industry that adequate and effective internal controls are necessary, particularly for systems supporting significant business processes.[58]

54.4.3 Achieving Compliance. SOX compliance should be approached by identifying key processes within the organization, documenting how they are implemented and controlled, and the defining or characterizing methods for reporting on their success or failure.

Coverage must include the entire system life cycle, and internal processes must include projects, design, architecture, system development, delivery, and operations. An auditor will be looking for no more than the assessment of core processes, the adequacy of associated controls, and whether those processes were followed, and controls executed, as stated. For more on SOX issues and regulations, see Chapter 64 in this *Handbook*.

54.4.3.1 Control Framework. Fortunately, the hard work of choosing a controls and assessment framework has already been done. The U.S. Securities and Exchange Commission (SEC) mandates the use of the internal control framework recommended by COSO,[59] and the Public Company Accounting and Oversight Board (PCAOB)[60] supports the SEC's choice as detailed in its *Auditing Standard No. 5, An Audit of Internal Control Over Financial Reporting Performed in Conjunction with an Audit of Financial Statements*.[61]

54.4.3.2 COSO. The COSO "Internal Control—Integrated Framework (2013)"[62] was sponsored by a consortium comprising:

- American Accounting Association (AAA)
- American Institute of Certified Public Accountants (AICPA)
- Financial Executives International (FEI)
- Institute of Internal Auditors (IIA)
- Institute of Management Accountants (IMA)

The Executive Summary discusses changes in the framework since the original 1992 version, including:

- Expectations for governance oversight
- Globalization of markets and operations
- Changes and greater complexities of business
- Demands and complexities in laws, rules, regulations, and standards
- Expectations for competencies and accountabilities

- Use of, and reliance on, evolving technologies
- Expectations relating to preventing and detecting fraud.

According to COSO, "Internal control is a process, effected by an entity's board of directors, management, and other personnel, designed to provide reasonable assurance regarding the achievement of objectives relating to operations, reporting, and compliance."

The Executive Summary continues:

> This definition reflects certain fundamental concepts. Internal control is:
>
> - *Geared to the achievement of objectives* in one or more categories—operations, reporting, and compliance
> - *A process* consisting of ongoing tasks and activities—a means to an end, not an end in itself
> - *Effected by people*—not merely about policy and procedure manuals, systems, and forms, but about people and the actions they take at every level of an organization to affect internal control
> - Able to *provide reasonable assurance*—but not absolute assurance, to an entity's senior management and board of directors
> - *Adaptable to the entity structure*—flexible in application for the entire entity or for a particular subsidiary, division, operating unit, or business process.

The "five integrated components" of internal control in the COSO framework can be summarized as follows:

- *Control environment:* "… [T]he set of standards, processes, and structures that provide the basis for carrying out internal controls across the organization. …"
- *Risk assessment:* Evaluation of probabilities for identified harmful events in the business context for the organization.
- *Control activities:* "[P]reventive or detective" actions taken to mitigate risks while achieving the corporate objectives.
- *Information and communication:* Organizations need current, accurate data about all aspects of operations, including monitoring for internal controls. "Communication is the continual, iterative process of providing, sharing, and obtaining necessary information."
- *Monitoring activities:* "Ongoing evaluations … provide timely information. Separate evaluations, conducted periodically, will vary in scope and frequency depending on assessment of risks, effectiveness of ongoing evaluations, and other management considerations. Findings are evaluated against criteria established by regulators, recognized standard-setting bodies or management and the board of directors, and deficiencies are communicated to management and the board of directors as appropriate."

54.4.3.3 COBIT. ISACA[63] was originally called the *Information Systems Audit and Control Association*; ISACA defined a practical framework from which to derive key processes and controls for SOX compliance activities using its COBIT (Control Objectives for Information and Related Technology) framework. ISACA describes the principles underlying the framework as follows:

> COBIT 5 is based on five key principles for governance and management of enterprise IT:
>
> - Principle 1: Meeting Stakeholder Needs
> - Principle 2: Covering the Enterprise End-to-End

- Principle 3: Applying a Single, Integrated Framework
- Principle 4: Enabling a Holistic Approach
- Principle 5: Separating Governance from Management

ISACA describes the benefits of COBIT 5 as follows:

COBIT 5 helps enterprises of all sizes:

- Maintain high-quality information to support business decisions
- Achieve strategic goals and realize business benefits through the effective and innovative use of IT
- Achieve operational excellence through reliable, efficient application of technology
- Maintain IT-related risk at an acceptable level
- Optimize the cost of IT services and technology
- Support compliance with relevant laws, regulations, contractual agreements and policies

The COBIT 5 framework describes seven categories of enablers:

1. Principles, policies, and frameworks are the vehicle to translate the desired behavior into practical guidance for day-to-day management.
2. Processes describe an organized set of practices and activities to achieve certain objectives and produce a set of outputs in support of achieving overall IT-related goals.
3. Organizational structures are the key decision-making entities in an enterprise.
4. Culture, ethics, and behavior of individuals and of the enterprise are very often underestimated as a success factor in governance and management activities.
5. Information is required for keeping the organization running and well governed, but at the operational level, information is very often the key product of the enterprise itself.
6. Services, infrastructure, and applications include the infrastructure, technology, and applications that provide the enterprise with information technology processing and services.
7. People, skills, and competencies are required for successful completion of all activities, and for making correct decisions and taking corrective actions.[64]

COBIT is a comprehensive framework for management of the governance of risk and control of IT, comprising four domains, 34 IT processes, and 215 control objectives.[65] Although it has a wider purpose than simply addressing SOX compliance, COBIT removes much of the guesswork by suggesting 12 out of the 34 available standard processes for inclusion in a SOX implementation:

1. Acquire and maintain application software. (AI2) The provision of line of business applications, whether custom or off the shelf, should be congruent with business requirements.
2. Acquire and maintain technology infrastructure. (AI3) Technology infrastructure should underpin the delivery of services required by the business and follow organizational standards.
3. Enable operations. (AI4) Support effective use of technology through knowledge transfer, agreed service levels, and properly integrated solutions.

4. Install and accredit solutions and changes. (AI7) Ensure that supplied systems are fit-for-purpose prior to delivery and that they function as expected post-installation.
5. Manage changes. (AI6) Provide an effective, formal change management system to reduce errors and defects that may impact successful operations and business processes.
6. Define and manage service levels. (DS1) Align key business processes with delivery of technology in a set of meaningful service definition documents, with a mechanism for reporting to stakeholders on performance and achievement of service levels.
7. Manage third-party services. (DS2) Ensure the delivery of essential third-party services to support business activities while remaining transparent with regard to cost, benefits, and risks.
8. Ensure systems security. (DS5) Maximize the integrity and availability of systems and the confidentiality of data stored thereon while minimizing the impact of vulnerabilities through the application of effective security policies, standards, and procedures.
9. Manage the configuration. (DS9) Maintain an accurate and readily accessible repository of application and system configuration information, baseline standards, and variations thereof.
10. Manage problems and incidents. (DS8, DS10) Provide formal problem and incident management for all operations, including identification of issues, root cause analysis, and end-to-end problem resolution.
11. Manage data. (DS11) Provide tried and tested backup, recovery, and disposal systems.
12. Manage the physical environment and operations. (DS12) Control access to facilities and to computing assets, to reduce the likelihood of business disruption resulting from data leakage or theft of assets.

Specific analysis may require the addition of further processes, and within each process, the addition or removal of specific controls to further tailor the framework for each organization. Process and control selection must be agreed on in collaboration with the internal-audit function and with external auditors before committing to a particular framework.

54.4.3.4 Testing. Of equal importance to process and control selection is the agreement of the testing plan and schedule, especially the number of tests and the associated sample sizes.

For most organizations, resources are not unlimited. It is likely that staff will be asked to assume responsibility for some portion of SOX activity in addition to their regular workload. Thus, achieving a balance between compliance and the number of controls associated with each process is critical, because it is the controls that will be tested throughout the year, with the test results supporting the SOX certification process. A reduction in the number of tests or sample sizes can directly affect the integrity and quality of the results and positively affect staff efficiency and productivity. Although testing will likely be seen as onerous, much of the control activity should be considered business as usual, and thus the day-to-day processes should yield much of the evidence required for testing.

This section focuses on the importance and impact of IT on the wider goal of SOX compliance, but not all processes, even within an IT organization, are technical. Many are activities such as director-level meetings, incident boards, recovery forums, project risk meetings, and so on, and all may be part of a process that is included under SOX and must therefore be tested.

Testing typically falls into two categories: examination and discussion. Examination requires that a representative sample of evidence showing that a control is operating properly be collated and verified as accurate. Discussion requires that understanding of the process and associated controls be confirmed through one-to-one or group meetings among responsible staff. Sample sizes will depend on the test population and the frequency of sampling, and probably on the importance of the desired degree of accuracy and precision of the results for statistical confidence levels.

54.4.4 Audit and Certification. There will be at least two independent audit processes at work: internal and external. Internal audit will occur at the culmination of SOX testing, as a final quality-assurance checkpoint that the organization is compliant. Any identified gaps at must either be remediated or officially acknowledged within a formal risk process prior to the arrival of the external auditors.

54.4.4.1 External Audit. External audit will occur close to the end of the year and is the final test of compliance. It is not acceptable to wait until the external audit function identifies a gap before carrying out remediation activities. Any areas of noncompliance at this stage will be officially reported and may be included in the final management letter.

54.4.4.2 Schedule. Certification requirements vary by organization, although obviously at least an annual certificate will be required. Many organizations certify quarterly or monthly as part of some other SOX-related or controls process, and use those certificates to supplement their final annual declaration (see Exhibit 54.4).

54.4.5 Sarbanes-Oxley Conclusion. SOX compliance activities should not stand alone within the organization. They should be considered part of a wider risk-management program, preferably one supported by an embedded, proactive, risk-aware control culture. Further, it is never recommended to execute a compliance program with the goal of simply meeting regulatory requirements. In reality, a program that is designed from the outset to exceed the current regulation, and be adaptable to changes

EXHIBIT 54.4 Typical Annual SOX Schedule

Period*	Activity
January/February	Create and agree on controls and associated tests, certification schedule, and testing plan based on agreed processes
March to August	Execute testing (typically by process)
September	Retest where necessary
October	Internal audit
November/December	External audit, produce certificates, publish management letter

*The actual dates for compliance activities will vary with each organization and its respective financial years and filing deadlines.

to existing or entirely new regulation, represents a much smarter investment of time and effort.

For additional discussion of SOX compliance, see Chapter 64 in this *Handbook.*

54.5 TECHNICAL FRAMEWORKS FOR IT AUDITS.

The best IT auditors struggle with the reality of acceptable risk and vague controls, looking for solid frameworks to help with their audit. Great research and a good framework can help determine the questions for many of the unique or new audits that have not been faced in the past. Three useful models, as discussed next, can be applied from a high-level perspective to make sure that all of the relevant questions have been covered. In addition to models, general best practices help round out the technical bases to make sure the audit reveals any material weaknesses in key controls.

54.5.1 Framework 1: People, Processes, Tools, and Measures.

The first useful framework—People, Processes, Tools, and Measures (PPTM)—is simple conceptually, but its wide scope digs quickly into often-overlooked critical processes and important controls. Take a randomly picked application about which nothing is known, and apply PPTM concepts to the application to understand it and to develop a series of controls to test, and useful information to gather.

1. **People** build the application, input data into the application, and use the output or storage of the data handled by the application. People are a component that touches or uses the application, and as such should have controls that govern the interaction. For example, how are the people authenticated or authorized as administrators or users of the application?
2. **Processes** surround the operations of the application. What processes govern standard operating practices, and how can they be validated?
3. **Tools** are the physical controls, such as other applications that might interface with the application or ensure the quality or validation of the application. Other types of tool controls include checking the platform that the application uses. What physical controls existed during the implementation or are currently in operations to make sure the application is in a secure environment?
4. **Measures** are often-overlooked metrics, although they represent some of the most useful data in thorough audits. They can verify that the application is performing its function in support of its assigned business role. For example, metrics can report on the operating efficiency of an application and how well it might scale to meet customer needs over time.

54.5.2 Framework 2: STRIDE.

STRIDE, an acronym based on the ordered list of issues shown below, encompasses six areas of risk common to different technologies. Much like PPTM, STRIDE will help in understanding how the area of risk might play a role in the technology to be audited and then in finding the controls that alleviate that risk. The keepers of the Open Web Application Security Project (OWASP, at www.owasp.com) provide an excellent example of applying STRIDE to Web applications.

1. **S—Spoofing** describes the risk of any user assuming the identity of another user or masking directly or indirectly the attributes of another user. For example, a user logging onto a banking Website should generally not be able to assume another user's identity.

2. **T—Tampering** with data describes the need for input validation, process validation, and output validation. The integrity of the data should be preserved at all times, and in some cases protected from tampering, with encryption or by independent verification.
3. **R—Repudiation** describes a scenario where a user can suggest that a transaction never occurred. Poor audit trails lead to this situation. Nonrepudiation is the control that protects against repudiation. It includes signing a message with date and time as a unique, nonduplicatable moment.
4. **I—Information** disclosure describes the additional controls to prevent information from leaving the system to unauthorized parties or programs.
5. **D—Denial** of service describes a condition where the application or technology could be maliciously or inadvertently removed from service. If this is a concern, controls should be in place such as redundant systems, backups, and measures to prevent denial-of-service events.
6. **E—Elevation** of privilege describes the situation where a user maliciously or inadvertently gains administrative rights.

For a more complete model of the elements of computer security incidents, see Chapter 8 in this *Handbook.*

54.5.3 Framework 3: PDIO. PDIO—*Plan, Design, Implement, and Operations*—borrows from Cisco System's project management processes and describes the life cycle of a technology.[66] This framework can be very powerful, especially when combined with PPTM.

Administrators address people, processes, tools, and measures at each step in a project's planning, designing, implementation, and operations. PDIO can be viewed from a macroperspective to understand an entire new project or from a microperspective to understand each smaller element. The big-picture understanding of an audit is the mark of a great result that provides incredibly valuable—and useful—information to customers so that they can strengthen their controls.

54.5.4 General Best Practices. This short list of common best practices should help with additional controls for testing. This is especially helpful during an audit of a new technology that does not yet have an appropriate audit program.

1. Apply defense in depth so that you have layered controls.
2. Use a positive security model. By default, deny actions and allow only a trusted or benign subset of available options. Negative security models trust everything by default and attempt to discover when to block offending behavior.
3. Fail safely so that people, equipment, data, and business processes are safe from harm.
4. Run with least privilege to prevent users from escalating their privileges above what is necessary to do their job.
5. Avoid security by obscurity. Try to hide data or options. Security by obscurity is setting up the technology for compromise.
6. Keep security simple. Overly complex systems are difficult to administer and often end up not secured.

7. Detect intrusions and keep logs. There should be an audit trail for everything important.
8. Never trust infrastructure and services, especially those coming from a third-party managed solution, where there might be different security policies and practices from the originating organization.
9. Establish secure defaults. Default to safe values and actions over defaulting to less secure values and actions. Another common mistake is not to specify an important value, causing issues later for the technology or application.
10. Use open standards because they are tested more thoroughly than proprietary technologies. Encryption in Digital Rights Management is an example where several purportedly secure private ciphers or cryptographic systems have been broken.

54.5.5 Technical Frameworks Conclusion. Frameworks can be valuable assets when approaching a technical audit, allowing quick determination of those areas where the audit is going to be most demanding and where compliance can be most effective.

54.6 FURTHER READING

Brotby, W. K., and G. Hinson. *PRAGMATIC Security Metrics: Applying Metametrics to Information Security*. Auerbach, 2013.

Cascarino, R. E. *Auditor's Guide to IT Auditing*, 2nd ed. Wiley, 2012.

Chorafas, D. *IT Auditing and Sarbanes-Oxley Compliance: Key Strategies for Business Improvement*. Auerbach, 2008.

Cox, F. D. *Information Security: Risk Management of GLBA Privacy and Service Provider Oversight*. Amazon Digital Services, 2011.

Davis, C., M. Schiller, and K. Wheeler. *IT Auditing Using Controls to Protect Information Assets*, 2nd ed. McGraw-Hill Osborne Media, 2011.

Davis, R. E. *IT Auditing: Assuring Information Assets Protection*. Amazon Digital Services, 2011.

Halpert, B. *Auditing Cloud Computing: A Security and Privacy Guide*. Wiley, 2011.

Hawker, A. *Security and Control in Information Systems: A Guide for Business and Accounting*. Routledge, 2000.

Hingarh, V., and A. Ahmed. *Understanding and Conducting Information Systems Auditing*. Wiley, 2013.

Moeller, R. R. *IT Audit, Control, and Security*. Wiley, 2012.

Moeller, R. R. *Executive's Guide to IT Governance: Improving Systems Processes with Service Management, COBIT, and ITIL*. Wiley, 2013.

Roebuck, K. *Information Security Audit: High-Impact Strategies—What You Need to Know: Definitions, Adoptions, Impact, Benefits, Maturity, Vendors*. Lightning Source, 2011.

Senft, S., F. Gallegos, and A. Davis. *Information Technology Control and Audit*, 4th ed. Auerbach, 2012.

Weiss, M., and M. G. Solomon. *Auditing IT Infrastructures for Compliance*. Jones & Bartlett Learning, 2010.

54.7 NOTES

1. S. Abelow, "Five Ways that an IT Audit Adds Value." Yahoo! Voices, January 13, 2011, http://voices.yahoo.com/five-ways-audit-adds-value-7567404.html
2. See, for example, "Guide for Assessing the Security Controls in Federal Information Systems and Organizations" NIST Special Publication SP 800-53A Rev. 1 (June 2010), http://csrc.nist.gov/groups/SMA/fisma/assessment.html
3. U.S. Department of Defence CSC, "Rainbow Series" (1980), available at www.fas.org/irp/nsa/rainbow.htm
4. National Information Assurance Partnership (NIAP), www.niap-ccevs.org
5. Information Assurance Support Environment (IASE), *STIGs: Security Technical Implementation Guides*, U.S. Department of Defense (DoD) Defense Information Systems Agency (DISA), http://iase.disa.mil/stigs
6. Computer Security Resource Center (CSRC) Special Publications (800 Series), National Institute of Standards and Technology (NIST) Information Technology Laboratory (ITL), http://csrc.nist.gov/publications/PubsSPs.html
7. Information Technology Infrastructure Library (ITIL), www.itil-officialsite.com
8. ISO is not an abbreviation of International Organization for Standardization but instead a shortened form of the Greek *isos*, meaning equal. The term was chosen to be understood in all translations and speak to the organization's intent of equal representation for all members regardless of their national economic status or country's level of development.
9. U.S. Senate Committee on Banking, Housing and Urban Affairs, Financial Services Modernization Act (1999), http://banking.senate.gov/conf/grmleach.htm
10. NIST, "Federal Information Security Management Act (FISMA) Implementation Project," http://csrc.nist.gov/groups/SMA/fisma/index.html
11. Federal Information Security Management Act of 2002 (FISMA), 44 USC 3541, *et seq.*, www.law.cornell.edu/uscode/text/44/3541
12. OMB, Circular A-130—Revised, Transmittal Memorandum No. 4, "Memorandum for Heads of Executive Departments and Agencies; Subject: Management of Federal Information Resources," www.whitehouse.gov/omb/circulars/a130/a130trans4.html
13. NIST, "FISMA Risk Management Framework," http://csrc.nist.gov/groups/SMA/fisma/framework.html
14. NIST, "FISMA Detailed Overview," http://csrc.nist.gov/groups/SMA/fisma/overview.html
15. Health Information Privacy, U.S. Department of Health & Human Services (HHS), www.hhs.gov/ocr/privacy
16. HIPAA, www.gpo.gov/fdsys/pkg/PLAW-104publ191/html/PLAW-104publ191.htm
17. PCI Security Standards Council—About Us, https://www.pcisecuritystandards.org/organization_info/index.php
18. "PCI DSS Quick Reference Guide," https://www.pcisecuritystandards.org/documents/PCI%20SSC%20Quick%20Reference%20Guide.pdf
19. PCI Security Standards Council—Documents Library, https://www.pcisecuritystandards.org/security_standards/documents.php?document=pci_dss_v2-0#pci_dss_v2-0

20. NIST, "Recommended Security Controls for Federal Information Systems," Special Publication 800-53 Revision 4 (April 2013), http://dx.doi.org/10.6028/NIST.SP.800-53r4
21. NIST, "Standards for Security Categorization of Federal Information and Information Systems (February 2004)," FIPS 199, http://csrc.nist.gov/publications/fips/fips199/FIPS-PUB-199-final.pdf
22. A *federal information system* is an information system used or operated by an executive agency, by a contractor of an executive agency, or by another organization on behalf of an executive agency.
23. NIST, "Guideline for Identifying an Information System as a National Security System (August 2004)," Special Publication 800-59, http://csrc.nist.gov/publications/nistpubs/800-59/SP800-59.pdf
24. NIST, "Minimum Security Requirements for Federal Information and Information Systems (March 2006)," FIPS-200, http://csrc.nist.gov/publications/fips/fips200/FIPS-200-final-march.pdf
25. NIST, "Federal Information Security Management Act (FISMA) Implementation Project," http://csrc.nist.gov/groups/SMA/fisma/index.html
26. NIST, "Draft Guide for Mapping Types of Information and Information Systems to Security Categories: Volume 1: Guide for Mapping Types of Information and Information Systems to Security Categories; Volume 2: Appendices," SP 800-60 Revision 1. http://csrc.nist.gov/publications/nistpubs/800-60-rev1/SP800-60_Vol1-Rev1.pdf and http://csrc.nist.gov/publications/nistpubs/800-60-rev1/SP800-60_Vol2-Rev1.pdf
27. NIST, "Risk Management Guide for Information Technology Systems (Sept 2012)," SP 800-30 Revision 1, http://csrc.nist.gov/publications/nistpubs/800-30-rev1/sp800_30_r1.pdf
28. NIST, "Guide for Developing Security Plans for Federal Information Systems (February 2006)," SP 800-18 Revision 1, http://csrc.nist.gov/publications/nistpubs/800-18-Rev1/sp800-18-Rev1-final.pdf
29. NIST, "Security and Privacy Controls for Federal Information Systems and Organizations," SP 800-53 Revision 4 (May 2013), http://dx.doi.org/10.6028/NIST.SP.800-53r4
30. NIST, "Guide for Applying the Risk Management Framework to Federal Information Systems: A Security Life Cycle Approach," SP 800-37 Revision 1 (Feb 2010). http://csrc.nist.gov/publications/nistpubs/800-37-rev1/sp800-37-rev1-final.pdf
31. NIST SP 800-37 and SP 800-53A (see previous notes).
32. See endnote 1.
33. For membership information, contact the Head of Membership, listed on the "Structure and governance page," www.iso.org/iso/home/about/about_governance.htm
34. All approved standards continue to be subject to periodic review to ensure timely update of industry requirements and technologies.
35. International Organization for Standardization, *Standards FAQ*. www.iso.org/iso/home/faqs/faqs_standards.htm
36. An ISMS includes any components necessary to maintain information assurance, including policies, plans, processes, roles, responsibilities, and so forth.
37. ISO/IEC 17799:2005 (superseded by ISO/IEC 27002:2005), www.iso.org/iso/home/store/catalogue_ics/catalogue_detail_ics.htm?csnumber=39612

38. International Organization for Standardization, "Improved ISO/IEC 17799 Makes Information Assets Even More Secure," www.iso.org/iso/home/news_index/news_archive/news.htm?refid=Ref963
39. ISO/IEC 27000:2012, http://standards.iso.org/ittf/PubliclyAvailableStandards/c056891_ISO_IEC_27000_2012(E).zip
40. Effective April 2007, ISO 17799 was superseded by ISO/IEC 27002.
41. OECD is an international cooperative committed to sharing information and developing accepted standards on economic and social issues related to trade, education, development, and science: www.oecd.org
42. IT Governance Ltd., "ISO 27001 & Information Security," www.itgovernance.co.uk/iso27001.aspx
43. IT Governance Ltd., *Information Security & ISO 27001: An Introduction*, www.itgovernance.co.uk/everything-you-want-and-need-for-iso27001.aspx
44. IT Governance Ltd., *ISO 27001 in North America*, www.itgovernance.co.uk/shop/p-1243-it-regulatory-compliance-in-north-america.aspx#.Udnt4UvDnsY
45. "Extended Mass Layoffs in 2011." Report 1039, U.S. Department of Labor and U.S. Bureau of Labor Statistics December 2012, www.bls.gov/mls/mlsreport1039.pdf (calculations based on data from Table 13, page 16).
46. C. Isidore, "Uncle Sam's outsourcing tab: $517 billion," CNNMoney June 10, 2013, http://money.cnn.com/2013/06/10/news/economy/outsourced-federal-government/index.html
47. AICPA, "SAS 70 Overview," http://sas70.com/sas70_overview.html
48. AICPA, "SSAE Overview," http://ssae16.com/SSAE16_overview.html
49. "Treadway" refers to the founding Chairman of the Commission, James C. Treadway, Jr. For a history and further details of COSO, see their "About" Web page: http://coso.org/aboutus.htm
50. AICPA, "ISAE 3402 Overview," http://isae3402.com/ISAE3402_overview.html
51. Ernst & Young, "Implementing and maintaining ISAE 3402" (2013).
52. Pub. L. 107-204, July 30, 2002, 116 Stat. 745; see *Legal Information Institute* entry for 15 USC 7201 ff, www.law.cornell.edu/topn/sarbanes-oxley_act_of_2002
53. M. Jickling, "The Enron Collapse: An Overview of Financial Issues." Congressional Research Service Report RS21135, February 4, 2002, http://fpc.state.gov/documents/organization/8038.pdf
54. M. Jickling, "Accounting Problems Reported in Major Companies Since Enron." Congressional Research Service Report RS21269, January 2002, http://congressionalresearch.com/RS21269/document.php
55. 15 USC 7241 (Section 302) (civil provision), www.law.cornell.edu/uscode/text/15/7241 and 18 USC 1350 (Section 906) (criminal provision), www.law.cornell.edu/uscode/text/18/1350
56. World Stock Exchanges, www.world-stock-exchanges.net/usa.html
57. MetricStream, "Ten Years On, Approach to SOX Shifts from Compliance to Better Governance," press release, July 24, 2012, www.metricstream.com/pressNews/pr_385_Ten-years-sox.html
58. A *significant business process* is one that accounts for a minimum portion of an organization's balance sheet. The actual threshold for inclusion will vary by organization.

59. Committee of the Sponsoring Organizations of the Treadway Commission, www.coso.org
60. Public Company Accounting Oversight Board (PCAOB). http://pcaobus.org/Pages/default.aspx
61. PCAOB Auditing Standard No. 5 superseded Auditing Standard No. 2 as of 15 November 2007. http://pcaobus.org/Standards/Auditing/Pages/Auditing_Standard_5.aspx
62. "Internal Control—Integrated Framework (2013)," COSO, May 2013. Available from "Guidance on Internal Control" page: http://coso.org/IC.htm with Executive Summary available at http://coso.org/documents/990025P_Executive_Summary_final_may20_e.pdf
63. History of ISACA, www.isaca.org/About-ISACA/History/Pages/default.aspx
64. COBIT 5, www.isaca.org/COBIT/Pages/default.aspx
65. COBIT documents in PDF are available to members and nonmembers of ISACA for free; printed copies are available at low cost (e.g., $50 for nonmembers and $35 for members). At the time of writing in July 2013, versions were available in Chinese, French, Spanish, and German, with other language translations under development. www.isaca.org/COBIT/Pages/Product-Family.aspx
66. As of the time of writing (July 2013), there were two dozen hits for the search on "PDIO" at the CISCO Website, http://tinyurl.com/l8fkvb6

CHAPTER 55

CYBER INVESTIGATION[1]

Peter Stephenson

55.1 INTRODUCTION. Cyber investigation (also widely known as *digital investigation*) as a discipline has changed markedly in the first two decades of the twenty-first century. In 1999, when *Investigating Computer Related Crime*[2] was published, practitioners in the field were just beginning to speculate as to how cyber investigations would be carried out. At that time, the idea of cyber investigation was almost completely congruent with the practice of computer forensics. Today (as this is being edited in July 2013), we know that such a view is too confining for investigations in the current digital environment.

Cyber investigation today is evolving into a discipline that is not only becoming commonplace in information technology but is also finding acceptance by both law enforcement and the forensic science community. The American Academy of Forensic Science, for example, now recognizes the forensic computer-related crime investigator as a legitimate discipline within its general category of membership.[3]

This chapter defines cyber investigation and examines some of its forensic components. It discusses a useful cyber investigation approach called *end-to-end digital investigation* (EEDI). Finally, the chapter explores some forensic tools and considers their usefulness both practically and theoretically.

55.1.1 Defining Cyber Investigation. Rogers, Brinson, and Robinson[4] approach the definition of cyber forensics in an ontology ("the question of how many fundamentally distinct sorts of entities compose the universe"[5]); it can also be viewed as a taxonomy ("the practice or principles of classification"[6]). Although their descriptive schema is not complete, it is informative. Most important, Rogers's approach recognizes that there is no simple definition of cyber investigation; ontology and taxonomy are therefore particularly useful in clarifying meaning and structure for such a field.

The *Rogers cyber forensic ontology* consists of five layers. Ontology generally contains classes, subclasses, slots, and instances. These elements also contain constraints and relations. Rogers's five layers can be considered to be a superclass with two classes and four nested subclasses. He does not define the other elements in his paper. The Rogers schema is easy to extend, however, to a proper ontology using a tool such as Protégé.[7] For our purposes, we will refer to his model as the *Rogers taxonomy*.

The core of the Rogers taxonomy as a definition resides in the relationships inherent in the various subclasses. Exhibit 55.1 presents the taxonomy as a hierarchy with two major classes, Profession and Technology.

Starting with *cyber forensics* at the top and with two classes represented in columns, the farther to the right in each class, the more granularity one adds to the characterization. Ontology supports understanding by providing a collection of characteristics that describe a concept; each class and nested subclass adds characteristics to that concept and contributes to a functional definition of cyber forensics. At the same time, concepts *not* included help to constrain the description and increase the precision of the ontological definition.

55.1.2 Distinguishing between Cyber Forensics and Cyber Investigation. *Cyber investigation* uses the tools of *cyber forensics* as part of investigative procedures. The Digital Forensics Research Workshop (DFRWS)[8] in 2001 developed a useful framework for digital investigation,[9] a version of which appears in Exhibit 55.2.

Although this framework appeared in 2001, it has not been improved on markedly in the intervening years.[10]

55.1.3 DFRWS Framework Classes. The DFRWS framework is a matrix. The columns are called *classes* and the cells are called *elements*. In the class descriptions that follow, the quoted italicized descriptions are taken verbatim from the original publication.[11]

The DFRWS framework classes contain key elements that are under constant review by the digital forensics community. The continuity among the classes is important; for example, the Preservation class continues as an element of the Collection, Examination, and Analysis classes. This indicates that *preservation* of evidence (as characterized by case management, imaging technologies, chain of custody, and time synchronization)

- Profession
  - Law
    - Enforcement
      - ✓ Evidence
      - ✓ Collection/Analysis
    - Courts
      - ✓ Laws
      - ✓ People
  - Academia
    - Research
      - ✓ Discipline definition
      - ✓ Problem solving
    - Education
      - ✓ Contributions
      - ✓ Professional outcome
  - Military
    - Offensive
      - ✓ Passive
      - ✓ Active
    - Defensive
      - ✓ Proactive
      - ✓ Reactive
  - Private sector
    - Industry
      - ✓ System admins
      - ✓ Legal contact
    - Consulting
      - ✓ Data recovery
      - ✓ Forensic analysis
      - ✓ Expert witness consultant
- Technology
  - Software
    - Analysis tools
      - ✓ Proprietary
      - ✓ Open-source tools
    - Operating systems
      - ✓ Proprietary OS
      - ✓ Open-source OS
      - ✓ Open source
    - File systems
      - ✓ Windows
      - ✓ UNIX/Linux
      - ✓ Mac
  - Hardware
    - Large-scale digital devices
      - ✓ Clusters
      - ✓ Grids
    - Small-scale digital devices
      - ✓ Cell phones
      - ✓ PDAa
      - ✓ SSD Operating software
    - Computers
      - ✓ Desktops
      - ✓ Laptops
      - ✓ Servers
      - ✓ Tablets
    - Storage devices
      - ✓ Thumb drive
      - ✓ Digital music player
      - ✓ External music player
      - ✓ External hard drives
    - Obscure devices
      - ✓ Gaming devices
      - ✓ Recording devices

EXHIBIT 55.1 Rogers Cyber Forensics Taxonomy

is an ongoing requirement throughout the digital investigative process. Thus, *preservation* is "a guarded principle across 'forensic' categories."[12] Traceability, likewise, is a guarded principle, but not across all forensic categories. The next topics discuss each of the DFRWS framework classes in more detail. Elements marked with an asterisk (*) in the discussions are *required* in all cyber investigations.

55.1.3.1 Identification Class.

The DFRWS defines the Identification class in this way:

> Determining items, components, and data possibly associated with the allegation or incident. Perhaps employing triage techniques.[13]

The Identification class describes the method by which the investigator is notified of a possible incident. Since about 50 percent of all reported incidents have benign

EXHIBIT 55.2 DFRWS Digital Investigation Framework

Identification	Preservation	Collection	Examination	Analysis	Presentation
Event/Crime detection	Case management	Preservation	Preservation	Preservation	Documentation
Resolve signature	Imaging technologies	Approved methods	Traceability	Traceability	Expert testimony
Profile detection	Chain of custody	Approved software	Validation techniques	Statistical	Clarification
Anomalous detection	Time synchronization	Approved hardware	Filtering techniques	Protocols	Mission impact statement
Complaints		Legal authority	Pattern matching	Data mining	Recommended countermeasure
System monitoring		Lossless compression	Hidden data discovery	Timeline	Statistical interpretation
Audit analysis		Sampling	Hidden data extraction	Link	
		Data reduction		Spatial	
		Recovery techniques			

explanations,[14] processing evidence in this class is critical to the rest of the investigation. Likewise, as it is the first step in the EEDI process, it is the only primary evidence not corroborated directly by other primary evidence. Therefore, a more significant amount of secondary evidence is needed to validate the existence of an actual event.

The author has adopted the next definitions of the individual framework classes for the purposes of EEDI. The DFRWS has, as of this writing, not developed such definitions. Elements marked with an asterisk (*) are required elements within the DFRWS class. The elements of the Identification class are:

- **Event/crime detection.*** This element implies direct evidence of an event. An example of such direct evidence is discovery that a large number of credit card numbers have been downloaded from a server.
- **Resolve signature.** This applies to the use of some automated event detection system, such as an intrusion system or anti-virus software program. The system in use must make its determination (of the presence of an event of interest) by means of signature analysis and mapping.
- **Profile detection.** Like signature resolution, profile detection usually relies on some automated event detection system. However, in this instance, the event will be characterized through matching with a particular profile as opposed to an explicit signature. Signatures generally apply to an individual event. Events, however, may come together in an *attack scenario* or *attack profile*. Such a profile may consist of a number of events, a pattern of behavior, or pattern of specific results of an attack.
- **Anomalous detection.** Again, like the preceding two elements, this usually relies on a detection system. However, in the case of anomalous detection, the event is deduced from the detection of patterns of behavior outside of the observed norm. Anomalies can include the presence of unusual behavior but also, as in the classic Sherlock Holmes case of the dog that "did nothing in the night-time," the absence of expected behavior.[15]
- **Complaints.** This element relies on the direct reporting of a potential event by an observer. This person may observe the event directly or simply the end result of the event.
- **System monitoring.** System monitoring explicitly requires some sort of intrusion detection, anti-virus, or similar system in place. It is less specific than other elements requiring a specific action (e.g., anomaly, profile of signature detection) and may be used together with another element of this class.
- **Audit analysis.** This element refers particularly to the analysis of various audit logs produced by source, target, and intermediate devices.

55.1.3.2 Preservation Class. The Preservation class deals with those elements that relate to the management of items of evidence. The DFRWS describes this class as "a guarded principle across 'forensic' categories." The requirement for proper evidence handing is basic to the digital investigative process as it relates to legal actions.

The DFRWS defines this class as "[e]nsuring evidence integrity or state."

- **Case management.*** This element covers the management of the investigative process by investigators and digital forensic examiners. Typical in this element are investigator notes, process controls, quality controls, and procedural issues.

- **Imaging technologies.** This element is separate from the elements in the Collection class, in that it does not refer to specific hardware, software, or techniques. The imaging technologies element refers to the *technology* used for imaging computer media. For example, physical imaging or bitstream backup may be considered an appropriate imaging technology whereas a logical backup would not be. The term *imaging* as used here is rather broad. It encompasses not only the technology used to create an image of computer media but also the technology used to extract such items as logs from a device. In this case, the log might be extracted from a bitstream image or it might be read out of the device to a peripheral as a result of a keystroke command issued by the investigator.
- **Chain of custody.*** This element refers to the process of limiting access to and subsequent alteration of evidence. In most jurisdictions chain of custody rules require that the evidence custodian be able to account for all accesses or possible accesses to items of evidence within his or her care from the time it is collected until the time it is used in a legal proceeding,
- **Time synchronization.*** This element refers to the synchronizing of evidence items to a common time base. Since logs and other evidence are collected from a number of devices during the conduct of an investigation, it is clear that those devices can differ from each other in terms of time base. If all devices are in a single time-synchronized network, they will not, of course, differ. However, that rarely is the case, and some effort must be made to obtain a common time base for all devices. There are two approaches one might take. The first is to adjust all times on evidence to a common device. The second is to use a common time zone (TZ), such as Universal Time (UT) or Greenwich Mean Time (GMT), as a baseline. No evidence is modified. The investigator simply notes the variance of a particular log or other piece of digital evidence from the predetermined time standard. This also is referred as *normalizing* time stamps.

55.1.3.3 Collection Class. The Collection class is concerned with the specific methods and products used by the investigator and forensic examiner to acquire evidence in a digital environment. As has been noted, the Preservation class continues as an element of this class. With the exception of the legal authority element, the elements of this class are largely technical.

The DFRWS defines this class as "[e]xtracting or harvesting individual items or groupings."

- **Approved methods.*** This element refers to the techniques used by the forensic examiner or investigator to extract digital evidence. The concept of being *approved* refers to the general acceptance in courts of the techniques and training or certifications of the individual performing the evidence collection. The most rigorous test of methods and technologies is the *Daubert* test. (For more information on expert testimony, see Chapter 73 in this *Handbook*.) However, due largely to the immaturity of digital forensic science, most court tests have not had this level of rigor applied. For this reason, those elements in this class that relate to approval derive their authority from cases where the technique, technology, or product has been challenged in a court of the same level as the case in question and has survived the test.
- **Approved software.** This element addresses the specific software product used to collect evidence. The discussion of the approval process in the last bullet point

applies. There is an issue specifically involving software used for digital forensic data collection. In order for a software program to be considered approved, it must be identical in every way to the software that has survived either a *Daubert* hearing or a court challenge. That means that the software source code must be in every way identical in both instances of the program. Failing that, the program may need to undergo its own court testing. For the purposes of the framework and subsequent EEDI procedures, however, a program that has any differences (e.g., version level, bug fixes, source code changes, etc.) from the program tested originally is not considered to be approved software.

- **Approved hardware.** This element describes the hardware, if any, used to collect evidence. Usually this is not an issue unless the hardware is designed specifically for use in a digital forensic evidence collection environment. To a lesser extent, the caveats of sameness that apply to approved software apply to approved hardware. The hardware device used must in every way be identical to instances of the device that have survived court challenges. The approved hardware element does not apply to simple computers, disks, or other media used by the examiner to collect evidence unless the device was developed explicitly for digital forensic evidence collection and contains special unique features for use in that environment only.
- **Legal authority.*** The legal authority element is the only element of this class that is nontechnical. In most jurisdictions, some legal authority is required prior to extracting information from computer media. This authority could be a policy, a subpoena, or a search warrant, for example. Failure to comply with applicable laws may render the evidence collected useless in a court of law.
- **Lossless compression.** This element refers to the compression techniques, if any, used by backup, encryption, or digital signature software used to collect and/or preserve evidence. If the software program uses compression, it must be proven to be lossless, that is, to cause no change whatever upon the integrity of the evidence on which it is used.
- **Sampling.** If sampling techniques are used to collect evidence, it must be shown that the technique causes no degradation of the evidence collected, or, if it has, that the effects can be demonstrated clearly and unambiguously. It must also be shown that the sampling method is valid (generally accepted by the mathematical community) and that the conclusions that may be drawn from the sample are defined clearly.
- **Data reduction.** When techniques and/or programs (such as normalization) are used to reduce data that contain or may contain evidence, it must be shown that such techniques or programs produce valid, repeatable, provable results that do not affect, in any way whatever, the evidence being collected. For example, using data reduction directly on evidence would alter the evidence and would not be acceptable. However, using such methods or tools on a *copy* of the evidence would have no direct affect on the evidence. Its affect on the analysis of the evidence (the validity of conclusions, for example) is an issue for the Examination and Analysis classes.
- **Recovery techniques.** This element refers to the recovery of data that may contain evidence from a digital device. It specifically describes the methods used by the forensic examiner to extract evidence using approved hardware, software, and methods. Whereas the elements of approved hardware, software, and methods refer to the naming (or brief description of) the element and the connection

between the element and the appropriate court test by which it is approved, *recovery techniques* describes in detail the actual process used to recover the evidence. By extension, when nonforensic methods are used to collect information (e.g., traditional investigation methods such as interviewing), we consider these techniques also to be recovery techniques and we apply the same rules to them (e.g., approved methods, legal authority, etc.) as we would in a digital environment. However, we apply the rules in the context of the technique used.

55.1.3.4 Examination Class. The Examination class deals with the tools and techniques used to examine evidence. The DFRWS gives describes the Examination class in this way: "Closer scrutiny of items and their attributes (characteristics)." It is concerned with evidence discovery and extraction rather than the conclusions to be drawn from the evidence (Analysis class). Whereas the Collection class deals with gross procedures to collect data that may contain evidence (such as imaging of computer media), the Examination class is concerned with the examination of those data and the identification and extraction of possible evidence from them. Note that the Preservation class continues to be pervasive in the Examination class.

- **Traceability.*** This element is, arguably, the most important element in the EEDI process. It is the traceability and continuity of a *chain of evidence* throughout an investigation that leads to the credibility and correctness of the conclusions. According to the DFRWS, "[t]raceability (cross referencing and linking) is key as evidence unfolds."
- **Validation techniques.** This element refers to techniques used to corroborate evidence. Evidence may be corroborated in a variety of ways. Traditionally, evidence is corroborated by other, relevant evidence. However, digital evidence may stand on its own merit if its technical validity can be established. For example, a fragment of text extracted from an image of a computer disk may be shown to be a valid piece of evidence through various technical validation techniques. Its applicability or usefulness as an element of proof in an investigation may be open to interpretation, but that it is *valid* data would not be in dispute. A log, however, if extracted from a device that had been penetrated by a criminal hacker, would require additional corroboration (validation) to show that the hacker had not altered its contents.
- **Filtering techniques.** When dealing with evidence acquired from certain types of digital systems (such as intrusion detection systems), it is not uncommon to find that the gross data have been filtered for expediency by the system. Although many intrusion detection experts would agree that filtering at the source (the incoming data flow from sensors) is not as appropriate as filtering the display while preserving the original data, such source filtering does occur. This element requires that the investigator and/or forensic examiner determine and describe the filtering techniques used, if any, and apply the results of that description to the determination of the validity of the data as evidence. Another application of filtering is the extraction of potential evidence from a gross data collection[16] such as a bit-stream image of digital media. Some digital forensic tools use filters to extract data of a particular type, such as graphical images. This element requires that the filtering technique be defined clearly and understood by the investigator or forensic examiner. These tools may also use the filtering technique of matching a known hash value to digital items on a gross data collection. Items that match

the known hash are presumed to be the same as the item for which the hash value was originally generated. Again, the techniques and tools applied must be clearly understood by the investigator or the forensic examiner.

- **Pattern matching.** This element addresses methods used to identify potential events by some predetermined signature or pattern. Examples are pattern-based intrusion detection systems and signature-based virus checkers. When the pattern or signature is unclear, ambiguous, or demonstrates a large number of false positives or negatives, the evidence and conclusion following from it are open to challenge.
- **Hidden data discovery.** This element refers to the discovery of evidence that is hidden in some manner on computer media. The data may be hidden using encryption, steganography, or any other data-hiding technique. It may also include data that have been deleted but are forensically recoverable.
- **Hidden data extraction.** This element addresses the extraction of hidden evidence from a gross data collection.

55.1.3.5 Analysis Class.

This class is described by the DFRWS as "[f]usion, correlation and assimilation of material for reasoned conclusions."

The Analysis class refers to those elements that are involved in the analysis of evidence collected, identified, and extracted from a gross data collection. The validity of techniques used in analysis of potential evidence impact as directly the validity of the conclusions drawn from the evidence and the credibility of the evidence chain constructed therefrom. The Analysis class contains, and is dependent on, the Preservation class and the Traceability element of the Examination class.

The various elements of the Analysis class refer to the means by which a forensic examiner or investigator might develop a set of conclusions regarding evidence presented from the other five classes. As with all elements of the framework, a clear understanding of the applicable process is required. Wherever possible, adherence to standard tools, technologies, and techniques is critical.

The link element is the key element used to form a chain of evidence. It is related to traceability and, as such, is a required element.

55.1.3.6 Presentation Class.

DFRWS describes the Presentation class in this way: "Reporting facts in an organized, clear, concise, and objective manner."

This class refers to the tools and techniques used to present the conclusions of the investigator and the digital forensic examiner to a court of inquiry or other finder of fact. Each of these techniques has its own elements, and a discussion of expert witnessing is beyond the scope of this chapter. However, for our purposes, we will stipulate that the EEDI process emphasizes the use of timelines as an embodiment of the clarification element of this class. For more information on expert witness testimony, see Chapter 73 in this *Handbook*.

55.2 END-TO-END DIGITAL INVESTIGATION.

The end-to-end digital investigation process takes into account a structured process including the network involved, the attack computer, the victim computer, and all of the intermediate devices on the network. Structurally, it consists of nine steps:

1. Collecting evidence
2. Analysis of individual events

3. Preliminary correlation
4. Event normalizing
5. Event deconfliction
6. Second-level correlation (consider both normalized and nonnormalized events)
7. Timeline analysis
8. Chain of evidence construction
9. Corroboration (consider only nonnormalized events)

55.2.1 Collecting Evidence.

A formal definition of the term *evidence collection* is:

> The use of approved tools and techniques by trained technicians to obtain digital evidence from computer devices, networks, and media. By *approved* we mean those tools and techniques generally accepted by the discipline and the courts where collected evidence will be presented.[17]

The collection of evidence in a computer security incident is time sensitive. When an event occurs (or when an expected event fails to occur), we have the first warning of a potential incident. An event may not be, by itself, particularly noteworthy. However, taken in the context of other events, it may become extremely important. From the forensic perspective, we want to consider all relevant events, whether they appear to have been tied to an incident or not. Events are the most granular elements of an incident.

We define an incident as a collection of events that lead to, or could lead to, a compromise of some sort. That compromise may include unauthorized change of control over data or systems; disclosure or modification of a system or its data; data or system destruction of the system; or unauthorized alterations in availability or utility or its data. An incident becomes a crime when a law or laws is/are violated.

Collecting evidence from all possible locations where it may reside must begin as soon as possible in the context of an incident. The methods vary according to the type of evidence (forensic, logs, indirect, traditionally developed, etc.). It is important to emphasize that EEDI is concerned not only with digital evidence. Gathering witness information should be accomplished as early in the evidence collection process as possible. Witness impressions and information play a crucial role in determining the steps the forensic examiner must take to uncover digital evidence.

Critical in this process are:

- Images of effected computers
- Logs of intermediate devices, especially those on the Internet
- Logs of effected computers
- Logs and data from intrusion detection systems, firewalls, and so on

55.2.2 Analysis of Individual Events.

An alert or incident is made up of one or more individual events. These events may be duplicates reported in different logs from different devices. These events and duplications have value both as they appear and after they are normalized. This analysis step examines isolated events and assesses what value they may have to the overall investigation and how they may tie into each other.

55.2.3 Preliminary Correlation.

The formal definition of the term *correlation* is:

> The comparison of evidentiary information from a variety of sources with the objective of discovering information that stands alone, in concert with other information, or corroborates or is corroborated by other evidentiary information.

Preliminary correlation examines the individual events to correlate them into a *chain of evidence*. The main purpose is to understand in broad terms what happened, what systems or devices were involved, and when the events occurred.

The term *chain of evidence* refers to the chain of events related in some consistent way that describes the incident. The relationship may be temporal or causal. Temporal chains are also called *timelines*. Essentially they say "This happened, *then* that happened." Causal relationships imply cause and effect. They say "That happened *because* this happened."

The term *chain of evidence* must not be used as a synonym for *chain of custody*, which this chapter defines in the discussion of the Preservation class of the DFRWS framework.

55.2.4 Event Normalizing.

The formal definition of *normalization* is:

> The combining of evidentiary data of the same type from different sources with different vocabularies into a single, integrated terminology that can be used effectively in the correlation process.

Some events may be reported from multiple sources. During part of the analysis (timeline analysis, e.g.), these duplications must be eliminated. This process is known as normalizing. EEDI uses both normalized and nonnormalized events.

55.2.5 Event Deconfliction.

The formal definition of *deconfliction* is:

> The combining of multiple reportings of the same evidentiary event by the same or different reporting sources, into a single, reported, normalized evidentiary event.

Sometimes events are reported multiple times from the same source. An example is a denial-of-service attack where multiple packets are directed against a target and each one is reported individually by a reporting resource. The EEDI process should not count each of those packets as a separate event. The process of viewing the packets as a single event instead of multiple events is called *deconfliction*.

55.2.6 Second-Level Correlation.

Second-level correlation is an extension of earlier correlation efforts. However, at this point, views of various events have been refined through normalization or deconfliction. For example, during the process of deconfliction or normalization, we have simplified the collection of events to eliminate redundancies and/or ambiguities. The resulting data set now represents the event universe at it simplest (or nearly simplest). These events (some of which actually may be compound events, i.e., events composed of multiple subevents) now represent the building blocks with which we may build chains of evidence.

55.2.7 Timeline Analysis. In this step, normalized and deconflicted events are used to build a timeline using an iterative process that should be updated constantly as the investigation continues to develop new evidence. The entire process is iterative: Event analysis, correlation, deconfliction, and timeline analysis are repeated in sequence as required.

55.2.8 Chain of Evidence Construction. Once there is a preliminary timeline of events, the process of developing a coherent chain of evidence begins. Ideally, each link in the chain, supported by one or more pieces of evidence, will lead to the next link. That rarely happens in large-scale network traces, however, because there often are gaps in the evidence-gathering process due to lack of logs or other missing event data.

Such problems do not invalidate this step, however. Although we may not always be able to construct a chain of evidence directly, we can nonetheless infer missing links in the chain. Now, an inferred link is not evidence: It is more properly referred to as a *lead*. Leads can point us to valid evidence and that valid evidence can, at some point, become the evidence link. Thus again, the iterative process of refinement of evidence makes it perfectly reasonable to start with a chain that is part evidence and part leads and refine it into an acceptable chain of evidence.

A second approach to handling gaps in evidence is to corroborate the questionable link very heavily. If all corroboration points to a valid link, it may be acceptable. For most purposes, however, the former approach is best.

55.2.9 Corroboration. In this stage, we attempt to corroborate each piece of evidence and each event in our chain with other, independent evidence or events. For this process, we use the noncorrelated event data as well as any other evidence developed either digitally or traditionally. The best evidence is that which has been developed digitally and corroborated through traditional investigation or vice versa. The final evidence chain consists of primary evidence corroborated by additional secondary evidence. This chain will consist of both digital and traditional evidence. The overall process does not differ materially between an investigation and an event postmortem except in use of the outcome.

55.3 APPLYING THE FRAMEWORK AND EEDI. The important issue in application is evidence management. Both the framework and EEDI help the investigator manage evidence. They do not substitute for good investigative techniques. The incident may or may not be a criminal act; even if it is such an act, it may not be treated as one. No matter. The approach to investigating is essentially the same in either case. To understand how these investigative tools might apply, it is useful to begin with a generalized framework for understanding the execution of a cyber incident.

55.3.1 Supporting the EEDI Process. Experienced traditional investigators often resist a process-based approach to investigation. However, in numerous interviews with such investigators, the author determined that what these investigators do by habit and experience is almost exactly the same process discussed in this chapter. Thus, it is convenient to view the DFRWS framework and EEDI as tools that investigators can use to apply past physical investigation experience to the more complicated requirements of digital investigation.

55.3.2 Investigative Narrative. The investigative narrative typically consists of the investigator's notes. The EEDI process supports the construction of an investigation around an investigative framework. For the purposes of this chapter, we use the DFRWS framework shown in Exhibit 55.2. The framework includes the basic areas where investigative and forensic controls are required. Once the narrative is complete, it can be translated into a more structured evidence support and management process using the framework and EEDI.

For example, under the Collection class, we find reference to approved software, hardware, and methods. This indicates that the forensic software, hardware, and methods used by the investigator or digital forensic examiner must meet some standard of acceptance within the investigative community. That standard usually refers to court testing. Should the investigator or forensic examiner not adhere to that standard, the evidence collected will be subject to challenge. At critical points in the investigation, such as the collection of primary evidence, such a lapse could jeopardize the outcome materially.

Again, the framework does not necessarily alter the generalized investigative techniques of experienced investigators and forensic examiners. Rather, it adds a dimension of rigor and quality assurance to the digital investigative process. It also ties the functions of the forensic examiner and the investigator tightly together, ensuring that the chain of evidence is properly supported, developed, and maintained.

55.3.3 Intrusion Process. Today, there are many ways in which an attack can occur. There has been a shift since about 2000 in types of incidents from manual hacking to automated malware-generated attacks. The sources of these attacks vary widely over time, and there is no definitive pattern to how they work. Today's assaults typically are some form of blended attack. Examples are botnets, spam, Trojan horses, rootkits, worms, and other malware. (See Chapters 2, 13, 15, 16, 17, and 18 in this *Handbook* for more details of attack methods.)

A *blended attack* is one in which various intrusion techniques are combined to deliver a payload. The payload can be a malicious outcome, such as damaging the target computer, or it can be more subtle, such as a spybot that harvests personal information and calls home periodically to deliver its collected information.

Regardless of the intrusion technique—manual hacking or automated malware—there is a generalized pattern of activities associated with a cyber attack. These steps are:

- **Information gathering.** Information gathering usually does not touch the victim. During this phase, the attacker selects his or her target, researches it, and determines such things as expected range of IP addresses exposed to the Internet. There is an exception to not touching the victim: Sometimes an attacker performs a scan of a block of IP addresses to determine whether there are any vulnerable devices in the IP block. This is what security professionals usually call a *script-kiddie* attack. The usual use for this step, however, is to select a victim for a targeted attack.
- **Footprinting.** Footprinting is the act of scanning a block of addresses owned by a victim for those that are online and may be vulnerable. The attacker is obtaining the *footprint* of the victim's presence online.
- **Enumerating.** *Enumerating* refers to the analysis of exposed addresses for potential weaknesses. In this step, the attack may grab banners to determine the versions

of various services running on the target. The objective is to understand what the victim is running on exposed machines. Once that information is gathered, the attacker can select potentially successful exploits based on published vulnerabilities. Although this process will leave a footprint on the target, it is likely to remain hidden in thousands of lines of logs (as in the footprinting phase). If these two steps (footprinting and enumerating) are performed carefully, they will not trigger most intrusion detection systems.

In a fully automated attack, such as one resulting from some form of social engineering (phishing, e.g.), these two steps are replaced by research that focuses on people and their access methods (e.g., email addresses). (For more information on social engineering, see Chapter 19 in this *Handbook*; for more on phishing, see Chapter 20.)

- **Probing for weaknesses.** In this step, the attacker may perform a vulnerability scan or some more stealthy probes to determine specific exploitable vulnerabilities. In an automated attack, this phase may consist of attempting to seduce large numbers of targets to give up important information that can be used in the next step. In this case, the probes consist of social engineering attempts.
- **Penetration.** This is the entry phase. It is essentially the same no matter if the attack is manual or automated. Only the penetration technique changes. The objective always is to reach into the victim system.
- **Backdoors, Trojans, rootkits, and so on.** In this phase, the attacker deposits the payload. The objective may be to reenter the target at some later date, plant some malware, or take the system down with a denial-of-service attack. Most experts seem to agree that denial-of-service attacks are on the decline. The objective of today's intruders is more frequently stealing information than damaging systems. (For more about denial-of-service attacks, see Chapter 18 in this *Handbook*.)
- **Cleanup.** In a traditional hack, this step is where the attacker removes tools from the target, alters logs, and performs other actions to cover his or her tracks and obscure his or her presence from system administrators and forensic analysts. In an automated attack, the tasks are similar and have similar objectives, but the techniques are a bit different and the forensics required to find evidence are a bit different.

55.3.4 Describing Attacks.

Three factors lead to a successful attack:

1. The attacker can access the target.
2. There is a significant vulnerability to attack, and that vulnerability can be identified by the attacker.
3. The attacker needs to have effective command and control and the prospects for attribution are minimized.

It is important to be able to describe a cyber event in clear terms. There are several attack taxonomies and descriptive languages available to help do that. However, these tools, while useful, are inconsistent with each other (there is no universally accepted descriptive language or taxonomy) and are often unnecessarily complicated for smaller investigations. The author recommends Howard's common language[18] as a good starting point for something simple and concise. Before applying a common language, however, there are several questions that need to be asked.

- **Description of the attack.** This is a narrative describing how the attack appeared when analyzed: What is happening? What service is being targeted? Does the service have known vulnerabilities or exposures?
- **Type of attack.** Is it benign, an exploit, a denial-of-service attack or reconnaissance?
- **Attack mechanism.** This is a narrative describing how the attack was carried out: How did the attacker do it?
- **Correlations.** How does this attack compare with other similar attacks? Are there any other attacks happening at the moment that might help trace/explain the attack?
- **Evidence of active targeting.** Is the attack leveled against one or more specific targets, or is it a generic *blast*?
- **Severity.**

  Severity = (Target Criticality + Attack Lethality) − (System Countermeasures + Network Countermeasures)

  Severity formula values usually are from 1 to 5, with 5 representing the highest measure. These computations are for heuristic purposes only and do not purport to be rigorous metrics.

In answering these questions, the analyst may apply the common language (or other formal approach) as appropriate.

There are also 10 generalized questions about the incident that need to be resolved early in the investigation. These can form an informal template for early interviews.

1. What is the nature of the incident?
2. How can we be sure that there even was an incident?
3. What was the entry point into the target system? Was there only one?
4. What would evidence of an attack look like? What are we looking for?
5. What monitoring systems were in place that might have collected useful data before and during the incident?
6. What legal issues need to be addressed (policies, privacy, subpoenas, warrants, etc.)?
7. Who was in a position to cause/allow the incident to occur?
8. What security measures were in place at the time of the incident?
9. What nontechnical (business) issues may have impacted the success or failure of the attack?
10. Who knew what about the attack, and when did they know it?

55.3.5 Strategic Campaigns. The steps in an attack are, largely, tactical. This is what may be expected from an attacker during an individual attack. Often the tactical attacks are part of larger strategic campaigns. Examples are spam, identity theft carried out by organized groups, and politically motivated cyber war. There are three important differences between a tactical attack and a strategic campaign:

1. Single objective versus ongoing objectives
2. Low-hanging fruit versus sustained effort to penetrate
3. Trivial versus complicated targets and objectives

Attacks may be part of campaigns. However, just because a company experiences a tactical attack does not mean that it is part of a sustained campaign. Campaigns have distinct phases:

1. Mapping and battle space preparation
2. Offensive and defensive planning
3. Initial execution
4. Probes, skirmishes
5. Adjustment and sustainment
6. Success and termination

55.4 USING EEDI AND THE FRAMEWORK.

Once we understand how attackers attack, we can see how EEDI and the framework can help us. The first, and most obvious, application of EEDI is the application of the investigative process to identify the results of each of the attack phases above. The act of collecting evidence, for example, may lead us to performing a forensic analysis of the target computer. When we do that, we will want to refer to the framework to ensure that we have not missed some important task. We may apply each step of the EEDI process to each step of the attack process to gather, correlate, and analyze evidence of an attack.

- **Collecting evidence.** Perform appropriate log collection, forensic imaging, and so on. Conduct interviews. There are 10 classes of evidence that the investigator should collect:
  1. Logs from monitoring devices
  2. Logs from hosts and servers
  3. Firewall and router (especially edge router) logs
  4. Interviews with involved personnel
  5. Interviews with business and technical managers
  6. Device configuration files
  7. Network maps
  8. Event observation timelines
  9. Notes of relevant meetings
  10. Response team notes and observations
- **Analysis of individual events.** Consider each of the events revealed by the collection and analysis of evidence in step one. Look for evidence of enumeration, penetration, and cleanup.
- **Preliminary correlation.** Tie together events from logs so that a smaller evidence set emerges. Consider each step of the attack process that applies to the device or system under analysis. Generate a straw-man chain of evidence.
- **Event normalizing.** The first and most important aspect of normalizing is time stamping. It is unlikely that all of the involved devices are on the same time tick. In this step, some allowance for differences in time zones and clocks must be made. Other normalizing tasks include combining different reports of the same events.
- **Event deconfliction.** This simply is an extension of event normalizing.

- **Second-level correlation.** This is a further refinement of the evidence and the straw-man chain of evidence. Here an important task is correlating log events, media forensic results, and results of interviews into a clear chain of evidence. This chain should be both causal and temporal, although the emphasis on the temporal chain is in the next step. This step is distinguished from the next two steps by level of detail. This correlation should offer significant detail. The next steps refine that detail making the results more comprehensible to laypeople.
- **Timeline analysis.** Refine the level of detail in the temporal chain of evidence.
- **Chain of evidence construction.** Refine the level of detail in the causal chain of evidence.
- **Corroboration.** Apply as much corroboration to evidence associated with each step of the attack process as you can.

55.5 MOTIVE, MEANS, AND OPPORTUNITY: PROFILING ATTACKERS.

Attacks, even automated ones, are performed by people. In order to understand attacks, we must understand the people who deliver them. We call those people *threat agents* because an attack simply is the delivery of a threat against a target. The act of delivering a threat is described concisely by Jones.[19] His model appears in Exhibit 55.3.

According to Jones, the threat agent first must have the capability of delivering the threat: The attacker must have access to the threat and know what to do with it. An example is an attacker who delivers a virus to a target system. The virus is the threat, and the attacker is the threat agent.

The threat agent then must be motivated to carry out the attack. However, just because motivation exists does not mean that a wily attacker will deliver the threat immediately. Usually, there needs to be a catalyst which tells the attacker that, for whatever reason, the time has come to attack.

The next step in the process, access, is the first place that we can manage the attack. Denying the threat agent access to the target denies the threat agent the ability to deliver the threat. However, assuming that the attacker can obtain access, the effectiveness of

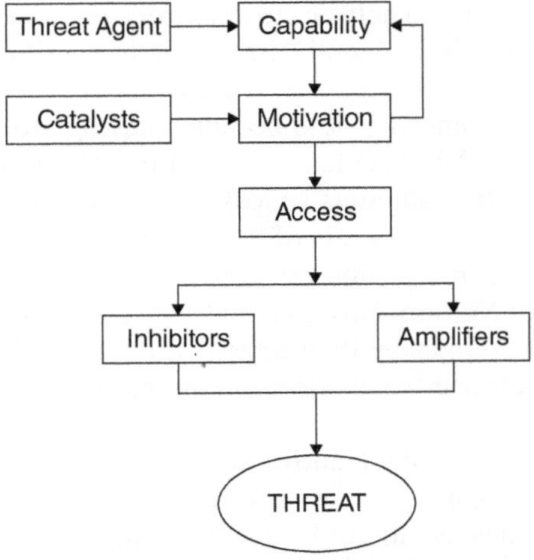

EXHIBIT 55.3 Jones's Threat Delivery Model

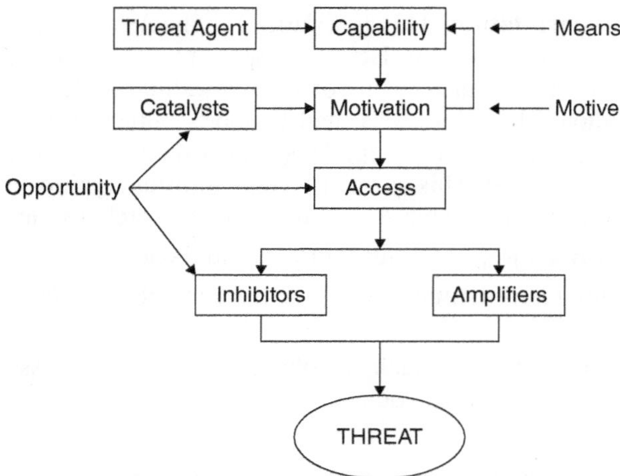

EXHIBIT 55.4 Jones's Model Showing Motive, Means, and Opportunity

the attack is now determined by the amplifiers and inhibitors present in the target system. These steps have direct analogs in the notion of motive, means, and opportunity, as Exhibit 55.4 shows.

55.5.1 Motive. Motive is critically important to understanding an attack. Why an attacker attacks often helps us understand the attack and, ultimately perhaps, who the attacker is. Traditional profiling matches evidence to known perpetrator profiles to understand the perpetrator. We do the same thing in cyber investigation.

An attacker with the motive of stealing personally identifiable information for the purpose of identity theft or credit card fraud may have an entirely different motive from a disgruntled employee who performs the same act to get even with his or her employer. In the former case, the attacker is motivated strictly by financial gain. In the latter, the attacker is motivated by a need for revenge.

Understanding the motivation helps us to determine the level of threat. In the former case, since the motivation is financial, the threat is significant and potentially far reaching because the attacker could attempt to maximize financial return. In the latter case, the threat could be somewhat less because, having stolen the information, the attacker might be likely to publicize his or her act in order to get the revenge desired. This might result in extortion attempts or leaks to the media but not in the attempt to sell or profit from the theft through sale of the information.

Additionally, analysis of motivation can help determine if the attacker is likely to be an individual or is part of a group. Groups tend to have somewhat different motivations from individuals, and they manage their attacks differently. There are several classes of threat agents, and each one has its own unique motive set. A summary appears in Exhibit 55.5.

The FBI, prior to 1995, described motive in general terms in its adversarial matrix.[20] Although this matrix needs updating for current trends and technology, it still is amazingly accurate and provides useful guidelines to the investigator. The behavioral characteristics appear in Exhibit 55.6, which is drawn from a British source.[21] This equates, approximately, to motive.

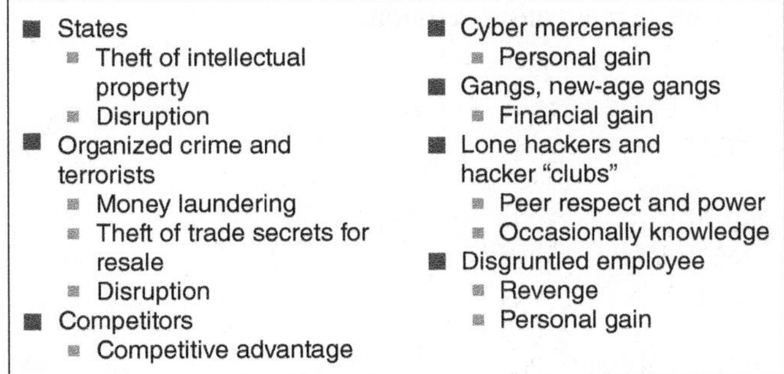

- States
  - Theft of intellectual property
  - Disruption
- Organized crime and terrorists
  - Money laundering
  - Theft of trade secrets for resale
  - Disruption
- Competitors
  - Competitive advantage
- Cyber mercenaries
  - Personal gain
- Gangs, new-age gangs
  - Financial gain
- Lone hackers and hacker "clubs"
  - Peer respect and power
  - Occasionally knowledge
- Disgruntled employee
  - Revenge
  - Personal gain

EXHIBIT 55.5 Types of Threat Agents and Their Motivations

EXHIBIT 55.6 Adversarial Matrix Behavioral Characteristics

Category of Offenders	Motivation	Personal Characteristics	Potential Weaknesses
Crackers			
Groups	Intellectual challenge; peer group fun; in support of a cause	Highly intelligent individuals, counterculture orientation	Do not consider offenses crimes, talk freely about actions
Individuals	Intellectual challenge; problem solving; power; money; in support of a cause	Moderately to highly intelligent	May keep notes and other documents of actions
Criminals			
Espionage	Money and a chance to attack the system	May be crackers operating in groups or as individuals	Become greedy for more information and then become careless
Fraud/Abuse	Money or other personal gain; power	Same personal characteristics as other fraud offenders	Become greedy and make mistakes
Vandals			
Strangers	Intellectual challenge; power; money	Same characteristics as crackers	May become too brazen and make mistakes
Users	Revenge against organization; problem solving; money	Usually have some computer expertise	May leave audit trail in computer logs

Jones also describes a motivation taxonomy:

- Political
- Secular
- Crime
- Personal gain
- Revenge
- Financial
- Knowledge or information
- Peer recognition
- Power
- Curiosity
- Religion
- Terrorism
- Competitive advantage
- Belief

55.5.2 Means. Means is a very important part of the profile. In cyber investigation, we generally equate means directly to the tools and techniques used in the attack. Indirectly we relate means to skill level of the attacker. We live in an Internet-enabled society. That state of affairs extends to computer-related crime. Relatively unskilled threat agents can deliver moderately sophisticated attacks simply because the means is readily available on the Internet to enable their actions. Analysis of evidence for indications of skill level helps us to eliminate suspects.

A word on investigative process is in order here. Although it may seem as if the right approach to an investigation is to focus on the probable perpetrator, in reality, it is far more productive, initially at least, to focus on those who absolutely could *not* be the perpetrator. This is an extension of the Sherlock Holmes' admonition: "It is an old maxim of mine that when you have excluded the impossible, whatever remains, however improbable, must be the truth."[22] The point here is that it is far more efficient to eliminate those who could not have participated in the attack. In cyber investigations, doing this becomes even more important because of the huge universe of possible participants in a network-based attack.

The FBI adversarial matrix of operational characteristics appears in Exhibit 55.7. Exhibit 55.8 extends the operational characteristics and includes specific tools, techniques, and support required. These equate, approximately, to means.

55.5.3 Opportunity. The Jones threat model describes the notion of opportunity. Considered with means, opportunity helps determine whether an attacker is a credible threat agent. Opportunity not only reflects Jones' threat model, it includes such things as knowledge of the victim system. The insider threat is an important piece of the opportunity puzzle. In this case, an insider can be the attacker him- or herself or a confederate of the threat agent. Besides insider help, the attacker may have the support of a group of some sort, such as a hacker gang, drug gang, or organized crime group.

EXHIBIT 55.7 FBI Adversarial Matrix of Operational Characteristics

Category of Offenders	Planning	Level of Expertise	Tactics/Method Used
Crackers			
Groups	May involve detailed planning	High	Each target computers via computer networks, exchange information with other crackers and groups
Individuals	Study networks before attempts are made	Medium to high, Experience gained through social networks	Use networks but more likely to use trial and error online than to do careful research and planning, use BBSs share accounts on other systems
Criminals			
Espionage	Same characteristics as crackers	High	May contract with crackers to conduct information and data collection
Fraud/Abuse	Careful planning prior to crime	Medium to high, although is typically more experienced at fraud than at computer programming	May use more traditional intrusion methods, such as wiretapping and trapdoors, will break into systems using basic methods
Vandals			
Strangers	Not much planning, more a crime of opportunity	Varies	Looks around until able to gain access to system
Users	May involve detailed planning and execution	Varies, may have high level of expertise	Trapdoors and Trojan horse programs, data modification

55.6 SOME USEFUL TOOLS. The usual tools for digital investigation include tools for:

- Computer forensic imaging and analysis
- Network forensic/log aggregation and analysis
- Malware discovery
- Media imaging (without analysis)
- Network discovery
- Remote (over-the-network) computer forensic analysis and imaging

These tools are well known in the cyber forensic community and do not warrant further elucidation here.[23] Specific products come and go so it is not appropriate to provide that level of detail here.

Exhibit 55.8 FBI Adversarial Matrix Resource Characteristics

Category of Offenders	Training Skills	Minimum Equipment Needed	Support Structure
Crackers			
Groups	High level of informal training	Basic computer equipment with modem	Peer group support
Individuals	Expertise gained through experience	Basic computer equipment with modem	BBS, information exchanges
Criminals			
Espionage	Various level of expertise	Basic computer equipment with modem, in some cases, uses more sophisticated devices	Support may come from sponsoring intelligence agency
Fraud/Abuse	Some programming experience	Computer with modem or access to target computer	Peer group support, possible organized crime enterprise
Vandals			
Strangers	Range from basis to highly skilled	Basic computer equipment with modem	Peer group support
Users	Some computer expertise, knowledge of programming ranges from basic to advanced	Access to targeted computer	None

In addition, there are some nonstandard tools that can make the EEDI process much easier. These include:

- Link analysis
- Attack-tree analysis
- Modeling
- Statistical analysis

Unlike the standard tools, these specialized requirements bear explanation. Again, however, specific products come and go. Where examples are provided, the specific product that generated the example will be listed along with its source at the time of writing.

55.6.1 Link Analysis. In this author's view, link analysis is the single most useful technique for cyber investigators. Link analysis allows the investigator to analyze large data sets for nonobvious relationships. Link analysis is used in the investigation of complicated criminal activities, such as fraud, drug-related activities and groups, terrorist acts and groups, and organized crime. It is used far less commonly in analysis of cyber crime, but it should be integrated into cyber investigations.

The core theory behind link analysis is that pairings of related items (e.g., people and addresses, source and destination IP addresses, hacker aliases and real names, etc.) can be analyzed to find relationships that are not immediately obvious. We do that by testing for associations in suitable pairs of data sets.

An example of such an analysis is an analysis of hackers and groups. We might start by pairing hacker aliases and real names. These can be collected in a simple spreadsheet in columns with the first column as hacker aliases. Through research, the real names of some of the hackers may be discovered and be placed into their own column next to their associated aliases. Next, research may reveal hacks associated with individual aliases or, perhaps, real names. These go into their own column in the same row with their associated hackers. Finally, perhaps the groups with which the hackers are associated can provide useful connections. These groups are researched and placed in their own column on the rows associated with the hackers who are members.

The link analyzer accepts the input two columns at a time and iteratively analyzes the relationships. Some of the things that the analysis might reveal are multiple aliases for the same hacker, multiple hackers participating in the researched hacks, and membership in various hacker groups. In turn, membership in a particular hacker group may imply participation in individual hacks by members of the group who were not initially reported as being involved.

A more difficult problem to solve is the relationship between attack source IP addresses and target addresses. Often these relationships are *clustered*. In link analysis language, a *cluster* is

> a group of entities that are bound more tightly to one another by the links between them than they are to the entities that surround them.[24]

Since the entities within a cluster are more tightly interconnected within the cluster than they are with entities outside of the cluster, these clustered entities usually represent activities of interest.

Applying this concept to a large log from a firewall, we might take all of the denied connections, place their source and destination addresses in the link analyzer, and look for relationships. That might yield a complicated pattern such as the one shown in Exhibit 55.9.

This map can be simplified by performing a cluster analysis as shown in Exhibit 55.10.

The clustering operation on the data in Exhibit 55.9 reveals the cluster in Exhibit 55.10. This simplified analysis in turn shows two interesting relationships:

1. It quickly identifies the IP addresses that are broadcasting.
2. It clearly shows several IP addresses that are receiving a lot of traffic as well as the sources of that traffic.

The cluster map in Exhibit 55.10 is far easier to read than the map in Exhibit 55.9. Considering that the original log had several thousand entries, this is a much improved way to see nonobvious relationships; it is much easier than reading the log data or manipulating a spreadsheet.

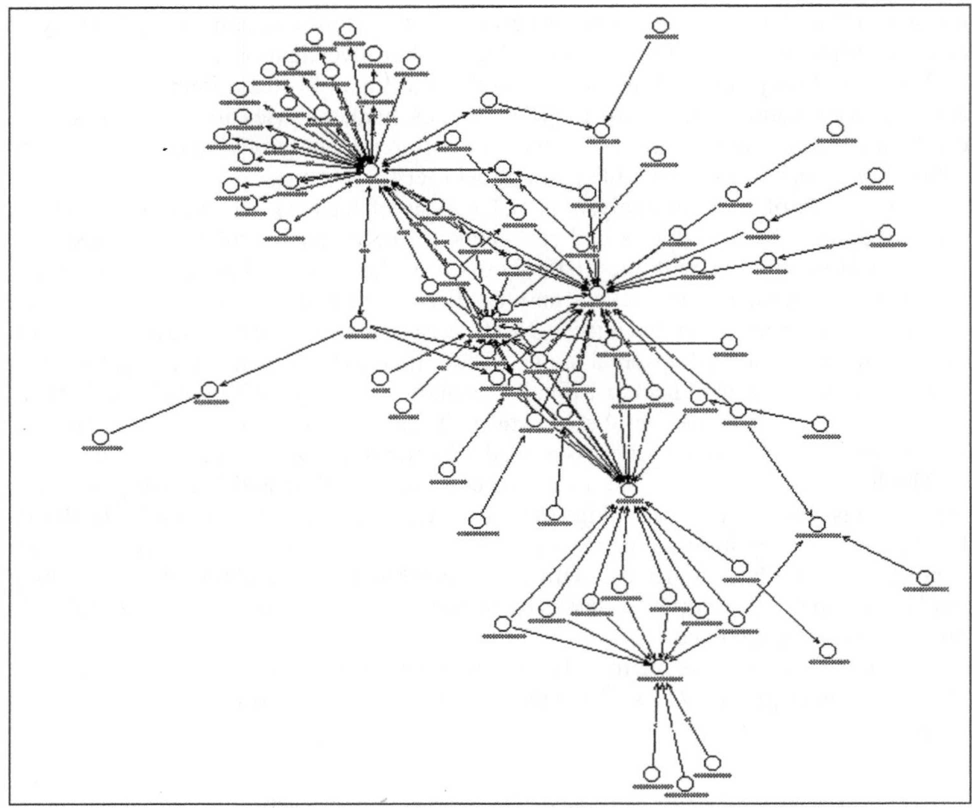

Exhibit 55.9 Link Analyzer Relationship Map of Source and Destination IP Addresses

55.6.2 Attack-Tree Analysis. *Attack-tree analysis* is a technique for analyzing possible attack scenarios on a compromised network. Its purpose is to hypothesize the attack methodology and calculate the probabilities of several possible scenarios. Once these probabilities are calculated, the investigator can hypothesize where to look for evidence. In a complicated attack on a large distributed network, having a set of these models on hand can be a big help. The analyst prepares various attack-tree models in advance and then modifies them to be consistent with the facts of a particular incident. This limits the number of high-probability attack paths and simplifies the evidence discovery process.

55.6.3 Modeling. *Attack modeling* is a broad term that refers to all of the techniques used to simulate attack behavior. The author uses Coloured Petri Nets (CPNets).[25] CPNets are a graphical representation of a mathematical formalism that allows the modeling and simulation of attack behavior on a network. To use CPNets effectively, the investigator must understand the enterprise in terms of its *security-policy domains*. The author defines security-policy domains in this way: "A security policy domain, E_p, consists of all of the elements, **e,** of an enterprise that conform to the same security policy, **p**."[26]

The policy domains are represented along with the communications links between them in a graphical chart. Once the mathematical definitions of the domains and the

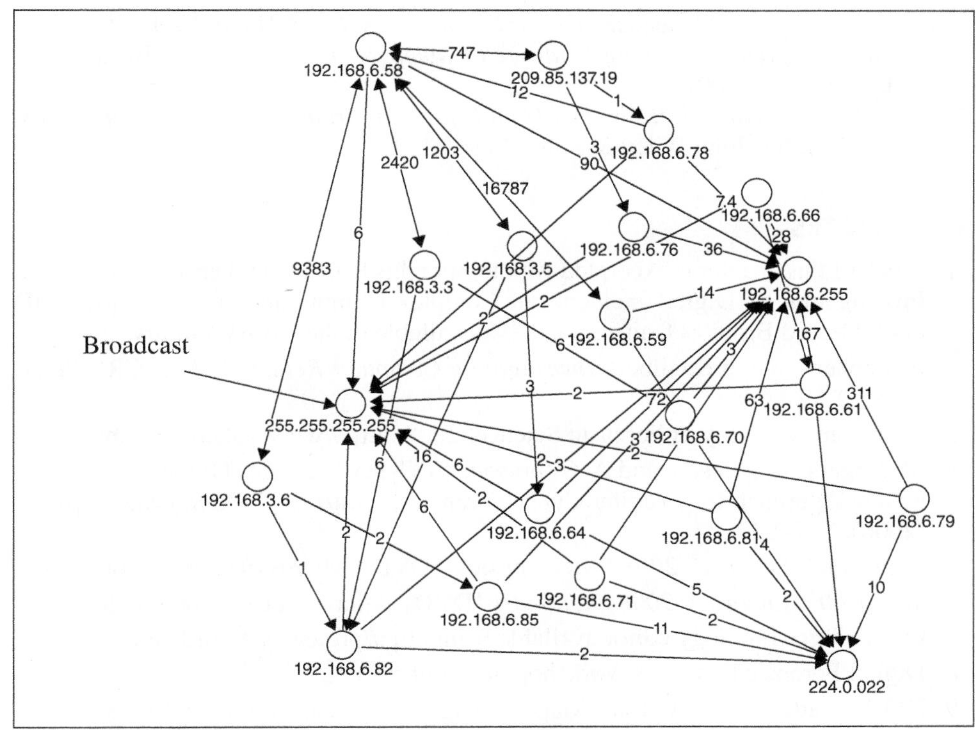

EXHIBIT 55.10 Map in Exhibit 55.9 Reduced through Cluster Analysis

communications conditions that exist between them have been defined, the behavior of the attack can be simulated. The simulations assist the investigator in tracing the attack source.

55.7 CONCLUDING REMARKS.

In this chapter, we discussed a structured approach to cyber investigation along with some of the tools and techniques that support such an approach. Nordby[27] suggests that reliable methods of inquiry possess the characteristics of "integrity, competence, defensible technique and relevant experience." The nature of cyber investigation and cyber forensics supports this through rigor, underlying models and frameworks, and investigators who adhere to those characteristics.

55.8 FURTHER READING

Brown, C. L. T. *Computer Evidence: Collection & Preservation*. Hingham, MA: Charles River Media, 2005.

Carrier. B. *File System Forensic Analysis*. Upper Saddle River, NJ: Addison-Wesley, 2005.

Carvey, H. *Windows Forensics and Incident Recovery*. Upper Saddle River, NJ: Addison-Wesley, 2004.

Farmer, D., and W. Venema. *Forensic Discovery*. Upper Saddle River, NJ: Addison-Wesley, 2005.

Jones, K. J., R. Beijtlich, and C. W. Rose. *Real Digital Forensics: Computer Security and Incident Response*. Upper Saddle River, NJ: Addison-Wesley, 2005.

Marcella, A., and D. Menendez. *Cyber Forensics: A Field Manual for Collecting, Examining, and Preserving Evidence of Computer Crimes*, 2nd ed. Boca Raton, FL: Auerbach, 2007.

Steel, C. *Windows Forensics: The Field Guide for Corporate Computer Investigations.* Hoboken, NJ: John Wiley & Sons, 2006.

55.9 NOTES

1. Much of this chapter is excerpted with minor edits from P. Stephenson, "Structured Investigation of Digital Incidents in Complex Computing Environments," PhD diss., Oxford Brookes University, 2004, available in the British Library.
2. P. Stephenson and K.Gilbert, *Investigating Computer Related Crime* (CRC Press, 1999).
3. American Academy of Forensic Science, 2008: http://www.aafs.org/membership
4. M. Rogers, A. Brinson, and A. Robinson, "A Cyber Forensics Ontology: Creating a New Approach to Studying Cyber Forensics," *Journal of Digital Investigation* (2006): S37–S43.
5. *Microsoft® Encarta® 2008*, "Metaphysics" [DVD] (Microsoft Corporation, 2008).
6. *Microsoft® Encarta® 2008 Dictionary* [DVD] (Microsoft Corporation, 2008).
7. Open-source ontology editor available from http://protege.stanford.edu/
8. Digital Forensic Research Workshop: http://dfrws.org/
9. DFRWS attendees, "A Road Map for Digital Forensic Research," Report from the First Digital Forensic Research Workshop, August 7–8, 2001, Utica, NY. Air Force Research Laboratory, Rome Research Site, Rome, NY, http://dfrws.org/2001/dfrws-rm-final.pdf
10. There have also been attempts to relate cyber investigation to the generalized Zachman Enterprise Architecture Framework: J. A. Zachman, "A Framework for Information Systems Architecture," *IBM Systems Journal* 26, No. 3 (1987), http://www.zachmanframework.com/images/ZI_PIcs/ibmsj2603e.pdf
11. DFRWS attendees, "A Road Map for Digital Forensic Research."
12. DFRWS attendees, "A Road Map for Digital Forensic Research."
13. The DFRWS definitions in these sections are from Digital Forensics Research Workshop, "Day 1-DF-Science, Group A Session 1 (D1-A1), Digital Forensic Framework," Work notes for the 2003 Digital Forensics Research Workshop, August 6, 2003. For more information on the DFRWS Framework, see DFRWS attendees, "Road Map for Digital Forensic Research."
14. Author's experience over 25 years of conducting incident response.
15. A. C. Doyle, "Silver Blaze." In: *The Memoirs of Sherlock Holmes* (Newnes, 1893). http://www.gutenberg.org/files/834/834-h/834-h.htm
16. A gross data collection is a file or files containing data collected from a digital source that may contain individual evidentiary data.
17. This and other formal definitions appear in Stephenson, "Structured Investigation of Digital Incidents in Complex Computing Environments."
18. See Chapter 8, Sections 8.1 to 8.6, in this *Handbook*.
19. Andrew Jones describes a cyber threat delivery model in his paper "Identification of a Method for the Calculation of Threat in an Information Environment," unpublished (April 2002, revised 2004). http://www.researchgate.net/publication/

228957980_Identification_of_a_method_for_the_calculation_of_threat_in_an_information_environment

20. D. Icove, K. Seger, and W. VonStorch, *Computer Crime: A Crimefighter's Handbook* (O'Reilly & Associates, 1995.
21. Stephenson, "Structured Investigation of Digital Incidents in Complex Computing Environments."
22. A. C. Doyle, *The Sign of Four* (Blackett, 1890). http://www.gutenberg.org/ebooks/2097
23. For more details, see the recommendations for further reading.
24. i2 Limited "About Clusters," Analyst's Notebook v6 Help file, August 9, 2005; http://www-03.ibm.com/software/products/us/en/analysts-notebook/
25. Coloured Petri Nets at the University of Aarhus: http://www.daimi.au.dk/CPnets
26. P. Stephenson and P. Prueitt, "Towards a Theory of Cyber Attack Mechanics," First IFIP 11.9 Digital Forensics Conference, 2005. http://www.ontologystream.com/gFT/Towards a Theory of Cyber Attack Mechanics.PDF
27. S. H. James and J. J. Nordby, *Forensic Science: An Introduction to Scientific and Investigative Techniques* (CRC Press, 2003).

INTRODUCTION TO PART VI

RESPONSE AND REMEDIATION

What are the options when security breaches or accidents occur? How do we prepare for trouble so that we can minimize the consequences and respond quickly and effectively? This part includes these chapters and topics:

56. **Computer Security Incident Response Teams.** Planning and rehearsing responses to a wide variety of security problems—in advance instead of on the fly
57. **Data Backups and Archives.** The essential tool for all forms of recovery, with new material on cloud backups
58. **Business Continuity Planning.** Systematic approach to analyzing the priorities for orderly recovery when anything interrupts the smooth operation of the organization
59. **Disaster Recovery.** Planning for rapid, cost-effective return to normal after a crisis is over
60. **Insurance Relief.** Using modern insurance services to reduce the consequences of disasters
61. **Working with Law Enforcement.** Establishing relations with all levels of law enforcement before there is a crisis, and coordinating efficiently and effectively to support investigation and prosecution of criminals

CHAPTER 56

COMPUTER SECURITY INCIDENT RESPONSE TEAMS[1]

Michael Miora, M. E. Kabay, and Bernie Cowens

56.1 OVERVIEW.

No matter how good one's security, at some point a security measure will fail. Knowing that helps organizations to plan for security in depth, so that a single point of failure does not necessarily result in catastrophe. Furthermore, instead of trying to invent a response when every second counts, it makes sense to have a competent team in place, trained, and ready to act. The value of time is not constant. Spending an hour or a day planning, so that an emergency response is shortened by a few seconds, may save a life or prevent a business disaster.

An essential element of any effective information security program today is the ability to respond to computer emergencies. Although many organizations have some form of intrusion detection in place, far too few take full advantage of the capabilities those systems offer. Fewer still consistently monitor the data available to them from automated intrusion detection systems, let alone respond to what they see.

The key is to make beneficial use of the knowledge that something has happened, that something is about to happen, or that something is perhaps amiss. Intrusion detection systems can be costly to implement and maintain. It therefore makes little business sense to go to the trouble of implementing an intrusion detection capability if there is not, at the same time, a way to make use of the data produced by these systems.

Computer emergency quick-response teams are generally called *computer security incident response teams* (CSIRTs, the abbreviation used in this chapter) or *computer incident response teams* (CIRTs). Sometimes one sees the term "computer emergency response team" (CERT), but that term and acronym are increasingly reserved for the Computer Emergency Response Team Coordination Center (CERT/CC®) at the Software Engineering Institute of Carnegie Mellon University, as explained in Section 56.1.3 of this chapter.

CSIRTs can provide organizations with a measurable return on their investment in computer security mechanisms and intrusion detection systems. Intrusion detection can indicate that something occurred; CSIRTs can do something about that occurrence. Often their value to an organization can be felt in more subtle ways as well. Many times computer emergencies and incidents cast an organization in an unfavorable light, and they can erode confidence in that organization. Efficient handling of computer emergencies can lessen the erosion of confidence, can help speed the organization's recovery, and in some cases can help restore its image. In addition, CSIRT postmortems (see Section 56.7) can provide information for process improvement (as discussed in Section 56.7.2).

When an incident occurs, the intrusion detection system makes us aware of the incident in one manner or another. We make use of this knowledge by responding to the situation appropriately. "Appropriately" can mean something different in different situations. Therefore, a well-trained, confident, authoritative CSIRT is essential.

Intrusion detection systems are not the only means by which we learn about incidents. In a sense, every component of a system and every person who interacts with the system forms a part of the overall defense and detection system. End users are often the first to notice that something is different. They may not recognize a particular difference as an incident; however, proper awareness and training will encourage them to report such situations to those who can make a determination and act on the information.

56.1.1 Description. CSIRTs are multifaceted, multitalented groups of individuals who are specially trained and equipped to respond quickly and effectively to computer emergencies.

CSIRTs come in a variety of forms and compositions. For example, while some teams are static, established groups, others are assembled dynamically to fit a specific mission or to deal with specific emergencies. Often the most effective teams are characterized as a mixture of these two approaches. These teams generally have a standing core membership made up of both technical and nontechnical members. When a situation arises that must be addressed by the CSIRT, additional members with specific skills are added to meet the requirements of handling the incident in progress. Once the incident is resolved, the team reverts to its core membership status.

56.1.2 Purpose. CSIRTs provide the first reaction to an incident. Their immediate goal should be to take control of a situation in order to contain the scope of a potential compromise, to conduct damage control, and to prevent the possible spread of a compromise to adjacent systems. Containing the scope of compromise is also synonymous with preventing or reducing loss.

Maintaining a dedicated CSIRT at the ready 24 hours a day is a costly proposition from many perspectives. Virtually any organization today, no matter its mission, will be hard pressed to justify funding such a team only to have the team stand by awaiting an emergency. The cost of maintaining a team of highly trained resources, with only emergency response roles, is a most difficult issue to overcome. Therefore, it is important to make use of team members and their skills during nonemergency periods. In many organizations, the teams have important security and awareness roles as integral parts of their charters. Carefully selected, these additional roles can benefit team readiness while at the same time providing tangible and often visible value to the organization.

For example, some CSIRTs spend their nonemergency days and nights monitoring security issues and developments for the latest trends, threats, and countermeasures. They analyze threat data and prepare reports for various levels of the organization on such topics as virus protection, password security, and emerging technology. Members of the team spend a significant amount of time and effort developing and maintaining leading-edge technical skills. They hone their response skills and procedures through continuous training. Training often is conducted in the classroom and through dry runs using a variety of response scenarios.

Often, response teams provide and maintain awareness programs for the organization. This serves several purposes. First, awareness programs benefit an organization by pointing out risks and ways to avoid them. Next, delivering awareness programs makes the team members more visible. As a result, should something unusual or out of the ordinary occur, members of the organization are not only more likely to notice it, they are also more likely to report the information, so that it winds up in the hands of the response team.

The teams respond to emergencies or incidents. An incident does not always indicate something unwanted; it also can be something that is merely unexplained, or out of the ordinary. A response acts not only to defend, or to fight back, or to prevent further damage, but also to discover more information or to verify facts—in essence, it is part investigation and part education. To keep in step with the rapid pace of change in technology, quick response teams must be learning constantly. These teams should strive to remain abreast of each new development and technology that impacts, or has the potential to impact, the systems under their care. Therefore, responding to incidents, whether actual attacks or benign anomalies, should be seen as opportunities to sharpen the CSIRT's skills. This need is also served by the additional responsibilities the team holds in nonemergency times, typically including ongoing security research and evaluation.

If locks and other preventive measures were foolproof, intrusion detection and incident response would be unnecessary. Banks put huge vault doors, time locks, and other seemingly impenetrable defenses into their buildings. But they recognize that these measures are insufficient to prevent completely any loss of their money or other valuables. So they also install alarm systems to detect when one of the defensive barriers has been breached. But that knowledge is of little value if no one hears the alarm or, if having heard it, does not act on the information. Therefore, organizations also put into place guards, night watchers, and others, including law enforcement, to monitor systems and to respond. CSIRTs are the response part of the secure + monitor + detect + respond equation. Because connected systems are under constant passive and active attack virtually 24 hours a day, emergency response teams are a necessary part of the security equation.

56.1.3 History and Background.

Help desks became popular in the 1960s for all kinds of organizations providing services and products; as computers grew in importance in the 1970s, manufacturers and users organized helpdesks specifically devoted to supporting computer users. With the increased access to the Internet in the 1980s and the arrival of the World Wide Web in the early 1990s, help desks added email, Websites and instant messaging (chat) to the range of options for customers.[2] A natural evolution of the helpdesk was to include security-incident response planning and execution; for example, the Federal Computer Incident Response Capability (FedCIRC) was proposed in April 1996 by the National Institute of Standards and Technology (NIST), the Department of Energy's Computer Incident Advisory Capability (CIAC), and the Computer Emergency Response Team Coordination Center (CERT/CC) (discussed below).[3]

The formal coordination of information from multiple CSIRTS can be traced back to one of the more notorious computer incidents of the late twentieth century. The infamous Morris Worm incident of November 2, 1988, wreaked havoc by disabling a significant portion, by some estimates as much as 10 percent, of the Internet. As organization after organization attempted to deal with the worm, it quickly became apparent that a coordinated response to such incidents would have helped to lessen the impact and speed recovery. There was no central place to report or disseminate information about the attack. Internally, few organizations were equipped with teams dedicated to responding to such attacks. As a result, they wasted time and resources duplicating efforts to identify the source of the attack, to formulate countermeasures, and finally to eradicate the worm.

At that time, the most common response was simply to disconnect from the Internet. That same response would carry unacceptable losses of revenues, confidence, and performance for today's organizations. As more commercial organizations, government agencies, and individuals became dependent on Internet-connected systems, the criticality of the need for teams capable of responding to emergencies quickly and effectively increased.

The Morris Worm incident and several other attacks on the Internet in November and December 1988 highlighted the need for a coordinated response to widespread computer emergencies. As a result, in December 1988, under the direction of the Defense Advanced Research Projects Agency (DARPA), security experts established the Computer Emergency Response Team Coordination Center (CERT/CC®) at the Software Engineering Institute of Carnegie Mellon University in Pittsburgh, Pennsylvania. The role of the CERT/CC was to coordinate communication among organizations during computer emergencies. Their role has since expanded dramatically to include, among other things, assisting with the establishment of other CSIRT teams, acting as a clearinghouse for threat and vulnerability data, and providing training and education programs relating to security incident handling. Many entities, both public and private, have since that time adopted CSIRT's incident-handling procedures.[4]

Since its inception, CERT/CC has provided invaluable services to the world community of Internet users and especially to system and security administrators. In addition to the archives of security alerts and incident analyses available online and via free email subscriptions, CERT/CC provides free electronic textbooks of great quality. One of these is the famous *Handbook for Computer Security Incident Response Teams (CSIRTs)* edited by Moira J. West-Brown and colleagues, and which is now in its second edition.[5] We strongly recommend this work to anyone concerned with establishing and managing a CSIRT.

West-Brown et al. describe the functions of the CSIRT in this way:

> For a team to be considered a CSIRT, it must provide one or more of the incident-handling services: incident analysis, incident response on site, incident response support, or incident response coordination.

They explain in detail all aspects of these functions, and they summarize their research on the range of services that CSIRTs actually provide, whether by themselves or in cooperation with other teams in the information technology sector. They provided a "List of Common CSIRT Services" as Table 4 in their *Handbook for CSIRTs*; we have reformatted it here:

- Reactive Services
  - Alerts and warnings
  - Incident handling
    - Incident analysis
    - Incident response on site
    - Incident response support
    - Incident response coordination
  - Vulnerability handling
    - Vulnerability analysis
    - Vulnerability response
    - Vulnerability response coordination
  - Artifact handling
    - Artifact analysis

    - Artifact response
    - Artifact response coordination
- Proactive Services
    - Announcements
    - Technology watch
    - Security audits or assessments
    - Configuration and maintenance of security tools, applications, and infrastructures
    - Development of security tools
    - Intrusion detection services
    - Security-related information dissemination
- Security Quality Management Services
    - Risk analysis
    - Business continuity and disaster recovery planning
    - Security consulting
    - Awareness building
    - Education and training
    - Product evaluation or certification

The only problematic term in this list is *artifact*, which the authors define as "any file or object found on a system that might be involved in probing or attacking systems and networks or that is being used to defeat security measures. Artifacts can include but are not limited to computer viruses, Trojan horse programs, worms, exploit scripts, and toolkits" (p. 28).

The specific combination of functions that a CSIRT will provide will be a function of personnel and budgetary resources, and of the maturity of the team. It is wise to focus a completely new CSIRT on essential services such as incident handling and analysis as their first priority. With time and experience, the team can add functions, such as coordinating with other security teams, with computer and network operations in the more proactive services, and with the security quality services that will lead to long-term reduction in security incidents and to lower damages and costs from such incidents.

For more extensive discussion of the possible factors in any computer-security incident, see Chapter 8 in this *Handbook.*

56.1.4 Types of Teams. The exact composition of a CSIRT depends on factors such as the size, type, complexity, budget, and location of its sponsoring organization. Some organizations might be able to justify and support a full-time, dedicated, in-house CSIRT with the very latest technology and training. Others might improvise teams once an incident occurs, or they might even hire outside expertise to handle computer emergencies on their behalf. Still others might use a combination of these approaches by having core CSIRT staff who can be augmented by other people as needed to manage incidents.

One viable alternative to developing in-house quick response teams is to take advantage of outsourced services in this area. Outsourced incident-handling services are becoming increasingly popular, and many security companies offer them to their customers. In some cases, this might be the most practical option for companies that lack the resources or desire to develop in-house response capabilities. Outsourcing computer emergency quick response efforts can be an effective, albeit somewhat costly, alternative to developing in-house response teams, for both short- and long-term incident handling.

However, for many organizations, establishing their own incident response capabilities can provide significant advantages. Internal teams generally know the organization and understand its goals, issues, and requirements. Outsourced responses are often mechanical and standardized. Vendors can take longer to respond since they are normally located off site and might even be a considerable distance away. Vendors may undergo frequent staff turnover, which can mean that those assigned to respond to incidents at an organization might be unfamiliar with that organization or its mission. As a result, outsiders might require precious time to "ramp up" before dealing effectively with a current incident or situation. The connected nature of today's organizations, and modern monitoring technologies, may make up for distance in some ways, but there is no substitute for an expert on site.

Some organizations are fortunate enough to have implemented formal, standing CSIRTs whose members are dedicated primarily to monitoring systems, preventing intrusions, and responding to computer emergency incidents. These teams are superior to ad hoc or outsourced teams in their ability to respond quickly with customized procedures acting from a deep and current knowledge base.

With the increased use of outsourced cloud services, it is important for in-house CSIRTs to coordinate closely with the CSIRTs at the service providers. Members of the in-house CSIRT should contact their corresponding colleagues at the service provider before there are incidents to handle; regular communication and collaboration will support smooth handling of cases involving both organizations.

56.2 PLANNING THE TEAM. Not every organization has a CSIRT already in place; not all CSIRTs are structured and managed in the most appropriate ways for an organization's specific needs. This section presents systematic approaches for rational design and implementation of a CSIRT.

Establishing a CSIRT is a complex process that must be given careful thought and must be based on comprehensive planning. Before establishing a CSIRT, the organization needs to determine exactly what it expects to accomplish. From this, the organization can decide on specific goals for the team, and perhaps most important, it can decide on policies that apply to the team. The team should be conceived and defined in terms of the organization to which it belongs. That is, the team should be tailored to achieving a specific mission. Clarity, vision, and focus are vital planning elements that ultimately will determine the success or failure of the CSIRT. Skimping during the planning stage will ensure failure. Devoting some extra effort to planning in this stage will help improve the chances of success.

56.2.1 Mission and Charter. The CSIRT should include members from every sector of the organization; key members include operations, facilities, legal staff, public relations, information technology, and at least one respected and experienced manager with a direct line to top management. The CSIRT should establish good relations with law enforcement officials and should be prepared to gather forensic evidence. The organization should have a policy in place on how to decide whether to prosecute malefactors if they can be identified. The CSIRT should be prepared to respond not only to external attacks but also to criminal activities by insiders. Proper logging at the operating system level and from intrusion-detection systems can be useful to the CSIRT. The CSIRT plays an important role in disaster prevention, mitigation, and recovery planning.

Organizing people to respond to computer security incidents is worth the effort not only when an incident occurs but also because the analysis and interactions leading to establishment of the CSIRT bring benefits even without an emergency. A CSIRT can provide opportunities for improving institutional knowledge, contributing to continuous process improvement and offering challenging and satisfying work assignments to technical and managerial staff, thus contributing to reduced turnover. A well-trained, professional, courteous CSIRT can improve relations between the entire technical support infrastructure and the user community. The team and its members often serve as key elements of business continuity and disaster recovery teams.

A clear, written mission and a charter establishing the CSIRT are essential to its success. These documents should establish why the team exists and what the organization expects from the team at a high level. Although the current security landscape provides compelling reasons for establishing an incident response capability, identifying organization-specific goals and expectations for the team remains an essential task.

RFC 2350, "Expectations for Computer Security Incident Response," provides a solid framework that can be used and adapted in creating the charter of a new CSIRT.[6] The document includes a template and a filled-in example to serve users. The template (Appendix D) is as follows:

> This outline summarizes in point form the issues addressed in this document, and is the recommended template for a CSIRT description document. Its structure is designed to facilitate the communication of a CSIRT's policies, procedures, and other relevant information to its constituency and to outside organizations such as other CSIRTs. …

1. Document Information
- **1.1.** Date of Last Update
- **1.2.** Distribution List for Notifications
- **1.3.** Locations where this Document May Be Found

2. Contact Information
- **2.1.** Name of the Team
- **2.2.** Address
- **2.3.** Time Zone
- **2.4.** Telephone Number
- **2.5.** Facsimile Number
- **2.6.** Other Telecommunication
- **2.7.** Electronic Mail Address
- **2.8.** Public Keys and Encryption Information
- **2.9.** Team Members
- **2.10.** Other Information
- **2.11.** Points of Customer Contact

3. Charter
- **3.1.** Mission Statement
- **3.2.** Constituency
- **3.3.** Sponsorship and/or Affiliation
- **3.4.** Authority

4. Policies
    4.1. Types of Incidents and Level of Support
    4.2. Co-operation, Interaction and Disclosure of Information
    4.3. Communication and Authentication
5. Services
    5.1. Incident Response
        5.1.1. Incident Triage
        5.1.2. Incident Coordination
        5.1.3. Incident Resolution
        5.1.4. Proactive Activities
6. Incident Reporting Forms
7. Disclaimers

Effective policies are essential for any organization. The CSIRT's mission and charter should be based on organizational policies, especially information security policies. Establishing a team without having appropriate policies in place is ineffective and can put the team at odds with its own organization. Without formal policies on which to base computer emergency response activities, the team can have no legitimate basis for deciding on courses of action that support the organization. During an incident, CSIRT decisions can be unpopular. Disconnecting systems from the Internet could prevent some, or perhaps all, of the organization from carrying out its mission. Without established policies both to define and to defend those decisions, often the team is viewed as an adversary.

Without this clear definition of mission and an idea of what can be expected from the CSIRT, internal cooperation and support for the team will be difficult to obtain and even more difficult to sustain. Without internal cooperation, the team's effectiveness will be diminished, which could exacerbate the impact of an incident or prevent the team from handling an incident in a timely manner.

The overarching goal of responding to an incident should always be to prevent further damage and to restore systems and operations to normal as expeditiously as possible, consistent with organizational policies. The CSIRT members must have a clear sense of the strategic and operational priorities of the organization, just as members of business continuity and disaster recovery teams do. Without a clear idea of what the organization expects the team to accomplish, the team is likely to waste the limited time and resources it usually has available.

For more information on business continuity planning, see Chapter 58 in this *Handbook*; for discussion of disaster recovery, see Chapter 59.

56.2.2 Establishing Policies and Procedures. As the U.S. Government Defense Information Systems Agency (DISA) training course on CD-ROM about CSIRTs succinctly puts it, "policies and procedures are not merely bureaucratic red tape."[7] They are the scaffolding on which one can establish clear understanding and expectations for everyone involved in incident response. These living, evolving documents are (quoting the CD-ROM notes) tools that provide guidance on:

- Roles and responsibilities
- Priorities
- Escalation criteria
- Response provided
- Orientation

Policies are the statements of desired goals; procedures are the methods for attaining those goals. Policies tend to be global and relatively stable; procedures can and should be relatively specific, and can be adapted quickly to meet changing conditions and to integrate knowledge from experience. Policies cannot be promulgated without the approval and support of appropriate authorities in the organization, so one of the first steps is to identify those authorities. Another step is to gain their support for the policy project.

All policies and especially CSIRT policies should be framed in clear, simple language so that everyone can understand them, and they should be made available in electronic form. Hypertext can make policies more understandable by providing pop-up comments or explanations of difficult sections or technical terms. Similarly, procedures show how to implement the policies in real terms. For example, a policy might stipulate: "All relevant information about the time and details of a computer incident shall be recorded with regard for the requirements of later analysis, and for possible use in a legal proceeding." That policy might spawn a dozen procedures describing exactly how the information is to be recorded, named, stored, and maintained through a proper chain of custody. For example, one procedure might start: "Using the Incident-Report form in the CSIRT Database accessible to all CSIRT members, fill in every required field. Use the pull-down menus wherever possible in answering the questions." Again, as the DISA CD-ROM points out, these procedures should minimize ambiguity and should help members of the team to provide a consistent level of service to the organization. A glossary of local acronyms and technical terms can be helpful as part of these procedures.

Whenever policies and procedures are changed in a way that may affect users, it is important to let people know about the changes so that their expectations can be adjusted. The DISA course recommends using several channels of communications to ensure that everyone gets the message; for example, send email, use phone and phone messages, send broadcast voicemail, announce the changes at staff meetings, and use posters and Websites.

For more information on developing and promulgating security policies, see Chapters 44 and 50 in this *Handbook*.

56.2.3 Interaction with Outside Agencies and Other Resources. No CSIRT can operate in a vacuum in an interconnected world. At some point, teams and their sponsors will require interaction with outside agencies, and even with other CSIRTs. Rather than wait until an emergency is under way, the team should establish and document contacts such as:

Internal Contacts

- **Management.** The team should establish and maintain management contacts who hold sufficient authority to make the tough business decisions that will inevitably arise during an emergency situation.
- **Systems.** The CSIRT should have a working relationship with those responsible for operating and maintaining the organization's information systems. These contacts will be necessary to allow CSIRT members appropriate system access during an emergency response situation.
- **Applications.** As with systems personnel, the CSIRT should have preestablished contact with those who manage and maintain applications. These individuals will

be able to provide CSIRT members with access to application logs, documentation, and with access to accounts during an emergency.

- **Business units.** CSIRT members should be familiar with and have established contacts with the various organizational business units they support. Having such contacts ahead of time will facilitate decision making and will avoid delays in gaining access to appropriate business personnel during an emergency.

External Contacts

- **CERT/CC.** The CERT/CC can provide valuable advice and assistance to the response team during an attack. Knowing before an emergency whom to contact, and how to reach them, will speed the process.
- **Consultants.** Often, organizations will rely on outside consultants to augment technical skills and knowledge. Therefore, it is important that the organization be able to contact these consultants during an emergency, in the event their expertise is required to respond to or to resolve a situation. Planning for such emergency contact ahead of time will avoid delays in responding to an emergency.
- **Vendors.** Responding to an emergency may require specialized information about hardware or software features and about specifications that might be available only from a vendor. Additionally, backup systems or software may need to be acquired in order to return systems to operational status during or after an incident. As mentioned in Section 56.1.4 in this chapter, coordination with CSIRTs at vendors providing services in the cloud is also essential.
- **Law enforcement.** Law enforcement agencies today frequently have specialized units capable of assisting an organization in tracing and identifying the perpetrator of an attack. However, it is important that law enforcement contacts be made in advance so that the organization can make sound decisions about whom to notify and how best to use such assistance. For more information about coordinating with law enforcement, see Chapter 61 in this *Handbook.*
- **Utilities.** Electrical power and similar infrastructure services are essential to any organization. Power outages and similar emergencies can have a devastating effect on operations. Maintaining contact with local utilities will help the organization plan for and mitigate impact from power outages. In the event of an outage, team members will know whom to contact, and they can gather information about the cause and duration of an outage more quickly. For more information on business continuity, see Chapter 58 in this *Handbook.*
- **Internet service providers.** Typically, vital connectivity is provided to the organization by one or more Internet service providers (ISPs). In many cases, ISPs are the first line of defense against some types of Internet-originated attacks, such as distributed denial of service. In addition, if an organization is attempting to track a suspected intruder, the Internet service provider will be pivotal. It is therefore vitally important that the CSIRT have pre-established contacts within the organization's ISPs in order to avoid wasting precious response time trying to get assistance during an emergency.
- **Other CSIRTs.** Other CSIRTs may well have faced the situation or emergency that another team might be facing. Other CSIRTs can provide advice and assistance, and some may even share resources and expertise to help an organization respond to an emergency. There is also an opportunity to share knowledge and conduct joint training with other teams. Information Sharing and Analysis Centers (ISACs)

in the United States are an ideal forum for such collaboration, and the National Council of ISACs provides a central source of information for locating a local ISAC.[8]

56.2.4 Establish Baselines. To be able to spot that which is out of the ordinary, the CSIRT must determine what *normal* looks like. False incidents have occurred because the observer did not have adequate knowledge to realize that the event was actually normal. Emergency response teams called into action without well-documented baselines, or detailed activity logs, must work very hard to determine whether the event is normal.

In either case, whether the triggering event turns out to be false or genuine, resources and time will have been wasted by this identification effort. A good baseline can reduce the resources expended on false positives, and can hasten the response to real events.

56.3 SELECTING AND BUILDING THE TEAM.

An effective CSIRT comprises these elements, dictated by the incident at hand:

- People
- Skills
- Knowledge
- Equipment
- Access
- Authority

The makeup of the team has everything to do with how effective and responsive it will be in an emergency. Careful selection of team members at the outset will provide for an effective, cohesive group with the right skills, authority, and knowledge to deal properly with a range of known and unknown incidents.

Frequently, the first inclination is to select the most technically knowledgeable individuals available as members of the team. Although technical ability is essential to a CSIRT, this should not be the overriding characteristic. Given aptitude and motivation, appropriate technical skills can be learned. Indeed, during the course of an incident situation, adept handlers can draw on the technical expertise of people, either internal or outside, to augment their own skills and knowledge.

Maturity and the ability to work long hours under stress and intense pressure are crucial characteristics. Integrity in the response team members must be absolute, since these people will have access and authority exceeding that given them in normal operations.

Exceptionally good communications skills are required because, in an emergency, quick and accurate communications are needed. Inaccurate communications can cause the emergency to appear more serious than it is and therefore escalate a minor event into a crisis. Conversely, proper communications can galvanize others into immediate and effective activity, without creating a panic reaction.

56.3.1 Staffing. The CSIRT may be a permanent, full-time assignment for a fixed group of experts, or it may be a part time role formed dynamically as conditions require. In either case, or for any of the intermediate arrangements, certain fundamentals will dictate the choice of staff members.

The DISA course on CSIRT management also addresses the question of the technical level required by CSIRT staff. The course authors suggest using a scale from 1 to 10, with 1 representing the novice or support staff and 10 representing the technical wizard. Individuals in the 1-to-3 technical range should be sufficient to handle the initial triage process, which involves separating service request into categories, and directing them to the appropriate team member.

Information requests can be handled by team members in the 1-to-5 range. For example, a support staff person can send out publications, while someone with greater expertise would be required to address questions about identifying spoofed email.

Team members in the 5-to-8 technical range are necessary to respond to actual incidents. This response can involve technical analysis and communicating with compromised sites, with law enforcement technical staff, and with other CSIRTs. In handling incidents that represent new attack types, it may be necessary to call "wizards" to help understand and analyze the activity.

Vulnerability handling requires the most proficient personnel, falling into the 8-to-10 range. These individuals must be able to work with software vendors, CSIRTs, and other experts to identify and resolve vulnerabilities. Many CSIRTs do not have access to this level of technical expertise.

CSIRT staff with the psychological flexibility to allow them to adapt quickly to changing requirements will do better than people who resist change or resent ambiguity. Ideally, the team will include problem solvers with an intuitive grasp of the differences between observation and assumption, hypothesis, and deduction. As always, team players committed to getting the problem solved will contribute more than people interested in acquiring personal credit for achievements. Having at least one person on the team with a penchant for meticulous note taking is a real benefit (see Sections 56.4.5.2 and 56.5.6).

56.3.2 Involve Legal Staff. As with any crisis event, every action carries with it a potential legal implication. This is especially true in a situation where an evidentiary chain may be required. Even if evidence is not a primary concern, due diligence requires that accurate records be kept of the incident costs, including response team costs, and of the scope of compromise and effect.

The corporate legal staff must play an important role in developing response team procedures, in training the response team, and in crisis resolution.

56.4 PRINCIPLES UNDERLYING EFFECTIVE RESPONSE TO COMPUTER SECURITY INCIDENTS. Some general considerations underlie effectiveness for all incident-handling teams.

56.4.1 Baseline Assumptions. The primary consideration in responding to any emergency situation must be given to preventing loss of human life. Following that, a comprehensive information security program will have included the identification and classification of the most sensitive data and systems. This classification should provide a clear prioritization of what should be protected first, in the event of an emergency. For example, a business's survival might depend on the confidentiality and integrity of some intellectual property, such as engineering diagrams. After the safety of personnel, those drawings, and the systems on which they are stored, would be the obvious first priority for protection. A network intrusion that threatened an email server located on a separate network segment would likely not warrant immediately disconnecting the entire network from the Internet. If the particular server containing the company's engineering drawings, or the network segment on which it sits, were under direct attack, however, an appropriate first response might well be to disconnect from the Internet.

In any case, there must be an unambiguous sense among the CSIRT that those responsible for taking actions in good faith will not suffer reprisals as a result of taking those actions. For example, based on facts in evidence at one time or another, a member of the team might decide to disconnect an operational system from the Internet because it appears to be under attack or compromised. Should this turn out to be a false alarm of some sort, the individual authorizing the action should suffer no reprisal or sanction by taking what he or she believed was a legitimate action to stop, or to respond to, an attack.

With appropriate plans in place before incidents happen, recovery can be effected much more quickly and with less residual damage.

Appropriate responses depend on the systems involved, and should be documented and agreed to before those systems are connected to the Internet. If a router, or a firewall protecting the outer perimeter of the network, becomes compromised, it may be necessary to disconnect the entire system in order to contain the situation.

If a Web server in an isolated part of the network becomes compromised, though, disconnecting only that system should be sufficient. However, any business-related activities carried out using that server might no longer be available. A loss of revenue or image might result from disconnecting the server. Business units and others that depend on these systems must be made aware of, and must agree to accept, the impact of proposed responses the CSIRT might take during an incident.

Planned responses, combined with the authority and confidence to execute them, can save the organization both time and money. As an example, if every incident requires the presence of senior business managers or executives, those leaders must be taken away from their normal duties during rehearsals and during actual events. If the CSIRT leader on duty or on call finds the incident to be routine, and if the incident has been well planned for, a simple notification of the facts can be sent to appropriate senior-level personnel, leaving them free to attend to their normal duties and to participate only in a major event at their appropriate level of management.

Planned, preapproved responses can speed reaction times, enhance security, and lessen impact of a given breach or incident. In most cases, the CSIRT leader will follow a series of commonsense steps to handle an incident from identification through resolution. As the leader progresses through each step, he or she may choose from one of the preapproved responses to handle the incident, or the situation may require the involvement of other people and resources for resolution. In either case, the basic flow of events should be similar to this list:

- **Triage.** Deciding how to direct calls for help or reports of a computer security incident
- **Technical expertise.** Assembling the different kinds of knowledge required to support an effective response
- **Tracking incidents.** Ensuring appropriate documentation to save time and reduce errors
- **Critical information.** Laying the ground rules for collecting the kinds of data needed for effective decisions
- **Telephone hotline.** Establishing protocol for real-time notification and response

56.4.2 Triage. The word *triage* itself comes from a French root meaning *to sort.* In medicine, triage is "prioritization of patients for medical treatment: the process of prioritizing sick or injured people for treatment according to the seriousness of the condition or injury."[9] Similarly, anyone receiving calls about computer security incidents must be able to classify the call right away, so that the right resources can be called into play. As the DISA course on CSIRT management suggests:

> The triage process recognizes and separates
>
> - new incidents,
> - new information for ongoing incidents,
> - vulnerability reports,
> - information requests, [and]
> - other service requests.[10]

We have altered the order of the original list to reflect a decreasing rank of importance for these factors in communicating and acting on calls.

Triage is common to ordinary help desks as well as to emergency hotlines. In general, there are two models for staffing the phones for such front-line functions: the "dispatch" model and the "resolve" model.[11]

1. The *dispatcher* has just enough technical knowledge to collect appropriate information about an incident and to assign a team member for investigation; the alternative is to assign someone with more expertise to answer the phone so that response can be even faster.
2. However, the *resolve* model risks wasting resources because the more experienced staff member may end up doing largely clerical work instead of focusing on applying expertise to problem analysis and resolution.

To support triage, staff members need explicit training on data collection and priorities. They need to record: who is calling; how to reach that person; what the caller thinks is happening; what the caller has observed; how serious the consequences are; how many people or systems are affected; whether the incident is in progress or is over, as far as they know; and how the caller and others are responding. The CSIRT procedures should include guidance on assigning priorities to incidents; factors can include:

- Security classifications (e.g., SECRET or COMPANY CONFIDENTIAL data under attack)
- Type of problem (e.g., breach of confidentiality, data corruption, loss of control, loss of authenticity, degradation of availability or utility)
- Possible direct costs (e.g., personnel downtime, costs of recovery, or loss of business)
- Possible indirect costs (e.g., damage to business reputation or legal liability and so on), as appropriate for each organization

Readers may find the work of John Howard relevant for such analysis; Dr. Howard established a useful taxonomy for discussing computer security incidents that can serve as a framework for establishing priorities.[12] See Chapter 8 in this *Handbook.*

We recommend an automated system for capturing information on all calls to the CSIRT. Using keywords "helpdesk software" and also "help desk software" in an online search brings up dozens of options for such programs. Readers with modest skills in database design can also create their own using a program such as Microsoft Access, but it may take a good deal of time to improve the home-grown system so that it matches commercial or freeware versions based on extensive experience of the user community. However, with appropriate locking strategies to permit safe concurrent access and with well-designed automated reports, your CSIRT can know and control the priorities of all the open incidents under investigation at any time.

For more about management perspectives on triage, see Section 56.6.3.

56.4.3 Technical Expertise.

The DISA CD-ROM course starts by classifying technical expertise in approximate ranges:

- **Low**, suitable for the triage function which involves determining who should best handle a specific call
- **Medium**, appropriate for answering requests for information
- **High**, suitable for technical problem solving
- **Expert**, suitable for handling problems that others have been unable to resolve and especially for issues involving vulnerability analysis and real-time response to attacks

As the DISA writers point out, "Vulnerability handling requires your most proficient personnel.… These individuals must be able to work with software vendors, CIRTs, and other experts to identify and resolve vulnerabilities. Many CIRTs don't have access to this level of technical expertise."

56.4.4 Training.

Teams that have no experience responding to incidents are of little value to an organization. Predictably, computer emergency responses by untrained or inexperienced teams result in loss or destruction of evidence, legal exposure by failing to properly protect individual rights, and failure to properly document and learn from the experience. To be most effective, training must be iterative (learn, exercise, review, analyze, repeat) and should involve as many realistic scenarios as possible, so that the CSIRT becomes exposed to a wide variety of potential emergency situations.

56.4.4.1 Rehearse Often.

Experience can be gained only by responding to incidents or through training with simulated attacks. While the time and resources required to practice responding to incidents might be costly, more costly still is the potential damage resulting from an uncontained or poorly handled breach of the system.

An excellent opportunity to practice response procedures, and to develop response teams, occurs during periodic security assessments, including penetration testing. Penetration tests simulate external and internal attacks on a system and offer a real yet controlled environment in which to exercise, train, and evaluate a CSIRT. The simulation is especially effective when an outside, independent team is engaged to conduct the penetration test and security assessment. With proper coordination, the test can provide an opportunity for the team to observe, and react to, many different types of incidents.

56.4.4.2 *Perform Training Reviews.* At the conclusion of any training exercise, it is important to reassemble the team as soon as possible, not only to review management's view of its performance but to reveal its own perspectives as well. Each of the participants should be asked what went right and what went wrong. Were necessary resources (information, decision makers, tools, software, equipment) unavailable when the team needed them? Did the team have, or was it able to obtain in a timely manner, the physical and system access it needed? Did it have the right documentation and access to other company personnel? Were systems for communicating among the team and with other company or external personnel adequate and efficient?

Video cameras are a useful tool for recording events during the training sessions; many employees will have such equipment available and can make inexpensive recordings that can be analyzed during the training reviews.

See Section 56.7.1 on postmortem analysis of real incidents for more ideas that can be applied to training reviews.

56.4.5 Tracking Incidents. This section focuses on some of the advantages, requirements, and tools for incident tracking. First, we establish why documentation in general is so important.

56.4.5.1 *Will This Have to Be Done Again?* When one of the authors (MK) joined Hewlett-Packard (Canada) Ltd. in 1980, he arrived on the job armed with a small, green, hard-covered book prominently labeled LOGBOOK in big black letters. From his first day as a member of the systems engineering organization, he wrote down what he learned; he logged how he spent his time. When he met clients, he took notes. When he installed new versions of the MPE operating system, he kept a chronological record of everything he did—including mistakes. When he taught courses, he kept a list of questions he could not answer right away.

Pretty soon, people began asking him what he thought he was doing, writing a novel?

His colleagues may have been puzzled by what they perceived as a mania for record keeping, but he was equally astonished that record keeping was not a normal part of their way of doing work. The reason for automatically kept records was his years in scientific research, where logbooks with hard covers, numbered pages, and even waterproof paper were just usual parts of doing serious work. The idea of doing anything of importance without keeping a concurrent record simply did not occur to anyone in research. One could not reproduce an experiment without knowing exactly what sequence one had used in accomplishing the steps. Even adding salts to solutions had to be done in a particular order.

So he just kept on keeping his little green logbooks.

56.4.5.2 *Why Document?* Documentation, far from being a sterile exercise done to conform to arbitrary requirements of nameless, faceless superiors, should be a vital part of any intellectual exercise. Documentation is simply writing down what we learn: the crucial step in human history that changed traditional cultures into civilizations. By keeping a record independent of any specific individual, we liberate our colleagues and our successors from dependence on our physical availability. Documentation is our assurance that work will continue without us; a kind of immortality, if you will.

We document what we do as a part of systematic problem solving. Writing forces us to identify the problem in words, instead of being content to define it in vague, unclear ideas. Writing down each idea we are in the process of testing helps us notice the ideas we missed the first time we tackled the problem. Keeping notes helps us pay attention to what we are doing.

Documenting what we do also helps us during training—both our own and that of the people we are helping to learn technical skills. Trainees can review their own notes on how to do something instead of relying entirely on someone else's description. If taking notes is viewed as a chance to engage one's mind more thoroughly in what we are learning, it can be stimulating and even fun.

Finally, accurate records can be a boon in legal wrangles. In a case one of us (MK) experienced, upper management seriously considered legal procedures against a supplier for supposed breach of contract. Careful records of exactly when meetings were held, and with whom, permitted us to analyze the problem and to resolve the issues by collaboration instead of by confrontation. Such records, if kept consistently, in good times and bad, can be accepted in a court of law as evidence—but only if everything points to a steady pattern of record keeping as events unfold. Records made long after a problem occurs are worthless.

56.4.5.3 Keep Electronic Records. The best way of keeping records on specific problems is an easy-to-use database. Such records help team members remember and share information that can help in solving new problems as they arise. With easily accessible records, it is possible to solve problems without the presence of specific team members. Such shared knowledge speeds problem resolution, improves the competence of all team members with access to the knowledge base, and provides a sound basis for training and integration of new team members. Sharing knowledge can be a liberation for key members of any organization by sparing them from the sense of obligation to be present at all times; it also supports management policies that enforce security principles by requiring employees to take vacation time. For a discussion of the dangers of allowing any employee to become indispensable, see Chapter 45 in this *Handbook* on employment practices and policies.

56.4.5.4 Advantages for Technical Support and CSIRTs. Keeping track of all of technical support calls is essential for effective incident handling. Having details available to all members of the CSIRT in real time, and for research and analysis later, serves many functions:

- **Communication among team members.** Having the details written down in one place means that team members can pass a case from one to another and share data efficiently.
- **Better client service.** Callers become frustrated when they have to repeat the same information to several people in a row; a good incident-tracking system reduces that kind of irritation.
- **Documentation for effective problem solving.** A good base of documented experience can help find the right procedure and the right solution quickly.
- **Institutional memory.** When experience is written down and accessible, the organization's capacity to respond quickly and correctly to incidents improves over time.
- **Follow-up with clients.** Managers can use the incident database to prepare management reports and to follow-up with specific clients to understand and resolve difficulties or complaints.

- **Forensic evidence.** Detailed, accurate, and correctly time-stamped notes can be a deciding element in successful prosecution of malefactors.

56.4.5.5 Requirements. Some of the more obvious requirements of any incident-handling system are:

- A unique identifier for each case
- Dates and times for all events
- Who currently controls the case: It should be instantly obvious who is in charge of solving the problem
- Keywords
- Contact information: Every person in the case should be listed with office phone, cell phone, email, and fax numbers
- Handover of control: Whenever someone takes over control of the case, that handover should be noted in the record
- Technical details, including:
  - Diagnostics
  - Tests of hypotheses
- Resolution: What was the outcome? When was the case closed?
- Search facilities: Full-text search capabilities
- Knowledge base: Ability to integrate vendor-supplied entries to speed research
- Industry-standard database engine: Easy to learn, maintain, and improve
- Accept input from comma-separated value (CSV) files: Import data from other systems

56.4.5.6 Tools. There is a wide range of software available for tracking incidents. One can build one's own, but then proper documentation and training materials must also be created, because turnover is a constant problem for CSIRTs. In addition, unless analysts have experience with the CSIRT function, they are likely to miss useful features that have accumulated over the years in products used by thousands of people.[13] Well-respected open-source tools are listed in the "Further Reading" section of this chapter.

All such tools can be complex. To prevent people from fumbling about in an emergency, a budget must be established adequate for staff training in implementation of the selected tool.

56.4.5.7 Get the Global Picture. When gathering information about an incident, staff members should establish a clear picture of what people were doing when they realized that there was a problem. For example, it may be important to know that someone was accessing a rarely used account and noticed that a file was not available because someone else had it open. Those details will help to characterize the attack and to provide clues that may lead to additional valuable data. However, the CSIRT investigator should also ask why the contact was accessing the rarely used account; it takes only a minute, but getting a wider picture may give the analyst another perspective that can also lead to new clues. In the scenario just sketched, one could imagine that a system administrator had become curious about some unexpected resource utilization in a supposedly dormant account. This simple fact might lead to additional exploration of system log files and questions about whether any other dormant accounts had sparked curiosity. So, in general, it is worthwhile to explore the situation more broadly at first, rather than driving down the very first avenue that presents itself in the initial questions.

For more information on using log files for analysis of problems, see Chapter 53 in this *Handbook*.

56.4.5.8 Distinguish Observation from Assumption. As the CSIRT member listens to the observations of other staff members, it is critically important to distinguish facts—that is, personal observations—from assumptions. Assumptions are ideas taken for granted or statements that are accepted without proof. For example, imagine the serious consequences of hearing someone say, "And so then they must have exploited a flaw in the firewall and then they..." and simply writing that assumption down as if it were a tested and validated explanation of the events. Such an assumption could profoundly distort the investigation, putting people's efforts onto the wrong track and diverting their attention from a more fruitful line of inquiry. Hearing such a statement, one should write down, "And so perhaps they exploited a flaw in the firewall and..." or "Bob thinks that they exploited a flaw in the firewall and..."

56.4.5.9 Distinguish Observation from Hearsay. Everyone has played the child's game of whispering a sentence to another person and then hearing the distorted version that come out the other end of a long chain of transmission without error correction. CSIRT staff must always distinguish between first-person observations ("I read the log file and found...") and hearsay ("Shalama read the log file and she found..."). Team members should not trust hearsay: They must check it out themselves by tracking down the source of the information. Even when someone is reporting a personal observation to a CSIRT member, it is important to weigh the cost of verifying the observation (when possible) against the consequences of branching off into the wrong part of the solution space.

56.4.5.10 Distinguish Observation from Hypothesis. Sometimes when people are careless or untrained, they do not distinguish between what they *saw* and an idea that might *explain* what they saw. In the previous example about a supposed flaw in a firewall, the person speaking seemed to take the flaw for granted; that was an assumption. A similar problem can occur when someone thinks that *maybe* there is a flaw in the firewall and then proceeds as if that were true without testing the hypothesis. "And so maybe they exploited a flaw in the firewall, so we should patch all the holes right away." Putting aside for the moment the advisability of patching holes in firewalls, merely hypothesizing an exploit does not make it true. Maybe it is a good thing to patch the firewall, but it does not follow that it is the top priority right now simply from having thought of the idea. CSIRT staff should be careful to think about what they are hearing and should note explicitly when people are proposing explanations rather than reporting facts.

56.4.5.11 Challenge Hypotheses. When CSIRT members develop hypotheses about what is happening in a breach of security, they have to do two things: see if the ideas are consistent with observation but also test those ideas to see if they are flawed.

Trying to show that an idea is *correct* is a natural response when solving problems. Especially when the clock is ticking and a critical process is stopped, the immediate need is to get the system running immediately, no matter what it takes. Unfortunately, doing something and having the system work afterward does not automatically mean that the solution being proposed actually fixed the problem—that is the fallacy known as *post hoc, propter hoc* (after the fact, because of the fact). It is possible that what we think fixed the problem simply preceded a change of state related to some other factor. The supposed fix may have nothing to do with the solution or may be only part of the solution. Even under pressure, technical support teams with experience go beyond the immediate fix to see if there are other factors that need to be controlled for long-term stability of the system.

In analyzing the behavior of a compromised system, the CSIRT is usually less concerned with restart than with forensic analysis. Who did what to which parts of the system? What do the log files tell us about the incident? How could the attacker have gotten in? What might (s)he have changed?

For that kind of analysis, it is especially important to find ways of testing our ideas before we go down a long chain of reasoning that may be flawed at its very start. Thus, just as in quality assurance, try to come up with ways of showing that our explanation is *wrong*. If we fail to disprove a hypothesis using genuine, thoughtful, intelligent tests of our ideas, maybe we have got something useful after all. In practice, the principle teaches us to go a step further when solving problems. Instead of stopping the testing as soon as we find supportive evidence, we can make it a habit to ask "Yes, but what if... ?"[14]

56.4.6 Telephone Hotline. Users should be trained and encouraged to call the telephone hotline—usually the helpdesk line—to report anomalies or suspected breaches of security. The helpdesk operator can route the call to the appropriate persons, including the CSIRT monitor.

Returning for a moment to the advice on staffing the CSIRT as discussed in Section 56.3.1, there are some additional requirements for the people involved in the CSIRT concerning their interpersonal relations. Not only should managers look for, and ensure, adequate technical knowledge, they should also enhance interpersonal skills and disciplined work habits.

CSIRT members inevitably work with some users who are stressed by the problems they are facing. It is no help to have a technical wizard who so offends the users that they stop cooperating with the problem-resolution team. Sometimes CSIRT staff members forget that their job includes not only resolving a technical issue but also keeping the clients as happy as possible under the circumstances—and the use of the word "clients" is deliberate here.

Here are some of the most irritating responses to users we have run across in several decades of technical support and client support followed by our comments in brackets:

- "No one has ever complained about this before." [So what? If the problem is real, we should thank the user for reporting it, not make veiled criticisms that imply that the problem cannot be real.]
- "I don't have time for this now." [That is a time management problem for the CSIRT, not for the client. Take responsibility for getting the right person to take charge of the problem in real time.]
- "Why don't you try calling... ?" [Same comment as last one.]
- "That's not my problem." [Just plain rude as well as irresponsible.]

- "Why don't you reload the operating system and call me back if it happens again?" [Significant risk and time cost for the client; often the first-line suggestion of the terminally incompetent technician.]
- "Just format your hard disk and see if it happens again." [Even worse than the previous suggestion if it is just a casual suggestion to get the client off the phone for now.]
- "Don't get mad at me—I just work here." [A professional will understand that there is a difference between criticism directed at the organization or its procedures versus a direct *ad hominem* attack. The former should be taken seriously and passed on to people who can evaluate the seriousness of the criticism; the latter can be unacceptable and should be passed on to a manager who can explain to the user the need for and value of civility even under stress.]

56.5 RESPONDING TO COMPUTER EMERGENCIES.

This section offers specific recommendations and comments on a structured response plan to help develop a systematic approach to CSIRTs.

56.5.1 Observe and Evaluate.

A response team leader must assess the situation as quickly as possible based on available information. The leader should make a preliminary estimate of the type of incident, its scope, the people involved, and the data or systems affected, and then begin formulating first responses. This is the point at which the team leader or other responsible person orders a move from a state of standby monitoring to one of active monitoring, focused on the particular event or events. It is important to maintain standby and baseline monitoring activities during an actual incident, because the obvious event might well be a ruse designed to divert attention from a more serious attack.

If proper planning has taken place, the team leader usually will be able to direct a specific course of action in response to a particular incident. The leader can choose from a menu of planned responses while drawing on only those resources necessary to execute that particular response. Doing this minimizes the impact on staff at all levels and allows the incident to be dealt with efficiently and effectively. However, the more unique or complex the situation, the more likely it is that a complete team response may be required.

Responses, the players involved, and the audience are obviously different when considering a data center–type situation as opposed to a user-reported situation. Often, formal handling procedures are pre-established for data centers, which generally are staffed by more technical personnel. The CSIRT can expect a higher level of response from data center personnel and will likely be able to communicate instructions more concisely and with more assured compliance.

Dealing with individual users, however, requires a greater degree of sensitivity and understanding. In most cases, the CSIRT will be moving quickly and enthusiastically when handling an incident, since this is what the team has trained so long and hard to do. Individual users often are stressed or bewildered when confronted by a computer emergency incident serious enough to warrant a response team. In these situations, users tend to be nervous rather than excited or confident. This can cause communication problems, especially when a team member converses with users over a phone. Instructions become garbled, or may not be carried out exactly as desired.

Team members must be trained to communicate clearly and calmly when dealing with individual users who may not have exceptionally well-developed technical skills.

This is especially important when giving end users instructions over the phone or via some remote means. A calm, careful conversation will lessen the amount of stress the individual feels while helping to ensure that the CSIRT member's instructions are carried out properly. Proper compliance with instructions can make or break an incident investigation, especially when forensic issues are to be considered, as in the case of known or suspected criminal activity. Failure to maintain the state of an attacked system properly can thwart any subsequent attempt at a successful prosecution.

56.5.2 Begin Notification. Once the team leader establishes that an incident is in fact in progress, notification must begin to appropriate individuals within the organization, consistent with the type of situation. Notification and actions should be carried out, whenever possible, according to existing plans.

In some cases, the CSIRT leader might be able to identify the incident as one calling for a prearranged response. The leader, having the authority and confidence to carry out such a preapproved response, will notify those appropriate to the incident and carry out the contemplated actions. In other cases, the situation might not be so clear, and the notification process might include additional personnel with authority to decide on various courses of action.

56.5.3 Set Up Communications. Team members, especially when dealing with remote or multiple sites, must be able to communicate easily and securely with one another as well as with management representatives. Team members need to be able to communicate data, status updates, actions, responses, and similar events. Communications should flow securely to the designated CSIRT leader for coordination. The team leader must be able to direct and advise other team members, but the potentially sensitive nature of an incident may require that these communications be handled out of band and through secure means. "Out of band" in this case refers to communication methods that are neither part of nor connected to the system believed to be under attack. For example, in communications regarding an attack, the use of unencrypted email that might be intercepted by an attacker, or by other unauthorized parties, should be avoided whenever possible.

56.5.4 Contain. The CSIRT's next course of action is to contain the incident. The goal is to limit the scope of any compromise as much as possible, by isolating the system under attack from other systems in order to prevent the problem, attack, or intrusion from spreading. Containment might involve steps such as disconnecting systems from the Internet. However, doing so might limit the organization's ability to catch an intruder who is currently active on the system. The priority level assigned to intruder identification and prosecution is a part of the mission and charter of the team, modified by the specific action plans in use for a particular incident.

56.5.5 Identify. Once the team has taken steps to contain the incident as much as possible, it should focus on identifying exactly what happened, why it happened, and how it happened, and then identify steps that can be taken to prevent a recurrence. This effort also might involve identifying who, if anyone, was or still is involved in the incident or attack.

56.5.6 Record. As discussed in Section 56.4.5 above, all CSIRT members should be trained to document everything during an incident. No relevant event or detail is too small to record when responding to computer emergencies. Always try to answer

"Who? What? Where? How? When? Why?" This is especially true when dealing with criminal activity, when there is the possibility or even an expectation that the intruder will be prosecuted. Keeping accurate records of what happened and the team's actions can prove pivotal in the organization's ability to identify positively the cause or source of an incident and to prevent similar incidents in the future.

In the case of criminal activity, with an expectation of prosecution, a legal representative should be kept informed so that appropriate forensic measures may be ordered at appropriate times and to avoid contaminating evidence through improper collection, storage, and analysis.

56.5.7 Return to Operations. For most business managers and executives, restoring operations is of paramount importance. Frequently, they will pressure the EDP people and the CSIRT to put off all other activities and to direct all resources to that end. Except in extreme cases, that pressure should be resisted, and the orderly carrying out of all preceding steps must be assured. As soon as possible, the CSIRT should assist operations personnel with bringing systems back online and returning them to full operating capacity. In some cases, hard drives, logs, and even entire systems may need to remain off-line until detailed forensics examinations can be completed. In these situations, backup systems should be used to bring systems and operating capabilities back online.

See Chapter 57 in this *Handbook* for a discussion of backups and Chapters 58 and 59 for extensive information about business continuity and disaster recovery.

56.5.8 Document and Review. While all CSIRT members should keep careful notes at all times, it is important to remember that formal procedures to document incidents and resulting actions are vital to the overall success of the incident response effort. This documentation can form the basis for new approaches, procedures, policies, awareness programs, and similar changes. Documenting successes and failures can provide the organization with a realistic view of its security posture and of its capability to respond to emergencies, and in some cases can justify the expenditure of additional funds on training or technology. This effort also ensures that the data captured can be used by the CSIRT to learn and to sharpen skills.

56.5.9 Involving Law Enforcement. The decision to involve law enforcement, or even when to involve law enforcement, in an incident response is one that must be given careful consideration. Although most organizations recognize the benefit of a close relationship with law enforcement, involving such agencies when responding to a computer emergency can have consequences beyond those that are immediately evident.

Clearly, local and national law enforcement agencies have a great deal to offer when establishing CSIRTs and developing incident handling capabilities. It is not uncommon these days to find that many law enforcement agencies have specialized units dedicated to computer crimes and issues. They can be a valuable resource, likely to have a wealth of threat data on hand. For this reason, it is important to partner with appropriate agencies to take advantage of their experience and to establish relationships. Knowing whom to contact in an emergency not only will save time and frustration, but may mean the difference between merely repelling an attack or catching and successfully prosecuting the perpetrator, which could help prevent future attacks.

Local laws and statutes may dictate specific notification requirements that an organization is obliged to follow in the event an actual or suspected incident occurs. Careful review of local laws, statutes, and ordinances should be undertaken to ensure that the organization complies with notification requirements and other legal requirements.

When there is a choice to be made, the organization must weigh carefully the decision to involve law enforcement, and especially the question of when to do so. In most cases, formally involving law enforcement means that the organization may have to turn control of the incident and subsequent investigation over to the agency whose jurisdiction it is to investigate the crime.

While most professional law enforcement agencies will work with an organization to minimize any adverse impact on normal operations, this may not always be feasible. Because the goals of law enforcement often are different from those of others, especially of commercial enterprises, law enforcement agencies may not consider the impact of their response on the organization under attack.

Since law enforcement's mission is to investigate criminal activity, its focus will naturally be on identifying, tracking, and locating the intruder. This can, in some cases, result in seizure and removal for forensic purposes of systems and data, even systems that may be critical to the continued operation of the organization. In the case of a business, this might well mean the loss of necessary servers or workstations while an investigation is under way, with a possibly devastating effect.

Indeed, decisions about a preferred response may be taken out of the hands of managers and executives when law enforcement enters into an incident response situation. A commercial business might focus on identifying the vulnerability that made the attack possible, protecting against that vulnerability, and restoring systems to full operating capability. If, during the course of these efforts, the perpetrator can be identified, law enforcement will be informed, but such identification is rarely the overriding objective of the business. For law enforcement, however, identification and prosecution of the perpetrator is the primary objective. Establishing contact with appropriate law enforcement agencies before the organization is forced to respond to an incident will help the CSIRT plan when to notify law enforcement and how most effectively to align both sets of objectives when dealing with an incident.

For more details of working with law enforcement agencies and personnel, see Chapter 61 in this *Handbook*. For additional discussion of data collection for forensic applications, see Section 56.6.9 in this chapter.

56.5.10 Need to Know. Protecting information about an incident in progress is essential, not only to a successful response but because it can have serious legal, privacy, and other ramifications as well. Those charged with handling an incident must use out-of-band communications, such as cellular telephones, pagers, and encrypted email systems not connected to the system under attack, to ensure that knowledge of the incident is restricted to those who need to know about it. Attackers could intercept team communications if passed through in-band or normal channels and use that information to cover their tracks or even to prolong an incident.

Responding to incidents always involves gathering information about systems, users, activities, and events. In most cases, sensitive system and even personal information may be collected. During the course of their response and investigation, members of the team frequently make assumptions about the identities of those responsible for the incident, These assumptions are based on data that are continually being collected, refined, modified, and frequently changed during the course of an emergency response. Should an unproven or interim assumption that a particular individual was involved in the incident be made public, that individual's reputation might become needlessly tarnished, and the organization might well find itself facing legal proceedings as a result.

It is therefore essential that the CSIRT disseminate information about the incident according to a strict need-to-know policy. Limiting knowledge about an incident will help ensure that sensitive information remains in the hands of those who need it to perform their duties.

56.6 MANAGING THE CSIRT.

All the work that goes into creating a CSIRT can be wasted if managers fail to lead. Sloppy management can result in degraded performance, alienation of the client base, staff frustration, sabotage, and employee turnover. Management plays a key role in the formation, operation, and support of a CSIRT. Ideally, teams should be composed not only of technical personnel, but also of managers with sufficient authority to assist the team in taking actions that contain an incident and that protect data and systems from further compromise. Outside of incident handling, management support for planning, establishing and enforcing policies, and preauthorizing responses is essential. Most important is management support of the CSIRT. Without solid backing from the highest levels of management, the CSIRT will be frustrated in its attempts to carry out its mission.

56.6.1 Professionalism.

The DISA course wisely emphasizes the importance of professional behavior by all members of the CSIRT. The authors write:

> The survival of your CIRT may well depend upon using a Code of Conduct, which will earn the trust and respect of the commands you support. The conduct of any single team member reflects upon the entire CIRT organization. If the commands don't trust your CIRT, they won't report to you. It is important, therefore, not only to have a Code of Conduct, but also to shake it out and dust it off every once in a while. Remind team members what it is and why it is important… and use it.[15]

Here are some of the practical recommendations from that course (although we have put them in our own words for the most part):

- Write down the rules—a code of conduct—that represent your ideals of courteous, professional service to your clients.
- Train the team to understand and apply the code.
- Review the code periodically with the team.
- Speak clearly and avoid technobabble.
- Tell people exactly what you intend to do.
- Never hesitate to say "I don't know—but I'll find out."
- Do not criticize other people in your interactions with clients.
- Respect the confidentiality of your clients.
- Be respectful of your callers; do not belittle them or make them feel bad.

Notice how consistently we refer to clients; this usage emphasizes that both technical support teams and CSIRTs all perceive users as people to whom we owe service. There is no benefit to allowing an adversarial relationship between the technical support team or a CSIRT and the client base. Managers must not allow a gulf to develop between the CSIRT and the client community; leaders should clamp down on disparaging terms and derogatory comments about users. Team members must understand why such language is harmful.

Managers should identify CSIRT members with a chip on their shoulder; they must not adopt defensive, arrogant, or aggressive attitudes toward the users. If a computer security incident can be traced to procedural errors (i.e., the procedures themselves rather than user error are causing problems), the person reporting the problem should be thanked for the information, not criticized for having experienced or identified the problem.

No one in a CSIRT has ever regretted being professional.

56.6.2 Setting the Rules for Triage. As we mentioned in Section 56.4.2, *triage* in French means *sorting*. The same concept has been applied to helpdesks. For example, the "Helpdesk triage policy" from Courtesy Computers illustrates how a helpdesk team can categorize problems to ensure that important issues receive faster service than less important problems.[16] Importance is defined in terms of the number of users affected, the effects on mission-critical functions, and the costs of downtime or of less-than-optimal functions. The five priority levels suggested in the document are typical of the kind of triage categories established in many helpdesk departments (adapted from a table in the Courtesy Computers document):

Priority 1

- Issues of the highest importance; mission-critical systems with a direct impact on the organization (Examples: widespread network outage, payroll system, sales system, telecom system, etc.)
- Contact: Immediate–5 minutes
- Resolution: 30 minutes

Priority 2

- Single-user or group outage that is preventing the affected user(s) from working (Examples: failed hard drive, broken monitor, continuous OS lockups, etc.)
- Contact: 15 minutes
- Resolution: 1 hour

Priority 3

- Single-user or group outage that can be permanently or temporarily solved with a workaround (Examples: malfunctioning printer, synchronization problem, PC sound problem, etc.)
- Contact: 30 minutes
- Resolution: Same day

Priority 4

- Scheduled work (Examples: new workstation installation, new equipment/software order, new hardware/software installation)
- Contact: 1 hour
- Resolution: 1–4 days

Priority 5

- Nonessential scheduled work (Examples: office moves, telephone moves, equipment loaners, scheduled events)

- Contact: Same day
- Resolution: 5 days

The particular structure and specific timelines are merely examples, not blanket recommendations. Every organization must determine its own version of such a table.

In his helpful overview, "CIRT—Framework and Models," Ajoy Kumar summarizes the functions of triage in this way:

> Triage: The actions taken to categorize, prioritize, and assign incidents and events. It includes the following sub-processes:

- Categorize events.
- Correlate various events. Personnel involved in such teams typically also belong to Forensic teams.
- Prioritize events.
- Assign events for handling and response.
- Communicate information to "Respond" process for further handling.
- Re-assign (and close) events not belonging to CIRT.[17]

The DISA training materials suggest three broader categories of interactions with helpdesks and CSIRTs: "incidents, vulnerabilities, and information requests."[18]

1. *Incidents* involve breaches of security
2. *Vulnerabilities* include reports of security weaknesses (and may be reported as part of an incident)
3. *Information requests* often are managed using lists of frequently asked questions (FAQs).

The DISA instructors go on to define factors that can help CSIRTs prioritize incidents:

- The sensitivity and/or criticality of the data affected
- The amount of data affected
- Which host machines are involved
- Where and under what conditions the incident occurred
- Effects of the incident on mission accomplishment
- Whether the incident is likely to result in media coverage
- Number of users affected
- Possible relationships to other incidents currently being investigated
- The nature of the attack
- Economic impact and time lost
- Number of times the problem has recurred
- Who reports the incident[19]

On this last point, the DISA writers point out that the organizational rank of someone calling in an incident *may* bear on its priority—but that it may be wise to cross-check the report with a security expert who can speak to whether the report is sound. Sometimes a high-level manager's sense of urgency may be rooted more in his sense of self-importance than in operational requirements.

In summary, it is important to establish a sound basis for staff members of the CSIRT to carry out triage effectively. Once the rules for evaluating incidents have been clarified, staff members should practice analyzing a number of cases to train themselves in applying the rules consistently. Role-playing exercises, based on historical records or on made-up examples, can provide an excellent and enjoyable mechanism for staff members to establish a common standard for this difficult and sensitive task.

For additional ideas on using ideas and lessons from social psychology in managing security personnel, see Chapter 50 in this *Handbook*.

56.6.3 Triage, Process, and Social Engineering. Sometimes staff (or even managers) question the value of strict adherence to policy. Policy is sometimes seen as the expression of unnecessary rigidity—an inability to respond quickly to changing or unexpected circumstances. However, in CSIRT management, knowing and adhering to well-thought-out policies and following a reliable process are particularly valuable, not only for information gathering, data recording, and analysis, but also to maintain strict security.

One of the well-known tricks used by criminal hackers and spies is to simulate urgency that supports demands for violations of normal security restrictions. For example, criminals will call a relatively low-status employee, such as a secretary, and pressure him into violating standard protocols to obtain the password of his boss by claiming extreme circumstances of great urgency. The criminal may escalate the pressure to outright bullying by threatening the employee with punishment.

A criminal determined to penetrate security barriers can manufacture an incident that leads to involvement of the CSIRT. Allowing such a person to apply pressure for violations of protocol is an invitation to compromise. Worse, such deviations from well-tried and well-justified procedures can add to the embarrassment caused by the compromise; it is bad enough to have someone breaking through our security without having to admit that we helped.

For additional information on social engineering, see Chapters 19 and 20 in this *Handbook*.

56.6.4 Avoiding Burnout. Much of the discussion that follows applies equally to CSIRTs and to helpdesks; in a sense, one can view the CSIRT as a specialized helpdesk. Many CSIRTs are specialized subsets of the helpdesk team.

Any organization, even one with a relatively small CSIRT or a small helpdesk, can suffer spikes in demand. Ordinary business cycles can influence network usage; for example, universities often see perfectly normal but large increases in call volumes at registration times as new students forget their passwords, try to connect unverified laptops to the university network, or get blocked for violating appropriate-use policies. At any site, a denial-of-service attack, a plague of computer virus infections, or an infestation of computer worms can cause a flood of calls.

Another trend is the ironic observation that the better a CSIRT (or helpdesk team, although the focus will continue on CSIRTs) becomes at handling problems, the more readily members of its community will turn to it to report problems or ask for help.

Thus, the better the CSIRT does its job, the heavier its workload can become, at least for a while. According to the DISA course:

> As a new CSIRT grows and the workload increases, and especially on those teams that provide 24-hour emergency response, burnout becomes quite common. By studying the issue, one national CSIRT determined that a full-time team member could comfortably handle one new incident per day, with 20 incidents still open and actively being investigated.[20]

Staff members who face increasing workloads may become stressed. Working long periods of overtime, missing time with family and friends, perhaps even missing regular exercise and food—these factors may lead to increased errors and turnover if people are forced to accept increasingly demanding conditions for long periods.

One of the most valuable organizational approaches to preventing burnout is to rotate staff from the IT group through the CSIRT function on a predictable schedule. For example, one can assign people to the CSIRT for three- or six-month rotations.

Such rotations require especially good training programs and particularly good documentation, to maintain efficiency as new people come on duty; in addition, the assignments must be staggered so that the CSIRT does not have to cope with large numbers of newcomers all at once. Ideally, there would not be more than one switch of personnel a week.

How should existing assignments be transferred within the CSIRT? *Difficult* existing cases should be transferred to staff members who have been on duty for a few weeks, not to the incoming staff member (even one with experience on the CSIRT). The incoming CSIRT member should be given a chance to get into (or get back into) the rhythm of the job before being hit with the most intractable problem or the most ornery client.

Every incident must have a case coordinator—the person who monitors the problem, aggregates information from varied resources, and serves as the voice of the CSIRT for that incident. When transferring responsibility for a case from one case coordinator to another, managers should ensure that the previous coordinator prepares clients for the transition and introduces the new coordinator to the key client contacts to ensure a smooth transition of control. Clients often come to depend on the person they have been working with to resolve an incident; an unexpected change can be unsettling and disturbing.

56.6.5 Many Types of Productive Work. The DISA course writers suggest:

> Allow team members to allocate time away from high stress incident response assignments and pursue broader interests in areas such as tool development, public education and presentations, research, and other professional opportunities.[21]

CSIRT members, by the nature of their work, will have a great deal to contribute to the awareness, training, and education of their colleagues.

In the technical support group for Hewlett-Packard Canada in the 1980s, managers exercised great care in preventing consistent overwork. In emergencies, employees all pitched in—including managers—to resolve the problem for clients; however, the policy on allocation of time was strictly enforced under normal circumstances. Everyone kept careful records of time worked—a habit everyone can usefully follow—so that managers could analyze where the burden was distributed, and to provide statistical information for load balancing and personnel planning. Employees who violated the policy that no more than 70 percent of their time in the system engineering group should be spent on billable hours were warned to ease off; the rationale was that it was *necessary* to maintain constant training and time for administration and just for thinking, to ensure long-term productivity of their specialists.

56.6.6 Setting an Example. The behavior of managers can greatly influence morale, motivation, and dedication among team members. For example, supervisors and upper managers can greatly motivate staff by pitching in to support them during emergencies or extraordinary demands, even if only by their presence. Making the CSIRT a stimulating and enjoyable duty that people *want* to be on is one of the best approaches to avoiding burnout and ensuring reliable response to computer-related problems.

56.6.7 Notes on Shiftwork. As discussed in Section 56.6.4, rotating assignments among CSIRT members can be an excellent idea. However, frequent changes in work schedules that involve changes in sleep cycles are *not* a good idea; for example, weekly changes in shift from day to night schedules can seriously disrupt the natural circadian wake/sleep cycle and have been shown to increase the rate of errors and accidents.[22] One authoritative resource states that there are "adverse health and safety effects to working shifts[:]"

> A shiftworker, particularly one who works nights, must function on a schedule that is not natural. Constantly changing schedules can:
>
> - upset one's circadian rhythm (24-hour body cycle),
> - cause sleep deprivation and disorders of the gastrointestinal and cardiovascular systems,
> - make existing disorders worse, and
> - disrupt family and social life.[23]

Scientific studies throughout the world have long shown that shiftwork, by its very nature, is a major factor in the health and safety of workers; LaDou writes in his abstract:

> Daily physiologic variations termed *circadian rhythms* are interactive and require a high degree of phase relationship to produce subjective feelings of wellbeing. Disturbance of these activities, circadian desynchronization, whether from passage over time zones or from shift rotation, results in health effects such as disturbance of the quantity and quality of sleep, disturbance of gastrointestinal and other organ system activities, and aggravation of diseases such as diabetes mellitus, epilepsy, and thyrotoxicosis.[24]

The U.S. National Institute for Occupational Safety and Health has published a monograph about shiftwork that contains this advice for improving shiftwork schedules:

- Avoid permanent (fixed or nonrotating) night shift
- Keep consecutive night shifts to a minimum
- Avoid frequent shift changes—provide enough stability to let employees adapt to their schedule
- Plan some free weekends

- Avoid several long days of work followed by four- to seven-day "mini-vacations"—such schedules are stressful because of the radical shifts of diurnal cycles in the two phases
- Keep long work shifts and overtime to a minimum
- Consider different lengths for shifts
- Examine start-end times to fit in better with life in the external world; for example, making it possible for parents on night shift to see their children before they leave for school
- Keep the schedule regular and predictable
- Examine rest breaks[25]

56.6.8 Role of Public Affairs. The nature of interconnected systems today—as well as some employees' practice of blurting out confidential information on their social-networking pages—all but guarantees that any incident will become obvious to partners, customers, clients, and others, including even the press. In many cases, the organization will be compelled to advise its constituents continuously of the status of any outage or degradation of services resulting from an incident, and the causes behind it. Therefore, it is crucial that information released for general consumption be properly screened and cleared prior to release.

It is equally important that such information be released through a single source, such as the public affairs office. Restricting release of incident-related information through the public affairs office, or other designated point, will help ensure that frequent, straightforward communications with stakeholders can take place, while at the same time controlling rumors and misinformation. This simple step can do much to lessen anxiety about an incident and to reassure members, partners, and customers that the situation is well in hand and will be resolved.

56.6.9 Importance of Forensic Awareness. As implied in Section 56.5.9, depending on the specific incident, the organization may desire not only to control the incident but also to trace and prosecute the perpetrators in the case of known or suspected criminal activity. It is therefore highly advisable that members of the CSIRT receive thorough training in procedures for collecting and preserving evidence. Mishandling of evidence can result in an inability to take successful legal action against an attacker or to recover damages following an incident. Computer forensics and evidence handling should be high on the CSIRT's list of training topics. Chapters 2 and 61 of this *Handbook* contain additional material on computer forensics and working with law enforcement.

56.7 POSTINCIDENT ACTIVITIES.

One of the most important principles of management in general, and operations management in particular, is that fixing a problem has two aspects: the short term and the long term. One must be able to solve problems quickly enough to be effective; that is, the speed of solution must be appropriate to the consequential costs of delay. However, we should not figuratively wipe our hands in satisfaction and walk away from a problem resolution without thinking about why it happened, how we fixed it, and whether we can do better to avoid repeats and to improve our response.[26]

The CSIRT's efforts do not end once the incident is resolved. Instead, the team should take a reasonable period to rest and recover. Then, while the details are still fresh in the team members' minds, they should examine the incident from start to finish, both formally and informally, asking questions such as "What happened? What went right? What went wrong?" This way, the team will learn from each incident and become more efficient and confident when handling new incidents in the future.

At the conclusion of each incident, the team should be assembled, and a formal debriefing and review of the incident should be carried out. This debriefing should include a complete review of the team and its handling of the incident, including its adherence to policy and its technical performance. Each team member should be individually debriefed following the incident. Their recollections, thoughts, ideas, and reactions as to how the incident was handled and how the team performed, should be documented and preserved. A management team might debrief members, and team members might debrief each other, or they might even debrief themselves using a checklist or form. Regardless of the method, the CSIRT members themselves are the best source of data about the weaknesses and strengths of the team, and that data must be captured if the team is to improve and grow in skills and confidence.

Once individual impressions are captured, it is often effective to assemble the team as a group for an incident postmortem session. Starting from the beginning of the incident, the team should examine whether it had adequate, workable policies on which to base its actions and decisions. The group should jointly evaluate each aspect of the team, its composition, skills, authority, and step-by-step handling of the incident. A list of lessons learned and action items for improvements should result from this review.

Data collected during this review process should form the basis for improving the team. This information provides input to what should be a continuous cycle involving planning, preparation, training, responding, and evaluating. Shortfalls in training, skills, equipment, access, policies, and authority will become evident through this process. These shortfalls can be corrected to improve the team's ability to respond effectively to incidents in the future.

The next sections provide additional insights into how to learn from the CSIRT's experiences.

56.7.1 Postmortem. As a matter of standard operating procedure, every technical support person and the CSIRT must schedule time to analyze the underlying factors that led to the problem they have just resolved. This analysis will likely involve operational staff outside the CSIRT; these are the people with line expertise who will be able to contribute their intimate knowledge of technical details that contributed to this security breach. These discussions can often lead to practical recommendations for improvement of the security architecture, such as its topology or firewall placement, operational procedures such as monitoring standards or vulnerability patching, and technical details such as configurations or parameter settings.

Similarly, it is a commonplace in discussions of disaster recovery and business continuity planning that every practice run, or real-life incident, should be analyzed to see where we have made errors or achieved less than our goals in performance. Managers must ensure that these analyses are not perceived as (or worse, really are) finger-pointing exercises for apportioning blame. In a column for *Network World*, M. E. Kabay has explained the concepts of *egoless work*; the postmortem analysis of an incident must be ego-free.[27] Managers can set the tone by responding positively to what might otherwise be perceived as criticism; "That's a good point" and "Very good observation" are examples of positive, encouraging responses to observations such as "We were too slow in getting back to the initial caller given that she clearly stated that the entire department was off-line." The meeting should focus on ways to improve the response, given the insights resulting from detailed analysis of successes and failures during an incident.

The other aspect that sometimes gets lost in such postmortems is exploring the reasons for the problems. If we do not pay attention to underlying causes, we may fix specific problems, and we may improve particular procedures, but we will likely encounter different consequences of the same fundamental errors that caused those particular problems. We must pursue the analysis deeply in order to identify structural flaws in our processes, so that we can correct those problems and thus reduce the likelihood of entire classes of problems.

The U.S. National Institute of Standards and Technology *Computer Security Incident Handling Guide* specifically recommends a postincident analysis in Section 3.4. We quote the authors' list of suggested questions verbatim:

- Exactly what happened, and at what times?
- How well did staff and management perform in dealing with the incident? Were the documented procedures followed? Were they adequate?
- What information was needed sooner?
- Were any steps or actions taken that might have inhibited the recovery?
- What would the staff and management do differently the next time a similar incident occurs?
- What corrective actions can prevent similar incidents in the future?
- What additional tools or resources are needed to detect, analyze, and mitigate future incidents?[28]

The authors also recommend these actions (paraphrasing and summarizing):

- Invite people to the postmortem with an eye to increasing cooperation throughout the organization.
- Plan the agenda by polling participants before the meeting.
- Use experienced moderators.
- Be sure the meeting rules are clear to everyone to avoid confusion and conflict.
- Keep a written record of the discussions, conclusions, and action items.

On this last point, we add that all action items should indicate clearly who intends to deliver precisely what operational result, to whom, in which form, and by when.

56.7.2 Continuous Process Improvement: Sharing Knowledge within the Organization. On page 3-23 of the *Computer Security Incident Handling Guide*, the authors make a series of recommendations on how to capitalize on the knowledge gained through systematic analysis of incidents.[29] We are commenting briefly on each of their suggestions (which are shown in quotation marks).

- "Reports from these meetings are good material for training new team members by showing them how more experienced team members respond to incidents." The incident reports that were used for discussion in the analytic meetings should be made available, perhaps as appendices, in a single report document so that all of the information about a specific incident or series of incidents can be accessed at one time. In what follows, such a dossier is referred to as the *follow-up report*.

- "Another important postincident activity is creating a follow-up report for each incident, which can be quite valuable for future use." The general principle is that without documentation, we lose the opportunity for increasing institutional knowledge. If we do not record what we have learned, transmission depends on luck: the haphazard contacts of people who need to know something with those who can help. Without documentation and efficient indexing, information transferred becomes an inefficient, random process of querying and guesswork. Informal knowledge sometimes remains limited to a few people or even a single individual; without these key resources, the information is unavailable. If the holders of undocumented information leave the organization, their knowledge is usually lost to the group.
- "First, the report provides a reference that can be used to assist in handling similar incidents." Why waste time reinventing solutions that have already been found? Why make the same errors and cause the same problems that have already been located and that could be avoided?
- "Creating a formal chronology of events (including time-stamped information such as log data from systems) is important for legal reasons, as is creating a monetary estimate of the amount of damage the incident caused in terms of any loss of software and files, hardware damage, and staffing costs (including restoring services)." One of the most important kinds of information for managing security is the cost estimate. Rational allocation of resources depends on knowing how often problems occur, and how much they cost, so that we can spend appropriate amounts of money for equipment, and for the time of our employees and consultants to prevent such problems.
- "This estimate may become the basis for subsequent prosecution activity by entities such as the U.S. Attorney General's office." Estimates of monetary consequences are also essential for civil torts in the calculation of restitution.
- "Follow-up reports should be kept for a period of time as specified in record retention policies." As the *Guide*'s authors discuss in their section 3.4.2, historical records become increasingly useful as they provide a statistical base for analyzing and predicting phenomena. The costs of saving such data (which have relatively small volumes) have dropped to virtually nothing given the huge digital storage capacities of today's archival media, and their extremely low cost.

56.7.3 Sharing Knowledge with the Security Community. One of the most valuable contributions we can make to each other is information sharing. The Computer Emergency Response Team Coordination Center (CERT/CC) offers an overview of why and how to report security incidents in its *Handbook for Computer Security Incident Response Teams*.[30] The CSIRT experts summarize the types of activity on which they would appreciate receiving reports; reasons for reporting security incidents; the variety of people and agencies who can benefit from such reports; extensive guidelines on what to include in the reports; and how to reach the CERT/CC securely.

The section "Why should I report an incident?" has these headers (and a paragraph or so of explanation of each point):

- You may receive technical assistance.
- We may be able to associate activity with other incidents.
- Your report will allow us to provide better incident statistics.
- Contacting others raises security awareness.
- Your report helps us to provide you with better documents.
- Your organization's policies may require you to report the activity.
- Reporting incidents is part of being a responsible site on the Internet.

Another way of contributing to the field is to speak at conferences. For example, the Forum of Incident Response and Security Teams (FIRST) organizes conferences, technical colloquia, and workshops.[31] The conferences are open to all, not just members of FIRST, and organizers want participants to:

- Learn the latest security strategies in incident management
- Increase their knowledge and technical insight about security problems and their solutions
- Keep up-to-date with the latest incident response and prevention techniques
- Gain insight on analyzing network vulnerabilities
- Hear how the industry experts manage their security issues
- Interact and network with colleagues from around the world to exchange ideas and advice on incident management best practices

Readers should think about contributing papers to such conferences. Anyone who has spoken at technical conferences will confirm that there is no better way to solidify one's expertise than marshaling information into a clear presentation and speaking before one's peers. Feedback from interested participants can improve not only the current presentation but also the process being described. Intelligent, enthusiastic interchange among practitioners of goodwill with varied experiences, and from different environments, is not only productive of new ideas, it is immense fun.

The FIRST event includes "Lightning Talks" which are described as "short presentations or speeches by any attendee on any topic, which can be scheduled into conference proceedings with the approval of the organisers." Participants with hot news can thus present their findings or their ideas without necessarily having to prepare a long lecture or submitting their work many months in advance.

Other conferences, such as those organized by the Computer Security Institute (CSI),[32] MIS Training Institute (MISTI),[33] and RSA Security,[34] among many others, usually offer opportunities for discussions of CSIRT management. Readers, if they can, should take advantage of these opportunities by registering for the calls for participation (CFPs) and responding to one or two a year.

56.8 CONCLUDING REMARKS. CSIRTs are an effective organizational tool for responding to computer emergencies. However, to be effective, these teams must be carefully planned, built, trained, and supported. Proper planning and the establishment of a clear set of organizational objectives for the CSIRT are key to ensuring success.

Teams that are well planned, well trained, confident, and that possess the authority and training to execute their stated mission, ultimately can provide a real return on investment for an organization. This return often can be measured in terms of limiting the impact and cost, both tangible and intangible, of a computer emergency.

56.9 FURTHER READING

Brownlee, N., and E. Guttman. "Expectations for Computer Security Incident Response," RFC 2350. IETF (June 1998), http://datatracker.ietf.org/doc/rfc2350/

Beisse, F. *A Guide to Computer User Support for Help Desk and Support Specialists*, 5th edition. Cengage Learning, 2012.

Czegel, B. *Running an Effective Help Desk*, 2nd ed. Wiley, 1998.

Gerbyshak, P., and J. M. Brooks. *Help Desk Manager's Crash Course*. BookSurge Publishing, 2009.

Johnson, L. R. *Computer Incident Response and Forensics Team Management: Conducting a Successful Incident Response*. Syngress, 2013.

Knapp, D. *A Guide to Service Desk Concepts*, 4th ed. Cengage Learning, 2013.

Lucas, J., and B. Moeller. *The Effective Incident Response Team*. Addison-Wesley Professional, 2003.

Mandia, K., C. Prosise, and M. Pepe. *Incident Response and Computer Forensics*, 2nd ed. McGraw-Hill/Osborne, 2003.

McCarthy, N. K., M. Todd, and J. Klaben. *The Computer Incident Response Planning Handbook: Executable Plans for Protecting Information at Risk*. McGraw-Hill Osborne Media, 2012.

Menken, I. *Transform and Grow Your Help Desk into a Service Desk within Service Operation: Service Desk, Help Desk Best Practice within Service Operation*. Emereo, 2010.

Rajnovic, D. *Computer Incident Response and Product Security*. Cisco Press, 2010.

Robertson, K. E. *Spectacular Support Centers*. Customer Service Press, 2007.

Online resources and some software links:

- BMC TrackIt!: www.numarasoftware.com/track-it
- CERT/CC. "Resources for Computer Security Incident Response Teams (CSIRTs)," 2012, www.cert.org/csirts/resources.html
- Help Desk Institute: www.thinkhdi.com
- HelpMaster Pro Suite: www.helpmasterpro.com
- Hesk Help Desk Software: www.hesk.com
- Open Source Ticket Request System (OTRS): http://otrs.org
- Request Tracker (RT): www.bestpractical.com/rt
- Zendesk: www.zendesk.com/help-desk-software

56.10 NOTES

1. Parts of this chapter are based on a long series of articles published over several years by M. E. Kabay in his *Network World Security Strategies* newsletter. To avoid cluttering the text with unnecessary endnotes and quotation marks, there are no further specific references to particular sources in the *Network World* series on CSIRT management. For an archive of Kabay's *Network World* newsletters in PDF, including a global index, see www.mekabay.com/nwss

2. T. Maleshefski, "Infographic: The History of Customer Support," www.zendesk.com/blog/the-history-of-customer-support
3. Computer Security Resource Center, "History of the Federal Computer Incident Response Capability (FedCIRC) Pilot," 1998, http://csrc.nist.gov/topics/incidentNIST/history.htm
4. www.cert.org
5. M. J. West-Brown, D. Stikvoort, K.-P. Kossakowski, G. Killcrece, R. Ruefle, and M. Zajicek, *Handbook for Computer Security Incident Response Teams (CSIRTs),* 2nd ed. (Computer Emergency Response Team Coordination Center [CERT/CC™], Carnegie Mellon University Software Engineering Institute, 2003); www.cert.org/archive/pdf/csirt-handbook.pdf
6. N. Brownlee and E. Guttman, "Expectations for Computer Security Incident Response," Internet Engineering Task Force Network Working Group Request for Comment (RFC) 2350 (June 1998), http://tools.ietf.org/html/rfc2350
7. DISA, "Introduction to Computer Incident Response Team (CSIRT) Management, v1.0" (CD-ROM), Defense Information Systems Agency, 2001. Available free for download as ZIP file with permission of the DISA Information Assurance Support Environment at www.mekabay.com/infosecmgmt/disa_cirtm_cdrom.zip
8. National Council of ISACs (Information Sharing and Analysis Centers) www.isaccouncil.org
9. Microsoft® Encarta® Reference Library 2008.
10. DISA, "Introduction to Computer Incident Response Team (CSIRT) Management, v1.0."
11. B. Czegel, *Running an Effective Help Desk*, 2nd ed. (Wiley, 1998).
12. J. D. Howard, "An Analysis of Security Incidents on the Internet, 1989–1995," Ph.D. diss., Department of Engineering and Public Policy, Carnegie Mellon University, Pittsburgh, PA, April 1997, www.cert.org/archive/pdf/JHThesis.pdf
13. For an extensive list of articles on this topic, use the Network World search function (www.networkworld.com/search) and enter the term "help desk."
14. M. E. Kabay, "The Art of Technical Support," www.mekabay.com/courses/academic/jac/TSP/index.htm
15. DISA, "Introduction to Computer Incident Response Team (CSIRT) Management, v1.0."
16. "Help Desk Triage Policy," Courtesy Care Services, www.courtesycare.net/Best%20Practices/help%20desk%20triage.doc
17. A. Kumar, "CIRT—Framework and Models." SecurityDocs.com, January 31, 2005, originally available at www.securitydocs.com/library/2964 and now available at www.docstoc.com/docs/84310604/CIRT—Framework-and-Models
18. DISA, "Introduction to Computer Incident Response Team (CSIRT) Management, v1.0."
19. DISA, "Introduction to Computer Incident Response Team (CSIRT) Management, v1.0."
20. DISA, "Introduction to Computer Incident Response Team (CSIRT) Management, v1.0."
21. DISA, "Introduction to Computer Incident Response Team (CSIRT) Management, v1.0."

22. A. Kerin and A. Aguirre, "Improving Health, Safety, and Profits in Extended Hours Operations (Shiftwork)," *Industrial Health* 43 (2005):201–208, www.jniosh.go.jp/en/indu_hel/pdf/43-1-28.pdf
23. Canadian Centre for Occupational Health and Safety, "Rotational Shiftwork," 2010, www.ccohs.ca/oshanswers/work_schedules/shiftwrk.html
24. J. LaDou, "Health Effects of Shift Work," *Western Journal of Medicine* 137, No. 6 (December 1982), www.ncbi.nlm.nih.gov/pmc/articles/PMC1274227
25. R. R. Rosa, "Plain Language about Shiftwork," U.S. Department of Health and Human Services, Public Health Service, Centers for Disease Control and Prevention, National Institute for Occupational Safety and Health, 2001. Available as a NOOK document from Barnes & Noble, www.barnesandnoble.com/w/plain-language-about-shiftwork-roger-rosa/1004120554?ean=9780160615603
26. M. E. Kabay, "On Not Knowing: Embracing the Opportunity to Learn," 2004, www.mekabay.com/opinion/not_knowing.pdf
27. M. E. Kabay, "Egoless Work: Take Your Ego out of the Equation," *Network World Security Strategies Newsletter*, February 2, 2006, www.mekabay.com/nwss/435_egoless_work.pdf
28. P. Cichonski, T. Millar, T. Grance, and K. Scarfone, *Computer Security Incident Handling Guide*, NIST Special Publication SP800-61 Rev. 2, August 2012. http://csrc.nist.gov/publications/nistpubs/800-61rev2/SP800-61rev2.pdf
29. Cichonski et al., *Computer Security Incident Handling Guide.*
30. M. J. West-Brown, D. Stikvoort, K.-P. Kossakowski, G. Killcrece, R. Ruefle, and M. Zajicek, *Handbook for Computer Security Incident Response Teams (CSIRTs)*, 2nd ed.
31. www.first.org
32. www.gocsi.com
33. www.misti.com
34. www.rsaconference.com

CHAPTER 57

DATA BACKUPS AND ARCHIVES

M. E. Kabay and Don Holden

57.1 INTRODUCTION. Nothing is perfect. Equipment breaks, people make mistakes, and data files become corrupted or disappear. Reliably dated backups can provide evidence of innocence (or guilt) in forensic examinations and for proof of legitimate authorship in copyright disputes. Everyone, and every system, needs a well-thought-out backup and retrieval policy. In addition to making backups, data processing personnel also must consider requirements for archival storage and for retrieval of data copies. Backups also apply to personnel, equipment, and electrical power; for other applications of redundancy, see Chapters 23 and 45 in this *Handbook*.

57.1.1 Definitions.

Backups are copies of data files or records, made at a moment in time, and primarily used in the event of failure of the active files. Normally, backups are stored on different media from the original data. In particular, a copy of a file on the same disk as the original is an acceptable backup only for a short time; the *.bak, *.bk!, *.wbk, and *.sav files created by programs such as word processors are examples of limited-use backups. However, even a copy on a separate disk loses value as a backup once the original file is modified, unless *incremental* or *differential* backups also are made. These terms are described in Section 57.3.3. Typically, backups are taken on a schedule that balances the costs and inconvenience of the process with the probable cost of reconstituting data that were modified after each backup; rational allocation of resources is discussed in Section 57.8.

Deletion or corruption of an original working file converts the most recent backup into the *de facto* original. Those who do not understand this relationship mistakenly believe that once they have a backup, they can safely delete the original file. However, before original files are deleted, as when a disk volume is to be formatted, there must be at least *double backups* of all required data. Double backups will usually ensure continued operations should there be a storage or retrieval problem on any one backup medium.

This chapter uses these **abbreviations** to denote *data storage capacities*:

KB = kilobyte = 1,024 bytes (characters) (approximately 10^3)
MB = megabyte = 1,024 KB = 1,048,576 bytes ($\sim 10^6$)
GB = gigabyte = 1,024 MB = 1,073,741,824 bytes ($\sim 10^9$)
TB = terabyte = 1,024 GB = 1,099,511,627,776 bytes ($\sim 10^{12}$)
PB = petabyte = 1,024 TB = 1,125,899,906,842,624 bytes ($\sim 10^{15}$)
EB = exabyte = 1,024 PB = 1,152,921,504,606, 846,976 bytes ($\sim 10^{18}$)[1]

Archives—Although backups are used to store and retrieve operational data chronologically, data archives are used to store data that is seldom or no longer used but, when needed for reference, compliance (e.g., Federal Drug Administration [FDA], Health Insurance Portability and Accountability Act of 1996 [HIPAA], Securities and Exchange Commission [SEC]), or legal actions such as e-discovery (turning over electronic evidence in a legal proceeding), must be retrieved in a quick, logical mode. Some new data storage management systems combine both backup and this expanded archival capability.

Cloud backups—Backup copies can also be kept on servers connected to the originating systems through the Internet; also known as *online storage*.

57.1.2 Need.

Backups and storage archives are used for many purposes:

- To replace lost or corrupted data with valid versions
- To satisfy audit and legal requirements for access to retained data
- In forensic examination of data to recognize and characterize a crime and to identify suspects

- For statistical purposes in research
- To satisfy requirements of due care and diligence in safeguarding corporate assets
- To demonstrate the authorship of documents or works of art through a chain of documented, dated copies
- To meet unforeseen requirements

57.2 MAKING BACKUPS.

Because data change at different rates in different applications, backups may be useful when made at frequencies ranging from milliseconds to years.

57.2.1 Fault-Tolerant Systems.

The ultimate backup strategy is to do everything twice at the same time. Computer systems such as HP NonStop (formerly Tandem) and Stratus use redundant components at every level of processing; for example, they use arrays of processors, dual input/output (I/O) buses, multiple banks of random access memory, and duplicate disk storage devices to permit immediate recovery should anything go awry. Redundant systems use sophisticated communications between processors to ensure identity of results. If any computational components fail, processing can continue uninterrupted while the defective components are replaced.

A similar approach duplicates disk I/O, as discussed below in Section 57.2.3 on disk mirroring.

57.2.2 Hierarchical Storage Systems.

Large computer systems with terabytes or petabytes of data typically use a *hierarchical storage system* to place often-used data on fast, relatively expensive disks while migrating less-used data to less expensive, somewhat slower storage media such as slower magnetic disks, optical media, or magnetic tapes. However, users need have no knowledge of, or involvement in, such migration; all files are listed by the file system and can be accessed without special commands. Because the secondary storage media are stored in dense cylindrical arrays, usually called *silos,* they may have total capacities in the PB per silo, with fast-moving robotic arms that can locate and load the right unit within seconds. Users may experience a brief delay of a few seconds as data are copied from the secondary storage units back onto the primary hard disks, but otherwise there is no problem for the users. This system provides a degree of backup simply because data are not erased from the silo media when they are copied to magnetic disk on the system, nor are data removed from disk when they are appended to the secondary storage; this data remanence provides a degree of temporary backup because of the duplication of data. For more information on disk-based storage systems, see Chapter 36 in this *Handbook.*

57.2.3 Disk Mirroring.

There are several methods for duplicating disk operations so that disk failures cause limited or no damage to critical data. *Continuous data protection* (CDP) provides infinitely granular *recovery point objectives* (RPO), and some implementations can provide near instant *recovery time objectives* (RTOs). This is because CDP protection typically is done on a write-transaction-by-write-transaction basis. Every modification of data is recorded, and the recovery can occur to any point, down to the demarcation of individual write operations.

The Continuous Data Protection Special Interest Group (CDP SIG) of the Storage Networking Industry Association (SNIA) defines CDP as:

> ...a methodology that continuously captures or tracks data modifications and stores changes independent of the primary data, enabling recovery points from any point in the past. CDP systems may be block-, file-, or application-based and can provide fine granularities of restorable objects to infinitely variable recovery points. So, according to this definition, all CDP solutions incorporate these three fundamental attributes:
>
> 1. Data changes are continuously captured or tracked
> 2. All data changes are stored in a separate location from the primary storage
> 3. Recovery point objectives are arbitrary and need not be defined in advance of the actual recovery[2]

57.2.3.1 RAID. *Redundant arrays of independent* (originally *inexpensive*) *disks* (RAID) were described in the late 1980s and have become a practical approach to providing fault-tolerant mass storage. The falling price of disk storage has allowed inexpensive disks to be combined into highly reliable units, containing different levels of redundancy among the components, for applications with requirements for full-time availability. The disk architecture involves special measures for ensuring that every sector of the disk can be checked for validity at every input and output operation. If the primary copy of a file shows data corruption, the secondary file is used and the system automatically makes corrections to resynchronize the primary file. From the user's point of view, there is no interruption in I/O and no error.

RAID levels define how data are distributed and replicated across multiple drives. The most commonly used levels are described in Exhibit 57.1.[3]

57.2.3.2 Storage Area Network and Network Area Storage. A storage area network (SAN) is a network that allows more than one server to communicate with more than one device via a serial Small Computer System Interface (SCSI) protocol. SANs share devices via the SCSI protocol, running on top of a serial protocol such as Fibre Channel or Internet SCSI (iSCSI). They offer multiple servers access to raw devices, such as disk and tape drives.

Network-Attached Storage (NAS) effectively moves storage out from behind the server and puts it directly on the transport network. Unlike file servers that have SCSI and local area network (LAN) adapters, an NAS appliance offers multiple servers access to a file or file system via standard file-sharing protocols: Network File System (NFS), Common Internet File System (CIFS), Direct Access File System (DAFS), or others. One NAS disadvantage is that it shifts storage transactions from parallel SCSI connections to the production network. Therefore, the backbone LAN has to handle both normal end user traffic and storage disk requests, including backup operations. For more information on SAN and NAS, see Chapter 36.

57.2.3.3 Workstation and Personal Computer Mirroring. Anyone who has more than one computer may have to synchronize files to make them the same on two or more computers. In addition to the simple matter of convenience, synchronizing the computers provides excellent backup, which supplements daily incremental backups (i.e., backups of all the files that have changed since the previous incremental backup) and periodic full backups. The inactive synchronized computers serve as daily full backups of the currently active computer. For example, FreeFileSync,

RAID Features and Performance

Comparison of RAID levels from the RAID Advisory Board.

Common Name	Description	Disks (cost)	Data Reliability	Data Transfer	Maximum I/O Rate
0 Disk Striping	Data is distributed across disks in the array. No redundant info provided.	*N*	Lower than single disk	Very high	Very high for read and write
1 Mirroring	All data replicated on *N* separate disks. *N* is almost always 2.	2*N* 3*N* etc.	Higher than RAID 2, 3, 4, or 5. lower than 6	R: higher than single disk W: similar to single disk	R: up to 2x single disk W: similar to single disk
2	Data are protected by Hamming code. Redundant information distribued across *m* disks (*m* = number of data disks in array).	*N*+*m*	Much higher than single disk; comparable to RAID 3, 4, or 5	Highest	Similar to 2x single disk
3 Parallel Transfer Disks with Parity	Each data sector is subdivided and distributed across all data disks. Redundant information normally stored on dedicated parity disk.	*N*+1	Much higher than single disk; comparable to RAID 2, 4, or 5	Highest	Similar to 2x single disk
4	Data sectors distributed as with disk striping. Redundant information stored on dedicated parity disk.	*N*+1	Much higher than single disk; comparable to RAID 2, 3, or 5	R: similar to disk striping W: much lower than single disk	R: similar to disk striping W: much lower than single disk
5	Data sectors distributed as with disk striping. Redundant information interspersed with user data.	*N*+1	Much higher than single disk; comparable to RAID 2, 3, or 4	R: similar to disk striping W: lower than single disk	R: similar to disk striping W: usually lower than single disk
6	As RAID Level 5, but with additional independently computed redundant information	*N*+2	Highest	R: similar to disk striping W: lower than RAID 5	R: similar to disk striping W: much lower than RAID 5

EXHIBIT 57.1 RAID Levels *Source*: Used with kind permission of Alan Freedman, Computer Desktop Encyclopedia (Computer Language Company, 2013), www.computerlanguage.com

Laplink Gold, SyncToy, and Viceversa software (see also Section 57.3.4.4) check files on the source and target machines and allow one to choose how to transfer changes:

- *Clone* the target machine using the source machine as the standard (i.e., make the target identical to the source, including deletions).
- Copy all new files from the source to the target without deleting any files on the target.
- Copy all new files from either machine to the other without deleting files.

Software solutions also can provide automatic copying of data onto separate internal or external disks. There are dozens of such utilities available, many of them free.[4] Examples include:

- SureSync software, which runs on most versions of Windows, and which can replicate and synchronize files on Windows, MAC, and Linux.
- NFTP 1.64, which runs on Windows, OS/2, BeOS, Linux, and UNIX; it includes "transfer resume, automatic reconnect, secure authentication, extensive firewall and proxy support, support for many server types, built-in File Transfer Protocol (FTP) search, mirroring, preserving timestamps and access rights, control connection history."[5]
- UnixWare Optional Services include Disk Mirroring software for what was originally the Santa Cruz Operation (SCO) UNIX.
- Double-Take software goes beyond periodic backup by capturing byte-level changes in real time and replicating them to an alternate server, either locally or across the globe.

Early users of software-based disk mirroring suffered from slower responses when updating their primary files because the system had to complete output operations to the mirror file before releasing the application for further activity. However, today's software uses part of system memory as a buffer to prevent performance degradation. Secondary (mirror) files are nonetheless rarely more than a few milliseconds behind the current status of the primary file.

57.2.4 Logging and Recovery. If real-time access to perfect data is not essential, a well-established approach to high-availability backups is to keep a log file of all changes to critical files. *Roll-forward* recovery requires:

- Backups that are synchronized with log files to provide an agreed-on starting point
- Markers in the log files to indicate completed sequences of operations (called *transactions*) that can be recovered
- Recovery software that can read the log files and redo all the changes to the data, leaving out incomplete transactions

An alternative to roll-forward recovery is *roll-backward* recovery, in which diagnostic software scans log files and identifies only the incomplete transactions and then returns the data files to a *consistent state*. For a detailed discussion of logging, see Chapter 53 in this *Handbook*.

Microsoft Windows XP and later versions include the *System Restore* function.[6] System Restore uses a disk buffer of at least 200 MB to store several time-stamped copies of critical executable files and settings, including system registry settings, when users install new software or patches. Users can also create restore points themselves. Users can thus return their operating system to a state consistent with that of a prior time. In addition, Windows offers a device driver rollback function for a single level of driver recovery.[7]

57.2.5 Backup Software. All operating systems have utilities for making backups. However, sometimes the utilities that are included with the installation sets are limited in functionality; for example, they may not provide the full flexibility required to produce backups on different kinds of removable media. Generally, manufacturers of removable media include specialized backup software suitable for use with their own products.

There are so many backup products on the market for so many operating environments that readers will be able to locate suitable candidates easily with elementary searches. When evaluating backup software, users will want to check for these minimum requirements:

- The software should allow complete control over which files are backed up. Users should be able to obtain a report on exactly which files were successfully backed up and detailed explanations of why certain files could not be backed up.
- Restore operations should be configurable to respect the read-only attribute on files or to override that attribute globally or selectively.
- Data compression should be available.
- A variety of standard, open (not proprietary) data encryption algorithms should be available.
- Backups should include full directory paths on demand, for all files.
- Scheduling should be easy, and not require human intervention once a backup is scheduled.
- Backups must be able to span multiple volumes of removable media; a backup must not be limited to the space available on a single volume.
- If free space is available, it should be possible to put more than one backup on a single volume.
- The backup software must be able to verify the readability of all backups as part of the backup process.
- It should not be easy to create backup volumes that have the same name.
- The *restore* function should allow selective retrieval of individual files and folders or directories.
- The destination of restored data should be controllable by the user.
- During the restore process, the user should be able to determine whether to overwrite files that are currently in place; the overwriting should be controllable both with file-by-file confirmation dialogs and globally, *without* further dialog.

57.2.6 Removable Media. The density of data storage on removable media has increased thousands of times in the last half century. For example, in the 1970s, an

8-inch word-processing diskette could store up to 128 KB. In contrast, at the time of writing (April 2008), a removable disk cartridge 3 inches in diameter stored 240 GB, provided data transfer rates of 30 MB per second, and cost around $100. Moore's Law predicts that computer equipment functional capabilities and capacity double every 12 to 18 months for a given cost; this relationship definitely applies to mass storage and backup media.[8]

57.2.6.1 External Hard Disk Drives. Many styles of portable, removable stand-alone disk drives with universal serial bus (USB) and FireWire connections are available at relatively low cost. For example, at the time of writing (July 2013), Western Digital USB 3.0 portable drives with 500 GB to 2 TB storage fit easily into a shirt pocket to provide backup and recovery for travelers with laptop computers and cost from $70 to $160.

For office or higher-volume applications, a 3 TB Western Digital MyBook USB 3.0 external hard drive cost about $130.

Such devices make it easy to create one or more encrypted clones (exact copies, although not necessarily bit-for-bit copies)[9] of all of one's laptop or tower computer data, and can allow one to synchronize the clones as often as necessary. The disadvantage compared with using multiple independent storage media is that if the unit fails, all the backup data are lost. However, with costs so low, it may be affordable to have several units and to synchronize a different one at every backup, allowing a collection of backups to accumulate.

57.2.6.2 Removable Hard Disk Drives. Hard disks configured so that they can slide into bays provide for both expansion of disk storage and for backups of critical data. For example, in July 2013, the Imation RDX Removable HDD Storage System USB 3.0 was selling for about $300 for a docking station plus one 750-GB cartridge; a 1.5 TB cartridge cost about $265. One of the advantages of these systems is that one can connect install bays for multiple drives, allowing concurrent I/O to multiple cartridges, thus increasing the speed of backup.

57.2.6.3 Optical Storage. Many users and systems now use optical storage for backups. Single-layer DVDs can store 4.7 GB, while dual-layer DVDs can store 8.5 GB on media that cost less than a dollar per disk. Write parameters in the optical drivers allow users to specify whether they intend to add to the data stored on disks or whether the disks should be closed to further modification at the end of the write cycle. Internal and external optical read/write drives cost as little as $20.

Blu-ray discs™ (BDs) are an optical disk alternative to the DVD format that won out over the competing High Definition (HD) DVD standard in 2008. Single-layer BDs can store 25 GB in the same size disk as CDs and DVDs; dual-layer BDs store 50 GB. BDXL triple-layer drives can store 100 GB per disk and BDXL quad-layer drives can store 128 GB per disk.

An upcoming technology to monitor is the *holographic* disk, with storage capacities of up to 1.6 TB. However, at the time of writing in July 2013, the technology was still viewed as experimental. The hVault company, a startup in 2011, was in beta-test of these devices for the commercial market (not personal use) in configurations supporting petabytes of storage. The company described how the system works:

> Holographic Storage is a totally new way of storing digital data. It works by splitting a blue laser beam in two, a reference beam and a data beam. The data beam is modulated with

a spatial light modulator (like in a digital projector) that creates a very high density array of 1.5 million pixels. Where the data beam and the reference beam intersect, a holographic interference pattern is formed. When focused on an unexposed, light sensitive holographic disk, a permanent 3D holographic image is formed in the light sensitive layer of the disk. To recover the data from the disk, a reference laser is focused on the disk and an image of the original digital array is formed and captured on a CCD image sensor.

Once the image containing 1.5Mbits of data is written to the disk, the angle of the reference beam is moved slightly and another 1.5Mbits can be written in the same 3D volume as the first image. This process is repeated many times with slightly different reference beam angles to create multiple, non-interfering data images in the same volume of the disk. Then the disk is rotated slightly to the next area of the disk and the multiple write sequence is repeated. Unlike magnetic Hard Drives and optical disks such as CD, DVD and Blu-Ray, where bits are written one bit at a time onto a spinning disk, holographic data storage reads and writes 1.5Mbits at a time on a stationary disk. This results in improved read and write speeds as well as much lower power consumption because there is no need to spin the disk constantly.

Once the disk is exposed with the data to be saved, the disk is cured with the laser which is analogous to developing and fixing photographic film. Once developed, black and white photographic film is no longer light sensitive and is relatively inert, which gives it very good long term image retention. Similarly, holographic disks become inert once they are cured they become unalterable by natural elements, human errors or tampering. Accelerated life testing indicates that holographic disks can store their digital data safely for over 50 years with no loss of data.[10]

hVault products were described as follows:

hVault provides complete holographic storage systems for any size archive. For small archives, the single drive, 15 disk slot, rack mount autoloader is a very cost effective way to create, store and retrieve Terabytes of digital data in compact, low cost unit. Larger archives can opt for the automated libraries that can be configured with 2 to 8 drives and up to 540 disk slots. Expansion cabinets can be added to increase the total slot count to 2140 disks. These robotic units provide very high system flexibility due to the ability to read and write simultaneously from multiple drives. hVault holographic storage systems provide expansion capability for your growing archive storage needs. hVault provides complete holographic storage systems for any size archive. For small archives, the single drive, 15 disk slot, rack mount autoloader is a very cost effective way to create, store and retrieve Terabytes of digital data in compact, low cost unit. Larger archives can opt for the automated libraries that can be configured with 2 to 8 drives and up to 540 disk slots. Expansion cabinets can be added to increase the total slot count to 2140 disks. These robotic units provide very high system flexibility due to the ability to read and write simultaneously from multiple drives. hVault holographic storage systems provide expansion capability for your growing archive storage needs.

All hVault storage systems are designed to plug in to existing network architectures with no disruption to existing workflows. Flexible control and data path options make integration easy. Whether your network uses Gigabit Ethernet or FibreChannel, hVault libraries are plug and play. Flexible control interfaces to the robotic controls make integration into your control architecture a snap.

With any hVault storage system, ANY content on ANY disk is accessible in less than 10 seconds. Once the disk is loaded into a drive, the read or write throughput is 20MB/sec. Caching provides a very high bandwidth input channel that allows bursting of very high speed data to the system.[11]

Prices were projected to start at about $50,000 for the low-end 15-disk autoloader. There were indications that the company might also offer consumer units capable of storing more than 1 TB per platter.

57.2.6.4 Tape Cartridge Systems. The old 9-track, reel-to-reel 6,250 bytes-per-inch (bpi) systems used in the 1970s and 1980s held several hundred MB. Today's pocket-size tape cartridges hold GBs. For example, the industry leader in this field, a

Sony LTO3 cartridge, has 400-GB native and 800-GB compressed maximum storage capacity per cartridge and a transport speed of 80 MB/s native and 160 MB/s compressed data transfer. Cartridges have mean-time-between-failure (MTBF) of 250,000 hours with 100 percent duty cycles and can tolerate 1 million tape passes. All such systems have streaming input/output (I/O) using random access memory (RAM) buffers to prevent interruption of the read/write operations from and to the tapes and thus to keep the tape moving smoothly to maximize data transfer rates.

Although this buffering is effective for directly attached tape systems, this is not effective for backing up data over an LAN. When backing up data over an LAN, users will probably experience *shoeshining* of the tape drive (rapid back-and-forth movement of the tape), which reduces the effective throughput rate significantly. For example, a 50 MB per second (ps) tape drive, receiving a data stream at 25 MBps, does not write at 25 MBps. Rather it fills a buffer and writes short bursts at 50 MBps. The mechanical motion of the tape moves empty tape over the read/write head after the data transfer ends. The tape motor then stops, rewinds to reposition the tape at the appropriate place on the tape for continued writing, and prepares itself to write another short burst at 50 MBps. This repositioning process of stopping, rewinding, and getting back up to speed is called *backhitching*. Each backhitch can take as long as a few seconds. Frequent backhitching is called *shoeshining* because the tape activity mimics the movement of a cloth being used to shine shoes. The farther one operates from the designed throughput rate, the less time one spends writing data and the more time backhitching. A 50-MBps tape drive that is receiving data at 40 MBps will actually write at 35 MBps because it is spending at least 20 percent of its time shoeshining. Similarly, a data stream at 30 MBps will actually be written at 20 MBps, a 20 MBps data stream at 10 MBps, and a 10 MBps data stream at less than 1 MBps.

In conjunction with automated tape library systems, holding many cartridges and capable of switching automatically to the next cartridge, tape cartridge systems are ideal for backing up servers and mainframes with TBs of data. Small library systems keep 10 to 20 cartridges in position for immediate access, taking approximately 9 seconds for an exchange. These libraries have approximately 2 million mean exchanges between failures, with MTBF of around 360,000 hours at 100 percent duty cycle.

The large enterprise-class library systems such as the 8-frame SpectraLogic's T950 can be configured with up to 10,050 slots and 120 LTO (Linear Tape-Open, the open-software alternative to DLT or Digital Linear Tape) drives. The 8-frame T950 offered a native throughput of 14.4 GB/second using LTO-4 drives. These library systems can encrypt, compress, and decrypt data using the strongest version of the Advanced Encryption Standard (AES), to meet regulatory and security compliance requirements. As another example, the Plasmon Ultra Density Optical (UDO) Library offered up to 19 TB of archival storage capacity for enterprise systems at a price of about $100,000.

57.2.6.5 *Virtual Tape Library.* A virtual tape library (VTL) is a disk-based system that emulates a tape library, tape drives, and media. These systems are used in disk-based backup and restore operations.[12] VTLs used for backup emulate tape drive and library functions and can provide a transition for legacy systems to an integrated disk-based backup and recovery. These units (e.g., the IBM Virtual Tape Server introduced in 1997) provide backward compatibility for older production systems by using optical, or modern high-capacity magnetic disk storage but presenting the data as if they were stored on magnetic tapes and cartridges. VTLs can use existing storage architecture and can be used remotely. Naturally, their throughput is far greater than the older tape-based backup systems.

As an example of technology available at the time of writing (July 2013), FalconStor VTL was described by the manufacturer as follows:

Ultra-fast, reliable backup and deduplication

There is a reason why FalconStor® Virtual Tape Library (VTL) is the industry's market-leading virtual tape solution: It provides enterprise-level disk-based backup and deduplication to organizations of all sizes at the fastest available speeds. FalconStor VTL optimizes backup speed, performance, and reliability without interrupting existing backup environments, minimizing backup windows and making data more available and secure.

Optimized

- Flexible, policy-based deduplication: Inline, post-process, concurrent, or no deduplication
- Fastest backup speeds: Up to 5.8TB/hr
- Fastest deduplication speeds: Up to 40TB/hr

Available

- Enhanced replication ensures efficient bandwidth usage in LAN and WAN environments
- Global deduplication scales to over 2PB of usable storage
- High-availability (HA) cluster configurations for large enterprises

Secure

- Sophisticated physical tape integration; automated, nondisruptive direct tape export
- Replication with Advanced Encryption Standard (AES) encryption
- Federal Information Processing Standards (FIPS) compliance support

Optimized, high-performance disk backup

By offering ultra-fast backup of up to 1.6GB/sec (5.8TB/hr), FalconStor VTL addresses the single biggest backup challenge: the backup window. When eight appliances are combined into one logical unit, speeds accelerate to 12.8GB/sec. Combined with high-speed protocols such as 8Gb Fibre Channel (FC) and 10Gb Ethernet, FalconStor VTL can sustain deduplication speeds of up to 40TB/hr—the fastest in the industry.

Highly flexible, FalconStor VTL enables you to set customized policies for deduplication, replication, and archiving. You can select from up to four deduplication types—inline, post-process, concurrent, or no deduplication—on a per-job basis.

Global deduplication ensures availability with efficiency

FalconStor VTL ensures the availability of critical data. It replicates data from across the globe to a central clustered repository of unique, deduplicated data. WAN-optimized replication ensures fast and reliable backup and recovery while reducing bandwidth requirements. Global deduplication simplifies storage management and reduces capacity requirements by up to 95%, shrinking the storage footprint at the data center.

Secure backup, recovery, and archiving

FalconStor VTL provides support for a broad range of systems, tapes, and tape libraries, including Symantec OST environments. FalconStor VTL ensures the safety and security of critical data through features such as extended tape management, encryption with Advanced

> Encryption Standard (AES), tape shredding, and Federal Information Processing Standards (FIPS) compliance support.
>
> **Flexible deployment options**
>
> FalconStor VTL is available in a variety of form factors, providing enterprise-class functionality to customers ranging from small-to-medium businesses (SMB) to large global enterprises with multiple remote and branch offices (ROBO).... [13]

VTLs may be offered by certain vendors as software only, purpose-built appliances, or virtual appliances for VMware environments. Pricing for virtual appliances generally start at $2,000–$3,000 per license and an additional cost for capacity.

57.2.6.6 Personal Storage Devices: Flash Memory. USB flash drives have become ubiquitous due to the decline in price and the vast amount of data that they can store. Cheap multi-MB and multi-GB USB flash drives (also called *memory sticks* and *thumb drives*) are available at drugstores, are given away at conferences, and are available in a variety of forms, such as pens, pocketknives, and supposedly amusing variants such as dolls and even sushi. Other personal devices using flash memory can also be used to store large amounts of data. These include music players, personal digital assistants, and mobile phones. For example, Secure Digital (SD) memory cards with 256 GB of storage were available at the time of writing (July 2013) for about $600; a 128-GB card sold for around $300; and a 64-GB card cost about $100.

Although these devices can provide a convenience for the user who wants to transfer large amounts of data, they pose a serious security risk to businesses, since sensitive company data can be easily removed, against company policy. Although some USB flash drives have built-in encryption to protect the contents from being exposed if the device is lost or stolen, most flash drives and other personal devices store data in unencrypted form—a serious problem if the device is lost or stolen. Some companies have implemented technical means (*data-loss prevention*, or DLP) to block the use of USB flash and other devices from downloading data from corporate PCs. Just as these devices can download data from a computer, they can also be a vector for transferring malware to a computer and to a network. User policies and education are the primary defenses to supplement technical controls.

Flash drives are sometimes recommended as a backup medium for end users. However, they suffer from a number of disadvantages:

- They are usually physically small and therefore easy to misplace or lose
- They are relatively fragile (e.g., their enclosures break easily if struck and may not be water resistant)
- They are relatively expensive per storage unit compared with magnetic or optical media

57.2.6.7 Developing Storage Technologies. IBM research scientists are working on *Millipede*, a method of storing data using an atomic-force microscope to punch nanometer-sized depressions in thin polymer films.[14] The storage density is about 100 GB per square cm.[15] It will be interesting to see if this technology develops into yet another order-of-magnitude increase in storage capacity and precipitous decline in storage costs.

Another astounding leap forward is the demonstration of multilayered nanostructured quartz glass, which has allowed storage of 360TB on a glass disk with expected lifetimes so long they have not yet been estimated accurately.[16]

57.2.7 Labeling. Regardless of the size of a backup, every storage device, from diskettes to tape cartridges to external or removal disk drives, should be clearly and unambiguously tagged, both electronically and with adhesive labels. Backups to hard drives can be placed in folders or files with as much detail as required; for example, *BU_2016-03-31_FULL* or *BU_2016-04-11_DB.ZIPX*.

Larger-capacity media, such as cartridges used for UNIX and mainframe systems, often have extensive bar-code or electronic labeling available. On some systems, it is possible to request specific storage media and have the system automatically refuse the wrong media if they are mounted in error. Tape library systems typically use optical bar codes that are generated automatically by the backup software and then manually or automatically affixed to each cartridge for unique identification. Magnetic tapes and cartridges have electronic labels written onto the start of the recording medium in each unit, with specifics that are particular to the operating system and tape-handling software.

An unlabeled storage medium or one with a flimsily attached label is evidence of a bad practice that will lead to confusion and error. Sticky notes, for example, are not a good way to label diskettes and removable disks. If the notes are taken off, they can get lost; if they are left on, they can jam the disk drives. There are many types of labels for storage media, including printable sheets suitable for laser or inkjet printers and using adhesive that allows removal of the labels without leaving a sticky residue. At the very least, an exterior label should include this information:

- Date the volume was created (e.g., *2016–09–08*)
- Originator (e.g., *Bob R. Jones, Accounting Dept.*)
- Description of the contents (e.g., *Engineering Accounting Data for 2016*)
- Application program (e.g., *FastAccounting v3.4.5*)
- Operating system (e.g., *Windows 9 v3.4.5.6*)

Storing files with *canonical names* (names with a fixed name or a defined structure) on the media themselves is also useful. An example of canonical files much used in installation packages is *READ.ME* or *README.TXT*. For example, an organization can mandate files such as the following as minimum standards for identifying and documenting its storage media:

- *ORIGIN.mmm* (where *mmm* represents a sequence number for unique identification of the storage set) indicating the originating system (e.g., the *ORIGIN.1234* file could contain data such as *Accounting Workstation number 3875-3* or *Bob Whitmore's SPARC in Engineering Rm 379 serial 98765*). This file can be written to every volume.
- *DATE.mmm* showing the date (preferably in year-month-day sequence) and time (usually 24-hour clock) on which the storage volume was created (e.g., *DATE.1234* could contain the data *2016–09–08 23:41*). Such a file can be written to each volume of the storage set.

- *SET.mmm* to describe exactly which volumes are part of a particular set; e.g., SET.1234 could include *SET 1234: VOL 444, VOL 445, VOL 446.* This kind of file is normally located on the last volume of the set.
- *INDEX.mmm*, an index file on the last volume listing all the files on all the volumes of that particular storage set; for example, INDEX.1234 could contain *SET 1234: VOL 444 – FIL F1, F2, F3; VOL 445 – FIL F4, F5, F6, F6; VOL 446 – FIL F7, F8.*
- *VOLUME.nnn* (where *nnn* represents a sequence number for unique identification of the medium) that contains an explanation; e.g., *VOLUME.444* could include data such as *VOL 444 SET 1232 NUMBER 1.*
- *FILES.nnn*, which lists all the files on that particular volume of that particular storage set; for example, contents of file FILES.444 could include *SET 1234: VOL 444 – Files F1, F2, F3.*

Such labeling is best handled by an application program; many backup programs automatically generate analogous files.

57.2.8 Indexing and Archives. As implied earlier, backup volumes need a mechanism for identifying the data stored on each medium. Equally important is the capacity to locate the storage media where particular files are stored; otherwise, one would have to search serially through multiple media to locate specific data. Although not all backup products for personal computers (PCs) include such functionality, many do; server and mainframe utilities routinely include automatic indexing and retrieval. These systems allow the user to specify file names and dates, using wild-card characters in the defined identification pattern to signify ranges and also to display a menu of options from which the user can select the appropriate files for recovery.

This file-level indexing, though, is not sufficient for retrieving unstructured content such as word processing documents, e-mails, instant messages, diagrams, Web pages, and images that may be required for regulators, business research, and legal subpoenas (e-discovery). The Federal Rules of Civil Procedure (FRCP) specifically address discovery and the duty to disclose evidence in preparation for trial.[17] Recent changes to FRCP specifically address electronic data.

Due to the cost of locating and retrieving data for litigation, companies are changing the way they manage the life cycle of data. For instance, the cost to do a forensics search of one backup tape to locate e-mails that contain certain relevant content can be $35,000 per tape. In some recent cases, a search of e-mail tapes has involved over 100 tapes. Companies are now implementing archiving systems to address this requirement.

A method of providing fast access to fixed content (data that are not expected to be updated) is *content-addressed storage* (CAS). CAS assigns content a permanent place on a disk. CAS stores content so that an object cannot be duplicated or modified once it has been stored; thus, its location is unambiguous.

When an object is stored in CAS, the object is given a unique name that also specifies the storage location. This type of address is called a *content address*. It eliminates the need for a centralized index, so it is not necessary to track the location of stored data. Once an object has been stored, it cannot be deleted until the specified retention period has expired. In CAS, data is stored on disk, not tape. This method streamlines the process of searching for stored objects. A backup copy of every object is stored to enhance reliability and to minimize the risk of catastrophic data loss. A remote monitoring system will notify the system administrator in the event of a hardware failure.

Combined archiving and backup systems can reduce the amount of stored data by reducing the amount of duplicate data, thereby reducing the storage cost and time to retrieve or restore data files.

EMC's Centera product first released in 2002 is an example of a CAS product. The product overview highlights the following features:

- **Content authenticity**: Centera ensures that your online, long-term archive data is authentic, cannot be overwritten, and is immutable with write-once, read-many (WORM) technology.
- **Governance and compliance**: Meet industry regulations and corporate requirements using a wide range of retention capabilities on a hardened platform with assured content authenticity and legal admissibility of content.
- **High availability**: Ensure data accessibility with redundant array of independent nodes (RAIN), flexible protection schemes, self-healing, and replication for unmatched protection and 99.999 percent availability.
- **Efficient operation**: Reduce total cost of ownership (TCO) with seamless, nondisruptive scale and location-independent storage. Automate storage management tasks including self-configuring, self-healing, and virtual storage pools. Ensure low-capacity overhead with single-instance storage.
- **Broad partner ecosystem**: Extend Centera investment value with more than 300 out-of-the box, integrated archiving applications to manage email, file, medical imaging, content management, video, and voice archiving on a single archiving platform.[18]

57.2.9 Registry Backups. On Windows systems, the central repository of settings for all installed programs and device drivers is the *registry*. The equivalent for Mac computers is the *system preferences*. On *nix systems, similar information is in files in specific folders such as */settings*.

For some operating systems, it may not be possible to make a usable copy of such data using file-system–based backup software. However, there may be options in some backup software to make bit-for-bit copies of the registry (or equivalent) so that settings can be restored to a system that has suffered catastrophic damage or that has been restored to a previous condition. Under Windows, a variety of registry-editors typically include options for automatically making restorable copies of the registry. Windows itself has functions for so doing; for example, the *Create a restore point* function allows one to store usable copies of the registry. The *Restore system files and settings from a restore point* or *Restore your computer to an earlier time* are pointers to returning to what one hopes will be a better version of the system configuration.

When creating restore point, it is wise to take advantage of options for storing information explaining why the restore point has been taken; for example, a description could be *2016-06-02 before installing BaffleGab 4.3.6.*

57.2.10 Bootable Versions. Registry backups can be useful, but what does one do if the operating system disk has been completely corrupted or if one has to initialize a new computer system? On Windows systems with hundreds of installed programs, recreating a work environment can take days of annoying installations, re-registration, and repeated boot cycles. To avoid such time-wasting labor, one should keep bootable versions of the entire system.

Most system-backup software today includes the option to allow restoration of the entire configuration, including the registry, every installed program, and all installed options for settings of those programs. Some packages allow access to individual folders and files for restoration and others don't; however, the key is that a bootable backup can save days of time and effort.[19]

The ultimate bootable backup is the *image backup* which is a bit-for-bit copy of the disk containing operating system files. Such files are commonly used in corporate environments to ensure easy restoration of all networked workstations to an authorized initial state. They can save enormous amounts of time for large networks by eliminating the need to install upgrades manually system by system; for example, a university network with 1,000 lab computers accessible to students could not possibly be managed without image backups to centralize the configuration updates of all those machines.

57.2.11 Cloud Backup. An alternative to making onsite backup copies is to pay a third party to make automatic backups via high-speed telecommunications channels and to store the data in a secure facility. Some firms involved in these services move data to magnetic or optical backup volumes, but others use RAID (see Section 57.2.3.1) for instant access to the latest backups. Additional features to look for when evaluating online backup facilities:

- Compatibility of backup software with the computing platform, operating system, and application programs
- Availability of different backup options: full, differential, incremental, and delta
- Handling of files that are held in an *open* state by application programs
- Availability and costs of sufficient bandwidth to support desired data backup rates
- Encryption of data during transmission and when stored at the service facility
- Strong access controls to limit access to stored data to authorized personnel
- Physical security at the storage site, and other criteria similar to those listed in Section 57.5.3.5
- Methods for restoring files from these backups, and the speed with which they can be accomplished

In a May 2013 forecast on global network bandwidth growth, Cisco's "Visual Networking Index" included the following predictions, among many others:

- Annual global IP traffic will surpass the zettabyte threshold (1.4 zettabytes) by the end of 2017. In 2017, global IP traffic will reach 1.4 zettabytes per year, or 120.6 exabytes per month. Global IP traffic will reach 1.0 zettabytes per year or 83.8 exabytes per month in 2015.
- Global IP traffic has increased more than fourfold in the past 5 years and will increase threefold over the next 5 years. Overall, IP traffic will grow at a compound annual growth rate (CAGR) of 23 percent from 2012 to 2017.
- Nearly half of all IP traffic will originate with non-PC devices by 2017. In 2012, only 26 percent of consumer IP traffic originated with non-PC devices, but by 2017 the non-PC share of consumer IP traffic will grow to 49 percent. PC-originated

traffic will grow at a CAGR of 14 percent, while TVs, tablets, mobile phones, and machine-to-machine (M2M) modules will have traffic growth rates of 24 percent, 104 percent, 79 percent, and 82 percent, respectively.

- Traffic from wireless and mobile devices will exceed traffic from wired devices by 2016. By 2017, wired devices will account for 45 percent of IP traffic, while Wi-Fi and mobile devices will account for 55 percent of IP traffic. In 2012, wired devices accounted for the majority of IP traffic at 59 percent.[20]

The global bandwidth of the Internet has been climbing steadily and is predicted to continue accelerated growth over the remainder of the 2010 decade:

> ...[I]nternational bandwidth availability has soared ("used bandwidth" refers to the capacity deployed by providers, rather than bandwidth consumed by end users). From 1.4 terabits per second in 2002, it steadily climbed to 6.7 terabits in 2006 and has now reached 92.1 terabits per second. TeleGeography expects that number to hit 606.6 terabits per second in 2018 and 1,103.3 terabits per second in 2020.[21]

The increasing availability of higher bandwidth connections is encouraging the growth of cloud-based file-sharing and backup services, especially for mobile computing platforms (laptops, tablets, phones). Although some services date back for decades (e.g., Asigra[22]), dozens of companies and their remote-backup services have appeared in the twenty-first century to date. The Storage Networking Industry Association (SNIA) convened a Cloud Storage Initiative (CSI) in 2010; members included Cisco Systems, Cleversafe, Inc., EMC, Evaluator Group, Hewlett-Packard, Hitachi Data Systems, IBM, Inktank, Mezeo Software, NetApp, Oracle, Scality, SpectraLogic, SwiftTest, Symantec, and Vedams, as of July 3, 2013.[23]

The SNIA CSI has defined the *Cloud Data Management Interface* (CDMI) cloud-storage standard, which

> ...defines the functional interface that applications will use to create, retrieve, update, and delete data elements from the Cloud. As part of this interface the client will be able to discover the capabilities of the cloud storage offering and use this interface to manage containers and the data that is placed in them. In addition, metadata can be set on containers and their contained data elements through this interface.
>
> This interface is also used by administrative and management applications to manage containers, accounts, security access, and monitoring/billing information, even for storage that is accessible by other protocols. The capabilities of the underlying storage and data services are exposed so that clients can understand the offering.[24]

Virtualization has also been implemented in cloud backups. For example, in early 2012,

> Amazon Web Services...launched a public beta test of AWS Storage Gateway, which allows enterprises to back up application data in Amazon's cloud using a software appliance.... The Storage Gateway appliance is a virtual machine that runs on VMware's virtualization software. It uses an iSCSI interface to integrate with applications. The appliance stores data on local storage hardware, while uploading backup snapshots to Amazon's cloud. This provides low-latency access to data and off-site backups in the cloud....
>
> Enterprises that want to use Storage Gateway pay a monthly fee of US$125 per activated gateway. Added to that is the cost of storage capacity used by the snapshots, and traffic out of Amazon's cloud.
>
> The snapshots are stored and billed as Amazon EBS (Elastic Block Store) snapshots, which cost from $0.14 per GB per month.

> The cost of data transfer drops as the amount of data increases: Up to 10 TB of transferred data in one month costs $0.12 per GB, and the next 40 TB costs $0.09 per GB. Rate tiers are chosen based on aggregate usage across multiple Amazon services, including EC2 (Elastic Compute Cloud), S3, and VPC (Virtual Private Cloud).[25]

One of the critical issues when choosing a cloud-backup service is quality of service: If the service goes offline, there can be serious problems both updating the backups and accessing backup files.[26]

Another consideration when deciding whether to use cloud-backup services is the consequences for court-ordered forensic seizure of the data. Gordon Merrill published a list of questions that should be discussed with possible vendors:

- Do we even know which specific drives were in use by XYZ before the crash at EC2?
- Would Amazon have the ability to remove those drives and replace with others if ordered to do so?
- How many other companies' data have been written on those drives in the interim?
- If the original XYZ data have been overwritten by other companies and the drives are removed for recovery attempts, does the removal mean that the later users have now lost control of their data?
- Do the current users of the removed drives have to be served with a notice that the drives are being forensically reviewed?
- Is there a legal requirement that the current users need to be notified?
- Are the current users due a description of how their data was handled during the recovery and how it was destroyed when the exam was complete in order for them to produce the same to their customers as ordered for compliance with applicable laws?

One last concern facing most companies legally is that of legal hold orders and/or search warrants.

- If XYZ is being investigated by the Department of Justice (DoJ) and they want to find out more during an investigation, can the DoJ serve a warrant to Amazon and search without ever notifying XYZ that the search is going on?
- If the same hard drives are now in use by company ABC, does ABC get notified of the search and seizure or is the warrant on Amazon enough to search without any notice to the companies involved?[27]

Finally, shared folders such as those on Dropbox must be backed up regularly in a separate way—whether on the local hard drives or using a different cloud-backup service. If any user of the shared folders deletes files, all the users will have their copies automatically deleted. Without explicit backups, valuable information can be destroyed.[28]

For an extensive review of cloud storage and backup, see the paper by Legendre.[29]

57.3 BACKUP STRATEGIES. There are different approaches to backing up data. This section looks at what kinds of data can be backed up and then reviews appropriate ways of choosing and managing backups for different kinds of computer systems. Some of the challenges that a backup strategy should address are:

- Rapid growth of electronic data
- Shrinking time for backing up data
- Increasing backup costs
- Performance bottlenecks
- Compliance and legal discovery

57.3.1 Exclusive Access. All backup systems have trouble with files that are currently in use by processes that have opened them with write access (i.e., which may be adding or changing data within the files). The danger in copying such files is that they may be in an *inconsistent state* when the backup software copies their data. For example, a multiphase transaction may have updated some records in a detail file, but the corresponding master records may not yet have been posted to disk. Copying the data before the transaction completes will store a corrupt version of the files and lead to problems when they are later restored to disk.

Backup software usually generates a list of everything backed up and of all the files *not* backed up; for the latter, there is usually an explanation or a code showing the reason for the failure. Operators always must verify that all required files have been backed up and must take corrective action if files have been omitted.

Workstation backups for operating systems such as Windows and Mac usually include options for using what is often called *volume shadow copy services* to provide access to files in current use. The Windows Volume Shadow Copy Service (VSS) is a feature of Windows 7, Windows Server 2003, Windows XP, and Windows Vista. VSS was removed from Windows in the development of Windows 8.[30]

Some high-speed, high-capacity backup software packages provide a buffer mechanism to allow high-availability systems to continue processing while backups are in progress. In these systems, files are frozen in a consistent state so that backup can proceed, and all changes are stored in buffers on disk for later entry into the production databases. However, even this approach cannot obviate the need for a minimum period of quiescence so that the databases can reach a consistent state. In addition, it is impossible for full functionality to continue if changes are being held back from the databases until a backup is complete; all *dependent* transactions (those depending on the previously changed values of records) also must be held up until the files are unlocked.

57.3.2 Types of Backups. Backups can include different amounts and kinds of data:

- *Full* backups store a copy of everything that resides on the mass storage of a specific system. To restore a group of files from a full backup, the operator mounts the appropriate volume of the backup set and restores the files in a single operation.
- *Differential* backups store all the data that have changed since a specific date or event; typically, a differential backup stores everything that has changed since the last full backup. The number of volumes of differential backups can increase with each additional backup. To restore a group of files from a differential backup, the

operator needs to locate the latest differential set and also the full backup on which it is based to ensure that all files are restored. For example, suppose a full backup on Sunday contains copies of files *A, B, C, D,* and *E*. On Monday, suppose that files *A* and *B* are changed to *A′* and *B′* during the day; then the Monday evening differential backup would include only copies of files *A′* and *B′*. On Tuesday, suppose that files *C* and *D* are changed to *C′* and *D′*; then the Tuesday evening backup would include copies of files *A′, B′, C′*, and *D′*. If there were a crash on Wednesday morning, the system could be rebuilt from Sunday's full backup (files *A, B, C, D,* and *E*), and then the Tuesday differential backup would overwrite the changed files and restore *A′, B′, C′*, and *D′*, resulting in the correct combination of unchanged and changed files (*A′, B′, C′, D′*, and *E*).

- *Incremental* backups are a more limited type of differential backups that typically store everything that has changed since the previous full or incremental backup. As long as multiple backup sets can be put on a single volume, the incremental backup requires fewer volumes than a normal differential backup for a given period. To restore a set of files from incremental backups, the operator may have to mount volumes from all the incremental sets plus the full backup upon which they are based. For example, using the same scenario as in the explanation of differential backups, suppose a full backup on Sunday contains copies of files *A, B, C, D,* and *E*. On Monday, suppose that files *A* and *B* are changed to *A′* and *B′* during the day; then the Monday evening incremental backup would include only copies of files *A′* and *B′*. On Tuesday, suppose that files *C* and *D* are changed to *C′* and *D′*; then the Tuesday evening backup would include copies only of files *C′* and *D′*. If there were a crash on Wednesday morning, the system could be rebuilt from Sunday's full backup (files *A, B, C, D,* and *E*) and then the Monday incremental backup would allow restoration of *A′* and *B′* and the Tuesday incremental backup would restore *C′* and *D′*, resulting in the correct combination of unchanged and changed files (*A′, B′, C′, D′*, and *E*).
- *Delta* backups store only the portions of files that have been modified since the last full or delta backup; delta backups are a rarely used type, more akin to logging than to normal backups. Delta backups use the fewest backup volumes of all the methods listed; however, to restore data using delta backups, the operator must use special-purpose application programs and mount volumes from all the delta sets plus the full backup upon which they are based. In the scenario used earlier, the delta backup for Monday night would have records for the changes in files *A* in *delta-A* and records for the changes in file *B* stored in file *delta-B*. The Tuesday night delta backup would have records for the changes in files *C* and *D* stored in files *delta-C* and *delta-D*, respectively. To restore the correct conditions as of Tuesday night, the operator would restore the *A* and *B* files from the Sunday night full backup, then run a special recovery program to install the changes from the *delta-A* and a (possibly different) recovery program to install the changes from *delta-B*. Then it would be necessary to load the Tuesday night delta backup and to run recovery programs using files *C* and *D* with corresponding files *delta-C* and *delta-D*, respectively.
- *Versions* of working files are essential to protect the creators or users in case data are accidentally deleted without notice. For example, suppose an author constantly opens and saves all changes in a new document to filename *manuscript.docx* but uses no version numbers. At one point, the author accidentally deletes a significant block of text written the day before without noticing or under the belief that the

deleted material is valueless. The author then continues working and eventually makes a backup—say, at the end of the week. There is therefore no backup of the deleted material: the *manuscript.docx* file overwrites the previous day's work. In contrast, the author may open yesterday's *manuscript_v32.docx* and immediately save it as *manuscript_v33.docx* for today's work. Even if a block of text written yesterday is deleted, it will be possible to open *manuscript_v32.docx* to recover the deleted text. In addition, having a consistent series of numbered, dated versions of a manuscript may serve to exonerate an author charged with plagiarism.[31]

Another aspect of backups is whether they include all the data on a system or only the data particular to specific application programs or groups of users:

- *System* backups copy everything on a system.
- *Application* backups copy the data needed to restore operations for particular software systems.

In addition to these terms, operators and users often refer to *daily, partial, weekly*, and *monthly* backups. These terms are ambiguous (they refer to the *frequency* of backups, not to the type) and could be used for any kind of backup; they should be used only in conjunction with the backup type (e.g., *monthly full backup* or *daily incremental backup*) when setting up procedures.

57.3.3 Computer Systems. Systems with different characteristics and purposes can require different backup strategies. This section looks at large production systems (mainframes), smaller computers used for distributed processing (servers), individual computers used primarily by one user (workstations), and portable computers (laptops) smartphones, or handheld computers and personal digital assistants (PDAs) which are still used by some corporations.

57.3.3.1 Mainframes. Large production systems using mainframes, or networks of servers, routinely do full system backups every day because of the importance of rapid recovery in case of data loss (see Chapters 42 and 43 of this *Handbook*). Using high-capacity tape libraries with multiple drives and immediate access to tape cartridges, these systems are capable of data throughput of up to 2 TB per hour. Some software vendors claim that they have been able to accelerate backups to 4 TB per hour. Symantec describes the increased throughput using their NetBackup Accelerator software as follows:

> One of the most painful parts of backup has always been the time required. It's a big deal—a recent Symantec survey revealed that 72 percent of enterprises would switch backup products if it would double their backup speed. Not content with simply doubling the speed, we implemented NetBackup Accelerator, which accelerates full backups by up to 100 times. This gives you the benefits of a full recovery image, instantly available, at the speed of performing an incremental backup.
>
> So what is the secret sauce? NetBackup Accelerator provides packaged in a single backup type the capability to read only changed files, dedupe these changed files, send only unique data from the client to the media server and from these unique changes, instantly make a full backup image available for recovery using NetBackup's synthesis engine.
>
> The results are astounding. Using old school backup, 1 TB of data could take up to 6 hrs to backup. With client deduplication alone, backup time is cut to 2 hours. With NetBackup Accelerator, backup time is cut to less than 15 minutes.[32]

Typically, all backups are performed automatically during the period of lowest system utilization. Because of the problems caused by concurrent access, mainframe operations usually reserve a time every day during which users are not permitted to access production applications. A typical approach sends a series of real-time messages to all open sessions announcing "Full Backup in xx minutes; please log off now." Operations staff have been known to phone offending users who are still logged on to the network when backups are supposed to start. To prevent unattended sessions from interfering with backups (as well as to reduce risks from unauthorized use of open sessions), most systems configure a time-out after a certain period of inactivity (typically 10 minutes). If users have left their sessions online despite the automatic logoff, mechanisms such as forced logoffs can be implemented to prevent user processes from continuing to hold production files open.

In addition to system backups, mainframe operations may be instructed to take more frequent backups of high-utilization application systems. Mission-critical transaction-processing systems, for example, may have several incremental or delta backups performed throughout the day. Transaction log files may be considered so important that they are also copied to backup media as soon as the files are closed. Typically, a log file is closed when it reaches its maximum size, and a new log file is initiated for the application programs.

57.3.3.2 Servers. Managers of networks with many servers have the same options as mainframe operations staff, but they also have increased flexibility because of the decentralized, distributed nature of the computing environment. Many network architectures allocate specific application systems or groups of users to specific servers; therefore, it is easy to schedule system backups at times convenient for the various groups. In addition to flexible system backups, the distributed aspect of such networks facilitates application backups.

Web servers, in particular, are candidates for high-availability clones of the entire Website. Some products provide for regeneration of a damaged Website from a read-only clone, one that includes hash totals allowing automatic integrity checking of all elements of the exposed and potentially damaged data on the public Website.[33]

57.3.3.3 Workstations. Individual workstations pose special challenges for backup. Although software and backup media are readily available for all operating systems, the human factor interferes with reliable backup. Users typically are not focused on their computing infrastructure; taking care of backups is not a high priority for busy professionals. Even technically trained users, who are aware of the dangers, sometimes skip their daily backups; many novice or technically unskilled workers do not even understand the concept of backups.

If the workstations are connected to a network, then automated, centralized, backup software utilities can protect all the users' files. However, with user disk drives containing as many as 500 GB of storage, and with the popularity of large files such as pictures and videos, storing the new data, let alone the full system, for hundreds of workstations can consume TBs of backup media and saturate limited bandwidths. It takes a minimum of 45 hours to transfer 1 TB over an OC-1 communications channel running at 51.84 megabits per second (Mbps); an OC48 running at 2,488.32 Mbps would transfer 1 TB in 56 minutes.[34] There are also privacy issues in such centralized backup if users fail to encrypt their hard disk files. In addition, it is impossible to compress encrypted data, so encryption and backup software should always compress *before* encrypting data.

57.3.3.4 Laptop Computers. A laptop computer is sometimes the only computer a user owns or is assigned; in other cases, the portable computer is an adjunct to a desktop computer. Laptop computers that are the primary system must be treated like workstations. Laptops that are used as adjuncts—for example, when traveling—can be backed up separately, or they can be synchronized with the corresponding desktop system.

Synchronization software offer a number of options to meet user needs:

- A variety of hardwired connection methods, including cables between serial ports, parallel ports, SCSI ports, and USB ports.
- Remote access protocols allowing users to reach their computer workstations via modem, or through TCP/IP connections via the Internet, to ensure synchronization or file access.
- Cloning, which duplicates the selected file structure of a source computer onto the target computer; cloning deletes files from the target that are not found on the source.
- Filtering, which prevents specific files, or types of files, from being transferred between computers.
- Synchronization, in which all changes on the source computer(s) are replicated onto the target computer(s). One-way synchronization updates the target only; two-way synchronization makes changes to both the target and the source computers.
- Compression and decompression routines to increase throughput during transfers and synchronizations.
- Data comparison functions to update only those portions of files that are different on source and target; for large files, this feature raises effective throughput by orders of magnitude.
- Security provisions to prevent unauthorized remote access to users' computers.
- Log files to record events during file transfers and synchronization.

In addition to making it easier to leave the office with all the right files on one's hard disk, synchronization of portable computers has the additional benefit of creating a backup of the source computer's files. For more complete assurance, the desktop system may be backed up daily onto one or two removable drives, at the same time that the portable computer's files are synchronized. If the portable is worked on overnight, all files should be synchronized again in the morning.

57.3.3.5 Mobile Computing Devices. Another area that is often overlooked is mobile computing devices: dedicated personal digital assistants (PDAs) and today's smart phones with calendars, contact lists, and so on. These devices often contain critically important information for their users, but not everyone realizes the value of making regular backups.

Mobile devices can usually be synchronized with a workstation file such as Outlook or Entourage. Synchronization programs for managing addresses, calendars, tasks, and so on can be configured to copy data unidirectionally from the workstation to the phone or from the phone to the workstation; bidirectional synchronization is also available. Android, Blackberry, iOS Nokia, Symbian, and Windows phones have a number of widely used synchronizing apps available free or at modest cost through the appropriate app stores.

Synchronizing a smart phone or PDA with a workstation has the added benefit of creating a backup on the workstation's disk. Security managers would do well to circulate an occasional reminder for users to synchronize or back up their PDAs and smart phones to prevent data loss should they lose or damage their valuable tool. USB or FireWire cable connections as well as Bluetooth links may be available on different phones. Some phone or PDA docking cradles have a prominent button that activates instant synchronization, which may be completed in only a minute or two (depending on what type of data flow is configured).

One other option for backing up smart phones is cloud-based repositories. For example, Android phones can upload their configuration to and from Gmail accounts.

57.3.4 Testing. Modern backup software can automatically verify the readability of backups as it writes them; this function should not be turned off in a misguided attempt to shorten the backup time.

As mentioned earlier, when preparing for any operation that destroys or may destroy the original data, two independent backups of critical data should be made, one of which may serve as the new original; it is unlikely that exactly the same error will occur in both copies of the backup. Such risky activities include partitioning disk drives, physical repair of systems, moving disk drives from one slot or system to another, and installation of new versions of the operating system.

57.3.5 Known-Good Boot Media. Production systems must take special care to create backup boot media that are known to be uncontaminated by malware or damage from faulty software. Therefore, immediately after the initial installation of a new operating system and its required patches, operators should create a *known-good boot medium* before any other changes are made to the system.

Before applying new patches to the operating system or installing a new program, the operators reboot the system from the previous known-good boot medium and then create the next generation once the patches or program have been installed.

57.4 DATA LIFE CYCLE MANAGEMENT.

Data management has become increasingly important in the United States with electronic discovery and with the passage of laws, such as the Gramm Leach Bliley Act (GLBA), Health Insurance Portability and Accountability Act (HIPAA), and the Sarbanes-Oxley Act (SOX), that regulate how organizations must deal with particular types of data. (For more on these regulations, see Chapter 64 in this *Handbook.*) Data life cycle management (DLM) is a comprehensive approach to managing an organization's data, involving procedures and practices as well as applications. DLM is a policy-based approach to managing the flow of an information system's data throughout its life cycle, from creation and initial storage, to the time when it becomes obsolete and is destroyed. DLM products automate the processes involved, typically organizing data into separate tiers according to specified policies, and automating data migration from one tier to another, based on those policies. As a rule, newer data, and data that must be accessed more frequently, are stored on faster but more expensive storage media, while less critical data are stored on cheaper but slower media.

Having created a backup set, what should be done with it? And how long should the backups be kept? This section looks at issues of archive management and retention from a policy perspective. Section 57.5 looks at the issues of physical storage of backup media, and Section 57.6 reviews policies and techniques for disposing of discarded backup media.

57.4.1 Retention Policies. One of the obvious reasons to make backup copies is to recover from damage to files. With the 2006 changes to the Federal Rules of Civil Procedure (FRCP), the corporate legal staff should provide advice regarding the retention period of certain data in order to comply with legal and regulatory requirements and to avoid potential litigation. In all cases, the combination of business and legal requirements necessitates consultation outside the information technology (IT) department; decisions on data retention policies must involve more than technical resources. Backup data may be used to retrieve files needed for regulatory and business requirements; the next section looks at archive systems as a more effective method of storing and retrieving data needed for business and legal purposes.

The probability that a backup will be useful declines with time. The backup from yesterday is more likely to be needed, and more valuable, than the same kind of backup from last week or last month. Yet each backup contains copies of files that were changed in the period covered by that backup but that may have been deleted since the backup was made. Data center policies on retention vary because of perceived needs and experience as well as in response to business and legal demands. The next sample policy illustrates some of the possibilities in creating retention policies:

- Keep daily backups for one month.
- Keep end-of-week backups for three months.

If your company does not have a data archive system, or if the backup system does not include archival features, you may need to keep the backup media for longer periods:

- Keep end-of-month backups for five years.
- Keep end-of-year backups for 10 years.

With such a policy in place, after one year there will be 55 backups in the system. After five years, there will be 108, and after 10 years, 113 backups will be circulating. Proper labeling, adequate storage space, and stringent controls are necessary to ensure the availability of any required backups. The 2006 changes to the FRCP may require the corporate legal staff to advise retention of certain data for even longer periods, as support for claims of patent rights, or if litigation is envisaged. In all cases, the combination of business and legal requirements necessitates consultation outside the IT department; decisions on data retention policies must involve more than technical resources and may include engineering, accounting, human resources, and so on.

Readers must note that these are merely examples, not fixed recommendations on the retention periods for any organization—those must be tailored to actual requirements.

57.4.2 Rotation. Reusing backup volumes makes economic and functional sense. In general, when planning a backup strategy, different types of backups may be kept for different lengths of time. To ensure even wear on media, volumes should be labeled with the date on which they are returned to a storage area of available media and should be used in order of first in, first out. Backup volumes destined for longer retention should use newer media. An expiry date should be stamped on all tapes when they are acquired so that operations staff will know when to discard outdated media.

57.4.3 Media Longevity and Technology Changes. For short-term storage, there is no problem ensuring that stored information will be usable. Even if a software upgrade changes file formats, the previous versions are usually readable. In one year, technological changes such as new storage formats will not make older formats unreadable.

Over the medium term—up to five years—difficulties of compatibility do increase, although not catastrophically. There are certainly plenty of 5-year-old systems still in use, and it is unlikely that this level of technological inertia will be seriously reduced in the future.

Over the longer term, however, there are serious problems to overcome in maintaining the availability of electronic records. During the last 10 to 20 years, certain forms of storage have become essentially unusable. As an example, the AES company was a powerful force in the dedicated word processor market in the 1970s; 8-inch disks held dozens or hundreds of pages of text and could be read in almost any office in North America. By the late 1980s, however, AES had succumbed to word processing packages running on general-purpose computers; by 1990, the last company supporting AES equipment closed its doors. Today it would be extremely difficult to find the equipment for reading AES diskettes.

The problems of obsolescence include data degradation, software incompatibilities, and hardware incompatibilities.

57.4.3.1 Media Degradation. Magnetic media degrade over time. Over a period of a few years, thermal disruption of magnetic domains gradually blurs the boundaries of the magnetized areas, making it harder for I/O devices to distinguish between the domains representing 1s and those representing 0s. These problems affect tapes, diskettes, and magnetic disks and cause increasing parity errors. Specialized equipment and software can compensate for these errors and recover most of the data on such old media.

Tape media suffer from an additional source of degradation: The metal oxide becomes friable and begins to flake off the Mylar backing. Such losses are unrecoverable. They occur within a few years in media stored under inadequate environmental controls and within five to 10 years for properly maintained media. Regular regeneration by copying the data before the underlying medium disintegrates prevents data loss.

Optical disks, which use laser beams to etch bubbles in the substrate, are much more stable than magnetic media. Current estimates are that CD-ROMs and CD-RW and DVD disks will remain readable, in theory, for at least a decade, and probably longer. However, they will remain readable in practice if, and only if, future optical storage systems include backward compatibility.

USB flash drives have largely replaced floppy diskettes and zip disks as a means of storing or transporting temporary data. Flash drives, similar to flash memory, have a finite number of cycles of writing and erasing before slowing down and failing. Typically, this is not an issue, as the number of cycles is in the hundreds of thousands.[35]

57.4.3.2 Software Changes. Software incompatibilities include the application software and the operating system.

The data may be readable, but will they be usable? Manufacturers provide backward compatibility, but there are limits. For example, Microsoft Word 2007 can convert files from earlier versions of Word—but only back to version 6 for Windows. Over time, application programs evolve and drop support of the earliest data formats. Database programs, e-mail, spreadsheets—all of tomorrow's versions may have trouble interpreting today's data files correctly.

In any case, all conversions raise the possibility of data loss since new formats are not necessarily supersets of old formats. For example, in 1972, RUNOFF text files on mainframe systems included instructions to pause a daisy-wheel impact printer so the operator could change daisy wheels—but there was no requirement to document the desired daisy wheel. The operator made the choice. What would document conversion do with that instruction?

Even operating systems evolve. Programs intended for Windows 3.11 of the early 1990s would not necessarily function on Windows 7 or 8 in 2013. Many older operating systems are no longer supported and do not even run on today's hardware.

Finally, even hardware eventually becomes impossible to maintain. As mentioned, it would be extremely difficult to retrieve and interpret data from word processing equipment from even 20 years ago. No one outside museums or hobbyists can read an 800 bpi 9-track 3/4-inch magnetic tape from the very popular 1980 HP3000 Series III minicomputer. Over time, even such parameters as data encoding standards (e.g., Binary Coded Decimal [BCD], Extended Binary Coded Decimal [EBCDIC], and American Standard Code for Information Interchange [ASCII]) may change, making obsolete equipment difficult to use even if they can be located.

The most robust method developed to date for long-term storage of data is COM (Computer Output to Microfilm). Documents are printed to microfilm, appearing exactly as if they had been printed on paper and then microphotographed. Storage densities are high, storage costs are low, and, if necessary, the images can be read with a source of light and a simple lens or converted to the current machine-readable form using optical character recognition (OCR) software.

57.5 SAFEGUARDING BACKUPS.

Where and how backup volumes are stored affects their longevity, accessibility, and usability for legal purposes.

57.5.1 Environmental Protection.

Magnetic and optical media can be damaged by dust, mold, condensation, freezing, and excessive heat. All locations considered for storage of backup media should conform to the media manufacturer's environmental tolerances; typical values are 40 to 60 percent humidity and temperatures of about 50 to 75° F (about 10 to 25° C). In addition, magnetic media should not be stacked horizontally in piles; the housings of these devices are not built to withstand much pressure, so large stacks can cause damaging contact between the protective shell and the data storage surface. Electromagnetic pulses and magnetic fields are also harmful to magnetic backup media; mobile phones, both wireless and cellular, should be kept away from magnetic media. If degaussers are used to render data more difficult to read before discarding media (see Section 57.6), these devices should never be allowed into an area where magnetic disks or tapes are in use or stored.

57.5.2 Onsite Protection.

It is obviously unwise to keep backups in a place where they are subject to the same risks of destruction as the computer systems they are intended to protect. However, unless backups are made through telecommunications channels to a remote facility, they must spend at least some time in the same location as the systems on which they were made.

At a minimum, backup policies should stipulate that backups are to be removed to a secure, relatively distant location as soon as possible after completion. Temporary onsite storage areas that may be suitable for holding backups until they can be moved offsite include specialized fire-resistant media storage cabinets or safes, secure media storage rooms in the data center, a location on a different floor of a multifloor building, or an appropriate location in a different building of a campus. What is *not* acceptable is to store backup volumes in a cabinet right next to the computer that was backed up. Even worse is the unfortunate habit of leaving backup volumes in a disorganized heap on top of the computer from which the data were copied.

In a small office, backups should be kept in a fire-resistant safe, if possible, while waiting to take the media somewhere else.

57.5.3 Offsite Protection. As mentioned, it is normal to store backups away from the computers and buildings where the primary copies of the backed-up data reside.

57.5.3.1 Care during Transport. When sending backup media out for storage, operations staff should use lockable carrying cases designed for the specific media to be transported. If external firms, specializing in data storage, pick up media, they usually supply such cases as part of a contract. If media are being transported by corporate staff, it is essential to explain the dangers of leaving such materials in a car: In the summer cars can get so hot that they melt the media, whereas in winter they can get so cold that the media instantly attract harmful water condensation when they are brought inside. In any case, leaving valuable data in an automobile exposes them to theft.

57.5.3.2 Homes. The obvious, but dangerous, choice for people in small offices is to send backup media to the homes of trusted employees. There are a number of problems with this storage choice:

- Although the employee may be trustworthy, members of that person's family may not be so. Especially where teenage and younger children are present, keeping an organization's backups in a private home poses serious security risks.
- Environmental conditions in homes may be incompatible with safe long-term storage of media. For example, depending on the cleaning practices of the household, storing backups in a cardboard box under the bed may expose the media to dust, insects, cats, dogs, rodents, and damage from vacuum cleaners. In addition, temperature and humidity controls may be inadequate for safe storage of magnetic media.
- Homeowner's insurance policies are unlikely to cover loss of an employer's property and surely will not cover consequential losses resulting from damage to crucial backup volumes.
- Legal requirements for a demonstrable chain of custody for corporate documentation on backup volumes will not be met if the media are left in a private home where unknown persons may have access to them.

57.5.3.3 Safes. There are no *fireproof* safes, only *fire-resistant* safes. Safes are available with different degrees of guaranteed resistance to specific temperatures commonly found in ordinary fires (those not involving arson and flame accelerants).

Sturdy, small safes of 1 or 2 cubic feet are available for use in small offices or homes; they can withstand the heat during the relatively short time required to burn a house or small building down. They can withstand a fall through one or two floors without breaking open. However, for use in taller buildings, only more expensive and better-built safes are appropriate to protect valuable data.

57.5.3.4 Banks. Banks have facilities for secured, environmentally controlled storage of valuables. Aside from the cost of renting and accessing such boxes, the main problem for backup storage in banks is that banks are open only part of the day; it is almost impossible to access backups in a safe deposit box after normal banking hours. In any case, it is impossible to rent such boxes with enough room for more than a few dozen small backup media. Banks are not usable as data repositories for any but the smallest organizations and should not be considered as a reasonable alternative even for them.

57.5.3.5 Data Vaults. Most enterprises will benefit from contracting with professional, full-time operations that specialize in maintaining archives of backup media. Some of the key features to look for in evaluating such facilities include:

- Storage areas made of concrete and steel construction to reduce risk of fire
- No storage of paper documents in the same building as magnetic or optical media storage
- Full air-conditioning, including humidity, temperature, and dust controls throughout the storage vaults
- Fire sensors and fire-retardant technology, preferably without the use of water
- Full-time security monitoring including motion detectors, guards, and tightly controlled access
- Uniformed, bonded personnel
- Full-time, 24/7/365 data pickup and delivery services
- Efficient communications with procedures for authenticating requests for changes in the lists of client personnel authorized to access archives
- Evidence of sound business planning and stability

References from customers similar in size and complexity to the inquiring enterprise will help a manager make a wise choice among alternative suppliers.

57.5.3.6 Backing Up Online Data. A related topic is the converse of online backups: backing up online services such as Gmail and AOL, where critical data reside on a server out of a user's control. For an e-mail service, use an e-mail client configured to access the service using Post Office Protocol (POP) or Internet Message Access Protocol (IMAP) (see Chapter 5 in this *Handbook*), or use scripting languages to extract data from the server to a hard disk.[36]

57.6 DISPOSAL.

Before throwing out backup media containing unencrypted sensitive information, operations and security staff should ensure that the media are unreadable. This section looks at the problem of data scavenging and then recommends methods for preventing such unauthorized data recovery.

57.6.1 Scavenging. Discarded disk drives with fully readable information have repeatedly been found for sale by computer resellers, at auctions, at used-equipment exchanges, on eBay, and at flea markets and yard sales.[37] In a formal study of the problem from November 2000 through August 2002, MIT scientists Simson Garfinkel and Abhi Shelat bought 158 used disk drives from many types of sources and studied the data they found on the drives. Using special analytical tools, the scientists found a total of 75 GB of readable data. They wrote:

> With several months of work and relatively little financial expenditure, we were able to retrieve thousands of credit card numbers and extraordinarily personal information on many individuals. We believe that the lack of media reports about this problem is simply because, at this point, few people are looking to repurposed hard drives for confidential material. If sanitization practices are not significantly improved, it's only a matter of time before the confidential information on repurposed hard drives is exploited by individuals and organizations that would do us harm.[38]

Computer crime specialists have described unauthorized access to information left on discarded media as scavenging, browsing, and Dumpster®-diving (from the trademarked name of metal bins often used to collect trash outside office buildings).

Scavenging can take place within an enterprise; for example, there have been documented cases of criminals who arranged to read *scratch tapes,* used for temporary storage of data, before they were reused or erased. Often they found valuable data left by previous users. Operations policies should not allow scratch tapes, or other media containing confidential data, to be circulated; all scratch media, including backup media that are being returned to the available list, should be erased before they are put on the media rack.

Before deciding to toss potentially valuable documents or backup media into the trash can, managers should realize that in the United States, according to a U.S. Supreme Court ruling, discarded waste is not considered private property under the law. Anything that is thrown out is fair game for warrantless searches or inspection by anyone who can gain access to it, without violating laws against physical trespass. Readers in other jurisdictions should obtain legal advice on the applicable statutes.

Under these circumstances, the only reasonable protection against data theft is to make the trash unreadable.

57.6.2 Data and Media Destruction. When a file is erased or purged from a magnetic disk, most operating systems leave the information entirely or largely intact, removing only the pointers from the directory. *Unerase* utilities search the disk and reconstruct the chain of *extents* (areas of contiguous storage), usually with human intervention to verify that the data are still good.

57.6.2.1 Field Research on Data Remanence. Garfinkel and Shelat reported on the many failed attempts to destroy (*sanitize*) data on disk drives, including erasure (leaves data almost entirely intact), overwriting (good enough or even perfect but not always properly applied), physical destruction (evidently, renders what is left of the drive unusable), and degaussing (using strong magnetic fields to distort the magnetic domains into unreadability).

With regard to ordinary file-system formatting, the authors noted:

> ...most operating system format commands only write a minimal disk file system; they do not rewrite the entire disk. To illustrate this assertion, we took a 10-Gbyte hard disk and filled every block with a known pattern. We then initialized a disk partition using the Windows 98 FDISK

> command and formatted the disk with the format command. After each step, we examined the disk to determine the number of blocks that had been written. . . . Users might find these numbers discouraging: despite warnings from the operating system to the contrary, the format command overwrites barely more than 0.1 percent of the disk's data. Nevertheless, the command takes more than eight minutes to do its job on the 10-Gbyte disk—giving the impression that the computer is actually overwriting the data. In fact, the computer is attempting to read all of the drive's data so it can build a bad-block table. The only blocks that are actually written during the format process are those that correspond to the boot blocks, the root directory, the file allocation table, and a few test sectors scattered throughout the drive's surface.[39]

57.6.2.2 Operating System Formatting. Multiuser operating systems remove pointers from the disk directory (*file allocation table*) and return all sectors in a purged file to a disk's *free space map*, but the data in the original extents (sections of contiguous disk space) persist until overwritten, unless specific measures are taken to obliterate them. Over time, as the disk continues to be used, some of the deleted file data are likely to be overwritten by chance as the free extents are assigned to new files and overwritten during file initialization and further data storage to these previously used sectors.

Formatting a hard disk using Windows' *Quick Format* option deletes no data except pointers to the file labels.[40] Full formatting does overwrite all the data on the disk, but not so thoroughly that the information cannot be read.

57.6.2.3 Clearing Data. *Erase* functions are widely available through free or purchased utilities; they typically not only remove entries in the file allocation table but actually overwrite the data up to the end-of-file using pseudorandom sequences in multiple passes. Some of these utilities explicitly overwrite slack space (the sectors between the end of file and the end of the last extent).

Even full formatting and explicit overwriting files on magnetic media do not make them unreadable to sophisticated equipment and forensic software. Since information on magnetic tapes and disks resides in the difference in intensity between highly magnetized areas (1s) and less-magnetized areas (0s), writing the same 0s or 1s in all areas to be obliterated merely reduces the signal-to-noise ratio. That is, the residual magnetic fields still vary in more or less the original pattern—they are just less easily distinguished. Using highly sensitive readers, a magnetic tape or disk that has been zeroed will yield much of the original information.

One way of *clearing* data[41] on magnetic media is to overwrite using several passes of random patterns. The random patterns make it far more difficult, *but not impossible*, to extract useful information from the discarded disks and tapes. For this reason, the U.S. Government no longer allows overwriting of classified media to obliterate data remanence when moving media to a lower level of protection. Small removable thumb drives of 2 GB and Advanced Technology Attachment (ATA) disk drives of 15 GB or more can use a *secure erase* to purge data.[42] ATA drives have secure erase in their firmware. Secure erase for thumb drives can be downloaded from the University of California, San Diego (UCSD) CMRR site.[43]

Degaussers can be used to remove data remanence physically. A degausser is a device that generates a magnetic field used to sanitize magnetic media. Degaussers are rated based on the type (i.e., low energy or high energy) of magnetic media they can purge. Degaussers operate using either a strong permanent magnet or an electromagnetic coil. These devices range from simple handheld units suitable for low-volume usage to high-energy units capable of erasing magnetic media, either oxide- or metal-based, up to 1,700 Oersteds (Oe). These devices remove all traces of previously recorded data, allowing the media to be used again. The U.S. Government has approved certain degaussers for secure erasure of classified data. Degaussing of any hard drive assembly usually destroys the drive, as degaussing also erases firmware that manages the device. There are other downsides to using degaussers.

57.6.2.4 Shredding.

Another solution is physical destruction[44] of magnetic or optical backup media before they are discarded. For end user departments, operations and security staff can provide identifiable secure collection receptacles (typically black) throughout the enterprise. Discarded media can be erased or destroyed by appropriate staff on a regular schedule. Hard disks, tapes, optical disks, and floppy disks can be cut into pieces, melted with oxyacetylene torches, crushed in large compactors, and incinerated, although proper incineration requires specialized equipment to prevent atmospheric release of toxic by-products. Some commercial companies specialize in secure destruction of sensitive records and can provide bonded pickup services, or mobile destruction units, that move from enterprise to enterprise on a regular schedule and handle paper as well as magnetic and optical media.

Ensconce Data Technology, a firm specializing in secure data destruction, has argued that software overwriting alone is not trustworthy because the choice of algorithm may be inadequate and because certain portions of the drive may not be overwritten at all. Degaussing is unreliable and even dangerous; sometimes drives are damaged so that they cannot be checked by users to evaluate the completeness of data wiping—even though expert data recovery specialists may be able to extract usable data from the degaussed disks. The strong magnetic fields can also unintentionally damage other equipment. Outsourcing degaussing introduces problems of having to store drives until pickup, losing control over data, and having to trust third parties to provide trustworthy records of the data destruction.

Physical shredders capable of securely destroying magnetic hard drive disks are expensive and usually offered only by outside companies, leading to similar problems of temporary storage, relinquishing control, and dubious audit trails. Ensconce Data Technology's *Digital Shredder* is a small, portable hardware device that provides a wide range of interfaces called *personality modules* that allow a variety of disk drives to be wiped securely. The design objectives, quoting the company, were to provide:

1. Destruction of data beyond forensic recovery
2. Retention of care, custody, and control
3. Certification and defendable audit trail
4. Ease of deployment
5. Ability to recycle the drive for reuse

The unit can wipe up to three disks at once. It includes its own touch screen; offers user authentication with passwords to ensure that it is not misused by unauthorized personnel; provides positive indications through colored light-emitting diodes (LEDs) to show the current status of each bay; can format drives for a range of file systems; and can be used to reimage a drive by making bitwise copies from a master drive in one bay to a reformatted drive in another.[45]

57.7 COSTS.

All data-center managers should be able to answer questions about the costs of the backups being made on their systems. Exhibit 57.2 presents the factors

Disk Costs, Variable	
a. Disks/Backup	______
b. Purchase Cost/Disk	______
c. Disk Cost/Backup (a*b)	______
Time Costs, Variable	
d. Hours/Backup Disk	______
e. Total Disks/Backup	______
f. Total Hours/Backup (d*e)	______
g. Operator Cost/Hour (Salary + Benefits)	______
h. Time Cost/Backup (f*g)	______
Total Variable Costs/Backup (f+h)	______
Fixed Costs	
i. Monthly costs of storage space, racks, insurance, transportation, hardware rental and maintenance, software rental and maintenance, cost of time to combine daily backups into weekly, weekly into monthly, etc.	______
j. Number of Backups/Month	______
k. Fixed Cost/Backup (i/j)	______
Total Variable and Fixed Costs/Backup (f+h+k)	______
Annualized Costs	
l. Backups/Year	______
m. Total Variable and Fixed Costs/Backup (f+h+k)	______
n. Total Cost/Year (l*m)	______

EXHIBIT 57.2 Calculating Costs of Backup

that should be included in a simple spreadsheet when calculating costs of backups, with disks as an example of backup media.

57.8 OPTIMIZING FREQUENCY OF BACKUPS.

Suppose a manager asks the security and operations staff these questions:

- "If backups are so important that you do a daily full backup, why don't you do a full backup twice a day?"
- "If taking a daily full backup is good enough for you, why don't you save money by doing a full backup only every other day?"

To answer such questions, managers must be able to adjust the frequency of backups to the perceived risk. One of the ways of approaching a rational allocation of resources when faced with random threats is to calculate the *expected value* of a strategy. The expected value is the average gain (if it is a positive quantity) or loss (if it is negative) that participants will incur in a process that involves random events. When this technique applies to losses over an entire year, it is called the *annualized loss expectancy*. Insurance companies use this approach to balance the costs of premiums against the disbursements to customers.

For backups, the principle is summarized by this equation:

$E(x) = P(u)^{*}C(u) - P(n)^{*}C(n)$

where:

x = Some particular strategy, such as doing a daily full backup.

$E(x)$ = Expected value or cost of the strategy.

$P(u)$ = Probability of having to use the backup within a single day; for example, 1 chance in 1,000, or 0.001.

$C(u)$ = Money saved by not having to redo all the work that would otherwise be lost if there were no backup; for example, the cost of paying for reconstruction of the previous day's data (e.g., \$9,000) + avoidance of lost business, wasted salary, and other expenses during 3 hours of downtime during reconstruction (e.g., \$30,000) for a savings of \$39,000 per incident when the backups are available.

$P(n)$ = Probability of not having to use the backups at all in a given day = 1 − $P(u)$ = 0.999.

$C(n)$ = Cost of making and storing a daily backup that will not be used (e.g., \$50).

The expected value of doing a single daily full backup using the figures used in the last example is

$E(x) = (0.001.\$39,000) - (0.990.\$50) = \$39 - \$49.95 = -\$10.95$

In other words, the daily full backup has an average cost of about \$11 per day when the likelihood of its use is factored into the calculations. This is equivalent to a self-insurance strategy to prevent larger disasters by investing money in preventive mechanisms and measures for rapid and less expensive recovery than possible without the backups.

If one adjusts the frequency of backups, the calculated loss expectancy can be forced to zero or even to a positive number; however, no self-insurer can make a profit from loss-avoidance measures. Nonetheless, adjusting the frequency and costs of backup strategies using the suggested factors and calculation of loss expectancies can help a data center manager answer questions from management about backup strategies in a rational manner. Since no one can estimate precisely how much a disaster costs or compute precise probabilities of having to use backups for recovery, these figures can serve only as rough guidelines.

In many organizations, the volume of changes follows a seasonal pattern. For example, 80 percent of all orders taken might come in two three-month periods spaced several months apart. For example, registration for college courses occurs mostly in the autumn, with another bulge in January. Boat, swimsuit, and ski sales follow seasonal variations. Despite this obvious variability, many organizations foolishly follow the same backup schedule regardless of date. It makes sense to adjust the frequency of backups to the volatility of data, since operations can schedule more frequent backups when there are many changes and fewer when the data are relatively stable.

57.9 CONCLUDING REMARKS. Backups are an essential component of operational security, and they play a crucial role in business resumption and disaster recovery. Backup policies should be developed rationally as a function of the specific requirements of each application, and of each computer system. Because conditions change, backup policies should be adjusted as needed to reflect changing requirements. Decisions on keeping archival copies of data should include consideration of legal requirements. Backup policies should include provisions for the full life cycle of the backup media, including acquisition, rotation, storage, and destruction.

57.10 FURTHER READING

Cosgrove, R. *Online Backup Guide for Service Providers—How to Start and Operate an Online Backup Service*. Lulu.com, 2010.

EMC Education Services. *Information Storage and Management: Storing, Managing, and Protecting Digital Information in Classic, Virtualized, and Cloud Environments*, 2nd ed. Wiley, 2012.

Kyriazis, D. *Data Intensive Storage Services for Cloud Environments*. IGI Global, 2013.

Landis, C., and D. Blacharski. *Cloud Computing Made Easy: An Easy to Understand Reference about Cloud Computing*. CreateSpace Independent Publishing Platform, 2013.

Little, D. B., and D. A. Chapa. *Implementing Backup and Recovery: The Readiness Guide for the Enterprise*. Wiley, 2003.

Mather, T., S. Kumaraswamy, and S. Latif. *Cloud Security and Privacy: An Enterprise Perspective on Risks and Compliance*. O'Reilly Media, 2009.

McGehee, S. *SQL Server Backup and Restore*. Red Gate Books, 2012.

Nelson, S. *Pro Data Backup and Recovery*. Apress, 2011.

Nielsen, L. *The Little Book of Cloud Computing, 2013 Edition: Including Coverage of Big Data Tools*. New Street Communications, 2013.

Preston, W. C. *Backup & Recovery: Inexpensive Backup Solutions for Open Systems*. O'Reilly Media, 2007.

Rhoton, J., J. De Clercq, and D. Graves. Cloud Computing Protected: Security Assessment Handbook. Recursive, 2013.

Schilling, C. O. *Online Backups and Cloud Computing: The Stupidly Simple Way To Backup Your Digital Life*. Amazon Digital Services, 2012.

Winkler, J. R. Securing the Cloud: Cloud Computer Security Techniques and Tactics. Syngress, 2011.

57.11 NOTES

1. According to a 1998 proposal from the International Electrotechnical Commission, the preferred prefixes should be KiB for kibibytes, MiB for mebibytes, GiB for gibibytes, and TiB for tebibytes to distinguish them from the powers-of-10 notations using kilo (103), mega (106), giga (109), and tera (1012), but this suggestion has not yet been accepted by the technical community. See NIST Reference on Constants, Units and Uncertainty. http://physics.nist.gov/cuu/Units/binary.html
2. SNIA CDP SIG, Continuous Data Protection Special Interest Group (2008), www.snia.org/forums/dmf/programs/data_protect_init/cdp (URL inactive). For information on Data Protection and Capacity Optimization Committee, www.snia.org/forums/dpco
3. For more extensive discussion of RAID levels, see IBM Technote, "About RAID levels and ClearCase" (2009), http://www-01.ibm.com/support/docview.wss?uid=swg21149421

4. 3D2F.com Software Directory, "Automatic Folder File Free Software" (2008), http://3d2f.com/tags/software/automatic/mirror/folder/file
5. 3D2F NFTP download, http://3d2f.com/programs/5-339-nftp-download.shtml
6. M. Wise, "Windows XP Systems Restore," Windows & .NET Magazine (September 2002), http://technet.microsoft.com/en-us/library/bb490854.aspx
7. Microsoft TechNet, "How to Roll Back a Device Driver, for the IT Pro" (2001), http://technet.microsoft.com/en-us/library/bb457021.aspx
8. In 1980, an HP7925 120 MB drive the size of a washing machine cost $25,000—about $213,333 per GB in 1980 dollars. In 2008, a Seagate 1 TB drive the size of a paperback book cost $237—about $0.23 per GB in 2008 dollars or roughly $0.07 in 1980 dollars. The compounded annual rate of decline in the cost of disk storage over 28 years was thus about 0.58 per year—pretty close to Moore's Law. See Intel Museum, "Moore's Law" (2008); www.intel.com/museum/archives/history_docs/mooreslaw.htm
9. Bit-for-bit copies are used in forensic analysis (see Chapter 55 in this Handbook) and include the entire contents of a storage medium, including control information and unused areas, in exactly the original layout found on the source device. In contrast, the term "clone" implies that all functional data are replicated but does not require identical distribution of those data on the physical media. Thus a bit-for-bit copy will include bad sectors and deleted files, but a clone will not.
10. hVault Holographic Storage Systems, "How It Works," http://hvault.com/a-brief-description-of-how-holographic-storage-works
11. hVault Holographic Storage Systems, "Products," http://hvault.com/solutions-for-any-size-application
12. SNIA, "Virtual Tape Library Buyer's Guide" (2006), www.snia.org/sites/default/files/SNIA_DMF_V6_DPI_Guide_4WEB.pdf
13. FalconStor, "Virtual Tape Library with Deduplication for the Fastest, Most Scalable Backup," www.falconstor.com/products/virtual-tape-library
14. P. Vettiger, et al., "The 'Millipede'—More than One Thousand Tips for Future AFM Data Storage," *IBM Journal of Research and Development* 44, No. 3 (2000): 323–340; http://ieeexplore.ieee.org/xpl/login.jsp?tp=&arnumber=5389137
15. M. Humprhies, "IBM Showcases Millipede Storage." *GEEK News*, March 16, 2005, www.geek.com/news/ibm-showcases-millipede-storage-559662
16. M. Gibbs, "Storage? You Want Storage? How about 360TB per Disk?" *Network World Gearhead* (2013-07-11). www.networkworld.com/community/toolshed/storage-you-want-storage-how-about-360tb-disk
17. Federal Rules of Civil Procedure, www.law.cornell.edu/rules/frcp
18. www.emc.com/archiving/centera.htm
19. E. Mendelson and M. Muchmore, "The Best Backup Software," *PC Magazine*, March 25, 2013, www.pcmag.com/article2/0,2817,2278661,00.asp
20. Cisco, "Cisco Visual Networking Index: Forecast and Methodology, 2012–2017," May 29, 2013, www.cisco.com/en/US/solutions/collateral/ns341/ns525/ns537/ns705/ns827/white_paper_c11-481360_ns827_Networking_Solutions_White_Paper.html
21. J. Brodkin, "Bandwidth Explosion: As Internet Use Soars, Can Bottlenecks Be Averted? Bandwidth Usage Is Soaring, Driven by the Proliferation of Internet-Connected Devices." *Ars|technica*, May 1, 2012, http://arstechnica.com/

business/2012/05/bandwidth-explosion-as-internet-use-soars-can-bottlenecks-be-averted

22. H. Marks, "New Cloud Backup Pricing Targets Recovery," *Network Computing*, July 10, 2013, www.networkcomputing.com/backup-recovery/new-cloud-backup-pricing-targets-recover/240158054
23. SNIA Cloud Storage Initiative, www.snia.org/forums/csi
24. SNIA CDMI Cloud Storage Standard, www.snia.org/cloud/newcontent
25. M. Ricknäs, "Amazon Web Services Moves Backups to Cloud with New Appliance: The Appliance Costs $125 per Month, While Storage Capacity and Data Transfer Is Extra," *Network World*, January 25, 2012, www.networkworld.com/news/2012/012512-amazon-web-services-moves-backups-255284.html
26. S. Bradner, "Cloud Services: Computus Interruptus: Hard To Get Work Done when Cloud Services Go Down," *Network World*, March 20, 2013, www.networkworld.com/columnists/2013/032013-bradner.html
27. G. Merrill, "Can You Comply with Court Orders for Data from the Cloud?" *Network World*, July 18, 2011, www.networkworld.com/newsletters/sec/2011/071811sec1.html
28. "Dave," "Dropping the Ball on Dropbox," M. E. Kabay's *InfoSec Perception* Website, April 19, 2013, http://resources.infosecskills.com/perception/dropping-the-ball-on-dropbox
29. J. Legendre, "Cloud Storage: The Risks and Rewards," Norwich University IS340 Term Paper, November 14, 2012, www.mekabay.com/infosecmgmt/cloud_storage.pdf
30. P. Bright, "A Step Back in Time with Window 8's File History: Microsoft Reinvents Time Machine for the Second Time," *Ars|technica*, July 10, 2012, http://arstechnica.com/information-technology/2012/07/a-step-back-in-time-with-windows-8s-file-history
31. M. E. Kabay, "Backups as an Anti-Plagiarism Tool," *Network World*, March 9, 2011, www.networkworld.com/newsletters/sec/2011/030711sec2.html
32. S. Jelley, "Information Anesthetic: Taking the Pain out of Backup," *Symantec | Connect*, January 22, 2013, www.symantec.com/connect/blogs/taking-pain-out-backup
33. SiteVault Site Backup Utility, www.site-vault.com
34. OC48 has a bandwidth of 2.49E3 Mbps, which is 2.61E9 bps; 1 TB, which is 8.80E12 bits, takes 8.80E12/2.61E9 = 3.37E3 seconds = 56.2 minutes.
35. G. Crump, "How Long Will Flash SSD Last?" *InformationWeek*, May 10, 2011, www.informationweek.com/storage/systems/how-long-will-flash-ssd-last/229403122
36. G. Trapani, "Geek to Live: Back up Gmail with Fetchmail," *Lifehacker* (2007), http://lifehacker.com/software/gmail/geek-to-live—back-up-gmail-with-fetchmail-235207.php
37. Parts of this section are taken and modified from M. E. Kabay, "Disk Data Remanence, Part 1: The Problem," and following parts. *Network World Security Strategies* (2007), www.networkworld.com/newsletters/sec/2007/0730sec2.html
38. S. L. Garfinkel and A. Shelat, "Remembrance of Data Passed: A Study of Disk Sanitization Practices," *IEEE Security & Privacy* (January/February 2003), www.myoops.org/twocw/harvard/distribution/lectures/8/articles8.pdf

39. Garfinkel and Shelat, "Remembrance of Data Passed."
40. Windows, "Formatting Disks and Drives," http://windows.microsoft.com/en-us/windows-vista/formatting-disks-and-drives
41. Clearing information is a level of media sanitization that would protect the confidentiality of information against a robust keyboard attack. Simple deletion of items would not suffice for clearing. Clearing must not allow information to be retrieved by data, disk, or file recovery utilities. It must be resistant to keystroke recovery attempts executed from standard input devices and from data scavenging tools. For example, overwriting is an acceptable method for clearing media. Most media can be cleared with one overwrite. (NIST DRAFT Guidelines for Media Sanitization, SP800-88 Rev. 1, September 6, 2012). http://csrc.nist.gov/publications/PubsDrafts.html#SP-800-88-Rev.%201
42. Purging information is a media sanitization process that protects the confidentiality of information against a laboratory attack. A laboratory attack would involve a threat with the resources and knowledge to use nonstandard systems to conduct data recovery attempts on media outside their normal operating environment. This type of attack involves using signal processing equipment and specially trained personnel. (NIST DRAFT Guidelines for Media Sanitization, SP800-88 Rev. 1, September 6, 2012). http://csrc.nist.gov/publications/PubsDrafts.html#SP-800-88-Rev.%201
43. Center for Magnetic Recording Research, University of San Diego, http://cmrr.ucsd.edu
44. Destruction of media is the ultimate form of sanitization. After media are destroyed, they cannot be reused as originally intended.
45. Ensconce Data Technology, "Digital Shredder," www.deadondemand.com/products/digitalshredder

CHAPTER 58

BUSINESS CONTINUITY PLANNING

Michael Miora

58.1 INTRODUCTION.

We are in an age where businesses and governments are turning in increasing numbers to high-technology systems, and to the Internet, to gain and maintain their competitive advantage. Businesses of all types are relying on high-technology products to build, promote, sell, and deliver their wares and services—as are government, educational, and nonprofit enterprises. All of these are dependent on technology to maintain their income, image, and profitability. Business continuity planning (BCP) is the process of protecting organizations from the deleterious effects on their missions that can result from outages in information systems.

The goal of BCP is to protect the operations of the enterprise, not just the computing systems. Prudent planning is not restricted to computer or telecommunications systems

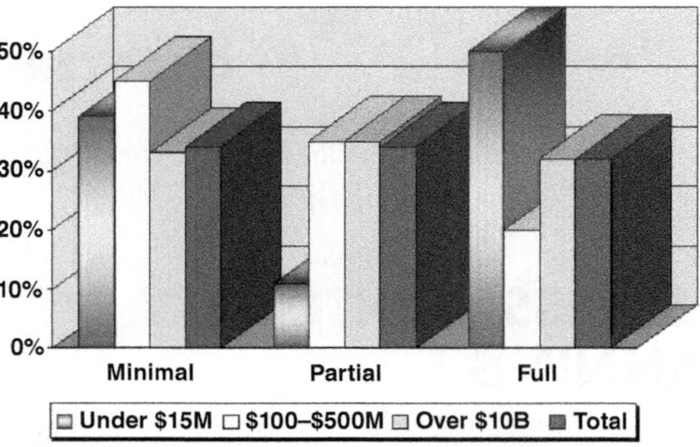

EXHIBIT 58.1 Corporate Preparedness
Source: BC Management, "2003 Benchmark Study Results."

but is enterprise wide. There lies the key difference between the traditional hot sites and service providers and the newer, self-contained, and supported backup and recovery capabilities. Without the people, procedures, and connectivity to keep the enterprise going, there is little point in restoring systems.

The enterprise has evolved to this dependency through the continual redefining of the word *fast* and the growing expectation of having access to information anywhere and at any time. In the 1960s and 1970s, fast turnaround meant a week or, with luck, a few days. In the 1980s, fast was redefined to mean *today*—the 1980s brought lower-cost computing and the beginning of high-speed communications. For the 1990s, fast meant *now*. The 1990s brought the Internet, intranets, and extranets, with distributed systems, sophisticated client/server architectures, and high-speed communications.

Today, information is predominantly collected and sent electronically, often without human intervention. Analyses have been automated and streamlined, strengthened by user-friendly tools and by expert systems. Data are requested, sent, and analyzed in minutes; reports are generated automatically; and presentations can be created, edited, and delivered in near–real time. Moreover, access to information is provided almost equally fast to internal corporate personnel, to business partners and allies, and to customers and consumers.

It should be self-evident to business owners and other stakeholders that planning is an important function and that no enterprise, large or small, should be without a plan. However, as shown in Exhibit 58.1, this is not the case. Regardless of the size of the enterprise, full readiness to handle disruptions is not universally achieved. For larger enterprises, only one-third of companies claim to be fully prepared. For smaller companies, the number is larger, but the validity of some of these responses may be questioned, given that this result is based on self-assessments reported to a survey organization.

At least one partial explanation for this lack of preparedness goes to the heart of how BCP is understood in the business community. It is not clearly understood that the goal of BCP is to protect the business, not simply its equipment or information; at least one goal of this chapter is to show that the focus of the planning should be on business issues.

58.1.1 Enterprise Risks and Costs. The overall risk is to the continued survival of the enterprise. A company weakened by a disaster and without adequate preparation may be unable to recover before failure or a hostile takeover occurs. In the

1970s, formal business continuity plans did not exist; only data backup and recovery procedures, with some disaster recovery planning for large systems, was considered. Today, companies without active and tested enterprise contingency plans are likely to fail in the event of a disaster. Such failures may have dire consequences for the board and corporate officers, whose lack of due diligence is demonstrated by the absence of planning. The need for planning may be well recognized, but protected companies are still in the minority.

There is abundant evidence that unprotected companies suffer greatly during major outages. In investment trading, time is crucial, yet many investment firms did not have a plan in place until late 1993, when a major hot-site provider first built a contingency trading facility in New York. Companies protected by disaster recovery plans can control their losses, holding them down to reasonable levels. Experts in the field believe that companies without such plans are likely to suffer significantly greater losses, with consequences so critical that almost 50 percent of firms that do not recover within 10 days never will recover.

R. A. Elbra, the author of "Contingency Planning," a technical report published in 1989 for the National Computing Center (London), demonstrated that if a critical system was inoperable without suitable backup for as few as six days, the cumulative loss could amount to 200 percent of the net daily income produced by that system. After 12 days, the cumulative loss could be 800 percent of the net daily income, as shown in Exhibit 58.2. In the years since that report was published, the reliance by large and small enterprises on their systems has grown significantly. As greater portions of corporate revenues are closely tied to systems and connectivity, these numbers take on even greater significance.

Even today, few industries have strict disaster recovery or business continuity planning regulations. The banking industry is subject to such regulations for portions of its systems only. Even Sarbanes-Oxley has minimal requirements, although there are other U.S. Federal and state laws that lay requirements on financial services organizations. The Health Insurance Portability and Accountability Act (HIPAA) contains security and privacy elements that make business continuity plans even more important than before, although full BCP is not a specific requirement.

There are many examples of serious downtime, including one instance of a construction crew repairing a nearby roadway and mistakenly damaging the power lines feeding a nearby set of buildings. Repairs required parts that delayed completion of

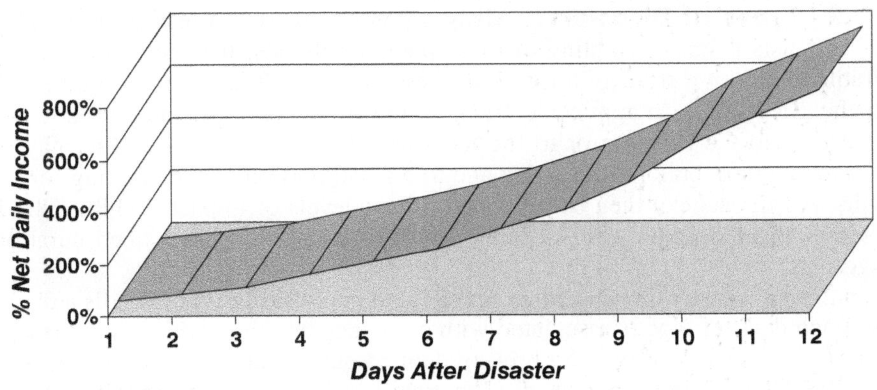

EXHIBIT 58.2 Fiscal Losses Caused by Disasters

repairs for almost 48 hours. One of the affected companies was an electrical supply company with revenues of approximately $50 million annually. The company felt safe because it had a plan that included reciprocal agreements to share spare computer time with other companies using similar equipment. Unfortunately, the company was unable to secure as much time as it expected because some of the other companies had changed equipment since the agreements were made, some were too busy with their own processing, and some simply did not abide by their agreements. To the chagrin of management, the replacement capability was limited to 30 percent of normal processing. Management reported that this outage cost the company over $250,000 in lost and unrecoverable sales. Although managers were unsure of their market share losses, they did know that two major customers subsequently split their orders between the affected company and another supplier. Although this is not a headline-grabbing disaster, it did significantly affect this financially healthy company.

A less healthy company might have been bankrupted by such a loss. Even surviving businesses experience significantly lower profits for the two-year period following a disaster. Reconstruction costs usually exceed insurance allowances and typically involve uninsured costs for modernization. Insurance premiums usually rise, and advertising budgets increase, to repair the corporate image. The largest problems, however, are due to productivity declines and inefficient operations caused by production restarts, debugging efforts, and the need to retrain newly hired staff to replace employees who departed in fear of corporate collapse or layoffs.

Cantor Fitzgerald, a bond company with a major office in the World Trade Center, lost 733 workers in the North Tower on September 11, 2001. The company's disaster recovery plans and mirroring sites enabled it to be back in action and taking orders just 47 hours after that loss. This was especially noteworthy because of the range of the disaster and the fact that the tragic loss of life included approximately 150 information technology workers.

Management's voice is needed to address another key issue. During natural disasters, employees at all levels of the corporate structure will make family and home their top priority. The successful recovery plan considers the need for employees with recovery responsibilities to ascertain first the condition of their own homes and families. Corporate management can make it clear to all employees that people come first. Recovery plans must provide participants with the time and the means to reach their loved ones. Once people are satisfied that families and homes are safe, then they can turn their full attention to corporate recovery.

58.1.2 Types of Disasters. Many different threats can lead to disasters. Exhibit 58.3 lists a small sampling of these potential threats. It is neither feasible nor desirable to design a strategy for each of these disasters. It is more important to consider the effects of each applicable potential threat. For example, a bomb threat may deny access to the building or to the local area for a time. A small fire may deny access to an entire building for a day and to a small portion of the building for a few months. All threats can then be grouped by their levels of impact. Exhibit 58.4 lists one hierarchical structure that maps the levels of impact to a predefined duration of outages.

Identifying disaster threats and grouping them into disaster types fulfills a planning need. Each disaster type is associated with an outage duration, which is the length of downtime expected, and with a set of predefined outage durations, such as indicated in Exhibit 58.4. Therefore, each disaster type can be mapped to specific corporate functions that will be affected.

♦ Accidents	♦ Equipment Problems
♦ Airports	♦ Fire
♦ Arson	♦ Flood
♦ Blackout	♦ Forced Evacuation
♦ Bomb Threat	♦ Hurricane
♦ Building/Facility Inaccessibility	♦ Ice Storms
♦ Chemical Spills	♦ Key Resource Loss
♦ Civil Disorders	♦ Labor Disputes
♦ Civil Disturbances	♦ Malicious Damage
♦ Computer Compromise	♦ Municipal Services Stoppages
♦ Computer Virus	♦ Postal Service Disruption
♦ Construction Damage	♦ Power Loss or Fluctuation
♦ Construction Obstruction	♦ Riot
♦ Data Diddling	♦ Security Breach
♦ Data Loss	♦ Strike
♦ Disgruntled Employee	♦ Terrorism
♦ Drug Abuse	♦ Tornado
♦ Earthquake	♦ Toxic Spills
♦ Elevator Failure	♦ Vandalism
♦ Embezzlement	♦ Volcano
♦ Environmental Control Failure	♦ Water

EXHIBIT 58.3 Disaster Threats

Area Affected	*Duration of Outage*
Partial Building	Less than 1 Day
	1–3 Days
	4–7 Days
	Week to Month
	More than Month
Full Building	Less than 1 Day
	1–3 Days
	4–7 Days
	Week to Month
	More than Month
Multi-Building (Campus Facility)	Less than 1 Day
	1–3 Days
	4–7 Days
	Week to Month
	More than Month
Local Area (Immediate)	Less than 1 Day
	1–3 Days
	4–7 Days
	Week to Month
	More than Month
Region	Less than 1 Day
	1–3 Days
	4–7 Days
	Week to Month
	More than Month

EXHIBIT 58.4 Levels of Impact and Durations

For example, a bomb threat may affect an entire building, but only for a fraction of a day. If this is so, then protecting against a bomb threat requires protecting only those corporate functions performed in that building whose survival time is one day or less. A toxic spill caused by a nearby train derailment may disrupt an entire facility, or campus of buildings, for several days. Protecting against a toxic spill requires protecting all functions whose survival time is less than several days. A regional disaster such as an earthquake, flood, or hurricane, however, disrupts operations for a longer period, and may prevent quick recovery anywhere within the affected area.

Business continuity plans need to be developed in a modular fashion so that modules can be activated depending on the disaster type. Assessing the expected duration of a disaster provides a means of determining which functions should be scheduled for recovery initiation; assessing the level of impact provides a mechanism for determining what type of recovery should be performed on each function. These are the two major factors that need to be identified promptly after a disaster: estimated duration and expected level of impact.

On September 11, 2001, there were many companies whose complete operations were destroyed. In one case, all of the staff perished. Yet, the companies that had made business continuity and disaster recovery in advance did recover, some with no discernable long-lasting impact to the client base or long-term profitability. The companies that survived and flourished had preplanned, prestaged, up-to-date hot sites, either through an external provider or internally.

The key point is that planning for specific threats is not necessary. Planning for types of outages is more efficient and more effective. It may not matter whether the building is damaged by fire, water, or terrorist attack, but the extent of damage and the duration of the outage are important, for those factors determine the types of recoveries to make. Traditionally, enterprise risks were calculated on a per-threat basis. Each threat was analyzed to determine the percentage probability of that threat occurring within a period. Those probabilities were then summed over all possible threats. The resulting figure was a representation of probability of some disaster having a significant impact on business operations over a period such as a year. The disadvantage of this method is that it misleads management into believing that the probabilities are so small as to be insignificant. A different and more streamlined analysis is more useful for the disaster recovery process. It is called the *Generalized Cost Consequence model* (GCC) and is described in Section 58.5.2.

58.1.3 Recovery Scenarios.

Recovery scenarios are the planned steps to be followed when disaster strikes. These scenarios are designed based on the various threat levels of impact and durations. All recovery scenarios are built in three phases, or sequences, of activities as shown in Exhibit 58.5.

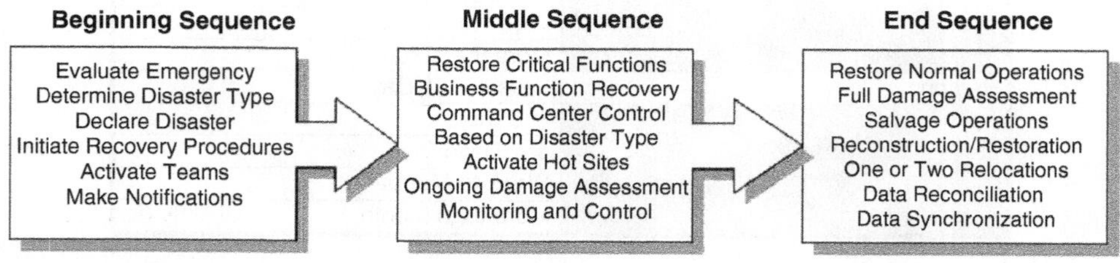

EXHIBIT 58.5 Phases of Recovery

The beginning sequence evaluates an emergency to determine the effect of the event on the enterprise. This can be an unhurried, deliberate activity when there is sufficient notice of an approaching problem. An example of this is a hurricane, where weather reports contain warnings days in advance and additional information can be evaluated as it becomes available. In contrast, the pace is highly fast and frenetic during an evacuation due to fire, flood, or earthquake. Achieving a safe position is always the first consideration; following that are the other steps: determining the disaster type and declaring a disaster; activating the disaster recovery teams; making legal, regulatory, and other notifications; and establishing command and control centers. This beginning sequence often involves top corporate management.

The middle sequence includes most of the major recovery activities. Whereas the beginning sequence determines the type of disaster in progress, this sequence provides procedures to the various functional groups based on the type of disaster in progress. One key element of the middle sequence is to perform ongoing damage assessments and maintain contact with salvage operations. Knowledgeable information technology personnel should be available to review salvage possibilities and rebuilding plans for information equipment.

The end sequence restores normal operating conditions. This phase of recovery is the least predictable of all, and is linked to disaster type and to specific threats. Therefore, this phase is planned in more general terms than the two preceding sequences. In the end sequence, detailed damage assessment is performed. Salvage operations for vital records, information equipment, data, and general facility equipment take place. Reconstruction or relocation activities are specified and executed. Finally, normal operations are restored. Often the end sequence includes two facility relocations. The first relocation moves operations from the emergency operations centers, including the command center, hot sites, work area recovery centers, and other offsite workplaces, to a longer-term interim operating area. This longer-term operating area may be a cold site or other temporary work area. The second relocation is from the interim facility back to the reconstructed, or to a newly constructed, permanent home.

Completion of the recovery plan occurs when normal operations are restored. Ending the formalized recovery procedures before then may introduce errors and may compromise integrity in the final move to the permanent facility. In this final move, large processing equipment is torn down and moved, just as it was during the initial disaster declaration, only in a more deliberate manner. Temporary operations may require use of the reserve systems as backup in case the move encounters problems. Often much of the equipment at the interim site is required at the permanent site. Finally, data reconciliation, the merging of data from different operating environments, and data synchronization require planning and careful implementation to prevent the destruction and replacement of good data with erroneous information.

The traditional disaster recovery strategies include hot sites for data centers and emergency services for employees. These sites have been effective and continue to be necessary, but not sufficient. New strategies are needed to consider the new ways of doing business: mobile computing, real-time sales and service support, client-server architectures, extensive telecommunications, real-time process controls, and online customer service support. Preplanned recovery capabilities can resurrect functions that depend on huge databases and large systems in hours rather than days. Connectivity can be restored in minutes, and the client base need never know that a disaster has occurred. Business can continue, no matter what has happened, so long as proper recovery precautions have been taken.

58.2 DEFINING THE GOALS. Defining the specific goals of a business continuity plan is a multistep process that correlates what is important to the enterprise with what the enterprise does, tempered by what is possible. A general goal for a plan may be stated in this way: Protect critical business functions so they will continue meeting minimum corporate objectives cost effectively during times of crises and disasters. This general statement describes (BCP) goals for many companies. Before building a plan, however, specific goals must be conjectured by the planner, evaluated by the planning team or steering committee, and validated by corporate management.

This section describes the specific elements and steps of defining the goal of the recovery and continuity plan, and identifying the specific objectives required to meet that goal. Succeeding sections describe how to determine the criticality and time sensitivity of various corporate business functions, how to gain and keep commitments from management, and how to define what protections are needed for each business function.

A business continuity plan may have many specific goals. For example, a central order entry and production scheduling system may reside at corporate headquarters or at the corporate sales office, while manufacturing may be dispersed geographically and by product across many facilities. One possible objective of the plan for such an enterprise is to maintain production levels at some fraction of normal levels even if the corporate center is damaged or destroyed.

A California manufacturer of custom filters devised exactly such an objective. For the vast majority of the firm's products, normal operating procedures were for a five-day cycle from order to shipment. Order entry was performed at corporate headquarters. Full material requirements planning (MRP) for all North American manufacturing sites, including purchasing, control, scheduling, and shipping, was performed on the same system. Corporate management determined that the company could not survive for more than a short time unless overall plant production capacity was maintained at 50 percent of normal levels. Production of less than 50 percent would make it infeasible for the company to survive more than two weeks. Production of more than 50 percent but less than 100 percent of normal levels would severely reduce or eliminate profits but would not cause corporate failure. The clear goal of this plan was to protect the functions required to meet the objective of achieving a minimum of 50 percent of normal levels.

The firm performed an analysis of products and revenues. It considered the quantity and cost of the various filters made, the resulting manufacturing load, and the customer base. Although the overall requirement was to maintain a manufacturing load of at least 50 percent of normal, the firm also wanted to make certain that major customers were served and that large contract commitments were met. All of these requirements were incorporated into the final BCP.

In another case, a major electronics manufacturer provided free, seven-day, 24-hour customer service and technical support to all customers. Two facilities in the United States provided support to customers worldwide. This support was a major competitive advantage and was believed to be a major contributing factor to the reputation and exceptional customer loyalty enjoyed by the manufacturer. During normal operations, the call center guidelines were:

- All incoming calls must be answered by the third ring.
- Average waiting times must be less than two minutes.
- Maximum waiting times would not exceed six minutes without operator intervention. Moreover, busy signals should not exceed one caller in 500. Communications systems linked technical support personnel with technical databases.

These were strict criteria for the company's service-level objectives, and traffic engineering studies carefully monitored busy signals and queuing delays to prevent violations of call center guidelines. Trunk lines were added or removed, and staff members were rescheduled to maintain this level of support, which far exceeded industry standards. The major goal for the call center business continuity plan was to maintain service-level objectives at a predefined minimum degradation level. The allowable queuing delay was increased significantly, and the busy signal allowance was increased slightly. A special message would play apologizing for any inconvenience, but all customers still would be served. The planning project identified what capabilities were needed to meet these requirements. The goal of this plan was to provide the backup capabilities needed to meet the reduced service-level objectives using a combination of the preexisting surviving call center and some emergency capability for the damaged or destroyed call center.

Corporate goals are independent of means and systems; they are stated in business terms. Top management must make decisions about what needs to be protected and how protected it needs to be. Often, though, this is an iterative process in which management designs some preliminary decisions and instructs analysts to confirm or refine those thoughts. The disaster recovery planning process includes steps to do just that during the business impact analysis (BIA) phase.

The goals of the plan are associated with the products and services that the enterprise or operating unit provides. In cases where the facility to be protected is a support facility, such as the corporate headquarters of a manufacturing conglomerate, the services provided are in support of the overall corporate operations, perhaps including banking and other support activities. In these cases, although the services are somewhat removed from actual production, they are still imperative to continuing production. Building the plan requires goals that are more specific in nature than those in the examples above. In this methodology, these lower-level goals are referred to as the plan objectives.

The BCP objectives are closely coupled with specific business functions and are not adequately defined until the conclusion of the business impact analysis. In order to begin this definition process, however, first the recovery problem must be constrained by defining the scope of the disaster recovery plan.

58.2.1 Scope. The scope of the plan is the definition of the environment to be protected. Before performing detailed analyses and interviewing management, decisions must be made regarding who and what is to be included in the plan. Specifying the systems, equipment, procedures, locations, and support capabilities that require protection identifies the scope. The corporate environment consists of people, information, facilities, and equipment. The plan focuses on a subset of the people, some of the information, selected facilities, and specific equipment. That constitutes the scope of the BCP. Stated more simply, no matter what the size or complexity of the enterprise, planning is performed on one part of the enterprise at a time.

The scope must be established in order to define the goals of the plan. However, during the planning process, the scope will be refined and redefined as the analysis progresses. Which facility is involved? Is part of a building being protected, such as the data center or the shop floor? Is it the entire facility, including a campus of buildings that fall into the scope of the plan? To perform a BIA, users must focus on the business elements that reside or utilize the people, information, facilities, and equipment that are in scope. However, sometimes it becomes clear during the analysis that the scope must be broadened or can be restrained to protect business functions adequately.

In a world of tight budgets, compressed schedules, and phased implementations, BCP usually is performed in stages. Perhaps the computer and telecommunications systems are protected first, followed later by other office support equipment such as copiers and hard copy files. No matter which elements are chosen for implementation, the scope must be clearly documented. For computer systems, the current systems in use must be identified. Hardware and software must be described in detail. Special equipment must be identified.

In the planning process, it sometimes becomes clear that important items have been excluded from the plan. Where those newly uncovered requirements prove to be critical, they must be included, but for all others, a well-defined scope will prevent creeping requirements that increase cost and lengthen implementation schedules. Requirements identified as desirable but not absolutely necessary can be recorded in an ongoing project log and scheduled for implementation in a later phase. It is better to put into place a plan that leaves out some capabilities while meeting basic objectives than to allow the planning scope to expand, thereby risking long delays or project abandonment. A clearly defined scope enables the planning team to communicate to management precisely what is and what is not protected or included in the planning process.

Major scope issues and disagreements sometimes can be resolved in this early phase of the planning project. If not, resolution of these issues is best delayed until the conclusion of the BIA, since that process reveals hidden functional interdependencies. For example, research and development (R&D) functions usually are longer-term projects that can be delayed without major impact on the enterprise. In many plans, R&D functions are relegated to low priority. Consider, however, the case of a customer service technical representative discussing the status of a custom-manufactured product with a key customer who is unhappy with the delivered prototype. If R&D technical personnel are required to resolve such issues, and resolution has an impact on production schedules, then R&D may be elevated to a higher priority. The BIA process usually reveals and prioritizes such hidden interdependencies.

58.2.2 Correlating Objectives to Corporate Missions and Functions.

It usually falls on the information systems and technology department to build the BCP. Naturally, then, most plans focus first on computers and telecommunications. While there is nothing intrinsically wrong with starting that way, it must be just the first step of the analysis. The danger is the potential for myopic views of corporate functions; corporate computer and telecommunications systems may be required for the successful execution of critical business functions, but usually they are only part of many needed capabilities. Desktop paper files, telephones, personal phone directories, and copying machines may be just as important as access to the corporate database or to some tailored vertical application. The list of functions and equipment to be investigated must be complete or the resulting plan will be inadequate.

The BIA provides a formal methodology for ranking business functions by criticality and time sensitivity. The process includes interviews with key personnel from each business function included in the scope of the planning project. There are two dangers inherent to an information technology–based approach to disaster recovery planning.

1. Business functions that do not use information systems may be inadvertently overlooked.
2. Noncomputer support structures and systems may not be recognized and, therefore, not brought into the protection definition process.

When the information systems department leads the disaster recovery project, it will naturally base the plan on a systems-based knowledge of the enterprise. The accounting department, a traditional heavy user of computer systems, will naturally be included among the functions that potentially need protection. Similarly, all other functions that use computers in their normal activities will likely be included in any list of functions requiring analysis. All organizational elements that use computer systems will be recognized and included precisely because they use computers and therefore are known to the systems department. However, there are many important functions that may not regularly use computers or may use them in ways that are only minimally visible to the systems people.

Mailroom operations are frequently omitted because often they are not computer users. Planning personnel are clearly well aware that mail operations exist; they just might forget to include them in the planning process even though mail operations are important to every organization. Planning mailroom recovery and continuation is simple before a disaster but very difficult after the fact.

Facilities management, maintenance, and plant engineering organizations are seldom intensive computer users in their daily activities. Nevertheless, in normal circumstances, operations in a large facility would deteriorate quickly without these functions. During a disaster, these are the people who can rapidly determine the nature and breadth of facility damage. They are the people who need to be instantly available to evaluate damage, hasten repairs, and estimate duration of outages. They are also the individuals who are often left off the disaster recovery team lists and phone rosters. Similarly, security forces are needed when building damage leaves valuable equipment and other assets vulnerable to theft or vandalism. They may be needed to protect employees who are working during civil disturbances or other such incidents. Corporate communications and public relations departments are also frequent computer systems users, but they are not very visible to the systems department as unique functions, although their contributions to a successful recovery are often essential.

The safest way to compile a list of business functions is to work from three documents: an organization chart, a corporate phone directory, and a list of corporate operations budget line items (see Exhibit 58.6). Using these three lists, the planner can develop a comprehensive list of business functions and can identify the manager or supervisor of each function. That comprehensive list should include every function performed, regardless of the perceived importance of that function. Criticality and time sensitivity will be determined during the BIA; leaving off any functions can lead to inaccurate BIA results.

Working from that comprehensive list, a second list should be compiled that includes or excludes each business function based on the defined scope of the BIA. When doubt exists, the function should be included. The BIA will be the final filter for out-of-scope functions. Therefore, for each function in the list, the planner must determine which of the included elements are relevant to the function under evaluation. Although this may seem to be a complicated process, it is usually straightforward. The golden rule is: When in doubt, include the function. It can always be excluded later if analysis shows that the function is really out of scope.

58.2.3 Validating Goals. A full disaster recovery plan must consider the contribution of each element of the organization to the overall corporate goals. Clearly, no single area is dispensable, for if it were, it would have been discarded already. Properly defined goals are independent of specific functions as they are stated in global terms. Validating the goals requires examining each function to determine how it contributes

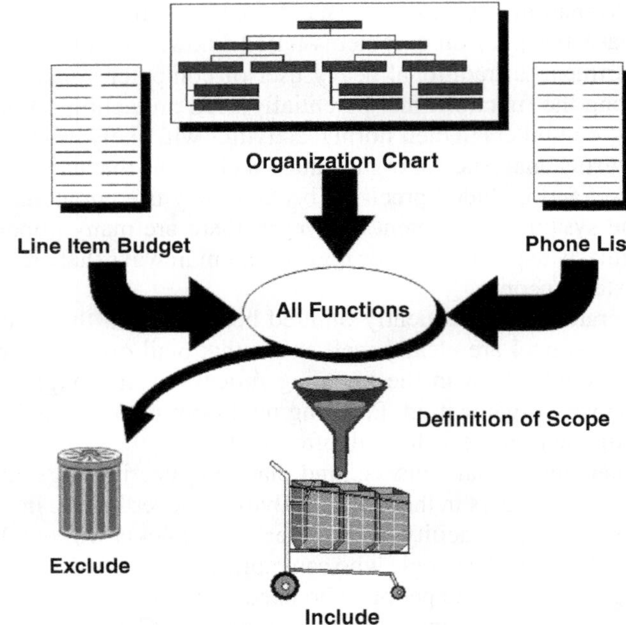

EXHIBIT 58.6 Building and Filtering the List of Functions

to the corporate objectives. It is necessary to distinguish between the importance of a function toward meeting specific disaster recovery goals and the overall importance of a function to an enterprise.

Even functions that are not relevant to any specific disaster recovery goals may be crucial to the overall operation of the enterprise. The BCP focuses on protecting selected corporate functions for a specified period of time, but it is a mistake to assume that a function whose importance to recovery goals is low is not important to the enterprise in the longer run. For example, during a crisis, the corporate tax accounting function often can cease operations with little impact to the enterprise. If this is true, then the continuation requirements for that department are minimal, and the recovery timeline can be extended. Clearly this does not mean that the corporate tax accounting function is unimportant. Other examples of longer-term requirements include fulfilling regulatory and legal requirements.

The goals of the BCP are associated with the products and services of the enterprise and are expressed in business terms. Validating those goals requires presenting management with options for levels of protection and their associated costs. Gross estimates are possible at the outset; refined presentations require a complete BIA. The goals should be clearly defined and presented to management. Although these goals are not addressed specifically by each procedure in the ultimate BCP, they drive the entire recovery strategy development. A clear and concise description of the goals must be presented to management and approved by them. After this approval, the disaster recovery planners can attempt to attain those goals. During the strategy development, other alternatives may appear and may be added for ultimate management consideration, but the initial goals become the operational baseline against which strategies and costs can be measured.

58.2.4 Mapping Goals to Recovery Phases. There are three phases to the recovery process:

1. Continuation activities
2. Resumption activities
3. Restoration activities

The continuation activities are those specific tasks and procedures that enable a very limited set of functions to continue operating with little or no interruption. The resumption activities provide for resuming a full, or almost full, range of business functions, even if that resumption means using backup methods and temporary operating procedures. The restoration activities are those that bring back a normal operating environment in a permanent facility.

The continuation and resumption activities occur during the middle sequence of activities and are the activities that must meet the short-term recovery goals that are within the domain of the recovery plan. The restoration activities occur during the end sequence and may include some long-term goals. The long-term goals may include decisions about rebuilding versus relocating and other major decisions that are beyond the province of BCP construction.

Each goal should be assigned to one of these three sets of activities. This assignment is based primarily on timeline considerations: what must be continued quickly versus what can wait a short while, and what can be delayed for the longer term. In the call center example, the number of rings, the allowable queuing delays, and the busy signal allowance were measurements of service levels. They constituted the goals for the recovery plan. After an interruption, the levels of service can be restored to normalcy gradually, as a function of time since the disaster. Stated differently, with each passing day, the level of service should improve. Therefore, the goal of the continuation activities may be for service within some stated parameters, and the goal of the resumption activities would be for improved levels of service. Normal levels may await the restoration activities.

Clearly, the same level of service can be attained at lower cost if the timing requirements are loosened. That is the reason it is important to assign each goal to a particular set of activities. Exhibit 58.7 illustrates a potential mapping of service levels to activity sets. In the first hours following a disaster, the continuation activities maintain a minimum required level of functionality, with some increases over time. The resumption activities dramatically increase functionality immediately and then bring functionality, over time, to an almost normal condition. The restoration function, shown as two bars to represent temporary and permanent facilities, achieves full levels of service.

58.2.5 Emergency Issues. A good plan includes provisions for ensuring the *safety* of all employees potentially affected by a disaster. This is especially true for employees working on site when a disaster occurs. Life safety issues include health and safety preparedness, shelter and care of employees caught in the enterprise facilities during a disaster, and search and rescue teams for employees in imminent danger. Some of these protections are required by various local, state, and federal regulatory agencies. Others are not mandated but are nonetheless important to the survival of the employees and the business.

Public relations is an important issue during any disaster. More than one enterprise has realized too late that neglecting the media can induce a second disaster, even

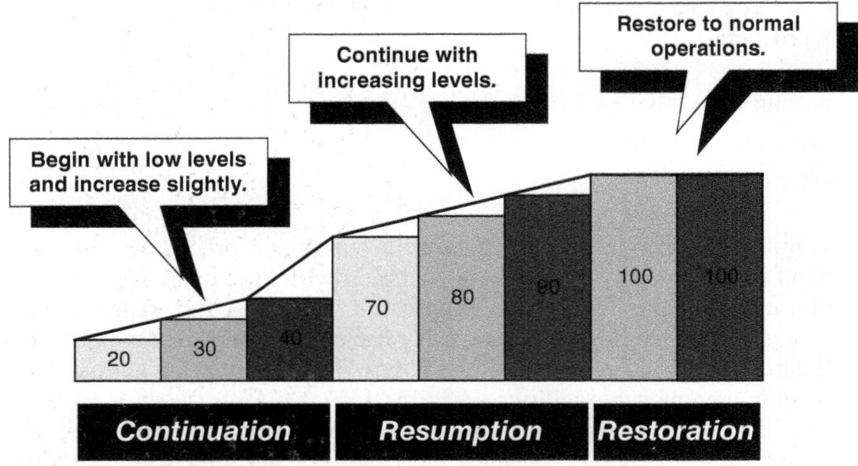

EXHIBIT 58.7 Service Levels Mapped to Recovery Activities

greater than the original one to which the media was responding. Even a small fire can make major news in the local community. The public relations aspect includes recovery actions. For example, one chemical company suffered a minor fire but refused to inform the media on the status of cleanup operations. The result was predictable: The media reported that a fire had potentially released toxic chemicals into the local environment and that the company had refused to comment. That report did more to damage the reputation of this chemical company than did the fire that caused the spill, which was not in fact toxic and was brought under control within hours of the fire.

58.3 PERFORMING A BUSINESS IMPACT ANALYSIS.

The business impact analysis comprises the heart of the planning process. It is here that the recovery planner determines what is important for inclusion into the BCP and what is not relevant to that effort. The BIA determines how far to go in protecting the people, information, and equipment that constitute the organization and its functions so that all survive to flourish another day.

The BIA assesses how unavailability of each system would affect the enterprise. The BIA is a multistep process that may be performed over a period of weeks or months, depending on the availability of various corporate personnel. Often, the BIA may be a first effort to determine the total cost and the schedule required for a full plan. In all cases, the BIA should precede any other planning activities since it will help determine the direction and strategies for prevention, mitigation, and recovery.

58.3.1 Establishing the Scope of the Business Impact Analysis.

To succeed, a project must be well defined in terms of work effort and work product. Just as the BIA helps bound the recovery problem in precise recovery terms so that the project may be successful, the BIA subproject also must be understood in terms of the work required and the product of the analysis. This requires establishing the scope of the BIA by deciding what equipment the BIA will investigate and what people to interview.

The BIA begins with an inventory process to catalog the various equipment and capabilities to be protected. As systems evolve to meet ever-increasing customer demands, equipment and management responsibilities change along with them. For example, a mainframe shop with large local area networks (LANs) and wide area networks (WANs) may be managed by the information technology department, whereas smaller LANs may be managed by individual departments such as accounting or engineering.

Without a comprehensive and constantly updated list of systems across departments and functional areas, systems can evolve quickly with little or no overall corporate knowledge. For the recovery planner, this means the plan will be incorrect at its outset, or will grow obsolete quickly.

The inventory should describe in detail the general hardware and software used in each included system, paying particular attention to special-purpose equipment, such as imaging equipment, custom equipment, and uncommon equipment.

The inventory must include communications links and equipment. A connectivity map showing LAN and WAN equipment and connections is useful; a cabling diagram with gateways, routers, bridges, firewalls, proxy servers, and other communication equipment is also important. General telephony diagrams and summaries of lines and capacities are required to bring voice communications systems into the recovery process.

The inventory provides an opportunity to decide what level of office equipment and supplies (e.g., paper, writing implements, staplers, note pads) should be protected by the recovery plan. Although staplers seldom will be critical, certain printed business forms might well require offsite storage for quick recovery. Boxes of corporate checks, for example, should be stored securely off site.

Security access controls and special alarm systems should be included in the inventory, along with current procedures for maintaining them. There have been instances in which recovery was hampered by inaccessibility to the building, caused by active alarm and access control systems. Inclusion of such systems into the inventory helps ensure that they will help rather than hinder the recovery process.

58.3.2 Interview Process. The best source of information about the work performed by the enterprise is the enterprise's own labor force. Corporate executives understand and control corporate goals; managers understand and control operations. Front-line supervisors and workers perform the daily tasks that bring revenue to the enterprise, and these are the people who have the knowledge needed for the BIA. The recovery planner must collect that information, understand it, and translate it into terms meaningful for disaster recovery planning. Exhibit 58.8 shows the three steps of interviewing.

The first step is to compile a list of all the departments that fall within the scope of the BIA. The term *department* is used here to describe an organizational entity that may not correspond with a specific organization chart position or with the use of the term within the enterprise. The term is meant to convey a functionally complete unit performing a task or a series of related tasks. It might well be that people from different organization chart departments work more closely with one another than they do with people in their own departments.

For example, the accounting department of an organization may handle all corporate accounting functions, including accounts receivable (A/R), accounts payable (A/P), general ledger (G/L), and payroll. However, for the purpose of the planning project, the planner may choose to group accounting into two departments: accounting and payroll. In this way, payroll can be separated from its organizational component and combined with other portions of the enterprise that provide the payroll data, with which the payroll department interacts daily.

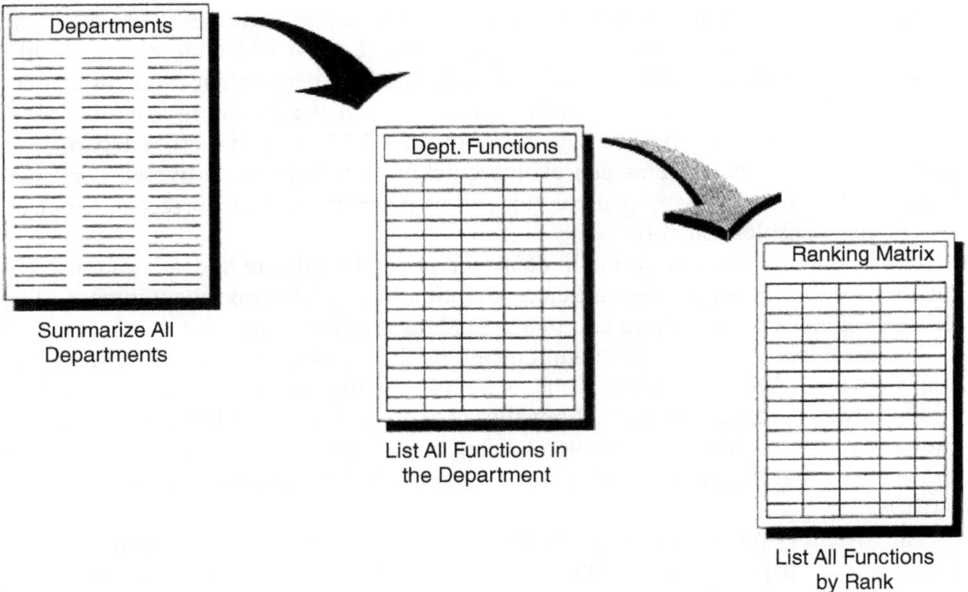

EXHIBIT 58.8 Three Steps of Interviewing

Once the list of departments is complete, the next step is to choose an individual in each department to be the primary interview candidate. Because the primary interviewee from each department will perform two functions—(1) identify all of the high-level functions performed within that department and (2) describe in detail many of those functions—that person should be an experienced and knowledgeable member of that department. It is neither necessary nor desirable to assign this interview position to a senior manager. Management interviews should be scheduled for a later phase that requires management insight. The first interviews should focus on daily task structures and purposes.

The recovery planner guides the interview. The first step of the interview is to describe the department in terms of its overall function and to list all the high-level functions performed. For example, in the accounting department, the high-level functions usually include accounts payable, accounts receivable, general ledger, and payroll. It may include corporate tax preparation, or that may be a completely separate function. It may include financial reporting for the Securities and Exchange Commission (SEC) and other filings, or a different department may perform those functions.

A corporate human resources department may include employee records, benefits management, payroll distribution, time sheet processing, and other common functions. For the planning project, the payroll distribution and time sheet processing functions may be more closely allied with the accounting department than with the human resources department.

During the interview process, the department expert will likely want to describe functions at a detailed level. For example, in the financial reporting area, the expert may want to list each and every report produced. While it may be useful for the planner to learn about the production of these reports, the BIA should categorize all related reporting functions into one function. Therefore, there is no function called *10K Reports*, but there may be an overall SEC Reporting function. It is not possible

Common Functions
◆ Accounts Payble
◆ Accounts Receivable
◆ Cash Accounting
◆ Customer Service
◆ Financial Analysis
◆ Financial Consolidation
◆ Financial Reporting
◆ General Ledger
◆ Inventory
◆ Invoicing
◆ Marketing Support
◆ Order Entry
◆ Parts Inventory
◆ Payroll
◆ POS, ATM and Related
◆ Process Control
◆ Purchase Order Generation
◆ SEC Reporting
◆ Tax
◆ Vital Records
◆ Work-In-Progress

EXHIBIT 58.9 Examples of High-Level Functions

to list all functions or potential functions here, but Exhibit 58.9 lists some examples. Each department should include several to a dozen functions. If a department contains only one function, it may be combined with another department, or it may be divided into lower-levels functions. If a department includes too many functions, then either the functions should be combined into a higher level, or that department can be divided into two departments.

The primary purpose of these interviews is to provide the information necessary to perform a matrix analysis that ranks all enterprise functions for recovery capabilities and timelines. An important secondary purpose is to raise corporate awareness of the recovery planning goals and preparations. During this interview process, the planner can explain that the overall purpose of the planning project is to protect employees and the business functions they perform. This is the opportunity to promulgate disaster preparedness as a normal and necessary part of the corporate business posture.

58.3.3 Describing the Functions. Once the functions have been listed, the interviewer must collect summary information about each function. This functional summary will be included in the BIA document, so that it will be clear to the reader precisely what the function entails. The description of no more than one or two paragraphs prevents misunderstandings and helps focus discussions during the interview. Along with the summary description, the interviewer can further describe the function by identifying the key and alternate individuals responsible for performing that

Department	Functions	Key Person	Key Alternate	Survival Days	Criticality	Ops Impact	Ranking Factor	No. Users	Category	Department Head	System Elements									

EXHIBIT 58.10 Blank, Sample BIA Matrix

function. These are not the managers of the functional areas; these are the people who do the work on a daily basis, enter the data, and perform the function. Each function should be associated with those individuals and with the functional area manager, and the information should be recorded in a matrix format.

This matrix format provides a single place to record all the nonnarrative information about the function. The matrix, which also will include quantitative data, will be combined with the narrative descriptions and some analysis to become the BIA document. The descriptions of each function identify the function clearly, assess the survivability factors of the function, and associate the function with the various existing corporate capabilities. The sections that follow describe the information to be collected about each function and suggest ways to encourage objectivity, even when collecting subjective quantification information. Exhibit 58.10 shows a blank, sample matrix.

58.3.4 Definition of Departments and Functions. The first column is entitled *Department,* such as Financial Reporting, Central Distribution Center, A/P, Merchandising, Planning, Distribution, and Purchasing. Although these are not necessarily equal in number or scope, they are units that need to be analyzed as groups. When unsure of organizational entities, the planner can use the organization chart as a starting point. The department title can always be modified and the functions expanded as the need arises during the development of the BIA.

The second column is the *Functions* list. The functions are the high-level groups of activities performed within the department. Each function is a group of activities related to a single purpose. In the accounting department, for example, there is an accounts payable function, which may include activities such as receiving invoices, requesting payment approval, scheduling payment, and printing checks. Although these detailed tasks are very important, they need not be described individually since they all follow a single thread and timeline. The aim of the BIA is to establish the time and processing needs; therefore, any series of tasks that occur in a closely connected chain can be addressed together. Exhibit 58.11 pictorially depicts the relationship between departments and functions.

Another example of a department is the distribution center of a warehousing operation. This may include functions commonly known as receiving, processing, shipping, quality control, and inventory control. Some of these are aggregates of lower-level tasks. Processing is a function that includes *pulls*, *moves*, and *put-aways*. If shipping, receiving, and processing are performed using the same resources according to a similar timeline, then they can be grouped as one function. Often the BIA calls this the

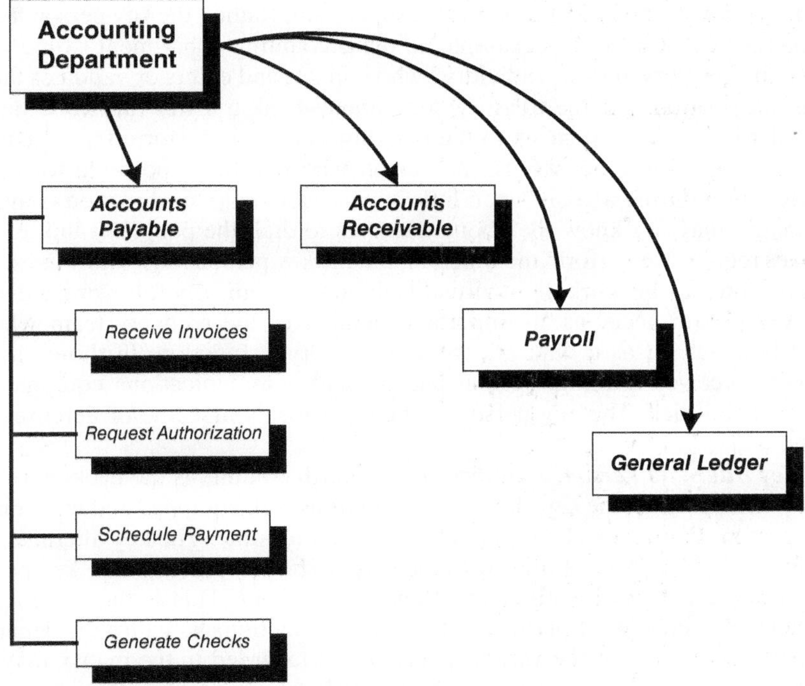

EXHIBIT 58.11 Departments and Functions

Shipping and Receiving function. If inventory control is an outcome or natural byproduct of the Shipping and Receiving function, then it need not be addressed individually. If inventory control includes special functions apart from the Shipping and Receiving function, however, it can be addressed separately.

One example of inventory as a separate function is regulated inventories. For example, alcohol storage requires careful scrutiny according to regulations of the Bureau of Alcohol, Tobacco, and Firearms. Inventories must be documented according to length of storage time, source, destination, and quantities. In this case, inventory control is a special function with its own resource and timeline requirements. Another example of inventory control as a separate function is the isolated customs areas in import and export centers, where inventory must be controlled according to source, arrival time, destination, departure time, and shipper.

If functions are defined too tightly, which means at too low a level of detail, then there will be a great many functions, thereby hiding the true set of functions requiring analysis. This will result in a large set of functions that are so interrelated that they cannot reasonably be separated for individual analysis. If the functions are defined too loosely, which means at too high a level, then there will be too few functions, thereby hiding the timelines and forcing all functions to be rated as time critical. During the interview process, it is likely that the definition of functions will be refined and redefined several times. The functional area experts should guide the definitions, with the recovery specialist helping formulate the ideas.

58.3.4.1 *Key Person, Key Alternate, and Department Head.* The third column in Exhibit 58.10 identifies the *Key Person* for each function. The key person is typically neither a manager nor a supervisor. Rather, the key person normally performs the task at hand. For example, in the accounting department's time-keeping function, the key person is the individual who collects and enters or validates the time-keeping information. For the treasury department, bank transfer function, this is the individual who calls or connects to the banking system to perform the transfers and manage accounts—in other words, the person who will be responsible for performing the function during a crisis when little supervision, help, or direction is available. The manager may not know the phone numbers to dial, the people to talk to, or the keystrokes required to perform the function, but the key person must know these things, for that person may be working in virtual isolation immediately following a disaster.

The key person becomes an important member of the recovery team when that function is identified as a time critical, or Category I, function. In those cases, the key person receives training, special backup and communications equipment, and extra responsibilities. The key person is the enterprise's first line of defense against disasters.

The *Key Alternate Person*, identified in the fourth column, is the backup to the key person. When possible, the key alternate should be as well equipped and well trained as the key person. In practice, however, this is seldom feasible. The key alternate should be an employee who is as familiar with the tasks to be performed as the key person.

The eleventh column identifies the *Department Head*. This is the one individual who is held accountable for performance of all the functions listed for the department. The department heads for the various departments recorded in the matrix may report at different levels on the organization chart; this is an acceptable situation so long as each department head has direct management control of all functions listed for the department.

58.3.4.2 Survival Time. The fifth column records the *Survival Days* as reported by the interviewee and discussed with the disaster recovery planner. The survival days are the length of time the enterprise can withstand the lack of a function with minimal impact. This length of time is measured in whatever units are appropriate to the enterprise, which may be minutes, hours, or months. This length of time is the maximum allowable downtime for the function, after which the enterprise begins to suffer serious repercussions. This measure does not determine the importance of the function to the enterprise; it only measures the time sensitivity of the function. Payroll, for example, is most often very time sensitive, affecting operations after only one or two days.

It may be possible to postpone tax accounting functions because there are alternative actions possible. Missing a filing deadline is avoidable by using past data and making reasonable, informal estimates of changes. Overpayments have few or no consequences. Underpayments may result in modest penalties and interest. Typically, payroll checks are generated close to the distribution date, with little spare time. However, most organizations can develop backup payroll procedures that can compress payroll processing into one or two days so that there is no delay in payroll distribution. Obtaining this information may require exploring past instances when the function had been postponed. The delay may have been due to illness, vacation, system downtime, or management direction. Inquiring about the effect of the delay may help refine the estimate of allowable down time for the BIA.

58.3.4.3 Criticality. The *Criticality* of a function, recorded in the sixth column, measures the magnitude of the immediate effect on the enterprise of function loss beyond the survival time. If payroll processing has been determined to have a one-day survival time, then criticality is the effect on the enterprise of payroll processing delays, beginning on the second day and continuing from there. If tax accounting has been assigned an allowable downtime of 30 days, then its criticality is the affect on the enterprise after 30 days.

Criticality is a measure of time-phased impacts. The criticality of a function is loosely based on fiscal impact to the enterprise. It is not identical with fiscal loss because indirect impacts are also important. A corporate image of reliability and strength may be lost forever if functional capabilities are not restored. NASA's *Challenger* disaster had an effect far beyond any fiscal estimate. The space program suffered a setback and a long delay. Some believe that NASA's loss of funding in subsequent years was attributable to this disaster. The value of lives lost in the disaster is, of course, immeasurable.

A major telephone common carrier once lost a major switching station, thereby causing all of its customers to be without long-distance phone capability for a significant time in the middle of a business day. Although the company lost only a relatively modest amount of money due to lost calls, the damage to its reputation lives on. Its loss of business is irreparable: Many of its dedicated customers decided to double-source their long-distance providers and now split their services between this company and its major competitor. This event constituted a permanent, unrecoverable loss of market share.

The Criticality column records an estimate of the impact of loss once the survival period has been exceeded. It is an estimate because it is not the result of a detailed analysis but rather is provided by the interviewee based on heuristic analyses and experience. The interviewee is asked to rank each function on a scale of 1 to 10, where 1 is the least critical, and 10 is the most critical. Exhibit 58.12 summarizes these level criticality ratings and provides brief descriptions. The recovery planner provides this information to the interviewee and solicits a response. These criticality ratings are subjective, so the planner and the expert must work together to attempt to smooth out individual prejudices and opinions as much as possible. However, the ratings are designed to work with the operational impact measure (described in Section 58.3.4.4) to minimize this problem.

On the rating scale, a value of 10 is the highest level of criticality possible. This value should be accepted only if it is clear that virtually all corporate functions will come to a standstill. Frequently, the payroll function for hourly employees fits this criterion. Hourly, unionized employees may be specifically barred from working by union rules if the enterprise cannot provide a paycheck within some number of hours after the checks are due. In the case of a manufacturing company, this could mean that all production, receiving, shipping, and related functions cease. This is tantamount to a company shutdown. The phrase *out of business* from the summary table (Exhibit 58.12) fits this scenario. This phrase does not mean that the company ceases to exist; it means only that company operations cease until this function is restored.

Range	Description
1 to 2	"Nobody would notice." Very minor inconvenience.
3 to 4	Minor inconvenience, virtually no fiscal impact.
5 to 7	Greater inconvenience, monetary impact.
8 to 9	Major problems, significant monetary impact.
10	"Out of business."

EXHIBIT 58.12 Criticality Ratings and Descriptions

The criticality range 8 to 9 often is used to signify that loss of a function will not drive an enterprise to close its doors but will cause severe damage or loss of confidence. Missed deliveries, loss of customer service functions, lower quality, and similar effects warrant a rating in this range. Functions such as corporate communications (e.g., press releases, customer relations, and shareholder notices), banking functions, some accounting filings, and order entry are examples of functions in this range.

The range of 5 to 7 is probably the criticality rating used most often. This range indicates considerable fiscal effect and significant inconvenience. If such a function were not recovered in time, the effect would be felt but would not be a major corporate event. Perhaps the significant difference between the range of 5 to 7 and the range of 8 to 9 can be summarized in this way: The former is an internal event that would be an internal problem. The latter would be reportable in annual reports and may require media involvement or public advertisements to explain the outage. The higher range has significance beyond corporate walls. Some functions that often meet the lower criteria are accounts payable, various reporting functions, and low-priority government regulatory requirements.

The criticality range of 3 to 4 identifies loss of a function as a minor inconvenience, with little or no monetary impact. Various filings, audits, and internal support functions often can be delayed, with no impact other than the need to perform the work later when functional capability is restored. These are not unimportant functions, but they are functions that can be delayed for a fixed interval with minimal impact on corporate operations. Examples of such functions are certifications, some SEC filings, electronic data processing (EDP) audit, financial audit, internal consulting, corporate directories, and ongoing training programs. Although these are important functions, sometimes significant to overall corporate survival, often they can be delayed without major problems.

The 1- to 2-criticality level indicates that loss of the function would be barely noticeable for the short term and would cause minimal inconvenience. Although these may be important, often regulated, functions, often they are fairly time independent. Examples include former employee tracking functions, claims management, charitable contributions, and equal employment opportunity/affirmative action plans. Although these are not necessarily level 1 to 2 functions in all companies, often they are functions that can be delayed for a significant time without jeopardizing the corporate mission.

58.3.4.4 Operational Impact, Ranking Factor, and Number of Users.

The *Operational Impact*, recorded in the seventh column, is an automated result that is a function of the criticality. Individuals within the enterprise will express their biases in the criticality ratings they assign to various functions. One employee may say that a function has a criticality rating of 7 and another may say 6 or 8. The operational impact measure lowers the granularity of the estimates by transforming a scale of 10 levels to a scale of 4 levels. In this way, individual biases can be normalized and the estimates adjusted to achieve a 4-level assessment of functional criticalities and impacts.

Operational impact is derived through a many-to-one mapping that transforms criticality to operational impact, as shown in Exhibit 58.13. This transformation achieves a data-smoothing function that removes discontinuities caused by individual or organizational biases. It also reverses the order of importance, making 1 the highest impact and 4 the lowest impact. Criticality measurements are transposed; where earlier a higher number meant higher criticality to a system, now a lower number means greater impact and higher priority. This provides a mathematical convenience for combining survival time and criticality into a single measure.

Criticality	Impact	Description
10–9	1	Critical operational impact or fiscal loss
8–7–6	2	Significant operational impact or fiscal loss
5–4–3	3	Some operational impact or fiscal loss
2–3	4	No short term impacts or fiscal losses

EXHIBIT 58.13 Transformation of Criticality to Operational Impact

The eighth column is the *Ranking Factor*, which is the combination of survival time and operational impact, and hence criticality. The ranking factor is the product of the survival time in days and the operational impact. A function with short survival time and high operational impact receives the highest-priority (lowest-number) ranking factor. For example, a function with a one-day survival time and level 1 operational impact receives a ranking factor of 1. Another function with seven-day survival time and operational impact of 3 earns a ranking factor of 21.

The purpose of the ranking factor is to provide a single measure that ranks all corporate functions from highest priority to lowest priority for recovery planning purposes. The compilation of all functions listed in ascending order of ranking factor will show functions in their order of priority for disaster recovery and restoration.

The ninth column of the matrix shown in Exhibit 58.10 is the *Number of Users*. This column simply records the number of employees involved in each function. Note that in most cases, individual employees perform multiple functions and, therefore, will be counted as users in several functional areas. As a result, the sum of users in this column may exceed the total employees of the enterprise. This duplication is acceptable and accounted for in the detailed plans.

58.3.4.5 Category. The tenth column is used to record the *Category* of the function. This column summarizes the analysis achieved through the assessment of survival time, identification of criticality, and computation of ranking factors. The category is simply a way of grouping functions with similar recovery periods. Once sorted by ranking factor in ascending order, the functions are then classified into several categories based on natural groupings.

Using heuristic techniques or more formal graphical ones, the survival times of the functions can be traced or mapped as they proceed from highest priority to lowest priority. The functions will naturally fall into groups or clusters. Often one category consists of functions requiring recovery within one to three days, which can be assigned Category I, and which form the foundation of functions requiring quick recovery. Another group, which can be assigned Category II, often consists of functions requiring recovery or resumption in one to two weeks. These are the highest-priority recovery functions, once all of the Category I items have resumed. Other categories are similarly assigned.

Exhibit 58.14 shows a sample translation of functions to a graph and the subsequent assignment of categories. Each function is represented by one tick mark on the horizontal axis, the x-axis. The corresponding survival time is the height, graphed on the y-axis. In the exhibit, there are four categories: Category I functions have survival periods of from 1 to 3 days. Category II functions have survival times of 7 to 14 days. Category III functions have survival times of 30 days, and Category IV have survival times of 60 days. Although there are usually more functions than those shown on the exhibit, the process is the same.

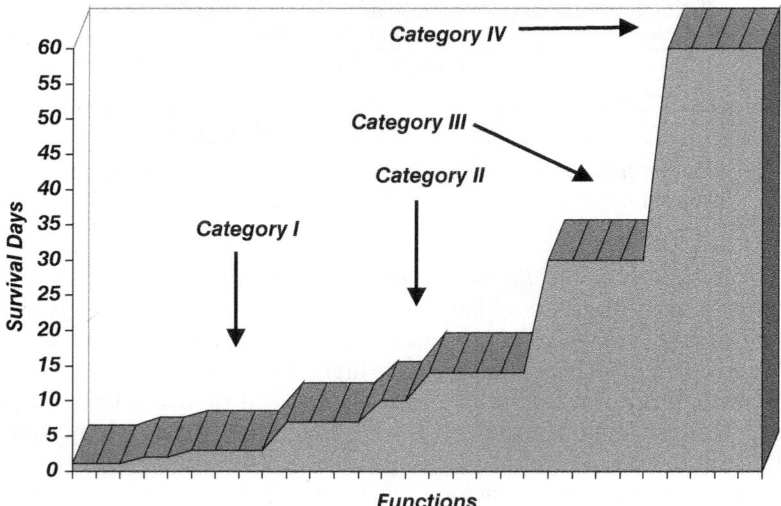

EXHIBIT 58.14 Category Assignment Curve

58.3.4.6 System Elements. The twelfth and final column is really a series of columns each representing a system element. The system elements consist of hardware, software, communications systems, and operating units. The purpose of these columns is to record which functions make use of which system elements. For each function, the disaster recovery planner marks the appropriate system element used in performing that function.

Columns may correspond to hardware devices or to a functional hardware description, such as an imaging system. Major software systems may be column headings, especially for custom-built or custom-tailored software systems, such as MRP or accounting systems. Office software systems such as word processors, spreadsheets, presentation software, databases, communication software, and many other software packages may each form column headings as well. Software packages that are always installed as a group may be described that way in the column. Several system elements may constitute one functional system. For example, the time-keeping and recording function may use electronic punch clocks, communication links between the clocks and a computer, and software to translate the electronic punch clock data into time sheets. This entire system may be labeled as the time-keeping system and be consolidated into one column.

This column also functions as a check and balance against the defined scope of the recovery plan. If columns are necessary for systems that are out of scope, then either the scope must be changed or important statements must be made regarding the limited recovery posture for those system elements not included in the plan.

58.4 BUSINESS IMPACT ANALYSIS MATRIX ANALYSIS.

The BIA matrix forms the heart of the business impact analysis. The matrix provides the basic information needed to establish recovery requirements and timelines, and to estimate costs of outages. The matrix can be manipulated to help the recovery planner perform the analyses required for translating the business objectives defined earlier in the process into the business continuity plan objectives.

58.4.1 Listing the Functions Organizationally. The major matrix manipulations that the planner will perform are a special set of sorts. Exhibit 58.15 shows a sample BIA matrix. This sample BIA matrix is representative of a corporate headquarters facility with some production and warehousing capabilities. The matrix shown is for illustrative purposes only and therefore is composed of only a selected subset of the columns found in an operational matrix. It also shows only a few of the many corporate functions that would normally comprise a full matrix.

Department	Functions	Survive Days	Criticality	Ops Impact	Ranking Factor	No. of Users	Category
Corp Accounting	Cash Management	1	10	1	1	2	
Corp Accounting	Benefits	1	5	3	3	1	
Corp Accounting	Payroll (Mgt)	2	9	1	2	2	
Corp Accounting	A/P	2	6	2	4	3	
Corp Accounting	Financial Planning	30	7	2	60	4	
Corp Accounting	Income Tax	30	7	2	60	2	
Corp Accounting	A/R	30	6	2	60	3	
Corp Accounting	G/L	30	5	3	90	2	
Corporate Services	Auto Fleet Mgt	30	6	2	60	1	
Corporate Services	Travel Administration	30	2	4	120	2	
Corporate Services	Facilities	1	10	1	1	2	
Customer Service	Order Entry	1	8	2	2	1	
Customer Service	Production Scheduling	2	9	1	2	1	
Human Resources	Payroll (Union)	1	10	1	1	2	
Human Resources	Workers Comp	10	8	2	20	1	
Human Resources	Benefits	15	3	3	45	1	
Human Resources	OSHA Compliance Programs	90	N/A	N/A	N/A	1	
Human Resources	Rideshare Program	90	1	4	360	1	
Marketing	Pricing Strategies	2	10	1	2	3	
Marketing	Strategic Product Development	14	9	1	14	5	
Marketing	Account Targeting	30	6	2	60	3	
Marketing	Advertising	90	3	3	270	2	
Materials	Production Scheduling	1	8	2	2	2	
Materials	Purchasing	1	8	2	2	3	
Materials	Bill & Materials	3	6	2	6	1	
Materials	Materials Planning	7	4	3	21	2	
Materials	Invoice I/F	14	8	2	28	2	
QA	Inspection Records	7	3	3	21	1	
QA	Project Tracking	14	4	3	42	4	
QA	Reporting	30	3	3	90	1	
R&D	CAE	1	7	2	2	4	
R&D	General Research	14	4	3	42	2	

EXHIBIT 58.15 Sample BIA Matrix

This matrix is sorted alphabetically by department. Within departments, it is sorted first by survival time of functions, starting with shortest survival. When the survival time of functions is equal, functions are sorted by criticality so that the most critical functions are listed first. This matrix sort, called the *organizational sort* because it follows corporate structures, frequently is the first one used, and is most useful for summarizing interviews and results. This sort is also the one that is most useful when meeting with department managers, for their concerns center on their own departments.

58.4.2 Finding Cross-Department Functions. A second useful view emphasizes similar functions across departmental boundaries. In this view, shown in Exhibit 58.16, functions that cross departments are grouped together. This matrix, which for simplicity is a subset of the matrix shown in Exhibit 58.15, provides facility for uncovering functions with similar titles performed by different departments. In the exhibit, there are three sets of functions with similar names but different departments.

The corporate accounting and human resources departments both perform functions named *Benefits*. However, the two departments describe the survival time and criticality of these functions very differently. Human resources considers this function a minor inconvenience with virtually no fiscal impact and an allowable downtime of more than two weeks. The accounting department tags this function with a downtime of only one day and a greater inconvenience with fiscal impact. The ranking factors of these two functions, both called *Benefits*, are widely different in value, showing at a glance that there is a discrepancy here. The planner must determine whether this discrepancy is the result of inconsistent descriptions, and therefore a problem, or the result of different functions with a similar name.

The other two sets of cross functions are the *Payroll* function, another overlap between the corporate accounting and human resources departments, and *Production Scheduling*, which is performed by both the materials department and customer service. In both cases, the survival time and criticality measures were assessed to be similar by both departments, with ranking factors that are close or the same.

Department	Functions	Survive Days	Criticality	Ops Impact	Ranking Factor	No. of Users	Category
Corporate Services	Auto Fleet Mgt	30	6	2	60	1	
Corp Accounting	Benefits	1	5	3	3	1	
Human Resources	Benefits	15	3	3	45	1	
Customer Service	Order Entry	1	8	2	2	1	
Human Resources	OSHA Compliance Programs	90	N/A	N/A	N/A	1	
Corp Accounting	Payroll (Mgt)	2	9	1	2	2	
Human Resources	Payroll (Union)	1	10	1	1	2	
Marketing	Pricing Strategies	2	10	1	2	3	
Materials	Production Scheduling	1	8	2	2	2	
Customer Service	Production Scheduling	2	9	1	2	1	
QA	Project Tracking	14	4	3	42	4	

Exhibit 58.16 Emphasizing Cross Departmental Functions

The matrix makes apparent the existing overlaps, but the planner must determine whether the overlaps are similar, overlapping functions, or different functions with similar names. In the first example, the function named *Benefits* is quite different. The human resources department views this function as a regular record-keeping function with occasional changes, and it includes tracking and managing employee health plan choices, usually offered annually. Short processing delays are usually inconsequential to the enterprise and its employees. For the corporate accounting department, however, the same named function includes making matching funds payments, exercising stock options, and calculating other financial disbursements based on existing benefits packages and agreements. The functions are similarly named but different in meaning.

The other two examples are similar functions with the same meanings but performed from different perspectives. *Payroll* for management and union personnel is performed differently due to union rules and regulations. Therefore, corporate accounting can calculate regular salaries and benefits for management employees and produce payroll checks. However, the human resources department must be involved in calculating pay for unionized, hourly employees to make certain that all rules and regulations are followed precisely.

Production Scheduling, performed by customer service and by materials, is a similar function with different perspectives. For customer service, production scheduling means setting requirements for customer deliveries and, thereby, determining production schedules. *Materials* finalizes the schedules to reconcile possibly conflicting production requirements for different customers by advancing or delaying schedules within corporate policy constraints.

The planner must understand the meaning of each function and recognize the differences between similarly named functions so that all recovery capabilities meet the true needs of the corporate users and customers.

58.4.3 Using the Ranking Factor. A third view, which is the most important part of the matrix analysis, is the ranking factor view. In this sort, shown in Exhibit 58.17, functions are listed in ascending order according to their ranking factor first and then in ascending sequence according to survival days. The purpose of this view is to assign *Category* designations to all functions and to establish specific timelines for the categories. These timelines become the disaster recovery plan *technical* objectives. Exhibit 58.17 consists of the same data as the previous exhibits but sorted differently.

A useful function of the ranking factor is to list functions in a reasonable priority order for recovery timeline planning. The primary purpose of the *Category* designation is to group functions by recovery requirement or timeline, as a function of short-term importance to the enterprise. Therefore, the ranking factor sort is ideal for determining functional categorizations. All Category I functions for this organization must be recovered in less than three days. For most of these functions, the criticality is high and the survival time is low. Category II functions begin when the survival time jumps to 14 days.

This type of orderly grouping is not exceptional; it occurs in most organizations. The natural organizational activity is to perform functions, generally in a regular, repeating pattern. Many functions are critical and performed almost daily. Other functions are performed weekly, monthly, quarterly, or annually. The ranking factor is a good tool for viewing functions according to their natural cycle. It works because this factor measures both cycles and relative importance. Either measure alone would be insufficient. Exhibit 58.18 graphs three basic measures: survival days, operational impact,

Department	Functions	Survive Days	Criticality	Ops Impact	Ranking Factor	No. of Users	Category
Human Resources	Payroll (Union)	1	10	1	1	2	I
Corporate Services	Facilities	1	10	1	1	2	I
Corp Accounting	Cash Management	1	10	1	1	2	I
R&D	CAE	1	7	2	2	4	I
Materials	Production Scheduling	1	8	2	2	2	I
Materials	Purchasing	1	8	2	2	3	I
Customer Service	Order Entry	1	8	2	2	1	I
Marketing	Pricing Strategies	2	10	1	2	3	I
Customer Service	Production Scheduling	2	9	1	2	1	I
Corp Accounting	Payroll (Mgt)	2	9	1	2	2	I
Corp Accounting	Benefits	1	5	3	3	1	I
Corp Accounting	A/P	2	6	2	4	3	I
Materials	Bill & Materials	3	6	2	6	1	I
Marketing	Strategic Product Development	14	9	1	14	5	II
Human Resources	Workers Comp	10	8	2	20	1	II
QA	Inspection Records	7	3	3	21	1	II
Materials	Materials Planning	7	4	3	21	2	II
Materials	Invoice I/F	14	8	2	28	2	II
R&D	General Research	14	4	3	42	2	II
QA	Project Tracking	14	4	3	42	4	II
Human Resources	Benefits	15	3	3	45	1	II
Marketing	Account Targeting	30	6	2	60	3	III
Corporate Services	Auto Fleet Mgt	30	6	2	60	1	III
Corp Accounting	Financial Planning	30	7	2	60	4	III
Corp Accounting	Income Tax	30	7	2	60	2	III
Corp Accounting	A/R	30	6	2	60	3	III
QA	Reporting	30	3	3	90	1	III
Corp Accounting	G/L	30	5	3	90	2	III
Corporate Services	Travel Administration	30	2	4	120	2	III
Marketing	Advertising	90	3	3	270	2	III
Human Resources	Rideshare Program	90	1	4	360	1	III
Human Resources	OSHA Compliance Programs	90	N/A	N/A	N/A	1	III

EXHIBIT 58.17 Ranking Factor View

and ranking factor. This graphical representation is based on the data contained in Exhibit 58.17.

Each item on the horizontal (x) axis represents one function from the matrix. The height of each of the three curves represents their numerical values. The ranking is an increasing curve because the data are presented according to the ranking factor view. The survival days is mostly increasing but does drop near the middle of the graph and then rises again. This dip corresponds to the two functions with seven-day

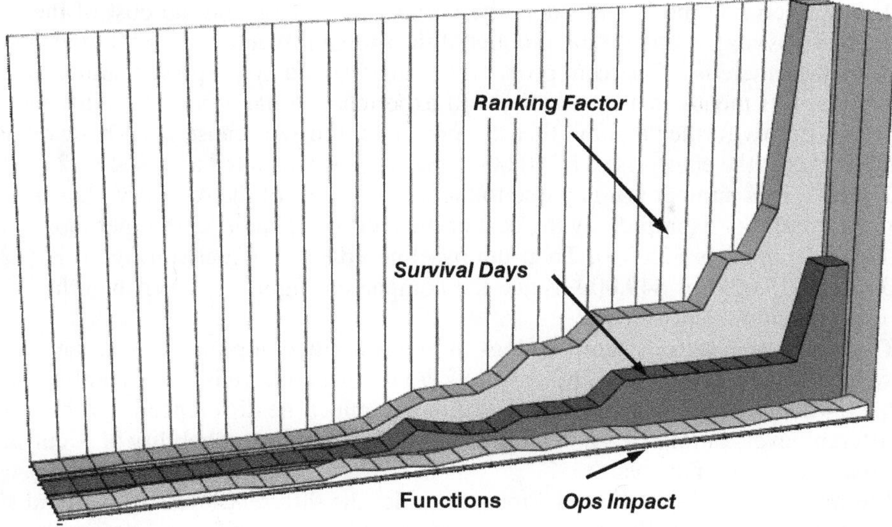

Exhibit 58.18 Graphing the Three Measures

survival times The rankings of the operational impact curve begin at fairly low values, corresponding to high levels of effects such as criticality 10 or 9, and end with fairly high values, corresponding to lower levels of effects, which are typically less than 5 or 6. This curve rises and falls but follows a generally increasing pattern.

Sorting this information according to operational impact would not yield sufficient information on which to base recovery timelines. Some functions with great detrimental effects only begin to have an effect after a longer time. Similarly, a simple sort of survival time may erroneously include functions as high priority whose operational impacts are too low to merit the quick recovery and expense associated with Category I functions. In both cases, the timeline would not be accurate because the sorting criteria exclude either levels of impact or time. Only the ranking factor is reliable since it reflects both time and effect simultaneously.

58.5 JUSTIFYING THE COSTS.

One of the most difficult aspects of the planning process is justifying the costs of the planning process, the reserve equipment, and the contract services. The cost justification is performed best and most efficiently using the generalized cost consequence model rather than the quantitative risk model. Both models are described in the sections that follow.

58.5.1 Quantitative Risk Model.

The quantitative risk model is a formal and rigorous methodology for analyzing expected losses that will be incurred over a predetermined time period. This procedure requires a significant amount of analysis and research. The model consists of three main factors: probability of loss, cost of loss, and annual loss expectancy (ALE). The probability of loss is really a sum of the probabilities of different catastrophic events that range from partial outages to severe interruptions. The cost of loss depends on the level of interruption. For example, a partial building loss affecting computer systems but leaving phone systems in operating condition has a much lower cost than a complete building destruction. Therefore, the cost of loss is dependent on the type of disaster.

A simplified risk model considers the probability of loss and the cost of the loss. The annual loss expectancy is the product of the probability and the cost. For example, let us assume there is a 5 percent probability (annual) of a major power failure. Stated differently, this means that the facility will experience a major power failure once in 20 years. Let us further assume that the power failure will cause a 72-hour outage, which will cost the enterprise $1,250,000. The ALE is calculated as 5% × $1,250,000, or $62,500. This number is compared to the baseline cost of the recovery plan and the cost of capital. For example, say the cost of the recovery plan is $2,000 per month and the cost of capital is $25,000. Then the baseline cost or comparison figure is (12 × $2,000) + $25,000, or $49,000. Since the comparison figure is lower than the ALE, recovery planning is justified.

There are some serious shortcomings in this simplified approach. First, the cost of the outage depends on the level of loss. A 72-hour power outage is significantly costlier than a 24-hour outage. Therefore, the ALE must reflect the difference in probabilities of different levels of impact. Another problem is defining the probability of occurrence for an aggregation of events.

The more acceptable risk model must consider the different levels of loss and sum the probabilities of all disasters that can cause that level of loss to define the true probability of loss for that loss level. This is accomplished for each loss level. First, a series of disaster events is defined. Each event is then refined into levels. For example, office buildings are susceptible to loss due to fire. Data on numbers of fires and amount of destruction (in predefined ranges) are available from various fire protection services. For a given facility, the total number of such buildings in the geographical vicinity is considered. Then the frequency or probability of a fire causing a range of damage is calculated. This calculation is performed for each defined range of damage. The level of loss for each range of damage is assessed, then the ALE is calculated for each range of damage by multiplying the probability of a fire causing that range of damage with cost of the loss if there is such a fire. All the ALE values are summed to calculate the total fire ALE. This calculation must be performed for all types of disasters that can affect the facility to determine the grand total ALE. For each level of impact for all disasters, the baseline costs also must be calculated. These figures are also summed to form a total baseline cost. The grand total ALE is then compared with this baseline cost figure.

This analysis is a complex process that requires great effort to generate and even greater patience to explain. However, there are two more important problems with the quantitative risk model.

1. Calculating all the outage costs is very difficult and subject to debate. Moreover, once the cost figures are finalized, they are subject to constant change due to the changing business climate and practices.
2. Calculating the probabilities is also very difficult and often requires many subjective conclusions. For example, what is the effect of modernizing the sprinkler system based on the level of damage experienced by a particular type of fire? Each countermeasure can significantly alter both the cost and the probability. Moreover, the probability of any particular event tends to be quite small—often less than 1 percent.

While the quantitative risk model is an interesting actuarial exercise, it is of marginal use in modern business continuity planning.

58.5.2 Generalized Cost Consequence Model. The generalized cost consequence (GCC) model (developed by this author between 1990 and 1995) does not consider probabilities of specific disaster events. Instead, it estimates the total cost of outages as a function of time after an event. This model is significantly simpler than the quantitative risk model: It is easier to build and simpler to explain. The GCC estimates the cost of an outage for each function and applies that cost to the total disaster cost after the maximum allowable down time has been exceeded.

For instance, assume the cost of delaying the treasury department's bank management function is $25,000 per day after the first day. Let us also assume that the cost of delaying the law department's general contract review is $5,000 per day after seven days. For the bank management function, the cost to the enterprise is calculated as $25,000 per day beginning on the second day. For the contract review function, the cost is calculated as $5,000 per day beginning on the eighth day. Therefore, the contract review function does not contribute to loss during the first seven days. This calculation is performed for each function, and then the costs are collected by category. This category cost summary is used to develop and present a graph that shows the total cost losses for each category level once they are activated and the total for all categories over time.

A sample graph of the contribution of functions aggregated by category level is shown in Exhibit 58.19. In this example, Category I functions cause slightly more than $120,000 of loss on a daily basis once the maximum allowable downtime has been exceeded. Category II functions contribute slightly under $60,000 in this example. It is likely that different functions will commence their loss contribution at various times after the disaster event. Therefore, the true Category I loss contribution may begin at a lower level and increase to its full level. That distribution of effect will occur beginning on the first day any function exceeds its allowable downtime and will continue to grow until the last day any function exceeds its downtime, at which point the effect will have achieved its full loss contribution. Since categorizations cluster functions with similar downtimes, the loss can be presented as a single, or point, value rather than as a value that varies over time.

The bars indicate that Category I has a higher value than Categories II and III. Category IV is also high. The U-shape is characteristic of this graph. No matter how many categories are used, the Category I functions tend to be quite high in their contributions. The next one or two categories are lower, but increasing in values until the lowest-priority category, which tends to be quite high. This shape results from the manner of the categorizations. The Category I functions are highly critical, with great

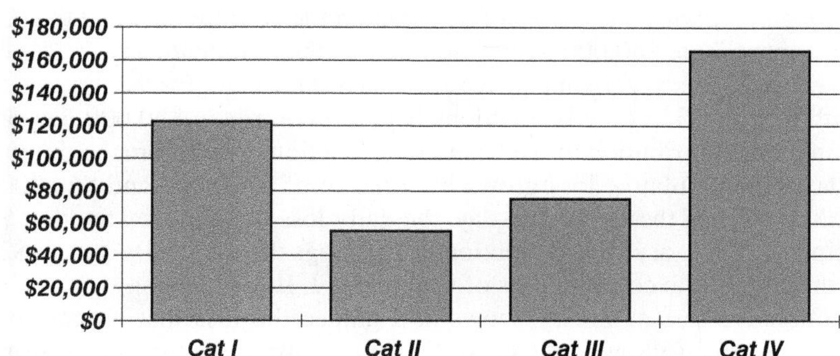

EXHIBIT 58.19 Summary of Loss Contribution

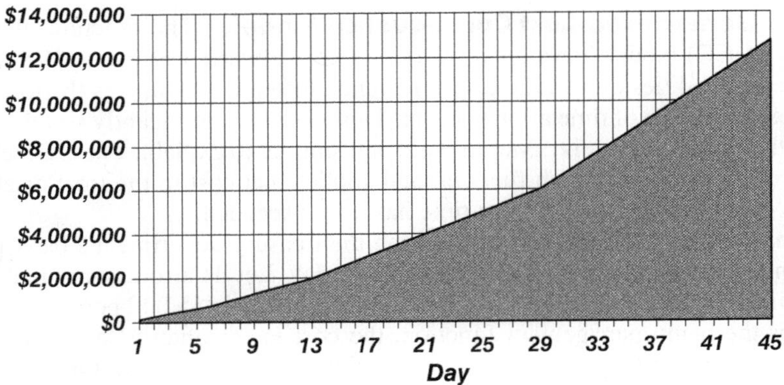

EXHIBIT 58.20 Cumulative Loss Summary

effects on corporate operations. Category I functions tend to be few in number, with each function contributing significantly. The middle categories tend to be larger in number than Category I, with the number increasing with each succeeding category, although still small compared to the overall set of organizational functions. The final category tends to contain the largest number of functions, each of which contributes less on a daily basis than the Category I functions, but the sheer magnitude of this set often causes it to be the largest overall contributor to loss. Of course, Category I functions begin their effects quickly, while loss of Category IV functions may be insignificant for weeks.

Exhibit 58.20 presents a sample graph showing the accumulation of losses from all categories following a disaster. This exhibit uses the same values as in Exhibit 58.19 but presents them in a different format and represents the losses accumulated after 45 days. Neither exhibit measures physical losses such as real property, capital equipment, and the like. Physical losses are not issues that affect the planning process; they affect the cost to recover and are independent of continuation measures. The horizontal (x) axis represents the number of days since the disaster event caused damage and cessation of corporate functions. The vertical (y) axis represents the total losses the enterprise will have sustained on the corresponding day represented on the x-axis.

At the time of the disaster occurrence, no losses will have accumulated. Thereafter, the accumulated loss is increased each day by the cost contribution of the category whose earliest start time has already been surpassed. Assume that Category I functions begin to contribute to corporate losses of $120,000 on the first day, that Category II functions begin to contribute losses of $60,000 on the seventh day, and that Category III functions contribute $80,000 daily beginning on the fourteenth day. In this case, the cumulative loss begins at zero and grows by $120,000 per day for the first six days. On the seventh day, the Category II functions begin to contribute $60,000 per day along with the ongoing contribution of the Category I functions. Therefore, beginning on the seventh day, the cumulative loss grows by the sum of $120,000 and $60,000, which is $180,000 daily. On the fourteenth day, the daily loss increases by another $80,000, representing the Category III contribution. This brings the total daily loss to $240,000, which is the sum of the contributions of Categories I, II, and III.

The cumulative loss summary shows at a glance the loss that an enterprise will experience over time following the disaster, if no recovery planning is performed. The active simplifications of this model are the grouping of functions by category and the

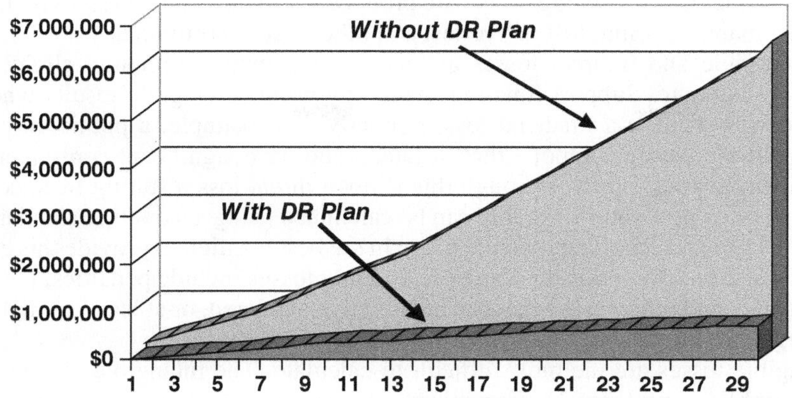

EXHIBIT 58.21 Cumulative Loss Summary With and Without Planning

subsequent representation of each category as a single value beginning at a fixed point in time. This may render the estimate slightly inaccurate at some local points, but the overall values are as accurate as the underlying estimates.

The generalized cost consequence model summarizes at a glance the effects of loss of functions. These loss figures can be affected by insurance reimbursements, legal liabilities, and overall management objectives.

A second model can be developed if the recovery planning is in place, showing the residual loss proposed. That model would be developed in a similar manner but with the assumption that certain functions are restored within established time parameters. There would be residual loss only if the restoration occurs later than the allowable downtime, which will almost certainly be the case for some functions. Exhibit 58.21 presents a graph that shows cumulative losses with and without a disaster recovery plan in place. The Without Plan curve is similar to the previous exhibit. The With Plan curve reflects the residual loss that would occur even if a plan were in place. This loss is normally dramatically lower but is seldom zero. Typically, a reduction to zero residual loss would require extraordinary and prohibitively expensive measures. Most organizations can benefit more from a substantial lowering of residual losses than from a full reduction to zero losses.

The estimation process itself is much simpler than for the quantitative risk model. For each function, the loss estimate is based on three criteria, or types of losses:

1. Tangible and direct losses
2. Tangible and indirect losses
3. Intangible losses

The tangible and direct losses are the easiest to calculate. These losses can be traced to specific revenue-producing functions. The results are direct because the loss occurs as a first-order effect, meaning that revenue stops because the function cannot be performed. The results are tangible because they can be measured easily. An example of such a function is automated production control of an assembly line. If the systems exceed their allowable downtime, then production will cease. The cost is the resultant loss of sales after inventory is depleted. Another example is loss of order entry functions. In this case, the result is similarly calculable: lost sales after in-stock items are depleted and existing orders are produced. Tangible, direct losses include lost sales, lost manufacturing, lost deliveries, and other lost opportunities.

The tangible and indirect losses are the most common, although slightly more difficult to estimate. Support functions generally produce tangible results whose deprivation would cause a financial loss indirectly. For example, a public corporation issues quarterly earnings reports that, if late, could have significant consequences on the company's stock value. Although this is not a direct loss resulting from cessation of sales or other production, the loss can be calculated using accounting standard practices. The internal accounting personnel are in the best position to provide this estimate to the disaster recovery planner. Tangible, indirect losses include penalties, fees, fines, market share, and other issues that can be directly calculated, or at least estimated with some degree of confidence.

Intangible losses are the most difficult to calculate. The intangible effects include reduced public confidence, compromised customer satisfaction, promises not kept, damaged reputation, and other losses that are general in nature and not easily calculable. Sometimes these losses are not translated into specific financial losses and are, therefore, not represented in the cost graphs. In such cases, prominent notations should be made explaining the additional but not quantified losses.

According to a study by Contingency Planning Research in their 2001 Cost of Downtime Study, hourly losses by major companies can range from a low of $12,000 for service-oriented organizations to over $7 million for a major brokerage firm. There are no strict rules for estimating losses. The timeline can be specified in increments of days, as shown in the preceding examples. It also can be as fine as hours or minutes. Some industries, such as hospitals and other acute care facilities, must measure loss in finer increments.

The generalized cost consequence model can solve the problem of cost justification. This model shows the potential, possibly catastrophic, losses without engaging in the analysis paralysis that can stem from a detailed quantitative risk model development effort.

58.6 PLAN PRESENTATION.

The development of a business continuity plan is an involved and somewhat complex process. Though there is the simplifying technique of the generalized cost consequence model, there is still significant work required to devise and implement a workable and resilient plan.

The complexity of the development process, however, must give way to simplicity in the final plan that is presented to the enterprise. Complex analyses and detailed descriptions must give way to simple and easy-to-read flows and action plans, for even after significant training, the people responsible for carrying out the plans need simple documentation to help them along.

Exhibit 58.22 provides on example of how to present the overall recovery flow. This one diagram can form the basis for a set of sections that describes each of the specific steps to be followed. Each decision point requires information and decision guidelines; the BCP document can describe each of these steps and can provide guidance for which path to follow. In this diagram, some recovery responses have *cases* that further define the steps to take. In this example, the cases are parameterized by the expected outage period or the actual outage duration.

Exhibit 58.23 illustrates the meaning of the cases in Exhibit 58.22. This illustration draws from the previously described concepts of function categories and lays those categories against their specific timeline requirements. The cases overlay time periods and make it clear which functions must be recovered and in which of the three cases

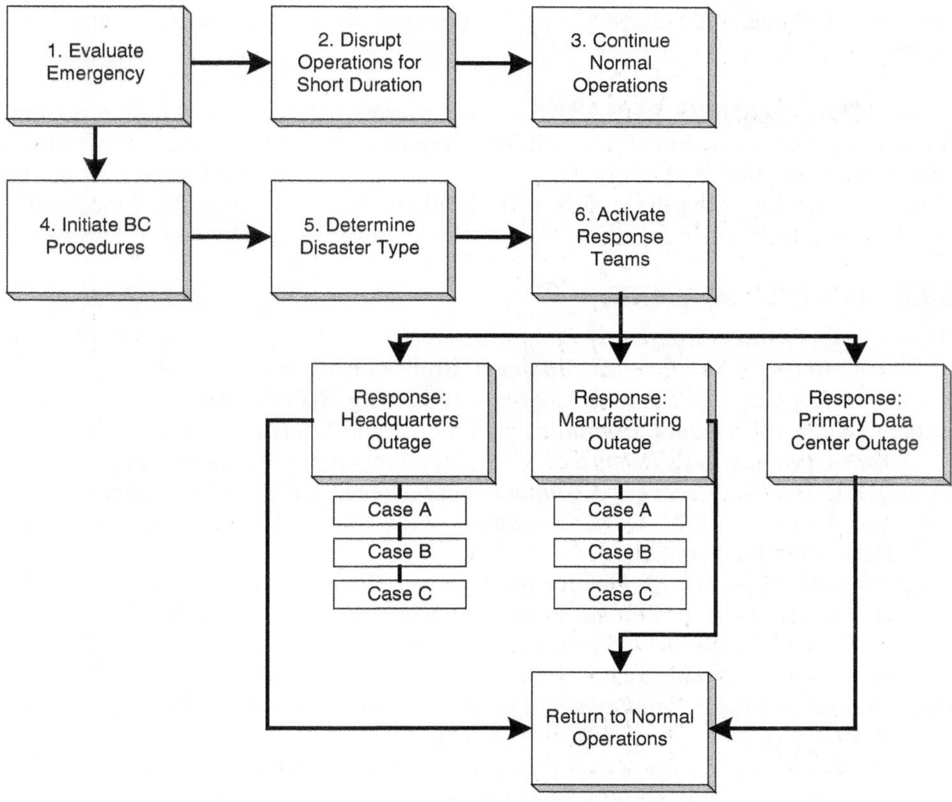

EXHIBIT 58.22 Recovery Flow

they reside. The diagram intends to clarify that categories of functions continue across time boundaries, and new categories are activated at their designated times.

In this example, Case A represents the time period from 1 hour after an event to 1/2 day after the event. In Case A, only Category 1 functions are activated. If the event lasts longer than 1/2 day, up to 2 days, then after the 1/2-day period, the organization enters Case B and activates Category 2 functions but leaves Category 1 functions active. If the event duration is greater than 2 days, then Case C shows that Category 1 and 2

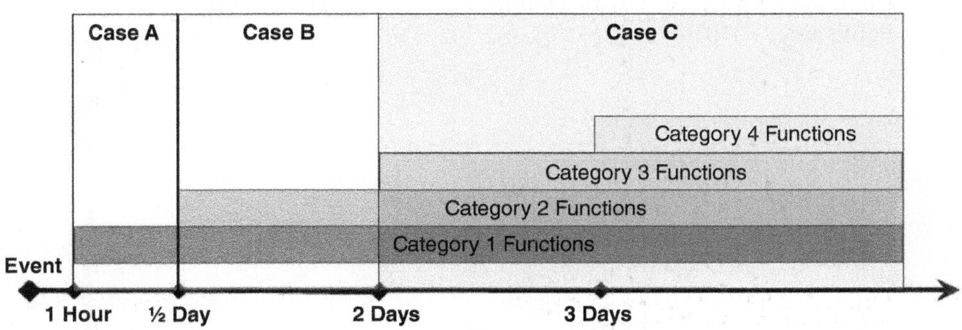

EXHIBIT 58.23 Cases and Categories

functions continue, and Category 3 and 4 functions are activated at the 2- and 3-day points.

58.7 CONCLUDING REMARKS.

This chapter has introduced a methodology for analyzing mission-critical functions in an organization and for structuring business continuity plans that reflect organizational needs and resources. Chapter 59 in this *Handbook* continues the discussion with details of how to recover full functionality should a disaster occur.

58.8 FURTHER READING

Barnes, J. C. *Business Continuity Planning and HIPAA: Business Continuity Management in the Health Care Environment*. Rothstein Associates, 2004.

Barnes, J. C. *A Guide to Business Continuity Planning*. Wiley, 2001.

Butler, J. G., and P. Badura. *Contingency Planning and Disaster Recovery: Protecting Your Organization's Resources*. Computer Technology Research Corp., 1997.

Cimasi, J. L. *Disaster Recovery & Continuity of Business: A Project Management Guide and Workbook for Network Computing Environments*. CreateSpace Independent Publishing Platform, 2010.

Engemann, K. J., and D. M. Henderson. *Business Continuity and Risk Management: Essentials of Organizational Resilience*. Rothstein Associates, 2011.

Fulmer, K. L. *Business Continuity Planning: A Step-by-Step Guide with Planning Forms on CD-ROM*, 3rd ed. Rothstein Associates, 2004.

Hiles, A. *The Definitive Handbook of Business Continuity Management*, 3rd ed. Wiley, 2010.

Hiles, A. *Business Continuity: Best Practices—World-Class Business Continuity Management*, 2nd ed. Rothstein Associates, 2003.

Hiles, A., ed. *The Definitive Handbook of Business Continuity Management*, 2nd ed. Wiley, 2008.

Myers, K. N. *Manager's Guide to Contingency Planning for Disasters: Protecting Vital Facilities and Critical Operations*, 2nd ed. Wiley, 1999.

Roebuck, K. *Business Continuity and Disaster Recovery: High-Impact Technology—What You Need to Know: Definitions, Adoptions, Impact, Benefits, Maturity, Vendors*. Tebbo (2011).

Sayed, A., and A. Sayed. *Business Continuity Planning Methodology*. Sentryx, 2003.

Snedaker, S. *Business Continuity and Disaster Recovery Planning for IT Professionals*, 2nd ed. Syngress, 2013.

Watters, J. *The Business Continuity Management Desk Reference: Guide to Business Continuity Planning, Crisis Management and IT Disaster Recovery*. Leverage Publishing, 2010.

CHAPTER 59

DISASTER RECOVERY

Michael Miora

59.1 INTRODUCTION. In Chapter 58 in this *Handbook*, the importance of a business impact analysis (BIA) and the method of preparing one were described. Once the preliminary groundwork is finished and the BIA analysis is complete, the next step is to design specific strategies for recovery and the tasks for applying those strategies. In this chapter, we discuss the specific strategies to recover the Category I functions, the most time-critical functions identified during the BIA, as well as the remaining lower-priority functions. We examine the traditional strategies of hot sites, warm sites, and cold sites as well as a more modern technique we call *reserve systems*. We describe how to make good use of Internet and client/server technologies and of high-speed connections for data backup, for making electronic journals, and for data vaulting. We develop the recovery tasks representing the specific activities that must take place to continue functioning and to resume full operations. These tasks begin with the realization that there is, or may be, a disaster in progress, continue through to full business resumption, and end with normalization, which is the return to normal operations. We examine a set of tasks taken from a real-world disaster recovery plan to illustrate how each task fits into an overall plan, accounting for anticipated contingencies while providing flexibility to handle unforeseen circumstances.

59.2 IDENTIFYING THREATS AND DISASTER SCENARIOS. Threat assessment is the foundation for discovery of threats and their possible levels of impact.

Threat assessments can vary from rigorous analyses of natural events and the probabilities associated with them to informal surveys of recent disasters and their regional characteristics. The rigorous analysis will yield detailed results but will require significant effort to perform the required research and to interpret the results. The informal survey can yield sufficient information for the disaster recovery planner, and it requires significantly less effort.

59.2.1 Threats. Local fire, police, and other emergency response services can provide the data needed for an informal survey. Flood district management agencies can provide data regarding floods of all types, whether caused by storms, draining, or other factors. Police departments can provide information about building or neighborhood closures due to man-made catastrophes, whereas city and county governments can provide information about emergency declarations over a period of years.

Compiling this list of threats accomplishes two objectives: It helps define the different levels of impact, and it helps to develop a risk mitigation plan. The mitigation techniques outlined in the plan are intended to lower the damage caused by the likeliest disasters. For example, an area prone to seasonal flooding can reduce the risk of computer outages by placing computer installations and important equipment above the flood level. Facilities located in areas prone to power failures can install UPS (uninterruptible power supply) equipment with higher capacities than usual for the type of equipment being protected.

Many threats can have important consequences to information-processing systems. Physical security risks stand out among them as the highest-profile disasters. These are also the most highly dependent on geography and include events such as fire, flood, and earthquake.

Exhibit 59.1 lists a large number of threats to help the disaster recovery planner begin the process of listing threats that apply to specific facilities.

EXHIBIT 59.1 List of Threats

Accidents	Denial-of-service attacks	Kidnapping/hostages
Acts of God	Disgruntled employees	Labor disputes
Aircraft accident	Drug abuse	Local area disaster
Alcohol abuse	Dust storms	Malicious damage
Area evacuation	Earthquakes	Mass illness
Arson	Elevator failure	Municipal service failure
Asbestos	Embezzlement	Nuclear accident
Boiler explosion	Environmental controls fail	Postal strike
Bomb threat	Evacuation	Power failure
Brownout	Falling object	Regional disaster
Building inaccessible	Fire	Sabotage
Chemical spill	Flood	Sanctions
Civil unrest riots	Fraud	Sandstorm
Cold weather	Hacker attack	Snowstorm
Communications failure	Hardware failures	Strike
Computer virus	Heat	Terrorism
Construction disturbance	Humidity	Tornado
Crime	Hurricane	Utility failure
Data diddling	Ice storms	Volcano
Delivery interruptions	Industrial espionage	Water damage
Demonstrations	Information compromise	Water supply failure

59.2.2 Disaster Recovery Scenarios. Each of the threats described in Exhibit 59.1 causes specific damage, with the scope of damage and damage characteristics well known and predefined. Once the characteristics of specific threats are known, then mitigation measures can be applied. One of the important mitigation techniques is the application of survivable technologies to mission-critical functions. Survivable technologies applied to the most critical of the functions (Category I) can prevent outages or at least significantly lower the probability and duration of the outage. For example, client/server and distributed architectures can be implemented with geographic data distribution, so that the loss of a single data center will not disrupt operations but may only degrade them. One such strategy is the geographically dispersed placement of two computers operating on a single main network with functionality shared between them. If backup data are regularly logged from one machine to another, then both systems maintain current databases. If one system is disrupted, then the other can assume full functions; the response times may degrade, but the functionality will not be lost. Replicated architectures with automatic failover are an even better alternative. The desirability of such measures was amply demonstrated by the catastrophe of September 11, 2001, again by Hurricane Katrina, and yet again in the Southern California fires of 2007.

Escalation scenarios are mechanisms that map the expected duration of failures against the requirements for operational continuity. With well-known threats as described, and the ensuing and defined outage durations that can be characterized, disaster declaration and escalation points can be calculated and presented. Timelines must be carefully constructed to leave little room for doubt.

Exhibit 59.2 provides an example of an escalation timeline. Note that the figure is based on data from Chapter 58, and from Exhibit 58.17 in particular. In this exhibit, the top, horizontal row of boxes corresponds to recovery time estimates. For each column, specific initiation parameters are established. The operators and engineers can, at a glance, determine whether this particular situation requires a disaster declaration. For example, an estimated downtime of less than one day requires no recovery, since in Exhibit 58.17 there are no functions requiring recovery in less than one day. The key factors are that the operations personnel must be trained in the use of the procedures and must have ready access to contact information for disaster recovery declaration authorities.

Disaster recovery scenarios and activities are dependent on the scope of the damage. Therefore, it is necessary to group specific events according to a classification of the damage they inflict on a facility. Once this is accomplished, the disaster recovery planner can identify declaration, escalation, and recovery activities based on the specific threats and their resulting disaster scenarios. Classifications of damage include the duration of an outage and the scope of its effects.

Exhibit 59.3 summarizes some threat durations and provides some sample classifications of damage. The first column of the exhibit lists a sampling of threats, and

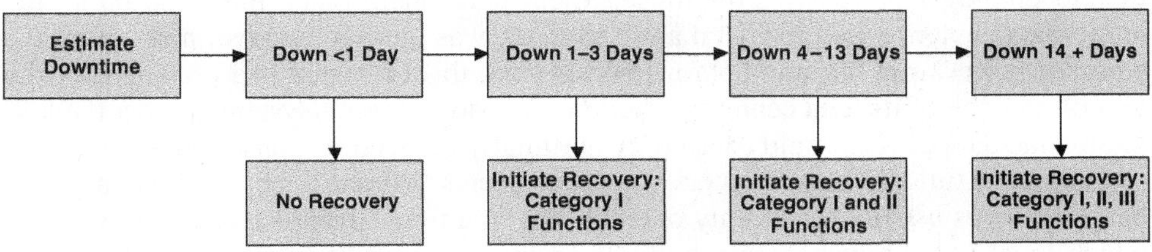

EXHIBIT 59.2 Escalation Timeline

EXHIBIT 59.3 Sample Classifications of Damage

Event Description	Possible Scope of Effect	Potential Duration of Effect
Aircraft accident	Building to local area	Hours to days
Asbestos	Partial to full building	Days to weeks
Bomb threat	Building to local area	Hours to days
Chemical spill	Building to lacal area	Hours to days
Civil unrest/riots	Local to regional	Days to weeks
Cold weather	Local to regional	Days
Communications failure	Building to regional	Hours to days
Computer virus	Systems	Hours to days
Data diddling	Systems	Hours to days
Earthquakes	Local to regional	Days to weeks
Environmental controls fail	Partial to full building	Hours to days
Fire	Partial to full building	Days to weeks
Flood	Local to regional area	Days to weeks
Hardware failures	Systems	Hours to days
Hurricane	Local to regional area	Days to weeks
Ice storms	Local to regional area	Days to weeks
Municipal service failure	Local	Hours to days
Nuclear accident	Regional area	Days to weeks
Snowstorm	Local to regional area	Days to weeks
Volcano	Regional area	Weeks
Water damage	Building to local area	Hours to days

the second column classifies each threat according to the possible scope of its effect. The set of possibilities contains systems only, partial or full building, local area, and regional area.

A systems-only disaster leaves the facility unaffected but partially or fully disables the system's operations. Breaches of logical security usually affect only systems, as do hardware failures. The exhibit does not attempt to differentiate between types of systems and number of systems affected, but the disaster recovery planner must do that classification for each facility and for the interactions of facilities. A characteristic of systems-only disasters is that sometimes they can travel across physical boundaries, such as when the incident involves a security breach, a connectivity disruption, or a software failure.

As an example of a system disaster, in 2007, one major company experienced just such a failure during the testing of a dry pipe sprinkler system. When the system was pressurized, the pipes burst. The data center was not serviced by the sprinkler system; it had its own system in place. However, one pipe crossed over the data center, a fact thereto unknown to the systems management personnel. When that pipe burst, the entire data center, which included a raised floor, was quickly flooded, making all the equipment wet from top and bottom. Fortunately, this company had prepared for the loss of any one of its data centers by building a load-balanced system, so that the loss of any one data center would cause only minimally reduced response times.

Partial- or full-building disasters consist of events that cause physical damage to a building. Fires usually affect only one building at a time. Even detection of asbestos, which most often occurs during building maintenance or improvement, is seldom a multibuilding affair. Local and regional area disasters are difficult to distinguish from each other. Generally, a disaster that affects a single geographic area, such as a city or neighborhood, is a local area disaster, whereas a disaster affecting more than one geographic entity is a regional disaster. The importance of this demarcation is that local area disasters at a company site may affect some of the employees personally, although most will be unaffected, except as it relates to company business. A regional disaster usually affects most employees' homes and families as well as the organizations that employ them. A municipal services failure clearly affects a single geographic entity, and employees living outside of that municipality are unlikely to be affected. Conversely, a major storm resulting in floods, or a large earthquake, will affect residents and businesses over a wide area, probably leaving employees at work concerned with the health and safety of their families and homes. The availability of employees to handle a disaster is much greater when the disaster is local, or of smaller scope, than during a regional disaster.

The third column in Exhibit 59.3 estimates the duration of the effect, ranging from hours to days to weeks. These are inexact and somewhat vague guidelines only. Although fire is listed as having a duration ranging from days to weeks, a very small fire may be managed and the building reoccupied in only a few hours. Similarly, an earthquake is listed as having a duration of days to weeks, yet a major earthquake may have large impacts lasting many months. After the 1994 Northridge earthquake in Southern California, for example, major highway arteries were closed for many months, requiring employees to telecommute or spend hours per day traveling. This affected the operations of many companies, forcing them to redesign their workflows. The Seattle earthquake of February 2001, however, had no such long-term effects. Many companies initiated disaster recovery procedures to handle the commuting problem, even when there had been no physical damage to the corporate facilities. The terrorist destruction of the World Trade Center twin towers in New York on September 11, 2001, is perhaps the most obvious example of how the destruction or closure of major roads and other transportation means affected operations of companies not otherwise affected by the terrorist act itself.

The disaster recovery planner must analyze enough specific threats against the corporate operations and physical plant to build a series of disaster scenarios, which become the guiding forces of the recovery activity definitions. Some planners design disaster recovery scenarios to suit each disaster threat. Floods call for one set of activities, fires another. This can result in an extensive set of scenarios, each requiring training, testing, and maintenance. This technique may be too complex. Another similar approach uses active scenarios chosen from a set of only five possible levels of disasters: systems only, partial building, full building, local, and regional. Each organization should try to reduce the number of disaster scenarios, generally to no more than three, and many can handle emergencies adequately using only two scenarios. For most organizations, a systems-only disaster is not restricted to computer systems, but may include phone systems and telecommunications systems. Systems-only cases must be defined in the context of the organization's unique structure.

For example, a manufacturing facility may require three scenarios: systems only, partial building, and full building. Perhaps for the manufacturer, a loss of systems can be handled with a hot site for computers and a fast, high-bandwidth connection to the shop floor. A partial building disaster, affecting only office space, can be handled similarly, but with additional office space for support functions. A full-building disaster that damages or destroys manufacturing capability requires a completely different set of continuation and recovery procedures. As another example, a corporate office facility may require just two scenarios—systems only and building disaster—where the building disaster is a combined building, local, and regional scenario. The systems hot site can handle the systems-only disaster. The building disaster scenario will require that all functions be restored at a hot site that provides full office functions from phone to fax to desks and copiers in addition to computer systems and networks.

The planner defines the sets of disasters and develops recovery scenarios for those sets. This defines the number of scenarios required; then the disaster recovery activities can be designed.

59.3 DEVELOPING RECOVERY STRATEGIES.

The BIA defines the timeline for recovery for each category of functions. The recovery strategies depend on factors such as: the complexity of the functions, the amount of information required to carry them out, the number of people involved in performing the function, and the amount of interaction between this function and other functions. The strategy of choice for each function is based on the timeline and the specific factors relating to it. The tasks required to activate the function immediately after a disaster follow directly from the BIA timeline and from the various factors that have been described.

Recovery strategies are defined differently from continuation strategies. The recovery strategy is the overall plan for resuming a function, or set of functions, in a near-normal work mode. The continuation strategy is the plan for immediate or nearly immediate operations of a key function, even if it results in significantly degraded performance or limited capability. The continuation strategy is most often applied to a small set of functions rather than to a more complete set, and it is often only temporary. Although the recovery strategy may be used for several weeks or longer, the continuation strategy typically survives for hours or days.

Traditional recovery strategies include hot sites, warm sites, and cold sites. The most common recovery strategy uses a commercial service provider to maintain an on-demand operating capability for well-defined systems. There are a variety of such companies, some of which provide a standby mainframe or midrange system, along with selected peripherals and telecommunications facilities on a first-come, first-served basis. Others guarantee availability by providing a dedicated facility.

The operating capability required is defined at the outset. Processor type is specified down to the model level. Required disk space, hard drives, tape drives, ports, connectivity, and all other required elements must be specified explicitly. Timeline requirements must be stated precisely, with rehearsal, practice, and drill times negotiated in advance. Geographic location of the backup systems is often determined at the time of disaster declaration, and connectivity is usually provided to corporate fixed facilities. The obvious advantage of this strategy is ready access to maintained systems and environments. The principal disadvantage is cost.

A continuation strategy usually depends on internal resources rather than on commercially available providers. Continuation strategy requires that equipment be available instantly, with current data. "*Instant availability*" means that the systems must be local, or at least connected, yet survivable. The continuation strategy is becoming more common as microcomputer-based systems assume greater roles in corporate computing structures. The continuation strategy often relies on reserve systems, a concept pioneered over the past five years. This strategy, described in Section 59.3.2.8, uses high-performance microcomputers residing off site at homes, branch offices, and other locations easily accessible to employees.

The reserve system provides immediate, but limited, functionality so that operations can be continued after a disaster while awaiting full restoration or recovery.

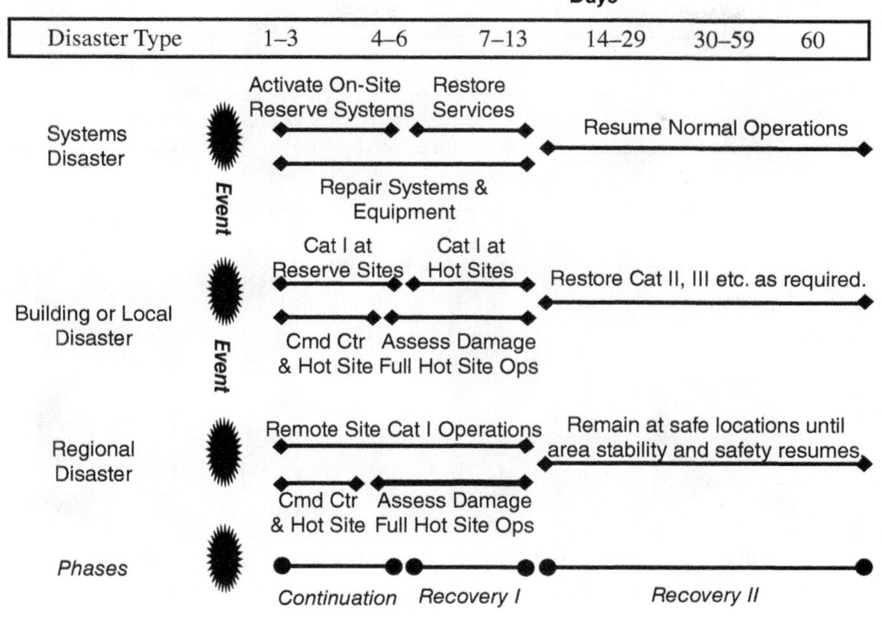

EXHIBIT 59.4 Recovery Phases

59.3.1 Recovery Phases. Orderly recovery requires organized processes and procedures. The BIA uncovers the time sensitivity and criticality of functions, so that continuation and recovery strategies can be designed. Activation of these strategies is performed systematically in time-phased increments.

Exhibit 59.4 shows an example of such phasing. The figure is based on Exhibit 58.17, and illustrates a common schema that consists of three scenarios. Each scenario represents a collection of disasters according to their effects on the company. The first, a systems disaster, represents an effect that has interrupted computer and related systems but has left basic services such as heating and air conditioning, water, power, and life safety intact. The second scenario is the building or local disaster. In this case, a major portion of the building, the entire building, or even several surrounding buildings are rendered unfit for occupancy. This may be due to a problem with the building or with the local area, including fire, toxic spills, minor flooding of surrounding areas, terrorist action, and other such events. The third scenario is the regional disaster, in which some calamitous event affects a wider geographic area. Examples of such catastrophes are earthquakes, hurricanes, floods, large fires or firestorms, and heavy ice and snowstorms.

Each of these scenarios requires different recovery strategies and tasks. However, the overall recovery phases remain similar. The exhibit shows that there are three basic phases: continuation of critical (Category I) functions, recovery of critical functions, and recovery of other functions. These are labeled near the bottom of the figure as "Continuation," "Recovery I," and "Recovery II."

The Continuation phase begins at the time of the disaster. For each scenario, the goal of the continuation phase is to support the Category I functions as best as possible and within the time frames defined by the BIA. In this example, the BIA timeline for Category I functions is one to three days. For the systems disaster and the building or

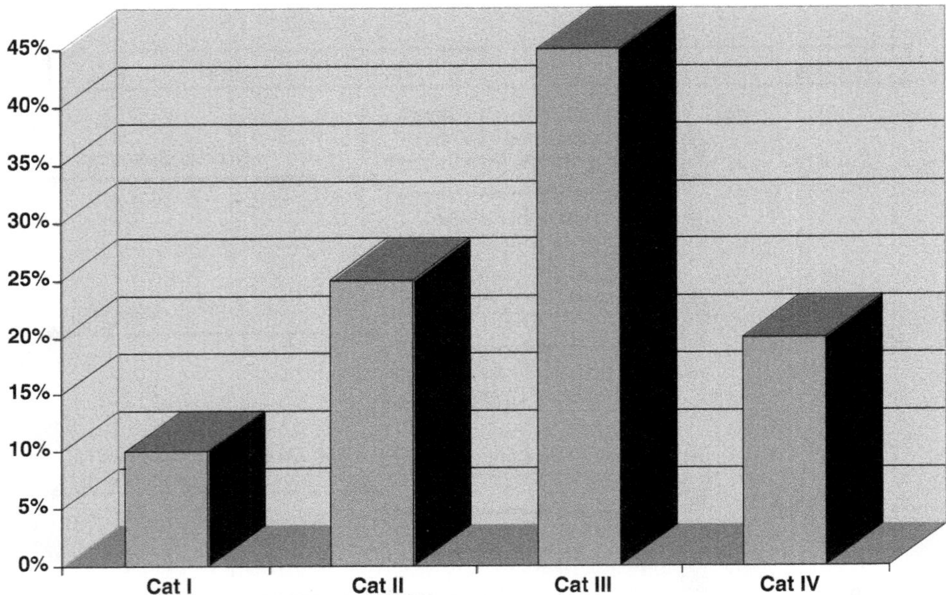

EXHIBIT 59.5 Spread of Functions across Categories

local disaster scenarios, the Continuation phase depends on the local or onsite reserve systems. For the regional disaster, where local functioning may be impossible, the Category I functions must be supported by remote sites.

The recovery phase is further divided into two subphases. Recovery I phase restores full or nearly full functionality to the Category I functions that were partially supported by the reserve systems. In the example, the Recovery I phase begins after all continuation functions have been stabilized. In practice, it is more common for the Recovery I phase to begin shortly after the disaster event in order to minimize the duration during which the Category I functions must operate in a degraded fashion. The Recovery II phase is used to recover other functions in the order they are needed, as defined by the BIA. Exhibit 59.5 shows the typical spread of functions across categories. Typically, Category I functions constitute approximately 10 to 15 percent of the functions performed in a facility or campus. The Category II functions consist of functions that are very important and time critical but can be delayed for a short time. These functions significantly outnumber the Category I functions, sometimes reaching 20 to 35 percent of facility functions. Category III and, if applicable, Category IV functions are much greater in number, often comprising more than half of the facility functions performed.

The BIA process assessed the cost contribution of each category of functions to the total losses the company would sustain after a disaster without a plan. Exhibit 59.6 compares the number of functions per category to the total impact of the functions in each category on operations in a typical organization. Although Category I functions number the fewest of all categories, their impact is the greatest. The Category III functions typically rank second in contributions to losses, with Category II third in rank. The critical functions that constitute Category I are ranked first precisely because of their high impact and time criticality. Category III is typically the largest group, so that even though the impact of each function may be small, the large number of

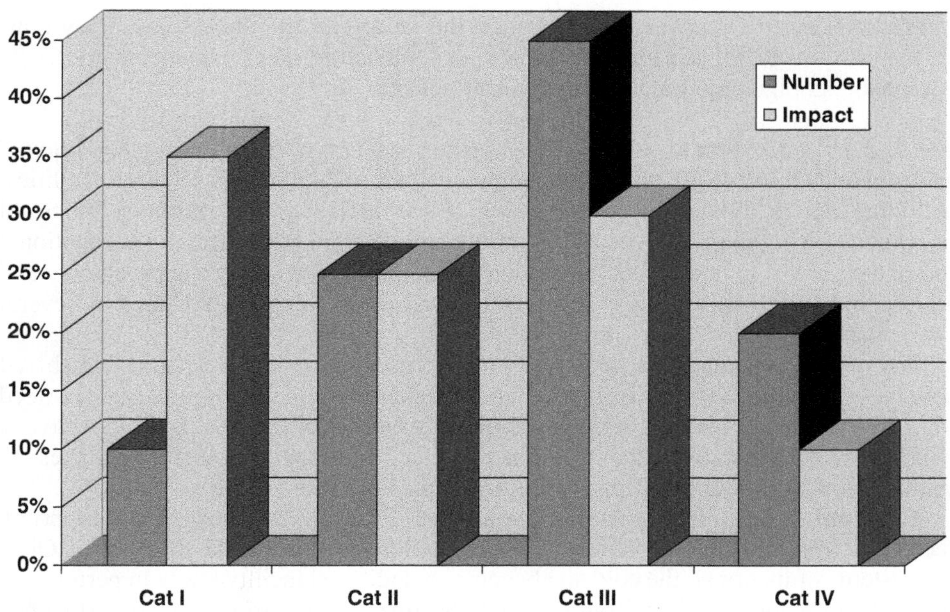

EXHIBIT 59.6 Number versus Impact of Functions

functions increases the total effect of that group. Category IV tends to be a fairly small set of functions, so typically it is small in number and last in impact.

In the example, the systems disaster phases reflect certain assumptions. The Continuation phase begins at the time of the disaster and continues for up to three days. The Recovery phase is scheduled to begin no later than the fourth day, with full recovery by the seventh day, at which time a return to normal operations is expected. The underlying assumption is that the off-site reserve systems have been replicated on site. This is shown by the caption "Activate On-Site Reserve Systems" in Exhibit 59.4. An additional assumption in this example is that the system can be recovered in less than seven days. Some analysis would have been performed to show that new equipment or equipment repairs could be obtained fairly early during the first seven days, leaving enough time for service restoration, including data recovery, to be completed by the seventh day. In this example, it is also clear that the Category II functions are required beginning on the seventh day. This is illustrated by the building or system disaster Recovery II phase, which begins on the seventh day and is labeled as restoring Category II, III, and other functions.

59.3.2 Range of Strategies. Three general areas of traditional recovery strategies address the needs of mainframes, midrange systems, and PC LAN systems. There is a rich history and many years of experience in providing recovery for large, mainframe systems, with strategies that include hot sites, cold sites, reciprocal or mutual aid agreements, and commercial recovery facilities, as will be described.

Strategies for recovery of midrange systems, including distributed systems, minicomputers, and workstations, include all the same strategies as those used for mainframe systems, along with mobile data centers, internal redundancy, failover arrangements, and agreements with manufacturers for priority shipping of replacement equipment.

PC LAN system recovery strategies are the newest of the three areas. They typically make use of combinations of capabilities, including quick replacement, off-site equipment storage (equipment sparing), and hot sites.

59.3.2.1 Cold Sites. A cold site is a room or set of rooms in a *ready-conditioned* environment. It is a fully functional computer room with all of the required facilities, including electrical power, air conditioning, raised floors, and telecommunications, all in operating condition and ready for occupancy. Missing from this fully functional room, because of high costs, is the computer equipment, including the processors and all required peripherals. Cold sites can be owned by one company or shared by several companies.

The major advantage of a dedicated cold site, somewhat diminished in the shared case, is simply that for a relatively low acquisition or leasing cost, the site is guaranteed to be available over the long term to the owner or lessee of the site. To be effective, a cold site must be distant enough from the main facility so that a disaster that makes the primary facility unusable will likely not affect the cold site.

There are several disadvantages to cold sites. First and foremost is that ordering, receiving, installing, and powering up the computer system can take many days. Once the system is functional, the cold site becomes a dedicated facility ready to perform all functions in a controlled environment, but the time required to achieve this state can stretch into a week or more. Few organizations can rely on a cold site as their primary vehicle for disaster recovery. A secondary disadvantage of cold sites is the inherent inability to test the recovery plan. An untested plan is an unreliable plan—testing a cold site would require obtaining all of the requisite equipment, installing the equipment, and performing operations on the new equipment. Few organizations can afford the costs associated with such testing. There are also hidden pitfalls with this strategy. Key equipment may be unavailable for immediate delivery. Communication lines may be untested and unreliable. This strategy is generally not a desirable first line of defense. It can, however, be a part of a larger overall strategy that includes other types of sites.

59.3.2.2 Hot Sites. A hot site is a facility ready to assume processing responsibility immediately. The term usually refers to a site that contains equipment ready to assume all hardware functions, but requiring massive restoration of data and an influx of personnel to operate the equipment. The hot site cannot, therefore, begin total processing instantaneously. In actuality, the site is only warm, with an ability to get hot fast. A hot site can be dedicated to one organization, shared by several organizations, or leased from a specialty company, called a *commercial recovery service provider*. The provider option is described in a later section.

The primary advantage of a hot site is the speed of recovery. The time to resume processing is defined as the time to reach the facility with people and backup media, plus the time to restore data and programs from the backup media, to test the operations, and to go live with a fully functional system. For larger systems, this period can range from less than two days to almost a week.

The primary disadvantage of a hot site is the cost associated with acquiring and maintaining the fully equipped site. For this reason, most organizations choose to share the cost of a hot site with other organizations, which may be sister companies or only neighbors. In any event, there is a large cost associated with maintaining the site and ensuring that it is updated with every change to each of the participant's requirements, while still maintaining compatibility with all of them. One of the most common solutions to this problem is to use a service provider.

59.3.2.3 Reciprocal Agreements. Reciprocal agreements were often used in the earlier decades of disaster recovery planning but are uncommon today. A reciprocal agreement is an arrangement between two or more companies in which each agrees to make excess capacity available to the others in case of a disaster. The major advantage is the apparent low cost of this solution. The major disadvantage is that these arrangements rarely provide the needed computing power. A major issue with these arrangements is maintaining compatible systems. If one company changes a processor, it may find that its partners' systems cannot perform adequately, even in degraded mode. If the host company faces a crisis or deadline of its own, a reciprocal company may find itself with no computer power at all. These arrangements are seldom testable, because it is the rare company willing to shut down operations to help a partner perform a disaster recovery test.

59.3.2.4 Internal Redundancy. A strategy of internal redundancy requires that a business have multiple facilities, geographically dispersed, with similar equipment in each site. If there are data centers at several sites, then the alternate data centers may be designed with excess capacity to support a potential failure at another site.

The major advantage of internal redundancy is that the organization maintains complete control of all equipment and data, without relying on any outside company to come to its aid. The excess capacity at the various alternate sites must be carefully protected, and management must exercise diligence in budgeting and operations. Careful intracompany agreements must be crafted to ensure that all parties are aware of, and agree to, the backup arrangements. Internal redundancy can be an effective solution in cases where temporarily degraded processing still can provide sufficient support to meet timeline requirements. If degraded performance is not an acceptable option, then the cost of the excess capacity will probably be too high. If reasonable degradation is acceptable, then those costs can be manageable.

Internal redundancy can also be difficult to test. Testing requires that processing be shifted to a recovery mode. Unlike external, separate computers, all of these redundant systems would be operational. Testing one disaster recovery plan requires affecting a minimum of two corporate locations. A failed test that causes a system crash or other problem can have damaging consequences.

Internal redundancy can overcome its difficulties if the redundancy is part of a load-balanced system with automatic or semiautomatic failover. In such cases, normal processing is already split between the primary and backup system so that both systems are fully operational at all times. The recovery requirements add an additional dimension to the nominal load-balancing configuration. Namely, there can be no system or system component that is unique to only one site. The most common load-balancing implementations may still rely, for example, on a database housed at only one site. This is insufficient for recovery purposes. If full duplication can be achieved, then the sudden loss of one of the systems causes degradation rather than loss of functionality. There are, however, often technical issues that many organizations must overcome prior to the implementation of such load balancing with full redundancy. For example, some legacy systems do not support multiple points of processing; some modern implementations may require a single database instead of multiple, overlapping databases, as is required for full load balancing with redundancy.

59.3.2.5 Mobile Data Centers. Mobile data centers are transportable units such as trailers outfitted with replacement equipment, air conditioning, electrical connections, and all other computer requirements. Mobile data centers are used most often for recovery of midrange and PC LAN systems. The primary advantage of the mobile data center is that it can be activated quickly at reasonably low cost. The primary disadvantages are the expense of testing such a facility and the possibility that a local or regional disaster will prevent successful activation. Deploying a mobile data center requires careful planning. Land must be available to accommodate the transportable units, with outside parking lots as the most common resource. Local government and municipal regulations must be researched in advance to ensure that such units do not violate ordinances, and can arrive as certified for immediate occupancy. External power and communications hookups also must be available.

59.3.2.6 Priority Replacement Agreements. Some computer vendors support priority equipment replacement agreements. These are arrangements in which the vendor promises to ship replacement equipment on a priority basis. For midrange systems, this is often an agreement to send the next-off-the-line system to the priority customer. The major advantage of this strategy is its low cost. However, if the vendor is not currently manufacturing the required system, or if the assembly line is down for any reason, and if equipment stocks are depleted, there may still be a significant delay in receiving the equipment. This is the major disadvantage. This strategy also assumes the disaster recovery plan makes an alternate facility available in case the primary facility is damaged along with the equipment being replaced.

59.3.2.7 Commercial Recovery Services. Commercial recovery service providers can support a combination of the strategies just discussed. These companies generally provide three major benefits: cost sharing, reduced management needs, and diminished risk of obsolescence. First, they spread facility costs across multiple subscribers so that each subscriber saves as compared with building and maintaining a comparable, privately held capability. Because all subscribers share the same physical space, each pays less than would be needed to maintain such a site independently.

The second major benefit of using a commercial provider is that these companies eliminate the need for the subscriber to manage backup resources. Management and maintenance of such a site by an individual business could be a heavy burden, but the provider's primary focus is on managing, maintaining, and upgrading the equipment and sites. The subscriber company can be assured that the equipment is exercised and serviced regularly and that peripheral equipment, power systems, and facility support structures are properly maintained. A properly run site will also provide security, safety, compliance with evolving rules and regulations, and competent staffing. The provider assumes full responsibility for these functions during normal operations and continues support during times of crisis. The subscriber brings its technical personnel, while the provider leaves its facilities staff in place.

The third major benefit centers around today's fast pace of hardware evolution. A subscriber company typically leases a hot site or other service for a five-year period. During that time, hardware platforms will evolve. The subscribing company can protect its lease investment by ensuring that system upgrades are reflected in the leased equipment configuration for reasonable extra charges. A business that provides its own hot site must upgrade the hot site whenever hardware, and sometimes software, changes are made to the operational systems.

The disadvantage of commercial recovery services is in the obvious risk that the hot site may not be available in an emergency. Indeed, if a local or regional disaster affects numerous subscribers, there could be significant contention for the provider's resources. To address this issue, providers typically maintain hot sites in geographically dispersed areas. Although it is likely that in the case of a local or regional disaster a subscriber would need to use a hot site farther away than planned, it is unlikely that the subscriber would be left completely without the prearranged resources.

59.3.2.8 *Reserve Systems.* The newest of strategies is the reserve system, which is a small replica of a portion of an operational system meant for use during the first few days following a disaster. The reserve system provides continuation of key functions for short durations, although in degraded mode. The reserve system usually resides off site at an employee's home or at another corporate office. Another version of the reserve system is also kept on site. A reserve site may be equipped with a microcomputer or a minicomputer ready to assume functioning in case the primary system becomes unavailable. This meets the important criteria of a reserve system, which must be fast and easy to activate, simple to move, low in cost, testable, available, and highly reliable.

The reserve system concept was not feasible until client/server technology emerged and telecommuting with high-speed communications became accepted and readily available. Many large organizations provide employees the option of telecommuting on a regular basis so that they work at home sometimes and in the office at other times. Web-centric processing and remote application server technologies can provide powerful reserve systems for disaster recovery.

Proper security precautions must be taken to protect proprietary, confidential, and critical information stored on these reserve systems. Strong encryption protects against theft, while redundant systems protect against other losses. The reserve system is a quick-response, short-term solution intended to solve the problem of immediate continuation, even in the case where employees may be unable to travel outside their immediate residence areas. See Exhibit 59.7 for an overview of different recovery strategies.

59.3.3 Data Backup Scenarios and Their Meanings. Data backup is a key function in all system installations. The best recovery strategy, chosen to meet recovery timelines according to the BIA, is useless without a backup from which to restore and resume operations. Data backup is perhaps the single most critical element of a disaster recovery plan, yet only 31 percent of U.S. companies have backup plans and equipment. See Chapter 41 in this *Handbook* for details of backup scenarios.

EXHIBIT 59.7 Strategy Overview

Strategy	Activation	Cost	Testability	Availability	Reliability
Ideal strategy	Fast	Low	Excellent	High	Excellent
Reserve systems	Fast	Low	Excellent	High	Excellent
Internal redundancy	Fast	Medium	Poor	Medium	Good
Commercial providers	Fast	Varies	Excellent	High	Excellent
Hot site	Fast	High	Excellent	High	Excellent
Mobile data centers	Medium	Low	Medium	High	Good
Reciprocal agreements	Slow	Low	Poor	Low	Poor
Priority replacement	Slow	Low	Poor	Low	Poor
Cold site	Slow	High	Poor	High	Poor

59.4 DESIGNING RECOVERY TASKS.

The disaster recovery plan becomes an operating document when the strategies and reserve capabilities are translated into specific actions to be performed during the disaster recovery process. These are the actions required to protect assets, mitigate damage, continue partial operations, and resume full operations. Most tasks begin with actions to evaluate the disaster and then to initiate recovery procedures. The example recovery task flow (Exhibit 59.8) lists a series of steps to evaluate the situation. These steps, numbered 1 through 5, determine whether to declare a disaster or not. The second set of steps, numbered 6 through 10, is used to initiate recovery procedures. These first two sets of steps are called the *beginning sequence*.

The beginning sequence leads to full activation of a disaster recovery effort. The next set of activities, called the *middle sequence*, institutes the actions necessary to perform business continuation and recovery. Usually multiple choices for the middle sequence correspond to the disaster scenarios developed. Each path in the middle sequence is executed for a particular scenario. At the end of the middle sequence, full operations are resumed as specified in the disaster recovery plan. In the exhibit, the middle sequence includes two distinct paths. The first path includes steps numbered 11 through 20, and the second path includes steps numbered 21 through 30.

The end sequence begins with damage assessments and continues through resumption of normal operations in the original facility, a semipermanent facility, or a new facility. The end sequence may begin while the middle sequence is still unfolding. The timing is dependent on the requirements specific in the BIA. The end sequence consists of two sets of activities performed in sequence. The first set consists of steps 31 through 38, and the second set consists of steps 39 through 59.

59.4.1 Beginning Sequence.

The beginning sequence (Exhibit 59.9) helps the disaster recovery team in its first two major actions: evaluation of the emergency and initiation of the recovery procedures. Box 1, labeled "Disaster Evaluation," begins the process with a set of actions whose end goal determines what actions to take to meet the upcoming emergency. In step 2, the disaster recovery team determines which course of action to take: continue normal operations, disrupt operations for a short while and then resume normal operations, or initiate a full- or partial-scale disaster recovery. The decision is based on a set of predetermined criteria.

Box 2 is labeled "Evaluate Emergency." This is the step in which the disaster recovery team assesses the expected duration and extent of the upcoming or existing outage. Using a set of criteria developed as part of the BIA, and based on the assessment of the outage, the team determines which course of action to take. For example, if the emergency is a power outage, the disaster recovery team will likely call the power utility to determine the cause. If the outage is expected to last less time than the shortest recovery requirement, then it may make the most sense simply to disrupt operations for a short time without initiating recovery procedures. The comprehensive disaster recovery procedures provide sufficient guidance in a simple form to support the team's decision-making process while leaving room for real-time evaluation and decision making.

If the decision is to initiate disaster recovery procedures, then the flow proceeds through box 5, "Initiate DR Procedure," to the initiation phase represented by the actions in boxes 6 through 9. In step 6, the disaster recovery team determines which of the disaster scenarios applies; the team formally declares that type of disaster in step 7, and, in step 8, notifies the disaster recovery team and others, as required, of the

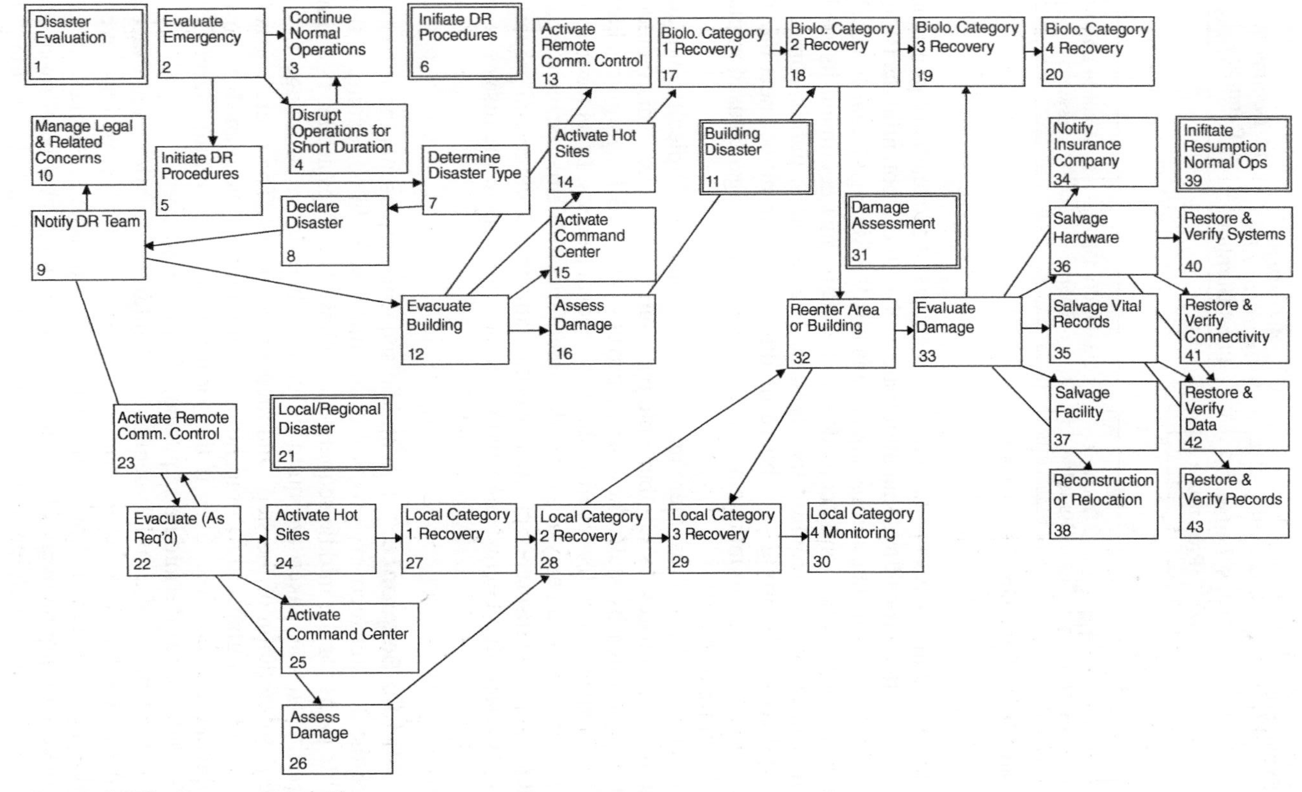

EXHIBIT 59.8 Recovery Task Flow

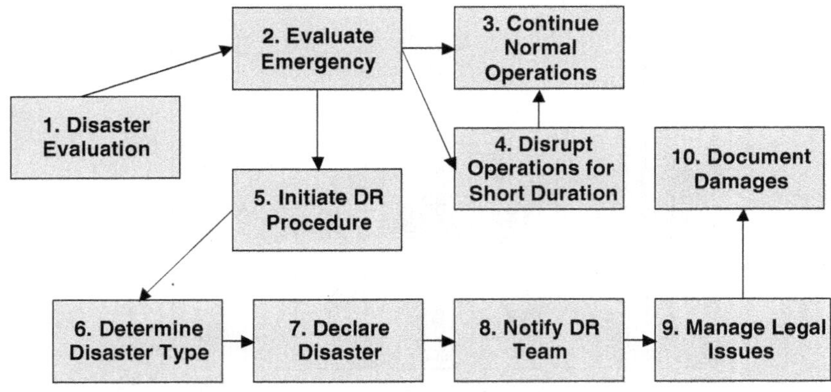

EXHIBIT 59.9 Beginning Sequence

decisions made and the next steps to take. All members of the team are pretrained and equipped with written procedures that anticipate each of these potential decisions. The only remaining step in the beginning sequence is box 9, "Manage Legal Issues." From the moment a disaster situation is considered, the team must document its decisions. In some industries, this is required by regulatory agencies; in public companies, it may be required for reporting to a board of directors' committee meeting. For all companies, it is important to maintain a clear record of the diligence used in planning and implementing recovery.

In addition to legal concerns, there are insurance concerns. Typically, money spent during the recovery process is reimbursable by insurance policies. This includes out-of-pocket expenditures by staff; the cost of travel, food, and lodging vouchers; and other allowed expenditures for meeting disaster recovery needs. In its haste to restore damaged systems, the team may neglect to document specific damages; once repaired, it is difficult to submit an insurance claim unless the damage is documented properly. Box 10 represents a step that begins early and continues throughout the disaster recovery process.

59.4.2 Middle Sequence. The middle sequence represents the activities that begin once the disaster recovery procedures are under way. In our example, there are two possible paths for the middle sequence to follow. The steps are labeled similarly, but the specific actions taken are quite different. There is an advantage to using a schematic representation of the steps and their relationships: The overall structure or shape can show at a glance the complexity or simplicity of the plan. It is best to be as uncomplicated as possible, even if the form and structure require larger content. Exhibit 59.10 describes the middle sequence, "Building Scenario."

The first step listed in the middle sequence, "Building Scenario," is to evacuate the building. Although this is clearly performed as early as possible, perhaps even early in the beginning sequence, it is presented here for completeness. Human safety is the primary concern of any recovery plan—no employee should ever be allowed to delay evacuation or reenter a building, except in the case of a qualified individual who is helping others evacuate or making a rescue attempt. The next four activities occur in parallel. They are represented by boxes 3 through 6, and include activation functions for remote communications, the hot sites, and the command center. These four steps also include a first effort at damage assessment.

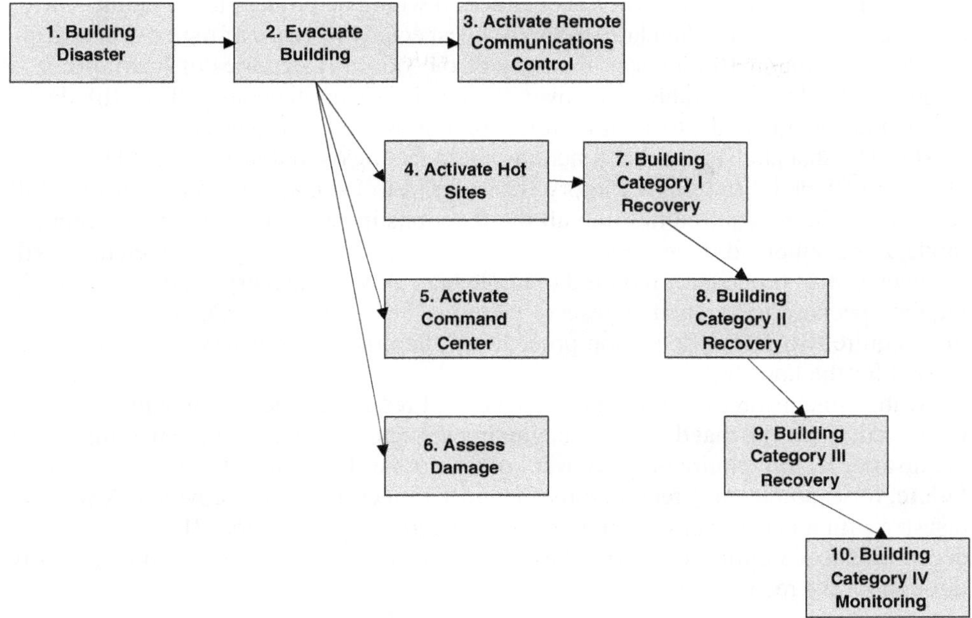

EXHIBIT 59.10 Middle Sequence, "Building Scenario"

Box 3 is labeled "Activate Remote Communications Control." This is the activity that reroutes digital and analog communications from their normal patterns to their emergency routes. This may include telecommunications lines, call center toll-free lines, normal business lines, data lines, and other communications media. Typically, arrangements are made in advance with the various telecommunications carriers so that a series of short phone calls can initiate the rerouting. If arrangements were not made in advance, then the rerouting will not meet timeline requirements and may significantly impair the efficiency of the disaster recovery team members.

Box 4, "Activate Hot Sites," represents the sets of actions required to inform the hot site provider that a disaster is in progress. Hot site activation must be performed at the earliest moment, so that the hot site can be available as soon as possible and so that, in cases of contention, the preferred hot site will be available.

Hot site activation usually obliges the company to pay certain activation costs and occasionally a minimum usage cost. If the disaster requires the hot site, then insurance often reimburses the company for related expenses, but if the declaration was erroneous, the company will suffer a financial loss.

The major hot site providers' services are quite reliable. There are few instances of hot site providers failing to meet their obligations, and many stories of near-heroic feats performed to meet customer needs. One provider even abandoned its own operations so that a client suffering from a regional disaster could occupy the provider's corporate space to continue its own operations. Hot site contracts usually include a proviso that in cases of contention, where more than one company is seeking the same disaster recovery space, the provider can send the late declarer to another, equivalent site. This means that the disaster recovery plan must include instructions for multiple hot sites. All maps, directions, instructions, and delivery requirements must be consistent with the assigned hot site location. Clearly, it is in the company's best interest to declare early so that the hot site of choice is obtained. It would be prudent to err on the side of early declaration rather than late declaration, especially in cases of regional disasters.

Boxes 7 through 10 represent recovery of the various categories of functions. It is seldom possible or desirable to recover all functions simultaneously. The BIA determined and documented the timelines for all functions needing recovery. The procedures must reflect that analysis so that functions are in fact recovered *just in time*. These four boxes are labeled "Building Category Recovery" I to IV. Each box represents the full set of procedures required to bring all the functions in each category into operational mode. For example, if there are seven functions in the Category I group, then there will be seven sets of procedures required to implement Box 7. Category I functions usually require special efforts, such as reserve systems. Therefore, each Category I function may require two sets of activation procedures: the first for the reserve system and the second for the hot site.

At the conclusion of the middle sequence, all required functions would have been recovered. It may be that during the beginning sequence a determination was made that the disaster would require only recovery of a subset of functions. A small-scale power failure, for example, may require only Category I functions to be recovered. A weather disaster with no lasting effects may require Category I and Category II functions. This decision is made during the early phases of the recovery, and reevaluated continually throughout the recovery process.

59.4.3 End Sequence. The end sequence represented in Exhibit 59.11 is the long path back to normal operations. The end sequence consists of two major phases. The "Damage Assessment" set of activities comprises the first phase and includes boxes 2 through 8. The "Initiate Resumption of Normal Operations" set of activities constitutes the second phase and includes boxes 10 through 13. Although there is an

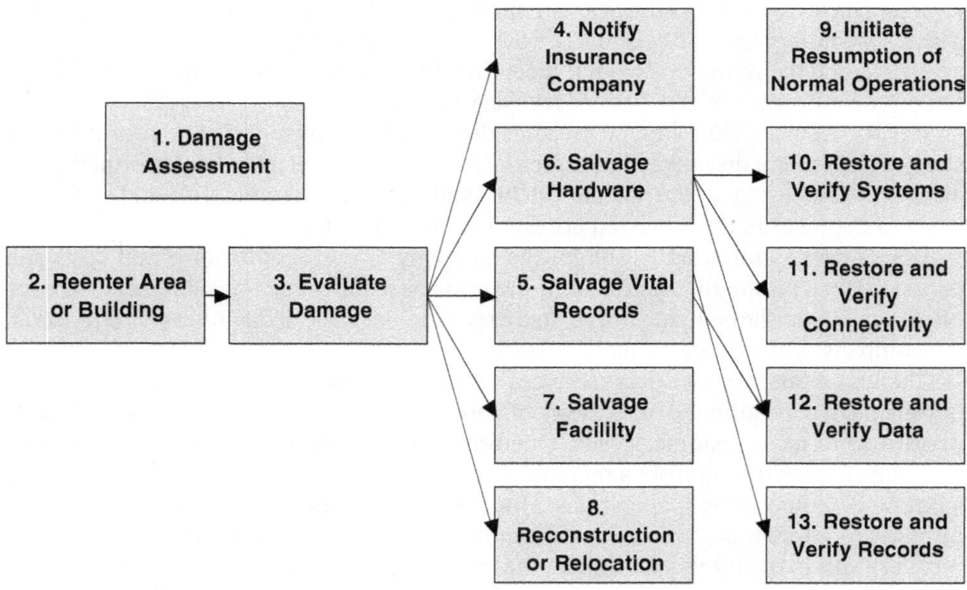

EXHIBIT 59.11 End Sequence

assess damage activity at the beginning of the middle sequence, that activity is a quick assessment of damage for the purpose of determining what recovery options need to be activated. This damage assessment activity is a comprehensive evaluation of damage to equipment, facilities, and records.

Box 2 is labeled "Reenter Area or Building." This activity needs supporting procedures to guide disaster recovery team members on what regulatory, municipal, state, and federal authorities control access into damaged facilities. Often access is restricted for long periods of time even when there is little or no apparent damage. For example, following an earthquake, structural engineers may tag a building as uninhabitable pending further analysis. As another example, after a fire, the fire marshal may prohibit entry pending analysis by chemical engineers to determine whether the fire produced hazardous materials. Fires often cause chemical reactions that transform normal, benign office materials into toxic chemicals. The procedures for box 2 should provide contact information for each major agency that may control the facility after a disaster.

Box 3 leads to five parallel activities. The first, "Notify Insurance Company," is related to the "Manage Legal and Other Concerns" activity in the beginning sequence. In this case, the various insurance carriers will need to send their own adjusters and engineers to help assess the damage.

The procedures for box 4 should provide the disaster recovery team with specific contact information for all insurance carriers with which the company has policies in force. The insurance company must be given the opportunity to investigate the premises before any salvage, repair, or cleanup operations begin. Unlike the period immediately following a disaster, when some cleanup may be required for safety and health reasons, the insurance company will look very unfavorably at any attempt to disturb the scene prior to it inspections. This does not mean that facility repairs must await a leisurely investigation and inspection by the insurance company; there are immediate steps to take to make preparations for salvage and repair. The procedure for box 4 will aid the disaster recovery team in deciding what they can do immediately, how they can document status prior to repairs, and what must await the approval of the insurance company and others.

Boxes 5 through 7 are the control procedures for salvaging hardware, records, and the facility. The procedures for "Salvage Hardware" must contain all the contact information for hardware vendors, including computer, communications, reproduction, and others. Each type of equipment requires different salvage operations; the best procedure for a computer may, for example, be the worst procedure for a magnetic tape drive. The salvage procedures should provide general guidelines and contact information for quick access to salvage experts. The same is true for facility salvage procedures.

Salvaging vital records is a complex and unpredictable process. For some records, drying is the top priority; for others, getting them into oxygen-free containers is far more important. The procedures supporting the "Salvage Vital Records" activity must provide contact points, general instructions, and guidance for making decisions about salvage possibilities. Unlike hardware, where the salvage decision is usually driven by cost considerations alone, salvaging vital records and legacy materials may be driven by other factors, such as corporate legacy and history considerations or legal issues. The salvage decision is often much more subjective in this area.

Box 8 is labeled "Reconstruction or Relocation." This task differs from the other tasks in three important ways. First, it is likely that the members of the disaster recovery team will not have the required authority to make this decision but will play an important role in presenting analyses to the decision-making top management people. Second, there are no specific company-external contacts to be made by the disaster recovery team as a part of this process. Although a real estate agent may be contacted for information, it is not likely that the disaster recovery team will undertake that task. The third difference is that the result of this activity is not some specific observable process but a set of recommendations made to top management. The procedures built to support this activity should provide guidance to the disaster recovery team so that they can develop the analyses and present the results in a timely fashion.

Box 9 represents the last phase of the disaster recovery process, initiating the process that returns operations to a normal operating environment. At the time the plan is written, there is no way to predict whether by following this step the company will be relocating to a new facility, or making minor repairs or none, and returning to the existing facility. The importance of these last steps is that they confirm the operability of the newly restored and operational systems. Each of these activities needs to be supported by a set of procedures that guide qualified personnel in their tasks of restoring and verifying systems, networks, data, and records.

59.5 IMPLEMENTATION AND READINESS. The final steps in preparing the disaster recovery plan are proving that the plan works and ensuring that the people understand their roles. This is performed through rehearsals, walk-throughs, and testing. Once the plan is completed and all of the reserve systems and capabilities have been installed, it is time to test whether these backup systems work as planned. There are a variety of testing phases, starting with extremely limited tests performed separately from ongoing operations and proceeding through full tests using live data.

The first set of tests is intended to prove that specific functions and capabilities are in place and available for use. These are the onsite and offsite limited tests, whose goal is to segregate tasks into small groups of related functions. With only a few functions per tests, there can be many tests that, in the aggregate, prove that each required function is successfully represented in the suite of recovery capabilities. The onsite portion of these tests will *disconnect* the users from normal operating capabilities such as LAN, WAN, and support staff.

This is best accomplished by setting up a testing room within the facility, but away from operations. Users are given the tools and instructions they would receive during a real disaster, and they attempt to perform their designated disaster recovery functions. An example of such a function is emergency payroll operations, where the outsource company is notified that this is only a test or the backup company facility is put on notice that a test is in progress. The tests would determine whether offline systems were able to process and transfer data as expected. It also may demonstrate that manual procedures work as written. In this testing, the keys are to set test objectives in advance, monitor test progress, ensure that users have only the expected disaster recovery tools at their disposal and no others, and document the results. After the onsite tests prove satisfactory, these same basic, limited procedures should be followed off site as they would be during an actual emergency. This requires some employees to stay away from the office, so the tests should be planned to avoid periods of expected high activity.

Once the functions have been tested, the next set of tests is intended to prove that the technical systems can be made operational in the planned time frame and that the systems can support users as expected. Two types of tests accomplish this: offsite network tests and hot site tests. These are discussed together because they are often overlapping capabilities performed at the same time. The offsite network and large-system hot site tests demonstrate that the systems and networks can each be restored within the time allotted and that the interface between them survives the transition to hot site operations. One of the primary advantages of performing the offsite network and hot site tests concurrently is that connectivity and intersystem functionality can be demonstrated.

The last test is a full operations test that attempts to show that all of these elements will work together. Just as in a real emergency, the test will focus on a subset of normal operations. Critical functions are tested first, and other functions are added according to the recovery timeline. For these operations, a test disaster is declared. Employees are notified that this is a test and that they are to cease normal operations and immediately implement their recovery procedures.

Most disaster recovery tests use simulated data or backup data that are real but are not the operational data. Changes made and transactions recorded during such tests are never brought back into the operational environment. Processing performed during the test is based on simulated business operations, with *representative* transactions rather than real ones. In the past decade, there has been a trend toward making final full operations tests online, using actual backup sites, systems, and procedures for processing real transactions. This makes the test process significantly more exciting, with a corresponding increase in stress, for employees and management. Mistakes made in this type of testing can cost the company dearly, but success can assure the company of a recovery plan that is much more likely to succeed during a real crisis.

Employees participating in full operations tests, using real data, are going to be much more serious, but employee rewards are also greater. There is more of a feeling of accomplishment if the test processed live data rather than simulated data. After the test, employees can return to work without needing to catch up on missed work. Management is also more likely to be directly involved in a live test than in a simulated test—because in a real test, management will be called on to make real decisions. They are more likely to be present, just as they would be during a real emergency. Not all organizations are structured in such a way as to make live tests possible. When they can be used, they are the most valid test of the recovery plan. However, they should never be attempted until the plan has been proven using multiple instances of the full complement of tests that should precede the live test.

59.6 CONCLUDING REMARKS. Over the past three decades, the very nature of the threats we considered, and the preparations we made, have changed dramatically. In the early days, major fears included equipment failures and minor geographic events, such as storms and small floods. In the event of a major catastrophe, we felt confident that our plans would unfold as well as those of our neighboring companies; perhaps there would even be some cooperation between companies.

In the decade of the 1990s, however, the criticality of systems combined with an upsurge in man-made disasters forced us to rethink our practices, scenarios, and procedures. The first bombing of the New York World Trade Center in 1993, the bombing of the Murrah Federal Building in Oklahoma City in 1995, the damage to the Pentagon and the heinous destruction of the World Trade Center twin towers in 2001, as well as attacks and failed attempts worldwide since then have finally led us to the point where we must include *artificial* disasters in our planning as well as natural ones. The disaster recovery planner must now consider disasters and recovery scenarios that include terrorism as well as tornadoes. The task is difficult, but the techniques and technologies are the same as before.

59.7 FURTHER READING.

See Chapter 58 in this *Handbook* for a list of suggested readings. Additional suggestions follow:

Websites

Disaster Recovery Institute International. *Education.* https://drii.org/education/education.php

Disaster Recovery Journal. www.drj.com

Disaster Recovery News. www.itworld.com/disaster-recovery

Disaster Recovery Overview. U.S. Economic Development Administration. www.eda.gov/disasterrecovery.htm

Disaster Recovery Resources. Clair B. Rubin. www.disasterrecoveryresources.net/aboutus.php

National Disaster Recovery Framework. Federal Emergency Management Agency (FEMA). www.fema.gov/national-disaster-recovery-framework

Books:

Gregory, P., and P. J. Rothstein. *IT Disaster Recovery Planning for Dummies.* Wiley, 2007.

Gustin, J. F. *Disaster and Recovery Planning: A Guide for Facility Managers*, 6th ed. Fairmont Press, 2013.

Hiatt, C. J. *A Primer for Disaster Recovery Planning in an IT Environment.* Information Science Reference, 1999.

López-Carresi, A., M. Fordham, B. Wisner, I. Kelman, and J. C. Gaillard, editors. *Disaster Management: International Lessons in Risk Reduction, Response and Recovery.* Routledge, 2013.

Rothstein, P. J., ed. *Disaster Recovery Testing: Exercising Your Contingency Plan.* Rothstein Associates, 2007.

Schreider, T. *Encyclopedia of Disaster Recovery, Security & Risk Management.* Crucible Publishing Works, 1998.

Stein, M. *Disaster Recovery 81 Success Secrets—81 Most Asked Questions On Disaster Recovery—What You Need To Know.* Emereo Publishing, 2013.

Toigo, J. *Disaster Recovery Planning: Getting to Business-Savvy Business Continuity*, 4th ed. Prentice-Hall, 2013.

Wallace, M., and L. Webber. *The Disaster Recovery Handbook: A Step-by-Step Plan to Ensure Business Continuity and Protect Vital Operations, Facilities, and Assets*, 2nd ed. AMACOM, 2010.

CHAPTER 60

INSURANCE RELIEF

Robert A. Parisi, Jr., John F. Mullen, and Kevin Apollo

60.1 INTRODUCTION.

This chapter presents an overview of traditional insurance products, and how they may or may not provide coverage for the risks associated with intellectual property and with computer and network security. It also addresses the new types of coverage that have been developed expressly to address those risks.

60.1.1 Historical Background.

Historically, people responded to the risks associated with commerce by finding ways to lessen the impact or severity of potential losses.

- Around 3000 BC, Chinese merchants cooperated by distributing cargo among several ships prior to navigating dangerous waterways, so that one ship's demise would not cause a total loss to any individual.
- Around 1700 BC, Babylonian merchant caravans were constantly imperiled by bandits. In addition to any risk-management practices they might have employed similar to those of Chinese merchants, the Babylonians opted for a risk transfer approach. ". . . Babylonian king Hammurabi developed a code of law, known as the *Code of Hammurabi*, which codified many specific rules governing the practices of early risk-sharing activities. For instance, the code dictated that traders had to repay merchants who financed trading voyages unless thieves stole goods in transit, in which case debts would be cancelled."[1]
- In addition to the well-known Colossus, the people of Rhodes created the *general average*—an insurance construct that survives to this day. The people of Rhodes were a superstitious lot, and would often attribute the fact that a voyage was not going well to some aspect of the cargo being cursed; once identified, the "cursed" cargo was heaved overboard—much to the chagrin of its owner. In response to this practice, which apparently became a burden on trade, Rhodes developed the general average, whereby all the noncursed stakeholders on the voyage contributed *pro rata* to making the unlucky soul whole—at least economically.
- Similarly, as Venice rose to power in the thirteenth century AD and began to venture farther afield in pursuit of commercial and political gain, it encountered such diverse problems as spoilage, pillage, and piracy. The clever Venetians established the practice of pooling their funds, and would then indemnify any losses from that pooled fund—essentially creating the first mutual insurance company.
- Finally, during the late seventeenth century, as international commerce grew, there developed the modern approach to risk transfer, whereby disinterested third parties put up financial capital against the likelihood of a loss of a ship or cargo. The third parties, who frequented Edward Lloyd's coffeehouse, were called *underwriters* because they would literally write their names on posted pieces of paper under the names of the ships they desired to insure.

60.1.2 Growing Recognition of the Need for Insurance. The theft or unintended disclosure of personally identifiable, sensitive, or confidential information led to increased concerns and ever expanding data breach regulations (state, federal, and non-U.S.) and litigation across the United States. First- and third-party liability exposure for data breaches, and related privacy risks, are mounting for all businesses that collect and maintain personal information about customers and/or employees. Individuals and business entities are facing new threats (in addition to ever-present threats of employee and vendor error) that may compromise data stored on computer systems, networks, and paper.

Among the many companies encountering higher-risk attendant to data breach are healthcare organizations, financial services entities, retail establishments, hospitality businesses, and professional service providers. Insurers are encountering data breach risks and cybersecurity concerns both in the context of underwriting and claims handling, given the significant, and ever-increasing, role of data and electronic commerce in the marketplace. The concomitant potential for significant, and costly, breaches of electronic and paper information cause a wide spectrum of public and private entities to recognize the need not only to manage these risks, but to insure against potential losses from them.

Even a perfect network-security infrastructure would be subject to human error. Every organization must integrate the more traditional ways that businesses manage the risks of simply doing business. A company does not decline to buy fire insurance because it installed a new sprinkler system; a bank does not refrain from purchasing crime coverage because it has the best available vaults and guards.

Companies traditionally bought insurance to protect against damage or loss of their principal assets—their plant, their fleet of vehicles, and so on. Where do they turn now that their principal assets are the data and information stored on their business networks?

60.1.3 General Liability Issues. Businesses traditionally managed risks through the purchase of insurance, principally *commercial general liability* (CGL), and property policies. Additional risks faced by financial institutions and professional services firms usually were addressed through a mix of fidelity/surety bonds and specialty insurance products, for example, errors-and-omissions insurance. What they have in common, however, is that all these lines of coverage were created before the widespread, commercial use of computers and networks, especially the Internet and the many statutes addressing data security. Not surprisingly, these traditional policies often fall short of addressing the increasingly complex data and network security exposures that companies face today.

The CGL policy is the most fundamental component of a corporation's insurance portfolio and, not surprisingly, the coverage that receives initial attention in the wake of a data loss or computer breach. Originally called *comprehensive general liability* (also CGL), such policies provide a wide range of coverage for the liability of an insured, because of bodily injury or property damage suffered by a third party as a result of the insured's action or inaction. This coverage, which is explored later in greater detail, is the perceived situs of coverage for intellectual property infringement claims—an issue of critical importance today, when so much of a company's worth, even its existence, is based on its rights under patents, copyrights, or trademarks.

The basic CGL policy provides coverage for all sums the insured is legally obligated to pay as a result of bodily injury, property damage, or personal and advertising injury.

However, the potential bodily injury associated with information technology is quite limited. There is also confusion due to the use of a common term, *privacy*. The CGL policy responds to a claim of *invasion* of privacy, but typically will not respond to a privacy *breach*, absent facts and circumstances that otherwise bring the event into the ambit of the CGL policy's terms and conditions.

60.2 INTELLECTUAL PROPERTY COVERAGE.

Of critical importance to a company dealing with new technologies is the potential that its new innovation is a variation on existing and protected intellectual property (as discussed in Chapter 11 in this *Handbook*). In such cases, the innovator may be forced to cease production, to obtain a license from the entity that owns the intellectual property at issue, or to seek to have the legal protections of the applicable area of intellectual property invalidated through the courts.

Alternatively, the company in possession of protected technology, created through the expenditure of millions of dollars for research and development (R&D), may suddenly find that such technology has been incorporated in the new product of a competitor. The victimized company is faced with loss of market share, and possibly with a threat to its very existence. It must enforce its legal property rights—either through a license to the offender, or by seeking to preclude the use of the technology. In both situations, all parties will be incurring significant legal fees to resolve the issue.

In CGL policies, coverage does not always exist (on a defensive basis) for the infringement of a third-party's intellectual property. Such coverage is neither a subject of a broad grant nor a particularly effective one. To trigger coverage, generally, the infringement must be deemed an offense under the policy's *Personal and Advertising Injury* coverage section. Even then, coverage is limited by applicable definitions, exclusions, and the restrictive insuring agreement.

60.2.1 Recent Developments in Comprehensive General Liability for Intellectual Property.

Two recent iterations of the *Insurance Services Office, Inc.* (ISO) language for the ISO CGL form CG 00 01 (July 1998) and (October 2001) highlight the significant differences to coverage that may be afforded depending on the policy language at issue. For example, the July 1998 version provides:

> **COVERAGE B. PERSONAL AND ADVERTISING INJURY LIABILITY**
>
> **1.** Insuring Agreement
>
> **a.** We will pay those sums that the insured becomes legally obligated to pay as damages because of "personal and advertising injury" to which this insurance applies. We will have the right and duty to defend the insured against any "suit" seeking those damages. . . .

By virtue of the use of the defined term—*advertisement*—the form is clear that advertising injury liability coverage is applicable solely to offenses committed in the course of advertising the insured's business (i.e., goods, products, or services).

This grant of coverage is conditioned by caveats that are restrictive in the old economy of brick-and-mortar commerce and are all the more troublesome when viewed in context of the Internet and potential Internet- and data-related liability. To understand the coverage that may or may not exist, it is first necessary to understand how the liability policy defines the operative terms.[2]

The July 1998 CGL policy includes the following terms:

> "Personal and advertising injury" means injury . . . arising out of one or more of the following offenses:
>
> f. The use of another's advertising idea in your "advertisement"; or
>
> g. Infringing upon another's copyright, trade dress, or slogan in your "advertisement."

As discussed, the grant of coverage is limited. There is no coverage for an infringement, for example, if it does not satisfy certain standards, such as the three-pronged test utilized in *New Hampshire Ins. Co. v. Foxfire*[3]:

1. Advertising activity of the policyholder;
2. A claim that falls within one or more of the enumerated advertising injury offenses; and
3. Causal nexus between the offense and the advertising activity.

This representative approach is merely one of several threshold requirements that must be satisfied before coverage will apply. The policy form requires that the advertising injury arise out of an enumerated offense and that the claim seeks damages recoverable under the policy. The question of coverage is further limited by several exclusions that serve to drive home the limited scope of coverage.

Of course, the terms of the specific policy at issue play a significant role in evaluating any claim scenario. The 2001 ISO CGL revision both clarifies and restricts coverage with respect to liability for an insured's Internet activities. For example, included in the definition of "advertisement" are notices that "include material placed on the Internet or on similar electronic means of communication;" and "[r]egarding websites, [are] only that part of a website that is about your goods, products, or services for purposes of attracting customers or supporters." In addition, the 2001 ISO CGL form modified and expanded the meaning of "coverage territory" to include personal and advertising injury offenses "that take place through the Internet or similar electronic means of communication."

However, the growth of Internet activity prompted a significant restriction in potential coverage, as the ISO CGL form explicitly states that "electronic data is not tangible property." Under this form, electronic data means "information, facts, or programs stored as or on, created or used on, or transmitted to or from computer software, including systems and applications software, hard or floppy disks, CD-ROMs, tapes, drives, cells, data processing devices, or any other media which are used with electronically controlled equipment." These provisions appear in subsequent versions of ISO's CGL forms.

The courts' disparate construction of the CGL policy form policies created some confusion in the marketplace. The situation worsens when applied to the Internet, depending on the policy language involved. More specifically, an exclusion regarding ". . . an offense committed by an insured whose business is advertising, broadcasting, publishing, or telecasting" makes the coverage particularly problematic.

If the policyholder specifically operates in the media business, such an exclusion's applicability is clear and unequivocal. However, what happens in the more likely scenario when the policyholder is not a multimedia service provider, but merely an e-tailer or an entity that maintains an informational Website? Not surprisingly, there are two schools of thought.

One group, championed by the plaintiff's coverage bar, argues that, unless the policyholder is actively engaged in the business of advertising, broadcasting, publishing, or telecasting as those industries have been traditionally defined, the exclusion is not applicable. This logic rests on the argument that computers and the Internet do not alter the fundamentals of how the world does business.

The second school of thought looks to the way that computers and the Internet blur the line between traditional media activities and a company's online presence. By maintaining any presence online, the policyholder's activities now fall within the parameters defined by the exclusion. This position bears further exploration.

It is rare for a Website not to contain a banner advertisement, hyperlink to a third-party's site, or material imported from sources other than the policyholder's cache of copyrights and trademarks. The presence of such content may place the policyholder in the shoes of an advertiser, broadcaster, or publisher. It is challenging to differentiate between the newspaper or television network that accepts advertisements, and the e-tailer that carries a banner ad.

The applicability of such an exclusion becomes less clear when a business Website carries no banner ads or hyperlinks, and contains no material beyond that which has sprung from the corporate mind of the policyholder. The question then becomes one that does not involve the misuse of a third-party's content. Does the simple maintenance of a Website presume a business is advertising, broadcasting, publishing, or telecasting? The logic behind that position argues that the insured, by maintaining a Website, is effectively sidestepping the services of publishers and broadcasters and doing the job itself.

Finally, another argument considers the manner, speed, and magnitude with which business is conducted via the Internet. The medium of the Internet was not contemplated when the insurance industry drafted some of the initial versions of the CGL policy. Similarly, premiums charged for most CGL policies do not reflect any actuarial data related to the Internet. In fact, the very nature of the Internet lies in direct opposition to most assumptions an insurance underwriter formulates when calculating a premium.

For instance, when a business contemplates launching an advertising campaign, a concept traditionally goes through some preliminary review or in-house analysis. That concept is then taken to an advertising agency, where, among other things, it would be reviewed for general propriety (whether it infringed another's copyright, trademark, etc.). The final product then would be marketed to either the print or broadcasting media, where the publisher would review the advertisement. In granting advertising injury/personal injury coverage, the insurance underwriter assumes the content has gone through similar independent reviews. On the Web, however, such levels of scrutiny are typically nonexistent.

It is unlikely that these arguments will be resolved definitively until more cases reach the courts. Even then, there will be issues surrounding the applicability of boilerplate policy language. Several carriers have either clarified the intent of the policy by expressly excluding some aspect of Internet activity or have simplified it by not offering such coverage to those entities that have an Internet exposure. Several companies have addressed the issue by creating a policy that affirmatively covers the risks associated with a company presenting information on the Internet, be it substantive content or just a banner advertisement.

It should be noted that the 2001 ISO form included several important exclusions to the personal and advertising liability coverage provided. An important exclusion bars coverage for personal and advertising injury arising out of the alleged infringement of copyright, patent, trademark, trade secret, or other intellectual property rights. This exclusion includes an exception for claims alleging infringement, in an insured's advertisement, of a copyright, trade dress, or slogan. The 2001 ISO form also sets forth an exclusion applicable to Internet communications, precluding coverage for certain personal and advertising injury claims against an insured who maintains an Internet business or an electronic chatroom or bulletin board. In addition to manuscript endorsements, liability policies may include versions of exclusions promulgated by ISO, such as ISO's 2007 standard form CG 00 01 12 07, that apply to (1) personal and advertising injury arising out of the unauthorized use of another's name or product in the course of the insured's Internet activities, or (2) claims resulting from a violation of applicable laws restricting/prohibiting communications involving facsimile machines, telephones, or computers.

60.2.2 Loss/Damage to Intangible Assets. Property damage is generally defined as physical injury to tangible property including all resulting loss of use of that property and loss of use of tangible property that is not physically injured. However, as discussed in Section 60.2, the 2001 ISO CGL form (and subsequent forms) states that electronic data is not tangible property. In addition, the 2004 version of ISO's CGL form restricts coverage in connection with a loss of electronic data, excluding from coverage "[d]amages arising out of the loss of, loss of use of, damage to, corruption of, inability to access, or inability to manipulate electronic data." These 2001 and 2004 revisions likewise appear in subsequent ISO-promulgated CGL forms, such as CG 00 01 12 07.

Several cases have looked at the nexus between the virtual world and property damage. In one case, a large assembler of personal computers purchased disk drives from a manufacturer and subsequently alleged that the disk drives were defective. It did not, however, allege that the defective drives caused any harm to the other components, nor did it claim any loss of use. The manufacturer presented the claim to its CGL carrier, which later denied the claim. In the resultant coverage litigation, the court ruled the claim did not involve property damage because "physical incorporation of a defective product into another does not constitute property damage unless there is a physical harm to the whole."[4] The implication is clear: The mere fact that a piece of hardware or application is defective will not trigger covered property damage. The importance of this distinction cannot be underestimated. This issue will be emphasized further in Section 70.0, which addresses first-party coverage as a result of direct loss.

However, some argue that coverage may exist under certain policies for loss of electronic data, even in the absence of loss of data due to physical injury to tangible property. For instance, ISO promulgated form CG 00 65 12 04 and form CG 00 65 12 07, which afford coverage on a claims-made basis for sums that an insurer becomes liable to pay as damages because of the loss of electronic data, caused by an electronic data incident. The 2007 version of this ISO form sets forth the following definitions:

> "Electronic data" means information, facts, or programs stored as or on, created, or used on, or transmitted to or from computer software (including systems and applications software), hard or floppy discs, CD-ROMs, tapes, drives, cells, data processing devices, or any other media which are used with electronically controlled equipment.
>
> "Electronic data incident" means an accident, or a negligent act, error or omission, or a series of causally related accidents, negligent acts, or errors or omissions, which results in "loss of electronic data."
>
> "Loss of electronic data" means, damage to, loss of, loss of use of, corruption of, inability to access, or inability to properly manipulate, "electronic data."

In addition, in connection with the 2004 revisions to ISO's CGL form, ISO included a CGL coverage endorsement relating to electronic data liability, form CG 04 37 12 04, which affords more limited coverage than the referenced claims-made coverage forms.

Of course, these types of coverages are subject to various restrictions and exclusions, including retroactive dates.

In most instances, the more critical and interesting issue remains whether damage to or loss of computer data is property damage not only in the context of third-party liability coverage, but also first-party property coverage (discussed in Section 60.3). Generally, courts that have looked at the issue have held that loss of data in isolation does *not* constitute damage to tangible property.[5] This conclusion is not universal and is under attack.[6] However, the failure of an insurer to define "tangible property" clearly in a liability policy may raise the risk of a court's finding coverage.[7]

60.2.3 Intellectual Property Policies. As a result of the emerging importance of technology and the increased recognition of the value of intangible assets, various insurance products have been developed to fill the void.

These policies fall within three general types:

1. Third-party liability;
2. Prosecution or abatement; and
3. First-party liability/loss.

The most common forms of insurance coverage available for intellectual property are third-party liability policies, including policies offering errors and omissions or professional liability coverage. In these policies, coverage may exist for an insured's liability to a third party for infringing on that party's intellectual property rights. There is a limitation on this coverage, though. Coverage usually is conditioned on the infringement's being part and parcel of the insured rendering the service that is the basis (or trigger) of the coverage. Additionally, coverage usually is restricted to claims for copyright or trademark infringement, but generally carries express exclusions relating to trade secrets and patents.

This sort of coverage is written either on a claims-made or occurrence basis. Traditionally, firms that provide content (e.g., advertising agencies, media firms, and publishing companies) have found coverage for copyright and/or trademark infringement in multimedia liability policies that are written on an occurrence basis. The policy language generally covers an insured for claims arising out of wrongful acts that occur during the policy period. In contrast, most other errors and omission/professional liability policies are written on a claims-made basis. They provide coverage for claims made and reported to the carrier during the policy period. The two types of policies can be distinguished further by the fact that claims-made policies may provide coverage for wrongful acts of the insured that occurred prior to the policy period, often dating back several years.

Firms looking for more explicit coverage for intellectual property infringement claims, including coverage for trade secrets and patents, usually are left to look to policies with the sole purpose of providing such coverage.

60.2.4 Claims Made versus Occurrence Coverages. Insurance policies generally fall into one of two types: claims-made or occurrence based. The differences in such policies are relatively simple to grasp.

An occurrence insurance policy provides coverage for claims that are made at any time so long as bodily injury or property damage, caused by wrongful, liability-producing acts of the insured, occurred during the policy period.

It generally does not matter if the claim is made long after the policy has expired. Traditionally, some CGL, and most media liability policies, have been written on an occurrence basis; this group of policies is often the first line of defense for claims of copyright and trademark infringement.

A claims-made insurance policy provides coverage for claims made during the policy period, regardless of when the wrongful acts giving rise to the claim occurred, unless the policy imposes a retroactive date. A claims-made policy would respond to a claim made against the policyholder only during the policy period, even if the wrongful acts complained of occurred several years prior to the inception of the policy. Nearly all professional liability/errors and omissions policies, and some hybrid CGL policies, are written on a claims-made basis. Nearly all policies that offer express and specialized coverage for intellectual property infringement liability are written on a claims-made basis.

How the occurrence/claims-made distinctions apply to these data and technology driven exposures is generally of interest only to insurance brokers and underwriters. Some insurance companies initially took the approach that the Internet was entirely a media risk and, as such, should be addressed by occurrence-based coverage. In contrast, other carriers viewed the exposure as entirely based in the services a Website provides, even if those services are media related, and offer only claims-made coverage to Internet businesses. Still another, smaller group of insurance carriers took the approach that the Internet presents risks that are best served by both types of coverage and have offered blended policies.

The benefits of occurrence versus claims-made policies really depends on whether the claimant is likely to discover and assert its claim soon after the wrongful act, and whether the policyholder has any existing insurance coverage that will respond to potential claims from its prior actions.

60.2.5 Duty to Defend versus Indemnity. Those policies providing express coverage for intellectual property are written on both a duty-to-defend and an indemnity basis. The differences between the two types of coverage are less subtle than the claims-made/occurrence distinction, although the two share some of the same history.

Generally, most liability policies written by domestic insurance companies today obligate the insurance company to defend the policyholder so long as the asserted claim alleges facts that might reasonably be expected to result in coverage under the policy. Different jurisdictions take different views on how to interpret if, and when, that duty is trigged and when the duty is no longer owed. The question is the subject of no small amount of case law and legal analysis. For purposes of this discussion, it need merely be noted that the general duty to defend under the law is broader than the insurer's duty to indemnify the policyholder for damages.

Some older policies, as well as those offered through Lloyds' of London, are written on an indemnity basis. The practical effect of this is that the policyholder must incur the cost of defending itself and paying damages for which it is held liable. The insured then must seek indemnity or reimbursement, subject to any retention or deductible, from the carrier.

Whether a policyholder is better served by purchasing an indemnity or a duty-to-defend policy depends not only on its ability to fund a defense but also on its desire to maintain complete control over that defense. Pursuant to a duty-to-defend policy, the carrier, subject to the deductible or retention, provides a defense for covered claims from day 1, including designating and appointing counsel.

Duty-to-defend policies usually are associated with a pay-on-behalf-of component. This element of coverage obligates the carrier to pay on behalf of the policyholder any covered damages for which the policyholder is held liable, subject only to the applicable deductible or retention.

In the case of an infringement liability policy, the duty to defend is triggered when a claim alleges that an insured has violated or infringed on the intellectual property rights of another in the course of its business or, if more narrowly underwritten, in the course of the expressly designated covered activity. It is important to note that the validity of the claim is often irrelevant to the duty of the carrier to provide a defense.

60.2.6 Who Is Insured? The typical policy generally provides coverage to the principal or named insured, and to subsidiaries of the named insured; the named insured usually is the entity that applied for the insurance and completed the application. Subsidiary coverage traditionally has been limited to actions taken while the entity at issue was actually a subsidiary of the named insured. Coverage is also customarily provided to any present or former partner, officer, director, or employee of the named insured or subsidiary, but only while acting in his or her capacity as such. Often it includes the estates, heirs, legal representatives, or assigns of deceased persons who were insureds at the time that the intellectual property infringement was alleged to have been committed, and the legal representatives or assigns of insureds in the event of the insured's incompetence, insolvency, or bankruptcy.

Persons that may qualify as insureds under a policy are potentially large in number and diverse. Traditionally, intellectual property infringement liability policies have focused not so much on the *who* but on the *what* of coverage. In this case, the *what* is the scope of the policyholder's business activity for which the insurance carrier has agreed to provide coverage. This can involve anything from a single product or service to the entire breadth of the policyholder's operations.

60.2.7 Definitions of Covered Claims. The value of intellectual property coverage can best be viewed by how it defines a claim. As illustrated by current cases, more often than not, the first salvo fired by a plaintiff is not one seeking damages, but rather one seeking to enjoin the infringer from further infringement. Many policies, however, require that the claimant seek monetary damages before coverage attaches. Thus, a company seeking broader coverage should make sure that the policy would respond to actions seeking:

- A demand for money, services, nonmonetary, or injunctive relief; or
- A suit(s), including a civil, criminal, or arbitration proceeding, for monetary or nonmonetary relief.

Integral to a covered claim is how the policy defines claims expenses. Simply offering coverage for those expenses incurred in defense of an infringement action often affords only half of an effective defense. Often the best defense really is a strong offense. In order for defensive coverage to be effective, it needs to incorporate coverage for expenses incurred in seeking to challenge the validity of the patent that a company's product or service is allegedly infringing.

60.2.8 Prior Acts Coverage. Obtaining coverage for prior acts can be crucial when the coverage is written on a claims-made basis. A company must consider how long it has been doing what it is seeking to protect. Ideally, coverage should go back to the inception of the company; unfortunately, such broad coverage is not always available. Carriers often limit coverage to a discrete number of years prior to policy inception—such as for the time when the policyholder instituted certain internal intellectual property controls and/or when it began the activities for which coverage is sought.

Prior acts coverage is not an issue for policies written on an occurrence basis, since, by definition, they provide coverage only for bodily injury or property damage that occurs within the policy period.

60.2.9 Extensions of Coverage. Most intellectual property insurance policies currently available are written to cover only a specific type of intellectual property infringement, chief among them a patent infringement policy. The typical company, assuming that such an entity even exists, does not have the luxury of being sued only for an isolated activity. It is more probable that a company, by its very existence, will be subject to potential exposures across the entire spectrum of intellectual property. As such, companies need coverage that will respond to an allegation of more than just patent infringement.

Several insurance carriers offer coverage options that address this broad range of intellectual property (IP) risks in a single policy form. Other carriers have addressed this issue by endorsing only that coverage that the company specifically requests. The most common coverage extensions available are for copyright and/or trademark infringement.

60.2.10 Common Exclusions. The most common exclusions considered when evaluating third-party liability coverage generally relate to intentional or criminal activities. Several policies contain absolute exclusions that bar coverage when the infringement is willful or intentional. Other carriers soften the impact by providing a defense until the prohibited conduct is proven. Even then it is possible that coverage will apply to those insureds under the policy that did not know of or participate in the willful conduct.

Along similar lines is an exclusion for punitive or exemplary damages. Historically, such damages have been excluded as a matter of course. Recently, however, some carriers have offered coverage for awards of such damages to the extent that to do so is not against public policy, or otherwise against the law.

Other common exclusions track with the principle that liability insurance is meant to cover fortuitous risks. They include claims arising out of breach of contract, antitrust activities, and infringements that existed prior to the inception of the policy. Liability policies are meant to cover unforeseen risks, not known claims or the cost of doing business.

60.2.11 First-Party Coverage and Other Key Provisions. One breed of coverage differs by its very nature. This *first-party coverage* reimburses the policyholder for the loss of the value of its intellectual property after it is declared invalid (patents) or misappropriated (trade secrets). In addition, coverage is available in the market for a policyholder's loss of a trade secret resulting from a computer attack.

At the moment, the number of carriers offering such coverage is very limited, and the underwriting is, in a word, intense. The first coverage mentioned is called *patent validity* coverage, which indemnifies buyers and/or sellers of patent rights for loss related to the patents subsequently being declared invalid or held unenforceable. Such coverage can be tailored to the premium that the company wants to pay. The basic coverage pays up to the purchase price of the patent rights. Expanded coverage pays for the loss of expected royalty income. This coverage is limited to patents only.

Another recent innovation provides first-party coverage for loss of a company's trade secrets. At least two Internet-focused policies also provide first-party coverage to a policyholder for the loss of its trade secrets. These policies provide coverage for the assets a policyholder has decided to treat as a trade secret. The policies generally require that the trade secrets be misappropriated through some deficiency in the security of the policyholder's computer system.

60.3 PROPERTY COVERAGE. Of particular importance to any commercial entity that values its information is the protection, or lack thereof, afforded under existing property policy forms.

60.3.1 Direct Physical Loss. Traditionally, such policies provide coverage for the direct financial loss suffered by the policyholder for *direct physical loss of or damage to* an entity's physical, covered property as a result of such brick-and-mortar perils, or covered causes of loss, as fire, windstorm, theft, and the like. ISO's "Causes of Loss—Basic Form" CP 10 10 04 02 provides a representative list of covered causes of loss. An *all risk* property policy provides coverage broader in scope, but it is still usually subject to the brick-and-mortar restraint.

The realities of how things work today, and the shift away from a company's worth being largely comprised of physical assets, suggests that such tangible property–based coverage is no longer adequate or sufficient, in and of itself. In today's economy, the lifeblood of an organization is not its buildings and equipment, although the events of September 11 and recent storms demonstrate how vital coverage for such assets is; in fact, a fairly standard business model is for a company to have elements of its infrastructure provided to it only virtually by any number of third-party service providers. The latter often replace many of the systems that a company would have leased or purchased outright only a few short years ago.

Such relationships create further problems when applied to the traditional property policy. The typical policy provides coverage for tangible, covered property at the physical locations of a business. As such, even if one overcomes the hurdle of whether intangible assets are or are not covered property under the policy, it is likely that such property is not resident at the locations covered under the policy.

60.3.2 Loss of Income. Often purchased in conjunction with the standard property policy is coverage for loss of income due to a business interruption. This coverage customarily has the same direct physical loss of or *damage to* trigger, but whereas the basic property policy seeks to indemnify the policyholder for the value of the actual lost or damaged property, business interruption coverage reimburses a policyholder for loss in the form of (1) the loss of net income plus normal operating expenses that continue during the covered period, or extended period, of interruption; and (2) the necessary extra expense incurred during the period of restoration in the effort to continue normal business operations. In addition, coverage often is extended to include an element of reimbursement for contingent or dependent business interruption. This provides coverage for a policyholder if a business that the policyholder depends on is interrupted by a peril covered under the policy, and subsequently causes the policyholder to suspend business as a result. Some recent property policies, such as policies based on ISO's "Business Income (and Extra Expense) Coverage Form," CP 00 30 04 02, set forth explicit limitations on business income and extra expense coverage when the suspension of operations is caused by an interruption of computer operations (such as from the destruction or corruption of data). In addition, forms such as ISO's "Business Income Form Dependent Properties—Broad Form" endorsement, CP 15 08 06 07, preclude dependent property business income coverage "when the only loss to 'dependent property' is loss or damage to electronic data," and impose other related restrictions on business income coverage as related to such lost or damaged electronic data and other property.

In today's world, most if not all, businesses rely on third parties to maintain some element of their network or computer systems, from the obvious application service provider (ASP), or hosting company (ISP), to the less obvious, but equally vital, outsourcing of network security. The concept of the weakest link applies not only to those allowed within a firewall—such as supply chain elements and extranet members, but also to backbone and infrastructure suppliers. A network or site will be just as inoperative whether the distributed denial-of-service attacks the business directly, or brings down its hosting company or ASP, backup and business continuity plans notwithstanding.

A case in Arizona called into question much of what the insurance industry felt was well settled on the issue of tangible versus intangible property. In *American Guarantee & Liab. Ins. Co. v. Ingram Micro, Inc.*,[8] a policyholder sought business interruption coverage under a property policy for loss of access, use and functionality of its computer systems, which resulted from the loss of custom programming information in the random access memory of three mainframe computers that occurred due to a brief power outage. In finding for the policyholder, this federal court based its decision largely on federal computer crime law and its belief that the continued distinction between *tangible* and *intangible* property, embodied in the policy term "physical damage," was not justified.

Not surprisingly, the *Ingram Micro* case has had a galvanizing effect on the legal and insurance community. The policyholder's bar has hailed it as a commonsense decision; whereas some carriers and some in the legal community at large have pointed at holes in the logic, personal opinion, and leaps of faith in the decision in criticizing the opinion. What all can agree on, however, is that it has created an increasing awareness and sensitivity by companies as to their insurance portfolios. In addition, subsequent case law has thrown the *Ingram Micro* decision into question, rejecting an expansive interpretation of what constitutes physical loss or damage to property. *See Ward Gen. Ins. Servs., Inc. v. Employers Fire Ins. Co.,* 7 Cal. Rptr. 3d 844 (Cal. Ct. App. 2003) (loss of computer data not direct physical loss). In addition, carriers have endeavored to include provisions in policies designed to exclude coverage for computer-related loss. For example, ISO-based exclusions, such as IL 09 35 07 02, exclude coverage for loss or damage due to the failure, malfunction, or inadequacy of computer hardware, software, operating systems, and networks, and any products, services, data, or functions that use or rely on any of those items, due to the inability to correctly process dates or times.

In addition to the efforts of commercial property insurers to manuscript endorsements that exclude coverage for loss of data, ISO introduced a revised "Building and Personal Property Coverage Form," in 2002, CP 00 10 04 02, which provided that electronic data was not covered property, except as provided in an additional coverage (subject to various policy conditions). The most recent version of the ISO "Building and Personal Property Coverage Form," CP 00 10 06 07, contains provisions similar to the 2002 version of the form. Covered property does not include "electronic data," defined as follows:

> Electronic data, except as provided under the Additional Coverage, Electronic Data. Electronic data means information, facts, or computer programs stored as or on, created or used on, or transmitted to or from computer software (including systems and applications software), on hard or floppy discs, CD-ROMs, tapes, drives, cells, data processing devices, or any other repositories of computer software that are used with electronically controlled equipment. The term *computer programs*, referred to in the foregoing description of electronic data, means a set of related electronic instructions that direct the operations and functions of a computer or device connected to it, which enable the computer or device to receive, process, store, retrieve, or send data.

60.3.3 Damage from Employees. This 2007 ISO form provides additional coverage for the cost to replace or restore destroyed or corrupted electronic data, but the coverage is subject to a $2,500 annual aggregate sublimit, as well as other limitations. In addition, this extended coverage is somewhat limited by its very terms. For example, the 2007 ISO form states as follows:

> The Covered Causes of Loss include a virus, harmful code or similar instruction introduced into or enacted on a computer system (including electronic data) or a network to which it is connected, designed to damage or destroy any part of the system or disrupt its normal operation. But there is no coverage for loss or damage caused by or resulting from manipulation of a computer system (including electronic data) by any employee, including a temporary or leased employee, or by an entity retained by you or for you to inspect, design, install, modify, maintain, repair, or replace that system.

A logical extension of increased interaction and dependencies between service providers and clients, as well as between co-venturers and simple conversants, is that, increasingly, businesses will come to hold, or at least touch, more and more information assets besides their own in their computer system. Such property, like its electronic brethren, tortured judicial logic notwithstanding, will not rise to the level of *covered property*, which generally is limited to tangible property located at, near, in, or on the policyholder's insured premises.

It has been suggested that coverage might be found under a property policy pursuant to a *valuable papers and records* extension. The problem with this argument is that, absent express endorsement to the contrary, valuable papers and records are usually defined as manuscripts and the like, not electronic data or the media used to store or record such data. However, different policy wording may yield different results. *NMS Servs. Inc. v. Hartford,* 62 F. App'x 511, 514-15 (4th Cir. 2003) (hacker erased vital computer files and databases; destroyed property constituted a "record" within the policy definition of "valuable papers and records").

60.3.4 Necessary and Reasonable Costs for Recovery. There also have been attempts to resurrect the notion that coverage might be found under the *sue and labor* aspect of first-party property coverage. This would result in affording coverage not for the actual property loss itself but for the necessary and reasonable costs associated with preventing or fixing the perceived problem. Much was made of this in numerous cases seeking coverage for year 2000 (Y2K) remediation efforts; these cases died quiet deaths due in large part to the *known* element of Y2K (the technological equivalent of a burning building in that programmers were well aware of the problem) and the nonevent that Y2K eventually proved to be. An analogy in relation to network and computer security would be for an insured to look to its insurance company to pay for the company's firewall and intrusion detection system, or for evaluating the effectiveness of those systems.

It is worth noting that a few carriers have expressly added coverage for loss or damage to intangible assets and resulting business interruption from nonphysical perils. This approach is decidedly in the minority but does highlight that when the markets want to address an issue, they do so directly and expressly.

60.4 CRIME/FIDELITY COVERAGE. Traditional crime and fraud policies have provided, and do provide, a certain level of coverage for direct financial loss due to computer fraud. These policies, however, have usually been limited to indemnifying a policyholder for loss of *money, securities, and other property.* Such policies also can contain limitations as to coverage involving both the intent and the identity of the thief, that is, whether an employee of the policyholder or a third party. However, these policies commonly fall short in offering protection or indemnification for the theft or misappropriation of information, and of intangible assets such as trade secrets, data, and technology—the essential elements of e-commerce.

Those policies that do afford express coverage for the loss suffered by a policyholder as a result of a computer crime generally limit that coverage to the loss of intangible property or information assets. In some instances, courts may focus on rules of insurance contract interpretation that result in a finding of coverage. For example, in *Retail Ventures, Inc. v. National Union Fire Ins. Co. of Pittsburgh, PA*, 691 F. 3d 821 (6th Cir. 2012), the Court of Appeals for the Sixth Circuit held, through a questionable analysis, that a commercial crime policy provided coverage for certain losses resulting from a hacking incident that occurred at DSW in which unauthorized access to a main computer system resulted in the downloading of credit card and checking account information pertaining to more than 1.4 million DSW customers. Construing the policy phrase "resulting directly from" very liberally in favor of DSW, the Court of Appeals ruled that the policy did not "unambiguously limit coverage" to loss resulting solely or immediately from the theft at issue, thereby affording coverage for direct financial loss sustained due to a hacker's infiltration of a main computer system. Time will tell whether this ruling will be generally applied. Not surprisingly, carriers have responded to the decision by adding language to their crime/fidelity wordings that attempt to plug the issues identified by the Court.

Common fidelity policies also can include loss that is other than the deprivation of the information asset, such as situations where the crime involves the copying of data. In today's economy, a company can effectively suffer a loss where its information assets are only copied—for example, the disclosure of a client list, business plan, vendor relationship details, and the like.

60.5 E-COMMERCE POLICIES. In the time since the 5th edition of this *Handbook* was published in 2009, the marketplace for ecommerce policies has matured, with considerably more uniformity among the competing insurance products. One of the things that the markets do agree on is a focus on all industries as opposed to simply concentrating on the technology, telecommunications, and financial sectors. The markets offering policies with definitive coverage for information technology, e-commerce, and network security have begun to grow to meet increasing demand in a technology-driven, increasingly regulated economy, though new entrants now come more from established carriers as opposed to small start-up entities—with over 30 markets now offering some sort of stand-alone e-commerce or "cyber" policy. What remains important to note is that all of these forms must, and will, continue to change with time as the technology, business practices, and regulations to which they are tied change and evolve. One need only look back to the early 1990s to find policies that spoke of the infinite channels of the Internet, and information security as part and parcel of the general content-related risks faced by publishers and broadcasters.

These e-commerce policies generally fall into two broad categories: (1) those that cover damage to third parties by the actions or failures of the policyholder's computer systems and/or its mishandling of confidential information, and (2) those that cover direct financial loss of the policyholder from certain specified cyber perils. Several carriers also offer loss prevention and loss mitigation services tied to covered claims or losses.

60.5.1 Damage to Third Parties. The most common e-commerce policy is that which would defend and indemnify a policyholder for claims made against it by others for damages allegedly suffered by those third parties. In addition to filling the gaps in traditional policies, such as a CGL policy, such policies also extend new coverage that is peculiar to the needs and exposures of information technology and computer system security.

Typical third-party exposures include the infringement of another's intellectual property, violation of privacy rights, content-based liability such as libel and slander, and professional malpractice. Claims alleging such wrongs are more often than not attributable to an error or act of negligence by an insured. They do not differ dramatically from their old economy cousins, with the exception of the myriad of privacy issues that recently have come to the fore in the form of general privacy, healthcare, and financial information.

The new exposures or risks that these policies respond to include the damage caused by the transmission of malicious code, the unwitting participation in a distributed denial of service attack as a zombie,[9] and others. These perils also can be the triggers for coverage for the direct loss suffered by the policyholder itself in the form of stolen information assets, corrupted data, network interruption, cyber extortion, and so on.

The more robust e-commerce policies have adapted and will continue to adapt to the inherent differences between the Old and the New Economy. Policyholders risk finding themselves bare at worst, or at best succeeding in forcing a settlement after protracted litigation, when they seek to shoehorn coverage for today's risks into hoary old policies from the days of black-and-white television and the Cold War. New coverages have always developed around new exposures, such as employment practices; so too have new coverages arisen to address the new exposures of: a company relying on a cloud service provider for elements of its infrastructure, divergent regulations either requiring proactive action to adopt a standard or imposing a penalty, and/or remedial response in the wake of a defined incident.

As these new e-commerce policies cover new risks, the due diligence performed by the insurance carrier in underwriting the risk must break new ground. The carriers that have taken the time to educate themselves about the risks inherent in computer and network security have turned to computer security professionals to assist in their due diligence. This due diligence generally takes the form of data security assessments, remote penetration testing, a holisitic security assessment, and a full-blown on-site security audit, or some combination. What is important to note is that these activities basically focus exclusively on the applicant's computer and network security issues and policies; as such, they represent a true value added to the applicant in the form of an additional set of eyes taking a critical look at its security.

60.5.2 Direct Financial Loss. In addition, companies have developed policies and marketed coverage that would allow individuals to cover the damages and costs associated with the loss and repair of their financial or credit identity. Such coverage also has been available to individuals under traditional personal lines policies, such as homeowner's insurance, although that capacity seems to be disappearing as the risks associated with such loss become more widespread and publicized.

Recent events continue to highlight the vulnerability of even the most robust computer, data, and network security. One need only check the news on any given day to learn of a cyber attack from organized crime or hostile state, a loss or mishandling of data by a major corporation, or other event highlighting the truly different way that the world works today. Apart from simply shutting down a business, the only way for a business to operate with the confidence that it will survive a computer attack and to instill that same confidence in its trading partners, be they customers or suppliers, is to have that traditional old risk-transfer vehicle, the insurance policy, sitting behind that business.

The issue of computer, data, and network security is itself changing. Accounting changes, shifts in asset composition, regulation, and the leveraging of intangible assets have caused network and computer security to evolve from a technology issue into a management liability issue. That evolution requires that companies address both the efficacy of their technology and internal policies and the completeness of their insurance portfolio. Of critical importance today is the issue of privacy.

In light of changing economic and regulatory realities, insurers have developed specialty insurance coverage products (using many different naming conventions) that afford consumers and businesses options to address various cyber data risks, including protecting against potential loss resulting from a security data breach. These so-called cyber security insurance policies sometimes offer a wide range of coverage to businesses, for example, offering coverage for third-party claims asserted by consumers affected by a data breach, or for costs incurred in responding to regulatory actions. Carriers are increasingly offering identity theft coverage to individuals, as well as other types of related coverage, as discussed more fully in Section 60.6.3. Cyber data security policies may also afford first-party coverage to protect against damage due to a theft or loss of data assets, cyber extortion, cyber terrorism, or even lost laptops. Of course, these types of policies may be subject to various limitations, restrictions, and exclusions on coverage, as is the case with traditional insurance policies.

60.6 PRIVACY AND IDENTITY THEFT EXPOSURES.

Businesses of all sizes across all industries hold both confidential commercial and personally identifiable, information in their care. Both businesses and consumers can take advantage of insurance to mitigate the consequences of an unauthorized disclosure or mishandling of confidential information, including the increasingly troublesome issues created by new and often confusing regulation from all levels of government and self-regulating industries.

60.6.1 Issues for Businesses. Consumers, employees, clients, vendors, merger partners, and other constituents expect the businesses they entrust with confidential information to safeguard it. Importantly, so do legislators and regulators. When a business fails to do so, the consequences can be severe.

60.6.2 Civil/Legal Liability. Companies may be held legally liable for losses that consumers or other third parties incur if information in their care is accessed or compromised, or if identity theft occurs. Even if a business has sound security practices in place, and is not negligent in handling private data, the cost of defending against the allegations and the settlements that often result can be significant. In addition, insurers providing noncyber policies will challenge claims for defense and indemnity coverage in response to a claim arising out of a data breach or hacking incident. Following are few of the many recent scenarios that have put companies at risk:

- In June 2005, victims of a massive compromise involving millions of credit card accounts stolen from payment-processor CardSystems Solutions[10] filed a class-action lawsuit demanding damages. Plaintiffs included not only individuals but also retailers affected by the breach.[11] CardSystems were also charged by the Federal Trade Commission (FTC) and agreed to comply with strict standards for security improvements and audits.[12]
- After a hacker stole debit card information in 2006 from TJX Companies, Inc., owners of T.J. Maxx and Marshalls stores across the United States, approximately a dozen banks had to reissue thousands of new cards to customers.[13] The banks sued the retailer for the cost of reissuance and fraud.[14] This case was deemed the largest security breach in history to that date.[15] A settlement agreement was negotiated in 2008 that offered "vouchers, cash benefits, credit monitoring, identity theft insurance, and reimbursements to eligible people affected by the intrusion(s). TJX will also hold a one-time special event reducing prices 15% for one day at T.J. Maxx, Marshalls, T. J. Maxx 'n More, Marshalls MegaStore, HomeGoods, A.J. Wright, Winners, and HomeSense stores on a future date not yet determined."[16] This incident emphasizes the potential, significant liability that may arise out of a data breach. In that regard, the United States Court of Appeals for the First Circuit permitted banks that issued credit and debit cards to customers affected by this security breach to proceed with various state law claims against TJX, and the processing bank for those credit/debit card transactions on TJX's behalf, based on claims that TJX failed to take adequate measures to protect data security.[17]
- In the past several years, carriers have filed declaratory judgment actions denying any CGL-based obligation to defend or indemnify numerous class action lawsuits (and other claims and potential regulatory matters) arising out of incidents in which cyber attacks resulted in the unauthorized access to and the theft of personal identification and financial information of millions.

60.6.3 Regulatory Issues. Various regulatory bodies may pursue administrative actions against entities experiencing a data or privacy breach. Actions may be brought by the Federal Trade Commission (FTC), Office of Civil Rights (OCR), the Securities and Exchange Commission (SEC), the Commodity Futures Trading Commission (CFTC), state insurance authorities, federal banking agencies, and state Attorneys General. Responding to these investigations require a significant amount of managerial time and legal expenses, and may result in costly settlements. In addition, companies may be forced to undertake lengthy, expensive, and ongoing corrective actions as a result of the investigations and settlements.

Illustrating the impact of a regulatory investigation is the widely publicized case of ChoicePoint, in which a major consumer data broker agreed to pay $10 million in civil penalties and $5 million for consumer redress in January 2006 to settle FTC charges arising from a data security breach. Under the terms of the settlement, the company was also required to implement new procedures to enhance information security and must undergo security audits by a third party every other year for decades. The breach compromised the personal financial records of more than 163,000 consumers and resulted in at least 800 cases of identity theft.[18]

In another example of the steep liability that a company may face as a result of an FTC investigation, in August 2012, Google agreed to pay a record $22.5 million civil penalty to settle charges that it violated an earlier privacy settlement with the FTC. This particular fine arose out of charges that Google had misrepresented to users of an Internet browser that Google would not place "tracking" cookies on a certain consumers' computers, or serve other targeted advertisements to those users. The FTC charged that Google not only circumvented default blocking settings, but made misrepresentations in that regard, thereby violating a prior settlement that barred Google from misrepresenting the extent to which consumers could control the collection of customer information. This is the largest fine that the FTC has ever issued for a violation of an FTC order.[19]

Regulatory requirements, investigations, and actions can affect a wide variety of industries, involving endless factual scenarios, and resulting in a variety of potential costs and penalties. For example, in January 2013, the FTC reached a settlement with the operator of a leading umbilical cord blood bank in response to charges that the company failed to protect the security of customers' personal information. According to the FTC, the company violated its own privacy policy by failing to use reasonable and appropriate procedures for handling customers' personal information. The company had sustained a security breach during which unencrypted backup tapes, a laptop, a hard drive, and a USB drive, all containing the personal data of approximately 300,000 customers, were stolen from an employee's personal vehicle. As part of this particular settlement, each future violation could result in a civil penalty of up to $16,000.[20]

Other security failures have resulted in the FTC filing a complaint against a global hospitality company (and subsidiaries) arising out of alleged data security failures that led to several data breaches. With respect to one of those incidents, the FTC alleged that inadequate security failures led to fraudulent charges appearing on consumers' accounts, millions of dollars in fraud loss, and the export of hundreds of thousands of consumers' payment card accounts to an Internet domain address registered in Russia.[21] Other companies that have faced FTC charges as a result of alleged security breaches include businesses that market products enabling employers to comply with federal immigration laws.[22]

Most states have enacted laws requiring companies to notify consumers if personal, sensitive, or confidential information has been, or may have been, compromised. These laws dictate under what circumstances a company must give notice, and what method of communication must be used.[23] Although requirements vary from state to state, the costs of legal guidance, forensics, and notification often can run into hundreds of thousands of dollars. As of early 2013, only four states have not enacted any such breach notification laws: Alabama, Kentucky, New Mexico, and South Dakota.

60.6.4 Recent Laws Governing Liability for Data Privacy Breaches. Over the past few years, there have been a number of federal and state initiatives that may govern the possible liability that holders of personally identifiable information may incur as a result of a breach.

60.6.4.1 Executive Order—Improving Critical Infrastructure Cybersecurity. On February 12, 2013, President Obama signed an Executive Order[24] designed to strengthen the cybersecurity of critical infrastructure by increasing information sharing regarding cyber threats (between the Federal Government and U.S. private sector entities). This Order defined the term "critical infrastructure" as a system/asset so vital to the United States that its incapacity or destruction would have a debilitating impact on national security, economic security, or public health or safety. The Order requires the Secretary of Commerce to direct the Director of the National Institute of Standards and Technology to lead the development of a baseline framework to reduce the threat of cyber risks to critical infrastructure, including developing "a set of standards, methodologies, procedures, and processes that align policy, business, and technological approaches to address cyber risks." According to the Order, this framework "shall focus on identifying cross-sector security standards and guidelines applicable to critical infrastructure" and "shall incorporate voluntary consensus standards and industry best practices to the fullest extent possible." In addition, this baseline framework "shall include methodologies to identify and mitigate impacts of the Cybersecurity Framework and associated information-security measures or controls on business confidentiality, and to protect individual privacy and civil liberties." As explained in the Order, the Federal Government will create these standards through consultation with owners and operators of critical infrastructure and other stakeholders, and an open public review and comment process. The establishment of these voluntary standards may provide a critical baseline that may lead to future regulations. However, courts or agencies currently evaluating a particular data breach may choose to consult these security standards, when developed, in order to evaluate and to resolve the alleged liability of a holder of personal information for a security breach.

60.6.4.2 SEC Disclosure Guidance. On October 13, 2011, the U.S. Securities and Exchange Commission, Division of Corporation Finance, released a disclosure guidance document, entitled CF Disclosure Guidance: Topic No. 2, which provides the SEC's views regarding disclosure obligations that relate to cybersecurity risks and cyber incidents.[25] Publicly traded businesses must be cognizant of these guidelines when reviewing the adequacy of disclosures that may relate to security risks and incidents. As emphasized in this guidance document, although current disclosure requirements may not explicitly refer to cybersecurity risks and incidents, federal securities laws are designed to elicit the disclosure of timely, comprehensive, and accurate information concerning risks and events that a reasonable investor would consider important to an investment decision. In addition, the disclosure of material information regarding cybersecurity risks and incidents may be required when necessary to make other required disclosure not misleading. Although various operational and financial considerations will impact the adequacy of any disclosure relating to cybersecurity, registrants should disclose such risks "if these issues are among the most significant factors that make an investment in the company speculative or risky." In that regard, registrants should take into account various factors, such as: (1) prior cyber incidents, and the severity and frequency of those incidents; (2) the probability of cyber incidents occurring, and the quantitative and qualitative magnitude of such an incident occurring; and (3) the adequacy of preventative actions taken to reduce cybersecurity risks in the context of the industry in which the registrant operates. Registrants should also address cybersecurity risks and incidents in presenting management's discussion and analysis of the financial conditions of a company's operations "if the costs or other consequences associated with one or more known incidents or the risk of potential incidents represent a material event, trend, or uncertainty that is reasonably likely to have a material effect on the registrant's results of operations, liquidity, or financial condition or would cause reported financial information not to be necessarily indicative of future operating results or financial condition." Other instances that may require a registrant to disclose such information include "if one or more cyber incidents materially effect a registrant's products, services, relationships with customers or suppliers, or competitive conditions." Thus, the SEC's guidance highlights the need for publicly traded companies to engage in a critical analysis regarding cybersecurity risk and assessment as a component of obligation relating to financial disclosure under federal securities laws. It is unclear if, and how, this SEC guidance affects the obligations of companies to comply with breach notification laws, including the need to inform shareholders concerning breach notifications by way of statements set forth in audited financial statements, or otherwise. However, depending on the registrant's circumstances, the SEC noted that appropriate disclosures may include a "[d]escription of relevant insurance coverage."

60.6.4.3 HIPAA/HITECH. The Department of Health and Human Services issued its 563 page HIPAA/HITECH final rule designed to strengthen the enforcement of rules promulgated under the Health Insurance Portability and Accountability Act (HIPAA).[26] The Health Information Technology for Economic and Clinical Health (HITECH) Act, enacted as part of the American Recovery and Reinvestment Act of 2009 and signed into law on February 17, 2009, was designed to promote the adoption and meaningful use of health information technology, and modified the authority of the Secretary of the Department of Health and Human Services to impose more stringent civil monetary penalties for violations of HIPAA rules. The recent HIPAA/HITECH modifications had several goals: (1) to strengthen privacy and security protections for individuals' health information established under HIPAA; (2) to modify breach notification rules relating to unsecured, protected health information; (3) to modify HIPAA's privacy rules, strengthening privacy protection for genetic information; and (4) to make certain modifications to improve the effectiveness of HIPAA's breach notification and enforcement rules, thereby increasing flexibility for and decreasing burden on regulated entities. It is anticipated that the effect of this final rule will result in a greater number of breaches that require reporting and in an increase in potential exposure to civil penalties and attendant risk. This final rule was published on January 25, 2013, becomes effective on March 26, 2013, and requires covered entities and business associates to come into compliance by September 23, 2013.

60.6.4.4 Gramm-Leach-Bliley Act. Federal law imposes obligations on financial institutions to ensure the security and confidentiality of personal customer information. Financial institutions include businesses significantly engaged in providing financial products and services. In connection with the implementation of the Gramm-Leach-Bliley Act, the FTC issued a final rule entitled "Standards for Safeguarding Customer Information," commonly referred to as the "Safeguards Rule." The Safeguards Rule requires financial institutions subject to the FTC's jurisdiction to develop a written pre-breach security plan composed of standards establishing administrative, technical, and physical safeguards for customers' information.[27] The FTC adopted the Safeguards Rule in order to "ensure the security and confidentiality of customer records and information; protect against any anticipated threats or hazards to the security or integrity of such records; and protect against unauthorized access to or use of such records or information that could result in substantial harm or inconvenience to any customer." The Safeguards Rule became effective on May 23, 2003.

60.6.4.5 Massachusetts Data Security Regulations. In addition to the federal government, state governments focus on imposing stringent requirements on those individuals and businesses that collect and retain personal information for purposes of engaging in commerce so as to protect against the unwanted and/or unauthorized disclosure of personal information. For example, Massachusetts enacted regulations, effective March 1, 2010, that established standards for persons and companies who collect and retain personal information about a resident of Massachusetts.[28] These regulations require the development and implementation of a written information security program that outlines administrative, technical, and physical safeguards appropriate to protect personal information. In addition, Massachusetts requires each person that owns or licenses personal information about a resident of Massachusetts (and that electronically stores or transmits that information) to include in the required written, comprehensive information-security program, the establishment (and maintenance) of a security system covering computers, including any wireless system.

60.6.4.6 Federal Statues under Consideration in 2013. Federal legislators have introduced a number of recent initiatives that, if passed, could change the landscape regarding liability and costs for data breaches, and have significant impact on possible liability implications for holders of personally identifiable information. At the time of writing (July 2013), the Library of Congress's *Thomas* system and *govtrack.us* provided the following statuses for some of the more significant publicized proposals[29]:

S.1193

Title: DATA SECURITY AND BREACH NOTIFICATION ACT OF 2012.

Full Title: A bill to require certain entities that collect and maintain personal information of individuals to secure such information and to provide notice to such individuals in the case of a breach of security involving such information, and for other purposes.

Sponsor: Sen. Toomey, Patrick [R-Pa].

Introduced: June 20, 2013.

Latest Major Action: This bill was assigned to a congressional committee on June 20, 2013, which will consider it before possibly sending it on to the House or Senate as a whole.

H.R. 1468

Title: SECURE IT.

Full Title: A bill to improve information security, and for other purposes.

Sponsor: Rep. Marsha Blackburn [R-TN7].

Introduced: April 10, 2013.

Latest Major Action: This bill was assigned to a congressional committee on April 10, 2013, which will consider it before possibly sending it on to the House or Senate as a whole.

S.1408

Title: DATA BREACH NOTIFICATION ACT OF 2011.

Full Title: A bill to require Federal agencies, and persons engaged in interstate commerce, in possession of data containing sensitive personally identifiable information, to disclose any breach of such information.

Sponsor: Sen. Dianne Feinstein [D-CA].

Introduced: July 22, 2011.

Latest Major Action: Feb 6, 2012 Placed on Senate Legislative Calendar under General Orders. Calendar No. 310.

S.1511

Title: PERSONAL DATA PRIVACY AND SECURITY ACT OF 2011.

Full Title: A bill to prevent and mitigate identity theft, to ensure privacy, to provide notice of security breaches, and to enhance criminal penalties, law enforcement assistance, and other protections against security breaches, fraudulent access, and misuse of personally identifiable information.

Sponsor: Sen. Patrick Leahy [D-VT].

Introduced: June 7, 2011.

Latest Major Action: Sep 22, 2011. Died (Reported by Committee).

S.3742

Title: DATA SECURITY AND BREACH NOTIFICATION ACT OF 2010.

Full Title: A bill to protect consumers by requiring reasonable security policies and procedures to protect data containing personal information, and to provide for nationwide notice in the event of a security breach.

Sponsor: Sen. Mark Pryor [D-AR].

Introduced: August 5, 2010.

Latest Major Action: August 5, 2010 Senate Commerce, Science and Transportation committee/subcommittee actions.

Status: Still under consideration.

H.R. 6236

Title: DATA BREACH NOTIFICATION ACT OF 2011.

Full Title: A bill to require Federal agencies, and persons engaged in interstate commerce, in possession of data containing sensitive personally identifiable information, to disclose any breach of such information.

Sponsor: Sen. Dianne Feinstein [D-CA]

Introduced: September 28, 2010.

Latest Major Action: September 22, 2011 Reported by committee.

Status: Died.

60.7 DAMAGES TO BRAND IMAGE, CONSUMER CONFIDENCE.

When private information in a company's care, custody, or control is accessed, compromised, or stolen, the company can sustain costs, damage to its reputation, and a decline in customer and employee confidence. How a company communicates the problem to those affected and manages the aftermath of an incident is critical.

If a company responds to a security breach or a potential security breach with rapid, effective, and accurate communications, and affords proactive, practical assistance for victims, it can generally mitigate damage to its public image. Companies that handle private or confidential data must plan, and prepare to mount, an appropriate response to potential security breaches, including considering the costs such a response will entail.

60.7.1 Special Considerations. All businesses that handle personal information are exposed to privacy- and identity theft–related liabilities. Certain businesses hold especially sensitive information, and have a particularly pronounced risk. They include:

- Any company that holds confidential information under a confidentiality agreement.
- Financial services companies that hold information concerning an individual that would be considered *nonpublic personal information* as defined under Title V of the Gramm-Leach-Bliley Act of 1999 (Pub. L. No. 106-102, 113 Stat. 1338), and the FTC's subsequent final Safeguards Rule. This definition encompasses all information on applications to obtain financial services, such as credit card or loan applications, bank or credit card account histories, and the fact that an individual is or was a customer of the financial institution.
- Healthcare companies and their business associates that handle information that could be considered *protected health information* within the meaning of the Health Insurance Portability and Accountability Act of 1996 (Pub. L. No. 104-191, 110 Stat. 1936) (HIPAA), and the HIPAA/HITECH final rule issued by the Department of Health and Human Services in early 2013. HIPAA defines protected health information to encompass all *individually identifiable health information* held or transmitted by a covered entity or its business associate in electronic, paper, or oral form. The new HIPAA/HITECH rules expand business associate obligations to certain subcontractors of business associates.

60.7.2 Business Insurance for Privacy Risks. Privacy insurance coverage enables businesses to manage the significant exposure associated with privacy breaches and identity theft. The insurance addresses the expenses and liability that can result when confidential information in a company's care, custody, and control is accessed, disclosed, compromised, or stolen. The same markets that provide e-commerce policies have responded with specialized coverage for privacy breaches. In evaluating this coverage, it is important to note that while the e-commerce policies generally require a computer malfunction of some sort, the privacy liability coverage responds to the claim regardless of how the privacy breach occurs—be it a computer glitch, Dumpster® diving, a lost laptop, or a rogue employee walking out the door with a thumb drive or paper file.

A sound insurance program should provide coverage for both claims-related expenses as well as out-of-pocket pre-claims expenses that are typically incurred as part of a privacy event. Coverage should also respond the risks and incidents that are caused by the policyholder's vendors. Termed "vicarious liability" or information holder coverage, privacy insurance has expanded to allow for a trigger that does not require any direct error or action by the policyholder; basically treating the breach occasioned by the vendor as if caused by the policyholder in order to protect the policyholder—with the carrier reserving the right to seek reimbursement from the actual party who caused the breach.

Coverage is available for the following:

- ***Legal liability and defense costs***. This includes judgments, settlements, and defense fees incurred as a result of a claim or civil litigation initiated by consumers, clients, organizations, or other businesses.
- ***Regulatory action expenses***. This includes legal expenses that result from investigations, negotiation of consent orders, and formal adversarial proceedings instituted by government or regulatory agencies. This is a critical privacy coverage, since the regulatory action will often precede the civil suit. It is in the insured's and insurer's best interests to have a favorable resolution of the regulatory action.
- ***Event Response Expenses:*** The costs incurred to hire forensic and legal experts to determine the cause and extent of the event, as well as any legal obligations that may flow from the forensic findings. This also includes the services of a breach coach, typically a law firm that will act as guide and counsel to the policyholder as it manages through the crisis. This is another element of coverage that is typically triggered long before a claim is alleged by a third party.
- ***Notification costs.*** The costs incurred to notify individuals or businesses whose information was compromised or stolen, including costs of mail, e-mail, telephone, or advertising. This is an interesting coverage enhancement, not generally found in other policy forms. It is, however, of growing importance as relates to current and pending state and federal regulations.
- ***Crisis communications management expenses.*** This includes the cost of public relations counsel to help a company shield its reputation during a pivotal period.
- ***Recovery services for victims***. This includes the costs of education, assistance, credit monitoring, and/or identity restoration for customers, employees, or others whose information was stolen or compromised. Providing these services can help a company to retain customers, maintain employee satisfaction, and prevent costly legal actions in the wake of an incident.

A recent and growing trend is for the carrier to provide elements of pre-claim expenses such as event response expenses, recovery services, and notification costs as part of a service offering, included as part of the coverage but sitting apart from the policy's aggregate financial limit as opposed to a simple monetary limit designated for the specific coverage elements. Such an event or breach response service offering approach has proven attractive to small and medium-sized entities, who often lack the sophistication or relationships to respond to an incident. The ability to simply call on the panel of experts assembled by the carrier enables the policyholder to manage the event and mitigate potential loss in a way that they could not do unaided.

60.7.3 Other Commercial Insurance Policies. Many companies operate under the risky and possibly inaccurate perception that traditional insurance policies, such as commercial general liability (CGL), directors & officers (D&O) liability, or errors and omissions (E&O) insurance, will adequately address their cyber, privacy and identity theft exposures. However, traditional commercial insurance policies are generally not designed to address risks related to computer networks and electronic information. Citing just one example, CGL policies typically do not define coverage *territory* to align with the global nature of the Internet, and do not contemplate the various privacy laws worldwide. These policies would not normally encompass coverage for expenses associated with victim notification, crisis management, and identity theft recovery either.

In fact, company management and other professionals who rely solely on traditional insurance will be surprised to find they have little or no insurance when a privacy breach or identity theft incident occurs. The specialized privacy and identity theft insurance discussed previously was designed expressly to fill this significant coverage gap.

60.7.4 Issues for Consumers. Identity theft, defined as the theft and fraudulent use of an individual's personal identification information, including a Social Security number, account numbers, or other personal data, is the fastest growing financial crime in America. One of every eight adults, or a family member, has been a victim of identity theft.[30] More than 9.3 million individuals were victimized in the United States in 2004.[31]

Identity theft is not only widespread; it is costly. Individuals use unlawfully obtained personal information to purchase goods and services, or to obtain new mortgages, lines of credit, or additional credit cards. A criminal may use a stolen identity to commit employment fraud or to escape criminal prosecution.

According to statistics gathered from consumer complaints filed with numerous state and federal organizations, and reported by the FTC, consumers reported 990,242 fraud-related complaints in 2011. Consumers reported paying over $1.5 billion in those fraud complaints. Categories of identity theft included: government documents/benefits (27%), credit card fraud (14%), utilities fraud (13%), bank fraud (9%), employment fraud (8%), and loan fraud (3%).[32] Medical identity theft is also increasing.

60.7.5 Insurance for Consumers. Consumers in the United States are well protected from the direct financial loss that can result from identity theft. If unauthorized credit card charges and electronic banking transactions are reported promptly, an individual has little financial liability. Still, individuals whose identities are stolen must undertake a time-consuming and often costly process to restore their names and credit. It can take six months to detect identity theft, and up to 600 hours to recover from the crime.[33] In some cases, individuals must pay to dispute fraudulent debts and accounts opened by an identity thief.

Insurance can help individuals alleviate the costs associated with the compromise of their personal information and identity theft. Such insurance is primarily geared to mitigate the costs of recovering from such incidents and to ease the recovery process. A typical policy might provide:

- **Expense Reimbursement,** encompassing numerous fees and expenses required to recover from identity theft
- **Income Protection,** which pays wages lost as a result of time off from work required to recover from identity theft
- **Identity Restoration Services,** including the services of a personal case manager to handle identity recovery work on the victim's behalf
- **Loss Prevention and Mitigation Services,** such as access to a customer service center to assist in preventing identity theft, and credit monitoring to promote early detection of problems

Many financial institutions, associations, employers, and service providers make this type of insurance available to customers, members, and employees.[34] Identity theft insurance may also be available to consumers in conjunction with homeowners' or business owners' policies.

60.8 CONCLUDING REMARKS. The significant exposures resulting from intellectual property and privacy breaches that companies and individuals face today have become serious boardroom concerns. To mitigate against these exposures, a comprehensive insurance program should be a critical component of the risk-management strategies put in place. While insurance for information systems exposures was once considered novel and limited in scope, it has quickly evolved, and new products in the marketplace offer broad and effective protection.

60.9 FURTHER READING

Dionne, G. *Handbook of Insurance*, 2nd ed. Springer, 2014.

Fordney, M. *Insurance Handbook for the Medical Office*, 12th ed. Saunders, 2011.

Ostrager, B. R., and T. R. Newman. *Handbook on Insurance Coverage Disputes*, 16th ed. Aspen Law & Business, 2013.

Sutcliffe, G. S. *E-Commerce Insurance and Risk Management*, 2nd ed. Standard Publishing, 2000. *Out of print.*

60.10 NOTES

1. Norma L. Nielson, "Insurance," *Microsoft® Encarta® 2008* [DVD] (Redmond, Washington: Microsoft Corporation, 2007).
2. Few cases have addressed coverage under common policy formulations defining the term "personal and advertising injury" in the context of an underlying data breach. The Court of Appeals for the Ninth Circuit held that a personal injury liability offense provision, covering claims alleging certain violations of a person's right of privacy, afforded coverage for underlying lawsuits complaining that an Internet provider interrupted and intentionally disseminated private online communications. *Netscape Commc'ns Corp. v. Federal Ins. Co.*, 343 F.App'x 271 (9th Cir. 2009). *Compare Novell, Inc. v. Federal Ins. Co.*, 141 F. 3d 983 (10th Cir. 1998) (software company claimed that general liability insurer failed to defend a prior action brought by an independent software developer; creation of a similar software program was not an offense committed in the course of advertising goods, products, or services). *Zurich Am. Ins. Co. v. Fieldstone Mortgage Co.*, Civil No. CCB-06-2055, 2007 WL 3268460 (D. Md. Oct. 26, 2007), *reconsideration denied*, 2008 WL 941627 (D. Md. Mar. 24, 2008) (underlying complaint alleged that a mortgage company improperly accessed and used customer credit information, without permissible consent, in order to solicit refinance business).
3. 820 F. Supp. 489 (N.D. Cal. 1993); *see also Zurich Ins. Co. v. Sunclipse, Inc.*, 85 F. Supp. 2d 842, 852 (N.D. Ill. 2000), *aff'd*, 241 F.3d 605 (7th Cir. 2001).
4. *Seagate Technology, Inc. v. St. Paul Fire & Marine Ins. Co.*, 11 F. Supp. 2d 1150, 1157 (N.D. Cal. 1998) (citation omitted).
5. *Rockford Pharmacy, Inc. v. Digital Simlistic, Inc.*, 53 F. 3d 195 (8th Cir. 1995).
6. *See, e.g., NMS Services, Inc. v. Hartford*, 62 F. App'x 511 (4th Cir. 2003) (first party coverage; software development company sought insurance coverage after a hacker erased vital computer files and databases from an internal computer network; the

company sustained "damage to its property" in the form of damage to computers); *State Auto Prop. & Cas. Ins. Co. v. Midwest Computers & More*, 147 F. Supp. 2d 1113 (W.D. Okla. 2001) (third-party coverage; data stored on a computer disk or tape was not "tangible property" within the meaning of a business owners' liability policy; however, the lost use of computers constituted a loss of use of tangible property within the loss of use of property damage coverage afforded); *see also America Online, Inc. v. St. Paul Mercury Ins. Co.*, 207 F. Supp. 2d 459 (E.D. Va. 2002) (third-party liability case; no duty to defend Internet service provider under CGL policy for loss of tangible property, as computer data, software, and systems were not tangible property; however, alleged loss of use of computers constituted property damage under a CGL policy that defined property damage as "physical damage to tangible property of others, including all resulting loss of use of that property.") *aff'd* 347 F. 3d 89 (4th Cir. 2003).

7. *Eyeblaster, Inc. v. Federal Ins. Co.,* 613 F. 3d 797, 802 (8th Cir. 2010) (the underlying complaint alleged repeatedly the "loss of use" of a computer; general liability and errors and omissions policies both provided coverage relating to underlying claims that consumer's computer was infected by spyware).
8. No. 99-185 TUC ACM, 2000 WL 726789 (D. Ariz., Apr. 18, 2000).
9. Zombies are computers that have been taken over by an attacker and used to transmit large volumes of traffic. See Chapters 18, 20, 30, and 41 in this *Handbook*.
10. R. Lemos, "MasterCard Warns of Massive Credit-Card Breach," *SecurityFocus*, June 17, 2005, www.securityfocus.com/news/11219
11. J. Evers, "MasterCard Data Breach: Lawsuit Demands Damages," *Silicon.com*, July 7, 2005, http://software.silicon.com/security/0,39024655,39150141,00.htm (URL inactive).
12. Federal Trade Commission, "CardSystems Solutions Settles FTC Charges," FTC Website, February 23, 2006, www.ftc.gov/opa/2006/02/cardsystems_r.shtm
13. T. Lewis, "TJX Sued for Loss of Consumer Data," *ConsumerAffairs.com*, January 29, 2007, www.consumeraffairs.com/news04/2007/01/tjx_folo.html; original article now replaced with M. Huffman, TJX Pays $9.75 Million to Settle Data Breach," *ConsumerAffairs,com*, July 27, 2009, www.consumeraffairs.com/tj-maxx-data-breach
14. R. Lemos, "New England Bankers Sue TJX for Breach," *SecurityFocus*, April 26, 2007, www.securityfocus.com/brief/490
15. J.Evers, "Revealed: World's Largest Security Breach," *Silicon.com*, March 30, 2007, www.silicon.com/retailandleisure/0,3800011842,39166613,00.htm (URL inactive).
16. *In re TJX Cos. Retail Sec. Breach Litig.*, 584 F. Supp. 2d 395, 398 (D. Mass. 2008) (although the court struck from the settlement the provision regarding the one-day special event sale); The TJX Companies, Inc. and Fifth Third Bancorp., Case No. 07-10162.
17. *In re TJX Cos. Retail Sec. Breach Litig.*, 564 F. 3d 489 (1st Cir. 2009); *Anderson v. Hannaford Bros. Co.,* 659 F. 3d 151 (1st Cir. 2011) (hackers stole up to 4.2 million credit and debit card numbers of grocery store customers; consolidated multidistrict litigation); *Pisciotta v. Old Nat'l Bancorp*, 499 F. 3d 629 (7th Cir. 2007) (putative class of consumers commenced a lawsuit against a bank based on the alleged failures of the bank to secure adequately personal information; bank's motion for judgment on the pleadings granted).

18. Federal Trade Commission, "ChoicePoint Settles Data Security Breach Charges; to Pay $10 Million in Civil Penalties, $5 Million for Consumer Redress: At Least 800 Cases of Identity Theft Arose From Company's Data Breach," FTC.gov, January 26, 2006, www.ftc.gov/opa/2006/01/choicepoint.shtm
19. Federal Trade Commission, "Google Will Pay $22.5 Million to Settle FTC Charges it Misrepresented Privacy Assurances to Users of Apple's Safari Internet Browser," FTC.gov, August 9, 2012, www.ftc.gov/opa/2012/08/google.shtm
20. Federal Trade Commission, "Cord Blood Bank Settles FTC Charges That It Failed to Protect Consumers' Sensitive Personal Information," FTC.gov, January 28, 2013, http://ftc.gov/opa/2013/01/cbr.shtm
21. Federal Trade Commission, "FTC Files Complaint Against Wyndham Hotels For Failure to Protect Consumers' Personal Information," FTC.gov, June 26, 2012, www.ftc.gov/opa/2012/06/wyndham.shtm
22. Federal Trade Commission, "FTC Settles Charges Against Two Companies That Allegedly Failed to Protect Sensitive Employee Data," FTC.gov, May 3, 2011, www.ftc.gov/opa/2011/05/ceridianlookout.shtm
23. Court decisions provide guidance on such issues. For example, the California Supreme Court held that a customer's ZIP code constitutes "personal identification information" under the Song-Beverly Credit Card Act, prohibiting merchants from requesting a credit card holder's ZIP code. *Pineda v. Williams-Sonoma Stores, Inc.*, 246 P. 3d 612 (Cal. 2011); *but see Feder v. Williams-Sonoma Stores, Inc.*, Civ. No. 2:11-03070 (WHW), 2011 WL 4499300 (D.N.J. Sept. 26, 2011) (oral request for a ZIP code as part of a credit card transaction did not violate New Jersey's Truth-in Consumer Contract, Warranty and Notice Act).
24. Executive Order: *Improving Critical Infrastructure Cybersecurity*, 2013 WL 503840 (February 12, 2013).
25. See www.sec.gov/divisions/corpfin/guidance/cfguidance-topic2.htm
26. 78 *Fed. Reg.* 5566 (January 25, 2013).
27. 67 *Fed. Reg.* 36484 (May 23, 2002).
28. 201 Mass. Code Regs. 17.00, *et seq.*
29. Library of Congress THOMAS system for tracking legislation: http://thomas.loc.gov
30. K. Gilpin, "Identity Theft Affects Millions, Survey Shows," *New York Times*, September 3, 2003.
31. M. T. Van Dyke, ed., "2005 Identity Fraud Report," Javeline Strategy and Research, January 2005.
32. *Federal Trade Commission, Consumer Sentinel Network Data Book January-December 2011* (February 2012) (Executive Summary).
33. L. Foley and J. Foley, "Identity Theft: The Aftermath 2003," Identity Theft Resource Center, September 2003.
34. M. E. Kabay, "Defending against Identity Theft: LifeLock," *Network World Security Strategies*, March 4, 2008, www.networkworld.com/newsletters/sec/2008/0303sec1.html and "Defending against Identity Theft: Identity Guard," *Network World Security Strategies*, March 6, 2008, www.networkworld.com/newsletters/sec/2008/0303sec2.html

CHAPTER 61

WORKING WITH LAW ENFORCEMENT

David A. Land

61.1 INTRODUCTION. The year 2012 must be recognized as the "Year of Intrusions." Threats to your organization may involve external threats from hackers, crackers, phreakers, and the like, or an internal threat involving a trusted employee(s) or a competitor attempting to steal, acquire, or otherwise damage information critical to your organization's viability. There appear to be two emerging trends. The first is politically driven attacks on organizations, where the attacker views an organization as being complicit in an event contrary to the criminal hackers' (sometimes called *hacktivists*) views. This is especially true where privacy on the Internet is concerned or viewed as being threatened. The other is financial motivation by individual(s) who have a plethora of agendas to support their illegal activity. Fraud, waste, and abuse by an individual who has legitimate and authorized access to organizational networks or computing systems is also big business for both foreign and domestic entities seeking to gain an intellectual or economic advantage.

Working with law enforcement at all levels, both nationally and internationally, is an important aspect of computer security and your collective need to protect your sites, your sites' information, and your organizations' enterprise infrastructure. The cybercrime paradigm has dramatically shifted to one in which we need law enforcement and they need us. The success of both sides not only depends on but demands collaboration and sharing.

Understanding the needs and constraints of law enforcement before, during, and after the commission of a cybercrime can significantly enhance an organization's opportunity to come back online quickly, with potentially little or no disturbance to users or customers. In contrast, failing to know your counterparts may ensure the attacker's success and escape from successful prosecution. Conveying your needs and the needs of your clients to law enforcement *before* an incident occurs will serve everyone well.

However, working with law enforcement is not an opportunity to assume the role of law enforcement. You must know your organization's limitations and at what point to engage your law enforcement contacts. It is equally beneficial to know the abilities of law enforcement, especially where it applies to your local law enforcement agency. In short, not all local law enforcement agencies are created equal when dealing with cybercrimes, and contacting the proper organization on the first call is critical. Involvement and coordination with your C-level leadership as well as legal and Human Resource staff are all critical players in any decisions made relative to sharing data.

Most organizations, whether they support the corporate or the government sector (e.g., .mil, .gov, .org, .com, or .edu), will at some point have a need to meet, or otherwise collaborate with, a local, state, or federal law enforcement or an intelligence agency. Intelligence agencies of the United States and of other nations are included here to remind the reader that there are 16 U.S. government entities, such as the Department of Homeland Security (DHS), Federal Bureau of Investigation (FBI), and other government departments within the United States, that have an intelligence role tied directly to computer incidents or cyber-related investigations. Furthermore, as cyber-related crimes know no geographical bounds, there is also the possibility that investigative agencies of other nations, such as the Royal Canadian Mounted Police, the German BSI ("Bundesamt für Sicherheit in der Informationstechnologie," also known as the Office for Security in Information Technology),[1] and Interpol, might need to become involved. Where investigations take on an international nexus, the FBI, the Department of Homeland Security, or Department of State will likely be one of the lead organizations conducting the investigation. The need for collaboration with any of these agencies is driven by the inevitable reality that at some point, a computer or cyber-related crime will be committed where the computers or information of an organization are the targets of unwelcome cyberattacks.

The goals of law enforcement, both foreign and domestic, as well as the various U.S. intelligence agencies, tend to vary based on jurisdiction and the mission of the investigating organization. Where a computer or cybercrime may be of little or no prosecutorial value to one agency, another may find there is significant value in pursuing an investigation. Keep that in mind when making your first contact. Likewise, there is absolutely nothing wrong with selling your company's desire to pursue an investigation to law enforcement or intelligence agencies. In some instances, it may be necessary for you to do some of the initial investigative legwork to make it more attractive for law enforcement to pursue. Much will depend on the nature of the crime and any losses your organization may have experienced. While the FBI states that they are concerned only with crimes that exceed $5,000, the reality is that the threshold for the FBI is much higher, especially given their current workload and the number of investigations they are currently working. Never assume that the FBI is the first, best organization to call. While they maintain investigative purview in many criminal areas, there are a multitude of other organizations, some of which may actually trump the FBI.

To address these inevitabilities, it is prudent to examine your organization for potential vulnerabilities and to develop a logical path forward in addressing any identified weaknesses. In the planning process, identify your supporting law enforcement organizations and meet with them in order to put in place some form of memorandum of agreement (MOA). This memorandum should clearly articulate the responsibilities of each entity; creating this document will save everyone a substantial amount of time, avoid potential miscommunications, and ensure that organizational information and assets are handled in an appropriate manner. As part of this agreement, make it clear what you as the impacted organization expect as part of any investigation, and that reciprocity is expected. Where there is a need to deem information as classified, intelligence organizations can facilitate the clearance of individuals to support the sharing of any evidence found. MOAs are discussed in detail in Section 61.4.

61.2 GUIDELINES

61.2.1 Relevant Laws. In examining computer crime laws, it is worthwhile to understand which laws, and which law enforcement agencies, are responsible for responding to you or your organization. It is equally necessary to know when the need for law enforcement involvement is warranted and unwarranted. When does a computer crime break a federal, state, or local law? Exhibit 61.1 lists crimes that should be reported whenever they are discovered or when there is any uncertainty as to their status as a crime. Exhibit 61.2 presents a list of activities you should not report.

61.2.2 Plan Ahead. When you know when and whom to call, dealing with any type of significant cyberincident can be manageable. Leaving things to chance or uncertainty or assuming that someone else is responsible and will take care of things can leave your organization in a very precarious situation. Know who is responsible for the conduct of a computer-related investigation and, where possible, train for such likelihoods. These efforts can greatly reduce the time from discovery to prosecution. Lastly, keep your senior management as well as your legal team in the loop regarding all contacts with law enforcement as well as what your intended plans are should the need arise.

61.2.3 Activities You Should Always Report. One checklist for activities you should always report is available online at http://i.i.com.com/cnwk.1d/i/tr/downloads/home/computer crime reporting checklist.pdf

61.2.3.1 Report Intrusions or Attacks on Major Networks or Networks that Deal with Sensitive or Classified Data. If sensitive data such as client financial information, medical records, customer credit card information, Social Security numbers, or other personally identifiable information are compromised, you should report it to the authorities. This is also true if the company has government/

Report intrusions or attacks on major networks, or those that deal with sensitive data.

If sensitive data such as client financial information, medical records, customer credit card information, social security numbers, and the like has been compromised, you should report it to the authorities. This is also true if the company has government/defense contracts or deals with other types of regulated information. The FBI's computer crime squad investigates major network intrusions and network integrity violations. You can report these types of attacks to federal, state, and local authorities and let them sort out the jurisdictional issues.

Report intrusions or attacks that result in large monetary losses.

The amount of monetary loss often determines whether a theft is considered a misdemeanor or felony. Felony offenses will get more attention from law enforcement agencies when they involve a bank or most any other type of financial institution. The following site enumerates the laws relative to financial institutions and the requirement to report: http://www.fdic.gov/news/news/financial/1997/fil97124.html

Report cases of suspected state-sponsored or Industrial espionage.

If an intruder goes after your company's trade secrets, or there are indications that individuals within your organization are the targets of a foreign intelligence service, this is a serious federal offense that will be investigated by the FBI who maintains the charter for all domestic counterintelligence investigations, and by other government and military agencies.

Report cases involving child pornography.

This is an offense that is taken very seriously by law enforcement. If child pornography was discovered on your company computers and was not promptly reported, you, as network administrator, may be implicated or held liable in a civil lawsuit. The possession of child pornography images on a computer, no matter who is in possession of the computer, is breaking the law and is subject to prosecution.

Report e-mailed or other digitally transmitted threats.

All states have laws against threatening and harassing communications. Physical threats against individuals, terrorist threats, bomb threats, blackmail, and similar electronic communications should be reported to security personnel and local police.

Internet fraud

If one of your users is a victim of "phishing" scams or other fraudulent activities perpetrated by an e-mail or unknown individuals on the Web, this information can be reported to one of many different Federal Agencies. Within the US you can report to the Federal Trade Commission, the FBI, the US Secret Service, the US Postal Service, the National Fraud Information Center, etc. A complete list of US Government and non-Government agencies as well as investigative organizations of other countries can be found at http://www.consumerfraudreporting.org/governments.php

Report suspected terrorist activities.

If you suspect that your network is being used for communications between terrorists, first and foremost do not attempt to investigate yourself. Report suspected activities to the U.S. Department of Homeland Security, or the FBI via the FBI's "tips" Website.

EXHIBIT 61.1 Activities That Should Be Reported

defense contracts or deals with other types of regulated or classified information. The FBI's computer crime squad investigates major network intrusions and network integrity violations. The Department of Homeland Security also has a vested interest in both national and international cybercrime, and should be contacted via their toll-free number, 1-866-DHS-2-ICE, or via their Cyber Crimes Website.[2] You can report these types of attacks to federal, state, and local authorities and let them sort out the jurisdictional issues, with the exception of classified information. This is directly reportable to the FBI, as well as the organization's intelligence and security personnel.

Don't report port scanning and similar "nonintrusive" activities.

Although port scanning is often a precursor to intrusion or attack, in most jurisdictions it's not, in itself, a crime. It's more like walking down a hallway in an apartment building and trying each door to see if it's locked. If you find an unlocked door and go inside, that is criminal trespass— but as long as you don't go in, you haven't committed a crime.

Don't report viruses, Trojans, worms, and spyware—at least, not to law enforcement agencies, although there are exceptions.

Malicious software is a huge and ever-growing problem that does a great deal of damage and costs companies millions of dollars. However, law enforcement agencies generally don't respond to individual malware reports. While those who release viruses and other malware can be prosecuted under Title 18 of the U.S. Code, prosecutors generally go after developers of malware that is widely distributed and causes a large amount of harm. If you encounter a new variety of malware, check the pages of popular anti-virus vendors and report to them if it isn't already listed. Remember that the sender of a virus often doesn't even know he or she is sending it. However, if you have evidence that a particular person wrote and intentionally released a piece of malware with the intent to cause harm or otherwise destroy data, you should contact local law enforcement or your local FBI cybercrime squad.

EXHIBIT 61.2 Activities That Should Not Be Reported

61.2.3.2 Report Intrusions or Attacks That Result in Large Monetary Losses. The amount of monetary loss often determines whether a theft is considered a misdemeanor or felony. Felony offenses will get more attention from law enforcement agencies when they involve a bank or most any other type of financial institution. The following site enumerates the laws relative to financial institutions and the requirement to report: www.fdic.gov/news/news/financial/1997/fil97124.html

61.2.3.3 Report Cases of Suspected State-Sponsored or Industrial Espionage and Potential Terrorism. If an intruder goes after your company's trade secrets, or there are indications that individuals within your organization are the targets of a foreign intelligence service activity, this is potentially a serious federal offense. The FBI or other government and military agencies that may have a vested interest in the matter should be contacted. The FBI maintains the charter for all domestic counterintelligence investigations; however, other government agencies may have an equal stake and thus should be notified. The most important part to take away from this subsection is to limit the number of people who are aware of any incident regarding the potential loss or theft of classified data!

61.2.3.4 Report Cases Involving Child Pornography. Child pornography is a criminal offense taken very seriously by law enforcement at all echelons. If child pornography is discovered on your company computers and is not promptly reported, you, as network administrator, may be implicated or held liable as part of the criminal investigation. The possession of child pornography, which can include images, or other forms of data found on a computer, no matter who is in possession of the computer, is a crime, and is subject to federal prosecution. Once discovered, this data should not be viewed by anyone and immediately reported to a federal law enforcement agency.

61.2.3.5 Report E-Mailed or Other Digitally Transmitted Threats. All states have laws against threatening and harassing communications. Physical threats against individuals, terrorist threats, bomb threats, blackmail, and similar electronic communications should be reported to security personnel, local police, and the Department of Homeland Security.

61.2.3.6 Internet Fraud. If one of your users is a victim of a "phishing" scam or other fraudulent activities perpetrated by an e-mail or unknown individuals on the Web, this information can be reported to one of many different federal agencies. Within the United States you can report to the Federal Trade Commission, the FBI, the U.S. Secret Service, the U.S. Postal Service, the National Fraud Information Center, and so on. A complete list of U.S. Government and non-Government agencies, as well as investigative organizations of other countries, can be found at www.consumerfraudreporting.org/governments.php

61.2.4 Activities You Should Not Report. http://i.i.com.com/cnwk.1d/i/tr/downloads/home/computer crime reporting checklist.pdf (URL inactive).

61.2.4.1 Do Not Report Port Scanning and Other Similar "Non-Intrusive" Activities. Although port scanning is often a precursor to intrusion or attack, in most jurisdictions it's not, in itself, a crime. It's more like walking down a hallway in an apartment building and trying each door to see if it's locked. If you find an unlocked door and go inside, that is criminal trespass—but as long as you don't go in, you haven't committed a crime. You can, however, collaborate with other similar organizations, and, using many different tools, you can develop a picture of what the scans may mean, and what information is being sought. This is where information sharing across similar organizations such as major banking institutions can be beneficial. It can be done in such a manner as to protect company information while still putting together potential threat vectors.

61.2.4.2 Don't Report Viruses, Trojans, Worms, and Spyware—At Least, Not To Law Enforcement Agencies, Although There Are Exceptions. Malicious software is a huge and ever-growing problem that does a great deal of damage and costs companies millions of dollars annually. However, law enforcement agencies generally don't respond to individual malware reports. While those who release viruses and other malware can be prosecuted under Title 18 of the U.S. Code, prosecutors generally go after developers of malware that is widely distributed, and causes a significant amount of harm. If you encounter a new variety of malware, check the pages of popular anti-virus vendors and report to them if it isn't already listed. Remember that the sender of a virus often doesn't even know he or she is sending it. However, if you have evidence that a particular person wrote and intentionally released a piece of malware with the intent to cause harm or otherwise destroy data, you should contact local law enforcement, the DHS Computer Crimes Unit, or your local FBI cybercrime squad. NOTE: Most FBI cybersquads will be located in major cities, and will not be found in local Resident Agencies, while DHS has an online presence for reporting viruses and malware.

61.2.5 Terrorism. If you suspect that your network is being used for communications between terrorists, first and foremost do not attempt to investigate this incident yourself. Report suspected activities to the U.S. Department of Homeland Security or the FBI via the FBI's "tips" Website, or through the DHS Website.

They can also reduce the potential of having agencies involved that would otherwise not have a need to know (e.g., the local press).[3]

- Local/State Law Enforcement: Call your local police department, county sheriff's agency. Do not call 9-1-1. Ask for the agency's high-tech crimes unit or, its smaller investigation division.
- FBI Computer Crimes Squad: nccs@fbi.gov or 202-324-9164
- FBI Tips site: https://tips.fbi.gov
- U.S. Secret Service Form 401—Cyber Threat/Network Incident Report: www.secretservice.gov/net.intrusionforms.shtml
- Internet Crime Complaint Center: www.ic3.gov
- National White Collar Crime Center (NW3C): www.nw3c.org
- FTC Scams and Identity Theft Website: www.consumer.gov/section/scams-and-identity-theft

61.3 LAW ENFORCEMENT RESOURCES

61.3.1 Federal Bureau of Investigation. The Federal Bureau of Investigation (FBI) is responsible for the investigation and prosecuting of more than 200 federal statutes. Relative to the cyberworld, the FBI has two primary responsibilities.

First, it is the lead law enforcement agency for investigating cyberattacks by foreign or state-sponsored espionage or terrorism. Second, the FBI and DHS also work to prevent criminals, sexual predators, and others intent on malicious destruction from using the Internet and online services to steal from, defraud, and otherwise victimize citizens, businesses, and communities.

The FBI retains jurisdiction over many types of cases, which include: national security, including counterintelligence and counterproliferation; terrorism; and organized crime. The U.S. Secret Service retains jurisdiction where the Treasury Department is victimized or whenever computers are attacked that are not under the purview of the FBI. In certain federal cases, the Customs Department, the Commerce Department, or military organizations such as the Air Force Office of Investigations, Naval Criminal Investigative Service, U.S. Army Intelligence, or U.S. Army Criminal Investigation Division, may also have jurisdiction.

In the United States and its territories, a number of federal laws protect against attacks on computers, misuse of passwords, electronic invasions of privacy, and other transgressions. The Computer Fraud and Abuse Act of 1986 is the statute governing most common computer crimes, although prosecutions may take place under other laws. The Computer Abuse Amendments Act of 1994 expanded the 1986 act to address the transmission of viruses and other harmful code.

Many of the states within the United States have adopted their own computer crime laws.

According to the Federal Investigative Guidelines, federal law enforcement can gather only proprietary information concerning an incident in four ways:

1. Request for voluntary disclosure of information
2. Court order
3. Federal grand jury subpoena
4. Search warrant

61.3.2 U.S. Postal Inspection Service.

The U.S. Postal Inspection Service is the federal law enforcement investigative arm of the U.S. Postal Service. Postal inspectors enforce over 200 federal laws in investigations of crimes that may adversely affect or fraudulently use the U.S. mail, the postal system, or postal employees. Many fraud schemes that originate over the Internet (such as auction fraud or multilevel marketing schemes) or that involve payment or delivery via the U.S. mail are under the jurisdiction of the Postal Inspection Service.

61.3.3 U.S. Secret Service.

The U.S. Secret Service began as a force investigating counterfeit currency; it still enforces all laws relating to "the counterfeiting of obligations and securities of the United States," which includes financial crimes, identity theft, computer fraud, and any computer-based attacks on the infrastructure of the United States. It is worth noting that the U.S. Secret Service is another investigative agency like the FBI. Both agencies work very well together and collaborate on many cyber-related investigations.

61.4 MEMORANDUM OF AGREEMENT.

A memorandum of agreement (MOA) between any organization and any law enforcement agency is a prudent measure. With an MOA in place, both sides of any investigation have a clear understanding of what to expect. Within the MOA, specific points enumerate the breadth and depth of responsibilities.

For those interested, the Department of Justice maintains a list of recent computer crimes cases and those involved in the litigation.[4]

Know your limitations. Know when to call law enforcement and when to deal with a situation yourself. Discuss the inherent problems on both sides, such as public disclosure of a confirmed intrusion and potential liabilities, which may follow any disclosure.

61.5 HANDLING EVIDENCE AND THE CHAIN OF CUSTODY.

Many different cyber-related investigative agencies and groups can be found on the Web. For 12 years, the author has been a member of the International Association of Computer Investigative Specialists (http://iacis.org), which offers to the public a comprehensive set of directions relative to computer forensics and the collection of electronic evidence. A step-by-step process for the examination and collection of electronic evidence follows.

61.5.1 Never Work from the Original Media.

Prior to any media examination, a bit-for-bit image should be made of the media. Never work from the original media.

1. Examine the media, logically and systematically, by starting where the data of evidentiary value is most likely to be found. These locations will vary depending on the nature and scope of the case. Examples of items to be noted might include:
   - If the media is a hard drive, the number and type of partitions should be noted.
   - If the media is an optical disc, then the number of sessions should be noted.
   - File systems on the media should be noted.
   - A full directory listing should be made to include folder structure, filenames, date/time stamps, logical file sizes, and so on.
   - Installed operating systems should be noted.

- User-created files should be examined using native applications, file viewers, or hex viewers. This includes such files as text documents, spreadsheets, databases, financial data, electronic mail, digital photographs, sound, and other multimedia files, and the like.
- Operating system files and application created files should be examined, if present. This includes, but is not limited to, boot files, registry files, swap files, temporary files, cache files, history files, and log files.
- Installed applications should be noted.
- File hash comparisons may be used to exclude or include files for examination.
- Unused and unallocated space on each volume should be examined for previously deleted data, deleted folders, slack space data, and intentionally placed data. Previously deleted filenames of apparent evidentiary value should be noted. Files may be automatically carved out of the unallocated portion of the unused space based on known file headers.
- Keyword searches may be conducted to identify files or areas of the drive that might contain data of evidentiary value and to narrow the examination scope.
- The system area of the volume (i.e., FAT, MFT, etc.) should be examined and any irregularities or peculiarities noted.
- Examination of areas of the media that are not normally accessible, such as extra tracks or sectors on a floppy disk, or a host-protected area on a hard drive, may be required.
- To facilitate examination of data, including user settings and device and software functionality, the computer may be booted using either a copy of the boot drive or by using a protected program to determine functionality of the hardware and/or software.
- The forensic software used during the examination should be noted by its version, and should be used in accordance with the vendor's licensing agreement. The software should also be properly tested and validated for its forensic use by the examiner or the examiner's agency.

2. At the conclusion of the examination process, provide sufficient notation of any discovered material of an apparent incriminating or exculpatory evidentiary nature.
3. Provide sufficient documentation of all standard procedures and processes initiated, as well as detailed notation of any variations made to the standard procedures.
4. Properly mark any output of the recovered data with appropriate identifiers in accordance with policies from the examiner's agency.

61.5.2 Issues of Liability. In examining any media or conducting any cybercentric investigation, consideration should be given to these areas:

- Proprietary information
- Business-sensitive information
- Export-controlled information
- Downloading copyrighted music or videos
- National defense information

61.5.3 Ask Law Enforcement To Give Back. In many situations where law enforcement is notified of an event requiring further investigation, the agency may ask you for everything even remotely connected to the investigation. At the same time, most law enforcement agencies have the ability to give back. They can provide training to key personnel and information on various topics, including identity theft, espionage, equipment theft, access control, and so on.

61.5.4 The Knock at the Door. What do you do if your first indication of a possible security incident is a law enforcement agent appearing at your office with a search warrant? In many cases, nothing could be more unnerving. However, if you have done your homework and you have an established rapport with this law enforcement agency, you have little to fear. You already have a plan in place for just such a situation, and you know the rights and obligations.

Although, under the best of circumstances, stress can still occur, it is important to remain unemotional and to express complete willingness to comply with the search warrant team. Avoid being defensive or giving the appearance that you are trying to hide anything. Offer all assistance possible and take these seven steps:

1. Read the warrant carefully and understand what the search warrant team wants to search or seize.
2. Notify both upper management and the legal department of current events.
3. If the authorities want to search a local machine, the impact on the organization may be minimal. Get the appropriate manager or supervisor to evaluate the impact and to assist the officers in securing the machine. In cases of child pornography, the police will take the entire computer. Work with them to see if backup copies can be made of critical data and programs prior to removal.
4. If a server is the target, see if copies of relevant portions of the hard drives will satisfy the requirements of the warrant. Where it is not possible to do this, involve your server and network administrators to bring down the server in an orderly fashion. Your plan should also include bringing online any backup server.
5. Rarely will an entire network have to be taken down. Have your network administrator work with law enforcement to ensure orderly access to parts of the network described in the search warrant.
6. After the search and seizure, the team will leave you "an officer's return" regarding what property was seized. Retain this document for review by your legal staff. Make arrangements with the team to follow up with them on the status of your equipment. Offer whatever technical assistance to law enforcement that your legal department deems advisable.
7. Meet with your management, legal counsel, and technical staff after the team leaves to assess the impact of the seizures on your operations. Also, consider what actions need to be taken for continued operations.

61.5.5 Keeping Your Operation Running during an Investigation. Any investigation that involves a continued law enforcement presence requires time and resources of the organization to ensure support to clients or customers. It is also important to anticipate such an occurrence and to develop a plan on how to cooperate with law enforcement without shutting down your operation. In most instances, a computer crime specialist can generate data dumps, make secure copies of files, and create logs without carting away all of your organization's computers. Administrators should however, have a plan in place to allocate requisite resources in a manner that will avoid, or at least minimize, disruptions in business operations. The following are some suggestions that may help to minimize the disruption caused by an onsite investigation:

Schedule meetings with key organizational members of your information technology organization, as well as other key legal and management employees, and develop a plan that can be implemented should a significant event take place during either normal or noncritical work periods. Once your plan is developed, *test it!*

If any part of the network needs to come down in support of investigative activities, arrange, where feasible, for this outage to take place during nonpeak hours. Your law enforcement counterparts may be of a different mind, with a greater sense of urgency to take down suspect systems. If possible, work out such details beforehand.

Depending on the operating system environment your organization works in, you will need to know where to acquire the necessary logs and audit files. These files should be identified now rather than during the heat of a significant investigation. In taking this extra step early on, you will help minimize the amount of staff time necessary to retrieve the files needed.

Make sure law enforcement does not take software or database files for which no copy or backup exists. Prior to this, and as a matter of policy, ensure that all organizational employees and contractors are following required backup and copying procedures to avoid any unnecessary loss of vital data. Should any law enforcement agency show up with a warrant or subpoena, you are compelled to provide any, and all, information clearly specified within those documents.

Keep the investigation compartmentalized, and on a need-to-know basis. This action will reduce the amount of staff involved and protect the continuity of the investigation. The more people cognizant of an ongoing investigation, the greater the possibility information central to the investigation may be compromised.

Keep the lines of communication open with law enforcement. Knowing about the needs for records or access to information systems in advance can save staff time and system downtime. In short, do not wait for law enforcement to visit you; visit them, and do it frequently. This will establish good rapport and create trust that may be needed at some future time.

Encourage onsite copying of memory and any magnetic media rather than their removal. Computer forensics specialists possess this capability (also known as *fly-away kits*), and not all cases require the removal of equipment to a forensics lab. With law enforcement's cooperation, you can schedule these procedures during nonpeak hours and keep your equipment on the premises and in service.

61.5.6 Using Log Records. Paper records, video surveillance tapes, proximity card records, and any other means of tracking employee activity can all play a significant role during the investigation of computer crimes and incidents. Admittedly, no one wants to assume the role of "Big Brother," but at the same time, an organization's livelihood may well depend on these methods of verifying access. No one metric exists that clearly demonstrates the true nature of insider threats. It is, however, reasonable to believe that greater than half of all computer crimes are committed by current or former organizational insiders. To assess, and perhaps better to detect, this threat to organizational computing systems, internal documentation and monitoring become important evidence trails.

For example, if video cameras monitor the entrances to the computer processing center or labs, the video surveillance tapes document the entrance and exit of any employee at a given time. If an entrance uses access cards, the reports or databases containing the access records document employee traffic into sensitive areas. The use of conventional access tracking is not by itself foolproof and will not, for example, preclude "piggybacking," which is the act of closely following another individual and gaining entry without proper authentication. Contradictions between access and video records can often document anomalies or possible misdeeds that will require further investigation. For example, if the access control report indicates John Jones entered the computer lab at 6:45 p.m. on 07-12-08, but the videotape for same time shows Sam Smith entering, there is clear indication that Sam has used John's card or access code. The question now remains: Why? Is there a need to call in law enforcement? At first blush, there is no apparent need to make such a call. Only after some initial investigation on the part of your security staff will this perhaps be necessary.

Paper files—personnel records, departmental documents, project logs, programming modification records, sign-out logs for software, and job assignment records—all tell a story. When you want to know who worked on what, or who had access to which project, paper records can often provide the needed history. Audit logs such as those stored on a UNIX or UNIX-type operating system within /var/log can provide even greater illumination. Using the same type of operating system, a system administrator can simply type "last", which will provide login information to that system. With this said, no effort should be made to verify this information on the original media. Doing so will modify files that may be potentially critical evidence. Thus, an original (bit-for-bit) image of any magnetic media should be made, and all investigation conducted on the imaged data and not the original media.

61.6 INFORMATION SHARING.

After 9/11, all law enforcement officers will agree that the sharing of information between any organization and law enforcement is critical to the success of cyber-related investigations. Working with any law enforcement agency has both benefits and consequences. Benefits accrue because:

- Most law enforcement agencies, as well as government and commercial entities have cyberinvestigative capabilities. Many of the federal agencies have taken steps to train and educate investigators to ensure that the most comprehensive investigation is conducted with the least amount of disturbance to the victim agency.
- Law enforcement agencies are also being funded to establish, or better train officers in, cyberinvestigative disciplines that, in most instances, facilitate the acquisition of personnel, equipment, and training.
- Working with law enforcement agencies can serve as a conduit to training and education for on-site first responders and cybersecurity personnel. The FBI or any other law enforcement agency benefits from better educating you as to what it wants and needs, as this helps to ensure that all evidence is properly collected and remains intact. Exhibit 61.3 is a draft example of how a memorandum of understanding (MOU) or an MOA between two or more entities might be constructed for the purpose of sharing law enforcement data.

61.6.1 InfraGard.

One of the resources in the United States for forming good relations with law enforcement agencies is the InfraGard. The regional meetings of InfraGard members offer an excellent opportunity for sharing information with trusted

EXHIBIT 61.3 Information-Sharing Example

Information-Sharing Initiative—Implementation Plan

Participating Sites

I. Objective
Implement a program to retrieve information of varying degrees of criticality from specified contributors for the purpose of establishing a repository of related data. This is to enable single search capability for the production of a single composite record. The record will be available as a tool to enhance operational needs of the participants. The record should support tactical operations as well as strategic, investigative, and analytical operations.

II. Participating Agencies

This should include, state, local, federal, and commercial law enforcement, investigative, and analytic entities.
Specific and detailed memorandums of understanding (MOU) will be entered into for each cooperating entity. The MOUs will specify the particular information and data for submission, the limitations or restrictions placed on the data by the subscribing entities, and the roles, responsibilities, and facts agreed upon. Each MOU will recognize and acknowledge the oversight and leadership responsibilities exercised by [your company or the agency taking lead responsibility].

III. Security and Location of Equipment
The system's "Data Warehouse" and IS equipment, including but not limited to computers, servers, printers, and peripherals, will be physically located in a secure facility on your location. The building should be a controlled and "Limited Access" facility, populated with data from three levels (described further below) of information from detailed investigative and analytical assessments.

The security of the system will be controlled and accredited in accordance with the "Organization's" Master Security Plan. (Your site here) is a tenant of the Master Plan. Systems maintenance (updates, backups, etc.) and password control will be regulated by the "Organization's" technical security personnel, who will produce quarterly reports articulating the usage and administration of the system.

The "Organization's" Accepted Use and Security banner will be displayed on all Web pages and sign-in screens.

Access to the system will be restricted to member agencies and their described representatives; the total to be determined by the Executive Management Team. Access levels will be defined as follows:

Level 1: Federal, State, and Local Law Enforcement (L/E) Information

This category is primarily concerned with the identification of persons and normally relates to public safety. Included are sensitive but unclassified law enforcement information such as police and related investigative and field reports, arrest and conviction data, identification databases, and the like.

Level 2: Analytical Access Data

Users in this category will have access to all unclassified tactical incident information available from typical federal government sources for the purpose of analyses based on the data that have been manually collated. Examples of this level of data are 1-94 Arr/Dpt Records, Visa Database accesses (Department of State), 1-20 Student and Visitor records, Custom's Treasury Enforcement Communications System (TECS) data, unclassified federal investigative data (Foreign Access Central Tracking System/FACTS and Personnel Access System).

(Continued)

EXHIBIT 61.3 *(Continued)*

Information-Sharing Initiative—Implementation Plan

Level 3: Classified and Security-Related Data Sources

Data not generally shared unless the inquiring entity maintains a clearance and a "need to know" the information. These data are normally derived from isolated databases in the control of the federal or contractor organization. Access to these systems will undergo a much higher screening and approval process. Examples of this level of data are the identity-sensitive documentation and classified systems within the FBI.

Sharing of Level 3 data is an additional phase for implementation after the initial system is operational. Submission of data concerning Levels 1 and 2 can be shared, based on the existing capabilities of joined database systems. However, Level 3 data loading presently can only be accomplished by stand-alone disk loading and by manual transport (sneaker net).

IV. Information to Be Shared

Each participating Agency will provide current data relating to Intelligence, Counterintelligence, Counterterrorism, Terrorist Matrixes, Threat Assessments, Law Enforcement (L/E) alerts, and other L/E sensitive activity reports. All participants will be specifically tasked with providing the elements of Homeland Security effecting Energy, Banking and Finance, Agriculture, Food, Water, Public Health, Information Technology and Telecommunications, Transportation and Border Security, Postal and Shipping, Defense, Government and Emergency Services, and Maritime Security.

Queries of the system by participating agencies will enable access of data on violent criminal gangs, information on persons in jail or prison, searches of criminal records, and other data related to criminal activity (arrest, citation, and booking information, and field and investigative reports). The Federal and DOE data available for review will consist of similar and related alerts, State Department Visa application data, Department of Commerce, Homeland Security data and assessments, as well as portions of the Personnel Access System (PAS) and defined Export Control data. Other initiatives include work authority statements and internal security reports concerning suspected attempts to breach security.

V. Proposed Date of Implementation

The time frame of implementation is best approximated to be a minimum of 6 months from date of contract.

VI. Administration Management

The Lead Agency [to be determined] will be responsible for overall management and administration of the system. Each individual agency will be responsible for day-to-day supervision and oversight of the review, as required to ensure the appropriate level of security of data submitted. Likewise, each participating site will ensure proper data integrity as outlined in MOU. This implies that each site will be responsible for ensuring that the data they upload is not infected with any form of virus or Trojan. While this may not be the most appropriate place for insertion, it must be covered.

The Lead Agency will coordinate with the other agencies the standards and compliance protocols, rules of access and operation, policies for dissemination of analytical reports, and security standards, and will specifically conduct periodic and cursory reviews, not less than monthly, to ensure appropriateness of participation and usage of system. Periodic audits will be conducted to ensure that the highest level of quality information is received, and that appropriate retrieval queries are being administered.

(Continued)

EXHIBIT **61.3** *(Continued)*

Information-Sharing Initiative—Implementation Plan

A management team of no less than the Lead Agency and (X) member agencies will be formed to execute the fundamental oversight operations described herein. Each participating agency will be represented by its Executive Manager (CIO or Organizational Investigator, Chief of Police, Sheriff, Commander, etc.) for all operations and decisions. Standards and protocols should be specified in any accompanying MOUs. However, full agency members will enjoy several perks. Most important is the notion of one agency, one vote, which covers development and structure processes relative to the oversight principals and directives.

The management team will define reporting processes to evaluate the program on a quarterly basis to ensure that system integrity is intact and to be cognizant of additional improvements that can be undertaken to provide a more thorough and user-friendly product and process.

members of critical infrastructure organizations and with law enforcement officials. The organization describes itself this way:

> InfraGard is an information-sharing and analysis effort serving the interests and combining the knowledge base of a wide range of members. At its most basic level, InfraGard is a partnership between the Federal Bureau of Investigation and the private sector. InfraGard is an association of businesses, academic institutions, state and local law enforcement agencies.[5]

61.6.2 Information-Sharing Initiative—Implementation Plan. The following sections provide guidance through examples of how one can prepare useful MOAs to foster appropriate collaboration between organizations and law enforcement agencies.

61.6.2.1 Objective. Implement a program to retrieve information of varying degrees of criticality from specified contributors for the purpose of establishing a repository of related data. This is to enable single search capability for the production of a single composite record. The record will be available as a tool to enhance operational needs of the participants. The record should support tactical operations as well as strategic, investigative, and analytical operations.

61.6.2.2 Participating Agencies. This should include, state, local, federal, and commercial law enforcement, investigative, and analytic entities. Specific and detailed MOUs will be entered into for each cooperating entity. The MOUs will specify the particular information and data for submission, the limitations or restrictions placed on the data by the subscribing entities, and the roles, responsibilities, and facts agreed upon. Each MOU will recognize and acknowledge the oversight and leadership responsibilities exercised by your company or the agency taking lead responsibility.

61.6.2.3 Security and Location of Equipment. The system's data warehouse and IS equipment, including but not limited to computers, servers, printers, and peripherals, will be physically located in a secure facility on your location. The building should be a controlled, limited-access facility, populated with data from three levels (described further below) of information from detailed investigative and analytical assessments.

The security of the system will be controlled and accredited in accordance with your organization's Master Security Plan. Your site is a tenant of the Master Plan. Systems maintenance (updates, backups, etc.) and password control will be regulated by the organization's technical security personnel, who will produce quarterly reports articulating the usage and administration of the system.

The organization's Accepted Use and Security banner will be displayed on all Web pages and sign-in screens.

Access to the system will be restricted to member agencies and their described representatives; the total to be determined by the Executive Management Team. Access levels will be defined as follows:

61.6.2.3.1 Level 1: Federal, State, and Local Law Enforcement (L/E) Information. This category is primarily concerned with the identification of persons and normally relates to public safety. Included are sensitive but unclassified law enforcement information, such as police and related investigative and field reports, arrest and conviction data, identification databases, and the like.

61.6.2.3.2 Level 2: Analytical Access Data. Users in this category will have access to all unclassified tactical incident information available from typical Federal Government sources for the purpose of analyses based on the data that have been manually collated. Examples of this level of data are I-94 Arr/Dpt Records, Visa Database accesses (Department of State), I-20 Student and Visitor records, Customs' Treasury Enforcement Communications System (TECS) data, and unclassified federal investigative data (Foreign Access Central Tracking System/FACTS and Personnel Access System).

61.6.2.3.3 Level 3: Classified and Security-Related Data Sources. Data not generally shared unless the inquiring entity maintains a clearance and a "need to know" the information. These data are normally derived from isolated databases in the control of the federal or contractor organization. Access to these systems will undergo a much higher screening and approval process. Examples of this level of data are the identity-sensitive documentation and classified systems within the FBI.

Sharing of Level 3 data is an additional phase for implementation after the initial system is operational. Submission of data concerning Levels 1 and 2 can be shared, based on the existing capabilities of joined database systems. However, Level 3 data loading presently can only be accomplished by stand-alone disk loading and by manual transport (sneaker net).

61.6.2.3.4 Information to Be Shared. Each participating agency will provide current data relating to intelligence, counterintelligence, counterterrorism, terrorist matrixes, threat assessments, law enforcement (L/E) alerts, and other L/E sensitive activity reports. All participants will be specifically tasked with providing the elements of Homeland Security affecting energy, banking and finance, agriculture, food, water, public health, information technology and telecommunications, transportation and border security, postal and shipping, defense, government and emergency services, and maritime security.

Queries of the system by participating agencies will enable access of data on violent criminal gangs, information on persons in jail or prison, searches of criminal records, and other data related to criminal activity (arrest, citation, and booking information, and field and investigative reports). The federal and DOE data available for review will consist of similar and related alerts, State Department Visa application data, Department of Commerce, Homeland Security data and assessments, as well as portions of the Personnel Access System (PAS) and defined Export Control data. Other initiatives include work authority statements and internal security reports concerning suspected attempts to breach security.

61.6.2.3.5 Proposed Date of Implementation. The time frame of implementation is best approximated to be a minimum of 6 months from date of contract.

61.6.2.3.6 Administration Management. The Lead Agency [to be determined] will be responsible for overall management and administration of the system. Each individual agency will be responsible for day-to-day supervision and oversight of the review, as required to ensure the appropriate level of security of data submitted. Likewise, each participating site will ensure proper data integrity as outlined in MOU. This implies that each site will be responsible for ensuring that the data they upload is not infected with any form of virus or Trojan. While this may not be the most appropriate place for insertion, it must be covered.

The Lead Agency will coordinate with the other agencies the standards and compliance protocols, rules of access and operation, policies for dissemination of analytical reports, and security standards, and will specifically conduct periodic and cursory reviews, not less than monthly, to ensure appropriateness of participation and usage of system. Periodic audits will be conducted to ensure that the highest level of quality information is received, and that appropriate retrieval queries are being administered.

A management team of no less than the Lead Agency and (X) member agencies will be formed to execute the fundamental oversight operations described herein. Each participating agency will be represented by its executive manager (CIO or organizational investigator, Chief of Police, Sheriff, Commander, etc.) for all operations and decisions. Standards and protocols should be specified in any accompanying MOUs. However, full agency members will enjoy several perks. Most important is the notion of one agency, one vote, which covers development and structure processes relative to the oversight principals and directives.

The management team will define reporting processes to evaluate the program on a quarterly basis to ensure that system integrity is intact and to be cognizant of additional improvements that can be undertaken to provide a more thorough and user-friendly product and process.

61.6.3 Additional Considerations. There is, however, another side to any relationship with law enforcement that must be considered. Despite your efforts to be as forthcoming as possible with law enforcement, situations may arise that will cause you and your organization great angst. There may be times when an investigator is simply not able to fully disclose all information gleaned during the conduct of an investigation. There also may be times when your efforts and your methodologies in investigating, prior to involving law enforcement, will come under scrutiny. Probably the most disconcerting of all situations is where law enforcement is compelled to make public disclosure of an incident. It is during these times that you want to work with your own management and legal staff as well as with the law enforcement agency conducting the investigation. Everyone concerned wants to make the public aware of any known or suspected threats, but this must also be weighed against the potential harm that might result from a public release. Another concern from the company's point of view is public perception of security measures within the organization, and to what extent they can protect information and thus customer investments.

61.7 CONCLUSION.

Trying to stay ahead of cybercriminals is not getting easier, though inroads are being made, especially into the group Anonymous. Attempts to understand their intent or motivations are rarely successful. The best chance any organization has is to come to know local law enforcement agencies and to help them know you. Articulate your expectations in the event of a significant cyberevent, and have them do the same. Working together is the only path to success. Given that not all computer security or cyberlaw enforcement entities are created equal, you have to be willing to share knowledge, all in pursuit of the same end goal.

61.8 FURTHER READING

Ballou, S., and K. Higgins, eds. *Electronic Crime Scene Investigation: A Guide for First Responders.* National Criminal Justice Reference Service of the Office of Justice Programs, U.S. Department of Justice, 2001. Available free from www.ncjrs.gov/pdffiles1/nij/187736.pdf

Computer Crime and Intellectual Property Section. Criminal Division, United States Department of Justice. "Searching and Seizing Computers and Obtaining Electronic Evidence in Criminal Investigations," 2002. Available free from www.cybercrime.gov/s&smanual2002.htm (URL inactive)

Web sites

InfraGard home page: www.infragard.org
www.fbi.gov/cyberinvest/cyberhome.htm
www.securityfocus.com/infocus/1523
www.ic3.gov/complaint/default.aspx

61.9 NOTES

1. Information provided by Jürgen Pabel, MSIA, Office for Security in Information Technology, Information Security Officer at Deutsche Post AG.
2. See www.ice.gov/cyber-crimes
3. See http://i.i.com.com/cnwk.1d/i/tr/downloads/home/computercrimereportingchecklist.pdf
4. www.usdoj.gov/criminal/cybercrime/cccases.html (URL inactive)
5. "Learn More About Infragard," Infragard Web site, December 9, 2011, www.infragard.org

INTRODUCTION TO PART VII

MANAGEMENT'S ROLE IN SECURITY

Management responsibilities include judgments of which resources can rationally be expended in defending against which threats. Managers must understand how to cope with the lack of quantitative risk estimates while using what information is available to guide investment decisions in personnel and technology. Their decisions are affected by regulatory and legal requirements and by the practical constraints of their relationships with other leaders within their organizations. This part includes chapters and topics that bear on information assurance managers' roles:

62. **Quantitative Risk Assessment and Risk Management.** Which vulnerabilities warrant repair? Which threats must be taken seriously? How much expense is justified on specific security measures?
63. **Management Responsibilities and Liabilities.** Roles, responsibilities, due diligence, staffing security functions, and the value of accreditation and education
64. **U.S. Legal and Regulatory Security Issues.** For U.S. practitioners especially, this chapter reviews the Gramm-Leach-Bliley Act and the Sarbanes-Oxley legislation
65. **The Role of the CISO.** The chief information security officer as an agent of change and as a strategist working to ensure that security fits into the strategic mission of the organization, and that it is communicated effectively to other C-level executives
66. **Developing Security Policies.** Approaches to creating a culture of security where policies grow organically from the commitment of all sectors of the organization, instead of being imposed unilaterally by security staff
67. **Developing Classification Policies for Data.** The essential role of data classification and how to implement systems that conform to regulatory and legal requirements
68. **Outsourcing and Security.** Security of outsourcing and outsourcing of security

CHAPTER 62

QUANTITATIVE RISK ASSESSMENT AND RISK MANAGEMENT

Robert V. Jacobson and Susan Baumes

62.1 AN INTRODUCTION TO RISK MANAGEMENT

62.1.1 What Is Risk? There is general agreement in the computer security community with the common dictionary definition of risk: *the possibility of suffering harm or loss*. The definition shows that there are two parts to risk: the *possibility* that a risk event will occur, and the harm or *loss* that results from occurrences of risk events. Consequently, the assessment of risk requires consideration of both factors: the frequency of threat events that cause losses, and the loss each such event causes. The product of the two factors, frequency and loss, is a *quantitative* measure of risk; for example, we might express a risk as an *Annualized Loss Expectancy* (discussed in Section 62.2) of, say, $100,000 per year. Risk is managed by taking actions that recognize and reduce these two factors.

Management of risk is important to the design, implementation, and operation of information technology (IT) systems because IT systems are increasingly an essential part of the operation of most organizations. As a result, both the size of the potential harm or loss and the possibility of a risk event occurring are increasing. In extreme cases, a risk loss may be large enough to destroy an organization. If an organization's risk-management program is deficient in some area, the organization may suffer excessive harm or loss, but at the same time the organization may be wasting resources on ineffective, excessive, or misdirected mitigation measures in other areas.

62.1.2 What Is Risk Management? This chapter discusses risk management with special emphasis on two aspects of risk management: risk assessment and risk mitigation. Exhibit 62.1 below suggests that risk management can be thought of as a four-step process.

Step 1: Identify and assess the risks. A risk assessment will only be as good as the inventory of systems and processes. If an organization does not have an adequate inventory, there may be systems or processes with significant risk that may not be reviewed. Once an inventory is complete, the organization can determine the risks associated with each.

Step 2: Identify the *optimum* set of risk-management measures.[1] In this context, *optimum* means making the best use of the resources available for risk

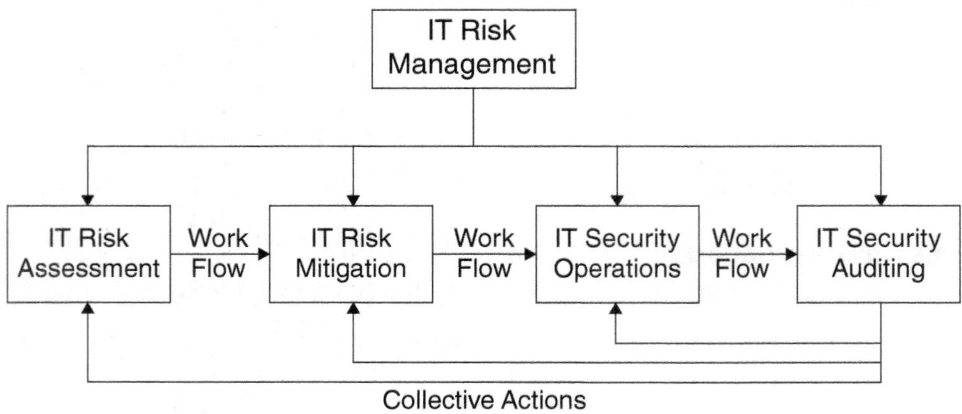

EXHIBIT 62.1 The Four IT Risk-Management Activities

management. Because no organization has infinite resources, risk management requires allocating finite resources by selecting from the broad range of IT risk mitigation measures, the *optimum* set. Since the resources being allocated are measured quantitatively in monetary terms, the risks must likewise be measured in monetary terms. A CIO can hardly expect to go to the CFO and announce that the risk assessment has identified a *high* risk, so a *high* security budget will be needed to address the risk. This issue is discussed in more detail in Section 62.4.3.

Step 3: Perform the ongoing, activities necessary for the effective functioning of the risk-management measures. Depending on the mitigating controls implemented, this could be ongoing log reviews of systems or quarterly meetings with local police. It will depend on the risk and the mitigating controls implemented.

Step 4: Security auditing is conducted to evaluate the effectiveness of IT security operations and to detect changing conditions that require a reassessment of risks, the implementation of new mitigation measures, or modifications to the security management program. Daily security management tasks and IT auditing are discussed elsewhere in this *Handbook* (see, for example, Chapters 23, 27, 40, 47, 52, 53, and 54), so this chapter will confine itself to the first two steps: *risk assessment* and *risk mitigation.*

62.1.3 Regulatory Compliance and Legal Issues. Increasing regulatory and legal issues are impacting risk management, most notably the Sarbanes-Oxley Act. More and more corporate officials are being sent to jail for infractions. As a result, it is not surprising that there may be an overreaction to compliance regulations, with excessive measures being recommended by auditors. Whenever implementation of a compliance recommendation does *not* include a cost justification, and the implementation cost is material, it may be a candidate for a simple risk analysis like this.

1. What effect does the recommended measure have on the probability of noncompliance? In other words, what will be the difference in the likely loss experience with and without the recommended measure?
2. Does this difference compare favorably with the cost to implement and maintain the recommended measure?

There are several points to be made.

- If the cost-benefit is marginal or negative, consideration should be given to alternate (and lower cost) ways to achieve the same end result.
- If the cost-benefit is strongly negative, consideration should be given to dropping the recommendation.
- Under no circumstances should an organization deliberately break the law.

For more about these issues, refer to Chapter 65.

Readers should note that there are strong disagreements about the validity of using quantitative risk-assessment and risk-management methods. For example, Donn Parker has argued for decades that quantitative estimates of risk are an illusion and that expert consensus on best practices provide a far more solid foundation for risk management.[2]

Chapter 10 in this *Handbook* includes discussion of the problems of ascertainment that complicate quantitative estimation of risk.

62.2 OBJECTIVE OF A RISK ASSESSMENT. This *Handbook* describes the pros and cons of a wide range of security measures that can be applied to an IT system. However, no organization has unlimited resources, and so it is necessary to decide which measures should be implemented.[3] It would be convenient if there were a set of security standards that applied equally to all IT systems, but as guidelines cited in Section 62.1.3 note, this is not the case for two basic reasons:

- Each IT system has its own particular risk environment.
- Each IT system has a unique workload. Although two or more IT systems may perform the same list of functions, it is highly unlikely that the systems will have exactly the same level of activity for each of the functions, and so the cost of lost data and service interruptions will not be the same.

Because of these differences, each IT system will have unique security requirements.[4] These two factors correspond to the two elements in the definition of risk:

- The risk environment determines the possibility of experiencing harm or loss.
- The characteristics of the system workload, and the associated IT system assets, determine the magnitude of the harm or loss.

The objective of a risk assessment is to generate information about risk exposures and the potential for loss associated with the workload in order to estimate the annualized loss expectancy (ALE) of the IT system under current conditions.

62.2.1 Qualitative versus Quantitative Risk Assessments. There are two basic types of risk assessments: *qualitative* and *quantitative*. The difference between them is substantial. A quantitative assessment provides a dollar figure associated with the loss. In the case of a qualitative risk assessment, the dollar figure may not be easy to obtain. The cost of the loss is difficult or in some cases impossible to quantify. As an example, if a retailer's database containing customer records is breached, how does one quantify the reputational impact in financial terms? The retailer may have significant losses associated with the breach, but for how long? Loyal customers may continue to frequent the business, but there may be a loss of new clients. Obviously, the impact will depend on the type of business and the relationship of the customer to the business.

In the example of the retailer performing a risk assessment, the customer impact may be rated as Low, Medium, or High with set boundaries. Oftentimes an organization will incorporate a combination of qualitative and quantitative risk-assessment properties in their final risk analysis. Certainly, organizational maturity plays a role in the type of risk assessment completed, particularly one that has never performed any type of risk analysis. In instances where no analysis has been completed, the firm may start with a qualitative analysis and then apply quantitative analysis to the top 10 risks to help prioritize a mitigation strategy.

A quantitative assessment provides a dollar figure associated with a loss. As organizations review their risk mitigation strategy, having the dollar figure is extremely

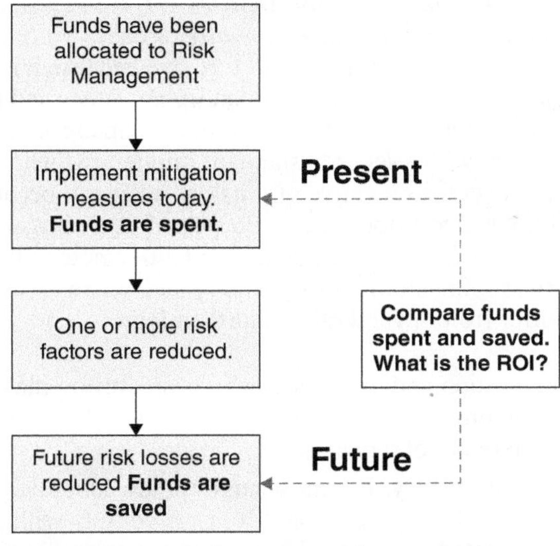

EXHIBIT 62.2 Evaluating an IT System Security Strategy

helpful. The dollar estimate is used to optimize the subsequent risk mitigation decisions and to validate decisions about existing security measures. In this context, *optimize* means to allocate the organization's resources to those actions that will yield the best overall performance. It would be suboptimum to spend \$10,000 to avert \$1,000 in expected losses. To avoid such wasteful expenditures, one must be able to estimate quantitatively both expected losses[5] and the effect of proposed mitigation measures. For this reason, in all but the simplest situations a risk assessment must produce a quantitative, monetary measure of risk, so that (a) risks can be compared with one another on a common basis and (b) the cost of risk mitigation measures can be related to the risks they are meant to address. Assessing a risk as *high*, *unacceptable*, or in other qualitative terms does not provide the information needed to support decisions to implement risk mitigation measures, which will always have quantitative implementation costs.

Exhibit 62.2 above shows why a quantitative estimate of ALE is an essential element in the optimization of the strategy. A sum of money has been budgeted for IT risk management for next year. A risk-management measure is selected and implemented, and so funds are expended. The implementation is expected to reduce one or more risk factors. As a result, we expect *future* risk losses will be reduced, and funds will be saved. By comparing the present values of the funds expended now and those saved in the future, we can estimate the return on investment (ROI) of the implemented measure. The goal is to maximize the ROI, and to avoid risk-management measures with small or negative ROIs. This is the essential character of businesslike IT system risk management. However, it is evident that we must be able to make credible estimates of expected risk losses under both conditions, and under the assumption that a proposed risk-management measure has been implemented to optimize our risk-management strategy.

It may be suggested that quantitative assessment of risk is *too complicated*, and so a simpler, qualitative method can be used instead. However, the complexity is inherent in risk itself, and any *simple* assessment technique will be inherently weak, and potentially misleading. This topic is discussed in more detail in Section 62.4.3.

62.3 LIMITATIONS OF QUESTIONNAIRES IN ASSESSING RISKS. One may be tempted to think of a *security questionnaire* or checklist as a valid risk assessment, but even if the checklist seems to be authoritative because it is automated, this is not the case. Typical questionnaires can help identify inventory and therefore potential areas of risk, but *not* expected loss. At best, a questionnaire can only compare the target of the questionnaire with a security standard implicit in the individual questions. Questionnaires do not meet the objective of a risk assessment, because the answers to a questionnaire will not support optimized selection of risk mitigation measures. The most a well-designed questionnaire can do is to identify potential risk areas, and so they can be of help in scoping and focusing a quantitative risk assessment.

Questionnaires suffer from several other shortcomings:

- The author of a question and the person who is answering the question may have different understandings of the meanings of key words. As a result, an answer may not match the intent of a question.
- Questions tend to be binary, but most answers are inherently quantitative. For example, consider the binary question "Do users comply with password policy?" Although the anticipated answer is either yes or no, a meaningful answer is likely to be much more complicated because each user will have a unique pattern of compliance. Some users will make every effort to be 100% compliant, some will make every effort to circumvent the policy, and the remaining users will comply to a greater or lesser extent. Note also that the question does not attempt to evaluate the appropriateness of the policy.
- Because questionnaires are inherently *open loop*, and because of the binary answer issue discussed above, questionnaires tend to miss important information that would be elicited by a risk analyst who interacts directly with respondents and responds to a quantitative answer with a new question.[6]

Questionnaires are appealing because they appear to relieve the risk assessor of the need to probe into the business system being assessed, but something better is needed for a valid risk assessment. The ensuing sections of this chapter will build a model of risk, and then show how to apply quantitative parameters to the model. Although a greater effort is required, far superior results are achieved.

62.4 A MODEL OF RISK. Exhibit 62.3 is a simplified model of threats and consequences devised by Robert Jacobson. The model takes the first steps toward quantification of risks. In this very simple model, all risk events are assumed to have either a low or high rate of occurrence, and all consequences of risk event impacts are assumed to be either low or high. Mr. William H. Murray, at the time an executive consultant at Deloitte & Touche, referred to this risk model as Jacobson's Window. Let us now consider the implications of the model.

62.4.1 The Two Inconsequential Risk Classes. The two-by-two empty matrix model implies that there are four classes of risk: low-low, high-low, low-high, and high-high. Exhibit 62.4 suggests that two of the classes can be ignored. The low-low class can be ignored because these risks do not matter. As an extreme example, it is obvious that a risk event that occurs at about 10,000-year intervals and causes a $1 loss each time can be ignored safely. Experience suggests that the high-high class can be assumed not to exist in the real world. If 50-ton meteorites crashed through the roofs

		Consequences	
		Low	High
Occurrence Rate	Low		
	High		

EXHIBIT 62.3 Jacobson's Window, A Simple Risk Model

of computer rooms every day, there would be no attempt to use computers. In practice, high-probability, high-loss risks just do not exist. Catastrophic events do occur, but not frequently.

62.4.2 The Two Significant Risk Classes. This analysis suggests that there are only two significant risk classes: high-low and low-high. Data entry keystroke errors are an example of a high-low risk: a high probability of occurring, and usually a low resulting loss. A major fire that destroys the building housing an IT system is an example of a low-high risk: a low probability of occurrence, and a high consequential loss. However, we know that real-world risks do not fall into just these two classes. Instead there is a spectrum of risks from high-low to low-high.

62.4.3 Spectrum of Real-World Risks. Exhibit 62.5 illustrates the distribution of representative risks from high-low (key stroke errors) to low-high (major fires). Conceptually, there is little difference between the high-low and low-high threats. Experience suggests that averaged over the long term the high-low and low-high threats will cause losses of similar magnitude to an organization. This concept is quantified by the notion of annualized loss expectancy (ALE). The ALE of a risk is simply the product of its rate of occurrence, expressed as occurrences per year, and the loss resulting from a single occurrence expressed in monetary terms, for example, dollars per year.

		Consequences	
		Low	High
Occurrence Rate	Low	Don't care	
	High		Doesn't happen

EXHIBIT 62.4 The Two Inconsequential Risk Classes

		Consequences	
		Low	High
Occurrence Rate	Low		"low-high" major fire flooding cash fraud
	High	power failure software bug key error "high-low"	

EXHIBIT 62.5 The Spectrum of Real-World Risks

Here is a simple example of ALE: Assuming that 100 terminal operators each work 2,000 hours per year and make 10 keystroke errors per hour, the occurrence rate of keystroke errors would be 2,000,000 per year. Next, assuming that 99.9% of the errors are immediately detected and corrected at an insignificant cost, 2,000 errors slip by each year (a high occurrence rate risk), which must be corrected later at a cost estimated to be $10 each, a low consequence for each occurrence. Thus, the ALE of the high-low risk: Keystroke error is estimated to be 2,000 occurrences per year × $10 per occurrence, or an ALE of $20,000/year.

Continuing our example, assume that the probability of a major fire in any one year is 1/10,000 (in other words the annualized probability of occurrence of a major fire is estimated to be 0.0001), and if the loss resulting from a major fire would be $200 million, then major fire is a low-high risk. These assumptions lead to an estimate of $20,000/year for the ALE of major fires.

Thus, the two risks from opposite ends of the risk spectrum are seen to have ALEs of about the same magnitude. Of course, we have manipulated the two sets of assumptions to yield similar ALEs, but the results are typical of the real world. However, note that we are assured of having a loss of $20,000 *every year* from keystroke errors, but a loss of $200 million in one of the next 10,000 years.

Exhibit 62.6 is a computer-generated[7] plot of threat occurrence rates and consequences (total single occurrence loss) taken from an actual quantitative risk analysis of a facility. Each of the numbered boxes represents a threat type. Because the two scales are logarithmic, the contours of constant ALE are diagonal straight lines. As expected there are no threats in the high-high (Doesn't Happen) and low-low (Trivial) zones.

While the ALEs span a range of about four orders of magnitude (from about $50 per year to about $500,000 per year), frequencies and consequences each span about seven orders of magnitude. This result is typical of the real world, and illustrates the fundamental flaw in High-Medium-Low risk models like the matrix in Exhibit 62.7. These models attempt to simplify risk assessments by defining a very limited range of values, three each, for frequency and consequence. As a result, threat event ALEs that differ by as much as two orders of magnitude, as illustrated in Exhibit 62.5, are given the same ranking when assessed using a high-medium-low matrix.

Proponents of this risk model are silent about the details. Firstly, as Exhibit 62.6 shows, the *Very High* and *Very Low* risks are meaningless in the real world. Secondly, the matrix requires users to compress numerical values with a range of almost seven

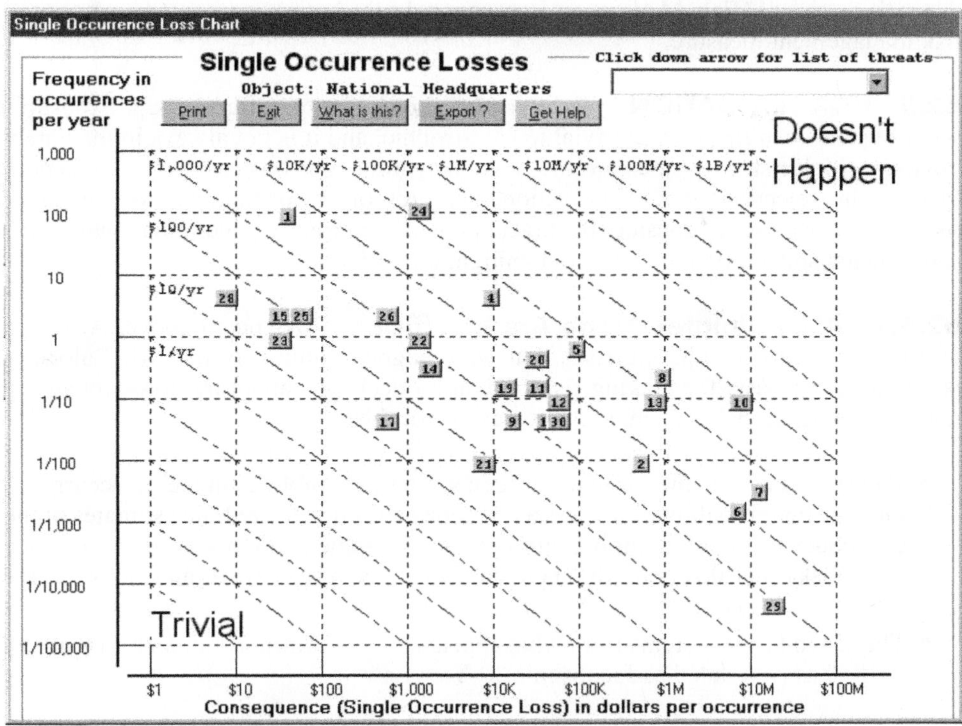

EXHIBIT 62.6 A Plot of Actual Threat Frequencies and Consequences

orders of magnitude, for example, from 100/year to 1/20,000 years, into only three values: Low, Medium, and High. In other words, two risks with same consequence but occurrence rates that differ by a factor of 100 might receive the same evaluation. Likewise, because of the arbitrary boundaries between low, medium, and high, two risks with the same consequence but with occurrence rates that differ by 1% could receive different ratings. These considerations defy common sense, and make it clear

		Threat Occ. Rate		
		Low	Medium	High
System Impact	High	Medium	High	Very High
	Med.	Low	Medium	High
	Low	Very Low	Low	Medium

EXHIBIT 62.7 A Typical Risk Matrix

that rating a risk as High, Medium, or Low cannot be the basis to cost-justify a proposed risk management measure.

62.5 RISK MITIGATION.

Exhibit 62.6 shows that the effect of risk exposures on IT systems can range from trivial to catastrophic, and it is not always immediately obvious which risk exposures are the most dangerous. For this reason, it is essential to base the selection of risk mitigation measures on a quantitative assessment of risks. In this section we consider the practical considerations in generating quantitative assessments and applying them to risk mitigation decisions.

62.5.1 ALE Estimates Alone Are Insufficient.

As noted above, ALE is a useful concept for comparing risks, but we recognize intuitively that ALE alone is not a sufficient basis for making risk mitigation decisions about the low-probability high-consequence risks. There are two reasons for this.

- The first reason is the difficulty in generating a credible estimate of occurrence rate for low-probability risks. As a rule, one can generate credible estimates of the consequences of a low-probability risk, but the same is not true of its occurrence rate. Risks that flow from human actions such as fraud, theft, and sabotage are also difficult to quantify credibly.
- The second reason stems from what appears to be a common human trait that this writer has postulated as Jacobson's 30-Year Law:

People (including risk managers) tend to dismiss risks that they have not *personally* experienced within the past 30 years.

Why 30 years? It is not clear, but it may be related genetically to human life expectancy, which until just a few generations ago was about 30 years. Possibly, people who were able to suppress anxiety about rare events were more successful than those who worried too much. Numerous instances of Jacobson's 30-Year Law can be found. For example, the United States Government has had a major fire at about 28-year intervals beginning in 1790, most recently at the Military Records Center. Presumably each new generation of federal property managers must relearn the lessons of fire safety by direct experience. The Northeast power blackout of 2003 followed a similar event in 1976, 27 years earlier.

It seems to be common for senior managers, particularly public officials, responding to a calamity such as the meltdown of the Fukushima nuclear plant in March 2011 following an earthquake and the resulting tsunami, to say something like this: "Who could have imagined that such a thing would happen? However, we have taken steps to see that it will never happen again."[8] This is an imprudent statement for two reasons. First, prudent managers will anticipate potential disasters. Second, saying *never* implies that perfect security is the goal. This is nonsensical, since perfect security is infinitely expensive, and so cannot be achieved.

62.5.2 What a Wise Risk Manager Tries to Do.

Unlike the senior managers quoted above, an organization's risk manager should be trying to imagine every possible *material* risk the organization faces, even those not personally experienced, and developing estimates of the impact of these risks. Next, the risk manager should strive to identify the optimum response to each material risk by identifying security measures that have a positive return on investment (ROI). Note that potentially fatal low-occurrence/high-consequence threats require treatment irrespective of ALE and ROI as discussed in Section 62.5.3.

Consider this example of cost effectiveness (presented as individual steps in reasoning):

- The ALE for keystroke errors was estimated in the Section 62.4.3 example as $20,000 per year, or $200 per operator.
- This estimate is credible because presumably there has been ample past experience with both the occurrence rate and impact cost of the keystroke-error risk.
- The risk manager considers how to treat this risk.
- Imagine that experience suggests that spending $100 each year on keyboard skills training for each operator would reduce the undetected error rate by 30%.
- Because the $100 per operator expense would yield a benefit of $60 in reduced ALE (30% of $200, the per-operator ALE), the ROI[9] of training would be –40%, clearly not a cost-beneficial mitigation measure.
- In effect we would be spending $10,000 to achieve a $6,000 loss reduction.
- However, if the error rate were reduced by 90% instead of 30%, the training would appear to be a good investment; spending $100 each to train operators, would produce a reduction in ALE per operator of $180, an ROI of +80%.
- The goal of the risk manager is to find the package of risk-management measures, which yields the greatest overall ROI.

62.5.2.1 The Three Risk-Management Regions. Basing risk-management decisions on ROI estimates, as described above, does not work for the low-probability, high-consequence risks because of two negative factors (1) the credibility of risk estimates and (2) management's concern about the risk consequences. End users commonly have a higher level of concern about risks than IT system managers, but as a rule it is the IT system managers who make the decisions about security measures. An IT system manager generally has no difficulty choosing between buying a faster server, and a more reliable server. The benefit of higher throughput is immediately evident. The benefit of higher reliability is not as obvious. Thus, although a risk manager may identify a significant low-occurrence, high-cost risk before it has occurred, an organization's senior managers probably would be unaware of these low-high risks, and would be genuinely surprised were a major loss to occur. Hence, the "Who could have imagined . . ." press releases. In other words, simply identifying an exposure might be thought to be enough to justify adoption of a mitigation measure to address the exposure. This suggests that the risk manager needs additional criteria for selecting risk mitigation measures. The next section presents an overview of mitigation measures to clarify the selection criteria.

It will help risk managers to understand the universe of risk events to which an organization is exposed, by dividing the total risk space into the three regions shown in Exhibit 62.8. The two axes are logarithmic, and the dots represent individual threats.

These regions help define appropriate risk-management actions. The bounders of the regions are defined by two senior management decisions.

1. The first decision is to define the *minimum significant threat event occurrence rate*. The concept is that it is reasonable to simply ignore the risk of threat events for which we have estimated occurrence rates less than some minimum rate. For

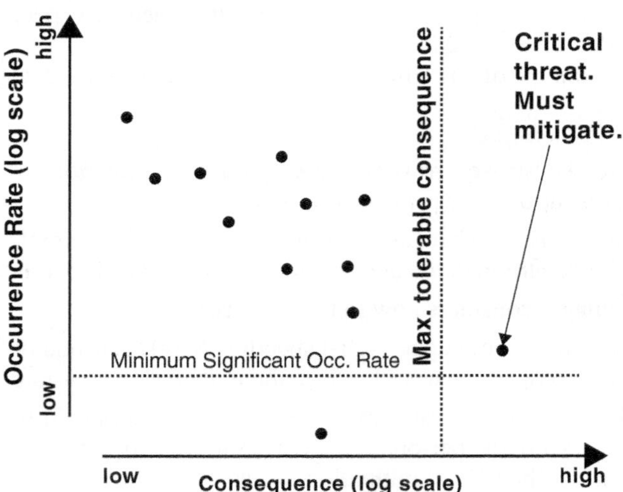

EXHIBIT 62.8 The Three Risk Zones

example, senior management may decide to ignore risks with occurrence rates estimated to be less than once in 20,000 years—that is, the probability of an occurrence of the threat next year is estimated to be less than 0.00005.

2. Senior management may also identify a loss level (consequence) that is *intolerably high.* Risk events of this type will appear in the upper right of Exhibit 62.6. The occurrence rate of these events is immaterial as long as they exceed the minimum consequence criterion and the minimum occurrence rate. If we estimate that the loss caused by an occurrence of a threat event (commonly referred to as the *single occurrence loss*, or SOL) exceeds the loss threshold *and* the occurrence rate exceeds the minimum material occurrence rate, then we *must* take steps to reduce the loss, perhaps by transferring the risk with an insurance policy, or by reducing the estimated occurrence rate to a value below the minimum material occurrence rate.

It is instructive to consider where to plot an unusual risk event like the attack on the World Trade Center on September 11, 2001. It is likely that many organizations have facilities that would generate losses in excess of their maximum tolerable loss if totally destroyed by a similar terrorist attack. This implies that such organizations should take steps to protect these facilities against terrorist attacks. However, we should also take into account the estimated rate of occurrence before making a decision. How can we make a credible estimate of such a rare event? We can begin by estimating how many such events will occur next year in the United States. For example, based on past experience we might assume that there will be about two such attacks each year. Secondly, we estimate the likelihood that, of all the facilities in the United States, our facility would be selected for attack. This will depend on the *attractiveness* of our facility to a terrorist group when compared with all other potential targets in the United States. For example, assume that there are 100 *attractive* buildings that are as widely recognized and as vulnerable as the WTC. If our facility is one of the hundred, then we might estimate the occurrence rate as $1/100 \times 2$, or a probable occurrence rate of

0.02/year. On the other hand, if our building is *not* one of the 100 high-profile buildings, then we might estimate that if there are 200,000 similar buildings in the United States, our occurrence rate is 1/200,000 × 2 or an occurrence rate of 1/100,000 years. In this latter case, our senior management probably would choose to ignore the risk.

The remaining portion of the Exhibit 62.6 graph, the mid- to upper-left-hand corner, is the zone where the risk manager attempts to find cost/beneficial risk-management measures as discussed in the sections that follow.

62.5.2.2 Where ROI-Based Risk Management Is Effective. ROI-based mitigation works well for high-probability, low-consequence risk exposures for two reasons: The manager who approves the expenditure believes that the risk exists and should be addressed, and believes further that the parameters used to generate estimates of ALE and the reduction in ALE, used to estimate ROI, are reasonable and credible.

62.5.2.3 Four Reasons for Adopting a Risk-Management Measure. There are four general tests of the utility of a risk-management measure:

1. The measure is required by law or regulation. In effect, a governing body has determined (one hopes) that the measure makes good public policy because it will always meet one of the remaining three tests. Exit door signs in public buildings are a good example. Sarbanes-Oxley may be an example of a bad (not cost-effective) law.
2. The cost of the measure is trivial, but its benefit is material. For example, a little-used door, which compromises physical access controls, is not being kept locked. One can institute a procedure and install security hardware to keep the door locked at very low cost.
3. The measure addresses a low-high risk that has an intolerable SOL, as discussed in Section 62.5.2.1. For example, it would be intolerable for a corporation to experience an SOL that exceeded owner equity or net worth. The failure several years ago of a prominent British merchant bank following unwise speculation by a staff member is a tragic example of an organization that failed to identify and address an intolerable SOL exposure.
4. The cost of the measure will be more than offset by the reduction in future losses (ALE) that it will yield. In other words, the mitigation measure has a positive ROI. This reason is commonly used to justify protection against the high-low risks. Operator keyboard training described in Section 62.5.2 is an example.

Procedures for managing the last two risk categories follow.

62.5.3 How to Mitigate Infrequent Risks.

After the high-low threats have been addressed using an ROI analysis, the risk manager considers all imaginable low-high risks, one by one, and makes for each such risk an estimate of the SOL and the rate of occurrence. The report of this analysis should describe for each threat the confidence level of the estimates of its SOL and occurrence rate. These estimates are arranged in descending order of SOL. The list is presented to senior management, who draws a line somewhere on the list and says, "The risks above the line are intolerably high. Do something about them." The risk manager then considers each of the unacceptable risks in two ways.

62.5.3.1 Reduce the Magnitude of High Single-Occurrence Losses. Sometimes the magnitude of an SOL can be reduced. There are several possibilities:

1. Transfer the risk by obtaining insurance against it. The premium will depend in part on the amount of the loss that is deductible. For example, one might obtain insurance against a $100 million SOL with a $10 million deductibility to minimize the insurance premium. In effect, the intolerable $100 million SOL has been reduced to a tolerable $10 million SOL at the cost of the insurance policy premium.
2. Disburse the risk exposure. For example, replace a single IT center with an intolerable SOL of $500 million of catastrophic physical damage, and service interruption losses, with three centers having SOLs of about $167 million each. The centers should be sufficiently isolated from one another to rule out shared disasters. The cost will be the incremental cost of the less efficient operation of three facilities.
3. Reduce the vulnerability of the IT system to the risk. For example, implementing an enhanced business resumption plan, at some additional cost, can speed up recovery off site. This will reduce the SOL associated with catastrophic service interruption losses. Notice that this an example of a risk mitigation measure that affects more than one threat.

The risk manager also may strive to reduce the occurrence rate of a high SOL. Because of the uncertainty of the estimates of low occurrence rates, this is less satisfactory. Nonetheless, even the uncertain occurrence rate estimates can be useful. If two risk exposures have the same SOL, but differ by an order of magnitude in estimated occurrence rate, it is reasonable to assume that the risk with the lower occurrence rate represents a lesser danger to the organization.

62.5.3.2 Risk-Management Measures Selection Process. Assume that the risk manager has presented a risk-assessment/risk mitigation report to senior management as described above. The report lists the low-high risks with one or more strategies for treating each risk.[10] The senior manager is responsible for selecting the mitigation measures for implementation because, as noted above, ROI-based justification is inappropriate for this class of risks.

1. If the risk manager is able to identify a relatively low-cost mitigation measure that reduces the rate of occurrence of a risk to a low enough value, senior management may elect to adopt the mitigation measure.
2. There is some rate of occurrence below which the senior manager is willing to ignore a risk, even if the estimate is low confidence. Typically, this applies to very low occurrence rate events. Extreme examples are a nuclear detonation or a crashing meteorite.
3. Risk transfer by insurance, or one of the other techniques listed above, reduces the SOL to a tolerable level, and the senior manager is willing to accept the cost of the insurance coverage.

A complete tabulation of occurrence rates, and the costs of mitigating actions for all the high-SOL risk exposures, will help senior management to prioritize the implementation of the mitigation measures.

62.5.4 The ROI-Based Selection Process. After the potentially fatal risks have been addressed as described in the preceding sections, the risk manager can turn to selection of measures to address the remaining high-low risks. A five-step procedure for selecting strategies on the basis of ROI is straightforward.

1. For each of the threats, identify possible risk-management measures. As noted above, some measures will affect more than one threat. There are four possible strategies:
   - *Threat mitigation*. Measures to reduce the occurrence rate and/or the impact of one or more of the threats.
   - *Risk transfer*. Use an insurance policy or other contractual means to transfer some or all of the risk to another party.
   - *Business resumption plans*. Take steps in advance of threat occurrences to decrease the time required to resume business operations. This type of strategy applies to non-IT business systems that are included in the scope of the risk-management project.
   - *IT system recovery plans*. Take steps in advance of threat occurrences to decrease the time required to resume operation of the IT system, and to reduce the amount of stored data lost. See Section 62.6.3.2 for details.
2. For each strategy, estimate the present value of the ***cost*** to implement and maintain the measure, taking into account the remaining life of the facility, the useful life of the measure, and the applicable time value of money. The organization will not enjoy the full benefit of a measure with a high initial cost and a low annual support cost if the life of the facility is less than the life of the measure.
3. For each strategy, estimate the effect of the measure on the occurrence rate and consequence of the threat(s) that the strategy addresses. Use these data to calculate total ALE, assuming the measure is implemented. Calculate the present value of the ***reduction in total ALE*** the strategy is expected to yield. This is the ***benefit*** of the measure. Note also that in addition to reducing risks a strategy may reduce operational costs. This cost saving should be added to the ongoing benefit (ALE reduction) of the strategy.
4. Using the values of cost and benefit, calculate ROI as follows:

   ROI = ((\$Benefit – \$Cost)/\$Cost) × 100%

   For example, using the data in Section 62.5.2, ROI is calculated as follows:

   ```
   ROI = (($6,000 - $10,000)/$1,000) x 100%
       = (-$4,000/$1,000) x 100%
       = 0.4 x 100% = -40%
   ```

   This equation normalizes the ROI and expresses it as a percentage. Zero percent represents a neutral ROI (benefit equals cost). One hundred percent would represent a very beneficial measure, and 1,000% would probably be a no-brainer. If the measure generates a cost saving, the saving is added to the ALE reduction benefit when calculating the ROI. *Note that the ROI analysis of a risk mitigation measure* ***will understate its benefit****, if the risk assessment does not include all the risk events that the measure will address.*

5. Make a list of the strategies in descending order of ROI after discarding the strategies with a negative ROI.

Presumably, management now selects for implementation the strategies in descending order of ROI until all available resources are allocated. However, if two or more strategies impact the same threat, it is possible that their effects may be partially overlapping. The risk manager can investigate this possibility the following way. Begin by assuming that the most attractive strategy has been implemented, and recalculate the *baseline ALE*. Next, verify the parameters for the remaining strategies, taking into account the effect of the measures assumed to have been implemented. Recalculate their ROIs as described above, and repeat the selection process. It would be convenient if there were an analytic way to do this, but this author has been unable to devise a practical way to do so because of the wide range and complexity of potential interactions.

62.5.5 Risk-Assessment/Risk-Management Summary.

The risk model illustrated by Jacobson's Window leads to the following conclusions:

1. Risks can be broadly classified as ranging from high-probability, low-consequence to low-probability, high-consequence events. In general, risk events in this range cause losses over a relatively narrow range of loss values when expressed as an annual rate or ALE.
2. Because of IT operating staff familiarity with the high end of the high-low risks, all available measures may already have been taken such that there may not be any cost-beneficial way to further reduce the ALE of some of these threats.
3. Midrange risks can be addressed by selecting mitigation measures with a positive ROI, based on the relationship between the cost to implement a mitigation measure and the reduction in ALE it is expected to yield.
4. Treatment of low-high risks requires the judgment of senior management, based on estimates of SOL and, to a lesser extent, estimates of rate of occurrence. Mitigation measures or risk transfer may reduce SOLs to acceptable levels or decrease occurrence rates to the level at which risks can be ignored.
5. To be effective, the risk-management function must be:
   - Performed by properly qualified persons
   - Independent of IT line management
   - Reported to senior management to ensure that all risks are recognized, and that resource allocation is unbiased

62.6 RISK-ASSESSMENT TECHNIQUES.

The first step in performing a risk assessment is to define the scope and focus of the assessment. The scope will define the IT functions or business processes, the physical assets, the intangible assets, and the liability exposures, which are to be included in the assessment. The focus means the kinds of risk events to be included in the analysis. Risk events may include failures of the IT hardware and software, software logical errors, deliberate destructive acts by both insiders and outsiders, and external events such as earthquakes, hurricanes, river floods, and so forth. Sometimes the focus is determined by the desire to evaluate a specific class of risk-management measures.

62.6.1 Aggregating Threats and Loss Potentials. Aggregation is a key concept of quantitative modeling, and refers to the practice of combining related items to keep the model at a manageable size. For example, one can define a single risk event (*IT Server Failure*) or two risk events (*Server01 Failure* and *Server02 Failure*) under the assumption that the two servers support different systems with different loss potentials) and so on in ever-increasing detail. The more risk events defined for a risk assessment, the greater will be the effort required to establish the risk parameters, and perform the calculations. However, *the individual risk events will not all have the same impact on the results of the assessment*. Indeed, some risk events will be found to be completely inconsequential, so the time expended to estimate their parameters will have been wasted. In other words, an appropriate degree of detail will not be immediately obvious.

This suggests that one should begin an assessment using highly aggregated risks, functions (typically business processes), and assets, perhaps no more than 10 to 15 of each in a typical situation, together with roughly prepared estimates of the risk parameters. This preliminary analysis will show which elements are important to the results. One can then add details to the important elements as appropriate, and refine the material estimates to improve the validity of the model. This approach works to concentrate the effort on the important issues, and avoids wasting time refining unimportant input data.

62.6.2 Basic Risk-Assessment Algorithms. It is generally accepted that ALE, in dollars (or other currency as appropriate) per year, is calculated as follows:

$$
\begin{aligned}
\text{ALE} = {} & \text{Threat Occurrence Rate (number per year)} \\
& \times \text{Threat Effect Factor (0.0 to 1.0)} \\
& \times \text{Loss Potential (in monetary units)}
\end{aligned}
$$

The term *threat occurrence rate* (TOR) is used to designate the estimate of the probability of occurrence of a threat event during a risk-management planning period, typically one year, thus the TOR is the probability of occurrence at an annualized *rate*. The functions and assets are characterized by their potential to trigger a loss when impacted by one or more of the threats. The term *potential for loss* or simply *loss potential* is used specifically to designate the **worst-case loss** a function or asset can generate. This implies that there is at least one threat event (the worst-case threat) that will trigger a loss equal to the loss potential. Other threats will cause lesser losses because they have a lesser effect on the function or asset. The *Threat Effect Factor* is used to quantify the relationship between a threat event and a function or asset. If the threat event has no impact on the function or asset, the corresponding Threat Effect Factor will be zero. If the threat event triggers the worst-case loss (the loss potential), the Threat Effect Factor will be 1.0. Threat Effect Factors will range from zero to 1.0 for all threats.

Exhibit 62.9 illustrates how each threat-function or threat-asset pair includes a Threat Effect Factor. The SOL, expressed in monetary units for each function or asset with respect to a given threat event, is calculated as follows:

```
SOL = Threat Effect Factor (0.0 to 1.0)
      x Loss Potential (monetary units)
```

	Process #1	Process #2	Process #3	Process #4
Threat #1	TEF_{11}	TEF_{12}	TEF_{13}	TEF_{14}
Threat #2	TEF_{21}	TEF_{22}	TEF_{23}	TEF_{24}
Threat #3	TEF_{31}	TEF_{32}	TEF_{33}	TEF_{34}
Threat #4	TEF_{41}	TEF_{42}	TEF_{43}	TEF_{44}

EXHIBIT 62.9 Threat Effect Factors Connect Threats and Processes, Functions, and Assets

The terms *loss potential* and *Threat Effect Factor* are as defined above. The sum of the SOLs for all the functions and assets with respect to a given threat is the consequence of an occurrence of the threat.

From these two definitions, we can see that:

```
ALE = SOL × Threat Occurrence Rate ($/year)
```

The sections that follow discuss these two equations in more detail and describe techniques for estimating values for TOR, loss potential, and Threat Effect Factor.

62.6.3 Loss Potential. There are four basic kinds of losses that contribute loss potential:

1. *Property damage losses.* Property damage losses occur when a threat event impacts an asset of the organization. The asset may be physical property damaged, for example, by a fire or flood, or the asset may be an intangible asset, such as a trade secret or a proprietary database, the improper disclosure, modification, or destruction of which causes a loss to the organization.
2. *Liability losses.* The operation of an IT system may expose the organization to liability for damage or injury. For example, improper operation of an IT-controlled process might release a toxic gas. Improper disclosure of personal information may cause the individual to sue the organization for damages. If third parties place reliance on data generated or maintained by an IT system, there may be an exposure to damage suits if the data are incorrect as a result, for example, of flaws in the IT system.
3. *Service interruption losses.* Service interruption losses occur when IT system services or other business functions are interrupted, or are not initiated in a timely manner because of the action of a threat event. In general, the longer the duration of an interruption, the greater will be the amount of the loss. This means that service interruption loss potential must be estimated in the form of a table of values appropriate to the expected range of interruption durations the threats are expected to generate. As a consequence, each threat that causes

service interruptions must be defined in terms of the percentage of the threat's occurrences that result in each of the interruption durations used to define service interruption loss potential.

4. *Lost data losses.* IT systems typically require stored data to function. If the primary copy of the stored data is lost, the data are recovered from the most recent backup copy, or reconstructed from paper records, if they exist, of prior transactions. The magnitude of the data loss will depend on the rate at which the stored data change, the frequency with which a backup copy is made, the accuracy of the backup copy process, and the frequency of the occurrences of the threat events that require data recovery of the stored data. The stored data used by some IT systems do not change continuously, and so a complete backup copy can be made after each update phase, and data loss thus avoided.

Loss potentials, as described in the three following subsections, are based on estimates of the worst-case losses with respect to the list of risk events.

62.6.3.1 Property and Liability Losses. These losses are treated the same way, so they can be discussed together. It is advisable to begin consideration of property damage losses by making an aggregated list of possible sources. For example, the initial list might consider together all the hardware in an IT facility, and similarly all of the databases needed to operate each of the principal IT applications. For each such asset[11], an estimate is made of the worst-case loss that the organization could experience with respect to that asset. For example, the worst-case loss for a set of stored data would be the cost to reconstruct the data from back-up copies, and the cost to recover any missing or corrupted data. There will be other losses resulting from interruptions to IT services that require the availability of the data, but these losses are described separately in the next subsection.

Liability[12] loss potentials, if included in the scope of the risk-management project, should be estimated in the same way. The first step is to determine which liabilities should be included in the risk assessment. The organization may already have a mechanism for addressing liability exposure, possibly through a risk transfer mechanism. However, the liability exposures that are unique to the IT operations should be included, and the worst-case loss potential estimated as described above.

62.6.3.2 Service Interruption Losses. Service interruption (sometimes referred to as *denial of service*[13]) losses refer to the losses experienced by end-users of an IT system when the service is not performed on time. The first step in estimating service interruption losses is to construct a list of the IT services for which there is a significant interruption loss potential. Here, too, it is desirable to aggregate individual applications in basic service areas. Examination of a wide range of functions suggests that there are six different classes of service interruption losses. Since each class of loss may begin after a different interruption duration, it is unlikely that there will be a single loss rate that begins at the instant the interruption begins, and has a fixed rate per hour of interruption duration into the indefinite future. Reviewing the causes with the persons most familiar with each service, typically the line-of-business managers, will determine which classes apply and what the loss potential factors are. By tabulating the losses associated with each of the classes, one can generate an overall loss potential for a suitable range of service interruption durations.

- ***Reduced productivity***. Would people be idled if there were a service interruption? If yes, how many and how soon? What, approximately, is their total pay, including benefits? If substantial production facilities would be idled, what is the approximate hourly cost of ownership of the facilities, computed as the total life-cycle cost of ownership divided by the total operating life in hours?
- ***Delayed collection of funds***. Does the IT system application trigger collection of funds for the organization, for example, a billing system, or a loan-notes-due collection system? If yes, determine the average amount collected each business day, which would be affected by a service interruption. Because in most cases it will be possible to do some manual processing of the high-value items, the affected amount may be less than the full daily processing dollar volume. Determine a suitable cost-of-money percentage for use in present-value calculations by consulting the organization's treasurer or controller. Alternatively, the current commercial bank prime rate plus one or two percentage points can be used. The total loss does not increase linearly with the duration of the interruption. For example, assume that the one-day loss is $100 due to delayed collection. After a two-day outage, the loss would be $300: $200 from the first day and $100 from the second day. A three-day outage would cost $600. $300 of accumulated losses for the first day, $200 for the second day of delayed collections, and $100 for the third day, and so on.
- ***Reduced income***. Will an interruption of the application impact sales revenue or other income receipts? If yes, estimate the amount of income lost both immediately, and over the long term, for a range of service interruption durations appropriate to the risk events included in the risk assessment. It may be difficult for the end user to make an estimate, unless it is possible to remember the last major service interruption, and to describe what happened. What would the organization do if a major competitor had a service outage? How would the outage become known, and how would it be exploited to increase income? These questions may help to determine the amount of reduced income to be expected.

  Along with reduced income, there would probably be a reduction in operating expenses, such as cost of sales, caused by the decreased activity. When the reduction in operating costs is subtracted from the reduced revenues, the result is the net loss. Estimates should be made for the shortest service interruption duration that the user believes would cause significant lost business; in addition, planning should include provisions for one or more service interruptions of greater duration.
- ***Extra expense***. How would the user respond to an outage? Would it be necessary to hire temporary help, or to work overtime? Could an outside service be used? Would there be an increased error rate, which would increase error research and correction expenses? Might there be increased fraud loss, and fraud investigation costs? The cost to catch up, after the outage ends, is often a major extra expense factor. Beginning with the shortest significant duration, several estimates should be made, including a worst-case scenario.
- ***Lateness penalties***. If the application entails any lateness penalties, contractual, regulatory, or legal, an estimate should be made of the amount of the penalties that would be triggered by an outage, and the outage duration that would trigger the penalties.
- ***Public perception***. Public perception, as a catchall term, refers to the indirect effects of a service interruption. Staff morale and customer attitudes may be

affected negatively by the impression that the organization's risks are not being effectively managed. The value of publicly traded stock may be adversely affected, and pending mergers or stock offerings may be derailed. The cost of borrowing may increase.

Note that this procedure does not involve asking end users to estimate the maximum *tolerable* service interruption duration. Asking for a tolerable duration is *not* a useful question. An attempt by end users to establish the value of *tolerable* is simply an opinion or subjective judgment call. The basic risk assessment will establish the expected annualized losses. Then, an evaluation of the cost-benefit or ROI of alternative risk mitigation measures, implemented to reduce the number and duration of service interruptions, will identify the optimum IT system configuration, including measures to control service interruptions.

62.6.3.3 IT Systems Interruption Mitigation. IT system service interruption mitigation is a special case because of the effect of lost-data losses. This is why.

The performance of IT system continuity plans is often characterized using two parameters, referred to as *Recovery Time Objective*[14] (RTO) and *Recovery Point Objective* (RPO). RTO is the maximum service interruption duration that will result from the action of threats on an IT system. The RTO of the continuity plan in place for an IT system will determine the expected losses of an IT system that result from the impact of the service interruption threats. Decreasing the RTO will decrease the expected loss, but will increase the cost to implement and maintain the IT system continuity plan.

The RPO is a measure of the frequency with which an IT system backs up stored data. The more frequently data are backed up, the lower will be the lost data losses, but the greater will be the cost to install and maintain the backup provisions.

The risk-management task is to pick the IT system continuity plan (RTO-RPO combination) that has the most favorable cost-benefit. The *cost* is the cost to install and maintain a given RTO-RPO combination. The *benefit* is the reduction in expected loss the RTO-RPO combination will achieve, compared with the RTO-RPO combination currently in use. This is why the question: "What is your maximum 'tolerable' outage duration, that is, your RTO?" is worthless. A rational selection depends on both cost and benefit, not the subjective appeal of any particular RTO.

Typically, there is an interaction between RTO and RPO. For example, tape is probably less expensive as a backup storage medium than disk, so we would expect a tape-based IT system continuity plan to be cheaper than a disk-based plan. However, tape will restrict the range of RPOs that can be implemented, and may control the best achievable RTO, both of which will increase expected loss. There is another important point.

There is no inherent connection between the service interruption loss potential of an IT system and the cost of RTO-RPO combinations for the system.

For example, a small inexpensive system (one with low RTO and RPO costs) might be running a very time-critical, high-value function, such as currency trading, while a large system with high RTO and RPO costs might be analyzing the works of William Shakespeare for the local college, a low criticality task.

62.6.4 Risk Event Parameters. As noted in the prior section, during the determination of loss potential, a list of significant risk events can be constructed. The list should be examined critically to determine if additional event types should be added to the list, bearing in mind the aggregation considerations discussed above and the defined scope of the project.

Once the risk events list has been completed, two parameters are estimated for each event as follows:

1. ***Occurrence rate***. There are several ways to estimate occurrence rates. If the event has had a relatively high occurrence rate in the past, typically more than once in 10 years, the organization is likely to have records of those events, from which the occurrence rate can be inferred with high confidence. However, there are two cautions. First, consideration must be given to any changes in the environment that would affect the occurrence rate. For example, the root cause of some system crashes may have been corrected, so that one would expect the future rate to be lower than in the past. Second, it is important to avoid double counting. For example, a system outage log may lump electric power failures into a catchall category: hardware failure. If electric power failure is included in the risk assessment as a separate risk event, its occurrences may be inadvertently counted twice.

   If the risk event is external to the IT facility, for example, river flooding and earthquake, one can usually find external sources of information about past occurrences. For example, one could use the NOAA National Hurricane Center's list of the United States' most intense hurricanes (www.nhc.noaa.gov/pastint.html) to determine if a given U.S. location has ever been impacted by a high-intensity hurricane. There are numerous Websites that can support a risk assessment. One also may find that past copies of local publications can help to determine the past local history. In some cases, there will be no meaningful past history for a risk event, particularly if the event is of recent origin, for example, e-business fraud and terrorism. In these cases, it may be possible to reason by analogy with other similar risk events to develop a reasonable estimate.

2. ***Outage duration***. The range of outage durations for each threat must be estimated in order to be able to estimate service interruption losses. If the outage duration is not the same for all the IT systems that the risk event impacts, one may either use an average value or define a separate risk event for each of the systems, keeping in mind the aggregation considerations discussed above.

Remember that until an initial overall risk assessment, like Exhibit 62.6, has been generated, the analysts do not know which of the input data are important. Consequently, it is counterproductive to devote effort to refining initial data. The wide range of values encountered in a typical risk assessment makes it clear that rough initial estimates of the risk parameters will be sufficiently accurate to identify the critical parameters.

62.6.5 Threat Effect Factors, ALE, and SOL Estimates. From the basic risk-assessment algorithms, it is possible to determine the risk event/loss potential pairs for which the Threat Effect Factor is greater than zero (see Section 62.6.2), and having done so, to estimate the value of the factor. It is then possible to use the risk data discussed above and the algorithms to calculate an estimate of the ALE and SOL for each of the pairs, and then to tabulate the individual ALE and SOL estimates to obtain a complete risk assessment for the IT organization. This is useful as a baseline because it provides an assessment against which to evaluate potential risk mitigation measures.

In other words, the benefit of a risk-management measure is the amount by which it reduces this baseline or current expected loss estimate.

In order to validate the assessment, it is necessary to identify the threat event/loss potential pairs that account for the majority of the expected losses. Typically, about 20 percent of the pairs cause 80 percent of the total expected loss. Reviewing the details of each input item, these questions should be asked: Were source data transcribed correctly? Are the assumptions reasonable? Were calculations made correctly? Does any threat event/loss potential pair account for so much of the expected losses that it should be disaggregated from other data items? Once the validation process is complete and indicated changes have been made, it is feasible to consider risk mitigation, but first one must gain acceptance of these data.

Field experience has disclosed a very powerful technique for gaining acceptance of estimates used in the risk assessment. First we gather data from knowledgeable people in the organization: line-of-business managers, IT specialists, audit, security, and so on. We use these data to make a preliminary baseline estimate of risks as described in the previous sections. We then convene a round table meeting of all the people who provided the data. We show them the results and the input data. This results in a useful discussion of the data, and tends to identify inputs based on faulty assumptions, personal biases, and misinformation. It is rather like an instant peer review. The agreed-upon changes to the input data are then used to make a final estimate of risks, which can be used to evaluate proposed mitigation measures.

62.6.6 Sensitivity Testing. The preceding discussion implies that a single value is to be estimated for each of the risk parameters included in the risk assessment. However, it may be thought that a parameter should not be limited to a single value, and that a Monte Carlo technique should be used to generate a set of ALE and SOL estimates. In a Monte Carlo approach, one generates random inputs into a model following specified probability distribution functions for each of the variables being studies. The outputs of the model then generate frequency distributions that allow one to evaluate the sensitivity of critical outputs to the precision of specific inputs. There are two obstacles to using this approach. Apart from the big increase in the complexity of the calculations, there is still a requirement to select a *single* risk mitigation strategy based on the set of ALE and SOL estimates. *It is not feasible to install a range of performance values for given mitigation measures* to match a range of loss estimates. As described previously, cost-beneficial risk mitigation measures are selected by calculating the baseline ALE, and then recalculating the ALE, assuming that the proposed mitigation measure has been installed. The difference between the two ALE estimates is taken to be a reasonable estimate of the return in the ROI calculation. Assuming two sets of 1,000 ALE estimates (without and with a proposed mitigation measure), which were generated by a Monte Carlo simulation, calculating all possible differences produces a set of 1,000,000 returns. Which one should be selected to calculate ROI?

Using the most likely value for each risk parameter, and generating only two ALE estimates, the difference between the two may be used to calculate ROI. Because the ROI typically flows from a relatively large number of parameters, the overall result will tend to average out any individual departures from the average values used, and so will be a fair representation of the actual risk losses that will occur.

However, if confidence in the accuracy of an estimate is extremely low, estimates using low, median, and high values of the parameters should be used to evaluate the effect on the overall results. Whenever a risk assessment includes a material low-confidence parameter, full disclosure should be made to the managers who review and act on the results. Risk analysts should bear in mind that almost all other decisions about resource allocations, which senior managers are regularly called on to make, are based on uncertain estimates of future events. There is nothing unique about the uncertainties surrounding risk mitigation decisions.

62.6.7 Selecting Risk Mitigation Measures. The objective of the risk mitigation process is to identify the optimum set of mitigation measures. The first step is to address the intolerable SOL exposures as discussed in Section 62.5.3. The risk assessment and the evaluation of potential risk mitigation measures provide the raw material on which to base an implementation strategy for the risk exposures in the midrange. Considerations include:

The mitigation measures with negative ROIs can be discarded.

The remaining mitigation measures can be tabulated in three ways:

1. In descending order of net benefit: ALE reduction minus the implementation cost
2. In ascending order of implementation cost
3. In descending order of ROI

Based on other considerations, senior management selects mitigation measures from one of the three lists. Other considerations include the following:

- The availability of resources for risk mitigation may be limited, in which case some mitigation actions must be deferred until the next budgeting period. In extreme cases, the lowest cost measures may be selected.
- The mitigation of risk exposures that have a particularly undesirable effect on marketing considerations, as compared with other loss categories, may be given priority.

62.7 SUMMARY.

This chapter has shown the tremendous advantage of having a detailed, quantitative assessment of the risk exposures leading to a quantitative evaluation of prospective mitigation measures. Senior managers will appreciate the advantage of using rational business judgment in place of seat-of-the-pants guesswork.

62.8 FURTHER READING

Anderson, E. *Business Risk Management: Models and Analysis*. Wiley, 2014.

Bhatia, M. *Handbook of Applied Risk Measurement*. Wiley, 2014.

Blundell, D. M., T. Cuthbertson, and J. Daniel. *Operational Risk Management*. Global Professional Publishing, 2013.

Coleman, T. S. *A Practical Guide to Risk Management*. Research Foundation of CFA Institute, 2011.

Crouhy, M., D. Galai, and R. Mark. *The Essentials of Risk Management*, 2nd ed. McGraw-Hill, 2013.

Gordon, L. A. *Managerial Accounting—Concepts and Empirical Evidence*, 6th ed. McGraw-Hill, 2005.

Lam, J. *Enterprise Risk Management: From Incentives to Controls*, 2nd ed. Wiley, 2014.

Louisot, J.-P. *ERM—Enterprise Risk Management: Issues and Cases*. Wiley, 2013.

McGill, W. L. *Math for Security*. CRC Press, 2014.

Moeller, R. R. *Executive's Guide to COSO Internal Controls: Understanding and Implementing the New Framework.* Wiley, 2013.

Mulcahy, R. *Risk Management Tricks of the Trade for Project Managers + PMI-RMP Exam Prep Guide*, 2nd ed. RMC Publications, 2010.

Siepman, F. *Managing Risk and Security in Outsourcing IT Services: Onshore, Offshore and the Cloud.* Auerbach, 2013.

Sweet, K. *Introduction to Security and Risk Management.* CRC Press, 2014.

Sunstein, C. R. *Risk and Reason: Safety, Law, and the Environment.* Cambridge University Press, 2002.

62.9 NOTES

1. The term *mitigation measure* is used here broadly to refer to all actions taken to manage risks, and may include logical controls over access to data, physical controls over access to IT hardware, facilities to monitor operations, selection and supervision of IT personnel, policy and procedures to guide operations, and so forth— in short, all of the security techniques described in this *Computer Security Handbook.*
2. Donn B. Parker, "What's Wrong with Information Security—and How to Fix It." Lecture at Naval Postgraduate School, April 28, 2005, www.youtube.com/watch?v=RW9hOBCSy0g
3. Another way of expressing this concept is as follows: Perfect security is infinitely expensive, and so it is not a rational goal of a risk-management program.
4. As a practical matter, it may become obvious that in some situations the differences between the members of a group of like IT systems are too small to be significant, and that a single set of security measures can be adopted for all of the systems.
5. "Expected loss" is a shorthand term for the losses an organization can reasonably expect to experience given its risk environment and the potential for loss of its functions and assets. It is the sum of the individual ALEs.
6. This author has made it a practice at the end of each interview to ask: "Is there something I should have asked about?" or words to that effect. In most cases, new information emerges as a result.
7. The plot was generated automatically by CORA® (Cost-Of-Risk Analysis), a risk-management software system.
8. D. McNeill, "With Fukushima Nuclear Plant Still Leaking, Japan Clean-Up Bill Soars to $50bn." *The Independent*, July 24, 2013, www.independent.co.uk/news/world/asia/with-fukushima-nuclear-plant-still-leaking-japan-cleanup-bill-soars-to-50bn-8730832.html
9. Return on investment is the ratio of the return received from an investment to the investment itself. If a bank pays back $1.05 one year after $1.00 has been deposited in the bank, the ROI is roughly 5%. To determine ROI accurately, one must take the ratio of the present value of the return to the present value of the investment.
10. A given measure may address more than one threat, so the total of the individual reductions in expected loss are used to evaluate the ROI of the measure.
11. This is an example of the advantage of aggregation. Rather than estimating the loss potential for individual physical item, it is much more efficient to aggregate the items into large classes. It may also be feasible to estimate loss potential on the basis of replacement cost per unit area.

12. The term *liability* is used here as a shorthand for *exposure to liability*. For example, an IT service performed for others might expose the organization to a liability action if the service was performed incorrectly resulting in a client loss. This potential risk exposure is referred to here simply as a liability.
13. The term *denial of service* implies that service interruptions are the result of deliberate attacks on an IT system, but, of course, there are many other threats that cause service interruptions. For this reason, the term may cause misunderstanding, and so should not be used.
14. The use of the word *objective* is unfortunate in this context. It would be more precise to use a term like *provision of performance* to make clear that the quantity is what a contingency plan is expected to achieve . . . not a vague goal. However, the terms *RTO* and *RPO* are widely used, so we will use them here.

CHAPTER 63

MANAGEMENT RESPONSIBILITIES AND LIABILITIES

Carl Hallberg, M. E. Kabay, Bridgitt Robertson, and Arthur E. Hutt

63.1 INTRODUCTION. This chapter reviews the critical roles of management in establishing, implementing, and maintaining information security (INFOSEC) policies in the modern enterprise. It also reviews some of the risks to management personnel in failing to ensure adequate standards of INFOSEC.[1]

63.1.1 Role of Management.

Organizations are unequally affected by the risk of loss. In certain government computer installations, matters of national security are at stake, and the measures required to protect such facilities are elaborate and costly. At the other end of the spectrum are computers used exclusively for word processing of unclassified materials, which are not connected to networks; these require few security precautions except for file backup and antivirus software. This chapter and this *Handbook* do not address either of these extremes, but rather the bulk of user organizations in business, government, and universities, where concentrations of information assets and dependence on computers create an exposure to loss, and managers must balance security with cost effectiveness and common sense while convincing colleagues with a superficial knowledge of security to pay attention to their recommendations.

Management provides the essential framework for accomplishing technical work. Whether it is drawing up a security policy, enforcing such policies, training the individuals who will implement and enforce those policies, or proposing a budget to get all this done, management plays an essential role. Information technology (IT) managers ensure the consistent functioning of the organizational computing environment. Ideally, they also provide insights and guidance to upper management in strategic planning to take advantage of new opportunities.

Many organizations, regardless of size and history, have heterogeneous networks with many different operating systems running different applications and serving many purposes and clients. Web servers sit next to email servers, which connect to outside networks, which then rely on connections to more than one third-party corporate network. The rapid pace of technological change impedes the IT manager's ability to keep the enterprise IT infrastructure running smoothly.

A key function of IT managers is loss avoidance by managing risk intelligently, in order to reduce the likelihood of trouble in the IT sector and to reduce the costs of coping with such trouble.[2] In a broader sense, this entire *Handbook* is designed to support management in these efforts.

IT managers must focus constantly on enabling business functions. Given that most enterprises do not consider security as their main task, IT managers must ensure that INFOSEC policies and technology support, rather than hinder, the principal business of the enterprise. It is equally important to impress this philosophy of service to the strategic and operational goals of the enterprise on all members of the security staff. Many of these members may have developed their careers entirely in the technical sectors, and they may not have developed a service orientation toward their nontechnical fellow workers, and toward the enterprise itself.

63.1.2 CISO.

In recent years, INFOSEC has been growing in visibility as a major business concern. IT managers are now being joined by INFOSEC managers. For example, a major bank responded to infiltration of its systems in the 1990s by naming a chief INFOSEC officer (CISO) reporting at the same level as officers such as the chief information officer (CIO), chief financial officer (CFO), chief operations officer (COO), chief technology officer (CTO), and chief executive officer (CEO). Together, the CIO and the CISO face complex responsibilities, and are increasingly visible in the corporate infrastructure.

Today, CISOs are increasingly found in all types of corporations. They may report to the CIO, or they may have a position on an equal level with the CIO. Some of the functions in a security organization are suggested in the hierarchy that follows. (These functions do not imply one team or one person per function, but simply illustrate the range of functions a CISO must coordinate.)

- CISO
  - Security policy team
    - Development
    - Awareness
    - Education
    - Update management
  - Access controls
    - Data classification functions
    - Identification, authentication, and authorization functions
  - Intrusion detection and prevention
    - Outward-facing intrusion detection systems
    - Gateway security devices
    - Malware control team
  - Security assessment
    - Security auditing
    - Penetration team
  - Engineering coordination
    - Software quality assurance coordination
    - Patch management review
    - Network security oversight
    - Control systems and logging management
  - Security incident response team
    - Planning and rehearsals management
    - First line response
    - Data gathering and forensic analysis
    - Coordination with internal functions (legal, public relations, human resources, etc.)
    - Coordination with law enforcement

One of the factors in this increased visibility of the CISO is the rapid growth in the popular press of technology issues coverage and of INFOSEC breaches in particular. For example, distributed denial-of-service attacks, malware infestations, breakdowns of privacy policies, theft of credit card numbers, loss of control of large volumes of personally identifiable information, identity theft, Website defacements, spam, phishing, and the other forms of abuse to information systems, described in several chapters of this *Handbook,* have kept the public aware of INFOSEC and its breaches.[3]

In some sense, publicity has helped the IT world, because some IT managers now have increased ammunition with which to argue for management support of the security function. Publicity has increased visibility, however, so that even a minor breach of security may spark an overreaction in the upper echelons of the enterprise. Indeed, in

California, it is now law (SB 1386) that companies that suffer from some forms of INFOSEC breaches must quickly advise their customers of these events.[4]

63.1.3 Information Security Integrating into Strategic Vision. IT security managers are now able to help their businesses achieve strategic goals and to further their responsibilities by showing that security involves more than just protecting assets, it is also potentially a business enabler. In the absence of a secure IT infrastructure, businesses may be slow to enter a given market for fear of losses and liabilities resulting from security breaches. However, with security integrated into the corporate culture, these enterprises can confidently enter new arenas and convince their potential clients that their data will be safe. The authors have personal experience from consulting assignments in which clients stated that their own potential customers were reluctant to do business with them because their security measures were inadequate.

George Lin describes the benefits of a business-focused IT organization:

> In a business-focused IT organization … IT staff are more interested in understanding the business—and the people, processes, and organization that make up the business—than they are in the technology for its own sake. These staff members possess a balanced set of soft skills, and business acumen as well as analytical and technical skills. They think about business processes first and technology second. The solutions they propose tend to be more complete, often involving people, process, and organization as well as technology, which is seen as simply a tool. Interacting with such an organization yields an experience similar to that expected from Big Four consulting firms, but with the added intimacy and insights only an internal organization can provide.
>
> More importantly, IT/business alignment becomes a nonissue because it is natural to a business-focused IT organization, the very DNA of its staff. There is no need to expend effort specifically on IT/business alignment because the business-focused IT organization thinks and acts like the business that it serves, and is an integral part of that business.[5]

In this framework, INFOSEC becomes not an afterthought, preventing loss, but part of the design strategy, which will help realize gain. This is a much more powerful, and positive, view of INFOSEC's role in the business world than is the traditional one. Using INFOSEC principles in the design of a product or service generally helps to create a more robust product or service, one that will be less prone to risk.

The National Institute of Standards and Technology has articulated a roadmap for integrating security considerations into the system development life cycle (SDLC)[6] (with addition of three more security objectives in compliance with the Parkerian hexad described in Chapter 3 in this *Handbook*):

> A general SDLC includes the following five phases: *initiation, acquisition/development, implementation/assessment, operations/maintenance, and sunset (disposition)*. Each of these five phases includes a minimum set of security tasks needed to effectively incorporate security in the system development process. Including security early in the information SDLC will usually result in less expensive and more effective security than adding it to an operational system.
>
> The following questions should be addressed in determining the security controls that will be required for a system:
>
> - How critical is the system in meeting the organization's mission?
> - What are the security objectives required by the system, e.g., integrity, confidentiality, and availability [and control, authenticity, and utility]?
> - What regulations and policies are applicable in determining what is to be protected?
> - What are the threats that are applicable in the environment where the system will be operational?

Integrating a security methodology into a product or service helps to defines roles and responsibilities and helps to manage expectations.

63.1.4 Net Present Value of Information Security. A paper from the late 1990s articulated the positive value of INFOSEC in a competitive economy. The summary included these conclusions:

> The news is that we can now go beyond gibbering and fist shaking. In today's e-commerce environment, effective information security can actually increase business and increase profits, not merely reduce risk. …
>
> Tom Nelson, VP and Chief Strategy Officer of AtomicTangerine, has defined the Net Present Value of Information Security (NPVSec) as follows: "NPVSec is the value protection and value creation that is realized when barriers to e-Business are removed through mechanisms that ensure business integrity, service availability, and customer/consumer confidentiality and privacy. Value creation examples include: new distribution channels, new revenue streams, new business models, among others."
>
> In other words, instead of viewing information security solely as a risk-avoidance measure—like a kind of insurance policy that never actually pays anything back—we are forced by the nature of e-business to accept that security actually *supports* and *enables* e-business.
>
> As we have seen … e-business has brought security to the forefront of strategic thinking for successful businesses. Business leaders can no longer tolerate the view that security is an add-on feature relegated to the end of the design process. Security is a process, not a product or a state; security affects every e-businesses bottom line in a positive way. Security is no longer a cost center; it's part of your repertoire for meeting the legitimate needs of your public. Instead of seeing security as solely the purview of the technical staff in your organization, you should ensure that your marketing and public relations departments are well versed in the principles of information security and can communicate effectively to an anxious public about the measures you are taking to safeguard your customers' privacy and their money.[7]

Another perspective on the value of integrating information security into a corporate culture argues that "the responsibility for protecting the organization's information assets is no longer restricted to the CSO [chief security officer]. Every employee has a responsibility to help protect the proprietary data they are entrusted with."[8] The authors write that:

> This approach:
>
> - Improves individual leadership through collaboration and team building
> - Strengthens corporate allegiance
> - Helps to provide a sense of community
> - Builds an intelligent workforce where every employee is recognized and watched by their peers for their individual contribution to the team's strength. …
>
> In addition, embedding security deep into every process of the corporation, starting at the executive level, is an extremely effective method of taking one problem and leveraging the success of that solution to correct other problems.

63.1.5 Case Study: Veterans Affairs. The next summary of a specific case of management failures will serve to help readers think about the management responsibilities for information assurance.[9]

63.1.5.1 Announcement without Taking Responsibility. In March 2007, *Network World* writer Jon Brodkin wrote an excellent analysis of 10 letters informing victims of data theft or loss of control of personally identifiable information (PII) that their data might be compromised.[10] He pointed out that almost all of the letters failed to express any responsibility for the loss of control over data stored on unencrypted disks that were lost or stolen or for poorly secured Websites that posted PII without protection, or with poor protection. Perhaps staff attorneys warned the public relations officials to avoid any implication of responsibility to avoid contributing anything that would exacerbate their liability in potential lawsuits. Passive voice is often used to shift responsibility from specific agents to the great gaseous cloud of the unnamable and unblamable. The classic example is "Mistakes were made."

In 2007, this letter was sent to physicians affected by a security breach.

DEPARTMENT OF VETERANS AFFAIRS

1615 Woodward St.

Austin, TX 78772

—, MD

Dear —, MD:

I am writing to you, as the Director of the Veterans Integrated Service Network (VISN) 7 in Atlanta, Georgia, to inform you that I have been notified that a portable computer hard drive used by an employee of the Birmingham Veterans Affairs (VA) Medical Center is missing. This portable hard drive was used to back-up information contained on a VA employee's office computer, related to research projects with which the employee was involved. A file on the portable hard drive included information from the Unique Physician Identification Number (UPIN) Directory dated 2004, which includes demographic information and identifiers, such as the UPIN, dates of birth, state license numbers, business addresses, and employer identification numbers (EIN). In the case of your information, we believe the EIN was your Social Security Number. This file was obtained by VA from the Centers for Medicare & Medicaid Services (CMS) for the purpose of conducting research on veterans' health care.

The Birmingham VA Medical Center has conducted extensive physical searches and has involved local police and Federal investigative resources, and a reward is being offered; however, the hard drive remains missing. To prevent further security breaches or losses, we have taken immediate measures to protect the integrity and security of all personally identifiable information including prohibition of the use of external drives and the required encryption of personally identifiable information when authorized distribution is required.

An independent risk analysis was conducted as required by law, and risk mitigation recommendations are being implemented immediately. VA will contact you shortly by mail to offer a credit monitoring service at no cost to you. In the mean time, one precaution we recommend is for you to request a free credit report from one or more of the three national credit bureaus by calling the toll free number 1-877-322-8228. The credit bureaus may also be contacted at:

Equifax
P.O. Box 740241
Atlanta, GA 30374
1-800-685-1111
Experian
P.O. Box 9554
Allen, TX 75013
1-888-397-3742

TransUnion
P.O. Box 2000
Chester, PA 19022
1-800-916-8800

More information about credit protection, including placing a "fraud alert" on your accounts, is available by calling the Federal Trade Commission at its toll free number, 1-877-438-4338, or by visiting its Website, http://www.ftc.gov/

If you have questions concerning this letter, the Birmingham VA Medical Center has established a dedicated call center to answer your questions. Please contact us toll free at 1-877-xxx-xxxx from 6:00 am to 9:00 pm CT, or email us at < address suppressed >.

We at VA take information security and privacy very seriously. We apologize for any inconvenience or concern this situation may cause, but we believe it is important for you to be fully informed of any potential risk to you.

Sincerely,

[digitized signature]

Lawrence A. Biro

Network Director, VISN 7

63.1.5.2 Initial Problems. On May 3, 2006, a career civil servant at the Department of Veterans Affairs (VA) violated official policy by taking computer disks containing PII about 26.5 million veterans home with him. The disks were stolen from his home.[11] Two weeks after officials learned of the theft, the VA disclosed the incident to the public and set up a Website and an 800-number to provide veterans and with information and a channel for reporting possible identity theft.[12]

The USA.gov Website put up a page called "Latest Information on Veterans Affairs Data Security"[13] with answers to frequently asked questions; the VA itself also continued issuing press releases.[14]

In early June 2006, the VA announced that the stolen data might include PII about up to 1.1 million active-duty troops, 430,000 members of the National Guard, and 645,000 members of the reserves.[15] Reactions from a coalition of veterans groups were immediate: They launched a class-action lawsuit demanding full disclosure of exactly who was affected by the theft and seeking $1,000 in damages for each victim.[16]

The VA struggled to cope with the bad publicity and potential legal liability resulting from the May theft. On May 26, 2006, Secretary of VAR James Nicholson issued a Directive to all VA supervisors, in which he wrote:

> Having access to such sensitive information brings with it a grave responsibility. It requires that we protect Federal property and information, and that it shall not be used for other than authorized activities and only in authorized locations. As managers, supervisors, and team leaders it is your responsibility to ensure that your staff is aware of and adheres to all Federal and VA policies and guidelines governing privacy protected material. I also expect each and every one of you to know what sensitive and confidential data your subordinates, including contractors, have access to and how, when and where that data is used, especially in those cases where it is used or accessed off-site.[17]

On May 30, 2006, the VA fired the analyst "responsible for data loss" and announced changes in the administration of INFOSEC in the organization.[18] The press release made no mention of who was responsible for allowing anybody to store unencrypted PII on VA computers or media.

Coincidentally, at the end of May, the Government Accountability Office (GAO) issued a report: "GAO-06-612: Homeland Security: Guidance and Standards Are Needed for Measuring the Effectiveness of Agencies' Facility Protection Efforts."[19] The report specifically named the VA as requiring "guidance and standards for measuring performance in federal government facility protection."

On June 21, 2006, the VA announced that it would provide free credit monitoring for everyone affected by the data theft in May.[20]

But worse was yet to come.

63.1.5.3 Systematic Management Failures.

On June 14, 2006, Linda D. Koontz, Director, Information Management Issues, and Gregory C. Wilshusen, Director, Information Security Issues of the Government Accountability Office of the United States, offered testimony before the Committee on Veterans' Affairs, House of Representatives. The GAO report on their analysis and recommendations later appeared as GAO-06-866.[21] Highlights of their analysis included these comments:

> For many years, significant concerns have been raised about VA's information security—particularly its lack of a robust information security program, which is vital to avoiding the compromise of government information, including sensitive personal information. Both GAO and the department's inspector general have reported recurring weaknesses in such areas as access controls, physical security, and segregation of incompatible duties. The department has taken steps to address these weaknesses, but these have not been sufficient to establish a comprehensive information security program. For example, it is still developing plans to complete a security incident response program to monitor suspicious activity and cyber alerts, events, and incidents. Without an established and implemented security program, the department will continue to have major challenges in protecting its information and information systems from security breaches such as the one it recently experienced.

Two related reports appeared about a week later with specific comments about the May 2006 data breach[22] and about the overall challenges facing the VA and the Department of Defense (DoD) in protecting PII of active-duty and retired military personnel.[23]

At the end of June 2006, the laptop and external hard drive stolen on May 3 from the consultant's home were recovered. Forensic examination suggested that the data had not been accessed. This good news suggested that the disaster might blow over.

It was not to be.

The Inspector General (IG) of the VA, George Opfer, released a report on July 11 severely criticizing senior managers of the VA for their lackadaisical response to the original theft of unencrypted PII. The inadequate data security policies had not yet been corrected.[24] VA secretary James Nicholson responded to the IG's report with assurances that the agency had "embarked on a course of action to wholly improve its cyber and information security programs."[25]

63.1.5.4 Continued Problems.

On Monday, August 7, 2006, Secretary Nicholson announced that a Unisys subcontractor working for the VA offices in Philadelphia and Pittsburgh had reported that his desktop computer was missing. The computer contained PII for 18,000 and possibly up to 38,000 veterans.[26]

A week later (August 14), the VA announced that it would spend $3.7 million on encryption software and would encrypt data on all the department's computers and external data storage media or devices. Installation would begin Friday, August 18.[27]

In mid-September, the stolen Unisys desktop computer with VA data was located and a temporary employee working on subcontract to Unisys was arrested and charged in the theft.[28]

In October 2006, the Congressional Committee on Oversight and Government Reform published a report on data losses in U.S. Government agencies since January 1, 2003.[29] There were 788 incidents in 19 agencies—in addition to hundreds of incidents at the VA. The report's findings included these bald assertions:

1. Data loss is a government-wide occurrence. …
2. Agencies do not always know what has been lost. The letters received by the Committee demonstrate that, in many cases, agencies do not know what information has been lost or how many individuals could be impacted by a particular data loss. Similarly, agencies do not appear to be tracking all possible losses of personal information, making it likely that their reports to the committee are incomplete. For example, the Department of Justice reports that, prior to the May 2006 Veterans Administration data breach, "the Department did not track the content of lost, stolen, or otherwise compromised devices."
3. Physical security of data is essential. Only a small number of the data breaches reported to the Committee were caused by hackers breaking into computer systems online. The vast majority of data losses arose from physical thefts of portable computers, drives, and disks, or unauthorized use of data by employees.
4. Contractors are responsible for many of the reported breaches. Federal agencies rely heavily on private sector contractors for information technology management services. Thus, many of the reported data breaches were the responsibility of contractors.

Alas, the best-laid plans of VA administrators gang aft agley, and on October 31, 2006, VA officials informed 1,400 veterans that their PII had been on unencrypted data disks sent by mail from the VA clinic in Muskogee, Oklahoma, on May 10, June 10, and July 10, which were lost. A spokesperson for the hospital explained the three-month delay as being due to the "wait for officials in Washington to approve the wording of the letter." Approval arrived October 26. There was no explanation of why the data were unencrypted, nor why two additional disks were mailed out after the May 10 disk was lost. A report on this incident dated November 3, 2006, by Rick Maze in the *Federal Times*[30] also indicated that a laptop computer from the VA hospital in Manhattan was stolen on September 8 from a computer locked to a cart in a locked room in a locked corridor—and that the data on the stolen machine was deliberately not encrypted despite policy because "a decision had been made not to encrypt data being used for medical purposes."

And more was to come in February 2007.

63.1.5.5 Analyses and Responses. On Friday, February 2, 2007, Secretary of Veterans Affairs Jim Nicholson announced that a VA employee in the VA medical center in Birmingham, Alabama, had reported an external hard drive as missing on January 22. According to Representative Spencer Bachus (R-AL), the backup hard drive contained PII on up to 48,000 veterans—and despite VA regulations promulgated in 2006, as many as 20,000 of those records were not encrypted.[31] A week later, the VA admitted that the hard drive actually contained PII about 535,000 patients and 1.3 million doctors.[32] It was that loss that led to the letter quoted in the first part of this section.[33]

A few weeks later, the GAO released the closest thing to an exasperated blast of which government workers are capable. In testimony before the Subcommittee on Oversight and Investigations, Committee on Veterans' Affairs, House of Representatives on February 28, 2007, GAO Director of Information Security Issues Gregory C. Wilshusen presented a report entitled "Veterans Affairs Needs to Address

Long-Standing Weaknesses."[34] The summary on page 2 of the PDF file includes this commentary:

> For many years, GAO has raised significant concerns about VA's information security—particularly its lack of a comprehensive information security program, which is vital to safeguarding government information. The figure below details information security weaknesses that GAO identified from 1998 to 2005. As shown, VA had not consistently implemented appropriate controls for (1) limiting, preventing, and detecting electronic access to sensitive computerized information; (2) restricting physical access to computer and network equipment to authorized individuals; (3) segregating incompatible duties among separate groups or individuals; (4) ensuring that changes to computer software were authorized and timely; or (5) providing continuity of computerized systems and operations. The department's IG has also reported recurring weaknesses throughout VA in such areas as access controls, physical security, and segregation of incompatible duties. In response, the department has taken actions to address these weaknesses, but these have not been sufficient to establish a comprehensive information security programs. As a result, sensitive information has remained vulnerable to inadvertent or deliberate misuse, loss, or improper disclosure. Without an established and implemented security program, the department will continue to have major challenges in protecting its systems and information from security breaches.

In early March 2007, the VA reacted to the January 22 loss of the portable hard drive. CIO Robert Howard promulgated a policy restricting the use of portable data storage devices. Only flash drives smaller than 2 GB—and only those issued by the VA's CIO office itself—would be permitted on the VA network or computers. Encryption would be used throughout the system, just like the assurance issued in August 2006 about spending $3.7 million on encryption tools.[35] In addition, the CIO announced sweeping changes in security administration, with promotion of five deputy CIOs to the rank of assistant secretaries for these functions: application development, information security, operations and maintenance, resource management, and strategic planning.

As of late May 2007, federal agencies announced that they would stop storing Social Security numbers and other PII wherever possible.[36]

For an extensive compilation of additional cases of interest, see the "Chronology of Data Breaches: Security Breaches 2005–Present," managed by the Privacy Rights Clearinghouse.[37]

63.2 RESPONSIBILITIES.

Modern information processing philosophy transcends the boundaries of the computer room and demands the consistent delivery and collection of data to and from remote sections of the organization. Once this operating mode is extensively used, the company becomes dependent on its continued availability. Any shutdown or cutoff in service can be disastrous, unless the company is able promptly to revise operations, in order to continue vital activities. Central computers, local servers, workstations, and the network are essential to the operating environment.

Computer security includes the protection of confidentiality, control, integrity, authenticity, availability, and utility of information.[38] Computer security encompasses the total infrastructure for maintenance and delivery of information, including physical computer hardware, supporting equipment, communication systems, logical processes defined by software, and the human factors that support and possibly threaten this infrastructure.

Computer security is inseparable from the basic structure of the information processing system; one cannot and should not design a system without including security as an underlying strategy. The objectives and properties of secure systems must be considered collectively from their inception.

Software, systems, and networks should be designed to ensure information protection that corresponds to business needs. There are many steps that can be taken to do this, but managers must place a high priority on making it happen. Managers are in a position to see what the business needs actually are, much more so than the typical INFOSEC analyst or engineer. A prime example is e-commerce Website management. No reputable site allows transactions without minimal SSL encryption. A savvy INFOSEC manager will track all information from the setting up of the SSL tunnel, all the way through the shipping process, and beyond into the storage of information gathered during any transaction, and ensure that security is not lacking at any juncture in the process. If the data are not securely stored while sitting in a database, the whole process falls apart.

The ability of a system to ensure accuracy, reliability, and confidentiality is a basic building block. The collective system (hardware, software, communications, and people) must be able to maintain and process data correctly, and move traffic (transactions, inquiries, commands, etc.) from its origins to the intended destinations, without unauthorized modification or disclosure and without misrepresentation, forgery, or other breaches of authenticity. Reliable performance is essential. Any failures should be orderly and predictable, with adequate detection methods to provide timely evidence of failure and to permit prompt corrective actions. Hardware/software limitations should be known and documented, as should load limits. Bounds checking, at a minimum, should be implemented in all software to avoid buffer overflows. Any inputs that are not checked should be documented, and measures should be put in place to detect possible abuses.

Suspicious user activity should be detectable through appropriate analysis of logfiles. The network and its data should be protected from contamination or outside interference using appropriate gateway security devices and other intrusion prevention systems. Firewalls must be present, updated, and frequently reviewed, along with intrusion detection systems and intrusion prevention systems (IDS/IPS), and all logs should be centralized and scrutinized. Measures should be put in place to ensure that data transmitted are the same as the data received and that error correction is used wherever possible.

Service-level agreements should define goals for efficient response and adequate capacity, in order to support acceptable performance. Systems should be able to recover quickly from either short-term or long-term disruptions. Backup measures, including data backup and equipment backup[39] and tested incident response, contingency, and recovery plans, should be in place.[40] Appropriate cost recovery measures should also be in place.[41] Prevention of harm is of primary importance.

Single points of failures should be avoided. Avoid dependence on single equipment devices or single communications pathways. Web servers should be clustered, and databases should be replicated across various servers and placed in different geographic regions. Avoid overloading the network at peak activity periods. Provide environmental backup (redundant power, air-conditioning, heating and other support systems, limited equipment access, etc.) to reduce other exposures.[42]

Management should have the capability to limit who can access the systems, how much capacity can be used for each purpose or function, what purposes are allowed, what data are accessible and transmittable for each user, and what connections can be made. Technical measures include access control (system access, resource restrictions), logon password control, alternative identification methods (personal tokens, digital signatures, biometric authentication), callback connections, network isolation from public networks, firewalls, and physical security of system components.[43]

Administrative measures include publication of policies, standards, and guidelines; screening of personnel; security awareness training; system change control procedures, including security criteria in system design; and monitoring system activity and quality.[44]

In addition, management should use the audit function as an independent arbiter to measure compliance with policies, standards, and guidelines as well as to assess the adequacy of technical protection. The system and its network should preserve and display evidence of use, behavior, and content, and should record deviations from expected use.[45]

Managers are responsible for specific tasks or functions to the extent that they make decisions about business processes and suffer the consequences or reap the benefits of those decisions.

63.2.1 Policy Management. Managers spend more time on people issues than on technical issues. The right people must be hired for each position.[46] Employees who do not work responsibly and competently must either be brought up to the proper standard or let go. Employees who do their jobs properly must be kept satisfied, lest they move to another organization. Management in the IT world must ensure compliance with corporate policies.[47] Compliance with policies includes motivation, supervision, judgment, and adaptation.

63.2.2 Motivation. Employees need motivation to pay attention to INFOSEC policies, which often are perceived as a nuisance, interfering with the fundamental goals of the enterprise. Upper management, in particular, must set an example by following enterprise policies; when top managers are seen to ignore policies, the people reporting to them quickly imitate their behavior, and the problem spreads throughout the organization. For example, if the CEO refuses to wear a picture badge, the vice presidents (VPs) will quickly follow suit because they will associate *not* wearing badges with high status. Similarly, the directors reporting to VPs will start dropping their badges, and so within a few months the entire hierarchy will be convinced that no one but stock clerks should wear badges. Sometime later, the stock clerks will be resisting badges too.

According to *Computerworld* writer Mary Pratt, writing in 2006:

> The risk that employees pose is significant. They can fall prey to social engineering, a fancy term for being conned. They can ignore company policy by failing to encrypt sensitive data. Or they might install unauthorized software that can corrupt the system.
>
> Think you're well protected? Recent findings from the Computing Technology Industry Association might convince you otherwise. In this year's CompTIA information security study, 59% of the organizations surveyed indicated that their latest security breaches were the result of human error alone. That's up from 47% last year.[48]

A survey by NFO Prognostics highlighted that 66 percent of the companies surveyed believe that staff training or certification has improved their IT security through increased awareness and proactive risk identification.[49]

Since people can be the company's greatest strength against attacks, training employees should be a high priority in any organization. At Stop and Shop, in February 2007, employees noticed suspicious activity; they saw four people tampering with the keypads for credit/debit card authorization units. The employees notified police at once, and the suspects were arrested. That kind of quick thinking and commitment can make an enormous difference in the effectiveness of security systems of all kinds—and it depends on management support and motivation.[50]

Some managers think that punishment is the only motivation that can change behavior; but everything known about human psychology shows that reward is more powerful.[51] Reward is not limited to salary increases and bonuses; sometimes the most effective way to keep IT employees satisfied and productive is to provide training. The IT world is evolving, and the demand for competent staff has never been higher. Most employees want to feel that their employers value their services and that they are worth an investment to improve staff competence. Training employees, and providing challenging opportunities for the exercise of intelligence, serves the interests of both employer and employee. See Section 63.5.3 for more details about education.

Challenging employees in other ways can be highly motivating. For example, managers can encourage staff to prepare and deliver presentations at internal meetings and at security conferences. Some examples of useful conferences are SecureWorld-Expo, InfoSecWorld, and NetSec. Motivated employees can lead special interest group discussions at conferences (such as RSA, SANS, etc.) and so develop a Web of relationships that promote sharing of knowledge, and that enhance their self-image. There are also security contests to test their skills, such as the Honeynet forensics contest.

The Honeynet Project provides archives of past security challenges that allow security staff to challenge their technical skills, as well as to learn and teach new tricks of the trade. The Honeynet Project posts these challenges on the Web,[52] and tasks would-be contestants to unravel what the hacks were and how they were performed. Along with finding out what had happened, judging was also based on how much information was uncovered and how this information was communicated. These challenges have been solved, but they are still valuable lessons for any INFOSEC staff. Many other challenges pop up frequently and easily can be found using Google.

Many journals and Web-based magazines are ready to accept articles written by professionals in the field. Not only does writing solidify employees' knowledge and build their own confidence, but it also instills confidence in the entire team. Writing and teaching help the enterprise, as well as its clients and partners, to view the security team as a real benefit, at the same time that the organization develops a strong reputation for excellence in security.

Another way for management to make the security team more cohesive is to build camaraderie. A monthly pizza party or an occasional outing to a sports event can do a lot to ease stress and to help everyone to know each other. Having good friends at work can reduce turnover and motivate employees to do their best, not only for the rather abstract goal of doing good for the enterprise, but also because of a commitment to their colleagues.

To help encourage a higher level of expertise and to establish a feeling of belonging, periodic "brown bag" lunch sessions can be effective. At each session, a different team member can be designated to present an informed talk or to lead a discussion on a topic of general interest. There could even be an informal call for papers, giving team members an opportunity to present valuable information in a professional manner.

At the same time, a little friendly competition can help as well. For example, if the enterprise has a training network that can be subdivided into several subnets, managers can organize a "tiger-team challenge." Each team will be responsible for securing a subnet or host and then given the opportunity to break into the subnet or host of another team. The winners would get both a reward and a responsibility. The reward can be as simple as pizza for the team or a modest trophy. The responsibility would be to present the exploits used and the ways to secure against them to the rest of the teams.

Another way to build the team is to support staff in choosing the areas in which they want to excel. There may be some overlap, but overlap can be good. Clearly, if there are two firewall experts, the enterprise is less vulnerable should one of them be absent. Furthermore, the firewall experts can provide better-quality assurance by discussing alternatives when planning a change and better-quality control by checking each other's work. It can also help to have the security team members switch roles periodically, both to ensure that no one gets into a rut and to contribute to the challenges presented when a change is made.

Last, almost nothing is more infuriating than being expected to accomplish a task without the necessary resources. Adequate time to get a task done is always an important issue, as many people have several tasks to do, and each of the tasks may be seen as critical by someone. A manager should be willing to give the team all of the resources it needs to complete a task in the allotted time, or it should be made clear to other departments, or to higher management, what the realistic expectations are for the completion of such tasks, if required resources are lacking. If expectations are properly managed, there should be less conflict and fewer problems.

It is useful to view management not as separate from the IT security team, but as an integral part of it. This allows management to contribute directly toward the employees' enthusiasm as well as to detect early warning signals of impending trouble. A manager who does not spend time listening to the team members, or who does not understand what their jobs involve at a technical level, will not be respected by the team. Lack of respect will block communication and keep the department from becoming a solid, effectively functioning unit.

63.2.3 Supervision. What we know about damage to computer systems indicates that errors and omissions are a major source of harm. Poorly trained employees make mistakes, but so do trained employees who have become careless. Managers should examine performance records as a normal part of their supervision of the security team. In particular, every incident that damages production systems should be analyzed to identify the *reasons* for the event. Careful technical support records and log files can help the team spot the crucial weaknesses, whether technical or human, that allowed compromise of the damaged systems.[53]

Analysis of security breaches of all kinds may reveal that certain employees are associated with unusually high or unusually low frequencies of particular problems. Careful analysis of both types of extremes can be helpful in spotting weaknesses for remediation and strengths from which to learn, so that the knowledge can be spread across the entire unit. However, managers must not assume that disproportionate numbers of problems are necessarily caused by the employees involved; for example, low rates of penetration during the day shift may be associated with lower rates of attack from hackers, who often work in the evenings or nights. Similarly, higher rates of security breaches may, after detailed study, be found to have been caused by factors entirely outside the control of a particular employee.

In addition to monitoring performance, managers must ensure that all employees know that they are being monitored. Warning notices, pre-employment agreements, and yearly policy reviews can ensure that staff develop no unwarranted expectation of privacy about their work.[54]

One of the most effective supervisory practices an INFOSEC team leader, or any other manager, can use is *managing by walking around*.[55] Managers should set aside time every week to observe the conditions and to absorb the atmosphere of the working areas. Visiting team members and hearing about their specific job experiences, both positive and negative, can only improve communications and motivation within the security team.

Not surprisingly, poor communication is a major enemy of effective team development. This poor communication can exist on multiple levels: among IT staff members, between staff members and IT management, and between IT and internal customers.[56]

Tools for enhancing communication include production control meetings, regular brief status review meetings, all-hands updates at which group members are required to give updates, and individual staff members to give technical updates, as well as establishing regular and thorough communication with internal customers and top management.

All members of the IT staff should be familiar with all lines of communication and with what behavior is expected of them in every scenario. Pushing communication awareness down through the organization appears to be an effective strategy.

63.2.4 Judgment and Adaptation. Management must not permit policies and procedures to keep the work from getting done. The comic strip *Dilbert*[57] has become popular largely because it caricatures managers who apply policy unintelligently; for example, in one real company known to the authors, managers decided to give the marketing department new laptops because of all the traveling they had to do. The managers then decided that to prevent theft, the laptops should be so securely fastened to the employees' desks that they could not be moved at all.

When security policies interfere with productivity, the correct solution is rarely black and white. Usually, neither dropping the policy nor enforcing it without change is appropriate. A hospital security administrator, for example, might note that a workstation in the emergency room is always logged on for the entire day, using the ID and password of the first person who logged on. Clearly, this violates the principle that everyone using the system must be positively identified and authenticated. Piggybacking on the first user damages the credibility of log files and makes it impossible to ascertain exactly which person is retrieving and modifying data at any time during the day. However, cracking down insensitively on the emergency room staff is a bad idea; chances are that the harried medical and support personnel are simply racing to get their work done saving lives. Logging off and on repeatedly is not a good method of identification and authentication in that environment. A reasonable security manager would listen to the employees, understand their point of view and their functional needs, and then explore technical alternatives to the usual ID-password technique. For example, the security manager might find that proximity cards or smart cards could meet the requirements at reasonable cost.[58]

Management must concern itself with safeguarding the resources under its jurisdiction. Just as investors seek both a high rate of return and reasonable safety for their investments, so must managers seek a high rate of return through the effective use of resources under their command and take adequate steps to protect the value of the resources.

The manager's function is essentially the management of resources: human resources and capital resources. In a computer operations environment, capital resources are represented by the investment in equipment and operating programs. Human resources are represented by the skills needed to operate and control both hardware and software facilities. Human capital resources are also represented by complete operating programs. Information is another form of resource, one that is often created as a product of data processing or concentrated at the computer facility, in order to utilize equipment resources better.

63.2.5 Management Failures. The most pervasive vulnerabilities in computer security are due to poor management. Efforts to contain or mitigate computer security exposures often fall short, or fail, because of management inadequacy, either of senior management or of operating management, or both. Sometimes the problem is simply inertia. Equally damaging is management lip service. In far too many instances, computer security is simply not taken seriously by senior management. Some of the most common management errors are listed next[59]:

- The belief that "if it hasn't been needed before, it probably will not be needed now." This is the default frame of mind, which is really self-insurance.
- Competition with other goals. Security measures use resources that are often needed for other activities. If security is regarded as an add-on burden rather than an integral part of the business process, it may be neglected or postponed.
- Lack of contribution to the bottom line. If security needs to be cost justified as an independent activity, it may be regarded as a target for elimination or reduction.
- Unwillingness properly to fund security activities. Far too often management is reluctant to commit all the resources needed for complete protection. A prime example is the lip-service contingency plan, published and display to the auditors, but never fully implemented.
- The explosive growth of the Internet and of the Web has increased the number of novice computer users into the hundreds of millions worldwide, cowering in fear at the latest hoax but cheerfully sending each other joke programs with embedded viruses. Some of these novices have taken on responsibilities for computer system management and have spread havoc within their organizations.
- The common occurrence of laptop theft has shown how vulnerable *any* kind of unencrypted removable media can be. Several companies have come under fire for not having a laptop encryption policy. This policy should be extended to any type of removable media (such as USB "thumb" drives) for certain types of information.
- Cell phones and PDAs are other technologies that need to be controlled. They are frequently connected to company computers, on the company network, to sync up with Microsoft Outlook email and calendars. These provide another potential point of entry for malicious software.
- Adults such as teachers and parents (many of them violating software copyrights without realizing they are breaking the law) have too often failed to teach children in their care how to resist the wiles of criminal hackers, virus writers, pornographers, and pedophiles. Some of these children have now grown up and become young managers who tolerate, encourage, or demand illegal acts by their employees.
- Some Websites are being managed by undertrained staff who know nothing about the years-old vulnerabilities they have left invitingly on their systems. These unfortunate people are stuck with inadequate resources and dismissive managers, who nevertheless blame them when the site is plastered with obscenities by teenagers with little or no conscience. Even worse, the Website may be used in a for-profit scheme by the ever-increasing legions of highly skilled professional hackers.
- In addition to the old vulnerabilities, these undertrained (or simply overworked) staff may also be introducing new vulnerabilities to their Websites by using new

tools or methodologies with no consideration of security. These new methodologies, such as the current AJAX (Asynchronous JavaScript and XML), may make use of old tools, but may do so in a new and insecure way.

- Some Web designers assume that users should trust mobile application programs (Java applets, ActiveX controls) whose origins are uncertain, whose documentation is unavailable, and whose actions may be pathological. Technically incompetent managers who take credit for their corporate Website may have no idea of what their Webmasters are doing—and failing to do—to protect their site.[60]
- Software makers, who ought to have known better, have blurred the distinction between document and program by adding automatic execution of macros to their word processors. Emailed Trojan horses are activated automatically when the message is opened. Bloated programs are routinely so full of bugs that consumers now think it is normal to pay money for a service release that fixes what never ought to have been released. Some managers with inadequate training take this situation as a given.
- Not necessarily a failure on just the part of management, software is often written without thought to security at all. Buffer overflows continue to be the "low-hanging fruit" for software hackers. Unfortunately, secure coding has been slow to catch on, but is showing signs of gaining traction today.[61] SANS has announced it will offer courses in secure coding, and there is an expanding list of books and papers on the subject. Perhaps as it becomes mainstream, universities will start requiring full courses in secure coding practices for computer programming degrees.
- We collectively continue to use Internet protocols devised decades ago and which have no provision for packet authentication. Criminals forge mail headers and packet headers with impunity, and use them for denial-of-service attacks and email spam. Network managers continue to avoid output filtering, which could reduce such attacks, because it is too low on their list of priorities, or because they have never considered their responsibility to other Internet users.
- Access control still relies largely on the outdated and ineffective use of passwords chosen by untrained users. Conveniently for criminal hackers, many users pick names of family members, people with whom they are having illicit romances, movie stars, pets, favorite sports teams, and the names of objects on their desks or visible from their windows. Some managers contribute to this situation by refusing to follow recommendations for better passwords and by refusing to consider better, or additional, authentication methods, such as tokens and biometrics.
- Some managers are loyal neither to colleagues nor to employers. The boom in firings and job-hopping has led to a shortsighted emphasis on the quarterly bottom line that makes investments in corporate security seem pointless.
- Security specialists still lack reliable data on network and computer intrusions. Although there are now some resources for information sharing, such as CERT/CC, many managers resist contributing to the knowledge base for fear that they and their enterprise will be embarrassed by their victimization.
- Social engineering is still one of the largest weaknesses of the security realm. Hackers really do not need to spend much time trying to break through defenses when so many users are perfectly willing to give them free access to go right through. While it is debatable whether training programs will ever be sufficient to overcome this, managers need to pay close attention to the "phishing" attacks that are now becoming more popular and more sophisticated.

Some organizations are taking steps to implement creative and memorable security awareness programs such as *Jeopardy*-style games, where workers compete to supply the right answers to security-related topics. Scavenger hunts on a company's Website are used to find the answers to 10 security-related questions.[62]

63.2.6 Risk Management.

Part of the data processing management task is to protect information resources and to safeguard the human capital resources that are essential to the services provided. Top management must concern itself with adequate recognition of the risks and must be assured that protective measures relative to these risks are in effect.[63]

In addition to the problems caused by management failures discussed in Section 63.2.5, managers should be aware of other risks in their work such as:

- **Physical hazards.** The likelihood of threats, whether accidental or intentional, that can result in physical damage. Fire, water, power loss, explosions, vandalism, terrorism, and civil disorder are all within this category.
- **Equipment malfunction.** The possibility of failures in computers and supporting equipment, such as printers, disk drives, and air conditioners.
- **Software malfunction.** The likelihood of loss and failures caused by computer programs, including operating system software and application programs.
- **Human error.** The threat of disruption or loss due to accidental or intentional action or inaction by employees. Computer operators, programmers, maintenance engineers, and service personnel can all precipitate loss.
- **Misuse of data.** The capacity for intentional misuse of information or facilities by perpetrators of crime, such as fraud, espionage, misrepresentation, forgery, or theft of data or other assets controlled by the data.
- **Loss of data.** The intentional or unintentional loss of information through disruption of the physical media on which the data resides, or the corruption or erasure of the data.

In addition to classifying risks by category of threats, it is useful to analyze risks by the magnitude of potential loss, the probability of loss, and the frequency and permanence of occurrence. Although magnitude of loss can be expressed in terms of time or dollars, it is more practical to use dollar cost as a common basis for measurement. Quantifications should be based on reasonable and supportable estimates of the costs associated with the actual occurrences of adverse events.

Threats must be evaluated in terms of probability or occurrence. True risk is difficult or impossible to measure, but a reasonable priority of risks may be established by evaluating the likelihood of occurrence in conjunction with the magnitude of potential loss for each threat. An aggregation of consequential costs for each threat, over a common time period, and based on the likelihood of occurrence for each threat, can serve to prioritize seemingly diverse risks.

Three convenient groupings for permanency of damage are disasters, solid failures, and transient failures. Disasters are serious and lengthy disruptions, usually resulting in costly reconstruction of data, alternative off-premises processing, loss of business, and high cost. Solid failures are those that require shutting down part or all of the system in order to take corrective action. Costs of solid failures may range from simple inconvenience to substantial loss of business. Transient failures are defined as temporary disruptions that do not recur regularly and therefore may be difficult to correct. Like solid failures, their costs can vary widely.

Quantification of risk is imprecise at best and varies greatly from one organization to another, and even among computer installations in the same organization. Nevertheless, quantification affords the means of ordering the relative importance of various threats and of substantiating the need for expenditure to counteract threats. In summary, even though probability estimates for specific events may represent intuitive feelings about likelihood, rather than actuarial knowledge, they can nonetheless serve as a basis for focusing discussion and planning.

An effective computer security program requires a balance of rationality and prudence. It also requires a continuing management commitment. Absolute security is an impossible dream unless one has unlimited resources—and even then, many responses would still have to be post hoc reactions to new threats, vulnerabilities, and attacks. Surprisingly, however, even on a modest budget, it is usually possible to achieve reasonable security. Many basic safeguards can be implemented for modest expenditures of time and effort. Many chapters in this *Handbook* discuss such basic safeguards.

63.3 LIABILITIES.

As discussed, security managers focus on minimizing liability by a practice generally known as *risk management*. Risk management is the traditional model for INFOSEC; ideally, one determines risk by identifying the threats and vulnerabilities and then evaluating the associated costs and probabilities of each type of incident. The probabilities are difficult to define, and as a result, much of risk management is, in practice, an intuitive, nonquantitative process.

Security managers face many liabilities. Some of the possible negative consequences of inadequate security include:

- Loss of revenue
- Loss of reputation
- Loss of business partner confidence
- Loss of consumer confidence
- Loss of enterprise valuation
- Failure of the entire enterprise

Each of these types of loss also involves a loss of trust. Trust is easy to lose, especially in uncertain economic climates, and it is, unfortunately, harder to regain trust than to establish and maintain it. It is necessary for managers to understand that security and privacy are integral to the services and products offered by the enterprise. Security and privacy must apply to data from customers, business partners, employees, and every other individual or entity with whom the enterprise comes into contact.

63.3.1 Stakeholders.

It is easy to think of only stockholders and customers when evaluating the potential costs of security breaches. However, it is useful to enumerate all of the people, and other entities, that are potentially affected by INFOSEC breaches. Such *stakeholders* can include:

- **Stockholders.** People and organizations owning stock in a privately held or publicly traded enterprise
- **Employees.** Managers and workers depending on an enterprise for their livelihood

- **Customers.** People and organizations depending on fulfillment of contractual obligations by the enterprise
- **Potential customers.** Those who might want to do business with the enterprise
- **Suppliers.** Those depending on the enterprise for acceptance of materials and services followed by payment as per contract
- **Data subjects.** People or other entities about whom an enterprise stores, manipulates, and reports data
- **Regulatory agencies and law enforcement.** People and organizations devoted to enforcing statutory regulations and laws
- **Users of other systems victimized by means of a compromised system.** Innocent bystanders who may be harmed, through no fault of their own, when a compromised system is used as an intermediary to launch attacks on an ultimate target

Managers must explore the potential consequences of specific types of security incidents with respect to all of the stakeholders. This wider analysis contributes significantly to effective risk management.

63.3.2 Due Diligence of Care. Due diligence of care in INFOSEC refers to the research and analysis carried out in establishing that risks have been minimized to an extent consistent with industry standards. Due diligence investigations, typically, are crucial in mergers and acquisitions, where unanticipated liabilities resulting can result in financial disaster and legal culpability.

Unfortunately, just as there is no sound basis for assertions about computer crime rates, there is not even the most rudimentary basis for asserting that any given level of security represents adequate care for information. What, precisely, is the right length for the asymmetric encryption key used in protecting confidential email sent across the Internet? Does failing to update antivirus signatures daily constitute a violation of due diligence, or is once a week good enough? Does due diligence in securing a manufacturing system require installation of an intrusion detection system? What about lacking an IDS in a hospital or a bank? Is a computer emergency response team a requirement to demonstrate due care in protecting information assets?

Attempts at defining security standards have not yet convinced more than a few enterprises to conform to their recommendations; the INFOSEC field is not yet at the point where quality assurance was a decade ago, when the International Standards Organization promulgated ISO 9000 certification, and it became widely used in manufacturing plants around the world.

Sensitivity to due diligence of care should, at a minimum, begin with consideration of legal and regulatory requirements for the protection of information. Contractual obligations with any and all stakeholders will determine the required degree of responsiveness to intrusion, and may help determine whether to cooperate with law enforcement authorities to investigate any breach of security.[64]

63.3.3 Downstream Liability. In recent years, a growing number of security experts and attorneys have predicted that the doctrine of downstream liability would become a significant factor in pushing management toward better security. Downstream liability is an application of the legal theory of contributory negligence as it applies to INFOSEC. In turn, contributory negligence refers to reckless endangerment of others, "reckless" meaning without consideration of the consequences and endangerment resulting from putting others at risk of harm. The term "downstream" refers to the conventional model in which the source of data is viewed as being upstream of the recipient of those data; thus if someone compromises a university computer system and uses those computers to launch an attack on a bank, the bank is viewed as downstream from the university. Conceivably, the bank's attorneys could accuse the university administrators of negligence for allowing their computers to be compromised and therefore claim damages.

Keeping in mind that the authors are not attorneys, and that the information being discussed here is in no sense legal advice (for legal advice, consult an attorney), examples of what might be construed in a court of law as downstream liability include:

- Distributing virus-infected documents through email because all antivirus mechanisms have deliberately been turned off
- Allowing a malefactor to install *zombie* software on a poorly configured system and involving that compromised system in a distributed denial-of-service attack[65]
- Failing to install patches for a well-known and years-old vulnerability, thus allowing a criminal hacker to attack a third party via a root compromise of the poorly secured system[66]
- Allowing private information such as credit card numbers belonging to thousands of people to be stolen and distributed on the Internet, for use in credit card fraud
- Providing an unsecured email server that provides an open spam-relay point for junk email, with a forged REPLY-TO address, to flood millions of mailboxes with unwanted email, thereby causing thousands of bounce messages and angry accusations to clog the mail system of the innocent owner of the forged REPLY-TO address
- Having an employee who sends out thousands of fraudulent notices using the employer's email system to libel a competitor, causing depression of that competitor's sales and stock price
- Configuring a *honey-pot* system on the enterprise network to attract the attention of criminal hackers—who then turn around and use the honey pot to attack a third party

It is important to note that *honey pots*, while used as security measures to attract a hacker to a specific server for the purpose of gathering data on an attack, do in fact introduce security holes. The honey pot is a live server, with intentional vulnerabilities built in, connected to a company's network. Once penetrated, an attacker may use it as a platform from which to launch future attacks. Special safeguards must be designed to prevent this.

One possible safeguard is to prevent any traffic that leaves the honey pot to actually go anywhere, or to trap it on what might be termed a "honey logger," a server designed to simply catch all the traffic for the purpose of analyzing it.

As of this writing, there appear to have been no cases in which a plaintiff has successfully sued an enterprise for damages on the basis of downstream liability linked to inadequate security. However, in December 2000, FirstNet Online (Management) Limited filed a lawsuit in the Court of Sessions in Edinburgh, Scotland, against Nike, Inc., apparently an innocent victim. The incident began in June 2000, when someone hacked the DNS (Domain Name System) by filing incorrect data for resolution of the nike.com domain with Network Solutions, Inc., which is charged with the responsibility of managing acquisition and retention of certain classes of domain names. All subsequent attempts to reach nike.com were redirected to the s11.org domain, an activist site devoted to fighting globalization. The redirection allegedly caused serious harm to the Web-hosting service for s11.org; according to the plaintiffs, FirstNET Online "experienced an 1800% increase of traffic over the 46 hours it took to correct the problem completely."[67] Blaming Nike administrators for failing to protect the password required for updating the DNS records at Network Solutions, the plaintiffs demanded compensation for the expenses incurred. Nike officials rejected such accusations and blamed Network Solutions for allowing the redirection of Internet traffic to the s11.org site. Readers will want to search the Web for later developments in this interesting case.

63.3.4 Audits. As managers attempt to manage security according to nebulous principles of due care, they must remember that in many enterprises, IT and INFOSEC departments are seen as being equivalent to the police. Many people in these departments have privileged access to other people's secrets; for example, they can read all email, and can often tell exactly what Websites' employees have been visiting. In some environments, network monitors allow administrators and security personnel to activate keystroke monitoring and to view in real time the appearance of any given terminal or workstation on the network. Because of the enormous power of these people, managers must ensure that their levels of access are not abused.

Information systems auditors are responsible for keeping the technical and security staff honest. In some larger enterprises, there is a department of internal audit whose director reports to the same level as other officers, such as the CEO and CFO. In other cases, third-party auditors monitor adherence to policy, standards, and procedures.[68]

Security audits are often feared, and with good reason. In general, many audits are performed with the focus of finding fault. This approach is counterproductive and unnecessarily stressful. The point of an audit should not be to find the maximum number of offenses but rather to assess the level of compliance. The most important outcome of an audit is finding areas of potential improvement. A nonadversarial style facilitates positive results; thus, an auditing team should provide constructive suggestions for improvement wherever possible.

An auditing team also needs to listen to those being audited. Although a particular network may not be configured to full compliance with security policy, there may be reasons for this apparent failure. For example, suppose a specific patch was required by security policy to have been installed on a Solaris server, but a particular Solaris server did not comply. An auditor might report a failure without further investigation even though, in reality, the patch might have been installed but found to be incompatible with a critical application. Just like managers, audit teams need to see the big picture, not just the rules and procedures. The main point is that all audits must be done with the needs of the business in mind. It does no good to have a process that gets in the way of the business at hand. Instead, to enable the business, alternative measures must be found. That is the job of the auditor—to help ensure compliance and to provide another set of eyes that can see to it that all needs are taken care of.

To prove due diligence, auditing is a must. Generally, third-party audits create more trust, as a third party has no bias about the findings. However, it is important to ensure that a third-party audit firm maintains its independence. It can be risky to use a small firm that bases more than a modest fraction of its revenue on income from any one client. However, it may be undesirable to have the same large firm perform accounting or auditing functions while also serving as security consultants.

63.4 COMPUTER MANAGEMENT FUNCTIONS.

The job of the manager is to provide leadership, and it must be provided in an organized and creative manner. Management is dynamic, not static, and the manager must deal with change—change in the organizational environment, change in people, and change in the methods of management. Unfortunately, the laws of inertia apply to management as to physics, and change will often be resisted. The challenge to the manager is to manage change.

Even a successful security program will usually result in higher costs, as well as in changes in the organizational structure and in the working environment. To compound the problems, the benefits of the security program are not highly visible. Security is essentially preventive and is often regarded as capital expenses and overhead of questionable value. Too often, upper managers dismiss proposals for better security by pointing out that there have been no breaches of security in the last year; thus the more successful the security program, the less evidence there is to support its usefulness. To counteract this circular and destructive reasoning, security managers should compile evidence of the numbers and types of attempted penetrations identified by intrusion detection systems[69] and attempted malfeasance by authorized users identified by system and application logging.[70]

The tools of the manager include planning, organizing, integrating, and controlling. These are not independent activities that can be completely separated; rather they represent a matrix. Taken as an interrelated process, they achieve balance and direction.

63.4.1 Planning for Computer Security.

The planning function of management includes the determination of objectives, policies, priorities, schedules, standards, and strategy.

It is important to define the scope and purpose of a computer security program in terms of objectives. There should be a clear statement of results to be achieved within a given period of time. Security objectives must be balanced with other organizational objectives, because conflicts may arise. As an example, the need for controlled access will naturally conflict with desires for user flexibility and convenience. Objectives should be imaginative and responsive to change and conflict.

Planning for computer security requires the participation of top management, so that security objectives can be reconciled with general organizational objectives and with financial priorities. It is also necessary to coordinate security activities between data processing and all the other areas of the organization. Auditing, insurance, legal, financial, and other groups are affected by, and should contribute to, a computer security program.[71]

The objectives, policies, schedules, and standards that result from the planning process need to be communicated throughout the organization. While this is generally true for all planning, it is especially crucial to the success of a security program, which may conflict with existing corporate culture.[72] Finally, feedback is essential to permit recognition of failures and departures from plans. Only by monitoring results is it possible to take corrective action or to readjust the objectives, policies, plans, schedules, and standards to the practicalities of the real world.

63.4.2 Organizing.

Organization is the process of marshaling resources, grouping activities and responsibilities, and establishing relationships that will enable people to work together most effectively in determining and accomplishing the objectives of an enterprise.

The important elements of organization for computer security include:

- Obtaining resources of personnel, money, and facilities adequate to accomplish the assigned mission
- Fitting responsibly into the organizational pattern
- Assigning responsibility and authority to individuals
- Formulating supporting methods and procedures
- Measuring organizational effectiveness

Traditionally, the organizing function is concerned with grouping activities into manageable components and grouping human resources into logical relationships to accomplish the desired results. It would be unusual to find an enterprise that was designed with an optimum structure to achieve security at the expense of other goals. Security is not an independent activity, nor does it represent the primary goal of a data processing organizational element. Data processing departments are usually organized into units that reflect the nature of the work performed, or user relationships, or some other structure designed to achieve an adequate service level for the end user. Security measures quite often conflict with the service objectives. That conflict is all the more reason why security must be managed in order to be effective. It is also motivation for creating a separate functional activity, particularly in large organizations, so that INFOSEC can be administered independently of competing activities.

63.4.3 Integrating. Computer security is frequently an afterthought to the organization of the data processing function. Security is also perceived as a passive activity. As a result, responsibility for security is often assigned haphazardly. Security should not merely be superimposed but, instead, should be carefully fitted into the organizational structure. Some important considerations are:

- Accountability for specific security tasks should be included in formal job definitions of every job level.
- Training programs should include a complete review of security objectives and policies, as well as details relating to assigned security tasks.
- Supervisory and management personnel should be assigned responsibility for both performance and attitude of staff with respect to security.
- Certain line or staff positions could include responsibility for overall security, or a grouping of security tasks, or measurement and monitoring of security. It may be convenient to combine security and control of data processing into a single function. Monitoring of security effectiveness is sometimes assigned to the data processing auditor.
- Primary responsibility for INFOSEC should not be assigned to those with inherently conflicting priorities; for example, it is a bad practice to assign major responsibility for security to the chief of operations, the director of software development, or the vice president of finance.
- Information systems security should be coordinated and reviewed with security specialists in other areas of the organization. In a manufacturing concern the plant security personnel, or in a bank the bank security officer, should be consulted. It

may be desirable to assign monitoring responsibility for security housekeeping tasks to these specialists.

- Whenever possible, policies should be translated into written guidelines and procedures to provide the detailed requirements for each task. Standards for performance of each activity must be formulated and applied.

Initiating and monitoring the accomplishment of objectives according to established plans requires skillful leadership. The integration function has a direct bearing on the success of a security program. Without effective leadership, security can become a farce. With leadership, a security program can overcome its basic passivity and truly enhance the utility of information systems. Management must embrace and inspire the concept of security as an everyday fact of life. But beyond transmitting a positive attitude of acceptance, management must also be concerned with testing and improving security. The security program is dynamic rather than static. Management's role must be one of continued concern in order to identify, adopt, and adapt better methods to accomplish corporate security objectives.

63.4.4 Controlling. The final process in the management cycle is measuring and controlling. It is the function that is concerned with achieving cost-effective results and includes establishing standards, improving methods, examining results, and adjusting the organizational mechanism for corrective action.

The basis for effective control is the use of consistent techniques for measurement and the application of standards for comparison and interpretation. Results should be analyzed promptly, as feedback to effect corrective action. Control systems need not be burdensome or elaborate, but they should be consistent, and they should allow for flexibility and adjustment. Management action is the end product of control. Mistakes in original objectives and plans are forgivable, but failure to recognize and react to mistakes can only compound the problem, add to costs, and undermine the effective use of valuable resources.

63.5 SECURITY ADMINISTRATION.

In large organizations, an independent security administration function is often the most effective method for accomplishing the overall objective of improved INFOSEC.

63.5.1 Staffing the Security Function. The importance of INFOSEC has given rise to a new management specialty, consisting of professionals involved in the planning and administration of protection for the integrity and security of automated information assets. Titles such as INFOSEC administrator, computer security manager, information systems security officer, and chief INFOSEC officer have been used to describe these roles.

Coordination of the INFOSEC function requires a combination of managerial and technical talents. The successful administrator must be a superior communicator capable of selling the concept of security and maintaining security awareness at all levels of the organization. Sufficient technical knowledge is important, so that the INFOSEC administrator can evaluate and initiate appropriate technological solutions to meet corporate INFOSEC policies and to counteract threats. While technical skill, in the form of a data processing background, is important, a broader range of capabilities is needed for maximum effectiveness. The ideal security administrator should possess the ability to communicate with all levels of management and should have good knowledge of related functions such as auditing, internal control, and general security. It is also important to have some knowledge of the industry within which the organization operates.

The administration of INFOSEC can be centralized or decentralized, depending on the needs of the organization. Where multiple data center locations are involved, the decentralized approach may be more appropriate to accomplish the details of administration. However, it is important to have one focal point for overall coordination of INFOSEC policy. It is also essential to understand that responsibility for INFOSEC rests with all members of the organization, and not just the security personnel. Security is a shared responsibility, and this concept must be widely promoted by the security administrator and strongly backed by senior management.

63.5.2 Authority and Responsibility. As in all management areas, INFOSEC administrators (ISAs) need not only specific responsibilities but also the authority to carry out their duties. Those duties are listed next:

- **Establish policy statements and guidelines for information protection.** Although policy is the primary responsibility of senior management, it is appropriate for the ISA to participate in the delineation of a formal policy statement covering this important organizational goal and to prepare appropriate guidelines.
- **Identify vulnerabilities and risks.** The ISA serves as a consultant and coordinator in the process of risk analysis. The sensitivity of data resources must be decided by senior management, but with full consensus and agreement by all affected sections of the organization. The ISA has a special responsibility to identify specific risks that affect the automated data resources. The ISA should then coordinate the process of quantifying or otherwise prioritizing the value of the vulnerable data, in order to establish a basis for selection and economic justification of protective measures.
- **Recommend protective measures.** Major responsibility for identification of economic solutions to INFOSEC vulnerabilities is usually assigned to the ISA. Requiring a combination of technical knowledge and management analysis, this process entails the evaluation of protective solutions for technological, operational, and economic effectiveness. Appropriate recommendations must be coordinated with other affected sections of the organization, including audit, data processing operations, software development, legal counsel, human resources, facilities security, public relations, and others. Implementation plans must also be developed, and there must be a management commitment to the implementation.
- **Control the implementation of protective measures.** Whether the final administration of the day-to-day security procedures is centralized or decentralized, the coordination and control of implementation for major protective measures should be centralized. A prerequisite for implementation is the development of standards for INFOSEC to ensure consistency in the application of protection. Important areas for standardization are security design for application systems, programming development, data sensitivity criteria, database access, and program maintenance. In general, security standards cover the entire systems life cycle.

- **Measure effectiveness of security precautions.** Feedback is essential to assess how effectively policies are being followed. Since the nature of INFOSEC is defensive, the measures adopted can easily fall into disuse unless there is ongoing confirmation of effectiveness. The ISA should have primary responsibility to conduct security audits for operational systems as well as for systems under development. Backup protection and disaster-recovery procedures are especially sensitive plans that must be tested periodically. Monitoring of variances in security procedures is also important, and is best controlled through the ISA function. In many organizations these activities are coordinated with the auditors. Finally, the ISA should provide senior management with reports on the effectiveness of security policy, with identification of weaknesses, and with recommendations for improvement.
- **Promote security awareness and security education.** Another important area of responsibility for the ISA is security education and awareness. The concept of security must be actively communicated to all members of the staff to maintain awareness of its importance. An effective program should achieve a workable balance between security and the utility of computer resources.
- **Ensure security awareness across cultures.** In today's global economy, many companies are located in various geographic regions. As a result, security professionals must understand the role that culture plays in the global enterprise. Different cultural perspectives exist regarding security, and these must be taken into consideration when developing a security-awareness program. Understanding the impact of culture on business operations will be very beneficial for the organization. For example, how should global enterprises create cross-border awareness strategies? How might the laws and regulations in various countries help or inhibit the creation of an awareness program?

  Although English is still a widely used language of business, U.S. security professionals are well advised to understand the cultural nuances of their foreign counterparts in order to protect their organization against increasing threats. The growing economic power of the European Union, China, and India, should prompt U.S. professionals to begin expanding their language competencies to match those of their global competitors.

63.5.3 Professional Accreditation and Education. Professional accreditation can provide managers with a basis of assurance that a common body of knowledge is applied to the requirements of INFOSEC in their enterprise. There are several professional societies and organizations that offer specialized certification to INFOSEC personnel. Such certification is voluntary, since there are no specific licensing requirements for INFOSEC practitioners. However, certification does signify serious professional intent on the part of the individual to acquire and maintain the needed knowledge and skills. In most cases, the certification process requires a combination of education, experience, and knowledge; knowledge is evaluated through written examinations. Once achieved, a professional certificate requires continuing education in the field to maintain its validity.

Unfortunately, some managers fear that after they provide training or support advanced education, their employees will leave and use their new skills to benefit some other organization—perhaps even a competitor. In reality, some employees are more likely to walk out if the investment is *not* made. Numerous studies have shown that if employees feel valued, they will be more willing to stay. For example, a summary of changing contributions to employee satisfaction specifically states that:

- Although money is clearly an important consideration, cash is not the primary factor that keeps people in their current job or attracts them away to a new job.
- Opportunity to grow and learn at work is emerging as a primary determinant of attracting and retaining employees. ...
- Although employees consistently indicate that education and training are key aspects of their willingness to stay at or leave their current job, employees also typically rank the quality of their employer's education and training function as low.[73]

Training need not be expensive, excessively time consuming, or difficult.[74] Online security training can be taken anytime and is self-paced. Training videos are also an excellent tool for stimulating employee knowledge and interest. The simplest way to locate such resources is to search on the Web with a good search engine using keywords such as "security training." A particularly helpful site is CCCure.org, which includes a wealth of self-study materials as well as links to many vendors.[75]

Another alternative is to have the employer use obsolete equipment for training, equipment that would otherwise lie idle in a storage area. Even small departments may have old PCs lying around dormant, as well as hubs and possibly router/switches. These can be used to create a network for testing and learning at little cost. Companies that do not have spare equipment can buy used equipment for less than the cost of a one-week intensive course. For an employee who wants to learn the basics of firewalls, Linux is a cheap (and even free) operating system that has just recently started supporting firewalls. Setting up a Linux firewall requires no expensive software or appliances. It can provide an effective way of encouraging employees to learn the practical details of configuring firewalls—a valuable skill set in any security department—while rewarding loyal employees by showing confidence in their commitment to learning, and to their continued employment in the enterprise.

Once the firewall is set up, other employees can use the testing and training network to learn about penetration testing, intrusion detection, and other security elements. Different operating systems can be installed, with various applications, all for a minimal investment. As technology, techniques, and tools change, this training network will be valuable in keeping skills up to date.

External, college-level undergraduate and graduate education also provides resources for employees and managers. Universities and colleges are increasingly recognizing the value and validity of educational programs centering on information assurance, both at the technical and managerial levels. Some offer noncredit courses or certificate courses in addition to degree programs. Some offer online programs that support the needs of working adults. Managers can take advantage of these opportunities to improve the knowledge base within their organizations and to increase employee loyalty and retention by supporting employees who want to further their careers in information assurance. Some programs include case studies that may, with permission, center on fieldwork within the students' own work environments, resulting in extensive analysis and recommendations of immense value to their employers.[76]

63.6 CONCLUDING REMARKS.

Society needs the insights of information assurance specialists. Managers with daily opportunities to think about the strategic implications of vulnerabilities, exploits, and, above all, about the business processes for which they are responsible are in an excellent position to contribute not only to the success of their own enterprises but also to the future of their societies. As Adam Shostack and Andrew Stewart have written in their future-pointing treatise, it is time for a new school of INFOSEC—one that involves:

> Learning from other professions, such as economics and psychology, to unlock the problems that stymie the security field. ...
>
> Sharing objective data and analysis widely. ...
>
> The embrace of the scientific method for solving important security problems. Analyzing real-world outcomes is the best way for information security to become a mature discipline.[77]

Readers should embrace every opportunity to bring their experience and wisdom to a wider audience, and by speaking and writing they should share their insights with each other and with the general public.

63.7 FURTHER READING

Calder, A., and S. Watkins. *IT Governance: An International Guide to Data Security and ISO27001/ISO27002*, 5th ed. Kogan Page, 2012.

Goddard, J., and T. Eccles. *Uncommon Sense, Common Nonsense: Why Some Organisations Consistently Outperform Others*. Profile Books, 2013.

Kouns, J., and B. L. Kouns. *The Chief Information Security Officer*. IT Governance Publishing, 2011.

Laplante, P., and T. Costello. *CIO Wisdom II: More Best Practices*. Prentice-Hall, 2005.

Mellado, D., L. E. Sanchez, E. Fernandez-Medina, and M. Piattini, eds. *IT Security Governance Innovations: Theory and Research*. IGI Global, 2012.

Moeller, R. R. *Executive's Guide to IT Governance: Improving Systems Processes with Service Management, COBIT, and ITIL*. Wiley, 2013.

Patterson, T. *Mapping Security*. Prentice-Hall, 2005.

Rees, M., and M. Kennedy. *Fraud and the Human Factor: Fighting the Greatest Threat to Today's Corporation*. Bloomsbury Information Ltd, 2013.

Solms, S. H., and R. Solms. *Information Security Governance*. Springer, 2008.

Swiderski, F., and W. Synder. *Threat Modeling*. Microsoft, 2004.

Talbot, J., and M. Jakeman. *Security Risk Management Body of Knowledge*, 2nd ed. Wiley, 2009.

Wheeler, E. *Security Risk Management: Building an Information Security Risk Management Program from the Ground Up*. Syngress, 2011.

Wibbeke, E. S., and S. McArthur. *Global Business Leadership*, 2nd ed. Routledge, 2013.

Wood, C. C. *Information Security Roles & Responsibilities Made Easy*, 2nd ed. Information Shield, 2005.

63.8 NOTES

1. Because this entire *Handbook* in a sense provides the underlying details for the management of information assurance, most cross-references to other chapters have been relegated to endnotes to avoid cluttering the text.
2. See Chapters 60 and 62 in this *Handbook*.

3. For an extensive discussion of the role of the CISO, see Chapter 65 in this *Handbook.*
4. California State Legislature (2002) Senate Bill SB 1386, http://info.sen.ca.gov/pub/01-02/bill/sen/sb_1351-1400/sb_1386_bill_20020926_chaptered.html
5. G. Lin, "The Tao Perspective," in D. Lane, ed., *CIO Wisdom* (Upper Saddle River, NJ: Prentice-Hall, 2003), Chapter 4.
6. NIST, "Information Security System in the Systems Development Lifecycle," 2004 [Brochure], http://csrc.nist.gov/groups/SMA/sdlc/index.html
7. M. E. Kabay, "The Net Present Value of Information Security: A Paradigm Shift for INFOSEC and E-commerce," vol. 17 (2006), www.mekabay.com/infosecmgmt/npvsec.pdf
8. J. Bassett and D. Rothman, *A Seat at the Table for CEOs and CSOs: Driving Profits, Corporate Performance & Business Agility* (Bloomington, IN: AuthorHouse, 2007), p. 111.
9. This section is based on the paper by M. E. Kabay, "The VA Data Insecurity Saga," 2008, www.mekabay.com/infosecmgmt/vasaga.pdf
10. J. Brodkin, "Rating Apologies: Deep Regrets, from TJX to ChoicePoint, about Data Leaks," *Network World,* March 14, 2007, www.networkworld.com/news/2007/031407-wider-net-apologies-letters.html
11. G. Gross, "U.S. Agency Loses Data Containing 26 Million IDs," *Network World,* May 22, 2006, www.networkworld.com/news/2006/052206-us-agency-loses-veterans-data.html
12. G. Gross, "Lawmaker Calls on VA Head to Resign after Data Theft," *Network World,* May 25, 2006, www.networkworld.com/news/2006/052506-lawmaker-calls-on-va-head.html
13. "FirstGov.gov," "Latest Information on Veterans Affairs Data Security," *Military.com | Money* (n.d.) www.military.com/money/personal-finance/credit-debt-management/latest-information-on-veterans-affairs-data-security.html
14. Using keyword "data" in the search field at http://www1.va.gov/opa/pressrel/index.cfm provides a reasonable chronology
15. U.S. Department of Veterans Affairs, "Secretary Nicholson Provides Update on Stolen Data Incident: Data Matching with Department of Defense Providing New Details," June 6, 2006, www.va.gov/opa/pressrel/pressrelease.cfm?id=1134
16. Associated Press, "Data on 2.2M Active Troops Stolen from VA," *USA TODAY,* June 7, 2006, www.usatoday.com/news/washington/2006-06-06-veterans-data_x.htm
17. U.S. Department of Veterans Affairs, "Directive by the Secretary of Veterans Affairs R. James Nicholson to All VA Supervisors on Information Security," May 26, 2006, www.va.gov/opa/pressrel/pressrelease.cfm?id=1128
18. U.S. Department of Veterans Affairs, "VA Secretary Inserts New Leadership in Policy & Planning Office," May 30, 2006, www.va.gov/opa/pressrel/pressrelease.cfm?id=1129
19. U.S. Government Accountability Office, "Homeland Security: Guidance and Standards are Needed for Measuring the Effectiveness of Agencies' Facility Protection Efforts," Report GAO-06-612, May 2006, www.gao.gov/cgi-bin/getrpt?GAO-06-612

20. U.S. Department of Veterans Affairs, "VA Secretary Inserts New Leadership in Policy & Planning Office."
21. U.S. Government Accountability Office, "Veterans Affairs: Leadership Needed to Address Information Security Weaknesses and Privacy Issues," Report GAO-06-866T, June 14, 2006, www.gao.gov/cgi-bin/getrpt?GAO-06-866T
22. U.S. Government Accountability Office, "Information Security: Leadership Needed to Address Weaknesses and Privacy Issues at Veterans Affairs," Highlights of GAO-06-897T, 2006, www.gao.gov/highlights/d06897thigh.pdf
23. U.S. Government Accountability Office, "Information Technology: VA and DOD Face Challenges in Completing Key Efforts," Highlights of GAO-06-905T, 2006, www.gao.gov/highlights/d06905thigh.pdf
24. Department of Veterans Affairs Office of Inspector General, "Review of Issues Related to the Loss of VA Information Involving the Identity of Millions of Veterans," Report No. 06-02238-163, July 11, 2006, www.va.gov/oig/pubs/VAOIG-06-02238-163.pdf
25. D. Pulliam, "Report: VA Treated Data Breach with 'Indifference'," Government Executive Website, July 11, 2006, www.govexec.com/technology/2006/07/report-va-treated-data-breach-with-indifference/22234
26. "Personal Data for 38,000 Veterans Missing, VA Says," *USA TODAY,* August 7, 2006, www.usatoday.com/tech/news/computersecurity/infotheft/2006-08-07-veterans-data_x.htm
27. G. Gross, "VA to Spend $3.7M on Encryption Tools: The Move Follows the Theft of a VA Laptop in May," *Computerworld,* August 14, 2006, www.computerworld.com/s/article/9002447/VA_to_spend_3.7M_on_encryption_tools
28. R. McMillan, "Update: Unisys Contractor Arrested in VA Theft: Investigators Do Not Believe 21-Year-Old Suspect Sought Agency's Data," *InfoWorld,* September 18, 2006, www.infoworld.com/d/security-central/update-unisys-contractor-arrested-in-va-theft-825
29. H. A. Waxman, "Committee Report Finds Data Breaches Throughout Federal Government," Committee on Oversight and Government Reform, 110th Congress, October 13, 2006, http://oversight-archive.waxman.house.gov/story.asp?ID=1127
30. R. Maze, "VA Reports Two More Data Security Lapses," *Federal Times,* November 3, 2006 (no longer available online).
31. A. Broache, "Hard Drive Vanishes from VA Facility," *C|Net News,* February 5, 2007, http://cnet.news.com/2100-1029_3-6156386.html
32. G. Keizer, "Lost VA Hard Drive May Have Held 1.8M IDs: Initially, the Agency Said Just 50,000 Were Potentially Affected," *Computerworld,* February 13, 2007, www.computerworld.com/s/article/9011218/Lost_VA_hard_drive_may_have_held_1.8M_IDs
33. M. E. Kabay, "PIIssed Off Yet?" *Network World | Security Strategies,* June 12, 2007, www.networkworld.com/newsletters/sec/2007/0611sec1.html
34. U.S. Government Accountability Office, "Information Security: Veterans Affairs Needs to Address Long-Standing Weaknesses," Report GAO-07-532T, February 28, 2007, www.gao.gov/new.items/d07532t.pdf
35. G. Gross, "VA to Spend $3.7M on Encryption Tools."
36. J. Vijayan, "OMB Sets 120-Day Deadline for Fed Breach-Notification Plans: Agencies Have the Summer To Develop and Implement First Phases of Policies,"

Computerworld, May 29, 2007, www.computerworld.com/s/article/9021544/OMB_sets_120_day_deadline_for_Fed_breach_notification_plans

37. Chronology of Data Breaches: Security Breaches 2005–Present," Privacy Rights Clearinghouse (2013-07-14), www.privacyrights.org/data-breach
38. See Chapters 1 and 3.
39. See Chapter 57.
40. See Chapters 56, 58, and 59.
41. See Chapter 60.
42. See Chapters 22 and 23.
43. See Chapters 24 through 37.
44. See Chapters 43 through 50.
45. See Chapters 51 through 55.
46. See Chapter 45 for more on employment practices and policies.
47. Policy issues are discussed in detail in Chapters 44, 45, 47, 48, 49, and 50 of this *Handbook*.
48. M. K. Pratt, "Employee Security Training: Beyond Posters," *Computerworld*, April 17, 2006, www.computerworld.com/s/article/110494/Employee_Security_Training_Beyond_Posters
49. G. G. Gross, "Study: Human Error Causes Most Security Breaches," *Computerworld*, March 18, 2003, www.computerworld.com/s/article/79485/Study_Human_error_causes_most_security_breaches
50. E. Dickson, "Could the Arrests in the Stop and Shop Data Breach Indicate a Tie to Armenian Mobsters?" Fraud, Phishing and Financial Misdeeds Blog (Feb 28, 2007), http://fraudwar.blogspot.com/2007/02/could-arrest-in-stop-and-shop-data.html
51. See Chapter 50 for more information about using social psychology to motivate compliance with security policies.
52. The Honeynet Project: Challenges, www.honeynet.org/challenges
53. For more about log files, see Chapters 52 and 53; on postmortem analysis, see Chapter 56.
54. See Chapters 49 and 50.
55. T. J. Peters and R. H. Waterman, *In Search of Excellence: Lessons from America's Best-Run Companies* (New York: HarperCollins, 1983). See also H. K. Jones, "Does MBWA (Management By Wandering Around) Still Work?" Self-Growth.com, 2007, www.selfgrowth.com/articles/Jones6.html
56. B. J. Fox, "Communications: Communication Excellence in IT Management," in D. Lane, ed., *CIO Wisdom,* (Upper Saddle River, NJ: Prentice-Hall, 2003), Chapter 5.
57. S. Adams, "Official Dilbert Website" (2008), www.dilbert.com
58. See Chapter 28.
59. M. E. Kabay, "A Rant about InfoSec: A Security Veteran in a Bad Mood Dumps on Everyone" (2004,; www.mekabay.com/opinion/rant.pdf
60. See Chapter 30.
61. See Chapter 38.
62. For more security-awareness ideas, see Chapter 49.

63. Chapter 62 of this *Handbook* discusses risk management in more detail.
64. See Chapter 61.
65. See Chapter 18.
66. See Chapters 15 and 40.
67. R. J. McGillivray and S. C. Lieske, "Webjacking," *The Computer & Internet Lawyer* 18, no. 7 (July 2001):1, www.hackerzvoice.net/ouah/webhijack.html
68. See Chapter 54.
69. See Chapter 27.
70. See Chapters 53 and 54.
71. See Chapter 56 for a more extensive discussion of these principles in connection with the computer emergency response team.
72. See Chapter 50 for a discussion of the psychology of implementing security policies.
73. L. J. Basai, "Employee Retention." Learning in the New Economy," *LineZine* (Summer 2000), www.linezine.com/3/themes/hardtalk.htm
74. M. R. Farnum, "Security Awareness Training Does Not Have to Be Hard," Hitting the Security Nerve—*Computerworld* Blogs (2006), http://blogs.computerworld.com/node/4175
75. www.cccure.org
76. For more details of United States–based certification and education in the security field, see Chapters 74 and 75.
77. A. Shostack and A. Stewart, *The New School of Information Security* (Upper Saddle River, NJ: Addison-Wesley, 2008), p. xiv.

CHAPTER 64

U.S. LEGAL AND REGULATORY SECURITY ISSUES

Timothy Virtue

64.1 INTRODUCTION. Since the previous edition of this *Handbook* was published in 2009 there have been significant technical, political, economic, legal, and regulatory changes that have complicated efforts to achieve compliance. In addition, the overall global economic downturn has made compliance more difficult.

With the global and U.S. economic downturn, many organizations were challenged to maintain or increase their compliance programs with fewer resources. In periods of economic decline, fraud and other criminal activities have a tendency to increase, requiring security leaders to focus on both security and regulatory issues simultaneously.

The rising use of social media, mobile devices, and cloud computing has complicated the application of security controls and strategies and increased regulatory and legal challenges. Security teams must apply flexible, innovative, and adaptive security solutions.

Many organizations are restructuring independent and isolated operational units (sometimes described as *silos*) and focusing on coordinated strategic risk management for the enterprise. Such changes support business values, achieve compliance, and reduce risk.

Another recurring theme of today's regulatory environment is accountability for, and protection of, sensitive or private information. Specific regulatory requirements and how an organization addresses the requirements will vary, based on industry, organizational structure, and internal processes. However, an effective enterprise-wide regulatory-governance model should incorporate two common elements:

1. The senior management team must create a compliance-driven culture by actively exercising leadership by example.
2. The team must actively support this culture of compliance by enabling computer security strategies, tactics, and technologies as discussed throughout this *Handbook*.

Compliance with regulatory requirements must include, but is not limited to, these computer security fundamentals:

- Program management
  - Policy and procedure design and implementation
- Risk assessment and management
  - Prevention
  - Detection
  - Response
- Implementation of safeguards
  - Administrative controls
  - Physical controls
  - Technical controls
- Awareness and training

Organizations must also keep in mind that vendor due diligence and management may play a more critical role as they adopt social media, mobile, and cloud-computing technologies within the organization. The same levels of management and oversight still need to exist; however, now they need to be applied outward.

Although there are a number of regulations that today's business leaders may be accountable for, these requirements vary from industry to industry. This chapter focuses on two important U.S. regulations: the Sarbanes-Oxley and the Gramm-Leach-Bliley Acts. These particular acts require a significant level of management involvement in order to validate that the organization adequately addresses the regulatory requirements.

64.2 SARBANES-OXLEY ACT OF 2002. The *Sarbanes-Oxley Act of 2002* (SOX), also sometimes referred to as the *Public Company Accounting Reform and Investor Protection Act of 2002*, comprises 11 titles and is administered by the Securities and Exchange Commission (SEC). The main goal of the legislation is to protect the public and shareholders from accounting errors and fraudulent practices by requiring that companies monitor and record any access to sensitive financial data. They must provide reports on their controls, and must respond in a timely and appropriate manner should an incident occur.[1]

EXHIBIT 64.1 Eleven Titles of SOX with Descriptions

Title #	Name	Description
I	Public Company Accounting Oversight Board	Establishment of a private nonprofit board. Duties of the board include establishing auditing, quality control, and independence standards for public accounting firms.
II	Auditor Independence	Prohibits certified public accountants from simultaneously performing audit and nonaudit services.
III	Corporate Responsibility	Requires that the Securities and Exchange Commission (SEC) order the national security exchanges and associations to bar the listing of an issuer that does not comply with the specific requirements set forth in Title III.
IV	Enhanced Financial Disclosures	Sets forth various requirements to validate the accuracy of financial statements and supporting disclosures.
V	Analyst Conflicts of Interest	Defines a code of conduct for security analysts and includes a measure to help restore confidence in their reporting.
VI	Commission Resources and Authority	Authorizes the SEC to hire staff to provide additional oversight of auditors and audit services. Also outlines the conditions a person can be prohibited from practicing as a broker, advisor, or dealer.
VII	Studies and Reports	Provides for research to be conducted for the enforcement of actions against violations by SEC registrants and auditors.
VIII	Corporate and Criminal Fraud Accountability	Defines penalties for the destruction of audit reports and the willful destruction, manipulation, or falsification of documents in federal investigations and bankruptcy proceedings.
IX	White Collar Crime Penalty Enhancements	Increases the penalties for white-collar crimes and requires that both the CEO and CFO of a corporation certify periodic financial statements.
X	Corporate Tax Returns	Requires that the CEO sign the corporation's federal income tax return.
XI	Corporate Fraud and Accountability	Establishes penalties for persons who manipulate or destroy documents or impede an official proceeding.

Exhibit 64.1 offers each title within SOX with a brief description added by the author.

All of the individual components from Exhibit 64.1 that specify the requirements for SOX must have the support and involvement of an organization's senior leadership team.

No single component of SOX is more important than any other component. However, the remaining discussion focuses on the part of the Act that affects computer security the most: Section 404.

The passage of SOX in 2002 led the way for an important change in how business leaders in today's public companies look at information security. This change has caused significant impact on today's information systems, the security that supports them, and management's perception of how the systems affect financial reporting.

Although SOX was primarily intended to enhance the integrity of financial reporting, it has broader implications. Specifically, the integrity of financial reporting can be accomplished only by ensuring the integrity of the source information used to complete financial reporting requirements. Management must therefore support the design, implementation, and continuous management of strong controls over the information systems that are the primary source for today's financial reporting requirements.

64.2.1 Section 404 of SOX. Since compliance with SOX is supported by the organization's ability to develop, implement, and manage a combination of business reporting requirements and management controls, many of the organization's information systems are directly or indirectly involved in the SOX-compliance process. The extent of involvement can range from end-user computing applications (e.g., spreadsheets) all the way to the data center. Business leaders must address these issues and must provide adequate support to achieve continuous compliance with SOX.

SOX addresses a number of areas requiring senior executive leadership and support. However, Section 404 of SOX is most relevant to information-security programs, and requires businesses to:

- Evaluate the adequacy of internal controls that impact financial reporting
- Implement new controls as necessary
- Annually test and report on the assessment results of internal controls

Section 404 requires the business to implement a comprehensive internal control framework sustainable throughout the enterprise. Furthermore, these controls must not only directly protect the integrity of financial data and indirectly protect the systems that support the data, but the business is also required to show that these controls are operational and are functioning as intended. Since compliance with SOX affects the organization at an enterprise-wide level, information-security protections should be designed, implemented, and managed from a holistic perspective supported by management as part of an overall business strategy, rather than as a single compliance activity.

In most organizations, almost all corporate information, including financial information, is linked to enterprise information systems. Many systems feed or share information with each other. Therefore, the organization must look at data origins, data flows, and data output to validate that they have adequately identified all of the information that could impact financial reporting. Management must provide the appropriate level of support for robust controls to protect the data resources of critical corporate information systems, which ultimately act as the primary data source the business must rely on when delivering and validating the integrity of the organization's financial statements.

With today's modern technologies pervasively deployed in business environments, organizations are likely to face a variety of SOX compliance challenges. These challenges result from the vast number of information systems, the associated supporting infrastructure, highly connected and communication intensive networks, and in many cases externally facing Web-based applications that are highly susceptible to exploitation.

Additional challenges come from inside as well. The insider threat is quickly becoming one of the most difficult security challenges to overcome, and causes the majority of security problems for many organizations (see Chapters 13 and 45 in this *Handbook*). Internal data protection challenges are further complicated by the increase in *privileged users* such as database administrators, system administrators, and a variety of other users with powerful access to critical information systems. Such users often unknowingly create significant SOX compliance risks for their organization. These powerful privileges are often overused, and ultimately can be the pathway to noncompliance or malicious activity within the organization. Furthermore, many of these privileged users can manipulate system log files so that their malicious activity goes unnoticed or in some cases becomes untraceable (see Chapter 53).

64.2.2 Management Perspectives on SOX. Properly administered compliance initiatives must strike a balance between information security and system usability, to support business and compliance objectives without creating an environment of distrust. Although the insider threat is a significant threat to many businesses, the senior leadership team must accept that employees are a critical component of business operations. Since management controls are intended to protect sensitive system data and not to create a hostile work environment, SOX-related corporate policies and standards must support the spirit of the act by ensuring that organizations closely monitor and control access to critical business systems while not impeding employee productivity. Achieving this balance is not always an easy task.

Regardless of the specific strategies organizations employ to design, implement, and manage, there are some fundamental operational policies and processes that should be put in place to protect the integrity of both the data and ultimately the organization's financial reporting.

Fortunately, many organizations may find they already have a majority of the required controls in place, because many of the control requirements can be accomplished through traditional information security best practices. Some of the more common examples include controls that address segregation of duties (e.g., among development, test, and production environments) and appropriate data-security controls and safeguards.

A list of more common database safeguard components that senior management should focus on when complying with Section 404 of SOX follows.

- Monitor database access by privileged users
- Monitor changes in privileges
- Monitor access failures
- Monitor schema changes
- Monitor direct data access

In order to get a better grasp on all of the complexity associated with database compliance challenges, senior leadership teams in many organizations elect to take a back-to-basics approach. One of the most effective strategies to deploying such a simplified approach is to use the traditional five *W*s. Specifically, organizations should be asking these questions in terms of database compliance:

1. Who did something to the database?
2. What did they do?
3. Which specific data component?

4. When was the activity performed?
5. Where was the information accessed?

When members of the organization's senior leadership team approach the SOX compliance issue in this manner, they are in a better position to understand and ultimately to assume the responsibility for the data security and integrity for which they are accountable.

The requirement of having an organization's senior management work with an external auditor to report on the internal control program is, unfortunately, the most costly requirement of SOX and requires an enormous effort.

However, organizations should also take note that there are a number of benefits from designing, implementing, and managing effective compliance strategies, beyond initial SOX compliance. Establishing a comprehensive internal controls program not only aids in SOX compliance but also forms a foundation for operational improvements. Anytime the organization's senior management team can institute an effective internal controls program, it is not only taking steps to compliance, but also building a solid foundation on which enterprise-wide data governance programs can follow.

64.3 GRAMM-LEACH-BLILEY ACT. One of the most significant pieces of legislation to affect the financial services industry was the *Financial Services Modernization Act* of 1999, commonly referred to as the *Gramm-Leach-Bliley Act* or GLBA.[2] It was enacted in response to the standardization of the U.S. banking and insurance industries in the late 1990s. The financial services industry was undergoing substantial change during this period. Since financial institutions and insurance companies were allowed to merge and consolidate their operations, legislators and industry observers were concerned about providing adequate protection of consumer rights and data protection. Specifically, significant concerns developed over the consolidation of consumer data. There was substantial fear that sensitive consumer data would be openly shared among financial organizations and their subsidiaries. This open environment would likely threaten consumer rights and the security of sensitive and personal financial data. The consolidation and reform within the financial services industry was enabling the creation of new financial services holding companies that could offer a full range of financial products. Prior to the passage of GLBA, some major financial institutions were selling personal and sensitive detailed customer information to business partners. This type of disclosure often included the disclosure of account numbers and other highly sensitive data to telemarketing firms. These telemarketing agencies often used the account numbers to charge customers for products and services they did not want and that had no value to customers.

64.3.1 Applicability. GLBA applies to U.S. domestic financial institutions; it defines financial institutions, as "companies that offer financial products or services to individuals, like loans, financial or investment advice, or insurance." GLBA coverage includes but is not limited to organizations that provide insurance, securities, payment settlement services, check cashing services, credit counselors, and mortgages.

GLBA is intended to address the proper handling of nonpublic financial information. However, senior management teams of financial institutions must acknowledge that the act also includes a wide range of information that is not obviously financial in nature.

This additional coverage is intended to offer further protections to the consumer and properly align with the spirit of the law. The additional types of information that must be protected include the consumer's name and address. However, protection may extend to:

- Information given to a financial institution in order to receive a financial product or service
- Information generated or remaining as a result of a transaction between a financial institution and a consumer
- Information obtained by the financial institution while providing a financial product or service to a consumer

GLBA requires financial institutions to safeguard nonpublic personal information (such as a Social Security number, credit card details, or a bank account number) provided by a consumer under various privacy rules or resulting from a transaction or other service performed on behalf of the consumer. This information is not necessarily considered financial information. For example, under GLBA, a consumer's name identifying a recipient of services from a specific institution is also considered nonpublic information that must be protected under GLBA. Specifically, GLBA mandates:

- Secure storage of consumer personal information
- Providing adequate and sufficient notice to consumers regarding how the financial institution shares their consumer personal and financial information
- Providing consumers with the choice to opt out of sharing their personal and financial information

64.3.2 Enforcement. GLBA is enforced by the Federal Trade Commission (FTC), various financial industry regulators, and state attorneys general. More stringent requirements may be placed on the financial institutions by individual states, because GLBA does not preempt state law.

Although current legislation does not offer a remedy of civil action, a financial institution's failure to comply with notice is considered a deceptive trade practice by both state and federal authorities. Some states do have specific legislation that offers a private right of action for consumers.

Title V of the act provides that financial institutions may share practically any information with affiliated companies but may share information with nonaffiliated companies for marketing purposes only after providing an opportunity for the consumer to *opt out* of the information sharing process. Management needs to play a proactive role in providing administrative, managerial, and technical support to achieve compliance with Title V of the Act. Consumers must be provided with easy-to-understand and easy-to-use opt-out choices. Organizations that make opting out difficult, or that otherwise appear to be duplicitous, are likely to be viewed as noncompliant with Title V of GLBA.

The provisions of Title V do not preempt or supersede state law. If organizations are conducting business in a state that has more stringent requirements, then those state requirements must be met, in addition to GLBA. Section 505 requires that the act and its associated regulations be enforced by various federal and state regulatory agencies having jurisdiction over financial institutions. This requirement of GLBA offers federal enforcement authority to a variety of enforcement agencies. The more common enforcement agencies include:

- Office of the Comptroller of the Currency
- Federal Reserve Board
- Federal Deposit Insurance Corporation
- Securities and Exchange Commission

An organization's senior leadership team should also note that the FTC has general enforcement authority for any financial institution that does not fall within the jurisdiction of any of the specific enumerated regulatory agencies.

As previously stated, the intent of GLBA is to offer adequate protection to consumers conducting business with financial services firms. Although the hope is that organizations will comply with GLBA on goodwill, the act was created with some serious repercussions to financial institutions that do not comply. GLBA does not include a private right of action, but financial institutions are required to give consumer notice, and they could face liability under deceptive trade practice statutes if the notices are determined to be deceptive or inaccurate. Furthermore, financial institutions that fail to comply with GLBA may also be subject to penalties under the *Financial Institution Reform Recovery and Enforcement Act* (FIRREA). FIRREA contains and offers penalties that range from up to $5,500 for violations of laws and regulations; up to $27,500 if violations are unsafe, unsound, or reckless; and up to $1.1 million for knowing violations. Given the consequences of noncompliance, organizations need to take the appropriate actions to obtain consumer protection and compliance with GLBA.

64.3.3 Consumers and Customers. One common misconception of GLBA is the interpretation of the legislation as it relates to the nonconsumer customers of financial institutions. This is likely to occur since the terms *consumer* and *customer* are often used interchangeably. However, in the context of GLBA, the critical distinction must be made. GLBA defines a *consumer* as "an individual who obtains, from a financial institution, financial products or services which are to be used primarily for personal, family, or household purposes, and also means the legal representative of such an individual." A *customer* is a type of consumer who has established some sort of ongoing relationship with an institution accountable to GLBA. An example of a customer would be an individual who has received credit financing to purchase a car. This individual would need to make monthly payments to a financial institution and hence has established an ongoing relationship. Under this definition, a business could not be defined either as a customer or as a consumer (since a business is not an individual[3]) and therefore does not fall under the protections of GLBA.

64.3.4 Compliance. Compliance with GLBA signifies that financial institutions must comply with a number of the act's provisions. From a high-level perspective, organizations must adhere to these points when seeking compliance with GLBA:

- Organizations must provide consumers with clear and conspicuous notice of the financial institution's information-sharing policies and practices.
- This notice must be given at the start of a new customer relationship and maintained on an annual basis.

- Organizations must provide customers with the right to opt out of having their nonpublic personal information shared with nonaffiliated third parties (unless the activity falls under one of the GLBA exceptions).
- They must refrain from disclosing to any nonaffiliated third-party marketer, other than a consumer reporting agency, an account number or similar form of access code to a consumer's credit card, deposit, or transaction account.
- Financial institutions must comply with the regulatory standards established to protect the security and confidentiality of customer records.
- Financial institutions must also protect against security threats and unauthorized access to such protected customer information.

64.3.5 Privacy Notices. As a part of GLBA, financial institutions are required to disseminate privacy notices to their consumers explaining what information the financial institution will collect about the consumer, whom the information may be shared with, and how the financial institution protects that information. The information the notice must refer to is the consumer's nonpublic personal information (such as a Social Security number, bank account number, or credit card number) collected, for example, during an application for auto financing. In an effort to help companies comply with this requirement in a consistent and effective manner, the FTC (in conjunction with various other financial regulators) established a GLBA privacy notice standard. Under this standard, financial institutions must provide a privacy notice at the inception of a relationship with a consumer and once a year for as long as the relationship persists. Furthermore, this notice must provide consumers with the option to declare within 30 days after the receipt of the notice that they do not want their information shared with the third parties mentioned in that privacy notice. Financial institutions must also mandate that the privacy notice itself be written in such a way that it is a clear and accurate statement of the company's privacy practices. Provided these requirements are met by the financial institution's privacy notice, the institution may share consumer information with its affiliated companies.

A financial institution may also share consumer information with nonaffiliated organizations provided it has clearly disclosed what information will be provided, to whom, and how it will be protected, and provided that consumers have a method of opting out clearly described in their privacy notices. However, GLBA prohibits financial institutions from disclosing consumer account numbers to nonaffiliated companies for purposes of telemarketing, direct-mail marketing (including through email), even if the consumer has not opted out of sharing the information for marketing purposes. There will be special circumstances in which consumers will not have the option to require that their information not be shared. Some of the more common occurrences of these special circumstances are:

- When a financial institution is required to share information with an outside organization as part of fulfilling its customer obligations (e.g., data processing services)
- When a financial institution is legally required to share the information
- When the information is shared with an outside service provider that market the products or services of the financial institution

64.3.6 GLBA Safeguards Rule. A significant component of GLBA is the *GLBA Safeguards Rule*. The Safeguards Rule is intended to support the privacy and protective rules within GLBA. In many organizations, it is the operational driver supporting the other components of GLBA. If the other components of GLBA are the *why* of the legislation, then the Safeguards Rule is the *how*.

GLBA contains specific requirements and safeguards that are applicable to both electronic and paper records. Management must protect records in both formats, even though the widespread use of electronic data processing makes it easy to overlook sensitive consumer information in hardcopy format because an increasing number of employees work almost exclusively with electronic representations of the data. GLBA requires financial institutions to develop, implement, and continuously manage a *comprehensive* information security program, which it defines as including administrative, technical, and physical safeguards to protect the security of customer information.

64.3.7 Flexibility. GLBA covers a broad array of financial institutions, and therefore mandates that an information security program be appropriate to the size, complexity, nature, and scope of the activities of each specific financial institution. This level of flexibility offers an organization's management team the flexibility to balance consumer protection against business objectives. However, it is critical that this flexibility not be abused and that the intent of the act be addressed. Furthermore, an organization's senior leadership team must not interpret the lack of specific safeguards as an opportunity for noncompliance with GLBA, but rather as an opportunity to provide consumer protection without impeding business operations.

Flexibility aside, certain key requirements must be followed to be compliant with the Safeguards Rule. The foundational security practices include having at least one designated employee to audit systems; determine risks; and develop, implement, and manage procedures to address information security. Specifically, a financial institution must provide three levels of security:

1. **Administrative security.** Includes program management of workforce risks, employee training, and vendor oversight
2. **Technical security.** Includes technical controls for computer systems, networks, applications, access controls, and encryption
3. **Physical security.** Includes safeguarding facilities, corresponding environmental protection, and disaster recovery protections

In order for financial institutions to be fully compliant with the Safeguards Rule, they need to create comprehensive internal controls for strong administrative, technical, and physical safeguards. To help guide an organization's senior leadership team toward GLBA compliance, some of the major requirements that financial institutions must keep in mind when building an organizational culture founded on consumer protection and GLBA compliance are listed next:

- Validate that consumer information is kept secure and confidential.
- Validate that consumer information is protected from likely threats to its security and integrity.
- Validate that consumer information cannot be accessed by any unauthorized entities, or accessed in a way that would result in substantial loss or in a way that would inconvenience the consumer.[4]

EXHIBIT 64.2 Recommended Evaluation Procedures

Key Questions or Considerations	
I.	**Determine the involvement of the board.**
A.	Has the board or its designated committee approved a written Corporate Information Security Program that meets the requirements of the Information Security Guidelines?
B.	If the board has assigned responsibility for program implementation and review of management reports to an individual or to a committee, is the necessary knowledge, expertise, and authority to perform the task available?
C.	Does the program contain the required elements? 1. If more than one information security program exists for the institution, are the programs coordinated across organizational units?
D.	Are the reports from management to the board (or its designated committee) useful? Does the report adequately describe the overall status of the program, including material risk issues, risk assessment, risk management, and control decisions, service provider oversight, results of testing, security breaches and management's response, and recommendations for program changes? 1. How often does the board (or its designated committee) review reports?
E.	Overall, do management and the board (or its designated committee) adequately oversee the institution's information security program?
II.	**Evaluate the risk assessment process.**
A.	Review the risk assessment program. 1. How does the institution assess risk to its customer information systems and nonpublic customer information? 2. Has the institution evaluated the risk to the entire customer information system? 3. Has the institution used personnel with sufficient expertise to assess the risk to its systems and customer information on an enterprise-wide basis? 4. Is the risk assessment part of a formal risk assessment process with timelines and milestones? If not, how will management ensure timely completion? 5. Does the institution have a process for identifying and ranking its information assets (data and system components) according to sensitivity? How does it use this process in its risk assessment?
B.	Assess adequacy and effectiveness of the risk assessment process. 1. Does the institution identify all reasonably foreseeable internal and external threats that could result in unauthorized disclosure, misuse, alternation, or destruction of customer information, or of customer information systems? 2. Does the institution support its estimate of the potential damage posed by various threats? 3. Review the institution's existing controls to mitigate risks. Does the institution's analysis consider the current administrative, physical, and technical safeguards that prevent or mitigate potential damage? 4. Does the institution use test results to support its assessment of the adequacy and effectiveness of those controls?

(continued)

EXHIBIT 64.2 *(Continued)*

Key Questions or Considerations	
C.	Does the institution identify and prioritize its risk exposure, decide on the risks it must mitigate, and create a mitigation strategy? Is the decision to accept risks documented and reported to the appropriate management levels? 1. Does the institution promptly act to mitigate risks that pose the immediate possibility of material loss? 2. How does the institution demonstrate that the mitigation strategy was reviewed by appropriate officials? 3. Does the risk assessment provide guidance for the nature and extent of testing? 4. Does the risk assessment include vendor oversight requirements?
III.	**Evaluate the adequacy of the program to manage and control risk.**
A.	Review internal controls and policies. Has the institution documented or otherwise demonstrated, at a minimum, that it considered the following controls, and adopted those it considered appropriate? 1. Access controls, such as controls to authenticate and permit access to customer information systems to authorized persons only. 2. Access restrictions at physical locations, such as buildings and computer facilities, to permit access to authorized persons only. 3. Encryption of electronically transmitted and stored customer data. 4. Procedures to ensure that systems modifications are consistent with the approved security program. 5. Dual control procedures, segregation of duties, and employee background checks. 6. Monitoring systems and procedures to detect actual and attempted attacks on, or intrusions into, customer information systems. 7. Response programs specifying actions to be taken by specific individuals when the institution suspects unauthorized access (i.e., incident response). 8. Measures to protect against destruction, loss, or damage of information from potential environmental hazards, such as fire and water damage or technological failures.
B.	Is staff adequately trained to implement the security program? 1. Obtain from management a listing of the training provided to all users of the institution's system.
C.	Determine whether key controls, systems, and procedures of the information security program are regularly tested by independent third parties, or by qualified independent staff, in accordance with the risk assessment. 1. Assess whether the nature and frequency of testing is consistent with the risk assessment. 2. Assess whether tests are conducted or reviewed by independent third parties or qualified staff independent of those that develop or maintain the security program. 3. Assess whether management reviews test results promptly. Assess whether management takes appropriate steps to address adverse test results.

EXHIBIT 64.2 *(Continued)*

Key Questions or Considerations	
IV.	**Assess the measures taken to oversee service providers.**
A.	Determine whether the institution exercises due diligence in selecting service providers.
B.	Determine what information is supplied to service providers.
C.	Obtain a copy of the contract(s) with the service provider(s). Determine whether contracts require service providers to implement appropriate measures to meet the objectives of the guidelines.
D.	If the institution's risk assessment requires monitoring a service provider, then perform the following steps for each applicable service provider.
	1. Determine whether the service provider contract provides for sufficient reporting from the service provider to allow the institution to evaluate appropriately the service provider's performance and security, both in ongoing operations, and when malicious activity is suspected or known.
	2. Determine whether the institution's actions adequately control information supplied to service providers, ensuring that the information is managed and secured properly.
	3. Review financial condition of service provider.
V.	**Determine whether an effective process exists to adjust the information security program.**
A.	Does the institution have an effective process to adjust the information security program as needed? Is the appropriate person assigned responsibility for adjusting the information security program?
B.	Review procedures that are in place to ensure that when the institution makes changes in technology, and in its business functions, the requirements of the guidelines are also considered. These changes can include:
	1. Technology changes (e.g., software patches, new attack technologies, and methodologies).
	2. Sensitivity of information.
	3. Threats (both as to nature and extent).
	4. Upcoming changes to the institution's business arrangements (e.g., mergers and acquisitions, alliances and joint ventures, outsourcing arrangements).
	5. Upcoming changes to customer information systems (e.g., new configurations or connectivity, new software).
C.	Determine whether appropriate expertise is applied to evaluate whether changes to the information security program are necessary.
D.	Determine whether appropriate controls exist to ensure that changes to the information security program are properly implemented in a timely, risk-minimized manner.
VI.	**Summarize and communicate your findings.**
A.	Discuss issues, conclusions, and potential violations with executive in charge.
B.	Discuss findings with institution management. If you have identified material issues, obtain and document management commitments to address those Issues.
C.	Complete work papers.
D.	Detail findings with support in a Summary Comment.

Fortunately, for many organizations, implementing the Safeguards Rule does not usually require significant structural changes to their information security program. This occurs because the principle of the Safeguards Rule requires compliance with basic information-security program elements. These elements are based on best practices that should already be a part of an effective information-security program.

Specifically, each financial institution must designate an employee to manage the programs safeguards. Depending on financial institution's size, culture, and organizational structure, the actual title and responsibilities of the position will vary significantly. However, at a high level, this function typically requires the identification and assessment of the organization's risk as it relates to consumer information. Furthermore, the organization's risk management must be carried out diligently, so that each relevant area of the institution's operation successfully completes a comprehensive evaluation of the effectiveness of its safeguards. In most cases, the effectiveness of the organization's safeguards can be measured by the organization's ability to manage risk successfully by designing, implementing, and managing adequate information security controls. This activity should further be supported by senior management's ability successfully to monitor and test the information risk-management program on a regular basis.

Finally, it is important that the financial institution's senior leadership team proactively protect customer information, even when working with third parties. Under GLBA, financial institutions must also select the appropriate service providers to support their GLBA requirements and to enter into security-minded agreements. Simply utilizing third parties does not free financial institutions from their GLBA obligations. The organization's senior leadership team must establish agreements in a manner that adequately protects consumer information and that requires the service provider to implement appropriate and GLBA-relevant safeguards. GLBA stresses that, at a minimum, the safeguards performed by the third party must be equal to the protections offered internally by the financial institution's senior leadership team.

64.4 EXAMINATION PROCEDURES TO EVALUATE COMPLIANCE WITH GUIDELINES FOR SAFEGUARDING CUSTOMER INFORMATION. The Office of the Controller of the Currency of the United States Department of the Treasury has published a useful table of recommended evaluation procedures that will help readers apply the principles discussed in this chapter.[5] A simplified and edited representation of the procedures is supplied in Exhibit 64.2.

64.5 CONCLUDING REMARKS. An overall increase in regulatory requirements is likely to emerge in coming years. Some of these requirements may be industry specific or broad enough to reach all organizations. Good security professionals will build and maintain comprehensive governance, risk, and control programs. This will give their organizations a strong foundation for any future regulatory requirements.

64.6 FURTHER READING

Anand, S. *Essentials of Sarbanes-Oxley*. Wiley, 2007.

Aspatore Publishers, eds. *Recent Trends in Privacy and Data Security: Leading Lawyers on Analyzing Information Storage Regulations and Developing Effective Data Protection Policies.* Thomson Reuters Westlaw, 2013.

Bianco, K. M., J. Hamilton, K. R. Benson, A. A. Turner, and J. M. Pachkowski. *Financial Services Modernization: Gramm-Leach-Bliley Act of 1999 Law and Explanation*. CCH Inc., 1999.

Buchanan, Jim "Cloud Computing: 4 Tips for Regulatory Compliance." *CIO.com* 2011. www.cio.com/article/687434/Cloud_Computing_4_Tips_for_Regulatory_Compliance

Cohen, H. R., and W. J. Sweet. *After the Gramm-Leach-Bliley Act: A Road Map for Banks, Securities Firms, and Investment Managers*. Practising Law Institute, 2000.

Cox, F. D. *Information Security: Risk Management of GLBA Privacy and Service Provider Oversight*. Amazon Digital Services, 2011.

Crosman, Penny. "Compliance Roadmap for Proposed Social Media Rules for Banks" *American Banker* (2013). www.americanbanker.com/issues/178_102/compliance-roadmap-for-proposed-social-media-rules-for-banks-1059418-1.html

Dunham, W. B. *After the Gramm-Leach-Bliley Act: A Road Map for Insurance Companies*. Practising Law Institute, 2000.

Greene, E. F., D. M. Becker, and L. N. Silverman. *Sarbanes-Oxley Act: Analysis and Practice*. Aspen Law & Business, 2003.

Hermann, D. S. *Complete Guide to Security and Privacy Metrics: Measuring Regulatory Compliance, Operational Resilience, and ROI*. CRC Press, 2006.

Kearney, E. F., R. Fernandez, J. W. Green, and D. M. Zavada. *Wiley Federal Government Auditing: Laws, Regulations, Standards, Practices, and Sarbanes-Oxley*, 2nd ed. Wiley, 2013.

Lekatis, G. *Understanding Sarbanes-Oxley: What Is Different after July 2013*. Amazon Digital Services, 2013.

Miles, B. L. *The Canadian Financial System*. Nova Science Publishers, 2004.

Moeller, R. R. *Executive's Guide to COSO Internal Controls: Understanding and Implementing the New Framework.* Wiley, 2013.

Tarantino, A. *Manager's Guide to Compliance: Sarbanes-Oxley, COSO, ERM, COBIT, IFRS, BASEL II, OMB's A-123, ASX 10, OECD Principles, Turnbull Guidance, Best Practices, and Case Studies*. Wiley, 2006.

White House. "Consumer Data Privacy in a Networked World: A Framework for Protecting Privacy and Promoting Innovation in the Global Digital Economy." White House Website, February 2012. www.whitehouse.gov/sites/default/files/privacy-final.pdf

64.7 NOTES

1. American Institute of Certified Public Accountants Center for Audit Quality, www.aicpa.org/INTERESTAREAS/CENTERFORAUDITQUALITY/RESOURCES/Pages/Resources.aspx; and see "Section 404(b) of Sarbanes-Oxley Act of 2002," www.aicpa.org/Advocacy/Issues/Pages/Section404bofSOX.aspx
2. Gramm-Leach-Bliley Act: 15 USC SubChapter 1, §§6801–6809, www.ftc.gov/privacy/glbact/glbsub1.htm
3. At least, not in this context. For a different perspective on the question of organizations as people, see discussions of Citizens United v. Federal Election Commission, www.scotusblog.com/case-files/cases/citizens-united-v-federal-election-commission

4. FTC, "Standards for Safeguarding Customer Information: Final Rule," May 23, 2002, 16 CFR §314 ¶1a, www.ftc.gov/os/2002/05/67fr36585.pdf
5. U.S. Department of the Treasury, Office of the Controller of the Currency, "Examination Procedures to Evaluate Compliance with the Guidelines to Safeguard Customer Information," OCC- 2001-35 (2001-07-18). www.occ.gov/news-issuances/bulletins/2001/bulletin-2001-35.html

CHAPTER 65

THE ROLE OF THE CISO

Karen F. Worstell

65.1 CISO AS CHANGE AGENT. The title of chief information security officer (CISO) has evolved because of the realization that the function of the chief information officer (CIO) is so broad as to require another person to focus specifically on the *security* elements of information. Another motivation derives from the fact that the CISO can perform functions that are not usually associated with the CIO. Our approach to information security needs to change in response to the disruptive events affecting the network and the boardroom. CISOs should be the change agents to make this happen. This is a shift from the majority of CISOs' emphasis today as senior managers of information technology (IT) security.

Today, CISOs are in the trust business, due to the need to create and maintain a network of trust among all the people, business processes, and technology of an enterprise and its partners. The interconnected ecosystem that developed since the commercialization of the Internet has seen dramatic shifts of trust: Consumers are thinking twice before conducting business transactions online, and governments have intervened with regulations to improve the trust environment. The shift has between toward less trust each time we encountered a *disruptive event*—an event that awakened us to the fact that things were not as they seemed and made us aware that protection of networked information and systems needed to address something we had not anticipated. The timeline of disruptive security events that began in 1986 with the promise of productivity by Macs and PCs worsened with the Brain virus (1986). Trust continued to decline with the Morris Worm (1988) and the Concept.A macro virus (1995). Our world became flatter,[1] and security became an entirely new kind of problem with the commercialization of the Internet and the introduction of the Web. In 1995, we still trusted the networked ecosystem. We saw the malicious works of nefarious individuals and groups, and we saw the future threat, but still did not fully realize how bad it would get.

Throughout this chapter, the author refers to *information security* and the *CISO*. This is not to the exclusion of aspects of security that do not deal directly with information systems; rather, it is intended in the broadest possible sense to address the interdependent disciplines that are required successfully to protect information in all its forms. It is in this context that the title *CISO* is used, inclusive of *CI* and *CSO* rather than exclusive.

In 2001, the horrific events of 9/11 rocked the planet, Enron collapsed, trust plummeted with Slammer (2002), and the insidious stealthy vectors that utilize port 80 to steal everything from personal identities to bank accounts and company data. The networked ecosystem has provided no end of new material for our profession while making *computer security*, *spyware*, and *identity theft* household terms.

Mark Twain once said the definition of insanity is to do the same thing over and over and expect different results. It is clear that we will need to apply a different way of thinking and new roles and responsibilities to the discipline of information security if we are to make progress in enabling the kind of protection that is required by businesses and agencies while enabling business agility and competitiveness. This is the opportunity of the CISO.

Trends reveal that we are just past the cusp of a new kind of *disruptive event* worldwide—the introduction of legislative and regulatory mandates to ensure effectiveness of controls for protection of consumers, critical infrastructures, and shareholder value. We deal today with a myriad of high-impact network-based crimes: extortion, corporate espionage, and massive fraud. Many experienced CISOs believe that a *cyber–Pearl Harbor* scenario is plausible. Since 2001, we are acutely aware of the vulnerability of critical infrastructures, at least 85 percent of which are owned and maintained by the private sector. Recent figures[2] indicate that new home PCs are compromised with anything from spyware to Trojans within 5 minutes of connecting to the Internet (it takes up to 60 minutes to download protective software). Although corporate PCs may enjoy a relative degree of protection, as many as 90 percent of home PCs have some kind of spyware. Corporations with the resources to address information security have doubled the use of IT security standards and guides since 2003. But the insidious attack on the home user is winning a game with serious stakes: Consumer confidence in the Internet is waning. Once *computer security* was the domain of techies and *geeks*; it is now pervasive enough to be a household concern.

Security has definitely reached the awareness of the C-level offices (chief executive officer, chief financial officer, etc.) on mahogany row, and there are articles in the popular press on a daily basis concerning information security around the world. This visibility ensures that no one can hide behind a plea of ignorance of security problems.

Legislators and regulators are more concerned than ever, and new statutes, codes, regulations, and guidelines have proliferated. In the face of huge threats and the need for a corporate duty of care, network security remains a concern, but compliance to regulations and statutes and the ability to demonstrate adherence have become mandatory.

Penalties for noncompliance to these recently established governing rules are setting breathtaking precedents: $1.2 billion for a large U.S. financial institution, $15 million for another. The U.S. Veteran's Administration admitted to the compromise of personal information, including Social Security numbers, of 26.5 million living American veterans.[3] It may be noted that even New Zealand was for sale on eBay® recently—reportedly the efforts of an unknown party in Queensland—and was taken off line after 22 bids had reached A$2,000.[4] The reserve, if any, was probably not met. We live in a new world. Trust is no longer assumed; it is easily broken in the most inadvertent to the most imaginative ways. The case law for settlements and summary judgments in information security matters is providing the basis for the best potential dollar-based impact analysis on business and information-security risk since Basel II, which is the second set of international guidelines on banking laws and regulations recommended by the Basel Committee on Banking Supervision.[5]

Companies, and clearly U.S. Government agencies, do not have control of intellectual property, employee data, or consumer data. The need to retain corporate records in the event of litigation regarding business matters, and to produce such information on demand under discovery, is infeasible for many firms with petabytes or more of structured and unstructured data. Recent legislation, regulations, and case law will drive the need for information security programs to solve this enormous data management and security problem and to demonstrate a level of effectiveness to a standard of care that will stand up to the scrutiny of opposing counsel. It is the role of the CISO to understand fully the implications of these new burdens and to incorporate them into a strategy along with the business strategy of each enterprise. Where information security spending was benchmarked by Gartner Group at 1 to 3 percent of overall IT budget in the mainframe days, and 5 to 7 percent at the dawn of distributed computing, the spending to resolve problems created by past failures to address solid controls and to be prepared for the threats of the future to any degree should well exceed 10 percent of an overall IT budget. This does not include the special allowances that will be required to treat some of the worst offenses. According to the 2004 Information Security survey conducted by PricewaterhouseCoopers and *CIO* magazine, the best-practices group spent 14 percent of their IT budgets on information security each year.[6] Companies must plan for these expenditures; the role of the CISO will be to help clarify obligations, business necessities, and strategic spending.

65.2 CISO AS STRATEGIST.

Information is the prize that motivates wrongdoers, perpetrators, and miscreants who tamper with, destroy, and penetrate systems that process, store, and transmit digital information. Phil Condit, former chairman of The Boeing Company, said it well at his keynote to the International Information Integrity Institute in 1995: "Information is the business."[7] His statement was visionary at the time. Indeed, since 1995, it is safe to say that information is the foundation of business, but it is the way it is used, combined, mined, shared, represented, accessed, and manipulated for business logic's sake that creates competitive advantage. And each of these areas of application logic and information requires rules-based protection to ensure that the business is basing decisions on sound knowledge.

There are three main drivers for CISOs to define a new strategy for information security:

1. Systems are inherently insecure as a result of enormous variations in configuration, sheer complexity, and volume of vulnerabilities. A risk-based approach using conventional methods is no longer valid (if it ever was).
2. The reach of global business processes, personnel, and business systems introduces new considerations into an already complex security problem.
3. The playing field between the *protectors* and the *interlopers* is dramatically uneven. There are literally hundreds of thousands, if not millions, of interlopers with a follow-the-sun 7×24×365 factory of attacks. Companies cannot afford any such investment to counter the attacks, even if it were possible with a combination of people and automation. The attack vectors change too quickly to be able to get ahead of the curve on the protection side of the equation. Nation-states, organized crime, terrorist organizations, fraudsters, and identity thieves are continuously developing ingenious models to attack, steal, and destroy precious assets of individuals as well as of enterprises.[8] Worse, professionals continue to consider trusted insiders as the most significant threat. With a globally distributed workforce of contractors, employees, and suppliers, it is necessary to have an approach to information protection controls that enables a reasonable assurance that both the external and insider threats are appropriately addressed.

The CISO as a strategist will be successful adopting and integrating new methods into the business, such as a rules-based standard of care and due diligence to that standard of care. This will necessarily include existing methods of network protection, data classification, and so forth—the standard of ISO/IEC 17799:2005 provides an excellent framework. It is the decision-making process about priorities that must change.[9]

As a strategist, the CISO will need to look at the security problem as an executive businessperson would. Adopting the kinds of strategic thinking described in classics such as *The Art of the Long View* is a key success factor.[10] A partial list of things to consider includes the reliance on information, why protection is important, the insecurity of systems, the futility of risk-based security, and world trends.

65.2.1 Reliance on Digital Information. Digital information is the lifeblood of our commerce, financial infrastructure, healthcare, transportation, energy, and even our very identities as citizens. In the United States alone there are 15 distinct critical infrastructures, vital to the interests of the country and to national security:

1. Information technology
2. Telecommunications
3. Chemicals
4. Transportation systems
5. Emergency services
6. Postal and shipping services
7. Agriculture and food
8. Public health and healthcare
9. Drinking water/water treatment

10. Energy
11. Banking and finance
12. National monuments and icons
13. Defense industrial base
14. Key industry/technology sites
15. Large gathering sites[11]

Eight-five percent of the systems that make up these critical infrastructures are owned by private enterprise. The systems that interconnect to deliver services require integrity, availability, the trusted relationships, and confidentiality. If we cannot trust the systems, we cannot trust the information. If we cannot trust the information, we cannot trust decisions based on that information. Information security also now requires us to be able to demonstrate digital ownership and even chain of possession. We have to maintain digital information in such a way that we know where our IP is at all times, what records our company must maintain, and how to store, label, and retrieve them. The definition of information security as CIA—confidentiality, integrity, and availability—is too simplistic.

65.2.2 Inherent Insecurity of Systems. Systems include hardware, software, utilities, scripts, and transport media, all of which are ultimately created by humans with scheduled deadlines and constrained budgets, and installed by organizations with scheduled deadlines and constrained budgets. It is all flawed. The vulnerabilities that exist today, let alone the ones we are going to learn about tomorrow and the next day, cannot all be addressed. Perfect security is a myth, unattainable, and arguably a waste of time to try. Risk-based methods for identifying required security tactics do not scale, nor is there meaningful data that describe probability and ALE (annualized loss expectancy) realistically for information security.

65.2.3 World Trends. Our world is changing. As summarized in a report titled "Ten Trends to Watch in 2006" published by McKinsey and Company,[12] trends that have already had significant implications for security professionals include:

- Dramatic geographic shifts in centers of economic activity, particularly in IT services, where labor and talent are increasing globally. Worldwide, distributed, and devolved security models will be required, as the supply chain and internal processes in a company's value chain are widely distributed. The implications of physical security, information systems protection, personnel practices, and the diversity of governing regulations and statutes require a much broader, business-based view of asset protection. Use of company-owned, leased, and outsourced facilities will prove to be a challenge to asset protection.
- Technological connectivity will transform the way we live and interact and will completely disrupt current security infrastructures. Enhanced connectivity and mobility using smaller (i.e., less observable), highly capable Internet-enabled devices requires access to enterprise information resources from anywhere, at any time, putting an enormous strain on rule sets designed to filter incoming and outgoing information, and where it travels. Peer-to-peer networking, tiny mass storage devices, blending of personal and enterprise computing on common devices—these are just a few of the near-term changes that will completely alter

the way enterprise rules are handled for information protection. Grid computing, virtual machines, work from home—all are issues that challenge the notion of comprehensive asset protection, both physical and logical.

- New models of in-the-cloud knowledge, including production, access distribution, and ownership are emerging, and fundamental trust models remain to be defined or even described. *Software as a service* (SAAS) is already enabled for consumers and small businesses, and, probably, enterprise services will follow. The download and introduction of software over the Web, and access to proprietary information in an anywhere-computing environment, requires redefinition of the way we think about intellectual property and data management.

A coordinated, interdisciplinary management approach to a proper set of controls based on business risk is essential to deal effectively with the enormous requirements to protect information in business today. Whether the enterprise is private or public, regardless of nationality, a solid information protection strategy must recognize the implications of that principle.

To summarize, successful use and management of information is the business. Setting priorities that demonstrate due diligence to a properly business-driven standard of care for the confidentiality, integrity, availability, ownership, and proper possession of information is the charge of the CISO. It is essential that the CISO function at the level of executive management and as a business strategist, participating with the executive leadership team to enable the integration of due diligence to a standard of care into all business streams.

65.3 STRATEGY, GOVERNANCE, AND THE STANDARD OF CARE. Recognizing the information security changes that drive the role of the CISO, what should be done to be successful? What are the key focus areas that should define the role of a CISO?

Success for information security professionals will depend on several key factors in this new world:

- Standard of care (e.g., rules-based) strategy
- Governance and accountability
- Clear roles and responsibilities
- Metrics, reporting, and executive visibility

The remainder of this section examines each of these more fully. For a general discussion of management's role in information assurance, see Chapter 63 in this *Handbook*.

65.3.1 Standard of Care. A CISO has one vision statement that drives strategy: to establish due diligence to a standard of care for the business; that is to say, to put in place the mechanisms (controls, oversight, monitoring, metrics, and reporting) that will enable the business to demonstrate due diligence to that standard of care. Instead such a standard of care is rules based, but it is not prescriptive in itself. The standard of care is the set of documented business risks from an information protection perspective, and the declaration of a set of rules in policy, that effectively mitigate those business risks. The standard of care declares *what* will be done. It is the governing book of policy to be reviewed and monitored by the executive leadership team, the audit committee of the board of directors, and senior management. It is the set of rules with which all internal standards and desktop procedures must comply.

Although a complete treatment of the identification of business risk is outside the scope of this chapter, it can be summarized in this way: Prior to identifying the controls within a standard of care, steps must be taken to qualify business risk relatively as *high*, *medium*, or *low* based on magnitude of potential business impact and perceived exposure. It does not use quantitative risk analysis methods such as those found in Octave, FAIR, or any other popular risk-based quantitative methodology. It does not use ALE. It does enable the business to defend the design of the standard of care, the controls of which are derived from the business risk analysis.

The standard of care derives its meaning from two primary sources: internationally accepted standards and the risk analysis that defines the business risks.

The basic set of internationally accepted standards is summarized in Exhibit 65.1. For more detailed analysis of security standards, see Chapters 44 and 51 in this *Handbook*.

It is important for these standards to be used as a foundation for the policy, to ensure that security policy is recognized by the larger body of security professionals, and to serve as an interchangeable trading partner agreement in the communication and enforcement of security expectations.

It is not in the scope of this chapter to go into the risk assessment methodology in detail; however, a general description will serve to indicate that this is not a vulnerability assessment. The risk assessment process is one used not to identify system vulnerabilities but to identify potential areas relating to people, process, and technology that could result in an exposure that reaches a defined threshold of business impact. For example, in a technology firm, one might align three major areas of concern: major inaccuracies in financial reporting (the domain of the Sarbanes-Oxley Act of 2002); failure to control IP adequately and the subsequent risk to trade secrets, patents, or copyrights; and failure to protect customer data adequately. Each of these slices of business risk can be the foundation for the questions in the risk assessment to ascertain major systems exposure, business process exposure, or exposure caused by people doing things incorrectly, such as human error or even malfeasance. Risk rankings will need to be on the basis of assumptions and figures acceptable to the senior leadership team; the wildcard in any risk ranking is probability. The business impact threshold will vary widely with each business. Thresholds may be set using the financials of the company. A company that has a *materiality threshold* (i.e., the minimum level of loss that matters significantly to the organization), for example, of $5 million that defines a material weakness in Sarbanes-Oxley compliance will prioritize its risks differently than a firm for which the materiality threshold is on the order of $500 million.[13]

With the risk analysis to use as a rationale, the road map to tailoring a book of policy derived from the international standards becomes a series of steps to take for each risk, to define the mitigating control, and to map that control to a control statement in, for example, ISO/IEC 17799:2005. Repeating this for all the risk categories and all the risk areas, one will have a foundation to demonstrate to any trading partner or outside party why the standard of care is relevant and appropriate to the company.

The next step is to help provide the translation of the high-level standard of care policy statements into action. Creating a set of implementation standards for the various controls described in the standard of care gives clear direction to all parties charged with ensuring that the needed controls are in place. The implementation standards also provide the foundation for a set of measurements and tests to determine that the controls are working as intended. This is the critical element that enables the executive

Exhibit 65.1 International Standards for Information-Security Governance

Basic set of internationally accepted standards includes	Useful in this context:
BS 7799	Replaced —see ISO/IEC 27001
ISO/IEC 17799:2005—Information technology. Security techniques. Code of practice for information-security management.	This universal standard provides a complete set of guidelines for an effective Information Security Management System (ISMS). It is essential guidance to help manage an effective information-security policy. It offers a common language and a common understanding to enable an organization to develop, implement, and measure effective security management practice, providing confidence in intercompany trading. ISO/IEC 17799 details a number of individual security controls, which may be selected and applied as part of the ISMS. ISO/IEC 17799, again based on a British standard, is scheduled to become ISO/IEC 27002 in a couple of years.
BS 7799-2:2005 (ISO/IEC 27001:2005) Information technology. Security techniques. Information-Security Management Systems. Requirements.	ISO/IEC 27001 specifies the requirements for the security management system itself. It is this standard, as opposed to ISO/IEC 17799, against which certification is offered. ISO/IEC 27001 has also been harmonized to be compatible with other management systems standards, such as ISO/IEC 9001 and ISO/IEC 14001. Organizations already certified under BS 7799- 2:2002 need to prepare for transition to ISO/IEC 27001 in order to meet its requirements.
BS ISO/IEC 13335-1:2004 Information technology. Guidelines for the management of IT security. Concepts and models for information and communications technology security management	This standard is useful to: • Define and describe the concepts associated with the management of IT security. • Identify the relationships between the management of IT security and management of IT in general. • Present several models that can be used to explain IT security. • Provide general guidance on the management of IT security.
IT Governance Institute's *Control Objectives for IT* (CoBIT®)	CoBIT® is a way to implement governance. It provides a tailorable set of controls.
ITIL—IT Infrastructure Library	ITIL® provides a cohesive set of best practice, drawn from the public and private sectors internationally. It is supported by a comprehensive qualifications scheme, accredited training organizations, and implementation and assessment tools. The best practice processes promoted in ITIL® support and are supported by the British Standards Institution's standard for IT service Management (BS15000). (OGC - ITIL)

team and the CISO to demonstrate that the controls are not only the right ones, but that they are working properly.

The CISO does not get involved in monitoring firewall rules or router configurations. This is work that is the domain of an operations security manager who is carrying out the standards established by the CISO. The CISO should review the reporting (once it is established) to ensure that the controls described for all Internet connectivity are in place and working, and to ensure that the handling of technical details is delegated to specialized technical staff and management.

65.3.2 Governance and Accountability. A recent research project completed by Booz Allen Hamilton reveals several factors that are changing the face of protecting enterprise assets, and ultimately adjusting the roles of the security profession. The information protection strategy is undergoing *convergence*, defined by ASIS International as "the identification of security risks and interdependencies between business functions and processes within the enterprise and the development of managed business process solutions to address those risks and interdependencies."[14] The role of the successful CISO is not only converging into an interdependent set of security specialties; it is also blending into business functions, intertwined into the fabric of decision-making processes throughout the life cycle of business strategy, plans, and execution.

Given the need for managing all the complexity recently introduced, security professionals must also adopt a different outlook—a more business-oriented than a protectionist position. Tim Mather, CISO of Symantec Corporation, describes it this way:

> For many information-security professionals, the urge is to promote information security—zealously. Many times too zealously. We often come to believe that security awareness equates to zealous promotion of information-security objectives, especially the deployment of (information) security technology—often at the "expense" of people, and policies and processes. However, that zealous promotion of information-security objectives tends to cloud our judgment as to the business considerations of the risks involved. Our information-security–colored glasses are polarized to security and tend to filter out business unit considerations. This leads to a loss of credibility with business unit personnel, hindering our ability to accomplish our information-security goals.
>
> Our challenge is to articulate our information-security objectives in terms of business risk that business unit personnel can understand and appreciate. That being said, it does not mean being "soft" on our objectives. We are not paid to install the "speed bumps" in enterprise hallways, but that articulation does mean translating information-security objectives into "business-speak." Only the combination of articulate translation and polite but firm emphasis on our information-security objectives will gain us the credibility that we need to accomplish our enterprise information-security goals. And that effort has to begin, and continue, at the top of the enterprise—with its executives.

Part of the reason security managers have had to take such hard positions in the past is that information-security practices have had a strong tendency to be in organizational silos: executive protection, IT, physical security, local business practices, policy management, HR investigations, fraud, and so on. Each of these practice areas is a specialty, to be sure, and will continue to require specialization. Independence can no longer be effective. Privacy, information security, data management, mobility, supply chain management, workforce management, human resources, facility management—the protection elements of these business domains, and so much more, must be coordinated to avoid weak links in the protection strategy that could prove disappointing if not devastating to a business, or to individuals.

With the need for an interdisciplinary approach at an executive level, with a broad reach across an enterprise, one might argue that the centralization of primary information security functions under a CISO would be one way to ensure that all information-security practice would be consistent and easily measured; on the contrary, the temptation to ensure the fidelity of an organizational mission through assembling affected functions under a single manager should be resisted. In a successful information-security strategy, it is far too easy for all enterprise management to think of security as *security's business* or as *the CISO's job*. In fact, the function of security should be emphasized as a business function, with accountability distributed in the business across all business unit executives, led by an executive-level security team. This has five advantages.

1. There will never be a security organization large enough to do the entire job of securing information assets in the new world. Security truly has to be everyone's job, in ways that are measured and tracked. Putting security accountability into the business units will leverage resources effectively.
2. Accountability is a good way to get someone's attention. Management is attentive to scorecards that are read at the top, with expectations for improvements that have been assigned to a responsible individual or group.
3. The interdisciplinary approach needed for the rapidly emerging challenges and competing priorities can best be addressed by an interdisciplinary team, including functions such as supply chain management, that have no reason to be merged into a security organization.
4. Being closely tied to the business allows for upstream integration into business processes, allowing security to be *built in* [versus an afterthought] when new business initiatives, strategies, and ventures are being designed.
5. The funding for proper protection of information assets is no longer a security problem or an IT problem, but it is a business problem, with the proper business visibility of what is and is not getting done, and what is the residual risk from funding decisions.

A simple policy-driven governance structure has been effective in many large-scale organizations to establish the necessary linkages with the business, to ensure consistency in strategy and approach, to gain executive buy-in on strategy through collective priority setting, and to gain visibility of progress and of unresolved issues on an ongoing basis. A basic governance structure can be tailored to fit corporate culture such as the number of representatives, and the layers of working groups. What is essential is the creation of a governance body to ensure corporate due diligence and to avoid conflicts of interest, such as are described further in Section 65.5.5.

A policy-driven approach to security and disaster recovery governance includes these components:

- Senior Leadership Team (C-level executives)
  - Authority for policy
  - Governance body
  - Program oversight
- Policy
  - Establishes accountability

- Establishes programs and program authority
- Establishes governance processes
- Publishes under authority of the senior leadership team
- Principles
  - Five to six high-level statements at a descriptive level
  - Separate from policy
  - Establishes guidance for business unit standards
- Business Unit Team
  - Provides staff support
  - Facilitates governance process
  - Provides technical leadership for security across business units
  - Consists of representatives from each business unit plus audit
  - CISO is chair
  - Coordinates policy principles for senior leadership team approvals
  - Establish standards at the prescriptive level
  - Implements standards
  - Monitors effectiveness of implementation (provides metrics and reports to senior leadership team)
  - Coordinates key initiatives for security and recovery improvement across business units

In this structure, the CISO can function as an agent of change for driving broad, funded, prioritized initiatives with true business impact.

Joel Scambray, coauthor of *Hacking Exposed* and senior security strategist at Microsoft, sees the need for CISOs as change agents:

> Information security is now such a very broad topic, the role of the senior security professional has to move away from implementation of the security technology to the role of change agent. Network issues are diminishing: so much can go through port 80 inbound and then by proxy to the application, the themes in the attack community are shifting and will always continue to do so as technology evolves. Attackers will strike a business through the path of least resistance and that is going to be throughout the business, not just in the network and applications. It is essential to have business group accountability to address risks in all areas, for each executive to think about risk and ensure they are taking informed steps to bring it to within acceptable levels.
>
> The CISO has to move up in the corporate structure—it's a revenue-protecting job and has to be supported at the highest levels of the company to get the company to focus on the right risks.[15]

65.3.3 Roles and Responsibilities. In general terms, there are a set of roles and responsibilities that support accountability that have been shown effective in practice. Some would require substantial change in the organizational responsibilities within a company or agency. That ISO is the change agent to make things better; once the foundation for security governance is in place, this should be a discussion topic. Outside professional opinions can be solicited. Refer to the practices documented at Institute of Internal Auditors (IIA), Information Systems Audit and Control Association (ISACA), and the IT Governance Institute (ITGI). Evaluate them in the context of your company; you may not be able to implement all 10 of these principles for accountability and reporting, but even some of them would demonstrate progress. The 10 principles for effective information-security control follow. For each item involving security, the CISO is the leader, or receives and acts on reports, or merely a participant and observer.

1. The CISO does not *own* IT assets but manages them on behalf of the business. Governance processes are in place for effective business management of IT.
2. An independent third party regularly reviews the implementation of each of these principles to verify control design and control effectiveness.
3. The expenditures on IT security are justified in terms of business value according to parameters established between the CISO and the business units.
4. IT security is actively monitored by an IT governance board consisting of IT, business management, and the CFO, and adjusted according to business needs.
5. Security, information assurance, and cybersecurity rules are tied to business rules in ways that are traceable, understandable, and agreed to by the business.
6. All IT security change is authorized by specifically designated IT management change boards.
7. Application development processes verify that applications perform only as intended, throughout the life cycle of the application, under the supervision of IT governance boards.
8. All IT security operations and processes are standardized, documented, and reviewed regularly for consistency by IT management and independent third parties.
   a. New processes are developed to accommodate business change.
   b. Existing processes are reviewed regularly for update, to accommodate business change. Consider having legal counsel review the documentation to determine if the records present unexpected legal risks or if they can provide legal advantage in any dispute over the standard of care.
9. All information systems assets (data, infrastructure, applications, processes, and services) have clear business owners with accountability to ensure:
   a. Assets are used only as intended.
   b. Assets are accessed only by those who are authorized according to defined business rules. (Access is defined as ability + opportunity.)
   c. Assets are available for use according to defined business rules.
10. Business and IT employees, contractors, vendors, and third parties have necessary documentation and training on a regular basis to carry out these principles in an effective, verifiable manner for the businesses in which they are engaged, and they have proof of training on a timely basis.

Generally, the business does not want to own IT. They see IT as a utility, the domain of IT staff, and too much work to understand. This is the major hurdle to be overcome in the change agent role of CISO. Remember, IT is the business. That is to say, IT today governs the systems that process the information that is the lifeblood of the business. Without the information, the business will stop. The logic applied to the information on behalf of the business should be owned by the business. It is worth the effort; once the business realizes its own accountability for the confidentiality, availability, integrity, ownership, and possession of business information, as well as for information-security practices and improvements, it will enjoy a whole new level of interest in, and responsibility for, the enterprise.

65.3.4 Reporting. With the governance structure established, the ability exists to assign accountability to the right places in the organization. The senior leadership team should identify how management will be held accountable. This is not a choice of *if* but of *how*. Without clear accountability, governance and policy will mean nothing because they will not be implemented or enforced effectively. The primary tools for enabling executive accountability are reporting, monitoring, and metrics.

65.3.5 Monitoring. Monitoring in the context of the standard of care is the set of processes, human resources, and automated and manual tools needed to ascertain how well the controls established by the standard of care are functioning. Key to monitoring success is to monitor meaningfully—monitor to determine that the set of controls established is, or is not, working as intended. This is a function that can easily be coordinated and shared with internal audit, and care must be taken to ensure that the monitoring is appropriate for the applicable standard of care rules. Monitoring should be done with an objective degree of proof—hearsay is not adequate monitoring. Monitoring will usually need to be automated to handle the scale and frequency required in most information systems environments.

65.3.6 Metrics. Metrics have been a difficult challenge for all CISOs. The generic advice is this: Choose metrics for reporting that are essential to (a) give the business a set of key performance indicators and (b) make a difference in a needed control area. We often measure something in security just because we can. This is a mistake. Measuring the number of viruses or number of penetration attempts is not meaningful because they are high-volume certainties. The measurement system has to ensure that good results could not be achieved from failing to look; a decline in security incidents from outside attacks may be truly declining, based on 100 percent visibility of the problem, or the problem may have shifted to a space that is not monitored. In most cases it is probably, the latter, given the changing vectors in the network attack space.

65.3.7 Executive Visibility. For executive visibility, experience indicates that a CISO executive scorecard, published with the support of the CEO, CFO, COO, or other executive sponsor, will drive behavior according to the metrics that are chosen and reported. Reporting should be at least quarterly—more frequent would be desirable, but may be difficult to achieve. Quarterly frequency allows for continuity of program management in making security improvements that require executive support for implementation.

65.4 SUMMARY OF ACTIONS.

In summary, the strategy for information security has to balance vulnerability management with a standard of care that is appropriate to all stakeholders. These stakeholders include business owners, trading partners, consumers, regulators, auditors, shareholders, and information owners whose membership in the interconnected community puts them at risk if any member has a breach. This requires coordination among diverse specialists and organizations. Security as a state of being is not feasible; due diligence to a standard of care is the approach CISOs should adopt.

The CISO has to develop a standard of care that answers to many demands. The Federal Information Security Management Act of 2002, EU Data Protection Act, Gramm-Leach-Bliley, HIPAA, Sarbanes-Oxley Act of 2002, Senate Bill 1386, BS 7799 certification, FIPS 199 and 200, as well as various NIST publications, and a host of local codes and statutes around the world greatly complicate the compliance function. It is best to adopt a standard-of-care approach that provides, based on international standards, a single comprehensive response to all queries. Expectations of records management, compliance with e-discovery, business continuance, disaster preparedness, IP and trade secret protections, sanctions for unfair information practices or advertising, and a burgeoning library of case law in matters related to security and privacy have become the drivers to which information-security professionals must respond. Clearly, information security has become a risk management role worthy of a C-level executive, working in a structured governance role to involve the business. Today, the transition from security director or even from today's CISO is not complete to the C-level role that the CISO name implies. The points made thus far indicate a real need to pursue this as a professional group and to adopt some generally accepted principles and standards so that businesses and agencies can enjoy the level of information protection that is required in this new world.

65.5 RECOMMENDATIONS FOR SUCCESS FOR CISOs. For all the interviews that I did at RSA in 2006, only one quote made it into the press. Under the title "Microsoft CISO Has a Sense of Humor," the reporter indicated that I had answered all their detailed questions with serious thoughtfulness. But when they asked me what would be the best advice to someone who aspires to be a CISO, they quoted, "Have a stiff drink until the feeling goes away." I actually said, "Have a lie-down somewhere," but no matter—the quip hit the papers.

It was seen as funny, but there is also a real need to consider the demands made on an individual who aspires to a C-level role in security, where there is so much at stake. Many technical security managers are chosen to fill the role but are ill equipped to transform into executive management. Even worse, a CISO who does understand the executive role and moves to perform it in an organization where CISO roles are not understood can easily fail. To quote Machiavelli:

> Let it be noted that there is no more delicate matter to take in hand, nor more dangerous to conduct, nor more doubtful in its success, than to set up as a leader in the introduction of changes. For he who innovates will have for his enemies all those who are well off under the existing order, and only lukewarm supporters in those who might be better off under the new.[16]

In this section, several pointers based on input from various CISOs are offered to help you assess whether an organization is ready for a CISO and whether you are ready. The areas include:

- Education and experience
- The *culture* of security in the business
- The alliance with corporate and outside counsel
- The partnership with internal audit
- The tension with IT and dealing with the potential conflict of interest
- Organizational structure
- Responsibilities and opportunities outside of CISO internal responsibilities

65.5.1 Education and Experience. First and foremost, do you have appropriate background to be able to lead with wise counsel and appropriate judgment? Do you feel you are better at tactical detail, or do you prefer the big picture? In a panel during a plenary session at RSA 2005, LJ (Lisa) Johnson, CISO of Nike, related that her MBA degree was very helpful in her role as CISO, and this sentiment echoes across others in similar positions; however, successful leaders in this space do not all have advanced degrees—life experience is a significant contributor. Reading the wealth of books on various aspects of business management, information systems, and information security is also a good way to expand one's background. Conferences are beginning to focus on the role of CISOs as the role is described in this chapter, but, for the most part, conferences are best at keeping up with technical or auditing trends.

One way to evaluate the background that is necessary, whether it be by experience, reading, or the classroom, is to evaluate the various stakeholders with whom a CISO must effectively communicate to one degree or another. Internal audit, legal counsel, business executives, and IT staff are the core stakeholders. Within the business units, finance, supply chain, and HR are areas with which the CISO will have frequent discussions. Do you know your company's value chain? Do you understand the major business processes? Have you read the company's disclosure statements, and annual report? Do you understand the major cost concerns and the revenue streams? What are the key risks, outside of security, that occupy the executive team's time? If you know the answers to these questions, you are in the minority of security professionals. If you do not create your own action plan to network with key individuals, then read, take a course, and create a career plan that will give you experience in these areas. Do not be afraid to admit that you are learning and interested in getting more information from the experts in a particular area.

Whether your education is a BS in computer science, an MBA, or high school, you can get a great education on the job in preparation to taking a leadership role in information security. Evaluate what it will take for success, and then make your plan to get that information on the job or in school.

Each company is unique, so each CISO job will have unique elements built on the basic CISO job description. A word of warning: As a new CISO, take the time to absorb the culture before launching major changes or initiatives. Remember Machiavelli—people need to know you care before they care what you know.

65.5.2 Culture of Security in the Business. The culture of security can be very difficult to ascertain. In a centralized security model that lends itself to top-down management, one at least knows where to look. In a company where security may be part of the company's core business, and many think of themselves as CISOs, the role is much more challenging. The culture can be defined as the set of attitudes toward accepting direction, allowing time and resources to be used in order to put proper controls in place. The next points will help you take a pulse check on culture and could be used for some due diligence prior to accepting a CISO role:

- **Risk appetite.** What is the materiality threshold (minimum significant loss) for risk management? It is important to understand this so that you can properly ascertain the importance of the issues you will encounter and thereby know whether they require an FYI or escalation as an urgent matter.
- **Cultural norms and attitudes.** Is the workforce dynamic, high rate of job turnover, low threshold of tolerance for change, autonomous? You would work

with this kind of workforce and the culture it engenders much differently than a company with a by the rule-book, policy-driven bureaucracy. There is no right answer, but you need to know how people receive security direction. Most people favor a carrot over a stick; it is a question of what kind of carrot.

- **Relevant regulations and statutes.** You will need an inventory and at least a basic understanding of the way regulations and statutes affect information security. If the company is multinational, this requires an understanding of local jurisdictions, local statutes, and local regulations as well. Find the people who can share with you what they know about this area.
- **Influence and awareness of the court of public opinion.** The court of public opinion is essentially a form of reputation risk and the impact that it can have on the organization. A decision about security, such as fixing a security bug in an online application, may not be governed by specific laws, but it could definitely create the perception of poor security practices in a way that influences other security issues that the company may have in the public eye. This area may be a major influence for highly visible companies, or less of a concern for others.
- **Influence of risk to reputation.** With consumer confidence at an all-time low for Internet security, this is an element of the company's risk profile that it is essential to define explicitly as much as possible. Would the company go so far as to achieve full transparency of its security controls and privacy statements as an approach to building trust as a competitive advantage? Or is it willing to take more reputation risk by obscuring the privacy statement because the security controls are not quite what they should be? As you discover security issues, knowing the company's posture relative to transparency and associated reputation risk will be useful to determine what to escalate.
- **Who else manages various aspects of risk?** Make it a point to build and maintain an active network of peers in these areas:
  - Financial
  - Legal
  - Corporate strategy and planning
  - Marketing
  - Other areas of security (consulting, product, customer support)
- **How is your role seen in relationship to those managers?** Who else should you be talking to? Keep asking the questions.

65.5.3 Alliance with Corporate and Outside Counsel. There are a few roles that merit special mention. Corporate counsel and outside counsel are becoming increasingly interdependent with the information security team. Historically, company policy, investigations, contracts, and incidents have all (or should be) coordinated with counsel. New developments in records management, e-discovery, third-party management, privacy, and case law relating to information-security breaches and losses have created a new role for counsel in defining protection of consumer and employee data and company IP. Counsel will be necessary to navigate the rule of law as it pertains to information, information systems, and associated business practices. This is an organization with which the CISO needs to be close.

65.5.4 Partnership with Internal Audit. While it is not uncommon to find IT personnel who assume that what audit does not know cannot hurt them, this attitude is a grave mistake. Internal audit is another special relationship for the CISO. A close IT–audit partnership is essential for these key reasons, and it should be the responsibility of the CISO to ensure that this partnership is in place and working smoothly:

- The rules for standard of care require demonstration that the controls are working effectively as designed. There is no better organization to provide clarity on what that entails than internal audit.
- Internal audit can collaborate with information security on the standard of care monitoring and reporting, thus effectively extending information protection resources.
- The CISO is accountable to ensure that control processes and policies that pertain are in place and working well. Internal audit should have full access to information-security processes to ensure compliance and to provide independent assurance against potential conflict of interest.
- By cultivating a close partnership (yet maintaining the arm's-length relationship), the CISO and an organization can exchange information, set priorities for the audit and security improvement programs, and provide support for each other on core issues to escalate.

65.5.5 Tension with IT. Many CISOs report to IT, and therein lies a potential for conflict of interest, or the appearance of conflict of interest. This is an area of increasing concern. The issue resides with the CISO needing to identify the security concerns and strategies for the company, including scope that extends beyond IT control, but doing so may be perceived as reflecting poorly on the IT management chain. Also, having a CISO report to the CIO creates an impression that the CISO is the IT security manager. Further, IT budgets are often calculated on the basis of run rates, assuming that it is an operational utility. Funding all the security effort out of an IT budget is a mismatch in two ways: Security is not a run-rate type of function, and taking what amounts to 10 percent or more of the IT budget for security is generally a significant hardship on other parts of IT that are critical to the business.

To address the conflict of interest concern, one could move the CISO role out of IT and have it reporting at the CFO, COO, or CEO level. The CISO in this regard would be a peer of the CIO. This has an advantage of removing the conflict of interest and the impression of IT security manager, but it also introduces the possibility of the CISO losing touch with the IT organization. Another alternative, if the CISO reports to the CIO, is to establish the governance structure and provide dotted-line relationships to the senior leadership on the governance board. Internal audit can monitor the relationships and processes to ensure that conflicts of interest are not developing. Politics being what they generally are, the latter choice seems the most difficult to implement well.

65.5.6 Organizational Structure. Organizational structure for the CISO will, of course, be heavily influenced by the company. We have already discussed some independent factors that argue against the CISO reporting to the CIO. Companies are moving away from the traditional model of having the senior information-security manager, or in some cases CISO, report directly to the CIO, opting instead to have the CISO report to the CEO, COO, or, in some cases, the CFO. In addition, a cross-functional, dotted-line relationship to key stakeholders may be required for adequate reporting and oversight.[17]

Aside from the question of to whom should the CISO report, what should the CISO manage? How should that be structured? The CISO's role as an executive should be focused on governance, policy management, and compliance monitoring and reporting. The CISO should establish parameters for IT security operations, information-security investigations, forensics and incident handing, identity and access management, business continuance, records management, and e-discovery but need not necessarily handle the day-to-day oversight of those functions. The CISO could also be responsible for physical security and executive protection or have oversight of those roles with other security managers.[18] The role has grown to become more than any single person can track if all these functions report directly to the CISO. It is incumbent on the CISO to set the strategy and the structure for all these related security functions and to monitor their progress against predefined performance objectives.

65.5.7 Responsibilities and Opportunities outside of CISO Internal Responsibilities. In this chapter, we have described CISOs as change agents and strategists, adopting a standard of care and strategies that both implement that standard of care and demonstrate due diligence to it. Such individuals have much to contribute to the profession, to the community at large, to the technical community, and even to the definitions being established by governing bodies at the local, state, federal, and international levels.

It would be unreasonable to try to prescribe what CISOs should do outside their direct internal responsibilities. Suffice it to say that CISOs should subscribe to a professional ethic to share what they have experienced, to codify security practice, and to bring about a better understanding of the problem space, so that defined problems can be solved with best practices that ultimately become standard protocols. Make it a practice to participate in professional organizations, to write, and to speak to community, professional, and trade organizations. Get the word out. Work to eliminate confusion. Define the role. There is much at stake for those who choose to wear this mantle—in the words of Theodore Roosevelt, "It behooves every man to remember that the work of the critic is of altogether secondary importance, and that in the end, progress is accomplished by the man who does things."

65.6 CONCLUDING REMARKS.

CISOs are strategic, executive agents of change for the protection of information that is the lifeblood of critical infrastructures and private enterprise. The realm of disciplines that CISOs must manage is expanding as the scope of security has broadened—an interdisciplinary approach that involves all aspects of the business to provide digital, physical, and personnel security is required with input from vital stakeholders.[19]

This role is different from that of technical security management in the near past, and involves tools that are different. The complexity and sheer insecurity of the interconnected ecosystem requires that we adopt a standard of care and that we be able to demonstrate due diligence to that standard of care—this is the mission of CISOs.

CISOs, to be successful, depend on strong governance, roles, and responsibilities; management accountability; and strong reporting practices (including monitoring, metrics, and executive visibility) to be successful. CISOs would necessarily provide oversight, direct or indirect, of functional roles such as technical security management functions.

CISOs are a rare breed and need to make their contributions to their respective organizations as well as to the larger set of professional, community, and industry groups that need guidance, clarity, and judgment in their movement forward to a trusted, interconnected ecosystem.

The challenge is huge—that is why CISOs like it. It is ever-changing, touches every part of business and technology, and is ultimately a people job. It is a very difficult job and, under the right circumstances, is a very rewarding one. It is a high position of trust and responsibility, and it finally has come into its own.

65.7 FURTHER READING

Brotby, W. K. *Information Security Governance: A Practical Development and Implementation Approach*. Wiley, 2009.

Brotby, W. K., and G. Hinson. *PRAGMATIC Security Metrics: Applying Metametrics to Information Security*. Auerbach Publications, 2013.

Fitzgerald, T. *Information Security Governance Simplified: From the Boardroom to the Keyboard*. CRC Press, 2011.

Fitzgerald, T., and M. Kraus. *CISO Leadership: Essential Principles for Success*. Auerbach Publications, 2007.

Harkins, M. *Managing Risk and Information Security: Protect to Enable*. Apress, 2012.

Kouns, J., and B. L. Kouns. *The Chief Information Security Officer*. IT Governance Publishing, 2011.

Oberlaender, M. S. *C(I)SO—And Now What?: How to Successfully Build Security by Design*. CreateSpace Independent Publishing Platform, 2013.

65.8 NOTES

1. Thomas L. Friedman, *The World Is Flat: A Brief History of the Twenty-First Century* (Farrar, Straus, and Giroux, 2005).
2. Eugene Spafford, "Information Security: Insanity Rules," AusCERT2006, AusCERT, Royal Pines Resort, Gold Coast, Australia, May 24, 2006.
3. Larry Greenemeier, "VA Had Many Security Warnings before Its 26.5 Million-Person Breach," *Information Week*, www.informationweek.com/va-had-many-security-warnings-before-its/188500807
4. T. Cooper, "NZ 'definitely not for sale': Ocker* tries to flog God's Own on eBay" *The Register*, May 12, 2006, www.theregister.co.uk/2006/05/12/nz_auctioned_on_ebay
5. Bank for International Settlements, "Basel II: Revised International Capital Framework" (2006), www.bis.org/publ/bcbsca.htm
6. Scott Berinato, with Lorraine Cosgrove Ware, "Six Secrets of Highly Secure Organizations," *CIO Magazine*, September 15, 2005, www.coresecurity.com/content/six-secrets-of-highly-secure-organizations
7. P. Condit, Keynote Speech, International Information Integrity Institute Forum 25, The Boeing Company, Seattle, WA (January 1995).
8. United States, Office of the National Counter-Intelligence Executive, *Annual Report to Congress on Foreign Economic Collection and Industrial Espionage—2004* (Washington, DC: ONCIX, 2005). www.fas.org/irp/ops/ci/docs/2004.pdf
9. Donn Parker, "Making the Case for Replacing Risk-Based Security," ISSA Journal (May 2001): 6–10.
10. P. Schwartz, *The Art of the Long View: Planning for the Future in an Uncertain World* (Doubleday, 1991).

11. P. W. Parfomak, "Guarding America: Security Guards and U.S. Critical Infrastructure Protection," Congressional Research Service Report for Congress, November 12, 2004, Order Code RL32670; http://ftp.fas.org/sgp/crs/RL32670.pdf
12. Ian Davis and Elizabeth Stephenson, "Ten Trends to Watch in 2006," *McKinsey Quarterly*, http://blog.jackvinson.com/archives/2006/01/19/the_mckinsey_quarterly_ten_trends_to_watch_in_2006.html
13. The concept of materiality threshold is widely used in accounting. For example, see the "Accounting Terminology Guide" from the New York State Society of CPAs, www.nysscpa.org/prof_library/guide.htm
14. Booz Allen Hamilton, "Convergence of Enterprise Security Organizations," ASIS (Alliance for Enterprise Security Risk Management) International, November 8, 2005, http://iris.nyit.edu/~kkhoo/Fall2008/755/Convergence EnterpriseSecurityOrg_08Nov05.pdf
15. Stuart McClure, Joel Scambray, and George Kurtz, *Hacking Exposed*, 5th ed. (Emeryville, CA: McGraw-Hill Osborne, 2005).
16. Niccolo Machiavelli, The Prince (1513), Chapter VI, Para 5, www.gutenberg.org/files/1232/1232-h/1232-h.htm
17. Scott Berinato, with Lorraine Cosgrove Ware, "Six Secrets of Highly Secure Organizations."
18. See, for example, Fran Howarth, "The Convergence of Physical and IT Security," IT-Director.com, September 11, 2006, www.it-director.com/business/regulation/content.php?cid=8743
19. Thomas L. Friedman, *The World Is Flat*.

CHAPTER 66

DEVELOPING SECURITY POLICIES

M. E. Kabay and Sean Kelley

66.1 INTRODUCTION.

This chapter reviews methods for developing security policies in specific organizations. Some of the other chapters of this *Handbook* that bear on policy content, development, and implementation are listed next:

- Chapter 23 provides an extensive overview of physical security policies.
- Chapter 25 discusses local area network security issues and policies.
- Chapter 39 reviews software development policies and quality assurance policies.
- Chapter 44 presents resources and standards for creating effective security policies.
- Chapter 49 looks at methods for enhancing security awareness.
- Chapter 45 provides guidance on employment policies from a security standpoint.
- Chapter 47 makes explicit recommendations about operations management policies.
- Chapter 48 reviews specific recommendations for email and Internet usage.
- Chapter 50 presents concepts and techniques from social psychology to make security policy implementation more effective.
- Chapter 52 discusses the policies that apply to application design.
- Chapter 72 looks at censorship and content filtering on the Internet.

66.2 COLLABORATING IN BUILDING SECURITY POLICIES.

Policies are the foundation of effective information security, but the task of policy creation is complicated by human and organizational resistance. Technology alone does not work. In changing human behavior, rationality and substance are not enough: The *process* of development affects how people feel about policies and whether they see these rules as needless imposition of power or as an expression of their own values.

Security is always described as being everyone's business; however, in practice, security *interferes* with everyone's business. For example, network managers work hard to make networks user friendly. They do everything they can to make life easier for users; they provide network access routines with a graphical user interface, client/server systems with hot links between local spreadsheets and corporate databases, and a gateway to the Internet for their users. Superficially, one might think that implementing network security would simply involve defining access controls, applying encryption, and providing people with handheld password generators. Unfortunately, as discussed in Chapter 50, security policies offend deep-seated self-conceptions. People form close-knit work groups in which they trust each other; they do not lock their desks when they leave them for a few minutes, so why should they obey the network security policy that dictates locking their sessions? They even lend people car keys in an emergency; why should it be such a terrible breach of security to lend access codes and passwords to trusted colleagues in an emergency?

Security policies challenge users to change the way they think about their own responsibility for protecting corporate information. Attempting to impose security policies on unwilling people results in resistance, both because more stringent security procedures make people's jobs harder and because people do not like being told what to do—especially by security officials perceived as being outside the chain of command.

The only approach that works in the long run is to present security to everyone in the organization in a way that causes recognition that each one, personally and professionally, has a stake in information protection. Security managers, to be successful, must involve employees from throughout the enterprise in developing security policies. Users must justifiably feel that they own their security procedures; employees with true involvement in the policy development process become partners, rather than opponents, of effective security.

66.3 PHASE 1: PRELIMINARY EVALUATION.

Studies of the extent to which information-security policies are in place consistently show that relatively few of the respondents have adequate policies in place. For example, the 2007 Global Security Survey run by *CIO Magazine* and PricewaterhouseCoopers was based on interviews and questionnaires involving 7,200 executives, security professionals, and technology managers "across all industries and more than 100 countries" about their organization's security and privacy policies and practices. According to the summary on page 2 of the report:

1. Only 6 out of 10 respondents worldwide (57 percent) say their organization has an information-security strategy in place. Only another 13 percent, however, consider putting one in place a "top priority."
2. Almost half of all respondents worldwide (48 percent) say their organization does not actively engage both business and information technology decision makers in addressing information security.
3. More than 7 out of 10 security managers, administrators, and technicians worldwide believe that their organization's security policies and spending can be improved.[1]

In what follows, it is assumed that a specific officer or manager (or group of officers or managers) in the enterprise has taken on the task of developing security policies. The group will be called the *policy development group.*

Before attempting to formulate policies, the policy development group needs formal authorization to use corporate resources in such a project. It should not be too difficult to obtain a short memorandum from top management to everyone in the organization that lays out the reasons for asking for their time and energy in gathering information about the current state of security. Such authorization and continuing top-level support are essential tools in convincing people to cooperate with the policy development group.

In the absence of existing or adequate security policies, a preliminary inventory is the first step in providing upper management with the baseline information that will justify developing a corporate information-security policy. The preliminary evaluation should be quick and inexpensive—perhaps days of work by a few people. There is no point in wasting time in expensive detail work before getting approval, support, and budget from upper management.

The goal of the preliminary evaluation is to ask the people who work with information resources what they believe are their most important-security needs. Even though they may not be conscious of security as a distinct need, in practice, employees and managers do have valuable insights that transcend theory and generalizations. Data entry clerks may tell the security staff about security violations that no one else has observed or even thought about; for example, they may observe that a bug in a particular program makes the previous operator's data entry screen available for unauthorized entries when the shift changes and a new operator sits at the same terminal.

The policy development group should work closely with human resources (HR) personnel in developing the research instruments for interviewing staff. HR members are likely to know the key managers to contact in each department. The managers have to be convinced to support the effort so researchers can interview willing staff. Some of the HR people are likely to have the professional skills and experience required to provide accurate and cost-effective evaluations of beliefs, attitudes, and behavior affecting security. They may be able to help construct unbiased questionnaires, organize focus groups, and guide interviews.

However, if the security staff and the HR staff are not confident about being able to handle this preliminary data collection, the policy development group should see if it can obtain authorization to hire a consultant with proven expertise in collecting and analyzing social attitudes. The policy development group might want to discuss such a study with a firm specializing in security audits and organizational analysis. If no one knows where to start looking for such resources, the policy development group can contact information security associations, security magazines, security Websites, and local universities and colleges to ask for suggestions.

These key issues should be part of the preliminary study:

- Introduction to the study
- State of current policy
- Data classification
- Sensitive systems
- Critical systems
- Authenticity
- Exposure
- Human resources, management, and employee security awareness
- Physical security
- Software development security
- Computer operations security
- Data access controls
- Network and communications security
- Antimalware measures
- Backups, archives, and data destruction
- Business resumption planning and disaster recovery

The next sections suggest some typical questions that would be helpful in gathering baseline data about the current state of security. All these questions (and more site-specific topics) should be asked of all the respondents in the preliminary evaluation. Applicable questions are not necessarily repeated in each section; instead, questions in the earlier parts of this list may be adapted for use in later sections. These suggestions are not intended to limit creativity but rather to stimulate development of more questions that would be particularly useful for a specific enterprise.

66.3.1 Introduction to the Study. Employees may perceive many of the questions as threatening. The preamble or introduction to the study, whether it is by survey or by interviews, should make it clear that this is *not an audit* and that its purpose is to establish the framework for an appropriate set of security policies—policies suited to the needs of the organization and its stakeholders. The information should be anonymized so that no person will be targeted for reprisal if the study discovers problems. Every effort should be made to reassure employees that the study is designed to learn about the facts of security with a view to improvement, rather than a search for culprits who will be punished.

66.3.2 State of Current Policy. The questions that follow not only gather baseline information about security policies but also determine whether employees have any idea about who is responsible for formulation of those policies.

- Does the enterprise have any security policies at all?
- Who developed them: an individual? a group?
- Where and how are the security policies available (paper, electronic)?
- When were the policies last updated? Last disseminated?
- Who, if anyone, has explicit responsibility for maintaining security policies?
- Who implements security policy at the enterprise level?
- To whom does the chief information security officer report within the enterprise?
- Who monitors compliance with security policies, standards, and compliance?

66.3.3 Data Classification. Questions to ask include:

- Are there levels of security classification that apply to your work? If so, what are they called?
- Are there rules for determining whether information you handle should be classified at a particular level of confidentiality?
- Are documents or files labeled to show their security classification?
- What is your opinion about the value of such classification?
- Do people in your group pay attention to security classifications?
- Do you have any suggestions for improvement of how data are classified?[2]

66.3.4 Sensitive Systems. The questions in this section focus on information that ought to be controlled against unauthorized disclosure and dissemination.

- In your work, are there any kinds of information, documents, or systems that you feel should be protected against unauthorized disclosure? If so, name them.
- How do you personally protect sensitive information that you handle?
- How do others in your department deal with sensitive information? No names, please.
- To your knowledge, have there been any problems with release of sensitive information in your department?
- Do you have any suggestions for improving the handling of sensitive data in your area?

66.3.5 Critical Systems. The questions in this section focus on information that requires special attention to availability and correctness.

- In your work, are there any kinds of information, documents, or systems that you feel are so critical that they *must* be protected against unauthorized modification or destruction? If so, name them.
- Are there any special precautions you use, or know of, to safeguard critical data in your area?

66.3.6 Authenticity. Questions to ask include:

- Do you know of any cases in which anyone has used someone else's identity in sending out messages such as letters, faxes, or email? If so, were there any consequences?
- Does everyone in your group use digital signatures on electronic documents?
- Does anyone in your group make or use unauthorized copies of proprietary software? If so, do you think there is any problem with that?

66.3.7 Exposure. Questions to ask include:

- What are the worst consequences you can realistically imagine that might result from publication in the newspapers of the most sensitive information you control?
- What might happen, in your opinion, if key competitors obtained specific confidential information that you use or control in your area?
- Can you estimate monetary costs associated with the scenarios you have just described?
- What would be the worst consequences you can foresee if critical information you work with were to be altered without authorization, or through accidental modification?
- What might happen if you could not access critical information quickly enough for your work?
- Can you estimate the costs of such breaches of data integrity and data availability?
- Could there be trouble if someone forged documents in your name, or in the enterprise's name? Can you sketch out some scenarios and associated costs resulting from such breaches of authenticity?

66.3.8 Human Resources, Management, and Employee Security Awareness

- As far as you know, who is responsible for developing security policies?
- Do you know where to find the security policies that apply to your work?
- When, if ever, did you last sign any documents dealing with your agreement to security policies?
- Who is responsible for monitoring compliance with security policy in your workgroup? In the enterprise as a whole?

- Have you ever received any training in security policies? If so, when was the last time?
- Have you ever seen any written materials circulating in your workgroup that discuss information security?
- Do you think of protecting corporate information as one of your official responsibilities?[3]

66.3.9 Physical Security

- Does anyone check your identity when you enter the building where you work? Always?
- Are there any electronic access-control systems limiting access to your work area? What are they?
- Do people hold a secured door open to let each other into your work area? Do you let people in after you open a secured door?
- Have you ever seen a secured door into your area that has been blocked open (e.g., for deliveries)?
- Do people leave your work area unlocked when everyone leaves?
- Do staff members wear identity badges at work? Are they supposed to? Do you wear your badge at work?
- Do visitors wear badges?
- Have you ever seen strangers in your area who are not wearing visitor badges?
- What would you do if you saw a stranger in your area who was not wearing a visitor's badge?
- Do you lock any parts of your desk when you leave your workspace?
- What would you do if you heard the fire alarm ring?
- Where is the nearest fire extinguisher?
- Who is the fire marshal for your floor?
- What would you do if someone needed emergency medical attention?
- Is there an emergency medical station in your area or on your floor?
- Do you know who is qualified in cardiopulmonary resuscitation (CPR) in your group or on your floor? Do such people wear identifying pins?
- Have you had recent training in what to do in the event of an emergency? Have you been trained in how to evacuate the building?
- Is there anything that comes to mind that you would like to see to improve physical security and safety in your work area?[4]

66.3.10 Software Development Security. These questions would be asked only of the software development team:

- Are there any security policies that apply to your work? What are they?
- Have you ever discussed security policies in your group?
- Is security viewed positively, neutrally, or negatively in your group? And by yourself?

- Do you and your colleagues discuss security during the requirements analysis and specification phases when developing software?
- How do you see quality assurance as part of the development process?
- Do you use automated software testing tools?
- Do you use automated version control software? If not, how do you exercise control?
- How do you document your systems?
- Do you think that your source code is adequately protected against unauthorized disclosure and modification?
- What is your opinion about Easter eggs (unauthorized code for an amusing picture or game)?
- Could anyone plant an Easter egg or a logic bomb (unauthorized, harmful functions) in code being developed in your group?
- Have you ever seen an Easter egg or a logic bomb in code from your group? Did it get through to production?
- Can you think of ways you would like to see better security in your work?[5]

66.3.11 Computer Operations Security. These questions would be asked only of the computer operations team:

- How long do you wait after initial release before installing new operating system versions on your production machines?
- How do you put new software into production?
- Can development personnel access production software? Production data?
- How do you handle problem reports? Do you have an automated trouble-ticket system?
- Can people from outside the operations group enter the operations center?
- Are contractors, including repair technicians, allowed to circulate in operations without being accompanied?
- Does the cleaning staff ever circulate within the secured areas of operations without operations staff present?
- Are system components labeled?
- Is there an emergency cutoff switch for main power to the entire data center? Does it include air conditioning?
- Are there uninterruptible power supplies for critical components of your systems?
- Do you keep records of system downtime? What is your downtime over the last three months? The last year?
- What accounts for most of the downtime? Have remedies been implemented?
- Who monitors system resource utilization? Are there automated reports showing trends in disk space usage? CPU utilization? Network bandwidth usage?
- What improvements in security would you like to see in operations?[6]

66.3.12 Data Access Controls

- Do you have to identify yourself to the computers and networks you work with?
- Do you have a user name (ID) that no one else shares?
- Are you required to use a password, passphrase, or personal identification number (PIN) as part of your routine when starting to use your computer?
- Have you ever shared your unique user ID and password or PIN with someone else? Or have you borrowed someone else's user ID and password to get some work done? If so, how often does this happen?
- Do you use a token, such as a physical key or a smart card, to prove who you are to the computer system? If so, have you ever lent or borrowed such tokens? What for? How often?
- In your work, are there any limitations on the data you are allowed to see, modify, add to, or delete?
- Are there data you can see but not change?
- Do you use encryption on any of the data you work with?
- Do you or members of your group use laptop computers? If so, do you encrypt sensitive data on the disks of those portable systems?
- Do you or anyone in your group take work home? If so, do you put corporate data on your own, personal (noncompany) computers? Does anyone else have access to those computers? Are there any controls on accessing corporate data on the home computers?[7]

66.3.13 Network and Communications Security. Most of the next questions would be appropriate only for network managers, administrators, and technicians. However, some of the questions are suitable for everyone.

- As a user, do you know what the rules are about using your employer's email system and Internet access?
- Do you know anyone who regularly violates system usage restrictions? No names, please.
- Have you ever seen pornography on corporate systems? Child pornography? Racist and other objectionable materials? If so, did you know what to do? And what did you do?
- Has anyone ever discussed rules for secure email with you? Do you know how to encrypt sensitive messages? Do you ever encrypt messages?
- As a network manager, do you have up-to-date network diagrams, or can you produce them on demand?
- Do you know which services are running on your Internet-connected systems? Are all of the running services needed?
- How do you determine which patches are appropriate for installation on your systems? How often do you check? Who is responsible for managing patches? How long does it take between notification of a vulnerability and installation of an appropriate patch?

- Does your security architecture include firewalls? If so, what determines the security policies you instantiate in the filtering rules?
- Do you have egress filtering enabled on your firewalls?
- Do you have intrusion detection systems? If so, who responds to apprehended intrusions? How are the responsible people notified of an intrusion?
- What are the procedures for responding to an intrusion?
- If your organization uses passwords, how do you handle requests for new passwords?
- Do you have centralized remote-access controls?
- Do remote users use virtual private networks (VPNs) to access corporate systems from outside the firewalls?
- Are your users supposed to use encryption for sensitive email that traverses the Internet? Do they? How do you know?
- Do your users apply digital signatures to all communications?
- Are your Web servers protected against intrusion and vandalism?
- Have you kept sensitive information off your Web servers?
- Do you encrypt all sensitive information stored on your Web servers?
- How long would it take you to recover a valid version of the Website if it were destroyed or vandalized?
- Do your telephone voicemail boxes have unique, nonstandard passwords? How do you know?
- How do you find out if an employee is being fired or has resigned? How long does it take between termination of employment of such an employee and deactivation of all system and network access?

66.3.14 Antimalware Measures

- Do you and all of your users have antimalware products installed on every workstation?
- How often are antimalware products updated? How are they updated?
- How long does it take for all vulnerable systems to be brought up to date?
- Do you or your users open unexpected, unsolicited email attachments?[8]

66.3.15 Backups, Archives, and Data Destruction

- How often do you do backups of your electronic data?
- Where do you store backup media? Are current copies retained off site as well as on? How do you know which media to use to restore a specific file?
- How long do you keep different types of backups? Why?
- How do you prevent unauthorized access to backup media?
- If you keep data backups for several years, how do you ensure that the old media will be readable and that the data developed for old applications will be usable?
- How do you dispose of magnetic and optical storage media after their useful life is over? Are the discarded media readable?

- Do you make backup copies of paper documents? Where are these copies kept? How would you locate a specific document you needed?
- How long do you keep various types of papers? Why?
- When you dispose of paper documents, does their content influence how they are destroyed? How do you dispose of sensitive paper documents?[9]

66.3.16 Incident Response

- Do you know what to do if you see a security problem such as strangers without badges in secured areas, threats of violence arriving by email, damaged company Web pages, bad data in files you use, missing files or data, or forged messages?
- Is there a specific team dedicated to responding to computer security breaches?
- Are you part of a computer security incident response team (CSIRT)? If so:
  - Is this a long-term assignment?
  - Do you have documentation and training on how to respond to specific types of incidents?
  - How are out-of-hours incidents handled?
  - Does your CSIRT hold practice drills?
  - Are there incident postmortems?
  - Do you have relations with local law enforcement officials? If so, which levels (municipal, state, federal)?
  - Have you ever experienced pressures from management to suppress incident reports of criminal activity to law enforcement?[10]

66.3.17 Business Resumption Planning and Disaster Recovery

- Do you have business resumption planning (BRP) or disaster recovery plans (DRP)? If so, where are they kept?
- Who is responsible for keeping BRP and DRP up to date?
- Have you ever participated in a BRP or DRP testing? If so, how long ago was the last one? When is the next scheduled test?
- During BRP and DRP tests, does anyone use video cameras or tape recorders to keep track of critical steps in the recovery?
- After a test, have you participated in analyzing the results of the tests to improve the plans?[11]

66.4 PHASE 2: MANAGEMENT SENSITIZATION. Support from upper management is essential for further progress. The goal in this phase is to get approval for an organization-wide audit and for a policy formulation project. In conjunction with the rest of the information-security project team, the responsible managers should plan on a meeting that lasts no more than one or two hours. The meeting should start with a short statement from a senior executive about the crucial role of information in the organization's business.

Professional aids, such as management-oriented training videos, are helpful to sensitize managers to the consequences of poor information security. For an up-to-date list of such videos, enter the keywords "information-security training video" into a search engine such as Google. After the video film, the team can present its findings from the preliminary evaluation. The immediate goal is to constitute an *information protection working group* to set priorities, determine an action plan, define a timetable and milestones, and formulate policies and procedures to protect corporate information resources. The presenters should name the people you want to see in your working group; all of these people should be contacted before the meeting to be sure that they have agreed in advance to participate in the working group.

The presenters should provide estimates of the time involved and the costs of in-house, and consulting, services, and software. To end the briefing, it is useful to offer upper managers a range of background reading about security. Some managers may be intrigued by this field; the more they learn, the more they will support security efforts. One of the best resources for such sensitization is "Managing Risk from Information Systems: An Organizational Approach."[12] This 67-page summary provides "guidelines for managing risk to organizational operations and assets, individuals, other organizations, and the nation resulting from the operation and use of information systems." The authors state: "The guidelines provided in this special publication have been broadly developed from a technical perspective to be generally useful across a wide range of organizations employing information systems to implement mission and business processes." They also provide extensive cross-indexing to other public documents issued by the National Institute of Standards and Technology (NIST), all of which are freely available online.[13]

66.5 PHASE 3: NEEDS ANALYSIS. The information protection working group should include representatives from every sector of the enterprise. As the group investigates security requirements, the participants' wide experience and perspective will be crucial in deciding which areas to protect most strongly. More important, their involvement is a concrete expression of corporate commitment to a fundamental attitude change in the corporate culture: Security is to be an integral part of the corporate mission.

For example, in a manufacturing firm, the team would include managers and staff from the factory floor, the unions, engineering, equipment maintenance, shipping and receiving, facilities management (including those responsible for physical security), administrative support, sales, marketing, accounting, personnel, the legal department, and information systems. Each of these members of the working group will help improve enterprise security.

If the organization is very large, the group may have to set up subcommittees to deal with specific sectors. Each subcommittee evaluates to what degree the systems and networks are vulnerable to breaches of security. For example, one group could focus on local and campus communications, another on wide area enterprise networks, and a third on electronic data interchange with clients and suppliers.

A typical audit covers the facilities, personnel policies, existing security, application systems, and legal responsibility to stakeholders (owners, shareholders, employees, clients, and the surrounding community). Based on the findings, the subcommittees formulate proposals for improving security. This is where the specialized knowledge obtained from information security specialists and information-security courses will prove especially useful.[14]

66.6 PHASE 4: POLICIES AND PROCEDURES. Once the information protection working group has built a solid floor of understanding of enterprise information security needs, the members are ready to construct the policies and procedures that meet those needs. The process should start from existing templates and normally takes weeks to months to complete a workable draft.[15]

Genuine participation by all the representatives from every sector of the enterprise is a critical element of success; without a thoroughgoing sense of ownership of the policies, working group members will fail to internalize the new policies. All the members of the working group must become enthusiasts for their collective efforts; in some sense, these people become missionaries engaged in the long-term conversion efforts of phase 5, the implementation of the policies.

66.7 PHASE 5: IMPLEMENTATION.

Once the working group members have defined the new or improved security policies, they are about halfway to their goal. The hardest part is ahead: explaining the need for security and the value of the new policies to fellow employees and convincing them to change. Even if they agree intellectually, there is a good chance that their ingrained social habits will override the new rules for at least months and possibly years. The challenge is to overcome these habits.

Chapter 50 shows in detail how to use the insights of social psychology to change corporate culture by working on beliefs, attitudes, and behavior. In addition to the suggestions in that chapter, the information protection working group should organize and deliver awareness and training sessions for all levels of the enterprise:

- Upper management
- Technical support
- Lower-level staff
- Other technical staff

The next sections offer some simple agendas for such preliminary sessions.

66.7.1 Upper Management.

Security policies and procedures require management support and sanctions. The transformation of corporate culture should begin at the top. Although it is difficult to coordinate the presence of top executives, the working group should try to organize a half-day executive briefing session on enterprise security. In practice, the group may be able to convince upper management to attend for one or two hours. The focus should be intensely practical, and should show executives how to protect themselves and the enterprise against common dangers. Suggested topics:

- **A review of the business case for improving security.** Industrial espionage, natural and manmade disasters, vandalism
- **Network security.** Protection against eavesdropping and tampering
- **Access controls.** Tokens, biometrics, passwords
- **Encryption.** Email, laptops, provision for emergency data recovery
- **Backup policies** for PCs, networks, and mainframes
- **Security agreements.** Summaries of the policies and procedures to be read and signed annually
- **Need for total support** to convince other staff to comply with security policies

66.7.2 Technical Support. The next target is the technical support group, the people who help explain security policies to users. In a one-day training session, the presentations can cover:

- Everything covered in the executive briefing
- Operating system security provisions
- Security software features
- Changes in operations to comply with new procedures

66.7.3 Lower-Level Staff. Lower-level staff need a half-day session that answers these questions in terms that apply directly to their own work:

- Why should I care about information security?
- What are my obligations as an employee?
- How do I protect the PC I am responsible for against viruses?
- How do I back up my data?
- How do I manage my passwords?
- What must I do if I see someone violating our security policies?

The class ends with participants signing the security agreement.

66.7.4 Other Technical Staff. More intensive training and education are needed for technical staff, such as members of the software development, operations, and network administration groups. More in-depth, specific material will have to be incorporated into their training; however, such training can be spread over a longer time than that for the groups already discussed, because of the rhythm of work and the crucial importance of technical competence for implementation of the policies. Most enterprises rely on outside trainers, specialized off-site or online courses, and certification programs to raise their staff to the appropriate levels of competence.

66.8 PHASE 6: MAINTENANCE.

Once the enterprise has begun to integrate a concern for security into every aspect of its work, the issue must be kept fresh and interesting. As described in Chapter 49, successful security awareness programs include amusing posters, interesting videos, occasional seminars on stimulating security topics such as recent frauds or computer crimes, and regular newsletters with up-to-date information. Finally, every employee should regularly reread and sign the annual security agreement. This practice ensures that no one can argue that the organization's commitment to security is a superficial charade.

66.9 CONCLUDING REMARKS.

For a secure installation, three things are essential:

1. Sound policies that have been developed with the cooperation of everyone concerned and that are updated periodically
2. Widespread dissemination of those policies, with ongoing observation of their implementation and with frequent training and continual reinforcement
3. Commitment to security on the part of everyone, from top management on down

When these essential elements are in place, the entire organization will function at a more productive level, one at which the possibilities of disruption and damage will have been reduced to a minimum. Nothing less is acceptable.

66.10 FURTHER READING

Barman, S. *Writing Information Security Policies*. New Riders Publishing, 2001.

Brotby, K. *Information Security Governance: A Practical Development and Implementation Approach.* Wiley, 2009.

Calder, A., and S. Watkins. *IT Governance: An International Guide to Data Security and ISO27001/ISO27002*, 5th ed. Kogan Page, 2012.

Fugini, M. G., and C. Bellettini. *Information Security Policies and Actions in Modern Integrated Systems*. IGI Global, 2004.

Greene, S. *Security Policies and Procedures: Principles and Practices*, 2nd ed. Pearson IT Certification, 2013.

Howard, P. D. *FISMA Principles and Best Practices: Beyond Compliance*. Auerbach Publications, 2011.

Jacobs, S. *Engineering Information Security: The Application of Systems Engineering Concepts to Achieve Information Assurance*. Wiley-IEEE Press, 2011.

Johnson, R., and M. Merkow. *Security Policies and Implementation Issues*. Jones & Bartlett Learning, 2010.

Peltier, T. R. *Information Security Policies and Procedures: A Practitioner's Reference*, 2nd ed. Auerbach Publications, 2004.

Smith, R. *The Definitive Guide to Writing Effective Information Security Policies and Procedures*. CreateSpace Independent Publishing Platform, 2010.

Williams, B. L. *Information Security Policy Development for Compliance: ISO/IEC 27001, NIST SP 800-53, HIPAA Standard, PCI DSS V2.0, and AUP V5.0*. Auerbach Publications, 2013.

Wood, C. C. *Information Security Policies Made Easy*, 12th ed. Information Shield, 2012.

Wood, C. C. *Information Security Roles & Responsibilities Made Easy*, 2nd ed. Information Shield, 2005.

66.11 NOTES

1. S. Berinato, "The Fifth Annual Global State of Information Security." *CIO*, August 27, 2007. www.cio.com/article/133600/The_Fifth_Annual_Global_State_of_Information_Security
2. See Chapter 67 in this *Handbook.*
3. For additional ideas in framing questions about security awareness, see Chapter 49. For ideas on appropriate questions dealing with employment practices and policies, see Chapter 45.
4. For more detail about physical security and additional ideas on appropriate questions, see Chapters 22 and 23.
5. For much more information suitable for devising questions about development security, see Chapters 38 and 39.
6. For more information suitable for devising questions about operations security, see Chapter 47.
7. For additional ideas on looking at identification and authentication, see Chapters 28 and 29.

8. See Chapter 41 for more ideas on checking for appropriate levels of antimalware precautions.
9. For additional suggestions to help in framing questions about data backups, see Chapter 57.
10. See Chapter 56.
11. For more ideas on questions that are appropriate in quickly evaluating the state of business resumption planning and disaster recovery, see Chapters 58 and 59.
12. R. Ross, S. Katzke, A. Johnson, M. Swanson, and G. Stoneburner, "Managing Risk from Information Systems: An Organizational Perspective," National Institute of Standards and Technology NIST SP 800-39, Second Public Draft (April 2008), http://csrc.nist.gov/publications/drafts/800-39/SP800-39-spd-sz.pdf
13. The *Further Reading* sections of chapters in this *Handbook* (as well as sections of the chapters themselves) provide a wealth of material for management sensitization.
14. Chapters 54, 63, and 62 have information that will help the information protection working group develop an evaluation plan.
15. Chapter 44 contains many practical suggestions and resources for the content and style of security policies.

CHAPTER 67

DEVELOPING CLASSIFICATION POLICIES FOR DATA

Karthik Raman, Kevin Beets, and M. E. Kabay

67.1 INTRODUCTION.

A figure appears from the bushes on a dark and stormy night. Silently, this figure slips past two crisscrossing guards marching in lock-step. Once past the guards and inside the building, a flashlight flickers to life and begins a slow dance around a cluttered office. The beam freezes. It illuminates an envelope that is stamped with large red letters:

TOP SECRET

The *Top Secret* label is likely the most recognized part of an oft-used schema for specifying the confidentiality requirements of data. This labeling is known as *data classification*. Data classification (DC) characterizes data so that its custodians can decide how to organize, view, edit, value, share, use, and protect data in compliance with security requirements.

Historically, data classification has been used by the government and military. Today however, DC has increasingly become a necessity for businesses as well.[1] The use of computers has only served to escalate this necessity. With data becoming available more readily and going to and from many widespread sources, it is imperative to be able to understand the aspects of these data so that they can be stored and controlled easily and securely.

This chapter highlights why DC is necessary, how it relates to information security, its design and implementation in an enterprise, hardware and software solutions that can assist in performing it, and some points to consider when implementing it.

67.2 WHY PERFORM DATA CLASSIFICATION?

Information life cycle management (ILM) is a combination of processes and technology that allow for the control of data throughout its life cycle.[2] This procedure ensures that information technology (IT) professionals can manage data from the point of its inception until the time the data has outlived its usefulness. DC is an important part of ILM.

For a real-world example, consider an audit on a business as part of a HIPAA-compliance check. If a data administrator has not spent the time to classify data, not only will the audit take longer than it should, but the company may be fined for lacking controls on this data simply because they do not understand what their data consists of. An example of such a sticky violation would be the posting of patient records by a clinic on a public-facing Website. If data custodians have not classified data types, how can they be expected to know what to protect and how to disseminate it securely and reliably?

Although legal requirements and compliance fines are a major reason that DC is performed, they are by no means the only motivators for a business to carry out DC. A business stands to gain increased productivity and cost savings using DC. Allowing data to flow freely yet securely is critical to business objectives and success.

One proposed solution to the problem of growing data volumes (and the energy required to run the systems that store the data) has been to reduce the amount of data being accessed on these hosts by purging the unnecessary and using only the requisite data. ILM including DC are essential to determine if a particular set of data has outlived its usefulness.

In summary, DC can bring an organization the following benefits:

- Compliance with data standards and legal requirements
- Streamlined and secure sharing of data
- More efficient data storage and retrieval
- Tracking of data through ILM

67.3 DATA CLASSIFICATION'S ROLE IN INFORMATION SECURITY.

Information security, including data classification, must consider the value of data. In addition to the operational value of data for the organization depending on it, data may be valuable to competitors or rapacious nation states with a policy of systematic industrial espionage. Disgruntled and dishonest employees may be able to sell it to a competitor. Data regarding an organization's clients and other data subjects, including personally identifiable information (PII) (e.g., credit card data) must be safeguarded against loss or theft; failure may result in legal action against that company. Data loss prevention (DLP) strategies and compliance hinge on accurate DC policies and DC implementation.

Guidelines such as those from the Federal Financial Institutions Examination Council (FFIEC) highlight the need to secure data as an integral part of DC:

> Classifying data allows the institution to ensure consistent protection of information and other critical data throughout the system. Classifying systems allows the institution to focus its controls and efforts in an efficient and structured manner. Systems that store or transmit data of different sensitivities should be classified as if all data were at the highest sensitivity. Classification should be based on a weighted composite of all relevant attributes.[3]

DC is an essential means to assist the data custodian to determine the type and value of specific data categories. DC thus helps determine how data will be protected during transport and in storage.

67.4 LEGAL REQUIREMENTS, COMPLIANCE STANDARDS, AND DATA CLASSIFICATION.

Legal requirements and compliance standards may make the marriage of DC and security a *mandatory* step for some businesses. A brief overview of such standards and compliance codes follows.

The amount of data that passes through an average-sized enterprise's computers and networks daily can run into terabytes. Regulations and compliance standards may make it necessary that the enterprise's IT staff be able to manage all of this data. Whatever the regulation or standard, an enterprise will need to be able search through all its data, no matter where it lies in the enterprise's computers, networks, or storage, to discover, preserve, and produce the data to meet a legal request or compliance requirement.

The use of DC to meet legal requests and for compliance has been hastened by the advent of the paperless office. Just 20 years ago, an enterprise could reasonably manage its data for compliance if its (physical) filing system were well organized. In today's digital office, however, an enterprise's data can be scattered over any number of hosts, in several geographic locations, across Storage Area Networks ensconced in offsite data centers, or any combination of each of these. Without a concerted enterprise-wide automation and DC implementation, meeting regulatory requirements will be nearly impossible.

Compliance to a number of laws and standards is facilitated by DC. Some of the key laws and standards requiring data classification are enumerated below.

67.4.1 Privacy Act of 1974.

The Privacy Act of 1974 aims to regulate the disclosure of records by government agencies. The Computer Matching and Privacy Protection Act of 1988 was grafted into the Privacy Act of 1974 and introduced provisions for "agencies to follow when engaging in computer-matching activities; provide matching subjects with opportunities to receive notice and to refute adverse information before having a benefit denied or terminated; and require that agencies engaged in matching activities establish Data Protection Boards to oversee those activities."[4]

67.4.2 Family Educational Rights and Privacy Act (FERPA).

Educational institutions that receive U.S. Government funding have to contend with the requirements of FERPA, which regulates the handling of educational data. There are many sections of FERPA on information disclosure that are relevant to DC. Here are some examples[5]:

- 99.12 What limitations exist on the right to inspect and review records?
- 99.33 What limitations apply to the re-disclosure of information?
- 99.34 What conditions apply to disclosure of information to other educational agencies or institutions?
- 99.35 What conditions apply to disclosure of information for Federal or State program purposes?
- 99.36 What conditions apply to disclosure of information in health and safety emergencies?
- 99.37 What conditions apply to disclosing directory information?

67.4.3 Health Insurance Portability and Accountability Act (HIPAA). One of the most important regulations that medical organizations must consider is the Health Insurance Portability and Accountability Act (HIPAA) of 1996. Title II of HIPAA, "Preventing Health Care Fraud and Abuse; Administrative Simplification; Medical Liability Reform," mandates a set of standards for the management of health information. The contents of Part C of Title II, "Administrative Simplification" address security[6]:

- Sec. 1171. Definitions.
- Sec. 1172. General requirements for adoption of standards.
- Sec. 1173. Standards for information transactions and data elements.
- Sec. 1174. Timetables for adoption of standards.
- Sec. 1175. Requirements.
- Sec. 1176. General penalty for failure to comply with requirements and standards.
- Sec. 1177. Wrongful disclosure of individually identifiable health information.
- Sec. 1178. Effect on State law.
- Sec. 1179. Processing payment transactions.

67.4.4 Gramm-Leach-Bliley Act. The Gramm-Leach-Bliley Act (GLBA) of 1999 introduced reform for the financial sector. Title V of GLBA imposes privacy requirements on the handling of information by financial organizations: "It is the policy of the Congress that each financial institution has an affirmative and continuing obligation to respect the privacy of its customers and to protect the security and confidentiality of those customers' nonpublic personal information." The contents of "Title V—Privacy" are as follows[7]:

- Subtitle A—Disclosure of Nonpublic Personal Information
  - Sec. 501. Protection of nonpublic personal information.
  - Sec. 502. Obligations with respect to disclosures of personal information.
  - Sec. 503. Disclosure of institution privacy policy.

- Sec. 504. Rulemaking.
- Sec. 505. Enforcement.
- Sec. 506. Protection of Fair Credit Reporting Act.
- Sec. 507. Relation to State laws.
- Sec. 508. Study of information sharing among financial affiliates.
- Sec. 509. Definitions.
- Sec. 510. Effective date.

- Subtitle B—Fraudulent Access to Financial Information
  - Sec. 521. Privacy protection for customer information of financial institutions.
  - Sec. 522. Administrative enforcement.
  - Sec. 523. Criminal penalty.
  - Sec. 524. Relation to State laws.
  - Sec. 525. Agency guidance.
  - Sec. 567. Reports.
  - Sec. 527. Definitions.

67.4.5 Sarbanes-Oxley Act. The Sarbanes-Oxley (SOX) Act was introduced in 2002 in the wake of a slew of accounting scandals involving a few large U.S. corporations. The scope of SOX is broad and many of its sections may have relevance for DC. For example, section 404, "Management assessment of internal controls," makes it the responsibility of management for "establishing and maintaining an adequate internal control structures and procedures for financial reporting."[8]

67.4.6 The Federal Rules of Civil Procedure. The Federal Rules of Civil Procedure (FRCP) are a set of rules for the trial of noncriminal cases in federal courts in the United States. The most recent editions of the FRCP include sections that address electronically stored information (ESI).[9]

Rule 26, "General Provisions Governing Discovery; Duty of Disclosure," states that a party should be able to provide[10]:

> ... a copy of, or a description by category and location of, all documents, electronically stored information, and tangible things that are in the possession, custody, or control of the party and that the disclosing party may use to support its claims or defenses, unless solely for impeachment; ...

Rule 34, "Production of Documents, Electronically Stored Information, and Things and Entry Upon Land for Inspection and Other Purposes," states:

> ... Any party may serve on any other party a request (1) to produce and permit the party making the request, or someone acting on the requestor's behalf, to inspect, copy, test, or sample any designated documents or electronically stored information ...

Further, Rule 34 states, "... a party who produces documents for inspection shall produce them as they are kept in the usual course of business or shall organize and label them to correspond with the categories in the request ..."

67.4.7 Compliance Standards. Many of the standards discussed in various chapters in this *Handbook* explicitly support DC. Examples include:

- ISO/IEC 27000 family of standards
- Control Objectives for Information and related Technology (COBIT)
- Federal Financial Institutions Examination Council (FFIEC) regulations for finances
- Department of Defense (DoD) issuances for defense contracting
- Media, Telecom: Federal Communications Commission (FCC) regulations
- Food and Drug Administration (FDA) regulations for the life sciences

67.5 DESIGNING AND IMPLEMENTING DC.

In this section we outline how a business can design and implement DC. Both tasks must be carried out by IT or INFOSEC staff with the support and collaboration of management. These tasks should be iterative.

The process to design DC can be modeled as follows:

- Obtain management approval.
- Study the organization's business continuity plan (BCP) and note the organization's current IT assets and storage-management processes.
- Present the benefits of DC to the heads of business units (BUs).
- Survey users in various BUs about how they store, retrieve, and edit data and how they would like to see their data organized and labeled.
- List the revenue-generating and mission-critical usage of each BU's data. Understand how each unit uses and manipulates data specific to their needs, and how those data may be shared across other units.

Once the above steps are undertaken, the DC team can devise a data-labeling scheme that takes into account all BUs and their interactions.

The process of implementation of DC can be modeled as follows:

- Obtain management approval
- Map data-labeling scheme to available hardware, networks, systems, and storage
- Apply automation or DC tools where relevant
- Guide users through adoption of new DC scheme and solicit feedback

Finally, the DC team should report the results of DC design and implementation to management. A refined data classification report would include a service-level agreement (SLA) for data usage as well as a comprehensive model of costs.[11] One of the major costs to announce would be for new hardware, networks, storage, or software needed to implement DC.

67.6 DATA CLASSIFICATION SOLUTIONS.

Software solutions for DC have been driven mostly by the advances in data-storage optimization. Some examples of the storage advances that helped to spark these solutions include the following:

- Virtualization—the ability to logically organize multiple physical locations
- De-duplication—technology to reduce duplicate data
- Serial Advanced Technology Attachment (SATA)-based disk arrays—cost-effective storage media

67.6.1 General Observations. Knowing the type of data being managed is imperative when deciding how to secure it, store it, and manage its information life cycle. This process can be involved and extremely time consuming.

There are several vendors who provide software solutions to assist in this classification process. Most of these solutions run on rack-mounted appliance. In fact, an entire market has sprung up—information and classification management (ICM)—to provide tools and consultation for DC.

Some of the features that a data custodian may want to consider when making a software solution decision include:

- Policy-based data-type discovery—DC based on the policies outlined by the data custodian. These policies can later be used to automatically enforce a business's storage policies
- File metadata classification—DC using a file's metadata and file content
- Multiple file system management—seamless classification across multiple file system types
- Compliance and legal considerations—DC that includes usage of legal metadata, retains file ownership chains, and uses pattern-matching for sensitive data such as Social Security numbers
- Report style—DC based on the utility of the reports on data that has been discovered, labeled, and classified

67.6.2 Varonis: Five Steps to Faster Data Classification. In a white paper, Varonis Systems, makers of the Varonis Data Governance suite, summarize their proposed five-step DC approach as follows:

1. **Identify Data Owners:** Use Varonis DatAdvantage to identify and assign data owners for important data without a known owner. In this example, we'll say "Dave Smith" was determined to be the owner for the SharePoint site "Project X Resources."
2. **Define Data of Interest:** Work with Dave Smith to define what he considers sensitive. In this example, Dave says data containing the phrase "Project Budget" or the word "Secret" is sensitive.
3. **Use Meta-Data to Focus and Accelerate**: Dave says the sensitive data on his site should not be accessible to the Marketing or Operations teams. Use Varonis IDU Data Classification Framework to find data on the Project X Resources SharePoint site that is accessible by the Marketing or Operations teams, and contains sensitive content.

4. **Report and Remediate**: Dave receives reports about sensitive data that is accessible by the Marketing and Operations team and works with IT Staff to change data permissions.
5. **Rescan Data**: The Project X Resources site is rescanned weekly, and Dave gets reports showing whether any newly added or modified data violates his specified access policies.[12]

67.6.3 Microsoft's Data Classification Toolkit.

Microsoft makes available a free "Data Classification Toolkit,"[13] which it introduces as follows:

> The Data Classification Toolkit for Windows Server 2012 is designed to help organizations:
>
> - Identify, classify, and protect data on file servers in private and public clouds.
> - Take advantage of new features and technologies in Windows Server 2012, as well as support hybrid environments with file servers running Windows Server 2012 and Windows Server 2008 R2 SP1.
> - Easily configure default central access policy across multiple servers.
> - Build and deploy policies cost-effectively to protect critical information.
>
> Use the Data Classification Toolkit to help your organization successfully plan and maintain data classification programs in these critical areas:
>
> - Identifying applicable IT GRC authority documents.
> - Defining corresponding classification policies.
> - Preserving evidence that demonstrates the implementation of effective controls.
>
> When used with the IT GRC Process Management Pack SP1 for System Center Service Manager, organizations can easily map classification requirements from various authority documents, such as PCI DSS and NIST 800-53. In addition, your organization can build and deploy its data classification policies, implement controls through Windows Server 2012 File Classification Infrastructure, and provide evidence of data classification policies to auditors. . . .
>
> Streamline your compliance experience with new features in the Data Classification Toolkit that will help you identify, classify, and protect data in private and public clouds. The toolkit supports file servers running Windows Server 2012 and Windows Server 2008 R2 SP1. In addition to configuring File Classification Infrastructure (FCI), the latest version of the toolkit allows you to manage Central Access Policy across file servers. The toolkit enhances the user experience by providing scenario-based wizards that you can use to configure, export, import, and compare file classifications, as well as manage central access policy on your file servers. It provides tools to provision user and device claim values and central access policy across a forest to help simplify configuring Dynamic Access Control in Windows Server 2012. The toolkit also provides a new report template that you can use to review existing central access policy on file shares. . . .[14]
>
> The Microsoft Data Classification Toolkit (the "software") is intended to help organizations simplify their ability to search, identify, and apply rules to data they specify. The software provides sample search expressions and rules that can be used to assist with compliance activities conducted by your organization's IT professionals, auditors, accountants, attorneys, and other compliance professionals. The software does not replace those professionals. . . .[15]

67.7 EXAMPLES OF DATA CLASSIFICATION SCHEMAS.

Security policy and practice can vary widely in design and implementation across different organizations. So too can DC design and implementations.

67.7.1 Universities. For example, here are some differences in the implementation of DC in four U.S. universities:

- The George Washington University's Data Classification Security Policy states, "Data is a critical asset of the University. All members of the University community have a responsibility to protect the confidentiality, integrity, and availability of data generated, accessed, modified, transmitted, stored, or used by the University, irrespective of the medium on which the data resides and regardless of format (such as in electronic, paper, or other physical form)." Three categories of data are defined, "Public," "Official Use Only," and "Confidential." The policy gives examples of each category.[16]
- Stanford University's Data Classification Guidelines Web page states the case for the classification of the University's data clearly and concisely. It defines three categories of data, "Public," "Sensitive," and "Restricted," and tabulates some legal requirements, reputation risks, other risks, access restrictions, and examples against these categories.[17]
- The University of Missouri's DC policy outlines the case for DC and defines four categories of data, "Public," "Confidential," "Restricted," and "National Security Interest." It lists three network zones, each with its own security requirements. It tabulates various set up and usage requirements for each data category.[18]
- Angelo State University's DC policy asks for three DC policies, provides examples of how data in each category can be lost, and sketches what the impact of losses could be.[19]

For each of the above examples, we can see that the DC policies and procedures could vary based solely on the labels chosen. Those entities that use fewer labels will most likely have fewer policies and procedures across a broader spectrum of data as opposed to those who choose to divide their data into more categories. For example, if a business chooses to label all data as "Classified," a single policy would be in place that all users would need to follow, as opposed to a business that chose to label data with many different labels. In practice, the number of labels or categories would most likely be somewhere between three and six.

67.7.2 U.S. Federal Government. The Federal Information Processing Standards Publication 199, "Standards for Security Categorization of Federal Information and Information Systems," provides the baseline for all U.S. Federal-Government agencies in their DC programs.[20] The standard is based on the outmoded C-I-A model (Confidentiality, Integrity, Availability)[21] and weighs the potential impact as low, moderate, or high. These levels are defined as follows:

> The potential impact is LOW if—
>
> —The loss of confidentiality, integrity, or availability could be expected to have a limited adverse effect on organizational operations, organizational assets, or individuals.
>
> AMPLIFICATION: A limited adverse effect means that, for example, the loss of confidentiality, integrity, or availability might: (i) cause a degradation in mission capability to an extent and duration that the organization is able to perform its primary functions, but the effectiveness of the functions is noticeably reduced; (ii) result in minor damage to organizational assets; (iii) result in minor financial loss; or (iv) result in minor harm to individuals.

The potential impact is MODERATE if—

—The loss of confidentiality, integrity, or availability could be expected to have a serious adverse effect on organizational operations, organizational assets, or individuals.

AMPLIFICATION: A serious adverse effect means that, for example, the loss of confidentiality, integrity, or availability might: (i) cause a significant degradation in mission capability to an extent and duration that the organization is able to perform its primary functions, but the effectiveness of the functions is significantly reduced; (ii) result in significant damage to organizational assets; (iii) result in significant financial loss; or (iv) result in significant harm to individuals that does not involve loss of life or serious life threatening injuries.

The potential impact is HIGH if—

—The loss of confidentiality, integrity, or availability could be expected to have a severe or catastrophic adverse effect on organizational operations, organizational assets, or individuals.

AMPLIFICATION: A severe or catastrophic adverse effect means that, for example, the loss of confidentiality, integrity, or availability might: (i) cause a severe degradation in or loss of mission capability to an extent and duration that the organization is not able to perform one or more of its primary functions; (ii) result in major damage to organizational assets; (iii) result in major financial loss; or (iv) result in severe or catastrophic harm to individuals involving loss of life or serious life threatening injuries.

Federal departments have references to internal policies that explicitly address data classification. Here are a few examples:

- **Agriculture**: "Sensitive Security Information means unclassified information of a sensitive nature, that if publicly disclosed could be expected to have a harmful impact on the security of Federal operations or assets, the public health or safety of the citizens of the United States or its residents, or the nation's long-term economic prosperity… ."[22]
- **Defense (DoD)**: A sample policy template available from the Defense Information Systems Agency has the following "Data Rules" governing the treatment of *sensitive* data from "Large Service Applications (LSAs)." The guidelines explicitly state that the references to LSA may be modified to suit each agency.

- All LSA data/information is highly sensitive and should be dated and marked as such. External labeling shall include special handling instructions (e.g., log/inventory identifiers, controlled access, special storage instructions, release, or destruction dates).
- All LSA information transported through the mail or courier/messenger service shall be double-sealed, the second envelope shall be marked "CONFIDENTIAL Designated Official Only."
- The receipt and delivery of sensitive data must be monitored and accounted for to ensure that data is not lost and potentially compromised while in transit.
- Sensitive data shall only be given to those employees with a need to know and who have authorized access in the performance of their official duties.
- Sensitive information must not be left unattended, even temporarily. Sensitive data must remain in the employee's physical control at all times. Sensitive material should be kept in a secure safe or a locked cabinet and returned to the safe each evening or during any lunch periods or breaks greater than 30 minutes.
- Sensitive information shall be turned over or be put out of sight when visitors are present.
- Physical, environmental protection controls shall be provided for sensitive data contained in a media storage vault or library.
- Sensitive information shall not be discussed outside LSA restricted areas.
- Sensitive information being hand-carried must be kept with the individual and protected from unauthorized disclosure… .[23]

- **Energy (DoE)**: "Security Framework for Control System Data Classification and Protection ... presents a data classification process that gives utility administrators, control engineers, and IT personnel a cohesive approach to deploying efficient and effective process control security."[24] The Executive Summary introduces the classification scheme as follows: "This document presents a data classification process that gives utility administrators, control engineers, and IT personnel a cohesive approach to deploying efficient and effective process control security. The fundamental goal is a clear delineation of control system data that will enable effective implementation of security techniques and technologies so the control system can function as required in the face of threats. Once created, the data classification security framework will help reduce the risk of energy disruptions due to control system failure by securing data critical to the operation of the control system."[25]
- **Health and Human Services (HHS)**: The *Federal Register* included a discussion in the "Health Insurance Reform: Security Standards" report in 2003 in which "One commenter stated that a data classification policy, that is a method of assigning sensitivity ratings to specific pieces of data, should be part of the final regulations." The response from HHS was, "We did not adopt such a policy because this final rule requires a floor of protection of all electronic protected health information. A covered entity has the option to exceed this floor. The sensitivity of information, the risks to and vulnerabilities of electronic protected health information and the means that should be employed to protect it are business determinations and decisions to be made by each covered entity."[26]
- **Homeland Security (DHS)**: Some of the relevant language pertaining to data classification includes the following definitions and orders:

> - *Confidential*: A level of classification applied to information, the unauthorized disclosure of which reasonably could be expected to cause damage to the national security that the original classification authority is able to identify or describe.
> - *Secret*: Level of classification applied to information, the unauthorized disclosure of which reasonably could be expected to cause serious damage to the national security that the original classification authority is able to identify or describe.
> - *Top Secret*: Level of classification applied to information, the unauthorized disclosure of which reasonably could be expected to cause exceptionally grave damage to the national security that the original classification authority is able to identify or describe.
> - *Top Secret Document Register*: A TOP SECRET Document Register will be maintained by the TSCO to record the receipt, disposition, and destruction of TOP SECRET information. DHS Form 11000-03, Document Control Register, Top Secret National Security Information, may be used for this purpose. Other forms or automated registers created by an organizational element may also be used, but, at a minimum, must contain the information included in DHS Form 11000-03. Electronic registers must be backed up after each transaction to ensure no loss of accountability.
> - *Secret and Confidential*: Except as required by the originator or as specified for certain categories of SECRET and CONFIDENTIAL information, there is no requirement to maintain accountability records or conduct inventories for SECRET and/or CONFIDENTIAL information. However, heads of organizational elements may mandate the use of accountability records within their respective elements at their discretion.[27]

- **State**: In the Department of State's "IT Strategic Plan: Fiscal Years 2006–2010," the authors discussed changes in the data-classification policies and access to different classification levels as follows:

The following list exemplifies the types of decisions that must be made now and in the future:

- Wireless laptops and networks, providing access from home and on travel
- Integration of voice mail and e-mail
- Cell phone access to e-mail
- Re-examination of data classification policies and practices to ensure that information is as accessible as possible
- Classified Instant Messaging
- PDA access to unclassified networks for e-mail and document browsing
- Laptop access to classified and unclassified networks
- PDA access to classified networks
- Inclusion of Sensitive But Unclassified (SBU)/NOFORN on OpenNet
- Inclusion of EXDIS on ClassNet
- Protection of Personal Identifiable Information; particularly on laptops and other remote devices[28]

67.7.3 State Governments. The following shows extracts from a few state government documents on DC.

New York:

> This document includes both the Information Classification and Control Policy and the Information Classification and Control Standard. The Policy is part of the broader Information Security Policy (P03-002) and is included in this document for ease of reference.
>
> In order to facilitate the process of classifying information assets an Information Classification Manual, Information Asset Classification Worksheet, Information Control Charts and Glossary of Information Security Controls are provided in the Appendices. The Information Classification Manual, in conjunction with the Worksheet, provides a process for classifying information assets and contains the minimum mandatory questions that must be answered when classifying information. The Control Charts contain the mandatory baseline controls that must be implemented based on the information classification. The Glossary contains explanations for each control. A SE [State Entity] may add more questions and/or controls but may not alter or remove the original questions and controls.
>
> Please note the Worksheet and the Control Charts and Glossary are available in an automated tool called the Information Asset Classification System (IACS). This application is available to all New York State governmental entities utilizing NYS Directory Services… .
>
> The classification of information pursuant to this Policy and application of appropriate controls to that information do not alter the responsibility of the SE to comply with the records retention and disposition requirements of the Arts and Cultural Affairs Law or its responsibility to make records available for public inspection and copying under the provisions of the Freedom of Information Law. The process of classifying information pursuant to this Policy may, however, serve as a basis for a SE to evaluate the retention and disposition schedules currently in effect for its records and, where appropriate, consider revising those schedules as a means of managing the records that must be protected by the SE. Similarly, the classification process can facilitate the accurate and efficient application of the exemptions from disclosure enumerated in the Freedom of Information Law by providing a framework for the comprehensive assessment of the SE's information assets.
>
> **A.** All information assets must have an information owner established within the SE's lines of business. The information owner will be responsible for assigning the information classification, determining access privileges of users or groups of users based on job duties, and overseeing daily decisions regarding information asset management. Periodic reviews will be performed by the information owner to confirm the classification of, or reclassify, the information asset.

B. Each classification will have an approved set or range of controls. If SE information is stored by a third-party, the information owner's SE is responsible for communicating requirements of this Policy and Standard to the third-party and addressing them in third-party agreements as they relate to the SE's data.

C. An information asset must be classified based on the highest level necessitated by its individual data elements.

D. All Personal, Private, or Sensitive Information (PPSI) shall be classified with a confidentiality of high.

E. Merging of information which creates a new information asset or situations that create the potential for merging (e.g., backup tape with multiple files) must be evaluated to determine if a new classification of the merged data is warranted.

F. If the SE is unable to determine the confidentiality classification of information stored on electronic storage media, the information must be assumed to have a high confidentiality classification and, therefore, is subject to high confidentiality controls.

G. All reproductions of information in its entirety must carry the same confidentiality classification as the original. Partial reproductions need to be evaluated to determine if a new classification is warranted.

H. A written or electronic inventory of all SE information assets must be maintained.[29]

Ohio:

This state policy provides a high-level data classification methodology to state agencies for the purpose of understanding and managing data and information assets with regard to their level of confidentiality and criticality. Accurate identification provides a basis to employ an appropriate level of security….

State agencies shall establish a data classification policy in compliance with this state policy. Each agency shall serve as a classification authority for the data and information that it collects or maintains in satisfaction of its mission….

Data Classification Labels. The classification of data is a critical tool in defining and implementing the correct level of protection for state information assets. Such classifications are a prerequisite to establishing agency guidelines and system requirements for the secure generation, collection, access, storage, maintenance, transmission, archiving and disposal of state data. Data classification shall be part of the agency's overall risk assessment process as outlined in Ohio IT Policy ITPB. 1, "Information Security Framework."

Agencies shall label data for both confidentiality and criticality. Such classification labels are defined at a high level and represent broad categories of information. State and federal law may also require specific labels.

Confidentiality. The confidentiality label identifies how sensitive the data is with regard to unauthorized disclosure. Data shall be assigned one of three labels for confidentiality:

- **Public**. The "public" label includes information that must be released under Ohio public records law or instances where an agency unconditionally waives an exception to the public records law.
- **Limited Access**. The "limited-access" label applies to information that an agency may release if it chooses to waive an exception to the public records law and places conditions or limitations on such a release.
- **Restricted**. The "restricted" label applies to information, the release of which is prohibited by state or federal law. This label also applies to records that an agency has discretion to release under public records law exceptions but has chosen to treat the information as highly confidential.

Criticality. The criticality label identifies the degree of need for data to maintain its integrity and availability. Data shall be assigned one of four labels for criticality:

- **Low.** The loss of data integrity or availability would result in insignificant or no financial loss, legal liability, public distrust, or harm to public health and welfare.

- **Medium.** The loss of data integrity or availability would result in limited financial loss, legal liability, public distrust, or harm to public health and welfare.
- **High.** The loss of data integrity or availability would result in significant financial loss, legal liability, public distrust, or harm to public health and welfare.
- **Very High.** The loss of data integrity or availability would result in catastrophic financial loss, legal liability, public distrust, or harm to public health and welfare.[30]

Texas:

Data Classification provides a framework for managing data assets based on value and associated risks and for applying the appropriate levels of protection as required by state and federal law as well as proprietary, ethical, operational, and privacy considerations. All [AGENCY] data, whether electronic or printed, should be classified. The data owner, who is responsible for Data Classification, should consult with legal counsel on the classification of data as Confidential, Agency-Sensitive, or Public. Consistent use of data classification reinforces with users the expected level of protection of [AGENCY] data assets in accordance with [AGENCY] security policies.

The purpose of the [AGENCY] Data Classification Policy is to provide a foundation for the development and implementation of necessary security controls to protect information according to its value and/or risk. Security standards, which define these security controls and requirements, may include: document marking/labeling, release procedures, privacy, transmission requirements, printing protection, computer display protections, storage requirements, destruction methods, physical security requirements, access controls, backup requirements, transport procedures, encryption requirements, and incident reporting procedures.

Data shall be classified as follows:

- Confidential.
  - Sensitive data that must be protected from unauthorized disclosure or public release based on state or federal law (e.g. the Texas Public Information Act) and other constitutional, statutory, judicial, and legal agreements.
  - Examples of "Confidential" data may include but are not limited to:
    - Personally Identifiable Information, such as: a name in combination with Social Security Number (SSN) and/or financial account numbers
    - Student Education Records
    - Intellectual Property, such as: Copyrights, Patents, and Trade Secrets
    - Medical Records
- Agency-Sensitive.
  - [optional AGENCY defined category that may be identified as: Agency "Security-Sensitive," "Privileged," or "Protected"].
  - Sensitive data that may be subject to disclosure or release under the Texas Public Information Act, but requires additional levels of protection.
  - Examples of "Agency-Sensitive" data may include but are not limited to:
    - [AGENCY] operational information
    - [AGENCY] personnel records
    - [AGENCY] information security procedures
    - [AGENCY] research
    - [AGENCY] internal communications
    - Public. Information intended or required for public release as described in the Texas Public Information Act[31]

West Virginia:

All State data requires classification, which is mandatory for more confidential and critical classes of data… .

- Level 1—Extremely Sensitive Data
  - Extremely sensitive data is the most sensitive data to integrity and confidentiality risks. Disclosure or corruption of this data could be hazardous to life or health… .

- Access is tightly restricted with the most stringent security controls at the system as well as the user level. Failure to maintain the integrity and confidentiality could have severe financial, health, or safety repercussions. Individuals must adhere to very strict rules in the usage of this data… .
  - Examples of extremely sensitive data may include the following: Contents of State law enforcement investigative records;
  - Child and adult protective services client data.
- Level 2—Very Sensitive Data
  - This data is only made available to authorized users and may be protected by federal and State regulations.
  - Access to very sensitive data is restricted to authenticated and authorized individuals who require access to that information in the course of performing their job duties. These are the data elements removed from responses to information requests for reasons of privacy.
  - Examples of very sensitive data may include the following:
    - Social Security numbers;
    - Credit card numbers;
    - Food assistance programs data;
    - Comprehensive law enforcement data;
    - Foster care data;
    - Health, mental health, acute medical care, and medical data;
    - Social Service or Temporary Assistance data; and
    - Tax information.
- Level 3—Sensitive Data
  - This data is made available through open record requests or other formal or legal processes; it includes the majority of the data contained within State government electronic databases.
  - Direct access is restricted to authenticated and authorized individuals who require access to that information in the course of performing their job duties.
  - Examples of sensitive data may include the following:
    - Most data elements in State personnel records;
    - Driver history records;
    - State/federal contracts data;
    - Employment and training program data;
    - Permits data; and
    - Historical records repository data.
- Level 4—Unrestricted Data
  - This data is characterized as being open, public data with no distribution limitations and to which anonymous access is allowed.
  - This type of information is: (1) actively made publicly available by State government; (2) published and distributed freely, without restriction; and (3) available in the form of physical documents such as brochures, formal statements, press releases, reports, web pages, and bulletin boards accessible with anonymous access.
  - Examples of unrestricted data may include the following:
    - Occupational licensing data excluding social security numbers;
    - Agency public websites; and
    - Statewide policies.[32]

67.8 CONCLUDING REMARKS.

This chapter has introduced DC, why it is relevant, how it relates to compliance and legal requirements, how one may design and implement it, and provided some examples of how a handful of entities have implemented their DC labeling schema.

In conclusion, here are some important points to remember when dealing with DC:

- A complete solution will most likely not be achieved by using software solutions alone. Since DC is still evolving, these solutions may require customization to fit what a business must accomplish. Thorough research will be required to find a best-fit solution.[33]

- In order to determine what type of data is used across an entire business, it is imperative to interview users from all segments of the business using surveys.
- Locations of data must be written into a DC policy. Since data can reside in many different locations, a policy must be drafted to account for geography and allow for proper storage and retrieval of these data from varied locations.
- An educational policy for users will need to be created for the "Important" data type (or equivalent) level and above. Creators and users of valuable data types must be educated about the policies and procedures that are put into place for the storage, retrieval, and use of their data.
- A complete DC solution will take some time to implement. Because of the complexity of DC, a complete and well-designed implementation will not happen overnight. A realistic estimate should be provided to management when undertaking a DC project.
- Compliance and legal requirements need to be understood well for a particular business. There are several compliance standards that make a business legally liable for certain data types. It is imperative that one understand which of those standards apply to their data when taking on the DC task. Remember too, that legal requirements may also cover investigations that require this data, so understanding data-handling laws is also important.

67.9 FURTHER READING

Anonymous. "Data Classification Methods and Policy." *ComputerWeekly*, April 2009. www.computerweekly.com/report/Data-classification-methods-and-policy

Anonymous, "Sensitive Data Classification and Protection: Overcoming the Challenges to Classify and Protect Sensitive Data at Federal Government Agencies." SECURE|IT, 2008. www.secureit.com/resources/WP_Data_Class_and_Protect.pdf

Buckley, S. "Data Classification." *Internal Auditor*, March 2011. www.theiia.org/intAuditor/itaudit/2011-articles/data-classification

Etges, R., and K. McNeil. "Understanding Data Classification Based on Business and Security Requirements." *ISACA Journal Online*, August 10, 2006. www.isaca.org/Journal/Past-Issues/2006/Volume-5/Documents/jopdf0605-understanding-data.pdf

Fowler, S. "Information Classification—Who, Why, and How." *GIAC Security Essentials Certification*, February 28, 2003. SANS Reading Room. www.sans.org/reading_room/whitepapers/auditing/information-classification-who_846

Heiser, J. "Data Classification Best Practices: Techniques, Methods and Projects." *SearchSecurity*, March 2009. Requires membership to view. http://searchsecurity.techtarget.com/magazineContent/Data-classification-best-practices-Techniques-methods-and-projects

Libicki, M. C., D. R. Frelinger, B. A. Jackson, B. E. Lachman, and C. Ip. *What Should Be Classified? A Framework with Application to the Global Force Management Data Initiative*. Rand Publishing, 2011.

Murray, W. H. "Classification and Labeling of Data." *Thinking About Security* blog, March 13, 2012. http://whmurray.blogspot.com/2012/03/classification-and-labeling-of-data.html

Reed, B. "Data-classification best practices." *NetworkWorld*, January 18, 2007. www.networkworld.com/news/tech/2007/012207-techupdate-data-classification.html

Vogel, V. "Data Classification Toolkit." In *Information Security Guide: Effective Practices and Solutions for Higher Education.* Internet2, last edited December 22, 2010. https://wiki.internet2.edu/confluence/display/itsg2/Data+Classification+Toolkit

67.10 NOTES

1. Dataglobal, "Dataglobal Announces dg classification 2.0, the Industry's First Unified Data Classification Solution," Press release via PRWeb, June 11, 2012, www.prweb.com/releases/2012/6/prweb9590296.htm
2. S. Duplessie, N. Marrone, and S. Kenniston, "The New Buzzwords: Information Lifecycle Management," *Computerworld*, March 31, 2003, www.computerworld.com/hardwaretopics/storage/story/0,10801,79885,00.html
3. Federal Financial Institutions Examination Council, "Information Security Booklet," July 2006, http://ithandbook.ffiec.gov/it-booklets/information-security.aspx
4. 5 U.S.C. §552a, U.S. Congress, The Privacy Act Of 1974, December 31, 1974, http://www.justice.gov/opcl/privstat.htm
5. 20 U.S.C. §1232g, U.S. Congress, Family Educational Rights and Privacy Act (FERPA), August 21, 1974, www.access.gpo.gov/nara/cfr/waisidx_04/34cfr99_04.html
6. 42 USC §201 *et seq*, U.S. Congress, Health Insurance Portability And Accountability Act of 1996, August 21, 1996, www.cms.hhs.gov/HIPAAGenInfo/Downloads/HIPAALaw.pdf
7. 15 USC §6801 *et seq*, U.S. Congress, Text of the Conference Report of Gramm-Leach-Bliley Bill, November 12, 1999, http://banking.senate.gov/conf/somfinal.htm
8. 15 U.S.C. §7241, 18 U.S.C. §1350, U.S. Congress, Sarbanes-Oxley Act of 2002, July 30, 2002, http://frwebgate.access.gpo.gov/cgi-bin/getdoc.cgi?dbname=107_cong_bills&docid=f:h3763enr.tst.pdf
9. Kahn Consulting, Inc., "The Federal Rules of Civil Procedure: Meeting the IT and Legal Challenges of the New E-Discovery Rules," Law.com, May 1, 2007, www.law.com/jsp/legaltechnology/detailWP.jsp?id=1190797378589 (registration required)
10. Committee on the Judiciary, One Hundred Ninth Congress, "Federal Rules of Civil Procedure," December 1, 2006, http://judiciary.house.gov/media/pdfs/printers/109th/31308.pdf
11. K. Langdon and J. Merryman, "Data Classification: Getting Started," TechTarget, July 1, 2005 http://searchstorage.techtarget.com/magazineFeature/0,296894,sid5_gci1258224,00.html (registration required).
12. Varonis, "5 Steps to Faster Data Classification," Varonis Website, January 22, 2010, www.varonis.com/go/resources/#Whitepapers (registration required).
13. R. Smith, "How to Use Microsoft's Data Classification Toolkit," *Biztech*, December 1, 2011, www.biztechmagazine.com/article/2011/12/how-use-microsofts-data-classification-toolkit
14. Microsoft, "Data Classification Toolkit," September 10, 2012, http://technet.microsoft.com/en-us/library/hh204743.aspx
15. Microsoft, "Important Information about the Data Classification Toolkit," September 10, 2012, http://technet.microsoft.com/en-us/library/hh367453.aspx

16. CIO, George Washington University, "Data Classification Security Policy," December 6, 2005, http://my.gwu.edu/files/policies/DataClassificationPolicy.pdf
17. Stanford University, "Classification of Data," November 6, 2007, www.stanford.edu/group/security/securecomputing/dataclass_chart.html
18. Division of Information Technology, University of Missouri, MU Data Classification System, August 3, 2007, http://doit.missouri.edu/security/data-classification/
19. Angelo State University, "Data Classification Standard," March 25, 2012, www.angelo.edu/services/technology/it_policies/dataClassificationStandard.php
20. NIST, "Standards for Security Categorization of Federal Information and Information Systems," FIPS PUB 199, February 2004, http://csrc.nist.gov/publications/fips/fips199/FIPS-PUB-199-final.pdf
21. This model omits consideration of control, authenticity, and utility as defined in Chapter 3 in this *Handbook*.
22. U.S. Department of Agriculture, "Control and Protection of 'Sensitive Security Information,'" Departmental Regulation 3440-002, January 30, 2003, www.fas.org/sgp/othergov/usda3440-02.html
23. NIST, "Sample Generic Policy and High Level Procedures for Marking, Handling, Processing, Storage, and Disposal of Data," August 2, 2000, http://csrc.nist.gov/groups/SMA/fasp/documents/production_io_controls/marking.doc
24. U. S. Department of Energy, "Security Framework for Control System Data Classification and Protection," Office of Electricity Delivery & Energy Reliability, 2013, http://energy.gov/oe/downloads/security-framework-control-system-data-classification-and-protection
25. B. T. Richardson and J. Michalski, "Security Framework for Control System Data Classification and Protection," Sandia National Laboratories Report SAND2007-3888P, July 2007, http://energy.gov/sites/prod/files/oeprod/DocumentsandMedia/21-Security_Framework_for_Data_Class.pdf
26. "45 CFR Parts 160, 162, and 164 Health Insurance Reform: Security Standards; Final Rule." *Federal Register* 68, no. 34 (February 20, 2003):8345, note m, www.hhs.gov/ocr/privacy/hipaa/administrative/securityrule/securityrulepdf.pdf
27. U. S. Department of Homeland Security, "Protection of Classified National Security Information: Accountability, Control, and Storage," Management Directive System MD Number 11045, October 4, 2004, www.dhs.gov/xlibrary/assets/foia/mgmt_directive_11045_protection_of_classified_national_security_information_accountability_control_and_storage.pdf
28. U. S. Department of State, "IT Strategic Plan: Fiscal Years 2006–2010," Information Resource Management, Department of State Publication Number 11455, December 2007, www.state.gov/m/irm/rls/92497.htm
29. T. D. Smith, "Cyber Security Policy & Standard PS08-001: Information Classification and Control," Office of Cyber Security, New York State Division of Homeland Security and Emergency Services, revised February 7, 2012, www.dhses.ny.gov/ocs/resources/documents/PS08-001-V1.2-February-7-2012.pdf
30. State of Ohio, "Data Classification." Statewide IT Policy Number ITP-B.11, March 19, 2008, www.oit.ohio.gov/IGD/policy/pdfs_policy/ITP-B.11.pdf
31. Texas Department of Information Resources, "IS Security Policies: Data Classification" template (Word .DOC file), Chief Information Security Office, March 30,

2010, http://www2.dir.state.tx.us/SiteCollectionDocuments/Security/Policies and Standards/data_classification_policy.doc

32. State of West Virginia, "Policy: Data Classification," Office of Technology Policy WVOT-PO1000, January 6, 2010, www.technology.wv.gov/SiteCollectionDocuments/ITC Policy Guidelines/Data Class PO.pdf
33. B. Reed, "Data-Classification Best Practices," *Network World*, January 18, 2007, www.networkworld.com/news/tech/2007/012207-techupdate-data-classification.html

CHAPTER 68

OUTSOURCING AND SECURITY

Kip Boyle, Michael Buglewicz, and Steven Lovaas

68.1 INTRODUCTION.

Since this chapter was first written in 2008, the world has seen significant transformation, driven to a large extent by economic factors, social networking phenomena, the cloud, and the increasingly pervasive need for always-on, always-available information and entertainment.

Global economic leadership is in transition. Europe and the European Union (EU) are locked in a struggle to remain economically viable, and EU leadership is forced into making decisions regarding who can stay in the EU. The BRIC countries (Brazil, Russia, India, and China) are all facing serious economic and political challenges and all the while unemployment in the United States remains at levels not seen since the Great Depression.

Global, regional, and local businesses around the world everyday work in this dynamic environment. Current multiyear contracts with outsourcers were likely executed in circumstances differing from today's rapidly evolving environment.

Outsourcing and security can mean outsourcing certain corporate activities to a third party and doing so in a security-conscious fashion; for example, business A hires business B to be business A's helpdesk. A second interpretation is that business A hires business B to provide corporate technology security.

The term "outsourcing" has come to identify several distinct concepts, each requiring a different risk-management strategy. In this chapter, we examine today's practice of outsourcing and the effects and considerations it has, or should have, on the work of information assurance professionals.

Organizations (companies, nonprofits, government agencies, etc.) outsource to gain efficiencies and effectiveness. The efficiencies gained, however, do have consequences. An outsourcing strategy of *implement-it-and-forget-it* is unwise, as the outsourcing environment can change quickly and dramatically. Within very recent history, outsourcing primarily referred to the movement of tasks from within a corporate environment to another corporation perhaps better suited or more efficient at those tasks. Now the term *outsourcing* also refers to transferring operations and ownership of portions of a corporate infrastructure, including key computing functions, to a cloud vendor, a solutions integrator, or other entity providing computing services. Thus, outsourcing no longer refers to a call center or provider, but instead covers data possession, movement, processing, protection, and retirement all done in a cloud spread across multiple servers in multiple data centers in multiple areas of the world.

Michael Cooney points out some of the significant considerations and problems facing the outsourcing world at end of the first decade of the twenty-first century:

- Security problems
- China's rise
- India's growth
- India's turmoil
- Blunders
- H-1B visa trials
- Small business outsourcing
- Managed services[1]

Despite the negative overtones that sometimes accompany the practice of outsourcing, there can be great benefits. Here are a few:

- A corporation's self-knowledge improves dramatically when it is compelled to articulate, explain, and define its corporate mission to others.

- Outsourcing clarifies and institutionalizes roles, goals, and measures of success.
- One of the largest and most important aspects is that outsourcing done successfully demands risk identification and formalized mitigation activities that might otherwise not occur within the corporation.
- Outsourcing allows a company to focus on corporate core competencies, thus making gains in:
  - Effectiveness (i.e., doing the tasks for which you have the potential to produce the desired results)
  - Efficiencies (i.e., using an optimal amount of time and energy to complete a task)
  - Focus (i.e., concentrating on key business objectives)
  - Discipline (i.e., holding the corporation accountable for corporate objectives, and holding the vendor to clearly and contractually defined objectives)
  - Appropriate utilization of high-value employees performing high-value business functions
- An organization gains or intends to gain financial improvements by moving work to vendors that can perform the work at a lower cost and/or at a greater level of specialization.

The outsourcing of operational computing functions to the cloud or solution providers allows a company to focus less on the tactical production of data for business analysis. Rather, when an organization doesn't need to focus on the tactical operation of keeping farms of data servers and complicated data storage techniques, that organization can focus on consumption and analysis of the data and the maturation of business knowledge and theoretically, business advantage.

68.1.1 Definitions

Vendor or contractor—an arm's-length entity providing an outsourced service

Organization or business—the entity contracting for its products or services with a vendor

Outsourcing—the fulfillment of a specific business function or functions by contracting with a vendor to perform within the vendor's own facilities

Insourcing—the commonplace use of contract or noncompany employees to fulfill certain business functions within the physical and logical corporate boundaries

Cloud services—data center and or software services offered by commercial computing corporation such as email, communications, collaboration technologies, and data services

68.1.2 Distinctions. The risks and considerations of outsourcing an inbound call center, outsourcing a corporate IT function, insourcing a corporate finance function, insourcing an HR function, outsourcing corporate email functions, or a combination of insourcing and outsourcing of a corporate security function all require different perspectives and tactical activities. Despite the commonalities among outsourcing functions (e.g., connectivity, user management, definition of task, measurements of effectiveness, goals and objectives), the same outsourcing blueprint for an inbound call center would not serve for outsourcing corporate security. The objectives, rules, policies, risks, and rewards for each scenario are distinct and require customized attention.

Outsourcing decisions depend on which functions an organization decides it should perform for itself to maintain effectiveness and which functions would be performed more efficiently or more effectively by a vendor. Outsourcing also implies that an organization does not have, does not want to have, and cannot or will not have a specific expertise as part of its core business missions.

68.1.3 Insourcing. Insourcing is an accepted business practice; the government and many of today's large corporations hire contractors who work as insourcers within the physical and logical boundaries of their organization.

Insourcing poses risks to an organization because the place of work for the insourcer (vendor) is often within the physical boundaries of the organization—well within the physical perimeter, and in many cases, inside the logical perimeter defenses of the corporation. The contract worker is not an employee, but in most cases the contractor enjoys the same accesses as employees for the duration of the contract.

The defenses used for external protection are not as effective (if at all) against an insider with malicious intent. Security considerations regarding an insourced contractor require a different approach, more similar to layered security strategies employed for internal company resources.

Besides traditional IT security concerns, for these outsiders with insider access, the problems of human error, omissions, or complete bungling must be addressed. Security from external sources does not normally include internal human-error considerations. Before considering insourcing, an organization should already have a formal risk-management strategy (quality control) for internal human errors as well as for insider espionage and other insider threats.

An insourced contractor is not a full-fledged member of an organization and frequently resides somewhat outside of internal controls, thus requiring a separate and recognized classification and specific handling appropriate to the role. The General Accounting Office recently conducted a study of four federal agencies that rely on contractors to collect certain data on American citizens. The study found that "[a]gencies often do not limit the collection or use of information as required by the Privacy Act of 1974, ... agencies don't ensure the accuracy of information ... [and] contractors are not bound by those fair information practices and they often don't comply with all of them."[2]

Sound risk management requires acknowledgment and recognition that significant and substantial risks exist when insourcing. Attention to detail, a reality-based risk assessment, clearly articulated risks, attainable observations, and concrete audit points are all essential to manage successfully the insourced contractors and their mission. (See Chapters 13 and 45 in this *Handbook*.)

With the proliferation of mobile devices (smartphones, tablets) as well as independent data connections via USB data cards that connect to major telecommunications companies (e.g., ATT, T-Mobile, etc.), an insourced vendor is able to communicate externally without any oversight or examination of the content of those communications. Thus, trade secrets, competitive advantage information, future marketing plans, or even mundane operations details that could be examined and potentially exploited are free to leave the confines of the corporation without the knowledge of anyone in the corporation.

It might be prudent to expand our consideration of insourcing to include any situation where an individual who is not a direct employee of a corporation or entity is granted the ability to work within a corporate environment. This could include interns, volunteers, and even maintenance staff. With the economic downturn late in the first decade of the twenty-first century, many corporations have learned to rely on interns and volunteers who are hopeful that their efforts will be duly noted and potentially result in an offer of permanent employment. However, the flip side of such an arrangement is that the intern or volunteer could indeed be keenly observant and equipped with a smartphone, tablet, or laptop with a camera and an independent data connection; some of these temporary workers may make more money by selling a corporation's intellectual property, marketing information, or financial data to the highest bidder. (See Chapter 13 for more details of insider threats.)

68.1.4 Nearshoring. *Nearshoring* is the outsourcing of a specific discrete business function to a vendor located within the same, a nearby, or a bordering geographic region.

In some cases, an international outsource vendor will place components of its business in a specific country to acquire work within that country. For example, a United States–based outsource vendor will often position its operations in the United States to fulfill contracts from companies in the United States. Nearshoring can also include outsourcing to a bordering or regional country that shares a common cultural knowledge and understanding, as when a U.S. organization outsources to a group in Canada or Mexico.

Many of the largest technology companies in the world are some of the largest nearsourcing vendors. "Productized offerings from the large outsourcers include service desks, desktop management, and specialized network offerings. Examples include EDS Agile, HP SMB Services, and IBM Express Advantage."[3]

During the opposition to outsourcing that occurred in the first few years of the twenty-first century, the negative connotations of outsourcing were sometimes blunted when organizations nearshored their outsourcing work. The move toward globalization, and the painful lessons it taught certain nation-centric IT organizations, seemed easier to comprehend and accept if those jobs went to vendors located within relative proximity.

68.1.5 Offshoring. *Offshoring* is the outsourcing of specific, discrete business functions to a vendor whose corporate headquarters, or employees who fulfill the outsourced function, reside and work on another continent, as when a European company outsources to a company based in India.

Perhaps the most controversial kind of outsourcing, offshoring evokes a strong response, both in countries that move work offshore and in offshoring destinations. Nationalism, job security, self-interest, and a host of other emotions, both rational and irrational, seem to be part of every discussion. Those concepts, along with many others, are examined in Thomas Friedman's cornerstone book on outsourcing, *The World Is Flat*.[4] Friedman's perspective organizes the many disparate elements converged to "flatten the world" and to create a truly global work environment.

Regardless of the reasoning behind the decision, offshoring involves different considerations from insourcing and nearshoring. Fundamental business tasks taken for granted in a single geopolitical environment require different considerations when offshoring. Many of the questions should be asked and answered long before addressing the ability of the offshore vendor and its employees simply to do the job.

Despite all of these complications, offshoring is an established business practice and successfully accomplished every day. However, the rules that make offshoring successful will make any other business successful:

- Clearly understand your business.
- Clearly articulate your outsourcing (insourcing, nearshoring, and offshoring) goals.
- Possess a razor-sharp understanding of all risks, and managing those risks in an effective and reasonable manner.

68.2 WHY OUTSOURCE? There are two main drivers behind the growth of outsourcing today: the never-ending quests for greater organizational *effectiveness* and for greater *efficiency*. These drivers have come to the forefront of our economy because of the shift in strategic business thinking, begun in the 1990s, that is still affecting the way organizations are managing their businesses and serving their customers.

With the economic downturn that occurred late in the first decade of the twenty-first century, the impetus to outsource at a more rapid rate to low cost labor markets reached a fever pitch. In an effort to squeeze out costs within the corporation in many cases simply for economic survival, outsourcing became even more frenzied, bordering on the desperate.

In an article published April 19, 2011, entitled "Top 'US' Corporations Outsourced More Than 2.4 Million American Jobs Over The Last Decade," author Zaid Jilani states that contrary to trends in the 1990s where large U.S. corporations were creating jobs in the United States, these same large corporations "… have been adding more jobs abroad than at home," as is illustrated here:

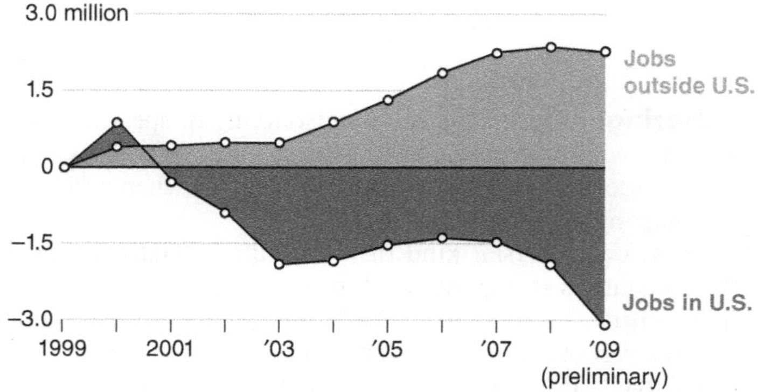

Source: Zaid Jilani, "Top 'US' Corporations Outsourced More Than 2.4 Million America Jobs over the Last Decade," Think Progress Economy, April 19, 2011, http://thinkprogress.org/economy/2011/04/19/159555/us-corporations- outsourced-americans/?mobile=nc

Mr. Jilani's article continues:

> Another question asked of the executives found that the top reason for companies to outsource was to "reduce operating costs" (46 percent of respondents). Only 12 percent of respondents said their reason for outsourcing was "access to world class capabilities." This means companies are outsourcing to save themselves money, not to make better products.

In addition to sending jobs overseas, Mr. Jilani as well points out that many of the large corporations who have sent jobs overseas are as well attempting to repatriate the profits they've made overseas at a reduced tax liability. Mr. Jiliani gives the example of Cisco Systems.

> ... which had 26 percent of its workforce abroad at the start of the decade but 46 percent of its workforce abroad by the end, is currently involved in a lobbying campaign titled "Win America" calling for a tax repatriation holiday that would let big corporations "bring money they have stashed overseas back to the US at a dramatically lower tax rate.[5]

68.2.1 Effectiveness versus Efficiency. Being *efficient* implies using an optimal amount of time and energy for getting a task done. In contrast, being *effective* means accomplishing the intended consequences of the task.

68.2.2 Being Effective. Historically, management has been primarily interested in increasing the efficiency of important business processes. But since the late 1980s, enlightened managers have realized that it can be very wasteful to try to optimize a process that does not lie within the core competency of the organization.

What are an organization's core competencies? A core competency is a *mission-critical* task or function that an organization is good at. "Mission-critical" refers to functions that are directly related to the strategic goals of the organization; for example, a hospital or a restaurant will consider cleanliness a mission-critical goal, whereas an automobile repair facility probably would not. Examples of core competencies may include reliable processes (e.g., Procter & Gamble's consumer brand management or Toyota's mantra of continuous improvement); a unique way of relating to customers (Nordstrom's superior retail service) or to suppliers (Boeing's supply chain management); or the particular look and feel of products or services (Apple's computers and iPods). A core competency also must meet these three conditions:

1. It can be used to develop entirely new products and services.
2. It provides significant customer benefits.
3. It is difficult for competitors to duplicate.[6]

If all three conditions are met, then a core competency can provide an organization with a true competitive advantage, which is a highly prized organizational asset, and which must be continuously guarded lest the competitive advantage be lost. A corollary is that all other functional areas, which are not within the core, are candidates for outsourcing.

By delegating tasks to vendors, an organization's management may concentrate more fully on its core business. Ideally, this will allow the organization to use its limited financial, talent, and other resources in the most productive manner. Knowing which activities an organization should perform, and which it should not, is the heart of being effective.

68.2.3 Being Efficient. Assuming one is doing the right things (i.e., being effective), the next logical question is whether one is doing them as efficiently as possible? Is the organization using the optimal amount of resources while still achieving quality and quantity goals? This question is important to both outsourcing organizations and to vendors performing outsourced work.

How can one measure efficiency? An often-sought-after outcome of efficiency is direct cost minimization. The idea of using outsourcing to achieve direct cost cutting is attractive. For example, according to a 2005 article appearing in *Mortgage Strategy*, British companies can save up to 40 percent by outsourcing all kinds of jobs to India. These companies report savings of a minimum £10 million pounds each year for every 1,000 jobs they outsource.[7]

In addition to direct cost reduction, other financial benefits of outsourcing to increase efficiencies include:

- **Decreased capital expenditure.** Because vendors utilize their own tools and infrastructure, there is no need for organizations to borrow money to purchase these items.
- **Decreased fixed costs.** Fewer fixed, lower, recurring payments allow an organization to manage its cash more easily because it would need less of it; fixed costs must be paid even when sales decrease, which may lead to a shortage of cash that could eventually bankrupt an organization.
- **Increased variable costs versus fixed costs.** If an organization pays a vendor based on units of work performed, then the costs of production become more variable, which is easier to manage as costs rise or fall based on the volume of goods or services required.

Another positive outcome of outsourcing is increased speed or work cycle time. By hiring a vendor located in India to test the quality of software written in the United States, an organization can perform software development work nearly 24 hours per day. Each morning on return to work, U.S. programmers would have the results of testing in India and could begin making corrections right away. By using this "follow the sun" approach, an organization can gain a speed advantage over its rivals.

Possibly the greatest aspect of efficiency that outsourcing can deliver is management focus. There can be great value in focusing a company's management team directly on those activities that differentiate it from the competition. Whenever a management team is focusing on noncore functions, it is usually operating not from a position of strength but from one of weakness. By definition, the team is not expert at noncore activities. In these cases, the team can spend too much time trying to understand and manage something that does not differentiate the organization from its competitors. If the noncore activities require too much management time and attention, there is a real risk that the core competencies of the organization may decrease in value. In the most serious of cases, an organization can lose its competitive edge completely, driving down sales, revenue, and profits.

68.3 CAN OUTSOURCING FAIL?

Yes, outsourcing can fail. For example:

> In 2004, J.P. Morgan Chase & Co. reassumed main technology functions following its merger with Bank One Corp., abandoning a US$5 billion pact with International Business Machines Corp. The same year, Electronic Data Systems Inc. abandoned a US$1 billion deal to run Dow Chemical Co.'s phone and computer networks.[8]

Deloitte Consulting's 2005 study, "Calling a Change in the Outsourcing Market," offers evidence that large organizations do not always achieve great efficiencies from outsourcing. The study, based on personal interviews with 25 of the largest organizations across eight industry sectors, reveals that:

- Seventy percent of participants have begun looking more cautiously at outsourcing after having negative experiences with outsourcing projects.
- One in four respondents have brought functions back in-house when outsourcing failed to deliver on promises of lower cost and more efficient operations.
- Forty-four percent of participants saw no cost savings as a result of outsourcing.[9]

It is important to keep in mind however, that for every outsourcing failure there are many other outsourcing successes. So then what separates successful from unsuccessful outsourcing/? Core to success are the following:

- A clear understanding of the corporation's business mission, and how the task to be outsourced contributes to that mission
- Rational and well-thought-out expectations of the outsourced function. If a corporation couldn't fully control the business function and continuously underperformed at the function, then don't expect outsourcing will be the panacea—unless there is corporate will (and dollars) to improve the function and the outsourcing includes hiring outside functional expertise for the function.
- Engagement with a world-class outsourcer. Unless a corporation has deep skills, knowledge, and insights in outsourcing, the risks of going with an untested or unknown outsourcing solution are simply too great. From infrastructure to data handling and security, there are simply too many moving parts for outsourcing to be a trivial task.

68.3.1 Why Does Outsourcing Fail? There are many risks to outsourcing, but direct cost reduction, often a top goal of outsourcing, can create the greatest risk of all. Indeed, "outsourcing deals most frequently stumble when they focus primarily on reducing costs."[10] Despite this observation, in a set of recent surveys, the rate of cost reduction as a driver for offshoring has been growing. From 2004 to 2006, the rate went from just over 70 percent of respondents to just over 80 percent.[11]

Total expenditure on outsourcing can meet or exceed the baseline of spending established prior to outsourcing. Although this may not be an inherently bad situation, management may perceive the experiment as a failure if the organization approaches outsourcing opportunities primarily to cut costs. However, if seen from a perspective of effectiveness rather than simply of efficiency, the outsourcing activities may be quite successful.

There are many other business reasons why outsourcing can fail. Looking more closely at the organization's perspective within the typical loss scenarios, in many cases the failure occurs because of one or more of these reasons:

- Monitoring and evaluating the performance of an outside vendor is a difficult task for many reasons, often due to inadequate selection and to monitoring of performance metrics.

- The outsourcing organization did not work hard enough to create a "win/win" opportunity for both itself and the vendor.
- Aligning the goals and priorities of the outside vendor with the organization's goals and priorities is rarely easy.
- Outsourcing requires an organization to master new and more complicated forms of communication, especially when outsourcing to a vendor in another country.
- It is challenging for an organization to ensure that the vendor's employees maintain sufficient knowledge and skill levels to do the work that has been delegated.
- Outsourcing usually introduces insecurity to the workforce and to the unions, as fear of job losses dominates their thinking. Terminating a contract usually requires a disruption in service continuity, and the quality of service can suffer, sometimes visibly to customers.[12]

Even when outsourcing appears to succeed from an operational perspective, there may be hidden inefficiencies in information protection that can decrease the overall value of the activity.

68.3.2 Intended and Unintended Consequences of Outsourcing. Now that the corporate world has experienced well over a decade of outsourcing, what in fact have we learned? In a lecture entitled "The Future of Outsourcing—Impact on Jobs," Patrick Dixon says:

> Outsourcing incentives are huge—and can lead to falls in service costs of 50–60%. Up to half of the $19 trillion spent every year by European companies on sales and administration could be outsourced.
>
> However, during 1995–2011 there has been a large migration of skilled, semi-skilled, and unskilled jobs from high-cost to low-cost nations. Outsourcing has produced labour shortages in many emerging economies. For example, China is now seeing 100% salary inflation at top end and India is not far behind—acute shortage of experienced business leadership. Some companies are now thinking of moving operations to places like Pakistan (50% lower costs and over 200,000 IT graduates looking for work), Bangladesh, or Vietnam. Changes are happening very quickly. But other corporations are already moving jobs back home—because cost savings have narrowed, and because outsourcing carries risks—in supply chain delays, language and culture challenges, distance management, loss of intellectual capital, and so on.[13]

Conversely, Mr. Dixon points out that many economists believe that while outsourcing does indeed move jobs to low-cost labor countries, there are subsequent higher-value jobs created in the original corporate country. Other cogent factors are:

- Outsourcing allows a company to control costs and by so doing stay in business.
- By staying in business the company can return value to shareholders.
- If the company remains economically viable it can as well live up to its obligations to its pensioners.
- By investing in low-cost labor markets, we are in effect helping those economies evolve and potentially become customers for our goods and services.[14]
- Reality, direct observation, and common sense tell us that moving from high-cost to low-cost labor markets creates the following cycle:
  - Technically skilled labor tasks move from high-cost (and experienced) labor markets to low- and mid-cost labor markets (with lower skills/less experience).

- The cost savings of moving from high-cost to low-cost labor can be significant on an hour to hour comparison, but because of the lack of experience and skill in the low-cost labor market, early savings are not as significant as expected. With less experienced labor, it simply takes longer to accomplish the same task as accomplished by experienced labor.
- Low-/mid-cost labor markets skills improve with experience. Those in high-cost labor markets that still remain focus on higher-level functions and much deeper technical expertise, and deeper skills transfer to the low-cost labor markets.
- As low-cost labor markets gain in experience and technical expertise, the high-cost labor teams grow smaller and smaller, and because the high-cost labor teams are no longer involved in the day-to-day technical operations, high-cost labor skills (especially experiential) begin an erosion cycle.

If we follow this cycle to its conclusion, given time, the technical and intellectual insights of a particular business now reside with an outsourcer, and the originating company has lost internal expertise to help lead and evolve the company into a viable future.

68.3.3 Universal Nature of Risk. Risk is inherent in virtually every human activity. One of the distinct advantages of an organized society is the ability of that society to distribute risk. Thus, not every member of society need manage every single risk.

When outsourcing, the greatest cost is that of ignorance, and the ultimate price is failure. Poorly defined expectations and poor planning resulting from a fundamental ignorance of a business will doom any corporate project, including outsourcing.

During early planning phases of the outsourcing project, it is prudent for the information assurance team to assess the entirety of the outsourcing project. However, information assurance does not have to own all aspects of the project; it is enough that the information assurance group should possess an end-to-end perspective, so that it can appropriately assess risk.

To relegate information assurance only to technical security tactics and practices is a serious error. Regardless of the vendor, the ultimate accountability (referred to as *responsibility*) stays with the firm. "One thing that can't be outsourced—responsibility . . . . Everything from employee policies to customer satisfaction to ethical and legal issues roots back to the impact on shareholder value. These responsibilities stay with the firm regardless of the functions that have been outsourced."[15]

The vendor, however, is accountable for carrying out all elements of the contractual agreement.

Thus, at the earliest planning stages, an information assurance review includes the overall scope of the outsourcing project. Questions should include:

- What information assets are at risk?
- What is the value and sensitivity of those assets?
- What current and future "risk shadow" will the outsourcing project cast on those corporate information assets?

The responses to these questions provide the foundation for the outsourcing project, as well as the degree of involvement from the information assurance community after that preliminary review.

Planning complex endeavors normally proceeds by careful identification and examination of concepts that move from general to specific. The sections that follow include broad categories for consideration at the onset of the outsourcing project. These categories require in-depth examination, as they relate to the specifics of each unique outsourcing project.

The outsource plan must include not only those tasks and security elements that are well known, but must as well consider the unthinkable. Amazon Corporation is an absolute pioneer and power in the cloud-computing world, providing hosting services to businesses large and small. As a cloud-computing provider, Amazon's Web services can have a direct impact on a business's revenue stream.

In an article entitled "Modern life halted as Netflix, Pinterest, Instagram go down" author Chris Matyszczyk describes how Netflix, Pinterest, and Instagram were completely unavailable: "The cause was reportedly an outage at Amazon's Elastic Compute Cloud in North Virginia, brought on by a thunder and lightning show."[16]

We need not look much further than very recent history to find other epic security incidents that involved corporations and outsourcers:

> ...Sony shut down its PlayStation Network and mustc-streaming service Qriocity after an attacker made off with passwords and personal data from 77 million customer accounts and possibly 10 million encrypted credit card files. The information was in an AT&T data center in San Diego but controlled by Sony, which on Monday also pulled its Sony Online Entertainment site and Station.com gaming site after discovering an issue while investigating the intrusions.[17]

Alex Pham of the *Los Angeles Times* provides us a glimpse into the fiscal impact of the breach:

> In addition to losing an estimated revenue stream of about $10 million a week, Sony will probably have to reimburse customers who pay for its premium service, rebuild its computer systems, and beef up security measures, said Michael Pachter, an analyst with Wedbush Securities who said the incident could cost the company $50 million.
>
> That doesn't take into account the cost of defending against lawsuits, including two filed in California that are seeking federal class-action status.
>
> "Even if everyone loses just $1, that's $70 million," said Mark Rasch, director of cybersecurity and privacy at CSC, a computer networking and security firm in Falls Church, Va. Rasch, a former federal prosecutor who prosecuted Kevin Mitnick, a once notorious computer hacker, added, "If it's $2, you're looking at $140 million. Even lawyers can do that kind of math."[18]

Explaining those volumes of losses to a Board of Directors and shareholders is not an easy or pleasant task—thus a very clear understanding of risk and risk management in any outsourcing agreement is key. As the Sony incident as well as the Amazon–Netflix/Pinterest/Instagram examples demonstrate, even when dealing with world-class outsourcing leaders, bad things can and do happen; thus, a well-thought-out mitigation plan is not only essential, it is a matter of survival.

68.3.4 Clarity of Purpose and Intent. To outsource, one must possess the ability to articulate the task and to focus on creating a mutually beneficial vendor relationship. Poorly defined tasks lead to frustration and to unstructured attempts to meet inchoate needs instead of to measurable objectives—limitations that cause both organization and vendor to fail.

Corporations should associate with outsourcers that possess depth expertise in the particular business function intended to be outsourced. If a corporation outsources a business function to an outsourcer that has to be told specifically how to fulfill the certain task, there is likely a disconnect. The purpose of outsourcing is to pay to have the function fulfilled by someone who can perform the function at more efficient and effective levels than the corporation itself.

Corporations depend on current employees to articulate the soon-to-be-outsourced task again, not the specific details of how they will attain the expected outcomes. Ironically, those employees best suited to articulate the task are frequently those whose jobs are most at risk after the successful implementation of the outsourcing project. This conflict of interest is a risk consideration.

Several phases of outsourcing include, but are not limited to, the collection and documentation of task knowledge for outsourced functions, vendor solicitation such as the request for information (RFI) or the request for proposal (RFP), vendor selection, and training.

Vendor selection is itself a key and integral part of the risk management of outsourcing, hence the importance of identifying, articulating, and quantifying the outsourcing goals. Once vendor selection occurs, corporate employees train vendor personnel on the outsourced functions. When the vendor personnel are trained and functional, most outsourcing results in the redeployment or release of corporate employees who fulfilled the specific task prior to outsourcing.

Risks related to clarity of purpose and intent include:

- Poor identification and definition of the outsourced task as well as clearly articulated success metrics results in an ineffective outsourcing program.
- Employees involved in the outsourcing project are aware that in many cases they are training their replacements.
- Any reduction in force regardless of the cause is a traumatic corporate event bringing unease and unrest to other employees.
- Unease and unrest can translate into lost productivity, poor morale, malaise, and corporate insider sabotage, all of which ultimately cause lost revenue.

Once outsource personnel are trained, especially if the technology/task is in high demand, the vendor must have safeguards in place to stem their attrition caused by their employees 'job hopping' to a more lucrative outsourcer.

68.3.5 Price. One of the largest risks of outsourcing is the formation of an unstable relationship with the vendor. When margins are paper thin, overall security practices often become the first victim. Recent findings from IT research firm Gartner indicate that a significant number of CIOs still look at outsourcing in terms of near-term profitability.

> As a result, they're setting themselves up for failure .... By 2008, more than 2.3 million offshore service workers will be employed by U.S. companies. But according to a recent Dun & Bradstreet survey, 20% of those outsourcing relationships will fail in the first two years, and 50% within five years.[19]

Risks related to price issues include:

- The vendor's culture must at least absorb, if not improve on, the originating company's corporate culture and do so in a fiscally responsible way.

- Defining outsourcing success by cost reduction alone introduces ongoing and increasing risk throughout the outsourcing relationship.
- Price and pricing are dependent on the ability to forecast business accurately. If the outsourced business does not have a perspective of historical trends, driving prices down at a vendor can actually have a negative effect on the outsourcer's outcomes and efforts.

Because outsourcers, like most businesses, seek to maximize profits in a low-margin industry, it is important to understand if the outsourcer actually outsources parts of their infrastructure (including security) to an even lower-cost outsourcer. For example, does an Indian outsourcing company outsource parts of their work (coding, reporting, training) to vendors in China, Vietnam, or other lower-cost labor markets? Understanding your outsourcer's business model and strategy is a key decision point.

68.3.6 Social Culture. The vendor must understand and address the social culture of the outsourced task and the differences from its own. Vendors must understand, absorb, and fulfill the outsourced task, under the same social norms as the sponsor organization. Cultures around the world have different societal norms, expectations, and nuances regarding confidentiality, possession, integrity, authenticity, availability, and utility. Vendors must be able to respond, react, and live within both the social culture they serve and their home culture.

Risks related to social culture include:

- Failure of the vendor to adapt to the social culture of the society served can result in lost money, wasted effort, potential legal issues, and customer dissatisfaction.
- Failure of organizations and vendors to anticipate, recognize, and mitigate problems arising from cultural differences regarding security, whether insourced or outsourced, poses a potentially catastrophic risk.
- Failure of the outsourcing corporation to understand the cultural nuances of the intended outsourcing country's social norms or the cultural nuances of the countries served by the outsourcer can drive out any potential gains of outsourcing with greater dissatisfaction in the outsourcing company, the outsourcer and the customer segments served

68.3.7 International Economics. The organization not only needs to understand its corporate and customer economics; it also must have a very deep and forward-looking view into the economic horizon of the vendor's geopolitical economy.

There are many willing vendors in emerging and low-cost labor markets. Without a clear understanding of the economic future of the vendor's country, a corporation can easily find itself tied to a vendor in an eroding or imploding economy.

Risks related to economic issues include:

- When the economy of a country collapses, any contractual relationship to an outsourcing vendor in that country will not survive.
- Forced into an evanescent relationship, a corporation may not have the ability to pull the outsourced task in-house, or to another vendor, quickly enough to save its own business.

In the second decade of the twenty-first century, China's economy contracts and wage growth increases, several European nations and the EU itself teeter on the verge of insolvency, and Vietnam and the Philippines see robust growth. Companies with long-term outsourcing contracts in highly changing regions may find themselves contractually locked into a difficult business climate for years to come.

68.3.8 Political Issues. Regardless of whether the vendor is nearshore or offshore, the client organization must have clear understanding, perspective, and acceptance of the political nuances in the vendor's country.

Political nuances and practices differ in every country. Acceptable behavior in one country may be reprehensible in another. Corporations must consider how political nuances intertwine with corporate objectives and policies.

Corporations must also be aware of and acknowledge the new risks and instabilities of the new century, and factor them into every nearshoring and offshoring outsourcing effort.

> The terrorist attacks Tuesday on trains in the western India city of Mumbai appeared unlikely to dampen investments and outsourcing to India .... The government also found evidence from terrorists killed in an encounter last year that they were targeting India's successful outsourcing industry.[20]

Risks related to political issues include:

- Are graft and bribery accepted or expected within the local political system? If so, how will such practices accord with national restrictions on the contracting organization? Will the outsourcing entity need to sponsor or participate in the political system of the vendor's country? How will such involvement be perceived nationally and internationally?
- Is the country politically stable? What are the opposing forces, and how do they see outsourcing vendors?
- Does the nearshoring or offshoring country possess an environment compatible with terrorist activities? What assurances of business continuity can the vendor make under such circumstances?

In mid-April 2012, the president of Argentina, Cristina Fernandez de Kirchner, announced "... a government plan to take YPF back through legislation that would expropriate a 51% share of the company. Through a decree, Fernandez immediately placed the leadership of YPF in the hands of Julio De Vido, the country's minister of planning and public investment."[21] Thus, the Spanish oil company Repsol lost its investment and purchase of Argentina's YPF, an oil and gas company. If a company outsources into a country where government seizures are acceptable and expected, the outsourcing company faces many risks related to infrastructure and, perhaps more importantly, intellectual property.

An energy crisis in India is having a significant impact on the Indian people and businesses. Contributing factors to the energy crisis include India's dependence on Iran for oil, yet U.S. and European sanctions are diminishing Iran's ability to deliver fuel to India. The diminished flow from Iran to India, as well as competition for oil and other fuels with China, Japan, and South Korea, leads commentators to suggest, "At stake is India's ability to bring electricity to 400 million rural residents—a third of the population—as well as keep the lights on at corporate office towers and provide enough fuel for 1.5 million new vehicles added the roads each month."[22]

68.3.9 Environmental Factors. Site selection is one of the fundamental building blocks in any outsourcing project and a topic worthy of careful examination by itself. (For additional details, see Chapter 23 in this *Handbook*.)

Risks related to environmental factors include:

- If nearshore or offshore, will the vendor's regional infrastructure predictably and reliably support the expected and required service levels for the outsourced task?
- How susceptible is the nearshore/offshore location to natural disaster?
- Could a natural disaster trigger debilitating political or economic events in the host country?
- Does the host country possess the ability to recover from an environmental disaster?
- Could the outbreak of an easily transmitted disease or illness affect the location? And does the host country have the medical, technical, and communications infrastructure to deal with a pandemic?
- Is the area prepared for the actual weather it receives? For example, it is well known that the monsoon season comes to India. One of the causes of absenteeism in monsoon season in Mumbai is street flooding.
- Does the proposed outsourcing location have the external technology infrastructure that would support a remote workforce? If an employee cannot go to work because of street flooding or a pandemic, does the outsourcing country's telecommunications infrastructure support continuity of operations?

68.3.10 Travel. Whether nearshore or offshore, outsourcing will likely, and with regularity, send employees to the vendor for training, quality control, and other management functions. Important travel considerations focus on the costs of travel as well as on employee safety and health, addressing such issues as travel safety, food safety, medical preparations (immunizations, malaria pills, etc.), and locally available medical care.

Risks related to travel include:

- Will foreign workers be able to obtain required travel documents (e.g., exit permits from their home country, working visas for the outsourcing organization's country), allowing them to work in the client's organization?
- Extensive travel is grueling, takes a toll on employees' personal lives, and can cause productivity and management issues.
- Travel is expensive. Failure to budget for appropriate amounts of travel to the vendor will result in budget overruns.
- In the post-9/11 world, the risks and stresses to travelers have increased. Depending on the vendor's location, exposure of corporate employees to terrorist threats, or the fear of terrorist threats, is a significant consideration.
- With the advent of airport body scanners, controversy still occurs as to the long-term health risks of multiple scans by frequent travelers

- Keeping employees on the road traveling for long periods of time leads to physical, mental, and family stresses, all of which can contribute to employee turnover.

Common sense reveals that in most companies, it is the more senior and experienced personnel who do in fact travel in support of outsourcers. However, by traveling, those senior personnel face more and more nonproductive hours in airports and airplanes. Given that more and more major airlines have wireless availability while in flight, productivity can increase. Conversely, the ability to eavesdrop and intercept corporate communications increases in public places like airports, and in a small, enclosed, and public Wi-Fi network on an airplane, the chances for corporate espionage increase significantly.

68.3.11 Labor. Labor and workforce risks occur everywhere from Detroit, Michigan, to the Philippines and Bangalore, India. Without a clear understanding of the risks particular to the vendor's region, a corporation could find itself in a quagmire of constant turnover, escalating wages, work stoppages, and unfettered cost growth.

Careful examinations of current and forecasted workforce trends are core to the vendor selection process. As outsourcing sites gain in popularity, wages escalate driven by competition for workers. Once a corporation moves key functions to a vendor, if workforce conditions negatively change, previous cost savings could be lost. Important considerations include current and forecasted worker supply, the vendor's ability to retain employees (as evidenced by annual turnover rates), a propensity for collective bargaining in the vendor's country, and the stability of the government and the opposition's tactics.

Additionally, understanding the history of strikes or work stoppages in the vendor's location is a necessary preparation. For example:

> Political strife led to a shutdown Oct. 4 of most major outsourcing companies in Bangalore .... In April, Bangalore shut down for two days when citizens rioted following the death of Indian film icon Rajkumar. Published reports said the country's software companies lost $40 million in revenue.[23]

As mentioned in Section 68.3.7, the economic conditions in the offshore location should be followed carefully. Some countries suffering inflation may push workers toward collective action. For example, in April 2008, 20,000 Vietnamese workers at a factory making shoes for Nike went on strike to demand increased wages to keep pace with inflation.[24]

Another issue is whether worker exploitation (e.g., wages below a reasonable minimum, child labor, slave labor, unhealthful working conditions) exists in the offshore location or is practiced by the outsourcing vendor. Do such practices pose a threat to morale and reputation of the outsourcing organization?[25]

As we examine years of outsourcing experience, it is not uncommon for those workforces originally involved in lower-skill call-center positions to acquire experiences and skills over time which should lead to better paying and more challenging positions. However, if those more challenging positions don't materialize in an outsourcing location, the workforce can become disillusioned and migrate to another environment where the potential to advance both career and salary are possible.

68.3.12 Intellectual Property Risks. Outsourcing can and does include work which itself contains corporate intellectual property. By exposing intellectual property to the outsourcer, that intellectual property can be easily copied and stolen. The U.S.-China Business Council noted,

> According to the release, six product areas are eligible for National Indigenous Innovation Product accreditation: computing and application hardware, telecom hardware, modern office equipment, software, new-energy products, and highly efficient energy-reducing products. These are the same six product areas outlined in the Notice Regarding the Launch of the National Indigenous Innovation Product Accreditation Work for 2009 (Circular 618), which was released in November 2009 . . . .
>
> Though the revised accreditation requirements are a step forward, several significant issues in China's indigenous innovation policies remain. In particular, the notice does not address the use of the product list or its link to government procurement preferences. Moreover, the proposed changes to the National Indigenous Innovation Product qualification criteria do not clear up questions about the relationship between the national product list and the continued validity and use of provincial- and local-level product lists that have been compiled based on discriminatory accreditation criteria. Finally, though the accreditation criteria no longer mention import substitution as a policy goal, the notice apparently does not change the November circular's application form, which asks whether an applicant's product can substitute for imports.[26]

In 2012, commentators reported that,

> It's no secret that China has been pressing multinationals to transfer more technology for accessing its huge market. Beijing now is turning another screw in its localization bid: requiring Chinese to run local operations of some foreign businesses.
>
> China in May ordered the Big Four auditors, Deloitte, PricewaterhouseCoopers, Ernst & Young, and KPMG, to have Chinese nationals manage their local units in three years . . . .
>
> As part of its "indigenous innovation" drive, Beijing in 2010 ordered that the technology of foreign firms must be registered in China, developed in China and, in some cases, made in China . . . .
>
> "We're fighting enough ghosts in China trying to protect our IP without having to intentionally share it," said Thomas Moga, an attorney at Shook, Hady & Bacon's Intellectual Property Section in Washington D.C . . . .
>
> While many emerging markets impose local content rules, none boasts China's economic weight. If Beijing continues to press, it could have a big impact on U.S. companies that rely on China for sales and manufacturing.[27]

Because foreign governments may have differing perspectives and practices around intellectual property, an assessment should be made of the financial consequences of losing control over intellectual property. A comparison of the size of the potential loss to the financial gains of outsourcing should be part of every outsourcing evaluation.

68.3.13 Additional Risks. Although the preceding lists may seem expansive, there are still many other fundamental and significant elements that must be part of any outsourcing decision-making process. Other complex and, in some cases, deeply fundamental considerations are:

- Loss of corporate expertise over tasks
- Loss of direct control
- Internal changes in corporate purpose (i.e., moving from a company of doers to a company that manages those who are doers)
- Overhead of ongoing contract management issues

- Currency fluctuations negatively impacting either the outsourcing corporation or the outsourcer
- Outsourcing staff turnover/retention
- Training (both failure to train, and failure to maintain training)
- Visa policies and the immigration of outsourced, highly skilled personnel to countries with permissive immigration policies for skilled labor
- Corporate espionage either directly or indirectly at an outsourcer

Understanding all of the risks allows the prepared organization to knowingly accept, mitigate, transfer, or ignore risks associated with the outsourcing project.

68.4 CONTROLLING THE RISKS. Outsourcing is an area in which the motto "Security transcends technology"[28] holds particularly true. Almost none of the threats to information itself, or information technology, is unique to an outsourced environment, although perhaps some may grow more dangerous in far-removed or foreign locales. Outsourcing does involve some serious security issues, but most—at first glance—might appear indirect threats to information assurance.

68.4.1 Controls on What? Most of the security issues of outsourcing involve people, corporations, societies, and governments. Security controls to mitigate the risks of outsourcing have little to do with technology such as computers and a great deal to do with organizational behavior. Since contractors perform crucial tasks but often are geographically far removed from those ultimately accountable for the tasks, the policies, contracts, agreements, and trust relationships that the organization has set up in advance will dictate the success of the endeavor. In particular, the organization's information-technology security policy takes on a much more visible role. The technological controls involve the assurance of interpersonal notions like trust and accountability, and are perhaps overshadowed by concern with legal matters, site selection, contractual obligations, politico-economics, and the impact of social networking and separation of duties.

68.4.2 Controlling Outsourcing Risk. Many of the risks described in Section 68.4 transcend the boundaries of individual risk types but are similar to other risk areas in the way they map to the six foundation elements of information security (the Parkerian Hexad).[29] It seems appropriate, then, to couch the discussion of controls in terms of the security foundations. This section focuses on controls that mitigate, for instance, confidentiality concerns in outsourced environments, touching on how the controls might affect the risk classes differently. Since part of the scope of this chapter is the outsourcing of security functions, some of the controls mentioned do not immediately appear to relate to information assurance but may affect other success metrics.

68.4.3 Availability Controls. When resources are local, the primary source of problems that can lead to a loss of availability has to do with physical and logical infrastructure. When resources are remote, the infrastructure issues are still important, and can indeed be more problematic. A good example of this difference is the February 2007 trans-Pacific cable cut that made much of Asia inaccessible over the Internet.[30] The farther the vendor from the home company, the more difficult and expensive it can be to acquire an alternate route for communications.

On June 29, 2012,

> ...[L]ightning in Virginia took out part of Amazon's cloud computing service, called Amazon Web Services, which hundreds of companies use for data storage and computation. Well-known sites like Netflix, Pinterest, and Instagram were not accessible for hours. There was little information for customers about what had happened, or even whether user data was safe.
>
> The interruption underlined how businesses and consumers are increasingly exposed to unforeseen risks and wrenching disruptions as they increasingly embrace life in the cloud. It was also a big blow to what is probably the fastest-growing part of the media business, start-ups on the social Web that attract millions of users seemingly overnight....
>
> The weekend's disruption happened after a lightning storm caused the power to fail at the Amazon Web Services center in Northern Virginia containing thousands of computer servers. For reasons Amazon was still unsure of on Sunday, the data center's backup generator also failed....
>
> It was at least the second major failure for Amazon in that area. In April 2011, a problem in Amazon's networking at a nearby data center took down a number of applications and popular Websites, including Reddit and Quora, for more than a day....[31]

Mitigation of availability risk revolves around planning. Sound backup strategies and business continuity plans should already be in place for the organization; the outsourcing project should also have these plans, both for the vendor site and for the staff at the home organization responsible for vendor communications. Given the economic, political, and environmental concerns that could lead to total (and possibly permanent) unavailability of the outsourced site, a backup vendor should be in place for disasters. These kinds of controls would be appropriate for natural disasters, labor strikes, terrorism, and a variety of other risks to availability. With the advent of cloud computing and, when ideally implemented, the geographical diversity of cloud computing providers, business continuity can benefit from the cloud computing platform, provided there are redundancies of path and infrastructure. (For details of backups, business continuity planning, and disaster recovery, see Chapters 57, 58, and 59 in this *Handbook*.)

If the vendor is in a foreign country where laws and contracts are enforced differently (or not at all), a service-level agreement incorporated into disaster planning might turn out to be a hollow, unenforceable contract.[32] Part of the evaluation of any outsourcing decision should be a visit to the site, including inspection of policy documents and physical tours of facilities. The organization needs to be sure that controls at the vendor site really do mirror the vendor's policy and contract documents and that the controls are instantiated contractually in an official statement of work. For example, it is a fairly common practice in outsourcing call centers that call center employees may not bring into the call center USB drives, recording devices, and the like. Yet, it has been these authors' first-hand experience that even in tightly controlled call centers, call-center employees routinely carry cell phones with gigabytes of memory and high-resolution cameras. Thus, not only is it important for controls to be contractually in place, but there must be the will and willingness on the part of the outsourcer to enforce the controls.

Beyond making sure that plans are in place against unavailability, the organization must be able to check up on the performance of the vendor. The agility required to switch to a backup vendor becomes much more possible with advance notice for at least some of the possible outages; however, this possibility must be evaluated with the knowledge that switching volumes or work between vendors is a complex task and should be field tested and validated on a regular basis. For instance, if the availability of a site relates to escalating economic problems causing workforce shortages, a periodic analysis of the regional news media, and of the vendor's work performance, might give hints of problems on the horizon. Automated checking is appropriate as well, especially to keep track of network resources when access traverses the public Internet. Ultimately, for both people and technology, mitigating the risks of outsourced availability comes down to planning and monitoring.

68.4.4 Utility Controls. The utility of information (and of remote resources) hinges mostly on communication—both format and process. Careful version control avoids incompatible data. Encryption recovery agents can avoid the loss of utility if a user forgets a decryption password, but national and international restrictions on encryption must be kept in mind when planning the use of encryption across national borders.[33] These utility issues are common to any organization. With outsourcing, incompatible formats become more of a problem, especially with offshoring. If an application written in the United States uses ASCII encoding, but the vendor has applications that use Unicode, format issues can arise that need to be accounted for and solved. Although these problems may not become apparent immediately, planning for them must occur well in advance.

Human communication is also an issue with outsourcing. Even if the organization's native language is spoken by employees in the outsource vendor's site, it may not be their first language. Spoken communication (e.g., at a helpdesk) can suffer greatly if a technician's accent is too difficult for employees and customers of the client organization to understand. Similarly, written documentation and regular reports can lead to misunderstandings if language skills are not adequate. Either of these situations becomes manageable through advance planning for workforce training and through onsite liaison from the home organization, especially early in the relationship.

Utility of information also hinges on the type of data and the location of the data. Some government entities around the world require that data particular to that government or government constituents reside only within that country. Although the information may indeed be held within a specific country, there are additional considerations if those accessing the information are not within the country boundaries. Thus, the information may indeed be useful, but may not be useful to all based on their location.

68.4.5 Integrity and Authenticity Controls. The risk that the organization's data might be changed unknowingly, or replaced with other data, hinges on trust. Any time crucial business functions are given to an outside entity, trust issues arise. The organization must understand how much information is being shared, and with whom. Role-based access control and the principle of least privilege are appropriate here: Based on its role of supporting a particular business function, what is the minimum amount of privilege the vendor needs to do its job? Nevertheless, to be an effective support organization, the vendor may need access to corporate information that could prove damaging if misused.

From the perspective of integrity and authenticity controls, the decision to outsource must be accompanied by a decision about levels of trust. This trust should include an analysis of the vendor's history and reputation as well as a visual inspection of the site. The "trust infrastructure," which would include access-control mechanisms as well as division of labor and delegation of responsibilities, must be designed by the organization. Importantly, the vendor must not be able to make changes in this structure. Changes to trust relationships must be driven by the organization.

Given fluctuation of economies, job markets, and international relations, the decision to trust the outsourced personnel and processes should not be a one-time event. Ongoing monitoring could reveal occasional lapses that might grow into bigger problems. How easy is it for the home organization to check up on the integrity and authenticity of data? Where are logs kept? Are backup copies of the logs (or the originals) sent to the home organization? What about change tracking on servers? How do technical personnel troubleshoot deeply technical issues that require access to protected information? Are all accesses of protected information logged and audited? What happens to protected customer information used in troubleshooting after it is no longer needed? Each of these questions should be addressed, and the answers should be written into the contractual language.

68.4.6 Confidentiality and Possession Controls. Merely making the decision to outsource partially compromises the confidentiality and possession of corporate information, just as the strength of a secret is decreased as soon as it is shared—even with a trusted confidante. The home organization must decide whether the loss of confidentiality and possession is balanced by the benefits of outsourcing. Within the United States, and in many countries with strong legal systems, laws protecting physical and intellectual property can help support this decision. The penalties enforced by the legal system serve as a deterrent to thieves and also serve to compensate damages in the event of a successful compromise. In countries where laws protecting intellectual property are weak (or absent), or where the rule of law is nominal or absent, this level of deterrent and compensation is not available, and the balance of risk shifts.

In June 2006, an employee at the HSBC bank call center in Bangalore, India, was arrested and charged with hacking into the bank's computers, breaching confidentiality agreements and privacy laws, and helping to steal £233,000. The accused was discovered to have been hired on the basis of forged school transcripts. According to news reports, the only criterion for hiring personnel into that call center was English-language skills.[34]

In the absence of strong legal backing, the organization can replace some of the deterrent normally provided by laws with language in the contract linking contractual compliance with payments and ongoing business relationships. The vendor should be required to meet security expectations, and the contract should specifically state that parts of the agreement (or the entire agreement) might be voided if security proves inadequate. Coupled with ongoing monitoring to catch problems before they become habitual or endemic, contractually tying security performance to the future of the relationship might prevent a damaging, large-scale loss of confidentiality or possession. And, although this kind of contractual language might not help in a foreign court, it should help protect the organization if the vendor manages to bring suit against the organization in the organization's home jurisdiction.

Outsourcing contracts should as well include specific requirements on the use of personal, portable electronic devices (smart phones, tablets, laptops, cameras) all of which are capable of independent data connections outside the purview of an outsourcer's technical infrastructure.

Additionally, rules regarding data exposure through social and professional networking sites should be written into outsourcing contracts. The personal use of sites such as Facebook or LinkedIn and the types of information that can be exposed by outsourced employees should be carefully considered as part of confidentiality and possession considerations in outsourcing contracts.

There are laws in the United States and other countries where governments may have access to confidential information when appropriate. Consider, for example, cloud-computing outsourcers operating with a global footprint and managing data for a European company, in a European data center, yet managing the data center in the United States using U.S. employees. In those situations, the European companies may not understand U.S. laws; because they are used to the stricter privacy controls defined by the European Privacy Directive, they may think that the U.S. Government could have easy access to European corporate data because of U.S. laws. Similar issues arise for U.S. corporations with respect to other nations. The outsourcing provider and the outsourcing client must clearly delineate the impact of local laws the countries involved in the business relationships.

68.4.7 Making the Best of Outsourcing. Controlling the risks of outsourcing any function involves planning and careful implementation, primarily focused on trust and monitoring. The advice to *trust, but verify* applies particularly to outsourcing situations, in which a vendor necessarily gains at least some level of access to the organization's internal information and systems. Planning for risks to availability requires adequate business continuity and disaster recovery planning. Training, liaison, and careful planning well in advance of the outsourcing move are required to mitigate risks to utility. Integrity and authenticity controls, as well as confidentiality and possession controls, hinge on monitoring and enforcement, which can become problematic in different legal climates. Making contracts include business consequences for falling short of security requirements can help control the shortfalls of foreign jurisdictions. The ability to quickly recognize and contain evolving risk is key to long-term success in outsourcing.

68.5 OUTSOURCING SECURITY FUNCTIONS. Delegating security functions to an outside vendor can increase the quality of an organization's overall security posture. This is done by leveraging the vendor's security expertise and perspective, which presumably it has acquired by providing a number of in-depth services to a large number of organizations.

Despite the media attention surrounding the outsourcing of some IT security functions, the use of a contracted guard force by organizations has been a common practice for years. As mentioned in Section 68.1.3, this is an example of insourcing: the use of contract or noncompany employees to fulfill certain business functions within physical and logical corporate boundaries.

In the last few years, organizations such as financial institutions have been nearshoring complex and costly IT security functions. This work is challenging for any organization, as the goal is to guard production networks against a never-ending stream of continuously changing threats. Also, these security functions usually do not pass the core competency tests described in Section 68.2.2, meaning they are good candidates for outsourcing. A leading example would be 24-hour-per-day monitoring and management of firewalls and intrusion-detection systems.

A new twist on a mature outsourcing tactic is offshoring software testing for security vulnerabilities. Assuming the vendor has the necessary tools and talent, outsourcing this function appears to make sense for many of the same reasons that organizations outsource quality assurance testing for any software development project. Not only is it an opportunity to gain effectiveness, but the efficiencies (e.g., faster cycle time and lower cost) can be compelling as well.

68.5.1 Who Outsources Security? A May 2013 report discussed the growth in security-outsourcing services:

> Despite some tumult, IT security outsourcing has been growing slowly but steadily during the last three years, with 38% of organizations outsourcing at least some element of this function in 2012. This growth will likely continue. More than one-fifth of survey respondents expect their IT security outsourcing to increase in the next year. At the same time, our outsourcing study shows strong cost benefits and service benefits to security outsourcing. In fact, the percentage of organizations that find outsourcing improves service is very high at 94%, tied for first place among the 11 IT functions included in our survey.
>
> Clearly, improving service is a strong factor motivating organizations to outsource their IT security functions. Why aren't more enterprise organizations doing so? Organizations are taking a measured approach to outsourcing the function because it is critical to the enterprise. The highly competitive outsourcing landscape could also be sowing uncertainty. Outsourcing partners need to do a better job of demonstrating their usefulness before the outsourcing of this vital IT function gains wider traction.[35]

68.5.2 Why Do Organizations Outsource Security? According to Levine, the top two reasons why organizations outsource network security are as a strategy for dealing with staffing challenges (effectiveness) and a desire for financial savings (efficiency).[36]

68.5.2.1 Staffing Challenges. Getting the most value from a security staff is an enduring challenge. Not only must talented people be found and retained, but they must be deployed so as to gain the greatest benefits. The highest value work for a security team includes those tasks that must be done from deep within the business context, such as policy setting, architecture, design, and risk management. These tasks require in-depth knowledge of a business's strategies, strengths, weaknesses, organizational structure, and culture. They are the core competencies of the corporate security team.

Given this situation, one of the best ongoing exercises a security officer or manager can perform to maximize the value of their team is to ask regularly, "Are my people exclusively working on tasks that cannot be delegated to anyone else?" Another way to ask this is, "Are my people doing any tasks that someone with less experience and organizational knowledge could perform at the same level of competency?"

Generally, such tasks are *not* mission-critical; they are *infrastructure* duties that support the key, distinguishing aspects of the organization's mission.

An example of a situation that can benefit from outsourcing security is protecting the network in an organization with limited technical resources.

Protecting the organizational network is a demanding job. Securing network connected digital assets (i.e., information systems) requires robust defenses against malicious hackers, viruses, worms, spyware, keystroke loggers, and denial of service attacks, just to name a few specific online threats. It may be difficult or impossible to find and employ enough security staff members who are both effective and efficient at dealing with all these threats. As well, threats and risk don't simplistically occur only during business hours. Maintaining adequate staff to manage and monitor 24 × 7 × 365 is both physically and financially challenging.

In addition, understanding and defending against the latest threats requires constant education of staff, proactive monitoring, maintenance, and patching of the organization's network defenses. The capital expenditure for the care and feeding of specialized software and equipment can be very high.

Due to the nature and rapid pace of the threats, and a chronic shortage of talented people, there is an ongoing need to replace security staff. This adds additional expense for contract workers, decreased productivity, and increased risk of mistakes. Keeping information assurance specialists around after you have trained them is not easy; other organizations want and need them too. Outsourcing offers one way to transfer the burden of staff training and retention to another organization.

Finally, security service providers offer competent handling of routine security activities (i.e., monitoring and maintenance of hardware and software), and they can prepare the many reports required to document compliance with corporate policies and outside regulations. With these tasks being taken care of by a vendor, organizations can focus their internal efforts and personnel on more critical, high-value IT security functions.

68.5.2.2 Financial Savings. Despite our admonition in Section 68.4.4 to avoid outsourcing as a primary means to achieve direct cost reduction, a managed security service provider (MSSP) can offer tremendous economic efficiencies. For example, full-time security monitoring can be outsourced for significant cost savings.

A substantial challenge for all but the largest organizations is monitoring IT security 24 hours per day, seven days a week. For financial institutions in particular, this level of monitoring has become the de facto standard of due care. But providing that kind of constant vigilance is nearly impossible for many small organizations, such as community banks.

To provide 24-hour-per-day coverage with internal staff, organizations have to hire at least three full-time professionals, but would likely require twice as many to prevent staff burnout and a high turnover rate over the long term. Having backup coverage in place would require even more employees.

Managing an average week of 24-hour-per-day monitoring and response takes a minimum of five fully trained people. To begin with, you need one person for each of the three 8-hour shifts during the week. For weekends, the most economical approach is to have one person for each of two 12-hour shifts. Realistically, due to sickness, vacation, holidays, training, and other demands on staff, there would need to be between 8 and 10 employees to provide reliable coverage. In addition, should an actual security event occur, with the minimal coverage model as described here, there simply will not be enough hands to manage and contain the event. Thus, the affected company may indeed appreciate the scope and impact of the event, but be quite limited in their response.

The economics of this situation are straightforward. In the United States, a nearshore vendor can be hired to manage a small organization's firewalls, as well as run host intrusion detection and perimeter intrusion detection, for between US$25,000 and $50,000 a year.[37] In contrast, any organization in the United States would likely spend at least six times that amount on salaries alone to perform those functions with minimal staff. It is common for a highly skilled, in-house security professional to be paid between US$70,000 and US$180,000 a year in salary alone.[38] Add money for benefits (20 to 50 percent of base salary) as well as facilities, equipment, and other employment costs (80 to 150 percent of base salary), and the fully burdened cost for each employee can be almost two times what they are paid in direct salary.

At one of our organizations, the fully burdened cost of all employees is calculated every quarter by taking their direct salary and adding 184 percent.[39] Using this formula, the fully burdened cost of a security professional paid US$100,000 a year in direct salary is US$284,000.

68.5.2.3 Threat Intelligence and Additional Perspectives. An organization is best positioned to make decisions regarding IT security when it has the freshest, most complete intelligence (information concerning an enemy or possible enemy[40]) about emerging threats.

However, the tremendous volume of threat data being released every day can overwhelm all but the largest organizations. Even national governments struggle to keep up, and they usually have dozens or hundreds of people dedicated to gathering and analyzing data. Beyond problems of volume, there is the question of scope: It is difficult to know how any given vulnerability will be applicable to a specific system, if at all. A software maker's estimation of vulnerability severity is generic in nature; it may be more or less severe within the context of another organization. This is where an MSSP can really help.

MSSPs typically have the ability to gauge severity and spot trends based on what is happening to its other customers. One MSSP advertises that it

> … process[es] over a billion security events every day across more than 7,000 devices, giving our security research group unprecedented internal and external threat visibility across the globe. Using this visibility, [this vendor] maps the latest vulnerabilities and real-world threats to your infrastructure, enabling your team to prevent attacks.[41]

In Section 68.3.11, "the loss of corporate expertise over tasks" was mentioned as one of the risks of outsourcing. If your organization takes advantage of an MSSP's intelligence capability, and you have the opportunity and resources, a valuable provision in an outsourcing contract would be to transfer the vendor's intelligence-gathering skills to one or more employees of your organization. However, vendors may view such knowledge as proprietary.

68.5.3 What Are the Risks of Outsourcing Security? Trust is at the heart of the question of outsourcing risks. Can you trust the vendor to whom you are outsourcing, and its employees? Internal employees cannot typically gain the kind of intimacy with these people that they can with each other. This is a barrier to the human desire and tendency to build trust with others through direct interaction and observation.

If trust is at the heart of outsourcing security, the remainder of the vital organs consists of competency, capability, scope, and the rapid adaptability of the outsourcer. Trust is of course key, but the ability of the outsourcer to remain cutting-edge relevant in the light-speed world of security threats must be present.

There are specific risks in outsourcing security functions. *Total* control of an organization's security should never be transferred to an outside vendor. Although it may be possible to delegate (i.e., outsource) some operational duties, most companies find that keeping control of critical functions is vital to a successful security program. Examples of critical functions include firewall administration, direct control over all administrative/root accounts, and direct control over security logging. However, depending on your ability to manage the risk to your organization, you may feel comfortable delegating any of these functions. At the end of the day, outsourcing IT security is a very personal decision.

Some specific risks for IT security outsourcing include:

- An intrusion-detection system (IDS) monitoring vendor is more profitable as the number of events it responds to decreases. If the vendor is also responsible for tuning your IDS, will your vendor tune the devices to produce the least number of events regardless of the actual threat environment?

- How can you ensure that in a significant customer-wide event, your organization will not be ignored or placed at a lower priority by your vendor?
- Is the vendor paid by "event" rather than by alert? If the answer is yes, what safeguards are in place to monitor potential abuse?
- Where are the outside vendor's personnel located: onshore, nearshore, offshore? Each would require specific contract language to accommodate language, cultural, and legal distinctions.
- Is the vendor vigilant about the background and expertise of its personnel?
- Who is monitoring the activities and behavior of the vendor's employees when they access your organization's data?
- Some countries are known as hotbeds of corporate espionage. Do you have strong control of your source code to ensure that the vendor's employees do not share the code with any other persons or entity?
- What are the vendor's source country's governmental policies on privacy and intellectual property?
- What is the vendor's employee turnover rate?
- What training takes place for each of the vendor's employees? Is the training frequently updated and refreshed? Do existing employees have access to the training as needed?
- An IT security outsourcer obviously serves many customers. In the case of a large-scale event, where will your corporation rank in order of importance, urgency, and response? Will your IT security outsourcer first attend to their largest clients, and eventually get to your corporation?

68.5.4 How to Outsource Security Functions. Although not very different from outsourcing any business process, there are some unique aspects to outsourcing IT security functions. This section describes what is different and provides specific examples. We encourage you to consult with your contracting office or other reputable and knowledgeable sources for a more thorough treatment.

68.5.4.1 Where to Begin. As with any outsourced work, first gather your business requirements and use them to define the outcomes you expect the vendor to deliver. Normally, this information is delivered to the vendor as a statement of work (SOW). Include in your SOW only those functions that do not require intimate knowledge and experience of the specific, mission-critical functions of the organization. As discussed in Section 68.2, outsourcing should allow management to focus on its mission-critical functions; thus it is inappropriate to outsource functions that require great experience and insight in those areas.

The following discussion includes examples from a specific case study on outsourcing user-account management.

68.5.4.2 Brief Case Study, Part I. One author of this chapter recently delegated responsibility for resetting passwords and creating user accounts to an outside vendor. The business driver to delegate was the result of an analysis of effectiveness of his internal team: There was just too much work to do for the number of employees authorized. In addition to asking whether a less experienced (i.e., less expensive) team could accomplish certain tasks, the security team also considered the risks to the organization if the work were not done correctly.

In a team decision meeting, we determined that resetting passwords and creating accounts for nonadministrative users was of sufficiently low risk that we could delegate those tasks. In contrast, we determined that performing these tasks on administrative and service accounts was too risky to delegate, so we continued to do that work. The fact that the daily volume of administrative account work was relatively low compared to nonadministrative accounts helped justify keeping those tasks in house.

68.5.4.3 Determining Desired Outcomes. When defining outcomes for operational IT security tasks, focus on the urgency and severity levels of the responses. This is typically driven by the response times required by the organization.

68.5.4.4 Brief Case Study, Part II. Once we decided to delegate resetting passwords and creating user accounts, we then asked operational business leaders what responsiveness they required. Based on their input, we assigned password resets as severity level 1, requiring no more than four hours to complete on receipt of request. User account creation is severity level 2, requiring no more than one business day to complete on receipt of request.

68.5.4.5 Choose a Reliable Vendor. Once your SOW is complete, choose a reliable IT security vendor. Consider these points before you make your final decision[42]:

- Financial health (e.g., annual revenues, longevity)
- Reliable infrastructure (e.g., state-of-the-art tools; disaster resistant)
- Competent staff (e.g., sufficient experience; appropriate credentials; access to global intelligence; original training plans; ongoing refresher training)
- Satisfied customers (e.g., talk with MSSP references; ask what they like the least about the MSSP)
- Vendor independence (e.g., no hidden financial motives to sell you solutions that are not appropriate for your organization; third-party attestations of effectiveness)
- Appropriate service-level agreement (e.g., contains requirements, outcomes desired, response times, roles and responsibilities, and metrics)
- Legal safeguards (e.g., recourse for your organization in the event of vendor breach of contract; if offshored, the applicable laws in the host country that might prevail in a contractual issue, or in a government "nationalization" situation)

68.5.4.6 Service-Level Agreements. Once a reliable vendor is chosen, a strong, precise service-level agreement (SLA) is required. The SLA must specify outcomes desired, response times, roles and responsibilities, metrics, and other requirements. Ideally, the SLA should be written to remain relatively stable over time. Realistically, an SLA needs reliable provisions for change and conflict resolution because the requirements will change over time, no matter how much homework you do.

SLAs need to be realistic given both the scope of the SLA and the financial underpinnings of the contract and statement of work. Demanding an SLA that could never be met, given contractually agreed-to staffing levels, would be useless.

68.5.4.7 Metrics. Include metrics in the SLA that will allow you to measure outcomes; install an independent monitoring system to validate reported metrics and to detect unauthorized behavior by vendor staff. Periodically (weekly at first, then monthly if performance warrants), review the metrics and activities with the vendor's management to ensure that work performed matches the requirements of the SLA; adjust the SLA as necessary to drop metrics that are not useful and add new metrics that are.

It is key to select performance metrics with great care. Reviewing metrics snapshots on a daily basis is important, but even more important is the trends in metrics over time. Many security incidents are not a "big bang," but instead are slowly expanding and growing "under the radar." Having carefully considered metrics that allow a window into both the vendor's adherence to the contract and a perspective of the health of the corporation are the ultimate goals.

68.5.4.8 Brief Case Study, Part III. We monitor the vendor response times for resetting passwords and creating user accounts by examining the time stamps in the vendor's ticketing system correlated with the events written in the system logs. To ensure the vendor does not tamper with the system logs, we have many events immediately forwarded to a centralized logging server to which the vendor has no access.

68.5.4.9 Gaining Maximum Efficiency. Unless you have a good reason not to do so, allow the vendor to determine how it will deliver your desired outcomes. This gives the vendor the ability to determine how to achieve maximize efficiency. Of course, a vendor is inherently motivated to do this in order to be competitive and maximize profits. Be aware that this also means the vendor has incentives to cut corners, which could result in security incidents for you.

Be clear on expected results while still allowing the vendor the flexibility to determine how they plan to deliver those results. However, you as the outsourcing corporation do have a responsibility as well to review and accept the final "how" the vendor will deliver to your result specifications.

68.5.4.10 How the Vendor Does the Work. Once the vendor has created its procedures, be sure to review and approve how the vendor will do the work. After all, security is based not just on what things you do but how you do them. The ultimate authority in the matter will be your organization's information-security policy. Be careful, though, not to criticize vendors just because they do not do things the way your team would. Your priorities are to get the right outcomes with the least risk at an affordable price. Be very careful not to upset your priorities over nothing more than personal preferences.

68.5.4.11 Brief Case Study, Part IV. In outsourcing password resets and account creation, we allowed the vendor to devise its own procedures. In our case, it made sense to permit this level of freedom because the vendor had tools and know-how that our team did not. For instance, we did not have an incident ticketing system, and the vendor already had one up and running. This allowed the vendor to receive, log, and assign work more efficiently than we could.

However, after some time, one of the risks we noted in Section 68.6.3.10 reared its ugly head. We found that the vendor sometimes placed passwords in the ticketing system because doing so saved time (it did not have to reset the passwords every time it went into an account) and allowed the ticket to be closed more quickly. Clearly, we were not as motivated by their profit motive as by preserving our security posture. This is why we regularly monitored the vendor's ticketing system by having a console installed directly in our work area.

68.5.4.12 *Holding the Vendor Accountable.* Finally, be sure to include a strong penalty provision in your SLA to deter careless mistakes by the vendor. If your monitoring tools are effective, you will know about mistakes before the vendor does. Be thoughtful, though, because you do not want to deter the vendor from reporting those mistakes. The point of discussing a mistake should not be to punish as a first recourse, but to correct the vendor in the hope that it will grow in competence and become a better steward of your security work.

68.5.5 Controlling the Risk of Security Outsourcing. Organizations should consider their decision to outsource security in terms of their organization's overall outsourcing strategy, and should determine if their organization has the skill sets and tools necessary to manage the outsourcing relationship. Also, they must realize that contract management skills will be the primary management tool, not IT management expertise.

Ongoing monitoring by the outsourcer will be required. Organizations cannot take for granted the presence and effectiveness of monitoring activity. Provisions must be made to ensure that organizations get the services they are paying for. Should the vendor fail to deliver the services, the organization should be prepared to perform the work once again, quickly and effectively. Once confidence in an IT security vendor has been lost, the vendor's administrative access should be revoked as soon as possible.

Refer to Section 68.4 of this chapter, controlling the risks of IT outsourcing, for more advice.

68.6 CONCLUDING REMARKS.

Outsourcing is a new term for an old concept: We humans have always liked to do what we are good at doing, relying on the skills of others to fill in the gaps in our competencies. We outsource tasks to concentrate on being more effective at our core skills, and we hope to become more efficient as a result. Types of outsourcing—insourcing, nearshoring, offshoring, cloud computing—differ based on how far from the parent organization the outsourcing vendor operates, but there are other much more significant differences when evaluating the risks of outsourcing.

Many organizations have saved significant amounts of money by outsourcing some functions both task and infrastructure. Hindsight, however, shows that many organizations that outsource solely to save money find themselves with significant problems caused by a lack of careful evaluation of outcomes and risks. Proper planning should include:

- Being clear about the purpose of the outsourcing
- Avoiding the tendency to focus only on cost
- Adequately understanding social culture
- Accounting for differences in politics and economics
- Analyzing potential problems in infrastructure and environment
- Anticipating travel and labor issues

Any organization that looks at all these issues well in advance of an outsourcing decision stands a good chance to succeed, despite the potential pitfalls.

The keys to mitigating risks in any outsourcing project—careful planning and constant vigilance—are particularly applicable if security functions are the subject of an outsourcing decision. Depending on the security stance and regulatory environment of the home organization, some security functions may be able to be outsourced in a way that does not put the organization at unacceptable risk. In the end, the great care required to outsource security functions properly has the potential to improve security throughout the organization, and perhaps even make security easier to do well at a vendor site than at the home organization.

68.7 FURTHER READING

Axelrod, C. W. *Outsourcing Information Security*. Artech House, 2004.

Carmel, E., and P. Tjia. *Offshoring Information Technology: Sourcing and Outsourcing to a Global Workforce*. Cambridge University Press, 2005.

Cohen, L., and A. Young. *Multisourcing: Moving Beyond Outsourcing to Achieve Growth and Agility*. Harvard Business School Press, 2005.

Cooney, M. "Can You Trust China for Outsourcing?" *Network World*, May 29, 2006. www.networkworld.com/columnists/2006/052906edit.html

Cullen, S. *Intelligent IT Outsourcing: Eight Building Blocks to Success*. Butterworth-Heineman, 2003.

Dara, N. "Cyber Crime Comes of Age as Foreign Plugs Sell Secrets," *DNA India*, October 19, 2005; www.dnaindia.com/india/6411/report-cyber-crime-comes-of-age-as-foreign-plugs-sell-secrets

Grance, T., J. Hash, M. Steven, K. O'Neal, and N. Bartol. *Guide to Information Technology Security Services*. NIST Special Publication SP 800-35 (October 2003). http://csrc.nist.gov/publications/nistpubs/800-35/NIST-SP800-35.pdf

Greaver, M. F. *Strategic Outsourcing: A Structured Approach to Outsourcing Decisions and Initiatives*. AMACOM, 1999.

Jansen, W., and T. Grance. *Guidelines on Security and Privacy in Public Cloud Computing*. NIST Special Publication SP 800-144 (December 2011). http://csrc.nist.gov/publications/nistpubs/800-144/SP800-144.pdf

Kendrick, R. *Outsourcing IT: A Governance Guide*. IT Governance Publishing, 2009.

Koulopoulos, T. M., and T. Roloff. *Smartsourcing: Driving Innovation and Growth Through Outsourcing*. Platinum Press, 2006.

Power, M. J., K. Desouza, and C. Bonifazi. *The Outsourcing Handbook: How to Implement a Successful Outsourcing Process*. Kogan Page, 2006.

Sood, R. IT, *Software and Services: Outsourcing and Offshoring*. AiAiYo Books, 2005.

Stees, J. *Outsourcing Security: A Guide for Contracting Services*. Butterworth-Heineman, 1998.

Vashistha, A. *The Offshore Nation: Strategies for Success in Global Outsourcing and Offshoring*. McGraw-Hill, 2006.

68.8 NOTES

1. M. Cooney, "Outsourcing Bonanza 2006: 8 Outsourcing Trends You Need to Know About," *Network World*, December 13, 2006; www.networkworld.com/news/2006/121306-outsourcing-trends.html

2. M. Cooney, "Government Agency Outsourcing Firms Don't Respect Private Data, GAO Reports," *Network World*, April 5, 2006; www.networkworld.com/news/2006/040506-gao-outsourcing.html
3. Dan Twing, "10 Reasons Why Small Businesses Should Consider Outsourcing," *Network World*, July 5, 2006; www.networkworld.com/newsletters/asp/2006/0703out1.html?page=1
4. T. L. Friedman, *The World Is Flat: A Brief History of the Twenty-First Century* (Farrar, Straus, and Giroux, 2006), 48–172.
5. Zaid Jilani, "Top 'US' Corporations Outsourced More Than 2.4 Million America Jobs Over The Last Decade," *Think Progress Economy*, April 19, 2011, http://thinkprogress.org/economy/2011/04/19/159555/us-corporations-outsourced-americans/?mobile=nc
6. G. Hamel and C. K. Prahalad, "The Core Competence of the Corporation," *Harvard Business Review* 68, No. 3 (May–June 1990): 79–93.
7. "Tempted by the Call of the East," *Mortgage Strategy* (August 22, 2005), 3.
8. S. Thurm, "Behind Outsourcing: Promise and Pitfalls," *Wall Street Journal* (February 27, 2007).
9. D. E. Levine, "Farming Out Network Security: Outsourcing Might Save You Money If You Choose Your Provider with Care," *Security Technology & Design*, May 2005, www.highbeam.com/doc/1G1-133132842.html
10. D. E. Levine, "Farming Out Network Security."
11. Duke University/Archstone Consulting LLC Offshoring Research Network 2004 and 2005 surveys; Duke University/Booz Allen Hamilton Offshoring Research Network 2006 survey. As reported by Mary Brandel, "Offshoring Grows Up," *Computerworld*, March 12, 2007, www.computerworld.com.au/article/174894/offshoring_grows_up
12. D. Winkelman, D. Dole, L. Pinkard, J. Molloy, D. Willey, and M. Davids, "The Outsourcing Source Book," *Journal of Business Strategy* 14, No. 3 (May–June 1993): 52.
13. P. Dixon, "The Future of Outsourcing—Impact on Jobs," Global Change.com; www.globalchange.com/outsourcing.htm
14. P. Dixon, "The Future of Outsourcing."
15. D. Twing, "Reviewing the Security Aspect of Outsourcing," *Network World Outsourcing Newsletter* (September 7, 2005).
16. Chris Matyszczyk, "Modern Life Halted as Netflix, Pinterest, Instagram Go Down," C|Net, June 30, 2012, http://news.cnet.com/8301-17852_3-57464342-71/modern-life-halted-as-netflix-pinterest-instagram-go-down
17. Donna Howell, "Security, Outages Gray Areas for Cloud Computing," *Investor's Business Daily* (May 3, 2011), A5.
18. Alex Pham, "PlayStation Network Security Break Will Cost Sony Much More than Money," *Los Angeles Times*, April 28, 2011, http://articles.latimes.com/2011/apr/28/business/la-fi-0428-ct-sony-hack-20110428
19. K. Evans-Correia, "Outsourcing on Verge of Cultural Evolution," SearchCIO.com, April 18, 2006, searchcio.techtarget.com/news/1179791/Outsourcing-on-verge-of-cultural-evolution
20. "Mumbai Blasts Should Not Affect Investments to India," IDG News Service, July 12, 2006, www.itworld.com/Man/2701/071206mumbai/pfindex.html

21. CNN Wire Staff, "Argentina, Spain at Odds over Oil Company Expropriation," CNN, April 17, 2012, http://articles.cnn.com/2012-04-17/americas/world_americas_argentina-ypf-repsol_1_ypf-julio-de-vido-argentine-government?_s=PM:AMERICAS

22. A. Sharma and M. Bahree, "Grinding Energy Shortage Takes Toll on India's Growth," *Wall Street Journal* (July 2, 2012), 1.

23. M. Cooney, "No Outsourcing Today: Strike Closes India's Tech Center," *Network World*, October 5, 2006; www.networkworld.com/news/2006/100506-strike-closes-india-tech-center.html

24. "20,000 Vietnamese Workers Go on Strike at Nike Contract Factory," Associated Press, April 1, 2008, usatoday30.usatoday.com/money/industries/retail/2008-04-01-vietname-nike-strike_N.htm

25. A. Fallone, "Overview Child Laborers," IHS Child Slave Labor News, 2005, http://ihscslnews.org/view_article.php?id=54

26. The US–China Business Council, "China Proposes Partial Solution to Indigenous Innovation Issues; USCBC Seeks Member Comments," USChina.org Website, April 12, 2010, https://www.uschina.org/public/documents/2010/04/indigenous-innovation-memo.html (URL inactive)

27. Doug Tsurruoka, "China Goes 'Local' On US Firms' Units," *Investor's Business Daily* (July 2, 2012), 1, http://finance.yahoo.com/news/china-goes-local-u-firms-222400546.html

28. (ISC)^2, International Information Systems Security Certification Consortium: www.isc2.org

29. We owe a lot to Donn Parker for this new way to look at information assurance. See Chapter 3 in this *Handbook* for his description of these security elements.

30. H. Timmons, "Cut Cable Disrupts Web and Phones in India and Middle East," *International Herald Tribune*, January 31, 2008, www.nytimes.com/2008/01/31/technology/31iht-net.4.9648965.html

31. Q. Hardy, "A Storm's Disruption Is Felt in the Technology Cloud," *The New York Times*, July 1, 2012, www.nytimes.com/2012/07/02/technology/amazons-cloud-service-is-disrupted-by-a-summer-storm.html

32. See, for example, A. Eunjung Cha, "New Law Gives Chinese Workers Power, Gives Businesses Nightmares," *Washington Post*, April 14, 2008; www.washingtonpost.com/wp-dyn/content/article/2008/04/13/AR2008041302214.html

33. See, for example, J. Markoff, "Encryption Tool Rekindles Security Debate," *International Herald Tribune*, May 21, 2006, www.nytimes.com/2006/05/21/technology/21iht-privacy.html

34. K. V. Subramanya, "HSBC Scam: U.K. recipient of data is of Indian origin," *The Hindu*, June 30, 2006, www.hindu.com/2006/06/30/stories/2006063002920700.htm

35. "IT Security Outsourcing Shows Steady Growth," *Computer Economics* (2013-05), www.computereconomics.com/article.cfm?id=1831

36. Levine, "Farming Out Network Security."

37. C. Costanzo, "Internet Security: Outsource or Go It Alone?" *Community Banker* 14, no. 6 (June 2005), http://findarticles.com/p/articles/mi_qa5344/is_200506/ai_n21373311/pg_1

38. "Information Security Officer Salaries," Glassdoor.com, July 2013, www.glassdoor.com/Salaries/information-security-officer-salary-SRCH_KO0,28.htm

39. This calculation was current in March 2007. The formula described and the 184 percent figure are the result of our consultation with the finance department at one of the authors' employers. The name of the employer is being withheld to protect their confidentiality.

40. *Merriam–Webster's Collegiate Dictionary*, 11th ed., 2004, p. 650. Also online at www.merriam-webster.com/dictionary/intelligence

41. Dell SecureWorks, "Threat Intelligence Service," www.secureworks.com/services/threat_intelligence.html

42. J. Mears, "Is Security Ripe for Outsourcing?" *Network World*, August 23, 2004, www.networkworld.com/news/2004/082304outsecure.html

INTRODUCTION TO PART VIII

PUBLIC POLICY AND OTHER CONSIDERATIONS

This edition of the *Handbook* ends with compelling issues in information security. Part VIII provides a basis for vigorous discussion about important and controversial topics such as:

69. **Privacy in Cyberspace: U.S. and European Perspectives.** With increasingly frequent losses of control over personally identifiable information, the public is ever more concerned about privacy, especially with recent revelations of widespread NSA surveillance and analysis of electronic communications
70. **Anonymity and Identity in Cyberspace.** How individuals are representing themselves in Internet-mediated communications; the social and legal consequences of completely anonymous interactions, and of untraceable but stable identifiers
71. **Healthcare Security and Privacy.** How the special requirements of high availability coupled with extreme sensitivity of medical information poses complex problems for security specialists in medical environments
72. **Legal and Policy Issues of Censorship and Content Filtering.** How corporations and governments around the world regulate access to information that violates social norms or is perceived as a potential threat to state power
73. **Expert Witnesses and the *Daubert* Challenge.** How security specialists should prepare for their day in court
74. **Professional Certification and Training in Information Assurance.** Benefits and costs of education, professional certifications, examinations, and commercial training
75. **The Future of Information Assurance.** A brilliant young computer scientist offers his take on possible directions of interest in our field

CHAPTER 69

PRIVACY IN CYBERSPACE: U.S. AND EUROPEAN PERSPECTIVES

Henry L. Judy, Scott L. David, Benjamin S. Hayes, Jeffrey B. Ritter, Marc Rotenberg, and M. E. Kabay

69.1 INTRODUCTION: WORLDWIDE TRENDS. As information technology continues to develop, increased opportunities and incentives are created to collect information about individuals and to use that personal information for diverse and lucrative purposes. Some believe that, in a global information economy, the most economically valuable electronic asset will be aggregations of information on individuals. For over two decades, concerns regarding the privacy of the individual and cross-border movement of personal information have been reflected in international policy frameworks, such as the *Organization for Economic Cooperation and Development* (OECD) *Privacy Guidelines*. In recent years, these concerns have escalated in Europe, the United States, and other economies, particularly due to the rapid commercialization of the Internet and the development of new and more powerful information technologies. There are also significant developments with DNA databases, RFID technologies, geopositioning data, and electronic health records. These concerns have accelerated the growth of privacy law, with recent enactments in the United States, Europe, and other areas of the world.[1] At the same time, new policy frameworks have emerged, most notably in the Asia-Pacific region.

As this chapter was going to press in July 2013, cyberprivacy issues in the United States and Europe were actively being covered by the news media and generating concern among civil liberties groups. The domestic spying programs of the U.S. National Security Agency and questions about illegal phone tapping in the United Kingdom were top news items.

69.1.1 Current Cyberprivacy Issues.

Several cases have caused interest among privacy advocates in the first decades of the twenty-first century.

69.1.1.1 NSA Domestic Spying.

The Electronic Frontier Foundation (EFF) page about extra-legal surveillance of U.S. residents includes this succinct summary:

> In October 2001, President Bush issued a secret presidential order authorizing the NSA to conduct a range of surveillance activities inside of the United States without statutory authorization or court approval, including electronic surveillance of Americans' telephone and Internet communications. This program of surveillance continues through today, although the legal justifications have changed over time, and works with the major telecommunications and Internet companies.
>
> In 2005, after the *New York Times* broke the story of the surveillance program, the President publicly admitted one portion of it—warrantless surveillance of Americans believed to be communicating with people connected with terrorism suspects—Senior Bush Administration officials later confirmed that the President's authorization went beyond the surveillance of terrorists and conceded that the program did not comply with the Foreign Intelligence Surveillance Act (FISA). The President, invoking a theory of limitless executive power to disregard the mandates of Congress, reauthorized this warrantless surveillance more than thirty times, including after the Department of Justice found the program to violate criminal laws. President Obama has continued the program, but with differing secret legal justifications. Obama has given no public legal justification for it and, in some situations, appears to be strategically denying certain portions of it. For other portions, including the collection of telecommunications records, the Obama Administration said it could neither confirm nor deny its actions until May 2013, when the DNI finally admitted additional portions of it. Members of Congress have confirmed that additional domestic surveillance by the NSA still remains a secret.[2]

69.1.1.2 NSA PRISM in the United States.

In July 2013, the Electronic Privacy Information Center (EPIC) reported on its efforts to block the widespread collection of call detail records (metadata) about phone calls originating or terminating in the United States:

> EPIC has filed a petition with the U.S. Supreme Court, asking the Court to vacate an unlawful order by the Foreign Intelligence Surveillance Court that enables the NSA's collection of all domestic phone records. On April 25, the secret court ordered Verizon to turn over all "call

detail records" for calls made "wholly within the United States, including local telephone calls."

The FISC's order is based on Section 215 of the USA PATRIOT Act, which allows the court to compel the disclosure of business records that are "relevant to an authorized investigation." The Verizon order, however, requires the disclosure of all telephone records in the company's database.

"It is simply not possible that every phone record in the possession of a telecommunications firm could be relevant to an authorized investigation," EPIC states. "Such an interpretation of [the law] would render meaningless the qualifying phrases contained in the provision and eviscerate the purpose of the Act. "To define the scope of the records sought as 'everything' nullifies the relevance limitation in the statute," EPIC continues. "If law enforcement has 'everything,' there will always be some subset of 'everything' that is relevant to something."

The call detail records provided to the NSA, called "telephony metadata," contain an immense amount of sensitive personal information. The records identify the phone numbers of both parties on a call, the call's time and duration, and the geographic location of each phone number. When aggregated, such records can map out "the daily activities, interactions, personal and business relationships, religious and political affiliations, and other intimate details of millions of Americans," says EPIC.

EPIC's petition asks the Supreme Court to issue a "writ of mandamus" vacating the Verizon Order issued by the FISC. Mandamus is a command from a higher court to a lower court or government official, used when a lower court extends beyond the scope of its legal authority. EPIC writes, "Mandamus relief is warranted because the FISC exceeded its statutory jurisdiction when it ordered the production of millions of domestic telephone records that cannot plausibly be relevant to an authorized investigation."

EPIC brought the petition directly to the Supreme Court because no other court has jurisdiction to address the unlawful order. The Foreign Intelligence Surveillance Act (FISA) allows only the government and the recipient of a production order (i.e., Verizon) to appear before the FISC or the Court of Review. Additionally, the law limits these courts to hearing only certain types of appeals. EPIC, a Verizon customer whose call records are subject to the order, would not be able to obtain relief from these courts.[3]

69.1.1.3 Phone Hacking in the United Kingdom. *The Telegraph* provides a detailed timeline of the events known as the U.K. phone-hacking scandal.[4] Key events include

- 2005 (November): The Royal Family complains about interception of private voicemail messages revealing a knee injury to Prince William.
- 2006 (August): "Detectives arrest the *News of the World*'s royal editor Clive Goodman and private investigator Glenn Mulcaire over allegations that they hacked into the mobile phones of members of the royal household."
- 2007 (January): "The *News of the World*'s royal affairs editor Clive Goodman is jailed for four months. Private investigator Glenn Mulcaire is given a six-month prison term. Goodman and Mulcaire admitted conspiring to intercept communications while Mulcaire also pleaded guilty to five other charges of intercepting voicemail messages."
- 2009 (July): "It emerges that *News of the World* reporters, with the knowledge of senior staff, illegally accessed messages from the mobile phones of celebrities and politicians while Coulson was editor from 2003 to 2007. It is also reported that News Group Newspapers, which publishes the *News of the World*, has paid out more than £1 million to settle cases that threatened to reveal evidence of its journalists' alleged involvement in phone hacking."

- 2011 (January): "British police open a new investigation into allegations of phone hacking at the tabloid called 'Operation Weeting' after actress Sienna Miller, MP George Galloway, and RMT union leader Bob Crow claim their phones were hacked."
- 2011 (February): "The Met Police release a statement saying officers have identified more potential victims of hacking while reviewing files relating to the original Goodman and Mulcaire case. They say they are urgently notifying people who had previously been told that police had 'little or no information' about them.

  "Former Deputy Prime Minister Lord Prescott, Labour MP Chris Bryant, ex-Scotland Yard commander Brian Paddick and journalist Brendan Montague, all alleged victims of phone hacking, win a High Court bid for a judicial review into the police inquiry. They believe their human rights were breached.

  "Lawyers for a football agent suing the *News of the World* claim Glenn Mulcaire passed information directly to the newsdesk rather than an individual reporter, Goodman. They say the desk could have been staffed by 'a number of journalists,' and suggest that this means knowledge of phone-hacking was more widespread than previously admitted. A judge rules that Mulcaire must provide information about whether other journalists at the *NoW* were involved in hacking. He had tried to claim he should be exempt from giving evidence for fear of incriminating himself."
- 2011 (March): "The BBC's Panorama reveals that in 2006, a then *News of the World* executive, Alex Marunchak, obtained e-mails belonging to an ex-British Army intelligence officer that had been hacked in to by a private detective."
- 2011 (April): "Former *News of the World* editor Ian Edmondson, chief reporter Neville Thurlbeck and senior journalist James Weatherup are arrested on suspicion of conspiring to intercept mobile phone messages. They are released on bail until September. The *News of the World* admits it had a role in phone hacking. The *News of the World* publishes apologies on both its website and newspaper. News International also announces it will set up a compensation scheme to deal with 'justifiable claims' fairly and efficiently. However, the publisher adds it will continue to contest cases 'that we believe are without merit or where we are not responsible.' "
- 2011 (May): "Former Deputy Prime Minister Lord Prescott, Labour MP Chris Bryant, ex-Scotland Yard commander Brian Paddick and journalist Brendan Montague, all alleged victims of phone hacking, win a High Court bid for a judicial review into the police inquiry. They believe their human rights were breached."
- In November 2012, Lord Justice Leveson released his report on the scandal.[5] Some of the key findings in the *Executive Summary* follow:
- "The evidence placed before the Inquiry has demonstrated, beyond any doubt, that there have been far too many occasions over the last decade and more (itself said to have been better than previous decades) when these responsibilities, on which the public so heavily rely, have simply been ignored. There have been too many times when, chasing the story, parts of the press have acted as if its own code, which it wrote, simply did not exist. This has caused real hardship and, on occasion, wreaked havoc with the lives of innocent people whose rights and liberties have been disdained. This is not just the famous but ordinary members of the public, caught up in events (many of them, truly tragic) far larger than they

could cope with but made much, much worse by press behaviour that, at times, can only be described as outrageous."

- "For many years, there have been complaints that certain parts of the press ride roughshod over others, both individuals and the public at large, without any justifiable public interest. Attempts to take them to task have not been successful. Promises follow other promises. Even changes made following the death of Diana, Princess of Wales, have hardly been enduring. Practices discovered by the Information Commissioner, during Operation Motorman, which led to the publication of two reports to Parliament,[6] revealed that large parts of the press had been engaged in a widespread trade in private and confidential information, apparently with little regard to the public interest. A private detective, Steve Whittamore, had certainly been engaged in wholesale criminal breaches of data protection legislation and, prima facie, journalists who engaged his services or used his products (and paid substantial sums for the privilege) must or should have appreciated that the information could not have been obtained lawfully."
- "When Clive Goodman, a journalist employed by the *News of the World* and Glenn Mulcaire, a private detective, were convicted of hacking into the telephone messages of members of the Royal Household and others, it was implicit during the course of the criminal prosecution that others must have been involved, whether knowingly or not, in using information that was the product of phone hacking. Most responsible corporate entities would be appalled that employees were or could be involved in the commission of crime in order to further their business. Not so at the *News of the World*. When the police had sought to execute a warrant, they were confronted and driven off by the staff at the newspaper. Cooperation, if provided, was minimal. The two that were sentenced to terms of imprisonment were paid very substantial sums as compensation for loss of employment when they were released."
- Then came exposure of the fact, albeit as long ago as March 2002, that the mobile phone of Milly Dowler had been hacked by someone at the *News of the World*. The information obtained had led the paper to publish false leads as a result of its misunderstanding of a message which had simply been left on the wrong phone in error. It was also believed that a message or messages had been deleted (thereby giving rise to a false moment of hope in her family). On 5 July 2011, these facts were reported by the *Guardian*. The outcry was immediate; two days later it was announced that the *News of the World* would close."
- "Phone hacking in itself, even if it were only in one title, would justify a reconsideration of the corporate governance surrounding the way in which newspapers operate and the regulatory regime that is required. Without making findings against anyone individually, the evidence drives me to conclude that this was far more than a covert, secret activity, known to nobody save one or two practitioners of the 'dark arts.' Yet it was illegal. And after the prosecution, at more than one title and more than one publisher, there was no in-depth look to examine who had been paid for what and why or to review compliance requirements."

69.1.2 Laws, Regulations, and Agreements. Across the emerging body of global privacy law, which varies substantially from jurisdiction to jurisdiction, general patterns are emerging. Virtually any piece of information related to an individual is defined as *personal information* (or *personally identifiable information,* PII) and, therefore, potentially subject to regulation with respect to its collection, storage, use, and transfer. Different types of personal information, and different uses of personal information, are subject to different levels of regulation. Typically, the collection and use of medical and other highly sensitive data are most highly regulated; for example, data revealing the subject's race, religion, political affiliation, sexual orientation, or data relating to children.

What conduct is regulated? Privacy laws are structured on the essential principle that the individual person—a *data subject*—should retain some control over the information about himself or herself that is collected or used by a person or organization, whether a business, a nonprofit organization, or a government. Privacy laws impose obligations that are intended to prevent the collection or use of information in any manner that is inconsistent with the expectations of the data subject. In effect, the data subjects' control of their own personal information cannot be circumvented or denied, except with their consent. Privacy laws impose obligations on organizations that collect personal information, and empower the data subject and the state to enforce the data subject's rights under that agreement.

In addition, across different legal systems and, particularly in the United States, across different regulatory schemes governing different industries, privacy laws embrace comparable core principles, commonly referred to as *fair information practices*. These practices include the concept of control by the data subject but also may embrace rules that prohibit or limit certain data practices regardless of the consent of, or other involvement by, the data subject. The Office of the Privacy Commissioner of Australia summarizes these emerging principles as its *National Privacy Principles* (NPPs), as follows (quoting directly):

- NPP 1: collection. Describes what an organisation should do when collecting personal information, including what they can collect, collecting from third parties and, generally, what they should tell individuals about the collection.
- NPP 2: use and disclosure. Outlines how organisations may use and disclose individuals' personal information. If certain conditions are met, an organisation does not always need an individual's consent to use and disclose personal information. There are also rules about direct marketing.
- NPPs 3–4: information quality and security. An organisation must take steps to ensure the personal information it holds is accurate and up-to-date, and is kept secure from unauthorised use or access.
- NPP 5: openness. An organisation must have a policy on how it manages personal information, and make it available to anyone who asks for it.
- NPP 6: access and correction. Gives individuals a general right of access to their personal information, and the right to have that information corrected if it is inaccurate, incomplete or out-of-date.
- NPP 7: identifiers. Generally prevents an organisation from adopting an Australian Government identifier for an individual (eg Medicare numbers) as its own.
- NPP 8: anonymity. Where possible, organisations must give individuals the opportunity to do business with them without the individual having to identify themselves.
- NPP 9: transborder data flows. Outlines how organisations should protect personal information that they transfer outside Australia.
- NPP 10: sensitive information. Sensitive information includes information relating to health, racial or ethnic background, or criminal records. Higher standards apply to the handling of sensitive information.[7]

For chief information officers, security officers, risk managers, general counsels, systems designers, and consultants of any company charged with assuring compliance with privacy laws, new technologies and new business practices are raising new challenges for the enforcement of privacy rules. Regulatory controls that target information assets such as personal information are transforming how information systems are designed and managed. Technology executives are required to assume increased responsibility for legal compliance across divergent legal regimes; business executives and legal officers are required to acquire significant new understandings of the technologies deployed in information management and the business relationships through which personal information is collected, used, and transferred in support of the execution of business relationships. In some circumstances, information technology is both a source and a means of addressing privacy issues.

What makes privacy law important to all of these participants is not the imposition of yet another set of regulations requiring compliance. Instead, privacy law tests companies in their ability to truly integrate business, law, and technology into the coherent planning and execution of their information systems. As the world's economy continues its remarkable transformation into a global environment in which information in electronic form is a significant measure of economic wealth, those companies that master privacy as a competitive opportunity, rather than as a regulatory cost without economic benefit, will be best positioned to safeguard the data of their customers and avoid the growing concerns about security breaches and identity theft.

However, although attention is increasingly paid to overcoming inadequate protection of personal privacy, there is a corresponding increase in the attention paid to the policy issues raised by the impact of new privacy practices. A few examples will suffice. Law enforcement and national security agencies are concerned about how increased privacy protection, including encryption and anonymizer techniques, will weaken their ability to detect crime and terrorism. Medical researchers are concerned about their ability to conduct statistically valid medical research. At the same time, the absence of effective privacy safeguards has led to growing concerns about identity theft and security breaches, particularly in the United States.

69.1.3 Sources of Privacy Law. The legal structures governing personal information use have developed along different lines concerning public and private entities. Typically, governments and other public-sector entities are restrained from undue intrusion into citizens' private lives by constitutional mechanisms.[8] Citizens typically are provided access to government-held personal information by statutes, although there has been an increase in constitutionally mandated access rights to personal information as formerly oppressive regimes give way to more democratic governments. The converse is equally true.[9]

By contrast, restraints and obligations placed on private uses of personal information derive almost exclusively from statutory law. However, the recent adoption of the European Charter of Fundamental Rights requires that nation-states treat personal data protection as a basic human right. Such a requirement will stand as a prerequisite for any new potential member of the European Union.[10]

This development suggests a new trend: that data protection may be enshrined into constitutions or supranational law. Indeed, certain developing nations that have recently enacted new constitutions have created bases for their private-sector data protection laws in them. Also, the new member states of the European Union have all adopted data protection rules to comply with the EU Data Directive. As a result, any attempt to master what privacy law is all about will demand, regrettably perhaps, complex legal analysis.

69.2 EUROPEAN APPROACHES TO PRIVACY

69.2.1 History and Organization for Economic Cooperation and Development Principles. Interest in the right of privacy increased in the 1960s and 1970s with the advent of information technology and new data processing techniques for records concerning the individuals. The surveillance potential of computers prompted public demands for specific rules governing the collection and handling of personal information. The genesis of legislation in this area usually is traced to the first modern data protection law, enacted in the German state of Hesse in 1970. That enactment was followed by national laws with differing objectives and scope in Sweden (1973), the United States (1974), Germany (1977), and France (1978).[11]

Two highly influential international instruments emerged following these enactments. The Council of Europe (COE) passed the *Convention for the Protection of Individuals with regard to the Automatic Processing of Personal Information* (the *COE Convention*) in 1981.[12] In the same year, the Organization for Economic Cooperation and Development (OECD) issued *Guidelines Governing the Protection of Privacy and Transborder Data Flows of Personal information* (the *OECD Guidelines*).[13] Both instruments articulate specific rules regarding the handling of personal information. Both present a comparable set of principles for fair information use that have since become the framework for the data protection laws of dozens of countries. These principles recognize personal information as data to be afforded legal protection at every step of their life cycle of collection, processing, storage, use, transfer, and destruction.

To date (July 2013), 46 countries have adopted the COE Convention.[14] In addition to being relied on by OECD nations to create data protection laws, the OECD Guidelines have been relied on by other nations that are not OECD members.[15] The OECD has continued to be involved in privacy issues and, indeed, makes available a privacy policy statement generator on the privacy page of its Website.[16]

69.2.2 European Union Data Protection Directive 95/46/EC. In 1990, both to (1) ensure that member states protected "fundamental" privacy rights when processing personal information, regardless of the national citizenship of the data subjects, and (2) prevent member states from restricting the free flow of personal information within the European Union (EU), the European Commission proposed the EU Directive on Data Protection. On October 24, 1995, following years of discussion and debate, the Council and Parliament of the EU adopted the final version of Directive 95/46/EC.[17] The directive became effective on October 25, 1998.

The directive is not self-executing. Instead, it requires EU member states to pass national legislation that transpose its terms. It is important to realize that the national laws that have been enacted in each of the EU member states are not identical. Indeed, there are fairly significant differences among these laws. Thus, having an understanding of the directive by no means guarantees that a business understands all of the steps it must take to comply with each national law.

69.2.2.1 European Union Directive Requirements. The EU Directive applies to all commercial uses of personal information. The directive establishes limitations and obligations on *controllers* (entities directing the collection, use, or transfer of personal information) and *processors* (those utilizing personal information at another party's direction) with respect to the processing (i.e., virtually any collection, use, transfer, or destruction of personal information) of personal information (any information that is readily traceable to a particular individual). The directive, like other privacy laws, is organized around certain key principles of information use. These can be summarized as follows:

- ***Notice.*** Data subjects, individuals to whom personal information relates, must be informed of:
  - The identity of the collector of the information;
  - The uses or purposes for which it is collected;
  - How they may exercise any available choices regarding its use;
  - Where and to whom it may be transferred; and
  - How data subjects may access information relating to themselves by an organization.
- ***Consent.*** Data subjects have the right, except under certain exceptions, not to have their personal information used without their consent, the right to opt out of having personal information used for direct marketing purposes, and the right not to have any "sensitive information" collected or used without express permission. Sensitive information includes information relating to race, religion, health, union membership, beliefs, and sex life.
- ***Consistency.*** Organizations may use personal information only in strict accordance with the terms of the notice given to the data subjects and any choices with respect to its use exercised by them.
- ***Access.*** Organizations must give data subjects access to the personal information held about them and must allow them to propose corrections to inaccurate information.
- ***Security.*** Organizations must provide adequate security, using both technical and other means, to protect the integrity and confidentiality of personal information. The sufficiency of such means is measured with respect to the state of the art.
- ***Onward Transfer.*** Personal information may not be transferred to a third party unless that third party has been contractually bound to use the data consistently with the notice given to data subjects, any choices they have exercised, and applicable law.
- ***Enforcement.*** The directive grants a private right of action to data subjects where organizations do not follow the law. In addition, each EU country has established a Data Protection Authority—a regulatory enforcement agency—that has the power to investigate complaints, levy fines, initiate criminal actions, and demand changes in information-handling practices of businesses.

69.2.2.2 International Data-Transfer Restrictions. While the directive governs much of the interaction between a business and its data subjects (i.e., its customers and employees), it also regulates how companies operating in multiple jurisdictions worldwide may move personal information within themselves and among their various affiliates or subsidiaries.

Transfers of personal information relating to EU-based data subjects to non-EU countries are *prohibited* unless the country of destination has *adequate legal protections for privacy*. Many countries, including the United States, are not considered by the EU to have adequate legal protection. Transfers to such countries may take place only with the consent of the data subject, or where other guarantees exist that personal information will be treated according to the EU standard. EU regulators have the legal authority to prohibit transfers of personal information where such guarantees cannot be demonstrated. This requirement is problematic for many businesses and may require significant technological, organizational, and/or contractual changes.

One possible solution to the directive's transfer restrictions is the United States/European Union "Safe Harbor." This arrangement is discussed in Section 69.3.3.5.

69.2.2.3 State of Implementation. As of July 2013, the 28 member countries of the European Union, including the new members states, have passed legislation fully implementing the Privacy Directive.[18]

In January 2012, the EU received a plan for improving privacy protection:

> The European Commission has … proposed a comprehensive reform of the EU's 1995 data protection rules to strengthen online privacy rights and boost Europe's digital economy. Technological progress and globalisation have profoundly changed the way our data is collected, accessed, and used. In addition, the 27 EU Member States have implemented the 1995 rules differently, resulting in divergences in enforcement. A single law will do away with the current fragmentation and costly administrative burdens, leading to savings for businesses of around €2.3 billion a year. The initiative will help reinforce consumer confidence in online services, providing a much needed boost to growth, jobs, and innovation in Europe.[19]

According to a press release,

> Key changes in the reform include:
>
> - A single set of rules on data protection, valid across the EU. Unnecessary administrative requirements, such as notification requirements for companies, will be removed. This will save businesses around €2.3 billion a year.
> - Instead of the current obligation of all companies to notify all data protection activities to data protection supervisors—a requirement that has led to unnecessary paperwork and costs businesses €130 million per year, the Regulation provides for increased responsibility and accountability for those processing personal data.
> - For example, companies and organisations must notify the national supervisory authority of serious data breaches as soon as possible (if feasible within 24 hours).
> - Organisations will only have to deal with a single national data protection authority in the EU country where they have their main establishment. Likewise, people can refer to the data protection authority in their country, even when their data is processed by a company based outside the EU. Wherever consent is required for data to be processed, it is clarified that it has to be given explicitly, rather than assumed.
> - People will have easier access to their own data and be able to transfer personal data from one service provider to another more easily (right to data portability). This will improve competition among services.
> - A "right to be forgotten" will help people better manage data protection risks online: people will be able to delete their data if there are no legitimate grounds for retaining it.
> - EU rules must apply if personal data is handled abroad by companies that are active in the EU market and offer their services to EU citizens.
> - Independent national data protection authorities will be strengthened so they can better enforce the EU rules at home. They will be empowered to fine companies that violate EU data protection rules. This can lead to penalties of up to €1 million or up to 2% of the global annual turnover of a company.
> - A new Directive will apply general data protection principles and rules for police and judicial cooperation in criminal matters. The rules will apply to both domestic and cross-border transfers of data.[20]

Readers committed to following the Directive will want to keep tabs on developments as these proposals wend their way through the EU deliberative process.

69.2.3 Harmonization of Non-EU Countries to the EU Directive. Largely due to the EU Directive's prohibition on the transfer of personal information to countries with lesser degrees of legal protection, and the fear in many countries of the potential adverse economic impact that could result from the interruption of data flows from EU countries, a number of other countries have passed essentially identical national legislation so as to assure adequate levels of legal protection. These countries can be roughly divided into two categories: EU trading partners that wish to ensure that data flows will not be interrupted[21] and countries actively conforming their national legislation to the EU model in hopes of gaining membership to the EU.[22]

69.2.4 European Union Telecommunications Directive. In addition to the general Data Protection Directive, the EU has enacted a second directive, imposing specific privacy-protective obligations on communications service providers. The *Telecommunications Directive*[23] obliges carriers and service providers to ensure technologically the privacy of the communications carried on their systems, including email and other Internet communications. This directive also restricts access to billing information, places limitations on marketing, allows for per-line blocking of caller ID, and requires that information gathered during a communication be deleted on the termination of the communication.[24] A new proposal would replace the Telecommunications Directive with a broader version affecting all "electronic communications" in the European Union.[25]

69.2.5 Establishment of the European Data Protection Supervisor. In 2002, the European Parliament and the European Council established the office of the *European Data Protection Supervisor* (EDPS), described as follows:

> The EDPS is an independent supervisory authority devoted to protecting personal data and privacy and promoting good practice in the EU institutions and bodies. He does so by:
>
> - monitoring the EU administration's processing of personal data;
> - advising on policies and legislation that affect privacy; and
> - cooperating with similar authorities to ensure consistent data protection. …
>
> The supervisory task is to ensure that the EU institutions and bodies process personal data of EU staff and others lawfully. The EDPS oversees Regulation (EC) 45/2001 on data protection, which is based on two main principles:
>
> The responsible data controller needs to respect a number of obligations. For instance, personal data can only be processed for a specific and legitimate reason which must be stated when the data are collected.
>
> The person whose data are processed—the data subject—enjoys a number of enforceable rights. This includes, for instance, the right to be informed about the processing and the right to correct data.
>
> Every institution or body should have an internal Data Protection Officer. The DPO keeps a register of processing operations and notifies systems with specific risks to the EDPS. The EDPS prior checks whether or not those systems comply with data protection requirements. The EDPS also deals with complaints and conducts inquiries.[26]

In July 2013, the EDPS issued a report strongly criticizing the European Commission's plans for implementing computer-assisted border checks (*smart borders*). Peter Hustinx, the Director of the EDPS, was quoted as saying,

> In the absence of such a policy, the creation of yet another large-scale IT database to store massive amounts of personal information is a disproportionate response to a problem that other recently created systems may be able to help solve. It would be prudent both economically and practically to evaluate the existing systems at least to ensure consistency and best practice.[27]

On July 31, 2013, the positions of EDPS and Assistant Supervisor became vacant.[28] It was not known whether there was a relationship between the EDPS criticism of smart borders and the vacancy.

69.3 UNITED STATES

69.3.1 History, Common Law Torts. The concept of privacy violations as a tort is a twentieth-century phenomenon. The framers of the U.S. Constitution did not recognize an explicit right to privacy, perhaps because privacy was intrinsic to an agrarian society. But the necessity for privacy protection under law gradually became apparent with urbanization and industrialization in the late nineteenth and early twentieth centuries. The concept of a "right to be left alone" was posited by Charles Warren and Louis Brandeis in an influential 1890 article in the *Harvard Law Review*.[29] Today, virtually every state recognizes a common law or statutory right of privacy.[30]

Like most common law torts, privacy law matured in a piecemeal fashion at the state level because there was no federal law on point. In 1960, the *Restatement of Torts* defined four *subtorts* that are generally held to comprise the common law of privacy. These are[31]:

1. **Intrusion.** The unreasonable intrusion, by physical or other means, upon the seclusion of another, if the intrusion is substantial and would be highly offensive to a reasonable person.
2. **Revelation of private facts.** The unauthorized and unreasonable publicity of facts about a person's private life, if the matter publicized is of a kind that would be highly offensive to a reasonable person, and which is not of legitimate concern to the public. These facts must be communicated to more than a single person or a small group in order to trigger this tort.
3. **False light.** Publicity that unreasonably places the other in a false light before the public. Essentially, a photo or story cannot be used if that photo or story conveys a false impression of someone. Note that this tort can be used if the person is cast in either a negative or *positive* false light.
4. **Misappropriation.** The unauthorized appropriation of another's name or likeness for benefit or gain. Misappropriation actions are most commonly brought by celebrities whose image is used without authorization in connection with advertising or promotion.

69.3.2 Public Sector. In the United States, government traditionally has been restrained from undue intrusion into the private lives of citizens by various provisions of the U.S. Constitution and similar provisions in the constitutions of many of the states of the Union. The Fourth Amendment to the U.S. Constitution, for instance, prohibits "unreasonable search and seizure" by the government. Fourth Amendment protection is also made applicable to the states by operation of the Fourteenth Amendment to the U.S. Constitution, which provides that "[n]o state shall make or enforce any law which shall abridge the privileges or immunities of citizens of the United States." Yet, except in certain state constitutions, there is no explicit right of privacy. Thus, many of the rules regarding how government may collect, maintain, and use personal information relating to citizens has been defined by case law and statutes. In the public sector, state governments may have greater privacy protection obligations to their employees than private sector businesses in the same states have to their employees.

69.3.2.1 Privacy Act of 1974 (Including the Freedom of Information Act). The most comprehensive privacy legislation in the United States, the Privacy Act of 1974,[32] placed limitations on how the Federal Government may use and transfer personal information, and gave individuals a right, subject to certain exceptions, to know what information is held about them by the Federal Government.[33] The Privacy Act incorporates the Freedom of Information Act (FOIA), which allows access to Federal Government records, except in certain situations.

The Act is intended to:

- Permit individuals to determine what records pertaining to them are collected, maintained, used, or disseminated by federal agencies
- Permit individuals to forbid records that are obtained by an agency for one purpose to be used for another purpose without consent
- Permit individuals to obtain access to agency records pertaining to them and to correct or amend such records as appropriate
- Ensure that agencies collect, maintain, and use personal information in a manner that ensures that the information is current, adequate, relevant, and not excessive for its intended use
- Create a private right of action for individuals whose personal information is not used in accordance with the act[34]

All provisions of the Act are subject to certain exceptions, such as criminal investigations or national security concerns. In addition, the Act protects each individual, so access to certain information can be limited where providing such information would compromise another individual's privacy.

69.3.2.2 Electronic Communications Privacy Act of 1986. The Electronic Communications Privacy Act (ECPA),[35] which amended the federal wiretap law of 1968, generally prohibits unauthorized and intentional "interception" of wire, oral, and electronic communications during the transmission phase, and unauthorized "accessing" of electronically stored wire or electronic communications. It is applicable in many connections. For example, it establishes standards for capturing telephone numbers through the use of pen registers and trap-and-trace devices. Pen registers record telephone numbers of outgoing calls; trap-and-trace devices record telephone numbers from which incoming calls originate, much like common caller ID systems. Although telephone numbers are not protected by the Fourth Amendment,[36] the ECPA requires law enforcement agencies to obtain court orders to install and use these devices. Rather than the strict probable cause showing the necessity for wiretaps, pen register orders require only certification from a law enforcement officer that "the information likely to be obtained is relevant to an ongoing criminal investigation."[37] It is also relevant to workplace invasions of privacy by electronic means (see Section 69.3.3.7).

69.3.2.3 Right to Financial Privacy Act of 1978. Under the Right to Financial Privacy Act,[38] the federal government is prohibited from obtaining the financial records of an individual, or information contained therein, from a financial institution without giving notice to the individual. Where the disclosure is sought via a subpoena, the required disclosure normally must be made within 90 days after the subpoena is served on the financial institution. Where the disclosure is sought by all other means, the required notice normally must be given prior to, or contemporaneously with, the disclosure request.

69.3.2.4 Driver's Privacy Protection Act. The Driver's Privacy Protection Act[39] marked the first time the U.S. Congress passed a law limiting how state governments may use personal information. Specifically, the Act prohibits disclosures of personal information obtained in connection with a motor vehicle record by state governments, except in order to facilitate legitimate government activities, facilitate recalls, and the like. This Act provides civil and criminal penalties as well as a private right of action. The Act survived a challenge to its constitutionality, brought by the state of South Carolina, by a 9-to-0 vote in the U.S. Supreme Court.[40]

69.3.2.5 Law Enforcement and National Security Surveillance. As technology has developed, crime and criminal activities have become increasingly sophisticated. Yet the same developments of technology have greatly facilitated information gathering and surveillance by law enforcement and national security organizations.

Law enforcement agencies have used technology to investigate crimes such as money laundering, narcotics trafficking, insider trading, and fraud. The technology used can be divided roughly into two categories: monitoring and surveillance. Monitoring technology is used to search for indicia of criminal behavior, without focusing on the activities of particular individuals. Examples of monitoring technologies used to detect crime online include:

- **Packet sniffers.** Programs that monitor all traffic flowing through a network, looking for keywords, phrases, email addresses, and the like. When a packet sniffer finds the type of data it is looking for, it saves the communication for later review.
- **"Black boxes."** Hardware installed by law enforcement agencies at Internet service providers (ISPs) in order to monitor communications or Web traffic. Typically, but not always, black boxes use packet-sniffing technology. In the United States, the Federal Bureau of Investigation (FBI) promoted the use of a black box system installed at ISPs called "carnivore" later renamed DCS1000[41]; currently the program is under review. In February 2001, the FBI renamed its software DCS1000.

Surveillance technology, by contrast, is used to eavesdrop on the communications or transactions of particular individuals. Monitoring technologies often are used or usable for this purpose. In addition, audio listening devices (bugs) and closed-circuit television (CCTV) are increasingly in use.[42]

National security agencies worldwide conduct monitoring and surveillance of communications, to varying degrees. The United States, United Kingdom, New Zealand,

Australia, and Canada are reputed to have an integrated global surveillance system known as Echelon. Although details of the Echelon system's capabilities are closely guarded state secrets, some reports indicate that the system is able to intercept virtually any electronic communication on earth.[43] Telecommunications operators in the United States should be aware that the Communications Assistance for Law Enforcement Act of 1994 (CALEA)[44] mandates certain technical standards for telecommunications networks in order to facilitate law enforcement interception of communications. Recent court decisions may, however, ultimately limit CALEA's application.[45] In 2005 the FCC's First Report and Order ruled that ISPs are "telecommunications carriers" under CALEA. This was challenged and upheld in the D.C. Circuit Court in 2006.

In 2001, the Council of Europe is developed, in consultation with the U.S. Department of Justice, an international Convention on Cyber-Crime which entered into force in 2004.[46] The Convention is controversial. As of September 2013, 40 countries have ratified the convention, and 11 are signatories but have not ratified the treaty.[47] Privacy advocates have also criticized this convention for being unduly intrusive.[48]

69.3.2.6 Foreign Intelligence Surveillance Act and Court. The Foreign Intelligence Surveillance Court (FISC) was established in 1978 as part of the Foreign Intelligence Surveillance Act (FISA). The Federal Judicial Center of the U.S. Government describes the origin and functioning of FISC and FISA as follows:

> Congress in 1978 established the Foreign Intelligence Surveillance Court as a special court and authorized the Chief Justice of the United States to designate seven federal district court judges to review applications for warrants related to national security investigations. Judges serve for staggered, non-renewable terms of no more than seven years, and until 2001 were drawn from different judicial circuits. The provisions for the court were part of the Foreign Intelligence Surveillance Act (92 Stat. 1783), which required the government, before it commenced certain kinds of intelligence gathering operations within the United States, to obtain a judicial warrant similar to that required in criminal investigations. The legislation was a response to a report of the Senate Select Committee to Study Governmental Operations with Respect to Intelligence Activities (the "Church Committee"), which detailed allegations of executive branch abuses of its authority to conduct domestic electronic surveillance in the interest of national security. Congress also was responding to the Supreme Court's suggestion in a 1972 case that under the Fourth Amendment some kind of judicial warrant might be required to conduct national security related investigations.
>
> Warrant applications under the Foreign Intelligence Surveillance Act are drafted by attorneys in the General Counsel's Office at the National Security Agency at the request of an officer of one of the federal intelligence agencies. Each application must contain the Attorney General's certification that the target of the proposed surveillance is either a "foreign power" or "the agent of a foreign power" and, in the case of a U.S. citizen or resident alien, that the target may be involved in the commission of a crime.
>
> The judges of the Foreign Intelligence Surveillance Court travel to Washington, D.C., to hear warrant applications on a rotating basis. To ensure that the court can convene on short notice, at least one of the judges is required to be a member of the U.S. District Court for the District of Columbia. The act of 1978 also established a Foreign Intelligence Surveillance Court of Review, presided over by three district or appeals court judges designated by the Chief Justice, to review, at the government's request, the decisions of the Foreign Intelligence Surveillance Court. Because of the almost perfect record of the Department of Justice in obtaining the surveillance warrants and other powers it requested from the Foreign Intelligence Surveillance Court, the review court had no occasion to meet until 2002. The USA Patriot Act of 2001 (115 Stat. 272) expanded the time periods for which the Foreign Intelligence Surveillance Court can authorize surveillance and increased the number of judges serving the court from seven to eleven. The eleven judges must be drawn from at least seven judicial circuits, and no fewer than three are to reside within twenty miles of the District of Columbia.[49]

Despite criticism by civil-liberties proponents, additional legislation was passed in 2007 and 2008 to strengthen the Executive Branch's powers to order wide-reaching surveillance without prior approval of the FISC.[50]

69.3.2.7 USA PATRIOT Act. The *Uniting and Strengthening America by Providing Appropriate Tools Required to Intercept and Obstruct Terrorism* (USA PATRIOT) Act, whose name was crafted to result in the positive-sounding acronym, was passed with minimal legislative review in October 2001 as a reaction to the terrorist attacks of September 11, 2001.[51]

The Electronic Frontier Foundation, a civil-liberties organization, summarizes its perception of the threats in the USA PATRIOT Act to online civil liberties as follows:

- The law dramatically expands the ability of states and the Federal Government to conduct surveillance of American citizens. The Government can monitor an individual's web surfing records, use roving wiretaps to monitor phone calls made by individuals "proximate" to the primary person being tapped, access Internet Service Provider records, and monitor the private records of people involved in legitimate protests.
- PATRIOT is not limited to terrorism. The Government can add samples to DNA databases for individuals convicted of "any crime of violence." Government spying on suspected computer trespassers (not just terrorist suspects) requires no court order. Wiretaps are now allowed for any suspected violation of the Computer Fraud and Abuse Act, offering possibilities for Government spying on any computer user.
- Foreign and domestic intelligence agencies can more easily spy on Americans. Powers under the existing Foreign Intelligence Surveillance Act (FISA) have been broadened to allow for increased surveillance opportunities. FISA standards are lower than the constitutional standard applied by the courts in regular investigations. PATRIOT partially repeals legislation enacted in the 1970s that prohibited pervasive surveillance of Americans.
- PATRIOT eliminates Government accountability. While PATRIOT freely eliminates privacy rights for individual Americans, it creates more secrecy for Government activities, making it extremely difficult to know about actions the Government is taking.
- PATRIOT authorizes the use of "sneak and peek" search warrants in connection with any federal crime, including misdemeanors. A "sneak and peek" warrant authorizes law enforcement officers to enter private premises without the occupant's permission or knowledge and without informing the occupant that such a search was conducted.
- The Department of Justice, with little input from Congress and the American people, is developing follow-on legislation—the Domestic Security Enhancement Act (nicknamed Patriot II)—which would greatly expand PATRIOT's already sweeping powers.[52]

69.3.3 Private Sector. Compared to other nations, the United States has been fairly slow to pass privacy laws affecting the private sector, preferring instead to rely on industry self-regulation (see Section 69.4.1). Nonetheless, the development of the Internet and electronic commerce, the integration of the financial services industries, and the integration of healthcare services have all spawned new private-sector legislation. Thus far, this legislation has concentrated on particular business sectors rather than regulating uses of personal information generally and has generally emphasized online business practices.

69.3.3.1 *Financial Services Sector.* The Gramm-Leach-Bliley Act (GLBA), enacted in 1999, requires every *financial institution* to:

- Protect the security and confidentiality of its customers' nonpublic personal information,
- Disclose its privacy policies to consumers, and
- Provide consumers with an opportunity to direct that the institution not share their nonpublic personal information with unaffiliated third parties.[53]

Violations of the privacy provisions of GLBA are subject to enforcement by various federal regulators; the specific sanctions that may be imposed vary according to the regulatory agency that has jurisdiction in a particular case.

Eight federal agencies have issued regulations enacting the privacy provisions of GLBA.[54] The Federal Trade Commission (FTC), among others, has acted aggressively to apply GLBA as broadly as possible. Specifically, the FTC defines *financial institution* by reference to a variety of other regulations:

> Under the Federal Trade Commission's Privacy Rule, a financial institution means "any institution the business of which is engaging in financial activities as described in § 4(k) of the Bank Holding Company Act of 1956 [12 U.S.C. § 1843(k)]." See 16 C.F.R. § 313.3(k)(1). (1) Further, you are not a financial institution unless you are significantly engaged in financial activities. Id. Moreover, the Commission's Rule covers only financial activities as of the date of enactment of the GLB Act. See 16 C.F.R. § 18(a)(2). Thus, financial activities added by regulation or order by the Federal Reserve Board or the Secretary of the Treasury after November 12, 1999, are not automatically covered by the Commission's Rule until the Commission so determines.[55]

This has the effect of causing a number of businesses not traditionally thought of as financial institutions, such as career counselors,[56] real estate settlement services, and property appraisers,[57] to be subject to GLBA's privacy regulations.

Another example of the broad application of these regulations is how *nonpublic personal information* is defined. In the case of certain agencies, it is defined as *any* personal information given by a consumer to an institution, whether the information is otherwise publicly available or not.

The regulations went into effect on July 1, 2001. All affected companies were required to have systems in place to comply with the regulations by that date. A list of the critical aspects of the GLBA regulations follows.

- *Customers*,[58] and in some instances *consumers*,[59] must receive initial and annual notices of how their personal information will be used by the financial institution and to which nonaffiliated third parties, other than service providers, it may be transferred.
- Where personal information is to be shared with nonaffiliated third parties other than service providers, the customer or consumer must be given an opportunity to *opt out* of having the personal information transferred.

- Appropriate security controls must be maintained, and specified procedures must be followed, for the adoption and testing of information-security protocols.
- Sharing of personal information among affiliates remains unaffected.

Some of the effects of GLBA that businesses should be aware of include:

- Systems must be created to capture a reliable record of a customer's opt-out (where applicable) at any time and to adopt controls to prevent that customer's personal information from being transmitted outside of a company or its affiliates.
- Systems must be created to deliver the appropriate notices to customers.
- Credit bureaus are no longer legally able to sell *credit header* information (i.e., as defined by the FTC in 1997, the identifying features of a credit report—name, aliases, date of birth, Social Security number, addresses current and prior, and current telephone number).
- Banks and other financial institutions are limited in their ability to sell or transmit lists of customers.
- Banks and other financial institutions must draft and execute, in most cases, detailed written information security policies.[60]
- Contract provisions governing the security of information transferred from financial institutions to other entities should be reviewed and may need to be amended.
- Where a particular company may be subject to GLBA regulation by more than one federal agency, particular care should be used to establish any differences in the different agencies' regulations and any provisions that may defer to a different agency's rules in such a situation.

There is an extensive series of practical questions and detailed answers about the Privacy Regulation on the FTC Website.[61] See Chapter 64 in this *Handbook* for a more extensive discussion of GLBA implications for security management.

69.3.3.2 Children's Online Privacy Protection Act. The Children's Online Privacy Protection Act of 1998 (COPPA) prohibits the collection, use, or disclosure of personally identifiable information from and about children under the age of 13 on the Internet without prior *verifiable parental consent*.[62]

The law firm of Kelly/Warner published an excellent summary of the COPPA provisions, including the following on the "Basic Provisions of COPPA:"

Who Must Abide by the COPPA Standards?

1. Anyone who operates an online service or commercial website that is attractive to children below the age of 13. Even if you don't mean to target kids, if they come to your site, you're responsible for knowing and following COPPA standards.
2. Anyone operating a website designed for general public consumption that collects information about users.
3. Anyone who develops plugins or add-ons that can be used on a site visited by minors.

Factors evaluated when determining if a website or software falls under COPPA's purview:

- Subject matter;
- Language;
- Advertising on the site, coupled with the intended target;

- Audio or visual content including animated characters;
- Age of the models;
- Information regarding the age of the intended or actual audience;
- Any features that may be child-oriented.

In addition, when determining who is and who isn't an "operator" under COPPA definitions, the FTC considers the quality of the information being collected. For example:

- Who owns and controls the information being collected?
- Who pays for the information and maintains it?
- What pre-existing contractual information exists? Is connected with that information?
- What is the role of the website under investigation in collecting and maintaining the information under review?

What Personal Information Are We Talking About When It Comes To COPPA?
COPPA's rules define what collected information is considered actionable under the law. Specifically:

- Full Name
- Home Address
- Email Address
- Telephone Number

Any other information that could be used to contact or identify a child is also covered, like interests and hobbies. Also covered under COPPA is digital info collected through Internet cookies or other tracking technologies, when are attached to personally identifying information. . . .

Basic Provisions of COPPA:
Under the Children's Online Privacy Protection Act a website's Privacy Notice must:

- include a link to the operation's information practices for each area where a child's personal information is collected.
- be posted prominently and clearly, using a font or text color distinctively different than the other text.
- be clearly stated without any confusing terminology or unrelated material that might distract from the intended message.
- sit on a contrasting background (i.e., dark text on a light background for easy reading).

Parental Notice Under COPPA
Privacy policies on websites should include a parental notice telling parents what, why and how information is being collected, in addition to what is done with the data. It must inform parents that the information can only be collected with verifiable parental consent. It should also instruct parents on how to submit consent as well as complaints.

Under COPPA, the terms or privacy notice should also include:

- The names of all website operators and the contact information of at least one;
- The information is being collected, with an explanation of how it's being collected;
- Explanation of how the collected data will be used;
- Third-party info: who they are, their business and how they will use the info;
- Clear notice on how parents can disallow third party access to the information;
- Instructions on how to get data deleted and the process of how to disallow further data collection.[63]

Obtaining verifiable parental consent has proven technologically challenging because of the ease with which children can deceptively click on confirmation of adult status on Website pages attempting to limit access by minors. Even attempts relating to provision of credit card numbers have proven ineffective in barring some children from accessing sites. See Chapter 72 in this *Handbook* for a discussion of parental controls on access to the Internet and the Web.

Violations of COPPA are enforced as *unfair* or *deceptive* trade practices by the Federal Trade Commission.[64] Website operators should refer to the FTC's informational Website[65] for more information.

69.3.3.3 Health Insurance Portability and Accountability Act. The Health Insurance Portability and Accountability Act of 1996 (HIPAA) mandated the establishment of standards to protect the privacy and confidentiality of individually identifiable health information.[66] Under HIPAA, the Department of Health and Human Services has adopted rules to implement the legislative mandate.[67] Both civil and criminal penalties can be assessed for violations.

The HIPAA regulations present significant challenges to "covered entities." A number of the key concepts embodied in the regulations are not clearly defined. The obligations created by the regulations required significant changes in the systems infrastructure and business processes of many affected entities. HIPAA dramatically affects any business dealing with personal information gathered in a healthcare setting. Compliance with the HIPAA privacy rules became mandatory for covered entities in April 2003, while the compliance deadline for small health plans was April 2004. Extensive interpretive guidelines were published by Health & Human Services (HHS) in 2009.[68]

The key features of the HIPAA privacy regulations include:

- Providers and health plans are required to give patients a clear written explanation of how they will use, keep, and disclose information.
- Covered entities must provide patients with access to their health records.
- Permitted uses and disclosures of personally identifiable health information must, subject to certain exceptions, be limited to the "minimum amount necessary to accomplish the purpose for which the information is used or disclosed."[69]
- Disclosure logs must be kept that record each entity to which personally identifiable health information has been disclosed, and individuals must have a right to access these logs.
- A provider or payer generally is not able to condition treatment, payment, or coverage on a patient's agreement to the disclosure of health information for other purposes.
- Federal criminal penalties will apply to obtaining health information under false pretenses, and knowing and improper disclosures of health information, with penalties set higher if the violation is done for "monetary gain."
- States are not preempted from further regulation of health information, so long as an affected entity could comply with both the federal and the state requirements.
- Violations of the regulations will be subject to substantial fines.

In 2005, the *Patient Safety and Quality Improvement Act* (PSQIA) established

> . . . a voluntary reporting system designed to enhance the data available to assess and resolve patient safety and health care quality issues. To encourage the reporting and analysis of medical errors, PSQIA provides Federal privilege and confidentiality protections for patient

safety information, called *patient safety work product*. PSQIA authorizes HHS to impose civil money penalties for violations of patient safety confidentiality. PSQIA also authorizes the Agency for Healthcare Research and Quality (AHRQ) to list patient safety organizations (PSOs). PSOs are the external experts that collect and review patient safety information. ...

The Patient Safety Rule implements select provisions of PSQIA.

Subpart C of the Patient Safety Rule establishes the confidentiality provisions and disclosure permissions for patient safety work product and the enforcement procedures for violations of confidentiality pursuant to section 922 of the statute. OCR [Office for Civil Rights[70]] enforces these confidentiality protections.[71]

The HIPAA regulations are complex with respect to privacy and electronic data transactions.[72] The HHS provides an extensive range of *Frequently Asked Questions* that provide guidance for implementation.[73]

For more information on medical records security, see Chapter 71 in this *Handbook*.

69.3.3.4 Cable and Video Acts. Although the United States has been very hesitant to pass private-sector legislation regulating how businesses use personal information, it has not altogether shied away from doing so. Two important exceptions to that general policy stance are in the form of federal legislation: the *Cable Communications Policy Act*[74] and the *Video Privacy Protection Act*.[75]

The Cable Communications Policy Act of 1984, section 551, governs the *protection of subscriber privacy*. This section requires that cable television companies give their customers initial and annual notice of what personal information the companies collect, to whom it is distributed, how customers may access it, and what other limitations the Act places on the companies. Cable companies are prohibited from using their cable systems to collect personal information without prior consent of customers. Companies are also prohibited from retransferring any personal information without customers' prior consent. Companies may retransfer names, addresses, and telephone numbers to other companies, but only after offering customers the chance to opt out of such disclosures. Law enforcement may obtain personal information from cable companies by court order. The Act creates a private right of action for customers, which includes the ability to recover punitive damages and attorneys' fees from companies that violate it. An ongoing question concerns the application of these privacy provisions to new services offered by cable companies.

The Video Privacy Protection Act of 1988 prohibits the transfer of videotape rental and sales records except for certain narrow exceptions, including permission of the customer. Transfers of such records may be made to law enforcement agencies enforcing a warrant. Customers may bring civil suits against violators of this Act. A case started in 2007 involving the social network service Facebook asserted that Blockbuster violated the Act when it disclosed video purchases to Facebook subscribers using that service's *Beacon* program.[76]

69.3.3.5 Privacy of Activity in Libraries and Bookshops. In sharp contrast with the privacy provisions of privacy protections for cable television and video rentals and sales discussed in Section 69.3.3.4, the USA PATRIOT Act (see Section 69.3.2.7) specifically allows intelligence and law enforcement agencies to monitor the use of libraries and booksellers by patrons. Specifically, librarians are required to submit detailed borrowing records on demand and may not reveal that these records were surrendered.

> The Patriot Act permits federal agents to secretly obtain information from booksellers and librarians about customers' and patrons' reading, internet, and book-buying habits, merely by alleging that the records are relevant to an anti-terrorism investigation. The act prohibits librarians and booksellers from revealing these requests, so they cannot be challenged in court. … A University of Illinois study . . . concludes that federal agents have sought records from about 220 libraries nationwide since September 2001 . . . [as of January 2002]. The Justice Department refuses to say how many times it has invoked this Patriot Act provision . . . But Assistant Attorney General Daniel Bryant says that people who borrow or buy books surrender their right of privacy. … Some libraries and bookstores unhappy with the law begin to fight back in a number of ways. Some libraries have posted signs warning that the government may be monitoring their users' reading habits. … Thousands of libraries are destroying records so agents have nothing to seize. … Many librarians polled say they would break the law and deny orders to disclose reading records.[77]

The American Library Association explains their perspective on why the provisions matter to the public:

> Libraries are key sources of information on all kinds of subjects and from all perspectives for their communities. Reading has always been one of our greatest freedoms. The written word is the natural medium for the new idea and the untried voice from which come the original contributions to social growth.
>
> Libraries provide a place to exercise intellectual freedom: a free and open exchange of knowledge and information where individuals may exercise freedom of inquiry as well as a right to privacy in regards to information they seek. Privacy is essential to the exercise of free speech, free thought, and free association. In a library, the subject of users' interests should not be examined or scrutinized by others.
>
> The ALA believes certain sections of the USA PATRIOT Act endanger constitutional rights and privacy rights of library users. Libraries cooperate with law enforcement when presented with a lawful court order to obtain specific information about specific patrons; however, the library profession is concerned some provisions in the USA PATRIOT Act go beyond the traditional methods of seeking information from libraries.[78]

69.3.3.6 United States/European Union Safe Harbor. The EU Directive restricts the export of personal information to only those nations with laws offering "adequate" privacy protection.[79] Since, as of 1998, no official body in the EU had determined U.S. law to be "adequate," ongoing data transfers from Europe to the United States across a wide number of significant industries (airlines, entertainment, credit cards, retailing) were in jeopardy of disruption.

In April 1998, United States and European Commission officials entered into negotiations to create a "Safe Harbor" for American companies desiring to import from Europe personal information relating to European citizens, by which American companies (and their trading counterparts) would not be required to prove the adequacy of American law as a condition to the execution of data transfers. Difficult negotiations ultimately produced, in July 2000, an arrangement under which transfers of personal information from the European Union to the United States will be allowed for those companies willing to comply with the "Safe Harbor" principles.[80] In substance, the principles are similar to the requirements of the directive. Under those principles, in the absence of committing to the jurisdiction of European officials, an American company importing personal information on European citizens must:

- Comply with the Safe Harbor principles, according to the guidance offered in the FAQs (see www.export.gov/safeHarbor for more details).

- Self-certify, on a voluntary basis, with the U.S. Department of Commerce its adherence to principles for the protection of personal information that are consistent with European legal principles, which adherence must be publicly announced.
- Provide for independent third-party verification that the company adheres to the Safe Harbor principles. This step can be accomplished by joining a self-regulatory privacy program that adheres to the Safe Harbor. Joining such an organization can, by itself, also qualify the company for the Safe Harbor. Examples such as TRUSTe or BBBOnline have been cited as representative of the types of programs contemplated; in effect, the U.S. and EU governments are encouraging self-regulation, deferring to nongovernment programs to enforce suitable standards on participating companies.[81]

Companies subject to explicit federal regulations regarding the privacy of personal information (e.g., HIPAA)[82] may in the future be eligible to self-certify their compliance with the applicable laws and gain the Safe Harbor recognition that would permit their transactions with European data to occur.[83] In the meantime, companies must be subject to the jurisdiction of the Federal Trade Commission for unfair or deceptive trade practices, under the U.S. Federal Trade Commission Act, or subject to the jurisdiction of the U.S. Department of Transportation in order to be eligible to join the Safe Harbor.[84] Failure of a company that has joined the Safe Harbor to abide by its stated privacy policy is actionable as an unfair or deceptive trade practice.[85] In addition, companies would be subject to sanctions under other applicable laws.[86]

Currently, European officials in those nations that have enacted laws responsive to the EU Directive are authorized to enforce those laws against U.S. companies, or their trading partners, involved in exporting personal information. To date, few conspicuous actions have been taken (largely as a result of an informal "standstill" agreed on during the pendency of the Safe Harbor negotiations).[87] As of July 2013, there were 4,091 organizations on the Safe Harbor List. However, 944 organizations were designated "not current" with respect to certification status.

The "US–EU Safe Harbor" pages at export.gov provide extensive resources for helping organizations comply with these agreements.[88]

69.3.3.7 Workplace Privacy. Software has been developed, and is increasingly used, to monitor employee email, voicemail, and Web usage. Some software can record every keystroke made by an employee,[89] or allow an employer to see what Web page the employee has on the screen in real time.

The area of workplace privacy presents an especially difficult Hobson's choice for employers. Monitoring gives rise to assertions of invasion of privacy, and the failure to monitor gives rise to claims of negligence in failing to detect and act on claims of maintaining a discriminatory work environment.

In the United States, the common law is fairly well established that because employers own the computer equipment and networks used by their employees, and particularly where employees have been given explicit notice that their Web usage or email may be subject to monitoring, employers may monitor such computer usage.[90]

The Electronic Communications Privacy Act (ECPA) (see Section 69.3.2.2) is the only federal statute relevant to claims of workplace invasions of privacy by electronic means. ECPA prohibits unauthorized and intentional "interception" of wire, oral, and electronic communications during the transmission phase and unauthorized "accessing" of electronically stored wire or electronic communications. An email is an "electronic communication."[91]

ECPA contains two important exceptions. The first is the "system provider" exception. There is considerable debate whether an employer who provides a company system for email and/or Internet access is covered by this exception. The second is the "consent" exception. Under this exception, an employer may intercept electronic communications if the prior consent of *one* of the parties to the communication has been obtained.[92] Hence, an employer needs the implied or express consent of *only* the employee. An employee probably will be considered to have given consent if he or she continues to use a communications system after having been advised of the employer's monitoring policy, although evidence of explicit consent through a signed writing, a returned email, or other technique is clearly preferable. For this reason, many companies require that employees agree to the company monitoring policy in writing as a condition of employment.

While voicemail is subject to employer monitoring by the same rules that apply to email, live employee telephone calls, even when made from company phones on company time, are subject to different rules. ECPA's prohibition on the "interception" of telephone calls during the transmission phase requires that employers not monitor employees' *non–work-related* telephone calls. Although it is awkward, the rule requires employers to cease monitoring of employees' telephone calls on the first indication that the call is made for personal purposes.[93]

In Florida and Maryland, state law requires that *both* parties to a communication consent to the monitoring of that communication.[94] Obtaining only an employee's consent therefore is unlikely to be legally sufficient to allow such monitoring in these states. In addition, other state laws governing the monitoring and interception of communications may apply. As of the publication deadline date of this chapter, however, there were no laws at either the state or the federal level prohibiting workplace email or Web usage monitoring in the United States.

In the European Union, all workplace monitoring is considered to be the collection of personal information and is subject to the terms of the Data Protection Directive, discussed earlier.

For additional discussions of employee management policies, see Chapter 45 in this *Handbook*.

69.3.3.8 Anonymity of Internet Postings and Defamation. Internet chat rooms, forums, and message boards have been used increasingly by disgruntled employees, customers, competitors, and others to attempt to damage or artificially elevate the stature of companies in the marketplace. Postings may include personal attacks; assertions about a company's business practices, the quality of its goods and services, or the worth of its stock. Such postings may be highly offensive to particular individuals, may result in intangible changes of perception about a company in the marketplace, or may result in a very real and measurable impact on the company's stock price. Understandably, companies that find themselves subject to such postings may wish to take action.

Options that a company may wish to consider when faced with negative or harmful Internet postings follow:

- **Do nothing.** Posters of negative messages may feed on the attention created by a public response. If ignored, they may become disinterested in pursuing the activity.

- **Utilize investigators to identify the poster.** If the poster's identity is known and the person is contacted by the company's counsel, the poster may cease the offending activity.
- **Contact law enforcement.** This option is appropriate where postings seem to have been intended to manipulate stock prices or where messages threaten or suggest harm to individuals or property.
- **File suit against "John Doe" and subpoena the relevant ISP to discover the identity of the poster.** This option is not as straightforward as it may seem. Many "John Doe" defendants have vigorously challenged such subpoenas,[95] and a recent court decision ruled that an ISP did not have to reveal the poster's identity.[96]

For a more detailed review of anonymity in cyberspace, see Chapter 70 in this *Handbook*.

69.3.3.9 Online Monitoring Technology. Much of the public concern surrounding privacy has derived from the use of various technologies to monitor Internet usage and compile information about users, often without clear notice to consumers. This section gives a brief description of the most prevalent technologies currently in use for online information gathering.

Cookies are small text files that are placed by a Web server onto the hard drive of an Internet user when that user visits a Website. Cookies allow Web servers to recognize computers bearing their cookies when users revisit Websites. Websites can use cookies to monitor what pages users view, what sites they come from to the Website, and where they go when they leave the site; cookies also can be used to trigger stored user settings and preferences at the Website. The use of cookies is almost ubiquitous on commercial Websites. Users have the ability, through browser software, to view and delete cookies or to set their browsers to reject them or warn them each time a cookie is placed.

The Electronic Privacy Information Center (EPIC) has a long history of what it defines as abuse of cookies:

> EPIC filed a complaint . . . with the Federal Trade Commission on February 10, 2000, concerning the information collection practices of DoubleClick Inc., a leading Internet advertising firm, and its business partners. The complaint alleges that DoubleClick is unlawfully tracking the online activities of Internet users (through the placement of cookies) and combining surfing records with detailed personal profiles contained in a national marketing database. EPIC's complaint follows the merger of DoubleClick and Abacus Direct, the country's largest catalog database firm. DoubleClick has announced its intention to combine anonymous Internet profiles in the DoubleClick database with the personal information contained in the Abacus database.[97]

For extensive resources about legal aspects of cookies, see the EPIC *Cookies* Web page.[98]

Web beacons, also called *Web bugs*, *single-pixel Graphics Interface Formats* (GIFs), or *clear GIFs*, are extremely small graphics files, generally invisible without magnification, that are used by online advertisers to gather marketing data. Web beacons function by recognizing cookies. When a user visits a Website bearing a company's Web beacon, that company can now learn that this is the same user who visited that company's own site earlier. Or, if the cookie was placed by an advertising company, the company can identify each site that the user visits that bears the company's Web beacons. This allows company to know more about users' exact Internet usage and surfing patterns than were possible using only cookies. Unlike the case with cookies, browsers do not readily detect the presence of Web beacons, nor do Website privacy policies typically disclose the use of Web beacons.[99]

Their use has provoked increasing consumer uneasiness; therefore, companies should proceed with care when electing to use or host Web beacons.[100]

69.3.3.10 Location Privacy. An explosion in the use of wireless devices, many of which are equipped with Global Positioning System (GPS) devices that allow for the identification or monitoring of the location of the device, has spurred corresponding public concern over how to protect the privacy of location information. Great marketing opportunities are envisioned, such as being able to extend special offers to consumers who are in the physical vicinity of a store or restaurant, but many people also have identified the potential for abuses.

A GPS-enabled receiver is the device that is commonly available through commercial retailers, and used by the general public to assist in navigation. The civilian GPS receivers deliver precise velocity and timing information, and very accurate location information. This device by itself does not transmit the data received from the satellite network to remote locations, nor is it typically capable of storing data regarding its long-term historical movements. However, most cell phones are now GPS-enabled and can transmit location data to the service provider or other third parties (such as Apps—see, e.g., Foursquare). Cell phones can also be used to track users even if they are not GPS-enabled. See Cell Phone Tracking Methods.

Because the technology that allows for the collection and use of this information is so new, industry best practices have not yet developed, and little legal guidance is available. It is expected, however, that location privacy will be the subject of intense policy and legislative debate over the next several years. Location-based advertising raises particular concerns when consumers are expected to pay the cost of incoming messages. There are also questions about the appropriate legal standards to access location information for law enforcement purposes. Because of consumer and media sensitivity to issues of location privacy, companies should carefully consider the legal and public relations aspects of collecting, using, or transferring such information.

A technology that was garnering a great deal of media attention as this chapter was going to press in July 2013 was *Google Glass*, a wearable, networked computer that includes a camera and projects information in the user's field of view. The device can not only record information from the user's environment, it can provide information about recognized people in the field of view.[101]

Great concern has been expressed by privacy advocates that information about individuals' every move will become available before any clear rules are established concerning the protection or use of that information. For example, EPIC writes,

> When individuals are moving about in public and private spaces, they do not expect to be tracked wherever they go. However, this expectation is being challenged as cell phones and other electronic devices now collect and store location data throughout the day. The expansion of location tracking technologies has significant implications for consumers and for their constitutional privacy rights.
>
> Over the last 10 years, law enforcement has stepped up its use of location tracking technologies, such as GPS (Global Positioning System) trackers and cell phones, to monitor the movements of individuals who may or may not be suspected of a crime. GPS is a geolocation network that consists of satellites and receivers that can calculate the precise location of a GPS device 24-hours a day (subject to environmental constraints). As of March 19, 2013, there are 31 satellites in the GPS constellation. The satellites and ground stations in the GPS network

are maintained by the U.S. Air Force Global Positioning Systems Wing. GPS satellites are designed to transmit three-dimensional location data (longitude, latitude, and altitude) as well as precise velocity and timing information to an unlimited number of users simultaneously. A GPS receiver is all that one needs to access the service. GPS satellites can not receive any data, they can only broadcast location and timing information.[102]

69.3.3.11 *Genetic Discrimination.* The collection and use of genetic information raises particular privacy concerns because this information can be used to determine whether individuals are prone to certain illnesses. This has implications for both employment and health insurance determinations. Among the most significant privacy bills recently enacted in the United States is the Genetic Information Nondiscrimination Act. The Act prohibits discrimination on the basis of genetic information with respect to health insurance and employment. From introduction to final passage, the bill took almost a dozen years.

69.3.3.12 *Social Network Sites and Privacy.* Among the most closely watched new areas of concern are the privacy impact of social network sites, such as Facebook and MySpace.[103] Concerns arise with respect to both the amount of personal information, particularly of minors, that is made available over the Internet, and also the advertising techniques that involve the collection and use of personal information. When Facebook introduced a revised News Feed service in 2006, the company was accused of invading the privacy of users and facilitating stalking. Over 700,000 users signed an online petition demanding the company discontinue the feature, stating that this compromised their privacy. Subsequently, Mark Zuckerberg, the CEO of Facebook, published an open letter apologizing for not having consulted with users prior to changing the service.

In 2007, the European Network and Information Security Agency issued a report on social networks and privacy. The paper concludes that social networks are a clear benefit to society; however, the study warns of the danger that new technologies pose in a world where there may be a false sense of intimacy created by social networks. The paper recommends government and corporate policy changes, increasing transparency of data handling practices, and encouraging social networking education rather than the banning of social networking sites in schools.[104] In 2008, the International Working Group on Data Protection in Telecommunications released a report and guidance on privacy in social networking services. The report identifies risks to privacy and security, and provides guidance to regulators, service operators, and users to counter these risks. Risks include the large amount of data collection; the misuse of profile data by third parties; insecure infrastructure and application programming interfaces. Regulators should ensure openness and require data breach notification. Providers must be transparent, live up to promises made to users, and use privacy friendly defaults. Privacy and consumer groups are also encouraged to raise the awareness of regulators, providers, and the general public.[105]

69.3.4 State Legislation. As noted in other sections, most federal privacy laws and regulations in the United States do not preempt state law. Most often, federal statutes set a "floor" on which states may create stricter rules. This approach to legislating is important because it reflects the federalism form of government that grants states significant power. It also allows the states to develop new approaches to emerging privacy challenges and to operate as "laboratories of democracy." Not surprisingly, in the absence of substantial federal legislation, U.S. states have acted aggressively to pass new legislation regarding personal information.

The important point regarding state privacy laws is that such laws are numerous and often organized by industry or commercial sector. A company always should research the laws of the state(s) in which it operates to determine whether there are state-level laws that affect its use of personal information.

States already have passed legislation concerning emerging privacy issues, such as DNA databases, RFID tags, and other new technologies. Examples of significant privacy state laws follow.

- California passed an influential security breach notification in 2003. SB 1386 requires "any person or business that conducts business in California, and that owns or licenses computerized data that includes personal information, [to] disclose any breach of the security system . . . to any resident of California whose unencrypted personal information was, or is reasonably believed to have been, acquired by an unauthorized person." The statute imposes specific notification requirements on companies in such circumstances. The statute applies regardless of whether the computerized consumer records are maintained in or outside California. Many states subsequently passed security breach laws similar to California, and California subsequently extended the legislation in 2007 to cover medical records.
- California also enacted strong consumer privacy legislation in 2003. The California Financial Information Privacy Act provides the strongest financial privacy protections in the United States. Among the key provisions, the law gives consumers greater control over their personal information held by businesses, requires simple and understandable notices, and includes strong penalties.[106]
- According to the National Conference of State Legislatures, the majority of state legislatures have taken steps to safeguard genetic information beyond the protections provided for other types of health information. The state of New Mexico, for example, grants the individual the right to access genetic information, requires consent for a wide range of purposes, and establishes specific penalties for violations of genetic privacy.[107]
- Several states have passed laws to regulate the use of RFID. Washington State passed a law in 2008 that makes it a felony to intentionally scan another person's identification remotely without his or her knowledge and consent, for the purpose of fraud, identity theft, or some other illegal purpose.[108] A 2006 law in Wisconsin prevents the forcible implementation of RFID tags into humans.

69.4 COMPLIANCE MODELS.

Responding to the challenges presented by rapidly developing privacy laws and the threats posed by hackers, requires the confrontation of complex new issues. A number of different paradigms are emerging. Each is interrelated, but for purposes of explanation, it may be best to consider each individually. Real-world solutions to privacy issues will, in almost every case, involve the use of multiple overlapping compliance models. This section illustrates, by providing a broad overview, the various models that are emerging as themes of privacy law compliance.

69.4.1 U.S. Legislation.

The primary compliance model for privacy protection is the enactment of law that makes clear the obligations of organizations that collect and use personal information and the rights of individuals who provide personal information. Privacy legislation is typically based on Fair Information Practices that are intended to promote the flow of personal data but to do so in a way that makes clear the purposes for which personal information is collected and will be used. Privacy legislation typically includes a variety of enforcement mechanisms, including a private right of action that allows an individual, or group of individuals, to file a lawsuit when a provision of the law has been violated; enforcement by the state of attorney generals, which can be particularly important when there is a pattern or practice of violation; as well as action by the Federal Trade Commission, which has the power to investigate unfair and deceptive trade practices.

69.4.2 U.S. Federal Trade Commission Section 5 Authority. The United States Federal Trade Commission has authority to investigate unfair or deceptive trade practices under Section 5 of the FTC Act. The FTC has applied this authority in a variety of privacy cases, involving primarily negligent security practices.

69.4.3 Self-Regulatory Regimes and Codes of Conduct. Self-regulatory regimes, including industry codes of conduct, are emerging as a means for achieving compliance with fair information practices among businesses. Self-regulation has two appealing aspects: (1) it minimizes the need for government to devote resources to enforcement, and (2) it allows the greatest degree of flexibility of business practices—important to those who stress that overregulation will stunt the growth of electronic commerce.

At the same time, self-regulatory approaches have come under increasing scrutiny from privacy officials, consumer organizations, and political leaders, particularly in the European Union. The EU national data protection commissioners (the Article 29 Committee) opposed the Safe Harbor proposal as inadequate. The Trans Atlantic Consumer Dialogue found that there was insufficient enforcement.[109] The European Parliament challenged the adequacy of the Safe Harbor Arrangement with the United States.[110]

Codes of conduct are explicitly contemplated by the EU Data Protection Directive as one means of compliance. The directive encourages EU member states to foster codes of conduct within self-policing industries as a means of ensuring compliance with data protection laws across entire business sectors.[111]

69.4.4 Contract Infrastructure. Several privacy laws contemplate the use of contracts to define how personal information will be collected, used, and/or transferred. Although the specific uses of contracts vary from law to law, an underlying trend is emerging: The rules governing the entire "life cycle" of personal information will be supplemented and maintained by a network of contracts.

Personal information, under most privacy laws, is collected from an individual subject to the terms of how that information will be used and to whom it may be transferred. In the absence of law, industry standards, or other guidelines, the rules for how personal information may be used are defined by the policies given to the data subject. Preferably, these policies will incorporate all of the elements of fair information practices. Once a company has collected personal information, it must process and use the data pursuant to the rules. Since personal information often passes from the collecting company to its affiliates, service providers, and others, additional contracts must be executed among and between all of these entities to ensure that the rules originally defined in the notice are followed.

Companies should begin to think about a "chain of contracts" that starts with fair information practices for the data subject—essentially a contract between the company and the individual. The terms of that contract are then enforced, by means of other contractual relationships, as personal information moves to different business entities, across national boundaries, and to third-party businesses.

69.4.5 Synthesis of Contracts, Technology, and Law. Contracts alone are not a complete solution to privacy issues. Although indemnity provisions and contractual warranties may, on paper, ensure that personal information has been properly collected, used, and transferred, the practical realities of the situation may be otherwise. Some points to consider:

- Policing such contracts may be beyond the means or the inclinations of many businesses.
- Most businesses are not likely to sue their trading partners to enforce these contracts, except in the most grievous cases.
- Most consumers do not perceive themselves as having enough at stake to bring actions on an individual level, but the possibility of class-action lawsuits may exist.
- The security of personal data, once compromised, is difficult to resecure—it is hard to unring the bell.
- Finally, given the massiveness of the data files typically involved, the speed with which data can be moved, and the multiplicity of jurisdictions into which it can be sent, governmental enforcement may face a larger challenge than governments will be willing to pay for.

Accordingly, technological controls on the collection, processing, access, storage, and transfer become a key element in the management of personal information.

Technology is the implementation of policy and business logic. For instance, when a customer makes a choice not to be included on a mailing list, it is technology that will segregate that person's information and ensure that the choice is honored. It is technology that will ensure that information relating to all the people who opted out of a proposed use of their data is not transferred to a third party for marketing uses. And it is, therefore, technology that ensures that the third party receiving personal information for marketing uses can use the information in those ways without incurring regulatory or public relations damage. Even simple policing techniques, such as the use of dummy names to detect unauthorized uses by onward transferees, can be administered more effectively using modern information technology. In this example, contracts and technology combine to add value. Contracts set terms of use for personal information that eliminate legal risk; technology ensures that the terms are followed. The end product is a valuable asset—usable personal information, the currency of the new economy.

It is vital that technological infrastructures embody both the specific legal rules that a company must observe with respect to personal information and the contracts created to manage that compliance process. Likewise, it is vital that the contracts themselves embody the legal requirements, the needs of the business, and the limitations of available technology. Business processes must adapt to the realities of the law, but must utilize technology and contractual relationships in order to maximize profits. To manage personal information assets effectively, technologists and businesspeople must begin to think about law, while lawyers must become familiar with technology and business.

69.4.6 Getting Started: A Practical Checklist. An outline of some of the practical steps that must be taken for an organization to begin to implement effective personal information management practices follows. This checklist is not all-inclusive but is designed to illustrate how the core privacy principles and different compliance models begin to interact in the management process.

- Achieve buy-in, at the highest level of the organization, to the idea that personal information management must be part of an organization's critical infrastructure.
- Perform due diligence to identify *all* types of personal information collected and the routes by which the data travel in and out of the organization.
- Identify all of the uses to which the information is put during its life cycle through collection, processing, use, transfer, storage, and destruction.
- Identify each law affecting the collection, use, and transfer of personal information to which the company is subject.
- Create an institutional privacy policy that accurately considers both a commitment to abide by various legal requirements and the legitimate business activities of the organization.
- Create supporting materials that educate employees and instruct on policy implementation.
- Implement consistent data transfer agreements with all data-trading partners, vendors, service providers, and others with whom personal information is acquired or transferred.
- Build privacy management into the organization's strategic planning, providing sufficient resources for personnel, training, technology, and compliance auditing.
- Hold employees accountable for implementation and compliance with the privacy policy and contract requirements.
- Consider innovative approaches to privacy protection and business development that limit or eliminate the collection of personally identifiable information.
- Periodically audit compliance.

69.5 FURTHER READING

Agre, P. E., and M. Rotenberg. *Technology and Privacy: The New Landscape*. MIT Press, 1998.

Bennett, C. J., and C. D. Raab. *The Governance of Privacy: Policy Instruments in a Global Perspective*. MIT Press, 2006.

Bygrave, L. A. *Data Protection Law: Approaching Its Rationale, Logic and Limits*. Kluwer Law International, 2002.

Garfinkel, S., and B. Rosenberg. *RFID Applications, Security, and Privacy*. Addison-Wesley, 2006.

Harvey, I., A. Cavoukian, G. Tomko, D. Borrett, H. Kwan, and D. Hatzinakos, editors. *SmartData: Privacy Meets Evolutionary Robotics*. Springer, 2013.

Hoepman, J.-H., and I. Verbauwhede, editors. *Radio Frequency Identification: Security and Privacy Issues: 8th International Workshop, RFIDSec 2012, Nijmegen, The Netherlands, July 2–3, 2012*. Springer, 2013.

Nehf, J. P. *Open Book: The Failed Promise of Information Privacy in America.* CreateSpace Independent Publishing Platform, 2012.

Rosen, J. *The Unwanted Gaze: The Destruction of Privacy in America.* Vintage, 2000.

Rosen, J., and B. Wittes, editors. *Constitution 3.0: Freedom and Technological Change.* Brookings Institution Press, 2013.

Solove, D. J., M. Rotenberg, and P. J. Schwartz. *Information Privacy Law.* Aspen, 2006.

Solove, D. J. *Understanding Privacy.* Harvard University Press, 2010.

Solove, D. J. *Nothing to Hide: The False Tradeoff between Privacy and Security.* Yale University Press, 2013.

Stewart, D., editor. *Social Media and the Law: A Guidebook for Communication Students and Professionals.* Routledge, 2012.

Ziegler, K. S. *Human Rights and Private Law: Privacy as Autonomy.* Hart, 2007.

Websites

American Civil Liberties Union: www.aclu.org

Electronic Privacy Information Center: http://epic.org

European Commission, Justice and Home Affairs, Protection of Personal Data: http://ec.europa.eu/justice/data-protection/index_en.htm

Federal Trade Commission, Privacy Initiatives: http://business.ftc.gov/privacy-and-security

National Conference of State Legislatures, NCSL 50—State Legislative Tracking Resources: www.ncsl.org/legislative-staff.aspx?tabs=856,34,736

Privacy, Business and Law—Pandab is an online newsletter summarizing the top news articles on privacy, law and business: www.pandab.org

Privacy Exchange—a global information resource on consumers, commerce, and date protection worldwide: www.privacyexchange.org

Privacy International—Privacy International (PI) is a human rights group formed in 1990 as a watchdog on surveillance and privacy invasions by governments and corporations: www.privacyinternational.org

69.6 NOTES

1. In this context, various non-U.S. legal systems, especially European law, tend to use the term *data protection*, while the law in the United States tends to use the term *privacy*. This chapter uses the terms interchangeably, although readers should be aware that *privacy* often is considered to be a broader concept than *data protection*.
2. "What Is the NSA Domestic Spying Program?" *NSA Spying on Americans*, Electronic Frontier Foundation, July 31, 2013, https://www.eff.org/nsa-spying/faq#37
3. "EPIC Urges US Supreme Court to Suspend NSA Domestic Surveillance." EPIC Alert 20.14, July 12, 2013, http://epic.org/alert/epic_alert_20.14.html
4. I. Chandrasekhar, M. Wardrop, and A. Trotman, "Phone Hacking: Timeline of the Scandal: The Key Events in the Phone Hacking Scandal, which Has Led to the Closure of the *News of the World*, Halted Rupert Murdoch's BSkyB Takeover Bid, and Prompted the Arrest of Several Key Figures," *The Telegraph*, July 23, 2012, www.telegraph.co.uk/news/uknews/phone-hacking/8634176/Phone-hacking-timeline-of-a-scandal.html
5. Lord Justice Leveson, *An Inquiry into the Culture, Practices and Ethics of the Press: Executive Summary,* http://media.ft.com/cms/643fca7e-3a2c-11e2-a00d-00144feabdc0.pdf

6. Parliamentary Reports What Price Privacy? The unlawful trade in confidential information May 13, 2006; What Price Privacy Now? December 13, 2006
7. According to the Australian Government, "The Privacy Amendment Act includes a set of new, harmonised, privacy principles that will regulate the handling of personal information by both Australian government agencies and businesses. These new principles are called the *Australian Privacy Principles* (APPs). They will replace the existing Information Privacy Principles (IPPs) that currently apply to Australian government agencies and the National Privacy Principles (NPPs) that currently apply to businesses.

   "Under the changes, there will be 13 new APPs. A number of the APPs are significantly different from the existing principles, including APP 7 on the use and disclosure of personal information for direct marketing, and APP 8 on cross-border disclosure of personal information." See www.oaic.gov.au/privacy/privacy-act/privacy-law-reform
8. E.g., the Fourth Amendment to the U.S. Constitution.
9. The U.S. Freedom of Information Act typifies the former trend; the constitutions of Argentina and South Africa typify the latter.
10. See Draft Charter of Fundamental Rights of the European Union, Charter 4487/00, Brussels, September 28, 2000: Article 7 ("Respect for Private and Family Life") of the charter states: "Everyone has the right to respect for his or her private and family life, home and communications." Article 8 ("Protection of Personal Data") states: "1. Everyone has the right to the protection of personal data concerning him or her. 2. Such data must be processed fairly for specified purposes and on the basis of the consent of the person concerned or some other legitimate basis laid down by law. Everyone has the right of access to data that has been collected concerning him or her, and the right to have it rectified. 3. Compliance with these rules shall be subject to control by an independent authority."
11. Sweden: The Data Act of 1973, found in Svensk Författningssamling (SFS; Swedish Code of Statutes) 1973: 289, amended at SFS 1982: 446; United States: The Privacy Act of 1974, P.L. 93-579, 5 USC §552a; Germany: The Federal Data Protection Act (BDSG), available in English in Ulrich Dammann, Otto Mallmann, and Spiros Simitis, eds., *Data Protection Legislation: An International Documentation* (Frankfurt am Main: [West] Germany, 1977); France: Loi No. 78-17 du 6 janvier 1978 relative à l'informatique, aux fichiers et aux libertés, *Journal Officiel de la République Française*, January 7, 1978.
12. ETS No. 108, Strasbourg, 1981. Available at: www.coe.fr/eng/legaltxt/108e.htm (URL inactive).
13. Paris, 1981. An important distinction in the activities of the OECD (as opposed to the activities of the COE) is the involvement and support of the U.S. Government. The OECD is supported by nearly 30 governments. For more information, see www.oecd.org
14. Council of Europe, Convention for the Protection of Individuals with regard to Automatic Processing of Personal Data (ETS No. 108): http://conventions.coe.int/Treaty/Commun/ChercheSig.asp?NT=108&CL=ENG
15. For example, Hong Kong, Estonia, and Lithuania seem to have based their privacy laws, in part, on the OECD Guidelines. Brazil, Malaysia, and Morocco are currently considering passage of privacy laws based on the OECD Guidelines. In April 2013, Uruguay ratified the Guidelines and they entered into effect on the 1st of August of that year.

16. See www.oecd.org/internet/ieconomy/oecdprivacystatementgenerator.htm
17. Directive 95/46/EC of the European Parliament and of the Council of October 24, 1995, on the protection of individuals with regard to the processing of personal information and on the free movement of such data, text available at http://europa.eu.int/eur-lex/en/lif/dat/1995/en_395L0046.html (URL inactive).
18. "Status of implementation of Directive 95/46 on the Protection of Individuals with regard to the Processing of Personal Data," European Commission, July 16, 2013, http://ec.europa.eu/justice/data-protection/law/status-implementation/index_en.htm
19. "Commission Proposes a Comprehensive Reform of the Data Protection Rules," European Commission Website, January 25, 2012, http://ec.europa.eu/justice/newsroom/data-protection/news/120125_en.htm
20. "Commission Proposes a Comprehensive Reform of Data Protection Rules To Increase Users' Control of Their Data and To Cut Costs for Businesses," EUROPA Press Releases, January 25, 2012, http://europa.eu/rapid/press-release_IP-12-46_en.htm?locale=en
21. Hong Kong, New Zealand, Chile, Argentina, and Canada have passed such laws; Japan, India, Brazil, and Australia, among others, have proposed new conforming legislation.
22. The Czech Republic, Hungary, Poland, Latvia, and Estonia have already passed national legislation that mimics the EU model. Romania, Turkey, and Russia, among others, have proposed such legislation.
23. Directive Concerning the Processing of Personal Data and the Protection of Privacy in the Telecommunications Sector (Directive 97/66/EC of the European Parliament and of the Council of December 15, 1997), available at www.ispo.cec.be/legal/en/dataprot/protection.html (URL inactive).
24. See David Banisar, *Privacy & Human Rights 2000*, EPIC and Privacy International, available at www.privacyinternational.org/survey/phr2000/threats.html (URL inactive).
25. European Commission, "Proposal for a Directive of the European Parliament and of the Council Concerning the Processing of Personal Data and the Protection of Privacy in the Electronic Communications Sector," available at http://europa.eu.institutionalize/comm/information_society/policy/framework/pdf/com2000385_en.pdf (URL inactive).
26. European Data Protection Supervisor. https://secure.edps.europa.eu/EDPSWEB/edps/EDPS
27. "EU Data Protection Supervisor Slams 'Smart Borders'," NewEurope Online, July 19, 2013, www.neurope.eu/article/eu-data-protection-supervisor-slams-smart-borders
28. https://secure.edps.europa.eu/EDPSWEB/webdav/site/mySite/shared/Documents/EDPS/MembersMission/Members/13-07-31_vacancies_EN.pdf
29. Charles Warren and Louis Brandeis, "The Right of Privacy," *Harvard Law Review* 4 (1890):193.
30. See, e.g., *Cox Broadcasting v. Cohn*, 420 US 469 (1975); *Time, Inc. v. Hill*, 385 US 374 (1967).
31. See Restatement (2d), Torts, § 652.
32. 5 USC § 552a. 5 USC § 552 incorporates the Freedom of Information Act (originally passed in 1966).

33. The Fair Credit Reporting Act of 1970 (15 USC § 1681 *et seq.*) was arguably the first sweeping privacy law.
34. P.L. 93-579, congressional finding and statement of purpose, paragraph (b).
35. 18 USC § 3121 *et seq.*
36. See *Smith v. Maryland*, 442 US 735, 742–45 (1979).
37. 18 USC § 3122(b)(2).
38. See 12 USC §§ 3401–22.
39. 18 USC § 2721 (1994).
40. See *Reno v. Condon*, 528 US 141 (2000).
41. "Earthlink Says It Refuses to Install FBI's Carnivore Surveillance Device," *Wall Street Journal*, July 14, 2000.
42. For more details on monitoring and surveillance, see Banisar, *Privacy & Human Rights*.
43. See "Interception Capabilities 2000" (Part 2/5: "The State of the Art in Communications Intelligence [COMINT] of the Automated Processing for Intelligence Purposes of Intercepted Broadband Multi-language Leased or Common Carrier Systems, and Its Applicability to COMINT Targeting and Selection, Including Speech Recognition"), European Parliament, PE 168. 184 Vol. 2/5.
44. 47 USC §1001 *et seq.*
45. See *United States Telecom Ass'n v. FCC*, 227 F.3d 450 (D.C. Cir. 2000).
46. Council of Europe, Convention on Cybercrime, CETS No. 185: http://conventions.coe.int/Treaty/Commun/QueVoulezVous.asp?NT=185&CM=8&DF=5/19/2008&CL=ENG
47. Council of Europe, Convention on Cybercrime, CETS No. 185, Status of May 19, 2008 http://conventions.coe.int/Treaty/Commun/ChercheSig.asp?NT=185&CM=8&DF=5/19/2008&CL=ENG
48. See, e.g., www.cdt.org/international/cybercrime/001211cdt.shtml (URL inactive).
49. "Foreign Intelligence Surveillance Court," Federal Judicial Center | History of the Federal Judiciary, www.fjc.gov/history/home.nsf/page/courts_special_fisc.html
50. "Beyond FISA," Electronic Frontier Foundation | Surveillance Self-Defense, 2013, https://ssd.eff.org/foreign/beyond-fisa
51. "The USA PATRIOT Act." Electronic Frontier Foundation (2005-08-03), http://w2.eff.org/patriot
52. "How PATRIOT Threatens Online Civil Liberties." Electronic Frontier Foundation (2013), http://w2.eff.org/patriot/why.php
53. Financial Services Modernization Act of 1999 (Pub.L. 106–102, 113 Stat. 1338). Signed into law on November 12, 1999; codified at 15 USC § 6801 et seq.
54. The Federal Deposit Insurance Corporation (FDIC), the Office of the Comptroller of the Currency (OCC), the Office of Thrift Supervision (OTS), and the Federal Reserve Board issued joint regulations. The Securities and Exchange Commission (SEC), the National Credit Union Administration (NCUA), the Commodity Futures Trading Commission (CFTC), and the Federal Trade Commission (FTC) have each issued separate sets of regulations.
55. "Who Must Comply with the Privacy Rule?" *Frequently Asked Questions for the Privacy Regulation*, Federal Trade Commission, Section A, Question 1, December 2001, www.ftc.gov/privacy/glbact/glb-faq.htm

56. See 47248 *Federal Register*, Vol. 61, No. 174, Friday, September 6, 1996.
57. See 12 CFR Ch. 11 § 211.5(d).
58. Individuals with whom a "financial institution" has an ongoing relationship.
59. All individuals who seek financial products or services for personal, family, or household purposes, whether or not those products or services are ever actually obtained.
60. A degree of variation has emerged concerning required information security standards under GLBA. The SEC and CFTC regulations set forth very general requirements; the OTS, OCC, FDIC and Federal Reserve Board jointly issued detailed information security guidelines (66 *Federal Register* 8615, February 1, 2001); the NCUA also issued guidelines paralleling those issued by the banking agencies (66 *Federal Register* 8152, January 29, 2001); the FTC issued a proposed regulation that represents a significant simplification of the banking agencies' guidelines (66 *Federal Register* 46112, August 7, 2001).
61. *Frequently Asked Questions for the Privacy Regulation*, Federal Trade Commission, December 2001, www.ftc.gov/privacy/glbact/glb-faq.htm
62. 15 USC § 6501 *et seq.*
63. Kelly/Warner Internet Law & Defamation Practice, "COPPA: Children's Online Privacy Protection Act Summary," 2012, www.aaronkellylaw.com/coppa-childrens-online-privacy-protection-act-summary/
64. 16 CFR § 312.9.
65. See www.ftc.gov/bcp/conline/pubs/buspubs/coppa.htm (URL inactive).
66. P.L. 104–191, August 21, 1996.
67. The final rule was published December 28, 2000, at 65 *Federal Register* 82,461 (2000).
68. Available at www.hhs.gov/ocr/privacy
69. See 45 CFR § 164.506
70. www.hhs.gov/ocr/office/index.html
71. *Patient Safety and Quality Improvement Act of 2005 Statute and Rule.* Health Information Privacy, US Department of Health & Human Services, www.hhs.gov/ocr/privacy/psa/regulation
72. More information about HIPAA's privacy regulations can be obtained at www.hhs.gov/ocr/hipaa or at hipaadvisory.com (URL inactive).
73. "*HIPAA—Frequently Asked Questions.*" Health Information Privacy, U.S. Department of Health & Human Services. www.hhs.gov/ocr/privacy/hipaa/faq/index.html
74. 47 USC § 551 (1984).
75. 18 USC § 2710 (1988).
76. *Harris v. Blockbuster*, Electronic Privacy Information Center, February 2, 2010, http://epic.org/amicus/blockbuster
77. "January 2002: Study Finds Agents Have Sought Records From 220 Libraries," *Profile: USA Patriot Act,* History Commons Website, 2002, www.historycommons.org/entity.jsp?entity=patriot_act
78. "The USA PATRIOT Act." American Library Association (2013), www.ala.org/advocacy/advleg/federallegislation/theusapatriotact
79. See Section 69.2.2.1 for more details.

80. The full text of the Safe Harbor Principles is available at www.ita.doc.gov/td/ecom/menu.html (URL inactive).
81. Additional information on TRUSTe and BBBOnline can be obtained at www.truste.org and www.bbbonline.org. Note that neither organization offers certification of offline privacy practices and is therefore not available as a complete solution to any company that engages in any type of offline collection or use of the personal information of EU residents.
82. The European Commission has deferred a review of whether the privacy provisions of GLBA are "adequate" pending implementation and possible further legislative action in the United States.
83. Although the Safe Harbor principles allow for adequacy determinations for U.S. business sectors that are subject to particular sectoral privacy laws, no determination has yet been made of the adequacy of any particular law.
84. See Introduction and Annex to Safe Harbor Principles: 15 USC § 45. Note that banks, savings and loans, and entities such as stockyards and meat packers are excluded from the scope of the FTC Act and are therefore not eligible for Safe Harbor membership.
85. See draft Safe Harbor FAQ No. 11: Dispute Resolution and Enforcement, available at www.ita.doc.gov/td/ecom/RedlinedFAQ11Enforc300.htm. (URL inactive). Note that entities that are eligible for Safe Harbor membership because they are subject to the jurisdiction of the Department of Transportation may be subject to enforcement actions brought by the department.
86. See draft Safe Harbor FAQ No. 11: Dispute Resolution and Enforcement.
87. The "Safe Harbor" came into effect in early November 2000. The informal stay of enforcement by EU Data Protection Authorities against U.S. companies was due to end in June 2001. Some enforcement actions have been brought against U.S. companies already; for instance, American Airlines was forced to change its practices with respect to passenger information by the Swedish authority and Microsoft was fined $60,000 in Spain.
88. *U.S.–EU Safe Harbor Overview*, http://export.gov/safeharbor/eu/eg_main_018476.asp
89. During 2001, such keystroke monitoring was the subject of increasing controversy. In the first case testing the use of such technology for law enforcement purposes, a federal judge in New Jersey recently ordered the U.S. government to reveal how it had performed keystroke monitoring of an alleged criminal. See Opinion and Order, August 7, 2001, *United States v. Nicodemo Scarfo et al.*, available at http://www2.epic.org/crypto/scarfo/order_8_7_01.pdf (URL inactive).

    In another incident, judges of the Ninth U.S. Circuit Court, based in San Francisco, ordered their information technology personnel to remove keystroke-monitoring software that had been installed on their computers by order of the Judicial Conference of the United States. See Neil Lewis, "Rebels in Black Robes Recoil at Surveillance of Computers," *New York Times*, August 8, 2001.
90. See, e.g., *Smyth v. Pillsbury Co.*, 914 F. Supp. 97 (E.D. Pa. 1996).
91. 18 USC § 2510.
92. 18 USC § 2511(2)(d).
93. See *Watkins v. L.M. Berry & Company*, 704 F.2d 577 (11th Cir. 1983); *Ali v. Douglas Cable Communications*, 929 F. Supp. 1362 (D. Kan. 1996); *US v.*

Murdock, 63 F.3d 1391 (6th Cir. 1995); *Deal v. Spears*, 980 F.2d 1153 (8th Cir. 1992).

94. Fla. Stat. 934.03-934.09; Md. Cts. & Jud. Proc.Code Ann. Sec.10-402 (1980). The Maryland law was the basis for the criminal investigation into Linda Tripp's recording of her conversations with Monica Lewinsky regarding then-president Clinton.
95. See www.johndoes.org for more information. (URL inactive).
96. See *Dendrite International, Inc. v. John Does 1-14, et al.*, New Jersey Superior Court (Morris/Sussex Vicinage), November 28, 2000, docket no. MRSC-129-00.
97. "EPIC Files FTC Privacy Complaint Against DoubleClick," *Cookies*, Electronic Privacy Information Center, http://epic.org/privacy/internet/cookies
98. *Cookies*, Electronic Privacy Information Center, http://epic.org/privacy/internet/cookies/
99. Free software that allows users to identify Web beacons on websites is available at www.bugnosis.com (URL inactive).
100. *Online Tracking and Behavioral Profiling*, Electronic Privacy Information Center, http://epic.org/privacy/consumer/online_tracking_and_behavioral.html
101. "Google Glass May Compromise Privacy of User and Others," KTVU TV, May 16, 2013, www.ktvu.com/news/news/special-reports/google-glass-may-compromise-privacy-user-and-other/nXtHx/
102. *Locational Privacy*, Electronic Privacy Information Center, http://epic.org/privacy/location_privacy
103. *Social Networking Privacy*, Electronic Privacy Information Center, http://epic.org/privacy/socialnet/default.html
104. "Security Issues And Recommendations for Social Networks," ENISA, October 2007, www.enisa.europa.eu/doc/pdf/deliverables/enisa_pp_social_networks.pdf (URL inactive).
105. International Working Group on Data Protection in Telecommunications, "Report and Guidance on Privacy in Social Network Services, 'Rome Memorandum'," March 2008, www.datenschutz-berlin.de/attachments/461/WP_social_network_services.pdf?1208438491
106. Privacy Rights Clearinghouse, "California Financial Information Privacy Act: Senate Bill 1, Speier & Burton," www.privacyrights.org/ar/SB1Info.htm
107. National Conference of State Legislatures, "State Genetic Privacy Laws," updated January 2008, www.ncsl.org/programs/health/genetics/prt.htm
108. "First of Its Kind RFID Law Prohibits Malicious Spying on Consumers," PRWeb Website, www.prweb.com/releases/2008/03/prweb803114.htm
109. Submission of the TACD, March 30, 2000 at: www.ita.doc.gov/td/ecom/Comments400/TACDComments1.htm (URL inactive).
110. European Parliament resolution on the Draft Commission Decision on the adequacy of the protection provided by the Safe Harbor Privacy Principles and related *Frequently Asked Questions* issued by the US Department of Commerce (C5-0280/2000–2000/2144(COS)): http://epic.org/privacy/intl/EP_SH_resolution_0700.html
111. Directive 95/46/EC, Article 27. The International Commercial Exchange provides an example of such an industry initiative; see www.icx.org for more information.

CHAPTER 70

ANONYMITY AND IDENTITY IN CYBERSPACE

M. E. Kabay, Eric Salveggio, Robert Guess, and Russell D. Rosco

70.1 INTRODUCTION.

As electronic communications technology is now commonplace among increasingly international populations of computer users, one of the most hotly debated questions is how to maintain the benefits of free discourse while simultaneously restricting antisocial communications and behavior on the Internet. The proliferation of pseudonymous blogging and anonymous or pseudonymous commenting and tweeting complicates and potentially degrades the level of discourse online. International and intercultural differences in communications complicate the issue of anonymity and identity online; what is viewed as freedom in some parts of the world is perceived as license in other communities. Conversely, what are conceived by some as attempts to impose civility on international discourse are sometimes rejected as gross interference in freedom of speech by others.

At the heart of much of the debate over the advisability and possibility of imposing limits on behavior in cyberspace is the question of identity. Some of the most egregious abuse of cyberspace seems reasonably to be attributable in part to the ease of concealing identity; using no names or false names, malefactors can often escape almost all of the consequences of their actions. Sophisticated attacks include propaganda meant to sway public opinion, whether in the political field or in commerce; anonymous criminal groups can mask nefarious and manipulative intent with a friendly and inviting countenance.

70.1.1 Identity Theft.

The FBI and other U.S. federal agencies consider identity theft a serious issue for law enforcement and national security: "Identity theft not only victimizes the individuals whose identity is stolen, but it can also pose a public safety and national security risk. … It is imperative that law enforcement know the true identity of the individuals they encounter while protecting our communities."[1]

70.1.2 Politics.

Under totalitarian regimes, masking identity while using the instantaneous communications capabilities of the Internet has permitted world awareness of atrocities in such countries as Egypt, China, and Syria. Anonymization of an identity becomes key to survival in such situations. In an acknowledgement of the power of instantaneous communications, China has instituted a user-registration process to thwart anonymization. In the January 18, 2012, edition of *The New York Times*, in an article entitled "China Expands Program Requiring Real-Name Registration Online," author Michael Wines writes:

> China will expand nationwide a trial program that requires users of the country's wildly popular microblog services to disclose their identities to the government in order to post comments online, the government's top Internet regulator said Wednesday.
>
> The official, Wang Chen, said at a news conference that registration trials in five major eastern Chinese cities would continue until wrinkles were worked out. But he said that eventually all 250 million users of microblogs, called weibos here, would have to register, beginning first with new users.
>
> Mr. Wang indicated that under the program, users could continue to use nicknames online, even though they would still be required to register their true identities.[2]

70.1.3 Harassment and Cyberbullying.

Corporations and individuals can suffer serious damage to their interests from abuse of anonymous communications. The availability of anonymous, highly critical postings to discussion groups about specific companies has resulted in problems in hiring new staff and depression of stock prices.[3]

One of the biggest issues facing law enforcement is how to deal with cyberthreats, especially anonymous threats. Many of the current laws, while similar in nature, are defused in court over technicalities by shrewd lawyers. It has been stated that new laws covering these new threats are sorely needed, but that the system is about five years behind the times.[4]

In an early case of cyberharassment, an innocent Florida businessman, Bruce Hovland, was harassed in 1997 by thousands of phone calls from angry strangers who complained about junk email that threatened to bill their credit cards for almost $200 in return for nonexistent pornographic videos they had never ordered and did not want. Hovland was the victim of a deliberate smear campaign, probably by a malefactor who had refused to pay rent at Hovland's marina and who had lost his boat in a seizure as a result. The anonymous malefactor spammed the 'Net in Hovland's name and suggested that people call his business number collect. Hovland guessed that he lost about two weeks of business because his phones were ringing off the hook. Hovland pointed out that his case was relatively minor; he imagined the mayhem if an emergency number were posted on the 'Net in such a fraud. The case illustrates the difficulty for victims in finding an agency willing to receive and follow up on complaints about such outrageous and dangerous attacks.[5]

Anonymous abuse of individuals can cause great personal distress; in 1997, for example, an Annapolis, Maryland, woman was mail-bombed after she warned other writers about extortionate fees from an author's agency; her name, phone number, and address were posted on alt.sex groups on the Usenet and resulted in floods of offensive phone calls.[6]

A woman in Atlanta was appalled when someone posted a photograph of an unknown anonymous woman with the victim's name and contact information; she received calls from men who told her the announcement claimed she was offering free sex. A victim of such anonymous harassment founded WHO@ (Working to Halt Online Abuse) to help victims fight this oppression.[7] The CyberAngels, an offshoot of the Guardian Angels vigilante group, claim to be willing and able to help victims of such harassment.[8]

In Florida, two students posted a picture of one of their high school classmates on a Website. The boy was pictured dancing with his prom date—but the girl's head was replaced by the picture of one of their male teachers. An electronic voice on the site announced that the teacher "must die." The student was profoundly disturbed by the intimations of homosexuality, as were the teacher and his colleagues. However, the state attorney's office reluctantly concluded that there is no valid state statute making it illegal for someone to publish libelous information anonymously on the 'Net. Although Florida does have a law forbidding "anonymous publication of material that holds a person up to ridicule or contempt," legal experts concluded that such a limitation on speech is unconstitutional.

In an article entitled "Web Plays Incendiary Role in Ohio High School Rape Case," from the January 7, 2013, edition of the *Los Angeles Times*, author Matt Pearce describes:

> The two high school football players accused of rape will get their day in court. The city of Steubenville, Ohio, however, will have to fight some of its battles online, where news of the case began.
>
> It's the story of a horrifying accusation met with small-town side-taking and blown up into a national scandal. Trent Mays and Ma'lik Richmond, both 16, are accused of raping a drunk and unconscious 16-year-old girl at a party on the night of Aug. 11 while other partygoers tweeted and Instagrammed about the attack.[9]

Pearce describes the ensuing cloud of information:

> The viral nature of the news was not limited to tweets on the night of the incident. The high-profile criminal case spotlighted by social media has put not only the defendants on trial but the culture surrounding them. Some town residents have compared the attention to a public lynching; others have said that without the attention, nothing would have been done.

Further exacerbating the situation,

> Hacker collective Anonymous recently posted video of youths who were said to be Steubenville High School students and alumni joking about the rape victim.

As a result of the varied and inaccurate information feeding angry public sentiment in the small town of Steubenville:

> The latest development in the case came Saturday as Steubenville Police Chief William McCafferty and City Manager Cathy Davison set up a blog dedicated solely to the case to "disseminate the most accurate information."

In this case, we have an alleged crime brought to light through real-time tweets and Instagrams; if the authors of these communications were witnessing a heinous crime such as this, why did no one take action to stop the crime, rather than to produce real-time tweets about it? Clearly, as a society, we have work to do with our children and ourselves.

Twenty years ago, a case like this would have played out in a court of law. Today, it plays out in a public forum with no rights afforded to any of those involved. The subsequent court case will be old news, with those involved already judged in unregulated public forums. The actual court results will hardly be noted except by the alleged suspects and victim, as the attention of tweeters, bloggers, and the public will have moved on to the next shiny and salacious topic.

In recent years, much has been written about cyberbullying of young people and tragedies that occurred as a result. However, in an article from the *Huffington Post* (www.huffingtonpost.com/larry-magid/cyberbullying_b_2162759.html) entitled "Researchers Dispel Myths About Cyber Bullying," technology journalist Larry Magid writes:

> A lot has been written about cyberbullying and I've seen some articles claiming that cyberbullying is more prevalent and more severe than in-person bullying. Some even refer to it as an "epidemic."
>
> But, in a presentation at the Family Online Safety Institute (FOSI) conference in Washington last week, a leading researcher on youth risk reported that the popular belief is actually a misconception. Compared to that bullying that takes place at school and other in-person venues, online bullying is both less prevalent and less distressing.

Magid brings us two key concepts to consider when thinking about media, cyberbullying, and anonymity; the first is from Michele Ybarra, President of the Center for Innovative Public Health, who states:

> . . . 17 percent of youth have reported online bullying compared to 39 percent who have experienced it "in person." Ten percent have been bullied by phone, according to Ybarra, while 14 percent have experienced bullying via text messaging.

Magid also brings forth another of Ybarra's key points, that is, the prevalent use of electronic communications among teens:

> For 12–17-year-olds, 95 percent are online, 77 percent have a cellphone, 23 percent have a smartphone, 63 percent text daily, and 76 percent use social media. Only 6 percent of teens use email on a daily basis.

Armed with that knowledge, Magid continues:

> Statistics from the U.S. Department of Health and Human Services also show that bullying—while still a significant problem—has not become more prevalent over the past few years. Bullying among high school students (Grades 9–12) remained flat (20 percent) between 2009 and 2011, with a slight decrease among boys and a slight increase for girls. The report found that in 2009, girls were twice as likely (22 percent vs. 11 percent) to be "electronically bullied" than boys.

Challenges remain. While most kids aren't bullied, a significant minority are, and the numbers are higher for lesbian, gay, bisexual, or transgender (LGBT) youth and those who are "perceived as different from their peers, such as being overweight or underweight, wearing glasses or different clothing, being new to a school, or being unable to afford what kids consider 'cool,'" according to the government Website StopBullying.gov.

70.1.4 Spam. Anonymity is fundamental to the abuse of the 'Net practiced by many spammers. Almost all spam contains forged headers in an attempt to escape retribution; in some cases the forgeries name real domains. One of the most significant early cases began in May 1997, when Craig Nowak, a college student, chose flowers.com at random as the fraudulent return address for his first attempt at junk email.[10] In so doing, he was merely following the suggestions of the unscrupulous purveyors of spam-distribution programs, who usually advise their naïve users to forge the headers of their junk email. Unfortunately for his victim, flowers.com is a legitimate business whose owner received 5,000 bounced messages and plenty of abuse for supposedly spamming the world. The enraged owner of flowers.com, Tracy LaQuey Parker, launched a lawsuit for damages and was supported by the Electronic Frontier Foundation (Austin chapter) and the Texas Internet Service Providers Association. In late September 1997, the plaintiffs won a temporary injunction against Nowak and his company, preventing him from further use of the appropriated domain name. In November 1997, Judge Suzanne Covington imposed a fine of over $18,000 on the defendants and added a particularly significant passage in her judgment that clearly enunciates the damages caused by forgery of return addresses:

> The Court additionally finds that the Plaintiffs have suffered, and will continue to suffer if [the defendant is] not enjoined, irreparable harm in the form of diminution in value of Plaintiffs' domain name; the possibility that Plaintiffs' reputation will be damaged forever by unauthorized use of a domain name associated with them in the controversial and hated practice of Internet spamming; and service disruptions. The potential harm to the Plaintiffs cannot be adequately valued in damages, and therefore the Plaintiffs have no adequate remedy at law. … The Court further finds that Plaintiffs … suffered actual damages from the unauthorized actions of the Defendants, including lost time, lost income, lost business opportunities, and lost use of their respective computer systems.[11]

In light of the seriousness of these abuses of inadequate identification in cyberspace, system managers and others concerned with the continued success of the Internet as an effective communications medium should consider the reasons for abusive behavior of anonymous individuals. Is such abuse an aberration particular to cyberspace, or are there precedents in history and in other areas of life that can provide insights to shape public and corporate policy toward identification in cyberspace?

See Chapter 20 in this *Handbook* for more details of spam.

70.1.5 Anonymous and WikiLeaks. Vigilante Internet groups (a good example of which is the loosely organized group Anonymous) use the shield of anonymity coupled with technical acumen and a propensity to use the world stage as a means of forwarding a particular political agenda or world view with little risk of legal prosecution. Anonymous has no central directorate or power structure; anyone can claim to be affiliated with this collective.

Even Anonymous members can be pushed too far—when colleagues stray from the path. From an article in the *Financial Times* entitled "Anonymous Withdraws Support for WikiLeaks," by Tim Bradshaw, we learn:

> WikiLeaks founder Julian Assange has lost another high-profile supporter as Anonymous, the hacking collective, said the whistleblowing site had been "ruined by egos."
>
> Anonymous, a loose group of internet "hacktivists," has been one of WikiLeaks' closest allies during the past two years, launching cyberattacks against the site's opponents and, some claim, becoming a source of its material.

The source of discontent according to Bradshaw is:

> "We have been worried about the direction WikiLeaks is going for a while," Anonymous wrote in an online statement published overnight on Friday. "In the recent month the focus moved away from actual leaks and the fight for freedom of information further and further while it concentrated more and more on Julian Assange ... But WikiLeaks is not—or should not be—about Julian Assange alone."
>
> The final straw for the shadowy group, which has also supported the Occupy Wall Street movement and the Arab Spring while at the same time attacking companies including Sony and News Corp, appears to have been Mr Assange's dinner this week with pop star Lady Gaga. ...
>
> "That's great for him but not much of our interest," Anonymous said. "We are more interested in transparent governments and bringing out documents and information they want to hide from the public."

So if we can extrapolate from the above, it appears that even those who employ tactics of anonymity, be they groups or Julian Assange prior to his discovery, have lines that should not be crossed. Once the line is crossed, justice will be meted out.

70.1.6 Chapter Plan. Understanding anonymity online and its intended and unintended consequences is a topic that should be understood by all Internet users and consumers of communications that either originate on the Internet, or traverse the Internet.

In a corporate world, a CISO, CSO, and Human Resources departments should form a partnership to educate their constituency into becoming intelligent and savvy consumers of information, as their organizations will benefit greatly from critical thinking. The ability to understand, analyze, and discuss issues related to anonymity in an accountable society should be part of every citizen's tool kit.

This chapter reviews some of the findings of social psychology that show how and why anonymity has generally been associated with anti-social behavior. In the political sphere, anonymity can be used to forward extremist agendas without accountability to fan the flames of hate or distrust based on falsehoods. It appears that anonymity on the 'Net will inevitably continue to spawn antisocial behavior in cyberspace and that we must somehow integrate this kind of abuse into plans for the further development of the Internet.

This chapter also touches on some positive uses of anonymity such as the use of anonymity in communications from inside repressive regimes to expose atrocities to the world. Additionally, some practical suggestions on how different degrees of tolerance for anonymity can be integrated into a cyberspace polity are discussed.

70.2 DEFINITIONS.

To explore anonymity in cyberspace, it is helpful to establish some common vocabulary. What is cyberspace? What are identity and its absence? What is pseudonymity?

70.2.1 Cyberspace.

In this chapter, *cyberspace* means the totality of electronic data storage and transmission; this chapter focuses on communications using the Internet. On the Internet, there are users of specific domains defined in the Domain Naming System (DNS), such as companies (those using addresses ending in *.com*); universities and other educational institutions (*.edu* addresses); U.S. Government agencies and departments (*.gov*); the U.S. military (*.mil*); and network service providers (*.net*); among others.[12] There are many geographical domain names, such as those ending in *.de* (Germany) or *.uk* (United Kingdom), which include users from commercial, educational, government, and military organizations. In addition, there are many Internet Service Providers (ISPs) in the *.net* and *.com* domains in the United States, and others throughout the world in geographical domains, whose members communicate through the Internet. Customers of value-added networks (VANs) such as America Online (AOL), MSN, Comcast, Cox Communications, Time Warner Cable, and a host of others communicate through the Internet as well as having restricted areas within their VANs where only members can post messages and files. Additionally, social media sites like Facebook, MySpace, LinkedIn, Google+, and Live.com can be manipulated to allow users of the service to post with real or imaginary names and as well to limit (or not) their audiences. All Internet users can post messages in public discussion lists on the Usenet or through remailing lists, which broadcast all inbound email to participants. Henceforth, for convenience, *the Internet* or *the 'Net* will include any of these users. Users of direct-dial bulletin board systems and modem-to-modem direct links are explicitly excluded from this discussion. For more details of data communications, see Chapter 5 in this *Handbook*.

70.2.2 The Real World.

As used here, *the real world* (sometimes referred to as *meatspace*) refers to the material world of everyday human interactions. Using *real world* in this way is not intended to imply that cyberspace is less significant, less useful, or even less real; it is merely a convenient reference to distinguish the physical from the electronic.

70.2.3 Identity in the Real World.

The key meanings of the noun *identity* for our purposes are:

- The collective aspect of the set of characteristics by which a thing is definitively recognizable or known

- The set of behavioral or personal characteristics by which an individual is recognizable as a member of a group
- The distinct personality of an individual regarded as a persisting entity; individuality

Roger Clarke summarizes the importance of personal identification in this way: The purposes of the interchange of identification include:

- to provide a gesture of goodwill,
- to develop mutual confidence, and
- to reduce the scope for dishonesty;
- to enable either person to initiate the next round of communications; and
- to enable either person to associate transactions and information with the other person.[13]

In line with these points, apparently ancient knights would tip their visor up for two reasons: for recognition as friend or foe, and out of respect for those being met.

70.2.4 Anonymity and Pseudonymity in the Real World. *Anonymity* can be defined simply as being without a name or with an unknown name. Someone who never uses the same unique identifier twice is anonymous. Notes left without any name are anonymous. Someone using a standard or canonical identifier ("student," "member," "guest," and so on) is also anonymous.

Pseudonymity is the *consistent* use of a false name that is not linked to personal details. When a musician chose to perform exclusively using the name *Sting*, it could have been an example of pseudonymity if the singer had concealed his usual name; however, in fact, Gordon Matthew Thomas Sumner never concealed his usual identifier.

These terms are imbued in English with negative connotations; nonetheless, anonymity has an honorable history in world philosophy and politics. In the United States, for example, the seminal *Federalist Papers*, which appeared in 1787 under the pen name "Publius," is held up as an outstanding example of anonymous contribution to political thought.[14]

Anonymity is protected in some government-sponsored monitoring programs, such as those supported by the Occupational Safety and Health Administration (OSHA) of the U.S. Department of Labor, where regulations stipulate for example that "Completed NETS Cards [hazard reports] can be given to a department manager or deposited, anonymously, into one of the drop boxes located throughout the facility."[15]

Clarke explores the concepts and history of human identity in a section of his paper on management and policy issues relating to human identification. Individuality has been a central concept in Western civilization since the Renaissance, says Clarke.[16] However, individuals can adopt more than one identity; for example, some women use their husband's surname in private life but maintain their original family name in their professions. Some people have several identities; for example, novelists with different styles sometimes use various pen names. The Danish philosopher Søren Kierkegaard wrote under 16 pseudonyms; Charles Dodgson wrote as Lewis Carroll; Eric Blair wrote as George Orwell. As the work of these writers illustrates, anonymity and pseudonymity are not inherently linked to anti-social behavior.

David G. Post wrote in a 1995 article,

> Should the government—can the government—control anonymity in cyberspace? Anonymity is pervasive in the "real world," to be sure; most of the encounters we have each day—on the bus, in the coffee shop, while shopping, etc.—are probably anonymous ones. But anonymity has perhaps never been quite so easy to achieve, and we have probably never been able to undertake so wide a range of anonymous transactions, as in cyberspace. For example, there are a number of "anonymous remailer" services now available on the Internet, computer systems where one can send an electronic mail message (addressed, say, to a friend across the country, to a list of individual addressees, or to an electronic bulletin board for public posting) in order to have the information identifying the computer from which the message was sent entirely stripped off and destroyed; the message, when it arrives at its destination, only contains information regarding the remailer from which it was sent, not the originator of the message. ...
>
> And anonymity is not without its costs. Most obviously, a truly anonymous regime makes it impossible for "law enforcement"—broadly defined to include both public and private enforcement of legal rules—to obtain information about the persons responsible for harmful behavior so as to punish wrongdoers or compensate the victims of that harm. Indeed, the wider availability of anonymous message capabilities may actually increase the amount of harmful activity; if, as the economists might say, individuals need not "internalize" the costs of the harm imposed on others by their actions because they will not be called to account, we might expect more such behavior to emerge.
>
> But there are benefits—possibly profound benefits—as well. There are, of course, perfectly legitimate, indeed laudable, reasons why individuals might want to engage in communicative activity without putting any aspects of their identity at risk; think, for instance, of a discussion group among HIV-positive individuals, or battered spouses. And think, in the example most likely to prove persuasive when this question arises in the constitutional context, of the Federalist Papers, arguably the greatest single work of political theory in history that may well never have seen the light of day had its authors had to reveal their true identities.[17]

70.3 SOCIAL PSYCHOLOGY OF ANONYMITY.

The popular mythology of the "Wild West" assumes that when large numbers of people migrated into western territories of the United States in the nineteenth century, they settled into new communities where few or no people knew about their neighbors' background. The anonymous or pseudonymous stranger is a staple of fiction; the assumption is that the lack of social ties increased the occurrence of lawlessness.

Technological change can have profound consequences on social behavior. For example, the development of mass-produced automobiles made possible the development of suburban shopping malls in the United States, which in turn led to an adolescent mall culture unimaginable in the 1920s.[18]

It seems quite likely that the pervasive spread of the Internet and the nature of anonymous and pseudonymous interactions is having equally profound effects on social organization and interactions.

The sections that follow review some well-established information on anonymity and social behavior from the social psychology literature. The implications of these principles for individuals, corporate policy makers, ISPs, and governments are discussed in the final section.

70.3.1 Deindividuation Theory.

What do scientists know about the behavior of anonymous people? In general, the findings are not encouraging for the future of cyberspace unless we can somehow avoid the known association of antisocial behavior and anonymity. Early work on people in groups focused on anonymity as a root of the perceived frequency of antisocial behavior.[19] The anonymous members of a crowd show reduced inhibition of antisocial and reckless, impulsive behavior. They are subject to increased irritability and suggestibility. One wonders if the well-known incidence of flaming (rude and largely *ad hominem* communications through email and postings on the Usenet and other public areas) may be traceable to the same factors that influence crowd behavior.

Later social psychologists formulated a theory of deindividuation[20] in which they proposed that one's personal sense of identity can be overwhelmed by the sense of belonging to a group.

Zimbardo suggested that anonymity, diffusion of responsibility, and arousal contributed to deindividuation and anti-sociality.[21] He noted that deindividuated people display reduced inhibitions, reduced reliance on internal standards that normally qualify their behavior, and little self-awareness.

70.3.1.1 Deindividuation and Technology. As mentioned briefly earlier, there is some reason to suppose that technology can contribute to the deindividuation of its users.

Anonymity has been postulated to account in part for the strong contrast between normal behavior and the behavior of those who become aggressive and hostile when driving cars. It seems intuitively plausible that being isolated in a tight personal space, a cocoon of glass and metal, gives some drivers a feeling of power precisely because of their (possibly temporary) anonymity. In addition, the anonymity of the other drivers may lead to a kind of dehumanization of the other. It would be interesting to study how many angry drivers refer to "that car" instead of "that driver" when they rail against some random act of road rudeness. Similarly, the isolation of an Internet user also may contribute to aggressivity; the object of wrath may, much like the driver of another car, be dehumanized.[22]

Sometimes it seems that email flamers are engaged in their version of a video game; they give the impression of losing sight of the real human beings on the other end of their verbal aggression.

Writers of computer viruses and others in the criminal computer underground may also focus so intensely on the challenge of defeating machines that they lose sight of their human victims. A commonplace informal interpretation of the insouciance of hackers and virus writers is that they are subject to the *video-game syndrome*: They seem to focus on their actions as if they were part of a game with only computers on the receiving end.

Criminal hackers have also expressed themselves as attacking systems, not people. At criminal-hacker conferences, it is commonplace to hear comments such as "Oh, I would never steal anything from a person, but if I found a radio in an office and it were labeled with a company sticker I wouldn't think twice about taking it."

Chapter 12 of this *Handbook* provides more detail on deindividuation theory.

70.3.1.2 Containment Theory. Walter Reckless[23,24] wrote about containment theory in a book entitled *The Crime Problem*. The theory addresses why people do not succumb to the pressure to commit crimes.[25,26] The theory includes external and internal containments that influence a person when making the decision to commit or not commit a crime.[27,28,29,30,31]

> External containments are external controls that "includes parental and school supervision and discipline, strong group cohesion, and a consistent moral front,"[32] "power of groups to make sure members comply with expected behavior,"[33] "external limits placed on children,"[34] or "forces that provide discipline and supervision including parents, police, schools, and the criminal justice system,"[35]

> Internal containments are a result of such things "as a positive self-concept, having a sense of direction in life, ability to tolerate frustration, and investment in and retention of group norms,"[36] "self-esteem, a strong sense of responsibility, internalized moral codes, tolerance of frustration, and positive goal orientations,"[37] or as simply "a strong conscience or a 'good self-concept,' "[38]

The inner containments are more important than external containments in determining whether a person commits a crime.[39] According to Taylor and colleagues,[40] containment theory consists of four processes: (1) "inner pushes and pulls lead an individual toward committing crime," (2) "inner containments inhibit criminal behavior ... internal personal controls that lead someone to not commit criminal acts," (3) "outer pressures and pulls which lead to criminal behavior," and (4) "outer containments inhibit criminal behavior."

Deviant actions that are contemplated but not attempted in the physical realm may actually be more readily attempted in cyberspace. This assumption is exemplified by a person who would like to rob but is not right for the job; for example, a five-foot-tall 98-pound person who is afraid of guns would not attempt to rob a six-foot 200-pound bodybuilder carrying a handgun. But whatever motivates this 98-pound person could be executed via the digital world of computer crime, because the 98-pound person would not have to face his/her victim and the accompanying physical risk at the crime site. Another way to view this increased execution of the crime is that the criminal actor achieves physical distance, possibly thousands of miles from the victim, and perceives an anonymity enabled by the use of a computer. In reality, computers do not provide anonymity; computers and the network infrastructure keeps many details which can betray the criminal actor. It is the perception of anonymity that facilitates the actions.

70.3.1.3 General Crime Theory. General crime theory also provides some insight into the effect of anonymity and computer usage. General crime theory is an extension of Hirschi's social bonding with some elements of rational choice theory.[41,42] Social bonding theory suggests that social control is due to people avoiding crime because it will damage their relationship with family and friends.[43] Social bonds are what prevent people from committing crimes and consist of four elements: attachment, commitment, involvement, and belief.[44,45,46]

When people interact primarily through pseudonyms or completely anonymously, their attachments may be limited, their commitments may be limited, their involvement in social structures may be weakened, and their belief in immunity to the consequences of their actions may facilitate anti-social behavior.

70.3.1.4 Social Learning Theory. Social learning had its start when Burgess and Akers[47] combined Sutherland's differential association theory with operant and respondent conditioning.[48,49,50,51,52] Akers[53] modified what Burgess and he had done by replacing operant conditioning with the social learning of Bandura.[54,55,56] Akers[57] states that social learning theory also incorporates neutralization theory; the neutralization techniques are used to create definitions favorable to deviant behavior.

Sutherland's differential association theory consisted of nine propositions premised on the belief that deviant behavior action is learned from the individuals one associates with; not the inability to obtain economic success.[58,59,60,61,62,63] The nine propositions are based on three interrelated concepts of normative conflict, differential association, and differential social organization.[64] Differential association addresses normative or cultural conflict and how this conflict influences whether or not an individual commits a crime or deviant behavior.[65,66,67]

A crime/deviant action is committed when the definitions favorable to crime/deviant behavior outweigh the definitions unfavorable to crime/deviant behavior.[68,69,70,71,72,73] Matsueda[74] emphasizes that "not all definitions receive equal weight … rather, each is weighted by four modalities: frequency, duration, priority, and intensity." Definitions are dependent on larger societal context and are thus the definitions are subject to change over time.[75]

70.3.1.5 Anonymity and Aggression. Sometimes, anonymous people go beyond verbal abuse and seem willing to inflict harm on others. Experimental work by Zimbardo suggested that anonymity can significantly decrease barriers to aggression.[76] For example, when women were asked to deliver electric shocks to victims, those who agreed to wear white lab coats and hoods administered what they thought were longer shocks to the supposed victims compared with women who wore their own clothes and nametags.

In a cross-cultural study, Watson analyzed the correlations between the ritual, anonymizing costumes and war paint of warriors and their style of battle and their postbattle treatment of prisoners.[77] He found a strong positive relationship between anonymity and brutality.

Violent soccer fans seem to be disinhibited in part because of the anonymity of the crowd.[78] In an undercover investigation, a journalist found that anonymity and pseudonymity are integral components of the anti-social behavior of soccer hooligans.[79]

These findings suggest that so-called dark-side hackers may be influenced significantly in their willingness to cause damage to computer systems and networks precisely because their very anonymity influences them to cross normal behavioral boundaries. These people may not be the permanently, irremediably damaged human beings they sometimes seem; they may, instead, be relatively normal people responding in predictable ways to the absence of stable identification and identity.

70.3.1.6 Anonymity and Dishonesty. Does anonymity increase the likelihood that people will transgress rules and laws? Apparently, yes.

In an experiment involving children, young trick-or-treaters were asked to take only one candy from a bowl and then left alone or in groups, supposedly unobserved. Those children who had given their names to adults were observed to be far less likely to take extra candy or to steal coins than those who had remained anonymous, even when the adults were apparently away.[80] (If these effects of anonymity on youngsters are consistent and widespread, they may contribute to the problems of system administrators who are under siege by underage hackers.)

70.3.1.7 Deindividuation and Self-Awareness. Why does anonymity change people's normal inhibitions and influence them to behave abnormally? It seems that the deindividuation of anonymous people lowers their self-reflective propensities.

Exploration of the inner world of deindividuated people suggests that they are less aware of themselves and may even enter a state of altered consciousness.[81] Prentice-Dunn and Rogers studied the behavior of college men who, as in the work of Zimbardo cited earlier, were asked to administer what they thought were electric shocks to confederates of the experimenters who were masquerading as victims.

- Some subjects were subjected to dim lighting and loud background noise; their names were not used; and they were told that the levels of the shocks they gave would not be recorded. These subjects were thought to be deindividuated.

- Other subjects experienced bright lights in quiet rooms; they were called by name; and they were told that the shock levels they delivered would be monitored.
- The deindividuated subjects administered more severe shocks to their victims than did the individuated students.

These observations may tie into the work on autotelic experiences.[82] Autotelic experiences are deeply satisfying activities that result in a temporary loss of self-awareness; they typically occur in repetitive, challenging, feedback-rich activities such as programming (or perhaps virus writing) and criminal computer hacking. Csikszentmihalyi studied people in a variety of work environments and in their home life and hobbies. The subjects reported on their attainment of a state of timelessness, where the passage of time was insensible. Many who have programmed know how easy it is to forget to eat or to go home when deeply involved in work; similarly, writers and musicians can lose track of time. The research suggested that some of the key attributes of an activity that leads to this autotelic experience are rapidity of feedback (e.g., seeing an article grow as one writes or running an increasingly complex program under development) and being at the limits of one's abilities. In contrast, challenges that are too easy or too hard tend not to result in the loss of self-awareness that defines the autotelic state.

Several recent popular books dealing with criminal hackers have mentioned the ability of legendary hackers to stick to their hacking for hours on end as if they were entranced. Combine the autotelic nature of hacking with the deindividuation associated with anonymity, and we have a prescription for trouble.

70.3.1.8 Triple A Engine. Triple A engine refers to access, affordability, and anonymity of computing. Cooper used the Triple A Engine in examining online sexual activities (OSA) at the workplace; 20 percent of 40,000 adults he surveyed enaged in OSA (any activity involving sexuality). Cooper wrote that there are three different profiles of people who engage in OSA (bullets added):

- The first and most common is the Recreational User, who engages in OSA in a nonproblematic manner.
- The second type, the Sexually Compulsive User, refers to those individuals who have an established pattern of unconventional and maladaptive sexual practices. When faced with the Triple A Engine, these individuals often transfer the locus of their pre-existing problems to Internet-based activities. These online activities may in turn reinforce and exacerbate the problematic behaviors.
- Finally, the third profile was labeled the At-Risk User. These individuals have no prior history of sexual compulsivity, but they too often find their better judgment, coping strategies, and impulse control are overwhelmed by the power of the Triple A Engine. Research has revealed that some employees continue to access forbidden sites and sexually explicit material, in defiance of workplace policies.[83]

70.3.1.9 Anonymity and Prosocial Behavior. The picture is not necessarily all bad, however. Sometimes a different environment actually can liberate anonymous subjects from their counterproductive inhibitions. For example, in some cases, it can be shown that anonymity has an unusual effect: It increases prosocial behavior instead of increasing anti-social behavior.[84] Gergen, Gergen, and Barton put people into brightly lit chambers or in totally dark chambers and monitored the behavior of the strangers they had put together; in the dark room, there was much more uninhibited and positive expression of physical contact such as hugs and of emotional openness such as discussions of personal matters.[85] However, directionality of these effects may be affected by the demand characteristics of the situation. That is, the way the experimental objectives were described could cause significant differences in the subjects' behavior.

The constructive, supportive communications often seen in discussion groups dealing with substance abuse, abusive relationships, and other personal and interpersonal problems illustrate the possible benefits of anonymity in a positive context.

70.3.2 Identity in Cyberspace. What exactly is meant by *identity* when using electronic communications? Is one's email address an identity? Could a made-up name be an identity?

Identity on the Internet is primarily the email address.[86] The email address sometimes provides crude and unreliable information about affiliation (e.g., domain names *.gov, .mil, .edu*) and geographic location (e.g., *.ca, .uk, .fr*).[87] Roger Clarke, a scholar with a long professional interest in questions of identity, identification, and privacy in cyberspace, has written an excellent introduction to these questions.[88] For discussions of information technology, Clarke defines *identification* as "the association of data with a particular human being."[89]

Identity now must also include Facebook, LinkedIn, MySpace, Google+, Live.com, sites such as Match.com, and any other host of Internet sites where identities real or imagined can exist. There are some identities in cyberspace where falsification and deception are actually part of the titillation of the business. Such a site is Ashley-Madison.com, where married individuals can register an identity of choice in order to arrange for an affair with another married person who too shares a desire for an extramarital affair.

Identities in other matchmaking sites, such as Match.com and eHarmony, are prone to falsification. In an article ("Online Dating Scams: Buyers Beware") from the *Huffington Post*, originally posted on February 14, 2012, and updated on May 15, 2012, author Ann Brenoffann writes:

> Online dating services are booming businesses, and the boomers who are joining them are doing so in big numbers. People aged 50 and older represent 25 percent of membership on the popular dating site Match.com—a 45 percent jump in the last five years, a spokesman said.
>
> But not everyone who hopes to find a mate online is falling blissfully in love. There have been a rash of complaints against online dating sites, according to the Better Business Bureau. And there is a class action lawsuit pending in the U.S. District Court that claims more than 60 percent of the profiles on Match.com are fraudulent—something Match.com spokesman Matthew Traub calls an "unfounded allegation in a money-seeking litigation."

Brennoffann continues:

> Then there is another, perhaps darker, side to the consumer complaints: People reporting that they were bilked out of money by those they connected with through an online dating site. The Better Business Bureau listed online dating sites among its top 10 scams for 2011, and one consumer advocacy group says its members have lost millions from online dating scams.... There is no attempt to verify the information someone posts—something the sites are generally upfront about.

Buyers beware indeed.

70.3.2.1 Theory of Nymity. There has been considerable discussion on the 'Net about the kinds of identity (sometimes called *nymity* in these discussions) that people assume in cyberspace. One of the best-known writers on this subject was "L. Detweiler," apparently a pseudonym that has never been traced to any other identifier. Detweiler suggested that identity on the Internet is amorphous and unstable because there is no one-to-one relationship between a person and an email address. One person may use multiple email addresses, and many people may share a single address.[90]

Detweiler conducted a vigorous battle against what he perceived as a sinister and deceptive practice he called *pseudospoofing*. Pseudospoofing, in Detweiler's conception, is the use of multiple aliases by an individual or a conspiracy; these aliases allow the perpetrators to deceive observers into misjudging the number of people agreeing or disagreeing over specific positions.[91] Current examples of such a system are online travel, services, and restaurant sites. Sites such as Trip Advisor, Yelp, Chowhound, and the like must be vigilant that owners of questionable businesses do not flood the review site with favorable reviews using a multitude of false personas. Such abusive pseudonyms are currently known as *sock puppets* and can be used as elements of dishonest *online reputation management*. Other abuses of pseudonymity include:

> Astroturfing (named after the synthetic grass, "AstroTurf") is the act of creating fake grassroots organizations to endorse a client or a client's point of view or criticize a political position or a competitor under the guise of pseudo-authenticity. Typically, these organizations are staffed with people directly involved with the company or industry they're promoting. In a notorious case of astroturfing, a public relations firm was hired by a coal company to lobby against a bill in the U.S. Congress that would have regulated coal-industry activities. They forged letters—including forged logos—claiming to be from various social-activism groups and were eventually discovered.
>
> Sock puppetry is the practice of pretending to be someone else and using the same techniques as astroturfing, the difference being the scale (sock puppetry is mainly done with individual reviews). For a hilarious send-up of sock puppetry, see the article in "Uncyclopedia, the content-free encyclopedia." Just don't take any of the content seriously.
>
> Flogging is, in current marketing parlance, a portmanteau term made up from the two words "fake" and "blogging," and refers to the practice of companies employing fake bloggers to write glowing reviews of certain products.[92]

A current illustration of the problems of pseudospoofing is the widespread difficulty experienced in online voting. The ease with which identity can be created, coupled with the ease of automatically scripting multiple votes, leads to unreliable tallies in almost all online polls. The only way to avoid such abuses is to enforce some tight coupling of real-world identity with the electronic identity registered for voting. Eventually, biometric identification may be the only acceptable form of authentication for voting online.[93]

70.3.2.2 Types of Anonymity and Pseudonymity. To understand the problem of anonymity and pseudonymity, it is useful to define varying degrees of the behavior. Froomkin distinguishes among four forms of imprecise or absent identification:

1. **Traceable anonymity.** Any anonymous remailer that keeps a record of the relation between the original message and the anonymized message allows tracing.
2. **Untraceable anonymity.** No record is kept or available showing the origin of an anonymized message.

3. **Untraceable pseudonymity.** A continuous identity or persona allows communication with a correspondent, but there is no way to link the pseudonym to the correspondent's real-world identity.
4. **Traceable pseudonymity.** Someone, somewhere has the information required to complete the link between a pseudonym and a real-world identity.[94]

The anonymizing remailer *anon.penet.fi* was actually a *traceable pseudonym remailer*. When a message was received by the server, its headers were stripped and it was assigned a fixed random pseudonym. In order to allow replies to the pseudonym to be forwarded to the original sender, every pseudonymous identity was linked in a table to the original email address. When Finnish police ordered Johan Helsingius in 1995 to identify the pseudonymous poster of copyrighted Scientology texts on the Usenet, Helsingius felt obliged to reveal the link.[95] Traceable online anonymity allows people to maintain their privacy by using screen identities, but many ISPs will furnish the real-world identity to law enforcement officials with a warrant or to tort lawyers with a subpoena. AOL, for example, furnished subscriber details to the lawyers for a Caribbean resort considering a lawsuit for defamation based on postings by "Jenny TRR."[96] All ISPs that charge money for access inherently provide traceable pseudonymity even when they permit false screen names.

Larry Lessig, David Post, and Eugene Volokh also distinguish between anonymity, pseudonymity, and traceability in their Internet course on cyberspace law.[97] They emphasize that private organizations, such as Internet service providers, can freely set terms of service that allow or forbid anonymity, but they may be required in the United States to provide traceability if the courts require it for individuals.[98] In general, it is difficult to see how the rule of law can apply to cyberspace without some form of traceability. Whether civil law or the criminal law is involved, the defendant must be found for court proceedings to have any effect. Untraceable anonymity and untraceable pseudonymity preclude justice for the aggrieved parties. Clarke points out that privacy interests are always to be balanced with other interests, such as the public good, commercial interests, and the interests of other individuals.[99] For example, the desire to post anonymous libel (construed as privacy of personal behavior) conflicts with the desire of the victim to be free from libel; anonymity makes it impossible to use the civil law for redress.

70.3.2.3 Why Anonymity and Pseudonymity Are Commonplace in Cyberspace. Surely anonymity and pseudonymity are possible using older means of communication: People have thrown rocks through windows, sent anonymous vituperation through postal mail, and harassed people with anonymous phone calls for millennia, centuries, and decades, respectively. Historically, such behavior has been of relatively minor importance. How is it that anonymity and pseudonymity seem so important in cyberspace?

One factor is the ease with which one can be untraceably anonymous in cyberspace. Many ISPs allow users to define screen names or aliases; some ISPs, such as AOL, distributed millions of trial subscription disks that allowed one to create an identity and then dispose of it after 50 hours online. Spammers often use disposable free accounts from such services as Hotmail, even defeating methods designed to stop them from abusing the services.[100]

Some moderated Usenet groups and email-based mailing lists require a real name, but there is little effort or even possibility, as things currently stand, for authentication of such names. Unmoderated groups, by definition, do not require real names at all; such groups allow postings by anyone. Almost all contributions to countercultural or frankly criminal Usenet groups and distribution lists are anonymous or at best pseudonymous.

In addition, some people systematically forge the headers of their email, often introducing completely false addresses for their origin but occasionally picking real addresses, whether by accident or design, as discussed earlier in the flowers.com case (Section 70.1.4).[101] Forging email headers can conceal the true origin of a message.[102] Junk email almost always includes false return addresses. Another way to generate false header information is to compromise someone's email account. If security on an email address is compromised, messages can be forged with a false ID. From a mobile media perspective, readily available software and services that allow phone and text spammers to alter the sending phone number displayed on mobile phones to one of a reputable or nonspam-associated telephone number are alive and well today—and harnessing the power of the cloud.

Anonymous remailers permit users to send email to a central address where all identifying information is stripped, and the original text is then retransmitted to the desired destination. In the wake of the tragic events of September 11, 2001, when terrorists killed thousands of people in attacks on the World Trade Center in New York City and on the Pentagon in Washington, D.C., commentators expressed doubts about the future of anonymizing services. "Using anonymizers at all raises all sorts of red flags," said John Young, operator of the Cryptome Website (www.cryptome.org), which covers intelligence matters. Even before the terrorist attacks, the well-respected Freedom Network operated by Zero-Knowledge Systems had experienced financial difficulties; that service shut down on October 22, 2001.[103]

In 2007, Dan Egerstad posted the user names and passwords for 100 email accounts of foreign embassies and human rights groups that used The Onion Router (Tor) network:

> Under Tor's architecture, administrators at the entry point can identify the user's IP address, but can't read the content of the user's correspondence or know its final destination. Each node in the network thereafter only knows the node from which it received the traffic, and it peels off a layer of encryption to reveal the next node to which it must forward the connection. (Tor stands for "The Onion Router.")
>
> But Tor has a known weakness: The last node through which traffic passes in the network has to decrypt the communication before delivering it to its final destination. Someone operating that node can see the communication passing through this server.[104]

The other factor that makes anonymity and pseudonymity especially significant in cyberspace is the ease of replication of messages. An anonymous communicator could hope to reach at best a few dozen or hundred people in a day with the phone system or by mail; in most areas, each phone call or letter would cost something to send. In contrast, spammers using botnets and those with large following on sites such as Twitter can reach countless people in seconds with very little effort and no cost at all.

70.4 BALANCING RIGHTS AND DUTIES.

Is there a basis for evaluating the ethics of using anonymous and pseudonymous communications? Are these modes of communications protected by principles of privacy, for example?

70.4.1 Benefits of Anonymity and Pseudonymity.

Historically, anonymity has been recognized as a benefit for acts of charity for those wishing to remain nameless for political, social, or personal reasons. Maimonides, the great twelfth-century rabbi, defined anonymous giving to anonymous recipients as the second-highest level of charity.[105]

In discussions of whether society ought to restrict anonymity and pseudonymity, a common argument is that these modes of communication are necessary to fight tyrannical corporate and political institutions. Anonymity and pseudonymity are, in this view, expressions of the right to privacy. Electronic Frontier Foundation has filed First Amendment friend-of-the-court briefs in support of anonymous speech in which even the plaintiff later stated that "anonymous speech is worth protecting."[106] Abuses are the price society has to pay to preserve the benefits of these tools of expression. The next sections examine the concepts of privacy and the resulting benefits of anonymity and pseudonymity.

70.4.2 Privacy in Cyberspace. If privacy rights are claimed to protect anonymous and pseudonymous communications, it is important to understand the concepts of privacy.

Clarke defines privacy as "the interest that individuals have in sustaining a 'personal space,' free from interference by other people and organizations." He analyses the concept further, naming four dimensions of privacy:

1. **Privacy of the person.** Freedom from compulsory tampering with one's body
2. **Privacy of personal behavior.** Freedom in such matters as sexual preferences, religion, and politics
3. **Privacy of personal communications.** Freedom from routine monitoring of interpersonal communications
4. **Privacy of personal data.** Control over who can obtain and what can be done with personal information[107]

Political discussion groups, resistance to totalitarian regimes, and discussions of socially embarrassing or traumatic problems are made easier for many people by the use of pseudonyms or of anonymity. Anonymity permits unrestricted political speech, whistleblowing with reduced likelihood of retaliation, and public or private discussions of potentially embarrassing personal problems.[108] Ubois writes:

> Anonymous communications are helpful in many ways. They've long been a tool of suicide prevention hotlines, suggestion boxes, and personal ads. Anonymity assures privacy, confidentiality, and security for individuals, but it also highlights the clash of interests between the individual and the community. Under a repressive government, it is a vital tool for keeping discourse alive. Just consider that Tom Paine would have landed in prison shortly after the publication of Common Sense if his identity hadn't been kept a secret.[109]

In chat rooms and multiuser dungeons, anonymity permits a flowering of imaginative departures from the strictures of a participant's real-world identity, social status, personality, gender and gender preferences, political affiliation, national origin, and religion. Multimedia environments such as WorldsAway (http://secondlife.com/) provide an imaginative pseudonymity by allowing players to select a name and a pictorial representation of themselves (an avatar) with amusing and fanciful features, such as various imaginary animal heads, skin colors, body shapes, and so on. Players adopt personae that can be quite different from their real-world identities, yet there is a consistent identity within the virtual world. Because of this consistency, social mechanisms have arisen in these worlds; for example, avatars can be invited to join parties if they are perceived as friendly or excluded and shunned if they have violated the norms of the imaginary world.

Anonymous, invisible electronic personalities can escape some of the damaging effects of intolerance and prejudice.[110] Everyone probably knows of Peter Steiner's famous *New Yorker* cartoon showing two dogs at a terminal, one of whom is saying "On the Internet nobody knows you're a dog."[111] Another current example is the country music video "Online" by Brad Paisley in which he sings "I'm much cooler online," and boasts about completely illusory qualities.[112]

For example, some professors may spend more time and effort in discussions with undergraduate students if they do not realize with whom they are corresponding.[113] At an intellectual level, stripping the authors of published materials of all details of their age, sex, race, national origin, and other attributes can reduce the effects of prejudice and focus discussion on substance. Absent such details, correspondents must perforce focus on the texts rather than on personalities.[114]

In electronic commerce, anonymity is a prerequisite for successful implementation of some trading systems.[115] All electronic or digital cash schemes (e-cash) emphasize the value of anonymous transactions for safeguarding consumer privacy.

In a legal sense, anonymity and pseudonymity are analogous to limited liability—a concept familiar from the business world. In business, people pool their assets into a limited liability partnership or other form of collectivity to prevent seizure of all their private assets if their collective entity becomes liable for debts or penalties.[116] Perhaps cyberspace anonymity and pseudonymity can encourage collective publications in an analogous way; for example, Post and others have formed the Cyberspace Law Institute. Some members would be reluctant to participate if their real-world identities were known to the public.

Thus, anonymity and pseudonymity cannot reasonably be forbidden without the loss of important benefits to individuals, corporations, and society at large.

70.4.3 Privacy and Freedom in Virtual Worlds. With the increasing growth of global access to the Internet, millions of people have joined virtual communities or *virtual worlds* where they can interact anonymously or pseudonymously. The freedom from discrimination based on physical, cultural, gender, and sociological attributes has proven liberating for many members of these virtual worlds; many participants have formed strong friendships that may even extend into the real world.[117] On the other hand, some critics argue that the avatars supplied by the owners of these virtual worlds reinforce conventional gender stereotypes.[118]

70.4.4 Defeating Dataveillance. Another area where anonymity and pseudonymity have marked benefits is in preventing intrusive monitoring of individual behavior in cyberspace. Clarke has defined dataveillance as surveillance using electronically compiled information about a person.[119]

The growth of some kinds of electronic commerce has increased pressures for strong identification and authentication[120]; anonymity serves to protect privacy in a world of electronic commerce. For example, without anonymous digital cash, it would be easy to accumulate detailed records of every electronic purchase made by an individual. Complete knowledge of purchasers' interests can be unfair for customers; for example, knowing that a user is addicted to fantasy simulation games, a retailer may neglect to offer that person a discount—or may even increase the price of the next game.[121]

Froomkin summarizes the issues well in his magisterial review of the challenges of anonymity in cyberspace:

> Anonymity lies at the heart of three interrelated problems arising from computer-aided communications over distributed networks (which I will call "the Internet" for short). First, communicative anonymity is an issue in itself: the Internet makes anonymous communication easy, and this has both good and bad consequences. …
>
> Second, the availability of anonymous electronic communication directly affects the ability of governments to regulate electronic transactions over the Internet (both licit and illicit).
>
> Third, anonymity may be the primary tool available to citizens to combat the compilation and analysis of personal profile data, although data protection laws also may have some effect. The existence of profiling databases, whether in corporate or public hands, may severely constrict the economic and possibly even the political freedoms of the persons profiled; although profiling may not necessarily change the amount of actual data in existence about a person, organizing the data into easily searchable form reduces her effective privacy by permitting "data mining" and correlations that were previously impossible.[122]

Froomkin discusses digital cash as an application of electronic anonymity and emphasizes the potential for abuse by "the Argus State" if anonymity is not guaranteed for readers. For example, he points out, in the absence of anonymous digital cash, reading texts on the Internet using micropayments for each access could provide a traceable record of a person's interests. Such records would be a gold mine for repressive regimes worldwide.

In June 2013, as this chapter was going to press, interest and debate were generated by the disclosure that the U.S. National Security Agency (NSA) had been using massive data capture under secret warrants issued by the Foreign Intelligence Surveillance Court to gather metadata about phone calls by hundreds of millions of American citizens. Decrying the abuse of the USA PATRIOT Act[123] to carry out dataveillance of such activities, the American Civil Liberties Union (ACLU) filed a lawsuit shortly after the revelations were published.[124]

These revelations suggested that anonymizing services that conceal all Internet activity, such as The Onion Router (Tor), would see an upsurge in use. The Tor Project describes its functions as follows:

> Tor is free software and an open network that helps you defend against a form of network surveillance that threatens personal freedom and privacy, confidential business activities and relationships, and state security known as traffic analysis.
>
> Tor protects you by bouncing your communications around a distributed network of relays run by volunteers all around the world: it prevents somebody watching your Internet connection from learning what sites you visit, and it prevents the sites you visit from learning your physical location. Tor works with many of your existing applications, including web browsers, instant messaging clients, remote login, and other applications based on the TCP protocol.[125]

Again, trying to ban anonymity and pseudonymity would have serious disadvantages for everyone, not just the benefits of impeding abuse by a minority of anti-social users.

Finally, police forces and intelligence agencies always recognize anonymity and pseudonymity as potentially important tools in specific investigations. Undercover or covert operations and agents can provide critically important evidence in anti-crime and anti-terrorist work. Even organizations such as the FBI-sponsored InfraGard recognize the value of anonymized information-sharing about attacks on computer systems.[126]

70.4.5 Disadvantages of Anonymity and Pseudonymity. Several commentators have reviewed the abuses of anonymous and pseudonymous modes of communication.

In considering the benefits of having a professor communicate with an anonymous student, misrepresentation of identity by such an undergraduate in one sense manipulates a professor into a decision based on a falsehood.[127] Contrary to the beliefs of many supporters of anonymity, social interactions are not necessarily equivalent to isolated streams of data interchange; conversing with a student can be enriched by having a sense of previous conversations, a picture of shared knowledge based on a relationship. Anonymity strips interactions of the deeper communication that is enhanced by such relationships.

Widespread use of untraceable e-cash may lead to increased fraud, tax evasion, money laundering, extortion, blackmail, and kidnapping.[128] Some crimes where solicitation leads to potential blackmail—for example, hiring a murderer—may become easier with anonymity and untraceable e-cash. Industrial sabotage by anonymous publication of trade secrets can damage organizations; for example, the publication of RC4 encryption algorithms from the respected company RSADSI has lowered the monetary value of the algorithm. Froomkin writes, "[The] inability to redress legitimate claims is, I believe, the strongest moral objection to the increase in anonymous interaction."[129]

Jurisprudence in the United States has generally supported claims to a right of anonymity in political speech. However, there have been several precedents where anonymity used to cloak socially harmful acts has been stripped from the perpetrators. Perfect (untraceable) anonymity prevents society from bringing sanctions to bear on malefactors.[130] Detweiler suggested "that Internet anonymity is a bad thing [and] that all user accounts should lead back to real users in the hopes of improving online behavior, especially in chat systems and the like." He responded to critics who claimed that "anonymity is an important part of life and ought to be part of the Internet as well" by pointing out that in real life, anonymous people cannot engage in such activities as opening a bank account, getting a driver's license, getting telephone service, or buying insurance coverage. He concluded, "So grow up and accept responsibility for what you do on the Internet."[131]

L. J. Rose, well known in cyberspace-law circles, writes scathingly of the seamier applications of online anonymity:

> People can anonymously transmit all sorts of illegal and injurious materials into public areas: copyright infringements, obscenity, stolen credit information, lies and slander, and so on. Individuals with a bone to pick against anyone else can get their licks in without fear of reprisal. Anonymous remailers are great for cowards. People who want to spread messages of hate and misunderstanding, but are unwilling to stand behind their views in public, can operate behind a wall of complete anonymity and inject a strong dose of thought pollution into the public arena.[132]

Another argument supporting disclosure of the origins of speech is quoted by Froomkin, ironically from an anonymous author: "'Disclosure advances the search for truth,' because when propaganda is anonymous it 'makes it more difficult to identify the self interest or bias underlying an argument.' "[133] Libel on the Internet is particularly pernicious, since once anything has been circulated via the 'Net, it becomes impossible to unring the bell of falsity.

The resurgence of hoaxes and rumors such as the Good Times virus[134] and the pathetic stories of Craig Shergold[135] and Jessica Mydek[136] illustrate the persistence of undated, unsigned, and untrue messages in cyberspace. These unfounded, exaggerated, or obsolete stories, threats, and appeals circulate endlessly among the gullible on the 'Net. There is no reason to suppose they will ever stop.

One of the significant lessons from email hoaxes and chain letters is that unsigned, undated correspondence is always to be treated with skepticism. This principle of devaluing anonymous or pseudonymous communications will be used later in this chapter in a model for categorizing and sequestering communications as a function of their traceability.

Another growing pseudonymity issue is the use of substitute students in online degree-granting programs. One type of scam involves hiring students to pretend to be online students so that the criminals running the scheme can collect student-aid money from governments. In one massive scam, an Arizona women used imposters to steal $539,000 in student aid from the U.S. Government.[137] The availability of online courses and degrees has raised serious questions about the use of imposters who take exams on behalf of incompetent but rich candidates.[138]

70.5 SYSTEMS ANALYSIS OF ANONYMITY.

Why can the usual protections of the criminal and civil law not deal with anonymous and pseudonymous communications? This problem is addressed by David Post and David Johnson.

Post and Johnson argue that geographically defined nation-states cannot reasonably cope with a virtual, boundaryless communications medium.[139] In the real world, geographical clustering combines with basic concepts of consent of the governed through some form of representation to legitimize the exercise of state power. Without the consent of the governed, state power fades insensibly into state tyranny. In their requirements analysis of possible systems of governance of cyberspace, they add that wherever possible, those affected by the conduct to be regulated have some say in framing the regulations.

However, in cyberspace, argue Post and Johnson, there is no geographical clustering. There is no "here" or "there" in cyberspace. "Location is indeterminate because there is no necessary relationship between electronic addressing ... and the location of the addressee (machine or user) in physical space."

Post and Johnson applied the work of the scientist Stuart Kauffman on self-organizing systems to study the nature of rule-making in a complex system that can model the interactions among users in cyberspace.[140] Research on self-organization of complex systems suggests that optimum configurations of constraints (regulations) can evolve when there is some degree of aggregation (they refer to "patches") in the population. These aggregates represent groups where individuals sacrifice some of their preferences in return for overall improvement in the way the whole society works. Members of a patch share responsibility for governing their behavior.

One of the most striking findings of Post's and Johnson's research is that systems where most of the effects of an individual's actions are felt by others, outside its decision-making unit, lead to chaos or to suboptimal configurations of rules. Contrariwise, a balance between bringing consequences to bear on individuals in a "patch" and allowing effects to propagate through the larger population leads to more optimal results in the system.

As a result of the experiments, Post and Johnson suggest that one of the most powerful tools for rebuilding comity in cyberspace is grouping users by their Internet Service Providers. Each ISP can develop its own rules governing the behavior of members; sanctions for transgression of these local rules would include banishment from the ISP.

The authors examine the case of spam. As long as each ISP enforces technical measures against allowing fraudulent origination addresses, everyone in cyberspace can decide whether to filter out messages from any given ISP or not. ISPs that allow behavior judged harmful by others will limit the range of communication of their members.

Those that are viewed as restrictive will self-select their own members accordingly. Thus, without any global legislation, simply allowing individuals to choose ISPs that have published rules they like could lead to an effective self-regulation of communications. In essence, loudmouthed rumormongers would end up talking only to each other; junk email could be identified simply from its provenance; and even copyright violations could be punished by collective banning of communications from the offending ISPs.

Such a model is an instance of the ideal market of ideas in that objectionable ideas are not forbidden, they are just ignored. Of course, admirable and desirable ideas may also be ignored, but at least there is a choice involved. Access for communication becomes a form of currency in such a model—perhaps appropriate for the governance of cyberspace, the realm of electronic communications.

70.6 IMPLICATIONS AND DISCUSSION.

Any attempt to restrict anonymity on the Internet would inevitably affect pseudonymity as well.[141] Anonymity and pseudonymity make law enforcement difficult enough, but these difficulties are exacerbated by the jurisdictional problems caused by a thoroughly decentralized communications medium like the Internet; "[W]ho should be setting the rules that apply to this new global medium?"[142] What, then, are some of the practical measures we can individually and collectively take to preserve the benefits of anonymity and pseudonymity without suffering the consequences of abuse?

70.6.1 Individuals, Families, and Schools.

Absorbing and applying normative behavior begins in earliest childhood and continues throughout the development of the child's capacity for rationality and ethical judgment. Children should be taught that anonymity and pseudonymity are not acceptable under normal circumstances. The same methods that parents, teachers, and other adults use to teach children a visceral dislike of anti-social behaviors such as lying, cheating, stealing, and bullying should be applied to behavior in cyberspace.

It takes time to integrate morality into our technological universe. Twenty years ago, many drivers felt that driving under the influence of alcohol was adventurous. Today most people feel that it is stupid and irresponsible. Smoking in public is becoming rare. Many of us in northern cities have witnessed exiled smokers huddled together in the cold outside buildings where they once lit up with impunity.

Similarly, we need a consensus on good behavior in cyberspace.

Criminal hackers who break into computer systems and roam through users' private files should be viewed as peeping Toms. Criminals using computers to steal services should be recognized as thieves. Those who destroy records, leave logic bombs, and write viruses should be viewed as vandals. Hackers who smear obscenities in source code should be seen as twisted personalities in need of punishment and therapy. Government agencies proposing to interfere in electronic communications should be subject to scrutiny and intense lobbying.

Government-sponsored cyberespionage/warfare has become a significant threat to all. With current trends in government-sponsored cyberspying, many government agencies and corporations are at risk of losing very hard won and expensive technology secrets to other countries who would rather anonymously and surreptitiously steal industrial secrets rather than to create the kind of economy that bears the fruits of innovation and technological earned advancement.

In a CNBC article entitled "Chinese Army Unit Is Seen as Tied to Hacking Against US" published on February 18, 2013, authors David E. Sanger, David Barboza, and Nicole Perlroth deliver a fascinating look at the Chinese Government's reported sponsorship of cyberspying.

> Unit 61398—formally, the 2nd Bureau of the People's Liberation Army's General Staff Department's 3rd Department—exists almost nowhere in official Chinese military descriptions. Yet intelligence analysts who have studied the group say it is the central element of Chinese computer espionage. The unit was described in 2011 as the "premier entity targeting the United States and Canada, most likely focusing on political, economic, and military-related intelligence" by the Project 2049 Institute, a nongovernmental organization in Virginia that studies security and policy issues in Asia.

The article contains specific information discovered by the security firm Mandiant; however, in the ultimate of ironies, several of the Chinese hackers (identified by nicknames) themselves use their very astute hacking skills to circumvent Chinese Government restrictions on access to social media sites:

> Mandiant discovered several cases in which attackers logged into their Facebook and Twitter accounts to get around China's firewall that blocks ordinary citizen's access ... an embarrassing inconsistency to be sure.

Beyond such prohibitions and inhibitions of taboos, cyberspace needs the electronic equivalent of Emily Post. We need to discuss the immorality of virus writing, the ethical implications of logic bombs, and the criminality of electronic trespassing. We should teach children how to be good citizens of cyberspace, and not just in schools. We should sit down with computer-using youngsters and follow them through their adventures in cyberspace. Parents should ask their teenage whiz kids about hacking, viruses, software theft, and telephone fraud. We must bring the perspective and guidance of adult generations to bear on a world that is evolving faster than most of us can imagine.

The adolescent confraternity of criminal hackers and virus writers has already begun developing totems: the personae of Dark Avenger and Acid Phreak loomed over youngsters in the 1990s much as Robin Hood once did for other generations.

What we need now are taboos to match the totems.[143]

70.6.2 Ethical Principles.

How do people make judgments about a course of action when there are no explicit guidelines? There are several kinds of principles that people use in reasoning about a new situation (see Chapter 43 of this *Handbook* for a more extensive discussion of ethical decision making).

70.6.2.1 Rights and Duties (Deontology).

The concepts of rights ("Something that is due to a person or governmental body by law, tradition, or nature") and duties ("An act or a course of action that is required of one by position, social custom, law, or religion," according to the 1992 edition of the *American Heritage Dictionary*) should influence one's decisions.

Are any rights abridged by anonymity? For example, the right to know the source of a warning so that we may judge the motives and credibility of the statement is infringed when such a message is posted anonymously or pseudonymously.

Personal duties at issue in a decision on posting anonymous warnings about a competitor's product include notions of trust, integrity, and truthfulness, all of which are violated by such an act. We lower the trust of technical advice when we use anonymous postings; we damage the integrity of an entire profession; and we implicitly betray truthfulness by failing to identify the source of such information.

Professional duties or responsibilities also apply. We are expected to maintain appropriate professional relationships, but anonymous posting does not further a Web of trust among colleagues. Posting anonymous messages casts doubt on the goodwill of all the innocent people who are perceived as possibly being the author of such messages. In terms of maintaining efficacy, anonymous postings reduce the flow of information among professionals by aborting the possibility of private communication with the authors of the anonymous messages.

70.6.2.2 Consequentialism (Teleology). One approach to evaluating the ethical dimensions of a proposed act is to look at the possible consequences of the act. Does the action minimize actual and potential harm? Egoism looks at what is good for me or does the least harm to me. Anonymous posting of critical information about a competitor's product offers the potential of benefits to one's employer with minimal direct consequences. However, such behavior opens up the organization to less obvious consequences, such as the risk of blackmail, degradation of trust within the group, lowered morale, and departure of employees whose moral sensibilities are outraged by what they see as unethical behavior.

Utilitarianism views decisions in terms of what is good for the group or does the least harm for the group. The question here is the inclusivity of the "group." If the group includes all users and potential users of the defective product, then posting the information serves a good purpose; the decision on whether to post anonymously resolves to the same questions as those raised in discussions of the consequences for an organization of having an employee post messages anonymously. The climate of trust, the credibility of warnings in general, and respect for the entire industry can be harmed by anonymous postings of warnings.

An altruistic approach to decisions accepts that what is good for all may be worth doing even if there is some harm to one's self. By this yardstick, posting a warning with full attribution is definitely the preferred way of communicating information about a problem. Another altruistic approach, however, would be to inform the competitor of the flaw in its product via private communications. The hope here is that such altruism will be reciprocated and that the industry as a whole can benefit from improvement in all products.

70.6.2.3 Kant's Categorical Imperative. At a different level, Immanuel Kant's principles for judging the ethical dimensions of an act are immensely useful in all aspects of life. The principle of consistency asks, "What if everyone acted this way?" In our example, if everyone posted anonymous warnings, the credibility of all warnings would be damaged. In the absence of a mechanism of redress, unscrupulous people would contaminate the alerts with false information, making it difficult to trust any warning. Since some people would retaliate for fraudulent postings about their products by posting equally fraudulent attacks on their competitors, the system of alerts would collapse, causing harm to users and to producers.

Another principle Kant enunciated was that of respect: Are people treated as ends rather than means? The author of an anonymous message may not be thinking about the people affected by that message; they remain ciphers—amorphous, unknown entities of no importance. In contrast, an empathic and ethical person remembers that every group consists of individual human beings with pretty much the same range of feelings as anyone else. Using them as a means of increasing market share is not respectful.

70.6.3 Corporations and Other Organizations. How can organizations contribute to the reduction of harmful anonymous or pseudonymous communications?

Every corporation, government department, nonprofit organization, educational institution, healthcare facility, banking or financial services organization, and so on should explicitly address the question of anonymity and forgery on the 'Net. Some practical guidelines to consider in setting organizational policy follow.

- No user of a corporate user ID should ever forge headers or use pseudonyms when communicating using corporate resources.
- Corporate firewalls should be configured to prevent all TCP/IP packets with forged origination IP addresses from passing outward through the firewall.
- SMTP servers should be configured to prevent any email from leaving a site with forged headers.
- All corporate email outbound from a site should be signed digitally by its author(s) to provide a basis, when necessary, for repudiation of unsigned and fraudulent email.

In addition, discussions of the ethical framework for making decisions about the use of technology should be integrated into employee training at all levels. Managers, in particular, ought to be cognizant of the principles of ethical decision making so that they can fluently guide their staff in practical problem solving.

As blogging, Twitter, and social networks (Facebook, LinkedIn, and others) allow for rapid and unmanaged corporate communications, written corporate policy on the use of blogging, Twitter, and social networking is a must.

Although sites like LinkedIn would traditionally not be anonymous, pseudo-personages are easy to construct and can be used for nefarious purposes. It does not take much of a stretch of the imagination to imagine a nefarious person/government constructing a series of false personas on LinkedIn and using those personas as a base from which to launch surveillance and information attacks on corporations through their employees who proudly proclaim their detailed information on LinkedIn.

70.6.4 Internet Service Providers. Because many users send email or post to Usenet groups, which with the growth of social media have seen a decline in use as social media sites have grown. Regardless, traffic still must traverse the Internet through accounts with ISPs, and these services have an obligation to become involved in preventing abuses of anonymity and pseudonymity. Except for some free services that are independently funded or that derive revenue from advertising rather than from user fees, ISPs must establish a relationship with their users in order to be paid; most use credit card accounts for this purpose. This method of billing inherently provides a link to the real-world identity of a user through the credit card issuers. Thus, for most ISPs, it is possible to enforce traceable anonymity and pseudonymity. Faced with a warrant or a subpoena duly issued by a judge, for example, most ISPs will be able to provide authorities with all the information needed to track down the person whose account was used to send a message. Linking a specific human being to the computer session used for sending that message is another matter.

70.6.5 A Free Market Model for Identity in Cyberspace. Some people use Caller-ID to refuse to accept phone calls from callers who mask their identities. Anyone who chooses not to be identified at the time of calling can simply leave a message.

What if users of ISPs could selectively reject communications from anonymous or unauthenticated pseudonymous sources? Email clients already allow users to reject or accept email from different top-level domains and to selectively block messages from specific sources known to generate enormous amounts of spam. The Chinese numerical domains of the form *nnn*.com (e.g., 123.com, 163.com), for example, are notorious for spewing spam messages written entirely in Chinese or which, using peculiar approximations to English, advertise concrete sewage pipes to information assurance professors; these nonsensical advertisements are delivered all over the world, probably due to the activities of swindlers who trick gullible neophytes into paying for supposedly targeted email campaigns.[144] Blocking all traffic from these domains is easy.

What might happen over time as a result of allowing communications only with selected ISPs, depending on their terms of service? Eventually, there would likely be an equilibrium in which those users who wished to send and receive anonymous, untraceable email could subscribe to those ISPs supporting that kind of communication. Others could automatically block email from unwanted ISPs. Furthermore, individuals who wished to use anonymity or pseudonymity sometimes could subscribe to more than one ISP and take advantage of their different policies. Computer systems managers who wanted to deal only with other professionals at work could use a restrictive ISP; however, they also could use a different ISP to post and read messages in a highly charged, free-wheeling discussion group about the politics of gun control, without having to reveal their real names or fear that they could ultimately be traced through a pseudonym.

As the forces of the marketplace continued to work on ISPs, there might be further evolution toward different degrees and types of communication blockage. ISPs with a reputation for harboring miscreants who libel and defame others without cause could find themselves being shut out of an increasing number of reputable communities of users. Those whose users exercised moderation and responsibility might find themselves being received by a widening circle of ISPs.

The advantage of this model is that individuals could exert power over their electronic environment by voting with their subscriptions, but no one would be censored by bureaucrats or tyrants. Just as Hyde Park in England allows both geniuses and crackpots to speak yet forces no one to listen, the electronic Hyde Park would provide a mechanism for shutting out the lunatics while letting the loonies talk to each other as they wish.

What this model would not permit is the imposition of unwanted communications on powerless victims. This model would spell the end of unsolicited commercial email. If digital signatures indicating the source ISP from which executable code was first distributed became commonplace, the same mechanism could seriously interfere with the distribution of viruses and other harmful programs. ISPs that became known for harboring virus writers or distributors would see their credibility as communications partners eroded. This model does not require individuals to sign their product or messages; the only constraint is that the ISP do so.

What about individuals who own their own domain on the 'Net? The same principles would apply. The modified SMTP software would automatically sign all output from their sites. Any site that refused to provide digital signatures could be excluded by any ISP that chose to apply such an exclusionary rule. Even postings to blogs and other discussion groups on the Web could be constrained by verification of the reliability of identities associated with the originators; those insisting on being anonymous or pseudonymous would have the freedom not to post on the sites demanding authentication.

70.6.6 Governments. The role of governments in cyberspace is complex. On one hand, several governments—notably that of the United States—have contributed to the development of the Internet through legislation and funding. On the other hand, many governments, especially totalitarian regimes, are intolerant of unfettered communications. Under the communist regimes, most countries in the Soviet Union and its satellites made ownership of unregistered spirit duplicators, photocopiers, fax machines, and modems illegal. Today, China, in the grip of a tyrannical regime, behaves equally rigidly with respect to electronic communications.

No matter how carefully crafted they are, attempts to apply legal constraints on anonymity in cyberspace will be undermined by inconsistent government regimes throughout the globe. The least restrictive geographical entities will subvert more restrictive jurisdictions.[145] If, say, Restrictopolis were to impose strictures on anonymous Internet use, its anonymity-seeking citizens might be able to use the ISPs in Liberalopolis, where the rules would be much freer.

On a less practical, more philosophic level, there are profound objections to any government regulation of the Internet. As Lewis writes: "We do not outlaw wig shops or Halloween masks just because some people use them for illegal or immoral purposes. We do not require caller-ID services for everyone just because some people make obscene or harassing phone calls. Nor should we strip the cloak of online anonymity from everyone, including those who legitimately need privacy, just to prevent sickos from abusing it."[146]

In the United States, the government would likely run up against strong constitutional guarantees of speech, especially political speech—and including anonymous political speech—if it tried to ban anonymity outright.[147] A particularly significant setback for government attempts to control anonymity in the United States came in June 1997. The case began in January 1997.[148] As Declan McCullagh described the judgment:

> In Georgia, Judge Marvin Shoob ruled that a state law forbidding anonymity online is unconstitutional since it violates free speech and free association rights. The law is so broadly written, the judge indicated, that even America Online screen names could be considered illegal. Judge Shoob "understood clearly the very strong need for our plaintiffs to communicate anonymously," the ACLU's Ann Beeson says. Both judges [in Georgia and in a similar case in New York] issued preliminary injunctions barring the state attorneys general from enforcing the laws. ...
>
> Georgia's Judge Shoob, in a 21-page opinion, ruled that the law—that the Democrat-controlled legislature passed in haste last year to muzzle a dissident Republican representative—violated the First Amendment.
>
> This echoes a recent Supreme Court case, *McIntyre v. Ohio*, in which the justices ruled that the right to anonymity extends beyond political speech; that requiring the author's name on a leaflet is unconstitutional; that writing can be more effective if the speaker's identity is unknown.[149]

Democratic governments worldwide would do better to stay out of cyberspace and allow users to develop their own transnational solutions for governing behavior, including the use of anonymity and pseudonymity.

For a discussion of the explosive revelations of massive data collection by the National Security Agency of the United States, see Chapter 69 in this *Handbook*.

70.7 CONCLUDING REMARKS.

Readers of this brief review of anonymity and pseudonymity are urged to consider these key observations and recommendations:

- Anonymous and pseudonymous communications are inherently associated with an increased incidence of antisocial behavior through deindividuation, social containment, general crime theory, and social learning.
- There are circumstances where anonymity and pseudonymity are useful tools in the defense of liberty and justice.
- Anonymous and pseudonymous electronic communications have already been used to harass victims, damage commercial interests, and launch hoaxes and rumors into cyberspace.
- The major problems of anonymity and pseudonymity in cyberspace can be avoided by the use of traceable identification.
- Making ISPs responsible for determining reasonable methods for enforcing their chosen level of strong identification and authentication will allow a nongovernmental, nonlegalistic approach to reducing abuse by anonymous and pseudonymous Internet users.
- All electronic communications ought to be tagged with unforgeable authenticators of identity.
- Individuals, families, and schools have a role to play in integrating cyberspace into the moral universe of children.
- Corporations and other organizations ought to integrate ethical decision making into their management procedures and corporate policies, and enforce those policies especially related to social media.
- Governments will continue to fail in their efforts to govern cyberspace because electronic communications networks are inherently divorced from geographical jurisdictions.
- A well-conceived, flexible strategy and resultant policies are essential as the instantaneous nature, growth, and evolution of social media and mobile computing exposes far more attack surface, which can be manipulated by anonymity and pseudoanonymity. Possessing the tools and vision to match the evolutionary pace of the Internet is key to managing the future.

70.8 SUMMARY.

The growth of the Internet has increased the use of anonymity and pseudonymity in electronic communications. Internet users must be able to preserve the benefits of privacy while fighting the abuses of anonymous and pseudonymous people. In the real world, identity resides in the ways that individuals are recognized and held responsible for their actions; in cyberspace, identity is potentially just a user ID. Social psychologists have found that anonymity can contribute to deindividuation—a state of loss of self-awareness, lowered social inhibitions, and increased impulsivity.

This chapter suggests practical applications of these insights from social psychology for managers concerned with reducing abusive behavior by their own employees. In addition, the chapter addresses the wider problem that, given the social psychology of anonymity, abuses of the Internet are certain to continue. There must develop a collective response to incivility and irresponsibility, without falling into authoritarian strictures on speech. This chapter further suggests that a free market approach using accessibility to communications as a kind of currency may help the 'Net evolve toward a more civil society. By blocking email from ISPs that fail to enforce acceptable standards for a given community of users, 'Net users can sort themselves into groups that tolerate or welcome different levels of anonymity and pseudonymity. No government intervention would be required under such a system.

In addition, this chapter suggests a framework for reaching into the early years of the educational system to help integrate cyberspace into the moral universe of children worldwide. In addition to being a moral imperative to support educational efforts on computer ethics, such programs are in the best economic interests of industry, academia, and government systems managers.

70.9 FURTHER READING

Bailey, M. *Complete Guide to Internet Privacy, Anonymity & Security*. Nerel Online, 2011.

Baggio, B., and Y. Beldarrain, eds. *Anonymity and Learning in Digitally Mediated Communications: Authenticity and Trust in Cyber Education*. IGI Global, 2011.

Boellstorff, T. *Coming of Age in Second Life: An Anthropologist Explores the Virtually Human*. Princeton University Press, 2008.

Eydie, A. *How to be Anonymous Online—A Quick Step-By-Step Manual*. Amazon Digital Services, 2013

Federrath, H., ed. *Designing Privacy Enhancing Technologies: International Workshop on Design Issues in Anonymity and Unobservability*, Berkeley, CA, July 25–26, 2000. Proceedings. Springer

Griffin, R. J. *The Faces of Anonymity: Anonymous and Pseudonymous Publication from the Sixteenth to the Twentieth Century*. New York: Palgrave Macmillan, 2003

Kjaerland, M. *Electronic Civil Disobedience. A Differentiation between "Hactivists" Based on Target and Message of Web Site Hacks*. Dissertation: The University of Liverpool, Department of Psychology, 2000.

Nicoll, C., J. E. J. Prins, and M. J. M. van Dellen, eds. *Digital Anonymity and the Law: Tensions and Dimensions*. Asser Press, 2003

Robbins, S., and M. Bell. *Second Life for Dummies*. Hoboken, NJ: John Wiley & Sons, 2008

Stryker, C. *Epic Win for Anonymous: How 4chan's Army Conquered the Web*. Overlook Hardcover, 2011

Stryker, C. *Hacking the Future: Privacy, Identity, and Anonymity on the Web*. Overlook Hardcover, 2012

Ziccardi, Giovanni. *Resistance, Liberation Technology and Human Rights in the Digital Age. Law, Governance and Technology Series*, Volume **7**, Pompeu Casanovas and Giovanni Sartor, eds. Springer Netherlands, 2013. http://cryptome.org/2013/03/hacking-digital-dissidence.pdf

70.10 NOTES

An asterisk (*) in notes marks a secondary reference to classic social psychology works drawn from D. G. Myers, *Social Psychology,* 4th ed. (New York: McGraw-Hill, 1993); R. A. Lippa, *Introduction to Social Psychology,* 2nd ed. (Pacific Grove, CA: Brooks/Cole Publishing, 1994); or D. O. Sears, L. A. Peplau, and S. E. Taylor, *Social Psychology,* 7th ed. (Englewood Cliffs, NJ: Prentice-Hall, 1991).

1. U.S. Department of Justice, United States Attorney's Office for the District of Maryland, "Identity Theft Working Group Increases Federal Prosecutions:

Maryland Crime Victims' Resource Center to Assist Victims," February 21, 2008, www.justice.gov/usao/md/news/archive/IdentityTheftWorkingGroupIncreasesFederalProsecutions.html

2. www.nytimes.com/2012/01/19/world/asia/china-expands-program-requiring-real-name-registration-online.html?_r=0&pagewanted=print
3. R. Abelson, "By the Water Cooler in Cyberspace, the Talk Turns Ugly," *New York Times*, www.nytimes.com/2001/04/29/technology/29HARA.html
4. R. D. Clifford, *Cybercrime: The Investigation, Prosecution and Defense of a Computer-Related Crime*, 3rd ed. (Carolina Academic Press, 2011)
5. J. Kornblum, "Net Crime Begs Questions: Who to Call?" C|Net News, August 5, 1997; http://news.cnet.com/2102-1023_3-202141.html
6. E. Kabay, "The INFOSEC Year in Review 1997", see www.mekabay.com/iyir/1997.pdf
7. WHO@ home page: www.haltabuse.org
8. CyberAngels home page: www.guardianangels.org/cyberangels.php
9. Matt Pearce, "Web Plays Incendiary Role in Ohio High School Rape Case," *Los Angeles Times*, January 7, 2013, http://articles.latimes.com/print/2013/jan/07/nation/la-na-nn-ohio-stuebenville-sexual-assault-20130106
10. J. Kornblum, "Antispam Efforts Heat Up," C|Net News, November 14, 1997, http://news.cnet.com/Antispam-efforts-heat-up/2100-1023_3-205363.html
11. Tracy Laquey Parker, Zilker Internet Park, Inc., Patrick Parker, Peter Rauch, Texas Internet Service Providers Association and EFF-Austin, Plaintiffs, v. C.N. Enterprises and Craig Nowak, Defendants, Final Judgement, No. 97-06273 (345th Judicial District of Texas, November 10, 1997), www.loundy.com/CASES/Parker_v_CN_Enterprises.html
12. Internet Corporation for Assigned Names and Numbers (ICANN). "Top-Level Domains (gTLDs)," 2013, www.icann.org/tlds
13. R. Clarke, "Human Identification in Information Systems: Management Challenges and Public Policy Issues," *Information Technology & People* 7, No. 4 (1994): 6–37, www.rogerclarke.com/DV/HumanID.html
14. A. M. Froomkin, "Anonymity and Its Enmities," *Journal of Online Law*, 1995, article 4, http://groups.csail.mit.edu/mac/classes/6.805/articles/anonymity/froomkin.html
15. OSHA, "Milliken & Company VPP Star Site." OSHA Voluntary Protection Programs, Success with VPP, 2006, www.osha.gov/dcsp/success_stories/vpp/reg4_ss_milliken_elm.html
16. Clarke, "Human Identification in Information Systems."
17. D. G. Post, "Knock Knock, Who's There?: Anonymity and Pseudonymity in Cyberspace."
18. Froomkin, "Anonymity and Its Enmities."
19. G. Le Bon, *The Crowd: A Study of the Popular Mind* (Macmillan, 1896).*
20. L. Festinger, A. Pepitone, and T. Newcomb, "Some Consequences of Deindividuation in a Group," *Journal of Abnormal and Social Psychology*, 47 (1952): 382–389.*
21. P. G. Zimbardo, "The Human Choice: Individuation, Reason and Order versus Deindividuation, Impulse, and Chaos," in *Nebraska Symposium on Motivation*, ed. W. J. Arnold and D. Levine (Lincoln: University of Nebraska Press, 1970).*

22. Montaldo, C. "The Growing Problem of Road Rage," About.com (2013), http://crime.about.com/od/victims/p/roadrage.htm
23. W. C. Reckless, *The Crime Problem*, Meredith Publishing Company, New York, 1967.
24. W. C. Reckless, *The Crime Problem*, Prentice-Hall, Inc., Englewood Cliffs, New Jersey, 1973.
25. C. H. McCaghy, T. A. Capron, J. D. Jamieson, and S. H. Carey, *Deviant Behavior: Crime, Conflict, and Interest Groups* (Boston: Pearson Education, Inc., 2006).
26. J. McGuire, *Understanding Psychology and Crime* (New York: Open University Press, 2004).
27. McCaghy et al., *Deviant Behavior.*
28. McGuire, *Understanding Psychology and Crime.*
29. R. W. Taylor, T. J. Caeti, D. K. Loper, E. J. Fritsch, and J. Liederbach, *Digital Crime and Digital Terrorism* (Upper Saddle River, New Jersey: Pearson Education, 2006).
30. R. L. Akers, *Criminological Theories: Introduction and Evaluation* (Los Angeles: Roxberry Publishing Company, 1994).
31. M. M. Lanier and S. Henry, *Essential Criminology* (Boulder, CO: Westview Press, 2004).
32. Akers, *Criminological Theories.*
33. McCaghy et al., *Deviant Behavior.*
34. McGuire, *Understanding Psychology and Crime.*
35. Taylor et al., *Digital Crime and Digital Terrorism.*
36. McGuire, *Understanding Psychology and Crime.*
37. Taylor et al., *Digital Crime and Digital Terrorism.*
38. Akers, *Criminological Theories.*
39. McCaghy et al., *Deviant Behavior.*
40. Taylor et al., *Digital Crime and Digital Terrorism.*
41. Taylor et al., *Digital Crime and Digital Terrorism.*
42. McGuire, *Understanding Psychology and Crime.*
43. Taylor et al., *Digital Crime and Digital Terrorism.*
44. Taylor et al., *Digital Crime and Digital Terrorism.*
45. McGuire, *Understanding Psychology and Crime.*
46. Akers, *Criminological Theories.*
47. R. L. Burgess and R. L. Akers, "A differential association-reinforcement theory of criminal behavior," *Social Problems* 14 (1966): 128–147.
48. Lanier and Henry, *Essential Criminology.*
49. McCaghy et al., *Deviant Behavior.*
50. McGuire, *Understanding Psychology and Crime.*
51. Akers, *Criminological Theories.*
52. S. Hinduja, *Music Piracy and Crime Theory* (New York: LFB Scholarly Publishing LLC, 2006).
53. R. L. Akers, *Social Learning and Social Structure: A General Theory of Crime and Deviance* (Boston: Northeastern University Press, 1998).

54. R. L. Matsueda, "The Current State of Differential Association Theory," *Crime and Delinquency* 34, no. 3 (1988): 277-306.

55. Akers, *Criminological Theories.*

56. Akers, *Social Learning and Social Structure.*

57. Akers, *Criminological Theories.*

58. Taylor et al., *Digital Crime and Digital Terrorism.*

59. McGuire, *Understanding Psychology and Crime.*

60. McCaghy et al., *Deviant Behavior.*

61. Akers, *Criminological Theories.*

62. R. White and F. Haines, *Crime and Criminology* (New York: Oxford University Press, 1996).

63. Lanier and Henry, *Essential Criminology.*

64. Matsueda, *The Current State of Differential Association Theory.*

65. K. Schuessler, *Edwin H. Sutherland on Analyzing Crime* (Chicago: The University of Chicago Press, 1973).

66. Matsueda, *The Current State of Differential Association Theory.*

67. C. S. Sellers, J. K. Cochran, and K. A. Branch, "Social Learning Theory and Partner Violence: A Research Note," *Deviant Behavior* 26, no. 4 (2005): 379–395.

68. Schuessler, *Edwin H. Sutherland on Analyzing Crime.*

69. Matsueda, *The Current State of Differential Association Theory.*

70. Sellers et al., "Social Learning Theory and Partner Violence."

71. Akers, *Social Learning and Social Structure.*

72. R. L. Akers and G. F. Jensen, eds., *Advances in Criminological Theory,* vol. 11, *Social Learning Theory and the Explanation of Crime: A Guide for the New Century* (New Brunswick, NJ: Transaction Publishers, 2003).

73. T. Thornberry, ed., *Advances in Criminological Theory,* vol. 7, *Developmental Theories of Crime and Delinquency* (New Brunswick, NJ: Transaction Publishers, 1997).

74. Matsueda, *The Current State of Differential Association Theory.*

75. Matsueda, *The Current State of Differential Association Theory.*

76. Zimbardo, "The Human Choice."

77. R. I. Watson, Jr., "Investigation into Deindividuation Using a Cross-Cultural Survey Technique," *Journal of Personality and Social Psychology* 25 (1973): 342–345.*

78. J. H. Kerr, *Understanding Soccer Hooliganism* (Buckingham: Open University Press, 1994).*

79. B. Buford, *Among the Thugs* (Mandarin Paperbacks, 1991). Also available via Kindle.

80. E. Diener, S. C. Fraser, A. L. Beaman, and R. T. Kelem, "Effects of Deindividuating Variables on Stealing by Halloween Trick-or-Treaters," *Journal of Personality and Social Psychology* 33 (1976): 178–183.*

81. S. Prentice-Dunn and R. W. Rogers, "Effects of Deindividuating Situation Cues and Aggressive Models on Subjective Deindividuation and Aggression," *Journal of Personality and Social Psychology* 39 (1980): 104–113*; and E. Diener,

"Deindividualtion, Self-Awareness, and Disinhibition," *Journal of Personality and Social Psychology* 37 (1979): 1160–1171.*

82. M. Csikszentmihalyi, *Flow: The Psychology of Optimal Experience* (Harper Perennial Modern Classics, 1990, republished 2008).
83. A. Cooper, M. P. Safir, and A. Rosenmann, "Workplace Worries: A Preliminary Look at Online Sexual Activities at the Office—Emerging Issues for Clinicians and Employers," *CyberPsychology & Behavior* 9 (2006): 22–29.
84. C. B. Spivey and S. Prentice-Dunn, "Assessing the Directionality of Deindividuation: Effects of Deindividuation, Modeling, and Private Self-Consciousness on Aggressive and Prosocial Responses," *Basic and Applied Social Psychology* 11 (1990): 387–403.*
85. K. J. Gergen, M. M. Gergen, and W. H. Barton, "Deviance in the Dark," *Psychology Today* (October 1973): 129–130.*
86. L. Detweiler, "Anonymity on the Internet FAQ" (1993), www.websteruniv.edu/~bumbaugh/net/anonfaq.html; and L. Detweiler, "The Joy of Pseudospoofing" (1993), *no longer available online;* but see L. Detweiler, "The Snakes of Medusa and Cyberspace: Internet Identity Subversion" *The Risks Digest* 15, no. 25 (November 10, 1993), http://catless.ncl.ac.uk/Risks/15.25.html#subj4
87. Detweiler, "Anonymity on the Internet FAQ."
88. R. Clarke, "Introduction to Dataveillance and Information Privacy, and Definitions of Terms," Roger Clarke's Web-Site, 1999, www.rogerclarke.com/DV/Intro.html
89. Clarke, "Human Identification in Information Systems."
90. Detweiler, "Joy of Pseudospoofing."
91. Detweiler, "Joy of Pseudospoofing."
92. Renner, T., and M. E. Kabay. "Dishonest Methods Involving Online Reputation Management," *Network World | Security Strategies Alert*, August 10, 2011, www.networkworld.com/newsletters/sec/2011/080811sec2.html
93. For current resources on electronic voting issues, see the Electronic Privacy Information Center's files at http://epic.org/privacy/voting/
94. Froomkin, "Anonymity and Its Enmities."
95. Froomkin, "Anonymity and Its Enmities."
96. C. Johnson, "Anonymity On-line? It Depends on Who's Asking," *Wall Street Journal*, November 24, 1995, p. B1.
97. L. Lessig, D. Post, and E. Volokh, "Cyberspace Law for Non-Lawyers. Lesson 23—Privacy 11: Privacy: Self-Help: Anonymity, Part 1," Originally available via the Social Science Research Network (SSRN) Website, 1997. Now available via the Internet Archive Wayback Machine: http://web.archive.org/web/19970416041146/http://www.ssrn.com/cyberlaw/
98. L. Lessig, D. Post, and E. Volokh, "Cyberspace Law for Non-Lawyers. Lesson 24—Privacy 12: Privacy: Self-Help: Anonymity, Part 2" Originally available via the Social Science Research Network (SSRN) Website, 1997. Now available via the Internet Archive Wayback Machine: http://web.archive.org/web/19970416041146/http://www.ssrn.com/cyberlaw/
99. Clarke, "Introduction to Dataveillance and Information Privacy."
100. E. Mahyuni, "Gone in 6 Seconds: Hotmail CAPTCHA Hacked by Spammers," *Tech.Blorge*, April 16, 2008, http://tech.blorge.com/Structure:%20/2008/04/16/gone-in-6-seconds-hotmail-captcha-hacked-by-spammers

101. C. Pappas, "The A to Z of Internet Sleaze," *Home Office Computing* 15, no. 8 (1997):70.
102. Detweiler, "Anonymity on the Internet FAQ."
103. W. Rodger, "Zero-Knowledge to Close Anonymity Service," SecurityFocus, 2001, www.securityfocus.com/news/262
104. K. Zetter, "Rogue Nodes Turn Tor Anonymizer into Eavesdropper's Paradise," Wired, September 10, 2007, www.wired.com/politics/security/news/2007/09/embassy_hacks?currentPage=all
105. "Maimonides' Eight Levels of Charity." Mishneh Torah, Laws of Charity, 10:7–14. Chabad.org Library, www.chabad.org/library/article_cdo/aid/45907/jewish/Eight-Levels-of-Charity.htm
106. Electronic Frontier Foundation, "Anonymous Critics' Identities Protected," Electronic Frontier Foundation Website, August 26, 2005, https://www.eff.org/press/archives/2005/08/26
107. Clarke, "Introduction to Dataveillance and Information Privacy."
108. Froomkin, "Anonymity and Its Enmities"; and A. M. Froomkin, "Flood Control on the Information Ocean: Living with Anonymity, Digital Cash and Distributed Databases," *University of Pittsburgh Journal of Law and Commerce* 15 (1996): 395, http://osaka.law.miami.edu/~froomkin/articles/ocean1.htm
109. J. Ubois, "Anonymity Has Its Place," *MIDRANGE Systems* 8, no. 8 (1995): 28.
110. Detweiler, "Anonymity on the Internet FAQ."
111. P. Steiner, "On the Internet, Nobody Knows You're a Dog." *New Yorker*, July 5, 1993, http://i2.kym-cdn.com/entries/icons/original/000/011/625/Internet_dog.jpg
112. B. Paisley, "Online" (2008), YouTube video of performance in Nashville: www.youtube.com/watch?v=UE6iAjEv9dQ
113. Detweiler, "Anonymity on the Internet FAQ."
114. Froomkin, "Flood Control on the Information Ocean."
115. Froomkin, "Flood Control on the Information Ocean."
116. D. Post, "Knock Knock, Who's There?: Anonymity and Pseudonymity in Cyberspace," 1995 [article not available online in June 2013, according to author].
117. G. Stringer, "Virtual Communities," course notes, "The Internet," Creative Media and Information Technology course MIT 2114/2214, 2005. University of Exeter (UK), Virtual Communities, http://services.exeter.ac.uk/cmit/modules/the_internet/webct/ch-communities.html
118. Ellen Gorsevski, "Running Free in Angelina Jolie's Virtual Body: The Myth of the New Frontier and Gender Liberation in Second Life," Chapter 8 in *Millennial Mythmaking: Essays on the Power of Science Fiction and Fantasy Literature, Films and Games*, John R. Perlich and David Whitt, eds. McFarland, 2009.
119. Clarke, "Introduction to Dataveillance and Information Privacy."
120. Detweiler, "Anonymity on the Internet FAQ."
121. Froomkin, "Anonymity and Its Enmities."
122. Froomkin, "Flood Control on the Information Ocean."
123. EPIC. "USA Patriot Act." Electronic Privacy Information Center, 2013, http://epic.org/privacy/terrorism/usapatriot

124. Brett Max Kaufman, "ACLU Files Lawsuit Challenging NSA's Patriot Act Phone Surveillance." ACLU Website, June 11, 2013, www.aclu.org/blog/national-security-technology-and-liberty/aclu-files-lawsuit-challenging-nsas-patriot-act-phone
125. The Tor Project, https://www.torproject.org
126. InfraGard home page: www.infragard.net
127. Detweiler, "Anonymity on the Internet FAQ."
128. Froomkin, "Anonymity and Its Enmities."
129. Froomkin, "Anonymity and Its Enmities."
130. Post, "Knock Knock, Who's There?"
131. Detweiler, "Anonymity on the Internet FAQ."
132. L. J. Rose, *NetLaw: Your Rights in the Online World* (New York: Osborne/McGraw-Hill, 1994), pp. 183–184.
133. Froomkin, "Flood Control in the Information Ocean."
134. Good Times Virus Hoax FAQ: www.cityscope.net/hoax1.html; but see also the satirical version at http://ifaq.wap.org/computers/goodtimesfaq.html
135. B. Mikkelson, "Craig Shergold," Snopes.com (2007): www.snopes.com/inboxer/medical/shergold.asp
136. B. Mikkelson, "American Cancer Society Hoax." Snopes.com (2006), www.snopes.com/inboxer/medical/cancer.asp
137. M. Parry, "Online Scheme Highlights Fears About Distance-Education Fraud," *Chronicle of Higher Education,* January 13, 2010, http://chronicle.com/article/Online-Scheme-Highlights-Fears/63517
138. M. E. Kabay, "Academic Dishonesty in Online Coursework," Presentation at 2012 eCampus Security Conference, Dartmouth College, http://www.ists.dartmouth.edu/docs/ecampus/2012/2012ecampus_kabay.pdf
139. D. Post and D. R. Johnson, "The New 'Civic Virtue' of the Internet: Lessons from Models of Complex Systems" (1997), http://journals.uic.edu/ojs/index.php/fm/rt/printerFriendly/570/491
140. Post and Johnson, "The New 'Civic Virtue' of the Internet"; and S. A. Kauffman, *The Origins of Order: Self-Organization and Selection in Evolution* (Oxford University Press, 1993).
141. Post, "Knock Knock, Who's There?"
142. Post and Johnson, "The New 'Civic Virtue' of the Internet."
143. M. E. Kabay, "Totem and Taboo in Cyberspace: Integrating Cyberspace into Our Moral Universe," Proceedings of the 17th National Computer Security Symposium, Baltimore, MD, October 11–14, 1994. Reprinted in NCSA News (June 1995): 4, online at www.mekabay.com//ethics/totem_taboo_cyber.pdf
144. M. E. Kabay, "Incomprensible Spam: Growing Global Economices Falling Prey to Scammers." *NetworkWorld | Security Strategies*, June 6, 2011, www.networkworld.com/newsletters/sec/2011/060611sec1.html
145. Froomkin, "Anonymity and Its Enmities."
146. P. Lewis, "Cloaks and Daggers: Online Anonymity Is a Blessing and a Curse," *Home Office Computing* 14(7):133 (1996).
147. Lessig et al., "Cyberspace Law for Non-Lawyers, Lesson 24."

148. D. McCullagh, "Brick by Brick," *The Netly News* (editorial), 1997, http://tech.groups.yahoo.com/group/cypherpunks/message/973?o=1&d=-1

149. D. McCullagh, "Courts Strike Down New York and Georgia Net-Censorship Laws," sent Friday, June, 1997, 13:49:06 -0700 (PDT), on fight-censorship-announce@vorlon.mit.edu mailing list. www.well.com/~declan/nym/georgia.0797.txt

CHAPTER 71

HEALTHCARE SECURITY AND PRIVACY

Paul Brusil

71.1 OVERVIEW/SYNOPSIS. Healthcare has become big business. In the United States it has grown to represent a very large fraction of the domestic economic output. The delivery of healthcare depends on use of personal healthcare and personal financial information. Threats to such information grow as information is aggregated into and used by various healthcare entities. Motives for compromising private healthcare-related information are evolving from sneaking celebrities' medical information to more serious, consequential, profit-driven motives such as medical identity theft.

Trust in the healthcare system is essential. Initially, the demands on protecting healthcare-relevant information were driven by simple, government-created, generalized regulations on privacy. They have since grown to significant, far-reaching, federal, state, and industry security and privacy regulations specific to both the healthcare-provisioning side and the business processing side of the healthcare system. Furthermore, as the healthcare system evolves to the use of always newer information technology (IT), IT service delivery paradigms and healthcare service delivery strategies, maintaining trust may not always be simple or straightforward.

The healthcare sector move to adopt IT is providing tectonic changes to the healthcare industry. As IT is embraced, the drive to lower healthcare costs will accelerate. A new healthcare business will capitalize on innovative use of IT. Big changes are in the offing as healthcare adopts technology.

First up is the current push to move to electronic patient records—so-called electronic health records (EHRs)—that will power the new digital healthcare sector. Next up is the electronic sharing of such EHRs and the personal healthcare data they contain among healthcare providers, specialists, and patients, in part via health information exchanges. Electronic data sharing will include real-time patient monitoring and patient/provider messaging.

Following the goal of electronic healthcare data sharing and the near-term focus on ensuring that healthcare IT meets the frantic pace of newly instituted government mandates, attention is expected to turn to adopting yet other new technologies. These technologies will offer the potential for big breakthroughs in personalized patient care outcomes and wellness. Analytics technologies[1] such as predictive analytics and big data analytics, as well as decision-support systems, expect to be key.

Such technologies will be essential in developing advanced medical knowledge from aggregated and mined healthcare data. Such knowledge can improve overall healthcare system quality and cost. On a case-by-case basis, such knowledge can be integrated with real-time, patient-specific data to diagnose and to treat individual patients in more efficacious ways. Today's advanced technologies, and other technologies yet to be conceived, will likely be slow in being incorporated across the board into routine medical workflows; provider trust in such technologies and associated ROI potentials will need to be sufficiently established.

As such, the ongoing and emerging dramatic shifts to reliance on new underlying IT is forcing equally significant attention to the security and privacy needs of the personal data fueling the healthcare sector's emerging digital industry. After all, lack of trust in the accuracy and completeness of shared personal healthcare information can jeopardize the delivery of quality care and have devastating consequences in the new healthcare system model, which depends on secure IT for the coordination of care and the advancement of healthcare knowledge.

The goal of this chapter is to provide a sense of the existing and emerging security and privacy issues facing the healthcare sector during the middle of the second decade of the 2000s.

It examines many of the more significant regulations, guidelines, and initiatives that progress the implementation and secure use of protected information to provide and to administer care in a healthcare environment.[2] References and links are provided for readers to learn more in-depth and evolving details themselves.

This chapter begins by summarizing the motivation for security and privacy in the handling of healthcare-related information. In Section 71.3 it provides a picture of the existing and emerging threats and vulnerabilities that exist in the healthcare sector. The requirements for healthcare sector privacy and security that have arisen from state laws and early Federal laws are identified in Section 71.4.

The significant and comprehensive HIPAA (Health Insurance Portability and Accountability Act of 1996) healthcare information protection "Rules" and follow-on HITECH (Health Information Technology for Economic and Clinical Health Act of 2009) modifications to these rules that emerged over the past 17 years are presented in Section 71.5. Initiatives related to demonstrating HIPAA compliance are considered in Section 71.5.7. A tabulation of government guidelines and emerging government initiatives that pertain to HIPAA and other aspects of protecting healthcare information is given in Section 71.5.8. Section 71.5.9 provides a comparison of HIPAA and the various other state and federal laws pertaining to privacy and security.

Other public sector initiatives pertaining to healthcare information privacy and security are considered in Section 71.6. Descriptions of the government-instigated HITECH push to move the United States toward so-called "meaningful use" of a new healthcare model that relies on secure, nation-wide, electronic sharing of protected healthcare information are given in Section 71.6.1. Section 71.6.2 provides an overview of the several other regulations and guidelines—other than HIPAA and HITECH—that can apply to healthcare information protection throughout the U.S. Defense Department (DoD). A glance at yet other government sector initiatives pertaining to healthcare information protection is given in Section 71.6.3.

Section 71.7 focuses on private sector initiatives pertaining to healthcare information privacy and security. The Health Information Trust Alliance (HITRUST) industry initiative that creates industry standards and compliance evaluations for the healthcare sector is described in Section 71.7.1, while industry efforts associated with medical device security are described in Section 71.7.2.

Finally, as technology evolves, healthcare security and privacy considerations and policies are impacted. Section 71.8 examines the healthcare information protection aspects of several emerging technologies that are likely to be introduced into the healthcare sector.

71.2 MOTIVATION FOR HEALTHCARE INFORMATION PRIVACY AND SECURITY.

There are many motivations for providing good security and privacy for the various types of transactions and information that flow through, or are stored, processed, and/or displayed by, different hardware, software, or virtual and human entities and services that are either within the healthcare sector or outsourced to parties outside the healthcare sector.

One motivation for a healthcare entity or individual provider to comply with applicable laws and regulations is to reduce the risks of financial and/or criminal penalties including regulatory fines and litigation fees. Such penalties may be incurred from (a) exposure of any patient's personal, private information, or (b) compromise of healthcare-related business transactions and business data. Government imposed penalties for either case can be extensive and provide motivation for improving healthcare privacy and security. Private litigations, especially class action privacy breach suites, can be even more costly. Summaries of total costs and penalties are examined in Section 71.3.2 (including Exhibit 71.1) and Section 71.5.6.4.

Consequences to legitimate patients can be extensive, ranging from financial liability for services fraudulently received by thieves, to higher insurance payments to cover stolen care services, to denials of care due to fraudulent attainment of care service limits. Patients want the privacy and security to prevent such financial tolls.

Another motivation is to reduce the risk of a provider, pharmacist, or carrier making potentially life-threatening (and litigable) medical diagnoses or treatment plans, prescription alterations, or service denials. Altered or missing medical information can lead to endangering patients via lower quality of care resulting from bad decision making and potentially devastating consequences.

Another motivation for a healthcare entity is to reduce the capital and labor costs associated with items such as additional security reviews, consulting fees, additional security awareness training, altered human processes, altered facility processes, and/or IT repairs necessitated by healthcare breaches. An associated motivation is to reduce the costs of providing timely notifications and possibly credit monitoring services to victims of information exposure.

While patients have not yet been studied as potentially fickle healthcare customers, a motivation to provide adequate privacy and security in other fields is to avoid the loss of customers when an information breach, or history of breaches, tarnishes a company's image and reputation.

The above motivators result from the existence of imposed negative consequences arising from exposing personal data. On the other hand, there are healthcare entities that are motivated by maintaining or enhancing their reputations as parties that provide superlative protection to healthcare information and transactions.

An exemplar sampling of the kinds of attacks, threats, and vulnerabilities that can provide such motives are shown in the exhibit in Section 71.3.

71.3 HEALTHCARE SECTOR THREATS AND VULNERABILITIES LANDSCAPE.

As the healthcare field embraces new networking and information handling technologies, vast sets of threats and vulnerabilities to health-related systems and information pose greater and greater risk to providing and administering patient care. A synopsis of the growing occurrence of healthcare data breaches appears in Section 71.0. As examined in Section 71.0, a wide spectrum of types of attacks are used to breach healthcare information and lead to several types and sizes of consequences. The attack landscape is constantly evolving and expanding (Section 71.0), keeping the healthcare sector in a nondiminishing state of risk.

Exhibit 71.1 Healthcare-Related Breaches

Responsible Organization and Partners	Date	Exposure Type	Exposed Data	Number of Records	Impact
Computer Sciences Corp (Medicaid contractor), NC & VA	3/1/13	Contractor employee lost USB drive with personal information of NC Medicaid providers	Provider names, SSNs, addresses, birth dates; no patient information	50,000	NC HHS directs CSC to conduct outside review of its security, provide victim notification and hotline for provider inquiries.
Lucile Packard Children's Hospital (LPCH), Stanford University, Palo Alto CA	1/13/13	Theft stole password-protected, unencrypted laptop from physician's car parked off-campus	Patient names, birth dates, med record numbers, med descriptors, clinical data from 2009 patient care and research	57,000 (approximate)	LPCH established investigation and strengthened data protection policies, controls, and encryption. Previous 2010 LPCH laptop theft resulted in $250 K fine (reduced to $1 K) issued by CA Department of Public Health after HHS investigation. Costs of investigations, patient-optional identity protection services, & call center for patient inquiries. Unknown potential future fine by CA Department of Public Health.
Utah Department of Health (UDOH)	1/13/13	Contractor employee loses unencrypted portable USB memory stick	Medicaid enrollee names, ages, prescriptions	6,000 (approximate)	Unknown. Potential impacts could be to improve employee awareness of security policies and/or to deploy technology to prevent copying of unencrypted sensitive files.
U.S. Air Force Health Longitudinal Technology Application clinic data repository	1/12/13	Bad software upgrade	Military personnel health records in 412 medical clinics and 65 military hospitals	9,000,000 (approximate)	Global health records system outage; service degraded; only local records available

(continued)

Exhibit 71.1 *(Continued)*

Responsible Organization and Partners	Date	Exposure Type	Exposed Data	Number of Records	Impact
Utah Department of Health (UDOH)	4/2/12	Thieves gained access to server with misconfigured authorization component and download healthcare client personal data	Medicaid claims & Children's Health Insurance Plan records, including patient names, SSNs, addresses, birth dates, provider names, & tax ID numbers	780,000	HHS investigation ongoing. UDOH reputation damaged, as clients feel violated by personal information loss; UDOH enhanced net monitoring & intrusion detection. Utah analyzing protection of all servers and IT policies & procedures. Public trust in emerging Utah statewide health information exchange needs rebuilding. Costs of victim mail notices + 1 year of free credit monitoring services. Utah Department of Technology Services head fired.
Emory Healthcare, Atlanta, GA	2/7/12	Emory lost 10 backup tapes containing data from an obsolete system deactivated in 2007	The backup contained 17 years of surgery patient data including names, SSNs, surgery dates, diagnoses, procedure codes, surgeon & anesthesiologist names, devices used in surgery	315,000	Emory paid costs of victim notification via postal service plus one year of credit monitoring and identity protection services. Emory reinforced, clarified security and privacy policies & procedures; conducted appropriate inventories.
St. Jute Medical Center, Mission Hospital, Queen of the Valley Medical Center, Santa Rosa Memorial Hospital, Petaluma Valley Hospital	Early 2011 through Feb 2012	Incorrect security settings allowed external Google and Yahoo! searches	Patient names, demographic data, medical info, (e.g., blood pressures, lab results, med allergies, BMI, etc.)	31,800	Cost of patient mail notification.

Howard University Hospital, Washington DC	1/25/12	Thief stole contractor's personal, password-protected laptop from car	Patient info including SSNs, addresses, ID numbers, medical record numbers, birthdates, admission & discharge dates, diagnosis medical codes, medical procedures & patient condition	66,601	Hospital strengthened policies regarding data & laptop encryption, usage and down loading. Costs of patient mail notices and identity theft alert coverage for 1 year.
Indiana University Health Goshen Hospital, South Bend ID	December 2011	Malware used to steal patient and job applicant data	Outpatient & maternity patient SSN, insurance & med service data; applicant name, address, SSN	500 patients; 12000 job applicants	Cost of patient mail notices; hospital provides one year of credit monitoring.
University of Miami, Miller School of Medicine, Miami FL	11/24/11	USB flash drive stolen from car	6 years of patient age, gender, diagnosis, treatment data	1,219	Cost of patient mail notices; theft reported locally and to HHS.
Sutter Health Network billing & managed care system, Sacramento, CA	10/1/11	Computer stolen with unencrypted data	6–16 years of patient names, addresses, birth dates, phone, email, medical records, service dates, diagnoses & procedures, insurance plan name	3.3M patients of Sutter Physician Services; 940 K patients of Sutter Medical Foundation	11 class-action lawsuits filed; rolled into one multi-billion-dollar suit. Voluntarily, Sutter expedites plans to encrypt all desktops while awaiting lawsuit outcome and likely associated monetary damage.
TRICARE Management Activity (TMA) Military health benefits provider for several military clinics & hospitals. Also named was the business partner, Science Application International Corporation (SAIC)	9/13/11	Unencrypted backup tapes stolen from the vehicle of an SAIC employee	The loss potentially exposed 19 years of patient SSNs, addresses, telephone numbers, clinical notes, lab test reports, and prescription information	4901,432	Plaintiffs filed a $4.9B class-action lawsuit against TRICARE, the Department of Defense, and Defense Secretary Leon Panetta for violation of Privacy Act of 1974, failure to encrypt, transport of data off government premises; victims experienced fraudulent financial transactions on credit cards and bank accounts.

(continued)

Exhibit 71.1 *(Continued)*

Responsible Organization and Partners	Date	Exposure Type	Exposed Data	Number of Records	Impact
Milton Pathology Associates, P.C. and their partner Goldthwait Associates.	7/26/10	Improper disposal of un-redacted, un-shredded medical records disposed into Georgetown, MA town dump	Patient names, SSNs, medical diagnoses, cancer & other pathology test results	11,000	Unknown. Potential impacts could be to conduct awareness training to follow state and federal health care data disposal laws. Jan '13 $140 K MA settlement for HIPAA and MA civil penalties by all 5 parties, attorney fees & contribution to MA healthcare and financial data protection improvement fund.
Alaska Department of Health and Social Services (DHSS)	10/12/09	Thief stole portable USB memory stick	Personal info of state Medicaid beneficiaries	501	DHSS investigation reveals inadequate information security practices that increased size of HHS fine. $1.7M settlement of HHS HIPAA civil fine + costs to institute risk analyses & management, conduct security awareness training, implement adequate IT security controls.
BlueCross BlueShield of Tennessee (BCBST)	10/7/09	Intruder stole 57 unencrypted hard drives from locked closet in training center in a leased facility	The hard drives contained customer support call recordings of BlueCross BlueShield Identifier, name, birth date, Medicare Health Insurance Claim number, SSN	1023,209	Department of Health and Human Services imposed HIPAA Security Rules & HITECH breach notification financial penalties and regulatory correction directives of $1.5 million. Additionally, BlueCross BlueShield of Tennessee spent $17 million on investigations, pen testing, notifications, employee awareness & security training, installation of data encryption, and free credit monitoring for victims.

APA Medical Practice, Atlanta GA	April 2010	Disgruntled former employee steals and deletes patient database	Patient names, telephone numbers, addresses	Unreported	APA database purged impacting provider patient care on case-by-case basis; APA database given to competitor for marketing campaign.
University of California at Los Angeles	2005–2009	Hospital staff snooped on medical records	Undisclosed amount of personal information viewed	2 celebrity patients	HHS imposed civil monetary penalty for HIPAA violation. $865 K penalty settlement and a multi-year program to prevent future violations.
Hospice of North Idaho	June 2010	Theft stole laptop from home hospice employee's car	Unencrypted sensitive personal patient info	441 patients	Hospice undertook several security and privacy improvement activities, e.g., risk analysis, stronger security controls, policies & procedures, laptop encryption, HIPAA training. Hospice undertook several security and privacy improvement activates, e.g., risk analysis, stronger security controls, policies & procedures, laptop encryption, HIPAA training.
Veterans Affairs	May 2012	Transmission of unprotected (i.e., unencrypted) electronic health records	Veterans' electronic health records from medical centers and outpatient clinics	Unknown	Veterans Affairs CIO Roger Baker and undersecretary Robert Petzel signed waivers delaying encryption. No immediate harm to patients known.
Accretive Health, Inc. (business associate)	7/1/11	Laptop stolen from Accretive Health employee	Unencrypted patient information	23,000 (approximate)	Minnesota Attorney General successfully sued Accretive Health, Inc. On July 30, 2012, Accretive Health agreed to pay $2.5 million in damages.

71.3.1 Healthcare Data Breaches are Growing. There is a growing body of evidence from the rise in healthcare information breaches that the need for comprehensive strategies for protecting healthcare-related data is aggressively growing. A snapshot of this accelerating need is presented in this section.

In the healthcare sector, a malware event occurs, on average, about once every four minutes with only modest variability from month to month.[3] Occasionally, healthcare sector attacks are event driven, such as the surge in healthcare sector malware attacks after China identified healthcare as one of its top priorities in its long-term science and technology development plan.[4]

As more medical records become electronic and as new IT storage, computing, and communication technologies appear in healthcare entities, the risk of healthcare breaches of personal health information (PHI) and/or breaches of other types of personally identifiable information (PII) found in a healthcare setting has increased in frequency and magnitude. The number of records stolen in a single breach has increased. Often months pass before a breach is discovered. It appears that the trend in focus of attacks in the healthcare sector is paralleling that seen in other sectors; namely personal data, especially medical identities, are being targeted more, while financial data are of less interest.

It is said "healthcare is one of the most-breached industries"; in the mid-2000s nearly 40 million patient records were breached in a four-year period.[5] But, in 2011 alone, breaches doubled from the previous year.[6] Typically, about three to nine[7] times more healthcare-related breaches occur than financial industry breaches. About 19 million patients' health records were breached via nearly 400 breach incidents. About 30 percent of healthcare entities experienced a data breach in 2012, with more than two-thirds experiencing more than one breach.[8] Furthermore, it is estimated that nearly all small healthcare offices have been breached. Medical identity theft occurred in nearly a third of these small office breaches.[9]

Motivations for initiating medical record breaches range from attackers seeking monetary gain for new employers[10] to attackers selling SSNs, medical IDs, and medical records. Indeed, in 2012 stolen medical records that include a health insurance ID number fetched $50[1] each on the underground market—an amount greater than the typical $1 value placed on stolen financial records that include a Social Security number. In 2012, each medical ID theft cost more than $20,000[11]—about ten times the cost of a regular identity theft—and took twice as long to discover and to resolve as regular ID theft.[12] All in all, though, it is believed the healthcare sector does not yet have a good picture of the major threat and attack motivators.[13]

The U.S. Department of Health and Human Services (HHS) maintains an extensive, formal list and synopses of healthcare information breaches.[14] Breaches affecting 500 or more people must now be reported to HHS. In practice, HHS postings appear to list many of the smaller healthcare-related data heists. The heists reported may not often appear in HHS's list in a timely fashion.

71.3.2 Scope of Attack Vectors and Breach Consequences Is Large. The numbers of healthcare information breaches and healthcare service identity thefts are enormous. Recently, the federal government investigated over 27,000 of the 77,000 complaints of healthcare information breaches it received; it monitored for misuse nearly 300,000 Medicare beneficiary IDs that were compromised.[15]

Exhibit 71.1 reveals examples of the diversity of types and sizes of data heists or exposures occurring in the healthcare sector. The exhibit includes many larger breaches not yet reflected in the HHS list. Many of the tabulated breaches are associated with some of the highest volumes of healthcare data compromise and the most significant associated remediation costs and penalty fines.

The exhibit shows the custodial source of the compromised data, characteristics of the data that were compromised, and the consequences of the data compromise. The characteristics of the data compromised include the date of the compromise, the type of data compromise that was experienced, the type of data that were exposed, and the number of records that were exposed. The consequences of the data compromise are described in terms of the impact of the compromise and financial penalties associated with the data compromise.

The exhibit shows that healthcare information breaches know no preferred source of compromised data; compromises occur in academia, private hospitals, military hospitals, small physician practices, large insurance carriers, small carriers, and more.

Inspection of the exhibit reveals the large diversity of threats and attacks that result in PHI loss. The threats and attacks range from social engineering attacks, to insider attacks, to poor patch management in medical device software, to outright theft, to ransom, and more. All too often, unauthorized requesters successfully extract the private, personal medical information of unsuspecting individuals—sometimes as easily as listening into minimally secured wireless networks in conjunction with a drive-by heist—or thieves steal patients' insurance billing information for financial benefit.

Common among the cause of many breaches is the theft or loss of portable devices (e.g., USB drive, laptop, backup media) that contain patient personal information. Missing devices with compromised PHI have been found in city dumps and pawn shops.

One of the underlying trends is that the data exposed by such breaches are often made available for exposure by unsuspecting healthcare entity employees who download PHI into less-protected, inadequately permissioned, poorly secured personal devices. Such downloads are typically not made for malicious reasons, but the data become more vulnerable nonetheless.

The exhibit also shows a frequently recurring commonality of the type of personal information exposed by the data that were compromised. Such common data items include name, SSN, birthday, address, and so on.

Ransoming healthcare information has emerged as a new threat that may be targeted[16] at small and midsize healthcare entities. In the future, as large volumes of medical data are aggregated into centralized, networked, health information exchanges, the potential for the formation of a cybercriminal's treasure trove bonanza increases dramatically.

Inspection of the exhibit also reveals a wide spectrum of consequences associated with PHI compromise. Lower price consequences include, for example, the costs of victim mailings, victim credit monitoring, and victim identity theft surveillance. On the other hand, the total cost of other breaches includes not only such victim-oriented remediation activities but also the costs incurred from federal or state regulators' penalties and fines. The average cost incurred by a custodian of breached health information is currently about $150 per record breached. But enterprising attorneys representing patients whose health information was breached are looking to set precedents for multimillion/multibillion dollar class-action lawsuits against covered entities that violate California's Confidentiality of Medical Information Act, which sets damages for health information exposure at $1,000 per person per privacy violation.[17] Such breaches can lead to very significant aggregate per-incident costs to the affected healthcare entity.

The consequences to a patient arising from a healthcare data breach are typically similar to consequences experienced in other industries. Often, stolen identity data are used to apply for credit consumed in the name of the victim from whom the identity information was stolen. In the case of stolen medical identity data such as carrier policy numbers associated with specific patients, the stolen data can be used illicitly to receive medical care billed to the person whose medical identity was stolen.

A new type of emerging consequence to a healthcare information breach is that individuals who received data breach notifications are also becoming victims of fraud. It was estimated in 2012 that 25 percent of breach victims become fraud victims, often because cyberthieves use stolen victims' Social Security numbers to defraud the victims' financial institutions. In the Utah Department of Health data breach, the $2 to $10 million being spent to recover from the breach is expected to be dwarfed by the more than $400 million lost in the expected 122,000 cases of fraud, where each case is expected to result in an average loss over $3,300.[18]

Reputation tarnish for a care provider that is a source for compromised PHI is a consequence that is hard to quantify; but consumers of services from the Oregon Health & Science University are likely to seek care elsewhere now that this covered entity has been involved with three significant breaches in four years.

The consequences of a PHI breach on a health entity's corporate executives can be significant. While C-level imprisonment is possible under Federal regulations specified in the Health Insurance Portability and Accountability Act (HIPAA) examined in detailed throughout this chapter, the consequences of healthcare data breaches on the sources of compromised data more typically range from expensive civil law suits, fines, and penalties to expensive changes in security and privacy policies and procedures.

The exhibit demonstrates that Federal authorities and state authorities are serious about enforcement of penalties for losing PHI. Indeed, HHS and other government agencies are providing precedents that government bodies will go after cases of large or small volumes of data compromised, as well as large or small violators, with equal vigor.

One of the first punitive actions of the HSS Office for Civil Rights (OCR) is shown via the BlueCross BlueShield of Tennessee (BCBST) entry in Exhibit 71.1. OCR applied the enforcement tool of the HIPAA Breach Notification Rule (described in Section 71.7). OCR used the precedent-setting BCBST medical record data breach penalty as a significant example to demonstrate to the healthcare community the very serious consequences of not having a high-priority, carefully designed, up-to-date, and monitored HIPAA compliance program.[19]

On the other hand, HHS also made an example of a small hospice that compromised personal information from only a very small number of patients.

The exhibit also reveals that in the case of Accretive Health, Inc., the state of Minnesota has established precedent that governments will undertake compliance enforcement actions with significant penalties against HIPAA-designated Business Associates of covered entities.

71.3.3 More Attack Vectors are Emerging. There are other attack vectors on health information and healthcare entities not shown in the table of examples. For example, thieves used fraudulent Automated Clearing House transactions though duped third parties to steal $1 million from a Washington State hospital.[20] Indeed, independent of applicability just to the healthcare sector, there is a constantly evolving and expanding threat landscape. As a consequence, new security approaches will likely be needed to respond effectively to the changing threat picture.

Furthermore, there will always be some new wave of vulnerabilities; the current wave of vulnerabilities associated with IT trends regarding mobility, social media, cloud computing, consumerization, and so on will undoubtedly be replaced by newly emerging vulnerabilities from other emerging IT trends.

For example, evidence is growing that in vivo electronic medical devices that communicate with external devices can become vulnerable to computer and/or process control attacks.[21] Researchers have shown that wearable and implantable medical devices such as insulin pumps, pacemakers, defibrillators, and more can be wirelessly hacked and device settings can be changed—even to the point whereby a rogue-controlled medical device can be configured to deliver fatal consequences to the associated patient. There is concern that constraints on in vivo power may limit the ability of an implanted or wearable medical device to provide the necessary security controls, such as encryption and authentication, to protect communications to/from the human body. Of further concern, the Department of Veteran Affairs within the U.S. Department of Defense (DoD) reported that hundreds of medical devices were infected with malware over a two-year period.

Other unexpected vulnerabilities that have the potential to be exploited include attacks on a healthcare entity's facility control systems, for example, those used in conjunction with electronic locks, surveillance cameras, lighting, alarms, hospital kitchen refrigeration, and so on.[22]

Drive-by thieves can eavesdrop on patient-specific information if such information is conveyed via an unprotected wireless network at a care provider's facility or home or a patient's home, or is displayed on an unattended computer screen. A lucrative primary target of such a healthcare-specific attack is the theft of patient-specific billing information. An unscrupulous care provider billing for unrendered services can use a patient's insurance ID number to perpetrate fraud. Alternatively, a patient without insurance can use a stolen patient ID number to obtain free, or nearly free, healthcare. Such fraudulent activity impacts healthcare premium costs, patient benefits, and patient medical histories needed for accurate, future diagnoses.

As patient medical records are made electronic and are aggregated into large data stores or healthcare information exchanges, the potential escalates for massive medical records losses to occur in one fell swoop. Challenges in maintaining care providers' patient care continuity and medical business continuity in response to potential cyber Pearl Harbors will take center stage.

Additionally, there is evidence that elements of the U.S. healthcare sector and the National Health Information Network being used to prototype the exchange of electronic medical records are under potentially coordinated attack by multiple government elements of a rogue nation state.[23] Primary attacks appear to include cyberspying on U.S. healthcare-related technology intellectual property and cyberespionage on healthcare business processes used by healthcare providers and insurance carriers. At risk are billions of dollars effectively being stolen, for example, via espionage and theft of pharmaceutical, medical device, and medical/biotechnology R&D and drug trials,[24] or via illegal pilfering and use of medical insurance. Furthermore, the potential exists for cyberadversaries to use such cyberpilfered knowledge to cause significant harm to patients—including loss of lives. Even more troubling is that there are emerging attacks, currently on other industries, where the motive for attack is solely to cause destruction.

71.3.4 The Bottom Line. Recent analyses[25] show that healthcare data breaches at the time of the writing of this chapter were, at least temporarily, diminishing in numbers of breach incidents and in the severity of the breaches in terms of the numbers of patient PHI records exposed. While providing an aurora of encouragement that perhaps the government regulations and imposed penalties described later in this chapter were starting to make improvements in protecting PHI, it is too early to conclude a corner has been turned in healthcare data protection or whether there was just a statistical calm before the next storm of exposures.

Whether there is or is not a long-term lull in healthcare data exposure, complacency about healthcare data protection is not an option. The prudent conservative approach is to assume that the historical epidemic of security will resume with a vengeance, that every healthcare entity is a target, and that the healthcare entity of concern to you will be the next target. Those charged with ensuring the security and privacy of healthcare-related information must be constantly vigilant about new threats and vulnerabilities that emerge in order to assess whether fielded security protections are adequate to withstand newly emergent threats and vulnerabilities.

Many organizations provide listings of recently discovered, general threats not necessarily specific to the healthcare sector; one,[26] for example, also enumerates costs incurred in recovery and information that can help in reducing risks. Furthermore, NIST maintains a database of discovered vulnerabilities (sometimes applicable to technology used in the healthcare sector) that can help guide vulnerability remediation efforts.

Perhaps most troubling is the emerging thought that privacy could be made impossible for certain types of medical information because of a new style of so-called "DNA hack."[27]

71.4 HEALTHCARE INFORMATION PROTECTION REQUIREMENTS IN U.S. LAWS.

This section contains brief descriptions of several of the state and federal laws in the United States that stipulate privacy and security requirements pertinent to patient care and healthcare sector business processes.

Privacy requirements were initially established for personal information maintained by the Federal Government. Privacy requirements were subsequently extended to applicability beyond government-held personal information.

Privacy of PII first became a requirement in the United States via The Privacy Act of 1974. This law applies only to those databases established, used, and maintained by any agency of the Federal Government. As such, this seminal law established privacy requirements pertaining to personally identifiable health information collected by any agency of the U.S. Government, such as Medicare treatment records entrusted to the HHS Centers for Medicare and Medicaid Services.

This law established the precedent that disclosure of PII (in this case by a federal agency) requires written individual consent of the person whose PII is to be disclosed. The law also specifies the few specific exception situations wherein disclosure consent is not required. The law specifies other privacy requirements and rights applicable to PII in databases wherein a Federal Government agency is the custodian of the database. The law also specifies the interworking with the Freedom of Information Act. The precedents established by the Privacy Act have since been incorporated into all subsequent public or private privacy rules applicable to a variety of industries, including healthcare.

Since the time that the Privacy Act was established, several presidential administrations have issued plans and policies pertaining to healthcare information entrusted to the Federal Government. For example,

- **Presidential administrations** issued policies, plans, and positions wherein the healthcare sector is deemed a critical national infrastructure. It needs to be protected. It needs to continue operating because the nation and economy depend on it.

- **The Health Care Finance Agency (HCFA)** established policy for incorporating security functionality and for appropriately using the Internet to convey healthcare information protected by the Privacy Act as well as other sensitive HCFA information.
- **The Office of Management and Budget** promulgated policy recommending all federal agencies, including those operating as healthcare entities for which HIPAA is also applicable, to implement protection mechanisms, including encrypting all data stored in mobile devices and establishing database access logging.
- **The Federal Acquisitions Regulation Council** issued a rule specifying that procurement officers at all federal agencies are required to incorporate IT security requirements in their IT acquisition planning. This policy applies to federal agencies that act as entities covered under HIPAA.
- **The Executive Branch** issued the Homeland Security Presidential Directive/HSPD-12 requiring government employees and contractors working at government agencies—including those operating as entities covered under HIPAA regulations—to use specific government IDs issued by trusted authorities only to identity-proven individuals.

There are yet other guidance and law that pertain to federal/DoD healthcare facilities and the healthcare information generated and used therein. These other healthcare information protection rules for government-entrusted personal healthcare data are presented in Section 71.6.2.

Some other laws are not specifically concerned with security, but compliance with such laws may infer the need for best-practice security implementations addressing implied security requirements associated with certain types of healthcare-related business information. For example, under the False Claims Act, healthcare providers submitting fraudulent claims can be punished with triple damages, penalties of $5,000 to $10,000 per wrongful billing, and exclusion from government insurance programs. Without implementation of adequate information security, electronic billing of health insurance carriers by healthcare providers can open doors to malicious attacks on healthcare claims so that they appear to be wrongful, prosecutable billing claims.

Currently, several other laws, standards, regulations, policies, and guidelines exist to protect the privacy of PII that is not maintained by the Federal Government. Such PII includes the specific PII used in healthcare.

Many of these rules and suggestions apply to protecting business processes, including the business processes associated with the delivery of healthcare. Some of the better-known guidance includes the Payment Card Industry (PCI) Data Security Standard (DSS) 2.0 and the Gramm-Leach-Bliley Act's (GLBA) Personal Financial Information (PFI).

Many of these overlap somewhat, giving the practitioner a point of reference when addressing healthcare data protection. HIPAA contains 18 distinct data elements. Some elements map closely to PCI and GLBA, in that HIPAA includes *name* as an element, whereas both PCI and GLBA are more specific. PCI and GLBA require first name or initial in conjunction with last name. Furthermore, PCI and GLBA must accompany a credit card number or financial account number respectively.

This minor difference broadens the scope of HIPAA such that either first name or last name could constitute *name* in the HIPAA context. This broadening extends to other, less standard, elements such as vehicle identification number (VIN) and telephone number. The key to understanding HIPAA's reach is to compare its purpose with PCI,

GLBA, or state data privacy laws like Massachusetts 201 CMR 17.00. HIPAA seeks to keep information about the patient private and knowledge of health data in and of itself is the act to be prevented. Others seek to prevent a subsequent action after an actor obtains vital combination data.

The HIPAA law and its various subsequent rules extend PII protection to personal healthcare information (PHI) created and used not necessarily just for healthcare business processes in both the private and public sectors but also for private sector and public sector patient care processes. The security, privacy, and breach notification requirements stipulated in HIPAA are examined in detail in the next section.

Additionally, recent updates and new state breach notification laws and state data protection laws govern much of the data considered PHI. Nearly all U.S. states and territories now have their own specific laws pertaining to breaches of PII.[28] Such laws typically specify requirements on notifications that must be provided when information breaches are detected, what specific types of PII disclosure require such notifications, and under what conditions (e.g., exposure of encrypted data) breach notifications are not required. For example, California's Security Breach Information Act (Senate Bill 1386) requires any company—including those that are entities covered under HIPAA—to disclose potential security breaches of specified types of PII such as a person's name, specified information about a person's various financial accounts, a person's Social Security number, specified information about a person's health insurance, and a person's driver's license and state ID number.

While many of these state laws maybe intended to be used when "consumer" PII is compromised, it is not far-fetched to expect that law enforcers may interpret patients as consumers (of healthcare) with which exposable healthcare-related PII is associated.

A comparison of portions of the laws identified in this section with the HIPAA law is given in Section 71.5.9.

71.5 THE HIPAA AND HITECH HEALTHCARE INFORMATION PROTECTION REGULATIONS.

The Health Insurance Portability and Accountability Act (HIPAA) of 1996[29] is a five-part U.S. federal law that pertains to many aspects of healthcare and its administration. HIPAA goals include (a) improving portability and continuity of healthcare insurance when a patient changes jobs, (b) minimizing waste, fraud, and abuse in healthcare insurance and healthcare delivery, (c) ensuring individual patient information privacy through security means, and (d) simplifying healthcare insurance administration. The Administrative Simplification (Title II, Subtitle F part of HIPAA) looked to improve the efficacy and reliability of the healthcare system and to reduce its costs.

The initial focus of HHS with regard to Administrative Simplification was to establish key pieces of an infrastructure for electronically exchanging certain healthcare-related financial and administrative transactions. The national standards[30] that were established included use of standard, specifically formatted electronic data interchange (EDI) transaction types with specific medical code sets for transaction contents, unique health identifiers for employers and care providers, health information security, and electronic signature. This portion of Administrative Simplification is administered and enforced by the Centers for Medicare and Medicaid Services.

But of interest to this chapter, Title II of HIPAA is one of several laws, standards, regulations, and guidelines that exist for protecting the healthcare information associated with patient-specific information. HIPAA in combination with the healthcare information protection aspects of the Health Information Technology for Economic and Clinical Health Act (HITECH) of 2009 provide federal standards and regulations, as well as legal underpinnings, for the provision of privacy and security protection to personal health information (PHI) and to medical identity.

HIPAA instigated moving the healthcare industry toward widespread use of information technology; personally identifiable electronic health information whose privacy was ensured by security technology and methods; the sharing of such information among authorized healthcare parties; and a single, common, secure electronic transaction environment for electronic billing.

To affect the intents of Administrative Simplification with regard to the topics of interest to this chapter, HHS developed several so-called HIPAA Rules. These HIPAA Rules are the regulations containing requirements that pertain to protecting PHI and to notifying individuals if their PHI was compromised to unauthorized parties.

The privacy and security regulations for protecting PHI apply to PHI while it is (a) in the custody of so-called covered entities and their business associates, (b) in transit between covered entities, and (c) in transit from covered entities to others such as business partners. Security and privacy are related in that in general, privacy depends on security: Appropriate security prevents theft or leakage of private data.

Regulations include developing, documenting, and implementing privacy, security, and breach notification policies and procedures (P&P) that meet HIPAA-stipulated requirements in these three areas, implementing technology and methods for addressing the specified HIPAA requirements, training staff about HIPAA requirements, guaranteeing patient rights regarding their PHI, and appointing privacy and security directors to monitor and to enforce privacy and security matters.

Summaries of the three specific HIPAA Rules appear below. First, the guiding principles for addressing healthcare information protection are given in Section 71.5.1. Descriptions of the original HIPPA Privacy Rule, the HIPAA Security Rule, and the HIPAA Breach Notification Rule are given in Sections 71.5.2, 5.3, and 71.5.4, respectively.[31] Regulations applying to the enforcement of the above three HIPAA Rules are given in Section 71.5.5.

These original HIPAA Rules were subsequently updated under the authority of the HITECH Act. The updates and modifications to the HIPAA Privacy Rule, the HIPAA Security Rule, the HIPAA Breach Notification Rule, and the enforcement of HIPAA Rules are described in Section 71.5.6.

Observations associated with the fielding of the HIPAA Rules and demonstrating compliance of various healthcare entities to these Rules appear in Section 71.5.7.

Various government-issued guidelines relevant to HIPAA and healthcare information protection exist. Examples are given in Section 71.5.8.

States within the United States can establish laws and regulations that are more, or less, comprehensive or restrictive than the federal HIPAA and HITECH laws and regulations. Examples of state-specific privacy and security laws are compared to HIPAA in Section 71.5.9.

Still other federal standards and guidelines exist that can impact the healthcare information security and privacy aspects of military hospitals (see Section 71.7.3). Standards developed by industry can impact the healthcare information security and privacy aspects of certain healthcare parties (see Section 71.7.4.1) as well as medical device manufacturing (see Section 71.7.4.2).

Finally, evolving and potentially emerging new government initiatives pertaining to security and privacy for healthcare information are identified and briefly examined in Section 71.7.8.

71.5.1 HIPAA's Privacy and Security Fundamental Principles. The HIPAA approach for healthcare information protection focuses on stipulating privacy and security requirements rather than specifying privacy and security solutions.

The privacy and security requirements apply to (a) "covered entities" and (b) to all individually identifiable, patient health information handled by such covered entities.

Covered entities include:

1. Health insurance carriers (sometimes referred to as "health plans," including private entities as well as government-funded entities such as the Centers for Medicare and Medicaid Service that act as insurance carriers);
2. Healthcare providers (including, e.g., institutions like medical centers, private physicians, dentists, pharmacies, and government agencies that provide healthcare services such as the Federal Employee Health Benefits Program, and DoD's TriCare Program), only if such healthcare providers conduct certain specified electronic transactions;
3. Healthcare billing clearinghouses (entities between providers and payers that can, if necessary, translate covered entities' transactions between HIPAA standard formats and nonstandard/proprietary, payer-specific or provider-specific formats);
4. Business associates, contractors, and service providers of covered entities (including government contractors such as those contracted for processing Medicare claims).

More detailed examples of which types of organizations are considered to be "covered entities" are given by HHS (www.hhs.gov/ocr/privacy/hipaa/understanding/coveredentities). Not every organization that generates, processes, or holds personally identifiable health information is a "covered entity" in the eyes of HIPAA. Tools to determine whether any specific entity is a "covered entity" exist.[32]

The privacy requirements stipulate how PHI is controlled. Legally authorized uses and disclosures are defined. Privacy requirements pertain to PHI created, stored, or conveyed in any form. For PHI in electronic form, privacy protection largely depends on HIPAA-stipulated security requirements.

The security requirements apply only to PHI in electronic, "computerized" form.[33] By securing electronic transactions that convey PHI between healthcare IT systems and by securing storage and processing of electronic PHI, abuse and fraud can be minimized and privacy of such information can be increased. The security requirements can be met by common, generally accepted, widely used security principles and practices.

HIPAA does not specify a one-size-fits-all privacy and security solution, applicable to all situations. Although every covered entity that electronically receives, maintains, processes, or transmits PHI must comply with applicable HIPAA privacy and security requirements, HIPAA does not specify how to meet these requirements. Privacy and security requirements may be met by covered entities by appropriate combinations of P&P, measures, security technology, and other ways deemed appropriate by each covered entity.

By focusing on privacy and security *requirements* rather than *solutions*, HIPAA offers (a) flexibility for differing covered entities to employ differing security solutions, (b) scalability of differing security solutions to work in covered entities of differing sizes, and (c) technology neutrality so that covered entities may use the newest applicable security solutions.

As such, HIPAA allows different covered entities to meet HIPAA information protection requirements by whatever strategy is reasonable and appropriate to each covered entity at any given point in time. Particular solutions may vary from situation to situation, but each solution must meet the HIPAA requirements. Some healthcare enterprises may need to implement more sophisticated information protection solutions than others. Small, less complex healthcare provider offices may have more limited privacy and security P&P and training requirements than those of large, more complex medical centers. Healthcare enterprises may need to change aspects of their information protection strategy as they change in size.

Covered entities must each assess their own potential risks to the PHI they handle. They must develop, document, implement, and maintain appropriate information protection P&P and measures to address their unique risks and situations. They can use risk-management techniques to help decide what strategy of potentially overlapping safeguards is reasonable and appropriate to their situations. All analyses, decisions, and rationale for decisions must be documented. HIPAA allows covered entities to select industry-acceptable, best-practice information protection strategies. Covered entities need periodic assessments to ensure continuing appropriateness and adequacy of their solutions to meet HIPAA requirements.

71.5.2 HIPAA Privacy Rule. HIPAA privacy regulations stipulate requirements for the use, disclosure, and dissemination of personally identifiable healthcare information as well as patient rights in such matters. A synopsis of the HIPAA Privacy Rule and its early corrections and modifications is given in this section. The more recent HITECH updates to the privacy rule appear in Section 71.5.6.2.

The HIPAA Privacy Rule[34] together with early modifications[35] establish a national floor of requirements pertaining to safeguarding privacy of PHI in any form—paper, oral, or electronic—from inappropriate or unauthorized disclosure or misuse. The Privacy Rule regulations apply to PHI created, stored, processed, used, transmitted, or received by covered entities. The privacy regulations limit sharing of PHI by covered entities. They also establish requirements pertaining to rights of patients with regard to understanding and controlling how their healthcare information is used, disclosed, and shared.

The purpose of HIPAA privacy requirements is to ensure patients' personal information is adequately protected and kept private without unduly disrupting the flow of healthcare information needed to provide, to oversee, and to pay for care, to assist healthcare research, and to improve the quality of the healthcare system. These requirements strike a balance between providing patients with greater peace of mind versus the public responsibility to support national medical priorities. Such priorities include protecting public health, identifying public health trends, conducting medical research, improving the quality of care available for the nation, and fighting healthcare fraud and abuse.

Given the massive extent, diversity, and complexity of the healthcare sector, the privacy requirements are comparably comprehensive—and appropriately flexible—to cover the plethora of uses of healthcare information by various covered entities and others outside the healthcare sector. Only a brief introduction and summary of the privacy requirements is given here.

The privacy regulations provide patients with rights to inspect and to correct their personal healthcare information. The original regulations require written patient consent for each covered entity to use a patient's PHI. Disclosure of PHI without patient consent was allowed for only a few, specified reasons. In the 2002 modification[36] of the HIPAA Privacy Rule, patients' rights of consent were stripped from the Privacy Rule. Patients can't specify who gets to see their PHI and why. But they can get to see their PHI held by all healthcare parties and a history of what disclosures of their PHI occurred without their authorization.

The regulations require business partners of each covered entity—via contracts or other similar mechanisms—to maintain the privacy of any patient information that is provided to them by the covered entity.

The regulations define the generally accepted set of information to be protected and kept private. It includes patient demographic information, common identifiers, insurance billing and payment information, symptoms, examination and test results, diagnoses, treatment, and future care plans that can be associated with or used to identify a patient, and so on. This information may be oral or recorded in any form or medium, such as paper, magnetic tape, computer drive, and so on. There are no privacy requirements that apply to healthcare information that is de-identified via specified ways.

A sampling of the privacy requirements follows. As readers' needs dictate, the full HIPAA Privacy Rule should be consulted for increasingly detailed descriptions of privacy requirements and exceptions that may apply to such requirements.

- **General use and disclosure requirements.** Other than information that is specifically permitted or under the written consent of the applicable patient, a covered entity cannot use or disclose PHI.
- **Specific permitted use and disclosure requirements.** Covered entities may share certain PHI without a patient's formal signed consent only under certain specified situations, including, for example, among healthcare providers involved in a patient's treatment, with third-party payers (e.g., insurance carriers), with the patient, with parties involved with medical reviews assessing the quality of patient care, with parties involved with assessing the performance of care providers and healthcare operations, and with regulatory and public health agencies, ethical researchers, and auditors. For certain specified reasons, a covered entity may share certain PHI with only informal patient permission not involving a signed, formal consent authorization.
- **Required use and disclosure requirements.** When some other law mandates a covered entity to disclose some specific PHI, the covered entity must disclose the PHI without obtaining authorization from impacted individual. Covered entities are permitted—but not required—to share PHI without a patient's consent or permission for 12 national priority purposes outside a patient's healthcare context. Examples of these purposes include public health activities, law enforcement, legal proceedings, protecting victims of abuse, workers' compensation, and so on. Otherwise, the covered entity must either obtain release authorization from the impacted individual or de-identify the individually identifiable health information before disclosing it.
- **Authorization requirements.** A patient-signed, written consent authorization with certain specified conditions and constraints is required by covered entities for any use or disclosure of PHI that is not for treatment, payment, or healthcare operations or otherwise permitted or required.
- **Minimum necessary data requirements.** Covered entities are required to develop and to use P&P to ensure that no more PHI is used or disclosed than the minimum amount needed for each purpose for which information is used or disclosed.

- **Privacy practices notice requirements.** Covered entities are required to develop privacy practice notices, to post these notices, and to collect individual patient acknowledgments of their receipt. These entities must abide by clearly stated procedures that (a) protect the privacy of patients' information, (b) describe how PHI is used and disclosed, and (c) describe how patients can access their PHI.
- **Patient access and control rights requirements.** Covered entities are required to give individual patients the rights to receive a copy of the entity's privacy practices notice and to specify how the entity should communicate with the patient. Patients have the right to inspect, and to obtain copies of, any disclosures and distributions of healthcare information about themselves. Patients have the right to get an accounting of the disclosures and to amend, correct, and restrict the uses, disclosure, and distribution of healthcare information about themselves.
- **Administrative requirements.** Covered entities are required to develop and to implement appropriate privacy P&P consistent with the HIPAA privacy regulations and tailored to fit their size and complexity, to train and to discipline employees regarding privacy P&P, and to designate a privacy official responsible for the entity's privacy practices and activities.
- **PHI safeguards requirements.** Covered entities are required to have reasonable and appropriate administrative, technical, and physical safeguards to prevent intentional or unintentional use or disclosure of PHI in violation of the HIPAA privacy regulations and to otherwise abide by all the allowed and disallowed uses and disclosures of PHI. The HIPAA security regulations (see Section 71.7.1.3) stipulate such safeguards for electronic PHI.

71.5.3 HIPAA Security Rule. The HIPAA Security Rule[37] is the regulation that stipulates national requirements for protecting electronic PHI that is created, stored, used, processed, displayed, maintained, or communicated by certain healthcare entities. The Security Rule does not apply to situations where PHI is in paper-based or oral form. A synopsis of the HIPAA Security Rule is given in this section. HITECH updates to the security rule appear in Section 71.5.6.1.

These security regulations establish requirements for safeguarding confidentiality, integrity, and availability of electronic PHI. PHI must be protected against reasonably expected threats, vulnerabilities, and hazards as well as against disclosures and inappropriate use not permitted by HIPAA's privacy regulations. The requirements also establish an organizational culture that facilitates the provisioning and maintenance of security safeguards.

There are linkages between HIPAA privacy requirements and HIPAA security requirements. Some requirements overlap or complement each other. For example, privacy and security regulations both contain awareness-training requirements. They can be combined so that employees of covered entities stay aware of both the importance of protecting PHI and the means by which PHI is protected. In other cases, a specific security requirement may need to be implemented to address a specific privacy requirement.

As outlined below, the security regulations stipulate various categories of administrative, technical, and physical security requirements as well as organizational, P&P, and documentation requirements. They require covered entities to assess risk and to provide for the safeguarding of electronic PHI at risk. For each covered entity, there must be fully auditable procedures for controlling access to PHI and for protecting PHI against compromise and misuse.

71.5.3.1 Administrative Safeguards Requirements. These requirements pertain to administrative P&P and actions targeted to manage (a) selection, deployment, and maintenance of security safeguards to protect electronic PHI and (b) roles of employees in protecting PHI. The requirements categories include:

- **Security management process.** Implement P&P for preventing, detecting, containing, and correcting security violations.
- **Assigned security responsibility.** Identify an individual responsible for developing and implementing security-oriented P&P.
- **Workforce security.** Implement P&P for ensuring appropriate employee access to, or denial of access to, PHI.
- **Information access management.** Implement P&P for authorizing access to PHI consistent with privacy access requirements.
- **Security awareness and training.** Implement a security awareness and training program for all employees.
- **Security incident procedures.** Implement P&P for handling incidents that impact systems associated with PHI.
- **Contingency plan.** Establish and implement P&P for responding to emergencies that damage systems containing PHI.
- **Evaluation.** Periodic assessments that the security P&P address the security requirements.
- **Business associate contracts and other arrangements.** Establish legally binding, chain-of-trust agreements with business partners for protecting PHI conveyed to such partners.

A synopsis of the implementation specifications associated with these administrative safeguards requirements appears in the Security Standards Matrix table in Appendix A of the HIPAA Security Rule.

71.5.3.2 Physical Safeguards Requirements. These requirements pertain to physical measures and associated P&P to protect IT systems, facilities, and applicable equipment from physical hazards, unauthorized physical access, and unauthorized intrusions. The requirements categories include:

- **Facility access controls.** Establish and implement P&P to control physical access to IT systems, related equipment, and the facilities that house them.
- **Workstation use.** Implement P&P regarding physical location and use of computers to access electronic PHI.
- **Workstation security.** Implement physical safeguards to control physical access to computers used to access electronic PHI.
- **Device and media controls.** Implement P&P regarding receipt, reuse, and disposal of hardware, software, and electronic media that handle electronic PHI.

A synopsis of the implementation specifications associated with these physical safeguards requirements appears in the Security Standards Matrix table in Appendix A of the HIPAA Security Rule.

71.5.3.3 Technical Safeguards Requirements. These requirements pertain to technological measures and associated P&P to protect and to control access to electronic PHI. A covered entity can determine which security will need to be implemented. The requirements categories include:

- **Access control.** Implement technical P&P for controlling access by people and software to IT systems that handle electronic PHI. Access must be appropriate to the role or job function of the entity seeking access. Subordinate requirements include (a) unique user identification to make users accountable by tracking their electronic activities, (b) emergency, possibly alternative, access procedures, (c) automatic user logoff to terminate inactive session, and (d) encryption and decryption to prevent view or use of PHI by unauthorized entities.
- **Audit controls.** Implement technical and procedural mechanisms that examine and record activities and accesses to IT systems that handle electronic PHI.
- **Integrity.** Implement P&P to ensure the validity of electronic PHI.
- **Person or entity authentication.** Implement procedures to verify legitimacy of people and software attempting to access electronic PHI.
- **Transmission security.** Implement technical security measures to control unauthorized access to electronic PHI in transit over computer networks. Subordinate requirements include reliance on (a) integrity controls to ensure PHI is not modified without detection, and (b) flexibility to establish compatible encryption/decryption methods between PHI senders and receivers.

A synopsis of the implementation specifications associated with these technical safeguards requirements appears in the Security Standards Matrix table in Appendix A of the HIPAA Security Rule.

71.5.3.4 Organizational Requirements. These requirements pertain to using business associate contracts or other official arrangements to establish trust that third parties associated with, or providing services to, covered entities will maintain HIPAA provisions.

71.5.3.5 Policies and Procedures and Documentation Requirements. These requirements pertain to developing all the requisite P&P (as outlined earlier), to developing and using all required documentation and documentation configuration control measures, and to implementing the P&P to comply with HIPAA security regulations.

71.5.3.6 Implementation Specifications. Each stipulated security requirement summarized above must be met by a defined implementation specification stipulated in the HIPAA security regulations, or, if no implementation specifications exist, by measures documented and implemented by each covered entity. NIST Special Publication 800-66[38] identifies (in Table 4 in Appendix D) implementation specifications and companion security controls (detailed in NIST Special Publication 800-53) accompanying each HIPAA Security Rule requirement.

For HIPAA Security Rule requirements met by HIPAA-stipulated implementation specifications, such implementation specifications are individually identified in the

HIPAA Security Rule (and in NIST SP 800-66) as either being "required" or "addressable." Covered entities must comply with all 13 *required* implementation specifications.

For "addressable" security implementation specifications, covered entities must document how they assessed and decided (a) whether each specific *addressable* implementation specification is reasonable and appropriate, or not; (b) whether it applies, or does not, to their specific environment; and (c) whether the covered entity implemented, or not, each addressable implementation specification (or some equivalent alternative measures).

For example, to meet HIPAA's contingency plan requirement, a covered entity is *required* to establish and to implement data backup, disaster recovery, and emergency mode operations plans; and it must also *address* procedures for testing and revising such plans.

Covered entities have options for how to field security solutions for addressable security implementation requirements that are deemed reasonable and appropriate in their environments. Risk, security, and financial analyses should help decide which security technologies or methods best address the security implementation requirements. Covered entities must document and periodically reassess their analyses and rationale for fielding specific security measures.

71.5.4 HIPAA Breach Notification Interim Rule. The U.S. HHS[39] and the Federal Trade Commission (FTC)[40] have companion, harmonized regulations pertaining to notifying individuals whose individually identified PHI is breached. A synopsis of the original Breach Notification Rule is given in this section. HITECH updates to the breach notification rule appear in Section 71.5.6.3.

The HHS regulations apply only to HIPAA-covered entities and to their business associates.

The FTC regulations apply only to certain Web-based businesses, such as vendors of personal health records, as well as certain other parties not stipulated in HIPAA, that provide individuals the voluntary ability to create, to collect, and to manage online stores of their own health information. The FTC regulations also apply to third-party applications that can be used by individuals voluntarily to interact with such health information stores, to create new individually identifiable content for such data stores (e.g., individually obtained blood pressure readings) or to process or to display existing individually identifiable content. The FTC regulations also specify other entities that fall within the jurisdiction of the FTC breach notice requirements.

The federal breach notice regulations specify what is a breach, under what conditions are breach notifications issued, who is responsible for issuing a breach notification, to whom breach notifications must be sent, timing constraints associated with the generation of breach notifications, what information must be contained in the breach notification, precedents among different breach notification laws, and penalties for not following the regulations. The various factors that compose the breach notification requirements are summarized below.

71.5.4.1 Breach Definition. According to the 2009 interim breach notification regulations, a breach occurs when a compromise of electronic PHI (and also paper-based PHI in the case of HHS) takes place and the breached information poses significant financial or reputational risk or other harm to the individual whose PHI was revealed, acquired, accessed, or used by an unauthorized party.

There are three exceptions to the definition of a breach. Breaches exclude inadvertent PHI disclosure between two authorized individuals in the same healthcare entity.

Breaches also exclude PHI disclosures to unauthorized individuals who are reasonably believed not to be able to retain such disclosed PHI. Also excluded are unintentional accesses, acquisition, or use of PHI if such actions were done in good faith within the scope of authority and such actions do not lead to further PHI use or disclosure.

71.5.4.2 Triggers for Breach Notifications. The required condition for generating a breach notification is when any part of any *unsecured* PHI within the domain of a PHI data custodian is exposed via a breach. The regulations stipulate that *unsecured* PHI is PHI that is decipherable, readable, and usable by parties that are not authorized to access such PHI. HHS has identified technologies and methodologies that can make PHI indecipherable, unreadable, and unusable.[41]

Use of such technologies and methodologies renders PHI adequately protected so that any breaches thereof do not require breach notifications. As such, for example, if encrypted PHI is stolen as a consequence of a breach, the custodians of the breached, encrypted PHI are not required to notify the individuals whose encrypted PHI was stolen. It is assumed that the parties stealing the breached encrypted PHI will not be able to decipher, read, or use the encrypted PHI.

There are other conditions, generally associated with the above breach exceptions, under which breach notices are not required. For one, any health information that has been de-identified according to methods specified in the HIPAA Privacy Rules does not constitute data for which breaches thereof require breach notification. For another, not all unauthorized accesses of PHI lead to unauthorized PHI acquisition and the need to provide breach notices. For example, inadvertent or unintentional access of PHI that does not lead to reading, using, or disclosing PHI may not constitute a breach. Furthermore, an impermissible disclosure of health information to an unauthorized individual who is not able to retain the disclosed health information may not constitute a breach. Similarly, a lost computer or storage device that houses PHI and is subsequently retrieved—and for which it can shown that PHI files were never opened, exchanged, or changed—also may not constitute a breach.

Custodians of breached PHI must be able to demonstrate that all required breach notifications have been sent or that disclosure of unsecured PHI did not meet the definition of a breach.

71.5.4.3 Issuers and Recipients of Breach Notifications. As to who is responsible for generating a breach notice, the HHS regulations require HIPAA-covered entities to notify individuals (and, under certain conditions, HHS and the media) when specified breach notification conditions are met. The FTC regulations require Web-based businesses under FTC jurisdiction to notify individuals (and FTC under certain conditions) when a breach of individually identifiable health information occurs.

When breaches occur within the domain of business associates of HIPAA-covered entities, the business associates are required to notify the covered entity with which a business agreement is established; the covered entities are then responsible for notifying the specific individuals whose PHI was compromised by the business associate.

Similarly, when breaches occur within the domain of service providers for businesses under the jurisdiction of the FTC regulations, such service providers are required to notify the businesses for which service is being provided; the businesses are then responsible for notifying their customers whose PHI was compromised by the service provider.

Several methods of conveying breach notices are permissible. Under certain conditions, custodians of breached PHI may use means other than direct communications to convey breach notices to specific individuals. Breach notices being sent to the HHS, or updates to previously submitted breach notices sent to HHS, must be submitted electronically via a specified HHS form.

71.5.4.4 Breach Timing Constraints. Breach notices that are to be sent to affected individuals and to the media must be sent as fast as is reasonably expected, but no later than 60 days after breach discovery.[42] Breach notifications issued by HHS business associates or by service providers to FTC-designated businesses must also abide by the as-soon-as-possible, -but-no-more-than-60-days, timing requirement.

The acceptable timing constraints of breach notices sent to HHS or the FTC vary with the number of individuals impacted by the breach. Breaches impacting more than 500 individuals must have breach notices sent within 60 days of breach discovery. Breaches impacting less than 500 individuals may be more leisurely treated in terms of notifying HHS or the FTC.

71.5.4.5 Breach Contents. The contents of breach notices to individuals, to the HHS or FTC and to the media serving the state or jurisdiction where the breach occurred must include: (a) a description of the breach event, including date of the breach occurrence and date of the discovery of the breach; (b) a synopsis of what unsecured PHI was compromised; (c) a statement of what impacted individuals should do to protect themselves from potential harm resulting from the PHI compromise; (d) a description of what the custodian of the breached PHI is doing to investigate the breach, to lessen potential losses that may result from the breach, and to bolster protection against future breach attempts; and (e) contact information for the custodian of the breached PHI.

Breach notices emanating from HHS-stipulated business associates or FTC-stipulated service providers must include a tabulation of the identity of all the individuals whose individually identifiable information was, or is reasonably believed to be, acquired during the health information compromise. These breach notices must also convey the information that is to be relayed to impacted individuals.

71.5.4.6 Breach Law Precedents. For entities that may be subject to both HHS and FTC breach notification rules, compliance with specific HHS requirements is sufficient to claim compliance with corresponding FTC requirements. Establishing such an order of precedent lowers the probability of duplicate breach notices being issued to the same individual.

There is also an order of precedence stipulated between breach notice requirements specified in both federal regulations and state regulations; federal requirements supersede any contrary state regulations. But federal requirements are additive to state regulations that do not conflict with federal regulations. Also, federal requirements do not supersede more stringent state requirements.

71.5.4.7 Breach Notification Policies, Procedures, and Penalties. Entities under the jurisdiction of HHS and FTC breach notification regulations must establish breach notification policies and procedures. Such policies and procedures should include educating employees as to what constitutes a breach, how to document and to analyze potential breaches of unsecured PHI, how to report actual breaches, the intricacies of sending breach notices, and what to do with PHI that employees may have acquired via inadvertent unauthorized access. Such entities must conduct policy and procedures training of employees, and must appropriately penalize noncompliant employees.

71.5.5 HIPAA Protection Rules Enforcement, Penalties, and Liabilities. HIPAA depends on a compliance-driven process to enforce the regulations established in the HIPAA Privacy, Security, and Breach Notification Rules. Victims of PHI disclosure and individuals believing there has been a violation of any of the HIPAA Rules can start the enforcement process by submitting a PHI disclosure or violation complaint to the HHS Office for Civil Rights (OCR). The required content of, and the rules governing, the complaint are specified.[43] Only certain types of complaints[44] will be considered for enforcement action.

The HHS OCR investigates complaints. It also may unilaterally initiate an HIPAA Rules compliance review of any covered entity. If it is determined that a potential criminal violation occurred, OCR can request the Department of Justice investigate the claim and impose any applicable penalties. The OCR can impose civil (monetary) penalties and the Department of Justice can impose criminal (prison) penalties.

The procedures performed during an OCR complaint investigation are stipulated.[45] OCR decides about the interpretation, implementation, and enforcement of HIPAA regulations. When it appears the covered entity that was the subject of the complaint was not in compliance with HIPAA Rules, OCR often attempts to seek resolution by letting the implicated covered entity take corrective actions to establish compliance.

If the actions are not satisfactory to resolve the disclosure compliant or noncompliance situation, OCR can impose civil sanctions. Covered entities can be penalized $100 per violation, up to $25,000 per year per HIPAA requirement not met.

However, there are large criminal penalties for those who wrongfully handle confidential PHI. Any person, who knowingly obtains, uses, causes to use, intends malicious harm, tries to sell or to transfer or to gain from, or discloses, patient information inappropriately, faces penalties. Penalties range from $50,000 to $250,000 and up to 10 years' imprisonment, depending on seriousness of the offense.

Some argue the real dangers of HIPAA enforcement may arise from loss of patient confidence in the implicated covered entity and possible litigation under contract law. When disclosure of personal information causes damage and the legal system is engaged, HIPAA penalties—especially the criminal penalties—can mean the difference between business failure and business survival for implicated entities. PHI disclosures, whether wrongful or unintentional, have potentials to be devastating. Some argue potential consequences of HIPAA litigation should be considered when developing disaster plans.

Other entities besides just covered entities can be implicated and at risk for PHI disclosure penalties. The "linked liability" concept may extend HIPAA-relevant liabilities and penalties to others. Covered entities forced into litigation for PHI privacy or security breaches may try to share blame or to pass it to others, such as the communications provider used to connect covered entity offices. Such other parties may also try to spread blame to yet others, such as negligent vendors of IT products with implementation errors, vulnerabilities, and less than adequate security. The ultimate assignment of liabilities may be legally tortious.

To minimize liability exposure, firms linked in even obtuse ways to covered entities are wise to be able to show (a) they exercised due diligence in establishing normal and customary privacy and security measures within their enterprises, services, or products; (b) their measures are in line with industry best practices and HIPAA requirements, and (as required by HIPAA) anticipate and address new threats; and (c) they made correct decisions regarding their privacy and security measures.

Some argue that employers offering health insurance also have implicit liabilities linked to HIPAA. It is argued that employers have a duty to ensure healthcare plans and associated care providers offered to employees are compliant with HIPAA. Second, when insurance carriers send enrollment and benefits data to employers, employers may be construed as acting as business associates subject to provisions that business associates of covered entities must also be HIPAA compliant.

A further class of entity not considered *covered* under HIPAA is the property and casualty insurance carrier. One can argue that even though the insurance carrier does not dispense treatment and is not in the treatment chain, it handles the same information that HIPAA regulates. Many make a successful argument in favor of this special class in that the patient relinquishes any expectation of privacy when the incident (i.e., accident) becomes part of a suit or arbitration. In that case the information becomes public record. However, property and casualty insurance carriers may simply pay as underwritten with no suit or arbitration. This constitutes a sufficient gray area in covered versus noncovered entities.

HITECH updates to legacy HIPAA enforcement regulations appear in Section 71.5.6.4.

71.5.6 HITECH's HIPAA Update.

The HITECH Act broadens and expands the scope of personal healthcare information (PHI) security and privacy beyond that stipulated by the original seminal HIPAA mandates. Changes to HIPAA regulations pertaining to healthcare information privacy, security, breach notification, and violation enforcement were recently issued in a so-called HIPAA Final Rule.[46] Of significance, the final rule now extends HIPAA's security and privacy requirements, HIPAA's compliance/penalty mandates, and liability risks to most business associates of HIPAA-covered entities.

71.5.6.1 *HIPAA Security Enhancements.*

HITECH extends the original HIPAA Security Rule to apply full-force to most of the business associates of the covered entities to which the original HIPAA Security Rule applies. The business associates that are affected are those who are exposed to any PHI in the covered entity's environment.

Business associates must comply with all aspects of the HIPAA Security Rule. They must develop, implement, and maintain security policies and address the same security requirements as the covered entity. Healthcare entities must conduct due diligence in evaluating the information protection capabilities of prospective business partners before business relationships are established and formally consummated by formal business associate agreements.

The business associates impacted are those corporate or individual bodies that in the course of their business with a HIPAA-covered entity create, receive, maintain, transmit, or have access to protected health information entrusted to the HIPAA-covered entity. Impacted business associates include such diverse entities as, for example, vendors of PHI records, providers of claims processing, medical equipment vendors, medical transcriptionists, benefits managers, lawyers, cloud service providers, billing, accounting, actuarial, and legal and financial services, as well as other kinds of contractors and subcontractors that perform services on behalf of a healthcare-covered entity.

Current legal analysis[47] expects that impacted subcontractors of business associates will also include the service providers and technology companies that service the business associates and that have access to PHI through their work for business associates as customers of their services or products. As such, HITECH stipulates that business associates will need to establish another tier of business associate agreements, namely business associate agreements with their subcontractors.

Further HHS guidance has been issued on how to secure protected health information.

71.5.6.2 HIPAA Privacy Enhancements. The HITECH enhancements to HIPAA privacy provide greater protection and control of PHI. HITECH extends all the use and disclosure provisions and limitations of HIPAA's original Privacy Rule to apply full-force to business associates of the covered entities to which the original HIPAA Privacy Rule applies.

Patient rights have been enhanced; patients have further control of the dissemination and use of their own PHI. For example, under specific patient payment conditions patients can prohibit providers from sending patient treatment information to health plan entities and insurance carrier entities. Patients can prohibit or authorize the sale of their PHI, the use or disclosure of their PHI for marketing and fundraising purposes, and/or the use of their PHI by researchers. Patients can authorize that certain of their minor children's PHI be provided to their children's school. Patients have the right to be notified of certain types of breaches of their PHI.

Providers' legacy privacy practice notices that were established in response to the original HIPAA Privacy Rule must be updated and posted to reflect the new HITECH HIPAA privacy mandates. All new patients must be given copies of such updated privacy notices.

71.5.6.3 HIPAA Breach Notification Enhancements. HITECH[48] and the FTC[49] updated and extended the breach notification requirements of the original HIPAA Breach Notification Rule. The original breach notification rule was based on the notion that breaches can pose a risk of harm to the individuals whose PHI was compromised. Such a risk of harm consideration was consistent with breach notification laws in several states. The new breach notification rule is based on the notion that there is risk that PHI is compromised instead of there being risk of harm to the individual.[50] The change to an *access* standard from a *harm* standard is intended to provide more objectivity in when to declare an incident to be a breach.

Furthermore, the applicability of breach rules now extends to the business associates of the covered entities to which the original HIPAA Breach Notification Rule applies. Business associates now have the same HIPAA liabilities and exposures as HIPAA-covered entities. As such, business associates must establish appropriate breach response policies and must respond to breach incidents in ways that are in full compliance with HIPAA regulations.

Legal analysis[51] of the extended breach notification requirements reveal that prudent covered entities and their business associates should move from a "risk of harm" standard to a "presumption of breach" standard. More specifically, parties impacted by HIPAA will move away from the original HIPAA position that a party that is the source of breached information is presumed innocent of harming patients when a breach occurs, until proven otherwise. They will move to the new HIPAA position that parties are presumed guilty of harming patients during a breach, unless the parties can prove their innocence. Impacted parties need to alter their incident response and breach notification strategies and processes, accordingly.

The new HITECH HIPAA requirements also modify what is classified as a breach and stipulate which breaches are reportable, under what conditions breach notifications must be issued, and to whom breaches must be reported.

The new requirements modify what risk assessments are required in order to initiate a breach incident response. Under the original HIPAA breach rules all unauthorized accesses to PHI were deemed breaches if such accesses posed significant risk of any financial or reputation consequences, or other type of harm, to the affected individual whose PHI was compromised. Under the new breach regulations, any access, disclosure, or use of PHI that is not allowed under the HIPAA Final Privacy Rule is a breach that must be reported unless the caretaker of the PHI in question can demonstrate that the probability of PHI exposure, via unauthorized PHI access or impermissible use by knowledgeable insiders, is too low to warrant a breach incident response.

The probability of PHI compromise demonstration must use a specific four factor risk assessment that must include factors like (a) whether the PHI in question was just viewed or whether a breach perpetrator actually acquired the PHI in question, and (b) the level of risk reduction brought about by efforts to mitigate the impact of the PHI exposure. Risk can be appropriately reduced, for example, by obtaining documented assurances from the breach perpetrator that the breached PHI has been destroyed, will not be further used, and/or will not be further disseminated.

Breaches that intentionally expose *unprotected,* personally identifiable PHI must be reported via breach notifications. Exposure of PHI that are *protected* by security such as encryption, but are nonetheless still compromised, do not require breach notifications.

Notifications of breaches affecting at least 500 individuals are to be conveyed to all individual victims as well as to HHS. Covered entities and their business associates have differing notification requirements that depend on which party discovers the breach. Notifications must be conveyed to at least each individual victim of unprotected PHI exposure, and possibly to other parties, within 60 calendar days after breach discovery. Only specified types of notification processes are permitted.

71.5.6.4 HIPAA Enforcement Enhancements. HIPAA enforcement actions are triggered by a written personal complaint that an HIPAA-covered entity or Business Associate violated some person's PHI privacy rights or otherwise committed some other violation of the HIPAA privacy or security rules. HITECH extended HIPAA civil and criminal penalties. Penalties for violations of noncompliance with any of the HIPAA Final Rules are now based on the level of negligence that occurred. The liabilities for Business Associates changed; the entire set of revised penalties, as well as HHS OCR audits and enforcement actions, is extended to apply full-force to Business Associates.

While business associates must now follow all HIPAA rules and can be held liable for an impermissible use or disclosure of PHI, the covered entities that receive services from their business associates are, nonetheless, still responsible for the actions of their business associates. As such, the chain of contracts—so-called Business Associate Agreements—from covered entities to business associates to business associates' subcontractors and so on must properly include provisions for appropriate assurances of HIPAA compliance.

Covered entities and their business associates must comply with all requirements stipulated in the HIPAA Final Rule by September 23, 2013. Any existing Business Associate Agreements between covered entities, business associates, or business associates' contractors or subcontracts that were in effect prior to January 26, 2013, must be modified by September 22, 2014, to reflect compliance with the new security, privacy, and breach notification rule changes. The new enforcement rules apply after September 23, 2013.

According to HITECH, State Attorneys General are given the power to undertake HIPAA civil enforcement actions for HIPAA violations that impact their state's residents. The AGs can now seek damages on behalf of state residents.

HITECH also specifies that criminal and civil violations of HITECH and HIPAA mandates can be punished by a four-tier set of increasingly onerous penalties based on increasingly greater levels of culpability.

Criminal violations of HITECH HIPAA mandates are prosecuted by the U.S. Department of Justice and can result in imprisonment as well as financial penalty. In 2005, the DOJ weakened the original HIPAA criminal statue by claiming that this statue does not apply to individuals. Some have argued that such a weakening allows miscreants (e.g., hackers who steal healthcare information or covered entity staff who might sell PHI), to walk away free of consequences because they do not violate HIPAA.

HITECH specifies that three types of specific violations are prosecutable. The prosecutable violations include inappropriate use of a medical ID, theft of PHI, or disclosure of PHI. Contrary to the seminal HIPAA strategy of there being a single level of punishment, HITECH now specifies that persons knowingly engaged in prosecutable violation activities can be assessed any of several different penalties. For example, they can be fined up to $50,000 and be imprisoned for up to one year. If the intent of disclosure is to sell or use PHI for commercial advantage, imprisonment can be as high as 10 years and fines may be as high as $250,000. Such HITECH criminal penalties are over and above any criminal penalties resulting from violation of the seminal HIPAA Law.

Financial penalties for civil violations of HITECH depend on the nature and intent of the PHI disclosure. Contrary to the seminal HIPAA provision, HITECH specifies three levels of penalties. They range from a $100 to $50,000 fine per unknowing violation (with a $25,000 to $1,500,000 yearly cap) up to a $10,000 to $50,000 fine per willful neglect violation (with a $250,000 to $1,500,000 yearly cap).

The consequences of noncompliance to the HIPAA Rules are many, not just possible federal penalties and state fines. Business associates can suffer the loss of contracts. Covered entities and business associates can expect to cover the costs associated with creating and sending notifications to all individuals whose PHI was compromised. They may have to cover the costs of credit monitoring services for victims of information exposure. They may have to incur costs to repair hacked IT. They may have to incur costs in revising existing, or in establishing new, protection policies, procedures, awareness training, and backup capabilities. There will be numerous legal and security review costs associated with supporting criminal or civil investigations. There may be legal costs and possible monetary settlements of private legal actions by individuals impacted by their PHI loss or compromise—especially if compromised PHI was unknowingly altered and led to erroneous medical decision making. Loss of reputation may impact future earnings.

71.5.7 Demonstrating HIPAA Compliance. Establishing whether a healthcare entity is compliant with HIPAA rules can be a daunting task. Determining compliance with all the other laws and regulations applicable to a healthcare entity complicates the compliance picture even more. Just for the case of HIPAA alone, an organization must initially determine many factors. It must identify which of its care and business activities are under the jurisdiction of HIPAA. It must find, identify, and document the totality of PHI created, stored, processed, and displayed in the organization. It must identify PHI flows, both those internal within the organization as well as external flows, to/from business associates and other third parties. Only then can an organization begin the process of assessing whether HIPAA rules are being followed in all situations.

As detailed elsewhere,[52] observations of the HIPAA compliance status of different healthcare entities in the healthcare sector show a mixed state of affairs. Large care providers (e.g., hospitals and medical centers) generally are complying in large numbers. The compliance story for other entities is mixed. Small care providers (single doctors and small offices of care providers) tend to be overwhelmed and minimally compliant. Insurance carriers are often not changing their legacy systems and procedures to adapt to HIPAA. Clearinghouses are trying to provide interfaces between providers and carriers, but these intermediaries are having troubles too.

Compliance-related initiatives associated with HIPAA-covered entities and business associates of covered entities are considered in Sections 71.5.7.1 and 71.5.7.2.[53]

71.5.7.1 HIPAA-Covered Entity Compliance. There are a number of organizations that support HIPAA compliance efforts. The organizations include the HHS Office of Civil Rights (Section 71.5.7.1.1), the healthcare accrediting commissions (Section 71.5.7.1.2), and the HITRUST industry group (Section 71.7.1.2).

71.5.7.1.1 HHS Office of Civil Rights (OCR). As required by HITECH, the HHS OCR established a compliance program for the HIPAA Privacy, Security, and Breach Notification Rules. The list of documents that may be requested by OCR during a HIPAA security onsite investigation and compliance review is extensive.[54] Compliance is assessed either by (a) OCR spot-checks of healthcare entities or (b) OCR targeted investigations triggered by reported incidents of PHI compromise.

71.5.7.1.2 Spot Checking. OCR must conduct spontaneous, spot-check, semi-random audits of healthcare-covered entities (and eventually business associates) to measure, against specified criteria, their compliance to the HIPAA Privacy Rule, Security Rule, and Breach Notification Rule. The spontaneous, spot-check audit is intended to result in a compliance improvement process whereby any deficiencies that are exposed can be fixed by the audited organization. Spot checks are repeated over time in order to assess changes in a healthcare entity's compliance status. Compliance status changes may arise from changes in healthcare business and care processes, personnel changes, HIPAA awareness changes, fielded technology changes, and so on.

However, it is possible that a spontaneous audit could unearth significant compliance shortcomings that could initiate a separate, targeted, OCR enforcement investigation (see below). The possible consequences of noncompliance discovered during a targeted investigation are many (see Section 71.5.6.4). As such, the threat of a spontaneous OCR audit may help[55] to improve an organization's compliance with HIPAA rules.

A pilot program to help OCR establish its HIPAA auditing role was recently completed. A wide range of large and small covered entities ranging from those using complex IT to those with paper-based workflows were included, including healthcare plans, clearinghouses, and individual and organizational providers. Each audit was completed within 30 business days. Each audit included onsite interviews and examinations of staff, equipment, facilities, and documents. Common shortcomings discovered[56] in this pilot included inadequate risk analyses, outdated HIPAA-related policies and procedures, and lack of contingency plans.

71.5.7.1.3 Targeted Investigations. OCR also conducts complaint-driven, targeted examinations (see Section 71.5.6.4) of specific covered entities purportedly suffering PHI loss incidents, as well as business associates (see Section 71.5.7.2), that purportedly exposed PHI. These examinations are HIPAA enforcement investigations that establish the level of compliance in place at the time of an incident of PHI exposure. Investigations also assess whether a specific incident was truly a breach, what intent (e.g., unsuspecting versus malicious) was associated with the breach, and whether any appropriate sanctions and penalties are warranted.

71.5.7.1.4 Healthcare Accrediting Commissions. Electronic Healthcare Network Accreditation Commission (EHNAC) and the Utilization Review Accreditation Commission (URAC) are healthcare accrediting organizations establishing roles in being federally recognized, independent third parties for demonstrating or testing HIPAA compliance.

With the advent of possible onsite visits from the OCR and the increasing risk of exposure to HIPAA penalties and breach handling costs, healthcare-covered entities are looking to get their HIPAA privacy and security ducks in order before an OCR audit commences. An EHNAC or URAC privacy and security accreditation can position the accredited healthcare-covered entity with more evidence to complete the OCR audit successfully.

EHNAC is an outside resource that can be used by a healthcare-covered entity to support its privacy and security compliance both to HIPAA and HITECH.[57] EHNAC can be contracted by a healthcare-covered entity to evaluate its privacy and security policies, procedures, and implemented controls that may likely be audited by OCR for HIPAA compliance. EHNAC is also looking to position itself as a third-party security and privacy certifier of healthcare entities seeking compliance to the Direct Messaging aspect of HITECH Stage 2 Meaningful Use.

Similarly, URAC operates HIPAA privacy and HIPAA security accreditation programs.[58] These programs are used by HIPAA-covered entities and business associates to help demonstrate their HIPAA compliance. Like the comparable EHNAC process, the URAC HIPAA privacy and HIPAA security accreditation processes consider industry best practices and examine a healthcare organization's operational policies and procedures to verify effective compliance to HIPAA rules.

A HIPAA Privacy and Security Accreditation by URAC or EHNAC demonstrates a healthcare organization's good faith efforts to abide by HIPAA requirements. Receiving such an accreditation also provides a measure of HIPAA compliance assurance to a healthcare organization's prospective business associates. Patients can also get comfort that their PHI will be safe at an accredited healthcare organization.

Other private organizations, not necessarily federally recognized, also provide HIPAA compliance auditing services that evaluate whether and why a healthcare organization is HIPAA compliant and if not, why not.

71.5.7.2 HIPAA Business Associate Compliance. According to HITECH, technology service providers who want to make themselves available as candidate business associates to HIPAA-covered entities, as well as to other HIPAA business associates, can become certified that they are compliant with HIPAA. The HIPAA compliance certification ensures that candidate business associates comply with all of HIPAA's privacy, security, and breach notification requirements so that a contracting HIPAA covered entity, or any contracting HIPAA business associate, is confident that when their PHI is exposed to a compliance-certified business associate, the PHI will be protected to the same level specified in HIPAA and that the compliance-certified business associate's protection solutions are HIPAA-compliant. The compliance-certification also ensures that candidate business associates conduct recurring evaluations that demonstrate that over time their privacy, security, and breach notification policies and procedures and associated awareness training meet all of HIPAA's privacy, security, and breach notification requirements.

71.5.8 Related Federal Guidelines. Various departments and agencies within the U.S. Government develop guidelines and other materials pertinent to the security and privacy within the healthcare sector. General guidelines are also available that apply across any industry or sector.

For example, HHS makes available several online healthcare security and privacy regulation summaries and guidelines, privacy and security tools, awareness and training materials, brochures, and videos.[59] Topics include, for example, providing guidance for planning implementation of solutions meeting HIPAA and Meaningful Use Privacy and Security requirements[60]; providing education about HIPAA-stipulated risk analysis[61]; providing guidance on using the HIPAA Privacy Rule when electronically exchanging PHI[62]; giving HIPAA Security Rule implementation support[63]; providing guidance on the remote use of PHI[64]; and providing guidance on protecting PHI.[65,66]

The National Institute of Standards and Technology (NIST) developed a number of white papers that provide insight into the HIPAA security rules.[67] NIST also published guidance to assist in understanding, implementing, and evaluating operational implementations of HIPAA security requirements.[68,69]

HHS also provides guidelines that specify basic steps for securing mobile devices that need to protect healthcare information.[70,71] The National Institute of Standards and Technology (NIST) has additional recommendations[72,73] for mobile devices. The NIST material is applicable across all fields of endeavor.

The Federal Trade Commission has developed guidance pertaining to several aspects of protecting healthcare information, including medical identity theft, risks of electronic file sharing, and electronic digital copiers.[74]

71.5.9 Comparing Federal and State Healthcare-Relevant Security and Privacy Laws. HIPAA provides a national floor for requirements for protecting PHI; state and other federal laws may provide even stronger protections. Examination of the mosaic of state laws introduced in Section 71.6 reveals that the existing state laws pertaining to PII are to some degree overlapping and sometimes inconsistent in terms of the enacted PII protections. In some cases, HIPAA may enhance the protections afforded by other laws. In other cases, other laws may deal with privacy and security more stringently than HIPAA.

So-called HIPAA preemption analyses are available in many states[75] to understand the relationship between state-specific privacy law and the HIPAA Privacy Rule. In general, the stronger information protection law should prevail. However, conflicts between state law and HIPAA are not always straightforward to resolve, especially when there are differences in limitations or restrictions that are, or are not, precisely stipulated in state and federal laws. Sometimes judicial ruling is needed.[76]

As the federal desire to implement a nationwide health information infrastructure based on sharing of person-specific EHRs progresses, differences among the state-specific laws need to be reconciled. The Harmonizing State Privacy Law Collaborative was formed as part of the Health Information Security & Privacy Collaboration (HISPC) to assist in such matters. The HISPC also considers federal–state healthcare coordination issues related to (a) harmonizing state-specific healthcare information release consent, (b) developing interorganization agreements pertaining to electronic healthcare information exchange, and (c) harmonizing certain aspects of security to facilitate secure PHI exchange between differing Health Information Exchange (HIE) models used in different states.[77]

The precedence between privacy and security requirements of state laws and the federal HIPAA law can have problematic consequences. Interoperability issues can arise between parties that have stronger protection methods and those that have the common, minimal level of protection stipulated by HIPAA. As such, there is the potential for problems with the concept of nationally networked EHRs, as described later in this chapter. Development and exchange of electronic healthcare records can be hampered by inconsistencies and variations in privacy and security policies and regulations between jurisdictions. The HISPC detailed variations in state laws and policies that pertain to the privacy and security of health information that is electronically exchanged.[78] Furthermore, there may be legal questions regarding how patient data can be shared across state lines. Some argue that HIPAA needs to be modified to provide more comprehensive national information protection standards that form a consistent, mandatory uniform ceiling above the growing hodgepodge of similar but potentially inconsistent state laws.

Exhibit 71.2 provides a comparison of the differing breach notification requirements in a representative example of three different laws: two federal laws (GLBA and HIPAA/HITECH) and one state law (Massachusetts). Covered entities have the burden to prove which law or laws pertain to each breached, individually identified data item. It is possible that a breached entity will be held accountable by several laws. Each law runs simultaneously. As such, a covered entity must respond to each breach law and in accordance with each law's timelines and other breach notification requirements.

Breach complaints, whistle blowers, or voluntary admission drive the enforcement of state breach laws and likewise the enforcement of federal breach regulations. Unlike the federal government, states typically do not have the resources to conduct active state-run policing through audits. Often, federal penalty assessments take precedent because states stand back as federal penalty actions occur. Sometimes, states still make penalty assessments that are additive to federal penalties.

Exhibit 71.3 provides an example comparison of a specific set of the privacy requirements appearing in many different laws. In particular, the exhibit identifies which specific date elements of PII have privacy requirements in the various laws. In particular, Table C1 identifies the eighteen primary HIPAA PHI data elements and compares them to the personal data elements identified in PCI DSS 2.0, GLBA, state of California breach notification, and the commonwealth of Massachusetts' 201 C.M.R. 17.00. Initially evident is that data included in HIPAA as PHI is far more inclusive. Regardless of this scope change, those practitioners charged with PHI care may note that there are many instances where data elements overlap.

In lines 1 and 2, the element "name" applies to all drivers listed. California, Massachusetts, GLBA, and PCI all specify a level of detail, whereas HIPAA does not. Using HIPAA's broad scope as a cue, it can be assumed that "names" includes either first or last name rather than the combination denoted in all other statutory and regulatory guidance listed. Of course, a name alone and outside the context of health information (or PII, PFI, PCI) is just a name. However, within the context of a healthcare record, even a first name requires protection.

For the practitioner charged with protecting healthcare information, the nuances of HIPPA data elements are important. Though, many of the controls already applied in other areas simply apply to a greater scope of data elements thus making the problem less overwhelming.

Exhibit 71.2 Comparison of Requirements in Various Breach Notification Laws

Requirement	GLBA	Massachusetts 201 C.M.R. 17.00	HIPAA/HITECH
Notification Exception	When no misuse of data has occurred or when reasonably assured that none will occur (e.g., encryption with proper key control).	If encrypted electronic data and the confidential process or key that is capable of compromising the security, confidentiality, or integrity of personal information not in question	Unintentional, but good faith access by employee or individual acting under covered entity that does not lead to further disclosure, inadvertent disclosure to otherwise authorized individuals does not constitute a breach and disclosure/notification not required. Additionally, breach must also actually compromise the security or privacy. Ostensibly encrypted information with adequate key management would not compromise security or privacy.
	Good encryption with adequate key control usually provides an exception to notification for electronic records. However, paper records have no such exception.		
Notification Timeline	Notify when an institution becomes aware of unauthorized access and misuse of data has occurred or reasonably possible	As soon as practicable and without unreasonable delay, when the Entity knows or has reason to know of a breach of security, or when the Entity knows or has reason to know that the PI of such resident was acquired or used by an unauthorized person or used for an unauthorized purpose.	Discovered is the first day the breach is known or when the entity should have known. From this point there should be "no unreasonable delay and in no case later than 60 days." Sec 13402 (c).
	There is no minimum threshold that changes the method or timing of notification.	HIPAA states that if breach affects 500 or more individuals, without unreasonable delay and in no case later than 60 days from discovery. Additionally, if breach affects less than 500 individuals, within 60 days of the end of the calendar year in which it occurred. HITECH does not make the size distinction. Rather HITECH requires no unreasonable delay and in no case later than 60 calendar days after discovery.	
	All provide for reasonable "law enforcement" delays to protect criminal investigations.		

Notification Recipients	To customer in a manner in which the customer can be reasonably expected to receive it.	MA Resident Affected MA Attorney General Director of consumer affairs and business regulation (who may notify others as necessary)	Written notification to individual (next of kin if individual is deceased). If contact information is insufficient or out of data for 10 or more individuals, prominent Web notification, local print or broadcast media shall be used. Notice to Secretary of HHS (Web form), Posting to HHS Public Website.
Notification Information	Description of incident including the kind of customer information compromised, what the institution has done to protect from further unauthorized access, contact information (e.g., telephone number) for assistance, a reminder to remain vigilant for 12 to 24 months, instructions to review and report any suspicious account activity, description of fraud alerts and how to place them in consumer credit reports, reminder to obtain credit reports and have fraudulent activity removed, and explanation of how to retrieve a free credit report. Attorney General & Director of Consumer Affairs: Above and Nature of the breach or unauthorized access or use	Resident: residents affected, and what actions the covered entity is taking to address the incident	Brief description of breach, date (if known), types of unsecured information (e.g., name, SSN, account number, etc.), steps individual should take to protect themselves, what the covered entity is doing to investigate the breach, mitigate losses, and prevent further breaches, and contact procedures.
	A common theme is that notification must include what the entity is doing currently to prevent further breaches.		
Breach Applies to Any Form Including Paper	Yes	Yes	Yes
	Breach notification most commonly applies to electronic records. However, most breach notification does not discern between paper records and electronic records.		

EXHIBIT 71.3 Comparison of Requirements in Various Privacy Laws

Data Element	HIPAA PHI	CA PII	MA PII	GLBA PII/PFI	PCI DSS PFI/PCI
1st Initial or Name & Last Name	Yes	Yes	Yes	Yes	Yes
Names	Yes			Must include first initial or name AND the last name whereas HIPAA has no such distinction.	
Account Number, Credit Card Number, Debit Card Number, with any required security code, access code, or password that would permit access	Only if it is associated with health care information	Yes	Yes	Yes	Yes
Account numbers	Yes			Only if the number is associated with personally identifiable information or personal financial information.	
All elements of dates (except year) for dates directly related to an individual, including birth date, admission date, discharge date, date of death; and all ages over 89 and all elements of dates (including year) indicative of such age, except that such ages and elements may be aggregated into a single category of age 90 or older	Yes	No			
All geographical subdivisions smaller than a state, including street address, city, county, precinct, ZIP code, and their equivalent geocodes, except for the initial three digits of a ZIP code if, according to the current publicly available data from the Bureau of the Census: (1) the geographic unit formed by combining all ZIP codes with the same three initial digits contains more than 20,000 people; and (2) the initial three digits of a ZIP code for all such geographic units containing 20,000 or fewer people is changed to 000.	Yes		No	This is partially applicable to GLBA and recent court cases indicated that postal code is private information in the context of a credit card transaction if not required as part of the transaction.[1]	

EXHIBIT 71.3 *(Continued)*

Data Element	HIPAA PHI	CA PII	MA PII	GLBA PII/PFI	PCI DSS PFI/PCI
Any other unique identifying number, characteristic, or code (note this does not mean the unique code assigned by the investigator to code the data)	Yes	No			
Biometric identifiers, including finger and voice prints	Yes	No			
Certificate/license numbers	Yes	No			
Device identifiers and serial numbers	Yes	No			
Electronic mail addresses	Yes	No			
Fax numbers	Yes	No			
Full-face photographic images and any comparable images	Yes	No			
Health plan beneficiary numbers	Yes	No			
Internet Protocol (IP) address numbers	Yes	No			
Medical record numbers	Yes	No			
Phone numbers	Yes	No			
Social Security Number	Yes	Yes	Yes	Yes	
Medical and/or Health Insurance Information	Yes	Yes		Yes	
Vehicle identifiers and serial numbers, including license plate numbers	Yes	No			
Web Universal Resource Locators (URLs)	Yes	No			
Information in Cookies	Not specifically listed; however, any information here in the context of healthcare information could be subject to regulation	No		Yes	No
Information on Consumer Reports	No	Yes	No		
State Driver's License Number	Yes	Yes			
State ID Number	Yes	Yes			

[1]Tyler v. Michaels Stores, Inc., No. 11-10920, 2012 WL 32208 (D. Mass. Jan. 6, 2012).

Operationally, the impact of a healthcare entity's need to comply with multiple laws and regulations arising from many jurisdictions can result in many complicating factors that a healthcare entity's information protection professionals must consider when managing PHI in a real operational environment.

The scope of HIPAA data elements extends beyond the boundaries of PII, PFI, and PCI. This only means that controls employed to protect other data elements necessarily apply. Erring on the side of caution by employing broader controls is prudent. Additionally, applying discrete controls in the absence of a data classification standard and risk-management program introduces complexities to an already complex arena. However, application of NIST 800-53 (see Section 71.6.2.2), or other risk frameworks (e.g., ISO 27001) generally provides adequate organization to address healthcare information security. There are pros and cons to each method and, like much guidance in information assurance; it must match the organization's culture and ability to execute given business and resource constraints.

There is immense value in information classification as an abstraction exercise. That is, classification, implemented as a means to determine the value of data and to identify the most appropriate way to store, to manipulate or to access data, brings immediate management value. It establishes classes and categories of like data for similar treatment. Classes establish a label whereby the healthcare entity can set policy, determine action, and protect assets based on known drivers. In effect, information classification can determine the minimum level of protection required based on the nature of the classification of the data. Furthermore, classification provides knowledge and guidance to determine the most effective course of action.

Where classification reveals that current systems, applications, processes, and procedures present risk, then risk remediation action is possible. Action will range from acceptance of risk, to implementation and fielding of additional controls, to redesign of IT systems or security protections. In the context of healthcare data, where controlled data have a wider scope than other statutory and regulatory edicts, classification serves to ensure that both security practitioners and nonsecurity employees understand data class, the driving regulation (e.g., HIPAA, PCI, etc.), and the required protection treatment (e.g., encryption at rest, in flight, or both, etc.).

As a practical matter, managing to compliance with HIPAA or any other statutory or regulatory driver diverts focus to the act of compliance rather than the act of managing risk associated with the data. HIPAA, as a driver, is one of many within the context of risk management within a healthcare entity. This is not to lessen its importance, but healthcare entity protection professionals must determine the most stringent of driver requirements and manage to that baseline. Each healthcare entity must write this most stringent baseline into its policies, standards, procedures, and enterprise awareness training. The minimum requirement becomes that of the entire enterprise and sufficiently covers all drivers, in all locations, and at all times.

71.6 OTHER PUBLIC SECTOR HEALTHCARE PRIVACY AND SECURITY INITIATIVES.

There are several government-instigated initiatives relevant to healthcare information privacy and security. HITECH efforts at pushing the United States toward so-called "meaningful use" of a new healthcare model that relies on secure, nationwide, electronic sharing of protected healthcare information are considered in Section 71.6.1. The several information protection regulations and guidelines that apply to DoD healthcare are considered in Section 71.6.2. Yet other government initiatives related to healthcare information protection are identified in Section 71.6.3.

71.6.1 The HITECH Act: Moving to Electronic Health Information. In part following on from a 2004 Presidential Executive Order,[79] the 2009 Health Information Technology for Economic and Clinical Health (HITECH) Act[80] funded and tasked the U.S. HHS to expand the adoption of health information technology and to create a national network of secure and private electronic health records (EHRs). In conjunction with its HITECH efforts, HHS also updated and expanded the HIPAA Rule of 1996 (see Section 71.5.6).

HITECH established an Office for a National Coordinator (ONC) for Health Information Technology (HIT). ONC established and guides the development of national HIT policy, standards, and certification testing associated with a national HIT infrastructure supporting the electronic use and secure exchange of privacy-protected EHRs. While ONC is currently incentivizing physicians and hospitals to adopt and to use certified EHRs, in 2015, healthcare entities and providers will receive Medicare financial penalties if EHRs are not used.

The ONC Meaningful Use (MU) initiatives are focused on the staged development, incentivized adoption, and meaningful use of protected EHRs. The MU initiatives are summarized in Section 71.6.1.1. The privacy and security aspects of the various stages of MU are described in Section 71.6.1.2.

71.6.1.1 HITECH's Meaningful Use Initiatives. Traditionally, the primary information that was exchanged among different parties in the healthcare sector was the exchange of batched billing information between providers and carriers, as well as the sending of prescriptions from providers to pharmacies. The primary way of communicating healthcare-related information among healthcare parties was fax exchanges of unstructured data.

HITECH's MU initiative[81] puts the U.S. healthcare system on a path leading to a nationwide network of interoperable, patient-specific protected EHRs. The EHRs will contain structured and unstructured medical information that can be electronically and securely processed, exchanged, and used by any care provider in the country. EHRs will contain all pertinent patient PHI. Subject to privacy constraints, trusted EHRs can be used to coordinate and to direct any patient's care among any set of care providers anywhere in the country.

MU's EHR efforts are looking to shift the healthcare delivery sector toward a new paradigm wherein a patient and all her/his applicable care providers get complete and secure visibility into all *appropriate, need-to-know,* private medical information of the patient. "Appropriate" information is the patient information applicable strictly and only to the specific patient conditions being treated by, and the services being provided by, each of a specific patient's various specific care providers. Furthermore, it will be possible to know who has accessed any particular patient data element.

The MU strategy is to move though various and expanding stages of capabilities that in aggregate build up to the ultimate goal of nationally interoperable and appropriately protected EHRs. Currently, three stages are specified.

71.6.1.1.1 Stage 1 MU. The goals of Stage 1 are to get providers and hospitals (a) to collect specified, relevant patient data electronically so as to be able to create EHRs, and (b) to use EHRs to meet a specified set of healthcare service requirements. Specific metrics were defined to evaluate whether fielded EHR technology met Stage 1 MU and, therefore, that healthcare entities could be awarded government incentive payments for fielding certified EHR technology.

71.6.1.1.2 Stage 2 MU. Stage 2 MU expands requirements on EHRs and creates the concept of Health Information Exchanges (HIEs). Again, metrics were established to define what it takes for a healthcare entity to claim that their fielded technology met Stage 2 MU.

The goal of MU Stage 2 is to start developing electronic capabilities to share, in real time and with sufficient security, protected clinical and patient care information as captured in an EHR. Such information sharing can increase the continuity of a patient's care among all providers seen by a patient. Stage 2 progresses through several steps toward demonstrated, bidirectional, more capable, interoperable, and secure exchange of ONC-specified standard patient records among different, disparate EHRs in disparate healthcare entity environments. Heretofore, interoperability among disparate EHRs was hampered because of environment-specific use of different vendor EHR products that create, store, display, communicate, or message EHR content data in different, sometimes proprietary ways.

Several federal, state, and industry groups[82] are working toward the Stage 2 goal of securely moving care data among disparate EHR systems. Interoperation can be via secure direct EHR to EHR interoperation, or it can be via an intervening Health Information Exchange. HIEs are trusted intermediary systems through which the data from the EHR system of one healthcare entity can move to the EHR system of another healthcare entity. States or regions within a state create and maintain state-specific HIEs. The aggregate of such HIEs are to form a Nationwide Health Information Network (NHIN)—aka the eHealth Exchange.

A certain portion of initially exchanged EHR data must consist of at least specific summary care records. Interoperation must be capable among and between several different groups. Such groups include (a) providers—both large (e.g., hospitals) and small (e.g., individual practitioners), (b) referred or referring providers, and (c) patients.

The strategy for ensuring interoperability relies on use of data transport, data structure, and data content standards[83] that are uniformly implemented by interacting parties. Interoperability is demonstrated and assured by formal EHR certification that arises from standard testing of EHR interoperation. Such testing is done in conjunction with a recognized, independent third party.

The focus on interoperation with patients is critical and essential, since a goal is to create the healthcare sector equivalent of a customer relationship management capability. But it is realized that electronic interoperation with patients and allowing patients to access their longitudinal health records or to send secure messages to care providers may be problematic. Certain patients may have less familiarity with Internet and computing technologies. As such, initial patient access to provider-created data may occur using air-gap technologies such as data exchange via the physical passing of a USB drive or a paper printout.

Of significance to this chapter, and as described below, all interoperations must be secure and private.

71.6.1.1.3 Stage 3 MU. The purpose of Stage 3 MU is to move the Medicare and Medicaid community to a new model of care made possible by meeting the Stage 2 goal of sharing patient EHRs. The new model is to be a collaborative model that focuses on care outcomes and shares care responsibility and care accountability among contributing providers, patients, and families. Where necessary the new model capitalizes on HIEs. The specific goals of Stage 3 MU, and the metrics to evaluate achieving Stage 3 MU, were not yet established at the time of the writing of this chapter. Indeed, the group that advises HHS on health IT sought community inputs to shape the Stage 3, and later-Stage, MU objectives during 2013.[84]

71.6.1.2 HITECH's Meaningful Use Security and Privacy Initiatives. In the course of pursuing Meaningful Use in the exchange of PHI via EHR technology, new healthcare information protection issues arose that were not anticipated in the HIPAA Privacy and Security Rules.

For example, HIPAA does not accommodate the situation where (a) a patient authorizes the sharing of EHR, (b) only a patient-authorized, specified portion of the PHI from a specific patient's EHR needs to be shared among multiple parties when multiple parties are involved with the care of a specific patient, and (c) mutual trust in the confidentiality of, and any assigned redisclosure rules associated with, shared PHI by all parties needs to be assured. Accordingly, the ONC initiated the Data Segmentation for Privacy Initiative (DS4P) to support the privacy and security aspects—such as exchange, adjudication, and enforcement of privacy consents—associated with sharing EHR PHI across the domains of different healthcare entities.

The DS4P used collaborative members of ONC's Standards and Interoperability Framework[85] to examine the use of data segmentation[86] to accomplish privacy consent management. Data segmentation ensures that any elements of PHI that are deemed unsuitable to share are indeed not shared. Segmentation is supported by privacy metadata tags that convey the disclosure policies associated with each tagged date element within PHI. These tags specify (a) the confidentiality that needs to be maintained on the PHI data element being shared, (b) all obligations (e.g., nonredisclosure) of the party receiving the shared PHI data element, and (c) the purposes (e.g., emergency treatment only) for which the shared PHI data element are allowed to be used.[87]

To encompass the new healthcare information protection requirements as well as the requirements within the HIPAA Privacy and Security Rules, the ONC developed a framework[88] that establishes the principles associated with a consistent national approach to privacy and security for the storage and exchange of EHRs. More recently, ONC developed guidance pertaining to MU privacy and security.[89] The guide also enumerates a plan for meeting MU privacy and security requirements.

In relation to the HITECH MU initiative and the three defined MU stages, the ONC has developed specific MU security and privacy requirements that pertain to EHRs.[90] It is specified that an EHR must provide adequate security and privacy protections for PHI by meeting nine security requirements: (1) access control, (2) emergency access, (3) automatic log-off, (4) audit log, (5) integrity, (6) authentication, (7) general encryption, (8) encryption when exchanging electronic health information, and (9) accounting of disclosures. The ways by which such requirements are to be met are not mandated.

ONC uses specified standard, implementation specification, and certification criteria to establish the technical capabilities of EHRs and to certify EHR products.[91] The scope of certification criteria includes privacy and security. The ONC Health Information Technology Certification Program maintains a list of EHR technology that has been tested and certified by an authorized body for achievement of Meaningful Use.[92]

As outlined below, different security and privacy requirements are required to achieve different stages of MU.

71.6.1.2.1 MU Stage 1 Security and Privacy Directives. In Stage 1, patient data must be protected to assure its privacy. As per the HIPAA Privacy Rule, patients must be able to obtain an electronic copy of their healthcare information. As per the HIPAA Security Rule, electronic PHI handled by EHR technology must implement policies and procedures for dealing with security violations. Healthcare entities looking to comply with Stage 1 must attest[93] that have met the specified HIPAA privacy and security requirements required for Stage 1.

Healthcare entities looking to comply with Stage 1 must engage in a continuing risk-management process. Periodically, one must conduct or review an EHR security risk-assessment, correct any security deficiencies that are found, and provide security updates.[94] While not mandated, possible ways of meeting such requirements are provided by the Centers for Medicare & Medicaid Services (CMS).[95]

In the field, however, astute healthcare parties are treating the risk analysis directive in various ways. Some see the risk analysis as nothing more than a be-all, end-all activity to meet the MU Stage 1 information protection directive. More astute parties use the risk analysis to identify, to understand, and to prioritize their healthcare information vulnerabilities and to initiate efforts to remedy discovered vulnerabilities.

71.6.1.2.2 MU Stage 2 Security and Privacy Directives. In Stage 2, complying providers and hospitals are required to attest that healthcare information at rest is encrypted.

In Stage 2, certified EHR products are required to include a secure, interoperable, email capability called the *Direct Secure Messaging protocol*. The Direct Project offers this email capability for point-to-point healthcare information exchange.[96] ONC's State Health Information Exchange Program runs the Direct Project.[97] Direct email has been demonstrated to exchange healthcare information among providers and hospitals in several states and across state borders.[98]

One possible Direct strategy for securing the privacy of information being messaged is use of a metadata wrapper around the message. The wrapper can stipulate message routing and the security needed to maintain privacy. Direct messages are transmitted via health information service providers (HISPs). HISPs are Internet Service Providers for the healthcare community.[99] They support the Direct email protocol and encrypt Direct messages. HISPs are registered with a registration authority and have digital certificates from a certificate authority. Authentication of Direct messages is done by the HISP. Vendors' EHR products must be certified in conjunction with one or more of such HISPs.

Another possible and more flexible Direct strategy relies on use of Web-focused SOAP (Simple Object Access Protocol) messaging services with digital signature, encryption, and authentication security services. SOAP-oriented security services are independent of HISPs and therefore do not require certification with specified HISPs or specified HIEs.

71.6.1.2.3 MU Stage 3 Security and Privacy Directions. The Stage 3 healthcare information protection goals were not yet stipulated at the time of the writing of this chapter. It appeared there was interest in considering issues of maintaining and managing healthcare information privacy and security, as well as consent information, as healthcare and consent information flows through HIEs from one domain of information protection capabilities to some other domain with potentially differing information protection capabilities.

A security goal that is likely to be incorporated into Stage 3 MU is that EHRs and providers should be able to conduct multifactor authentication, meeting NIST 800-63-1 Assurance Level 3,[100] for providers looking to access remote PHI outside the domain of the provider's healthcare entity. Also under consideration for inclusion in Stage 3 directives are requiring attestation that (a) certain aspects of security awareness, and training, are performed, and (b) logs of authorized and unauthorized access to PHI are maintained.

71.6.2 Healthcare Information Protection in the U.S. DoD Healthcare Environment. Certain government agencies provide healthcare, or otherwise handle PHI. In particular, the U.S. DoD operates several hospitals and medical facilities that create, store, process, manage, and transmit personal healthcare information. The DoD also exchanges PHI among different facilities. It is also looking to transition to unified medical records that are shared across DoD as well as its Veterans Affairs programs and hospitals. As such, all HIPAA, HITECH, and MU rules, standards, and directives pertaining to security and privacy of healthcare information, to reporting of healthcare information breaches, and to the pursuit of breach enforcement actions must be upheld in the DoD healthcare sector.

However, all government agencies—whether civil, intelligence, or defense—must also comply with the Federal Information Security Management Act of 2002 (FISMA). Accordingly, any government agencies that deal with the creation, processing, storage, and transmission of healthcare information must comply with multiple regulatory laws and multiple regulatory authorities for the purpose of protecting healthcare patient information and healthcare business processes. Such agencies must comply with both HIPAA, as administered by HHS, OCR, and DOJ, and the Federal Information Security Management Act of 2002 (FISMA), as administered by object management group (OMG).[101] And, in certain instances such agencies can also be compliant to yet more regulations and standards such as, for example, the Federal Risk and Authorization Management Program (FedRAMP) and Common Criteria.

71.6.2.1 FISMA. FISMA requires all federal agencies to adopt and to demonstrate use of NIST-specified IT security processes and procedures that include categorizing risks associated with IT systems, developing and maintaining minimum controls to protect information systems, verifying and monitoring the effectiveness of their security controls via a specified certification and accreditation framework, and taking corrective actions when necessary.

71.6.2.2 NIST 800-53. FISMA requires that all Federal agencies, including Federal healthcare entities, as well as their contractors and service providers, must adopt and demonstrate use of NIST Special Publication (SP) 800-53, as well as other specified NIST Federal Information Processing Standards and Special Publications. NIST SP 800-53[102] establishes a unified information security framework that applies across the entire Federal Government. It specifies that parties that need information protection must use information assurance best practices. Such practices provide and demonstrate the due care and diligence necessary to fulfill their fiduciary responsibilities associated with being custodians of PII, in general, or PHI, more specifically.

The best practices[103,104,105,106] stipulated in NIST SP 800-53 include the following information protection processes and procedures:

1. Use of a specified risk-management framework and process to achieve appropriate information protection sufficient for the situation wherein information protection is needed;

2. Use of specified, customizable, policy-neutral, security[107] and privacy controls from extensive, periodically evolving catalogs of augmentable security and privacy controls:
   (a) to provide information-specific, technical, and operational information protection safeguards and countermeasures that meet the identified security and privacy requirements and the risks, threats, exploits, and vulnerabilities associated with the environment in which the security and privacy requirements exist, and
   (b) to protect organizational-level programs for managing information protection activities;
3. Use of specified, consistent, repeatable guidelines for selecting the best information protection controls to meet specific information protection requirements;
4. Assurance requirements for establishing confidence in the correct selection, implementation, and operation of the selected information protection controls;
5. Use of a catalog of customizable, extendable assurance assessment actions to stipulate actions that provide evidence that the risk-management processes and information protection controls used are correctly implemented, operate as intended, produce the desired outcomes, are otherwise effective, and may be worthy of receiving security accreditation; and
6. Procedures for periodically demonstrating at a point in time—and eventually continuously demonstrating (e.g., via a potential DHS Continuous Monitoring as a Service capability)—the confidence and effectiveness of the selected information protection controls meeting the identified information protection requirements.

The FISMA/NIST 800-53 approach has its detractors who (a) identify possible problems and costs of using single-point-in-time compliance-oriented strategies to provide information protection and (b) propose use of a smaller set of security controls. Having seen disconnects between FISMA compliance reports to the OMB and an agency's actual security posture, such individuals believe that compliance is a deception. They believe that information protection efforts must be solely focused on providing good security controls rather than on demonstrating point-in-time compliance to regulations.

Regardless of differing views, information assurance does improve when rigorous information protection processes and procedures are followed. It is reasonable to expect that a combined approach that depends on building security features correctly from the get-go (the NIST 800-53 strategy) and then continuously monitoring fielded products and systems will be an approach that most everyone can support.

71.6.2.3 FedRAMP. It is reasonable to expect that in time government agencies that provide healthcare, or otherwise handle PHI, will adopt use of contracted, cloud-based technologies and services. Such government agencies can choose to use the Federal Risk and Authorization Management Program[108] (FedRAMP) to address the security needs of PHI that is processed, stored, or exchanged in cloud-based environments.

FedRAMP extends FISMA and NIST SP 800-53 applicability to cloud computing situations. In particular, FedRAMP provides a government-wide, unified risk management program that (a) establishes unified, government-wide security requirements for cloud technologies and services, (b) authorizes the security capabilities provided by specific cloud computing products and services for government agency use, and (c) uses accredited third parties to assess, via continuous security monitoring, the security protections provided by such products and services.

The IBX Vault (www.ibxvault.com) is an example of an external, third-party facility that can be used to provide contracted managed hosting, data center, and cloud services that are compliant to several government mandates including FISMA, the DOD Information Assurance Certification and Accreditation Process (DIACAP), FedRAMP, HIPAA, HITECH, PCI, and Sarbanes-Oxley (SOX).

71.6.2.4 Common Criteria. DoD's National Security Agency is party to a multicountry agreement to develop Common Criteria–specified profiles of security requirements and accompanying product implementation assurance requirements for specified types of commercial, off-the-shelf, IT products. A list is available of third-party–evaluated IT products that claim conformance to specific information protection requirements profiles and that have been independently validated[109] to comply with the claimed profiles. Such products were evaluated by any of several specifically certified evaluation laboratories that use a Common Criteria–specified standard international security testing and evaluation scheme. U.S. Government agencies that provide healthcare or otherwise handle PHI may choose to deploy such evaluated and validated products to meet those of their healthcare information security requirements that are consistent with the validated information protection solutions implemented by such products.

Historically, in the late 1990s NIST was looking to assist the healthcare community (both public and private), as well as the companion healthcare accreditation and certification community, by supporting a cross-healthcare-industry effort to develop profiles of HIPAA-based security and implementation assurance requirements of value to the healthcare community. Such requirement profiles were based on the international Common Criteria standards. The proposed strategy was for healthcare entities and vendors to use certified Common Criteria testing labs to verify the correctness and completeness of their HIPAA-based healthcare information protection solutions to specified HIPAA-based healthcare security and assurance requirements profiles. Accreditation and certification of healthcare entity use of such solutions would be straightforward as healthcare accrediting and certification agencies, such as EHNAC and URAC, would recognize and approve the use of such verified solutions.

This NIST-supported effort was not successful. Perhaps it was too early in the life cycle of healthcare information protection regulations. Apparently, healthcare corporate managers were not yet prepared to commit or, in their eyes, divert sufficient healthcare entity resources into healthcare information protection. They may have been reluctant due to the newness of government regulations and the unknown seriousness with which the government would police and enforce such regulations.

Perhaps now that the seriousness of widespread government regulation enforcement and the associated enormity of imposed penalties and fines are realized, the healthcare sector will consider revisiting such a standards-based approach to verifying the correctness and completeness of their information protection solutions.

71.6.3 Evolving and Emerging Government Healthcare Information Protection Initiatives. Many government bodies are pursuing, or seem poised to initiate, other security and privacy initiatives of relevance to the healthcare sector. Examples that existed at the time of the writing of this chapter appear below. It is not clear which—if any—of these examples will become fruitful initiatives.

The HHS ONC continues to pursue security and privacy initiatives related to HIPAA, HITECH, and Meaningful Use.

The Information Security and Privacy Advisory Board (ISPAB)[110] has lobbied for some Federal Government body such as the FDA to initiate a program to evaluate the security provisions of medical devices before they can be brought to market. Compromise of patient information and medical device control messages will likely become a big problem (see Section 71.7.2). The Federal Government may provide assistance in reducing security and privacy issues in the medical device field by establishing a program to provide some sort of "Seal of Approval" for successfully assessed medical device products.[111] Such a seal could alert buyers that specific products are approved for the security provisions they provide. How such a seal might differ from HITRUST-certified assessments or any Common Criteria certifications has not yet been addressed

The ISPAB is also pushing for the Feds to create a United States Computer Emergency Readiness Team for reporting and tracking security vulnerabilities within medical devices as well as security incidents associated with medical devices. Whether or not the government will undertake any ISPAB-requested initiatives is not known at this time.

In early 2013, the U.S. President issued an Executive Order[112] and a companion Presidential Directive.[113] This order tasks the NIST to develop a cybersecurity framework for protecting critical infrastructure in the United States. It is expected that this Executive Order and the ensuing activities will lead to new cybersecurity legislation. The United States considers the healthcare sector to be part of the U.S. critical infrastructure. Whether any dramatically new U.S. cybersecurity framework will emerge in the near term or whether any new legislation arising as a result of the NIST efforts will make changes to existing healthcare-related security and privacy laws and regulations is unknown. Readers are encouraged to stay abreast of any such new legislation.

Furthermore, as the threat landscape in the healthcare sector evolves and as new combative protection strategies emerge, it can be expected that government rules impacting healthcare information protection requirements will be updated. Readers responsible for healthcare sector security and privacy need to stay abreast of all such federal, state, or local government updates and make appropriate changes to their fielded security and privacy policies, procedures, and technologies as needed to meet new requirements.

71.7 PRIVATE SECTOR HEALTHCARE PRIVACY AND SECURITY INITIATIVES. Various industry parties in the healthcare sector are engaging in industry initiatives and developing industry standards that pertain to healthcare information protection. The HITRUST efforts are examined in Section 71.7.1. Efforts focused on privacy and security as they apply to medical devices are described in Section 71.7.2.

71.7.1 HITRUST. The Health Information Trust Alliance (HITRUST)[114] is an industry organization that creates industry standards for information security for various parties in the healthcare sector. HITRUST arose from an early initiative, the eHealth Vulnerability Reporting Program, that focused on finding, publicizing, and fixing vulnerabilities in healthcare application software, especially those software packages that were large and for which software development errors were more numerous, on average.

As presented below, HITRUST member organizations collaborated in developing a healthcare sector security framework, security specifications, and solutions for assessing and assuring compliance with claimed security implementations. HITRUST deliverables reflect best practices fielded in the healthcare industry.

HITRUST member organizations represent in-the-field private healthcare sector organizations that work directly with creating, managing, and exchanging electronic healthcare information as it flows through the healthcare sector.

71.7.1.1 HITRUST Security Initiatives. HITRUST looks to replace the existing hodgepodge of various commercial and/or proprietary silos of differing security and security assurance solutions currently used by employers, healthcare providers, and health insurance carriers. Instead, standard, comprehensive security, as well as security assessment practices, are specified for protecting, and assuring the protection of electronic healthcare information storage, access, and exchange.

The HITRUST Common Security Framework (CSF) is touted to provide for just this type of reasonable, flexible, trustworthy protection of healthcare information. Protection is provided by a common baseline of security capabilities plus, as appropriate, other additional, scaled, and/or emergent capabilities. The strategy is to make sure:

1. That a specific healthcare entity's security solution is appropriate and scaled to the specific healthcare entity's business and technology realities, to the specific risks to be managed, and to the specific healthcare entity's resources available to manage the risk, and
2. That the security solution can adapt to changing healthcare needs and evolving information and security technologies.

The CSF provides a harmonized approach for healthcare information security and privacy that reflects an amalgamation of protection concepts that have emerged across several parties, including federal laws and regulations (HIPAA, HITECH), federal government standards and guidelines (NIST, FTC, CMS), industry standards and regulations (ISO, PCI, COBIT), and state regulations. The CSF is available to HITRUST member organizations and to individuals from qualified organizations that do not provide security products or services.

71.7.1.2 HITRUST Compliance and Assurance Initiatives. HITRUST pursues a CSF compliance and assurance program,[115] According to HITRUST, the program is motivated and driven by:

1. The worsening threat landscape in the healthcare sector,
2. The cost of conducting various, multiple, often proprietary and inconsistent, conformance tests to satisfy different parties, and
3. The increasing penalties being levied on healthcare sector entities for non-compliance to various security and privacy specifications.

HITRUST compliance assurance is intended to elevate a healthcare entity's level of due diligence that appropriate security and privacy measures have been implemented in the conforming healthcare entity's environment. Of course, compliance to a comprehensive, appropriate, and adequate set of security mechanisms is key.

The HITRUST compliance and assurance program focuses on developing, and fostering healthcare sector use of HITRUST-standard assessment and reporting processes. These standard processes are used to determine and to document single-point-in-time compliance to any of several different federal and state security and privacy regulations, requirements and assurance laws, international standards, third-party standards, healthcare entity business associate healthcare information protection requirements, CSF security controls, auditors' requirements, and more.

HITRUST offers different types of assessments to provide any of three different levels of assurance. For the first level of assurance, HITRUST makes available a Web-based tool to perform HITRUST-standardized self-assessments of various factors associated with a healthcare entity's security program. The factors include:

1. A healthcare entity's, or its business associates', security program's alignment with the compliance requirements associated with any variety of the several different security regulations and standards that may be applicable to the party whose conformance is being assessed,
2. The maturity of the security program, and
3. The program's ability to protect healthcare information in a sustainable way.

For use in higher risk environments, HITRUST supports two other levels of assurance—evaluated by either remote assessment or onsite assessment. All three HITRUST assessments are recognized across the healthcare sector.

The result of a compliance assessment is a report. HITRUST vets all conformance reports. Such reports include identification of any corrective actions needed to achieve compliance. CSF conformance assessment reports can be sent to various governing bodies for proof of compliance to required security and privacy measures.

To increase assurance/confidence that an HITRUST compliance assessment report is appropriate, accurate, and comprehensive, the assessment report can additionally be (a) validated by a periodically requalified third-party CSF assessor, as well as (b) certified by HITRUST.

71.7.1.3 *Other HITRUST Initiatives.*

HITRUST runs a Cyberthreat Intelligence and Incident Coordination Center[116] and a Cyberthreat Analysis Service.[117] Together, these initiatives provide reports of emerging general threats and vulnerabilities, as well as threats and vulnerabilities specific to healthcare information protection. These initiatives also coordinate healthcare sector responses to potential cyberattacks on the healthcare sector. In addition, education is provided on pertinent topics such as healthcare technology risk analysis, healthcare business risk analysis, and more.

HITRUST efforts are also focused on developing healthcare sector-specific–guidelines, business partner contract templates, and protocols pertaining to physical, administrative, and technical security for healthcare sector information. Other HITRUST initiatives include providing healthcare information security education and awareness, analysis of evolving threats and solutions, commenting on and supporting the development of new federal rules applicable to healthcare information security, and more.

71.7.2 Medical Devices Security Initiatives.

Medical devices are fixed function, electronic medical diagnosis, or treatment devices. Despite their limited function, such devices are susceptible to attack. Since medical devices often create, store, and convey PHI, they are under the jurisdiction of HIPAA and other information protection regulations. The risk of attack on medical devices will likely only escalate as more medical devices leave the confines of healthcare providers and become assigned to remote telemedicine workers or directly to patients.

Significant threats to PHI exposure from medical devices and to alteration of patient-specific treatment control signals executed by medical devices have been demonstrated or speculated.[118] It has been shown that a wireless insulin pump that exchanges unencrypted healthcare information and pump controls with an external monitor or an external control system could be directed by a hacking intruder to be turned off or to dispense its entire insulin tank immediately. Defibrillators and pacemakers have allowed PHI to be compromised. They have also been remotely reprogrammed by intruders to permit denial-of-service attacks or to deliver hacker-directed high-voltage shocks. Networked medical devices that use commercial operating systems and are exposed to the Internet can be vulnerable to the same kinds of evolving vulnerabilities seen throughout all other industries. Lack of sufficient authentication and any encryption, use of software or firmware not tested for information protection, inability to patch software, use of unsupported legacy operating systems, and limited battery power, as well as limited CPU, memory, and storage to support the execution of security code, and more are all potentially suspect.

At the time of the writing of this chapter, the U.S. General Accountability Office examined what role the U.S. Food and Drug Administration should initiate to inspect fielded medical devices and to evaluate the security provided by new medical devices before they are released into the marketplace.

A trio of standards[119] from the International Electrotechnical Commission (IEC 62304) and the International Organization for Standardization (ISO 14971 and ISO 18348) specify a number of requirements pertaining to the development and testing of medical software, including application as well as security-related software within medical devices. IEC 62304 standardizes life cycle software requirements and software processes for medical device software development. ISO 14971 specifies a process for identifying medical device hazards and a companion risk-management process including, for example, creating and monitoring risk control mechanisms and evaluating control effectiveness. ISO 13485 specifies an organization's quality management needs for demonstrating the organization's ability to develop medical devices conformant to regulatory requirements such as HIPAA.

Also of value to the security and privacy accompanying medical devices, at the time of the writing of this chapter academic researchers were prototyping and investigating the feasibility of a firewall to observe communications to/from a medical device and to block external attacks on, or hijacking of, wireless, implantable or wearable, medical devices.[120]

71.8 SECURITY AND PRIVACY IMPACTS OF TECHNOLOGY TRENDS.

Like all other industries, the healthcare sector has embraced technology, in part to improve the efficacy of its care and business models. What appears to be emerging is that parts of the healthcare delivery model are evolving from a provider-centric model, where patients come to a care provider, to a patient-centric model, where providers electronically come to and interact with remote patients. New to this model is the emergence of patient-facing technologies that will generate, store, process, display, and communicate patient-specific data and treatment plans, as well as associated billing.

Due to the often conservative nature of many healthcare parties, emerging, cutting-edge technology may not always be rapidly adopted. Nonetheless, many leading-edge healthcare entities and/or individual employees and care providers are quickly adopting emerging IT infrastructure or medical device technologies that can impact the efficacy of healthcare.

But, the acceptance of new technology and its introduction to routine healthcare operations often increases the complexity of providing and managing protection. New technologies will have their own threats and vulnerabilities. Furthermore, government regulations on providing healthcare sector information protection may likely move from today's point-in-time compliance demonstration toward a continuous compliance demonstration model. As such trends occur, healthcare entity security and privacy policies will need to be updated, more protection gaps will open in fielded security technologies, eventually fielded security technologies will become useless for new breeds of stealthier attackers and malware, and new strategies and implementations for protecting healthcare information will need to be developed and fielded.

There are many kinds of new technologies that are being introduced and that are starting to impact the security and privacy considerations and policies of the healthcare sector. Indeed, there is evidence that introduction of new technologies, together with any new health information breaches that arise from such new technologies, is overtaking regulation compliance as the main driver for organizations to provide information protection.[121] With rapid technology evolution and changes, organizations are beginning to recognize that information protection regulations may not be able to evolve fast enough to handle newer technologies and the new risks they may impose. Correspondingly, organizations are realizing that compliance to static or more slowly evolving regulations alone can be insufficient to provide information protection within their organizations.[122] Some feel that ongoing security testing is key to maintaining reasonable information protection in quickly evolving threat landscapes.[123]

All such technology introduction trends lead to companion trends in new forms of risks to, and attacks on, healthcare information. A common principle that appears to be emerging is that as healthcare information flows to and through ever newer IT technologies, the healthcare sector security model is moving more toward a data-centric security model wherein a healthcare entity's security perimeter is positioned at the data level rather than at a facility or network or server or IT service provider or mobile device level.

Examples of the kinds of new technologies that are emerging appear below.

71.8.1 Mobile and Personal Technology. With the proliferation of new patient-facing technologies, patients are taking more responsibility for their healthcare. Indeed, they are also offloading some of the administrative, triage, and care follow-up tasks previously under the responsibility of providers' staff. Such patient-side technologies are leading to a new style of digital relationship between patients, providers, and insurance carriers. New patient-facing technologies will support remote, personal, tele-health sessions, tele-medicine sessions, provider-patient consultations, provider-to-home-caregiver consultations, test results tracking, automatic invoicing and bill paying, and much more.

While potentially improving provider or patient experiences, use of nomadic, mobile personal devices such as tablet computers and smart phones are leading the way to a so-called post-PC world wherein the so-called Bring Your Own Device (BYOD) movement that relies on mobile and personal technologies presents new challenges to healthcare entities' security and privacy posture. The emergence of ever-newer mobile operating systems, mobile health applications, and communication mechanisms adds to security and privacy challenges. Social media use also presents security and privacy concerns.

State-of-the-art support of evolving, enhanced mobile and personal technologies appears certain as the healthcare sector will continue to evolve toward younger personnel steeped in use of such technologies.

71.8.2 Virtualized Technology. Software-as-a-service (SaaS), IT virtualization, and the outsourcing of healthcare applications and data storage to technology providers in any of the various different types of ever-more complex clouds are virtual technologies that may be adopted by healthcare entities. Such technologies may increase the overall complexity of a healthcare entity's IT environment and can present yet other security and privacy challenges. Such challenges, such as identity and access management issues, are often not unique to the healthcare sector. Challenges exist; for example, if no agreements are made about matters such as (a) what privacy, security, and security assurance accompany external or virtualized third-party software, host computers and/or services, (b) how compliance of the external third-party's security provisions to HITECH/HIPAA can be monitored or verified in real time by the contracting healthcare entity, and (c) how HIPAA/HITECH liabilities and penalties will be apportioned between the contracting healthcare entity and the outsourced entity. Indeed, some authorities argue that as of the time of the writing of this chapter, the cloud is not yet ready for mission-critical applications—healthcare or otherwise—in part because no universal security and security vetting standards yet exist across all private and public[124] healthcare environments. Nevertheless, vendors are beginning to offer HIPAA/HITECH-compliant cloud services and companion secure access from any device, including personal, mobile devices; and they are doing so as full-fledged business associates to healthcare entities.[125]

71.8.3 Personalized Medical Technology. With regard to healthcare information and healthcare information databases, considerations regarding new security and privacy requirements and policies will accompany the introduction of new personally wearable or implantable healthcare technology that creates and communicates PHI or is reactive to patient-specific external controls. Security, privacy, and individual data element masking considerations must also accompany the introduction of individual-patient-centric, personal health information databases.

71.8.4 Big Data Trends. Government authorities envision that significant benefit will arise from the HITECH push toward new healthcare system models. Patient medical information, as well as carrier payment data, across the country can be aggregated, as needed, into or from new, enormously sized, massively horizontal, deeply longitudinal, highly distributed, potentially replicated data stores of heterogeneous data that can be stored, organized, integrated, and used in new ways. The expectation is to analyze such data, coupled with research data, pharmaceutical data, bioinformatics data, and more, to improve care; to lower healthcare costs; to analyze disease trajectories; to hone diagnostic and predictive abilities; to identify emerging pharmaceutical and medical device opportunities; to identify best practices; to improve underperforming facilities, techniques, or providers; to enhance disease research, public health research, medical treatment research, direct patient care, and treatment outcome analysis; and to uncover many more opportunities that have yet to be envisioned.

For such mammoth healthcare information databases, data may reside in traditional database systems or an array of different unstructured data stores; the specific PHI data elements from a specific patient may be copied, moved, and/or repositioned in ad hoc ways; the data acquisition velocity across all patients is extraordinarily high; and the location of healthcare data can be very broadly distributed among a large array of loosely federated, potentially self-organizing, data stores. Traditional database and analysis approaches are being replaced by new database and analytic technologies and methods for capturing, storing, managing, and orchestrating the processing and analysis of such complex, migrating, mammoth data—colloquially called "big data."

Privacy and security for big data in the healthcare sector is an ongoing challenge. There is no question that such a vast store of information provides a huge target and challenge to would-be "big score" data attackers. Traditional perimeter-oriented security and privacy may not apply. Establishing, sharing, and enforcing privacy consents (potentially among multiple copies of personal healthcare information), stifling ways of inferring personal identity from anonymized (e.g., partially redacted) PHI, and otherwise maintaining privacy in parallel and distributed healthcare information processing are examples of challenging privacy issues. Establishing security interoperability, data access knowledge, and end-to-end trust among a diverse array of differing, potentially self-organizing security technologies that may be sequentially used by differing parties with fluid boundaries to meet common security requirements espoused in government regulations is also nontrivial.

71.8.5 Other Factors Associated with Technology Trends. Large, potentially virtual, health information research databases will arise by using big data technologies to integrate and to aggregate the PHI of millions of patients nationwide. Appropriate methods of de-identifying personally identifiable healthcare information data elements need to accompany the introduction of big data technologies. Correspondingly, data mining technologies will need to be coupled with data element masking or other patient de-identification approaches when extracting healthcare knowledge from such massive aggregated healthcare information databases. Appropriate privacy and security measures need to accompany use of such technologies.

The opening of APIs and portals for accessing certain packages of health information from databases of aggregated health information will also have ramifications on the need for updated, flexible security and privacy policies and technologies. For example, in support of ONC goals to enhance patient engagement with electronic healthcare information, individual patients will likely rely on database portal technology to access their own information within the sea of healthcare data; but individual patients who have access to some specific small portion of healthcare data must not be allowed to access larger, cross-patient datasets that may be available to a public health researcher, to an insurer, or to appropriate government bodies for regulation refinement or law enforcement.

While the security and privacy challenges associated with emerging technology trends may not be insurmountable, healthcare sector parties do need to stay alert of emergent technology trends so that their security and privacy programs can be appropriately adjusted to accommodate technology trends being incorporated into the healthcare sector. Furthermore, while the emerging technologies used by the healthcare sector will change and potentially need new security and privacy mechanisms, the security and privacy capabilities in fielded security tools used by the healthcare community may also need to evolve. Over time, as common attack vectors evolve, or as one-of-a-kind, individually targeted attacks emerge, fielded security tools may no longer be able to keep healthcare information protected. New or updated security tools will need to be fielded.

However, healthcare sector parties need to stay aware of the possibility that even new fielded protection technologies and procedures may not completely be able to protect against the release of PHI. As security becomes more of a risk-management activity, it is envisioned that there can be a growing role for insurance in transferring or mitigating the risk and associated consequences and penalties of healthcare information theft and leakage due to inadequate protection. The cost and amount of insurance coverage made available by an insurance carrier should be commensurate with the level of due diligence associated with a healthcare entity's fielded security policies and solutions.[126]

The bottom line is that creation, storage, communication, sharing, and use of healthcare information wherever it will exist will occur by means of an IT infrastructure with constantly moving parts operating under a growing number of government and industry compliance requirements. Healthcare sector parties will need to stay vigilant and nimble in terms of protecting their evolving technologies and processes and the PHI entrusted to them. Some may consider outsourcing their need for appropriately compliant security solutions to an MSSP (Managed Security Solutions Provider), that is, a business associate in the eyes of HIPAA/HITECH that specializes in providing compliant information protection services to the healthcare sector. However, the cost of maintaining information protection in the face of evolving technologies, risks, and regulations will compete with several other line items in a healthcare entity's budget. Corporate officers need to be properly engaged to allocate sufficient resources to keep up with evolving information protection needs.

71.9 SUMMARY. Appropriately protected personal healthcare information and healthcare business processes are at the heart of proper healthcare. But, there are innumerable and growing threats to their security and privacy.

Through regulations, the government is pushing the healthcare sector in two directions: (1) HIPAA and other government regulations are pushing to keep patient records safe, and (2) HITECH MU regulations are pushing to make patient records more accessible and broadly available.

The first direction leads to more frequently recurring, so-called "living," risk assessments by healthcare entities. Such continuous risk assessments will be driven as government steps up regulatory enforcement, as patient demand for information safety and protection increases, as private lawsuits against healthcare information custodians liable for personal information compromise catch on, and as contract law legal proceedings arise between covered entities and business associates.

The second direction leads toward migration to broad dissemination technologies, such as mobile, cloud, and regional health exchange technologies.

But, the combined impact of both directions is to increase vulnerabilities to data exposure and to expand the required breadth of protection for healthcare information. Increased vulnerabilities couple with evolving, more sophisticated, more diverse targeted threats and attacks to increase the amount of healthcare information being compromised.

There are multitudes of government and industry laws, regulations, and initiatives pertinent to protecting healthcare information. However, traditionally the healthcare sector has focused on acquiring ever-newer revenue-generating medical technologies. It has been slow to turn its corporate attention and funds toward information protection, often doing just the minimum in terms of complying with government laws and regulations.

Ironically, looking across the healthcare sector, compliance with government information protection regulations has not seemed to have had a profound impact on personal healthcare information privacy protection: Healthcare information breaches are rampant despite adherence to government security regulations. The focus on compliance has not always led to better healthcare information protection.

Patient care typically trumps healthcare information protection, both in terms of capital and labor expenditures. In fact, the fraction of a typical healthcare organization budget allocated to information protection tends to be half, if not less, than that seen in other industries.[127] Even government compliance and breach enforcement fines on healthcare entities do not necessarily prevent repeat offenses of healthcare information compromise.

Privacy and security leaders serving healthcare entities must be able to express healthcare information protection needs in ways to gain healthcare entity executive support. For example, they must show executives how information protection critically supports the primary, moneymaking, care delivery business of the healthcare entity.

The current government drive for healthcare improvements while forcing reductions in healthcare costs and insurance carrier reimbursements does not help the government-mandated healthcare information protection situation. Healthcare organizations and professionals are caught in a bind and are under pressure to work out their corporate and Hippocratic priorities and regulatory responsibilities.

71.10 FURTHER READING

Anderson, R. *Personal Medical Information: Security, Engineering, and Ethics.* Springer, 1997 (reprinted 2008).

Casscells, S. W. *DoD Health Information Security Regulation.* U.S. Department of Defense (July 12, 2007).

Davis, N. A., and M. LaCour. *Health Information Technology*, 3rd ed. Saunders, 2013.

Jones, E. D., and C. P. Hartley. *Policies and Procedures for the Electronically Connected Medical Office*. American Medical Association, 2009.

Kabay, M. E. "Medical Informatics Security." (May 2004). www.mekabay.com/overviews/medical.pdf

Nelson, R., and N. Staggers. *Health Informatics: An Interprofessional Approach.* Mosby, 2013.

Shoniregun, C. A., K. Dube, and F. Mtenzi. *Electronic Healthcare Information Security.* Springer, 2010 (reprinted 2013).

Trotter, F., and D. Uhlman. *Hacking Healthcare: A Guide to Standards, Workflows, and Meaningful Use*. O'Reilly Media, 2011.

Wager, K. A., F. W. Lee, and J. P. Glaser. *Health Care Information Systems: A Practical Approach for Health Care Management*, 3rd ed. Jossey-Bass, 2013.

71.11 NOTES

1. "ACO Participants Investing in Analytics, Survey Finds," *Healthcare IT News | HIEWatch*, March 15, 2013, www.hiewatch.com/news/aco-participants-investing-analytics-survey-finds
2. A more extensive listing of many more of the federal laws and regulations addressing privacy and security in the healthcare sector together with brief summaries is available at www.healthit.gov/sites/default/files/federal_privacy_laws_table_2_26_10_final_0.pdf
3. "FireEye Advanced Threat Report 2 H 2012," http://www2.fireeye.com/rs/fireye/images/fireeye-advanced-threat-report-2h2012.pdf
4. R. Rachwald, "The New FireEye Advanced Threat Report," FireEye Blog, Advanced Malware, Threat Intelligence, April 3, 2013, www.fireeye.com/blog/technical/malware-research/2013/04/the-new-fireeye-advanced-threat-report.html

5. Thor Olavsrud, "Healthcare Industry CIOs, CSOs Must Improve Security," *Network World* newsletter, March 6, 2012.
6. Nicole Lewis, "Health Data Breaches Up 97% in 2011," *InformationWeek | Healthcare*, February 13, 2012, www.informationweek.com/healthcare/security-privacy/health-data-breaches-up-97-in-2011/232600746?cid=nl_IW_healthcare_2012-02-15_html&elq=022382be2aa443e9a3b3fd4dba6ce46f
7. Identity Theft Resource Center, "2012 Data Breach Stats," December 26, 2012, www.idtheftcenter.org/images/breach/Breach_Stats_Report_2012.pdf
8. M. Millard, "Breaches epidemic despite efforts at compliance, says Kroll," *Healthcare IT News*, April 10, 2012, www.healthcareitnews.com/news/breaches-epidemic-despite-efforts-compliance-says-kroll
9. Kelly Jackson Higgins, "Most Small Healthcare Practices Hacked in the Past 12 Months," *Dark Reading | Database | News*, February 16, 2012, www.darkreading.com/database-security/167901020/security/news/232601045/most-small-healthcare-practices-hacked-in-the-past-12-months.html?cid=nl_DR_daily_2012-02-17_html&elq=eeb7dbbf00374e629c9db74fae6ebf54
10. Nicole Lewis, "Patient Data Theft Sends IT Specialist to Jail," *InformationWeek | Healthcare*, January 17, 2012, www.informationweek.com/healthcare/security-privacy/patient-data-theft-sends-it-specialist-t/232400459?cid=nl_IW_healthcare_2012-01-18_html&elq=ab0ba4c34056469798ce4eb49d3fb11 d
11. D. Walker, "Medical Identity Theft To Be Explored at FTC Hearing," *SC Magazine*, May 3, 2013, www.scmagazine.com/medical-identity-theft-to-be-explored-at-ftc-hearing/article/291780/?DCMP=EMC-SCUS_Newswire
12. RSA, The Security Division of EMC^2, "Cybercrime and the Healthcare Industry," White Paper, 2010, www.rsa.com/products/consumer/whitepapers/11030_CYBHC_WP_0710.pdf (URL inactive).
13. Ericka Chickowski, "Healthcare Unable to Keep Up With Insider Threats," *Dark Reading | Insider Threat, | News*, May 1, 2012, www.darkreading.com/insider-threat/healthcare-unable-to-keep-up-with-inside/232901235
14. U. S. Department of Health and Human Services, "Health Information Privacy: Breaches Affecting 500 or More Individuals," HHS Website, www.hhs.gov/ocr/privacy/hipaa/administrative/breachnotificationrule/breachtool.html
15. J. Taitsman, C. M. Grimm, and S. Agrawal, "Protecting Patient Privacy and Data Security," *New England Journal of Medicine* 368 (2013):977–979, March 14, 2013, www.nejm.org/doi/full/10.1056/NEJMp1215258
16. Mathew J. Schwartz, "Hackers Holds Australian Medical Records Ransom," *InformationWeek | Security*, December 11, 2012, www.informationweek.com/security/attacks/hackers-hold-australian-medical-records/240144164?cid=nl_IW_healthcare_2012-12-12_html&elq=f71d081ae23a4929bdc01e6b0c9b37f1
17. T. Armerding, "Law Firms See Big Money in Healthcare Breach Cases," *CSO Online | Data Protection*. April 16, 2012, www.csoonline.com/article/704288/law-firms-see-big-money-in-healthcare-breach-cases?page=1
18. A. Pascual, "Financial Pain Ensues When Custodians of Health Fail to be Good Stewards of Privacy," Javelin Strategy & Research Blog, April 28, 2013, https://www.javelinstrategy.com/blog/2013/04/28/financial-pain-ensues-when-custodians-of-health-fail-to-be-good-stewards-of-privacy (see also E. McCann, "Link Between Breaches and Fraud on the Rise," *Healthcare IT News*

| *HIEWatch*, April 30, 2013, www.hiewatch.com/news/link-between-breaches-and-fraud-rise)

19. Ericka Chickowski, "$1.5M Fine Marks a New Era in HITECH Enforcement," *Dark Reading | Database | News*, March 21, 2012, www.darkreading .com/database/15 m-fine-marks-a-new-era-in-hitech-enfor/232700031
20. J. Robbins, "Cybertheft Heists $1 Million from Leavenworth Hospital," *The Wenatchee World*, April 26, 2013, www.wenatcheeworld.com/news/2013/ apr/26/cybertheft-heists-1-million-from-leavenworth
21. Ken Terry, "Should FDA Assess Medical Device Defenses against Hackers?" *InformationWeek | Healthcare*, April 24, 2012, www.informationweek.com/ healthcare/security-privacy/should-fda-assess-medical-device-defense/2329008 18?cid=nl_IW_healthcare_2012-04-25_html&elq=b34ee79cddae4a828974ed65 33178f9 a
22. Kim Zetter, "Vulnerability Lets Hackers Control Building Locks, Electricity, Elevators and More," *Wired | Threat Level*, February 6, 2013, www.wired.com/ threatlevel/2013/02/tridium-niagara-zero-day
23. Kelly Jackson Higgins, "Medical Industry Under Attack By Chinese Hackers," *Dark Reading | Threat Intel | News*, March 14, 2013, www.darkreading.com/ threat-intelligence/167901121/security/attacks-breaches/240150858/medical-industry-under-attack-by-chinese-hackers.html?cid=nl_DR_daily_2013-03-15_html&elq=da19ca4090704bcd87b093ad6ea14710
24. Cyber², "Medical Industry—A Cyber Victim: Billions Stolen and Lives at Risk," White Paper, March 14, 2013, www.cybersquared.com/wp-content/ uploads/downloads/2013/03/Medical-Industry-A-Cyber-Victim-Billions-Stolen-and-Lives-At-Risk.pdf
25. E. Chickowski, "Healthcare Securing Improving But Still Needs Treatment," *Dark Reading | Database Security | News*, March 27, 2013, www.darkreading. com/database-security/167901020/security/news/240151816/in-spite-of-improv ement-healthcare-security-still-needs-treatment.html?cid=nl_DR_daily_2013-03-27_html&elq=7a12116be5bc4b20b2b318a4ebf967 dd
26. Solutionary, "2013 Global Threat Intelligence Report (GTIR)."
27. Kevin Fogarty, "DNA Hack Could Make Medical Privacy Impossible," *NetworkWorld | Security*, March 11, 2013, www.networkworld.com/news/ 2013/031113-dna-hack-could-make-medical-267569.html?source=NWWNLE_ nlt_daily_pm_2013-03-11
28. National Conference of State Legislatures, "Security Breach Notification Laws," NCSL Website, August 20, 2012, www.ncsl.org/issues-research/telecom/ security-breach-notification-laws.aspx
29. 104th Congress of the USA, "Health Insurance Portability and Accountability Act of 1996," Public Law 104-191, Code of Federal Regulations (CFR) Title 45 Part 164 (August 21, 1996), http://frwebgate.access.gpo.gov/cgi-bin/getdoc.cgi? dbname=104_cong_public_laws&docid=f:publ191.104.pdf or http://tinyurl .com/5z4 csd
30. U. S. Department of Health and Human Services, OCR, "HIPAA Administrative Simplification Statute and Rules," HHS.gov Website, http://www.hhs.gov/ ocr/privacy/hipaa/administrative
31. HIPAA security requirements for specified types of healthcare transactions were described in Chapter 71 of the 5th edition of the *Computer Security Handbook*.

32. CMS.gov, Centers for Medicare & Medicaid Services, "Are You a Covered Entity?" www.cms.gov/Regulations-and-Guidance/HIPAA-Administrative-Simplification/HIPAAGenInfo/AreYouaCoveredEntity.html, and "Covered Entity Charts," www.cms.gov/Regulations-and-Guidance/HIPAA-Administrative-Simplification/HIPAAGenInfo/Downloads/CoveredEntitycharts.pdf
33. Analog forms of information such as paper-to-paper fax, voice telephony, mail, and so on are not within HIPAA's scope.
34. U.S. Department of Health and Human Services, Office of the Secretary, "Standards for Privacy of Individually Identifiable Health Information," 45 CFR Parts 160 and 164, *Federal Register* 65, no. 250 (December 28, 2000), www.hhs.gov/ocr/privacy/hipaa/administrative/privacyrule/prdecember2000all8parts.pdf
35. U.S. Department of Health and Human Services, Office of the Secretary, "Standards for Privacy of Individually Identifiable Health Information," 45 CFR Parts 160 and 164, *Federal Register* 67, no. 157 (August 14, 2002), www.hhs.gov/ocr/privacy/hipaa/administrative/privacyrule/privruletxt.txt
36. H. Hayes, "HIPAA: Best if Used By," *Government Health IT*, June 12, 2006, www.govhealthit.com/news/hipaa-best-if-used
37. U.S. Department of Health and Human Services, Office of the Secretary, "Health Insurance Reform: Security Standards," 45 CFR Parts 160, 162, and 164, *Federal Register* 68, no. 34 (February 20, 2003), www.hhs.gov/ocr/privacy/hipaa/administrative/securityrule/securityrulepdf.pdf
38. M. Scholl, K. Stine, J. Hash, P. Bowen, A. Johnson, C. D. Smith, and D. I. Steinberg, "An Introductory Resource Guide for Implementing the Health Insurance Portability and Accountability Act (HIPAA) Security Rule," NIST Spec Pub 800-66 Rev1, October 2008, www.hhs.gov/ocr/privacy/hipaa/administrative/securityrule/nist80066.pdf
39. U.S. Department of Health and Human Services, OCR, "Breach Notification for Unsecured Protected Health Information," 45 CFR Parts 160 and 164, *Federal Registry* 74, no. 162 (August 24, 2009): 42740–42770, www.gpo.gov/fdsys/pkg/FR-2009-08-24/pdf/E9-20169.pdf
40. Federal Trade Commission, "Health Breach Notification Rule; Final Rule," 16 CFR Part 318, *Federal Register* 74, no. 163 (August 25, 2009), http://www2.ftc.gov/os/2009/08/R911002hbn.pdf
41. U.S. Department of Health and Human Services, Office of the Secretary, "Guidance Specifying Technologies and Methodologies That Render Protected Health Information Unusable, Unreadable or Indecipherable to Unauthorized Individuals for Purposes of the Breach Notification Requirements," 45 CFR Parts 160 and 164, *Federal Register* 74, no. 79 (April 27, 2009), www.hhs.gov/ocr/privacy/hipaa/understanding/coveredentities/federalregisterbreachrfi.pdf
42. It is possible that breach detection may arise as a consequence of a formal complaint of a HIPAA privacy or security rules violation filed with the HHS OCR.
43. U.S. Department of Health and Human Services, "How to File a Complaint," HHS.gov | Health Information Privacy, www.hhs.gov/ocr/privacy/hipaa/complaints/index.html
44. U.S. Department of Health and Human Services, "What OCR Considers During Intake & Review," HHS.gov | Health Information Privacy, www.hhs.gov/ocr/privacy/hipaa/enforcement/process/whatocrconsiders.html

45. U.S. Department of Health and Human Services, "How OCR Enforces the HIPAA Privacy Rule," HHS.gov | Health Information Privacy, www.hhs.gov/ocr/privacy/hipaa/enforcement/process/howocrenforces.html

46. U.S. Department of Health and Human Services, "Modifications to the HIPAA Privacy, Security, Enforcement, and Breach Notification Rules Under the Health Information Technology for Economic and Clinical Health Act and the Genetic Information Nondiscrimination Act; Other Modifications to the HIPAA Rules," *Federal Register*, Document Citation 78 FR 5565, Doc No. 2013-01073 (January 24, 2013): 5565–5702, https://federalregister.gov/a/2013-01073

47. Goodwin Procter LLP, "HHS Issues Long-Awaited Final HIPAA Omnibus Rule," *Legal Alert Newsletter*, January 30, 2013.

48. U.S. Department of Health and Human Services, Office of the Secretary, "Modifications to the HIPAA Privacy, Security, Enforcement, and Breach Notification Rules Under the Health Information Technology for Economic and Clinical Health Act and the Genetic Information Nondiscrimination Act; Other Modifications to the HIPAA Rules, Final Rule," 45 CFR 160 and 164, *Federal Register*, Document Citation 78 FR 5565, Doc No. 2013-01073 (January 25, 2013): 5565–5702, https://federalregister.gov/a/2013-01073

49. FTC Breach Notification Rule.

50. A. Smith, "HIPAA Rule Alters Definition of 'Breach,'" Society for Human Resource Management | Legal Issues | Federal Resources, January 28, 2013, www.shrm.org/LegalIssues/FederalResources/Pages/HIPAA-rule-breach.aspx

51. Legal & Regulatory Affairs Staff, "HIPAA Final Rule Highlights for Practitioners," Practice Central, March 14, 2013, www.apapracticecentral.org/update/2013/03-14/final-rule.aspx

52. P. Brusil, "Medical Records Protection," Chapter 71, Section 71.6.6.3, in *Computer Security Handbook*, 5th ed., ed. S. Bosworth, M. E. Kabay, and E. Whyne, Hoboken, NJ: John Wiley & Sons, Inc., 2009.

53. Healthcare entities often have to demonstrate compliance to several other regulations. Bodies associated with the different regulations may provide guidance on how best to meet such other compliance requirements. For example, the PCI Security Standards Council publishes such guidelines for the various updates to the PCI DSS. As needed, interested readers should examine such other documents.

54. HIPAA Certification, "HIPAA Compliance Certification: Covered Entity," www.hipaacertification.net/HIPAA-compliance-certification.htm

55. Some observers argue that going through a spot-check OCR audit or enduring the consequences of an OCR or Attorney General investigation into a reported breach has not always been shown to alter the information protection behavior of the impacted healthcare entity.

56. J. Roman, "HIPAA Audits: The Next Phase; OCR's Leon Rodriguez Offers Compliance Tips," Healthcare Info Security, January 2, 2013, www.healthcareinfosecurity.com/hipaa-audits-next-phase-a-5397

57. ENHAC, "ENHAC to Fill HIPAA, Meaningful Use Compliance Gaps," www.ehnac.org/press-news/press-articles/194-hopkinson (URL inactive).

58. URAC, Healthcare Organizations, "Welcome to the Health IT Resource Center," https://www.urac.org/infoTech (see also "HIPAA Privacy Accreditation Program Overview," https://www.urac.org/programs/prog_accred_HIPAAP_po.aspx?

navid=accreditation&pagename=prog_accred_HIPAAP and "HIPAA Security Accreditation Program Overview," https://www.urac.org/programs/prog_accred_HIPAAS_po.aspx)

59. "Health IT Privacy and Security Resources," HealthIT.gov | Providers & Professionals | Privacy & Security, www.healthit.gov/providers-professionals/ehr-privacy-security/resources
60. "Health Information Privacy and Security: A 10 Step Plan," HealthIT.gov | Providers & Professionals | Privacy & Security, www.healthit.gov/providers-professionals/ehr-privacy-security/10-step-plan
61. U.S. Department of Health and Human Services, "[Final] Guidance on Risk Analysis Requirements under the HIPAA Security Rule," Office for Civil Rights, www.hhs.gov/ocr/privacy/hipaa/administrative/securityrule/rafinalguidancepdf .pdf
62. U.S. Department of Health and Human Services, "Health Information Technology," HIPAA Privacy Components of the ONC Privacy and Security Toolkit, Office for Civil Rights | Health Information Privacy, www.hhs.gov/ocr/privacy/hipaa/understanding/special/healthit
63. U.S. Department of Health and Human Services, "Security Rule Guidance Material," Office for Civil Rights | Health Information Privacy, www.hhs.gov/ocr/privacy/hipaa/administrative/securityrule/securityruleguidance.html
64. U.S. Department of Health and Human Services, "HIPAA Security Guidance," Office for Civil Rights, www.hhs.gov/ocr/privacy/hipaa/administrative/securityrule/remoteuse.pdf
65. U.S. Department of Health and Human Services, "Health IT Privacy and Security Resources," HealthIT.gov | Privacy & Security, www.healthit.gov/providers-professionals/ehr-privacy-security/resources
66. U.S. Department of Health and Human Services, "Your Mobile Device and Health Information Privacy and Security," HealthIT.gov | Privacy & Security, www.healthit.gov/providers-professionals/your-mobile-device-and-health-information-privacy-and-security
67. U.S. Department of Health and Human Services, Security Rule Educational Paper Series, HHS.gov | Health Information Privacy, www.hhs.gov/ocr/privacy/hipaa/administrative/securityrule/securityruleguidance.html
68. National Institute of Standards and Technology, " HIPAA Security Rule Toolkit," NIST Information Technology Laboratory | Security Content Automation Protocol, http://scap.nist.gov/hipaa
69. M. Scholl et al., "An Introductory Resource for Implementing the Health Insurance Portability and Accountability (HIPAA) Security Rule."
70. U.S. Department of Health and Human Services, "How Can You Protect and Secure Health Information When Using a Mobile Device?" HealthIT.gov | Providers & Professionals | Mobile Device Privacy and Security, www.healthit.gov/providers-professionals/how-can-you-protect-and-secure-health-information-when-using-mobile-device
71. U.S. Department of Health and Human Services, "Your Mobile Device and Health Information Privacy and Security," HealthIT.gov | Providers & Professionals, | Privacy & Security, www.healthit.gov/providers-professionals/your-mobile-device-and-health-information-privacy-and-security

72. M. Souppaya and K. Scarfone, "Guidelines for Managing and Securing Mobile Devices in The Enterprise," National Institute of Standards and Technology, NIST Special Publication 800-124, July 2012 (or succeeding revisions thereof).

73. L. Chen, J. Franklin, and A. Regenscheid, "Guidelines on Hardware-Rooted Security in Mobile Devices," National Institute of Standards and Technology, NIST Special Publication 800-164, October 2012 (or succeeding revisions thereof).

74. U.S. Department of Health and Human Services, "Other Security Rule Notices and Materials," Office for Civil Rights | Health Information Privacy, www.hhs.gov/ocr/privacy/hipaa/administrative/securityrule/index.html

75. American Hospital Association, "HIPAA Staté Preemption Analysis," HIPAA Privacy Standards, www.aha.org/content/00-10/preemption.pdf

76. A. Brino, "When HIPAA and States Collide," Healthcare IT News | HIE Watch, April 18, 2013, www.hiewatch.com/perspective/when-hipaa-and-states-collide

77. U.S. Department of Health and Human Services, "Health Information Security & Privacy Collaboration (HISPC)," HealthIT.gov/Policymaking, Regulation, & Strategy | Federal-State Health care Coordination, www.healthit.gov/policy-researchers-implementers/health-information-security-privacy-collaboration-hispc

78. U.S. Department of Health and Human Services, "Health Information Security & Privacy Collaboration (HISPC)."

79. George W. Bush, "Incentives for the Use of Health Information Technology & Establishing the Position of the NHI IT Coordinator," Executive Order EO 13335, April 27, 2004. Follow-on to Bush, "Transforming Health Care: The President's Health Information Technology Plan," http://georgewbush-whitehouse.archives.gov/infocus/technology/economic_policy200404/chap3.html

80. Health Information Technology for Economic and Clinical Health Act, Title XIII of the American Recovery and Reinvestmant Act of 2009, Public Law 111-5.

81. The MU initiative was created by the American Recovery Act of 2008. The ONC administers and leads the MU initiative. The MU program incorporates government-paid incentive payments through 2015 to coax providers to adopt technologies and processes that meet MU requirements and goals.

82. Such groups include, for example, the ONC Information Exchange Working Group (IEWG), the Massachusetts eHealth Collaborative, the electronic Health Record Association (EHRA), and the CommonWealth Health Alliance.

83. Ken Terry, "EHRA Guides Vendors on Data Transport Mechanism," *InformationWeek* | Healthcare, March 5, 2013, www.informationweek.com/healthcare/electronic-medical-records/ehra-guides-vendors-on-data-transport-me/240149830?cid=nl_IW_healthcare_2013-03-06_html&elq=bac8e913933c4b41952210a6b85116b0

84. U.S. Department of Health and Human Services, Office of the National Coordinator for Health Information Technology, Health Information Technology Policy Committee, "Request for Comment Regarding the Stage 3 Definition of Meaningful Use of Electronic Health Records (EHRs)," for comments to be delivered by January 14, 2013, www.healthit.gov/sites/default/files/hitpc_stage3_rfc_final.pdf

85. S&I Framework, "Data Segmentation for Privacy Charter and Members," S&I Framework Wiki, http://wiki.siframework.org/Data+Segmentation+for+Privacy+Charter+and+Members

86. "Roberta," "Electronically Exchanging Sensitive Health Information", HIE Answers Website, September 19, 2012, www.hieanswers.net/electronically-exchanging-sensitive-health-information

87. J. Coleman and D. Decouteau, ONC, "Use of Interoperability Standards and Data Segmentation to Support Patient Privacy," presentation to HIMSS13 Conference, New Orleans, LA, 2013, http://wiki.siframework.org/file/view/DS4P%20Showcase_v3FINAL.pdf/418765700/DS4P%20Showcase_v3 FINAL.pdf

88. U.S. Department of Health and Human Services, Office of the National Coordinator for Health Information Technology, "Nationwide Privacy and Security Framework for Electronic Exchange of Individually Identifiable Health Information," December 15, 2008, www.healthit.gov/sites/default/files/nationwide-ps-framework-5.pdf

89. U.S. Department of Health and Human Services, Office of the National Coordinator for Health Information Technology, "Guide to Privacy and Security of Health Information," Version 1.2 060112, www.healthit.gov/sites/default/files/pdf/privacy/privacy-and-security-guide.pdf

90. U.S. Department of Health and Human Services, Office of the National Coordinator for Health Information Technology, "Guide to Privacy and Security of Health Information," Chapter 2 "Privacy & Security and Meaningful Use," www.healthit.gov/sites/default/files/pdf/privacy/privacy-and-security-guide-chapter-2.pdf

91. U.S. Department of Health and Human Services, Office of the Secretary, "Health Information Technology: Standards, Implementation Specifications, and Certification Criteria for Electronic Health Record Technology, 2014 Edition; Revisions to the Permanent Certification Program for Health Information Technology" (Final Rule), *Federal Register* 77, no. 171 (September 4, 2012), www.gpo.gov/fdsys/pkg/FR-2012-09-04/pdf/2012-20982.pdf

92. U.S. Department of Health and Human Services, Office of the National Coordinator for Health Information Technology, "Certified Health IT Product List," HealthIT.gov Website, http://oncchpl.force.com/ehrcert

93. Critics of the Meaningful Use program point out that "attesting" to MU requirements pertaining to HIPAA is not as strong a show of compliance to HIPAA than,for example, demonstrating Meaningful Use of privacy and security capabilities that meet HIPAA requirements. Furthermore, attestation can lead to fraud if providers falsely attest to MU capabilities and inappropriately obtain MU incentive payments from the Centers for Medicare and Medicaid Services.

94. U.S. Department of Health and Human Services, "How Do I Comply with Meaningful Use Requirements," Health Resources and Service Administration Website, www.hrsa.gov/healthit/toolbox/HIVAIDSCaretoolbox/SecurityAndPrivacy Issues/howdoicomplywitmu.html

95. Centers for Medicare & Medicaid Services.

96. "The Direct Project," http://wiki.directproject.org/home

97. U.S. Department of Health and Human Services, "State Health Information Exchange," HealthIT.gov | Providers & Professionals | Help Center, www.healthit.gov/providers-professionals/state-health-information-exchange

98. B. Andriesen, "Bright Spots of the Direct Project Adoption," HealthIT.gov | HealthIT Buzz blog, June 18, 2012, www.healthit.gov/buzz-blog/state-hie/the-direct-project-adoption

99. K. Terry, "Healthcare Directed Exchange Gets Big Government Push," *InformationWeek* | Healthcare | News, April 16, 2013, www.informationweek.com/healthcare/interoperability/healthcare-directed-exchange-gets-big-go/240152932?cid=nl_IW_healthcare_2013-04-17_html&elq=1bfc583e686e4c96a60149885848e530

100. W. Burr, D. Dodson, E. Newton, R. Perlner, T. Polk, S. Gupta, and E. Nabbus, "Electronic Authentication Guideline," NIST Special Publication 800-63-1, December 2011, http://csrc.nist.gov/publications/nistpubs/800-63-1/SP-800-63-1.pdf

101. Federal Information Security Management Act of 2002, Title III of the E-Government Act of 2002, Pub.Law 107-347, December 17, 2002, http://csrc.nist.gov/drivers/documents/FISMA-final.pdf

102. Joint Task Force Transformative Initiative, "Security and Privacy Controls for Federal Information Systems and Organizations," NIST Special Publication 800-53 Rev 4, Final Public Draft (to be superseded by the final version), February 5, 2013, http://csrc.nist.gov/publications/drafts/800-53-rev4/sp800_53_r4_draft_fpd.pdf

103. M. E. Kabay, "NIST SP800-53 Rev. 3: Key to Unified Security Across Federal Government and Private Sectors" (Part 1), *NetworkWorld* | Security Strategies Alert, October 26, 2009, www.networkworld.com/newsletters/sec/2009/102609sec1.html

104. M. E. Kabay, "NIST SP800-53 Rev. 3: Risk Management Framework Underpins the Security Life Cycle" (Part 2), *NetworkWorld* | Security Strategies Alert, October 28, 2009, www.networkworld.com/newsletters/sec/2009/102609sec2.html

105. M. E. Kabay, "Extensive Catalog Provides Security Controls for Contemporary Security Requirements" (Part 3), *NetworkWorld* | Security Strategies Alert, November 2, 2009, www.networkworld.com/newsletters/sec/2009/110209sec1.html

106. M. E. Kabay, "SP 800-53 is Essential for Security in Federal Government IT Systems" (Part 4), *NetworkWorld* | Security Strategies Alert, November 4, 2009, www.networkworld.com/news/2009/110209-applicability-government.html

107. Many NIST SP 800-53 security controls map to security controls defined in international security standard ISO/IEC 27001.

108. FedRAMP, "Ensuring Secure Cloud Computing for the Federal Government," U.S. General Services Administration Website, www.gsa.gov/portal/category/102371

109. See, for example, www.niap-ccevs.org/CCEVS_Products/pcl.cfm or www.commoncriteriaportal.org/products

110. Kim Zetter, "Board Urges Feds to Prevent Medical Device Hacking," *Wired* | Threat Level: Cybersecurity, April 10, 2012, www.wired.com/threatlevel/2012/04/security-of-medical-devices

111. Such a program was attempted by NIST in the late 1990s, whereby health-care security requirements would be specified by Common Criteria methods; government-sanctioned, third-party, security testing labs would evaluate products to verify that the stipulated security requirements were met; and the government would validate the product evaluations and provide a product evaluation certificate.
112. Barack Obama, "Executive Order 13636—Improving Critical Infrastructure Cybersecurity," February 12, 2013, www.whitehouse.gov/the-press-office/2013/02/12/executive-order-improving-critical-infrastructure-cybersecurity
113. Barack Obama, "Critical Infrastructure Security and Resilience," Presidential Policy Directive PDD-21, February 12, 2013, www.fas.org/irp/offdocs/ppd/ppd-21.pdf
114. Information about HITRUST and its programs and deliverables is available at the HITRUST Website, www.hitrustalliance.net
115. HITRUST, "HITRUST CSF Assurance Program," Brochure, www.hitrustalliance.net/HIT_Bro_CSF_Assure_v2_Feb_2013.pdf
116. HITRUST, "HITRUST Cyber Threat Intelligence and Incident Coordination Center," www.hitrustalliance.net/c3
117. HITRUST, "HITRUST Cyber Threat Analysis Service," www.hitrustalliance.net/ctas
118. D. Bradbury, "The Prognosis for Medical Device Security," Infosecurity Magazine Q2 (2013):41–43, http://content.yudu.com/Library/A24a1q/InfoSecMagQ2V2/resources/42.htm
119. American National Standards Institute (ANSI), "ANSI/AAMI/ISO 13485, ANSI/AAMI/IEC 62304 and ANSI/AAMI/ISO 14971—Software, Quality and Risk Management of Medical Devices," Medical Devices Package, ANSI eStandards Store, http://webstore.ansi.org/RecordDetail.aspx?sku=ANSI%2fAAMI%2fISO+13485+%2f+ANSI%2fAAMI%2fIEC+62304+%2f+ANSI%2fAAMI%2fISO+14971+-+Medical+Devices+Package#.UUmyu6VXL8 t
120. United Press International, "Firewall Can Stop Medical Device 'Hacking,' " UPI.com | Science News, April 12, 2012, www.upi.com/Science_News/2012/04/12/Firewall-can-stop-medical-device-hacking/UPI-19931334276290
121. Vormetric, "New Technologies Surpass Compliance as Driver for Organizations to Secure Data," ITBusinessEdge, May 8, 2013, www.itbusinessedge.com/slideshows/new-technologies-surpass-compliance-as-driver-for-organizations-to-secure-data.html
122. With the advent of FISMA, it was first realized that regulated organizations were focusing more on regulatory compliance and the fear of regulatory audit rather than on security and actual risk reduction. Apparently, executives in affected organizations found compliance easier to measure. They also had penalties assessed based on lack of compliance not on appropriate risk management in an environment of advancing technology and complexity changes.
123. Spirent, "Achieving Cyber Security Readiness Within an Evolving Threat Landscape," February 13, 2013, in SC Magazine | White Paper Roundup, May 17, 2013, http://forms.madisonlogic.com/FormConfirmation.aspx?pub=18&pgr=259&src=2318&cmp=5303*=25776&frm;=446&pd=161275-9-6886-57-321-0 (URL inactive).

124. FedRAMP provides security assessment standards only for cloud software providers serving government clients.
125. T. Olavsrud, "Box Takes Electronic Health Records to the Cloud", CIO.com | Applications, April 25, 2013, www.cio.com/article/732375/Box_Takes_Electronic_Health_Records_to_the_Cloud?page=1&taxonomyId=600000
126. Bill Brenner, "Video: David Navetta on Cyber Insurance, Risk Management," CSO | Security and Risk | Salted Hash blog, March 15, 2013, http://blogs.csoonline.com/security-industry/2620/video-david-navetta-cyber-insurance-risk-management?source=CSONLE_nlt_update_2013-03-17
127. Karen Epper Hoffman, "Urgent Care—Health Providers Have Pressing Reasons to now Embrace Security," SC Magazine, April 1, 2013, www.scmagazine.com/urgent-care-safeguarding-data-at-health-care-providers/article/284420

CHAPTER 72

LEGAL AND POLICY ISSUES OF CENSORSHIP AND CONTENT FILTERING

Lee Tien, Seth Finkelstein, and Steven Lovaas

72.1 INTRODUCTION

Everyone has the right to freedom of opinion and expression; this right includes freedom to hold opinions without interference and to seek, receive, and impart information and ideas through any media and regardless of frontiers.[1]

One might think that the Internet will make this ringing proclamation a reality. Like no other technology, the Internet transcends national borders and eliminates barriers to the free flow of information. Governments, however, are controlling speech on the Internet.

72.1.1 Scope of This Chapter: Government Intervention. Many nations protect rights of free speech and free expression. The *First Amendment to the U.S. Constitution* provides that "Congress shall make no law ... abridging the freedom of speech or of the press." The *Canadian Charter of Rights and Freedoms* protects freedom of speech and press in Article 2 as fundamental rights. Although Great Britain has no formal constitution, the *Magna Carta* of 1215, the *1512 Privilege of Parliament Act*, the *1689 Bill of Rights*, and the *1911 Parliament Act* all protect aspects of the freedom of speech.[2]

Despite such constitutional protections, speech is regulated everywhere. Article 1 of the Canadian Charter of Rights and Freedoms permits "demonstrably reasonable" limitations on freedom of expression. Great Britain and Canada have promulgated legislation regulating racially defamatory speech, group defamation, or speech that incites racial hatred. Although American law is far more protective of speech, some expression is deemed unprotected by the First Amendment, and even protected speech can be regulated in a variety of circumstances.

Accordingly, some governments have enacted laws prohibiting certain content on the Internet and have sought to prosecute users and service providers. Others have tried to control access by insisting on the installation of national *proxy servers* and blocking targeted Websites. Governments also have encouraged *self-regulation* intended to enlist service providers to control customer behavior.

Readers from North America should also understand that in most of the developing world, access to the Internet is primarily through mobile phones. For example, at the time of writing (August 2013) in developing nations in the year 2012, mobile phone subscriptions for Internet access registered at 89.4 percent (5.2 billion subscriptions) of the population, whereas only 6.2 percent of the population (0.4 billion subscriptions) had fixed broadband subscriptions.[3] Thus, restrictions on Internet access include restrictions on mobile-device usage in many countries.

72.1.2 Whose Laws? Whose Standards? It is often thought that governments cannot successfully censor the Internet. After all, one nation's laws may be unenforceable elsewhere. But national laws can be applied to communication intermediaries like Internet service providers (ISPs), blocking access by people in that country.

Moreover, just as speech originating in one nation can reach a worldwide audience, one nation's laws can have powerful effects in other nations. As commentators have put it, "[t]he reach of the Internet multiplies both the number of laws and the number of jurisdictions applicable to speech transmitted on-line."[4] Indeed, "[b]ecause content posted on the Internet is instantaneously transmitted worldwide, Internet users and providers almost automatically face potential liability in any country to which the Internet is connected—not just the nation where the speech was created or where the author lives."[5]

A prominent example is the case in which a French court ordered the United States–based Yahoo! to "take all necessary measures to dissuade and make impossible any access via Yahoo.com to the auction service for Nazi merchandise as well as to any other site or service that may be construed as an apology for Nazism or contesting the reality of Nazi crimes."[6] The French court held that "the simple act of displaying [Nazi artifacts] in France violates Article R645-1 of the Penal Code and therefore [is] a threat to internal public order."[7] It described the mere availability of such information to be "a connecting link with France, which renders our jurisdiction perfectly competent to rule in this matter."[8] After the French order was handed down, Yahoo! filed suit in the United States seeking a judgment that it need not comply with the French order.[9] The French parties moved to dismiss the U.S. case for lack of personal jurisdiction, but the U.S. district court denied the motion, allowing Yahoo! to proceed.[10] In 2004, however, the U.S. Appellate Court overturned the district court's decision, ruling that the district court judge lacked the authority to hear the case, but also noting that Yahoo! should not expect both to benefit from the worldwide availability of its product and to avoid the possible consequences of that availability.

Resolving international jurisdiction in cyberspace is one of the most difficult and important issues for the Internet, but it is beyond the scope of this chapter. Moreover, the ways in which the laws of one nation may affect Internet speech in another extend beyond the topic of this chapter: state-backed censorship. Even when governments do not themselves target particular kinds of speech, their laws may give private parties legal rights against expression originating overseas, as in the area of defamation.[11] Laws relating to commerce also may raise free speech concerns, as in the areas of intellectual property[12] and privacy regulation. For instance, the 1995 European Union Data Protection Directive generally regulates all *processing* of *personal data*, giving data subjects legal rights quite different from those found in the United States.[13] See Chapter 69 in this *Handbook* for discussion of the Privacy Directive and other regulations affecting the handling of personally identifiable data.

72.1.3 Defining Objectionable Material: International Differences.

For most countries, the major concerns stem from the increased availability of objectionable content over the Internet. This section focuses on how the meaning of *objectionable* differs from country to country.

72.1.3.1 Sexuality.

A common type of objectionable material is speech about sex. In the United States, a series of attempts have been made to regulate the availability of sexually oriented speech over the Internet, although with little success.[14]

Several Middle Eastern nations also block pornographic sites.[15]

In 1995, the Bavarian Justice Ministry informed the value-added network CompuServe that senior company officials could face prison terms for violation of German antipornography laws. German police provided CompuServe a list of the discussion groups that contained potentially objectionable material.[16] In February 1997, Germany indicted Felix Somm, head of CompuServe's German subsidiary, for failure to prevent the dissemination of illegal material on its online service; with this Germany became the first Western democracy to prosecute an official of an online service for illegal Internet content.[17] German prosecutors argued that because CompuServe had access to screening software, the company had the opportunity to block the offending material but failed to do so. Soon thereafter, Germany enacted its *Information and Communications Services Act of 1997* (ICSA). The ICSA, however, has been sharply criticized for failing to resolve the uncertainties faced by ISPs.[18]

72.1.3.2 Hate.

Another major category of objectionable speech is what is loosely called *hate speech*.[19] American hate sites include sites promoting white supremacy, promoting Nazi or neo-Nazi views, supporting skinheads, and promoting the Christian Identity Movement.[20] Internet content that promotes Nazi views and Holocaust denial has attracted considerable international attention.

For instance, the German constitution, known as the *Basic Law*, incorporates freedom of expression as a fundamental individual right. But Article 5, the main provision concerning free speech, expressly provides that the government may limit an individual's expressive right if it conflicts with other people's rights, public order, or criminal laws. Thus, under Germany's general laws and the laws protecting youths, publishing or distributing neo-Nazi or Holocaust denial literature is a criminal offense.[21]

In February 1996, German prosecutors in Mannheim investigated several ISPs, including America Online, regarding alleged distribution of neo-Nazi material on the Internet in violation of anti-Nazi laws.[22] In 2000, German-born Frederick Toben, who used the Website of his Australian-based Adelaide Institute to advocate Holocaust denial, was found guilty of offending the memory of the dead.[23] The lower court had ruled "that German law against inciting racial hatred could not be applied to content on a foreign website."[24] Germany's Federal Court of Justice, the Bundesgerichtshof, overturned the lower court ruling and found that German law applies to Internet content that originates outside the country's borders, so long as people inside of Germany can access that content.[25]

In a 2002 study, Harvard Law School professor Jonathan Zittrain found that Google was systematically excluding search results containing banned content in the French and German versions of its site and that this was apparently "because of pressure applied or perceived by the respective governments."[26]

Canadian law directs courts to balance an individual's free speech rights with societal equality interests. Thus, Canadian courts have upheld hate speech convictions under laws that criminalize the willful promotion of hatred.[27] The Canadian Supreme Court held the statute constitutional.[28] The Court defined hate speech as including a requirement that "the accused 'promote' hatred against an identifiable group, indicating more than simple encouragement or advancement and rather required that the hate monger intend or foresee as substantially certain a direct and active stimulation of hatred against an identifiable group."[29]

The Internet has raised new issues in Canada regarding hate speech. In the 1990s, Bernard Klatt ran the *Fairview Technology Center* out of his home in British Columbia, and about a dozen neo-Nazi, white supremacist, and skinhead clients used his server to publish material against immigration and homosexuality while celebrating Hitler's accomplishments and "Euro-Christianity." The Canadian government attempted to shut down Klatt, but he and his clients insisted that they had not broken any laws.[30] The site suspended its services in 1998.[31] As of the time this chapter was updated (August 2013), the Website consisted of a single page with contact information and had not been updated since 2002.

The Zündelsite, a multilingual archive and news service, may be the most prominent Holocaust-denial Website run by an individual. Its administrator, German Canadian Ernst Zündel, became one of the denial movement's martyrs when he was convicted in Canada for his Holocaust denial pamphlets.[32] The Canadian Supreme Court later overturned his conviction.[33] Zündel's United States–based Web page then became the target of an official inquiry by the Canadian Human Rights Commission.[34] Zündel was deported from the United States to Canada in 2003. The Canadian government determined that he represented a risk to national security, and deported him to Germany, where he was sentenced in 2007 for the maximum term of five years on outstanding charges of incitement for Holocaust denial but was released in March 2010.[35]

72.1.3.3 Politics and Culture. Various countries also regulate Internet content that generally threatens their government or political, social, and cultural values.

72.1.3.3.1 People's Republic of China. At the end of 2006, there were approximately 137 million Internet users in China, an increase of 34 million over the previous year.[36] The Chinese government, although eager to capitalize on the Internet, feels that the "Internet is a very real threat to the hold their dictatorial regime has over the country."[37] Accordingly, China severely restricts communication via the Internet, including much dissent and the free reporting of news. The *Measures for Managing Internet Information Services* prohibit private Websites from publishing news without prior approval from Communist Party officials.[38]

A major obstacle for would-be Chinese Internet users is the registration process required to get online. One must pick an ISP and provide identification. One must also fill out a *Police File Report Form* that will be sent to the ISP, the local *Public Security Bureau* (PSB), and the provincial-level PSB *Computer Security and Supervision Office*. In addition, users must complete a Net Access Responsibility Agreement, pledging "not to use the Internet to threaten state security or reveal state secrets" or to read, reproduce, or transmit material that "endangers the state, obstructs public safety, or is obscene or pornographic."[39] The ISP application itself requests information such as employer's address, home address, and profession; home, office, cell phone, and pager numbers; as well as details about the computer, the modem type, and permit number, which is assigned by the PSB.[40]

The following news summaries from 2001 were posted on the *Digital Freedom Network* site, which no longer has any of the original reports online; however, the original article is available on the Internet Archive.[41]

- In January 2000, the Chinese newspaper the *People's Daily* published new Internet regulations issued by China's State Secrecy Bureau. These laws "ban the release, discussion, or transfer" of "state secret information" on bulletin board systems, chat rooms, or Internet news groups. Email users were banned from sending or forwarding state secrets by email. In addition, all Websites are required to undergo a security check. A provision requiring that anyone using encryption technology register with the government was later rescinded.
- In May 2000, after the *China Finance Information Network*, a financial Website, republished a Hong Kong newspaper about corruption by a provincial official, Chinese public security officials suspended the site for 15 days and fined the site 15,000 yuan (US$1,800). On August 3, 2000, state security officials forced a Chinese ISP to shut down the Xinwenming (New Culture Forum) site run by a group of dissidents in Shandong Province for posting "reactionary content."
- The following month, China's State Council passed Internet laws that limited foreign investment and imposed strict surveillance requirements on Internet content by mandating that Internet content providers monitor both the material they publish and the people who access that material, including the times users log onto the Internet, their account numbers, their Internet addresses, and the phone numbers they are dialing in from.
- On November 7, 2000, the Ministry of Information Industry and the Information Office of the State Council released new laws banning commercial media organizations from setting up independent news sites; prohibiting commercial portals from carrying news items based on their own sources; and requiring China-based Websites to obtain permission from the State Council Information Office before linking to overseas news sites or carrying news from overseas news media. The new Internet laws also restrict the content of online chat rooms and bulletin boards.

- In December 2000, the National People's Congress passed a new law to foster Internet safety. This law criminalizes several forms of online political activity, including using the Internet to "incite the overthrow of state power, topple the socialist system, or ... destroy national unity," promote "cults," or support the independence of Taiwan.
- The Ministry of Public Security announced on February 27, 2001, that it released Internet filtering software called *Internet Police 110* on February 26. The software comes in three versions for households, Internet cafés, and schools that can monitor Web traffic and delete or block messages from sources deemed "offensive." According to a news report published in the China Securities News, it can send text or voice warnings to network administrators about any unauthorized Internet surfing.
- On March 20, 2001, official Chinese media reported that China is developing a surveillance system to monitor activities on the Internet, which will be similar to the data-recording "black box" installed in commercial airplanes. According to Hong Kong *iMail,* it will be able to record all communications through the Internet.
- In April 2001, the official Chinese news agency Xinhua reported that China would impose a three-month ban on the opening of new Internet cafés. This is part of "a major offensive against unchecked use of the Internet. Xinhua said authorities are to conduct a massive probe into existing Internet outlets, which it views as potential hotbeds of dissent and vice."
- In addition, after January 2000, the Chinese government began arresting individuals who use the Internet in a manner they deem dangerous, often for online political or religious activity. Qi Yanchen, sentenced to four years in prison on September 19, 2000, is the first Chinese convicted of subversion for material he wrote that was published on the Internet. Qi was officially charged for writing articles in the May 6, 1999, and May 17, 1999, United States–based Chinese dissident email publication *Dacankao* (V.I.P. Reference). Guo Qinghai, a freelance writer, was arrested in September 2000 for "subverting state power." Guo published articles on the Internet that discussed Qi Yanchen's case. He also posted, on overseas online bulletin boards, essays promoting political reforms in China. He was sentenced to four years in prison.
- Zhang Haitao, creator of the only China-based Website on the outlawed Falun Gong, was charged with subversion on October 11, 2000, and is accused of establishing a site promoting Falun Gong and of posting an online petition urging followers to protest the government ban on the group. Zhang Ji, a college student in Heilongjiang Province, was charged on November 8, 2000, with "disseminating reactionary documents via the Internet." Authorities say Zhang had emailed information to United States– and Canada-based Websites of the Falun Gong religious group as well as downloaded news about the group and shared it with others in China.

Google has had a rocky relationship with the Chinese government, with its entire service being blocked several times for serving information critical of government policy. In January 2006, Google agreed to block a list of search terms that would be provided by the Chinese government and limit searches from within China to this partial set of results at google.cn. The independence of Taiwan and the 1989 Tiananmen

Square massacre remain on the list of forbidden topics. Given the history of outright bans, Google seems to have decided that some content was better than none.[42]

In May 2011, a new body, the State Internet Information Office (SIIO), was created to coordinate state control over all aspects of Internet usage. Within weeks, the SIIO had shut down over 6,000 sites offering reputation-management services (some of them allegedly fraudulent).[43]

In December 2012, reports from Beijing indicated that "China unveiled tighter Internet controls on Friday, legalizing the deletion of posts or pages which are deemed to contain 'illegal' information and requiring service providers to hand over such information to the authorities for punishment." A Reuters report included this summary:

> "Service providers are required to instantly stop the transmission of illegal information once it is spotted and take relevant measures, including removing the information and saving records, before reporting to supervisory authorities," the rules state.
>
> The restrictions follow a series of corruption scandals amongst lower-level officials exposed by Internet users, something the government has said it is trying to encourage.
>
> Li Fei, deputy head of parliament's legislative affairs committee, said the new rules did not mean people needed to worry about being unable to report corruption online. But he added a warning too.
>
> "When people exercise their rights, including the right to use the Internet, they must do so in accordance with the law and constitution, and not harm the legal rights of the state, society ... or other citizens," he told a news conference.
>
> Chinese Internet users already cope with extensive censorship measures, especially over politically sensitive topics like human rights and elite politics, and popular foreign sites Facebook, Twitter, and Google-owned YouTube are blocked.
>
> Earlier [in 2012], the government began forcing users of Sina's wildly successful Weibo microblogging platform to register their real names.[44]

The *New York Times* maintains an extensive and up-to-date compilation of its articles about Internet censorship in China.[45]

72.1.3.3.2 Islamic Countries. According to *Human Rights Watch*, the United Arab Emirates (UAE) is "the regional leader in advocating censorship of the Web through the use of high-tech means."[46] Dial-up users in the UAE do not access the Internet directly; they dial into a proxy server maintained by *Etisalat*, the state telecommunications company, in collaboration with a U.S. firm that is contracted to maintain and update the software. Although UAE officials have insisted that the proxy server's sole purpose is to block pornographic sites, at least one nonpornographic site, that of the *Gay and Lesbian Arabic Society* (www.glas.org) is blocked. When asked about the site, an Information and Culture Ministry official explained that there had been complaints about it.

Saudi Arabia bans publishing or even accessing various types of online expression, including "[a]nything contrary to the state or its system"; "[n]ews damaging to the Saudi Arabian armed forces"; "[a]nything damaging to the dignity of heads of states"; "[a]ny false information ascribed to state officials"; "[s]ubversive ideas"; and "[s]landerous or libelous material."[47]

All 30 of the country's ISPs are linked to a ground-floor room at the Riyadh Internet entranceway, where all of the country's Web activity is stored in massive cache files and screened for offensive or sacrilegious material before it is released to individual users.

The central servers are configured to block access to "sensitive" sites that might violate "the social, cultural, political, media, economic, and religious values of the Kingdom."[48]

According to Human Rights Watch, although official Saudi explanations of Internet censorship focus on materials deemed offensive to conservative Muslim sensibilities, Saudi blocking apparently extends to political sites. In early 1999, the site of at least one exiled dissident group, the Committee against Corruption in Saudi Arabia (www.saudhouse.com), was reportedly blocked.

Yemen's telecommunications service provider, *Teleyemen*, told Human Rights Watch that there is a "general requirement … to limit information which is considered to be undesirable in terms of causing offenses against social, religious, or cultural standards" (Eric Goldstein, The Internet in the Mideast and North Africa: Free Expression and Censorship, p. 24) and that Teleyemen uses the Surfwatch censorware program in conjunction with a proxy server.

More recently, controversies have erupted when Middle Eastern and other Islamic groups or nations have protested content offensive to Islam that was hosted outside their own borders. In 2005, a Danish newspaper published caricatures of the prophet Muhammad, which many Muslims found to be offensive. The cartoonist, the newspaper, and the Danish people as a whole were targeted with boycotts and death threats. Imams in Denmark brought suit to have the government punish the newspaper but had no success in the courts. In 2007, Turkey briefly blocked all access to YouTube in protest of a video insulting the nation's founder, Mustafa Kemal Atatürk. Google, which had purchased YouTube earlier that year, quickly removed the video in question, and Turkey revoked the ban.[49]

A report from *Freedom House* in 2012 analyzing Internet censorship around the world listed 47 countries; notably, predominantly Muslim countries differed in the direction of their controls, with some becoming more restrictive and other becoming more liberal. Highlights from the organization's press release[50] and the full report[51] (662 pages) include detailed, country-by-country reports spanning several pages each and including extensive reference material. Additional commentary on countries of interest in this section includes:

- **Bahrain**: "Following the February 14, 2011, protests, the government intensified censorship and surveillance of advanced Web 2.0 applications and blocked interactive exchanges online, particularly when its political agenda was not supported. Internet connections became very slow, making it difficult to upload media, and some locations were entirely offline. Since February 2011, most live broadcasting websites that were popular among protesters have been blocked. PalTalk, a chatting service that was used to conduct political seminars with prominent guests and mass online audiences, has been blocked since June 2011, while many blogs critical of government views were also blocked in 2011, particularly those that documented the protests and government crackdown. …"
- **Egypt**: "The Supreme Council of the Armed Forces (SCAF) maintained many of its predecessor's tactics of internet control, while intensifying others. Mobile phones, the internet, and social media remained under vigorous surveillance, bandwidth speeds were throttled during specific events, and SCAF-affiliated commentators manipulated online discussions. Several activists and bloggers were intimidated, beaten, shot at, or tried in military courts for "insulting the military power" or "disturbing social peace." Despite recent elections, the future trajectory of internet freedom in Egypt remains precarious and uncertain."

- **Ethiopia**: "In 2011, in the wake of the Arab Spring protests in the Middle East and several online calls for similar demonstrations in Ethiopia, … the government reacted by strengthening internet censorship and carrying out a systematic crackdown on independent journalists, including at least one blogger. Beginning in June 2011, over ten journalists were sentenced to long prison terms, … mostly on questionable charges of terrorism. Among them was the editor of an exiled online news Website who was sentenced in absentia to life imprisonment. A prominent dissident blogger based in Ethiopia was also arrested in September 2011 and sentenced to 18 years in prison in July 2012. … The latest crackdown is part of a broader trend of growing repression against independent media since the 2005 parliamentary elections, in which opposition parties mustered a relatively strong showing. …"
- **Indonesia**: "Since 2010, internet and mobile phone usage has continued to grow at a fast pace. Meanwhile, the popularity of social-networking applications has increased exponentially, with Indonesia becoming home to some of the largest contingents of Twitter and Facebook users in the world. The authorities have subsequently sought to regulate online content, citing fears of the internet's use for the spread of pornographic, blasphemous, and terrorism-related content. In the process, a number of actions taken, including passage of the Law on Information and Electronic Transactions (ITE Law) of 2008, have fallen short of international democratic standards. This trend continued in 2011 with the passage of the State Surveillance Law and increased filtering of content loosely defined as sexually explicit. Meanwhile, a surprising criminal conviction under the ITE Law of a housewife who disseminated critical information about a hospital and a series of other questionable criminal cases filed under the ITE exacerbated the atmosphere of legal uncertainty surrounding freedom of expression online and raised concerns of greater restrictions on internet freedom in the future."
- **Iran**: "The Iranian authorities used more nuanced tactics in a continued campaign against internet freedom that began after disputed elections in 2009. These tactics included: upgrading content filtering technology, hacking digital certificates to undermine user privacy, and moving closer to establishing a National Internet. Iranian judicial authorities also meted out some of the harshest sentences in the world for online activities, including imposing the death penalty on three bloggers and IT professionals."
- **Jordan**: "Jordan, a small kingdom of about six million people, prides itself on offering relatively broad freedom to use the internet and officially blocks only one Website. The Jordanian government's response to public protests in 2011 was relatively mild compared to neighboring countries. Moreover, the king and parliament passed a set of constitutional amendments that could improve human rights protections and free expression. Nevertheless, restrictions on internet freedom exist and have increased since January 2011. News Websites, which have become a vital source of information in a country where traditional media freedom is limited, often face pressure from state actors to delete articles deemed politically sensitive. In April 2012, a government council passed a resolution that could require online news Websites to register with the government, a policy that if implemented risks curbing their independent reporting and analysis. Meanwhile, surveillance, physical attacks against bloggers and online journalists, and hacking attacks against prominent news Websites also present a threat."

- **Libya**: "The political unrest and armed conflict that occurred in Libya in 2011, which resulted in the death of Muammar al-Qadhafi after over 40 years in power, led to a dramatic regime change. The country shifted from being one of the world's harshest dictatorships to a postconflict aspiring democracy. As of May 2012, the government of Libya was comprised of a National Transitional Council (NTC) formed during the conflict and an appointed interim government mandated to steer the country towards elections scheduled for July 2012, after which a new constitution will be drafted. These political changes were also reflected in the internet freedom landscape. As such, this report straddles three radically different periods: a highly restrictive environment under Qadhafi, a partial internet and telephone blackout for much of 2011, and a relatively open online information landscape since the rebel victory in October 2011."
- **Pakistan**: "Disconcerting recent developments in Pakistan include a ban on encryption and virtual private networks (VPNs), a death sentence imposed for transmitting allegedly blasphemous content via text message, and a one-day block on all mobile phone networks in Balochistan province. Several other initiatives to increase censorship—including a plan to filter text messages by keyword and a proposal to develop a nationwide internet firewall—were officially shelved in response to civil society advocacy campaigns, although some suspect that the government is still working on them behind closed doors."
- **Saudi Arabia**: "While the recent wave of protests and demonstrations in the Kingdom of Saudi Arabia has not changed the political landscape in the country as in other Arab countries such as Tunisia, Egypt, and Libya, the internet freedom landscape in the Kingdom has no doubt changed considerably over the past year. Inspired by the Arab Spring events in 2011, millions of people in Saudi Arabia flooded social media sites such as Facebook, YouTube, and Twitter, and hundreds, if not thousands, participated in political campaigns to demand political, social, and economic reforms, fostering the emergence of innumerable political activists on social media. However, as soon as Saudis went online to express their opinions, demand actions, and organize demonstrations, the Saudi government took immediate steps to respond to what it regarded as a national security threat. The government issued warnings banning protests, reminded people via email of the ban, and threatened the youth through the BlackBerry multimedia message service (MMS) to discourage them from participating in demonstrations. The authorities also detained and intimidated hundreds of online political activists and online commentators, implemented strict filtering mechanisms to block sensitive political content from entering the Saudi internet, recruited thousands of online supporters to warn against the call for protests and demonstrations as a counter measure, and continued to apply its excessive monitoring of internet users."
- **Syria**: "The Syrian government engages in extensive filtering of Websites related to politics, minorities, human rights, and foreign affairs, and such censorship has expanded in recent years. Tests conducted by the OpenNet Initiative (ONI) in 2008–2009 found pervasive blocking of Websites related to opposition to the Assad regime, human rights groups, the Muslim Brotherhood, and activism on behalf of the Kurdish minority. A range of Websites related to regional politics were also found to be blocked, including several Lebanese newspapers and the Websites of groups campaigning to end Syrian influence in Lebanon, as well as the prominent London-based Arabic newspapers Al-Quds al-Arabi and Al-Sharq

al-Awesat. Access to the entire Israeli domain name ".il" was also restricted. Internet censorship continued to worsen in 2011 and early 2012. Activists and average users consistently complained about the extensive and unprecedented blocking of circumvention tools, internet security software, and applications that enable anonymous communications. Websites used to mobilize people for protests or resistance against the regime, including those of the network of Local Coordination Committees (LCCs) that emerged as the uprising progressed, were blocked. Online initiatives to gather information and raise public awareness, such as the Mondaseh Website, were blocked as well. However, the Websites of most international news sources and human rights groups have remained accessible."

72.1.3.3.3 Burma (Myanmar). In 1988, a new military clique called the *State Law* and *Order Restoration Council* (SLORC) took power in Burma, now known as *Myanmar*. They managed to achieve cease-fires with 15 armed organizations, but they refused to step down, asserting that only "the military can ensure national unity and solidarity,"[52] even after the National League for Democracy's overwhelming victory in the 1990 election. In 1997, the SLORC was renamed the State Peace and Development Council (SPDC), but the membership remained largely unchanged.

SLORC/SPDC maintains power partly by controlling access to information. In January 2000, the Myanmar Post and Telecommunication (MPT), then the only ISP in Myanmar, passed a measure that forbids Internet users from posting political speech on the Web, such as writings "detrimental to the interests of the Union of Myanmar" or "directly or indirectly detrimental to the current policies and secret security affairs of the government of the Union of Burma."[53] Only the person granted an Internet account may use it, and the account holder is held responsible for all use of that account. Web pages may not be created without government permission, and violation of any regulation is subject to legal action.[54] In 2005, Myanmar's only private ISP, Bagan Cybertech, was nationalized under the control of the MPT, and the government has entered into an agreement with U.S. Web content filtering company Fortinet in order to better control Web access from within Myanmar.[55]

The Burmese military has been effective at "warding off any Internet revolution by limiting the rights of its citizens."[56] The Freedom House report cited in Section 72.1.3.3.2 identifies persistently weak infrastructure for both standard computer-based Internet connectivity and for mobile-phone access to the Internet as barriers to Internet access and usage.[57]

72.1.3.3.4 Russia. The Freedom House report[58] describes the situation in Russia at the end of 2012 as follows:

> After independent television channels were eliminated and press regulations tightened from 2000–2001, the internet became Russia's last relatively uncensored platform for public debate and the expression of political opinions. In response, the government has tried various tactics to suppress citizens' right to free speech online over the years. In 2009–2010, many bloggers were harassed and opposition blogs were hacked. While these incidents still occurred in 2011, the tactics to restrict freedom of expression online have slightly changed, with the deployment of distributed denial-of-service (DDoS) attacks ... and various smear campaigns ... to discredit online activists becoming more common. Extralegal intimidation of social network activists and independent forum moderators ... has become another line of pressure over the online world through strategies such as informal meetings with the security services, calls from the Federal Security Service (FSB) to the parents of activists, ... or the sudden refusal of forum ad sponsors to buy advertisements.

In May 2013, a wide range of Websites were blocked in central Russia after a district court responded to a prosecutor's claim that they were making available instructions on how to bribe officials. However, none of the Website owners were informed of the decision, some of the sites were for independent news organizations (rather than state-controlled outlets), and the blockage even included information such as employment advertisements. Activists described the incident as "Internet censorship on a whim."[59]

72.2 U.S. CONTEXT: FIRST AMENDMENT RIGHTS. The First Amendment of the U.S. Constitution strongly protects freedom of speech in the United States. In several ways, the right to speak is the most powerful of all U.S. constitutional rights. First Amendment scrutiny can be much stricter than in other areas of constitutional law. It is usually easier to get in front of a court when "speech" is at issue, and to win, because many technical legal requirements are relaxed.

Thus, although the right to speak is not constitutionally absolute, and may be restricted by government, several basic principles limit governmental authority to restrict freedom of speech, more than it is limited from restricting other activities. These principles have been articulated through a variety of legal doctrines.

72.2.1 What Does the First Amendment Protect? Today, the First Amendment generally protects all forms of communicative or expressive activity[60] from "state action" or governmental interference.[61] Courts generally presume that linguistic acts or visual depictions are covered by the First Amendment but require litigants to show that nonlinguistic acts are speech unless the law has already so held.[62]

Nevertheless, the coverage of the First Amendment is quite broad. It includes not only the right to speak but also the right *not* to speak, or against "compelled" speech,[63] the right to speak or associate anonymously,[64] and the right to read or to receive information.[65] Often, activity that is not necessarily communicative is protected because it enables or facilitates expression. Highly discretionary city licensing of newsstands was found to be an invalid scheme of licensing that affected liberty of circulation.[66] Money is not speech, but election campaign contributions and expenditures are protected as speech.[67]

In addition, the First Amendment requires that the government observe some degree of neutrality in its treatment of speakers[68] and speech media[69]; it cannot arbitrarily prefer one speaker or one medium to another.

72.2.2 Basic First Amendment Principles. There is no consensus or accepted theory underlying U.S. protection of free speech. The different rationales for freedom of speech can be categorized as more or less "positive" or "negative." Positive justifications identify speech as related to some special moral, social, or political value. For example, the "marketplace of ideas" theory is based on the notion that "the best test of truth is the power of the thought to get itself accepted in the competition of the market."[70] Courts also have defended the right to free expression as embodying the value of "speaker autonomy,"[71] thus "putting the decision as to what views shall be voiced largely into the hands of each of us, in the hope that use of such freedom will ultimately produce a more capable citizenry and more perfect polity, *and in the belief that no other approach would comport with the premise of individual dignity and choice upon which our political system rests*."[72]

Negative theories presume the value of speech and focus instead on the dangers of government regulation of speech. The main idea here is that speech is as vulnerable to threats of punishment as to punishment itself. "It is characteristic of freedoms of expression in general that they are vulnerable to gravely damaging yet barely visible encroachments."[73] This fear of "chilling effects" on speech sometimes is associated with the possibility that juries may not treat unpopular speakers or unorthodox ideas fairly, but it also reflects a concern that individuals may censor themselves. Such self-censorship can harm public debate while being almost "invisible" to the courts because it occurs through many small individual choices.[74]

72.2.2.1 Harm/Causation. Perhaps the most important First Amendment principle is that the government has the burden to show that the speech it wishes to regulate truly causes significant harm. This principle was not accepted for many years; in the early days of First Amendment law, speech could be punished as an "attempt" if the natural and reasonable tendency of what was said would be to bring about a forbidden effect. Thus, for instance, individuals who had mailed circulars to draftees arguing that conscription was unconstitutional and urging them to assert their rights were convicted for conspiring to attempt to obstruct the draft.[75]

Today, courts are far more skeptical about government claims of harm. If speech could be restricted merely because the mathematical expectation of harm were significant, speech would be easier to restrict as it were more widely disseminated. Such a result is inconsistent with the First Amendment's protection of open, public discourse. As a classic opinion stated, "no danger flowing from speech can be deemed clear and present, unless the incidence of the evil apprehended is so imminent that it may befall before there is opportunity for full discussion. If there be time to expose the evil by the processes of education, the remedy to be applied is more speech, not enforced silence."[76]

The concern here is not only for the speech itself; it includes a concern that the speaker can properly be held responsible for harm. The modern approach is exemplified by a case where a speaker was convicted for advocating violence. The Supreme Court reversed the conviction because the law did not require the government to show both that the speaker intended to produce "imminent lawless action" and that the speech was "likely to incite or produce such action."[77] The requirement of intent helps protect speakers from being held responsible for the acts of others. As one court put it, "Much speech is dangerous. Chemists whose work might help someone build a bomb, political theorists whose papers might start political movements that lead to riots, speakers whose ideas attract violent protesters, all these and more leave loss in their wake."[78] Without careful attention to harm and causation, the right to speak would mean little.[79]

72.2.2.2 Neutrality. Not all reasons that government might use to restrict speech are valid. Thus, a second basic First Amendment principle is governmental neutrality as to speech content. Government is likely to have illegitimate reasons for wishing to restrict speech, such as the desire to suppress political criticism, but it may be able to disguise such hostility by claiming that less selfish interests, such as "public order" or the civility of discourse, are truly at stake.[80] Also, because public officials may have a strong self-interest in stifling dissent, they are likely to ignore or undervalue the social interest in free speech. Such motivations may lead to regulation that skews or distorts public debate. In general, then, government may not regulate speech based on its substantive content or the message it conveys.[81]

72.2.2.3 Precision. Third, all speech regulation must be precise. "Because First Amendment freedoms need breathing space to survive, government may regulate in the area only with narrow specificity."[82] Much of the First Amendment's force stems from this principle. Imprecise regulation not only chills speech but also gives officials too much discretion to discriminate on the basis of content. Without clearly stated standards, courts cannot easily ferret out content-based discrimination.[83] Insisting on precision also allows courts to avoid assessing the importance of the legislature's goals; they need only say that the means are too blunt.

72.2.2.4 Background Doubt-Resolution Principles. Adding to the strength of First Amendment protection for speech are several principles for resolving uncertainty. Speech regulation generally requires knowledge or intent on the speaker's part, which protects bookstores and others that "carry" others' speech.[84] Moreover, the factual burden of proof is usually on the person or entity seeking to restrict speech.[85] Finally, speech that in itself might be disfavored receives "strategic" protection in order to protect undue chill to public discourse; for instance, while false statements of fact may be considered of little First Amendment value, permitting the punishment of mere falsehood would overly burden speakers.[86] Put simply, doubts generally are called in favor of speech.

72.2.3 Limitations on Government Interference with Speech

72.2.3.1 Distinction between Substantive Tests and Procedural Safeguards: Example of Prior Restraints. A critical distinction in First Amendment (and other) law is between substantive and procedural review. The difference is best explained by reference to "prior restraints," which are presumed unconstitutional.

Most people are familiar with prior restraints as judicial orders preventing speech or publication. In such cases, government "carries a heavy burden of showing justification for the imposition of such a restraint."[87] For instance, the Supreme Court required the government to demonstrate that publication of the *Pentagon Papers* "will surely result in direct, immediate, and irreparable damage to our Nation or its people."[88] Judicial "gag orders" on press publication are subject to similarly searching scrutiny.[89] In these cases, courts are concerned with whether the particular restraint on speech is sufficiently justified.

A second line of prior restraint doctrine illustrates procedural scrutiny. American hostility to prior restraints is a reaction to English press licensing systems under which nothing could be printed without the prior approval of government or church authority. The fear is that discretionary permit schemes make freedom of speech "contingent upon the uncontrolled will of an official."[90] Thus, the law authorizing such a licensing scheme must provide "narrowly drawn, reasonable and definite standards for the [administering] officials to follow."[91] Thus, licensing schemes, such as for screening obscene movies, are constitutional only if accompanied by procedural safeguards necessary "to obviate the dangers of a censorship system."[92] There must be a "prompt final judicial decision" reviewing any "interim and possibly erroneous denial of a license." Moreover, "because only a judicial determination in an adversary proceeding ensures the necessary sensitivity to freedom of expression," the censor must, "within a specified brief period, either issue a license or go to court."[93] In such cases, the particular restraint is relatively unimportant: The issue is whether the statute itself contains sufficient procedural safeguards.

72.2.3.2 Levels of Substantive Scrutiny and the Issue of Content Neutrality. First Amendment cases typically feature three levels of substantive scrutiny, turning mainly on how the statute regulates the meaning of speech: by subject, by viewpoint, or without reference to meaning at all. In general, strict scrutiny applies to laws that attempt to stifle "speech on account of its message."[94] In such situations, the government must demonstrate both that there is a compelling interest in restricting the speech and that it has chosen the least restrictive means of furthering that compelling interest.

When the government targets not subject matter but particular views taken by speakers on a subject, the violation of the First Amendment is all the more blatant.[95] Viewpoint discrimination is thus an egregious form of content discrimination. The government must abstain from regulating speech when the specific motivating ideology or the opinion or perspective of the speaker is the rationale for the restriction.[96] Such scrutiny is so stringent that it applies to otherwise "unprotected" speech.[97]

However, the government often regulates speech without reference to its meaning or communicative impact. So-called content-neutral speech regulation is subject to intermediate rather than strict scrutiny "because in most cases they pose a less substantial risk of excising certain ideas or viewpoints from the public dialogue."[98] Such laws "do not pose such inherent dangers to free expression, or present such potential for censorship or manipulation, as to justify application of the most exacting level of First Amendment scrutiny."[99]

Intermediate scrutiny comes in two main flavors. Content-neutral regulation of the time, place, or manner of speech must be narrowly tailored to serve a significant government interest and leave open ample alternative channels for communication.[100] Content-neutral regulation in other contexts must further a substantial government interest and not burden substantially more speech than necessary to further that interest.[101]

A third type of intermediate scrutiny is the "secondary effects" doctrine, which operates as an exception to the general rule that content-based speech regulation is subject to strict scrutiny. The doctrine asks whether the harm is attributable to the communicative aspects of the speech; if not, the regulation is said to be aimed not at speech but rather at its "secondary effects," and the regulation is deemed content-neutral.[102] Thus, city zoning ordinances have been upheld even though they applied only to theaters that showed adult films because their purposes of preventing crime and protecting property values and the quality of urban life were deemed unrelated to speech content. This doctrine has been criticized for permitting speech suppression "whenever censors can concoct 'secondary' rationalizations for regulating the content of political speech."[103] The main limit on the doctrine is the rule that "listeners' reaction to speech is not a content-neutral basis for regulation."[104]

72.2.3.3 Types of Procedural Scrutiny: Vagueness and Overbreadth. Laws generally may not "set a net large enough to catch all possible offenders, and leave it to the courts to step inside and say who could be rightfully detained, and who should be set at large."[105] This hostility to vague laws is greater when speech is concerned; courts will assume that ambiguous legal language will be used against speech.[106] The void-for-vagueness doctrine emphasizes both fair notice to citizens of what conduct is prohibited and clear standards for law enforcement to follow.[107]

A closely related doctrine is that of overbreadth. A law is overbroad when it "does not aim specifically at evils within the allowable area of [government] control, but … sweeps within its ambit other activities that constitute an exercise" of First Amendment rights.[108] The danger is "not merely the sporadic abuse of power by the censor" but the "continuous and pervasive restraint on all freedom of discussion that might be reasonably regarded as within its purview."[109] Accordingly, the overbreadth doctrine permits facial[110] invalidation of laws that inhibit speech if impermissible applications of the law are substantial, when "judged in relation to the statute's plainly legitimate sweep."[111] Both doctrines exemplify the basic precision principle.

72.2.4 Exceptions Where Speech Can Legally Be Limited. The government can restrict speech both directly and indirectly. Roughly speaking, the government is more limited in direct regulation of speech than in indirect regulation. First Amendment law also contains many subdomains with their own special rules, such as over-the-air broadcasting,[112] government enterprises,[113] and government subsidies.[114]

72.2.4.1 Neutral Laws of General Applicability. Many laws, in some sense, restrict speech to an extent. Absent special circumstances, "generally applicable" laws can be applied to speech without triggering First Amendment scrutiny. Classic examples are laws against speeding applied to a news reporter hurrying to file a story or taxes that apply to books and newspapers as well as other goods.

The "generally applicable" doctrine contains its own limits. Courts will look to see whether the law appears to be a pretext for targeting speech and whether it was based on perceived secondary effects.[115] If so, then there will be some level of First Amendment scrutiny.

72.2.4.2 Constitutionalization of Crimes and Torts: Advocacy of Illegality, Threats, and Defamation. Another major category of First Amendment doctrines relates to crimes and torts directed at speech. In general, the First Amendment does not prevent the application of criminal law to speech simply because it is speech. Although agreeing to participate or assist in doing an unlawful act is usually accomplished through "speech," the larger course of conduct in which that speech is integrated overrides any potential First Amendment applicability.[116] Even so, there can be concern for speech-suppressive effects.

Criminal laws that are likely to involve speech "must be interpreted with the commands of the First Amendment clearly in mind."[117] As discussed in Section 72.2.2.1, laws that criminalize incitement to unlawful action must require proof of both intent and harm. Similarly, threatening may be criminally punished if the law is carefully defined and applied to "true threats" but not "political hyperbole."[118] Recently, the Supreme Court held that federal law prohibiting the disclosure of unlawfully intercepted communications could not be applied to those who had innocently acquired the information of public concern.[119]

Tort laws that target speech also must be construed and applied in light of First Amendment concerns. The prime example is libel or defamation law. For many years, the First Amendment simply did not apply to libel suits. In 1967, however, the Supreme Court held that libel suits were a form of government action because courts must enforce libel judgments, and thus imposed First Amendment restrictions on such lawsuits.[120]

72.2.4.3 Unprotected Speech. Certain categories of speech, such as *obscenity, child pornography, fighting words, sedition, defamation*, and so on, are considered unprotected even though they are linguistic or pictorial. Here the issue is not that the speech is not communicative but that its value is low; *fighting words*, for instance, are deemed "utterances [that] are no essential part of any exposition of ideas, and are of such slight social value as a step to truth that any benefit that may be derived from them is clearly outweighed by the social interest in order and morality."[121]

Even so, the definition of *fighting words* is closely limited. First, the words must "by their very utterance inflict injury or tend to incite an immediate breach of the peace."[122] Second, they must be "directed to the person of the hearer."[123]

The Supreme Court defines obscenity as works that, (1) taken as a whole, appeal to the prurient interest of the average person in sex, (2) portray sexual conduct in a patently offensive way, and (3) taken as a whole, lack serious literary, artistic, political, or scientific value.[124] This definition illustrates how the Supreme Court has sought to ensure that even laws that target unprotected speech do not reach too far. In particular, the first prong of the obscenity test is evaluated with reference to "contemporary community standards." As the Supreme Court observed, "It is neither realistic nor constitutionally sound to read the First Amendment as requiring that the people of Maine or Mississippi accept public depiction of conduct found tolerable in Las Vegas, or New York City."[125] Moreover, any statute regulating obscenity must define the "sexual conduct" at issue.

Child pornography is defined generally as works that visually depict sexually explicit conduct by children below a specified age.[126] As with obscenity, the statute must clearly define the conduct that may not be depicted[127] and must require some element of knowledge or intent. Unlike obscenity, however, legally regulated child pornography need not appeal to the prurient interest of the average person, need not portray sexual conduct in a patently offensive manner, and need not be considered as a whole.[128] Child pornography is the least protected type of speech. Note that *virtual* child pornography (i.e., child pornography with adults representing children or with digital modifications to give the impression that children are involved) is not regulated. The U.S. Supreme Court clarified the distinction, noting that in actual child pornography, the perpetrator commits child abuse in the creation of the pornography; no such abuse is present in the virtual version.[129]

But even unprotected speech is not entirely invisible to the First Amendment. Regulations that target such speech must be based on the reason why the speech is categorized as unprotected; thus, even though fighting words may be regulated because of their potential to generate violence, regulating only "fighting words" that relate to race, color, creed, religion, or gender would "impose special prohibitions on those speakers who express views on disfavored subjects," amounting to unconstitutional viewpoint discrimination.[130]

72.2.4.4 Less-Protected Speech, Media, and Recipients. Other categories of speech are protected by the First Amendment but may be regulated more easily. The main examples are commercial speech, broadcast speech, and speech that is *indecent* or *harmful to minors*.[131]

Commercial speech is defined as speech that proposes a commercial transaction; the main example is advertising. Originally, such speech was considered unprotected, but today its regulation is subject to a form of intermediate scrutiny.[132]

Broadcast speech is also subject to a form of intermediate scrutiny.[133] The Supreme Court has long adhered to the view that different media of expression may require different First Amendment analyses. The standard for regulating the speech of cablecasters is not entirely clear.[134]

With regard to sexual content, there are three forms of less-protected speech. First, although nonobscene sexual expression is in a sense "fully" protected, cities may rely on "secondary effects" analysis to regulate the location of bookstores and theaters that sell "adult" material or offer "adult" entertainment like nude dancing.[135]

Second, the Supreme Court has permitted substantial regulation of indecent speech over the airwaves[136] and on cable TV.[137] Indecency regulation is closely tied to the interest of preventing minors' access to sexual material. As that interest varies, so does the latitude for regulation. For example, the regulation of indecent speech delivered telephonically was not permitted.[138] Thus, indecency is an odd speech category that is regulated primarily with respect to the audience: The government has a strong interest in regulating minors' access to indecency, but it has no such interest in regulating adults' access.

Closely related to the category of *indecency* is materials judged *harmful to minors* (HTM). Roughly speaking, this category is like obscenity, but geared to those under the age of 17.[139] This category has become increasingly important in the censorware context given the full protection accorded to speech over the Internet. Courts have narrowly tailored HTM-based access restrictions to their constitutional boundaries. This point was made clear in *Reno v. ACLU*, where the Supreme Court held unconstitutional a general prohibition of indecent speech on the Internet. The Court found:

- Parents may disseminate HTM speech to their children.[140]
- The HTM concept applies only to commercial transactions.[141]
- The government may not simply ban minors' exposure to a full category of speech, such as nudity, when only a subset of that category can plausibly be deemed HTM.[142]
- The government interest is not equally strong throughout the HTM age range.[143]

72.2.5 Legislation and Legislative Initiatives in the United States. Since the advent of the Internet, there have been many attempts to regulate access to Internet speech. Such legislation can be divided into two basic categories. In the first category, the law imposes liability for communicating certain kinds of material over the Internet. Such laws did not require the use of software to block Internet sites or to filter their content because they focused on the conduct of the speaker or publisher. In the second category, the law requires or encourages the use of filtering software by those who make Internet content available.

In 1996, Congress enacted the *Communications Decency Act* (CDA), which sought to regulate the communication of "indecent" material over the Internet. The CDA prohibited Internet users from using the Internet to communicate material that, under contemporary community standards, would be deemed patently offensive to minors under the age of 18. In holding that the CDA violated the First Amendment, the Supreme Court explained that without defining key terms, the statute was unconstitutionally vague. Moreover, the Court noted that the breadth of the CDA was "wholly unprecedented" in that, for example, it was "not limited to commercial speech or commercial entities" but rather embraced "all nonprofit entities and individuals posting indecent messages or displaying them on their own computers."

In response to the Supreme Court's invalidation of the CDA, Congress in 1998 enacted the *Child Online Protection Act*[144] (COPA). The COPA scaled down the restrictions of the CDA by using the "harmful to minors" category of speech. The COPA was found unconstitutional by a district court because it failed the strict scrutiny test for content-based regulation of speech.[145] That holding was affirmed on appeal, although on a different rationale—that because "harmful to minors," like obscenity, must be defined by reference to discrete, diverse, geographically defined communities,

COPA's attempt to promulgate a national "harmful to minors" standard was necessarily unconstitutional.[146] States also have attempted to control access to Internet speech by using the "harmful to minors" concept, but these attempts have proven similarly unsuccessful.[147]

The second category is exemplified by the *Child Internet Protection Act* (CIPA),[148] which, roughly speaking, requires all schools and libraries that receive certain types of federal funding to adopt and implement an Internet safety policy and to use "technology protection measures" on all computers that offer Internet access. Such measures must block or filter Internet access to visual depictions that are obscene, child pornography, or harmful to minors. Libraries must also regulate access by minors to "inappropriate material." Thus, the CIPA effectively requires the use of filtering software, sometimes referred to as *censorware*.

72.2.6 Attempts to Control Access: Case Law. The American Library Association has taken a firm stance against censorware in libraries[149] and has committed itself to challenging federal censorware requirements. To date, though CIPA applies to both libraries and schools, the legal battle over the use of censorware to control access to speech on the Internet has primarily involved libraries. The plaintiffs in these cases have library and librarian associations, including the American Library Association, library patrons and users, and entities and individuals whose Websites are likely to be blocked by censorware.

72.2.6.1 Public Libraries. On one hand, public libraries must be concerned that, by implementing censorware, they violate patrons' First Amendment right to receive information. On the other hand, public libraries also face liability for encouraging a hostile workplace for their employees by not implementing censorware on library Internet terminals.

As to the first concern, libraries face a conflict between not censoring adults' access to constitutionally protected material on the Internet and protecting children from inappropriate content. In a 1998 case involving a Virginia library, a federal district court found the library's blocking policy unconstitutional.[150] The challenged policy required that "site-blocking software ... be installed on all [library computers]" so as to block child pornography, obscene material, and harmful-to-minors material.[151] The defendants implemented the policy by installing the commercial filtering software X-Stop on all public library terminals in the county.

The court first concluded that the public libraries were limited public forums and then subjected the defendants' indisputably content-based filtering policy to strict constitutional scrutiny.[152] Assuming that the library's interests were compelling, the court found that its policy was not the least restrictive means of furthering those interests. First, the court held that the library had not even considered less restrictive means, including privacy screens, library staff monitoring of Internet use (which had been used to enforce other library policies), and filtering software installed only on Internet terminals used by minors or only when minors are using them.

More important, the court found that the censorware-based policy violated the First Amendment because censorware is both overbroad and overinclusive. On one hand, the X-Stop censorware blocked more speech than that targeted by the policy.[153] On the other hand, even if censorware could somehow be tailored to exclude only restricted materials, it unconstitutionally "limit[s] the access of all patrons, adult and juvenile, to material deemed fit for juveniles."[154]

Finally, the court found that the library policy violated the doctrine barring prior restraints. Mandatory filtering policies that rely on commercial blocking software arguably constitute prior restraints because, as in *Mainstream Loudoun*, they "entrust all ... blocking decisions ... to a private vendor" whose standards and practices cannot be monitored by the filtering library.[155]

In a notable departure from this line of argument, the U.S. Supreme Court found in a 2003 case from Pennsylvania that CIPA was constitutional because the library's interest in preventing minors from accessing obscene material "outweighs the free speech rights of library patrons and website publishers."[156]

As to the second concern, libraries are unlikely to face liability from patrons for failing to use censorware. For example, in *Kathleen R. v. City of Livermore*,[157] a woman sued a public library, complaining that her 12-year-old son was able to view and download pornography at a public library in Livermore, California. The plaintiff sought an injunction that would prohibit the library "from maintaining any computer system on which it allows people to access ... obscene material or on which it allows minors to access ... sexual material harmful to minors." The plaintiff also claimed that the library had a constitutional duty to "protect" library patrons from unwanted and "harmful" sexually explicit materials. The California court of appeals rejected all of the plaintiff's claims.

A different concern here is library liability to employees for failing to use censorware under sexual harassment *hostile work environment* theories. Federal civil rights laws and many states' parallel civil rights laws afford employees the "right to work in an environment free from discriminatory intimidation, ridicule and insult."[158] Arguably, access to materials over the Internet that are offensive due to their sexually explicit nature or messages regarding race, religion, or ethnicity may subject a library to liability for a hostile environment under these laws. In 2001, employees of a Minnesota library brought a successful complaint before the Equal Employment Opportunity Commission claiming that the library failed to prevent a hostile work environment by failing to prevent the viewing of objectionable material on library computers.[159]

Such complaints and resulting lawsuits are common in many workplaces. For example,

- In 2009, a Utica, NY, woman was awarded $580,000 in damages because she was harassed and fired after she began an "interracial" relationship with a colleague while working as a security hospital treatment assistant at the Central New York Psychiatric Center:

  > Bergerson's complaint also listed several other harassing behaviors that allegedly took place, such as the use of "sexually oriented" posters and inappropriate computer screensavers in the work area, and said male coworkers told her that women were not wanted there and started rumors regarding her sex life.[160]

- A posting on the *Illinois Sexual Harassment Attorney Blog* in May 2013 argued that offensive text messages may be a form of harassment that is actionable:

  > So your boss keeps sending you sexual type text messages. He tells you how sexy you look and what he would like to do to you after work. Is this a hostile work environment in Chicago? The answer is yes. In fact this would be considered sexual harassment and you would have a claim against both the supervisor and the company. Under state law, there is strict liability against the company if a supervisor engages in sexual harassment. That means there is no requirement that the employee report the conduct before liability attaches.[161]

72.2.6.2 Public Schools. There are no cases involving the use of censorware in public schools. Schools traditionally have been considered places where the government has a strong interest in regulating speech,[162] particularly with respect to curricular materials.[163] Prevailing cases emphasize the importance of inculcating values and maintaining civility in schools, along with the risk that the viewpoints expressed by student speech would be attributed to the school. Moreover, most public school students are too young to enjoy the same constitutional rights as adults.

Nevertheless, the First Amendment should place significant limits on public schools' use of censorware. In general, students do not "shed their constitutional rights to freedom of speech or expression at the schoolhouse gate."[164] Thus, while schools have maximum authority over curriculum and school-sponsored activities and substantial authority to regulate student speech, they have less authority to regulate students' right to receive information. Despite schools' "comprehensive authority" to prescribe and control student conduct, "students may not be regarded as closed-circuit recipients of only that which the State chooses to communicate."[165]

Moreover, the extent of governmental power to regulate conduct of minors not constitutionally regulable when committed by adults is a "vexing" question, "perhaps not susceptible of precise answer."[166] Although the government has a general interest in regulating schools, the interest in regulating students' access to "objectionable" extracurricular information is of uncertain pedigree. For instance, the Supreme Court has characterized the government interest in protecting children against "harmful to minors" material as derivative of or secondary to parents' interests.[167] Thus, "[s]peech that is neither obscene as to youths nor subject to some other legitimate proscription cannot be suppressed solely to protect the young from ideas or images that a legislative body thinks unsuitable for them."[168] This characterization suggests that the state has no interest in blocking a minor's access to HTM material to which parents do not object.[169]

Moreover, the state's interest is not uniformly strong across all minors. In general, minors' fundamental rights, including the right to receive information, strengthen as they grow older; "constitutional rights do not mature and come into being magically only when one attains the state-defined age of majority."[170] Moreover, some high school students are 18 or 19 and thus not minors for HTM purposes.

The Electronic Freedom Foundation published a report in 2003 that examined the issue of Internet content filtering in public schools. Based on the state of current filtering technology, which significantly underblocks material that would be considered harmful to minors and significantly overblocks some material that would be considered protected by the First Amendment, the EFF recommended that schools should use other, less restrictive methods.[171]

In 2006, the EFF and the ALA strongly opposed a bill passed by the House of Representatives, the *Deleting Online Predators Act*[172] (DOPA). The bill would have blocked federal funding for IT in any school allowing the use of "commercial social-networking sites" such as Facebook or Myspace. The bill died in the Senate.[173]

72.3 PARENTAL INVOLVEMENT/RESPONSIBILITY.

Although the technical issues of censorware are identical regardless of whether it is being applied by government, employers, or parents, the parent–child case generates much of the political discussion. Two conflicting mental models are at work in the debate.

The primary impetus for censorware arises out of an idea that might be called the "toxic material" theory, under which viewing certain information has a toxic effect, akin to a harmful drug or a poison. As was stated in a lawsuit seeking an injunction against a library with unrestricted Internet access: "Children such as Brandon P. who view obscenity and pornography on the library's computers can and have sustained emotional and psychological damage in addition to damage to their nervous systems. It is highly likely that such damage will occur given the library's policy."[174] The outcome of the toxic material threat model has been legislation such as the CIPA.

In contrast, theoretical discussion typically takes place in a model that can be termed the "control-rights" theory. This is concerned primarily with authority relationships within some framework. One paper submitted to a government commission stated:

> [T]he decision by a third party that a person may not use a computer to access certain content from the Internet demands some sort of justification. The burden should be on the filterer to justify the denial of another person's access. The most plausible justifications for restricting access are that the third party owns the computer or that the third party has a relation of legitimate authority over the user.[175]

However, the control-rights discussion does not address the assumptions and threat model inherent in the toxic material theory. A belief in harmful information logically requires restrictions to be as extensive and widespread as possible. In fact, this is an instance of typical security practices, where the potential attack is viewed along the lines of dangerous contamination. All possible environments where the subject may be located then need to be secured to the greatest extent possible. This social need is similar to the technical requirement regarding banning privacy, anonymity, and even language-translation Websites. It is all a matter of security holes.

72.4 SUMMARY.

Although the Internet has the technological potential to create a global forum for free expression, one must not underestimate the political and technological barriers at work.

Internet-specific laws. Some governments have criminalized certain types of Internet speech. Such criminal penalties may come in the form of laws intended to protect minors from "harmful" material. Under U.S. law, however, requiring Internet speakers to shield certain populations from their speech has been found to effect a ban on that speech.[176]

Application of existing laws. Governments need not specifically enact laws targeting Internet-based speech. For example, the German government action against CompuServe for providing access to illegal material merely applied existing laws to the Internet.

Content-based license terms applied to Internet users and service providers. Some countries have established licensing systems that require Internet users and/or service providers to agree to refrain from certain kinds of speech or that block access to speech as a condition of having, or using, or providing access to the Internet. For instance, China has issued rules requiring anyone with Internet access to refrain from proscribed speech.

Compelled use of computerized censorship, rating, or content labeling tools. Various techniques can prevent individuals from using the Internet to exchange information on topics that may be controversial or unpopular, may enable certain governments to enforce their own ratings systems, and may (through overblocking by overly broad filtering techniques) inappropriately block access to significant amount of nonobjectionable content.

72.5 FURTHER READING

Brown, I., and C. T. Marsden. *Regulating Code: Good Governance and Better Regulation in the Information Age*. MIT Press, 2013.

Hill, S. *Digital Revolutions: Activism in the Internet Age*. World Changing, 2013.

Howard, P. N., and M. H. Hussain. *Democracy's Fourth Wave? Digital Media and the Arab Spring*. Oxford University Press, 2013.

Kiethman, V. *Banned Websites*. Ox Books Publishing (OxBo), 2013.

Kolbert, K., and Z. Mettger. *Justice Talking From NPR (National Public Radio): Censoring the Web—Leading Advocates Debate Today's Most Controversial Issues*. The New Press, 2002.

Lessig, Lawrence. *Code and Other Laws of Cyberspace*. New York: Basic Books, 1999.

Pager, S. A., and A. Candeub, eds. *Transnational Culture in the Internet Age*. Edward Elgar Publishers, 2012.

Reed, C. *Making Laws for Cyberspace*. Oxford University Press, 2012.

Russomano, J. *Defending the First: Commentary on First Amendment Issues and Cases*. Routledge, 2013.

Youngs, G., editor. *Digital World: Connectivity, Creativity and Rights*. Routledge, 2013.

Ziccardi, G. *Resistance, Liberation Technology and Human Rights in the Digital Age*. Springer, 2012.

72.6 NOTES

1. Universal Declaration of Human Rights, art. 19, G.A. Res 217A, U.N. GAOR, 3d Sess., U.N. Doc. A/810 (1948).
2. Thomas D. Jones, "Human Rights: Freedom of Expression and Group Defamation Under British, Canadian, Indian, Nigerian and United States Law—A Comparative Analysis," 18 *Suffolk Transnat'l L. Rev*. 427, 428 (1995) (footnotes omitted).
3. "Mobile subscribers worldwide." *Global Mobile Statistics 2013 Part A: Mobile Subscribers; Handset Market Share; Mobile Operators*. mobiThinking (2013). http://mobithinking.com/mobile-marketing-tools/latest-mobile-stats/a#subscribers
4. Samuel Fifer and Michael Sachs, "The Price of International Free Speech: Nations Deal With Defamation on the Internet," 8 *DePaul-LCA J. Art & Ent. L.* 1, 2 (1997).
5. Samuel Fifer and Michael Sachs, "The Price of International Free Speech: Nations Deal With Defamation on the Internet."
6. Order of the County Court of Paris, at 2, in *La Ligue Contre Le Racisme Et L'Antisemitisme v. Yahoo! Inc.*, No. RG: 00/05308 (Nov. 20, 2000) (translated).
7. Order of the County Court of Paris, at 4.
8. Order of the County Court of Paris, at 4.
9. *Yahoo! Inc. v. La Ligue Contre le Racisme et L'Antisemitisme, et al.*, 145 F. Supp. 2d 1168 (N.D. Cal. 2001). www.cdt.org/jurisdiction/010607yahoo.pdf; Retrieved from WayBackMachine: http://web.archive.org/web/20011001001826/http://www.cdt.org/jurisdiction/010607yahoo.pdf
10. *Yahoo! Inc. v. La Ligue Contre le Racisme et L'Antisemitisme, et al.*
11. See note 4 generally.

12. Jane Ginsburg, "Copyright Without Borders? Choice of Forum and Choice of Law for Copyright Infringement in Cyberspace," 15 *Cardozo Arts & Ent. L.J.* 153 (1997).
13. Peter Swire, "Of Elephants, Mice, and Privacy: International Choice of Law and the Internet," 32 *Int'l Law*. 991 (1998).
14. *See* text at Section 72.2.5.
15. *See* text at Section 72.1.3.3.2.
16. John T. Delacourt, "Recent Development: The International Impact of Internet Regulation," 38 *Harv. Int'l L. J.* 207, 212 (1997).
17. Kim Rappaport, Note, "In the Wake of Reno v. ACLU: The Continued Struggle in Western Constitutional Democracies with Internet Censorship and Freedom of Speech Online," 13 *Am. U. Int'l L. Rev*. 765, 791 (1998).
18. Kim Rappaport, Note, at 795–799.
19. Some observers reported that the Internet seems to foster "hate" sites. Laura Leets, "Responses to Internet Hate Sites: Is Speech Too Free in Cyberspace?" 6 *Comm. L. & Pol'y* 287, 288 (2001) (noting that watchdog groups have documented about 2,800 hate sites).
20. Laura Leets, "Responses to Internet Hate Sites," at 291–294.
21. Kim Rappaport, Note, at 785–786 (footnotes omitted).
22. Kim Rappaport, Note, at 789 (footnotes omitted).
23. Steve Kettmann, "German Hate Law: No Denying It," December 15, 2000, www.wired.com/politics/law/news/2000/12/40669
24. Kettmann, "German Hate Law."
25. Kettmann, "German Hate Law."
26. J. Zittrain and B. Edelman, "Localized Google Search Result Exclusions," 2002, http://cyber.law.harvard.edu/filtering/google
27. Canadian Criminal Code §319(2), R.S.C. 1985, c. C-46 (willful promotion of hatred against an identifiable group); see *id*. at §181 (willful publication of false statements likely to injure a public interest).
28. *R. v. Keegstra*, 3 S.C.R. 697 (1990).
29. *R. v. Keegstra*, 3 S.C.R. 697 (1990).
30. Robert Cribb, "Canadian Net Hate Debate Flares," March 25, 1998, www.wired.com/news/news/politics/story/11195.html; Retrieved from *WayBack-Machine*, http://web.archive.org/web/19990203162438/http://www.wired.com/news/news/politics/story/11195.html
31. R. Howard, "Notorious Internet Service Closes; BC to continue probe of Klatt." *The Globe and Mail* (1998-04-28), www.nizkor.org/hweb/orgs/canadian/bc/fairview-technologies/press/globe-and-mail-980428.html
32. Zündel was charged with spreading "false news" in violation of §181 of the Canadian Criminal Code.
33. *R. v. Zündel* [1992] 2 S.C.R. (Can.) 731.
34. Credence Fogo-Schensul, "More Than a River in Egypt: Holocaust Denial, the Internet, and International Freedom of Expression Norms," 33 *Gonz. L. Rev*. 271, 245 n.32 (1997–1998) (citation omitted).
35. "Ernst Zündel Sentenced to 5 Years in Prison for Holocaust Denial," *Winnipeg Free Press*, February 15, 2007, online edition, www.winnipegfreepress.com/

breakingnews/world/story/3881650p-4489229c.html; Retrieved from *WayBack Machine*, http://web.archive.org/web/20070927194246/http://www.winnipegfree press.com/breakingnews/world/story/3881650p-4489229c.html

36. Internet World Stats, March 24, 2007, www.internetworldstats.com/asia/cn .htm
37. "China Begins Push for Internet Censorship," *BizAsia*, August 23, 2000. Retrieved from *WayBackMachine*, http://web.archive.org/web/20000823190350/ http://www.bizasia.com/gen/articles/stand_art.htm
38. Managing Internet Information-Release Services, P.R.C. Ministry of Information Industry Regulation, November 7, 2000; see also "China Issues Regulations on Managing Internet Information-Release Services," *China Online*, November 13, 2000. Retrieved from *WayBackMachine*, http://web.archive.org/ web/20010628140620/http://www.chinaonline.com/issues/internet_policy/News Archive/Secure/2000/November/C00110604.asp. Other restrictions target a variety of disfavored groups, particularly supporters of the Falun Gong spiritual movement. See "China Passes Internet Security Law," China Online, December 29, 2000, www.chinaonline.com/issues/Internet_policy/NewsArchive/Secure/ 2000/December/C00122805.asp (URL inactive).
39. Geremie R. Barme and Sang Ye, "The Great Firewall of China," *Wired*, June 1997, www.wired.com/wired/archive/5.06/china_pr.html
40. Geremie R. Barme and Sang Ye, "The Great Firewall of China."
41. Digital Freedom Network, "Attacks on the Internet in China," April 30, 2001, www.dfn.org/focus/china/netattack.htm; Retrieved from *WayBackMachine*, http://web.archive.org/web/20010506184353/http://www.dfn.org/focus/china/ netattack.htm
42. Michael Liedtke, "Google Agrees to Censor Results in China," *Associated Press Business Wire*, January 24, 2006, via AnandTech Forums, http://forums .anandtech.com/archive/index.php/t-1795022.html
43. M. Murphy, "China's State Internet Information Office Flexes Its Muscles," *Bloomberg Law*, 2011, http://about.bloomberglaw.com/practitioner-contributions/chinas-state
44. B. Blanchard and S. Huang, "China Tightens Internet Controls, Legalizes Post Deletion," *Reuters*, December 28, 2012, www.reuters.com/article/2012/ 12/28/net-us-china-internet-idUSBRE8BO01320121228
45. "Internet Censorship in China." *The New York Times*, http://topics.nytimes.com/ topics/news/international/countriesandterritories/china/internet_censorship/index .html
46. Human Rights Watch, "The Internet in the Middle East and North Africa: Free Expression and Censorship," July 1, 1999, www.hrw.org/reports/1999/07/01/ internet-middle-east-and-north-africa-free-expression-and-censorship
47. Saudi Internet regulations, Saudi Arabia Council of Ministers Resolution, February 12, 2001, www.al-bab.com/media/docs/saudi.htm
48. Human Rights Watch World Report 1999, "Freedom of Expression on the Internet," No longer available and not stored in *WayBackMachine*.
49. "Turkey Revokes YouTube Ban" *The Age.com*, March 10, 2007, www.theage .com.au/news/Technology/Turkey-revokes-YouTube-ban/2007/03/10/11731670 25391.html

50. Freedom House, "New Report: Governments Grow Increasingly Repressive Online, Activists Fight Back," 2012, www.freedomhouse.org/article/new-report-governments-grow-increasingly-repressive-online-activists-fight-back
51. Freedom House, *Freedom on the Net 2012: Summary of Findings*, www.freedomhouse.org/sites/default/files/inline_images/FOTN%202012%20FINAL.pdf
52. Christina Fink, "Burma: Constructive Engagement in Cyberspace?" *Cultural Survival Quarterly* 21 no. 4 (Winter 1997), www.culturalsurvival.org/ourpublications/csq/article/burma-constructive-engagement-cyberspace
53. Digital Freedom Network, "The New Net Regulations in Burma," January 31, 2000, www.dfn.org/voices/burma/webregulations.htm; Retrieved from *WayBackMachine*, http://web.archive.org/web/20030701231239/http://www.dfn.org/voices/burma/webregulations.htm
54. Digital Freedom Network, "The New Net Regulations in Burma."
55. Alison Hunter, "Burma's Internet Censorship Worsening," October 12, 2005, www.mizzima.com/mizzima/archives/news-in-2005/News-in-Oct/12-Oct-05-40.htm
56. Digital Freedom Network, "Burma Wards Off the Internet Revolution," January 31, 2000; www.dfn.org/focus/burma/Web-crackdown.htm; Retrieved from *WayBackMachine*, http://web.archive.org/web/20011030171711/http://www.dfn.org/focus/burma/web-crackdown.htm
57. Freedom House, *Freedom on the Net 2012: Summary of Findings.*
58. Freedom House, *Freedom on the Net 2012: Summary of Findings.*
59. "In Russia, Internet Censorship 'on a Whim.'" Committee to Protect Journalists Website, June 26, 2013, http://cpj.org/2013/06/in-russia-internet-censorship-on-a-whim.php
60. The notion of "unprotected" speech is discussed in Section 72.2.4.3.
61. In the context of the right to speak, the requirement of state action is somewhat relaxed compared to other constitutional rights. For example, when private persons—not the government—use the courts against another private person's speech, "state action" is usually found. *E.g., New York Times Co. v. Sullivan*, 376 US 254 (1964) (defamation); *Hustler Magazine, Inc. v. Falwell*, 485 US 46 (1988) (intentional infliction of emotional distress).
62. *Texas v. Johnson*, 491 US 397, 403 (1989).
63. *W. Va. Bd. of Educ. v. Barnette*, 319 US 624, 632 (1943).
64. *McIntyre v. Ohio Elections Comm'n*, 514 US 334 (1995).
65. *Lamont v. Postmaster General*, 381 US 301, 307 (1965) (invalidating law requiring willing recipient to request that certain, state-defined materials be sent to him); *Virginia Pharmacy Bd. v. Virginia Consumer Council*, 425 US 748, 756 (1974).
66. *City of Lakewood v. Plain Dealer Publishing Co.*, 486 US 750 (1988).
67. *Buckley v. Valeo*, 424 US 1, 19 (1976).
68. *Simon & Schuster, Inc. v. Members of N.Y. State Crime Victims Bd.*, 502 US 105, 117 (1991).
69. *City of Ladue v. Gilleo*, 512 US 43 (1994).
70. *Abrams v. United States*, 250 US 616, 630 (1919) (Holmes, J., dissenting).
71. *Hurley v. GLIB*, 515 US 557 (1995).

72. *Cohen v. California*, 403 US 15, 24 (1971) (emphasis added).
73. Bantam Books, Inc. v. Sullivan, 372 US 58, 66 (1963).
74. *Thornhill v. Alabama*, 310 US 88, 97 (1940). ("It is not merely the sporadic abuse of power by the censor but the pervasive threat inherent in its very existence that constitutes the danger to freedom of discussion.")
75. *Schenck v. United States*, 249 US 47, 52 (1919).
76. *Whitney v. California*, 274 US 357, 377 (1926) (Brandeis, J., concurring).
77. *Brandenburg v. Ohio*, 395 US 444, 447 (1969).
78. *American Booksellers Assn., Inc. v. Hudnut*, 771 F.2d 323, 333 (7th Cir. 1985), aff'd. mem. 475 US 1001 (1986).
79. See also *Planned Parenthood v. American Coalition of Life*, 244 F.3d 1007 (9th Cir. 2001).
80. *New York Times Co. v. Sullivan*, 376 US 254, 292 (1964).
81. *Police Dept. of Chicago v. Mosley*, 408 U. S. 92, 96 (1972).
82. *NAACP v. Button*, 371 US 415, 433 (1963).
83. *City of Lakewood v. Plain Dealer Publishing Co.*, 486 US 750 (1988).
84. *Smith v. California*, 361 US 147 (1959).
85. *Speiser v. Randall*, 357 US 513 (1958).
86. *Gertz v. Robert Welch, Inc.*, 418 US 323 (1974).
87. *Organization for a Better Austin v. Keefe*, 402 US 415, 419 (1971).
88. *New York Times Co. v. United States*, 403 US 713, 729 (1971) (Stewart, J., concurring).
89. *Nebraska Press Ass'n v. Stuart*, 427 US 539 (1976).
90. *Staub v. Baxley*, 355 US 313, 322 (1958).
91. *Niemotko v. Maryland*, 340 US 268, 271 (1951).
92. *Freedman v. Maryland*, 380 US 51, 58 (1965).
93. *Freedman v. Maryland* at 58–59.
94. *See, e.g., United States v. Playboy Entertainment Group, Inc.*, 120 S. Ct. 1878, 1880 (2000); *Reno v. ACLU*, 521 US 844 (1997).
95. *R.A.V. v. St. Paul*, 505 U. S. 377, 391 (1992).
96. *Perry Ed. Assn. v. Perry Local Educators' Assn.*, 460 U. S. 37, 46 (1983).
97. *R.A.V., supra* (government may not regulate otherwise unprotected "fighting words" based on viewpoint).
98. *Turner Broadcasting System, Inc. v. FCC*, 512 US 622, 642 (1994) (citations omitted).
99. *Turner Broadcasting System, Inc. v. FCC* at 661.
100. *Clark v. Community for Creative Non-Violence*, 468 US 288, 293 (1984).
101. *United States v. O'Brien*, 391 US 367, 376–77 (1968).
102. *City of Renton v. Playtime Theatres, Inc.*, 475 US 41, 47 (1986).
103. *Boos v. Barry*, 485 US 312, 335 (1988) (Brennan, J., concurring).
104. *Forsyth County v. Nationalist Movement*, 505 US 123, 135 (1992).
105. *United States v. Reese*, 92 US 214, 221 (1876).
106. *NAACP v. Button*, 371 US at 337.
107. *Kolender v. Lawson*, 461 US 352, 357–358 (1983).

108. *Thornhill v. Alabama*, 310 US 88, 97 (1940).
109. *Thornhill v. Alabama* at 97–98.
110. Often, laws are struck down only "as applied," that is, the particular application of the law to a particular person is found to violate the Constitution. Facial invalidation, on the other hand, is not limited to the particular application but to the entire law, roughly speaking. *See, e.g.*, Richard H. Fallon, Jr., "As-Applied and Facial Challenges and Third-Party Standing," 113 *Harv. L. Rev.* 1321 (2000).
111. *Broadrick v. Oklahoma*, 413 US 601, 612–615 (1973).
112. *Red Lion Broadcasting Co. v. FCC*, 395 US 367 (1969).
113. *Int'l Soc'y for Krishna Consciousness, Inc. v. Lee*, 505 US 672, 678 (1992).
114. *Legal Services Corporation v. Velazquez*, 531 US 533, (2001).
115. *Arcara v. Cloud Books, Inc.*, 478 US 697, 707 n.4 (1986).
116. *Giboney v. Empire Storage & Ice Co.*, 336 US 490, 502 (1949).
117. *Watts v. United States*, 394 US 705, 707 (1969).
118. *Watts v. United States*, 394 US at 707–8.
119. *Bartnicki v. Vopper*, 121 S.Ct. 1753, 1765 (2001).
120. *New York Times Co. v. Sullivan*, 376 US 254 (1964).
121. *Chaplinsky v. New Hampshire*, 315 US 568, 571 (1942).
122. *Chaplinsky v. New Hampshire*, at 572.
123. *Cohen v. California*, 403 US 15, 20 (1971).
124. *Miller v. California*, 413 US 15, 24 (1973).
125. *Miller v. California*, 413 US at 32.
126. *New York v. Ferber*, 458 US 747, 764 (1982).
127. The federal child pornography statute reaches "any visual depiction" of a minor under 18 years old engaging in "sexually explicit conduct," which includes "actual or simulated" sexual intercourse, bestiality, masturbation, sadistic or masochistic abuse, or "lascivious exhibition of the genitals or pubic area." 18 USC. §2256.
128. *Ferber*, 458 US at 764–765. Notably, the rationale for regulating child pornography is not content-based. Instead, it is based on the harm to children from being subjects of sexual performances, as well as the harm from the distribution of such photographs.
129. *Ashcroft v. The Free Speech Coalition*, 122 S. Ct. 1389 (2002).
130. *R.A.V. v. City of St. Paul*, 505 US 377, 391 (1992).
131. *Ginsberg v. New York*, 390 US 629 (1968).
132. *Liquormart, Inc. v. Rhode Island*, 517 US 484 (1996).
133. *Red Lion Broadcasting Co. v. FCC*, 395 US 367 (1969).
134. Speech on the Internet, however, is entitled to "full" First Amendment protection.
135. *City of Erie v. Pap's A.M.*, 120 S.Ct. 1382 (2000).
136. *FCC v. Pacifica*, 438 US 726 (1978).
137. *Denver Area Educ. Telecom. Consortium v. FCC*, 518 US 727 (1996); but *see* note 94.
138. *Sable Communications v. FCC*, 492 US 115 (1989).
139. Speech is "harmful to minors" if it (i) is "patently offensive to prevailing standards in the adult community as a whole with respect to what is suitable … for

minors"; (ii) appeals to the prurient interest of minors; and (iii) is "utterly without redeeming social importance for minors." *Ginsberg v. New York*, 390 US 629, 633 (1968) (upholding conviction of magazine vendor for selling adult magazine to 16-year-old).

140. *Reno*, 521 US at 865.
141. *Reno*, 521 US.
142. *Erznoznik v. City of Jacksonville*, 422 US 205, 212–214 (1975).
143. *Reno*, 521 US at 878. Lower courts have held that "if a work is found to have serious literary, artistic, political or scientific value for a legitimate minority of normal, older adolescents, then it cannot be said to lack such value for the entire class of juveniles taken as a whole." *American Booksellers Ass'n v. Webb*, 919 F.2d 1493, 1504–5 (11th Cir. 1990) (quoting *American Booksellers Ass'n v. Virginia*, 882 F.2d 125, 127 (4th Cir. 1989) (other citations omitted).
144. Pub. L. No. 105-277, 112 Stat. 2681 (1998) (codified at 47 USC. §231).
145. *ACLU v. Reno*, 31 F. Supp. 2d 473 (E.D. Pa. 1999).
146. *ACLU v. Reno*, 217 F.3d 162, 177 (3d Cir. 2000), cert. granted sub. nom. *Ashcroft v. ACLU*, [121 S.Ct. 1997] (2001), argued Nov. 28, 2001.
147. *E.g., ACLU v. Johnson*, 194 F.3d 1149 (10th Cir. 1999) (affirming injunction against enforcement of New Mexico statute criminalizing dissemination by computer of material harmful to minors); *American Libraries Ass'n v. Pataki*, 969 F. Supp. 160 (S.D. N.Y. 1997) (enjoining a New York statute similar to the CDA that criminalized the use of a computer to disseminate sexually explicit materials to minors).
148. Codified at 47 USC. §254(h) and 20 USC. §9134.
149. "The ALA's Resolution on the Use of Filtering Software in Libraries" is available from the ALA Office for Intellectual Freedom.
150. *Mainstream Loudoun v. Bd. of Trustees of the Loudoun County Library*, 2 F. Supp. 2d 783 (E.D. Va.1998) (*Mainstream Loudoun I*); *Mainstream Loudoun v. Bd. of Trustees of the Loudoun County Library*, 24 F. Supp. 2d 552 (E.D. Va. 1998) (*Mainstream Loudoun II*).
151. *Mainstream Loudoun I*, 2 F. Supp. 2d at 787.
152. *Mainstream Loudoun II*, 24 F. Supp. 2d at 564–565.
153. *Mainstream Loudoun II*, 24 F. Supp. 2d at 556 ("undisputed" that "sites that do not contain any material that is prohibited by the Policy" were blocked).
154. *Mainstream Loudoun II*, 24 F. Supp. 2d at 567.
155. *Mainstream Loudoun II*, 24 F. Supp. 2d at 569.
156. Electronic Freedom Foundation, "Supreme Court Supports Library Internet Blocking Law: Damages Free Speech of Library Patrons and Web Publishers," EFF.org Website, June 23, 2003, www.eff.org/Censorship/Censorware/20030623_eff_cipapr.php; Retrieved from *WayBackMachine*: http://web.archive.org/web/20080907201038/http://www.eff.org/Censorship/Censorware/20030623_eff_cipapr.php
157. 87 Cal. App. 4th 684 (1st Dist. 2001).
158. *Meritor Savings Bank FSB v. Vinson*, 477 US 57, 65 (1986).
159. "EEOC Determination that Net Porn Leads to Library Hostile Working Environment," EFF.org Website, May 23, 2001, www.eff.org/Censorship/Censorware/

20010523_eeoc_determination.html; Retrieved from *WayBackMachine*: http://web.archive.org/web/20010723005939/http://www.eff.org/Censorship/Censorware/20010523_eeoc_determination.html

160. C. Potts, "Woman Awarded $580,000 in Hostile Work Environment Case," *Utica Observer Dispatch*, October 20, 2009, www.uticaod.com/news/x536357184/Woman-awarded-580-000-in-hostile-work-environment-case
161. P. M. LaSorsa, "Are Sexy Text Messages a Form of a Hostile Work Environment in Chicago?" *Illinois Sexual Harassment Attorney Blog*. May 11, 2013, http://www.illinoissexualharassmentattorneyblog.com/2013/05/are_sexy_text_messages_a_form.html
162. *Bethel School District No. 403 v. Fraser*, 478 US 675 (1986) (upholding suspension of high school student for making sexually suggestive speech at school assembly).
163. *Hazelwood Sch. Dist. v. Kuhlmeier*, 484 US 260 (1988) (upholding teacher's censorship of articles destined for newspaper prepared by journalism class).
164. *Tinker v. Des Moines Indep. Community School Dist.*, 393 US 503, 506 (1969).
165. *Tinker v. Des Moines Indep. Community School Dist.* at 511. Schools may [, however,] regulate students' First Amendment rights if the prohibited speech would "materially and substantially interfere with the requirements of appropriate discipline in the operation of the school." *Id.* at 509. This burden cannot be satisfied by "undifferentiated fear or apprehension of disturbance"; the school must show "something more than a mere desire to avoid the discomfort and unpleasantness that always accompany an unpopular viewpoint." *Id.* at 508.
166. *Carey v. Population Servs. Int'l*, 431 US 678, 692 (plurality opinion) (1977).
167. *Reno v. ACLU*, 521 US 844 (1997); *Ginsberg v. New York*, 390 US 629 (1968); *Prince v. Massachusetts*, 321 US 158, 166 (1944).
168. *Erznoznik*, 422 US at 213–214.
169. In other contexts, schools often accommodate or try to accommodate parental wishes as to the exposure of their children in school to undesired material, even when the material is part of the school's chosen curriculum. Catherine J. Ross, "An Emerging Right for Mature Minors to Receive Information," *2 U. Pa. J. Const. L.* 223, 247 n.119 (1999) ("nearly every school district in the country allows parents 'to opt their own children out of sexuality and AIDS education, as well as out of specific activities or assignments that conflict with their religious beliefs.'"), *quoting* People for the American Way, *A Right Wing and a Prayer: The Religious Right and Your Public Schools* 60 (1997). In some states, such accommodation with respect to all or specified categories of curricular materials is required. *Minn. Stat. Ann.* §126.699 (West 1994) (schools must allow parents to review curricular materials and must provide alternative materials to replace those that parents find objectionable for any reason); *Mass. Gen. Laws Ann.* ch. LXXI 32A (West 1998) (requiring that school districts notify parents of the content of any curriculum primarily involving "human sexual education or human sexuality" and afford parents a flexible way of exempting their children from such curricula upon written notice to the school); *Va. Code Ann.* §22.1-207-2 (Michie 1998) (giving public school parents the right to review "the complete family life curricula [sic], including all supplemental materials").
170. *Planned Parenthood of Cent. Mo. v. Danforth*, 428 US 52, 74 (1976) (minors' right to abortion).

171. Electronic Freedom Foundation, "Internet Blocking in Public Schools," EFF.org Website, June 23, 2003, https://www.eff.org/node/67552
172. H.R. 5319 (109th): Deleting Online Predators Act of 2006. www.govtrack.us/congress/bills/109/hr5319
173. S. O'Hear, "Deleting Online Predators Act: R.I.P." ZDNET, January 4, 2007, www.zdnet.com/blog/social/deleting-online-predators-act-r-i-p/55
174. *First Amended Complaint in Kathleen R. v. City of Livermore*, www.techlawjournal.com/courts/kathleenr/19981103.htm
175. Members of the Information Society Project at Yale Law School, "Filtering the Internet: A Best Practices Model," September 15, 1999, www.copacommission.org/papers/yale-isp.pdf
176. *Reno v. ACLU*, 521 US 844 (1997).

CHAPTER 73

EXPERT WITNESSES AND THE *DAUBERT* CHALLENGE

Chey Cobb

73.1 INTRODUCTION. Whenever science or technology enters the courtroom, there must surely be an expert who can give clear and proper explanations of the subject matter to the judge and jury. As new sciences and technologies have emerged, the courts have had to decide if a person is, indeed, an expert and whether or not the science is real and admissible.[1]

In 1923, the United States courts began accepting scientific evidence based on a new rule. That rule used the "general acceptance" test to determine if evidence was legitimate. This test was based on the rulings in *Frye v. United States*, which declared that if a scientific practice was generally accepted among the scientific community in which it was practiced, it could be admitted in court. This has become generally referred to as the *Frye test*.[2]

In 1975, the federal government made the scientific assertions a bit stronger by issuing the Federal Rules of Evidence No. 702 (FRE 702), which states in part:

> If scientific, technical, or other specialized knowledge will assist the trier of fact to understand the evidence or to determine a fact in issue, a witness qualified as an expert by knowledge, skill, experience, training, or education, may testify.[3]

About the same time that FRE 702 was created, various states started changing laws to include the "theft of computer services" as a punishable offense, but it was not until 1984 that the Counterfeit Access Device and Computer Fraud and Abuse Law (18 U.S.C. § 1030) was created, officially making it a federal offense to play fast and loose with computer systems of any kind.[4]

Computers had been accepted as a science, crimes could be committed on or with a computer, and someone would be needed to explain computers and their workings to the courts. Enter the digital expert witness. Although it is difficult to say when the first computer expert was used as a witness in a computer crime trial, it is fair to say that such experts soon began playing an important part in the judicial process.

Since computer crimes became "official" in 1984, computer experts are often needed in trials in which the examination of a computer or computer component is crucial to proving the case. For example, in 1991, Special Agent Jim Christy of the Air Force Office of Special Investigations (OSI) became involved in a murder case on an Air Force base where the suspect had physically destroyed two floppy disks by cutting them into many pieces. Agent Christy and a deputy played with the pieces like a jigsaw puzzle until they eventually recovered 95 percent of the data on the disks. Those data were key to obtaining a conviction.[5] Following that case, computer forensics became a hot topic and a new industry soon followed.

The computer crime laws have been updated many times in the ensuing decades, evidence rules have changed, and computer forensics are considered a solid science, but it was the *Daubert v. Merrell Dow Pharmaceuticals* case in 1993 that really began to have an effect on expert witness testimony in cases where a computer or related technology is involved.[6]

73.2 DAUBERT. In 1974, a boy name Jason Daubert was born with a severely disfigured right arm and hand. His mother had taken Bendectin, an anti-nausea medication made by Merrell Dow Pharmaceutical, to combat the morning sickness she experienced while pregnant. This particular drug had been taken by tens of millions of women over the course of more than two decades, and a considerable number of children were born with significant birth defects. Many thousands of families took Merrell Dow to court over this problem, but Daubert's case was not decided until 1993.

73.2.1 Expert Witnesses' Testimony. Merrell Dow stated that the drug was not the problem, and worked to get the case thrown out of court. Merrell Dow presented the court an affidavit, given by a medical doctor, stating that he had reviewed many studies that indicated that the drug offered no risks in *humans* when taken during the first trimester of pregnancy. The Daubert family countered with eight affidavits from other experts that indicated there was a significant risk of birth defects in *animal* tests.

Sadly, the court did dismiss the case. In simple terms, the court felt that the Dauberts' affidavits did not compare apples to apples (i.e., animal studies were not the same as human studies). More importantly, however, the court also said that Dauberts' experts' findings were not admissible because they were neither published nor had they been subjected to peer review.

73.2.2 *Daubert* Challenge. The *Daubert* decision was heralded by many in the legal system as one of the most important findings by the Supreme Court in decades, because it went straight to the heart of the question of expert witnesses and testimony concerning science of one type or another. Many attorneys felt that juries were not capable of understanding new sciences or able to find flaws in scientific methods. With the *Daubert* case, however, the judges become "gatekeepers" of admissible evidence and, as gatekeepers, they decide whether scientific evidence could be admissible at all, based on these considerations:

- Whether the theory or technique used by the expert has been tested or *can* be tested
- Whether the theory or technique has ever been published and subjected to peer review
- Whether there is a known or potential rate of error for the method used
- The degree of acceptance within the relevant scientific community
- Whether standards exist for the method or technique used

73.3 WHETHER THE *DAUBERT* CHALLENGE IS APPLICABLE: REFINING *DAUBERT*.

It is hard to imagine any legal ruling in a U.S. court ever going unchallenged for very long, and so it went with *Daubert*. When lawyers refer to a *Daubert* challenge today, they are more likely making reference to the *Daubert* trilogy, which are the rulings in *Daubert* plus two other subsequent cases: *General Electric Co. v. Joiner*[7] and *Kumho Tire Co. v. Carmichael*.[8] In these cases, the judges made rulings that were an attempt to further define and refine the original *Daubert* rulings.

73.3.1 *General Electric Co. v. Joiner*. The 1997 Joiner case was one concerning product liability. Experts were called up to testify to the cancer-causing abilities of a certain fluid that Mr. Joiner came in contact with on a daily basis. Ultimately, the ruling made changes to the original *Daubert* ruling by adding that the *Daubert* challenge should be used not just for scientific testimony but for *all* testimony that could be described as "scientific, technical, or other specialized knowledge" under FRE 702.

Additionally, in *Joiner* it was ruled that the judge's scrutiny is not limited to methodology but can extend to the expert's analysis. This puts another strain on expert witnesses because the science, technology, and methodologies of collecting the evidence can be fine, but the interpretation of that evidence can be called into question.

73.3.2 *Kumho Tire Co. v. Carmichael*. Last in the *Daubert* trilogy is *Kumho Tire,* which was another product liability case tried in 1999. The science in question here revolved around tire failure, and *Daubert* challenges abounded. The final ruling in this case decreed that a trial judge is vested with broad authority to determine whether and to what extent the enumerated *Daubert* factors are applicable to a case.

To clarify: Technical and nontechnical testimony can be challenged, the expert witness's findings can be challenged, and, finally, the judge can decide that all, some, or none of the *Daubert* challenges apply.

Computers are sometimes easier to understand than U.S. law.

73.4 DIVIDED WE FALL? Since *Joiner* and *Kumho Tire,* there have been other decisions concerning *Daubert*, admissibility of evidence, and expert witnesses, but the *Daubert* trilogy seems to be the standard—at least for federal courts. (*Daubert* and subsequent decisions were made in federal courts.) State courts, however, seem to have a lot more leniency in deciding what rules to use to determine admissibility. If you are an expert witness in a federal trial, there is a good chance you may have to face a *Daubert* challenge. If the case is at the state level or lower, you will likely experience an unusual mix of rules and challenges. The next list shows which standards apply in different states of the United States.

States Accepting *Daubert*	States Accepting *Frye*	States with Their Own Rules
Connecticut	Alaska	Arkansas
Indiana	Arizona	Delaware
Kentucky	California	Georgia
Louisiana	Colorado	Iowa
Massachusetts	Florida	Military
New Mexico	Illinois	Minnesota
Oklahoma	Kansas	Montana
South Dakota	Maryland	North Carolina
Texas	Michigan	Oregon
West Virginia	Missouri	Utah
	Nebraska	Vermont
	New York	Wyoming
	Pennsylvania	
	Washington	

If you are called as an expert witness in any case, it is best to know what rules and challenges the court may be considering in the case. Leave no doubt; talk to your attorney and, if he or she has not considered a possible *Daubert* (or other) challenge, it could mean a tough road ahead. A competent attorney will be able to give you guidance on what testimony is likely to be challenged, and an excellent attorney will spend a long time with you going over your questions and concerns.

73.5 BEING THE BEST YOU CAN BE. Being an expert witness in a trial means more than just sitting in the stand and letting your expertise and knowledge flow. You need to be on the top of your game and know absolutely all you can possibly know about the subject matter in which you are to give testimony. One court recently dismissed an expert witness's opinion in digital forensics because he had *heard* of a certain book but had not personally read it.[9]

Although there are no hard-and-fast guidelines to being a good expert witness, you can use some general stratagems that have worked well for others. Certainly, if the list of books in online bookstores is any indication, the market for expert witnesses is strong.[10]

73.5.1 Prepare Your Résumé. The first step in becoming an expert witness is to have a very strong résumé that is completely and totally factual. The résumé will be entered in the trial records, so this is no time for elaboration of the facts. Expert testimony is allowed only if the court declares a witness to be an expert in a specified field, and your résumé will help establish the facts of the matter.

Highlight these items in your résumé to indicate your areas of expertise:

- Education
- Training
- Certificates
- Licenses
- Employment
- Lists of published articles, books, opinions
- Lists of speaking engagements and titles of talks

Once the court has examined your résumé, oral examination by the attorneys and the judge will likely follow. This can be quite easy, or it can be long and arduous.

73.5.2 Find Out Exactly What Testimony Is Expected. When contacted by an attorney to be an expert witness, do not be too fast to accept or decline. Most likely the attorney will be fishing at this point and will discuss things only in broad, general terms. It is also likely that your contact has limited knowledge of the subject matter. Find out as much as you can about the charges and what the attorney needs (or wants) to make the case.

Once you have reached an understanding with your contact, get everything in writing and make it a contract. This will be a statement of what is expected of you and what expertise is required to give the testimony. Your contract should also list your fees and payment schedule. This is where TV and reality take different roads. You have probably seen televised courtroom dramas where the opposing counsel undermines an expert witness by asking "How much were you paid for your testimony today?" Although that makes good television, in reality the courts *expect* that an expert witness is paid, and a fee actually lends credibility to the witness.

Also, look for any legal protections you will be offered for your testimony. You might be asked to do or say something that is a potential breach of ethics or confidentiality, and this could result in a loss of certain types of certification.

73.5.3 Examine the Paperwork. As soon as you are under contract, review the paperwork. If you discover there have been misrepresentations and you no longer want the job, you can back out at this point with no hard feelings. Of course, you may want to remain on the case, but you will need to discuss any concerns or questions with the attorney and possibly make an amendment to your contract.

Go over the paperwork as many times as you can until you are completely familiar with all aspects of the case. If the trial is particularly contentious, your familiarity with the case will certainly come into question.

73.5.4 Start Reading. Now is a good time to start brushing up on your knowledge base. Dig into your library of industry standard books and give them a review. Look for recent books on the subjects and articles in reputable journals. The more you are able to quote facts and figures, the better you will look on the stand.

73.5.5 Prepare a Written Report. Whether or not a written report is required should be a condition of your contract, but it is always a good idea to write up a report, even if it is just for your own use. While on the stand, you will be allowed to refer to your notes and to your report, although the court may want to examine them. Notes prepared at the time observations were made have stronger evidentiary value than statements from memory. This is a good strategy and makes you look very professional, and strong in your opinions.

It is a good idea to list all your sources and resources in your report, as well as your methodologies. This is an area where the *Daubert* challenge can get sticky, and the veracity of your opinion, based on what you have used and how you have used it, may come into question.

73.5.6 Ask for Pretrial Meetings. It is always a good idea to practice what you need to say, especially when it is to be delivered to a large group of people. Just as you would practice giving a lecture or speech, you should practice what you are going to say on the stand. You will need to appear to be confident at trial, so ask the attorney for assistance in preparing for trial. There is always the possibility that new questions or concerns may arise during the pretrial meeting, but it is better that these come up in the meetings than in front of the court.

73.5.7 Be Professional. Everyone is familiar with the geek stereotype—long hair, torn jeans, T-shirt, and sandals—but that is totally inappropriate. Dress professionally for court. When giving your testimony, use language that the layperson can understand. Do not let your ego show, and certainly contain your temper.

73.5.8 Accept the Oddities. No one expects you to understand everything that happens in a court proceeding. Simply answer the questions directly, and do not be afraid to say you do not know. (If you do not know because it cannot be known, however, that is important to relate.) You do not have to justify anything you say unless you are asked to. If an objection is raised, stop speaking and wait for the judge to ask you to continue. Last, do not be afraid to ask questions yourself if you are unclear on questions or procedures.

73.6 SUMMARY. It is certainly an ego boost to be considered enough of an expert in your field to be called as an expert witness, and some people have made successful careers of it. If you do make a career of being an expert witness, however, you cannot justify being an expert if you do not continually upgrade your expertise through industry experience. In any case, whether you are an expert, or whether your testimony is acceptable, is ultimately up to the court.

If you are called to be an expert witness and agree to the job, you do not really need to know the legal ins and outs of the *Daubert* challenge (or any other challenge); that is the attorney's job. The best plan is to know your subject matter better than anyone else and to be completely firm in your opinions and conclusions. If there is a challenge, do not take it personally. More often than not, the challenge has more to do with the methodology used in coming to your conclusions or with the science itself. To be prepared, it is best to keep detailed notes of everything you read and every step you take in coming to your opinions.

73.7 FURTHER READING

Brodsky, S. L. *Testifying in Court: Guidelines and Maxims for the Expert Witness*, 2nd ed. American Psychological Association, 2012.

Eastman, G., V. M. Howell, and M. Salgado. "A Primer on When to Use Expert Witnesses and How to Find Them." *Bloomberg Law* (2013). http://about.bloomberglaw.com/practitioner-contributions/a-primer-on-when-to-use-expert-witnesses-and-how-to-find-them/

Hallberg, B. J. *How To Be An Effective Litigation Consultant And Expert Witness*. AuthorHouse, 2010.

Lubet, S. and E. Boals. *Expert Testimony: A Guide for Expert Witnesses and the Lawyers Who Examine Them*, 2nd ed. LexisNexis/National Institute for Trial Advocacy, 2009.

Poynter, D. *The Expert Witness Handbook: Tips and Techniques for the Litigation Consultant*, 3rd ed. Para Publishing, 2007.

Sennewald, C. A. *From the Files of a Security Expert Witness*. Butterworth-Heinemann, 2013.

73.8 NOTES

1. The author is not a lawyer, and the facts presented here are a layperson's interpretation of the laws concerning digital evidence and expert witnesses.
2. *Frye v. United States,* 293 F. 1013 (D.C. Cir. 1923), www.daubertontheweb.com/frye_opinion.htm
3. Federal Rules of Evidence (amended to December 1, 2011), www.law.cornell.edu/rules/fre/rules.htm
4. Counterfeit Access Device and Computer Fraud and Abuse Act of 1984, www.answers.com/topic/counterfeit-access-device-and-computer-fraud-and-abuse-act-of-1984
5. Robin Mejia, "CSI: TCP/IP." *Wired*, Issue 15.01, January 2007, www.wired.com/wired/archive/15.01/cybercop.html
6. *Daubert v. Merrell Dow Pharmaceuticals,* 509 U. S. 579 (1993), www.law.cornell.edu/supct/html/92-102.ZS.html
7. *General Electric v. Joiner,* 522 U. S. 136 (1997), www.law.cornell.edu/supct/html/96-188.ZO.html
8. *Kuhmo Tire v. Carmichael,* 526 U. S. 137 (1999), www.griffithlaw.net/research.database/uploads/DAUBERT%20CHALLENGES%20IN%20GOVERNMENTAL%20LITIGATION%20final%20draft.pdf
9. Daniel J. Ryan and Gal Shpantzer, "Legal Aspects of Digital Forensics," n.d., http://euro.ecom.cmu.edu/program/law/08-732/Evidence/RyanShpantzer.pdf
10. Malack Amenya, "Recovering, Examining and Presenting Computer Forensic Evidence in Court," n.d., http://lib.convdocs.org/docs/index-267264.html

CHAPTER 74

PROFESSIONAL CERTIFICATION AND TRAINING IN INFORMATION ASSURANCE

M. E. Kabay, Christopher Christian, Kevin Henry, and Sondra Schneider

74.1 INCREASING COMPETENCE AND CONFIDENCE IN CYBERSECURITY PROFESSIONALS. Information assurance (IA) has grown into one of the most important and sought-after fields in the job market today. This is not a market saturated with professionals. Security professionals are well paid right out of college. And at the time of writing (August 2013), there is still a large demand for IA practitioners.

Persons responsible for a company's information security are given a lot of power. With this in mind, a company should hire only those whom it can trust to do the job right and who are ethical. Certifications provided by security groups and societies support management's quest for trustworthy, competent employees. Through rigorous examinations, adherence to approved protocols, and standards of ethics, a security professional can achieve one or many professional security-related certifications.

Perhaps one of the most critical decisions an organization has to make today is how to invest in its staff. Technology, policies, and well-defined processes are all important elements of an organization's infrastructure, but the most valuable and versatile asset that any company has today is its personnel.

How do we recruit, develop, and maintain a skilled and professional staff with other organizations competing for our trained experts, and how do we maintain their level of proficiency despite the rapid changes in technology and the many pressures of keeping the business operating?

Many companies struggle with the need to provide opportunity for their staff, while realizing that training and educating their staff makes these people attractive to other organizations.

Government regulations and legislation as well as increasing expectations from customers, suppliers, and business partners require information technology (IT) staff who are up to date with the latest technologies and who can provide assurance of reliable and stable IT operations. In most cases, a company is required either to develop internal resources to meet these demands or to pay a large price to recruit such people from external sources. More and more organizations are building relationships with universities and technical colleges to ensure that a ready supply of new graduates is available for their use. However, to retain good employees, it is necessary to make expensive investments in their further education. This is money and time that is hard to justify in some cases, and there are numerous options when it comes to registering for a professional training or educational program.

74.1.1 Recognition by Government Agencies. Upon taking office in 2009, U.S. Department of Homeland Security (DHS) Secretary Janet Napolitano recognized the urgency of the situation in cybersecurity. In October 2010 she announced a new hiring authority to enable DHS "to recruit the best cyber analysts, developers and engineers in the world to serve their country by leading the nation's defenses against cyber threats."[1]

In 2009 President Obama declared cybersecurity to be one of the nation's most serious economic and security challenges. The federal government needs a coordinated, sustained effort to build the capability of a qualified and validated cybersecurity workforce to combat cyberthreats and ensure the nation's safety.[2]

Finding the people with the needed skills is not easy. According to the DHS *Cyber-Skills Task Force Report* of Fall 2012,

> Finding the people with the needed skills, however, poses a dilemma. The numbers of professionals with these mission-critical skills are so limited that government contractors and federal agencies compete with one another and the private sector to hire them. Not surprisingly, a recent article in *Bloomberg News* reports that "the competition is fiercest for workers with hands-on experience defending systems against hackers and malicious viruses that can steal sensitive

government data."[3] For DHS to acquire sufficient talent in such a competitive environment, it needs to radically expand the national pipeline of professionals with sophisticated technical cybersecurity skills.[4]

Key recommendations from the DHS CyberSkills Task Force include the following:

- Adopt and maintain an authoritative list of mission-critical cybersecurity jobs, particularly in areas like penetration testing, security monitoring, and incident response, and modify that list in the face of changing threats and technologies.
- Develop training scenarios that allow it to properly evaluate cybersecurity talent for each of the mission-critical tasks.
- Adopt a sustainable model for assessing the competency and progress of existing and future cybersecurity talent.
- Establish a department-level infrastructure that oversees the development of the cybersecurity workforce.
- Streamline the hiring process and make government cybersecurity jobs more enticing by emphasizing the service, skills, and growth potential in the Federal Government.
- Establish a two-year, community-college-based program that identifies and trains large numbers of students for in-demand cybersecurity jobs.
- Raise the eligibility criteria for schools that participate in the Centers for Academic Excellence and Scholarship for Service programs to ensure that graduates are better prepared to perform in-depth cybersecurity work.
- Launch a major initiative to enhance the opportunities for U.S. veterans to be trained for and hired in mission-critical cybersecurity jobs.
- Use the large majority of its direct hiring authority to bring on people with critical cyber-skills, until at least 600 of those workers are fully on board.
- Specify the skills and level of proficiency needed in all cybersecurity-related contracting.
- Establish a pilot DHS CyberReserve program that ensures former DHS cybersecurity workers and other cyberprofessionals outside of government are known and available to DHS in times of need.[5]

How do we identify and capture those skilled IA professionals? How do we assess the current workforce to become the next qualified and validated cybersecurity workforce? What are the best ways to develop a national security workforce capable of meeting current and future IA challenges; how do we maintain their level of proficiency despite the rapid changes in technology and the many pressures of keeping the business operating; and, lastly, how do we improve capability to recruit and retain that sophisticated IA talent, because training makes these people attractive to other organizations?

Information-security certification has never been more important. Certification is one of the hottest topics in information security. Educating the workforce is the glue that reduces risk across the enterprise. Without hands-on education and training, daily threats and network vulnerabilities increase risk.

What are the ways to boost the nation's overall ability to develop professionals with the advanced IA skills needed to protect the information, systems, and networks that enable effective and secure operation of government and commercial elements of critical national infrastructure?

Companies need to focus the large majority of near-term efforts in IA hiring, training, and human-capital development to build teams with mission-critical IA skills.

74.1.2 Certification, Qualification, and Validation of Hands-on Skills.

The plain-English definition of a *certificate* is "document providing official evidence:

an official document that gives proof and details of something such as personal status, educational achievements, ownership, or authenticity."[6]

Certificates and certification are important in affirming the qualifications of IA professionals.

1. Any program that does not have an examination is a *certificate-of-participation* program.
2. Any examination that measures learning objectives is a part of a *certification* program.
3. A *professional certificate* program is an academic or commercial effort that awards a certificate from attending or participating in a course and *may or may not* measure the learning objectives with an examination at the course's conclusion.

Professional certificates are a way to move a career forward. Typically, certificate programs are a multiclass offering designed to expand expertise in a specific subject. They comprise required courses that cover areas of interest in more granular topics of specialization. Knowledge and hands-on skills gained can be immediately applied in the workplace.

Certification is even more valuable. Doctors take examinations to determine book or course knowledge, plus a residency to do surgery without harming anyone; pilots take courses and go through flight time to show that they can fly a plane without crashing. In IA, finding people who actually have qualified and validated cybersecurity skills is a challenge. As one commentator wrote in August 2013,

> Cybersecurity is one of the most high-demand, lucrative careers in the current IT job market. According to a report by Burning Glass Technologies, the total number of available jobs in IT security has grown by 73% from 2007 to 2012. That's 3.5 times faster than other IT disciplines and 12 times faster than the average for all other jobs. . . .
>
> There are a number of information security certifications, with broad and magnified focuses, that are imperative for any cybersecurity professional worth his or her salt to know. Security certifications provide a potential employer with a twofold incentive for adding you to the team. One, it shows that an impartial board of accredited professionals is willing to stake their reputations on your subject matter mastery. Two, it shows that you've been schooled in a high standard, ethical approach to your job. That way, they'll feel assured that you're not a Black Hat masquerading as a cybersecurity tech for just long enough to infiltrate their system and gorge yourself on the data held inside.[7]

Are there differences in certifications? Yes, there are hands-on skills *performance-based* certifications and *theory-based* certifications.

- *Theory-based* certification can be instructor-led lectures, and online or self-paced instruction. These programs end with an examination to measure the learning outcomes but are not intended to qualify or validate the participants' hands-on skills.
- *Performance-based* certifications are instructor-led, with daily labs, an examination to measure the learning outcomes, and written practical exams to qualify and validate that the participant has learned the intended outcome objectives.

  Today's cybersecurity workforce must become qualified and validated by a common set of cybersecurity roles/tasks/jobs standards for educating and building the cybersecurity workforce.

74.1.3 Effective Workforce Training. There is a significant difference between training and education. In this chapter, the emphasis is on training; in Chapter 75 of this *Handbook*, it is on education.

When a company invests in a technology such as firewalls or wireless systems, it often has to provide training to the people responsible for managing the devices. Such training is best provided through official sources approved of by the vendors, because product vendors can often arrange for training as a part of the purchase price; in addition, there is a certain assurance that the training materials are up to date if they are provided by the vendors or by an official source coordinating with the vendors.

74.1.3.1 Effective Training Programs. A common mistake companies make is to send one person to the official training program, trusting that person to pass the knowledge gained to their peers. What usually happens is that the person who attends the course provides a 10-minute overview or one page review to management and the rest of the staff when she returns. In theory this might work, but the knowledge transfer is limited because many organizations have no systematic way of sharing knowledge or evaluating a training program to ensuring that they receive value for their investment.

All worthwhile education and training programs should go beyond merely passing on information passively; they should provide the students with some form of practical work—whether through labs, a case study, or the need to prepare for and pass a difficult project or an extensive examination. It is too easy to have programs that are not really effective—the students can easily slip into a state of *death by PowerPoint* or *lecture hypnosis*, where they are following along with the program but not really absorbing or digesting the material. It is only when they are challenged to answer questions about the material or to use it in a practical manner that most people will truly grasp and retain the information. The goal is to integrate knowledge into the participants' world-view, not simply to pass an exam.[8]

74.1.3.2 Supporting Participants. One factor to consider is the location of the class. Ideally, a student should not be continuously distracted or pulled from the program to address issues back at the office or to handle email during the class. Distraction during class makes what is being presented or discussed in the class difficult to absorb. Lack of concentration causes the organization to lose the investment it made in the class; students may ask questions that were addressed earlier and thus frustrate other students; and distracted students may do poorly in the lab work or examinations and cause conflict by blaming the course or the instructor. While a student is assigned to a training class, she should be solely focused on the class and not participate in activities back at the office except in an emergency. Training should be held at facilities that enable serious study and learning. The courses themselves should not be just interesting hot topics, but rather those that will directly benefit in their work—and as soon as possible. Avoid educating someone in skills they will not use for several months: they will probably have forgotten most of the information by the time they try to use it.

Education and training are sometimes seen as a reward for an employee or a measure of respect for the staff. Although reward and respect are important, it is inappropriate to hand out training assignments as if they were perquisites of rank or signs of management favor. Courses should be focused on meeting specific behaviorally defined objectives.[9] In addition, to emphasize that learning is legitimate work and not a perk, employees who take assigned courses on weekends or outside their normal work shifts should be assigned compensatory time to make up for the use of their personal time.

74.1.4 Career Value of Certification.

In the *2007 SC Magazine/EC-Council Salary Survey*, a key finding was that "[w]hile not a mainstream occurrence, many companies are striving to ensure they're viewed as being proactive about securing digital assets by asking that new hires have a certification."[10] Indeed, there has been a steady increase in the acceptance of certification as a credible indicator of professional competence in the information assurance field. For example, even by 2003, the information technology industry had recognized the value of the *Certified Information Systems Professional* (CISSP) designation. A writer for the prestigious *SC Magazine* wrote:

> The CISSP designation from the International Systems Security Certification Consortium—or (ISC)^2—is often referred to as the de facto standard when it comes to information security certifications. It is described as the "International Gold Standard," according to (ISC)^2. But companies and government agencies also place importance on more technical certifications, such as the SANS Institute's Global Information Assurance Certification (GIAC).[11]

In June 2004, the CISSP designation was accredited by the International Standards Organization under the ISO/IEC 1702 standard, making it a globally recognized security-professional certification.[12]

In August 2004, the United States Department of Defense issued DoD Directive 8570.1. The DoD Fact Sheet from (ISC)^2 is provided in full as an appendix to this proposal.[13] The key points of this development are:

- "... requires any full- or part-time military service member, contractor, or foreign employee with privileged access to a DoD information system, regardless of job or occupational series, to obtain a commercial information security credential accredited by ANSI or equivalent authorized body under the ANSI/ISO/IEC 17024 Standard... ."
- The CISSP designation was recognized at the highest levels of both the technical and management categories.

The *Fact Sheet* continues with a discussion of "the significance of this mandate and of commercial certification in general." The authors wrote:

> This mandate will have far-reaching implications, including:
>
> - The Directive is viewed as a government endorsement of the effectiveness and cost-efficiency of commercial certification.
> - It provides military and civilian personnel with a certification that is professional, internationally recognized, and vendor-neutral (not tied to any agency, technology, or product).
> - It provides a portable certification that is recognized in both the public and private sectors.
> - It mandates and endorses a global standard (ANSI/ISO/IEC 17024).
> - It positions the information security profession as a distinct job series.

In a 2008 survey sponsored by (ISC)^2, analysts found that "[t]he clear differentiator in terms of career advancement and professional growth lies in certifications such as the CISSP. 'Certifications are a measure of experience and knowledge, and businesses increasingly like to see that certification... .' "[14]

Lauren Gibbons Paul wrote in April 2013,

> When it comes to education, most people agree, more is better.... Anyone who puts in the time and spends the money to get certified is showing they care about staying current with security trends and techniques. That quality makes someone more desirable to an employer....
>
> As a practical matter, many of today's information security certifications require much hands-on application of skills.... Being able to pass proves to a potential employer that you can do certain things, potentially giving you an edge over those who do not hold the certification.
>
> For some jobs, obtaining a particular security certification,,, is a [pre]requisite for even being considered.... Beyond that, however, attaining certifications is generally a matter of personal and/or employer choice. Some certifications require a great deal of work both in and out of the classroom, as well as sitting for the test....
>
> Whether or not security certification will earn you more, now or in the future, depends a lot on the organization, the job, and the industry. If your company values continuing education (and will help foot some of the bill for the training), that is a good indication that certification will elevate your status. If not, you may still want to pursue certification if ... [for you] education is its own reward, or you need to build up your resume in anticipation of a making a move.[15]

The 2011 (ISC)^2 Global Information Security Workforce Study reported,

> According to the 74 percent of respondents who were involved in hiring information security staff, the importance of information security certifications as a hiring criterion remains high, with just less than 90 percent of respondents ranking security certifications very or somewhat important.....[16]

However, the authors of that *Study* warned,

> Complexity has been added to the hiring process through the years due to the sheer number and qualitative differences of certifications offered in the marketplace. The list of vendor-neutral and vendor-specific security certifications grows every year, making it difficult for employees, hiring managers, and their organizations to discern which certifications carry the greatest value for them. Today, the number has significantly grown to more than 40 vendor-neutral and vendor-specific certifications. Frost & Sullivan [the firm conducting the research for (ISC)^2] first reported the perception of the dilution effect in the marketplace in the 2008 study. This trend continues to challenge certification vendors to differentiate themselves. The concern is that certifications considered of high value today may be perceived to be devalued and, consequently, less significant to information security professionals and, more importantly, their employers. Frost & Sullivan believes that many vendors are addressing the current skills gap increasing the complexity and continuing education requirements of their certifications.[17]

Figure 27 from the *Study* shows that 69 percent of the 10,413 respondents rated employee competence to be a contributing reason to hire a certified employee; 54 percent reported their quality of work as a positive factor.[18]

The 2013 version of the *Workforce Study* reported,

> Slightly more than 46 percent of all survey respondents indicated that their organizations require certification, and among those respondents, 50 percent of member and 39 percent of nonmember indicate certification is a requirement. Government-defense is most emphatic on this point; 84 percent state certification is required, and a distant, but still high, second is info tech at 47 percent.[19]

The 2013 *Study* found that 68 percent of the 12,396 respondents[20] accepted employee competence and 53 percent reported quality of work as reasons for requiring information-security certifications. This consistency between 2011 and 2013 supports

EXHIBIT 74.1 Comparison of Certification and Certificates

Certification	Certificate
Results from an assessment process that recognizes an individual's knowledge, skills, and competency in a particular specialty	Results from educational process
Typically requires professional experience	For newcomers and experienced professionals
Awarded by a third-party, standard-setting organization	Awarded by educational programs or institutions often for profit
Indicates mastery/competency as measured against a defensible set of standards, usually by lab, application, and exam	Indicates completion of a course or series of courses with a specific focus (different from a degree-granting program)
Standards set through a defensible, industry-wide process (job analysis/role delineation) that results in an outline of required knowledge and skills	Course content determined by the specific provider or institution, not standardized
Typically results in credentials to be listed after one's name (e.g., CISM, CISSP, GIAC, C—EH, Q/ISP, Security+)	Usually listed on a resume detailing education
Has ongoing requirements in order to maintain; holder must demonstrate (s)he continues to meet requirements	Demonstrates knowledge of course content at the end of a set period in time

the view that certification plays a valuable role in improving job prospects for IA personnel.

74.1.5 Summary Chart. Exhibit 74.1 provides a comparison of certification and certificates.

74.2 ACCREDITATION.

The next sections explain the three most important accreditation organizations and processes for information assurance: ANSI/ISO/IEC 17024, ICE/NOCA/NCCA, and IACE.

74.2.1 ANSI/ISO/IEC 17024:2012 Accreditation of Personnel Certification. The Accreditation Program for Personnel Certification Bodies under ANSI/ISO/IEC 17024, the International Organization for Standardization (ISO), and the International Electrotechnical Commission (IEC) have developed a global, voluntary benchmark for organizations responsible for certification of personnel. Fully enacted as of April 1, 2003, this international standard (ANSI/ISO/IEC 17024) was designed to harmonize personnel certification processes worldwide and create global standards for certifying the workforce in a wide range of fields. A new version (ANSI/ISO/IEC 17024:2012) was approved in July 2012.[21]

ANSI accreditation process involves both a review of a paper application and the performance of an audit (on-site visit) to validate information provided by each applicant organization with regard to the process and delivery of the examination. ANSI does not accredit/review or otherwise value the content of the certification program.

ANSI operates the Program in accordance with *ISO/IEC 17011, Conformity assessment—General requirements for accreditation bodies accrediting conformity assessment bodies.*[22] The requirements of this document provide the basis for a nationally recognized, open, transparent, and credible accreditation activity that requires applicants' certification programs to demonstrate integrity and technical and administrative quality.

Certifications accredited by ANSI are marked with asterisks (*) below.

74.2.2 ICE/NOCA/NCCA. The *Institute for Credentialing Excellence*,[23] formerly the *National Organization for Competency Assurance* (NOCA), founded in 1977, promotes excellence in credentialing worldwide through these services:

- Education
- Research
- Advocacy
- Standards
- Accreditation

The organization provides annual conferences, Webinars, and publications. In 1987, NOCA created the *National Commission for Certifying Agencies* (NCCA) to formalize the process of accreditation of certification programs and organizations.[24]

NCCA uses a peer review process to:

- Establish accreditation standards
- Evaluate compliance with the standards
- Recognize organizations/programs that demonstrate compliance
- Serve as a resource on quality certification

Certification organizations that submit their programs for accreditation are evaluated based on the process and products, not the content, and are therefore applicable to all professions and industries.

NCCA-accredited programs certify individuals in a wide range of professions and occupations, including nurses, automotive professionals, respiratory therapists, counselors, emergency technicians, crane operators, and more. As of August 2013, NCCA had accredited 297 certification programs, mostly in the healthcare professions, but including:

- American Board for Certification in Homeland Security (ABCHS)[25]
- American Health Information Management Association (AHIMA)[26]
- Defense Security Service (DSS)[27]

74.2.3 CNSS Standards. A set of standards used in accreditation, as shown in Section 74.2.2, are defined by the *Committee on National Security Systems* (CNSS), a U.S. interagency group which describes its mission as follows:

> The CNSS provides a forum for the discussion of policy issues, and is responsible for setting national-level Information Assurance policies, directives, instructions, operational procedures, guidance, and advisories for U.S. Government (USG) departments and agencies for the security of National Security Systems (NSS) through the CNSS Issuance System. The CNSS is directed to assure the security of NSS against technical exploitation by providing: reliable and

continuing assessments of threats and vulnerabilities and implementation of effective countermeasures; a technical base within the USG to achieve this security; and support from the private sector to enhance that technical base assuring that information systems security products are available to secure NSS.[28]

The CNSS focuses on *national security systems,* which it defines as follows:

- National security systems are information systems operated by the U.S. Government, its contractors, or agents that contain classified information or that:
  - involve intelligence activities;
  - involve cryptographic activities related to national security;
  - involve command and control of military forces;
  - involve equipment that is an integral part of a weapon or weapons system(s); or
  - are critical to the direct fulfillment of military or intelligence missions (not including routine administrative and business applications).

The definition for a National Security System, along with other applicable terms used in the National Security Community, are found in CNSSI 4009, "Information Assurance Glossary."[29,30]

Some of the key standards defined by the CNSS[31] include

- NSTISSI-4011: National Training Standard for Information Systems Security (INFOSEC) Professionals, dated 20 June 1994[32]
- CNSSI-4012: National Information Assurance Training Standard for Senior Systems Managers, dated June 2004; Supersedes NSTISSI No. 4012, dated August 1997[33]
- CNSSI-4013: National Information Assurance Training Standard for System Administrators (SA), dated March 2004[34]
- CNSSI-4014: Information Assurance Training Standard for Information Systems Security Officers, dated April 2004; supersedes NSTISSI No. 4014, dated August 1997[35]
- NSTISSI-4015: National Training Standard for Systems Certifiers, dated December 2000[36]
- CNSSI-4016: National Information Assurance Training Standard for Risk Analysts, dated November 2005[37]

For further discussion of certification of academic institutions involved in IA, see Chapter 75 in this *Handbook*.

74.3 IA CERTIFICATIONS.

IA has grown into one of the most important and sought-after career fields in the job market today. Security professionals are well paid, based on knowledge and experience. The demand has grown for qualified and validated IA practitioners.[38]

Persons responsible for a company's information security are given a lot of responsibility and power. An organization should hire only those whom it can trust to do the job right, and who are ethical. Certifications provided by security groups and societies support management's quest for trustworthy, competent employees. Through rigorous examinations, adherence to approved protocols and standards of ethics, a security professional can achieve one or many professional security-related certifications.

What follows are brief summaries of some of the key security-related certifications including basic, intermediate, advanced, forensics, anti-hacking, and specialized. For those starting up the information-security career ladder or who already have security experience and wish to hone their skills in some specialized area, these resources are of great value. The sections are in alphabetical order of the certification bodies.[39]

74.3.1 ACFE. The nonprofit *Association of Certified Fraud Examiners* (ACFE)[40] offers the *Certified Fraud Examiner* (CFE) certification. The CFE demonstrates ability to detect financial fraud and other white-collar crimes. This credential is of primary interest to full-time security professionals in law or law enforcement, or those who work in organizations with legal mandates to audit for possible fraudulent or illegal transactions and activities (such as banking, securities trading, or classified operations). The ACFE notes that "According to the *2013/2014 Compensation Guide for Anti-Fraud Professionals*, CFEs earn 25 percent more than their noncertified colleagues."[41] In addition,

> To become a CFE, an individual must pass a rigorous test on the four major disciplines that comprise the fraud examination body of knowledge:
>
> - Fraud Prevention and Deterrence
> - Financial Transactions and Fraud Schemes
> - Investigation
> - Law[42]

74.3.2 ASIS. ASIS International (in 1955, founded as the nonprofit *American Society for Industrial Security*) certifications are accredited by ANSI.[43]

- *Certified Protection Professional:* The CPP from *ASIS International*[44] (originally called the *American Association for Industrial Security*) demonstrates a thorough understanding of physical, human, and information-security principles and practices. The most senior and prestigious security professional certification covered in this article, the CPP requires extensive on-the-job experience (nine years or seven years with a college degree) including "at least three of those years in responsible charge of a security function," as well as a profound knowledge of technical and procedural security topics and technologies—not just IT security. Only those who have worked with and around security for much of their careers qualify for this credential.[45]
- *Professional Certified Investigator:* The PCI credential focuses on knowledge of legal and evidentiary matters required to present investigations in a court of law, including case management, evidence collection, and case presentation. It requires five years of investigation experience, with at least two years in case management, a high school diploma (or GED), and a clean criminal record.[46]

74.3.3 Brainbench Basic Security Certifications. *Brainbench,* a for-profit private company, offers 640 exams (as of August 2013) in a wide range of subjects including several basic-level security certifications, each requiring the candidate to pass one exam costing about $50.[47] Some of these exams may be useful for new entrants into the job market, for nonprofessionals looking to improve their career prospects, and for organizations seeking to measure the competence of applicants and employees claiming specific areas of knowledge. A career-development professional wrote about these low-level certifications in 2012,

> You can take a number of exams to meet their requirements on getting certified for a job role. They run specials and offer exams to take for free for a limited time. Most people wait to see when an exam they want to take becomes available for free and then they take the exam. Brainbench offers a yearly membership that cost about $200 dollars [sic] and you can take as many exams as you want. This is good value for the cost and the number of certifications that you can earn.[48]

Examples of these certifications relevant for IA include:

- *Computer Forensics (U.S.):* The Computer Forensics (U.S.) certification is designed for experienced individuals who can prepare for an investigation, analyze and collect evidence, recognize data types, follow proper examination procedures, and initial analysis, use forensic tools, provide initial analysis, and prepare for an investigation and report findings.[49]
- *Firewall Administration Concepts:* "… Audits, Core Technologies, Internals, Maintenance, Network Address Translation (NAT), Optimization, Piercing, Policies, Security Vulnerabilities, and Types."[50]
- *HIPAA (Privacy):* Tests "… knowledge of HIPAA Standards for Privacy. Designed for all professionals who are affected by the HIPAA Standards for Privacy, this test covers the following topics: General Knowledge, Impacted Areas, Implementation, Interactions with External Parties, Regulatory Environment, and Workplace Privacy."[51]
- *HIPAA (Security):* Tests "knowledge of compliance with the standards required by the Security and Electronic Signature Standards as they apply to HIPAA. Designed for healthcare professionals and focusing on nontechnical as well as technical aspects of the HIPAA Standards for Security and Electronic Signatures, this test includes the following topics: Computer Mechanisms, Computer Models, General Knowledge, Implementation, Medical Records, Organization, Security Basics, and Setup."[52]
- *Information Security Administrator:* This certification tests knowledge of networking and Internet security, including authorization, authentication, firewalls, encryption, disaster recovery, and more. Candidates must pass eight exams to obtain this certification.
- *Information Technology Security Fundamentals:* Topics evaluated include "Application Security, Architecture Security, Common Security Services, Data Security, Infrastructure Security, Network Security, Operating System Security, and Threats and Countermeasures."[53]
- *Internet Security:* "Communications, Electronic Mail, Encryption, Identity and Access Management, Malicious Programs, Network Devices and Services, Security Management, Threats, and World Wide Web."[54]
- *ITAA Information Security Awareness:* Information Technology Association of America test for general computer users. Topics include "Computer Best Practices, Computer Ethics & Misuse, ID & Data Information Theft, Internet Best Practices, Passwords, Physical Security, Sensitive Information, and Viruses & Other Harmful Software."[55]

- *Microsoft Security:* Tests "... knowledge of various aspects of security including networks, operating systems, security control concepts, servers, and client computers. Designed for experienced administrators, this test includes the following topics: Networks, Operating Systems, Patch Management, Security Best Practices, Security Controls, Security Incidents, Security Tools, and Servers."[56]
- *Network Authentication:* Tests "... knowledge of authentication protocols, policies, and configuration and audit techniques. Designed for experienced network administrators, this test includes the following topics: Authentication Methods, Encryption, Network Design and Architecture, Protocols, Risk Mitigation, User Accounts, Virtual Private Networking (VPN), and Web Server Authentication."[57]
- *Network Monitoring:* Tests "... knowledge of the core aspects of monitoring and troubleshooting networks. Designed for experienced network administrators, this test covers the following topics: Architecture and Terminology; SNMP Background, Components and Commands; RMON Background, Components and Commands; Other Monitoring and Troubleshooting Tools; System Design and Implementation; and Using SNMP and RMON Tools."[58]
- *Network Security:* Tests "... knowledge of the technical issues involved in maintaining network security. Designed for experienced network administrators, this test covers the following topics: Access Control, Cryptography, Infrastructure, Security Policy and Procedures, System Management, Threats, and Tools."[59]

74.3.4 CyberSecurity Institute. The *CyberSecurity Institute* is a "Noncommercial Research Organization"[60] that provides several courses of interest in addition to certifications:

- Computer Forensics Core Competencies (5 days)[61]
- Computer Forensics for Attorneys (1 day)[62]
- Packet Analysis and Intrusion Detection (5 days)[63]
- Computer Forensics Fundamentals (1 day)[64]
- Windows Forensics Essentials (2 days)[65]

The *CyberSecurity Forensic Analyst* (CSFA)[66] certification aims to identify individuals who can perform a comprehensive and sound forensic examination of a computer system and other digital/electronic devices within a limited time frame. Suggested prerequisites include attendance of the CyberSecurity Institute's *Computer Forensics Core Competencies* course and/or at least one of the following certifications:

- AccessData Certified Examiner (ACE)[67]
- Certified Forensic Computer Examiner (CFCE)[68]
- Certified Computer Examiner (CCE)[69]
- Computer Hacking Forensic Investigator (CHFI)[70]
- EnCase Certified Examiner (EnCE)[71]
- GIAC Certified Forensics Analyst (GCFA)[72]

In addition, candidates should have at least two years of experience performing forensic analysis of Windows FAT and NTFS file systems and writing forensic analysis reports. Candidates must have no criminal record and must pass an FBI background check.[73]

74.3.5 CERT. *CERT-Certified Computer Security Incident Handler:* The CERT-CCSIH credential is managed by the nonprofit Software Engineering Institute[74] of Carnegie Mellon University, home of the *Computer Emergency Response Team Coordination Center* (CERT/CC).[75]

The CERT-Certified Computer Security Incident Handler (CSIH) certification program has been created for:

- Computer network incident handling and incident responder professionals
- Computer security incident response team (CSIRT) members and technical staff
- System and network administrators with incident handling experience
- Incident handling educators
- Cybersecurity technical staff

The certification is recommended for those computer security professionals with one or more years of experience in incident handling and/or equivalent security-related experience. Although completion of training is not a requirement, we highly recommend that each applicant ensure they have studied appropriately for the examination.[76]

74.3.6 CompTIA. CompTIA is "a nonprofit trade association advancing the global interests of IT professionals and companies …" They "focus our programs on four main areas: education, certification, advocacy, and philanthropy."[77] They provide "four IT certification series that test different knowledge standards, from entry-level to expert."[78]

- Certified Advanced Security Practitioner Certification: CompTIA describes CASP as follows:

  > The CASP certification is an international, vendor-neutral exam that proves competency in enterprise security; risk management; research and analysis; and integration of computing, communications, and business disciplines.
  >
  > The exam covers the technical knowledge and skills required to conceptualize, design, and engineer secure solutions across complex enterprise environments. It involves applying critical thinking and judgment across a broad spectrum of security disciplines to propose and implement solutions that map to enterprise drivers. For more detailed information, download the exam objectives.[79]

- *Cloud+:* This certification "validates the knowledge and best practices required of IT practitioners working in cloud computing environments, who must understand and deliver cloud infrastructure. Recommended experience includes at least 24–36 months of work experience in IT networking, storage, or data center administration, and familiarity with any major hypervisor technologies for server virtualization."[80]
- *Mobile App Security+:* "The idea behind CompTIA Mobile App Security+ is to ensure that developers have the knowledge and skills to design and build applications with security built in from the start." In addition, "There are two editions of CompTIA Mobile App Security+ —one for Android and one for iOS.

Only one exam is required for certification. The exams cover web service and network security, data security and implementing encryption, and other aspects of mobile application security." At the time of writing (August 2013), this exam was under development.[81]

- *Security+:* This security certification focuses on important security fundamentals related to security concepts and theory, as well as best operational practices. Topics include:
  - Access control and identity management
  - Application, data, and host security
  - Compliance and operational security
  - Cryptography
  - Network security
  - Threats and vulnerabilities[82]
- *Social Media Security Professional:* "The SMSP certification designates professionals with demonstrated knowledge of the technical composition of social networking platforms and skills to effectively mitigate risks in order to safeguard organizations' critical information from social media hackers … The SMSP exam is delivered by Ultimate Knowledge Institute (UKI)."[83]

CASP and Security+ are ANSI-accredited.[84]

74.3.7 EC-Council. The for-profit *International Council of E-Commerce Consultants* (EC-Council) was founded in 2001:

> …[EC-Council] is a member-based organization that certifies individuals in various information-security and e-business skills. EC-Council has been certified by American National Standards Institute to meet its ANSI 17024 standard. It is the owner and creator of the world famous Certified Ethical Hacker (CEH), Computer Hacking Forensics Investigator (CHFI) and EC-Council Certified Security Analyst (ECSA)/License Penetration Tester (LPT) programs, and as well as many others programs, that are offered in over 87 countries through a training network of more than 450 training partners globally.
>
> As of January 1st, 2012 EC-Council has trained over 120,000 individuals and certified more than 50,000 security professionals… .[85]

Among the certifications managed by EC-Council[86] are the following. Only the C|EH is accredited by ANSI.[87]

- Certified Chief Information Security Officer (C|CISO)
- Certified Disaster Recovery Professional (EDRP)
- Certified Encryption Specialist (E|CES)
- Certified Ethical Hacker (C|EH)
- Certified Hacking Forensic Investigation (C|HFI)
- Certified Incident Handler (E|CIH)
- Certified Network Defense Architect (C|NDA)
- Certified Secure Programmer .NET (E|CSP .NET)
- Certified Security Analyst (E|CSA)
- Certified Security Specialist (E|CSS)

- Certified VoIP Professional (E|CVP)
- Computer Hacking Forensic Investigator (C|HFI)
- Licensed Penetration Tester (L|PT)
- Network Security Administrator (E|NSA)
- Security|5
- Secure Computer User (C|SCU)

74.3.8 CWNP. The *Certified Wireless Security Professional* (CWSP) certification from *Certified Wireless Network Professional* (CWNP),[88] which was founded in 1999, recognizes individuals who can design, implement, and manage wireless LAN security. To obtain this credential, candidates must pass two exams: one for network administration and the other for wireless LAN security.[89]

Other certifications available from CWNP as shown on the cited page include:

- Entry level—CWTS: Certified Wireless Technology Specialist
- Administrator level—CWNA: Certified Wireless Network Administrator
- Professional level—CWDP: Certified Wireless Design Professional
- Professional level—CWAP: Certified Wireless Analysis Professional
- Expert level—CWNE: Certified Wireless Network Expert

74.3.9 GIAC. The for-profit SANS Institute well known for its contributions to research and education in IA.

> The *Global Information Assurance Certification* (GIAC) was founded in 1999 to validate the real-world skills of IT security professionals. GIAC's purpose is to provide assurance that a certified individual has practical awareness, knowledge, and skills in key areas of computer and network and software security. GIAC currently offers certifications for over 20 job-specific responsibilities that reflect the current practice of information security.[90]

A GIAC designation is not a set standard of practiced and learned protocols. Instead SANS offers a number of certifications and certificates that are dedicated to different areas that require information security and different skill sets. Divided into divisions—Audit, Legal, Management, Operations, Security Administration—the certificates are further divided into levels (basic to more advanced skill sets).[91] To attain a GIAC certification, a five- or six-day SANS Training course must be taken followed by an exam. The exam can be taken within a six-month period from the end of the course.

For *Silver Certification*, the exam is taken online and consists of 150 to 200 multiple-choice questions. The cost of a GIAC certification is the same whether the candidate chooses self-study or conference training. Upon successful completion of the exam, a Silver Certification is given to the candidate.[92]

The Silver certification can be further upgraded to a *Gold Certification* two years or more after completing the Silver certification process. Upgrading requires completion of a technical paper related to the candidate's Silver certification. The paper must be completed in a six-month period, although a three-month extension can be added for an extra fee. When the paper is submitted, it is reviewed using a number of criteria:

- Technical—errors
- Education—clarity of thought and advanced knowledge of subject matter

- Extension—a topic outside the box of normal course studies
- Organization—paper clarity, setup, and professional work[93]

The *Global Information Assurance Certification Program* is described by Ed Tittel and Mary Lemons as follows:

> This program seeks to identify individuals who can demonstrate both knowledge of and the ability to manage and protect important information systems and networks. The SANS organization is well known for timely, focused, and useful security information and certification programs. A beacon on this landscape, GIAC now offers regular online classes and uses such classes to draw attendees to their frequent well-situated week-long conferences. Overall, the GIAC program aims at serious, full-time security professionals responsible for designing, implementing, and maintaining a state-of-the-art security infrastructure, which may include incident handling and emergency response team management. Available intermediate-level GIAC credentials include the following:
>
> - GIAC Security Essentials Certification (GSEC)
> - GIAC Information Security Professional (GISP)
> - GIAC Certified ISO-27000 Specialist (G2700)

Available advanced certifications from GIAC include the following 25 (those marked with an asterisk are ANSI-accredited),[94] all of which have links for details on the GIAC home page[91]:

- Assessing and Auditing Wireless Networks (GAWN)
- Certified Enterprise Defender (GCED*)
- Certified Firewall Analyst (GCFW)
- Certified Forensic Analyst (GCFA*)
- Certified Forensic Examiner (GCFE)
- Certified Incident Handler (GCIH*)
- Certified Intrusion Analyst (GCIA*)
- Certified ISO-27000 Specialist (G2700)
- Certified Project Manager (GCPM)
- Certified UNIX Security Administrator (GCUX)
- Certified Web Application Defender (GWEB)
- Certified Windows Security Administrator (GCWN)
- Exploit Researcher and Advanced Penetration Tester (GXPN)
- Information Security Fundamentals (GISF)
- Information Security Professional (GISP)
- Legal Issues in Information Technology & Security (GLEG)
- Mobile Device Security Analyst (GMOB)
- Penetration Tester (GPEN*)
- Reverse Engineering Malware (GREM)
- Secure Software Programmer- .NET (GSSP-.NET)
- Systems and Network Auditor (GSNA*)
- Secure Software Programmer-Java (GSSP-JAVA)

- Security Essentials (GSEC*)
- Security Leadership (GSLC*)
- Web Application Penetration Tester (GWAPT)

A particularly difficult and respected certification is the *GIAC Security Expert* (GSE), which the organization describes as follows:

> The GSE certification is the most prestigious in the IT Security industry. The current exam was developed by subject matter experts and top industry practitioners. The GSE's performance based, hands-on nature sets it apart from any other certifications in the IT security industry. The GSE will determine if a candidate has truly mastered the wide variety of skills required by top security consultants and individual practitioners.
>
> The GSE exam has two parts. The first is a multiple choice exam which may be taken at a proctored location just like any other GIAC exam. The current version of the GSE multiple choice exam has the passing score set at 75% and a time limit of 3 hours. Passing this exam qualifies a person to sit for the GSE hands-on lab. The first day of the two day GSE lab consists of an incident response scenario that requires the candidate to analyze data and report their results in a written report. The second consists of a rigorous battery of hands-on exercises... .[95]

74.3.10 HTCN. The High-Tech Crime Network (HTCN) includes:

> ...law enforcement agencies and corporate security professionals from 15 (fifteen) countries. Our membership includes prestigious agencies such as Royal Canadian Mounted Police, Federal Bureau of Investigation, Internal Revenue Service, US Customs, Alcohol Tobacco & Firearms, US Marshals, Department of Defense, National Security Agency, Naval Criminal Investigative Service, Federal Aviation Administration, Department of the Army, and many other law enforcement agencies from Belgium, Canada, England, Germany, Switzerland, and the United States, as well as major telecommunication corporations from across the nation.[96]

HTCN offers four computer-forensic certifications aimed at law enforcement and private-sector IT professionals seeking to specialize in the investigative side of the field.

- Certified Computer Crime Investigator (Basic)
- Certified Computer Crime Investigator (Advanced)
- Certified Computer Forensic Technician (Advanced)
- Certified Computer Forensic Technician (Basic)

The certifications require from three to five years of experience plus 40 to 80 hours of approved training courses plus written reports on from 10 to 40 specific criminal investigations and forensic analyses. Details are available on the organization's Website.[97]

74.3.11 IACIS. The *International Association of Computer Investigative Specialists* (IACIS) offers the *Computer Forensic Computer Examiner* (CFCE) credential to law enforcement and private industry personnel alike. Candidates must have broad knowledge, training, or experience in computer forensics, including forensic procedures and standards, as well as ethical, legal, and privacy issues. Certification requires an intensive peer review, hands-on performance-based testing, as well as a written exam.[68]

A feature of this certification program is its *peer review phase* which must be completed successfully before the candidates can attempt the *Certification phase*:

> The CFCE Program is a two-part process, consisting of a "Peer Review" phase and a "Certification" phase.... Upon entry, each candidate is assigned a "coach" who mentors the candidate through a series of practical exercises (also known as problems) which are based on the CFCE core competencies. Candidates are required to successfully complete the entire peer review phase in order to qualify for the CFCE Certification phase. Candidates who fail the peer review process, or otherwise fail to meet deadlines and other requirements, will not qualify for entry into the CFCE Certification phase.
>
> ...The CFCE Certification phase is an independent exercise and not led by a coach. During this phase the candidate is required to demonstrate their knowledge of the CFCE core competencies and practical skills by successfully completing the practical and written examination instruments. Once entry has been approved, the candidate is provided with a forensic image of some type of electronic media (typically a hard disk device) and a practical written examination based on the image (or other media). The candidate must successfully pass the practical examination to qualify for the final examination. Once the candidate has successfully completed the practical examination, they are provided with the final examination. The final examination is a comprehensive written examination consisting of one hundred (100) questions. The questions are based on the CFCE core competencies and deal with a variety of fundamental computer forensic/digital evidence issues.[98]

74.3.12 IIA. The *Institute of Internal Auditors* (IIA) membership (180,000 members worldwide as of August 2013) includes experts "in internal auditing, risk management, governance, internal control, information technology audit, education, and security."

Among the five certifications offered by the IIA is the *Certification in Risk Management Assurance* (CRMA), which began testing in July 2013. The IIA describes the program as follows:

> The CRMA is designed for internal auditors and risk-management professionals with responsibility for and experience in providing risk assurance, governance processes, quality assurance, or control self-assessment (CSA). It demonstrates an individual's ability to evaluate the dynamic components that comprise an organization's governance and enterprise risk-management program and provide advice and assurance around these issues.
>
> The CRMA is one more mark of professional distinction for internal audit practitioners. Earning the CRMA will assist you in demonstrating your ability to:
>
> - Provide assurance on core business processes in risk management and governance.
> - Educate management and the audit committee on risk and risk-management concepts.
> - Focus on strategic organizational risks.
> - Add value for your organization.[99]

74.3.13 ISACA. The nonprofit *ISACA* (formerly known as the *Information Systems Audit and Control Association*)[100] manages several respected certifications. Those marked with an asterisk are ANSI-accredited.

- *Certified in the Governance of Enterprise:* The CGEIT* reflects successful candidates' "knowledge and application of enterprise IT governance principles and practices."[101] ISACA adds that recent studies "ranked CGEIT among the most sought-after and highest-paying IT certifications."[102]
- *Certified Information Systems Auditor:* "The CISA* designation is a globally recognized certification for IS audit control, assurance, and security professionals.

Being CISA-certified showcases your audit experience, skills and knowledge, and demonstrates you are capable to manage vulnerabilities, ensure compliance, and institute controls within the enterprise."[103]

- *Certified Information Security Manager:* "The ... CISM* certification promotes international security practices and recognizes the individual who manages designs, and oversees and assesses an enterprise's information security."[104]
- *Certified in Risk and Information Systems Control* (CRISC) was awarded the Best Professional Certification Award from *SC Magazine* in February 2013.[105] "CRISC ... is the only certification that positions IT professionals for future career growth by linking IT risk management to enterprise risk management, and positioning them to become strategic partners to the business."[101]

74.3.14 (ISC)². The nonprofit *International Information Systems Security Certification Consortium* (ISC)² is a nonprofit professional organization[106] providing "vendor-neutral education products, career services, and Gold Standard credentials to professionals in more than 135 countries." As of August 2013, there were 90,000 professionals worldwide certified by (ISC)². The organization offers a range of certifications that are accredited under ANSI/ISO/IEC Standard 17024.[107]

The certifications are based on elements of the *Common Body of Knowledge* (CBK) defined by (ISC)². Each certification uses a subset of the CBK, which is kept updated yearly by expert committees to adapt to changing environments. The CBK domains are

- Access Control Systems and Methodology
- Application Development Security
- Business Continuity and Disaster Recovery Planning
- Certification and Accreditation (C&A)
- Communications and Network Security
- Cryptography
- Information Security Governance and Risk Management
- Initiate the Preparation Phase
- Law, Investigation, Forensics, and Ethics
- Legal, Regulations, Investigations, and Compliance
- Malicious Code and Activity
- Monitoring and Analysis
- Networks and Communications
- Operations Security
- Perform Execution Phase
- Perform Maintenance Phase
- Physical (Environmental) Security
- Recovery Planning (DRP)
- Risk, Response and Recovery
- Secure Software Concepts
- Secure Software Design

- Secure Software Implementation/Coding
- Secure Software Requirements
- Secure Software Testing
- Security Architecture Analysis
- Security Architecture and Design
- Security Compliance Management
- Security Management Practices
- Security Operations and Administration
- Software Acceptance
- Software Deployment, Operations, Maintenance, and Disposal
- Systems Development Security
- Systems Security Engineering
- Technical Management
- Technology Related Business Continuity Planning (BCP) and Disaster
- Telecommunications and Network Security
- U.S. Government Information Assurance (IA) Governance
- Understand Business Continuity Planning (BCP) and Disaster Recovery Planning (DRP)
- Understand the Purpose of Security Authorization[108]

The certifications offered by (ISC)^2 are as follows and generally require a minimum of three years of field experience in information-security–related jobs. The certifications marked by the asterisk (*) are ANSI-accredited.[109]

- Certified Authorization Professional (CAP*)[110]
- Certified Cyber Forensic Professional (CCFPSM)[111]
- Certified Information Systems Security Professional (CISSP*)[112]
- Certified Secure Software Lifecycle Professional (CSSLP*)[113]
- HealthCare Information Security and Privacy Practitioner Information Security and Privacy Practitioner (HCISPP): available November 2013[114]
- Systems Security Certified Practitioner (SSCP*): requires only one year of professional experience in a security-related job[115]

In addition, there are three additional certifications for holders of the CISSP:

- Information Systems Security Architecture Professional (ISSAP*)[116]
- Information Systems Security Engineering Professional (ISSEP*)[117]
- Information Systems Security Management Professional (ISSMP)*[118]

All (ISC)^2 certifications require Continuing Professional Education (CPE) credits:

> Credential holders must earn the minimum number of Continuing Professional Education credits (CPEs) annually during each year of the three-year certification cycle. Although members may earn more than the minimum number of CPE credits required for credential maintenance

for the three-year cycle, they are still required to earn and submit the minimum annual number to maintain their certification in "good standing."[119]

CPEs fall into several categories and each certification has different requirements.[120]

Finally, (ISC)^2 offers a program for students and other newcomers to the IA field to benefit from membership in and resources of the association. Such candidates can be certified as *Associate of (ISC)^2* for the CAP, CCFP, CISSP, CSSLP, or SSCP certifications by passing the appropriate exam, paying a modest fee, and accumulating the appropriate number of CPE credits. After the requisite number of years of experience have been accumulated, the *Associate* status is converted to full certification.[121]

74.3.15 mile2. The for-profit mile2 training firm offers a "...worldwide network of Authorized Training Partners provides Cybersecurity training and consulting services that meet military, government and corporate specifications." Certifications listed on their home page include:

- C)DFE Certified Digital Forensics Examiner
- C)DRE Certified Disaster Recovery Engineer
- C)IHE Certified Incident Handling Engineer
- C)ISSO Certified Information Systems Security Officer
- C)NFE Certified Network Forensics Examiner
- C)PTC Certified Penetration Testing Consultant
- C)PTE Certified Penetration Testing Engineer
- C)SLE Certified Secure Linux Engineer
- C)SLO Certified Security Leadership Officer
- C)SS Certified Security Sentinel
- C)SWAE Certified Secure Web Applications Engineer
- C)VA Certified Vulnerability Assessor
- C)WSE Certified Wireless Security Engineer
- IS20 Security Controls
- ISCAP Information Systems Certification and Accreditation Professional[122]

74.3.16 Security University. The for-profit *Security University* (SU) was established in 1999 and offers several security certifications and a wide range of classes, most of which involve hands-on training.

Security University is accredited by ACCET, the *Accrediting Council for Continuing Education and Training*; ACCET is listed by the U.S. Department of Education as a nationally recognized accrediting agency and is a recognized member of the *Council for Higher Education Accreditation.* Security University is an institute of higher education in the State of Virginia certified to operate by the *State Council of Higher Education for Virginia.* SU classes and certifications are GI Bill Approved. The National Security Agency has authorized Security University to award the *CNSS National Standard 4011, 4012, 4013, 4015*, and *4016E, I* and *A* certifications.

- *Q/ISP Qualified/ Information Security Professional:* complies with CNSS 4011/ 4102/4013/4015/4016A standards. Requires demonstration of both knowledge and proficiency in information security, including hands-on skills. Maintenance of the certification requires "participation in research or study, attendance at recognized subject-matter training and professional educational programs, presentation or publication of information security papers, contributions to the information security Q/ISP Body of Knowledge, or service in professional organizations."[123]

- *Q/IAP Qualified/ Information Assurance Professional:* for IT security professionals, system administrators, auditors, CISOs, and others "looking to build tactical security skills and improve their career and income."[124] This certification requires successful completion of three SU courses:
  - Qualified Access, Authentication & PKI Professional (a hands-on course)
  - Qualified Security Policy Admin & (SOA) Security Oriented Architect
  - Qualified Security Certification and Accreditation Process
- *Q/SSE Qualified/Software Security Expert:* This certificate is for everyone concerned with securing program code[125]
- *Q/WNP™ Wireless Certifications:* "The CWTS certification is the entry-level wireless certification for the IT industry designed for WLAN sales and technical support professionals. This certification will get you started in your IT career by ensuring you have a solid base of applicable knowledge of: fundamentals of RF behavior, can describe the features and functions of wireless components, and have the skills needed to install and configure wireless network hardware components."[126]

Security University has a complete list of its 60 courses (most of them 40 hours or more) available in its online catalog, with details available for every course.[127]

74.4 PREPARING FOR SECURITY-CERTIFICATION EXAMS.

The key to passing the security-certification exams is daily attention to expanding one's exposure to interesting and thought-provoking information and ideas in the field. Cramming does not work; it is not possible to remember what is learned in a rush for very long. Indeed, all students should learn to use SQ3R (survey/question, read/recite, review) a well-established study method that pays off with long-term integration and retention of knowledge.

Even when participating in serious, extended courses lasting many days, participants should review constantly and challenge themselves with questions about concepts, terminology, and subtleties. If the course material or the instructor's comments don't make sense on a particular point, the student must not let the mystery pass, but should question authority if necessary to ensure that every point is understood and integrated into a coherent picture of the issues. Students can also look online for recorded lectures[128] and slide presentations from academic or professional meetings and courses.[129]

Granted, some test takers may enroll in short courses (boot camps) devoted to preparing for specific certifications, but without long-term commitment to professionalism, such efforts result in a certificate that raises eyebrows among employers and clients when the crammer fails to display an ingrained understanding of soon-forgotten concepts and terminology.

Anyone committed to professionalism and long-term success in a field should read a wide range of reputable publications and participate in serious discussion groups where participants exchange real-world experiences and analysis.

74.5 CONCLUDING REMARKS.

This chapter cannot provide an exhaustive listing of training and certification resources. Practitioners should monitor the trade press for indications of trends in acceptance of new certifications and should judge how to keep themselves at the forefront of the field through continued professional development. In addition, professionals may find it satisfying, personally educational, and even moderately lucrative to involve themselves in training and certification as teachers and proctors.

74.6 FURTHER READING

@RISK: The Consensus Security Vulnerability Alert: www.sans.org/newsletters/risk

Armstrong, I., ed. *SC Magazine.* www.scmagazine.com/#

Bunting, S. *EnCase Computer Forensics—The Official EnCE: EnCase Certified Examiner Study Guide*, 3rd ed. Sybex, 2012.

Chapple, M. *The GSEC Prep Guide: Mastering SANS GIAC Security Essentials.* Wiley, 2003.

Computer Security Portal from the National Institute of Standards and Technology Information Technology Laboratory Computer Security Division's Computer Security Resource Center: www.nist.gov/computer-security-portal.cfm

Computerworld Newsletters: www.computerworld.com/s/newsletters

Conrad, E., S. Misenar, and J. Feldman. *CISSP Study Guide*, 2nd ed. Syngress, 2012.

Conrad, E., S. Misenar, and J. Feldman. *Eleventh Hour CISSP Study Guide*, 2nd ed. Syngress, 2013.

CRYPTO-GRAM from Bruce Schneier: www.schneier.com/crypto-gram.html

Daily Open Source Infrastructure Report: https://www.dhs.gov/dhs-daily-open-source-infrastructure-report

Docter, Q., E. Dulaney, and T. Skandier. *CompTIA A+ Complete Deluxe Study Guide Recommended Courseware: Exams 220-801 and 220-802*, 2nd ed. Sybex, 2012.

Docter, Q., E. Dulaney, and T. Skandier. *CompTIA A+ Complete Study Guide Authorized Courseware: Exams 220-801 and 220-802* 2nd ed. Sybex, 2012.

EFFector from the Electronic Frontier Foundation: www.eff.org/effector

EPIC Alert from the Electronic Privacy Information Center: www.epic.org/alert

Harris, S. *CISSP All-in-One Exam Guide*, 6th ed. McGraw-Hill Osborne Media, 2012.

Harris, S. *CISSP Boxed Set*, 2nd ed. (All-in-One). McGraw-Hill Osborne Media, 2012.

Hernandez, S., ed. *Official (ISC)^2 Guide to the CISSP CBK,* 3rd ed. Auerbach, 2012.

Information Systems Security Association. *The ISSA Journal.* www.issa.org/?page=ISSAJournal

ITL Security Bulletins from the National Institute of Standards and Technology Information Technology Laboratory Computer Security Division's Computer Security Resource Center http://csrc.nist.gov/publications/PubsITLSB.html

Krutz, R. L., and A. J. Fry. *The CSSLP Prep Guide: Mastering the Certified Secure Software Lifecycle Professional.* Wiley, 2009.

Lammle, T. *CompTIA Network+ Study Guide Authorized Courseware: Exam N10-005*, 2nd ed. Sybex, 2012.

Miller, L., and P. H. Gregory. *CISSP for Dummies*, 4th ed. For Dummies, 2012.

Network World Security Research Center: www.networkworld.com/topics/security.html

RISKS FORUM DIGEST from the Association for Computing Machinery Committee on Computers and Public Policy: http://catless.ncl.ac.uk/Risks

SANS newsletters: www.sans.org/newsletters

Special Publications (800 Series) from the National Institute of Standards and Technology Information Technology Laboratory Computer Security Division's Computer Security Resource Center: http://csrc.nist.gov/publications/PubsSPs.html

Stewart, J. M., M. Chapple, and D. Gibson. *CISSP: Certified Information Systems Security Professional Study Guide*, 6th ed. Sybex, 2012.

Walker, M. *CEH Certified Ethical Hacker Boxed Set* (All-in-One). McGraw-Hill Osborne Media, 2013.

74.7 NOTES

1. DHS Press Release, "Secretary Napolitano Announces New Hiring Authority for Cybersecurity Experts," October 1, 2009, www.dhs.gov/news/2009/10/01/secretary-napolitano-announces-new-hiring-authority-cybersecurity-experts
2. National Security Council, "Cybersecurity," May 29, 2009, www.whitehouse.gov/administration/eop/nsc/cybersecurity (URL inactive).
3. E. Engleman, K. Riddel, A. Holmes, and Raytheon, "SAIC Vie with U.S. in 'Fratricide' Over Cyberworkers." *Bloomberg News*, March 29, 2011 (reference #13 in original document), www.bgov.com/news_item/HMRFKLKr4Dj_sBtkxFos-Q (URL inactive) (registration required).
4. Homeland Security Advisory Council, "CyberSkills Task Force Report, Fall 2012," www.dhs.gov/sites/default/files/publications/HSAC%20CyberSkills%20Report%20-%20Final.pdf
5. B. Ballenstedt, "Eleven Tips for Building a Stronger Cybersecurity Workforce," *Nextgov Wired Workplace*, October 3, 2012, www.nextgov.com/cio-briefing/wired-workplace/2012/10/eleven-tips-building-stronger-cybersecurity-workforce/58564/
6. *Microsoft Encarta 2008*. © 1993–2007 Microsoft Corporation.
7. J. Walsh, "6 Essential Skills for Cyber Security Professionals," AE ashley ellis, August 2, 2013, www.ashleyellis.com/2013/08/6-essential-skills-for-cyber-security-professionals
8. A one-page summary of the useful Survey-Question-Read-Recite-Review (SQ3R) technique is available from one of the authors: www.mekabay.com/methodology/sq3r.pdf
9. A behaviorally defined learning objective is something that can be observed or measured; for example, "understanding firewall configuration parameters" is not a behavioral objective, whereas "configuring firewalls to meet defined goals" is a behavioral objective.
10. I. Armstrong, "Money Matters: SC Magazine/EC-Council Salary Survey 2007," *SC Magazine*, April 1, 2007, www.scmagazineus.com/Money-matters-SC-MagazineEC-Council-Salary-Survey-2007/article/34874/
11. M. Savage, "Get Qualified: Certification—That's the Name of the Game," *SC Magazine*, November 1, 2003, http://scmagazine.com/asia/news/article/419631/get-qualified-certification-thats-name-game (URL inactive).
12. A. Saita, "The CISSP Receives International Standardization," *SearchSecurity.com*, June 23, 2004, http://searchsecurity.techtarget.com/original-Content/0,289142,sid14_gci989901,00.html (URL inactive).
13. $(ISC)^2$, "DoD Fact Sheet," 2007, https://www.isc2.org/dod-fact-sheet.aspx?terms=DoD%20Fact%20Sheet%2c%202007

14. C. Hildebrand, "Forecast 2008: Information Security Goes Strategic," *InfoSecurity Professional* (Spring 2008): 4–7, www.isc2.org/uploadedFiles/(ISC)2_Member_Content/Member_Resources/infosecuritypro2008spring(1).pdf
15. L. G. Paul, "How Valuable Are Security Certifications Today?" *CSO Security Leadership*, April 1, 2003, www.csoonline.com/article/731010/how-valuable-are-security-certifications-today-
16. *2011 (ISC)2 Global Information Security Workforce Study* p 22. https://www.isc2.org/uploadedFiles/Industry_Resources/FS_WP_ISC%20Study_020811_MLW_Web.pdf
17. *2011 (ISC)2 Global Information Security Workforce Study*, p. 23.
18. *2011 (ISC)2 Global Information Security Workforce Study*, Fig. 27.
19. *2013 (ISC)2 Global Information Security Workforce Study* p 14. https://www.isc2.org/uploadedFiles/(ISC)2_Public_Content/2013%20Global%20Information%20Security%20Workforce%20Study%20Feb%202013.pdf
20. M. Suby. Personal communication, August 16, 2013.
21. "Accreditation Program for Personnel Certification Bodies under ANSI/ISO/IEC 17024," ANSI Website, https://www.ansica.org/wwwversion2/outside/PERgeneral.asp; see also E. Gasiorowski-Denis, "New and Improved ISO/IEC 17024 Standard for Personnel Certification Programmes," ISO Website, July 24,2012, www.iso.org/iso/home/news_index/news_archive/news.htm?refid=Ref1625
22. "ISO/IEC 17011:2004 Conformity Assessment—General Requirements for Accreditation Bodies Accrediting Conformity Assessment Bodies," ISO Website, Standard reviewed and confirmed in 2008, www.iso.org/iso/catalogue_detail?csnumber=29332
23. Institute for Credentialing Excellence, www.credentialingexcellence.org
24. NCCA Accreditation, www.credentialingexcellence.org/ncca
25. American Board for Certification in Homeland Security, www.abchs.com
26. American Health Information Management Association, www.ahima.org
27. Defense Security Service, www.cdse.edu/about.html
28. CNSS, "CNSS History," https://www.cnss.gov/history.html
29. CNSS,"Frequently Asked Questions | What are National Security Systems?" https://www.cnss.gov/faq.html
30. CNSS, CNSSI 4009, "National Information Assurance Glossary," CNSS Instruction No. 4009 (2010-04-26), https://www.cnss.gov/Assets/pdf/cnssi_4009.pdf
31. CNSS, "Unclassified Index," https://www.cnss.gov/full-index.html
32. NSTISSI 4011, https://www.cnss.gov/Assets/pdf/nstissi_4011.pdf
33. CNSSI 4012, https://www.cnss.gov/Assets/pdf/cnssi_4012.pdf
34. CNSSI 4013, https://www.cnss.gov/Assets/pdf/cnssi_4013.pdf
35. CNSSI 4014, https://www.cnss.gov/Assets/pdf/cnssi_4014.pdf
36. NSTISSI 4015, https://www.cnss.gov/Assets/pdf/nstissi_4015.pdf
37. CNSSI 4016, https://www.cnss.gov/Assets/pdf/CNSSI-4016.PDF
38. J. Vijayan, "Demand for IT Security Experts Outstrips Supply: Employers Will Pay More for Certified—and Experienced—IT Security Pros, Studies Find," *Computerworld*, March 7, 2013, www.computerworld.com/s/article/9237394/Demand_for_IT_security_experts_outstrips_supply

39. A particularly valuable publication that was immensely helpful in organizing the following information was written by Ed Tittel and Mary Lemons in May 2013. The authors express their gratitude to these colleagues. Reference: E. Tittel and M. Lemons, "SearchSecurity.com's IT Security Certifications Guide," *Search-Security,* May 2013, http://searchsecurity.techtarget.com/tip/SearchSecuritycom-guide-to-information-security-certifications
40. ACFE, "About the ACFE," www.acfe.com/about-the-acfe.aspx
41. ACFE, "2013/2014 Compensation Guide for Anti-Fraud Professionals." http://www.acfe.com/uploadedFiles/ACFE_Website/Content/documents/2013-comp-guide.pdf
42. ACFE, "The CFE Credential," www.acfe.com/cfe-credential.aspx
43. ANSI Accreditation Services: "ASIS International," https://www.ansica.org/wwwversion2/outside/ALLdirectoryDetails.asp?menuID=2&prgID=201&orgID=90&status=4
44. ASIS International, "About ASIS," https://www.asisonline.org/About-ASIS/Pages/default.aspx
45. ASIS International, "Certified Protection Professional," https://www.asisonline.org/Certification/Board-Certifications/CPP/Pages/default.aspx
46. ASIS International, "Professional Certified Investigator," https://www.asisonline.org/Certification/Board-Certifications/PCI/Pages/default.aspx
47. Brainbench Test Center, www.brainbench.com/xml/bb/common/testcenter/alltests.xml
48. G. Singh, "Boost Your Resume with Brainbench Certifications," *Examiner.com*, September 20, 2012, www.examiner.com/article/boost-your-resume-with-brainbench-certifications
49. Brainbench, "Computer Forensics (U.S.)," http://brainbench.com/xml/bb/common/testcenter/consumer/taketest.xml?testId=2516
50. Brainbench, "Firewall Administration Concepts," http://brainbench.com/xml/bb/common/testcenter/consumer/taketest.xml?testId=2581
51. Brainbench, "HIPAA (Privacy)," http://brainbench.com/xml/bb/common/testcenter/consumer/taketest.xml?testId=1489
52. Brainbench, "HIPAA (Security)," http://brainbench.com/xml/bb/common/testcenter/consumer/taketest.xml?testId=1143
53. Brainbench, "Information Technology Security Fundamentals," http://brainbench.com/xml/bb/common/testcenter/consumer/taketest.xml?testId=1542
54. Brainbench, "Internet Security," http://brainbench.com/xml/bb/common/testcenter/consumer/taketest.xml?testId=110
55. Brainbench, "ITAA Information Security Awareness," http://brainbench.com/xml/bb/common/testcenter/consumer/taketest.xml?testId=1349
56. Brainbench, "Microsoft Security," http://brainbench.com/xml/bb/common/testcenter/consumer/taketest.xml?testId=2723
57. Brainbench, "Network Authentication," http://brainbench.com/xml/bb/common/testcenter/consumer/taketest.xml?testId=2636
58. Brainbench, "Network Monitoring," http://brainbench.com/xml/bb/common/testcenter/consumer/taketest.xml?testId=424
59. Brainbench, "Network Security," http://brainbench.com/xml/bb/common/testcenter/consumer/taketest.xml?testId=30

60. CyberSecurity Institute, www.csisite.net
61. CyberSecurity Institute, "Digital Forensic Examiner," www.csisite.net/training/core.htm
62. CyberSecurity Institute, "Computer Forensics for Attorneys," www.csisite.net/training/attorneys.htm
63. CyberSecurity Institute, "Packet Analysis and Intrusion Detection," www.csisite.net/training/packetanalysis.htm
64. CyberSecurity Institute, "Computer Forensics Fundamentals," www.csisite.net/training/computerforensicsfundamentals.htm
65. CyberSecurity Institute, "Windows Forensics Essentials," www.csisite.net/ training/wfe.htm
66. CyberSecurity Institute, "CSFA," www.cybersecurityforensicanalyst.com
67. AccessData, www.accessdata.com/training/certifications
68. International Association of Computer Investigative Specialists (IACIS), https://www.iacis.com/certification
69. International Society of Forensic Computer Examiners (ISFCE), https://www.isfce.com/certification.htm
70. EC-Council, www.eccouncil.org/certification/computer-hacking-forensics-investigator
71. Guidance Software, www.guidancesoftware.com/computer-forensics-training-ence-certification.htm
72. Global Information Assurance Certification (SANS Institute), www.giac.org/certification/certified-forensic-analyst-gcfa
73. CyberSecurity Institue, "FBI Background Check," www.cybersecurityforensicanalyst.com/background.htm
74. Software Engineering Institute, www.sei.cmu.edu
75. CERT® Coordination Center (CERT/CC), www.cert.org/certcc.html
76. Software Engineering Institute, "CERT-Certified Computer Security Incident Handler," www.sei.cmu.edu/certification/security/csih
77. CompTIA, "About CompTIA," www.comptia.org/aboutus.aspx
78. CompTIA, "CompTIA Certifications," http://certification.comptia.org/getCertified/certifications.aspx
79. CompTIA, "CompTIA Advanced Security Practitioner," http://certification.comptia.org/getCertified/certifications/casp.aspx
80. CompTIA, "CompTIA Cloud+," http://certification.comptia.org/getCertified/certifications/cloudplus.aspx
81. CompTIA, "CompTIA Mobile App Security+," http://certification.comptia.org/getCertified/certifications/mobile_app_security.aspx
82. CompTIA, "CompTIA Security+," http://certification.comptia.org/getCertified/certifications/security.aspx
83. CompTIA, "Social Media Security Professional," http://certification.comptia.org/getCertified/certifications/smsp.aspx
84. ANSI Accreditation Services, "CompTIA," https://www.ansica.org/wwwversion2/outside/ALLdirectoryDetails.asp?menuID=2&prgID=201&orgID=93&status=4

85. EC-Council, "About EC-Council," www.eccouncil.org/about-us
86. EC-Council, "Certification," www.eccouncil.org/Certification
87. ANSI Accreditation Services, "International Council of E-Commerce Consultants (EC-Council)," https://www.ansica.org/wwwversion2/outside/ALLdirectoryDetails.asp?menuID=2&prgID=201&orgID=211&status=4
88. CWNP, "About CWNP," www.cwnp.com/about
89. CWNP, "About CWSP," www.cwnp.com/certifications/cwsp
90. SANS, "Certification," www.sans.org/help/site-network
91. GIAC, "Global Information Assurance Certification," www.giac.org
92. Jeff Pike, "GIAC: The Hands-On IT Security Certification," *Certification Magazine*, n.d., www.certmag.com/read.php?start=0&in=3469
93. GIAC, "Certifications: Gold Overview," www.giac.org/certifications/gold
94. ANSI Accreditation Services, "Global Information Assurance Certification (GIAC)," https://www.ansica.org/wwwversion2/outside/ALLdirectoryDetails.asp?menuID=2&prgID=201&orgID=98&status=4
95. GIAC, "GIAC Security Expert (GSE) Overview," www.giac.org/certification/security-expert-gse
96. HTCN, "History," www.htcn.org
97. HTCN, "Certification Requirements," www.htcn.org/cert.htm#
98. IACIS, "Overview of the CFCE Program," https://www.iacis.com/certification/external_overview
99. IIA, "Certification in Risk Management Assurance," https://na.theiia.org/certification/CRMA-Certification/Pages/CRMA-Certification.aspx
100. ISACA, "History of ISACA," www.isaca.org/About-ISACA/History/Pages/default.aspx
101. ISACA, "ISACA Certification: IT Audit, Security, Governance and Risk," www.isaca.org/CERTIFICATION/Pages/default.aspx
102. ISACA, "Foote Partners Report: ISACA Certifications Earn Top Pay Premiums," Press Release, September 8, 2011, www.isaca.org/About-ISACA/Press-room/News-Releases/2011/Pages/Foote-Partners-Report-ISACA-Certifications-Earn-Top-Pay-Premiums.aspx
103. ISACA, "Certified Information Systems Auditor (CISA)," www.isaca.org/Certification/CISA-Certified-Information-Systems-Auditor/Pages/default.aspx
104. ISACA, "Certified Information Security Manager," www.isaca.org/Certification/CISM-Certified-Information-Security-Manager/Pages/default.aspx
105. ISACA, "ISACA's CRISC Certification Wins Best Professional Certification Award from SC Magazine," Press Release, February 27, 2013, www.isaca.org/About-ISACA/Press-room/News-Releases/2013/Pages/ISACA-CRISC-Certification-Wins-Best-Professional-Certification-Award.aspx
106. The acronym is a geek joke: The original acronym was IISSCC which someone collapsed into the algebraic equivalent $(ISC)^2$ shortly after the organization was founded in1989.
107. $(ISC)^2$. "About $(ISC)^2$," https://www.isc2.org/aboutus/default.aspx
108. $(ISC)^2$. "The Compendium of Information Security Topics," https://www.isc2.org/uploadedFiles/Education/Review_Seminars/CBK.pdf

109. ANSI Accreditation Services, "International Information Systems Security Certification Consortium, Inc. (ISC)^2," https://www.ansica.org/wwwversion2/outside/ALLdirectoryDetails.asp?menuID=2&prgID=201&orgID=97&status=4
110. (ISC)^2, "CAP," https://www.isc2.org/cap/default.aspx
111. (ISC)^2, "CCFP," https://www.isc2.org/ccfp/default.aspx
112. (ISC)^2, "CISSP," https://www.isc2.org/cissp/default.aspx
113. (ISC)^2, "CSSLP," https://www.isc2.org/csslp/default.aspx
114. (ISC)^2, "HCISPP," https://www.isc2.org/hcispp/default.aspx
115. (ISC)^2, "SSCP," https://www.isc2.org/sscp/default.aspx
116. (ISC)^2, "About ISSAP," https://www.isc2.org/issap.aspx
117. (ISC)^2, "About ISSEP," https://www.isc2.org/issep.aspx
118. (ISC)^2, "About ISSMP," https://www.isc2.org/issmp/default.aspx
119. (ISC)^2, "Maintaining Your Credential," https://www.isc2.org/maintaining-your-credential.aspx
120. (ISC)^2, "Continuing Professional Education," https://www.isc2.org/uploadedFiles/Credentials_and_Certifcation/About_Our_Credentials_and_Process/CPE.pdf (URL inactive).
121. (ISC)^2,"Associate of (ISC)^2," https://www.isc2.org/associates/default.aspx
122. mile2 home page, http://mile2.com
123. Security University, "What is a Q/ISP 'Qualified' Information Security Professional?" www.securityuniversity.net/QISP.php
124. Security University, "What is a Q/IAP 'Qualified" Information Assurance Professional?" www.securityuniversity.net/QIAP.php
125. Security University, "Q/SSE Qualified/ Software Security Expert Certification," www.securityuniversity.net/QSSE.php
126. Security University, "CWTS Wireless LAN Technology," www.securityuniversity.net/classes_wireless_cert.php
127. Security University, "Roadmap," www.securityuniversity.net/classes.php
128. A useful tool when searching YouTube for lectures on specific topics is to append ", long" to the search string. For example, searching for "authentication" on YouTube in August 2013 resulted in 87,400 hits, but "authentication, long" resulted in 4,230 results, most of which were 20 minutes or longer.
129. See, for example, Professor Kabay's freely available course materials, www.mekabay.com/courses/index.htm

CHAPTER 75

THE FUTURE OF INFORMATION ASSURANCE

Jeremy A. Hansen

75.1 INTRODUCTION. As previous installments of this final chapter have done in other editions of this *Handbook*, I take a moment to tip my hat to the authors of the previous chapters for their informative coverage of topics in information assurance (IA). This chapter will be much less precise than earlier chapters for reasons that will become obvious, but hopefully no less informative.

In a departure from the typical academic style that I am comfortable with, I hope to dabble a bit in the dangerous game of predicting the future. I'll also make this a highly personal work and will address the reader directly.

Attempts to predict the future tend to extrapolate a spectrum of outcomes that we, residents of the present, should look out for. Others try to be more specific and try to lead the target and guess a single plausible outcome, like a hunter taking a careful shot at a running deer. I intend to find a middle ground here by considering specific possible outcomes, but select them in a spectrum narrow enough to group them together in a loosely logical whole.

75.2 COMPLEXITY. It is important to distinguish here between the real world and the constrained world of information assurance (IA) that appears in many academic sources, popular security sites, and best practices. Like many scientific treatments, the constrained world in its many forms requires us to make certain assumptions for certain conclusions to be true. If the compression function of a cryptographic hash algorithm acts like a random oracle, then we can conclude that some specified construction is secure. This is useful! The trouble with systems with constraints and assumptions is that they are often pressed into service as subsystems of a larger solution. Even then, they can be useful, but may now be working in applications where their constraints are violated and their assumptions no longer hold. The more complex the systems become, the more buried the subsystems become. At a certain point of high complexity, the number of vulnerabilities of a system becomes greater than the sum of the vulnerabilities of its parts.

We live in a complex civilization, with increasingly complex interconnections between the different moving parts: government, industry, utilities, technological advances, culture, and so on. The cultural, physical, and electronic infrastructure required to maintain what we have is immense.

Here is a thought exercise: look to your left and pick out something you see. Consider its component parts and the process required to construct it. Now pick any one of those component parts or one of the technologies used in its construction. Consider its component parts and the process required to construct it. Do this recursively until you get bored or happen upon some primitive component.

Consider how many of the processes and technologies that you identified in that technological family tree that we no longer have access to. Our modern technologies are being built on an increasingly narrow set of parent technologies, the loss of which could shake the supply chain of the descendant technologies.

Now we circle back to IA. The information systems that we have constructed are brittle and porous, no matter how many layers of steel we bolt on or how many fingers we hire to press in the holes of the dam. It is not possible to secure perfectly all the various component parts of the systems we rely on. We spend an awful lot of money doing this, and spending money protecting our systems with brittle and porous countermeasures will continue to be necessary (but not sufficient) for the foreseeable future.

And that is OK.

It is OK because you are already compromised, or will be shortly. Perhaps not in a big way, perhaps not in a detectable way, it has happened or it will happen. I am asking you for a moment to take a deep breath and let the waves of terror at the thought of this drift away. I am asking you to sit up straighter, take another breath, and change your mental posture when it comes to information assurance. Accept that you have been or will be compromised.

Changing one's (or one's organization's) security posture will likely be awkward and greeted with suspicion. Embracing the possibility (indeed, the likelihood) of failure can be perceived as cowardly. However unpalatable the idea of compromise, not having a post-compromise plan of action is the sort of irresponsibility that can sink an organization. On a personal level, if you have a lot of assets, it makes sense to have a will! This change in posture is also not likely to please developers of security software and devices—silver-bullet security promises move much more product and result in more subscribers per month than the compromise-anticipating approach.

Please do not misunderstand—you should not run out and turn off all your antivirus software to free up the processor cycles. As a matter of fact, your antivirus software is a sensible place to start, since its quarantine offers an easily understood approach to accepting compromise that I'll explore shortly.

75.3 CHANGING POSTURE. An attacker usually must expend fewer resources to compromise a target than a defender must expend defending that target. Realizing this cost asymmetry must force us to reconsider our approach to protecting information. Like previous attempts at handling asymmetric threats, we should not expect our approach to be successful all of the time. Nor should we expect that simply spending more money will necessarily lead to better results.

Your organization does not and cannot spend enough money on information security. Some managers, directors, and C-level executives realize this and are satisfied with *good enough* (not that they would probably say so), but are often aggressively confronted by employees and vendors with horror stories and dire warnings. You might know this as fear, uncertainty, and doubt, or FUD, and most would agree that though it can be effective, it is inappropriate and can distract from proper allocation of resources. Because resources are limited (and in spite of the cloud of FUD), one basic question needs to be answered to evaluate your current and future security postures: *What is your information security team's job?*

What is it now and what should it be? Is it to prevent all threats, external and internal (or foreign and domestic, if you prefer)? Is it to ensure that PCI, HIPAA, or whatever regulatory compliance checklist applies to you stays completely checked? Is it to avoid a public breach?[1]

75.3.1 Quarantine, DMZ, and Honeycombs. You don't get a towel-wrapped bottle of champagne, party favors, and an oversized check that says "Congratulations! You're compromised!" Almost everyone can agree that a compromise is a demoralizing event, usually resulting in a period of uncertainty and a raft of questions: Why didn't our PCI auditor point this out? Why did our Senior Technical Analyst put that USB drive into his system while he was running the weekly batch job? Where else did the bad actors go on the network?

Answers to the first two questions are not particularly helpful. The last question is often the most troubling and long-lasting. It is also a question you should spend some resources answering with a proper post-mortem. Once you have the answer (as little consolation as it might be), consider what you could have done to (a) make the post-mortem easier and (b) how you could have more effectively restricted the movements of the intruder.

Making the post-mortem easier requires good data-collection and analysis tools, which are available, but may not be accessible to organizations with small budgets. Much more interesting is how intruders can be confined to a small portion of the network, database, or application space without compromising usability by legitimate users. The demilitarized zone (DMZ) model, where Internet-facing servers are segregated from the internal network, is quite popular, but reinforces the *hard-crunchy-shell-with-a-soft-chewy-center* architecture. A better architecture would have pockets of chewy where access to related resources can be shared or simplified (using single sign on or the like), with crunchy boundaries between these pockets. I envision this as a honeycomb, with access compartmentalized inside each cell of the honeycomb, and each cell separated by rigid firewall rules or other access control. Compromising one of the cells, as damaging as that might be, would not lead to an organization-wide crisis. When compromise is detected, the affected cell may be quarantined from the rest of the network until a proper response can be mobilized.

A similar approach is used in companies that connect to the networks of partners via virtual private networks (VPNs). Legitimate bidirectional access is necessary, but restrictions on traffic entering the organization's network keep a partner's compromise from spilling over.

75.3.2 BYOD. Another effect of tightly segregated access is to mitigate the security concerns of a permissive Bring-Your-Own-Device (BYOD) policy. When a company supports BYOD, its information technology (IT) infrastructure is expected to allow, if not support, personally owned devices on the corporate network. Naturally, it gives security folks a headache. Taking BYOD to a logical (but conceivable) extreme, let's look at a somewhat ridiculous expectation for a network: BED, or Bring Every Device, where a network accepts and offers connectivity to every device requesting such access. Note that this is how many Internet service providers operate as impartial carriers of data.

BED means that devices known to be malicious will use the network. Trusted devices will use the network, too, and they might receive preferential access even before any user authentication takes place. In fact, separating device authentication from user authentication provides for access to legitimate users who may be using an untrusted personal device, and can restrict untrusted users who gain access to a trusted device.

Current network access control (NAC) techniques seem to be part of the solution, as they allow for authentication of devices and can properly isolate unauthenticated devices. The rest of the solution includes integrating NAC more tightly with LDAP or Kerberos in order to construct the requisite cells of the honeycomb architecture.

75.4 SOME SPECIFIC SLICES OF THE FUTURE.

With the *change your security posture* lecture over, I'd like to reflect on a few areas that I believe will become more important or change the way we think about assurance in the future:

- Quantum computing
- Healthcare
- Legal and jurisdictional issues
- Ubiquitous technologies

75.4.1 Quantum Computing.

This field is poorly understood by the majority of IT and security practitioners, and not well understood by most computer scientists. There is a good reason for this: It involves a physics and mathematics (primarily linear algebra) background to manage. Learning how these systems operate, much less how to secure them, will remain a formidable challenge should quantum computers see widespread deployment. I will provide an extremely brief overview here (paraphrased from Scott Aaronson's 2008 *Scientific American* article), but suggest Michael Nielsen's terrific video course[2] for those interested in more depth.

The basic idea of quantum computing is that subatomic particles relate to other particles in interesting and useful ways. If we have 1000 of these particles, they can be in a superposition that can represent 2^{1000} (about 10^{300} if you prefer that notation) different values—simultaneously.

I'll let Scott Aaronson take over:

> Then, by performing various operations on the particles and on some auxiliary ones—perhaps hitting them with a sequence of laser pulses or radio waves—we can carry out an algorithm that transforms all 10^{300} numbers (each one a potential solution) at the same time. If at the end of doing that we could read out the particles' final quantum state accurately, we really would have a magic computer: it would be able to check 10^{300} possible solutions to a problem, and at the end we could quickly discern the right one.[3]

There are catches. Among them, it is only possible to measure one of these solutions and there is no certainty that a computer operating on 1000 particles can even be built. Should these obstacles be overcome, one of the best-known security implications of such computers is that cryptographic algorithms that rely on factoring integers or calculating the discrete logarithm may be dramatically weakened. *Post-quantum cryptography* is a reasonably new[4] subfield of cryptography that investigates cryptographic systems that can remain strong even when attackers have quantum computers.

75.4.2 Healthcare. Consider healthcare security as broadly having two components:

1. Medical records and medical data security
2. Medical systems security

Though the Health Information Technology for Economic and Clinical Health (HITECH) Act and Health Insurance Portability and Accountability Act of 1996 (HIPAA) are not new or remotely futuristic, the implications of moving to an all-digital medical records system are. Medical records are inextricably linked to a single patient, so a disclosure of any sort can linger with that patient for the rest of his or her life. Chapter 71 in this *Handbook*, "Medical Records Security" covers this topic in much more detail.

The security of medical systems, on the other hand, is among the most interesting (to me) topics in the future of security. As computers become smaller and medical devices more sophisticated, digital logic will come to control, monitor, and interface with our bodies with increasing frequency. Exhibit 75.1 has a few examples of these devices and possible adverse events that may be caused by their failure or compromise. For example, at least one model of implantable cardioverter-defibrillators may be remotely reprogrammed or activated (!) with fairly inexpensive equipment.[5]

As computer systems that process data (often communicating this data wirelessly), these devices require traditional countermeasures to threats. The implications of compromise are much more severe than in other information systems, and may include the death of the patient. Consequently, controls that are strictly detective or respond after a compromise are less appropriate here.

Some interesting legal questions arise. Consider for a moment if an employee's implant required a reliable Wi-Fi connection to the Internet and a future interpretation of the United States' Americans With Disabilities Act required employers to provide such access as a reasonable accommodation. That could certainly force the affected organization toward support of a more broad BYOD policy. Consider now a different employee's *elective* implant, and whether that implant could be provided access, too.

The security lessons stretch beyond implantable medical devices (IMDs). Once surgically implanted, it may be infeasible, dangerous, or impossible to replace or remove an IMD. Consider the security posture required to deploy some nonimplanted IT system that might not be replaced or upgraded for five years (or ever[6]). I suspect that we can build effective systems with these constraints given that IT professionals have become used to supporting legacy systems for almost the entirety of the industry. When we assume that systems are legacy by design, can security, fault tolerance, and usability be maintained at a high level of service and performance? A redundant belt-and-suspenders approach may be more expensive initially, but the costs amortized over a very long life span can make sense.

75.4.3 Legal & Jurisdictional Issues. The law is not perfect, and neither are prescribed compliance requirements. While I do not intend to repeat material from

Exhibit 75.1 Potential Adverse Events in Various Implantable Medical Devices[a]

Device	Adverse Events
Pacemaker, implanted cardioverter defibrillator,[b] ventricular assist device[c]	Heart failure, tachycardia, bradycardia, arrhythmia[b and d]
Cochlear implant	Deafness, phantom sounds, distraction/confusion[e]
Prosthetic limb control system[f]	Injury, damage to prosthetic limb, inadvertent movement
Spinal cord stimulator[g]	Loss of pain relief, inappropriate stimulation
Sacral anterior root stimulator[h]	Infection from inability to void, inappropriate stimulation
Retinal prosthesis,[i] implanted contact lens, intraocular lens	Blindness, phantom images, distraction/confusion
Implanted infusion pump	Inappropriate dosage/timing
Brain-machine interface,[j] other neuroprosthesis[k]	Loss of consciousness, neural effects[l]
Responsive neurostimulator, other deep brain stimulator[m]	Inappropriate stimulation, failure to stimulate
Implanted monitor or sensor	Incorrect readings
Implanted radio frequency identification (RFID) tag[n]	Loss of privacy, data leakage
Implanted dynamic Light-Emitting Diode (LED) tattoo	Inappropriate display

[a] Jeremy A. Hansen and Nicole M. Hansen, "A Taxonomy of Vulnerabilities in Implantable Medical Devices," in *Proceedings of the Second Annual Workshop on Security and Privacy in Medical and Home-Care Systems* (SPIMACS '10) (New York: ACM, 2010): 13-20. DOI=10.1145/1866914.1866917

[b] M. Mirowski, M. M. Mower, W. S. Staewen, B. Tabatznik, and A. I. Mendeloff, "Standby Automatic Defibrillator: An Approach to Prevention of Sudden Coronary Death." *Arch Intern Med* 126, No. 1 (1970), 158–161.

[c] B. Glenville and D. Ross, "Ventricular Assist Devices," *British Medical Journal* 292 (February 1986): 361–362.

[d] S. Lee, K. Fu, T. Kohno, B. Ransford, and W. H. Maisel, Clinically Significant Magnetic Interference of Implanted Cardiac Devices by Portable Headphones," *Heart Rhythm* (October 2009).

[e] J. Robert, E. Morley, and E. J. Richter. Final Report on Measurements of Static Electricity Generated from Plastic Playground Slides, March 2006, www.access-board.gov/research/play-slides/report.htm (URL inactive).

[f] M. Velliste, S. Perel, M. C. Spalding, A. S. Whitford, and A. B. Schwartz, "Cortical Control of a Prosthetic Arm for Self-Feeding," *Nature* 453, No. 7198 (May 2008): 1098–1101.

[g] R. B. North, D. H. Kidd, M. Zahurak, C. S. Jones, and D. M. Long, Spinal Cord Stimulation for Chronic, Intractable Pain: Experience over Two Decades," *Neurosurgery* 32, No. 3 (1993):384–395.

[h] G. S. Brindley, C. E. Polkey, and D. Rushton. "Sacral Anterior Root Stimulators for Bladder Control in Paraplegia," *Paraplegia* 6, No. 20 (1982):365–381.

[i] A. Y. Chow, V. Y. Chow, K. H. Packo, J. S. Pollack, G. A. Peyman, and R. Schuchard, "The Artificial Silicon Retina Microchip for the Treatment of Vision Loss from Retinitis Pigmentosa," *Archives of Ophthalmology* 122, No. 4 (2004):460–469.

[j] G. Santhanam, S. I. Ryu, B. M. Yu, A. Afshar, and K. V. Shenoy, "A High-Performance Brain-Computer Interface," *Nature* 442, No. 7099 (2006):195–198.

[k] Dong Song, Rosa H. M. Chan, Vasilis Z. Marmarelis, Robert E. Hampson, Sam A. Deadwyler, Theodore W. Berger, "2009 Special Issue: Nonlinear Modeling of Neural Population Dynamics for Hippocampal Prostheses," *Neural Networks* 22, No. 9 (November 2009), 1340–1351.

[l] T. Denning, Y. Matsuoka, and T. Kohno. "Neurosecurity: Security and Privacy for Neural Devices," *Neurosurgical Focus* 27, No. 1 (July 2009).

[m] F. T. Sun, M. J. Morrell, and R. E. Wharen, "Responsive Cortical Stimulation for the Treatment of Epilepsy," *Neurotherapeutics* 5 (January 2008):68–74.

[n] J. Halamka, A. Juels, A. Stubblefield, and J. Westhues, The Security Implications of VeriChip Cloning," *Journal of the American Medical Informatics Association* 13, No. 6 (2006):601–607.

Chapter 64, "US Legal and Regulatory Security Issues," I do want to look toward some unresolved issues that will become more important. Even when laws are effective in achieving their stated goals, laws, like ethical guidelines for use, can rarely keep up with the breakneck pace of changes in technology. To choose a single example, emails older than 180 days on a service provider's server are considered abandoned by the Electronic Communications Privacy Act of 1986, which, despite multiple updates in the meantime, stands as current U.S. law at the time of this writing. Abandoned messages of this sort may be requested by any law enforcement agency without a warrant. This may have made sense in 1986, but with a significant portion of U.S. Internet users relying on Web- or cloud-based email, it no longer does.

Aside from the law's inability to keep up with technology, a few major issues come to mind:

- The increasing disconnect between policy makers and technology—policy makers are rarely knowledgeable enough to make decisions related to science and technology.
- Partly due to the previous point, and partly due to the increasing complexity of laws, rules, policies, and procedures, the increasing burden of regulatory compliance.
- Patchworks of changing state, national, and international laws can make compliance quite challenging, especially with the difficulty of pinning down data to a single location. Identical data on two different servers may fall into two jurisdictions, with different or conflicting regulations.
- The United States government's willingness to collect data on traffic (inadvertently or not) passing through its borders may violate privacy expectations of non-U.S. endpoints.

I admit that I don't have any suggestions here: tread carefully in this minefield, or get a job as a lawyer to get paid to hold the mine-detector for someone else!

75.4.4 Ubiquitous Technologies. With computers everywhere, the attack surface changes to everywhere. Where risks and the effects of exploitation were previously localized, these effects become equally pervasive and ubiquitous. Not only does each new device require security, but so do their future communications protocols. The devices' increasingly complex interactions in the Internet of Things make securing such interactions very difficult.[7] Not only does the number of targets increase, but so do the number of possible attack origins. Imagine a piece of malware that infects all the networked lightbulbs on the Internet and launches a distributed denial of service attack. Even if each bulb only produced a small bit of traffic, the number of bulbs might be staggering. The silver lining (if you can call it that) is that the number of easily compromised targets will also increase, making well-secured hosts less attractive.

While our information systems are becoming more numerous and complex, they are also becoming more autonomous. When data is processed faster than a human operator can react, computers often become decision makers with real-world impacts and consequences. Probably the best-known negative result of computerized decision making is the 2010 Flash Crash.[8] For whatever reason, algorithms monitoring and trading in the stock market decided that something (heuristically) bad was happening, and a feedback loop of sales and declining prices resulted in a drop of several percent in exchange-wide stock prices over about five minutes. Human administrators briefly halted trading to stop the freefall, and prices recovered about fifteen minutes later. In 2013, rules to prevent such crashes went into effect,[9] but it is not clear that they will be effective at preventing future events, especially considering *mini flash crashes* seem to happen with great frequency.[10]

Among the lessons the Flash Crash offers, I would like to highlight three:

1. Increasingly fast and complex automated systems will require increasingly fast and complex automated security.
2. Automated systems must fail safely. Clearly defining the parameters of safety in large systems is as necessary as defining reasonable inputs to a function in a programming project.
3. We should not expect automated systems to work perfectly all the time. Human-operated fail-safes with useful and responsive interfaces are necessary for oversight.

To illustrate these lessons, consider the lessons in the context of a self-driving car:

1. Built into the car's driving algorithms are a multitude of collision avoidance, location, and speed sensors to keep passengers safe. Security systems that act as a supervisor must ensure that these systems are not disabled and should have the authority to revert those systems to a basic feature set, provide appropriate alerts, or initiate a response to failure.
2. A human passenger or remote human monitor must have the ability to seize control of a misbehaving vehicle.
3. Every failure condition must be handled and result in the safe stopping of the vehicle or other safe, correct behavior.

75.5 NEW DIRECTIONS. I explored a handful of technologies that may prove to be disruptive to our current information assurance paradigm, and before that, I suggested a skeleton for that future paradigm. Rather than wrapping up the chapter with restatement of those discussions or offering some witty sendoff, I will conclude with a not-fully-baked pitch for decentralized security that I hope will encourage you to continue to consider alternative and new directions in information assurance.

Empowering individual users of information systems is one way to deal with a fast-moving environment and ubiquitous attack surfaces. Despite each user's capacity to be a malicious actor, their supervisors should also trust them enough to be part of the solution. People can make mistakes, but people can also be terrific first responders to an incident.

Distributing responsibility to the users resembles peer-to-peer or crowdsourced applications, so each user can be responsible for his or her own job tasks and security tasks, the results of which may then be shared with other users, possibly without a centralized controller. Using these combined findings, we end up with ensemble forecasting[11] for security.

As the user interacts with the information systems, feedback about their interactions both automatically generated and user-triggered can shape the reputation of individual systems and users both in terms of performance and how well they support or provide the services they advertise. I like to think of this as an informal way to provide feedback with a *thumbs down* or *one out of five stars* in lieu of opening a formal trouble ticket. In this way, the network behaves much more like a recommender system with real-time feedback and decision making. Since each system or user is dynamically assigned a reputation on the network, fuzzy authorization based on previous interactions with no a priori configuration is possible. When each device is a possibly malicious party, past behavior can be used as a predictor.

A related approach is to take advantage of existing social network relationships, such that individual users can be vetted by evaluating the links they share with previously trusted parties.[12] This mimics the trust and community interactions of the real world which, while imperfect, has evolved to be resilient to malicious and irresponsible parties, self-corrects, and requires no centralized authority. If we can strive for an imperfect by compromise-tolerant, disruption-tolerant, and flexible security posture, we will have a chance to ensure that technologies that move faster than we can keep up with will remain usable and effective at making our lives better. (That is what they're supposed to do, right?)

75.6 NOTES

1. Remember that according to the breach notification law SB1386: In California, everyone can hear you scream!
2. http://michaelnielsen.org/blog/quantum-computing-for-the-determined/
3. Aaronson, S. "The Limits of Quantum Computers." *Scientific American* 298(3):62-69, March 2008, http://www.scientificamerican.com/article.cfm?id=the-limits-of-quantum-computers
4. The first PQCrypto conference was held in 2006. See http://pqcrypto.org/
5. Halperin, Daniel, et al. "Pacemakers and implantable cardiac defibrillators: Software radio attacks and zero-power defenses." *Security and Privacy*, 2008. SP 2008. IEEE Symposium on. IEEE, 2008.
6. http://marsrovers.nasa.gov/overview/
7. http://www.wired.com/opinion/2013/01/securing-the-Internet-of-things/
8. http://www.bloomberg.com/news/2012-05-07/flash-crash-story-looks-more-like-a-fairy-tale.html
9. http://www.marketwatch.com/story/jitters-as-flash-crash-response-rules-take-effect-2013-04-08
10. http://money.cnn.com/2013/03/20/investing/mini-flash-crash/index.html
11. Michael Jahrer, Andreas Töscher, and Robert Legenstein. 2010. Combining predictions for accurate recommender systems. In *Proceedings of the 16th ACM SIGKDD international conference on Knowledge discovery and data mining* (KDD '10). ACM, New York, NY, USA, 693-702. DOI= 10.1145/1835804.1835893 http://doi.acm.org/10.1145/1835804.1835893
12. Beach, Aaron, Mike Gartrell, and Richard Han. "Solutions to security and privacy issues in mobile social networking." *Computational Science and Engineering, 2009. CSE'09. International Conference on.* Vol. 4. IEEE, 2009.

INDEX